Troubleshooting Nexus Switches and NX-OS

Vinit Jain, CCIE No. 22854
Brad Edgeworth, CCIE No. 31574
Richard Furr, CCIE No. 9173

Cisco Press

800 East 96th Street

Indianapolis, Indiana 46240 USA

Troubleshooting Cisco Nexus Switches and NX-OS

Vinit Jain, Brad Edgeworth, and Richard Furr

Copyright © 2018 Cisco Systems, Inc.

Published by:
Cisco Press
800 East 96th Street
Indianapolis, IN 46240 USA

All rights reserved. No part of this book may be reproduced or transmitted in any form or by any means, electronic or mechanical, including photocopying, recording, or by any information storage and retrieval system, without written permission from the publisher, except for the inclusion of brief quotations in a review.

34 2023

Library of Congress Control Number: 2018931070

ISBN-13: 978-1-58714-505-6
ISBN-10: 1-58714-505-7

Warning and Disclaimer

This book is designed to provide information about Cisco switches and NX-OS. Every effort has been made to make this book as complete and as accurate as possible, but no warranty or fitness is implied.

The information is provided on an "as is" basis. The authors, Cisco Press, and Cisco Systems, Inc. shall have neither liability nor responsibility to any person or entity with respect to any loss or damages arising from the information contained in this book or from the use of the discs or programs that may accompany it.

The opinions expressed in this book belong to the author and are not necessarily those of Cisco Systems, Inc.

Trademark Acknowledgments

All terms mentioned in this book that are known to be trademarks or service marks have been appropriately capitalized. Cisco Press or Cisco Systems, Inc., cannot attest to the accuracy of this information. Use of a term in this book should not be regarded as affecting the validity of any trademark or service mark.

Special Sales

For information about buying this title in bulk quantities, or for special sales opportunities (which may include electronic versions; custom cover designs; and content particular to your business, training goals, marketing focus, or branding interests), please contact our corporate sales department at corpsales@pearsoned.com or (800) 382-3419.

For government sales inquiries, please contact governmentsales@pearsoned.com.

For questions about sales outside the U.S., please contact intlcs@pearson.com.

Feedback Information

At Cisco Press, our goal is to create in-depth technical books of the highest quality and value. Each book is crafted with care and precision, undergoing rigorous development that involves the unique expertise of members from the professional technical community.

Readers' feedback is a natural continuation of this process. If you have any comments regarding how we could improve the quality of this book, or otherwise alter it to better suit your needs, you can contact us through email at feedback@ciscopress.com. Please make sure to include the book title and ISBN in your message.

We greatly appreciate your assistance.

Editor-in-Chief: Mark Taub

Alliances Manager, Cisco Press: Arezou Gol

Product Line Manager: Brett Bartow

Managing Editor: Sandra Schroeder

Development Editor: Marianne Bartow

Senior Project Editor: Tonya Simpson

Copy Editors: Barbara Hacha, Krista Hansing

Technical Editor(s): Ramiro Garza Rios, Matt Esau

Editorial Assistant: Vanessa Evans

Cover Designer: Chuti Prasertsith

Composition: codemantra

Indexer: Cheryl Lenser

Proofreader: Jeanine Furino

Americas Headquarters	Asia Pacific Headquarters	Europe Headquarters
Cisco Systems, Inc.	Cisco Systems (USA) Pte. Ltd.	Cisco Systems International BV Amsterdam,
San Jose, CA	Singapore	The Netherlands

Cisco has more than 200 offices worldwide. Addresses, phone numbers, and fax numbers are listed on the Cisco Website at www.cisco.com/go/offices.

Cisco and the Cisco logo are trademarks or registered trademarks of Cisco and/or its affiliates in the U.S. and other countries. To view a list of Cisco trademarks, go to this URL: www.cisco.com/go/trademarks. Third party trademarks mentioned are the property of their respective owners. The use of the word partner does not imply a partnership relationship between Cisco and any other company. (1110R)

About the Authors

Vinit Jain, CCIE No. 22854 (R&S, SP, Security & DC), is a technical leader with the Cisco Technical Assistance Center (TAC) providing escalation support in areas of routing and data center technologies. Vinit is a speaker at various networking forums, including Cisco Live events globally on various topics. Prior to joining Cisco, Vinit worked as a CCIE trainer and a network consultant. In addition to his CCIEs, Vinit holds multiple certifications on programming and databases. Vinit graduated from Delhi University in Mathematics and earned his Master's in Information Technology from Kuvempu University in India. Vinit can be found on Twitter as @VinuGenie.

Brad Edgeworth, CCIE No. 31574 (R&S & SP), is a systems engineer at Cisco Systems. Brad is a distinguished speaker at Cisco Live, where he has presented on various topics. Before joining Cisco, Brad worked as a network architect and consultant for various Fortune 500 companies. Brad's expertise is based on enterprise and service provider environments with an emphasis on architectural and operational simplicity. Brad holds a Bachelor of Arts degree in Computer Systems Management from St. Edward's University in Austin, Texas. Brad can be found on Twitter as @BradEdgeworth.

Richard Furr, CCIE No. 9173 (R&S & SP), is a technical leader with the Cisco Technical Assistance Center (TAC), supporting customers and TAC teams around the world. For the past 17 years, Richard has worked for the Cisco TAC and High Touch Technical Support (HTTS) organizations, supporting service provider, enterprise, and data center environments. Richard specializes in resolving complex problems found with routing protocols, MPLS, multicast, and network overlay technologies.

About the Technical Reviewers

Ramiro Garza Rios, CCIE No. 15469 (R&S, SP, and Security), is a solutions integration architect with Cisco Advanced Services, where he plans, designs, implements, and optimizes IP NGN service provider networks. Before joining Cisco in 2005, he was a network consulting and presales engineer for a Cisco Gold Partner in Mexico, where he planned, designed, and implemented both enterprise and service provider networks.

Matt Esau, CCIE No. 18586 (R&S) is a graduate from the University of North Carolina at Chapel Hill. He currently resides in Ohio with his wife and two children, ages three and one. Matt is a Distinguished Speaker at Cisco Live. He started with Cisco in 2002 and has spent 15 years working closely with customers on troubleshooting issues and product usability. For the past eight years, he has worked in the Data Center space, with a focus on Nexus platforms and technologies.

Dedications

This book is dedicated to three important women in my life: my mother, my wife, Khushboo, and Sonal. Mom, thanks for being a friend and a teacher in different phases of my life. You have given me the courage to stand up and fight every challenge that comes my way in life. Khushboo, I want to thank you for being so patient with my madness and craziness. I couldn't have completed this book or any other project without your support, and I cannot express in words how much it all means to me. This book is a small token of love, gratitude and appreciation for you. Sonal, thank you for being the driver behind my craziness. You have inspired me to reach new heights by setting new targets every time we met. This book is a small token of my love and gratitude for all that you have done for me.

I would further like to dedicate this book to my dad and my brother for believing in me and standing behind me as a wall whenever I faced challenges in life. I couldn't be where I am today without your invincible support.

—*Vinit Jain*

This book is dedicated to David Kyle. Thank you for taking a chance on me. You will always be more than a former boss. You mentored me with the right attitude and foundational skills early in my career.

In addition to stress testing the network with Quake, you let me start my path with networking under you. Look where I am now!

—*Brad Edgeworth*

This book is dedicated to my loving wife, Sandra, and my daughter, Calianna. You are my inspiration. Your love and support drive me to succeed each and every day. Thank you for providing the motivation for me to push myself further than I thought possible. Calianna, you are only two years old now. When you are old enough to read this, you will have long forgotten about all the late nights daddy spent working on this project. When you hold this book, I want you to remember that anything is possible through dedication and hard work.

I would like to further dedicate this book to my mother and father. Mom, thanks for always encouraging me, and for teaching me that I can do anything I put my mind to. Dad, thank you for always supporting me, and teaching me how to be dedicated and work hard. Both of you have given me your best.

—*Richard Furr*

Acknowledgments

Vinit Jain:

Brad and Richard: Thank you for being part of this yearlong journey. This project wouldn't have been possible without your support. It was a great team effort, and it was a pleasure working with both of you.

I would like to thank our technical editors, Ramiro and Matt, for your in-depth verification of the content and insightful input to make this project a successful one.

I couldn't have completed the milestone without the support from my managers, Chip Little and Mike Stallings. Thank you for enabling us with so many resources, as well as being flexible and making an environment that is full of opportunities.

I would like to thank David Jansen, Lukas Krattiger, Vinayak Sudame, Shridhar Dhodapkar, and Ryan McKenna for your valuable input during the course of this book.

Most importantly, I would like to thank Brett Bartow and Marianne Bartow for their wonderful support on this project. This project wouldn't have been possible without your support.

Brad Edgeworth:

Vinit, thanks again for asking me to co-write another book with you. Richard, thanks again for your insight. I've always enjoyed our late-night conference calls.

Ramiro and Matt, thank you for hiding all my mistakes, or at least pointing them out before they made it to print!

This is the part of the book that you look at to see if you have been recognized. Well, many people have provided feedback, suggestions, and support to make this a great book. Thanks to all who have helped in the process, especially Brett Bartow, Marianne Bartow, Jay Franklin, Katherine McNamara, Dustin Schuemann, Craig Smith, and my managers.

P.S. Teagan, this book does not contain dragons or princesses, but the next one might!

Richard Furr:

I'd like to thank my coauthors, Vinit Jain and Brad Edgeworth, for the opportunity to work on this project together. It has been equally challenging and rewarding on many levels.

Brad, thank you for all the guidance and your ruthless red pen on my first chapter. You showed me how to turn words and sentences into a book. Vinit, your drive and ambition are contagious. I look forward to working with both of you again in the future.

I would also like to thank our technical editors, Matt Esau and Ramiro Garza Rios, for their expertise and guidance. This book would not be possible without your contributions.

I could not have completed this project without the support and encouragement of my manager, Mike Stallings. Mike, thank you for allowing me to be creative and pursue projects like this one. You create the environment for us to be our best.

Contents at a Glance

Foreword xxvi

Introduction xxvii

Part I   **Introduction to Troubleshooting Nexus Switches**

Chapter 1   Introduction to Nexus Operating System (NX-OS)   1

Chapter 2   NX-OS Troubleshooting Tools   53

Chapter 3   Troubleshooting Nexus Platform Issues   95

Part II   **Troubleshooting Layer 2 Forwarding**

Chapter 4   Nexus Switching   197

Chapter 5   Port-Channels, Virtual Port-Channels, and FabricPath   255

Part III   **Troubleshooting Layer 3 Routing**

Chapter 6   Troubleshooting IP and IPv6 Services   321

Chapter 7   Troubleshooting Enhanced Interior Gateway Routing Protocol (EIGRP)   393

Chapter 8   Troubleshooting Open Shortest Path First (OSPF)   449

Chapter 9   Troubleshooting Intermediate System-Intermediate System (IS-IS)   507

Chapter 10   Troubleshooting Nexus Route-Maps   569

Chapter 11   Troubleshooting BGP   597

Part IV   **Troubleshooting High Availability**

Chapter 12   High Availability   689

Part V   **Multicast Network Traffic**

Chapter 13   Troubleshooting Multicast   733

Part VI Troubleshooting Nexus Tunneling

Chapter 14   Troubleshooting Overlay Transport Virtualization (OTV)   875

Part VII Network Programmability

Chapter 15   Programmability and Automation   949

Index   977

Reader Services

Register your copy at www.ciscopress.com/title/9781587145056 for convenient access to downloads, updates, and corrections as they become available. To start the registration process, go to www.ciscopress.com/register and log in or create an account*. Enter the product ISBN 9781587145056 and click Submit. When the process is complete, you will find any available bonus content under Registered Products.

*Be sure to check the box that you would like to hear from us to receive exclusive discounts on future editions of this product.

Contents

Foreword xxvi

Introduction xxvii

Part I   **Introduction to Troubleshooting Nexus Switches**

Chapter 1 **Introduction to Nexus Operating System (NX-OS)** 1

Nexus Platforms Overview 2

　Nexus 2000 Series 2

　Nexus 3000 Series 3

　Nexus 5000 Series 4

　Nexus 6000 Series 4

　Nexus 7000 Series 5

　Nexus 9000 Series 6

NX-OS Architecture 8

　The Kernel 9

　System Manager (sysmgr) 9

　Messages and Transactional Services 11

　Persistent Storage Services 13

　Feature Manager 14

　NX-OS Line Card Microcode 17

　File Systems 19

　Flash File System 21

　Onboard Failure Logging 22

　Logflash 23

Understanding NX-OS Software Releases
and Packaging 25

　Software Maintenance Upgrades 27

　Licensing 28

NX-OS High-Availability Infrastructure 28

　Supervisor Redundancy 29

　ISSU 34

NX-OS Virtualization Features 35

　Virtual Device Contexts 35

　Virtual Routing and Forwarding 37

　Virtual Port Channel 37

Management and Operations Capabilities   39
    NX-OS Advanced CLI   39
    Technical Support Files   44
    Accounting Log   45
    Feature Event-History   46
    Debug Options: Log File and Filters   47
    Configuration Checkpoint and Rollback   48
    Consistency Checkers   49
    Feature Scheduler, EEM, and Python   50
    Bash Shell   51
  Summary   51
  References   51

Chapter 2   NX-OS Troubleshooting Tools   53
  Packet Capture: Network Sniffer   53
    Encapsulated Remote SPAN   57
    SPAN on Latency and Drop   60
    SPAN-on-Latency   60
    SPAN-on-Drop   61
  Nexus Platform Tools   63
    Ethanalyzer   63
    Packet Tracer   71
  NetFlow   72
    NetFlow Configuration   73
    Enable NetFlow Feature   74
    Define a Flow Record   74
    Define a Flow Exporter   75
    Define and Apply the Flow Monitor   76
    NetFlow Sampling   77
    sFlow   78
  Network Time Protocol   81
  Embedded Event Manager   83
  Logging   87
    Debug Logfiles   90
    Accounting Log   91
    Event-History   92
  Summary   93
  References   93

Chapter 3	**Troubleshooting Nexus Platform Issues** 95
	Troubleshooting Hardware Issues 95
	Generic Online Diagnostic Tests 98
	Bootup Diagnostics 98
	Runtime Diagnostics 100
	GOLD Test and EEM Support 107
	Nexus Device Health Checks 108
	Hardware and Process Crashes 108
	Packet Loss 110
	Interface Errors and Drops 110
	Platform-Specific Drops 116
	Nexus Fabric Extenders 124
	Virtual Device Context 130
	VDC Resource Template 131
	Configuring VDC 133
	VDC Initialization 134
	Out-of-Band and In-Band Management 137
	VDC Management 137
	Line Card Interop Limitations 141
	Troubleshooting NX-OS System Components 142
	Message and Transaction Services 144
	Netstack and Packet Manager 148
	Netstack TCPUDP Component 156
	ARP and Adjacency Manager 160
	Unicast Forwarding Components 167
	Unicast Routing Information Base 167
	UFDM and IPFIB 171
	EthPM and Port-Client 175
	HWRL, CoPP, and System QoS 179
	MTU Settings 192
	FEX Jumbo MTU Settings 193
	Troubleshooting MTU Issues 194
	Summary 195
	References 196

Part II	**Troubleshooting Layer 2 Forwarding**
Chapter 4	**Nexus Switching 197**

    Network Layer 2 Communication Overview   197
    Virtual LANs   200
        VLAN Creation   201
        Access Ports   203
        Trunk Ports   204
        Native VLANs   206
        Allowed VLANs   206
        Private VLANS   207
        Isolated Private VLANs   208
        Community Private VLANs   212
        Using a Promiscuous PVLAN Port on Switched Virtual Interface   215
        Trunking PVLANs Between Switches   217
    Spanning Tree Protocol Fundamentals   218
        IEEE 802.1D Spanning Tree Protocol   219
        Rapid Spanning Tree Protocol   220
        Spanning-Tree Path Cost   221
        Root Bridge Election   222
        Locating Root Ports   224
        Locating Blocked Switch Ports   225
        Verification of VLANS on Trunk Links   227
        Spanning Tree Protocol Tuning   228
        Multiple Spanning-Tree Protocol (MST)   236
        MST Configuration   236
        MST Verification   237
        MST Tuning   240
    Detecting and Remediating Forwarding Loops   241
        MAC Address Notifications   242
        BPDU Guard   243
        BPDU Filter   244
        Problems with Unidirectional Links   245
        Spanning Tree Protocol Loop Guard   245
        Unidirectional Link Detection   246
        Bridge Assurance   250
    Summary   252
    References   254

Chapter 5 **Port-Channels, Virtual Port-Channels, and FabricPath** 255
  Port-Channels 255
    Basic Port-Channel Configuration 259
    Verifying Port-Channel Status 260
    Verifying LACP Packets 262
    Advanced LACP Configuration Options 265
      Minimum Number of Port-Channel Member Interfaces 265
      Maximum Number of Port-Channel Member Interfaces 267
      LACP System Priority 268
      LACP Interface Priority 268
      LACP Fast 269
      Graceful Convergence 270
      Suspend Individual 271
      Port-Channel Member Interface Consistency 271
      Troubleshooting LACP Interface Establishment 272
      Troubleshooting Traffic Load-Balancing 272
  Virtual Port-Channel 274
    vPC Fundamentals 275
    vPC Domain 275
    vPC Peer-Keepalive 276
    vPC Peer Link 277
    vPC Member Links 277
    vPC Operational Behavior 277
    vPC Configuration 278
    vPC Verification 280
      Verifying the vPC Domain Status 280
      Verifying the Peer-Keepalive 282
      vPC Consistency-Checker 283
    Advanced vPC Features 288
      vPC Orphan Ports 288
      vPC Autorecovery 289
      vPC Peer-Gateway 289
      vPC ARP Synchronization 291
      Backup Layer 3 Routing 292
      Layer 3 Routing over vPC 293

FabricPath 294
    FabricPath Terminologies and Components 296
    FabricPath Packet Flow 297
    FabricPath Configuration 300
    FabricPath Verification and Troubleshooting 303
    FabricPath Devices 310
Emulated Switch and vPC+ 310
    vPC+ Configuration 311
    vPC+ Verification and Troubleshooting 314
Summary 320
References 320

Part III **Troubleshooting Layer 3 Routing**

Chapter 6 **Troubleshooting IP and IPv6 Services 321**
IP SLA 321
    ICMP Echo Probe 322
    UDP Echo Probe 324
    UDP Jitter Probe 325
    TCP Connect Probe 328
Object Tracking 329
    Object Tracking for the Interface 330
    Object Tracking for Route State 330
    Object Tracking for Track-List State 332
    Using Track Objects with Static Routes 334
IPv4 Services 335
    DHCP Relay 335
    DHCP Snooping 341
    Dynamic ARP Inspection 345
    ARP ACLs 348
    IP Source Guard 349
    Unicast RPF 351
IPv6 Services 352
    Neighbor Discovery 352
    IPv6 Address Assignment 357
    DHCPv6 Relay Agent 357
    DHCPv6 Relay LDRA 360
    IPv6 First-Hop Security 362

RA Guard   363

                    IPv6 Snooping   365

                    DHCPv6 Guard   368

               First-Hop Redundancy Protocol   370

                    HSRP   370

                    HSRPv6   376

                    VRRP   380

                    GLBP   385

               Summary   391

Chapter 7   **Troubleshooting Enhanced Interior Gateway Routing Protocol (EIGRP)   393**

               EIGRP Fundamentals   393

                    Topology Table   395

                    Path Metric Calculation   396

                    EIGRP Communication   399

                    Baseline EIGRP Configuration   399

               Troubleshooting EIGRP Neighbor Adjacency   401

                    Verification of Active Interfaces   402

                    Passive Interface   403

                    Verification of EIGRP Packets   405

                    Connectivity Must Exist Using the Primary Subnet   409

                    EIGRP ASN Mismatch   412

                    Mismatch K Values   413

                    Problems with Hello and Hold Timers   414

                    EIGRP Authentication Issues   416

                    Interface-Based EIGRP Authentication   418

                    Global EIGRP Authentication   418

               Troubleshooting Path Selection and Missing Routes   419

                    Load Balancing   421

                    Stub   421

                    Maximum-Hops   424

                    Distribute List   426

                    Offset Lists   427

                    Interface-Based Settings   430

                    Redistribution   430

                    Classic Metrics vs. Wide Metrics   433

Problems with Convergence   439
  Active Query   441
  Stuck in Active   443
Summary   446
References   447

Chapter 8 Troubleshooting Open Shortest Path First (OSPF)   449
OSPF Fundamentals   449
  Inter-Router Communication   450
  OSPF Hello Packets   450
  Neighbor States   451
  Designated Routers   452
  Areas   453
  Link State Advertisements   453
Troubleshooting OSPF Neighbor Adjacency   456
  Baseline OSPF Configuration   456
  OSPF Neighbor Verification   458
  Confirmation of OSPF Interfaces   460
  Passive Interface   461
  Verification of OSPF Packets   463
  Connectivity Must Exist Using the Primary Subnet   468
  MTU Requirements   469
  Unique Router-ID   471
  Interface Area Numbers Must Match   471
  OSPF Stub (Area Flags) Settings Must Match   473
  DR Requirements   474
  Timers   476
  Authentication   478
Troubleshooting Missing Routes   482
  Discontiguous Network   482
  Duplicate Router ID   485
  Filtering Routes   487
  Redistribution   487
  OSPF Forwarding Address   488
Troubleshooting OSPF Path Selection   494
  Intra-Area Routes   494
  Inter-Area Routes   495

External Route Selection   495
E1 and N1 External Routes   496
E2 and N2 External Routes   497
Problems with Intermixed RFC 1583 and RFC 2328 Devices   499
Interface Link Costs   500
Summary   504
References   505

Chapter 9   Troubleshooting Intermediate System-Intermediate System (IS-IS)   507

IS-IS Fundamentals   507
Areas   508
NET Addressing   509
Inter-Router Communication   511
IS Protocol Header   511
TLVs   512
IS PDU Addressing   512
IS-IS Hello (IIH) Packets   513
Link-State Packets   515
LSP ID   515
Attribute Fields   515
LSP Packet and TLVs   516
Designated Intermediate System   516
Path Selection   517

Troubleshooting IS-IS Neighbor Adjacency   518
Baseline IS-IS Configuration   518
IS-IS Neighbor Verification   520
Confirmation of IS-IS Interfaces   523
Passive Interface   526
Verification of IS-IS Packets   528
Connectivity Must Exist Using the Primary Subnet   535
MTU Requirements   537
Unique System-ID   539
Area Must Match Between L1 Adjacencies   539
Checking IS-IS Adjacency Capabilities   541
DIS Requirements   543
IIH Authentication   544

Troubleshooting Missing Routes   546
   Duplicate System ID   546
   Interface Link Costs   549
   Mismatch of Metric Modes   553
   L1 to L2 Route Propagations   556
   Suboptimal Routing   562
   Redistribution   566
Summary   567
References   568

Chapter 10 Troubleshooting Nexus Route-Maps   569

Conditional Matching   569
   Access Control Lists   569
   ACLs and ACL Manager Component   570
   Interior Gateway Protocol (IGP) Network Selection   576
   BGP Network Selection   577
   Prefix Matching and Prefix-Lists   577
   Prefix Matching   578
   Prefix Lists   580
Route-Maps   581
   Conditional Matching   582
   Multiple Conditional Match Conditions   584
   Complex Matching   585
   Optional Actions   586
   Incomplete Configuration of Routing Policies   586
   Diagnosing Route Policy Manger   586
Policy-Based Routing   591
Summary   594
References   595

Chapter 11 Troubleshooting BGP   597

BGP Fundamentals   597
   Address Families   598
   Path Attributes   599
   Loop Prevention   599
BGP Sessions   600
   BGP Identifier   601
   BGP Messages   601

OPEN   601
UPDATE   602
NOTIFICATION   602
KEEPALIVE   602
BGP Neighbor States   602
Idle   603
Connect   603
Active   604
OpenSent   604
OpenConfirm   604
Established   605
BGP Configuration and Verification   605
Troubleshooting BGP Peering Issues   609
   Troubleshooting BGP Peering Down Issues   609
      Verifying Configuration   610
      Verifying Reachability and Packet Loss   611
      Verifying ACLs and Firewalls in the Path   613
      Verifying TCP Sessions   615
      OPEN Message Errors   617
      BGP Debugs   618
   Demystifying BGP Notifications   619
   Troubleshooting IPv6 Peers   621
   BGP Peer Flapping Issues   622
   Bad BGP Update   622
   Hold Timer Expired   623
   BGP Keepalive Generation   624
   MTU Mismatch Issues   626
BGP Route Processing and Route Propagation   630
   BGP Route Advertisement   631
   Network Statement   631
   Redistribution   633
   Route Aggregation   634
   Default-Information Originate   636
   BGP Best Path Calculation   636
   BGP Multipath   640
   EBGP and IBGP Multipath   640

BGP Update Generation Process 643
BGP Convergence 646
Scaling BGP 649
    Tuning BGP Memory 650
    Prefixes 650
    Paths 651
    Attributes 652
    Scaling BGP Configuration 653
    Soft Reconfiguration Inbound Versus Route Refresh 654
    Scaling BGP with Route-Reflectors 657
    Loop Prevention in Route Reflectors 658
    Maximum Prefixes 659
    BGP Max AS 662
BGP Route Filtering and Route Policies 662
    Prefix-List-Based Filtering 663
    Filter-Lists 669
BGP Route-Maps 673
    Regular Expressions (RegEx) 676
    _ Underscore 677
    ^ Caret 679
    $ Dollar Sign 679
    [ ] Brackets 680
    - Hyphen 680
    [^] Caret in Brackets 681
    ( ) Parentheses and | Pipe 681
    . Period 682
    + Plus Sign 682
    ? Question Mark 683
    * Asterisk 683
    AS-Path Access List 684
    BGP Communities 684
Looking Glass and Route Servers 687
Logs Collection 687
Summary 687
Further Reading 688
References 688

Part IV	**Troubleshooting High Availability**
Chapter 12	**High Availability 689**

    Bidirectional Forwarding Detection   689
        Asynchronous Mode   691
        Asynchronous Mode with Echo Function   693
        Configuring and Verifying BFD Sessions   693
    Nexus High Availability   707
        Stateful Switchover   707
        ISSU   713
    Graceful Insertion and Removal   719
        Custom Maintenance Profile   727
    Summary   731
    References   732

Part V	**Multicast Network Traffic**
Chapter 13	**Troubleshooting Multicast 733**

    Multicast Fundamentals   734
        Multicast Terminology   735
        Layer 2 Multicast Addresses   738
        Layer 3 Multicast Addresses   739
    NX-OS Multicast Architecture   741
        Replication   744
        Protecting the Central Processing Unit   745
        NX-OS Multicast Implementation   747
        Static Joins   748
        Clearing an MROUTE Entry   748
        Multicast Boundary and Filtering   748
        Event-Histories and Show Techs   749
    IGMP   750
        IGMPv2   751
        IGMPv3   752
        IGMP Snooping   756
        IGMP Verification   761
    PIM Multicast   771
        PIM Protocol State and Trees   772
        PIM Message Types   773

PIM Hello Message   775
PIM Register Message   775
PIM Register-Stop Message   776
PIM Join-Prune Message   776
PIM Bootstrap Message   777
PIM Assert Message   778
PIM Candidate RP Advertisement Message   779
PIM DF Election Message   779
PIM Interface and Neighbor Verification   780
PIM Any Source Multicast   785
PIM ASM Configuration   787
PIM ASM Verification   788
PIM ASM Event-History and MROUTE State Verification   789
PIM ASM Platform Verification   795
PIM Bidirectional   799
BiDIR Configuration   803
BiDIR Verification   805
PIM RP Configuration   811
Static RP Configuration   812
Auto-RP Configuration and Verification   813
BSR Configuration and Verification   820
Anycast-RP Configuration and Verification   830
Anycast RP with MSDP   831
PIM Anycast RP   838
PIM Source Specific Multicast   841
SSM Configuration   843
SSM Verification   845
Multicast and Virtual Port-Channel   848
vPC-Connected Source   849
vPC-Connected Receiver   861
vPC Considerations for Multicast Traffic   870
Duplicate Multicast Packets   870
Reserved VLAN   870
Ethanalyzer Examples   871
Summary   871
References   872

Part VI   **Troubleshooting Nexus Tunneling**

Chapter 14   **Troubleshooting Overlay Transport Virtualization (OTV)**   875

     OTV Fundamentals   875

         Flood Control and Broadcast Optimization   877

         Supported OTV Platforms   878

         OTV Terminology   878

         Deploying OTV   881

         OTV Deployment Models   *881*

         OTV Site VLAN   *882*

         OTV Configuration   *882*

     Understanding and Verifying the OTV Control Plane   885

         OTV Multicast Mode   887

         OTV IS-IS Adjacency Verification   888

         OTV IS-IS Topology Table   898

         OTV IS-IS Authentication   905

         Adjacency Server Mode   907

         OTV Control Plane Policing (CoPP)   912

     Understanding and Verifying the OTV Data Plane   913

         OTV ARP Resolution and ARP-ND-Cache   915

         Broadcasts   917

         Unknown Unicast Frames   918

         OTV Unicast Traffic with a Multicast Enabled Transport   919

         OTV Multicast Traffic with a Multicast Enabled Transport   924

         OTV Multicast Traffic with a Unicast Transport
            (Adjacency Server Mode)   932

     Advanced OTV Features   937

         First Hop Routing Protocol Localization   938

         Multihoming   939

         Ingress Routing Optimization   940

         VLAN Translation   941

         OTV Tunnel Depolarization   942

         OTV Fast Failure Detection   944

     Summary   946

     References   947

Part VII   **Network Programmability**

Chapter 15   **Programmability and Automation   949**

    Introduction to Automation and Programmability   949

    Introduction to Open NX-OS   950

        Shells and Scripting   951

        Bash Shell   951

        Guest Shell   957

        Python   960

    NX-SDK   964

    NX-API   968

    Summary   975

    References   975

    Index   977

Icons Used in This Book

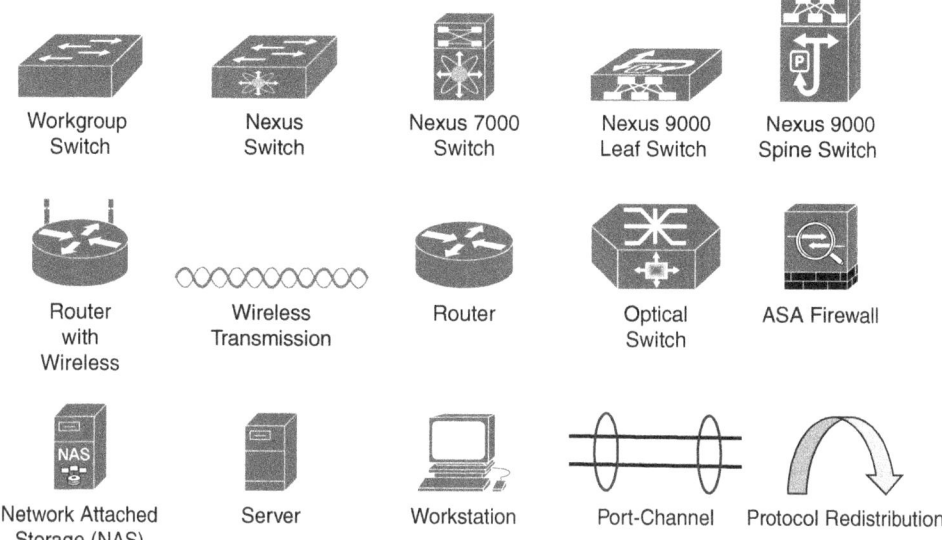

Command Syntax Conventions

The conventions used to present command syntax in this book are the same conventions used in the IOS Command Reference. The Command Reference describes these conventions as follows:

- **Boldface** indicates commands and keywords that are entered literally as shown. In actual configuration examples and output (not general command syntax), boldface indicates commands that are manually input by the user (such as a **show** command).
- *Italic* indicates arguments for which you supply actual values.
- Vertical bars (|) separate alternative, mutually exclusive elements.
- Square brackets ([ ]) indicate an optional element.
- Braces ({ }) indicate a required choice.
- Braces within brackets ([{ }]) indicate a required choice within an optional element.

Note This book covers multiple Nexus switch platforms (5000, 7000, 9000, etc). A generic NX-OS icon is used along with a naming syntax for differentiation of devices. Platform-specific topics use a platform-specific icon and major platform number in the system name.

Foreword

The data center is at the core of all companies in the digital age. It processes bits and bytes of data that represent products and services to its customers. The data storage and processing capabilities of a modern business have become synonymous with the ability to generate revenue. Companies in all business sectors are storing and processing more information digitally every year, regardless of their vertical affiliation (construction, medical, entertainment, and so on). This means that the network must be designed for speed, capacity, and flexibility.

The Nexus platform was built with speed and bandwidth capacity in mind. When the Nexus 7000 launched in 2008, it provided high-density 10 Gigabit interfaces at a low per-port cost. In addition, the Nexus switch operating system, NX-OS, brought forth evolutionary technologies like virtual port channels (vPC) that increased available bandwidth and redundancy while overcoming the inefficiencies of Spanning-Tree Protocol (STP). NX-OS introduced technologies such as Overlay Transport Virtualization (OTV), which revolutionized the design of the data center network by enabling host mobility between sites and allowing full data center redundancy. Today, the Nexus platform continues to evolve by supporting 25/40/100 Gigabit interfaces in a high-density compact form factor, and brings other innovative technologies such as VXLAN and Application Centric Infrastructure (ACI) to the market.

NX-OS was built with the mindset of operational simplicity and includes additional tools and capabilities that improve the operational efficiency of the network. Today, websites and applications are expected to be available 24 hours a day, 7 days a week, and 365 days a year. Downtime in the data center directly translates to a financial impact. The move toward digitization and the potential impact the network has to a business makes it more important than ever for network engineers to attain the skills to troubleshoot data center network environments efficiently.

As the leader of Cisco's technical services for more than 25 years, I have the benefit of working with the best network professionals in the industry. This book is written by Brad, Richard, and Vinit: "Network Rock Stars," who have been in my organization for years supporting multiple Cisco customers. This book provides a complete reference for troubleshooting Nexus switches and the NX-OS operating system. The methodologies taught in this book are the same methods used by Cisco's technical services to solve a variety of complex network problems.

Joseph Pinto
SVP, Technical Services, Cisco, San Jose

Introduction

The Nexus operating system (NX-OS) contains a modular software architecture that primarily targets high-speed/high-density network environments like data centers. NX-OS provides virtualization, high availability, scalability, and upgradeability features for Nexus switches.

In particular, the NX-OS is expected to have a measure of resilience during software upgrades or hardware upgrades (failover, OIR), with both sets of operations not affecting nonstop forwarding. NX-OS is required to scale to very large multichassis systems and still operate with the same expectations of resilience in the face of outages of various kinds. The NX-OS feature set includes a variety of features and protocols that have revolutionized data center designs with virtual port channels (vPC), Overlay Transport Virtualization (OTV), and now virtual extensible LAN (VXLAN).

The Nexus 7000 switch debuted in 2008, providing more than 512 10 Gbps ports. Over the years, Cisco has released other Nexus switch families that include the Nexus 5000, Nexus 2000, Nexus 9000, and virtual Nexus 1000. NX-OS has grown in features, allowing Nexus switch deployments in enterprise routing and switching roles.

This book is the single source for mastering techniques to troubleshoot various features and issues running on Nexus platforms with NX-OS operating system. Bringing together content previously spread across multiple sources and Cisco Press titles, it covers updated various features and architecture-level information on how various features function on Nexus platforms and how one can leverage the capabilities of NX-OS to troubleshoot them.

Who Should Read This Book?

Network engineers, architects, or consultants who want to learn more about the underlying Nexus platform and NX-OS operating system so that they can know how to troubleshoot complex network issues with NX-OS. This book also provides a great reference for those studying for their CCIE Data Center Certification.

How This Book Is Organized

Although this book could be read cover to cover, it is designed to be flexible and allow you to easily move between chapters and sections of chapters to cover just the material that you need more work with.

Part I of the book, "Introduction to Troubleshooting Nexus Switches" provides an overview on the Nexus platform and the components of NX-OS used for troubleshooting network events.

- **Chapter 1, "Introduction to the Nexus Operating System (NX-OS)":** This chapter introduces the Nexus platform and the major functional components of the Nexus operating system (NX-OS). The chapter discusses the four fundamental pillars of NX-OS: resiliency, virtualization, efficiency, and extensibility.

- **Chapter 2, "NX-OS Troubleshooting Tools":** This chapter explains the history of packet capture, NetFlow, EEM, logging, and event history.

- **Chapter 3, "Troubleshooting Nexus Platform Issues":** This chapter examines various Nexus platform components and commands to troubleshoot issues with the supervisor cards and line cards, hardware drops, and fabric issues. This chapter also examines how to troubleshoot interface and PLIM-level issues on the line card. This chapter also covers issues related to CoPP policies and how to troubleshoot CoPP-related issues.

Part II of the book, "Troubleshooting Layer 2 Forwarding," explains the specific components for troubleshooting Nexus switches during the switching of network packets.

- **Chapter 4, "Nexus Switching":** This chapter explains how Nexus switches forward packets and explains switch port types, private VLANs, and Spanning-Tree Protocol (STP).

- **Chapter 5, "Port Channels, Virtual Port-Channels, and FabricPath":** This chapter covers in great detail how vPC, Fabric Path, and vPC+ works and how they add value to the next generation DC design. This chapter focuses on designing, implementing, and troubleshooting issues related to vPC and vPC+.

Part III of the book, "Troubleshooting Layer 3 Routing," explains the underlying IP components of NX-OS. This includes the routing protocols EIGRP, OSPF, IS-IS, BGP, and the selection of routes for filtering or path manipulation.

- **Chapter 6, "Troubleshooting IP and IPv6 Services":** This chapter explains how various IPv4 and IPv6 services work and how to troubleshoot the same on Nexus platforms. This chapter also covers FHRP protocols, such as HSRP, VRRP, and Anycast HSRP.

- **Chapter 7, "Troubleshooting Enhanced Interior Gateway Routing Protocol (EIGRP)":** This chapter explains how to troubleshoot various issues related to EIGRP, including forming EIGRP neighborships, suboptimal routing, and other common EIGRP problems.

- **Chapter 8, "Troubleshooting Open Shortest Path First (OSPF)":** This chapter explains how to troubleshoot various issues related to OSPF, including forming OSPF neighbor adjacencies, suboptimal routing, and other common OSPF problems.

- **Chapter 9, "Troubleshooting Intermediate System–Intermediate System (IS-IS)":** This chapter explains how to troubleshoot various issues related to IS-IS, including forming IS-IS neighbor adjacencies, suboptimal routing, and other common IS-IS problems.
- **Chapter 10, "Troubleshooting Nexus Route-Maps":** This chapter discusses various network selection techniques for filtering or metric manipulation. It explains conditional matching of routes using access control lists (ACL), prefix-lists, and route-maps.
- **Chapter 11, "Troubleshooting BGP":** This chapter explains how to troubleshoot various issues related to BGP, including BGP neighbor adjacencies, path selection, and other common issues.

Part IV of the book, "Troubleshooting High Availability," discusses and explains the high availability components of NX-OS.

- **Chapter 12, "High Availability":** This chapter explains how to troubleshoot high availability components such as bidirectional forward detection (BFD), Stateful Switchover (SSO), In-service software upgrade (ISSU) and Graceful Insertion and Removal (GIR).

Part V of the book, "Multicast Network Traffic," explains the operational components of multicast network traffic on Nexus switches.

- **Chapter 13, "Troubleshooting Multicast":** This chapter explains the various components of multicast and how multicast network issues can be identified and resolved.

Part VI of the book, "Troubleshooting Nexus Tunneling," discusses the various tunneling techniques that NX-OS provides.

- **Chapter 14, "Troubleshooting Overlay Transport Virtualization (OTV)":** This chapter explains the revolutionary overlay transport virtualization technology and how it operates, along with the process for troubleshooting issues with it.

Part VII of the book, "Network Programmability," provides details on the methods that NX-OS can be configured with APIs and automation.

- **Chapter 15, "Programability and Automation":** This chapter examines various application programming interfaces (APIs) that are available with NX-OS and how they enable network operations to automate their network.

On the product web page you also will find a bonus chapter, "Troubleshooting VxLAN and VxLAN BGP EVPN."

Additional Reading

The authors tried to keep the size of the book manageable while providing only necessary information for the topics involved.

Some readers may require additional reference material and may find the following books a great supplementary resource for the topics in this book.

- Fuller, Ron, David Jansen, and Matthew McPherson. *NX-OS and Cisco Nexus Switching.* Indianapolis: Cisco Press, 2013.

- Edgeworth, Brad, Aaron Foss, and Ramiro Garza Rios. *IP Routing on Cisco IOS, IOS XE, and IOS XR.* Indianapolis: Cisco Press, 2014.

- Krattiger, Lukas, Shyam Kapadia, and David Jansen. *Building Data Centers with VXLAN BGP EVPN.* Indianapolis: Cisco Press, 2017.

Chapter 1

Introduction to Nexus Operating System (NX-OS)

This chapter covers the following topics:

- Nexus Platforms
- NX-OS Architecture
- NX-OS Virtualization Features
- Management and Operations Capabilities

At the time of its release in 2008, the Nexus operating system (NX-OS) and the Nexus 7000 platform provided a substantial leap forward in terms of resiliency, extensibility, virtualization, and system architecture compared to other switching products of the time. Wasteful excess capacity in bare metal server resources had already given way to the efficiency of virtual machines and now that wave was beginning to wash over to the network as well. Networks were evolving from traditional 3-Tier designs (access layer, distribution layer, core layer) to designs that required additional capacity, scale, and availability. It was no longer acceptable to have links sitting idle due to Spanning Tree Protocol blocking while that capacity could be utilized to increase the availability of the network.

As network topologies evolved, so did the market's expectation of the network infrastructure devices that connected their hosts and network segments. Network operators were looking for platforms that were more resilient to failures, offered increased switching capacity, and allowed for additional network virtualization in their designs to better utilize physical hardware resources. Better efficiency was also needed in terms of reduced power consumption and cooling requirements as data centers grew larger with increased scale.

The Nexus 7000 series was the first platform in Cisco's Nexus line of switches created to meet the needs of this changing data center market. NX-OS combines the functionality of Layer 2 switching, Layer 3 routing, and SAN switching into a single operating system.

From the initial release, the operating system has continued to evolve, and the portfolio of Nexus switching products has expanded to include several series of switches that address the needs of a modern network. Throughout this expansion, the following four fundamental pillars of NX-OS have remained unchanged:

- Resiliency
- Virtualization
- Efficiency
- Extensibility

This chapter introduces the different types of Nexus platforms along with their placement into the modern network architecture, and the major functional components of NX-OS. In addition, some of the advanced serviceability and usability enhancements are introduced to prepare you for the troubleshooting chapters that follow. This enables you to dive into each of the troubleshooting chapters with a firm understanding of NX-OS and Nexus switching to build upon.

Nexus Platforms Overview

The Cisco Nexus switching portfolio contains the following platforms:

- Nexus 2000 Series
- Nexus 3000 Series
- Nexus 5000 Series
- Nexus 6000 Series
- Nexus 7000 Series
- Nexus 9000 Series

The following sections introduce each Nexus platform and provide a high-level overview of their features and placement depending on common deployment scenarios.

Nexus 2000 Series

The Nexus 2000 series is a group of devices known as a fabric extender (FEX). FEXs essentially act as a remote line card for the parent switch extending its fabric into the server access layer.

The FEX architecture provides the following benefits:

- Extend the fabric to hosts without the need for spanning tree
- Highly scalable architecture that is common regardless of host type

- Single point of management from the parent switch
- Ability to upgrade parent switch and retain the FEX hardware

The Nexus 2000 FEX products do not function as standalone devices; they require a parent switch to function as a modular system. Several models are available to meet the host port physical connectivity requirements with various options for 1 GE, 10 GE connectivity as well as Fiber Channel over Ethernet (FCoE). On the fabric side of the FEX, which connects back to the parent switch, different options exist for 1 GE, 10 GE, and 40 GE interfaces. The current FEX Models are as follows:

- 1 GE Fabric Extender Models: (2224TP, 2248TP, 2248TP-E)
- 10 GBase-T Fabric Extender Models: (2332TQ, 2348TQ, 2348TQ-E, 2232TM-E, 2232TM)
- 10 G SFP+ Fabric Extender Models: (2348UPQ, 2248PQ, 2232PP)

When deciding on a FEX platform, consider the host connectivity requirements, the parent switch connectivity requirements, and compatibility of the parent switch model. The expected throughput and performance of the hosts should also be a consideration because the addition of a FEX allows oversubscription of the fabric-side interfaces based on the front panel bandwidth available for hosts.

Nexus 3000 Series

The Nexus 3000 series consists of several models of high performance, low-latency, fixed configuration switches. They offer a compact 1 or 2 RU (rack unit) footprint with a high density of front panel ports ranging in speed from 1 GE, 10 GE, 40 GE, to 100GE. These switches are not only high performance but also versatile because they support a wide range of Layer 2 features as well as support for Layer 3 routing protocols and IP Multicast. The model number is a combination of the platform series, the number of ports or the total bandwidth of the ports, and the type of interfaces.

The current Nexus 3000 models are as follows:

- Nexus 3000 Models: (3064X, 3064-32T, 3064T, 3048)
- Nexus 3100 Models: (3132Q/3132Q-X, 3164Q, 3172PQ, 3172TQ, 31128PQ)
- Nexus 3100V Models: (31108PC-V, 31108TC-V, 3132Q-V)
- Nexus 3200 Models: (3232C, 3264Q)
- Nexus 3500 Models: (3524/3524-X, 3548/3548-X)
- Nexus 3600 Models: (36180YC-R)

Each of these models has advantages depending on the intended role. For example, the Nexus 3500 series are capable of ultra-low-latency switching (sub-250ns), which makes them popular for high-performance computing as well as high-frequency stock trading environments. The 3100-V is capable of Virtual Extensible Local Area Network (VXLAN) routing, the 3200 offers low-latency and larger buffers, while the 3000 and 3100 series are good all-around line rate Top of Rack (ToR) switches.

> **Note** All Nexus 3000 series, with the exception of the Nexus 3500 series, run the same NX-OS software release as the Nexus 9000 series switches.

Nexus 5000 Series

The Nexus 5000 series support a wide range of Layer 2 and Layer 3 features, which allows versatility depending on the network design requirements. The Nexus 5500 series require the installation of additional hardware and software licensing for full Layer 3 support, whereas the Nexus 5600 series offers a native Layer 3 routing engine capable of 160 Gbps performance. The Nexus 5600 also supports VXLAN and larger table sizes compared to the 5500 series.

The current Nexus 5000 models are as follows:

- Nexus 5500 Models: (5548UP, 5596UP, 5596T)
- Nexus 5600 Models: (5672UP, 5672UP-16G, 56128P, 5624Q, 5648Q, 5696Q)

The Nexus 5000 series is well suited as a Top of Rack (ToR) or End of Row (EoR) switch for high-density and high-scale environments. They support 1 GE, 10 GE, and 40 GE connectivity for Ethernet and FCoE. Superior port densities are achieved when used as a parent switch for FEX aggregation. The 5696Q supports 100 GE uplinks with the addition of expansion modules. The platform naming convention is the model family, then the supported number of ports at 10 GE or 40 GE depending on the model. A Nexus 5672 is a 5600 platform that supports 72 ports of 10 GE Ethernet, and the *UP* characters indicate the presence of 40 GE uplink ports.

The support for Layer 3 features combined with a large number of ports, FEX aggregation, and the flexibility of supporting Ethernet, FCoE, and Fibre Channel in a single platform make the Nexus 5000 series a very attractive ToR or EoR option for many environments.

Nexus 6000 Series

The Nexus 6001 and Nexus 6004 switches are suited for ToR and EoR placement in high-density data center networks. The 6001 is a 1RU chassis that supports connectivity to 1 GE to 10 GE servers, and the 6004 is a 4RU chassis suited for 10 GE to 40 GE server connectivity or FCoE. FEX aggregation is also a popular application of the Nexus 6000 series. The Nexus 6000 series offers large buffers and low latency switching to meet the needs of high-performance computing environments. They support robust Layer 2, Layer 3, and storage feature sets with the appropriate feature license installed. The Nexus 6000 series has reached end of sale in its product life cycle as of April 30, 2017. The Nexus 5600 platform is designated as the replacement platform because it offers similar benefits, density, and placement in the data center.

Nexus 7000 Series

The Nexus 7000 series first shipped nearly 10 years ago, and it continues to be a very popular option for enterprise, data center, and service provider networks around the world. There are many reasons for its success. It is a truly modular platform based on a fully distributed crossbar fabric architecture that provides a large number of features. The Nexus 7000 series is categorized into two chassis families: the 7000 and the 7700. The 7000 series chassis are available in the following configurations, where the last two digits of the platform name represent the number of slots in the chassis:

- Nexus 7000 Models: (7004, 7009, 7010, 7018)
- Nexus 7700 Models: (7702, 7706, 7710, 7718)

The different chassis configurations allow for optimal sizing in any environment. The 7000 series has five fabric module slots, whereas the 7700 has six fabric module slots. The 7004 and the 7702 do not use separate fabric modules because the crossbar fabric on the Input/Output (I/O) modules are sufficient for handling the platform's requirements. Access to the fabric is controlled by a central arbiter on the supervisor. This grants access to the fabric for ingress modules to send packets toward egress modules. Virtual output queues (VOQ) are implemented on the ingress I/O modules that represent the fabric capacity of the egress I/O module. These VOQs minimize head-of-line blocking that could occur waiting for an egress card to accept packets during congestion.

The Nexus 7000 and 7700 utilize a supervisor module that is responsible for running the management and control plane of the platform as well as overseeing the platform health. The supervisor modules have increased in CPU power, memory capacity, and switching performance, with each generation starting with the Supervisor 1, then the Supervisor 2, and then the current Supervisor 2E.

Because the Nexus 7000 is a distributed system, the I/O modules run their own software, and they are responsible for handling all the data plane traffic. All Nexus 7000 I/O modules fall into one of two families of forwarding engines: M Series or F Series. Both families of line cards have port configurations that range in speed from 1 GE, 10 GE, 40 GE, to 100 GE. They are commonly referred to by their forwarding engine generation (M1, M2, M3 and F1, F2, and F3), with each generation offering improvements in forwarding capacity and features over the previous. The M series generally has larger forwarding table capacity and larger packet buffers. Previously the M series also supported more Layer 3 features than the F series, but with the release of the F3 cards, the feature gap has closed with support for features like Locator-ID Separation Protocol (LISP) and MPLS. Figure 1-1 explains the I/O module naming convention for the Nexus 7000 series.

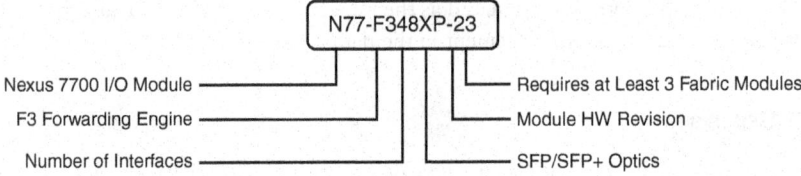

Figure 1-1 *Nexus 7000 Series I/O Module Naming Convention*

The Nexus 7000 is typically deployed in an aggregation or core role; however, using FEXs with the Nexus 7000 provides high-density access connectivity for hosts. The Nexus 7000 is also a popular choice for overlay technologies like MPLS, LISP, Overlay Transport Virtualization (OTV), and VXLAN due to its wide range of feature availability and performance.

Nexus 9000 Series

The Nexus 9000 Series was added to the lineup in late 2013. The Nexus 9500 is a modular switch and was the first model to ship with several innovative features. The modular chassis was designed to minimize the number of components so it does not have a mid-plane. The line-card modules interface directly to the fabric modules in the rear of the chassis. The switching capacity of the chassis is determined by adding up to six fabric modules that are designed to be full line rate, nonblocking to all ports. Recently the R-Series line cards and fabric modules were released, which feature deep buffer capabilities and increased forwarding table sizes for demanding environments. The Nexus 9500 is a modular switching platform and therefore has supervisor modules, fabric modules, and various line-card options. Two supervisor modules exist for the Nexus 9500:

- Supervisor A with a 4 core 1.8 GHz CPU, 16 GB of RAM, and 64 GB of SSD storage
- Supervisor B with a 6 core 2.2 GHz CPU, 24 GB of RAM, and 256 GB of SSD storage

The Nexus 9000 series uses a mix of commodity merchant switching application-specific integrated circuits (ASIC) as well as Cisco's developed ASICs to reduce cost where appropriate. The Nexus 9500 was followed by the Nexus 9300 and Nexus 9200 series. Interface speeds of 1 GE, 10 GE, 25 GE, 40 GE, and 100 GE are possible, depending on the model, and FCoE and FEX aggregation is also supported on select models. The 9500 is flexible and modular, and it could serve as a leaf/aggregation or core/spine layer switch, depending on the size of the environment.

The 9300 and 9200 function well as high-performance ToR/EoR/leaf switches. The Nexus 9000 series varies in size from 1RU to 21RU with various module and connectivity options that match nearly any connectivity and performance requirements. The available models are as follows:

- Nexus 9500 Models: (9504, 9508, 9516)
- Nexus 9300 100M/1G Base-T Models: (9348GC-FXP)
- Nexus 9300 10 GBaseT Models: (9372TX, 9396TX, 93108TC-FX, 93120TX, 93128TX, 93108TC-EX)
- Nexus 9300 10/25 GE Fiber Models: (9372PX, 9396PX, 93180YC-FX, 93180YC-EX)
- Nexus 9300 40 GE Models: (9332PQ, 9336PQ, 9364C, 93180LC-EX)
- Nexus 9200 Models: (92160YC-X, 9272Q, 92304QC, 9236C, 92300YC)

The Nexus 9000 platform naming convention is explained in Figure 1-2.

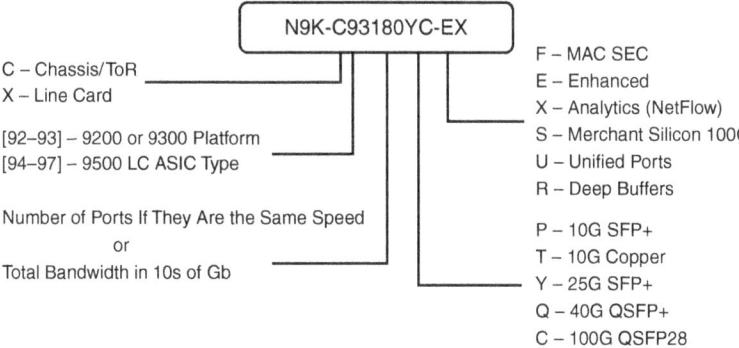

Figure 1-2 *Nexus 9000 Series Naming Convention*

The Nexus 9000 series is popular in a variety of network deployments because of its speed, broad feature sets, and versatility. The series is used in high-frequency trading, high-performance computing, large-scale leaf/spine architectures, and it is the most popular Cisco Nexus platform for VXLAN implementations.

Note The Nexus 9000 series operates in standalone NX-OS mode or in application-centric infrastructure (ACI) mode, depending on what software and license is installed. This book covers only Nexus standalone configurations and troubleshooting.

The portfolio of Nexus switching products is always evolving. Check the product data sheets and documentation available on www.cisco.com for the latest information about each product.

NX-OS Architecture

Since its inception, the four fundamental pillars of NX-OS have been resiliency, virtualization, efficiency, and extensibility. The designers also wanted to provide a user interface that had an IOS-like look and feel so that customers migrating to NX-OS from legacy products feel comfortable deploying and operating them. The greatest improvements to the core operating system over IOS were in the following areas:

- Process scheduling
- Memory management
- Process isolation
- Management of feature processes

In NX-OS, feature processes are not started until they are configured by the user. This saves system resources and allows for greater scalability and efficiency. The features use their own memory and system resources, which adds stability to the operating system. Although similar in look and feel, under the hood, the NX-OS operating system has improved in many areas over Cisco's IOS operating system.

The NX-OS modular architecture is depicted in Figure 1-3.

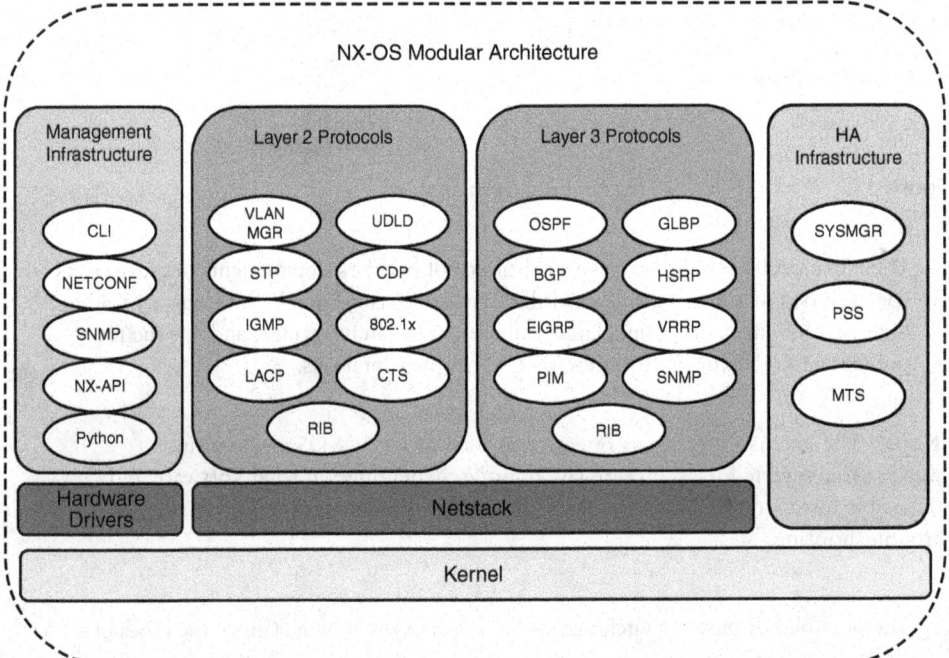

Figure 1-3 *NX-OS Modular Architecture*

Note The next section covers some of the fundamental NX-OS components that are of the most interest. Additional NX-OS services and components are explained in the context of specific examples throughout the remainder of this book.

The Kernel

The primary responsibility of the kernel is to manage the resources of the system and interface with the system hardware components. The NX-OS operating system uses a Linux kernel to provide key benefits, such as support for symmetric-multiprocessors (SMPs) and pre-emptive multitasking. Multithreaded processes can be scheduled and distributed across multiple processors for improved scalability. Each component process of the OS was designed to be modular, self-contained, and memory protected from other component processes. This approach results in a highly resilient system where process faults are isolated and therefore easier to recover from when failure occurs. This self-contained, self-healing approach means that recovery from such a condition is possible with no or minimal interruption because individual processes are restarted and the system self-heals without requiring a reload.

Note Historically, access to the Linux portion of NX-OS required the installation of a "debug plugin" by Cisco support personnel. However, on some platforms NX-OS now offers a **feature bash-shell** that allows users to access the underlying Linux portion of NX-OS.

System Manager (sysmgr)

The system manager is the NX-OS component that is responsible for the processes running on the system. That means that the system manager starts the processes and then monitors their health to ensure they are always functional. If a process fails, the system manager takes action to recover. Depending on the nature of the process, this action could be restarting the process in a stateful or stateless manner, or even initiating a system switchover (failover to the redundant supervisor) to recover the system if needed.

Processes in NX-OS are identified by a Universally Unique Identifier (UUID), which is used to identify the NX-OS service it represents. The UUID is used by NX-OS because a process ID (PID) may change, but the UUID remains consistent even if the PID changes.

The command **show system internal sysmgr service all** displays all the services, their UUID, and PID as shown in Example 1-1. Notice that the Netstack service has a PID of 6427 and a UUID of 0x00000221.

Example 1-1 show system internal sysmgr service all *Command*

```
NX-1# show system internal sysmgr service all
! Output omitted for brevity
Name                 UUID         PID    SAP    state      Start  Tag   Plugin ID
count
----------------     ----------   ----   ----   --------   -----  ---   ---------
aaa                  0x000000B5   6227   111    s0009      1      N/A   0
ospf                 0x41000119   13198  320    s0009      2      32    1
psshelper_gsvc       0x0000021A   6147   398    s0009      1      N/A   0
platform             0x00000018   5817   39     s0009      1      N/A   0
radius               0x000000B7   6455   113    s0009      1      N/A   0
securityd            0x0000002A   6225   55     s0009      1      N/A   0
tacacs               0x000000B6   6509   112    s0009      1      N/A   0
eigrp                0x41000130   [NA]   [NA]   s0075      1      N/A   1
mpls                 0x00000115   6936   274    s0009      1      N/A   1
mpls_oam             0x000002EF   6935   226    s0009      1      N/A   1
mpls_te              0x00000120   6934   289    s0009      1      N/A   1
mrib                 0x00000113   6825   255    s0009      1      N/A   1
netstack             0x00000221   6427   262    s0009      1      N/A   0
nfm                  0x00000195   6824   306    s0009      1      N/A   1
ntp                  0x00000047   6462   72     s0009      1      N/A   0
obfl                 0x0000012A   6228   1018   s0009      1      N/A   0
```

Additional details about a service, such as its current state, how many times it has restarted, and how many times it has crashed is viewed by using the UUID obtained in the output of the previous command. The syntax for the command is **show system internal sysmgr service uuid** *uuid* as demonstrated in Example 1-2.

Example 1-2 show system internal sysmgr service *Command*

```
NX-1# show system internal sysmgr service uuid 0x00000221
UUID = 0x221.
Service "netstack" ("netstack", 182):
        UUID = 0x221, PID = 6427, SAP = 262
        State: SRV_STATE_HANDSHAKED (entered at time Fri Feb 17 23:56:39 2017).
        Restart count: 1
        Time of last restart: Fri Feb 17 23:56:39 2017.
        The service never crashed since the last reboot.
        Tag = N/A
        Plugin ID: 0
```

Note If a service has crashed, the process name, PID, and date/time of the event is found in the output of **show cores**.

For NX-OS platforms with redundant supervisor modules, another important role of the system manager is to coordinate state between services on the active and standby supervisors. The system manager ensures synchronization in the event the active fails and the standby needs to take over.

Messages and Transactional Services

The modular and self-contained nature of NX-OS services necessitates that processes have a way for messages and data to be exchanged between processes while maintaining the self-contained architecture mentioned previously. The operating system component responsible for this service-to-service communication is the Messages and Transactional Services (MTS).

As the name implies, MTS is used for interprocess communication in NX-OS. This is facilitated using service access points (SAP) to allow services to exchange messages. To use an analogy, if the MTS is the postal service, think of the SAP as a post office box for a process. Messages are sent and received by a process using its SAP over MTS.

The system manager table output referenced previously is used again to reference a service name and find its UUID, PID, and the SAP. This SAP number is then used to get details from MTS on the number of messages exchanged and what the state of the MTS buffers are for this service. To illustrate this, an OSPF process is configured with a process tag of 32. Example 1-3 shows the OSPF process in the output of **show system internal sysmgr service all**. This output is used to locate the UUID 0x41000119, the PID of 13198, and the SAP of 320.

Example 1-3 *Locate the UUID for a Service Name*

```
NX-1# show system internal sysmgr service all
! Output omitted for brevity
Name                UUID        PID     SAP     state       Start   Tag     Plugin ID
count
----------------    ----------  ------  -----   ---------   ------  ---     ---------

aaa                 0x000000B5  6227    111     s0009       1       N/A     0
ospf                0x41000119  13198   320     s0009       2       32      1
psshelper_gsvc      0x0000021A  6147    398     s0009       1       N/A     0
platform            0x00000018  5817    39      s0009       1       N/A     0
```

In Example 1-4, the **show system internal mts sup sap** *sap-id* [**description** | **uuid** | **stats**] command is used to obtain details about a particular SAP. To examine a particular SAP, first confirm that the service name and UUID match the values from the **show system internal sysmgr services all** command. This is a sanity check to ensure the correct SAP is being investigated. The output of **show system internal mts sup sap** *sap-id* [**description**] should match the service name, and the output of **show system internal mts sup sap** *sap-id* [**UUID**] should match the UUID in the sysmgr output. Next examine the MTS statistics for the SAP. This output is useful to determine what the maximum value of the

MTS queue was (high-water mark), as well as examining the number of messages this service has exchanged. If the *max_q_size ever reached* is equal to the *hard_q_limit* it is possible that MTS has dropped messages for that service.

Example 1-4 *Examining the MTS Queue for a SAP*

```
NX-1# show system internal mts sup sap 320 description
Below shows sap on default-VDC, to show saps on non-default VDC, run
        show system internal mts node sup-<vnode-id> sap ...
ospf-32
NX-1# show system internal mts sup sap 320 uuid
Below shows sap on default-VDC, to show saps on non-default VDC, run
        show system internal mts node sup-<vnode-id> sap ...
1090519321
NX-1# show system internal mts sup sap 320 stats
Below shows sap on default-VDC, to show saps on non-default VDC, run
        show system internal mts node sup-<vnode-id> sap ...
msg tx: 40
byte tx: 6829
msg rx: 20
byte rx: 2910

opc sent to myself: 32768
max_q_size q_len limit (soft q limit): 1024
max_q_size q_bytes limit (soft q limit): 50%
max_q_size ever reached: 13
max_fast_q_size (hard q limit): 4096
rebind count: 0
Waiting for response: none
buf in transit: 40
bytes in transit: 6829

NX-1# hex 1090519321
0x41000119
NX-1# dec 0x41000119
1090519321
```

Note In the output of Example 1-4, the UUID is displayed as a decimal value, whereas in the output from the system manager it is given as hexadecimal. NX-OS has a built-in utility to do the conversion using the **hex** *value* or **dec** *value* command.

The NX-OS MTS service is covered in more detail in Chapter 3, "Troubleshooting Nexus Platform Issues," along with additional troubleshooting examples.

Persistent Storage Services

To achieve the level of resilience desired for NX-OS, its designers needed a way for services to be recovered by the system with minimal disruption. This necessitates a way of not only monitoring and restarting a failed service, but also restoring its run-time state so the restarted service can resume functioning after a restart or failure. The system manager, MTS, and the Persistent Storage Service (PSS) provide the NX-OS infrastructure requirements to achieve high availability. The system manager is responsible for starting, stopping, and monitoring heartbeats from services to ensure they are functioning correctly. The PSS service provides a way of storing run-time data so that it is available during recovery of a failed or restarted process.

The PSS provides reliable and persistent storage for NX-OS services in a lightweight key/value pair database. Two types of storage are offered by PSS, *volatile* and *nonvolatile*. The volatile storage is in RAM and is used to store service state that needs to survive a process restart or crash. The second type is nonvolatile, which is stored in flash. Nonvolatile PSS is used to store service state that needs to survive a system reload. Example 1-5 uses the **show system internal flash** command to examine the flash file system and demonstrates how to verify the current available space for the nonvolatile PSS.

Example 1-5 *Verify the Size and Location of PSS in the Flash File System*

```
NX-1# show system internal flash
Mount-on                    1K-blocks      Used   Available   Use%  Filesystem
/                              409600     65624      343976    17   /dev/root
/proc                               0         0           0     0   proc
/sys                                0         0           0     0   none
/isan                         1572864    679068      893796    44   none
/var                            51200       488       50712     1   none
/etc                             5120      1856        3264    37   none
/nxos/tmp                      102400      2496       99904     3   none
/var/log                        51200      1032       50168     3   none
/var/home                        5120        36        5084     1   none
/var/tmp                       307200       744      306456     1   none
/var/sysmgr                   3670016       664     3669352     1   none
/var/sysmgr/ftp                819200    219536      599664    27   none
/var/sysmgr/srv_logs           102400         0      102400     0   none
/var/sysmgr/ftp/debug_logs      10240         0       10240     0   none
/dev/shm                      3145728    964468     2181260    31   none
/volatile                      512000         0      512000     0   none
/debug                           5120        32        5088     1   none
/dev/mqueue                         0         0           0     0   none
/debugfs                            0         0           0     0   nodev
/mnt/plog                      242342      5908      223921     3   /dev/sdc1
/mnt/fwimg                     121171      4127      110788     4   /dev/sdc3
/mnt/cfg/0                      75917      5580       66417     8   /dev/md5
```

/mnt/cfg/1	75415	5580	65941	8	/dev/md6
/bootflash	1773912	1046944	636856	63	/dev/md3
/cgroup	0	0	0	0	vdccontrol
/var/sysmgr/startup-cfg	409600	15276	394324	4	none
/dev/pts	0	0	0	0	devpts
/mnt/pss	38172	9391	26810	26	/dev/md4
/usbslot1	7817248	5750464	2066784	74	/dev/sdb1
/fwimg_tmp	131072	508	130564	1	tmpfs

An NX-OS service utilizes volatile and nonvolatile PSS to checkpoint its run-time data as needed. Consistent with the modular nature of NX-OS, PSS does not dictate what is stored in which type of PSS and leaves that decision to the service. PSS simply provides the infrastructure to allow services to store and retrieve their data.

Feature Manager

Features in NX-OS are enabled on-demand and only consume system resources such as memory, CPU time, MTS queues, and PSS when they have been enabled. If a feature is in use and is then later shut down by the operator, the resources associated with that feature are freed and reclaimed by the system. The task of enabling or disabling features is handled by the NX-OS infrastructure component known as the *feature manager*. The feature manager is also responsible for maintaining and tracking the operational state of all features in the system.

To better understand the role of the feature manager and its interaction with other services, let's review a specific example. An operator wants to enable BGP on a particular Nexus switch. Because services in NX-OS are not started until they are enabled, the user must first enter the **feature bgp** command in configuration mode. The feature manager acts on this request by ensuring the proper license is in place for the feature, and then feature manager sends a message to the system manager to start the service. When the BGP service is started, it binds to an MTS SAP, creates its PSS entries to store run-time state, and then informs the system manager. The BGP service then registers itself with the feature manager where the operational state is changed to *enabled*.

When a feature is disabled by a user, a similar set of events occur in reverse order. The feature manager asks the service to disable itself. The feature empties its MTS buffers and destroys its PSS data and then communicates with the system manager and feature manager, which sets the operational state to *disabled*.

It is important to note that some services have dependencies on other services. If a service is started and its dependencies are not satisfied, additional services are started so the feature operates correctly. An example of this is the BGP feature that depends on the route policy manager (RPM). The most important concept to understand from this is that services implement one or multiple features and dependencies exist. Except for the fact that a user must enable features, the rest of this is transparent to the user, and NX-OS takes care of the dependencies automatically.

NX-OS Architecture

Certain complex features require the user to specifically install a *feature set* before the associated feature is enabled. MPLS, FEX, and Fabricpath are a few examples. To enable these features, the user must first install the feature set with the **install feature-set** [*feature*] command. The feature set is then enabled with the **feature-set** [*feature*] command.

Note The license manager tracks all the feature licenses on the system. When a license expires, the license manager notifies the feature manager to shut down the feature.

In Example 1-6, the current state of a feature is verified using the **show system internal feature-mgr feature state** command. The output is provided in a table format that lists the *feature name*, along with its *UUID*, *state*, and *reason* for the current state. In Example 1-6, several features have been enabled successfully by the feature manager, including two instances of EIGRP. The output also displays instances of a feature that have not yet been enabled, such as EIGRP instance 3 through 16.

Example 1-6 *Checking the Feature Manager State for a Feature*

```
NX-1# show system internal feature-mgr feature state
! Output omitted for brevity
Feature              UUID         State     Reason
--------------------  ----------  --------  --------------------
bfd                  0x000002c2   enabled   SUCCESS
bfd_app              0x000002c9   enabled   SUCCESS
bgp                  0x0000011b   disabled  feature never enabled
cts                  0x0000021e   disabled  feature never enabled
dhcp                 0x000001ba   enabled   SUCCESS
dot1x                0x0000017d   disabled  feature never enabled
__inst_1__eigrp      0x41000130   enabled   SUCCESS
__inst_2__eigrp      0x42000130   enabled   SUCCESS
__inst_3__eigrp      0x43000130   disabled  feature never enabled
__inst_4__eigrp      0x44000130   disabled  feature never enabled
__inst_5__eigrp      0x45000130   disabled  feature never enabled
__inst_6__eigrp      0x46000130   disabled  feature never enabled
__inst_7__eigrp      0x47000130   disabled  feature never enabled
__inst_8__eigrp      0x48000130   disabled  feature never enabled
__inst_9__eigrp      0x49000130   disabled  feature never enabled
__inst_10__eigrp     0x4a000130   disabled  feature never enabled
__inst_11__eigrp     0x4b000130   disabled  feature never enabled
__inst_12__eigrp     0x4c000130   disabled  feature never enabled
__inst_13__eigrp     0x4d000130   disabled  feature never enabled
__inst_14__eigrp     0x4e000130   disabled  feature never enabled
__inst_15__eigrp     0x4f000130   disabled  feature never enabled
__inst_16__eigrp     0x50000130   disabled  feature never enabled
..
```

Although problems with feature manager are not common, NX-OS does provide a way to verify whether errors have occurred using the command-line interface (CLI). Although no error codes are present in this output, Example 1-7 shows how to obtain an error code for a specific feature if it existed, using the **show system internal feature-mgr feature action** command.

Example 1-7 *Check for Feature Manager Errors*

```
NX-1# show system internal feature-mgr feature action
Feature                 Action    Status    Error-code
--------------------    --------  --------  --------------------
tacacs                  none      none      SUCCESS
scheduler               none      none      SUCCESS
bgp                     none      none      SUCCESS
pim                     enable    none      SUCCESS
msdp                    none      none      SUCCESS
pim6                    none      none      SUCCESS
__inst_1__eigrp         enable    none      SUCCESS
__inst_2__eigrp         enable    none      SUCCESS
__inst_3__eigrp         none      none      SUCCESS
__inst_4__eigrp         none      none      SUCCESS
__inst_5__eigrp         none      none      SUCCESS
__inst_6__eigrp         none      none      SUCCESS
__inst_7__eigrp         none      none      SUCCESS
__inst_8__eigrp         none      none      SUCCESS
__inst_9__eigrp         none      none      SUCCESS
__inst_10__eigrp        none      none      SUCCESS
__inst_11__eigrp        none      none      SUCCESS
__inst_12__eigrp        none      none      SUCCESS
__inst_13__eigrp        none      none      SUCCESS
__inst_14__eigrp        none      none      SUCCESS
__inst_15__eigrp        none      none      SUCCESS
__inst_16__eigrp        none      none      SUCCESS
lacp                    none      none      SUCCESS
dot1x                   none      none      SUCCESS
glbp                    none      none      SUCCESS
```

Note NX-OS maintains a running log of events for many features and services referred to as *event history logs*, which are discussed later in this chapter and referenced throughout this book. Feature manager provides two event history logs (errors and messages) that provide additional detail for troubleshooting purposes. The output is obtained using the **show system internal feature-mgr event-history** [*msgs* | *errors*] command.

NX-OS Line Card Microcode

Distributed line cards run a microcode version of the NX-OS operating system, as depicted in Figure 1-4. The modular architecture of NX-OS allows the foundational concepts and components of the software to be applied consistently to the line card as well as the system overall.

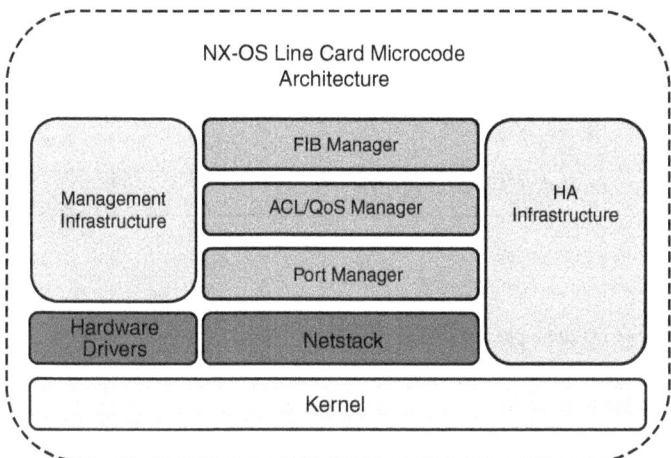

Figure 1-4 *NX-OS Modular Line Card Microcode Architecture*

During system boot, or if a card is inserted into the chassis, the supervisor decides if it should power on the card or not. This is done by checking the card type and verifying that the required power, software, and hardware resources are in place for the card to operate correctly. If so, the decision to power on the card is made. From that point, the line card powers on and executes its Basic Input/Output System (BIOS), power-on self-tests, and starts its system manager. Next, all the line card services are started that are required for normal operation. Communication and messaging channels are established to the supervisor that allow the supervisor to push the configuration and line card software upgrades as needed. Additional services are started for local handling of exception logging, management of environmental sensors, the card LEDs, health monitoring, and so on. After the critical system services are started, the individual ASICs are started, which allow the card to forward traffic.

In the operational state packets are forwarded and communications occur as needed with the supervisor to update counters, statistics, and environmental data. The line card has local storage for PSS as well as for On-Board Failure Logging (OBFL). The OBFL data is stored in nonvolatile memory so that it can survive reloads and is an excellent source of data for troubleshooting problems specific to the line card. Information such as exception history, card boot history, environmental history and much more is stored in the OBFL storage.

For day-to-day operations, there is typically no need to enter the line card CLI. The NX-OS operating system and distributed platforms are designed to be configured and managed from the supervisor module. There are some instances where direct access to the CLI of a line card is required. Typically, these scenarios also involve working with Cisco TAC to collect data and troubleshoot the various line card subsystems. In Example 1-8, the line card CLI is entered from the supervisor module using the **attach module** command. Notice that the prompt changes to indicate which module the user is currently connected to. After the user has entered the line card CLI, the **show hardware internal dev-port-map** command is issued, which displays the mapping of front panel ports to the various ASICs of the card on this Nexus 7000 M2 series card.

Example 1-8 *Use of the* **attach module** *CLI from the Supervisor*

```
NX-1# attach module 10
Attaching to module 10 ...
To exit type 'exit', to abort type '$.'
module-10# show hardware internal dev-port-map
--------------------------------------------------------------
CARD_TYPE:          24 port 10G
>Front Panel ports:24
--------------------------------------------------------------
  Device name             Dev role               Abbr num_inst:
--------------------------------------------------------------
> Skytrain                DEV_QUEUEING           QUEUE   4
> Valkyrie                DEV_REWRITE            RWR_0   4
> Eureka                  DEV_LAYER_2_LOOKUP     L2LKP   2
> Lamira                  DEV_LAYER_3_LOOKUP     L3LKP   2
> Garuda                  DEV_ETHERNET_MAC       MAC_0   2
> EDC                     DEV_PHY                PHYS    6
> Sacramento Xbar ASIC    DEV_SWITCH_FABRIC      SWICHF  1
+------------------------------------------------------------+
+-----------------+++FRONT PANEL PORT TO ASIC INSTANCE MAP+++------------+
+------------------------------------------------------------+
 FP port |  PHYS | SECUR | MAC_0 | RWR_0 | L2LKP | L3LKP | QUEUE |SWICHF
    1       0       0       0      0,1      0       0      0,1     0
    2       0       0       0      0,1      0       0      0,1     0
    3       0       0       0      0,1      0       0      0,1     0
    4       0       0       0      0,1      0       0      0,1     0
    5       1       0       0      0,1      0       0      0,1     0
    6       1       0       0      0,1      0       0      0,1     0
    7       1       0       0      0,1      0       0      0,1     0
    8       1       0       0      0,1      0       0      0,1     0
```

```
 9     2    0    0    0,1    0    0    0,1    0
10     2    0    0    0,1    0    0    0,1    0
11     2    0    0    0,1    0    0    0,1    0
12     2    0    0    0,1    0    0    0,1    0
13     3    1    1    2,3    1    1    2,3    0
14     3    1    1    2,3    1    1    2,3    0
15     3    1    1    2,3    1    1    2,3    0
16     3    1    1    2,3    1    1    2,3    0
17     4    1    1    2,3    1    1    2,3    0
18     4    1    1    2,3    1    1    2,3    0
19     4    1    1    2,3    1    1    2,3    0
20     4    1    1    2,3    1    1    2,3    0
21     5    1    1    2,3    1    1    2,3    0
22     5    1    1    2,3    1    1    2,3    0
23     5    1    1    2,3    1    1    2,3    0
24     5    1    1    2,3    1    1    2,3    0
+---------------------------------------------------------------------+
+---------------------------------------------------------------------+
```

Note A common reason to access a line card's CLI is to run embedded logic analyzer module (ELAM) packet captures on the local forwarding engine. ELAM is a tool used to troubleshoot data plane forwarding and hardware forwarding table programming problems. ELAM capture is outside the scope of this book.

File Systems

The file system is a vital component of any operating system, and NX-OS is no exception. The file system contains the directories and files needed by the operating system to boot, log events, and store data generated by the user, such as support files, debug outputs, and scripts. It is also used to store the configuration and any data that services store in non-volatile PSS, which aids in system recovery after a failure.

Working with the NX-OS file system is similar to working with files in Cisco's IOS, with some improvements. Files and directories are created and deleted from *bootflash:* or the external USB memory referred to as *slot0:*. Archive files are created and compress large files, like show techs, to save space. Table 1-1 provides a list of file system commands that are needed to manage and troubleshoot an NX-OS switch.

Table 1-1 *File System Commands*

Command	Purpose
pwd	Displays the name of the current directory
cd {*directory*	*filesystem:*[*//module/*][*directory*]}	Changes to a new current directory
dir [*directory*	*filesystem:*[*//module/*][*directory*]]	Displays the directory contents
mkdir [*filesystem:*[*//module/*]]*directory*	Creates a new directory
rmdir [*filesystem* :[*//module/*]]*directory*	Deletes a directory
move [*filesystem:*[*//module/*][*directory* /]	*directory/*] *source-filename* {[*filesystem:*[*//module/*][*directory* /]	*directory/*][*target-filename*]	*target-filename*}	Moves a file
copy [*filesystem:*[*//module/*][*directory/*]	*directory/*] *source-filename*	{[*filesystem:*[*//module/*][*directory/*]]	*directory/*][*target-filename*]	Copies a file
delete {*filesystem:*[*//module/*][*directory/*]	*directory/*} *filename*	Deletes a file
show file [*filesystem:*[*//module/*]][*directory/*]*filename*	Displays the contents of a file
gzip [*filesystem:*[*//module/*][*directory/*]	*directory/*] *filename*	Compresses a file
gunzip [*filesystem:*[*//module/*] [*directory/*]	*directory/*]*filename.gz*	Uncompresses a file
tar create {**bootflash:**	**volatile:**}*archive-filename* [**absolute**] [**bz2-compress**] [**gz-compress**] [**remove**] [**uncompressed**] [**verbose**] *filename-list*	Creates an archive file and adds files to it
tar append {**bootflash:**	**volatile:**}*archive-filename* [**absolute**] [**remove**] [**verbose**] *filename-list*	Adds files to an existing archive
tar extract {**bootflash:**	**volatile:**}*archive-filename* [**keep-old**] [**screen**] [**to** {**bootflash:**	**volatile:**} [*/directory-name*]] [**verbose**]	Extracts files from an existing archive

Note The **gzip** and **tar** options are useful when working with data collected during troubleshooting. Multiple files are combined into an archive and compressed for easy export to a central server for analysis.

Flash File System

The flash file system is used to store the system image and user-generated files. To see the contents of a directory in the file system, use the **dir** [*directory* | *filesystem*:[*//module/*] [*directory*]] command. In Example 1-9, notice the NX-OS image files are present in the *bootflash:* directory.

Example 1-9 *Output of the* **dir bootflash:** *Command*

```
NX-1# dir bootflash:
      4096    May 02 18:57:24 2017  .patch/
      7334    Jan 26 00:57:28 2017  LDP.txt
      1135    Mar 02 02:00:38 2016  MDS201309060745595990.lic
       580    Mar 02 02:00:12 2016  MDS201309060748159200.lic
       584    Mar 02 01:59:01 2016  MDS201309060749036210.lic
       552    Mar 02 01:56:02 2016  MDS201309071119059040.lic
      1558    Apr 21 05:21:39 2017  eigrp_route_clear.txt
      4096    Apr 29 09:37:44 2017  lost+found/
 425228450    Jun 30 01:27:40 2017  n7000-s2-dk9.6.2.12.bin
 580426199    Apr 06 20:08:12 2017  n7000-s2-dk9.7.3.1.D1.1.bin
  67492267    Dec 06 02:00:13 2016  n7000-s2-epld.6.2.14.img
  36633088    Jun 30 01:29:42 2017  n7000-s2-kickstart.6.2.12.bin
  36708352    May 24 01:43:48 2017  n7000-s2-kickstart.6.2.18.bin
  37997056    Apr 18 22:37:46 2017  n7000-s2-kickstart.7.2.2.D1.2.bin
  46800896    Apr 06 20:07:20 2017  n7000-s2-kickstart.7.3.1.D1.1.bin
      3028    Jun 13 00:06:22 2017  netflow_cap.pcap
         0    Apr 21 02:11:19 2017  script_out.log
        13    Apr 21 03:15:32 2017  script_output.txt
      4096    Apr 18 19:35:28 2016  scripts/
     17755    Mar 20 05:36:52 2016  startup-config-defaultconfig-DONOTDELETE
      4096    Nov 11 00:30:10 2016  vdc_2/
      4096    Apr 21 02:25:04 2017  vdc_3/
      4096    Dec 05 19:07:18 2016  vdc_4/
      4096    Apr 03 04:31:36 2016  vdc_5/
      4096    Apr 12 22:26:42 2013  vdc_6/
      4096    Apr 12 22:26:42 2013  vdc_7/
      4096    Apr 12 22:26:42 2013  vdc_8/
      4096    Apr 12 22:26:42 2013  vdc_9/
      4096    Apr 18 19:33:57 2016  virtual-instance/
      4096    Apr 18 20:36:58 2016  virtual-instance-stby-sync/
       664    Jun 30 02:17:45 2017  vlan.dat
     45137    Jun 30 01:33:45 2017  vtp_debug.log

Usage for bootflash://sup-local
 1370902528 bytes used
  445583360 bytes free
 1816485888 bytes total
```

This provides the list of files and subdirectories on the currently active supervisor. For platforms with redundant supervisors, directories of the standby supervisor are accessed as demonstrated in Example 1-10 by appending **//sup-standby/** to the directory path.

Example 1-10 *Listing the Files on the Standby Supervisor*

```
NX-1# dir bootflash://sup-standby/
      4096    Jun 12 20:31:56 2017  .patch/
      1135    Mar 03 00:07:58 2016  MDS201309060745595990.lic
       580    Mar 03 00:08:09 2016  MDS201309060748159200.lic
       584    Mar 03 00:08:20 2016  MDS201309060749036210.lic
       552    Mar 03 00:08:32 2016  MDS201309071119059040.lic
      4096    May 24 01:27:09 2017  lost+found/
 580426199    Apr 14 20:53:14 2017  n7000-s2-dk9.7.3.1.D1.1.bin
 579340490    Jun 13 19:40:12 2017  n7000-s2-dk9.8.0.1.bin
  36633088    Jun 30 01:49:14 2017  n7000-s2-kickstart.6.2.12.bin
  36708352    May 24 01:17:23 2017  n7000-s2-kickstart.6.2.18.bin
  37997056    Apr 18 22:37:46 2017  n7000-s2-kickstart.7.2.2.D1.2.bin
  46800896    Apr 14 20:50:38 2017  n7000-s2-kickstart.7.3.1.D1.1.bin
      8556    May 05 10:57:35 2017  pim-2nd.pcap
         0    May 05 10:05:45 2017  pim-first
      3184    May 05 10:12:24 2017  pim-first.pcap
      4096    Apr 18 20:28:05 2016  scripts/
      4096    May 19 22:42:12 2017  vdc_2/
      4096    Jul 18 21:22:15 2016  vdc_3/
      4096    Jul 18 21:22:49 2016  vdc_4/
      4096    Mar 02 08:23:14 2016  vdc_5/
      4096    Nov 28 05:52:06 2014  vdc_6/
      4096    Nov 28 05:52:06 2014  vdc_7/
      4096    Nov 28 05:52:06 2014  vdc_8/
      4096    Nov 28 05:52:06 2014  vdc_9/
      4096    Apr 18 19:46:52 2016  virtual-instance/
      4096    Apr 18 20:40:29 2016  virtual-instance-stby-sync/
       664    Jun 30 02:17:45 2017  vlan.dat
     12888    Jun 12 20:34:40 2017  vtp_debug.log

Usage for bootflash://sup-standby
 1458462720 bytes used
  315793408 bytes free
 1774256128 bytes total
```

Onboard Failure Logging

Onboard failure logging (OBFL) is a persistent storage available on Nexus platforms and is used to store operational information local to the card. Example 1-11 displays the different options that are enabled by default on a Nexus 7000 platform for an M2 I/O module. Having this persistent historical information is extremely useful for troubleshooting a module problem.

Example 1-11 *Confirm OBFL Is Enabled on a Module*

```
NX-1# show logging onboard module 10 status
---------------------------
OBFL Status
---------------------------
    Switch OBFL Log:                                    Enabled

    Module: 10 OBFL Log:                                Enabled
    counter-stats                                       Enabled
    cpu-hog                                             Enabled
    credit-loss                                         Enabled
    environmental-history                               Enabled
    error-stats                                         Enabled
    exception-log                                       Enabled
    interrupt-stats                                     Enabled
    mem-leak                                            Enabled
    miscellaneous-error                                 Enabled
    obfl-log (boot-uptime/device-version/obfl-history)  Enabled
    register-log                                        Enabled
    request-timeout                                     Enabled
    system-health                                       Enabled
    stack-trace                                         Enabled
```

Note The output in Example 1-11 is from a distributed platform; however, OBFL data is available for nondistributed platforms as well. The items enabled depend on the platform. Configure the OBFL options using the **hw-module logging onboard** configuration command with various subcommand options. There is typically no reason to disable OBFL.

Logflash

Logflash is a persistent storage location used to store system logs, syslog messages, debug output, and core files. On some Nexus platforms the logflash is an external compact flash or USB that may have not been installed, or was removed at some point. The system prints a periodic message indicating the logflash is missing to alert the operator about this condition so that it can be corrected. It is recommended to have the logflash mounted and available for use by the system so that any operational data is stored there. In the event of a problem, the persistent nature of logflash means that this data is available for analysis. Example 1-12 uses the **show system internal flash** to verify that *logflash:* is mounted and how much free space is available.

Example 1-12 *Verifying the State and Available Space for the logflash:*

```
NX-1# show system internal flash | egrep Filesystem|logflash
Filesystem       1K-blocks    Used Available Use% Mounted on
/dev/sda7         8256952   164288   7673236   3% /logflash
```

The contents of the logflash directory is examined using the **dir logflash:** as shown in Example 1-13.

Example 1-13 *Verifying the Contents of the logflash: Directory*

```
NX-1# dir logflash:
       4096    Jun 05 17:43:10 2017  ISSU_debug_logs/
       4096    May 19 13:00:36 2017  controller/
       4096    Mar 30 14:03:38 2017  core/
       4096    Mar 30 14:03:38 2017  debug/
       4096    Jul 10 16:43:33 2017  debug_logs/
     413807    Mar 30 14:02:21 2017  dme.log.2017.03.30.21.02.21.tar.gz
     148751    Mar 31 12:21:01 2017  dme.log.2017.03.31.19.21.01.tar.gz
     144588    May 19 12:58:31 2017  dme.log.2017.05.19.19.58.31.tar.gz
       4096    Mar 30 14:03:38 2017  generic/
       4096    Mar 30 13:58:28 2017  log/
      16384    Mar 30 13:57:52 2017  lost+found/
       4096    Jun 13 21:29:33 2017  vdc_1/

Usage for logflash://sup-local
  597725184 bytes used
 7857393664 bytes free
 8455118848 bytes total
```

Example 1-14 demonstrates using the **show file** command to print the contents of a file in *logflash:*.

Example 1-14 *Viewing the Contents of a Specific File in logflash:*

```
NX-1# show file logflash://sup-local/log/messages
2017 Mar 30 20:58:30  %VDC_MGR-5-VDC_STATE_CHANGE:
vdc 1 state changed to create in progress
2017 Mar 30 20:58:30  %VDC_MGR-5-VDC_STATE_CHANGE:
vdc 1 state changed to create pending
2017 Mar 30 20:58:31  Mar 30 20:58:30 %KERN-3-SYSTEM_MSG: [ 2726.358042]
biosinfo checksum failed expected ff Got 8    - kernel
2017 Mar 30 20:58:31  Mar 30 20:58:30 %KERN-3-SYSTEM_MSG: [ 2726.358044]
read_from_biosinfo: No Valid biosinfo - kernel
2017 Mar 30 20:58:31  %VMAN-2-INSTALL_STATE: Installing virtual service
'guestshell+'
```

```
2017 Mar 30 20:58:33   netstack: Registration with cli server complete
2017 Mar 30 20:58:48   %USER-2-SYSTEM_MSG:
ssnmgr_app_init called on ssnmgr up - aclmgr
2017 Mar 30 20:58:54   %USER-0-SYSTEM_MSG: end of default policer - copp
2017 Mar 30 20:58:54   %COPP-2-COPP_NO_POLICY: Control-plane is unprotected.
2017 Mar 30 20:58:56   %CARDCLIENT-2-FPGA_BOOT_PRIMARY: IOFPGA booted from Primary
2017 Mar 30 20:58:56   %CARDCLIENT-2-FPGA_BOOT_PRIMARY: MIFPGA booted from Primary
```

Understanding NX-OS Software Releases and Packaging

The publishing of a new NX-OS software version is categorized into one of three types of releases (Major/Minor/Maintenance). In general:

- Major releases introduce significant new features, functions, and platforms.
- Minor releases enhance the features and functions of an existing major release.
- Maintenance releases address product defects in a minor release.

Depending on the Nexus platform and release, the naming convention of the software version varies. In early versions of NX-OS, each platform was built on its own NX-OS operating system code base. Today the majority of platforms use a NX-OS common base operating system. This common base code is then modified or augmented as needed to meet the feature requirements or hardware support of a specific platform. The advantage of this approach is that fixes for software defects in the platform independent base code are now incorporated back into the common base, and all platforms benefit from those fixes.

Figure 1-5 explains how to interpret the NX-OS software naming convention to recognize the Major/Minor/Maintenance release portions of the image name for a 6.2 release of NX-OS for the Nexus 7000 platform.

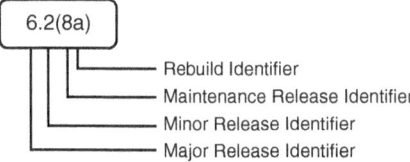

Figure 1-5 *NX-OS Software Naming Convention*

Figure 1-6 explains how to interpret the NX-OS software naming convention with the common platform independent base code and platform dependent release details for the Nexus 7000 platform.

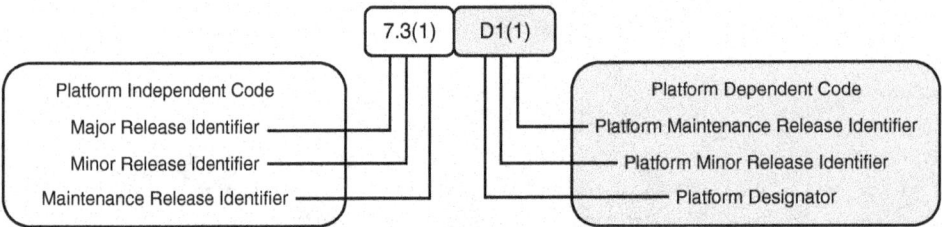

Figure 1-6 *NX-OS Software Naming Convention with Platform Designator*

The current NX-OS Platform Designators are as follows:

- I—Nexus 9000 and 3000 common code base
- D—Nexus 7000/7700
- N—Nexus 5000/6000
- U—Nexus 3000 for releases before the common code base
- A—Nexus 3548

Note The Nexus 3000 and Nexus 9000 series platforms now share a common platform-dependent software base, and the image name begins with *nxos*; for example, *nxos.7.0.3.I6.1.bin*.

In addition to the Major/Minor/Maintenance designation, releases are also classified as *long-lived* or *short-lived* releases, which describe their development life cycle. Long-lived releases are typically recommended over short-lived releases for most deployments when the required features and hardware are supported. Long-lived releases typically have more maintenance rebuilds that harden the software and add bug fixes with each new rebuild. Short-lived releases introduce new hardware or software features and receive maintenance releases as needed. Short-lived releases do not receive the same duration of support and have fewer maintenance rebuilds when compared with long-lived releases. The recommendation is to migrate away from a short-lived release when the feature requirements and hardware support are available in a long-lived release.

The NX-OS operating system is available on www.cisco.com; it consists of a kickstart image and a system image. Exceptions are the Nexus 9000 and Nexus 3000, which use a single system image file. For platforms that utilize the kickstart image, the kickstart image is booted first by the BIOS, and then the kickstart image loads the system image. For Nexus 3000 and Nexus 9000 platforms, a single binary file is booted directly.

Upgrading the Erasable Programmable Logic Device (EPLD) image is also possible on some platforms. The EPLD image is packaged separately from the NX-OS operating system. The EPLD image upgrades firmware on the hardware components of the I/O modules or line cards to offer new hardware functionality or to resolve known problems without having to replace the hardware.

> **Note** Not every NX-OS system upgrade requires an EPLD upgrade. The procedure for installing NX-OS software and EPLD images are documented with examples for each Nexus platform on www.cisco.com. Refer to the Software Upgrade and Installation Guides for more details.

Software Maintenance Upgrades

A recent addition to NX-OS is the capability to apply specific bug fixes as a patch to the currently installed software. This concept is familiar to those with experience on the Cisco IOS-XR platforms. NX-OS uses the same terminology.

The Software Maintenance Upgrade (SMU) feature allows network operators to apply a specific bug fix to their Nexus switch without requiring a system reload or in-service software upgrade (ISSU). Critical network environments do not upgrade software without extensive qualification testing specific to their architecture and configured features.

Previously if a bug fix was needed, a new maintenance release of NX-OS had to undergo qualification testing and then be rolled out to the network. This obviously adds delay waiting for the fix to be released in a maintenance release of NX-OS, as well as the delay accrued during qualification testing before the network was finally patched to eliminate the problem. This delay is solved with the SMU concept because only the SMU changes are applied to the already qualified base image. The SMU installation procedure leverages process restart or ISSU when possible to minimize impact to the network during installation. The Nexus switch then runs with the SMU applied until the specific bug fix is available in a qualified NX-OS maintenance release on Cisco.com.

> **Note** An SMU is valid only for the image it was created for. If the NX-OS software is upgraded to another release, the SMU is deactivated. It is critical to ensure any applicable software defects are fixed in the new version of software before performing an upgrade.

The SMU files are packaged as a binary and a README.txt that detail the associated bugs that are addressed by the SMU. The naming convention of the SMU file is *platform-package_type.release_version.Bug_ID.file_type*. For example, *n7700-s2-dk9.7.3.1.D1.1.CSCvc44582.bin*. The general procedure for installing a SMU follows:

Step 1. Copy the package file or files to a local storage device or file server.

Step 2. Add the package or packages on the device using the **install add** command.

Step 3. Activate the package or packages on the device using the **install activate** command.

Step 4. Commit the current set of packages using the **install commit** command. However, in case of the reload or ISSU SMU, commit the packages after the reload or ISSU.

Step 5. (Optional) Deactivate and remove the package, when desired.

> **Note** Before attempting the installation of an SMU, please review the detailed examples on www.cisco.com for the platform.

Licensing

NX-OS requires that the operator obtain and install appropriate license files for the features being enabled. Typically, Nexus platforms support a base feature set with no additional license requirements. This includes most Layer 2 functionality and generally some form of Layer 3 routing support. To enable advanced features, such as MPLS, OTV, FabricPath, FCoE, advanced routing, or VXLAN, additional licenses may need to be installed depending on the platform. In addition to feature licenses, several Nexus platforms also offer licenses to provide additional hardware capabilities. For example, *SCALEABLE_SERVICES_PKT* on the Nexus 7000 series enables XL-capable I/O modules to operate in XL mode and take full advantage of their larger table sizes. Another example is the port upgrade licenses available for some Nexus 3000 platforms.

License enforcement is built in to the NX-OS operating system by the feature manager, which disables services if the appropriate licenses are not present. If a specific feature is not configurable, the most likely culprit is a missing license. Cisco does allow for feature testing without a license by configuring the **license grace-period** in global configuration, which allows features to function for up to 120 days without the license installed. This does not cover all feature licenses on all platforms, however. Most notably the Nexus 9000 and Nexus 3000 do not support license grace-period.

License files are downloaded from www.cisco.com. To obtain a license file you need the serial number that is found with the **show license host-id** command. Next, use the product authorization key (PAK) from your software license claim to retrieve the license file and copy it to your switch. Installation of a license is a nondisruptive task and is accomplished with the **install license** command. For platforms that support virtual device contexts (VDC) the license is installed and managed on the default VDC and applies for all VDCs present on the chassis. The license installation is verified with the **show license** command.

NX-OS High-Availability Infrastructure

The system manager, MTS, and PSS infrastructure components that were described previously in this chapter provide NX-OS with the core of its high-availability infrastructure. This high-availability infrastructure enables NX-OS to seamlessly recover from most failure scenarios, such as a supervisor switchover or a process restart.

NX-OS is capable of restarting a service to recover and resume normal operation while minimizing impact to the data plane traffic being forwarded. This process restart event is either *stateful* or *stateless* and occurs when initiated by the user, or automatically when the system manager identifies a process failure.

In the event of a stateless restart, all the run-time data structures associated with the failed process are lost, and the system manager quickly spawns a new process to replace the one that failed. A stateful restart means that a portion of the run-time data is used to recover and seamlessly resume functioning where the previous process left off after a process failure or restart. Stateful restart is possible because the service updates its state in PSS while active and then recovers the important run-time data structures from PSS after a failure. Persistent MTS messages left in the process queue are picked up by the restarted service to allow a seamless recovery. The capability to resume processing persistent messages in the MTS queue means the service restart is transparent to other services that were communicating with the failed process.

NX-OS provides the infrastructure to the individual processes so that they can choose the type of recovery mechanism to implement. In some cases, a stateful recovery does not make sense, because a recovery mechanism is built in to the higher layers of a protocol. Consider a routing protocol process, such as OSPF or BGP, that has a protocol level graceful restart or nonstop forwarding implementation. For those protocols, it does not make sense to checkpoint the routing updates into the PSS infrastructure because they are recovered by the protocol.

Note The reason for a reset is reviewed in the output of **show system reset-reason**. Process crash or restart details are viewed with the **show processes log pid** and **show cores** commands.

Supervisor Redundancy

Nexus platforms with redundant supervisor modules operate in an Active/Standby redundancy mode. This means that only one of the supervisors is active at a time, and the standby is ready and waiting to take over when a fatal failure of the active occurs. Active/Standby supervisor redundancy provides a fully redundant control plane for the device and allows for stateful switchover (SSO) and in-service software upgrades (ISSU). The current redundancy state and which supervisor is active is viewed in the output of **show module**, as well as the output of **show system redundancy status**, as shown in Example 1-15.

Example 1-15 *Determining the Current Supervisor Redundancy State*

```
NX-1# show system redundancy status
Redundancy mode
---------------
       administrative:   HA
          operational:   HA
This supervisor (sup-1)
-----------------------
```

```
         Redundancy state:    Active
         Supervisor state:    Active
          Internal state:     Active with HA standby

Other supervisor (sup-2)
------------------------
         Redundancy state:    Standby
         Supervisor state:    HA standby
          Internal state:     HA standby
NX-1# show module
Mod  Ports  Module-Type                          Model              Status
---  -----  -----------------------------------  -----------------  ----------
3    32     10 Gbps Ethernet Module              N7K-M132XP-12      ok
5    0      Supervisor Module-2                  N7K-SUP2E          active *
6    0      Supervisor Module-2                  N7K-SUP2E          ha-standby
8    48     1000 Mbps Optical Ethernet Module    N7K-M148GS-11      ok
9    48     1/10 Gbps Ethernet Module            N7K-F248XP-25E     ok
10   24     10 Gbps Ethernet Module              N7K-M224XP-23L     ok
```

When a redundant supervisor boots, the following events occur:

1. The Supervisor Active/Standby election is done.

2. The system manager process on the standby announces itself to the system manager process of the active.

3. The system manager of the standby synchronizes the startup configuration from the active and starts all services on the standby to mirror the active.

4. The services on the standby synchronize state with a snapshot of the services state on the active.

5. MTS messages from the services on the active are copied to the standby.

6. Services on the standby are now in sync with the active.

7. Process events are now copied to the standby so the services on both supervisors remain in sync during normal operation (event-based synchronization).

In the event of a supervisor switchover, services on the standby supervisor are notified by the system manager to recover state and prepare to take over the active role. Because the process events are synchronized to the standby by MTS during normal operation, the recovery occurs quickly. After the switchover is complete, the supervisor that was previously active is restarted, and it undergoes normal boot diagnostic tests. If diagnostic tests pass, and it boots successfully, it synchronizes using the same procedure previously outlined to synchronize with the current active supervisor. Figure 1-7 shows the relationship of the NX-OS services that make up the supervisor redundancy model.

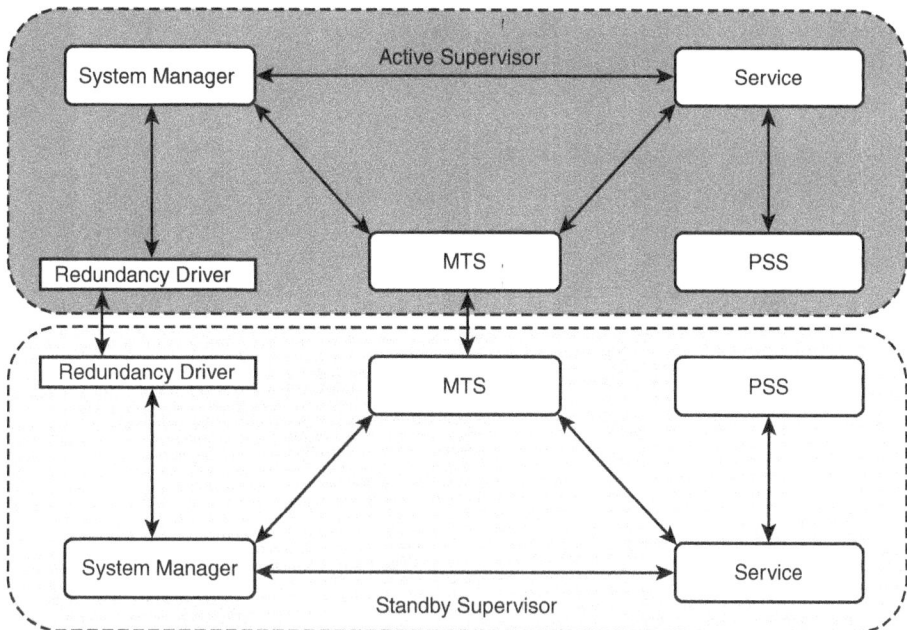

Figure 1-7 *Supervisor Redundancy Model*

In rare circumstances, the standby supervisor may fail to reach the *HA Standby* state. One possible reason is that a service on the standby is not able to synchronize state with the active. To check for this condition, verify the sysmgr state on the active and standby supervisor to confirm which service is not able to synchronize state. If multiple VDCs are configured, perform this verification for each VDC. To verify the synchronization state of the supervisors, use the **show system internal sysmgr state** command, as shown in Example 1-16.

Example 1-16 *Confirm the Redundancy and Synchronization State*

```
NX-1# show system internal sysmgr state
The master System Manager has PID 4862 and UUID 0x1.
Last time System Manager was gracefully shutdown.
The state is SRV_STATE_MASTER_ACTIVE_HOTSTDBY entered at time Fri Jun 30
01:48:40 2017.
The '-b' option (disable heartbeat) is currently disabled.
The '-n' (don't use rlimit) option is currently disabled.
Hap-reset is currently enabled.
Watchdog checking is currently enabled.
Watchdog kgdb setting is currently disabled.
        Debugging info:
```

```
The trace mask is 0x00000000, the syslog priority enabled is 3.
The '-d' option is currently disabled.
The statistics generation is currently enabled.

     HA info:

slotid = 5    supid = 0
cardstate = SYSMGR_CARDSTATE_ACTIVE .
cardstate = SYSMGR_CARDSTATE_ACTIVE (hot switchover is configured enabled).
Configured to use the real platform manager.
Configured to use the real redundancy driver.
Redundancy register: this_sup = RDN_ST_AC, other_sup = RDN_ST_SB.
EOBC device name: veobc.
Remote addresses:   MTS - 0x00000601/3      IP - 127.1.1.6
MSYNC done.
Remote MSYNC not done.
Module online notification received.
Local super-state is: SYSMGR_SUPERSTATE_STABLE
Standby super-state is: SYSMGR_SUPERSTATE_STABLE
Swover Reason : SYSMGR_UNKNOWN_SWOVER
Total number of Switchovers: 0
Swover threshold settings: 5 switchovers within 4800 seconds
Switchovers within threshold interval: 0
Last switchover time: 0 seconds after system start time
Cumulative time between last 0 switchovers: 0
Start done received for 1 plugins, Total number of plugins = 1
     Statistics:
Message count:           0
Total latency:           0           Max latency:    0
Total exec:              0           Max exec:       0
```

The **show system internal sysmgr gsync-pending** command is used to verify that synchronization is complete. Any services that are still pending synchronization are listed in the output. Example 1-17 confirms that no services are pending synchronization on the active supervisor.

Example 1-17 *Verify There Are No Services Pending Synchronization*

```
NX-1# show system internal sysmgr gsync-pending
Gsync is not pending for any service
```

The sysmgr output confirms that the *superstate is stable* for both supervisors, which indicates there is no problem currently. If there was a problem, the superstate displays as *unstable*. The superstate on the standby supervisor is verified by attaching to the standby supervisor module, as shown in Example 1-18.

Example 1-18 *Verifying the Sysmgr State on the Standby Supervisor*

```
NX-1# attach module 6
Attaching to module 6 ...
<output removed for brevity>
NX-1(standby)# show system internal sysmgr state
The master System Manager has PID 4708 and UUID 0x1.
Last time System Manager was gracefully shutdown.
The state is SRV_STATE_MASTER_HOTSTDBY entered at time Fri Jun 30 01:49:50 2017.
The '-b' option (disable heartbeat) is currently disabled.
The '-n' (don't use rlimit) option is currently disabled.
Hap-reset is currently enabled.
Watchdog checking is currently enabled.
Watchdog kgdb setting is currently disabled.

        Debugging info:

The trace mask is 0x00000000, the syslog priority enabled is 3.
The '-d' option is currently disabled.
The statistics generation is currently enabled.

        HA info:

slotid = 6    supid = 0
cardstate = SYSMGR_CARDSTATE_STANDBY .
cardstate = SYSMGR_CARDSTATE_STANDBY (hot switchover is configured enabled).
Configured to use the real platform manager.
Configured to use the real redundancy driver.
Redundancy register: this_sup = RDN_ST_SB, other_sup = RDN_ST_AC.
EOBC device name: veobc.
Remote addresses:   MTS - 0x00000501/3      IP - 127.1.1.5
MSYNC done.
Remote MSYNC done.
Module online notification received.
Local super-state is: SYSMGR_SUPERSTATE_STABLE
Standby super-state is: SYSMGR_SUPERSTATE_STABLE
Swover Reason : SYSMGR_UNKNOWN_SWOVER
Total number of Switchovers: 0
Swover threshold settings: 5 switchovers within 4800 seconds
Switchovers within threshold interval: 0
Last switchover time: 0 seconds after system start time
Cumulative time between last 0 switchovers: 0
Start done received for 1 plugins, Total number of plugins = 1

        Statistics:

Message count:            0
Total latency:            0          Max latency:             0
Total exec:               0          Max exec:                0
```

The superstate is stable, and the redundancy register indicates that this supervisor is redundancy state standby (RDN_ST_SB). Verify there are no services pending synchronization on the standby, as shown in Example 1-19.

Example 1-19 *Verify There Are No Services Pending Synchronization*

```
NX-1(standby)# show system internal sysmgr gsync-pending
Gsync is not pending for any service
```

If a service that was pending synchronization was found in this output, the next step in the investigation is to verify the MTS queues for that particular service. An example of verifying the MTS queues for a service was demonstrated earlier in this chapter and is also shown in Chapter 3. If the MTS queue had messages pending for the service, further investigation into why those messages are pending is the next step in solving the problem. Network or device instability could be causing frequent MTS updates to the service that is preventing the synchronization from completing.

ISSU

NX-OS allows for in-service software upgrade (ISSU) as a high-availability feature. ISSU makes use of the NX-OS stateful switchover (SSO) capability with redundant supervisors and allows the system software to be updated without an impact to data traffic. During an ISSU, all components of the chassis are upgraded.

ISSU is initiated using the **install all** command, which performs the following steps to upgrade the system.

Step 1. Determines whether the upgrade is disruptive and asks if you want to continue

Step 2. Ensure that enough space is available in the standby bootflash

Step 3. Copies the kickstart and system images to the standby supervisor module

Step 4. Sets the KICKSTART and SYSTEM boot variables

Step 5. Reloads the standby supervisor module with the new Cisco NX-OS software

Step 6. Reloads the active supervisor module with the new Cisco NX-OS software, which causes a switchover to the newly upgraded standby supervisor module

Step 7. Upgrades the line cards

Step 8. The Connectivity Management Processor (CMP) on both supervisors get upgraded (Sup1 on Nexus 7000 only)

For platforms that do not have a redundant supervisor, such as the Nexus 5000 series, a different method is used to achieve ISSU. The control plane becomes inactive while the data plane continues to forward packets. This allows the supervisor CPU to reset without causing a traffic disruption and load the new NX-OS software version. After the CPU is booted on the new software release, the control plane is restored from the previous configuration and run-time state. The switch then synchronizes the control plane state to the data plane.

Nexus 9000 and Nexus 3000 platforms introduced an *enhanced ISSU* feature beginning in release 7.0(3)I5(1). Normally the NX-OS software runs directly on the hardware. However, with enhanced ISSU, the NX-OS software runs inside of a separate Linux container (LXC) for the supervisor and line cards. During enhanced ISSU, a third container is created to act as the standby supervisor so that the primary supervisor and line cards are upgraded without disruption to data traffic. This feature is enabled with the **boot mode lxc** configuration command on supported platforms.

Note ISSU has restrictions on some platforms, and ISSU may not be supported between certain releases of NX-OS. Please reference the documentation on www.cisco.com to ensure ISSU is supported before attempting an upgrade with this method.

NX-OS Virtualization Features

As a modern data center class operating system, NX-OS and the Nexus switch platforms must provide support for virtualization of hardware and software resources to meet the demands of today's network architectures. These features are introduced in this section and are explained in additional detail throughout this book.

Virtual Device Contexts

The Nexus 7000 platform allows the operator to partition a physical switch into multiple virtual switches known as Virtual Device Contexts (VDC). VDCs are an important virtualization feature where a physical switch is divided into multiple logical switches, and each logical switch serves a different role in the topology.

A common use case for VDC is with OTV or LISP, where a dedicated VDC is configured for the overlay encapsulation protocol, and another VDC serves to function as a distribution layer switch performing traditional Layer 2 and Layer 3 functions. Another popular use of the VDC concept is to have a production VDC and a test/development VDC to allow separation of these different environments in a single chassis. After appropriate planning and VDC creation, operators allocate ports to each VDC and then interconnect those ports to allow control plane protocols and data plane traffic to be exchanged between the VDCs.

The VDC architecture inherently means that some resources are global to the switch; other resources are shared between VDCs or dedicated to a specific VDC. For example, an OSPF process in VDC-1 is independent of an OSPF process in VDC-2, although they share the common CPU resources of the switch. The management Ethernet on the supervisor is shared among all VDCs. Specific ports on an I/O module are dedicated to a VDC, whereas the NX-OS kernel is global to the switch.

The logical separation between VDCs extends to the protocol stack; however, all VDCs on the switch share the same kernel resources and infrastructure. The system infrastructure is designed to allow fair resource allocation of shared resources, as well as the control plane queues from the kernel to the protocol stack of each VDC. Other resources are dedicated to a particular VDC, such as VLANs and routing table space. Figure 1-8 provides a visual representation of the VDC architecture of the Nexus 7000 series.

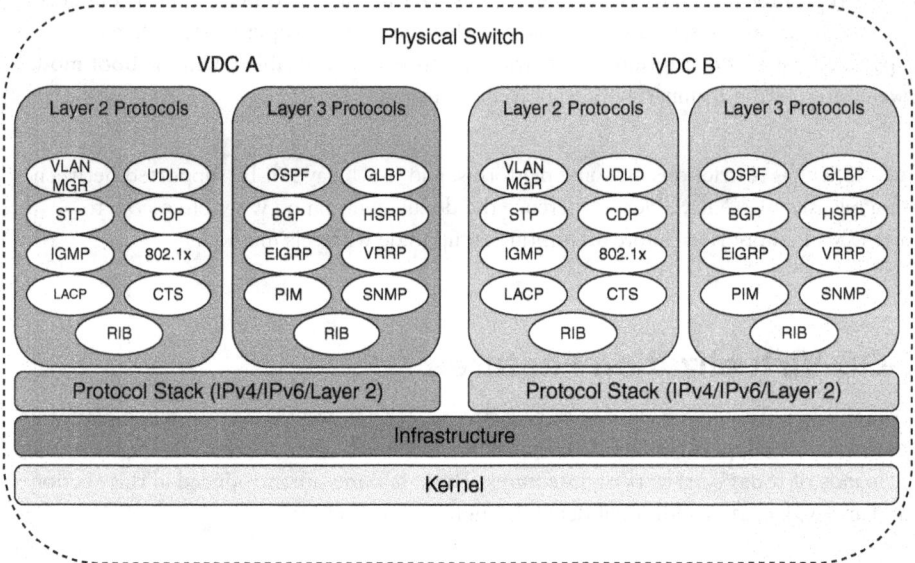

Figure 1-8 *Nexus 7000 VDC Architecture*

With appropriate licenses, the Supervisor 1 and Supervisor 2 allow for four VDCs plus an admin VDC. The Supervisor 2E allows for eight VDCs plus an admin VDC. The admin VDC does not handle any data plane traffic and serves only switch management functions. In the context of operating or troubleshooting in a VDC environment, note that certain tasks can be performed only from the default VDC.

1. In-service software upgrade/downgrade (ISSU/ISSD)
2. Erasable programmable logic devices (EPLD) upgrades
3. Control-plane policing (CoPP) configuration
4. Licensing operations
5. VDC configuration, including creation, suspension, deletion, and resource allocation
6. Systemwide QoS policy and port channel load-balancing configuration
7. Generic online diagnostics (GOLD) configuration
8. Ethanalyzer captures

Although VDCs allow additional versatility, some restrictions exist. For instance, all VDCs run on the same NX-OS version and kernel. Restrictions also exist on which I/O modules can be in the same VDC, and which ports of a line card can be allocated to a VDC based on the hardware application-specific integrated circuit (ASIC) architecture of the I/O module and forwarding engine. Before attempting to create VDCs, check the documentation for the specific supervisor and I/O modules that are installed in the switch so that any limitations are dealt with in the design and planning phase.

Note At the time of this writing, multiple VDCs are supported only on the Nexus 7000 series.

Virtual Routing and Forwarding

Virtual Routing and Forwarding (VRF) instances have proven very useful for logical separation of network resources. The purpose of a VRF is to allow multiple instances of control plane and data plane forwarding tables to operate simultaneously on a single device while remaining logically separated.

The concept of VRF-lite defines multiple routing and forwarding tables with logical separation on a single device without a Multiprotocol Label Switching (MPLS) transport. MPLS VPNs use VRFs on provider edge (PE) nodes to separate multiple routing and forwarding tables logically with an MPLS transport between PEs.

NX-OS supports both VRF-lite and MPLS VPN for virtualization and separation of routing tables and forwarding state. Importing and exporting routes between VRF contexts is supported, as well as import and export from the global routing table to a VRF table. In addition to the user-defined VRFs, NX-OS puts the management Ethernet interface of the switch into its own management VRF by default. This provides a desirable separation of data plane and management plane services.

In the virtualization hierarchy, a VRF exists locally within a VDC, and multiple VDCs can exist in a physical switch. If VRFs configured in different VDCs need to communicate, a control plane routing protocol is required to exchange information between the VRFs in different VDCs. This is done in the same manner as routing between VDCs using the default VRF. Routing traffic between VRFs is achieved with a control plane protocol to exchange routing information, or if the VRFs exist in the same VDC, route leaking is used to exchange routes between them.

Note Support for MPLS VPN is dependent upon the capabilities of the platform and the installed feature licenses.

Virtual Port Channel

Virtual port channels (vPC) allow a pair of peer switches to connect to a third device and appear as a single switch. The only requirement for the third device is that it must support IEEE 802.3ad port channels. No special configuration is needed to operate with a vPC switch pair, which makes this technology a very attractive option to remove STP blocking ports from the access layer. When two switches are configured as a vPC pair, one switch is elected primary (lowest priority wins). The primary role comes into play for STP, as well as during certain failure scenarios.

Figure 1-9 is an example of a vPC-enabled switch pair connected with two additional switches using vPC.

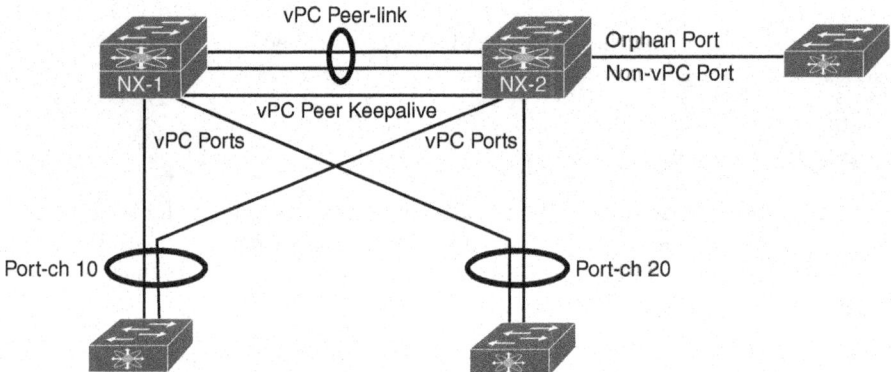

Figure 1-9 *The vPC Architecture*

In Figure 1-9, the vPC pair is using vPC Port-channel 10 and vPC Port-channel 20 to connect with two access switches. A third access switch to the right of NX-2 is not connected in vPC mode. This non-vPC enabled interface is known as an orphan port in vPC terminology. Each of the vPC terms in Figure 1-9 are as follows:

- **vPC Peer-link** is configured to carry all user-defined VLANs. It is also used to forward BPDUs, HSRP hellos, and CFS (Cisco Fabric Services) protocol packets between vPC peer switches. It should be a port channel with member links on different modules for redundancy purposes.

- **vPC Peer Keepalive** link should be a separate path from the peer-link. It does not have to be a point-to-point link and can traverse a routed infrastructure. The peer keepalive link is used to ensure liveness of the vPC peer switch.

- **Orphan Port** is a non-vPC port connected to a device in the vPC topology.

- **vPC Port (vPC member ports)** are ports assigned to a vPC Port-channel group. The ports of the vPC are split between the vPC peers.

Because all links are up and forwarding in vPC, the decision of which vPC member-link interface to forward a packet on is made by the port-channel load-balance hash of the device sending the packet. The sending switch looks at the frame source and destination addresses of a traffic flow and feeds these details into an algorithm. The algorithm performs a hash function and returns a selected member port of the port-channel for the frame to exit on. This allows all member link interfaces of the port-channel to share the load of traffic.

Historically, routing protocol adjacencies had limitations when configured to operate over a vPC topology. Recent versions of NX-OS have made changes that allow dynamic unicast routing protocols to operate over vPC without the limitations that existed previously. Check the vPC configuration guide of the platform to ensure support exists before attempting this configuration.

With each vPC peer making independent frame forwarding decisions, there is a need for state synchronization between the peers. CFS is the protocol that is used to synchronize Layer 2 (L2) state. It operates over the peer-link and is enabled automatically. Its role is to ensure compatibility of the vPC member ports between vPC peers. It is also used to synchronize MAC address tables and IGMP snooping state between vPC peers so that any table entries exist on both vPC peers. Layer 3 (L3) forwarding tables and protocol state are independent on each vPC peer.

Note vPC is introduced here as a virtualization concept and is covered in detail later in this book.

Management and Operations Capabilities

The following section introduces some of the operational, serviceability, and usability features of the Nexus switching platforms. These features were designed to improve the user experience and ease operational tasks associated with configuring, troubleshooting, and performing maintenance on Nexus switches.

NX-OS Advanced CLI

The NX-OS CLI was originally designed to have an IOS-like look and feel. At a high level the two CLI interfaces are very similar. IOS and NX-OS both have the concept of an executive mode, different user privileges, a running configuration, and a startup configuration, to name a few. NX-OS and IOS show commands and debugs are in many cases the same from one operating system to the other. However, NX-OS includes additional command-line enhancements and utilities that make operating and troubleshooting easier and more productive on NX-OS.

During the process of investigating a problem, data is often collected for offline analysis. This means that the user needs to execute commands, capture the output, and then transfer that output from the device to somewhere else for review. NX-OS provides the **>** and **>>** operators, as shown in Example 1-20, which allow output to be redirected to a new file or appended to an existing file, respectively. This is especially useful when collecting a lengthy show tech support file.

Example 1-20 show *Command Output Redirection*

```
NX-1# show tech netstack > bootflash:tech_netstack.txt
NX-1# dir bootflash: | inc netstack
   23144888    Jul 13 16:09:09 2017  tech_netstack.txt
```

The use of the parsing utilities (i.e. "| count" and "| wc") provide a way of counting the number of lines or words in the show command being executed. Example 1-21 shows how to use this for situations where a simple count provides verification of the current state; for example, comparing the number of lines in **show ip ospf neighbor** before and after a configuration change.

Example 1-21 *Using the Count or WC Utilities*

```
NX-1# show ip ospf neighbor | count
6
```

There are many troubleshooting scenarios where command output needs to be taken multiple times and compared to see what has changed or which counters have incremented since the previous execution. Example 1-22 demonstrates the use of the **diff** utility. Do not use this for large outputs such as show tech, because it consumes system resources while retaining the output for comparison. It is better to compare large outputs after transferring the data off-box.

Example 1-22 *The Diff Utility*

```
NX-1# show int e3/19 | diff
22,24c22,24
<      30 seconds input rate 360 bits/sec, 0 packets/sec
<      30 seconds output rate 112 bits/sec, 0 packets/sec
<      input rate 360 bps, 0 pps; output rate 112 bps, 0 pps
---
>      30 seconds input rate 336 bits/sec, 0 packets/sec
>      30 seconds output rate 72 bits/sec, 0 packets/sec
>      input rate 336 bps, 0 pps; output rate 72 bps, 0 pps
34,35c34,35
<      468 unicast packets  183033 multicast packets  1 broadcast packets
<      183506 input packets  18852532 bytes
---
>      468 unicast packets  183034 multicast packets  1 broadcast packets
>      183507 input packets  18852610 bytes
```

In some cases it is desirable to obtain only the last few lines of a command instead of paging through the output or using an include/exclude utility option. The **last** *count* utility displays the last few entries and is used when parsing the accounting log, system log buffer, or event history logs. Example 1-23 shows how to print only the last line in the log buffer.

Example 1-23 *The Last Utility*

```
NX-1# show logging logfile | last 1
2017 Jul 13 21:57:15 F340-35-02-N7K-7009-A %VSHD-5-VSHD_SYSLOG_CONFIG_I:
Configured from vty by admin on console0
```

Another nice feature is the "," utility, which is used to execute a command with multiple arguments. Example 1-24 shows how this is useful for checking the interface rate simultaneously on two different ports when combined with **egrep**.

Example 1-24 *Executing a Command with Multiple Arguments*

```
NX-1# show interface e3/18 , ethernet 3/19 | egrep "30 seconds"
  Load-Interval #1: 30 seconds
    30 seconds input rate 64680 bits/sec, 11 packets/sec
    30 seconds output rate 67304 bits/sec, 11 packets/sec
  Load-Interval #1: 30 seconds
    30 seconds input rate 66288 bits/sec, 11 packets/sec
    30 seconds output rate 64931 bits/sec, 11 packets/sec
```

The **egrep** and **grep** utilities are extremely useful for removing clutter in a command output to show only the character pattern of interest. Example 1-25 demonstrates a common use for **egrep**, which is to review an event history log and look for a specific event. In this example, **egrep** is used to find each time OSPF has run its shortest path first (SPF) algorithm. The **prev 1** option is used so that the line previous to the pattern match is printed, which indicates a full or partial SPF run. The **next** option is used to get lines after the **egrep** pattern match.

Example 1-25 *Using Egrep to Parse an Event History*

```
NX-1# show ip ospf event-history spf | egrep prev 1 STARTED
2017 Jul  9 23:46:00.646652 ospf 12 [16161]: : Examining summaries
2017 Jul  9 23:46:00.646644 ospf 12 [16161]: : SPF run 12 STARTED with flags
0x4, vpn superbackbone changed flag is FALSE
--
2017 Jul  9 23:44:05.194089 ospf 12 [16161]: : This is a full SPF
2017 Jul  9 23:44:05.194087 ospf 12 [16161]: : SPF run 11 STARTED with flags
0x1, vpn superbackbone changed flag is FALSE
--
2017 Jul  9 23:44:00.094088 ospf 12 [16161]: : This is a full SPF
```

```
2017 Jul  9 23:44:00.094085 ospf 12 [16161]: : SPF run 10 STARTED with flags
0x1, vpn superbackbone changed flag is FALSE
--
2017 Jul  9 23:43:56.074094 ospf 12 [16161]: : This is a full SPF
2017 Jul  9 23:43:56.074091 ospf 12 [16161]: : SPF run 9 STARTED with flags
0x1, vpn superbackbone changed flag is FALSE
--
```

Egrep has several other useful options that you should become familiar with. They are **count**, which returns a count of the number of matches, **invert-match**, which prints only lines that do not match the pattern, and **line-number**, which appends the line number of the match to each line.

Table 1-2 provides information on additional command utilities available in NX-OS.

Table 1-2 *Additional Command Utilities*

Utility	Purpose
no-more	Command output pages without the need to press return or space when the terminal length is reached.
json	Command output is printed as JSON. This is useful when data will be collected and then consumed by a script or software application because the output is structured data.
xml	Prints the output in XML format.
email	Command output is sent via email.
include	Only lines that match the pattern are printed.
exclude	Only lines that do not match the pattern are printed.
section	The section of output containing the pattern is printed.

Example 1-26 demonstrates **show cli list** [*string*], which returns all CLI commands that match the given string input. This saves time over using the "?" to figure out which commands exist.

Example 1-26 *Using* **show cli list** *Command*

```
NX-1# show cli list ospf
<! output omitted for brevity>
MODE exec
show logging level ospf
show tech-support ospf brief
show tech-support ospf
show ip ospf <str> vrf <str>
```

```
show ip ospf <str> vrf <str>
show ip ospf <str> vrf all
show ip ospf <str>
show ip ospf <str> neighbors <if> <ip>
show ip ospf <str> neighbors <if> <str>
show ip ospf <str> neighbors <if>
show ip ospf <str> neighbors <ip> vrf <str>
show ip ospf <str> neighbors <ip> vrf <str>
show ip ospf <str> neighbors <ip> vrf all
```

Complementary to the previous example, the syntax for the identified CLI commands are available with the **show cli syntax** [*string*] command, as shown in Example 1-27.

Example 1-27 *Using* **show cli syntax** *Command*

```
NX-1# show cli syntax ospf
<! output omitted for brevity>
MODE exec
(0) show logging level ospf
(1) show tech-support ospf [ brief ]
(2) show ip ospf [ <tag> ] [ vrf { <vrf-name> | <vrf-known-name> | all } ] [ ]
(3) show ip ospf [ <tag> ] ha [ vrf { <vrf-name> | <vrf-known-name> | all } ] [ ]
(4) show ip ospf [ <tag> ] neighbors [ { { <interface> [ <neighbor> | <neighbor-
    name> ] } | { [ <neighbor> | <neighbor-name> ] [ vrf { <vrf-name> | <vrf-known-
    name> | all } ] } } ] [ ]
```

The **show running-config diff** command is useful to quickly compare the running-configuration and the startup-configuration of the switch. In Example 1-28 a logging logfile was configured and is highlighted with the "!" in the output as a changed line between the two files.

Example 1-28 *Using* **show running-config diff**

```
NX-1# show running-config diff
*** Startup-config
--- Running-config
***************
*** 318,328 ****
  boot kickstart bootflash:/n7000-s2-kickstart.7.2.2.D1.2.gbin sup-2
  boot system bootflash:/n7000-s2-dk9.7.2.2.D1.2.gbin sup-2
  mpls ldp configuration
    router-id Lo0 force
  no system auto-upgrade epld
! no logging logfile
```

```
  logging level user 5
  router ospf 12
    router-id 172.16.0.1
--- 317,327 ----
  boot kickstart bootflash:/n7000-s2-kickstart.7.2.2.D1.2.gbin sup-2
  boot system bootflash:/n7000-s2-dk9.7.2.2.D1.2.gbin sup-2
  mpls ldp configuration
    router-id Lo0 force
  no system auto-upgrade epld
! logging logfile log 6 size 4194304
  logging level user 5
  router ospf 12
    router-id 172.16.0.1
```

Cisco IOS requires that you prepend any user or exec level command with **do** while in the configuration mode. NX-OS eliminates the need for the **do** command because it allows the execution of exec level commands from within the configuration mode.

Technical Support Files

The concept of a **show tech-support** CLI command is likely familiar to anyone who has worked on Cisco router or switch platforms. The general idea of a show tech support file is to capture common outputs related to a problem for offline analysis. NX-OS offers a very useful show tech support hierarchy. At the top level is the **show tech details**, which obtains and aggregates many commonly needed feature show tech files, event histories, and internal data structures with a single CLI command. Another useful command is the **tac-pac**, which collects the **show tech details** output and automatically stores it as a compressed file in *bootflash:*.

Each feature enabled in NX-OS has the capability to provide a tech-support file that obtains the most useful information about that specific feature. The **show tech-support [feature]** obtains the feature configuration, show commands, data structures, and event histories needed for offline analysis of a problem with a specific feature. Be aware of feature dependencies when performing data collection so that all relevant information about the problem is gathered.

For example, a unicast routing problem with OSPF as the routing protocol requires you to collect **show tech-support ospf**, but for a complete analysis the output of **show tech-support routing ip unicast** is also needed to get Unicast Routing Information Base (URIB) events. Feature dependency and what to collect is determined on a case-by-case basis, depending on the problem under investigation. Many feature show tech-support outputs do not include a full **show running-config**.

It is always a good idea to collect the full show running-config along with any specific feature show techs that are needed. Example 1-29 shows the collection of

show tech-support commands and the running-configuration to investigate a unicast routing problem with OSPF.

Example 1-29 *Collecting Show Tech-Support to Investigate an OSPF Problem*

```
NX-1# show tech-support forwarding l3 unicast detail > tech_l3_unicast.txt
NX-1# show tech-support routing ip unicast > tech_routing.txt
NX-1# show tech-support ospf > tech_ospf.txt
NX-1# show running-config > bootflash:running-config
NX-1# tar create bootflash:routing-issue-data bootflash:tech_l3_unicast.txt
  bootflash:tech_ospf.txt bootflash:tech_routing.txt bootflash:running-config
NX-1# dir | inc routing|tech|running
     578819    Jul 13 00:15:24 2017  routing-issue-data.tar.gz
       2743    Jul 13 00:12:38 2017  running-config
    8357805    Jul 12 23:57:46 2017  tech_l3_unicast.txt
     151081    Jul 12 23:58:04 2017  tech_ospf.txt
     396743    Jul 12 23:58:39 2017  tech_routing.txt
```

Notice that each show tech is collected as an individual file by redirecting the output to *bootflash:* with the "**>**" operator. After collecting all the relevant feature show techs, they are combined into an archive using the **tar** command, which makes the data easy to copy from the switch for later analysis.

Note In addition to the **show tech-support** [*feature*], NX-OS also provides **show running-config** [*feature*], which prints only the running-configuration of the given feature.

Accounting Log

NX-OS keeps a history of all configuration changes made to the device in the accounting log. This is a useful piece of information to determine what has changed in a switch, and by whom. Typically, problems are investigated based on the time when they started to occur, and the accounting log can answer the question, *What has changed?* An example of reviewing the accounting log is shown in Example 1-30. Because only the last few lines are of interest, the **start-seqnum** option is used to jump to the end of the list.

Example 1-30 *Examining the Accounting Log*

```
NX-1# show accounting log ?
  <CR>
  <0-250000>   Log Size(in bytes)
  >            Redirect it to a file
  >>           Redirect it to a file in append mode
```

```
  all            Display accounting log including show commands (Use <terminal
                 log-all> to enable show command accounting)
  last-index     Show accounting log last index information
  nvram          Present in nvram
  start-seqnum   Show messages starting from a given sequence number
  start-time     Show messages from a given start-time
  |              Pipe command output to filter
NX-01# show accounting log last-index
accounting-log last-index : 25712
NX-01# show accounting log start-seqnum 25709
Last Log cleared/wrapped time is : Fri Sep  9 10:14:48 2016
25709:Thu Jul 13 00:04:41 2017:update:console0:admin:switchto ; dir | inc routin
g|tech (SUCCESS)
25710:Thu Jul 13 00:13:30 2017:update:console0:admin:switchto ; dir | inc routin
g|tech|running (SUCCESS)
25711:Thu Jul 13 00:15:24 2017:update:console0:admin:switchto ; tar create bootf
lash:/routing-issue-data bootflash:/tech_l3_unicast.txt bootflash:/tech_ospf.txt
 bootflash:/tech_routing.txt bootflash:/running-config (SUCCESS)
25712:Thu Jul 13 00:15:30 2017:update:console0:admin:switchto ; dir | inc routin
g|tech|running (SUCCESS)
```

The accounting log is stored persistently in *logflash:* so that it is available even if the switch is reloaded.

Note The **terminal log-all** configuration command enables the logging of show commands in the accounting log.

Feature Event-History

One very useful serviceability feature of NX-OS is that it keeps circular event-history buffers for each configured feature. The event-history is similar in many ways to an always-on debug for the feature that does not have any negative CPU impact on the switch. The granularity of events stored in the event-history depends on the individual feature, but many are equivalent to the output that is obtained with debugging. In many cases, the event-history contains enough data to determine what sequence of events has occurred for the feature without the need for additional debug logs, which makes them a great troubleshooting resource.

Event-history buffers are circular, which means that the possibility exists for events to be overwritten by the time a problem condition is recognized, leaving no event history evidence to investigate. For some features, the event-history size is configurable as [small | medium | large]. If a problem with a particular feature is occurring regularly, increase the event-history size to improve the chance of catching the problem sequence in the buffer. Most feature event-histories are viewed with the **show** {*feature*} **internal event-history** command, as shown in Example 1-31.

Example 1-31 *Reviewing the OSPF Adjacency Event History*

```
NX-1# show ip ospf internal event-history adjacency
Adjacency events for OSPF Process "ospf-1"
2017 Jul 12 23:30:55.816540 ospf 1 [5817]: : Nbr 192.168.1.2: EXCHANGE --> FULL,
 event EXCHDONE
2017 Jul 12 23:30:55.816386 ospf 1 [5817]: :   seqnr 0x385a2ae7, dbdbits 0, mtu
1500, options 0x42
2017 Jul 12 23:30:55.816381 ospf 1 [5817]: : Got DBD from 192.168.1.2 with 0
entries
2017 Jul 12 23:30:55.816372 ospf 1 [5817]: :   seqnr 0x385a2ae7, dbdbits 0, mtu
1500, options 0x42
2017 Jul 12 23:30:55.816366 ospf 1 [5817]: : Got DBD from 192.168.1.2 with 0 ent ries
2017 Jul 12 23:30:55.814575 ospf 1 [5817]: :   mtu 1500, opts: 0x42, ddbits: 0x1,
seq: 0x385a2ae7
2017 Jul 12 23:30:55.814572 ospf 1 [5817]: : Sent DBD with 0 entries to
192.168.1.2 on Vlan2
2017 Jul 12 23:30:55.814567 ospf 1 [5817]: : Sending DBD to 192.168.1.2 on Vlan2
```

Note Troubleshooting scenarios may require a periodic dump of the feature tech support file. This is done with Embedded Event Manager (EEM), or another method of scripting the data collection. **bloggerd** is another tool for such scenarios, but it is recommended for use only under guidance from Cisco Technical Assistance Center (TAC).

Debug Options: Log File and Filters

If a feature's event history is not granular enough to troubleshoot a problem, or if you are not able to capture the event history before the relevant events are lost due to roll over, feature-specific debugs can be used. Debugs are enabled with filters and logged to a debug log file. Example 1-32 demonstrates a debug filter and debug log file to filter the output for only a particular OSPF neighbor.

Example 1-32 *Debug Log File and Debug Filter*

```
NX-1# debug-filter ip ospf neighbor 192.168.1.2
NX-1# debug logfile ospf-debug-log
NX-1# debug ip ospf adjacency detail
NX-1# dir log: | inc ospf
       1792     Jul 13 00:49:40 2017  ospf-debug-log
NX-1# show debug logfile ospf-debug-log
2017 Jul 13 00:49:14.896199 ospf: 1 [5817] (default)    Nbr 192.168.1.2
FSM start: old state FULL, event HELLORCVD
```

```
2017 Jul 13 00:49:14.896376 ospf: 1 [5817] (default)    Nbr 192.168.1.2:
FULL --> FULL, event HELLORCVD
2017 Jul 13 00:49:14.896404 ospf: 1 [5817] (default)    Nbr 192.168.1.2
FSM start: old state FULL, event TWOWAYRCVD
2017 Jul 13 00:49:14.896431 ospf: 1 [5817] (default)    Nbr 192.168.1.2:
FULL --> FULL, event TWOWAYRCVD
```

Configuration Checkpoint and Rollback

NX-OS supports the capability to create configuration checkpoints. These checkpoints are a way of storing a known good configuration for the system so that if a configuration change is made that introduces an undesirable behavior, it is quickly rolled back to a known good configuration without a system reload. This approach removes the error-prone human element and saves you from having to copy and paste the previous configuration back into the device. There are four types of configuration rollback.

- **Atomic:** Perform the rollback only if no errors occur. This is the default option.
- **Best-effort:** Perform the rollback and skip any errors.
- **Stop-at-first-failure:** Perform the rollback but stop if an error occurs.
- **Verbose mode:** Shows the detailed execution log during the rollback operation.

When performing a configuration rollback, the changes to be applied are viewed with the **show diff rollback-patch checkpoint** command. This allows a checkpoint file to be compared to another checkpoint file, or to the running configuration. During a rollback, if an error is encountered, you need to decide to cancel or continue. If the rollback is canceled, a list of changes that were applied is provided, and those changes need to be backed out *manually* to return to the pre-rollback configuration. Example 1-33 provides an example of a configuration checkpoint and rollback operation.

Example 1-33 *Configuration Checkpoint and Rollback*

```
NX-1# checkpoint known_good
...............Done
NX-1# show diff rollback-patch checkpoint known_good running-config
Collecting Running-Config
#Generating Rollback Patch
Rollback Patch is Empty
NX-1# conf t
Enter configuration commands, one per line. End with CNTL/Z.
NX-1(config)# no router ospfv3 1
NX-1(config)# end
NX-1# show diff rollback-patch checkpoint known_good running-config
Collecting Running-Config
#Generating Rollback Patch
```

```
!!

no router ospfv3 1
NX-1# rollback running-config checkpoint known_good
Note: Applying config parallelly may fail Rollback verification
Collecting Running-Config
#Generating Rollback Patch
Executing Rollback Patch
Generating Running-config for verification
Generating Patch for verification
Verification is Successful.

Rollback completed successfully.
NX-1# show diff rollback-patch checkpoint known_good running-config
Collecting Running-Config
#Generating Rollback Patch
Rollback Patch is Empty
```

In Example 1-33, an OSPFv3 process was deleted after creating the initial configuration checkpoint. The difference between the checkpoint and the running configuration was highlighted with the **show diff rollback-patch checkpoint** command. The configuration change was then rolled back successfully and the OSPFv3 process was restored.

Consistency Checkers

Consistency checkers are an example of how NX-OS platforms are improving serviceability in each release. Certain software bugs or race conditions may result in a mismatch of state between the control plane, data plane, or forwarding ASICs. Finding these problems is nontrivial and usually requires in-depth knowledge of the platform. Consistency checkers were introduced to deal with these situations, and they are the result of feedback from TAC and customers. Example 1-34 shows the usage of the forwarding consistency checker on a Nexus 3172 platform.

Example 1-34 *Executing the Consistency Checker*

```
NX-1# test consistency-checker forwarding ipv4
NX-1# show consistency-checker forwarding ipv4
IPV4 Consistency check : table_id(0x1)
Execution time : 73 ms ()
No inconsistent adjacencies.
No inconsistent routes.
Consistency-Checker: PASS for ALL
```

The type of consistency checkers that are available vary by platform. In addition, the capabilities are continuing to evolve, and support is being added for new protocols and platforms with each release. Consistency checkers are run on-demand while investigating a problem that has been isolated to the specific device. They quickly validate that a problem is not caused by a state mismatch in the platform.

Feature Scheduler, EEM, and Python

NX-OS supports a scheduler feature that allows commands or scripts to be executed in a non-interactive mode at a defined start time and frequency. The scheduler does not require any special license to run.

The scheduler is a useful feature for backing up configurations, copying files, or collecting data at a specified time interval. The scheduler feature can be combined with the NX-OS python or Embedded Event Manager (EEM) to provide a powerful method of automating tasks. In Example 1-35, a scheduler *job* is defined that executes a python script every day at midnight. The scheduler configuration requires that **feature scheduler** is enabled. The job and schedule for the job is then configured to determine when the job executes.

Example 1-35 *Configuring a Scheduler Job*

```
NX-1# show run | sec scheduler
feature scheduler
scheduler job name run_script
source /bootflash/scripts/snapshot_compare.py
end-job
scheduler schedule name at_midnight
  job name run_script
  time daily 00:00
```

NX-OS provides access to the python interpreter from the exec mode CLI by using the **python** command, as shown in Example 1-36.

Example 1-36 *NX-OS Python Interpreter*

```
NX-1# python
Python 2.7.5 (default, Jun  3 2016, 03:57:06)
[GCC 4.6.3] on linux2
Type "help", "copyright", "credits" or "license" for more information.
>>> print "hello world!"
hello world!
>>> quit()
```

In addition to python, NX-OS also supports EEM, which is another way of automating tasks such as data collection, or dynamically modifying the configuration if a defined event has occurred.

Note Chapter 15, "Programmability and Automation," covers the programming and automation capabilities of NX-OS in more detail.

Bash Shell

A recent addition to NX-OS is the *bash shell* feature. After **feature bash-shell** is enabled, the user can enter the Linux bash shell of the NX-OS operating system. Example 1-37 shows how to access the bash shell from the exec prompt.

Example 1-37 *Entering the Bash Shell*

```
NX-1# run bash
bash-4.2$ pwd
/bootflash/home/admin
bash-4.2$ uname -srvo
Linux 3.4.43-WR5.0.1.13_standard #1 SMP Thu Apr 7 08:39:09 PDT 2016 GNU/Linux
bash-4.2$
```

To gain access to the bash shell, your user account must be associated to the *dev-ops* or *network-admin* role. Bash commands can also be run from the exec mode CLI of the switch with the **run bash** [*command*] option. This command takes the command argument specified, runs it in the bash shell, and returns the output. Python scripts can run from within the bash shell as well. It is recommended to use caution while utilizing the bash shell to manage the device.

Summary

NX-OS is a powerful, feature-rich network operating system that is deployed in thousands of networks around the world. For the past 10 years, it has remained under constant development to meet the needs of those networks as they evolve over time. The modular architecture allows for rapid feature development and source code sharing between the different Nexus switching platforms. NX-OS and Nexus switches are designed for resilience of both the hardware and software to allow for uninterrupted service even in the event of a component failure.

The important management and operational features of NX-OS were introduced in this chapter. That foundational knowledge enables you to apply the troubleshooting techniques from the remaining chapters to your own network environment.

References

Fuller, Ron. "Virtual Device Context (VDC) Design and Implementation" (presented at Cisco Live, San Francisco 2014).

Fuller, Ron. "Cisco NX-OS Software Architecture" (presented at Cisco Live, Orlando 2013).

Esau, Matthew and Souvik Ghosh. "Advanced Troubleshooting Cisco 7000 Series" (presented at Cisco Live, Las Vegas 2017).

Fuller, Ron, David Jansen, and Matthew McPherson. *NX-OS and Cisco Nexus Switching*. Indianapolis: Cisco Press, 2013.

Cisco. Cisco Nexus Platform Product Data Sheets, www.cisco.com.

Cisco. Cisco Nexus Platform Configuration Guides, www.cisco.com.

Cisco. Cisco Nexus Platform Software Upgrade and Installation Guides, www.cisco.com.

Chapter 2

NX-OS Troubleshooting Tools

This chapter covers the following topics:

- Packet Capture: Sniffer
- Nexus Platform Tools
- NetFlow
- Network Time Protocol (NTP)
- Embedded Event Manager (EEM)

Troubleshooting is an art that requires both in-depth knowledge on the subject and the ability to verify operations and isolate the incorrect behavior. If a network problem arises and an engineer has a topology of hundreds or thousands of devices, troubleshooting seems difficult at first glance. When *part* of the problematic topology is presented, troubleshooting the network issue becomes much easier. Proper tools and the right view of the problematic topology can quickly isolate the problem, thereby reducing large-scale network impact. This chapter focuses on the various tools available on the Nexus platform that can help in troubleshooting and day-to-day operation.

Packet Capture: Network Sniffer

NX-OS provides a *command-line interface (CLI)* that assists with troubleshooting various complex issues. However, in some scenarios, the **show** and **debug** commands do not yield sufficient information to isolate the problematic direction of the packet flow. In such situations, performing a packet capture helps. Forwarding issues require isolating the direction of the problem and understanding whether the packet is actually reaching the far end device. Understanding the packet flow between two directly connected devices requires taking three perspectives:

- Determining whether the originating router is transmitting the packet across the network medium
- Determining whether the packet is being received on the destination router
- Examining packets flowing across the network medium

This is where concept of network sniffing comes into play. Network sniffing is the technique of intercepting the traffic that passes over the transmission medium for the protocol and for deep packet analysis. Not only does packet sniffing help with troubleshooting packet forwarding issues, but security experts also heavily use it to perform deep analysis of the network and find security holes.

Performing a network sniffer capture requires a PC with a packet capture tool, such as Wireshark, attached to the switch. A mirror copy of the relevant traffic is copied and sent to the destination interface, where it is captured by the packet capture tool and is available for analysis. Figure 2-1 shows a Nexus switch connected between two routers and a capture PC that has Wireshark installed to capture the traffic flowing between routers R1 and R2.

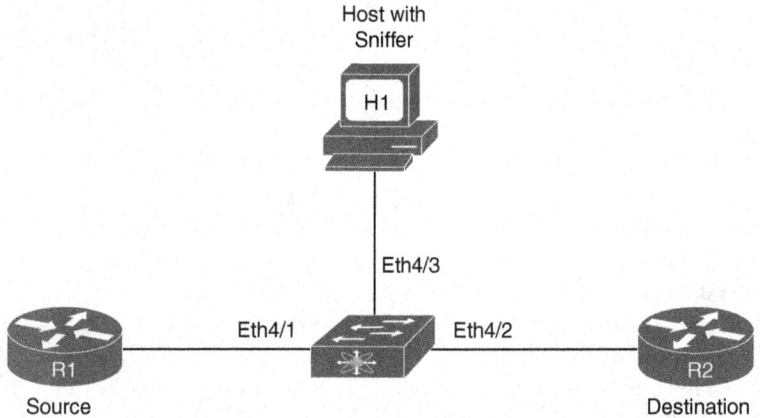

Figure 2-1 *Sniffer Setup on Nexus Switch*

On Cisco devices, the sniffing capability is called a Switched Port Analyzer (SPAN) feature. The source port is called the monitored port and the destination port is called the monitoring port. The SPAN feature on NX-OS is similar in Cisco IOS, but different Nexus switches have different capabilities, based on the hardware support. The following source interfaces can be used as SPAN source interfaces:

- Ethernet
- Fabric Expander (FEX) ports/Fabric port-channels
- Port-channel

- VLAN, or VLAN-based SPAN (VSPAN)
- Remote SPAN (RSPAN) VLAN
- Inband interfaces to the control plane CPU (on Nexus 7000, this feature is supported only on default virtual device context [VDC])
- FCoE ports

Note These features can vary on each Nexus platform, based on the hardware support. The number of active sessions and the source and destination interfaces per session vary on different Nexus platforms. Be sure to verify relevant Cisco documentation before configuring a SPAN session on any Nexus switch.

To enable a port to forward the spanned traffic to the capture PC, the destination interface is enabled for monitoring with the interface parameter command **switchport monitor**. The destination ports are either an Ethernet or Port-Channel interface configured in access or trunk mode. The SPAN session is configured using the command **monitor session** *session-number*, under which the source interface is specified with the command **source interface** *interface-id* [**rx**|**tx**|**both**]. The **rx** option is used to capture the ingress (incoming) traffic, whereas the **tx** option is used to capture the egress (outgoing) traffic. By default, the option is set to both, which captures both ingress and egress traffic on the configured source interface. The destination interface is specified with the command **destination interface** *interface-id*. By default, the monitor session is in shutdown state and must be manually un-shut for the SPAN session to function.

Note The SPAN features can vary across different Nexus platforms. For instance, features such as SPAN-on-Drop and SPAN-on-Latency are supported on Nexus 5000 and Nexus 6000 series but not on Nexus 7000 series. Refer to the platform documentation for more about the feature support.

Example 2-1 illustrates a SPAN session configuration on a Nexus switch. Notice that, in this example, the **source interface** is a range of interfaces, along with the direction of the capture.

Example 2-1 *SPAN Configuration on NX-OS*

```
NX-1(config)# interface Ethernet4/3
NX-1(config-if)# switchport
NX-1(config-if)# switchport monitor
NX-1(config-if)# no shut
NX-1(config)# monitor session 1
NX-1(config-monitor)# source interface Ethernet4/1-2 both
NX-1(config-monitor)# source interface Ethernet5/1 rx
NX-1(config-monitor)# destination interface Ethernet4/3
NX-1(config-monitor)# no shut
NX-1(config-monitor)# exit
```

> **Note** On FCoE ports, the SPAN destination interface is configured with the command **switchport mode SD**, which is similar to the command **switchport monitor**.

Example 2-2 displays the status of the monitor session. In this example, the rx, tx, and both fields are populated for interface Eth4/1 and Eth4/2, but the interface Eth5/1 is listed only for the rx direction. There is also an option to filter VLANS under the monitor session using the **filter vlan** *vlan-id* command.

Example 2-2 *Verifying SPAN Session*

```
NX-1# show monitor session 1
   session 1
---------------
type                  : local
state                 : up
source intf           :
    rx                : Eth4/1      Eth4/2      Eth5/1
    tx                : Eth4/1      Eth4/2
    both              : Eth4/1      Eth4/2
source VLANs          :
    rx                :
    tx                :
    both              :
filter VLANs          : filter not specified
destination ports     : Eth4/3

Legend: f = forwarding enabled, l = learning enabled
```

The default behavior of a SPAN session is to mirror all traffic to the destination port, but NX-OS also provides the capability to perform a filter on the traffic to be mirrored to the destination port. To filter the relevant traffic, an access control list (ACL) is created, to be referenced in the SPAN session configuration by using the **filter access-group** *acl* command. Example 2-3 illustrates the filtering configuration on the SPAN session and verification using the **show monitor session** command.

> **Note** ACL filtering varies on different Nexus platforms. Refer to the CCO documentation for ACL filtering support on respective Nexus platforms.

Example 2-3 *Filtering SPAN Traffic: Configuration and Verification*

```
NX-1(config)# ip access-list TEST-ACL
NX-1(config-acl)# permit ip 100.1.1.0/24 200.1.1.0/24
NX-1(config-)# exit
NX-1(config)# monitor session 1
NX-1(config-monitor)# filter access-group TEST-ACL
NX-1(config-monitor)# exit

NX-1# show monitor session 1
   session 1
---------------
type             : local
state            : up
acl-name         : TEST-ACL
source intf      :
   rx            : Eth4/1     Eth4/2     Eth5/1
   tx            : Eth4/1     Eth4/2
   both          : Eth4/1     Eth4/2
source VLANs     :
   rx            :
   tx            :
   both          :
filter VLANs     : filter not specified
destination ports : Eth4/3

Legend: f = forwarding enabled, l = learning enabled
```

Note Nexus platforms do not support Remote SPAN (RSPAN).

Encapsulated Remote SPAN

Encapsulated Remote SPAN (ERSPAN) is a SPAN feature in which the SPAN traffic is encapsulated to IP-GRE frame format, to support remote monitoring traffic over an IP network. ERSPAN enables monitoring of multiple remote switches across the network—that is, the ERSPAN spans traffic from source ports across multiple switches to the destination switch, where a network analyzer is connected. An ERSPAN session consists of the following components:

- ERSPAN ID
- ERSPAN source session
- GRE-encapsulated traffic
- ERSPAN destination session

The ERSPAN ID is used to distinguish among multiple source devices, sending spanned traffic to one single centralized server.

Figure 2-2 shows a network topology with ERSPAN setup. Two Nexus switches are connected by a routed network. The N6k-1 switch is configured as the ERSPAN-source with a local source SPAN port, and the destination port is located in an IP network on the N7k-1 switch. The GRE-encapsulated packets are transmitted across the IP network toward the destination switch, where they are decapsulated and sent to the traffic analyzer.

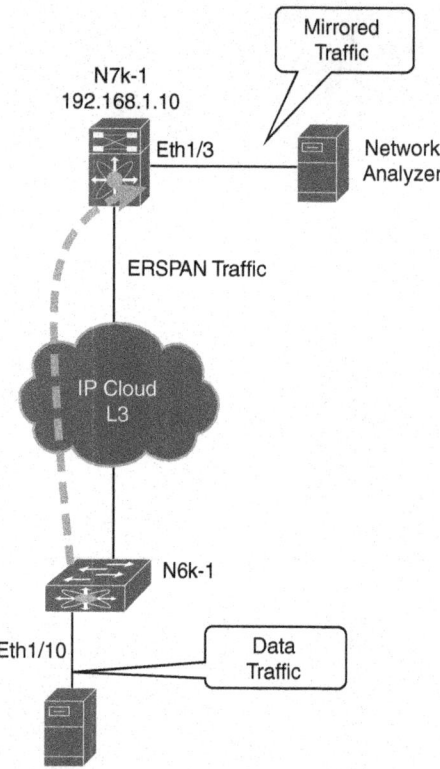

Figure 2-2 *ERSPAN Deployment*

The source and destination sessions can be configured on different switches separately for the source traffic in ingress, egress, or both directions. The ERSPAN is configured to span traffic on Ethernet ports, VLANs, VSANs, and FEX ports. The destination port remains in monitoring state and does not participate in the spanning tree or any Layer 3 protocols. Example 2-4 illustrates the configuration of both the source ports and destination ports on two different Nexus switches. Note that the ERSPAN-ID should be the same on both switches.

Example 2-4 *ERSPAN Configuration*

```
! ERSPAN Source Configuration
N6k-1(config)# monitor session 10 type erspan-source
N6k-1(config-erspan-src)# erspan-id 20
N6k-1(config-erspan-src)# vrf default
N6k-1(config-erspan-src)# destination ip 192.168.1.10
N6k-1(config-erspan-src)# source interface ethernet 1/10
N6k-1(config-erspan-src)# no shut
N6k-1(config-erspan-src)# exit
N6k-1(config)# monitor erspan origin ip-address 192.168.1.1 global
```

```
! ERSPAN Destination Configuration
N7k-1(config)# monitor session 10 type erspan-destination
N7k-1(config-erspan-dst)# erspan-id 10
N7k-1(config-erspan-dst)# source ip 192.168.1.10
N7k-1(config-erspan-dst)# destination interface e1/3
N7k-1(config-erspan-dst)# no shut
```

For the ERSPAN source session to come up, the destination IP should be present in the routing table. The ERSPAN session status is verified using the command **show monitor session** *session-id*. Example 2-5 demonstrates the verification of both the source and destination ERSPAN sessions.

Example 2-5 *ERSPAN Session Verification*

```
N6k-1# show monitor session 10
   session 10
---------------
type              : erspan-source
state             : up
erspan-id         : 20
vrf-name          : default
destination-ip    : 192.168.1.10
ip-ttl            : 255
ip-dscp           : 0
acl-name          : acl-name not specified
origin-ip         : 192.168.1.1 (global)
source intf       :
   rx             : Eth1/10
   tx             : Eth1/10
   both           : Eth1/10
source VLANs      :
   rx             :
source VSANs      :
   rx             :
```

```
N7k-1# show monitor session 10
   session 10
---------------
type                 : erspan-destination
state                : up
erspan-id            : 10
source-ip            : 192.168.1.10
destination ports    : Eth1/3

Legend: f = forwarding enabled, l = learning enabled
```

> **Note** Refer to the Cisco documentation before configuring ERSPAN on any Nexus switch, to verify any platform limitations.

SPAN on Latency and Drop

Both SPAN and ERSPAN provide the capability to apply filters to SPAN-specific traffic based on protocol and IP addressing. Often users or applications report high latency or experience traffic drops between the source and destination, making it hard to figure out where the drop is happening. In such instances, gaining visibility of traffic that is impacting users is always helpful during troubleshooting and can both minimize the service impact and speed up the troubleshooting process.

NX-OS provides the capability to span the traffic based on the specified latency thresholds or based on drops noticed in the path. These capabilities are available for both SPAN and ERSPAN.

SPAN-on-Latency

The SPAN-on-Latency (SOL) feature works a bit differently than the regular SPAN session. In SOL, the source port is the egress port on which latency is monitored. The destination port is still the port where the network analyzer is connected on the switch. The latency threshold is defined on the interface that is being monitored using the command **packets latency threshold** *threshold-value*. When the packets cross or exceed the specified threshold, the SPAN session is triggered and captures the packets. If the threshold value is not specified under the interface, the value is truncated to the nearest multiple of 8.

Example 2-6 illustrates the SOL configuration, in which packets are sniffed only at the egressing interface Eth1/1 and Eth1/2 for flows that have latency more than 1μs (microsecond). The **packet latency threshold** configuration is per port for 40G interfaces but if there are 4x10G interfaces, they share the same configuration. For this reason, Example 2-6 displays the log message that interfaces Eth1/1 to Eth1/4 are configured with a latency threshold of 1000 ns.

Example 2-6 *SPAN-on-Latency Configuration*

```
N6k-1(config)# monitor session 20 type span-on-latency
N6k-1(config-span-on-latency)# source interface ethernet 1/1-2
N6k-1(config-span-on-latency)# destination interface ethernet 1/3
N6k-1(config-span-on-latency)# no shut
N6k-1(config-span-on-latency)# exit
N6k-1(config)# interface eth1/1-2
N6k-1(config-if-range)# packet latency threshold 1000

Interfaces Eth1/1, Eth1/2, Eth1/3 and Eth1/4 are configured with latency
  threshold 1000
```

The SOL-ERSPAN is configured by specifying the type as **span-on-latency-erspan** in the **monitor session** command.

The few limitations with the SOL or SOL-ERSPAN are as follows:

- Only the Ethernet source is supported. Port-channel is not supported as the source port.
- The source cannot be part of any other session.
- The direction of SPAN is not allowed with SOL.
- ACL filtering is not supported with SOL.

SPAN-on-Drop

SPAN-on-Drop is a new feature that enables the spanning of packets that were dropped because of unavailable buffer or queue space upon ingress. This feature provides the capability to span packets that would otherwise be dropped because the copy of the spanned traffic is transferred to a specific destination port. A SPAN-on-Drop session is configured by specifying the type as **span-on-drop** in the **monitor session** configuration. Example 2-7 demonstrates the SPAN-on-Drop monitor session configuration. The source interface Eth1/1 specified in the configuration is the interface where congestion is present.

Example 2-7 *SPAN-on-Drop Configuration*

```
N6k-1(config)# monitor session 30 type span-on-drop
N6k-1(config-span-on-latency)# source interface ethernet 1/1
N6k-1(config-span-on-latency)# destination interface ethernet 1/3
N6k-1(config-span-on-latency)# no shut
N6k-1(config-span-on-latency)# exit
```

Note The SPAN-on-Drop feature captures only drops in unicast flows that result from buffer congestion.

Unlike other SPAN features, SPAN-on-Drop does not have any ternary content addressable memory (TCAM) programming involved. Programming for the source side is in the buffer or queue space. Additionally, only one instance of SPAN-on-Drop can be enabled on the switch; enabling a second instance brings down the session with the syslog message "No hardware resource error." If the SPAN-on-Drop session is up but no packets are spanned, it is vital to verify that the drop is happening in the unicast flow. This is verified by using the command **show platform software qd info interface** *interface-id* and checking that the counter IG_RX_SPAN_ON_DROP is incrementing and is nonzero. Example 2-8 shows the output for the counter IG_RX_SPAN_ON_DROP, confirming that no drops are occurring in the unicast flows.

Example 2-8 *Verifying Ingress L3 Unicast Flow Drops*

```
N6k-1# show plat software qd info interface ethernet 1/1 | begin BM-INGRESS
BM-INGRESS                               BM-EGRESS
------------------------------------------------------------------------
IG_RX                          364763|TX                          390032
SP_RX                            1491|TX_MCAST                         0
LB_RX                           15689|CRC_BAD                          0
IG_RX_SPAN_ON_DROP                  0|CRC_STOMP                        0
IG_RX_MCAST                     14657|DQ_ABORT_MM_XOFF_DROP            0
LB_RX_SPAN                      15689|MTU_VIO                          0
IG_FRAME_DROP                       0|
SP_FRAME_DROP                       0|
LB_FRAME_DROP                       0|
IG_FRAME_QS_EARLY_DROP              0|
ERR_IG_MTU_VIO                      0|
ERR_SP_MTU_VIO                      0|
ERR_LB_MTU_VIO                      0|
```

SPAN-on-Drop ERSPAN is an extension of the SPAN-on-Drop feature in which the dropped frames are spanned and sent to a remote IP where the network analyzer is attached.

Note At the time of writing, SOL and SPAN-on-Drop are supported only on Nexus 5600 and Nexus 6000 series switches.

Nexus Platform Tools

Nexus switches are among the most powerful data center switches in the industry. This is partly because of the CPU and memory available in the switch, but also because of the wide range of integrated tools that the NX-OS offers. These tools provide the capability to capture packets at different ASIC levels within the switch and help verify both hardware programming and the action taken by the hardware or the software on the packet under investigation. Some of these tools include the following:

- Ethanalyzer
- Embedded Logic Analyzer Module (ELAM)
- Packet Tracer

These tools are capable of performing packet capture for the traffic destined for the CPU or transit hardware-switched traffic. They are helpful in understanding the stages the packet goes through in a switch, which helps narrow down the issue very quickly. The main benefit of these features is that they do not require time to set up an external sniffing device.

Note The ELAM capture is supported on all Nexus switches, but because it requires deeper understanding of the ASICs and the configuration differs among Nexus platforms, it is outside the scope of this book. Additionally, ELAM is best performed under the supervision of a Cisco Technical Assistance Center (TAC) engineer. ELAM also is not supported on N5000 or N5500 switches.

Ethanalyzer

Ethanalyzer is an NX-OS implementation of TShark, a terminal version of Wireshark. TShark uses the libpcap library, which gives Ethanalyzer the capability to capture and decode packets. It can capture inband and management traffic on all Nexus platforms. Ethanalyzer provides the users with the following capabilities:

- Capture packets sent and received by the switch Supervisor CPU
- Define the number of packets to be captured
- Define the length of the packets to be captured
- Display packets with very detailed protocol information or a one-line summary
- Open and save captured packet data
- Filter packets capture on many criteria (capture filter)
- Filter packets to be displayed on many criteria (display filter)
- Decode the internal header of control packet
- Avoid the requirement of using an external sniffing device to capture the traffic

Ethanalyzer does not allow hardware-switched traffic to be captured between data ports of the switch. For this type of packet capture, SPAN or ELAM is used. When the interfaces are configured with ACLs with ACEs configured with the log option, the hardware-switched flows gets punted to the CPU and thus are captured using Ethanalyzer. However, this should not be tried in production because the packets could get dropped as a result of CoPP policies or the excessive traffic punted to the CPU could impact other services on the device.

Ethanalyzer is configured in three simple steps:

Step 1. Define capture interface.

Step 2. Define Filters: Set the capture filter or display filter.

Step 3. Define the stop criteria.

There are three kinds of capture interfaces:

- **Mgmt:** Captures traffic on the Mgmt0 interface of the switch
- **Inbound-hi:** Captures high-priority control packets on the inband, such as Spanning Tree Protocol (STP), Link Aggregation Control Protocol (LACP), Cisco Discovery Protocol (CDP), Data Center Bridging Exchange (DCBX), Fiber Channel, and Fiber Channel over Ethernet (FCOE)
- **Inbound-low:** Captures low-priority control packets on the inband, such as Internet Group Management Protocol (IGMP), Transmission Control Protocol (TCP), User Datagram Protocol (UDP), Internet Protocol (IP), and Address Resolution Protocol (ARP) traffic

The next step is to set the filters. With a working knowledge of Wireshark, configuring filters for Ethanalyzer is fairly simple. Two kinds of filters can be set up for configuring Ethanalyzer: capture filter and display filter. As the name suggests, when a capture filter is set, only frames that match the filter are captured. The display filter is used to display the packets that match the filter from the captured set of packets. That means Ethanalyzer captures other frames that do not match the display filter but are not displayed in the output. By default, Ethanalyzer supports capturing up to 10 frames and then stops automatically. This value is changed by setting the **limit-captured-frames** option, where 0 means no limit.

Note All in-band Ethernet ports that send or receive data to the switch supervisor are captured with the **inbound-hi** or **inbound-low** option. However, display or capture filtering can be applied.

Ethanalyzer is part of the software running on the supervisor, so it is important to understand its effects on the supervisor's CPU. Normally, Ethanalyzer does not have much impact, but sometimes it can increase the CPU utilization up to 5%. Utilization can be reduced by 1% to 2% by saving the capture data in a file using the **write** option with Ethanalyzer to save the capture in a file.

To start a packet capture with Ethanalyzer, use the command **ethanalyzer local interface [inbound-hi | inbound-lo | mgmt]** *options*, with the following options:

- **Autostop:** Capture autostop condition
- **capture-filter:** Filter on Ethanalyzer capture
- **capture-ring-buffer:** Capture ring buffer option
- **decode-internal:** Include internal system header decoding
- **detail:** Display detailed protocol information
- **display-filter:** Display filter on frames captured
- **limit-captured-frames:** Indicates the maximum number of frames to be captured
- **limit-frame-size:** Capture only a subset of a frame
- **write:** Identifies the filename to save capture to

While using Ethanalyzer, specifying the filters is easier for someone who is familiar with Wireshark filters. The syntax for both the capture filter and the display filter is different. Table 2-1 lists some of the common filters and their syntax with the **capture-filter** and **display-filter** options.

Table 2-1 *Ethanalyzer Capture and Display Filters*

	Capture Filter	**Display Filter**
Operators		And - &&
		Or - ||
		Equal - ==
		Not equal - !=
VLAN	vlan *vlan-id*	vlan.id==*vlan-id*
Layer 2	ether host *00:AA:BB:CC:DD:EE* ether dst *00:AA:BB:CC:DD:EE* ether src *00:AA:BB:CC:DD:EE* ether broadcast ether multicast ether proto *protocol*	eth.addr==*00:AA:BB:CC:DD:EE* eth.src==*00:AA:BB:CC:DD:EE* eth.dst==*00:AA:BB:CC:DD:EE* Match first 2 bytes: eth.src[0:1]==*00:AA* Filter on manufacturer: eth.src[0:2]==*vendor-mac-addr* e.g., Cisco: eth.src[0:2]==**00.00.0c** eth.addr contains aa:bb:cc

	Capture Filter	Display Filter
Layer 3	ip (filters out lower-level protocols such as ARP and STP)	IP address:
		ip.addr==*192.168.1.1*
	host *192.168.1.1*	
	dst host *192.168.1.1*	Source IP:
	src host *192.168.1.1*	ip.src==*192.168.1.1*
	net *192.168.1.0/24*	Dest IP:
	net *192.168.1.0* netmask *24*	ip.dst==*192.168.10.1*
	src net *192.168.1.0/24*	
	dst net *192.168.1.0/24*	Subnet:
	ip broadcast	ip.addr==*192.168.1.0/24*
	ip multicast	
	not broadcast	Fragmentation:
	not multicast	Filter on DF bit set (0 = may fragment)
	icmp	
	udp	ip.flags.df==*1*
	tcp	
	ip proto 6 (udp)	TCP Sequence:
	ip proto 17 (tcp)	tcp.seq==*TCP-Seq-Num*
	ip proto 1 (icmp)	
	Packet length:	
	less *length*	
	greater *length*	
Layer 4	udp port *53*	tcp.port==*53*
	udp dst port *53*	udp.port==*53*
	udp src port *53*	
	tcp port *179*	
	tcp portrange *2000-2100*	
FabricPath	proto 0x8903	Dest HMAC/MC destination:
		cfp.d_hmac==*mac*
		cfp.d_hmac_mc==*mac*

Capture Filter		Display Filter
		EID/FTAG/IG Bit:
		cfp.eid==
		cfp.ftag==
		cfp.ig==
		Source LID/OOO/DL Bit/Source HMAC:
		cfp.lid==
		cfp.ooodl==
		cfp.s_hmac==
		Subswitch ID/Switch ID/TTL:
		cfp.sswid==
		cfp.swid==
		cfp.ttl==
ICMP	icmp	icmp==*icmp-type*
		ICMP-Types:
		icmp-echoreply
		icmp-unreach
		icmp-sourcequench
		icmp-redirect
		icmp-echo
		icmp-routeradvert
		icmp-routersolicit
		icmp-timxceed
		icmp-paramprob
		icmp-tstamp
		icmp-tstampreply
		icmp-ireq
		icmp-ireqreply
		icmp-maskreq
		icmp-maskreply

Example 2-9 illustrates the use of Ethanalyzer to capture all packets hitting the inbound-low as well as inbound-hi queue on Nexus 6000. From the following outputs, notice that the TCP SYN/SYN ACK packets even for a BGP peering are part of the inbound-low queue, but the regular BGP updates and keepalives (such as the TCP packets after the BGP peering is established) and the acknowledgements are part of the inband-hi queue.

Example 2-9 *Ethanalyzer Capture*

```
N6k-1# ethanalyzer local interface inbound-low limit-captured-frames 20
Capturing on inband
2017-05-21 21:26:22.972623 10.162.223.33 -> 10.162.223.34 TCP bgp > 45912 [SYN,
ACK] Seq=0 Ack=0 Win=16616 Len=0 MSS=1460
2017-05-21 21:26:33.214254 10.162.223.33 -> 10.162.223.34 TCP bgp > 14779 [SYN,
ACK] Seq=0 Ack=0 Win=16616 Len=0 MSS=1460
2017-05-21 21:26:44.892236 8c:60:4f:a7:9a:6b -> 01:00:0c:cc:cc:cc CDP Device ID:
  N6k-1(FOC1934R1BF)  Port ID: Ethernet1/4
2017-05-21 21:26:44.892337 8c:60:4f:a7:9a:68 -> 01:00:0c:cc:cc:cc CDP Device ID:
  N6k-1(FOC1934R1BF)  Port ID: Ethernet1/1
2017-05-21 21:27:42.965431 00:25:45:e7:d0:00 -> 8c:60:4f:a7:9a:bc ARP 10.162.223
  .34 is at 00:25:45:e7:d0:00
! Output omitted for brevity
N6k-1# ethanalyzer local interface inbound-hi limit-captured-frames 10

Capturing on inband
2017-05-21 21:34:42.821141 10.162.223.34 -> 10.162.223.33 BGP KEEPALIVE Message
2017-05-21 21:34:42.932217 10.162.223.33 -> 10.162.223.34 TCP bgp > 14779 [ACK]
Seq=1 Ack=20 Win=17520 Len=0
2017-05-21 21:34:43.613048 10.162.223.33 -> 10.162.223.34 BGP KEEPALIVE Message
2017-05-21 21:34:43.814804 10.162.223.34 -> 10.162.223.33 TCP 14779 > bgp [ACK]
Seq=20 Ack=20 Win=15339 Len=0
2017-05-21 21:34:46.005039     10.1.12.2 -> 224.0.0.5    OSPF Hello Packet
2017-05-21 21:34:46.919884 10.162.223.34 -> 10.162.223.33 BGP KEEPALIVE Message
2017-05-21 21:34:47.032215 10.162.223.33 -> 10.162.223.34 TCP bgp > 14779 [ACK]
Seq=20 Ack=39 Win=17520 Len=0
! Output omitted for brevity
```

As stated earlier, optimal practice is to write the captured frames in a file and then read it after the frames are captured. The saved file in a local bootflash is read using the command **ethanalyzer local read** *location* [**detail**].

Nexus 7000 offers no option for inbound-hi or inbound-low. The CLI supports captures on the mgmt interface or the inband interface. The inband interface captures both high- and low-priority packets. Example 2-10 illustrates how to write and read the saved packet capture data. In this example, Ethanalyzer is run with a capture-filter on STP packets.

Example 2-10 *Ethanalyzer Write and Read*

```
N7k-Admin# ethanalyzer local interface inband capture-filter "stp" write
  bootflash:stp.pcap
Capturing on inband
10
N7k-Admin# ethanalyzer local read bootflash:stp.pcap
2017-05-21 23:48:30.216952 5c:fc:66:6c:f3:f6 -> Spanning-tree-(for-bridges)_00
 STP 60 RST. Root = 4096/1/50:87:89:4b:bb:42  Cost = 0  Port = 0x9000
2017-05-21 23:48:30.426556 38:ed:18:a2:27:b0 -> Spanning-tree-(for-bridges)_00
 STP 60 RST. Root = 4096/1/50:87:89:4b:bb:42  Cost = 1  Port = 0x8201
2017-05-21 23:48:30.426690 38:ed:18:a2:27:b0 -> Spanning-tree-(for-bridges)_00
 STP 60 RST. Root = 4096/1/50:87:89:4b:bb:42  Cost = 1  Port = 0x8201
2017-05-21 23:48:30.426714 38:ed:18:a2:17:a6 -> Spanning-tree-(for-bridges)_00
! Output omitted for brevity
```

```
! Detailed output of ethanalyzer
N7k-Admin# ethanalyzer local read bootflash:stp.pcap detail
Frame 1: 60 bytes on wire (480 bits), 60 bytes captured (480 bits)
    Encapsulation type: Ethernet (1)
    Arrival Time: May 21, 2017 23:48:30.216952000 UTC
    [Time shift for this packet: 0.000000000 seconds]
    Epoch Time: 1495410510.216952000 seconds
    [Time delta from previous captured frame: 0.000000000 seconds]
    [Time delta from previous displayed frame: 0.000000000 seconds]
    [Time since reference or first frame: 0.000000000 seconds]
    Frame Number: 1
    Frame Length: 60 bytes (480 bits)
    Capture Length: 60 bytes (480 bits)
    [Frame is marked: False]
    [Frame is ignored: False]
    [Protocols in frame: eth:llc:stp]
IEEE 802.3 Ethernet
    Destination: Spanning-tree-(for-bridges)_00 (01:80:c2:00:00:00)
        Address: Spanning-tree-(for-bridges)_00 (01:80:c2:00:00:00)
        .... ..0. .... .... .... .... = LG bit: Globally unique address (factory
  default)
        .... ...1 .... .... .... .... = IG bit: Group address (multicast/broadcast)
    Source: 5c:fc:66:6c:f3:f6 (5c:fc:66:6c:f3:f6)
        Address: 5c:fc:66:6c:f3:f6 (5c:fc:66:6c:f3:f6)
        .... ..0. .... .... .... .... = LG bit: Globally unique address (factory
  default)
        .... ...0 .... .... .... .... = IG bit: Individual address (unicast)
    Length: 39
    Padding: 00000000000000
```

```
Logical-Link Control
    DSAP: Spanning Tree BPDU (0x42)
    IG Bit: Individual
    SSAP: Spanning Tree BPDU (0x42)
    CR Bit: Command
    Control field: U, func=UI (0x03)
        000. 00.. = Command: Unnumbered Information (0x00)
        .... ..11 = Frame type: Unnumbered frame (0x03)
Spanning Tree Protocol
    Protocol Identifier: Spanning Tree Protocol (0x0000)
    Protocol Version Identifier: Rapid Spanning Tree (2)
    BPDU Type: Rapid/Multiple Spanning Tree (0x02)
    BPDU flags: 0x3c (Forwarding, Learning, Port Role: Designated)
        0... .... = Topology Change Acknowledgment: No
        .0.. .... = Agreement: No
        ..1. .... = Forwarding: Yes
        ...1 .... = Learning: Yes
        .... 11.. = Port Role: Designated (3)
        .... ..0. = Proposal: No
        .... ...0 = Topology Change: No
    Root Identifier: 4096 / 1 / 50:87:89:4b:bb:42
        Root Bridge Priority: 4096
        Root Bridge System ID Extension: 1
        Root Bridge System ID: 50:87:89:4b:bb:42 (50:87:89:4b:bb:42)
    Root Path Cost: 0
    Bridge Identifier: 4096 / 1 / 50:87:89:4b:bb:42
        Bridge Priority: 4096
        Bridge System ID Extension: 1
        Bridge System ID: 50:87:89:4b:bb:42 (50:87:89:4b:bb:42)
    Port identifier: 0x9000
    Message Age: 0
    Max Age: 20
    Hello Time: 2
    Forward Delay: 15
    Version 1 Length: 0
! Output omitted for brevity
```

The saved .pcap file can also be transferred to a remote server via File Transfer Protocol (FTP), Trivial File Transfer Protocol (TFTP), Secure Copy Protocol (SCP), Secure FTP (SFTP), and Universal Serial Bus (USB), after which it can be easily analyzed using a packet analyzer tool such as Wireshark.

Note If multiple VDCs exist on the Nexus 7000, the Ethanalyzer runs only on the admin or default VDC. In addition, starting with Release 7.2 on Nexus 7000, you can use the option to filter on a per-VDC basis.

Packet Tracer

During troubleshooting, it becomes difficult to understand what action the system is taking on a particular packet or flow. For such instances, the packet tracer feature is used. Starting with NX-OS Version 7.0(3)I2(2a), the packet tracer utility was introduced on the Nexus 9000 switch. It is used when intermittent or complete packet loss is observed.

Note At the time of writing, the packet tracer utility is supported only on the line cards or fabric modules that come with Broadcom Trident II ASICs. More details about the Cisco Nexus 9000 ASICs can be found at http://www.cisco.com.

The packet tracer is configured in two simple steps:

Step 1. Define the filter.

Step 2. Start the packet tracer.

To set up the packet tracer, use the command **test packet-tracer** [src-ip *src-ip* | dst-ip *dst-ip*] [**protocol** *protocol-num* | **l4-src-port** *src-port* | **l4-dst-port** *dst-port*]. Then start the packet tracer, using the command **test packet-tracer start**. To view the statistics of the specified traffic and the action on it, use the command **test packet-tracer show**. Finally, stop the packet tracer using the command **test packet-tracer stop**. Example 2-11 illustrates the use of the packet tracer to analyze the ICMP statistics between two hosts.

Example 2-11 *Packet Tracer Configuration and Verification*

```
! Defining the Filter in Packet-Tracer
N9000-1# test packet-tracer src-ip 192.168.2.2 dst-ip 192.168.1.1 protocol 1

! Starting the Packet-Tracer
N9000-1# test packet-tracer start

! Verifying the statistics
N9000-1# test packet-tracer show

 Packet-tracer stats
 ---------------------

Module 1:
Filter 1 installed:   src-ip 192.168.2.2 dst-ip 192.168.1.1 protocol 1
```

```
ASIC instance 0:
Entry 0: id = 9473, count = 120, active, fp,
Entry 1: id = 9474, count = 0, active, hg,
Filter 2 uninstalled:
Filter 3 uninstalled:
Filter 4 uninstalled:
Filter 5 uninstalled:
! Second iteration of the Output
N9000-1# test packet-tracer show

 Packet-tracer stats
 --------------------

Module 1:
Filter 1 installed:  src-ip 192.168.2.2 dst-ip 192.168.1.1 protocol 1
ASIC instance 0:
Entry 0: id = 9473, count = 181, active, fp,
Entry 1: id = 9474, count = 0, active, hg,
Filter 2 uninstalled:
Filter 3 uninstalled:
Filter 4 uninstalled:
Filter 5 uninstalled:
! Stopping the Packet-Tracer
N9000-1# test packet-tracer stop
```

Even if the incoming traffic is dropped because of an ACL, the packet tracer helps determine whether the packet is reaching the router incoming interface. To remove all the filters from the packet tracer, use the command **test packet-tracer remove-all**.

NetFlow

NetFlow is a Cisco feature that provides the capability to collect statistics and information on IP traffic as it enters or exits an interface. NetFlow provides operators with network and security monitoring, network planning, traffic analysis, and IP accounting capabilities. Network traffic is often asymmetrical, even on small networks, whereas probes typically require engineered symmetry. NetFlow does not require engineering the network around the instrumentation; it follows the traffic through the network over its natural path. In addition to traffic rate, NetFlow provides QoS markings, TCP flags, and so on for specific applications, services, and traffic flows at each point in the network. NetFlow assists with validating traffic engineering or policy enforcement at any point in the topology.

Cisco NX-OS supports both traditional NetFlow (Version 5) and Flexible NetFlow (Version 9) export formats, but using flexible NetFlow is recommended on Nexus platforms. With traditional NetFlow, all the keys and fields exported are fixed and it supports only IPv4 flows. By default, a flow is defined by seven unique keys:

- Source IP address
- Destination IP address
- Source port
- Destination port
- Layer 3 protocol type
- TOS byte (DSCP markings)
- Input logical interface (ifindex)

The user can select a few other fields, but NetFlow Version 5 has limitations on the details it can provide. Flexible NetFlow (FNF) is standardized on Version 9 NetFlow and gives users more flexibility on defining flows and the exported fields for each flow type. Flexible NetFlow provides support for IPv6 as well as L2 NetFlow records. The NetFlow version is template based, so users can specify what data has to be exported.

The FNF design gives the following levels benefits:

- Flexibility to choose the definition of a flow (the key and nonkey fields)
- Flexibility to selectively apply different flow definitions to different interfaces
- Flexibility to choose the exporter interface
- Extensibility to future improvements, such as IPFIX

Network operators and architects often wonder where to attach the NetFlow monitor. For such challenges, answering the following questions can assist:

- What type of information are users looking for? MAC fields or IPv4/v6 fields?
- What kind of interfaces are present on the box? L3 or L2 interfaces?
- Is the box switching packets within VLANs or routing them across VLANs using Switched Virtual Interfaces (SVI)?

NetFlow Configuration

These questions help users make the right choice of applying a Layer 3 or Layer 2 NetFlow configuration. Configuring NetFlow on a Nexus switch consists of following steps:

Step 1. Enable the NetFlow feature.

Step 2. Define a flow record by specifying key and nonkey fields of interest.

Step 3. Define one or many flow exporters by specifying export format, protocol, destination, and other parameters.

Step 4. Define a flow monitor based on the previous flow record and flow exporter(s).

Step 5. Apply the flow monitor to an interface with a sampling method specified.

Enable NetFlow Feature

On NX-OS, the NetFlow feature is enabled using the command **feature netflow**. When the feature is enabled, the entire NetFlow-related CLI becomes available to the user.

> **Note** NetFlow consumes hardware resources such as TCAM and CPU. Thus, understanding the resource utilization on the device is recommended before enabling NetFlow.

Define a Flow Record

A flow record is defined by specifying the different match keys and parameters NetFlow uses to identify the packets. A flow record is created using the command **flow record** *name*. NX-OS enables the following match fields by default when a flow record is created:

- Match interface input
- Match interface output
- Match flow direction

A flow record also specifies the fields of interest that has to be collected for a flow. The following match keys are supported for identifying flows in NetFlow:

- IPv4 source/destination address
- IPv6 source/destination address
- IPv6 flow label
- IPv6 options
- ToS field
- L4 protocol
- L4 source/destination ports

The following match key is provided for Layer 2 NetFlow:

- Source/destination MAC address
- Ethertype
- VLAN

A user has the flexibility to select the collect parameters that can be used in either Version 5 or Version 9, except for IPv6 parameters, which can be used only with Version 9. The following parameters are collected using NetFlow:

- Number of L3 bytes (32 bit or 64 bit)
- Number of packets (32 bit or 64 bit)
- Direction of the flow
- Sampler ID used for the flow
- Interface info (input and/or output)
- Source/destination AS number of the local device or the peer
- Next-hop IPv4/IPv6 address
- System uptime for the first or last packet
- TCP flags

Example 2-12 shows the configuration for a flow record for both Layer 3 and Layer 2 traffic. In this flow record, multiple match entries are created, along parameters to be used for collection.

Example 2-12 *NetFlow Flow Record*

```
! Flow Record for Layer 3 Traffic
flow record FR_V4
  match ipv4 source address
  match ipv4 destination address
  match ip protocol
  match ip tos
  collect timestamp sys-uptime last
  collect flow sampler id
  collect ip version
! Flow record for Layer 2 Traffic
flow record FR_L2
  match datalink mac source-address
  match datalink mac destination-address
  match datalink vlan
  match datalink ethertype
  collect counter packets
  collect flow sampler id
```

Define a Flow Exporter

The next step is to define a flow exporter. NetFlow data is exported to a remote collector using UDP frames. The data is exported periodically upon expiration of a flow timeout that is configurable by the user. The default flow timeout value is 30 minutes. Under the flow export, the following fields are defined:

- Collector IPv4/IPv6 address
- Source interface
- Virtual Routing and Forwarding (VRF)
- Version
- UDP port number

Example 2-13 demonstrates the configuration of the flow exporter.

Example 2-13 *NetFlow Flow Exporter*

```
flow exporter FL_Exp
  destination 100.1.1.1 use-vrf management
  transport udp 3000
  source mgmt0
  version 9
```

Define and Apply the Flow Monitor

After the flow exporter is defined, it is time to bind the flow record and the flow exporter to a flow monitor. When the flow monitor is defined, the flow monitor can be attached to an interface for collecting NetFlow statistics. Example 2-14 displays the configuration of the flow monitor and illustrates enabling NetFlow under the interface. To apply NetFlow for IPv4/IPv6/Layer 2 traffic, use the command [**ip** | **ipv6** | **layer2-switched**] **flow monitor** *name* [**input** | **output**].

Example 2-14 *NetFlow Flow Monitor and Interface Configuration*

```
flow monitor FL_MON
  record FR_V4
  exporter FL_Exp
!
interface Eth3/31-32
ip flow monitor FL_MON input
ip flow monitor FL_MON output
```

The NetFlow configuration is viewed using the command **show run netflow**. To validate the NetFlow configuration, use the command **show flow** [**record** *record-name* | **exporter** *exporter-name* | **monitor** *monitor-name*].

To view the statistics of the flow ingressing and egressing the interface E1/4 as configured in the previous example, use the command **show hardware flow** [**ip** | **ipv6**] [**detail**]. Example 2-15 displays the statistics of the ingress and egress traffic flowing across the interfaces Eth3/31-32. This example shows both ingress (I) and egress (O) traffic. NetFlow displays the statistics for OSPF and other ICMP traffic, along with the protocol number and packet count.

Example 2-15 *NetFlow Statistics*

```
N7k-1# show hardware flow ip
slot  3
=======
D - Direction; L4 Info - Protocol:Source Port:Destination Port
IF - Interface: ()ethernet, (S)vi, (V)lan, (P)ortchannel, (T)unnel
TCP Flags: Ack, Flush, Push, Reset, Syn, Urgent

D IF         SrcAddr          DstAddr          L4 Info           PktCnt       TCPFlags
-+----------+----------------+----------------+----------------+----------+--------
I 3/31      010.012.001.002 224.000.000.005 089:00000:00000 0000000159 ......
I 3/32      010.013.001.003 224.000.000.005 089:00000:00000 0000000128 ......
I 3/32      003.003.003.003 002.002.002.002 001:00000:00000 0000000100 ......
I 3/31      002.002.002.002 003.003.003.003 001:00000:00000 0000000100 ......
O 3/31      003.003.003.003 002.002.002.002 001:00000:00000 0000000100 ......
O 3/32      002.002.002.002 003.003.003.003 001:00000:00000 0000000100 ......
```

The statistics in Example 2-15 are collected on the N7k platform, which supports hardware-based flows. However, not all Nexus platforms have support for hardware-based flow matching. Nexus switches such as Nexus 6000 do not support hardware-based flow matching. Thus, a software-based flow matching must be performed. This can be resource consuming and can impact performance, however, so such platforms support only Sampled NetFlow (see the following section).

Note Nexus 5600 and Nexus 6000 support only ingress NetFlow applied to the interface; Nexus 7000 supports both ingress and egress NetFlow statistics collection.

NetFlow Sampling

NetFlow supports sampling on the data points to reduce the amount of data collected. This implementation of NetFlow is called Sampled NetFlow (SNF). SNF supports M:N packet sampling, where only *M* packets are sampled out of *N* packets.

A sampler is configured using the command **sampler** *name*. Under the sampler configuration, sampler mode is defined using the command **mode** *sample-number* **out-of** *packet-number*, where *sample-number* ranges from 1 to 64 and the *packet-number* ranges from 1 to 65536 packets). This is defined using the sampler subcommand **mode** *sampler-number* **out-of** *packet-number*. After the sampler is defined, it is used in conjunction with the flow monitor configuration under the interface in Example 2-16.

Example 2-16 *NetFlow Sampler and Interface Configuration*

```
sampler NF-SAMPLER1
 mode 1 out-of 1000
!
interface Eth3/31-32
 ip flow monitor FL_MON input sampler NF-SAMPLER1
```

Users can also define the active and inactive timer for the flows using the command **flow timeout [active | inactive]** *time-in-seconds*.

Starting with NX-OS Version 7.3(0)D1(1), NetFlow is also supported on the control plane policing (CoPP) interface. NetFlow on the CoPP interface enables users to monitor and collect statistics of different packets that are destined for the supervisor module on the switch. NX-OS allows an IPv4 flow monitor and a sampler to be attached to the control plane interface in the output direction. Example 2-17 demonstrates the NetFlow configuration under CoPP interface and the relevant NetFlow statistics on the Nexus 7000 platform.

Example 2-17 *CoPP NetFlow Configuration and Verification*

```
Control-plane
 ip flow monitor FL_MON output sampler NF-SAMPLER1
```

> **Note** In case of any problems with NetFlow, collect the output of the command **show tech-support netflow** during problematic state.

sFlow

Defined in RFC 3176, sFlow is a technology for monitoring traffic using sampling mechanisms that are implemented as part of an sFlow agent in data networks that contain switches and routers. The sFlow agent is a new software feature for the Nexus 9000 and Nexus 3000 platforms. The sFlow agent on these platforms collects the sampled packet from both ingress and egress ports and forwards it to the central collector, known as the sFlow Analyzer. The sFlow agent can periodically sample or poll the counters associated with a data source of the sampled packets.

When sFlow is enabled on an interface, it is enabled for both ingress and egress directions. sFlow can be configured only for Ethernet and port-channel interfaces. sFlow is enabled by configuring the command **feature sflow**. Various parameters can be defined as part of the configuration (see Table 2-2).

Table 2-2 *sFlow Parameters*

sFlow Parameter Configuration	Description
sflow sampling rate *rate*	The sampling rate for packets. The default is 4096. A value of 0 implies that sampling is disabled.
sflow max-sampled-size *sampling-size*	The maximum sampling size for packets. The default is 128 bytes. The value ranges from 64 to 256 bytes.
sflow counter-poll-interval *poll-interval*	The polling interval for an interface. The default is 20 seconds.
sflow max-datagram-size *size*	The maximum datagram size. The default is 1400 bytes.
sflow collector-ip *ip-address* **vrf** *vrf-context*	The sFlow collector/analyzer IP address.
sflow collector-port *port-number*	The UDP port number of the sFlow analyzer.
sflow agent-ip *ip-address*	The address of the sFlow agent. This is the local and valid IP address on the switch.
sflow data-source interface *interface-type interface-num*	The sFlow sampling data source.

Example 2-18 illustrates the configuration of sFlow on a Nexus 3000 switch. The running configuration of sFlow is viewed using the command **show run sflow**.

Example 2-18 *sFlow Configuration*

```
feature sflow
sflow sampling-rate 1000
sflow max-sampled-size 200
sflow counter-poll-interval 100
sflow max-datagram-size 2000
sflow collector-ip 172.16.1.100 vrf management
sflow collector-port 2020
sflow agent-ip 170.16.1.130
sflow data-source interface ethernet 1/1-2
```

To verify the configuration, use the command **show sflow**. This command output displays all the information that is configured for the sFlow (see Example 2-19).

Example 2-19 show sflow *Command Output*

```
N3K-1# show sflow
sflow sampling-rate : 1000
sflow max-sampled-size : 200
sflow counter-poll-interval : 100
sflow max-datagram-size : 2000
sflow collector-ip : 172.16.1.100 , vrf : management
sflow collector-port : 2020
sflow agent-ip : 172.16.1.130
sflow data-source interface Ethernet1/1
sflow data-source interface Ethernet1/2
```

When sFlow is configured, the sFlow agent starts collecting the statistics. Although the actual flow is viewed on the sFlow collector tools, you can still see the sFlow statistics on the switch using the command **show sflow statistics** and also view both internal information about the sFlow and statistics using the command **show system internal sflow info**. Example 2-20 displays the statistics for the sFlow. Notice that although the total packet count is high, the number of sampled packets is very low. This is because the configuration defines sampling taken per 1000 packets. The system internal command for sFlow also displays the resource utilization and its present state.

Example 2-20 *sFlow Statistics and Internal Info*

```
N3K-1# show sflow statistics
Total Packets         : 1053973
Total Samples         : 11
Processed Samples     : 11
Dropped Samples       : 0
Sent Datagrams        : 56
Dropped Datagrams     : 13
N3K-1# show system internal sflow info
sflow probe state -> RUN
sflow inband sflow is valid
sflow inband driver -> UP
sflow IPv4 socket fd 47
number of sflow sampled packets : 11
number of sflow dropped packets : 0
number of sflow datagram sent : 56
number of sflow datagram dropped : 13
sflow process cpu usage 0.86
sflow process cpu limit 50
```

Note In case of any problems with sFlow, collect the output of the command by using **show tech-support sflow** during problematic state.

Network Time Protocol

While troubleshooting, network operators often run through the logs to understand the symptoms of the problem and the timeline of the problem so they can find the relevant trigger of the problem. If the time is not synced on the devices, correlating the event across multiple devices becomes difficult. To overcome this problem, it is recommended to have the clock on the Nexus device synced with NTP throughout the network. NTP is used to synchronize clocks of devices in the network and on the Internet. NTP uses predefined UDP port number 123.

To configure NTP on the devices, enable NTP by using the command **feature ntp**. The Nexus device is configured for NTP depending on its role in the network (as either an NTP client or an NTP server). An NTP server receives its time from a time source that is attached to a time server and distributes the time across the network. As with distance-vector protocols, NTP uses a stratum value to describe the distance between a network device and an authoritative time source.

An NX-OS device can be configured as an NTP server and also an NTP peer. An NTP peer relationship enables network engineers to designate another host to consider synchronizing the time with in case a failure event occurs on the NTP server. The NTP server or NTP peer is defined using the command **ntp [server | peer]** [*ip-address* | *ipv6-address*] **[prefer] [use-vrf** *vrf-name*]. The configured NTP servers and peers are viewed using the command **show ntp peers**.

Additionally, users can configure a Nexus switch as an authoritative time server using the command **ntp master**. NX-OS also allows the users to specify the source interface or IP address of the NTP packets on the switch. The source of NTP packets is defined using the commands **ntp source** *ip-address* and **ntp source-interface** *interface-id*. If the configuration is specified, ensure that the NTP server is reachable via the specified IP address. These configurations are useful especially on a Nexus 7000 switch with multiple VDCs configured. On a multi-VDC Nexus 7000 switch, the hardware clock is synchronized in the default VDC, and a nondefault VDC can get the timing update from the default VDC. The nondefault VDC also acts as the server for other clients in the network after the **ntp master** command is configured under the VDC.

Example 2-21 demonstrates the NTP configuration on the Nexus device as a server and as a client.

Example 2-21 *NTP Configuration*

```
! NTP Server Configuration
ntp peer 172.16.1.11 use-vrf management
ntp source-interface  mgmt0
ntp master 8
```

```
! NTP Client Configuration
ntp server 172.16.1.10 prefer use-vrf management
ntp server 172.16.1.11 use-vrf management
ntp source-interface  mgmt0
```

When the NTP is configured, the NTP is automatically synchronized on the client from the server. To check the status of the NTP server or peer, use the command **show ntp peer-status**. The * beside the peer address indicates that the NTP has synchronized with the server. Example 2-22 displays the output from both the server and the client. On the NTP server, notice that the peer address is 127.127.1.0, which means that the device itself is the NTP server. On the client, the * is beside 172.16.1.10, which is configured as the preferred NTP server in the configuration. Note that all the devices in this example are part of the same management subnet.

Example 2-22 *NTP Configuration*

```
! NTP Server Verification
NX-1# show ntp peers
--------------------------------------------------
 Peer IP Address                 Serv/Peer
--------------------------------------------------
 127.127.1.0                     Server (configured)
 172.16.1.11                     Peer (configured)

NX-1# show ntp peer-status
Total peers : 2
* - selected for sync, + - peer mode(active),
- - peer mode(passive), = - polled in client mode
    remote              local              st    poll   reach delay     vrf
--------------------------------------------------------------------------
*127.127.1.0            0.0.0.0             8    16     377   0.00000
+172.16.1.11            0.0.0.0            16    16     0     0.00000  management

! NTP Client Verification
NX-3(config)# show ntp peer-status
Total peers : 2
* - selected for sync, + - peer mode(active),
- - peer mode(passive), = - polled in client mode
    remote              local              st    poll   reach delay     vrf
--------------------------------------------------------------------------
*172.16.1.10            0.0.0.0             9    16     77    0.00197  management
=172.16.1.11            0.0.0.0            10    16     0     0.00000  management
```

After the NTP has been synchronized, the time is verified using the **show clock** command.

NX-OS also has a built-in proprietary feature known as Cisco Fabric Services (CFS) that can be used to distribute data and configuration changes to all Nexus devices. CFS distributes all local NTP configuration across all the Nexus devices in the network. It applies a network-wide lock for NTP when the NTP configuration is started. When the configuration changes are made, users can discard or commit the changes, and the committed configuration replicates across all Nexus devices. The CFS for NTP is enabled using the command

ntp distribute. The configuration is committed to all the Nexus devices by using the **ntp commit** command and is aborted using the **ntp abort** command. When either command is executed, CFS releases the lock on NTP across network devices. To check that the fabric distribution is enabled for NTP, use the command **show ntp status**.

NX-OS also provides a CLI to verify the statistics of the NTP packets. Users can view input-output statistics for NTP packets, local counters maintained by NTP, and memory-related NTP counters (which is useful in case of a memory leak condition by NTP process), and per-peer NTP statistics. If the NTP packets are getting dropped for some reason, those statistics can be viewed from the CLI itself. To view these statistics, use the command **show ntp statistics** [**io** | **local** | **memory** | **peer ipaddr** *ip-address*]. Example 2-23 displays the IO and local statistics for NTP packets. If bad NTP packets or bad authentication requests are received, those counters are viewed under local statistics.

Example 2-23 *NTP Statistics*

```
NX-1# show ntp statistics io
time since reset:        91281
receive buffers:         10
free receive buffers:    9
used receive buffers:    0
low water refills:       1
dropped packets:         0
ignored packets:         0
received packets:        9342
packets sent:            9369
packets not sent:        0
interrupts handled:      9342
received by int:         9342
NX-1# show ntp statistics local
system uptime:           91294
time since reset:        91294
old version packets:     9195
new version packets:     0
unknown version number:  0
bad packet format:       0
packets processed:       4
bad authentication:      0
```

Embedded Event Manager

Embedded Event Manager (EEM) is a powerful device- and system-management technology integrated in NX-OS. EEM helps customers harness the network intelligence intrinsic to Cisco's software and give them the capability to customize behavior based on the network events as they happen. EEM is an event-driven tool that takes various types of trigger input and enables the user to define what actions can be taken. This includes capturing various **show** commands or performing actions such as executing a Tool Command Language (TCL) or Python script when the event gets triggered.

An EEM consists of two major components:

- **Event:** Defines the event to be monitored from another NX-OS component
- **Action:** Defines action to be taken when the event is triggered

Another component of EEM is the EEM policy, which is nothing but an event paired with one or more actions to help troubleshoot or recover from an event. Some system-defined policies look out for certain system-level events such as a line card reload or supervisor switchover event and then perform predefined actions based on those events. These system-level policies are viewed using the command **show event manager system-policy**. The policies are overridable as well and can be verified using the previous command. The system policies help prevent a larger impact on the device or the network. For instance, if a module has gone bad and keeps crashing continuously, it can severely impact services and cause major outages. A system policy for powering down the module after N crashes can reduce the impact.

Example 2-24 lists some of the system policy events and describes the actions on those events. The command **show event manager policy-state** *system-policy-name* checks how many times an event has occurred.

Example 2-24 *EEM System Policy*

```
NX-1# show event manager system-policy
          Name : __lcm_module_failure
   Description : Power-cycle 2 times then power-down
   Overridable : Yes


          Name : __pfm_fanabsent_any_singlefan
   Description : Shutdown if any fanabsent for 5 minute(s)
   Overridable : Yes


          Name : __pfm_fanbad_any_singlefan
   Description : Syslog when fan goes bad
   Overridable : Yes


          Name : __pfm_power_over_budget
   Description : Syslog warning for insufficient power overbudget
   Overridable : Yes


          Name : __pfm_tempev_major
   Description : TempSensor Major Threshold.  Action: Shutdown
   Overridable : Yes
```

```
            Name : __pfm_tempev_minor
     Description : TempSensor Minor Threshold.  Action: Syslog.
     Overridable : Yes
NX-1# show event manager policy-state __lcm_module_failure
Policy __lcm_module_failure
  Cfg count :   3
    Hash         Count       Policy will trigger if
-----------------------------------------------------------------
    default        0         3 more event(s) occur
```

An event can be either a system event or a user-triggered event, such as configuration change. Actions are defined as the workaround or notification that should be triggered in case an event occurs. EEM supports the following actions, which are defined in the **action** statement:

- Executing CLI commands (configuration or **show** commands)
- Updating the counter
- Logging exceptions
- Reloading devices
- Printing a syslog message
- Sending an SNMP notification
- Setting the default action policy for the system policy
- Executing a TCL or Python script

For example, an action can be taken when high CPU utilization is being seen on the router, or logs can be taken when a BGP session has flapped. Example 2-25 shows the EEM configuration on a Nexus platform. The EEM has the trigger event set for the high CPU condition (for instance, the CPU utilization is 70% or higher); the actions include BGP **show** commands that are captured when the high CPU condition is noticed. The policy is viewed using the command **show event manager policy internal** *policy-name*.

Example 2-25 *EEM Configuration and Verification*

```
event manager applet HIGH-CPU
 event snmp oid 1.3.6.1.4.1.9.9.109.1.1.1.1.6.1 get-type exact entry-op ge
       entry-val 70 exit-val 30 poll-interval 1
 action 1.0 syslog msg High CPU hit $_event_pub_time
 action 2.0 cli command enable
 action 3.0 cli command "show clock >> bootflash:high-cpu.txt"
 action 4.0 cli command "show processes cpu sort >> bootflash:high-cpu.txt"
 action 5.0 cli command "show bgp vrf all all summary >> bootflash:high-cpu.txt"
 action 6.0 cli command "show clock >> bootflash:high-cpu.txt"
 action 7.0 cli command "show bgp vrf all all summary >> bootflash:high-cpu.txt"
```

86 Chapter 2: NX-OS Troubleshooting Tools

```
NX-1# show event manager policy internal HIGH-CPU
                    Name : HIGH-CPU
             Policy Type : applet
  action 1.0 syslog msg "High CPU hit $_event_pub_time"
  action 1.1 cli command "enable"
  action 3.0 cli command "show clock >> bootflash:high-cpu.txt"
  action 4.0 cli command "show processes cpu sort >> bootflash:high-cpu.txt"
  action 5.0 cli command "show bgp vrf all all summary >> bootflash:high-cpu.txt"
  action 6.0 cli command "show clock >> bootflash:high-cpu.txt"
  action 7.0 cli command "show bgp vrf all all summary >> bootflash:high-cpu.txt"
```

In some instances, repetitive configuration or **show** commands must be issued when an event is triggered. Additionally, using an external script makes it difficult to continuously monitor the device for an event and then trigger the script. For such scenarios, a better solution is to use automation scripts and tools that are available with NX-OS. NX-OS provides the capability to use TCL and Python scripts in the EEM itself, which allows those scripts to be triggered only when an event is triggered.

Consider an example software problem in which any link shutdown on the switch causes the switching to get disabled on all the VLANs present on the switch. Example 2-26 demonstrates triggering the TCL script for a link shutdown. The TCL is saved on the bootflash with the .tcl extension. The TCL file iterates over all the VLAN database and performs a **no shutdown** under the VLAN configuration mode.

Example 2-26 *EEM with TCL Script*

```
! Save the file in bootflash with the .tcl extension
set i 1
while {$i<10} {
cli configure terminal
cli vlan $i
cli no shutdown
cli exit
incr i
}

! EEM Configuration referencing TCL Script
event manager applet TCL
event cli match "shutdown"
 action 1.0 syslog msg "Triggering TCL Script on Module Failure Event"
 action 2.0 cli local tclsh EEM.tcl
```

Similarly, a Python script can be referenced in the EEM script. The Python script is also saved in the bootflash with the .py extension. Example 2-27 illustrates a Python script and its reference in the EEM script. In this example, the EEM script is triggered when the traffic on the interface exceeds the configured storm-control threshold. In such an event, the triggered Python script collects multiple commands.

Example 2-27 *Python Script with EEM*

```
! Save the Python script in bootflash:
import re
import cisco
cisco.cli ("show module >> bootflash:EEM.txt")
cisco.cli ("show redundancy >> bootflash:EEM.txt")
cisco.cli ("show interface >> bootflash:EEM.txt")

! EEM Configuration referencing Python Script
event manager applet Py_EEM
event storm-control
 action 1.0 syslog msg "Triggering TCL Script on Module Failure Event"
 action 2.0 cli local python EEM.py
```

Note Refer to the CCO documentation at www.cisco.com for more details on configuring EEM on various Cisco Operating Systems. If any behavioral issues arise with EEM, capture the **show tech-support eem** output from the device.

Logging

Network issues are hard to troubleshoot and investigate if the device contains no information. For instance, if an OSPF adjacency goes down and no correlating alert exists, determining when the problem happened and what caused the problem is difficult. For these reasons, logging is important. All Cisco routers and switches support logging functionality. Logging capabilities are also available for specific features and protocols. For example, logging can be enabled for BGP session state changes or OSPF adjacency state changes.

Table 2-3 lists the various logging levels that can be configured.

Table 2-3 *Logging Levels*

Level Number	Level Name
0	Emergency
1	Alert
2	Critical
3	Errors
4	Warnings
5	Notifications
6	Informational
7	Debugging

When the higher value is set, all the lower logging levels are enabled by default. If the logging level is set to 5 (Notifications), for example, all events falling under the category from 0 to 5 (Emergency to Notifications) are logged. For troubleshooting purpose, setting the logging level to 7 (Debugging) is good practice.

Multiple logging options are available on Cisco devices:

- Console logging
- Buffered logging
- Logging to syslog server

Console logging is important when the device is experiencing crashes or a high CPU condition and access to the terminal session via Telnet or Secure Shell (SSH) is not available. However, having console logging enabled when running debugs is not a good practice because some debug outputs are chatty and can flood the device console. As a best practice, console logging should always be disabled when running debugs. Example 2-28 illustrates how to enable console logging on Nexus platforms.

Example 2-28 *Configuring Console Logging*

```
NX-1(config)# logging console ?
  <CR>
  <0-7>   0-emerg;1-alert;2-crit;3-err;4-warn;5-notif;6-inform;7-debug
NX-1(config)# logging console 6
```

NX-OS not only provides robust logging, but it also is persistent across reloads. All the buffered logging is present in the /var/log/external/ directory. To view the internal directories, use the command **show system internal flash**. This command lists all the internal directories that are part of the flash along with their utilization. The buffered log messages are viewed using the command **show logging log**.

Example 2-29 displays the directories present in the flash and the contents of the /var/log/external/ directory. If the **show logging log** command does not display output or the logging gets stopped, check the /var/log/ directory to ensure that space is available for that directory.

Example 2-29 *Internal Flash Directories*

```
NX-1# show system internal flash
Mount-on                1K-blocks        Used   Available  Use%  Filesystem
/                          409600       69476      340124    17  /dev/root
/proc                           0           0           0     0  proc
/sys                            0           0           0     0  none
/debugfs                        0           0           0     0  nodev
/cgroup                         0           0           0     0  vdccontrol
/isan                      716800      519548      197252    73  none
```

```
/etc                         5120      1632      3488     32   none
/nxos/tmp                   20480      1536     18944      8   none
/var/log                    51200       108     51092      1   none
/var/home                    5120         0      5120      0   none
/var/tmp                   307200       460    306740      1   none
/var/sysmgr               1048576       144   1048432      1   none
/var/sysmgr/ftp            409600        80    409520      1   none
/dev/shm                  1048576    353832    694744     34   none
/volatile                  204800         0    204800      0   none
/debug                       2048        28      2020      2   none
/dev/mqueue                     0         0         0      0   none
/mnt/cfg/0                 325029     12351    295897      5   /dev/sda5
/mnt/cfg/1                 325029     12349    295899      5   /dev/sda6
/mnt/cdrom                    350       350         0    100   /dev/scd0
/var/sysmgr/startup-cfg     40960      4192     36768     11   none
/dev/pts                        0         0         0      0   devpts
/mnt/pss                   325061      8898    299380      3   /dev/sda3
/bootflash                3134728    202048   2773444      7   /dev/sda4
/smack                          0         0         0      0   smackfs
NX-1# show system internal dir /var/log/external/
                                              ./            240
                                             ../            300
                                    libfipf.5834              0
                                     l2fm_ut.txt            774
                                     plcmgr.dbg              21
                                        snmp_log            180
                                    libfipf.3884              0
                                    libfipf.3855              0
                               syslogd_ha_debug          11221
                                        messages          25153
                                    startupdebug           3710
                                          dmesg@             31
```

The logging level is also defined for various NX-OS components so that the user can control logging for chatty components or disable certain logging messages for less chatty or less important components. This is achieved by setting the logging level of the component using the command **logging level** *component-name level*. Example 2-30 demonstrates setting the logging level of the ARP and Ethpm components to 3 to reduce unwanted log messages.

Example 2-30 *NX-OS Component Logging Level*

```
NX-1(config)# logging level arp 3
NX-1(config)# logging level ethpm 3
```

The most persistent form of logging is to use a syslog server to log all the device logs. A syslog server is anything from a text file to a custom application that actively stores device logging information in a database.

Example 2-31 illustrates the syslog logging configuration. Before configuring syslog-based logging on NX-OS, the command **logging timestamp [microseconds | milliseconds | seconds]** must be enabled for the logging messages so that all log messages have time stamps. This helps when investigating the log messages. Generally, management interfaces are configured with a management VRF. In such cases, the syslog host must be specified using the **logging server** *ip-address* **use-vrf** *vrf-name* command on NX-OS so that the router knows from which VRF routing table the server is reachable. If the VRF option is not specified, the system does a lookup in default VRF (the global routing table).

Example 2-31 *Syslog Logging Configuration*

```
NX-1(config)# logging timestamp milliseconds
NX-1(config)# logging server 10.1.1.100 7 use-vrf management
```

Debug Logfiles

NX-OS provides the user with an option to redirect debug output to a file. This is useful when running debugs and segregating debug outputs from regular log messages. Use the **debug logfile** *file-name* **size** *size* command. Example 2-32 demonstrates using the **debug logfile** command to capture debugs in a logfile. In this example, a debug logfile named bgp_dbg is created with a size of 10000 bytes. The size of the logfile ranges from 4096 bytes to 4194304 bytes. All the debugs that are enabled are logged under the logfile. To filter the debug output further to capture more precise debug output, use the **debug-filter** option. In the following example, a BGP update debug is enabled and the update debug logs are filtered for neighbor 10.12.1.2 in a VRF context VPN_A.

Example 2-32 *Capturing Debug in a Logfile on NX-OS*

```
NX-1# debug logfile bgp_dbg size 100000
NX-1# debug ip bgp updates
NX-1# debug-filter bgp neighbor 10.12.1.2
NX-1# debug-filter bgp vrf VPN_A
```

The NX-OS software creates the logfile in the log: file system root directory, so all the created logfiles are viewed using **dir log:**. After the debug logfile is created, the respective debugs are enabled and all the debug outputs are redirected to the debug logfile. To view the contents of the logfile, use the **show debug logfile** *file-name* command.

Accounting Log

During troubleshooting, it is important to identify the trigger of the problem, which could be normal **show** command or a configuration change. For such issues, examining all the configuration and **show** commands during the time of the problem provides vital information.

NX-OS logs all this information into the accounting logfile, which is readily available to the users. Using the command **show accounting log**, users capture all the commands executed and configured on the system, along with the time stamp and user information. The accounting logs are persistent across reloads. By default, the accounting logs capture only the configuration commands. To allow the capture of **show** commands along with configuration commands, configure the command **terminal log-all**. Example 2-33 displays the output of the accounting log, highlighting the various configuration changes made on the device.

Note The accounting logs and **show** logging logfiles are both stored on logflash and are accessible across reloads.

Example 2-33 *Accounting Log*

```
NX-1# show accounting log
Sun Apr  2 01:09:02 2017:type=update:id=vsh.12412:user=admin:cmd=configure terminal ;
  version 6.0(2)U6(9) (SUCCESS)
Sun Apr  2 01:09:03 2017:type=update:id=vsh.12412:user=admin:cmd=interface-vlan
  enable
Sun Apr  2 01:09:03 2017:type=update:id=vsh.12412:user=admin:cmd=configure terminal ;
  feature interface-vlan (SUCCESS)
Sun Apr  2 01:09:38 2017:type=update:id=vsh.12963:user=admin:cmd=configure terminal ;
  control-plane (SUCCESS)
Sun Apr  2 01:09:38 2017:type=update:id=vsh.12963:user=admin:cmd=configure terminal ;
  control-plane ; service-policy input copp-system-policy (SUCCESS
)
Sun Apr  2 01:09:38 2017:type=update:id=vsh.12963:user=admin:cmd=configure terminal ;
  hardware profile tcam region arpacl 128 (SUCCESS)
Sun Apr  2 01:09:38 2017:type=update:id=vsh.12963:user=admin:cmd=configure terminal ;
  hardware profile tcam region ifacl 256 (SUCCESS)
Sun Apr  2 01:09:38 2017:type=update:id=vsh.12963:user=admin:cmd=configure terminal ;
 ip ftp source-interface mgmt0 (SUCCESS)
! Output omitted for brevity
```

Event-History

NX-OS provides continuous logging for all events that occur in the system for both hardware and software components as event-history logs. The event-history logs are VDC local and are maintained on a per-component basis. These logs reduce the need for running debugs in a live production environment and are useful for investigating a service outage even after the services are restored. The event-history logs are captured in the background for each component and do not have any impact on CPU utilization to perform this task.

The event-history log size is configurable to three sizes:

- Large
- Medium
- Small

The event-history logs are viewed from the CLI of each component. For instance, the event-history is viewed for all ARP events using the command **show ip arp internal event-history event**. Example 2-34 displays the event-history logs for ARP and shows how to modify the event-history size. Disable the event-history logs by using the **disabled** keyword while defining the size of the event-history. Disabling event-history is not a recommended practice, however, because it reduces the chances of root causing a problem and understanding the sequence of events that occurred.

Example 2-34 *ARP Event-History Logs and Buffer Size*

```
NX-1# show ip arp internal event-history event
1) Event:E_DEBUG, length:143, at 449547 usecs after Mon May 29 11:11:38 2017
    [116] [4201]: Adj info: iod: 2, phy-iod: 2, ip: 172.16.1.11, mac: fa16.3ee2.
b6d3, type: 0, sync: FALSE, suppress-mode: ARP Suppression Disabled

2) Event:E_DEBUG, length:193, at 449514 usecs after Mon May 29 11:11:38 2017
    [116] [4201]: Entry added to ARP pt, added to AM for 172.16.1.11, fa16.3ee2.
b6d3, state 2 on interface mgmt0, physical interface mgmt0, ismct 0. R
earp (interval: 0, count: 0), TTL: 1500 seconds

3) Event:E_DEBUG, length:79, at 449432 usecs after Mon May 29 11:11:38 2017
    [116] [4201]: arp_add_adj: Updating MAC on interface mgmt0, phy-interface mgmt0
! Output omitted for brevity
NX-1(config)# ip arp event-history event size ?
  disabled  Disabled
            *Default value is small
  large     Large buffer
  medium    Medium buffer
  small     Small buffer
NX-1(config)# ip arp event-history event size large
```

Summary

This chapter focused on various NX-OS tools that can be used to troubleshoot complex problems. It examined various packet capture capabilities with Nexus platforms, including SPAN and ERSPAN. NX-OS provides the following capabilities, which are useful for troubleshooting latency and drops from buffer congestion:

- SPAN-on-Latency
- SPAN-on-Drop

The chapter explained how to use internal platform tools such as Ethanalyzer and packet tracer; it also described NetFlow and sFlow use cases, deployment, and configuration for collecting statistics and network planning. NTP ensures that all clocks are synchronized across multiple devices, to properly correlate timing of events across devices. EEM scripts are useful for troubleshooting on a daily basis or collecting information after an event. Finally, the chapter looked at the logging methods available with NX-OS, including accounting and event-history logging.

References

RFC 3176, InMon Corporation's sFlow: A Method for Monitoring Traffic in Switched and Routed Networks. P. Phaal, S. Panchen, and N. McKee. IETF, https://www.ietf.org/rfc/rfc3176.txt, September 2001.

BRKARC-2011, Overview of Packet Capturing Tools, Cisco Live.

Cisco, sFlow Configuration Guide, http://www.cisco.com/c/en/us/td/docs/switches/datacenter/nexus3000/sw/system_mgmt/503_U4_1/b_3k_System_Mgmt_Config_503_u4_1/b_3k_System_Mgmt_Config_503_u4_1_chapter_010010.html.

Chapter 3

Troubleshooting Nexus Platform Issues

This chapter covers the following topics:

- Troubleshooting Line Card Issues
- Troubleshooting Nexus Fabric
- Troubleshooting Hardware Drops
- Virtual Device Context
- System QoS and CoPP
- NX-OS

Chapter 1, "Introduction to Nexus Operating System (NX-OS)," explored the various Nexus platforms and the line cards supported on them. In addition to understanding the platform and the architecture, it is vital to understand what system components are present and how to troubleshoot various hardware-level components on the Nexus platforms. This chapter focuses on platform-level troubleshooting.

Troubleshooting Hardware Issues

Nexus is a modular platform that comes in either a single-slot or multiple-slot chassis format. In a single-slot chassis, the Nexus switch has a supervisor card with the physical interfaces integrated into it. A multislot chassis supports supervisor engine cards (SUP cards), line cards, and fabric cards. Each type plays an important role in the Nexus forwarding architecture and makes it a highly available and distributed architecture platform. Trouble with any of these cards leads to service degradation or service loss in part of the network or even within the whole data center. Understanding the platform architecture and isolating the problem within the Nexus device itself is important, to minimize the service impact.

Before delving into troubleshooting for Nexus platform hardware, it is important to know which series of Nexus device is being investigated and what kinds of cards are present in the chassis. The first step is to view the information of all the cards present in the chassis. Use the command **show module** [*module-number*] to view all the cards present on the Nexus device; here, *module-number* is optional for viewing the details of a specific line card. Examine the output of the **show module** command from Nexus 7009 and Nexus 3548P in Example 3-1. The first section of the output is from Nexus 7000. It shows two SUP cards in both active and standby state, along with three other cards: One is running fine, and the other two are powered down. The command output also shows the software and hardware version for each card and displays the online diagnostic status of those cards. The command output shows the reason the device is in a powered-down state. At the end, the command displays the fabric modules present in the chassis, along with the software and hardware versions and their status.

The second section of the output is from a Nexus 3500 switch that shows only a single SUP card. This is because the Nexus 3548P is a single rack unit (RU) switch. The number of modules present in the chassis depends on the device being used and the kind of cards it supports.

Example 3-1 show module *Command Output*

```
Nexus 7000
N7K1# show module
Mod  Ports  Module-Type                      Model            Status
---  -----  -------------------------------  ---------------  ----------
1    0      Supervisor Module-2              N7K-SUP2E        active *
2    0      Supervisor Module-2              N7K-SUP2E        ha-standby
5    48     10/100/1000 Mbps Ethernet XL Module                powered-dn
6    48     1/10 Gbps Ethernet Module        N7K-F248XP-25E   ok
7    32     10 Gbps Ethernet XL Module                         powered-dn

Mod  Power-Status  Reason
---  ------------  -------------------------
5    powered-dn    Unsupported/Unknown Module
7    powered-dn    Unsupported/Unknown Module

Mod  Sw               Hw
---  ---------------  ------
1    8.0(1)           0.403
2    8.0(1)           1.0
6    8.0(1)           1.2

Mod  MAC-Address(es)                         Serial-Num
---  --------------------------------------  ----------
1    6c-9c-ed-48-0d-9f to 6c-9c-ed-48-0d-b1  JAF1608AAPL
2    84-78-ac-10-99-cf to 84-78-ac-10-99-e1  JAF1710ACHA
```

```
5     00-00-00-00-00-00 to 00-00-00-00-00-00    JAF1803AMGR
6     b0-7d-47-da-fb-04 to b0-7d-47-da-fb-37    JAE191908QG
7     00-00-00-00-00-00 to 00-00-00-00-00-00    JAF1553ASRE


Mod  Online Diag Status
---  ------------------
1    Pass
2    Pass
6    Pass


Xbar Ports  Module-Type                         Model              Status
---- -----  ----------------------------------  -----------------  ----------
1    0      Fabric Module 2                     N7K-C7009-FAB-2    ok
2    0      Fabric Module 2                     N7K-C7009-FAB-2    ok
3    0      Fabric Module 2                     N7K-C7009-FAB-2    ok
4    0      Fabric Module 2                     N7K-C7009-FAB-2    ok
5    0      Fabric Module 2                     N7K-C7009-FAB-2    ok


Xbar  Sw                Hw
----  ---------------   ------
1     NA                2.0
2     NA                3.0
3     NA                2.0
4     NA                2.0
5     NA                2.0


Xbar MAC-Address(es)                          Serial-Num
---- --------------------------------------   ----------
1    NA                                       JAF1621BCDA
2    NA                                       JAF1631APEH
3    NA                                       JAF1621BBTF
4    NA                                       JAF1621BCEM
5    NA                                       JAF1621BCFJ
```

Nexus 3500
```
N3K1# show module
Mod  Ports  Module-Type                         Model                    Status
---  -----  ----------------------------------  -----------------------  -----------
1    48     48x10GE Supervisor                  N3K-C3548P-10G-SUP       active *


Mod  Sw               Hw      World-Wide-Name(s) (WWN)
---  ---------------  ------  ------------------------------------------------
1    6.0(2)A6(8)      1.1     --


Mod  MAC-Address(es)                          Serial-Num
---  --------------------------------------   ----------
1    f872.ea99.6468 to f872.ea99.64a7         FOC17263D71
```

> **Note** A fabric module is not required for all Nexus 7000 chassis types. The Nexus 7004 chassis has no fabric module, for example. However, higher slot chassis types do require fabric modules for the Nexus 7000 switch to function successfully.

One of the most common issues noticed with Nexus 7000/7700 installations or hardware upgrades involves interoperability. For example, the network operator might try to install a line card in a VDC that does not function well in combination with the existing line cards. M3 cards operate only in combination with M2 or F3 cards in the same VDC. Similarly, Nexus Fabric Extender (FEX) cards are not supported in combination with certain line cards. Refer to the compatibility matrix to avoid possible interoperability issues. The **show module** command output in Example 3-1 for Nexus 7000 switches highlights a similar problem, with two line cards powered down because of incompatibility.

> **Note** Nexus I/O module compatibility matrix CCO documentation is available at http://www.cisco.com/c/dam/en/us/td/docs/switches/datacenter/nexus7000/sw/matrix/technical/reference/Module_Comparison_Matrix.pdf.
>
> The referenced CCO documentation also lists the compatibility of the FEX modules with different line cards.

The **show hardware** command is used to get detailed information about both the software and the hardware on the Nexus device. The command displays the status of the Nexus switch, as well as the uptime, the health of the cards (both line cards and fabric cards), and the power supply and fans present in the chassis.

Generic Online Diagnostic Tests

Similar to Cisco 6500 series switches, Nexus devices have support for the Generic Online Diagnostic (GOLD) tool, a platform-independent fault-detective framework that helps in isolating any hardware as well as resource issues on the system both during bootup and at runtime. The diagnostic tests can be either disruptive or nondisruptive. Disruptive tests affect the functionality of the system partially or completely; nondisruptive tests do not affect the functionality of the system while running.

Bootup Diagnostics

Bootup diagnostics detect hardware faults such as soldering errors, loose connections, and faulty module. These tests are run when the system boots up and before the hardware is brought online. Table 3-1 shows some of the bootup diagnostic tests.

Table 3-1 *Nexus Bootup Diagnostic Tests*

Test Name	Description	Attributes	Hardware
ASIC Register Test	Tests access to all the registers in the ASIC	Disruptive	SUP and line card
ASIC Memory Test	Tests access to all the memory in the ASICs	Disruptive	SUP and line card
EOBC Port Loopback	Test the loopback of Ethernet out-of-band connection (EOBC)	Disruptive	SUP and line card
Port Loopback Test	Tests the port in internal loopback and checks the forwarding path by sending and receiving data on the same port	Disruptive	Line card
Boot Read-Only Memory (ROM) Test	Tests the integrity of the primary and secondary boot devices on the SUP card	Nondisruptive	SUP
Universal Serial Bus (USB)	Verifies the USB controller initialization on the SUP card	Nondisruptive	SUP
Management Port Loopback Test	Tests the loopback of the management port on the SUP card	Disruptive	SUP
OBFL	Tests the integrity of the onboard failure logging (OBFL) flash	Nondisruptive	SUP and line card
Federal Information Processing Standards (FIPS)	Verifies the security device on the module	Disruptive	Line card

Note The FIPS test is not supported on the F1 series modules on Nexus 7000.

Bootup diagnostics are configured to be performed and supported at one of the following levels:

- **None (Bypass):** The module is put online without running any bootup diagnostic tests, for faster card bootup.
- **Complete:** The entire bootup diagnostic tests are run for the module. This is the default and the recommended level for bootup diagnostics.

The diagnostic level is configured using the command **diagnostic bootup level [bypass | complete]** in global configuration mode. The diagnostic level must be configured within individual VDCs, where applicable. The bootup diagnostic level is verified using the command **show diagnostic bootup level**.

Runtime Diagnostics

The runtime diagnostics are run when the system is in running state (that is, on a live node). These tests help detect runtime hardware errors such as memory errors, resource exhaustion, and hardware faults/degradation. The runtime diagnostics are further be classified into two categories:

- Health-monitoring diagnostics
- On-demand diagnostics

Health-monitoring (HM) tests are nondisruptive and run in the background on each module. The main aim of these tests is to ensure that the hardware and software components are healthy while the switch is running network traffic. Some specific HM tests, marked as HM-always, start by default when the module goes online. Users can easily enable and disable all HM tests except HM-always tests on any module via the configuration command-line interface (CLI). Additionally, users can change the interval of all HM tests except the fixed-interval tests marked as HM-fixed. Table 3-2 lists the HM tests available across SUP and line card modules.

Table 3-2 *Nexus Health-Monitoring Diagnostic Tests*

Test Name	Description	Attributes	Hardware
ASIC Scratch Register Test	Tests the access to a scratch pad register of the ASICs	Nondisruptive	SUP and line card (all ASICs that support scratch pad register)
RTC Test	Verifies that the real-time clock (RTC) on the Supervisor is ticking	Nondisruptive	SUP
Nonvolatile Random Access Memory (NVRAM) Sanity Test	Tests the sanity of NVRAM blocks on the SUP modules	Nondisruptive	SUP
Port Loopback Test	Tries to loop back a packet to check the forwarding path periodically without disrupting port traffic	Nondisruptive	Line card (all front-panel ports on the switch)
Rewrite Engine Loopback Test	Tests the integrity of loopback for all ports to the Rewrite Engine ASIC on the module	Nondisruptive	Line card

Test Name	Description	Attributes	Hardware
Primary Boot ROM Test	Tests the integrity of the primary boot devices on the card	Nondisruptive	SUP and line card
Secondary Boot ROM Test	Tests the integrity of the secondary boot devices on the card	Nondisruptive	SUP and line card
CompactFlash	Verifies the access to internal CompactFlash on the SUP card	Nondisruptive	SUP
External CompactFlash	Verifies the access to external CompactFlash on the SUP card	Nondisruptive	SUP
Power Management Bus Test	Test the standby power management control bus on the SUP card	Nondisruptive	SUP
Spine Control Bus Test	Tests and verifies the availability of the standby spine module control bus	Nondisruptive	SUP
Standby Fabric Loopback Test	Tests the packet path between the standby SUP and fabric	Nondisruptive	SUP
Status Bus (Two Wire) Test	Checks the two wire interfaces that connect the various modules (including fabric cards) to the SUP module	Nondisruptive	SUP

The interval for HM tests is set using the global configuration command **diagnostic monitor interval module** *slot* **test** [*name* | *test-id* | **all**] **hour** *hour* **min** *minutes* **second** *sec*. Note that the name of the test is case sensitive. To enable or disable an HM test, use the global configuration command [**no**] **diagnostic monitor module** *slot* **test** [*name* | *test-id* | **all**]. Use the command **show diagnostic content module** [*slot* | **all**] to display the information about the diagnostics and their attributes on a given line card. Example 3-2 illustrates how to view the diagnostics information on a line card on a Nexus 7000 switch and how to disable an HM test. The line card in the output of Example 3-2 is the SUP card, so the test names listed are relevant only for the SUP card, not the line card. For example, with the ExternalCompactFlash test, notice that the attribute in the first output is set to *A*, which indicates that the test is Active. When the test is disabled from the configuration mode, the output displays the attribute as *I*, indicating that the test is Inactive.

Example 3-2 show diagnostic content module *Command Output*

```
Nexus 7000
N7K1# show diagnostic content module 1
Diagnostics test suite attributes:
B/C/*   - Bypass bootup level test / Complete bootup level test / NA
P/*     - Per port test / NA
M/S/*   - Only applicable to active / standby unit / NA
D/N/*   - Disruptive test / Non-disruptive test / NA
H/O/*   - Always enabled monitoring test / Conditionally enabled test / NA
F/*     - Fixed monitoring interval test / NA
X/*     - Not a health monitoring test / NA
E/*     - Sup to line card test / NA
L/*     - Exclusively run this test / NA
T/*     - Not an ondemand test / NA
A/I/*   - Monitoring is active / Monitoring is inactive / NA
Z/D/*   - Corrective Action is enabled / Corrective Action is disabled / NA


Module 1: Supervisor Module-2 (Active)

                                                    Testing Interval
 ID      Name                            Attributes  (hh:mm:ss)
____   _____           _____  _____

  1)   ASICRegisterCheck-------------->  ***N******A*   00:00:20
  2)   USB--------------------------->   C**N**X**T**   -NA-
  3)   NVRAM------------------------->   ***N******A*   00:05:00
  4)   RealTimeClock----------------->   ***N******A*   00:05:00
  5)   PrimaryBootROM---------------->   ***N******A*   00:30:00
  6)   SecondaryBootROM-------------->   ***N******A*   00:30:00
  7)   CompactFlash------------------>   ***N******A*   00:30:00
  8)   ExternalCompactFlash---------->   ***N******A*   00:30:00
  9)   PwrMgmtBus-------------------->   **MN******A*   00:00:30
 10)   SpineControlBus--------------->   ***N******A*   00:00:30
 11)   SystemMgmtBus----------------->   **MN******A*   00:00:30
 12)   StatusBus--------------------->   **MN******A*   00:00:30
 13)   PCIeBus----------------------->   ***N******A*   00:00:30
 14)   StandbyFabricLoopback--------->   **SN******A*   00:00:30
 15)   ManagementPortLoopback-------->   C**D**X**T**   -NA-
 16)   EOBCPortLoopback-------------->   C**D**X**T**   -NA-
 17)   OBFL------------------------->    C**N**X**T**   -NA-
N7K1# config t
N7K1(config)# no diagnostic monitor module 1 test ExternalCompactFlash
N7K1# show diagnostic content module 1
! Output omitted for brevity
Module 1: Supervisor Module-2 (Active)
```

```
                                                   Testing Interval
   ID    Name                           Attributes    (hh:mm:ss)
   ___   _____ _____ _____

   1)    ASICRegisterCheck------------> ***N******A*  00:00:20
   2)    USB--------------------------> C**N**X**T**  -NA-
   3)    NVRAM------------------------> ***N******A*  00:05:00
   4)    RealTimeClock----------------> ***N******A*  00:05:00
   5)    PrimaryBootROM---------------> ***N******A*  00:30:00
   6)    SecondaryBootROM-------------> ***N******A*  00:30:00
   7)    CompactFlash-----------------> ***N******A*  00:30:00
   8)    ExternalCompactFlash---------> ***N******I*  00:30:00
   9)    PwrMgmtBus-------------------> **MN******A*  00:00:30
   10)   SpineControlBus--------------> ***N******A*  00:00:30
   11)   SystemMgmtBus----------------> **MN******A*  00:00:30
   12)   StatusBus--------------------> **MN******A*  00:00:30
   13)   PCIeBus----------------------> ***N******A*  00:00:30
   14)   StandbyFabricLoopback--------> **SN******A*  00:00:30
   15)   ManagementPortLoopback-------> C**D**X**T**  -NA-
   16)   EOBCPortLoopback-------------> C**D**X**T**  -NA-
   17)   OBFL-------------------------> C**N**X**T**  -NA-
```

The command **show diagnostic content module** [*slot* | **all**] displays not only the HM tests but also the bootup diagnostic tests. In the output of Example 3-2, notice the tests whose attributes begin with *C*. Those tests are complete bootup-level tests. To view all the test results and statistics, use the command **show diagnostic result module** [*slot* | **all**] [**detail**]. When verifying the diagnostic results, ensure no test has a Fail (F) or Error (E) result. Example 3-3 displays the diagnostic test results of the SUP card both in brief format and in detailed format. The output shows that the bootup diagnostic level is set to *complete*. The first output lists all the tests the SUP module went through along with its results, where "." indicates that the test has passed. The detailed version of the output lists more specific details, such as the error code, the previous execution time, the next execution time, and the reason for failure. This detailed information is useful when issues are observed on the module and investigation is required to isolate a transient issue or a hardware issue.

Example 3-3 *Diagnostic Test Results*

```
N7K1# show diagnostic result module 1
Current bootup diagnostic level: complete
Module 1: Supervisor Module-2   (Active)

        Test results: (. = Pass, F = Fail, I = Incomplete,
        U = Untested, A = Abort, E = Error disabled)
```

```
         1) ASICRegisterCheck------------->  .
         2) USB-------------------------->  .
         3) NVRAM------------------------>  .
         4) RealTimeClock---------------->  .
         5) PrimaryBootROM--------------->  .
         6) SecondaryBootROM------------->  .
         7) CompactFlash----------------->  .
         8) ExternalCompactFlash--------->  U
         9) PwrMgmtBus------------------->  .
        10) SpineControlBus-------------->  .
        11) SystemMgmtBus---------------->  .
        12) StatusBus-------------------->  .
        13) PCIeBus---------------------->  .
        14) StandbyFabricLoopback-------->  U
        15) ManagementPortLoopback------->  .
        16) EOBCPortLoopback------------->  .
        17) OBFL------------------------->  .
N7K1# show diagnostic result module 1 detail
Current bootup diagnostic level: complete
Module 1: Supervisor Module-2  (Active)

  Diagnostic level at card bootup: complete

        Test results: (. = Pass, F = Fail, I = Incomplete,
        U = Untested, A = Abort, E = Error disabled)


     1) ASICRegisterCheck .

            Error code ------------------> DIAG TEST SUCCESS
            Total run count -------------> 38807
            Last test execution time ----> Thu May  7 18:24:16 2015
            First test failure time -----> n/a
            Last test failure time ------> n/a
            Last test pass time ---------> Thu May  7 18:24:16 2015
            Total failure count ---------> 0
            Consecutive failure count ---> 0
            Last failure reason ---------> No failures yet
            Next Execution time ---------> Thu May  7 18:24:36 2015


     2) USB .

            Error code ------------------> DIAG TEST SUCCESS
            Total run count -------------> 1
```

```
                    Last test execution time ----> Tue Apr 28 18:44:36 2015
                    First test failure time -----> n/a
                    Last test failure time ------> n/a
                    Last test pass time ---------> Tue Apr 28 18:44:36 2015
                    Total failure count ---------> 0
                    Consecutive failure count ---> 0
                    Last failure reason ---------> No failures yet
                    Next Execution time ---------> n/a
! Output omitted for brevity
```

On-demand diagnostics have a different focus. Some tests are not required to be run periodically, but they might be run in response to certain events (such as faults) or in an anticipation of an event (such as exceeded resources). Such on-demand tests are useful in localizing faults and applying fault-containment solutions.

Both disruptive and nondisruptive on-demand diagnostic tests are run from a CLI. An on-demand test is executed using the command **diagnostic start module** *slot* **test** [*test-id* | *name* | **all** | **non-disruptive**] [**port** *port-number* | **all**]. The *test-id* variable is the number of tests supported on a given module. The test is also run on a port basis (depending on the kind of test) by specifying the optional keyword **port**. The command **diagnostic stop module slot test** [*test-id* | *name* | **all**] is used to stop an on-demand test. The on-demand tests default to single execution, but the number of iterations can be increased using the command **diagnostic ondemand iteration** *number*, where *number* specifies the number of iterations. Be careful when running disruptive on-demand diagnostic tests within production traffic.

Example 3-4 demonstrates an on-demand PortLoopback test on a Nexus 7000 switch module.

Example 3-4 *On-Demand Diagnostic Test*

```
N7K1# diagnostic ondemand iteration 3
N7K1# diagnostic start module 6 test PortLoopback
N7K1# show diagnostic status module 6
            <BU>-Bootup Diagnostics, <HM>-Health Monitoring Diagnostics
            <OD>-OnDemand Diagnostics, <SCH>-Scheduled Diagnostics


============================================
Card:(6) 1/10 Gbps Ethernet Module
============================================
Current running test              Run by
PortLoopback                      OD


Currently Enqueued Test           Run by
PortLoopback                      OD (Remaining Iteration: 2)
```

```
N7K1# show diagnostic result module 6 test PortLoopback detail
Current bootup diagnostic level: complete
Module 6: 1/10 Gbps Ethernet Module

  Diagnostic level at card bootup: complete

       Test results: (. = Pass, F = Fail, I = Incomplete,
       U = Untested, A = Abort, E = Error disabled)

_____


     6) PortLoopback:

        Port   1  2  3  4  5  6  7  8  9 10 11 12 13 14 15 16
        ------------------------------------------------------
               U  U  U  U  U  U  U  U  U  U  U  U  U  .  .  .

        Port  17 18 19 20 21 22 23 24 25 26 27 28 29 30 31 32
        ------------------------------------------------------
               U  U  .  .  U  U  U  U  U  U  U  U  U  U  U  U

        Port  33 34 35 36 37 38 39 40 41 42 43 44 45 46 47 48
        ------------------------------------------------------
               U  U  U  U  U  U  U  U  U  U  U  U  U  U  U  U

        Error code ------------------> DIAG TEST SUCCESS
        Total run count -------------> 879
        Last test execution time ----> Thu May  7 21:25:48 2015
        First test failure time -----> n/a
        Last test failure time ------> n/a
        Last test pass time ---------> Thu May  7 21:26:00 2015
        Total failure count ---------> 0
        Consecutive failure count ---> 0
        Last failure reason ---------> No failures yet
        Next Execution time ---------> Thu May  7 21:40:48 2015
```

During troubleshooting, if the number of iterations is set to a higher value and an action needs to be taken if the test fails, use the command **diagnostic ondemand action-on-failure** [**continue failure-count** *num-fails* | **stop**]. When the **continue** keyword is used, the **failure-count** parameter sets the number of failures allowed before stopping the test. This value defaults to 0, which means to never stop the test, even in case of failure. The on-demand diagnostic settings are verified using the command **show diagnostic ondemand setting**. Example 3-5 illustrates how to set the action upon failure for on-demand diagnostic tests. In this example, the action-on-failure is set to continue until the failure count reaches the value of 2.

Example 3-5 *Action-On-Failure for On-Demand Diagnostic Tests*

```
! Setting the action-on-failure to continue till 2 failure counts.
N7K1# diagnostic ondemand action-on-failure continue failure-count 2
N7K1# show diagnostic ondemand setting
      Test iterations = 3
      Action on test failure = continue until test failure limit reaches 2
```

Note Diagnostic tests are also run in offline mode. Use the command **hardware module** *slot* **offline** to put the module in offline mode, and then use the command **diagnostic start module** *slot* **test** [*test-id* | *name* | **all**] **offline** to execute the diagnostic test with the *offline* attribute.

GOLD Test and EEM Support

The diagnostic tests help identify hardware problems on SUP as well as line cards, but corrective actions also need to be taken whenever those problems are encountered. NX-OS provides such a capability by integrating GOLD tests with the Embedded Event Manager (EEM), which takes corrective actions in case diagnostic tests fail. One of the most common use cases for GOLD tests is conducting burn-in testing or staging new equipment before placing the device into a production environment. Burn-in testing is similar to load testing: The device is typically under some load, with investigation into resource utilization, including memory, CPU, and buffers over time. This helps prevent any major outages that result from hardware issues before the device starts processing production traffic.

NX-OS supports corrective actions for the following HM tests:

- RewriteEngineLoopback
- StandbyFabricLoopback
- Internal PortLoopback
- SnakeLoopback

On the Supervisor module, if the StandbyFabricLoopback test fails, the system reloads the standby supervisor card. If the standby supervisor card does not come back up online in three retries, the standby supervisor card is powered off. After the reload of the standby supervisor card, the HM diagnostics start by default. The corrective actions are disabled by default and are enabled by configuring the command **diagnostic eem action conservative**.

Note The command **diagnostic eem action conservative** is not configurable on a per-test basis; it applies to all four of the previously mentioned GOLD tests.

Nexus Device Health Checks

In any network environment, the network administrators and operators are required to perform regular device health checks to ensure stability in the network and to capture issues before they cause major network impacts. Health checks are performed either manually or by using automation tools. The command line might vary among Nexus platforms, but a few common points are verified at regular intervals:

- Module state and diagnostics
- Hardware and process crashes and resets
- Packet drops
- Interface errors and drops

The previous section covered module state and diagnostics. This section focuses on commands used across different Nexus platforms to perform health checks.

Hardware and Process Crashes

Line card and supervisor card reloads or crashes can cause major outages on a network. The crashes or reloads happen because of either hardware or software issues. NX-OS has a distributed architecture, so crashes can happen even on the processes. In most hardware or process crashes, a core file is generated after the crash. The Cisco Technical Assistance Center (TAC) can use that core file to identify the root cause of the crash. Core files are found using the command **show cores vdc-all**. On the Nexus 7000 switch, run the **show cores vdc-all** command from the default VDC. Example 3-6 displays the cores generated on a Nexus 7000 switch. In this example, the core file is generated for VDC 1 module 6 and for the RPM process.

Example 3-6 *Nexus Core Files*

```
N7k-1# show cores vdc-all
VDC   Module   Instance   Process-name      PID        Date(Year-Month-Day Time)
---   ------   --------   ---------------   --------   --------------------------
1     6        1          rpm               4298       2017-02-08 15:08:48
```

When the core file is identified, it can be copied to bootflash or any external location, such as a File Transfer Protocol (FTP) or Trivial FTP (TFTP) server. On Nexus 7000, the core files are located in the core: file system. The relevant core files are located by following this URL:

   core://<module-number>/<process-id>/<instance-number>

For instance, in Example 3-6, the location for the core files is *core://6/4298/1*. If the Nexus 7000 switch rebooted or a switchover occurred, the core files would be located in the **logflash://[sup-1 | sup-2]/core** directory. On other Nexus platforms, such as Nexus

5000, 4000, or 3000, the core files would be located in the **volatile:** file system instead of the logflash: file system; thus, they can be lost if the device reloads. In newer versions of software for platforms that stores core files in volatile: file system, the capability was added to write the core files to bootflash: or to a remote file location when they occur.

If a process crashed but no core files were generated for the crash, a stack trace might have been generated for the process. But if neither a core file nor a stack trace exists for the crashed service, use the command **show processes log vdc-all** to identify which processes were impacted. Such crashed processes usually are marked with the *N* flag. Using the process ID (PID) values from the previous command and using the command **show processes log pid** *pid* can identify the reason the service went down. The command output displays the reason the process failed in the *Death reason* field. Example 3-7 displays using the **show processes log** and **show processes log pid** commands to identify crashes on the Nexus platform

Example 3-7 *Nexus Process Crash*

```
N7k-1# show processes log
VDC Process         PID      Normal-exit  Stack  Core   Log-create-time
--- ---------------  ------  -----------  -----  -----  ---------------
  1 ascii-cfg        5656                 N      Y      N  Thu Feb 23 17:10:43 2017
  1 ascii_cfg_serve  7811                 N      N      N  Thu Feb 23 17:10:43 2017
  1 installer        23457                N      N      N  Tue May 23 02:00:00 2017
  1 installer        25885                N      N      N  Tue May 23 02:28:23 2017
  1 installer        26212                N      N      N  Tue May 23 15:51:19 2017
! Output omitted for brevity
N7k-1# show processes log pid 5656
======================================================
Service: ascii-cfg
Description: Ascii Cfg Server
Executable: /isan/bin/ascii_cfg_server

Started at Thu Feb 23 17:06:20 2017 (155074 us)
Stopped at Thu Feb 23 17:10:43 2017 (738171 us)
Uptime: 4 minutes 23 seconds

Start type: SRV_OPTION_RESTART_STATELESS (23)
Death reason: SYSMGR_DEATH_REASON_FAILURE_HEARTBEAT (9)
Last heartbeat 40.01 secs ago
RLIMIT_AS: 1936268083
System image name: n7000-s2-dk9.7.3.1.D1.1.bin
System image version: 7.3(1)D1(1) S19

PID: 5656
Exit code: signal 6 (core dumped)
```

```
cgroup: 1:devices,memory,cpuacct,cpu:/1


CWD: /var/sysmgr/work

RLIMIT_AS:        1936268083
! Output omitted for brevity
```

For quick verification of the last reset reason, use the **show system reset-reason** command. Additional commands to capture and identify the reset reason when core files were not generated follow:

- **show system exception-info**
- **show module internal exceptionlog module** *slot*
- **show logging onboard** [**module** *slot*]
- **show process log details**

Packet Loss

Packet loss is a complex issue to troubleshoot in any environment. Packet happens because of multiple reasons:

- Bad hardware
- Drops on a platform
- A routing or switching issue

The packet drops that result from routing and switching issues can be fixed by rectifying the configuration. Bad hardware, on the other hand, impacts all traffic on a partial port or on the whole line card. Nexus platforms provide various counters that can be viewed to determine the reason for packet loss on the device (see the following sections).

Interface Errors and Drops

Apart from platform or hardware drops, interface issues can lead to packet loss and service degradation in a data center environment. Issues such as flapping links, links not coming up, interface errors, and input or output discards are just a few of the scenarios that can have a major impact on the services. Deciphering fault on the link can be difficult on a switch, but NX-OS provides CLI and internal platform commands that can help.

The **show interface** *interface-number* command displays detailed information regarding the interface, such as interface traffic rate, input and output statistics, and error counters for input/output errors, CRC errors, overrun counters, and more. The NX-OS CLI also provides different command options (including the **show interface** command) that are useful for verifying interface capabilities, transceiver information, counters, flow control,

MAC address information, and switchport and trunk information. Example 3-8 displays the output of the **show interface** command, with various fields highlighting the information to be verified on an interface. The second part of the output displays on information on the various capabilities of the interface.

Example 3-8 *Nexus Interface Details and Capabilities*

```
N9k-1# show interface Eth2/1
Ethernet2/1 is up
admin state is up, Dedicated Interface
  Hardware: 40000 Ethernet, address: 1005.ca57.287f (bia 88f0.31f9.5710)
  Internet Address is 192.168.10.1/24
  MTU 1500 bytes, BW 40000000 Kbit, DLY 10 usec
  reliability 255/255, txload 1/255, rxload 1/255
  Encapsulation ARPA, medium is broadcast
  full-duplex, 40 Gb/s, media type is 40G
  Beacon is turned off
  Auto-Negotiation is turned on
  Input flow-control is off, output flow-control is off
  Auto-mdix is turned off
  Rate mode is dedicated
  Switchport monitor is off
  EtherType is 0x8100
  EEE (efficient-ethernet) : n/a
  Last link flapped 2d01h
  Last clearing of "show interface" counters never
  2 interface resets
  30 seconds input rate 64 bits/sec, 0 packets/sec
  30 seconds output rate 0 bits/sec, 0 packets/sec
  Load-Interval #2: 5 minute (300 seconds)
     input rate 32 bps, 0 pps; output rate 32 bps, 0 pps
  RX
     950396 unicast packets  345788 multicast packets  15 broadcast packets
     1296199 input packets  121222244 bytes
     0 jumbo packets  0 storm suppression packets
     0 runts  0 giants  0 CRC  0 no buffer
     0 input error  0 short frame  0 overrun  0 underrun  0 ignored
     0 watchdog  0 bad etype drop  0 bad proto drop  0 if down drop
     0 input with dribble  0 input discard
     0 Rx pause
  TX
     950398 unicast packets  2951181 multicast packets  19 broadcast packets
     3901598 output packets  396283422 bytes
     0 jumbo packets
     0 output error  0 collision  0 deferred  0 late collision
```

```
         0 lost carrier    0 no carrier   0 babble   0 output discard
         0 Tx pause
N9k-1# show interface Eth2/1 capabilities
Ethernet2/1
    Model:                   N9K-X9636PQ
    Type (SFP capable):      QSFP-40G-CR4
    Speed:                   40000
    Duplex:                  full
    Trunk encap. type:       802.1Q
    FabricPath capable:      no
    Channel:                 yes
    Broadcast suppression:   percentage(0-100)
    Flowcontrol:             rx-(off/on/desired),tx-(off/on/desired)
    Rate mode:               dedicated
    Port mode:               Routed,Switched
    QOS scheduling:          rx-(none),tx-(4q)
    CoS rewrite:             yes
    ToS rewrite:             yes
    SPAN:                    yes
    UDLD:                    yes
    MDIX:                    no
    TDR capable:             no
    Link Debounce:           yes
    Link Debounce Time:      yes
    FEX Fabric:              yes
    dot1Q-tunnel mode:       yes
    Pvlan Trunk capable:     yes
    Port Group Members:      1
    EEE (efficient-eth):     no
    PFC capable:             yes
    Buffer Boost capable:    no
    Speed group capable:     yes
```

To view just the various counters on the interfaces, use the command **show interface counters errors**. The **counters errors** option is also used with the specific **show interface** *interface-number* command. Example 3-9 displays the error counters for the interface. If any counter is increasing, the interface needs further troubleshooting, based on the kind of errors received. The error can point to Layer 1 issues, a bad port issue, or even buffer issues. Some counters indicated in the output are not errors, but instead indicate a different problem: The Giants counter, for instance, indicates that packets are being received with a higher MTU size than the one configured on the interface.

Example 3-9 *Interface Error Counters*

```
N9k-1# show interface Eth 2/1 counters errors
--------------------------------------------------------------------------------
Port           Align-Err    FCS-Err    Xmit-Err    Rcv-Err  UnderSize OutDiscards
--------------------------------------------------------------------------------
Eth2/1                 0          0           0          0          0           0


--------------------------------------------------------------------------------
Port          Single-Col  Multi-Col   Late-Col  Exces-Col  Carri-Sen       Runts
--------------------------------------------------------------------------------
Eth2/1                 0          0          0          0          0           0


--------------------------------------------------------------------------------
Port              Giants SQETest-Err Deferred-Tx IntMacTx-Er IntMacRx-Er Symbol-Err
--------------------------------------------------------------------------------
Eth2/1                 0         --           0          0          0           0
```

To view the details of the hardware interface resources and utilization, use the command **show hardware capacity interface**. This command displays not only buffer information but also any drops in both the ingress and egress directions on multiple ports across each line card. The output varies a bit among Nexus platforms, such as between the Nexus 7000 and the Nexus 9000, but this command is useful for identifying interfaces with the highest drops on the switch. Example 3-10 displays the hardware interface resources on the Nexus 7000 switch.

Example 3-10 *Hardware Interface Resources and Drops*

```
N7k-1# show hardware capacity interface
Interface Resources

  Interface drops:
    Module  Total drops             Highest drop ports
         3  Tx: 0                   -
         3  Rx: 101850              Ethernet3/37
         4  Tx: 0                   -
         4  Rx: 64928               Ethernet4/4

  Interface buffer sizes:
    Module   Bytes:  Tx buffer       Rx buffer
         3            705024          1572864
         4            705024          1572864
```

One of the most common problems on an interface is input and output discards. These errors usually take place when congestion occurs on the ports. The previous interface commands and the **show hardware internal errors** [**module** *slot*] command are useful in identifying input or output discards. If input discards are identified, you must try to discover congestion on the egress ports. Input discards can be a problem even if SPAN is configured on the device if oversubscription on egress ports is taking place. Thus, ensure that SPAN is not configured on the device unless it is required for performing SPAN captured; in that case, remove it afterward. If the egress-congested port is a Gig port, the problem could result from a many-to-one unicast traffic flow causing congestion. This issue can be overcome by upgrading the port to a 10-Gig port or by bundling multiple Gig ports into a port-channel interface.

The output discards are usually caused by drops in the queuing policy on the interface. This is verified using the command **show system internal qos queueing stats interface** *interface-id*. The queueing policy configuration information is viewed using the command **show queueing interface** *interface-id* or **show policy-map interface** *interface-id* [**input** | **output**]. Tweaking the QoS policy prevents the output discards or drops. Example 3-11 displays the queueing statistics for interface Ethernet1/5, indicating drops in various queues on the interface.

Example 3-11 *Interface Queueing Statistics*

```
N7k-1# show system internal qos queuing stats int eth1/5
Interface Ethernet1/5 statistics

Transmit queues
-----------------------------------------
   Queue 1p7q4t-out-q-default
        Total bytes                      0
        Total packets                    0
        Current depth in bytes           0
        Min pg drops                     0
        No desc drops                    0
        WRED drops                       0
        Taildrop drops                   0
   Queue 1p7q4t-out-q2
        Total bytes                      0
        Total packets                    0
        Current depth in bytes           0
        Min pg drops                     0
        No desc drops                    0
        WRED drops                       0
        Taildrop drops                   0
   Queue 1p7q4t-out-q3
        Total bytes                      0
        Total packets                    0
```

```
        Current depth in bytes    0
        Min pg drops              0
        No desc drops             0
        WRED drops                0
        Taildrop drops            0
    Queue 1p7q4t-out-q4
        Total bytes               0
        Total packets             0
        Current depth in bytes    0
        Min pg drops              0
        No desc drops             0
        WRED drops                0
        Taildrop drops            81653
    Queue 1p7q4t-out-q5
        Total bytes               0
        Total packets             0
        Current depth in bytes    0
        Min pg drops              0
        No desc drops             0
        WRED drops                0
        Taildrop drops            35096
    Queue 1p7q4t-out-q6
        Total bytes               0
        Total packets             0
        Current depth in bytes    0
        Min pg drops              0
        No desc drops             0
        WRED drops                0
        Taildrop drops            245191
    Queue 1p7q4t-out-q7
        Total bytes               0
        Total packets             0
        Current depth in bytes    0
        Min pg drops              0
        No desc drops             0
        WRED drops                0
        Taildrop drops            657759
    Queue 1p7q4t-out-pq1
        Total bytes               0
        Total packets             0
        Current depth in bytes    0
        Min pg drops              0
        No desc drops             0
        WRED drops                0
        Taildrop drops            0
```

Platform-Specific Drops

Nexus platforms provide in-depth information on various platform-level counters to identify problems with hardware and software components. If packet loss is noticed on a particular interface or line card, the platform-level commands provide information on what is causing the packets to be dropped. For instance, on the Nexus 7000 switch, the command **show hardware internal statistics [module** *slot* **| module-all] pktflow dropped** is used to identify the reason for packet drops. This command details the information per line card module and packet drops across all interfaces on the line card. Example 3-12 displays the packet drops across various ports on the line card in slot 3. The command output displays packet drops resulting from bad packet length, error packets from Media Access Control (MAC), a bad cyclic redundancy check (CRC), and so on. Using the **diff** keyword along with the command helps identify drops that are increasing on particular interfaces and that result from specific reasons, for further troubleshooting.

Example 3-12 *Nexus 7000 Packet Flow Drop Counters*

```
N7k-1# show hardware internal statistics module 3 pktflow dropped


|---------------------------------|
|Executed at : 2017-06-02 10:09:16.914   |
|---------------------------------|
Hardware statistics on module 03:
|---------------------------------------------------------------------|
| Device:Flanker Eth Mac Driver    Role:MAC              Mod: 3       |
| Last cleared @ Fri Jun  2 00:28:46 2017
|---------------------------------------------------------------------|
Instance:0
Cntr  Name                                         Value              Ports
----- -----                                        -----              -----
    0 igr in upm: pkts rcvd, len(>= 64B, <= mtu) with bad crc 0000000000000001
3 -
    1 igr rx pl:  received error pkts from mac     0000000000000001   3 -
    2 igr rx pl:  EM-IPL i/f dropped pkts cnt      0000000000000004   3 -
    3 igr rx pl:  cbl drops                        0000000000002818   3 -
    4 igr rx pl:  EM-IPL i/f dropped pkts cnt      0000000000000002   4 -




Instance:1
Cntr  Name                                         Value              Ports
----- -----                                        -----              -----
    5 igr in upm: pkts rcvd, len > MTU with bad CRC 0000000000000001  10 -
    6 igr in upm: pkts rcvd, len > MTU with bad CRC 0000000000000001  11 -
    7 igr rx pl: EM-IPL i/f dropped pkts cnt       0000000000000002   9 -
    8 igr rx pl: EM-IPL i/f dropped pkts cnt       0000000000000011   10 -
```

```
    9 igr rx pl: cbl drops                             0000000000000004   10 -
   10 igr rx pl:  received error pkts from mac         0000000000000001   11 -
   11 igr rx pl: EM-IPL i/f dropped pkts cnt           0000000000000017   11 -
   12 igr rx pl: cbl drops                             0000000000002812   11 -


Instance:3
Cntr  Name                                             Value              Ports
----- -----                                            -----              -----
   13 igr rx pl: EM-IPL i/f dropped pkts cnt           0000000000000003   26 -
   14 igr rx pl: cbl drops                             0000000000000008   26 -
   15 igr rx pl: EM-IPL i/f dropped pkts cnt           0000000000000001   31 -


Instance:4
Cntr  Name                                             Value              Ports
----- -----                                            -----              -----
   16 igr in upm: pkts rcvd, len > MTU with bad CRC 0000000000000027     35 -
   17 igr in upm: pkts rcvd, len > MTU with bad CRC 0000000000000044     36 -
   18 igr in upm: pkts rcvd, len(>= 64B, <= mtu) with bad crc 0000000000000001
 36 -
   19 igr in upm: pkts rcvd, len > MTU with bad CRC 0000000000005795     37 -
   20 igr in upm: pkts rcvd, len > MTU with bad CRC 0000000000000034     38 -
   21 igr rx pl: EM-IPL i/f dropped pkts cnt           0000000000000008   33 -
   22 igr rx pl: cbl drops                             0000000000002801   33 -
   23 igr rx pl: EM-IPL i/f dropped pkts cnt           0000000000000004   34 -
   24 egr out pl: total pkts dropped due to cbl        0000000000001769   34 -
   25 igr rx pl:  received error pkts from mac         0000000000000003   35 -
   26 igr rx pl: EM-IPL i/f dropped pkts cnt           0000000000000200   35 -
   27 igr rx pl: cbl drops                             0000000000002813   35 -
   28 igr rx pl: dropped pkts cnt                      0000000000000017   35 -
   29 igr rx pl:  received error pkts from mac         0000000000000093   36 -
   30 igr rx pl: EM-IPL i/f dropped pkts cnt           0000000000002515   36 -
   31 igr rx pl: cbl drops                             0000000000002894   36 -
   32 igr rx pl: dropped pkts cnt                      0000000000000166   36 -
   33 igr rx pl: EM-IPL i/f dropped pkts cnt           0000000000047337   37 -
   34 igr rx pl: dropped pkts cnt                      0000000000001371   37 -
   35 igr rx pl: EM-IPL i/f dropped pkts cnt           0000000000000212   38 -
   36 igr rx pl: dropped pkts cnt                      0000000000000012   38 -


! Output omitted for brevity
```

```
|--------------------------------------------------------------------|
| Device:Flanker Xbar Driver      Role:XBR-INTF         Mod: 3       |
| Last cleared @ Fri Jun  2 00:28:46 2017                            |
|--------------------------------------------------------------------|
|--------------------------------------------------------------------|
| Device:Flanker Queue Driver     Role:QUE              Mod: 3       |
| Last cleared @ Fri Jun  2 00:28:46 2017                            |
|--------------------------------------------------------------------|
Instance:4
Cntr  Name                                      Value           Ports
----- -----                                     -----           -----
    0 igr ib_500: pkt drops                     0000000000000003  35 -
    1 igr ib_500: pkt drops                     0000000000000010  36 -
    2 igr ib_500: vq ib pkt drops               0000000000000013  33-40 -
    3 igr vq: 12 pkt drop count                 0000000000000013  33-40 -
    4 igr vq: total pkts dropped                0000000000000013  33-40 -


Instance:5
Cntr  Name                                      Value           Ports
----- -----                                     -----           -----
    5 igr ib_500: de drops, shared by parser and de 0000000000000004  41-48 -
    6 igr ib_500: vq ib pkt drops               0000000000000004  41-48 -
    7 igr vq: 12 pkt drop count                 0000000000000004  41-48 -
    8 igr vq: total pkts dropped                0000000000000004  41-48 -


|--------------------------------------------------------------------|
| Device:Lightning               Role:ARB-MUX           Mod: 3       |
| Last cleared @ Fri Jun  2 00:28:46 2017                            |
|--------------------------------------------------------------------|
```

Communication among the supervisor card, line card, and fabric cards occurs over the Ethernet out-of-band channel (EOBC). If errors occur on the EOBC channel, the Nexus switch can experience packet loss and major service loss. EOBC errors are verified using the command **show hardware internal cpu-mac eobc stats**. The Error Counters section displays a list of errors that occur on the EOBC interface. In most instances, physically reseating the line card fixes the EOBC errors. Example 3-13 displays the EOBC stats for Error Counters on a Nexus 7000 switch. Filter the output for checking just the error counters by using the **grep** keyword (see Example 3-13).

Example 3-13 *EOBC Stats and Error Counters*

```
N7k-1# show hardware internal cpu-mac eobc stats | grep -a 26 Error.counters
Error counters
-------------------------------+--
CRC errors ..................... 0
Alignment errors ............... 0
Symbol errors .................. 0
Sequence errors ................ 0
RX errors ...................... 0
Missed packets (FIFO overflow)   0
Single collisions .............. 0
Excessive collisions ........... 0
Multiple collisions ............ 0
Late collisions ................ 0
Collisions ..................... 0
Defers ......................... 0
Tx no CRS ...................... 0
Carrier extension errors ....... 0
Rx length errors ............... 0
FC Rx unsupported .............. 0
Rx no buffers .................. 0
Rx undersize ................... 0
Rx fragments ................... 0
Rx oversize .................... 0
Rx jabbers ..................... 0
Rx management packets dropped .. 0
Tx TCP segmentation context .... 0
Tx TCP segmentation context fail 0
```

Nexus platforms also provide in-band stats for packets that the central processing unit (CPU) processes. If an error counter shows the inband stats increasing frequently, it could indicate a problem with the supervisor card and might lead to packet loss. To view the CPU in-band statistics, use the command **show hardware internal cpu-mac inband stats**. This command displays various statistics on packets and length of packets received by or sent from the CPU, interrupt counters, error counters, and present and maximum punt statistics. Example 3-14 displays the output of the in-band stats on the Nexus 7000 switch. This command is also available on the Nexus 9000 switch, as the second output shows.

Example 3-14 *Nexus 7000/Nexus 9000 In-Band Stats*

```
N7k-1# show hardware internal cpu-mac inband stats


RMON counters                          Rx                    Tx
-----------------------+---------------------+--------------------
total packets                       1154193               995903
good packets                        1154193               995903
64 bytes packets                          0                    0
65-127 bytes packets                 432847               656132
128-255 bytes packets                429319                 8775
256-511 bytes packets                236194               328244
512-1023 bytes packets                  619                   18
1024-max bytes packets                55214                 2734
broadcast packets                         0                    0
multicast packets                         0                    0
good octets                       262167681            201434260
total octets                              0                    0
XON packets                               0                    0
XOFF packets                              0                    0
management packets                        0                    0


! Output omitted for brevity

Interrupt counters
-------------------+--
Assertions         1176322
Rx packet timer    1154193
Rx absolute timer  0
Rx overrun         0
Rx descr min thresh 0
Tx packet timer    0
Tx absolute timer  1154193
Tx queue empty     995903
Tx descr thresh low 0

Error counters
-------------------------------+--
CRC errors ..................... 0
Alignment errors ............... 0
Symbol errors .................. 0
Sequence errors ................ 0
RX errors ...................... 0
Missed packets (FIFO overflow)   0
```

```
Single collisions .............. 0
Excessive collisions ........... 0
Multiple collisions ............ 0
Late collisions ................ 0
Collisions ..................... 0
Defers ......................... 0
Tx no CRS ...................... 0
Carrier extension errors ....... 0
Rx length errors ............... 0
FC Rx unsupported .............. 0
Rx no buffers .................. 0
Rx undersize ................... 0
Rx fragments ................... 0
Rx oversize .................... 0
Rx jabbers ..................... 0
Rx management packets dropped .. 0
Tx TCP segmentation context .... 0
Tx TCP segmentation context fail 0

Throttle statistics
------------------------------+---------
Throttle interval ........... 2 * 100ms
Packet rate limit ........... 64000 pps
Rate limit reached counter .. 0
Tick counter ................ 193078
Active ...................... 0
Rx packet rate (current/max)  3 / 182 pps
Tx packet rate (current/max)  2 / 396 pps

NAPI statistics
----------------+---------
Weight Queue 0 ........ 512
Weight Queue 1 ........ 256
Weight Queue 2 ........ 128
Weight Queue 3 ........ 16
Weight Queue 4 ........ 64
Weight Queue 5 ........ 64
Weight Queue 6 ........ 64
Weight Queue 7 ........ 64
Poll scheduled . 1176329
Poll rescheduled 0
Poll invoked ... 1176329
Weight reached . 0
```

```
Tx packets ..... 995903
Rx packets ..... 1154193
Rx congested ... 0
Rx redelivered . 0

qdisc stats:
----------------+---------
Tx queue depth . 10000
qlen ........... 0
packets ........ 995903
bytes .......... 197450648
drops .......... 0

Inband stats
----------------+---------
Tx src_p stamp . 0
N9396PX-5# show hardware internal cpu-mac inband stats
================ Packet Statistics ======================
Packets received:              58021524
Bytes received:                412371530221
Packets sent:                  57160641
Bytes sent:                    409590752550
Rx packet rate (current/peak): 0 / 281 pps
Peak rx rate time:             2017-03-08 19:03:21
Tx packet rate (current/peak): 0 / 289 pps
Peak tx rate time:             2017-04-24 14:26:36
```

Note The output varies among Nexus platforms. For instance, the previous output is brief and comes from the Nexus 9396 PX switch. The same command output on the Nexus 9508 switch is similar to the output displayed for the Nexus 7000 switch. This command is available on all Nexus platforms.

In the previous output, the in-band stats command on Nexus 9396, though brief, displays the time when the traffic hit the peak rate; such information is not available on the command for the Nexus 7000 switch. Nexus 7000 provides the **show hardware internal cpu-mac inband events** command, which displays the event history of the traffic rate in the ingress (Rx) or egress (Tx) direction of the CPU, including the peak rate. Example 3-15 displays the in-band events history for the traffic rate in the ingress or egress direction of the CPU. The time stamp of the peak traffic rate is useful when investigating high CPU or packet loss on the Nexus 7000 switches.

Example 3-15 *Nexus 7000 In-Band Events*

```
N7k-1# show hardware internal cpu-mac inband events

1) Event:TX_PPS_MAX, length:4, at 546891 usecs after Fri Jun  2 01:34:38 2017
   new maximum = 396


2) Event:TX_PPS_MAX, length:4, at 526888 usecs after Fri Jun  2 01:31:57 2017
   new maximum = 219


3) Event:TX_PPS_MAX, length:4, at 866931 usecs after Fri Jun  2 00:31:30 2017
   new maximum = 180


4) Event:RX_PPS_MAX, length:4, at 866930 usecs after Fri Jun  2 00:31:30 2017
   new maximum = 182


5) Event:TX_PPS_MAX, length:4, at 826891 usecs after Fri Jun  2 00:30:47 2017
   new maximum = 151


6) Event:RX_PPS_MAX, length:4, at 826890 usecs after Fri Jun  2 00:30:47 2017
   new maximum = 152
! Output omitted for brevity
```

NX-OS also provides with a brief in-band counters CLI that displays the number of in-band packets in both ingress (Rx) and egress (Tx) directions, errors, dropped counters, overruns, and more. These are used to quickly determine whether the in-band traffic is getting dropped. Example 3-16 displays the output of the command **show hardware internal cpu-mac inband counters**. If nonzero counters appear for errors, drops, or overruns, use the **diff** keyword to determine whether they are increasing frequently. This command is available on all platforms.

Example 3-16 *Nexus In-Band Counters*

```
N7k-1# show hardware internal cpu-mac inband counters
eth0      Link encap:Ethernet   HWaddr 00:0E:0C:FF:FF:FF
          inet addr:127.5.1.5  Bcast:127.5.1.255  Mask:255.255.255.0
          inet6 addr: fe80::20e:cff:feff:ffff/64 Scope:Link
          UP BROADCAST RUNNING PROMISC MULTICAST  MTU:9338  Metric:1
          RX packets:2475891 errors:0 dropped:0 overruns:0 frame:0
          TX packets:5678434 errors:0 dropped:0 overruns:0 carrier:0
          collisions:0 txqueuelen:10000
          RX bytes:799218439 (762.1 MiB)  TX bytes:1099385202 (1.0 GiB)
```

Packet drops on the Nexus switch happen because of various errors in the hardware. The drops happen either at the line card or on the supervisor module itself. To view the various errors and their counters across all the modules on a Nexus switch, use the command **show hardware internal errors** [**all** | **module** *slot*]. Example 3-17 displays the hardware internal errors on the Nexus 7000 switch. Note that the command is applicable for all Nexus platforms.

Example 3-17 *Hardware Internal Errors*

```
N7k-1# show hardware internal errors
|------------------------------------------------------------------|
| Device:Clipper MAC           Role:MAC              Mod: 1        |
| Last cleared @ Wed May 31 12:59:42 2017                          |
| Device Statistics Category :: ERROR                              |
|------------------------------------------------------------------|
Instance:0
Cntr  Name                                       Value        Ports
----  ----                                       -----        -----
 148  GD GMAC rx_config_word change interrupt    0000000000000001  - I1
2196  GD GMAC rx_config_word change interrupt    0000000000000003  - I2
2202  GD GMAC symbol error interrupt             0000000000000002  - I2
2203  GD GMAC sequence error interrupt           0000000000000002  - I2
2207  GD GMAC transition from sync to nosync int 0000000000000002  - I2


|------------------------------------------------------------------|
| Device:Clipper XBAR          Role:QUE              Mod: 1        |
| Last cleared @ Wed May 31 12:59:42 2017                          |
| Device Statistics Category :: ERROR                              |
|------------------------------------------------------------------|
|------------------------------------------------------------------|
| Device:Clipper FWD           Role:L2               Mod: 1        |
| Last cleared @ Wed May 31 12:59:42 2017                          |
| Device Statistics Category :: ERROR                              |
|------------------------------------------------------------------|
! Output omitted for brevity
```

Note Each Nexus platform has different ASICs where errors or drops are observed. However, these are outside the scope of this book. It is recommended to capture **show tech-support detail** and **tac-pac** command output during problematic states, to identify the platform-level problems leading to packet loss.

Nexus Fabric Extenders

Fabric Extender (FEX) is a 1RU fixed-configuration chassis designed to provide top-of-rack connectivity for servers. As the name suggests, FEX does not function on its own. It is specifically designed to extend the architecture and functionality of the Nexus switches. FEX is connected to Nexus 9000, 7000, 6000, and 5000 series parent switches. The uplink ports connecting the FEX to the parent switch are called the Fabric ports or network-facing interface (NIF) ports; the ports on the FEX module that connect the servers (front-panel ports) are called the satellite ports or host-facing interface (HFI) ports. Cisco released FEX models in three categories, according to their capabilities and capacity:

- 1 GE Fabric Extender
  - N2224TP, 24 port
  - N2248TP, 48 port
  - N2248TP-E, 48 port
- 10GBASE-T Fabric Extender
  - N2332TQ, 32 port
  - N2348TQ, 48 port
  - N2348TQ-E, 48 port
  - N2232TM, 32 port
  - N2232TM-E, 32 port
- 10G SFP+ Fabric Extender
  - N2348UPQ, 48 port
  - N2248PQ, 48 port
  - N2232PP, 48 port

Note Compatibility between an FEX and its parent switch is based on the software release notes of the software version being used on the Nexus switch.

Connectivity between the parent switch and an FEX occurs in three different modes:

- **Pinning:** In pinning mode, a one-to-one mapping takes place between HIF ports and uplink ports. Thus, traffic from a specific HIF port can traverse only a specific uplink. Failures on uplink ports bring down the mapped HIF ports.
- **Port-channeling:** In this mode, the uplink is treated as one logical interface. All the traffic between the parent switch and FEX is hashed across the different links of the port-channel.
- **Hybrid:** This mode is a combination of the pinning and port-channeling modes. The uplink ports are split into two port-channels and the HIF ports are pinned to a specific uplink port-channel.

Note Chapter 4, "Nexus Switching," has more details on the FEX supported and nonsupported designs.

To enable FEX, NX-OS first requires installing the feature set using the command **install feature-set fex**. Then the feature set for FEX must be installed using the command **feature-set fex**. If the FEX is being enabled on the Nexus 7000, the FEX feature set is installed in the default VDC along with the command **no hardware ip verify address reserved**; the **feature-set fex** then is configured under the relevant VDC. The command **no hardware ip verify address reserved** is required only when the intrusion detection system (IDS) reserved address check is enabled. This is verified using the command **show hardware ip verify**. If the check is already disabled, the command **no hardware ip verify address reserved** is not required to be configured.

When the **feature-set fex** is enabled, interfaces are enabled as FEX fabric using the command **switchport mode fex-fabric**. The next step is to assign an ID for the FEX, which is further used to distinguish an FEX on the switch. Example 3-18 illustrates the configuration on the Nexus switch for connecting to an FEX.

Example 3-18 *FEX Configuration*

```
N9k-1(config)# install feature-set fex
N9k-1(config)# feature-set fex
N9k-1(config)# interface Eth3/41-44
N9k-1(config-if)# channel-group 1
N9k-1(config-if)# no shutdown
N9k-1(config-if)# exit
N9k-1(config)# interface port-channel1
N9k-1(config-if)# switchport
N9k-1(config-if)# switchport mode fex-fabric
N9k-1(config-if)# fex associate 101
N9k-1(config-if)# no shutdown
```

When FEX configuration is complete, the FEX is accessible on the parent switch and its interfaces are available for further configuration. To verify the status of the FEX, use the command **show fex**. This command shows the status of the FEX, along with the FEX module number and the ID associated by the parent switch. To determine which FEX interfaces are accessible on the parent switch, use the command **show interface** *interface-id* **fex-intf**. Note that the *interface-id* in this command is the NIF port-channel interface. Example 3-19 examines the output of the **show fex** and the **show interface fex-intf** commands to verify the FEX status and its interfaces.

Example 3-19 *FEX Verification*

```
Leaf1# show fex
  FEX         FEX              FEX                       FEX
 Number      Description      State          Model              Serial
---------------------------------------------------------------------------
 101         FEX0101          Online         N2K-C2248TP-1GE    JAF1424AARL
Leaf1# show interface port-channel 1 fex-intf
 Fabric           FEX
 Interface        Interfaces
--------------------------------------------------
 Po1              Eth101/1/48   Eth101/1/47   Eth101/1/46   Eth101/1/45
                  Eth101/1/44   Eth101/1/43   Eth101/1/42   Eth101/1/41
                  Eth101/1/40   Eth101/1/39   Eth101/1/38   Eth101/1/37
                  Eth101/1/36   Eth101/1/35   Eth101/1/34   Eth101/1/33
                  Eth101/1/32   Eth101/1/31   Eth101/1/30   Eth101/1/29
                  Eth101/1/28   Eth101/1/27   Eth101/1/26   Eth101/1/25
                  Eth101/1/24   Eth101/1/23   Eth101/1/22   Eth101/1/21
                  Eth101/1/20   Eth101/1/19   Eth101/1/18   Eth101/1/17
                  Eth101/1/16   Eth101/1/15   Eth101/1/14   Eth101/1/13
                  Eth101/1/12   Eth101/1/11   Eth101/1/10   Eth101/1/9
                  Eth101/1/8    Eth101/1/7    Eth101/1/6    Eth101/1/5
                  Eth101/1/4    Eth101/1/3    Eth101/1/2    Eth101/1/1
```

Further details on the FEX are viewed using the command **show fex** *fex-number* **detail**. This command displays the status of the FEX and all the FEX interfaces. Additionally, it displays the details of pinning mode and information regarding the FEX fabric ports. Example 3-20 displays the detailed output of the FEX 101.

Example 3-20 *FEX Detail*

```
Leaf1# show fex 101 detail
FEX: 101 Description: FEX0101    state: Online
  FEX version: 6.2(12) [Switch version: 6.2(12)]
  FEX Interim version: (12)FH_0_171
  Switch Interim version: 6.2(12)
  Extender Serial: FOC1710R0JF
  Extender Model: N2K-C2248PQ-10GE,   Part No: 73-14775-03
  Card Id: 207, Mac Addr: f0:29:29:ff:8e:c2, Num Macs: 64
  Module Sw Gen: 21  [Switch Sw Gen: 21]
  Pinning-mode: static    Max-links: 1
  Fabric port for control traffic: Eth3/41
  FCoE Admin: false
  FCoE Oper: false
  FCoE FEX AA Configured: false
```

128 Chapter 3: Troubleshooting Nexus Platform Issues

```
  Fabric interface state:
    Po1 - Interface Up. State: Active
    Eth3/41 - Interface Up. State: Active
    Eth3/42 - Interface Up. State: Active
    Eth3/43 - Interface Up. State: Active
    Eth3/44 - Interface Up. State: Active
  Fex Port        State    Fabric Port
      Eth101/1/1  Down         Po1
      Eth101/1/2  Up           Po1
      Eth101/1/3  Down         Po1
      Eth101/1/4  Down         Po1
      Eth101/1/5  Down         Po1
      Eth101/1/6  Down         Po1
      Eth101/1/7  Down         Po1
      Eth101/1/8  Down         Po1
      Eth101/1/9  Down         Po1
      Eth101/1/10 Down         Po1
! Output omitted for brevity
```

When the FEX satellite ports are available, use them to configure these ports as either Layer 2 or Layer 3 ports; they also can act as active-active ports by making them part of the vPC configuration.

If issues arise with the fabric ports or the satellite ports, the state change information is viewed using the command **show system internal fex info fport** [all | *interface-number*] or **show system internal fex info satport** [all | *interface-number*]. Example 3-21 displays the internal information of both the satellite and fabric ports on the Nexus 7000 switch. In the first section of the output, the command displays a list of events that the system goes through to bring up the FEX. It lists all the finite state machine events, which is useful while troubleshooting in case the FEX does not come up and gets stuck in one of the states. The second section of the output displays information about the satellite ports and their status information.

Example 3-21 *FEX Internal Information*

```
Leaf1# show system internal fex info fport all
   intf     ifindex    Oper chass module-id       Sdp Rx Sdp Tx State AA mode
       Po1 0x16000000    Up 101 0x000000000000        0       0 Active       0
Interface :      Po1 - 0x16000000 Up Remote chassis: 101
    satellite: 0x0,   SDP state Init, Rx:0, Tx:0
    Not Fabric mode. satellite Not Bound. Fport state: Active
    fabric slot:33, SDP module id:0x0, rlink: 0x0
    parent:0x0 num mem: 4 num mem up: 4
    Active members(4): Eth3/41, Eth3/42, Eth3/43, Eth3/44,
    Flags: , , , ,
```

```
   Fcot: Not checked, Not valid, Not present
 Fex AA Mode: 0
 Err disable Mode: 0
 Oper fabric mode: 0
Logs:
06/04/2017 15:30:19.553797: Remote-chassis configured
   Eth3/41  0x1a128000    Up 101 0xc08eff2929f0       169      175 Active      0
Interface : Eth3/41 - 0x1a128000 Up Remote chassis: 101
    satellite: 0xc08eff2929f0,  SDP state Active, Rx:169, Tx:175
    Fabric mode. satellite Bound. Fport state: Active
    fabric slot:33, SDP module id:0xc08eff2929f0, rlink: 0x20000000
    parent:0x16000000 num mem: 0 num mem up: 0
     Active members(0):
    Flags: , Bundle membup rcvd, , Switchport fabric,
    Fcot: Checked, Valid, Present
 Fex AA Mode: 0
 Err disable Mode: 0
 Oper fabric mode: 2
Logs:
06/04/2017 15:29:32.706998: pre config: is not a port-channel member
06/04/2017 15:29:32.777929: Interface Up
06/04/2017 15:29:32.908528: Fcot message sent to Ethpm
06/04/2017 15:29:32.908649: Satellite discovered msg sent
06/04/2017 15:29:32.908744: State changed to: Discovered
06/04/2017 15:29:32.909163: Fcot response received. SFP valid
06/04/2017 15:29:38.931664: Interface Down
06/04/2017 15:29:38.931787: State changed to: Created
06/04/2017 15:29:40.852076: Interface Up
06/04/2017 15:29:42.967594: Fcot message sent to Ethpm
06/04/2017 15:29:42.967661: Satellite discovered msg sent
06/04/2017 15:29:42.967930: State changed to: Discovered
06/04/2017 15:29:42.968363: Fcot response received. SFP valid
06/04/2017 15:29:45.306713: Interface Down
06/04/2017 15:29:45.306852: State changed to: Created
06/04/2017 15:29:45.462260: pre config: is not a port-channel member
06/04/2017 15:30:15.798370: Interface Up
06/04/2017 15:30:15.801215: Port Bringup rcvd
06/04/2017 15:30:15.802072: Suspending Fabric port. reason: Fex not configured
06/04/2017 15:30:15.802106: fport bringup retry end: sending out resp
06/04/2017 15:30:17.413620: Fcot message sent to Ethpm
06/04/2017 15:30:17.413687: Satellite discovered msg sent
06/04/2017 15:30:17.413938: State changed to: Discovered
06/04/2017 15:30:17.414382: Fcot response received. SFP valid
```

```
06/04/2017 15:30:19.554112: Port added to port-channel
06/04/2017 15:30:19.554266: State changed to: Configured
06/04/2017 15:30:19.554874: Remote-chassis configured
06/04/2017 15:30:19.568677: Interface Down
06/04/2017 15:30:19.685945: Port removed from port-channel
06/04/2017 15:30:19.686854: fport phy cleanup retry end: sending out resp
06/04/2017 15:30:19.689911: pre config: is a port-channel member
06/04/2017 15:30:19.689944: Port added to port-channel
06/04/2017 15:30:19.690170: Remote-chassis configured
06/04/2017 15:30:19.690383: Port changed to fabric mode
06/04/2017 15:30:19.817093: Interface Up
06/04/2017 15:30:19.817438: Started SDP
06/04/2017 15:30:19.817495: State changed to: Fabric Up
06/04/2017 15:30:19.817991: Port Bringup rcvd
06/04/2017 15:30:19.923327: Fcot message sent to Ethpm
06/04/2017 15:30:19.923502: Fcot response received. SFP valid
06/04/2017 15:30:19.923793: Advertizing Vntag
06/04/2017 15:30:19.924329: State changed to: Connecting
06/04/2017 15:30:21.531270: Satellite connected. Bind msg sent
06/04/2017 15:30:21.532110: fport bringup retry end: sending out resp
06/04/2017 15:30:21.534074: State changed to: Active
06/04/2017 15:30:21.640543: Bundle member bringup rcvd
! Output omitted for brevity
N7kA-1-N7KA-LEAF1# show system internal fex info satport ethernet 101/1/1
  Interface-Name   ifindex    State Fabric-if  Pri-fabric Expl-Pinned
       Eth101/1/1 0x1f640000 Down       Po1        Po1       NoConf
  Port Phy Not Up. Port dn req: Not pending
```

Note If any issues arise with the FEX, it is useful to collect **show tech-support fex** *fex-number* during the problematic state. The issue might also result from the Ethpm component on Nexus as the FEX sends state change messages to Ethpm. Thus, capturing the **show tech-support ethpm** output during problematic state could be relevant. Ethpm is discussed later in this chapter.

Virtual Device Context

Virtual Device Contexts (VDC) are logical partitions of a physical device that provide software fault isolation and the capability to manage each partition independently. Each VDC instance runs its own instance of routing protocol services, resulting in better utilization of system resources. Following are the few points to remember before creating VDCs:

- Only users with the network-admin role can create a VDC and allocate resources it.

- VDC1 (default VDC) is always active and cannot be deleted.

- The name of the VDC is not case sensitive.
- VDC is supported only on Nexus 7000 or 7700 series switches.
- Supervisor 1 and Supervisor 2 support a maximum of four VDCs; Supervisor 2E supports a maximum of eight VDCs.
- Nexus switches running Supervisor 2 or 2E cards and beginning with NX-OS version 6.1(1) support the Admin VDC.

Three primary kinds of VDCs are supported on the Nexus 7000 platform:

- **Ethernet:** Supports traditional L2/L3 protocols.
- **Storage:** Supports Fibre Channel over Ethernet (FCoE)–specific protocols, such as FCoE Initialization Protocol (FIP).
- **Admin:** Provides administrative control to the complete system and helps manage other VDCs configured on the system.

VDC Resource Template

A VDC resource template enables users to assign resources to a VDC with the same resource requirements. Unless the resource templates are assigned to a VDC, these templates do not take effect. Using resource templates minimizes the configurations and, at the same time, eases manageability on a Nexus platform. Limit the following resources in each VDC resource template with the following:

- **Monitor-session:** Number of span sessions
- **Port-channel:** Number of port-channels
- **U4route-mem:** IPv4 route memory limit
- **U6route-mem:** IPv6 route memory limit
- **M4route-mem:** IPv4 multicast memory limit
- **M6route-mem:** IPv6 multicast memory limit
- **Vlan:** Number of VLANs
- **Vrf:** Number of Virtual Routing and Forwarding (VRF) instances

The VDC resource template is configured using the command **vdc resource template** *name*. This puts you in resource template configuration mode, where you can limit the resources previously mentioned by using the command **limit-resource** *resource* **minimum** *value* **maximum** *value*, where *resource* can be any of the six listed resources. To view the configured resources within a template, use the command **show vdc resource template** [**vdc-default** | *name*], where **vdc-default** is for the default VDC template. Example 3-22 demonstrates configuration of a VDC template and the **show vdc resource template** command output displaying the configured resources within the template.

Example 3-22 *VDC Resource Template*

```
! Default VDC Template
N7K-1# show vdc resource template vdc-default

  vdc-default
  -------------

    Resource                            Min          Max
    ----------                          -----        -----
    monitor-rbs-product                   0           12
    monitor-rbs-filter                    0           12
    monitor-session-extended              0           12
    monitor-session-mx-exception-src      0            1
    monitor-session-inband-src            0            1
    port-channel                          0          768
    monitor-session-erspan-dst            0           23
    monitor-session                       0            2
    vlan                                 16         4094
    anycast_bundleid                      0           16
    m6route-mem                           5           20
    m4route-mem                           8           90
    u6route-mem                           4            4
    u4route-mem                           8            8
    vrf                                   2         4096
N7K-1(config)# vdc resource template DEMO-TEMPLATE
N7K-1(config-vdc-template)# limit-resource port-channel minimum 1 maximum 4
N7K-1(config-vdc-template)# limit-resource vrf minimum 5 maximum 100
N7K-1(config-vdc-template)# limit-resource vlan minimum 20 maximum 200
N7K-1# show vdc resource template DEMO-TEMPLATE

  DEMO-TEMPLATE
  ---------------

    Resource            Min          Max
    ----------          -----        -----
    vlan                 20          200
    vrf                   5          100
    port-channel          1            4
```

If the network requires all the VDCs on Nexus to be performing different tasks and have different kind of resources allocated to them, it is better not to have VDC templates configured. Limit the VDC resources using the **limit-resource** command under **vdc** configuration mode.

Configuring VDC

VDC creation is broken down into four simple steps:

Step 1. Define a VDC. A VDC is defined using the command **vdc** *name* [**id** *id*] [**type** **Ethernet** | **storage**]. By default, a VDC is created as an Ethernet VDC.

Step 2. Allocate interfaces. Single or multiple interfaces are allocated to a VDC. The interfaces are allocated using the command **allocate interface** *interface-id*. Note that the **allocate interface** configuration is mandatory; the interface allocation cannot be negated. Interfaces are allocated only from one VDC to another and cannot be released back to the default VDC. If the user deletes the VDC, the interfaces also get unallocated and are then made part of VDC ID 0.

For the 10G interface, some modules require all the ports tied to the port-ASIC to be moved together. This is done so as to retain the integrity where each port group can switch between dedicated and shared mode. An error message is displayed if not all members of the same port group are allocated together. Beginning with NX-OS Release 5.2(1), all members of a port group are automatically allocated to the VDC when only a member of the port group is being added to the VDC.

Step 3. Define the HA policy. The high availability (HA) policy is determined based on whether Nexus is running on a single supervisor or a dual supervisor card. The HA policy is configured using the command **ha-policy** [**single-sup** | **dual-sup**] *policy* under the VDC configuration. Table 3-3 lists the different HA policies based on single or dual supervisor cards.

Table 3-3 *HA Policies*

Single SUP	Dual SUP
Bringdown	Bringdown
Restart (default)	Restart
Reset	Switchover (default)

Step 4. Limit resources. Limiting resources on VDC is done by either applying a VDC resource template or manually assigning the resource using the **limit-resource** command. Certain resources cannot be assigned as part of the template; thus, the **limit-resource** command is required. The **limit-resource** command also enables you to define the type of modules that are supported in the VDC. When the VDC is initialized, its resources are modified only by using the **limit-resource** command. The template option then becomes invalid.

Example 3-23 demonstrates the configuration of creating an Ethernet VDC. Notice that if a particular interface is added to the VDC and other members of the port-group are not part of the list, NX-OS automatically tries to add the remaining ports to the VDC. The VDC defined in Example 3-23 limits only for F3 series modules; for instance, adding ports from an F2 or M2 series module would result in an error.

Example 3-23 *VDC Configuration*

```
N7K-1(config)# vdc N7K-2
Note:  Creating VDC, one moment please ...
2017 Apr 21 03:51:55  %$ VDC-5 %$ %SYSLOG-2-SYSTEM_MSG : Syslogs wont be logged into
  logflash until logflash is online

N7K-1(config-vdc)#
N7K-1(config-vdc)# limit-resource module-type f3
This will cause all ports of unallowed types to be removed from this vdc. Continue
  (y/n)? [yes] yes
N7K-1(config-vdc)# allocate interface ethernet 3/1
Entire port-group is not present in the command. Missing ports will be included
  automatically
Additional Interfaces Included are :
    Ethernet3/2
    Ethernet3/3
    Ethernet3/4
    Ethernet3/5
    Ethernet3/6
    Ethernet3/7
    Ethernet3/8
Moving ports will cause all config associated to them in source vdc to be removed.
  Are you sure you want to move the ports (y/n)?  [yes] yes
N7K-1(config-vdc)# ha-policy dual-sup ?
  bringdown   Bring down the vdc
  restart     Bring down the vdc, then bring the vdc back up
  switchover  Switchover the supervisor
N7K-1(config-vdc)# ha-policy dual-sup restart
N7K-1(config-vdc)# ha-policy single-sup bringdown
N7K-1(config-vdc)# limit-resource port-channel minimum 3 maximum 5
N7K-1(config-vdc)# limit-resource vlan minimum 20 maximum 100
N7K-1(config-vdc)# limit-resource vrf minimum 5 maximum 10
```

VDC Initialization

VDC is initialized before VDC-specific configuration is applied. Before VDC initialization, perform a **copy run start** after the VDC is created so that the newly created VDC is part of the startup configuration. The VDC is initialized using the **switchto vdc** *name* command from the default or admin VDC (see Example 3-24). The initialization process of the VDC has steps similar to when a new Nexus switch is brought up. It prompts for the admin password and then the basic configuration dialog. Use this option to perform basic configuration setups for the VDC using this method, or follow manual configuration by replying with *no* for the basic configuration dialog. The command **switchback** is used to switch back to default or admin VDC.

Example 3-24 *VDC Initialization*

```
N7k-1# switchto vdc N7k-2
         ---- System Admin Account Setup ----

Do you want to enforce secure password standard (yes/no) [y]:

  Enter the password for "admin":
  Confirm the password for "admin":

         ---- Basic System Configuration Dialog VDC: 2 ----

This setup utility will guide you through the basic configuration of
the system. Setup configures only enough connectivity for management
of the system.

Please register Cisco Nexus7000 Family devices promptly with your
supplier. Failure to register may affect response times for initial
service calls. Nexus7000 devices must be registered to receive
entitled support services.

Press Enter at anytime to skip a dialog. Use ctrl-c at anytime
to skip the remaining dialogs.

Would you like to enter the basic configuration dialog (yes/no): yes


  Create another login account (yes/no) [n]:

  Configure read-only SNMP community string (yes/no) [n]:

  Configure read-write SNMP community string (yes/no) [n]:

  Enter the switch name : N7k-2

  Continue with Out-of-band (mgmt0) management configuration? (yes/no) [y]:

    Mgmt0 IPv4 address : 192.168.1.10

    Mgmt0 IPv4 netmask : 255.255.255.0

  Configure the default gateway? (yes/no) [y]:

    IPv4 address of the default gateway : 192.168.1.1
```

```
    Configure advanced IP options? (yes/no) [n]:

    Enable the telnet service? (yes/no) [n]: yes

    Enable the ssh service? (yes/no) [y]: yes

      Type of ssh key you would like to generate (dsa/rsa) [rsa]:

      Number of rsa key bits <1024-2048> [1024]:

    Configure default interface layer (L3/L2) [L3]:

    Configure default switchport interface state (shut/noshut) [shut]:

The following configuration will be applied:
  password strength-check
  switchname N7k-2
vrf context management
ip route 0.0.0.0/0 192.168.1.100
exit
  feature telnet
  ssh key rsa 1024 force
  feature ssh
  no system default switchport
  system default switchport shutdown
interface mgmt0
ip address 192.168.1.1 255.255.255.0
no shutdown

Would you like to edit the configuration? (yes/no) [n]:
Use this configuration and save it? (yes/no) [y]:

! Output omitted for brevity
N7k-1-N7k-2#
N7k-1-N7k-2# switchback
N7k-1#
```

In Example 3-24, after the VDC is initialized, the host name of the VDC is seen as N7k-1-N7k-2—that is, the hostnames of both the default VDC and the new VDC are concatenated. To avoid this behavior, configure the command **no vdc combined-hostname** in default or admin VDC.

Out-of-Band and In-Band Management

The Cisco NX-OS software provides a virtual management interface for out-of-band management for each VDC. Each virtual management interface is configured with a separate IP address that is accessed through the physical mgmt0 interface. Using the virtual management interface enables you to use only one management network, which shares the AAA servers and syslog servers among the VDCs.

VDCs also support in-band management. VDC is accessed using one of the Ethernet interfaces that are allocated to the VDC. Using in-band management involves using only separate management networks, which ensures separation of the AAA servers and syslog servers among the VDCs.

VDC Management

NX-OS software provides a CLI to easily manage the VDCs when troubleshooting problems. The VDC configuration of all the VDCs is seen from default or admin VDC. Use the command **show run vdc** to view all the VDC-related configuration. Additionally, when saving the configuration, use the command **copy run start vdc-all** to copy the configuration done on all VDCs.

NX-OS provides a CLI to view further details of the VDC without looking at the configuration. Use the command **show vdc [detail]** to view the details of each VDC. The **show vdc detail** command displays various lists of information for each VDC, such as ID, name, state, HA policy, CPU share, creation time and uptime of the VDC, VDC type, and line cards supported by each VDC (see Example 3-25). On a Nexus 7000 switch, some VDCs might be running critical services. By default, NX-OS allocates an equal CPU share (CPU resources) to all the VDCs. On SUP2 and SUP2E supervisor cards, NX-OS allows users to allocate a specific amount of the switch's CPU, to prioritize more critical VDCs.

Example 3-25 show vdc detail *Command Output*

```
N7k-1# show vdc detail
Switchwide mode is m1 f1 m1x1 f2 m2x1 f2e f3 m3


vdc id: 1
vdc name: N7k-1
vdc state: active
vdc mac address: 50:87:89:4b:c0:c1
vdc ha policy: RELOAD
vdc dual-sup ha policy: SWITCHOVER
vdc boot Order: 1
CPU Share: 5
CPU Share Percentage: 50%
vdc create time: Fri Apr 21 05:57:30 2017
vdc reload count: 0
vdc uptime: 1 day(s), 0 hour(s), 35 minute(s), 41 second(s)
vdc restart count: 1
```

Chapter 3: Troubleshooting Nexus Platform Issues

```
vdc restart time: Fri Apr 21 05:57:30 2017
vdc type: Ethernet
vdc supported linecards: f3

vdc id: 2
vdc name: N7k-2
vdc state: active
vdc mac address: 50:87:89:4b:c0:c2
vdc ha policy: RESTART
vdc dual-sup ha policy: SWITCHOVER
vdc boot Order: 1
CPU Share: 5
CPU Share Percentage: 50%
vdc create time: Sat Apr 22 05:05:59 2017
vdc reload count: 0
vdc uptime: 0 day(s), 1 hour(s), 28 minute(s), 12 second(s)
vdc restart count: 1
vdc restart time: Sat Apr 22 05:05:59 2017
vdc type: Ethernet
vdc supported linecards: f3
```

To further view the details of resources allocated to each VDC, use the command **show vdc resource [detail]**. This command displays the configured minimum and maximum value and the used, unused, and available values for each resource. The output is run for individual VDCs using the command **show vdc** *name* **resource [detail]**. Example 3-26 displays the resource configuration and utilization for each VDC on the Nexus 7000 chassis running two VDCs (for instance, N7k-1 and N7k-2).

Example 3-26 show vdc resource detail *Command Output*

```
N7k-1# show vdc resource detail

  vlan              34 used     8 unused   16349 free   16341 avail   16383 total
  ------
         Vdc                  Min         Max        Used       Unused       Avail
         ---                  ---         ---        ----       ------       -----
         N7k-1                16          4094       26         0            4068
         N7k-2                16          4094       8          8            4086

  monitor-session    0 used     0 unused       2 free       2 avail       2 total
  -----------------
         Vdc                  Min         Max        Used       Unused       Avail
         ---                  ---         ---        ----       ------       -----
         N7k-1                0           2          0          0            2
         N7k-2                0           2          0          0            2
```

Virtual Device Context   139

```
    vrf                  5 used      0 unused    4091 free   4091 avail   4096 total
    -----
            Vdc                      Min         Max         Used        Unused       Avail
            ---                      ---         ---         ----        ------       -----
            N7k-1                    2           4096        3           0            4091
            N7k-2                    2           4096        2           0            4091

    port-channel         5 used      0 unused     763 free    763 avail    768 total
    -------------
            Vdc                      Min         Max         Used        Unused       Avail
            ---                      ---         ---         ----        ------       -----
            N7k-1                    0           768         5           0            763
            N7k-2                    0           768         0           0            763

    u4route-mem          2 used    102 unused     514 free    412 avail    516 total
    -------------
            Vdc                      Min         Max         Used        Unused       Avail
            ---                      ---         ---         ----        ------       -----
            N7k-1                    96          96          1           95           95
            N7k-2                    8           8           1           7            7
! Output omitted for brevity
```

Based on the kind of line cards the VDC supports, interfaces are allocated to each VDC. To view the member interfaces of each VDC, use the command **show vdc membership**. Example 3-27 displays the output of the **show vdc membership** command. In Example 3-27, notice the various interfaces that are part of VDC 1 (N7k-1) and VDC 2 (N7k-2). If a particular VDC is deleted, the interfaces become unallocated and are thus shown under the VDC ID 0.

Example 3-27 *R1 Routing Table with GRE Tunnel*

```
N7k-1# show vdc membership
Flags : b - breakout port
---------------------------------

vdc_id: 0 vdc_name: Unallocated interfaces:

vdc_id: 1 vdc_name: N7k-1 interfaces:
        Ethernet3/9             Ethernet3/10            Ethernet3/11
        Ethernet3/12            Ethernet3/13            Ethernet3/14
        Ethernet3/15            Ethernet3/16            Ethernet3/17
        Ethernet3/18            Ethernet3/19            Ethernet3/20
        Ethernet3/21            Ethernet3/22            Ethernet3/23
        Ethernet3/24            Ethernet3/25            Ethernet3/26
```

```
            Ethernet3/27          Ethernet3/28          Ethernet3/29
            Ethernet3/30          Ethernet3/31          Ethernet3/32
            Ethernet3/33          Ethernet3/34          Ethernet3/35
            Ethernet3/36          Ethernet3/37          Ethernet3/38
            Ethernet3/39          Ethernet3/40          Ethernet3/41
            Ethernet3/42          Ethernet3/43          Ethernet3/44
            Ethernet3/45          Ethernet3/46          Ethernet3/47
            Ethernet3/48

vdc_id: 2 vdc_name: N7k-2 interfaces:
            Ethernet3/1           Ethernet3/2           Ethernet3/3
            Ethernet3/4           Ethernet3/5           Ethernet3/6
            Ethernet3/7           Ethernet3/8
```

NX-OS also provides internal event history logs to view errors or messages related to a VDC. Use the command **show vdc internal event-history** [**errors** | **msgs** | **vdc_id** *id*] to view the debugging information related to VDCs. Example 3-28 demonstrates creating a new VDC (N7k-3) and shows relevant event history logs that display events the VDC creation process goes through before the VDC is created and active for use. The events in Example 3-28 show the VDC creation in progress and then show that it becomes active.

Example 3-28 *VDC Internal Event History Logs*

```
N7k-1(config)# vdc N7k-3
Note:  Creating VDC, one moment please ...
2017 Apr 25 04:19:03  %$ VDC-3 %$ %SYSLOG-2-SYSTEM_MSG : Syslogs wont be logged into
  logflash until logflash is online
N7k-1(config-vdc)#
N7k-1# show vdc internal event-history vdc_id 3

1) Event:VDC_SEQ_CONFIG, length:170, at 74647 usecs after Tue Apr 25 04:20:31 2017
    vdc_id = 3    vdc_name = N7k-3    vdc_state = VDC_ACTIVE
    desc = VDC_CR_EV_SEQ_DONE


2) Event:VDC_SEQ_CONFIG, length:170, at 74200 usecs after Tue Apr 25 04:20:31 2017
    vdc_id = 3    vdc_name = N7k-3    vdc_state = VDC_CREATE_IN_PROGRESS
    desc = VDC_SHARE_SEQ_CHECK


3) Event:VDC_SEQ_PORT_CONFIG, length:216, at 74130 usecs after Tue Apr 25 04:20:31
 2017
    vdc_id = 3    vdc_name = N7k-3    vdc_state = VDC_CREATE_IN_PROGRESS
    Dest_vdc_id = 3   Source_vdcs =    Num of Ports = 0
```

```
4) Event:E_MTS_RX, length:48, at 73920 usecs after Tue Apr 25 04:20:31 2017
   [RSP] Opc:MTS_OPC_VDC_PRE_CREATE(20491), Id:0X0047D41A, Ret:SUCCESS
   Src:0x00000101/179, Dst:0x00000101/357, Flags:None
   HA_SEQNO:0X00000000, RRtoken:0x0047D40D, Sync:UNKNOWN, Payloadsize:4
   Payload:
   0x0000:  00 00 00 00


5) Event:E_MTS_TX, length:50, at 36406 usecs after Tue Apr 25 04:20:31 2017
   [REQ] Opc:MTS_OPC_VDC_PRE_CREATE(20491), Id:0X0047D40D, Ret:SUCCESS
   Src:0x00000101/357, Dst:0x00000101/179, Flags:None
   HA_SEQNO:0X00000000, RRtoken:0x0047D40D, Sync:UNKNOWN, Payloadsize:6
   Payload:
   0x0000:  00 03 00 00 00 05
```

Note If a problem arises with a VDC, collect the **show tech-support vdc** and **show tech-support detail** command output during problematic state to open a TAC case.

Line Card Interop Limitations

Creating VDCs is simple. The challenge arises when interfaces are allocated from different module types present in the chassis. The operating modes of the line cards change with the different combination of line cards present in the chassis. While limiting the module-type resource for the VDC, be careful of the compatibility between M series line cards and F series line cards. Also keep the following guidelines in mind when both F and M series line cards are present in the chassis:

- Interfaces from F2E and M3 series line cards cannot coexist.
- If M2 module interfaces are working with M3 module interfaces, interfaces from the M2 module cannot be allocated to the other VDC.
- If interfaces from both M2 and M3 series line cards are present in the VDC, the M2 module must operate in M2-M3 interop mode.
- If interfaces from both F2E and M2 series line cards are present in the VDC, the M2 module must operate in M2-F2E mode.
- The M2 module must be in M2-F2E mode to operate in the other VDC.

The M2 series line cards support both M2-F2E and M2-M3 interop modes, with the default being M2-F2E mode. M3 series line cards, on the other hand, support M2-M3 interop mode only. To allocate interfaces from both M2 and M3 modules that are part of same VDC, use the command **system interop-mode m2-m3 module** *slot* to change the operating mode of M2 line cards to M2-M3. Use the **no** option to disable M2-M3 mode and fall back to the default M2-F2E mode on the M2 line card.

To support both M and F2E series modules in the same VDC, F2E series modules operate in proxy mode. In this mode, all Layer 3 traffic is sent to the M series line card in the same VDC.

Table 3-4 reinforces which module type mix is supported on Ethernet VDCs.

Table 3-4 *Module Type Supported Combinations on Ethernet VDC*

Module	M1	F1	M1XL	M2	M3	F2	F2e	F3
M1	Yes	Yes	Yes	Yes	No	No	Yes	No
F1	Yes	Yes	Yes	Yes	No	No	No	No
M1XL	Yes	Yes	Yes	Yes	No	No	Yes	No
M2	Yes	Yes	Yes	Yes	Yes	No	Yes	Yes
M3	No	No	No	Yes	Yes	No	No	Yes
F2	No	No	No	No	No	Yes	Yes	Yes
F2e	Yes	No	Yes	Yes	No	Yes	Yes	Yes
F3	No	No	No	Yes	Yes	Yes	Yes	Yes

Note For more details on supported module combinations and the behavior of modules running in different modes, refer to the CCO documentation listed in the "References" section, at the end of the chapter.

Troubleshooting NX-OS System Components

Nexus is a distributed architecture platform, so it runs features that are both platform independent (PI) and platform dependent (PD). In troubleshooting PI features such as the routing protocol control plane, knowing the feature helps in easily isolating the problem; for features in which PD troubleshooting is required, however, understanding the NX-OS system components helps.

Troubleshooting PD issues requires having knowledge about not only various system components but also dependent services or components. For instance, Route Policy Manager (RPM) is a process that is dependent on the Address Resolution Protocol (ARP) and Netstack processes (see Example 3-29). These processes are further dependent on other processes. The hierarchy of dependency is viewed using the command **show system internal sysmgr service dependency srvname** *name*.

Example 3-29 *Feature Dependancy Hierarchy*

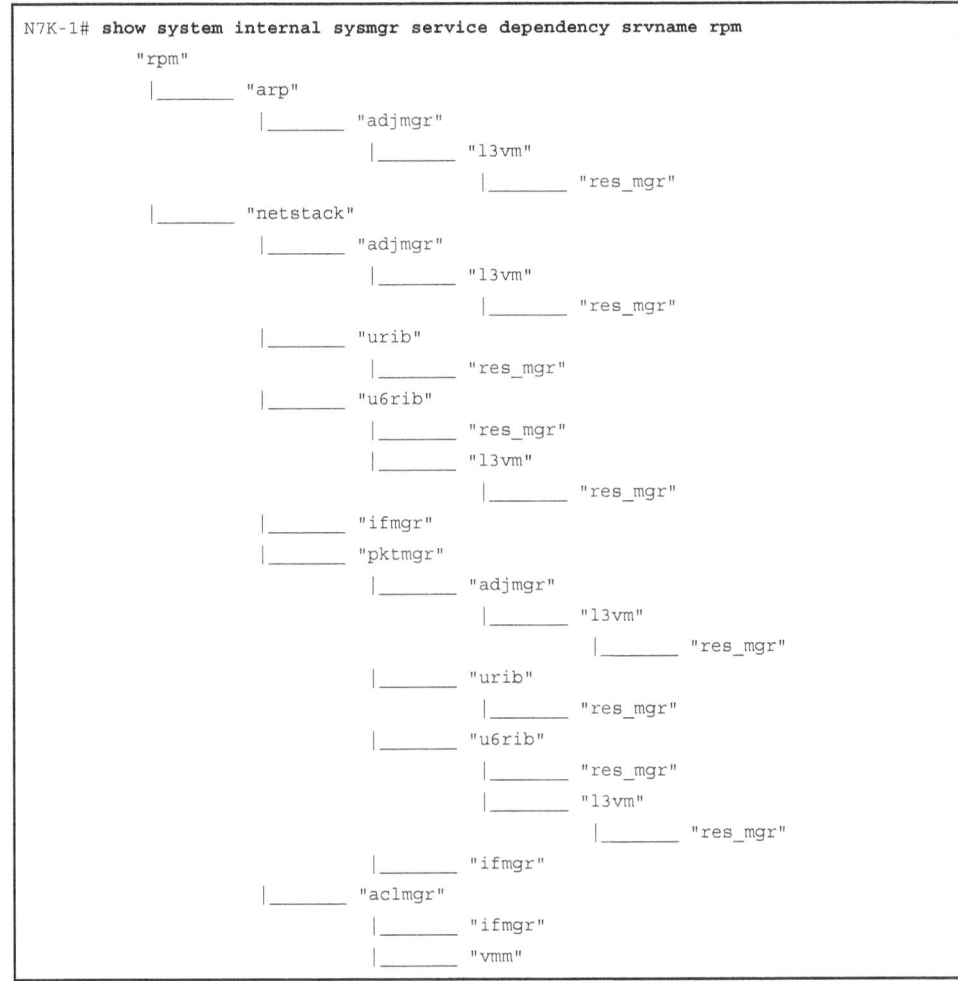

Of course, knowledge of all components is not possible, but problem isolation becomes easier with knowledge of some primary system components that perform major tasks in the NX-OS platforms. This section focuses on some of these primary components:

- Message and Transaction Services (MTS)
- Netstack and Packet Manager
- ARP and AdjMgr
- Forwarding components
  - Unicast Routing Information Base (URIB), Unicast Forwarding Information Base (UFIB), and Unicast Forwarding Distribution Manager (UFDM)
- EthPM and Port-Client

Message and Transaction Services

Message and Transaction Service (MTS) is the fundamental communication paradigm that supervisor and line cards use to communicate between processes. In other words, it is an interprocess communications (IPC) broker that handles message routing and queuing between services and hardware within the system. On the other hand, internode communication (for instance, communication between process A on a supervisor and process B on a line card) is handled by Asynchronous Inter-Process Communication (AIPC). AIPC provides features such as reliable transport across Ethernet Out of Band Channel (EOBC), fragmentation, and reassembly of packets.

MTS provides features such as the following:

- Messaging and HA infrastructure
- High performance and low latency (provides low latency for exchanging messages between interprocess communications)
- Buffer management (manages the buffer for respective processes that are queued up to be delivered to other processes)
- Message delivery

MTS guarantees independent process restarts so that it does not impact other client or nonclient processes running on the system and to ensure that the messages from other processes are received after a restart.

A physical switch can be partitioned to multiple VDCs for resource partitioning, fault isolation, and administration. One of the main features of the NX-OS infrastructure is to make virtualization transparent to the applications. MTS provides this virtualization transparency using the virtual node (vnode) concept and an architecturally clean communication model. With this concept, an application thinks that it is running on a switch, with no VDC.

MTS works by allocating a predefined chunk of system memory when the system boots up. This memory exists in the kernel address space. When applications start up, the memory gets automatically mapped to the application address space. When an application tries to send some data to the queue, MTS makes one copy of the data and copies the payload into a buffer. It then posts a reference to the buffer into the application's receive queue. When the application tries to read its queue, it gets a reference to the payload, which it reads directly as it's already mapped in its address space.

Consider a simple example. OSPF learns a new route from an LSA update from its adjacent neighbor. The OSPF process requires that the route be installed in the routing table. The OSPF process puts the needed information (prefix, next hop, and so on) into an MTS message, which it then sends to URIB. In this example, MTS is taking care of exchanging the information between the OSPF and the URIB components.

MTS facilitates the interprocess communication using Service Access Points (SAP) to allow services to exchange messages. Each card in the switch has at least one instance of MTS running, also known as the MTS domain. The node address is used to identify which MTS domain is involved in processing a message. The MTS domain is kind of a logical node that provides services only to the processes inside that domain. Inside the MTS domain, a SAP represents the address used to reach a service. A process needs to bind to a SAP before it communicates with another SAP. SAPs are divided into three categories:

1. **Static SAPs:** Ranges from 1 to 1023

2. **Dynamic SAPs:** Ranges from 1024 to 65535

3. **Registry SAP:** 0 (reserved)

> **Note** A client is required to know the server's SAP (usually a static SAP) to communicate with the server.

An MTS address is divided into two parts: a 4-byte node address and a 2-byte SAP number. Because an MTS domain provides services to the processes associated with that domain, the node address in the MTS address is used to decide the destination MTS domain. Thus, the SAP number resides in the MTS domain identified by the node address. If the Nexus switch has multiple VDCs, each VDC has its own MTS domain; this is reflected as SUP for VDC1, SUP-1 for VDC2, SUP-2 for VDC3, and so on.

MTS also has various operational codes to identify different kinds of payloads in the MTS message:

- **sync:** This is used to synchronize information to standby.
- **notification:** The operations code is used for one-way notification.
- **request_response:** The message carries a token to match the request and response.
- **switchover_send:** The operational code can be sent during switchover.
- **switchover_recv:** The operational code can be received during switchover.
- **seqno:** The operational code carries a sequence number.

Various symptoms can indicate problems with MTS, and different symptoms mean different problems. If a feature or process is not performing as expected, high CPU is noticed on the Nexus switch, or ports are bouncing on the switch for no reason, then the MTS message might be stuck in the queue. The easiest way to check is to check the MTS buffer utilization, using the command **show system internal mts buffer summary**. This output needs to be taken several times to see which queues are not clearing. Example 3-30 demonstrates how the MTS buffer summary looks when the queues are not clearing. The process with SAP number 2938 seems to be stuck because the messages are stuck in the receive queue; the other process with SAP number 2592 seems to have cleared the messages from the receive queue.

Example 3-30 *MTS Message Stuck in Queue*

```
N7k-1# show system internal mts buffers summary
node    sapno   recv_q  pers_q  npers_q log_q
sup     2938    367     0       0       0
sup     2592    89      0       0       0
sup     284     0       10      0       0
N7k-1# show system internal mts buffers summary
node    sapno   recv_q  pers_q  npers_q log_q
sup     2938    367     0       0       0
sup     2592    27      0       0       0
sup     284     0       10      0       0
```

Table 3-5 gives the queue names and their functions.

Table 3-5 *MTS Queue Names and Functions*

Abbreviation	Queue Name	Function
recv_q	Receive Queue	
pers_q	Persistent Queue	Messages in this queue survive through the crash. MTS replays the message after the crash.
npers_q	Nonpersistent Queue	Messages do not survive the crash.
log_q	Log Queue	MTS logs the message when an application sends or receives the message. The application uses logging for transaction recovery in restart. The application retrieves logged messages explicitly after restart.

Messages stuck in the queue lead to various impacts on the device. For instance, if the device is running BGP, you might randomly see BGP flaps or BGP peering not even coming up, even though the BGP peers might have reachability and correct configuration. Alternatively, the user might not be able to perform a configuration change, such as adding a new neighbor configuration.

After determining that the messages are stuck in one of the queues, identify the process associated with the SAP number. The command **show system internal mts sup sap** *sapno* **description** obtains this information. The same information also can be viewed from the sysmgr output using the command **show system internal sysmgr service all**. For details about all the queued messages, use the command **show system internal mts buffers detail**. Example 3-31 displays the description of the SAP 2938, which shows the statsclient process. The statsclient process is used to collect statistics on supervisor or line card modules. The second section of the output displays all the messages present in the queue.

Example 3-31 *SAP Description and Queued MTS Messages*

```
N7k-1# show system internal mts sup sap 2938 description
Below shows sap on default-VDC, to show saps on non-default VDC, run
        show system internal mts node sup-<vnode-id> sap ...
statscl_lib4320
N7k-1# show system internal mts buffers detail
Node/Sap/queue   Age(ms)         SrcNode   SrcSAP   DstNode   OPC    MsgSize
sup/3570/nper    5               0x601     3570     0x601     7679   30205
sup/2938/recv    50917934468     0x802     980      0x601     26     840
sup/2938/recv    50899918777     0x802     980      0x601     26     840
sup/2938/recv    50880095050     0x902     980      0x601     26     840
sup/2938/recv    46604123941     0x802     980      0x601     26     840
sup/2938/recv    46586081502     0x902     980      0x601     26     840
sup/2938/recv    46569929011     0x802     980      0x601     26     840
! Output omitted for brevity
N7k-1# show system internal mts sup sap 980 description
Below shows sap on default-VDC, to show saps on non-default VDC, run
        show system internal mts node sup-<vnode-id> sap ...
statsclient
```

Note The SAP description information in Example 3-31 is taken from the default VDC. For the information on the nondefault DVC, use the command **show system internal mts node sup-[*vnode-id*] sap** *sapno* **description**.

The first and most important field to check in the previous output is the SAP number and its age. If the duration of the message stuck in the queue is fairly long, those messages need to be investigated; they might be causing services to misbehave on the Nexus platform. The other field to look at is OPC, which refers to the operational code. After the messages in the queue are verified from the buffers detail output, use the command **show system internal sup opcodes** to determine the operational code associated with the message, to understand the state of the process.

SAP statistics are also viewed to verify different queue limits of various SAPs and to check the maximum queue limit that a process has reached. This is done using the command **show system internal mts sup sap** *sapno* **stats** (see Example 3-32).

Example 3-32 *MTS SAP Statistics*

```
N7k-1# show system internal mts sup sap 980 stats
Below shows sap on default-VDC, to show saps on non-default VDC, run
        show system internal mts node sup-<vnode-id> sap ...
msg tx: 14
byte tx: 1286
```

```
msg    rx: 30
byte rx: 6883

opc sent to myself: 0
max_q_size q_len limit (soft q limit): 4096
max_q_size q_bytes limit (soft q limit): 15%
max_q_size ever reached: 3
max_fast_q_size (hard q limit): 4096
rebind count: 0
Waiting for response: none
buf in transit: 14
bytes in transit: 1286
```

Along with these verification checks, MTS error messages are seen in OBFL logs or syslogs. When the MTS queue is full, the error logs in Example 3-33 appear. Use the command **show logging onboard internal kernel** to ensure that no error logs are reported as a result of MTS.

Example 3-33 *MTS OBFL Logs*

```
2017 Apr 30 18:23:05.413 n7k 30 18:23:05 %KERN-2-SYSTEM_MSG: mts_is_q_space_
  available_old():1641: regular+fast mesg total = 48079,
 soft limit = 1024  - kernel
2017 Apr 30 18:23:05.415 n7k 30 18:23:05 %KERN-2-SYSTEM_MSG: mts_is_q_space_
  available_old(): NO SPACE - node=0, sap=27, uuid=26, pid=26549,
 sap_opt = 0x1, hdr_opt = 0x10, rq=48080(11530072), lq=0(0), pq=0(0), nq=0(0),
 sq=0(0), fast:rq=0, lq=0, pq=0, nq=0, sq=0 - kernel
```

The MTS errors are also reported in the MTS event history logs and can be viewed using the command **show system internal mts event-history errors.**

If the MTS queue is stuck or an MTS buffer leak is observed, performing a supervisor switchover clears the MTS queues and helps recover from service outages from an MTS queue stuck problem.

Note If SAP number 284 appears in the MTS buffer queue, ignore it: It belongs to the TCPUDP process client and is thus expected.

Netstack and Packet Manager

Netstack is the NX-OS implementation of the user-mode Transmission Control Protocol (TCP)/Internet Protocol (IP) stack, which runs only on the supervisor module. The Netstack components are implemented in user space processes. Each Netstack component runs as a separate process with multiple threads. In-band packets and features specific to NX-OS, such as vPC- and VDC-aware capabilities, must be processed in software. Netstack is the NX-OS component in charge of processing software-switched packets. As stated earlier, the Netstack process has three main roles:

- Pass in-band packets to the correct control plane process application
- Forward in-band punted packets through software in the desired manner
- Maintain in-band network stack configuration data

Netstack is made up of both Kernel Loadable Module (KLM) and user space components. The user space components are VDC local processes containing Packet Manager, which is the Layer 2 processing component; IP Input, the Layer 3 processing component; and TCP/UDP functions, which handle the Layer 4 packets. The Packet Manager (PktMgr) component is mostly isolated with IP input and TCP/UDP, even though they share the same process space. Figure 3-1 displays the Netstack architecture and the components part of KLM and user space.

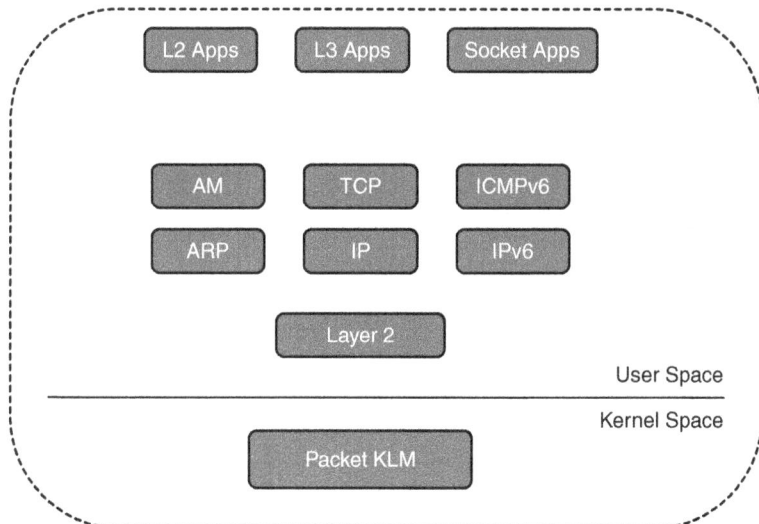

Figure 3-1 *Netstack Architecture*

Troubleshooting issues with Netstack is easiest by first understanding how Netstack forms the packet processing. The packets are hardware switched to the supervisor in-band interface. The packet KLM processes the frame. The packet KLM performs minimal processing of the data bus (DBUS) header and performs the source interface index lookup to identify which VDC the packet belongs to. The KLM performs minimal processing of the packet, so exposure is limited to crashes at the kernel level and no privilege escalation occurs. Most of the packet processing happens in the user space, allowing multiple instances of the Netstack process (one per each VDC) and restartability in case of a process crash.

Netstack uses multiple software queues to support prioritization of critical functions. In these queues, Bridge Protocol Data Units (BPDU) are treated under a dedicated queue, whereas all other inband traffic is separated into Hi or Low queues in the kernel driver. To view the KLM statistics and see how many packets have been processed by different queues, use the command **show system inband queuing statistics** (see Example 3-34). Notice that the KLM maps the Address Resolution Protocol (ARP) and BPDU packets separately. If any drops in the BPDU queue or any other queue take place, those drop counters are identified in the Inband Queues section of the output.

Example 3-34 *In-Band Netstack KLM Statistics*

```
N7k-1# show system inband queuing statistics
  Inband packets unmapped to a queue: 0
  Inband packets mapped to bpdu queue: 259025
  Inband packets mapped to q0: 448
  Inband packets mapped to q1: 0
  In KLM packets mapped to bpdu: 0
  In KLM packets mapped to arp : 0
  In KLM packets mapped to q0  : 0
  In KLM packets mapped to q1  : 0
  In KLM packets mapped to veobc : 0
  Inband Queues:
  bpdu: recv 259025, drop 0, congested 0 rcvbuf 33554432, sndbuf 33554432 no drop 1
  (q0): recv 448, drop 0, congested 0 rcvbuf 33554432, sndbuf 33554432 no drop 0
  (q1): recv 0, drop 0, congested 0 rcvbuf 2097152, sndbuf 4194304 no drop 0
```

The PktMgr is the lower-level component within the Netstack architecture that takes care of processing all in-band or management frames received from and sent to KLM. The PktMgr demultiplexes the packets based on Layer 2 (L2) packets and platform header information and passes them to the L2 clients. It also dequeues packets from L2 clients and sends the packets out the appropriate driver. All the L2 or non-IP protocols, such as Spanning Tree Protocol (STP), Cisco Discovery Protocol (CDP), Unidirectional Link Detection (UDLD), Cisco Fabric Services (CFS), Link Aggregation Control Protocol (LACP), and ARP, register directly with PktMgr. IP protocols register directly with the IP Input process.

The Netstack process runs on the supervisor, so the following packets are sent to the supervisor for processing:

- L2 clients – BPDU addresses: STP, CDP, and so on
- EIGRP, OSPF, ICMP, PIM, HSRP, and GLBP protocol packets
- Gateway MAC address

- Exception packets
  - Glean adjacency
  - Supervisor-terminated packets
  - IPv4/IPv6 packets with IP options
  - Same interface (IF) check
  - Reverse Path Forwarding (RPF) check failures
  - Time to live (TTL) expired packets

The Netstack process is stateful across restarts and switchovers. The Netstack process depends on Unicast Routing Information Base (URIB), IPv6 Unicast Routing Information Base (U6RIB), and the Adjacency Manager (ADJMGR) process for bootup. Netstack uses a CLI server process to restore the configuration and uses persistent storage services (PSS) to restore the state of processes that were restarted. It uses RIB shared memory for performing L3 lookup; it uses an AM shared database (SDB) to perform the L3-to-L2 lookup. For troubleshooting purpose, Netstack provides various internal **show** commands and debugs that can help determine problems with different processes bound with Netstack:

- Packet Manager
- IP/IPv6
- TCP/UDP
- ARP
- Adjacency Manager (AM)

To understand the workings of the Packet Manager component, consider an example with ICMPv6. ICMPv6 is a client of PktMgr. When the ICMPv6 process first initializes, it registers with PktMgr and is assigned a client ID and control (Ctrl) SAP ID and Data SAP ID. MTS handles communication between the PktMgr and ICMPv6. The Rx traffic from PktMgr toward ICMPv6 is handed off to MTS with the destination of the data SAP ID. The Tx traffic from ICMPv6 toward PktMgr is sent to the Ctrl SAP ID. PktMgr receives frame from ICMPv6, builds the correct header, and sends it to KLM to transport to the hardware.

To troubleshoot any of the PktMgr clients, figure out the processes that are clients of PktMgr component. This is done by issuing the command **show system internal pktmgr client**. This command returns the UUIDs and the Ctrl SAP ID for the PktMgr clients. The next step is to view the processes under the Service Manager, to get the information on the respective Universally Unique Identifier (UUID) and SAP ID. Example 3-35 illustrates these steps. When the correct process is identified, use the command **show system internal pktmgr client** *uuid* to verify the statistics for the PktMgr client, including drops.

Example 3-35 *In-Band Netstack KLM Statistics*

```
N7k-1# show system internal pktmgr client | in Client|SAP
Client uuid: 263, 2 filters, pid 4000
  Ctrl SAP: 246
 Total Data SAPs : 1 Data SAP 1: 247
Client uuid: 268, 4 filters, pid 3998
  Ctrl SAP: 278
 Total Data SAPs : 2 Data SAP 1: 2270    Data SAP 2: 2271
Client uuid: 270, 1 filters, pid 3999
  Ctrl SAP: 281
 Total Data SAPs : 1 Data SAP 1: 283
Client uuid: 545, 3 filters, pid 4054
  Ctrl SAP: 262
 Total Data SAPs : 1 Data SAP 1: 265
Client uuid: 303, 2 filters, pid 4186
  Ctrl SAP: 171
 Total Data SAPs : 1 Data SAP 1: 177
Client uuid: 572, 1 filters, pid 4098
  Ctrl SAP: 425
 Total Data SAPs : 1 Data SAP 1: 426
! Output omitted fore brevity
N7k-1# show system internal sysmgr service all | ex NA | in icmpv6|Name|--
Name          UUID        PID    SAP    state      Start count   Tag       Plugin ID
-------       ----------  -----  -----  ---------  -----------   ------    ----------
icmpv6        0x0000010E  3999   281    s0009      1             N/A       0
! Using the UUID value of 0x10E from above output
N7k-1# show system internal pktmgr client 0x10E
Client uuid: 270, 1 filters, pid 3999
   Filter 1: EthType 0x86dd, DstIf 0x150b0000, Excl. Any
   Rx: 0, Drop: 0
   Options: TO 0, Flags 0x18040, AppId 0, Epid 0
   Ctrl SAP: 281
   Total Data SAPs : 1 Data SAP 1: 283
   Total Rx: 0, Drop: 0, Tx: 0, Drop: 0
   Recirc Rx: 0, Drop: 0
   Input Rx: 0, Drop: 0
   Rx pps Inst/Max: 0/0
   Tx pps Inst/Max: 0/0
   COS=0 Rx: 0, Tx: 0     COS=1 Rx: 0, Tx: 0
   COS=2 Rx: 0, Tx: 0     COS=3 Rx: 0, Tx: 0
   COS=4 Rx: 0, Tx: 0     COS=5 Rx: 0, Tx: 0
   COS=6 Rx: 0, Tx: 0     COS=7 Rx: 0, Tx: 0
```

If the packets being sent to the supervisor are from a particular interface, verify the PktMgr statistics for the interface using the command **show system internal pktmgr interface** *interface-id* (see Example 3-36). This example explicitly shows how many unicast, multicast, and broadcast packets were sent and received.

Example 3-36 *Interface PktMgr Statistics*

```
N7k-1# show system internal pktmgr interface ethernet 1/1
Ethernet1/1, ordinal: 10  Hash_type: 0
  SUP-traffic statistics: (sent/received)
    Packets: 355174 / 331146
    Bytes: 32179675 / 27355507
    Instant packet rate: 0 pps / 0 pps
    Packet rate limiter (Out/In): 0 pps / 0 pps
    Average packet rates(1min/5min/15min/EWMA):
    Packet statistics:
      Tx: Unicast 322117, Multicast 33054
          Broadcast 3
      Rx: Unicast 318902, Multicast 12240
          Broadcast 4
```

PktMgr accounting (statistics) is useful in determining whether any low-level drops are occurring because of bad encapsulation or other kernel interaction issues. This is verified using the command **show system internal pktmgr stats [brief]** (see Example 3-37). This command shows the PktMgr driver interface to the KLM. The omitted part of the output also shows details about other errors and the management driver.

Example 3-37 *PktMgr Accounting*

```
N7k-1# show system internal pktmgr stats
Route Processor Layer-2 frame statistics

  Inband driver: valid 1, state 0, rd-thr 1, wr-thr 0, Q-count 0
  Inband sent: 1454421, copy_drop: 0, ioctl_drop: 0, unavailable_buffer_hdr_drop: 0
  Inband standby_sent: 0
  Inband encap_drop: 0, linecard_down_drop: 0
  Inband sent by priority [0=1041723,6=412698]
  Inband max output queue depth 0
  Inband recv: 345442, copy_drop: 0, ioctl_drop: 0, unavailable_buffer_hdr_drop: 0
  Inband decap_drop: 0, crc_drop: 0, recv by priority: [0=345442]
  Inband bad_si 0, bad_if 0, if_down 0
  Inband last_bad_si 0, last_bad_if 0, bad_di 0
  Inband kernel recv 85821, drop 0, rcvbuf 33554432, sndbuf 33554432


-------------------------------------------
  Driver:
-------------------------------------------
    State:               Up
    Filter:              0x0


! Output omitted for brevity
```

For IP processing, Netstack queries the URIB—that is, the routing table and all other necessary components, such as the Route Policy Manager (RPM)—to make a forwarding decision for the packet. Netstack performs all the accounting in the **show ip traffic** command output. The IP traffic statistics are used to track fragmentation, Internet Control Message Protocol (ICMP), TTL, and other exception packets. This command also displays the RFC 4293 traffic statistics. An easy way to figure out whether the IP packets are hitting the NX-OS Netstack component is to observe the statistics for exception punted traffic, such as fragmentation. Example 3-38 illustrates the different sections of the **show ip traffic** command output.

Example 3-38 *PktMgr Accounting*

```
N7k-1# show ip traffic


IP Software Processed Traffic Statistics
-----------------------------------------
Transmission and reception:
  Packets received: 0, sent: 0, consumed: 0,
  Forwarded, unicast: 0, multicast: 0, Label: 0
  Ingress mcec forward: 0
Opts:
  end: 0, nop: 0, basic security: 0, loose source route: 0
  timestamp: 0, record route: 0
  strict source route: 0, alert: 0,
  other: 0
Errors:
  Bad checksum: 0, packet too small: 0, bad version: 0,
  Bad header length: 0, bad packet length: 0, bad destination: 0,
  Bad ttl: 0, could not forward: 0, no buffer dropped: 0,
  Bad encapsulation: 0, no route: 0, non-existent protocol: 0
  Bad options: 0
  Vinci Migration Packets : 0
   Total packet snooped : 0
   Total packet on down svi : 0
    Stateful Restart Recovery: 0,  MBUF pull up fail: 0
  Bad context id: 0, rpf drops: 0 Bad GW MAC 0
  Ingress option processing failed: 0
  NAT inside drop: 0, NAT outside drop: 0
  Ingress option processing failed: 0  Ingress mforward failed: 0
  Ingress lisp drop: 0
  Ingress lisp decap drop: 0
  Ingress lisp encap drop: 0
  Ingress lisp encap: 0
```

```
    Ingress Mfwd copy drop: 0
    Ingress RA/Reass drop: 0
    Ingress ICMP Redirect processing drop: 0
    Ingress Drop (ifmgr init): 0,
    Ingress Drop (invalid filter): 0
    Ingress Drop (Invalid L2 msg): 0
    ACL Filter Drops :
        Ingress - 0
        Egree -   0
        Directed Broadcast - 0
Fragmentation/reassembly:
    Fragments received: 0, fragments sent: 0, fragments created: 0,
    Fragments dropped: 0, packets with DF: 0, packets reassembled: 0,
    Fragments timed out: 0
Fragments created per protocol

ICMP Software Processed Traffic Statistics
------------------------------------------
Transmission:
    Redirect: 0, unreachable: 0, echo request: 0, echo reply: 0,
    Mask request: 0, mask reply: 0, info request: 0, info reply: 0,
    Parameter problem: 0, source quench: 0, timestamp: 0,
    Timestamp response: 0, time exceeded: 0,
    Irdp solicitation: 0, irdp advertisement: 0
    Output Drops - badlen: 0, encap fail: 0, xmit fail: 0
    ICMP originate Req: 0, Redirects Originate Req: 0
    Originate deny - Resource fail: 0, short ip: 0, icmp: 0, others: 0
Reception:
    Redirect: 0, unreachable: 0, echo request: 0, echo reply: 0,
    Mask request: 0, mask reply: 0, info request: 0, info reply: 0,
    Parameter problem: 0, source quench: 0, timestamp: 0,
    Timestamp response: 0, time exceeded: 0,
    Irdp solicitation: 0, irdp advertisement: 0,
    Format error: 0, checksum error: 0
    Lisp processed: 0, No clients: 0: Consumed: 0
    Replies: 0, Reply drops - bad addr: 0, inactive addr: 0


Statistics last reset: never

RFC 4293: IP Software Processed Traffic Statistics
--------------------------------------------------
Reception
    Pkts recv: 0, Bytes recv: 0,
```

```
        inhdrerrors: 0, innoroutes: 0, inaddrerrors: 0,
        inunknownprotos: 0, intruncatedpkts: 0, inforwdgrams: 0,
        reasmreqds: 0, reasmoks: 0, reasmfails: 0,
        indiscards: 0, indelivers: 0,
        inmcastpkts: 0, inmcastbytes: 0,
        inbcastpkts: 0,
Transmission
      outrequests: 0, outnoroutes: 0, outforwdgrams: 0,
      outdiscards: 0, outfragreqds: 0, outfragoks: 0,
      outfragfails: 0, outfragcreates: 0, outtransmits: 0,
      bytes sent: 0, outmcastpkts: 0, outmcastbytes: 0,
      outbcastpkts: 0, outbcastbytes: 0
```

Netstack TCPUDP Component

The TCPUDP process has the following functionalities:

- TCP
- UDP
- Raw packet handling
- Socket layer and socket library

The TCP/UDP stack is based on BSD and supports a standards-compliant implementation of TCP and UDP. It supports features such as window scaling, slow start, and delayed acknowledgment. It does not support TCP selective ACK and header compression. The socket library is Portable Operating System Interface (POSIX) compliant and supports all standard socket system calls, as well as the file system-based system calls. The Internet Protocol control block (INPCB) hash table stores the socket connection data. The sockets are preserved upon Netstack restart but not upon supervisor switchover. The process has 16 TCP/UDP worker threads to provide all the functionality.

Consider now how TCP socket creation happens on NX-OS. When it receives the TCP SYN packet, Netstack builds a stub INPCB entry into the hash table. The partial information is then populated into the protocol control block (PCB). When the TCP three-way handshake is completed, all TCP socket information is populated to create a full socket. This process is verified by viewing the output of the debug command **debug sockets tcp pcb**. Example 3-39 illustrates the socket creation and Netstack interaction with the help of the debug command. From the debug output, notice that when the SYN packet is received, it gets added into the cache; when the three-way handshake completes, a full-blown socket is created.

Example 3-39 *TCP Socket Creation and Netstack*

```
N7k-1# debug sockets tcp pcb
2017 May  4 00:52:03.432086 netstack: syncache_insert: SYN added for
   L:10.162.223.34.20608 F:10.162.223.33.179, tp:0x701ff01c inp:0x701fef54
2017 May  4 00:52:03.434633 netstack: in_pcballoc: PCB: Allocated pcb, ipi_count:6
2017 May  4 00:52:03.434704 netstack: syncache_socket: Created full blown socket
   with F:10.162.223.34.20608 L:10.162.223.33.179 peer_mss 1460
2017 May  4 00:52:03.434930 netstack: in_setpeeraddr: PCB: in_setpeeraddr
   L 10.162.223.33.179 F 10.162.223.34.20608 C: 3
2017 May  4 00:52:03.435200 netstack: in_setsockaddr: PCB: in_setsockaddr
   L 10.162.223.33.179 F 10.162.223.34.20608 C: 3
```

Necessary details of the TCP socket connection are verified using the command **show sockets connection tcp [detail]**. The output with the **detail** option provides information such as TCP windowing information, the MSS value for the session, and the socket state. The output also provides the MTS SAP ID. If the TCP socket is having a problem, look up the MTS SAP ID in the buffer to see whether it is stuck in a queue. Example 3-40 displays the socket connection details for BGP peering between two routers.

Example 3-40 *TCP Socket Creation and Netstack*

```
N7k-1# show sockets connection tcp detail
Total number of tcp sockets: 6
Local host: 10.162.223.33 (179), Foreign host: 10.162.223.34 (20608)
  Protocol: tcp, type: stream, ttl: 1, tos: 0xc0, Id: 15
  Options:  REUSEADR, pcb flags none, state:  | NBIO
  MTS: sap 14545
  Receive buffer:
    cc: 0, hiwat: 17520, lowat: 1, flags: none
  Send buffer:
    cc: 19, hiwat: 17520, lowat: 2048, flags: none
  Sequence number state:
    iss: 1129891008, snduna: 1129891468, sndnxt: 1129891487, sndwnd: 15925
    irs: 3132858499, rcvnxt: 3132858925, rcvwnd: 17520, sndcwnd: 65535
  Timing parameters:
    srtt: 3500 ms, rtt: 0 ms, rttv: 1000 ms, krtt: 1000 ms
    rttmin: 1000 ms, mss: 1460, duration: 49500 ms
  State: ESTABLISHED
  Flags:  NODELAY
No MD5 peers   Context: devl-user-1
! Output omitted for brevity
```

Netstack socket clients are monitored with the command **show sockets client detail**. This command explains the socket client behavior and shows how many socket library calls the client has made. This command is useful in identifying issues a particular socket client is facing because it also displays the Errors section, where errors are reported for a problematic client. As Example 3-41 illustrates, the output displays two clients, syslogd and bgp. The output shows the associated SAP ID with the client and statistics on how many socket calls the process has made. The Errors section is empty because no errors are seen for the displayed sockets.

Example 3-41 *Netstack Socket Client Details*

```
N7k-1# show sockets client detail
Total number of clients: 7
client: syslogd, pid: 3765, sockets: 2
  cancel requests:      0
  cancel unblocks:      0
  cancel misses:        0
  select drops:         0
  select wakes:         0
  sockets: 27:1(mts sap: 2336), 28:2(mts sap: 2339)
  Statistics:
    socket calls: 2    fcntl calls: 6    setsockopt calls: 6
    socket_ha_update calls: 6
  Errors:

! Output omitted for brevity

client: bgp, pid: 4639, sockets: 3
  fast_tcp_mts_ctrl_q: sap 2734
  cancel requests:      0
  cancel unblocks:      0
  cancel misses:        0
  select drops:         0
  select wakes:         0
  sockets: 49:13(mts sap: 2894), 51:14(mts sap: 2896), 54:15(mts sap: 14545)
  Statistics:
    socket calls: 5    bind calls: 5    listen calls: 2
    accept calls: 14    accept_dispatch errors: 14    connect_dispatch: 3
    close calls: 16    fcntl calls: 9    setsockopt calls: 31
    getsockname calls: 11    socket_ha_update calls: 38    Fast tcp send requests: 207802
    Fast tcp send success: 207802    Fast tcp ACK rcvd: 203546
  Errors:
    connect errors: 3
    pconnect_einprogress errors: 3    pclose_sock_null errors: 14

Statistics: Cancels 100811, Cancel-unblocks 100808, Cancel-misses 1
           Select-drops 2, Select-wakes 100808.
```

Netstack also has an accounting capability that gives statistics on UDP, TCP, raw sockets, and internal tables. The Netstack socket statistics are viewed using the command **show sockets statistics all**. This command helps view TCP drops, out-of-order packets, or duplicate packets; the statistics are maintained on a per-Netstack instance basis. At the end of the output, statistics and error counters are also viewed for INPCB and IN6PCB tables. The table statistics provides insight into how many socket connections are being created and deleted in Netstack. The Errors part of the INPCB or IN6PCB table indicates a problem while allocating socket information. Example 3-42 displays the Netstack socket accounting statistics.

Example 3-42 *Netstack Socket Accounting*

```
N7k-1# show sockets statistics all

TCP v4 Received:
     402528 total packets received,     203911 packets received in sequence,
     3875047 bytes received in sequence,     8 out-of-order packets received,
     10 rcvd duplicate acks,     208189 rcvd ack packets,
     3957631 bytes acked by rcvd acks,     287 Dropped no inpcb,
     203911 Fast recv packets enqueued,     16 Fast TCP can not recv more,
     208156 Fast TCP data ACK to app,
TCP v4 Sent:
     406332 total packets sent,     20 control (SYN|FIN|RST) packets sent,
     208162 data packets sent,     3957601 data bytes sent,
     198150 ack-only packets sent,

! Output omitted for brevity

INPCB Statistics:
in_pcballoc: 38 in_pcbbind: 9
in_pcbladdr: 18 in_pcbconnect: 14
in_pcbdetach: 19          in_pcbdetach_no_rt: 19
in_setsockaddr: 13        in_setpeeraddr: 14
in_pcbnotify: 1 in_pcbinshash_ipv4: 23
in_pcbinshash_ipv6: 5    in_pcbrehash_ipv4: 18
in_pcbremhash: 23
INPCB Errors:

IN6PCB Statistics:
in6_pcbbind: 5
in6_pcbdetach: 4          in6_setsockaddr: 1
in6_pcblookup_local: 2
IN6PCB Errors:
```

Multiple clients (ARP, STP, BGP, EIGRP, OSPF, and so on) interact with the Netstack component. Thus, while troubleshooting control plane issues, if you are able to see the packet in Ethanalyzer but the packet is not received by the client component itself, the issue might be related to the Netstack or the Packet Manager (Pktmgr). Figure 3-2 illustrates the control plane packet flow and placement of the Netstack and Pktmgr components in the system.

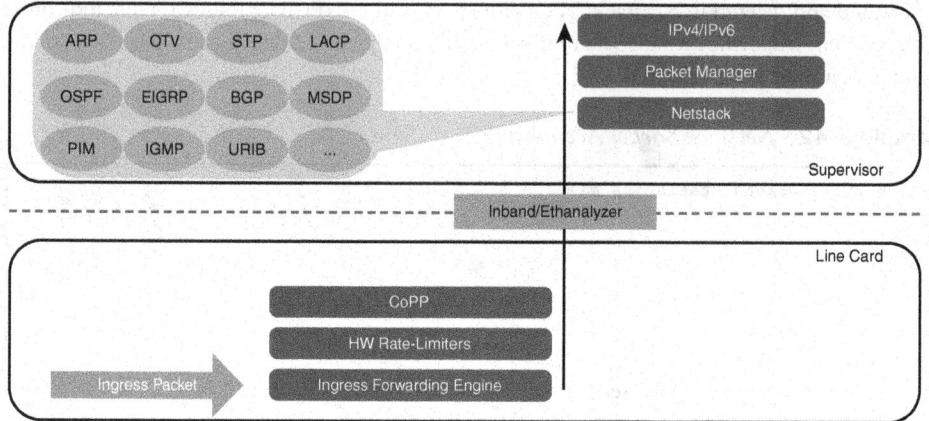

Figure 3-2 *Control Plane Troubleshooting—Traffic Path*

Note If an issue arises with any Netstack component or Netstack component clients, such as OSPF or TCP failure, collect output from the commands **show tech-support netstack** and **show tech-support pktmgr**, along with the relevant client **show tech-support** outputs, to aid in further investigation by the Cisco TAC.

ARP and Adjacency Manager

The ARP component handles ARP functionality for the Nexus switch interfaces. The ARP component registers with PktMgr as a Layer 2 component and provides a few other functionalities:

- Manages Layer 3–to–Layer 2 adjacency learning and timers
- Manages static ARP entries
- Punts the glean adjacency packets to the CPU, which then triggers ARP resolution
- Adds ARP entries into the Adjacency Manager (AM) database
- Manages virtual addresses registered by first-hop redundancy protocols (FHRP), such as Virtual Router Redundancy Protocol (VRRP), Hot Standby Router Protocol (HSRP), and Gateway Load-Balancing Protocol (GLBP)
- Has clients listening for ARP packets such as ARP snooping, HSRP, VRRP, and GLBP

All the messaging and communication with the ARP component happens with the help of MTS. ARP packets are sent to PktMgr via MTS. The ARP component does not support the Reverse ARP (RARP) feature, but it does support features such as proxy ARP, local proxy ARP, and sticky ARP.

> **Note** If the router receives packets destined to another host in the same subnet and local proxy ARP is enabled on the interface, the router does not send the ICMP redirect messages. Local proxy ARP is disabled by default.
>
> If the Sticky ARP option is set on an interface, any new ARP entries that are learned are marked so that they are not overwritten by a new adjacency (for example, gratuitous ARP). These entries also do not get aged out. This feature helps prevent a malicious user from spoofing an ARP entry.

Glean adjacencies can cause packet loss and also cause excessive packets to get punted to CPU. Understanding the treatment of packets when a glean adjacency is seen is vital. Let's assume that a switch receives IP packets where the next hop is a connected network. If an ARP entry exists but no host route (/32 route) is installed in the FIB or in the AM shared database, the FIB lookup points to glean adjacency. The glean adjacency packets are rate-limited. If no network match is found in FIB, packets are silently dropped in hardware (known as a FIB miss).

To protect the CPU from high bandwidth flows with no ARP entries or adjacencies programmed in hardware, NX-OS provides rate-limiters for glean adjacency traffic on Nexus 7000 and 9000 platforms. The configuration for the preset hardware rate-limiters for glean adjacency traffic is viewed using the command **show run all | include glean**. Example 3-43 displays the hardware rate-limiters for glean traffic.

Example 3-43 *Hardware Rate-Limiters for Glean Traffic*

```
N7k-1# show run all | in glean
hardware rate-limiter layer-3 glean 100
hardware rate-limiter layer-3 glean-fast 100
hardware rate-limiter layer-3 glean 100 module 3
hardware rate-limiter layer-3 glean-fast 100 module 3
hardware rate-limiter layer-3 glean 100 module 4
hardware rate-limiter layer-3 glean-fast 100 module 4
```

The control plane installs a temporary adjacency drop entry in hardware while ARP is being resolved. All subsequent packets are dropped in hardware until ARP is resolved. The temporary adjacency remains until the glean timer expires. When the timer expires, the normal process of punt/drop starts again.

The ARP entries on the NX-OS are viewed using the command **show ip arp** [*interface-type interface-num*]. The command output shows not only the learned ARP entries but also the glean entries, which are marked as incomplete. Example 3-44 displays the ARP table for VLAN 10 SVI interface with both learned ARP entry and INCOMPLETE entry.

Example 3-44 *ARP Table*

```
N7k-1# show ip arp vlan 10
Flags: * - Adjacencies learnt on non-active FHRP router
       + - Adjacencies synced via CFSoE
       # - Adjacencies Throttled for Glean
       D - Static Adjacencies attached to down interface

IP ARP Table
Total number of entries: 2
Address          Age         MAC Address       Interface
10.1.12.10       00:10:20    5087.894b.bb41    Vlan10
10.1.12.2        00:00:09    INCOMPLETE        Vlan10
```

When an incomplete ARP is seen, the internal trace history is used to determine whether the problem is with the ARP component or something else. When an ARP entry is populated, two operations (Create and Update) occur to populate the information in the FIB. If a problem arises with the ARP component, you might only see the Create operation, not the Update operation. To view the sequence of operations, use the command **show forwarding internal trace v4-adj-history [module** *slot*] (see Example 3-45). This example shows that for the next hop of 10.1.12.2, only a Create operation is happening after the Destroy operation (drop adjacency); no Update operation occurs after that, causing the ARP entry to be marked as glean.

Example 3-45 *Adjacency Internal Forwarding Trace*

```
N7k-1# show forwarding internal trace v4-adj-history module 4
HH 0x80000018
       Time                   if           NH              operation
    Sun May  7 06:43:10 2017   Vlan10       10.1.12.10      Create
    Sun May  7 06:43:10 2017   Vlan10       10.1.12.10      Update
! History for Non-Working host i.e. 10.1.12.2
    Sun May  7 06:43:10 2017   Vlan10       10.1.12.2       Create
    Sun May  7 06:43:10 2017   Vlan10       10.1.12.2       Update
    Sun May  7 06:53:54 2017   Vlan10       10.1.12.2       Destroy
    Sun May  7 06:56:03 2017   Vlan10       10.1.12.2       Create
```

To view the forwarding adjacency, use the command **show forwarding ipv4 adjacency** *interface-type interface-num* **[module** *slot*]. If the adjacency for a particular next hop appears as unresolved, there is no adjacency; FIB then matches the network glean adjacency and performs a punt operation. Example 3-46 illustrates the output of the **show forwarding ipv4 adjacency** command with an unresolved adjacency entry.

Example 3-46 *Verifying Forwarding Adjacency*

```
N7k-1# show forwarding ipv4 adjacency vlan 10 module 4
IPv4 adjacency information

next-hop          rewrite info      interface
--------------    --------------    ------------
10.1.12.10        5087.894b.bb41    Vlan10
10.1.12.2         unresolved        Vlan10
```

The ARP component also provides an event history to be used to further understand whether any errors could lead to problems with ARP and adjacency. To view the ARP event history, use the command **show ip arp internal event-history [events | errors]**. Example 3-47 displays the output of the command **show ip arp internal event-history events**, displaying the ARP resolution for the host 10.1.12.2/24. In the event history, notice that the switch sends out an ARP request; based on the reply, the adjacency is built and further updated into the AM database.

Example 3-47 *ARP Event History*

```
N7k-1# show ip arp internal event-history event
1) Event:E_DEBUG, length:144, at 720940 usecs after Sun May  7 17:31:30 2017
    [116] [4196]: Adj info: iod: 181, phy-iod: 36, ip: 10.1.12.2, mac: fa16.3e29
.5f82, type: 0, sync: FALSE, suppress-mode: ARP Suppression Disabled

2) Event:E_DEBUG, length:198, at 720916 usecs after Sun May  7 17:31:30 2017
    [116] [4196]: Entry added to ARP pt, added to AM for 10.1.12.2, fa16.3e29.5f
82, state 2 on interface Vlan10, physical interface Ethernet2/1, ismct 0. Rearp
(interval: 0, count: 0), TTL: 1500 seconds

3) Event:E_DEBUG, length:86, at 718187 usecs after Sun May  7 17:31:30 2017
    [116] [4196]: arp_add_adj: Updating MAC on interface Vlan10, phy-interface
Ethernet2/1

4) Event:E_DEBUG, length:145, at 713312 usecs after Sun May  7 17:31:30 2017
    [116] [4200]: Adj info: iod: 181, phy-iod: 181, ip: 10.1.12.2, mac: 0000.000
0.0000, type: 0, sync: FALSE, suppress-mode: ARP Suppression Disabled

5) Event:E_DEBUG, length:181, at 713280 usecs after Sun May  7 17:31:30 2017
    [116] [4200]: Entry added to ARP pt, added to AM for 10.1.12.2, NULL, state
1 on interface Vlan10, physical interface Vlan10, ismct 0. Rearp (interval: 2,
count: 4), TTL: 30 seconds
```

```
 6) Event:E_DEBUG, length:40, at 713195 usecs after Sun May  7 17:31:30 2017
    [116] [4200]: Parameters l2_addr is null

 7) Event:E_DEBUG, length:40, at 713154 usecs after Sun May  7 17:31:30 2017
    [116] [4200]: Parameters l2_addr is null

 8) Event:E_DEBUG, length:59, at 713141 usecs after Sun May  7 17:31:30 2017
    [116] [4200]: Create adjacency, interface Vlan10, 10.1.12.2

 9) Event:E_DEBUG, length:81, at 713074 usecs after Sun May  7 17:31:30 2017
    [116] [4200]: arp_add_adj: Updating MAC on interface Vlan10, phy-interface Vlan10

10) Event:E_DEBUG, length:49, at 713054 usecs after Sun May  7 17:31:30 2017
    [116] [4200]: ARP request for 10.1.12.2 on Vlan10
```

Note The ARP packets are also captured using Ethanalyzer in both ingress and egress directions.

The ARP component is closely coupled with the Adjacency Manager (AM) component. The AM takes care of programming the /32 host routes in the hardware. AM provides the following functionalities:

- Exports Layer 3 to Layer 2 adjacencies through shared memory

- Generates adjacency change notification, including interface deletion notification, and sends updates via MTS

- Adds host routes (/32 routes) into URIB/U6RIB for learned adjacencies

- Performs IP/IPv6 lookup AM database while forwarding packets out of the interface

- Handles adjacencies restart by maintaining the adjacency SDB for restoration of the AM state

- Provides a single interface for URIB/UFDM to learn routes from multiple sources

When an ARP is learned, the ARP entry is added to the AM SDB. AM then communicates directly with URIB and UFDM to install a /32 adjacency in hardware. The AM database queries the state of active ARP entries. The ARP table is not persistent upon process restart and thus must requery the AM SDB. AM registers various clients that can install adjacencies. To view the registered clients, use the command **show system internal adjmgr client** (see Example 3-48). One of the most common clients of AM is ARP.

Example 3-48 *Adjacency Manager Clients*

```
N7k-1# show system internal adjmgr client
Protocol Name    Alias    UUID
netstack         Static   545
rpm              rpm      305
IPv4             Static   268
arp              arp      268
IP               IP       545
icmpv6           icmpv6   270
```

Any unresolved adjacency is verified using the command **show ip adjacency** *ip-address* **detail**. If the adjacency is resolved, the output populates the correct MAC address for the specified IP; otherwise, it has 0000.0000.0000 in the MAC address field. Example 3-49 displays the difference between the resolved and unresolved adjacencies.

Example 3-49 *Resolved and Unresolved Adjacencies*

```
! Resolved Adjacency
N7k-1# show ip adjacency 10.1.12.10 detail
No. of Adjacency hit with type INVALID: Packet count 0, Byte count 0
No. of Adjacency hit with type GLOBAL DROP: Packet count 0, Byte count 0
No. of Adjacency hit with type GLOBAL PUNT: Packet count 0, Byte count 0
No. of Adjacency hit with type GLOBAL GLEAN: Packet count 0, Byte count 0
No. of Adjacency hit with type GLEAN: Packet count 0, Byte count 0
No. of Adjacency hit with type NORMAL: Packet count 0, Byte count 0

Adjacency statistics last updated before: never

IP Adjacency Table for VRF default
Total number of entries: 1

Address :            10.1.12.10
MacAddr :            5087.894b.bb41
Preference :         50
Source :             arp
Interface :          Vlan10
Physical Interface : Ethernet2/1
Packet Count :       0
Byte Count :         0
Best :               Yes
Throttled :          No
! Unresolved Adjacency
N7k-1# show ip adjacency 10.1.12.2 detail
! Output omitted for brevity
```

```
Adjacency statistics last updated before: never

IP Adjacency Table for VRF default
Total number of entries: 1

Address            : 10.1.12.10
MacAddr            : 5087.894b.bb41
Preference         : 50
Source             : arp
Interface          : Vlan10
Physical Interface : Ethernet2/1
Packet Count       : 0
Byte Count         : 0
Best               : Yes
Throttled          : No
! Unresolved Adjacency
N7k-1# show ip adjacency 10.1.12.2 detail
! Output omitted for brevity

Adjacency statistics last updated before: never

IP Adjacency Table for VRF default
Total number of entries: 1

Address            : 10.1.12.2
MacAddr            : 0000.0000.0000
Preference         : 255
Source             : arp
Interface          : Vlan10
Physical Interface : Vlan10
Packet Count       : 0
Byte Count         : 0
Best               : Yes
Throttled          : No
```

The AM adjacency installation into URIB follows these steps:

Step 1. The AM queues an Add adjacency request.

Step 2. The AM calls URIB to install the route.

Step 3. The AM appends new adjacency to the Add list.

Step 4. URIB adds the route.

Step 5. The AM independently calls the UFDM API to install the adjacency in the hardware.

The series of events within the AM component is viewed using the command **show system internal adjmgr internal event-history events**. Example 3-50 displays the output of this command, to illustrate the series of events that occur during installation of the adjacency for host 10.1.12.2. Notice that the prefix 10.1.12.2 is being added to the RIB buffer for the IPv4 address family.

Example 3-50 *Hardware Rate-Limiters for Glean Traffic*

```
N7k-1# show system internal adjmgr internal event-history events
1) Event:E_DEBUG, length:101, at 865034 usecs after Tue May  9 05:21:19 2017
    [117] [4017]: Appending ADD 10.1.12.2 on Vlan10 (TBL:1) AD 250 to rib buffer
 for Address Family :IPv4

2) Event:E_DEBUG, length:84, at 845226 usecs after Tue May  9 05:21:19 2017
    [117] [4043]: Add 10.1.12.2 on Vlan10 to rib work queue for afi: IPv4with wo
rk bit: 1
3) Event:E_DEBUG, length:61, at 845128 usecs after Tue May  9 05:21:19 2017
    [117] [4043]: is_mct 0, entry_exists 1, iod 0x85 phy_iod 0x85

4) Event:E_DEBUG, length:61, at 840347 usecs after Tue May  9 05:21:19 2017
    [117] [4043]: is_mct 0, entry_exists 0, iod 0x85 phy_iod 0x85
Adjacency related errors could be verified using the event-history logs as well by
using the command show system internal adjmgr internal event-history errors.
```

Note If an issue arises with any ARP or AM component, capture the **show tech arp** and **show tech adjmgr** outputs during problematic state.

Unicast Forwarding Components

The IP/IPv6 packet-forwarding decisions on a device are made by the Routing Information Base (RIB) and the Forwarding Information Base (FIB). In NX-OS, the RIB is managed by the Unicast Routing Information Base (URIB), and the FIB is managed by the IP Forwarding Information Base (IPFIB) component. URIB is the software perspective of the routing information on the supervisor, whereas the IPFIB is the software perspective of the routing information on the line card. This section discusses these components that manage the forwarding on NX-OS platforms.

Unicast Routing Information Base

The URIB component in NX-OS is responsible for maintaining SDB for all Layer 3 unicast routes installed by all the routing protocols. The URIB is a VDC local process—that is, routes cannot be shared across multiple VDCs unless a routing adjacency exists between them. The URIB process uses several clients, which are also viewed using the command **show routing clients** (see Example 3-51):

- Routing protocols—Enhanced Interior Gateway Routing Protocol (EIGRP), Open Shortest Path First (OSPF), Border Gateway Protocol (BGP), and so on
- Netstack (updates URIB for static routes)
- AM
- RPM

Example 3-51 *URIB Clients*

```
N7k-1# show routing clients
CLIENT: static
 index mask: 0x0000000000000080
 epid: 4059     MTS SAP: 266     MRU cache hits/misses:      1/1
 Stale Time: 30
 Routing Instances:
  VRF: "default"  routes: 0, rnhs: 0, labels: 0
 Messages received:
  Register       : 1     Convergence-all-nfy: 1
 Messages sent:

CLIENT: ospf-100
 index mask: 0x0000000000008000
 epid: 23091    MTS SAP: 320     MRU cache hits/misses:      2/1
 Stale Time: 2100
 Routing Instances:
  VRF: "default"  routes: 1, rnhs: 0, labels: 0
 Messages received:
  Register       : 1     Convergence-notify: 1     Modify-route      : 1

 Messages sent:
  Modify-route-ack : 1

! Output omitted for brevity
```

Each routing protocol has its own region of shared URIB memory space. When a routing protocol learns routes from its neighbor, it installs those learned routes in its own region of shared URIB memory space. URIB then copies updated routes to its own protected region of shared memory, which is read-only memory and is readable only to Netstack and other components. The routing decisions are made from the entry present in URIB shared memory. It is vital to note that URIB itself does not perform any of the add, modify, or delete operations in the routing table. URIB clients (the routing protocols and Netstack) handle all updates, except when the URIB client process crashes. In such a case, URIB might then delete abandoned routes.

OSPF CLI provides users with the command **show ip ospf internal txlist urib** to view the OSPF routes sent to URIB. For all other routing protocols, the information is viewed using event history commands. Example 3-52 displays the output, showing the source SAP ID of OSPF process and the destination SAP ID for MTS messages.

Example 3-52 *OSPF Route Distribution to URIB*

```
N7k-1# show ip ospf internal txlist urib


ospf 100 VRF default
ospf process tag 100
ospf process instance number 1
ospf process uuid 1090519321
ospf process linux pid 23091
ospf process state running
System uptime 4d04h
SUP uptime 2 4d04h


Server up        : L3VM|IFMGR|RPM|AM|CLIS|URIB|U6RIB|IP|IPv6|SNMP
Server required  : L3VM|IFMGR|RPM|AM|CLIS|URIB|IP|SNMP
Server registered: L3VM|IFMGR|RPM|AM|CLIS|URIB|IP|SNMP
Server optional  : none
Early hello : OFF
Force write PSS: FALSE
OSPF mts pkt sap 324
OSPF mts base sap 320

 OSPFv2->URIB transmit list: version 0xb

        9: 10.1.12.0/24
       10: 1.1.1.1/32
       11: 2.2.2.2/32
       11: RIB marker
N7k-1# show system internal mts sup sap 320 description
ospf-100
N7k-1# show system internal mts sup sap 324 description
OSPF pkt MTS queue
```

The routes being updated from an OSPF process or any other routing process to URIB are recorded in the event history logs. To view the updates copied by OSPF from OSPF process memory to URIB shared memory, use the command **show ip ospf internal event-history rib**. Use the command **show routing internal event-history msgs** to examine URIB updating the globally readable shared memory. Example 3-53 shows the learned OSPF routes being processed and updated to URIB and also the routing event history showing the routes being updated to shared memory.

Example 3-53 *Routing Protocol and URIB Updates*

```
N7k-1# show ip ospf internal event-history rib
OSPF RIB events for Process "ospf-100"
2017 May 14 03:12:14.711449 ospf 100 [23091]: : Done sending routes to URIB
2017 May 14 03:12:14.711447 ospf 100 [23091]: : Examined 3 OSPF routes
2017 May 14 03:12:14.710532 ospf 100 [23091]: : Route (mbest) does not have any
   next-hop
2017 May 14 03:12:14.710531 ospf 100 [23091]: : Path type changed from nopath to
   intra
2017 May 14 03:12:14.710530 ospf 100 [23091]: : Admin distance changed from 255
   to 110
2017 May 14 03:12:14.710529 ospf 100 [23091]: : Mbest metric changed from 429496
   7295 to 41
2017 May 14 03:12:14.710527 ospf 100 [23091]: : Processing route 2.2.2.2/32
   (mbest)
2017 May 14 03:12:14.710525 ospf 100 [23091]: : Done processing next-hops for
   2.2.2.2/32
2017 May 14 03:12:14.710522 ospf 100 [23091]: : Route 2.2.2.2/32 next-hop
   10.1.12.2 added to RIB.
2017 May 14 03:12:14.710515 ospf 100 [23091]: : Path type changed from nopath to
   intra
2017 May 14 03:12:14.710513 ospf 100 [23091]: : Admin distance changed from 255
   to 110
2017 May 14 03:12:14.710511 ospf 100 [23091]: : Ubest metric changed from 429496
   7295 to 41
2017 May 14 03:12:14.710509 ospf 100 [23091]: : Processing route 2.2.2.2/32 (ubest)
! Output omitted for brevity
2017 May 14 03:12:14.710430 ospf 100 [23091]: : Start sending routes to URIB and
summarize
N7k-1# show routing internal event-history msgs
! Output omitted for brevity
6) Event:E_MTS_TX, length:60, at 710812 usecs after Sun May 14 03:12:14 2017
   [NOT] Opc:MTS_OPC_URIB(52225), Id:0X0036283B, Ret:SUCCESS
   Src:0x00000101/253, Dst:0x00000101/320, Flags:None
   HA_SEQNO:0X00000000, RRtoken:0x00000000, Sync:NONE, Payloadsize:312
   Payload:
   0x0000:  04 00 1a 00 53 0f 00 00 53 0f 00 00 ba 49 07 00
7) Event:E_MTS_RX, length:60, at 710608 usecs after Sun May 14 03:12:14 2017
   [NOT] Opc:MTS_OPC_URIB(52225), Id:0X00362839, Ret:SUCCESS
   Src:0x00000101/320, Dst:0x00000101/253, Flags:None
   HA_SEQNO:0X00000000, RRtoken:0x00000000, Sync:NONE, Payloadsize:276
   Payload:
   0x0000:  04 00 19 00 33 5a 00 00 33 5a 00 00 ba 49 07 00
N7k-1# show system internal mts sup sap 253 description
URIB queue
```

After the routes are installed in the URIB, they can be viewed using the command **show ip route** *routing-process* **detail**, where *routing-process* is the NX-OS process for the respective routing protocols, as in Example 3-53 (*ospf-100*).

Note URIB stores all routing information in shared memory. Because the memory space is shared, it can be exhausted by large-scale routing issues or memory leak issues. Use the command **show routing memory statistics** to view the shared URIB memory space.

UFDM and IPFIB

After the URIB has been updated with the routes, update the FIB. This is where UFDM comes into picture. UFDM, a VDC local process, primarily takes care of reliably distributing the routes, adjacency information, and unicast reverse path forwarding (uRPF) information to all the line cards in the Nexus chassis where all the FIB is programmed. UFDM maintains prefix, adjacency, and equal cost multipath (ECMP) databases, which are then used for making forwarding decisions in the hardware. UFDM runs on the supervisor module and communicates with the IPFIB on each line card. The IPFIB process programs the forwarding engine (FE) and hardware adjacency on each line card.

The UFDM has four sets of APIs performing various tasks in the system:

- **FIB API:** URIB and U6RIB modules use this to add, update, and delete routes in the FIB.
- **AdjMgr notification:** The AM interacts directly with the UFDM AM API to install /32 host routes.
- **uRPF notification:** The IP module sends a notification to enable or disable different RPF check modes per interface.
- **Statistics collection API:** This is used to collect adjacency statistics from the platform.

In this list of tasks, the first three functions happen in a top-down manner (from supervisor to line card); the fourth function happens in a bottom-up direction (from line card to supervisor).

Note NX-OS no longer has Cisco Express Forwarding (CEF). It now relies on hardware FIB, which is based on AVL Trees, a self-balancing binary search tree.

The UFDM component distributes AM, FIB, and RPF updates to IPFIB on each line card in the VDC and then sends an acknowledgment *route-ack* to URIB. This is verified using the command **show system internal ufdm event-history debugs** (see Example 3-54).

Example 3-54 *UFDM Route Distribution to IPFIB and Acknowledgment*

```
N7k-1# show system internal ufdm event-history debugs
! Output omitted for brevity
807) Event:E_DEBUG, length:94, at 711536 usecs after Sun May 14 03:12:14 2017
    [104] ufdm_route_send_ack(185):TRACE: sent route nack, xid: 0x58f059ec,
v4_ack: 0, v4_nack: 24



808) Event:E_DEBUG, length:129, at 711230 usecs after Sun May 14 03:12:14 2017
    [104] ufdm_route_distribute(615):TRACE: v4_rt_upd # 24 rt_count: 1, urib_xid
: 0x58f059ec, fib_xid: 0x58f059ec recp_cnt: 0 rmask: 0


809) Event:E_DEBUG, length:94, at 652231 usecs after Sun May 14 03:12:09 2017
    [104] ufdm_route_send_ack(185):TRACE: sent route nack, xid: 0x58f059ec,
v4_ack: 0, v4_nack: 23


810) Event:E_DEBUG, length:129, at 651602 usecs after Sun May 14 03:12:09 2017
    [104] ufdm_route_distribute(615):TRACE: v4_rt_upd # 23 rt_count: 1, urib_xid
: 0x58f059ec, fib_xid: 0x58f059ec recp_cnt: 0 rmask: 0
```

The platform-dependent FIB manages the hardware-specific structures, such as hardware table indexes and device instances. The NX-OS command **show forwarding internal trace v4-pfx-history** displays the create and destroy history for FIB route data. Example 3-55 displays the forwarding IPv4 prefix history for prefix 2.2.2.2/32, which is learned through OSPF. The history displays the Create, Destroy, and then another Create operation for the prefix, along with the time stamp, which is useful while troubleshooting forwarding issues that arise from a route not being installed in the hardware FIB.

Example 3-55 *Historical Information of FIB Route*

```
N7k-1# show forwarding internal trace v4-pfx-history
PREFIX 1.1.1.1/32 TABLE_ID 0x1
     Time                    ha_handle    next_obj    next_obj_HH   NH_cnt    operation
   Sun May 14 16:42:47 2017   0x23d6b     V4 adj         0xb          1       Create
   Sun May 14 16:42:47 2017   0x23d6b     V4 adj         0xb          1       Update

PREFIX 10.1.12.1/32 TABLE_ID 0x1
     Time                    ha_handle    next_obj    next_obj_HH   NH_cnt    operation
   Sun May 14 16:42:39 2017   0x21d24     V4 adj         0xb          1       Create
```

```
PREFIX 2.2.2.2/32 TABLE_ID 0x1
      Time                    ha_handle   next_obj   next_obj_HH   NH_cnt   operation
   Sun May 14 16:44:08 2017   0x23f55     V4 adj     0x10000       1        Create
   Sun May 14 16:44:17 2017   0x23f55     V4 adj     0x10000       1        Destroy
   Sun May 14 16:45:02 2017   0x23f55     V4 adj     0x10000       1        Create


PREFIX 10.1.12.2/32 TABLE_ID 0x1
      Time                    ha_handle   next_obj   next_obj_HH   NH_cnt   operation
   Sun May 14 16:43:58 2017   0x21601     V4 adj     0x10000       1        Create
```

After the hardware FIB has been programmed, the forwarding information is verified using the command **show forwarding route** *ip-address/len* [**detail**]. The command output displays the information of the next hop to reach the destination prefix and the outgoing interface, as well as the destination MAC information. This information is also verified at the platform level to get more details on it from the hardware/platform perspective using the command **show forwarding ipv4 route** *ip-address/len* **platform** [**module** *slot*].

Then the information must be propagated in the relevant line card. This is verified using the command **show system internal forwarding route** *ip-address/len* [**detail**]. This command output also provides interface hardware adjacency information; this is further verified using the command **show system internal forwarding adjacency entry** *adj*, where the *adj* value is the adjacency value received from the previous command.

Note Note that the previous outputs can be collected on the supervisor card as well as at the line card level by logging into the line card console using the command **attach module** *slot* and then executing the forwarding commands as already described.

Example 3-56 displays step-by-step verification of the route programmed in the FIB and on the line card level.

Example 3-56 *Platform FIB Verification*

```
N7k-1# show forwarding route 2.2.2.2/32 detail
slot  3
=======

Prefix 2.2.2.2/32, No of paths: 1, Update time: Sun May 14 21:29:43 2017
   10.1.12.2         Vlan10            DMAC: 5087.894b.c0c2
     packets: 0         bytes: 0
N7k-1# show forwarding ipv4 route 2.2.2.2/32 platform module 3
```

```
 Prefix 2.2.2.2/32, No of paths: 1, Update time: Sun May 14 21:16:20 2017
    10.1.12.2           Vlan10              DMAC: 5087.894b.c0c2
      packets: 0              bytes: 0
 HH:0x80000026  Flags:0x0  Holder:0x1  Next_obj_type:5
 Inst :     0    1    2    3    4    5    6    7    8    9    10   11
 Hw_idx:  6320   N/A  N/A  N/A  N/A  N/A
N7k-1# show system internal forwarding route 2.2.2.2/32
slot  3
=======




Routes for table default/base

----+---------------------+----------+----------+-----------
Dev | Prefix              | PfxIndex | AdjIndex | LIF
----+---------------------+----------+----------+-----------
  0   2.2.2.2/32            0x6320     0x5f       0x3


N7k-1# show system internal forwarding route 2.2.2.2/32 detail
slot  3
=======
 RPF Flags legend:
          S - Directly attached route (S_Star)
          V - RPF valid
          M - SMAC IP check enabled
          G - SGT valid
          E - RPF External table valid
        2.2.2.2/32          , Vlan10
   Dev: 0 , Idx: 0x6320 , Prio: 0x8507 , RPF Flags: V     , DGT: 0 , VPN: 9
        RPF_Intf_5:  Vlan10       (0x3      )
        AdjIdx: 0x5f   , LIFB: 0    , LIF: Vlan10       (0x3     ), DI: 0x0
        DMAC: 5087.894b.c0c2 SMAC: 5087.894b.c0c5
N7k-1# show system internal forwarding adjacency entry 0x5f
slot  3
=======


Device: 0   Index: 0x5f     dmac: 5087.894b.c0c2  smac: 5087.894b.c0c5
              e-lif: 0x3      packets: 0            bytes: 0
```

Note In case of any forwarding issues, collect the following show tech outputs during problematic state:

- show tech routing ip unicast
- show tech-support forwarding l3 unicast [module slot]
- show tech-support detail

EthPM and Port-Client

NX-OS provides a VDC local process named Ethernet Port Manager (EthPM) to manage all the Ethernet interfaces on the Nexus platforms, including physical as well as logical interfaces (only server interfaces, not SVIs), in-band interfaces, and management interfaces. The EthPM component performs two primary functions:

- **Abstraction:** Provides an abstraction layer for other components that want to interact with the interfaces that EthPM manages
- **Port Finite State Machine (FSM):** Provides an FSM for interfaces that it manages, as well as handling interface creation and removal

The EthPM component interacts with other components, such as the Port-Channel Manager, VxLAN Manager, and STP, to program interface states. The EthPM process is also responsible for managing interface configuration (duplex, speed, MTU, allowed VLANs, and so on).

Port-Client is a line card global process (specific to Nexus 7000 and Nexus 9000 switches) that closely interacts with the EthPM process. It maintains global information received from EthPM across different VDCs. It receives updates from the local hardware port ASIC and updates the EthPM. It has both platform-independent (PI) and platform-dependent (PD) components. The PI component of the Port-Client process interacts with EthPM, which is also a PI component, and the PD component is used for line card-specific hardware programming.

The EthPM component CLI enables you to view platform-level information, such as the EthPM interface index, which it receives from the Interface Manager (IM) component; interface admin state and operational state; interface capabilities; interface VLAN state; and more. All this information is viewed using the command **show system internal ethpm info interface** *interface-type interface-num*. Example 3-57 displays the EthPM information for the interface Ethernet 3/1, which is configured as an access port for VLAN 10.

Example 3-57 *Platform FIB Verification*

```
N7k-1# show system internal ethpm info interface ethernet 3/1


Ethernet3/1 - if_index: 0x1A100000
Backplane MAC address: 38:ed:18:a2:17:84
Router MAC address:    50:87:89:4b:c0:c5

Admin Config Information:
  state(up), mode(access), speed(auto), duplex(Auto), medium_db(0)
  layer(L2), dce-mode(edge), description(),
  auto neg(on), auto mdix(on), beacon(off), num_of_si(0)
  medium(broadcast), snmp trap(on), MTU(1500),
  flowcontrol rx(off) tx(off), link debounce(100),
  storm-control bcast:100.00% mcast:100.00% ucast:100.00%
  span mode(0 - not a span-destination)
  delay(1), bw(10000000), rate-mode(dedicated)
  eee(n/a), eee_lpi(Normal), eee_latency(Constant)
  fabricpath enforce (DCE Core)(0)
  load interval [1-3]: 30, 300, 0 (sec).
  lacp mode(on)
  graceful convergence state(enabled)
  Ethertype 0x8100
  Slowdrain Congestion : mode core timeout[500], mode edge [500]
  Slowdrain Pause : mode core enabled [y] timeout[500]
  Slowdrain Pause : mode edge enabled [y] timeout[500]
  Slowdrain Slow-speed : mode core enabled [n] percent[10]
  Slowdrain Slow-speed : mode edge enabled [n] percent[10]
  Monitor fp header(included)
  shut lan (disabled)
  Tag Native Mode (disabled)

Operational (Runtime) Information:
  state(up), mode(access), speed(10 Gbps), duplex(Full)
  state reason(None), error(no error)
  dce-mode(edge), intf_type(0), parent_info(0-1-5)
  port-flags-bitmask(0x0) reset_cntr(4)
  last intf reset time is 0 usecs after Thu Jan  1 00:00:00 1970
  secs  flowcontrol rx(off) tx(off), vrf(disabled)
  mdix mode(mdix), primary vlan(10), cfg_acc_vlan(10)
  access vlan(10), cfg_native vlan(1), native vlan(1)
  eee(n/a), eee_wake_time_tx(0), eee_wake_time_rx(0)

  bundle_bringup_id(5)
  service_xconnect(0)
```

```
  current state [ETH_PORT_FSM_ST_L2_UP]
  xfp(inserted), status(ok) Extended info (present and valid)

Operational (Runtime) ETHPM_LIM Cache Information:
  Num of EFP(0), EFP port mode (0x100000), EFP rewrite(0),
  PORT_CMD_ENCAP(9), PORT_CMD_PORT_MODE(0),
  PORT_CMD_SET_BPDU_MATCH(2)
  port_mem_of_es_and_lacp_suspend_disable(0)

MTS Node Identifier: 0x302

Platform Information:
  Local IOD(0xd7), Global IOD(0) Runtime IOD(0xd7)

Capabilities:
  Speed(0xc), Duplex(0x1), Flowctrl(r:0x3,t:0x3), LinkDebounce(0x1)
  udld(0x1), SFPCapable(0x1), TrunkEncap(0x1), AutoNeg(0x1)
  channel(0x1), suppression(0x1), cos_rewrite(0x1), tos_rewrite(0x1)
  dce capable(0x4), l2 capable(0x1), l3 capable(0x2) qinq capable(0x10)
   ethertype capable(0x1000000), Fabric capable (y), EFP capable (n)
   slowdrain congestion capable(y),  slowdrain pause capable (y)
   slowdrain slow-speed capable(y)
  Num rewrites allowed(104)
  eee capable speeds () and eee flap flags (0)
  eee max wk_time rx(0) tx(0) fb(0)

Information from GLDB Query:
  Platform Information:
    Slot(0x2), Port(0), Phy(0x2)
    LTL(0), VQI(0xc), LDI(0), IOD(0xd7)
  Backplane MAC address in GLDB: 38:ed:18:a2:17:84
  Router MAC address in GLDB:    50:87:89:4b:c0:c5

Operational Vlans: 10

Operational Bits: 3-4,13,53
  is_link_up(1), pre_cfg_done(1), l3_to_l2(1), pre_cfg_ph1_done(1),
Keep-Port-Down Type:0 Opc:0 RRToken:0X00000000, gwrap:(nil)
   Multiple  Reinit: 0 Reinit when shut: 0
   Last    SetTs: 487184 usecs after Sun May 14 18:54:29 2017
   Last ResetTs: 717229 usecs after Sun May 14 18:54:30 2017

DCX LAN LLS enabled: FALSE
```

```
  MCEC LLS down: FALSE
Breakout mapid 0

  User config flags:   0x3
    admin_state(1), admin_layer(1), admin_router_mac(0) admin_monitor_fp_header(0)

Lock Info: resource [Ethernet3/1]
  type[0]  p_gwrap[(nil)]
      FREE @ 528277 usecs after Sun May 14 21:29:05 2017
  type[1]  p_gwrap[(nil)]
      FREE @ 528406 usecs after Sun May 14 21:29:05 2017
  type[2]  p_gwrap[(nil)]
      FREE @ 381980 usecs after Sun May 14 18:54:28 2017
0x1a100000

Pacer Information:
  Pacer State: released credits
  ISSU Pacer State: initialized

Data structure info:
  Context: 0xa2f1108
  Pacer credit granted after:   4294967295 sec 49227 usecs
  Pacer credit held for:  1 sec 4294935903 usecs
```

The port-client command **show system internal port-client link-event** tracks interface link events from the software perspective on the line card. This command is a line card-level command that requires you to get into the line card console. Example 3-58 displays the port-client link events for ports on module 3. In this output, the events at different time stamps are seen for various links going down and coming back up.

Example 3-58 *Port-Client Link Events*

```
N7k-1# attach module 3
Attaching to module 3 ...
To exit type 'exit', to abort type '$.'
module-3# show system internal port-client link-event
*************** Port Client Link Events Log ***************
----                       ------       -----  -----  -------
Time                       PortNo       Speed  Event  Stsinfo
----                       ------       -----  -----  -------
May 15 05:53:01 2017   00879553  Ethernet3/1    10G    UP     Autonegotiation
    completed(0x40e50008)


May 15 05:52:58 2017   00871071  Ethernet3/1    ----   DOWN   SUCCESS(0x0)
```

```
May 15 05:47:35 2017   00553866   Ethernet3/11   ----   DOWN   Link down debounce
timer stopped and link is down

May 15 05:47:35 2017   00550650   Ethernet3/11   ----   DOWN   SUCCESS(0x0)

May 15 05:47:35 2017   00454119   Ethernet3/11   ----   DOWN   Link down debounce
timer started(0x40e50006)
```

For these link events, relevant messages are seen in the port-client event history logs for the specified port using the line card-level command **show system internal port-client event-history port** *port-num*.

Note If issues arise with ports not coming up on the Nexus chassis, collect the output of the command **show tech ethpm** during problematic state.

HWRL, CoPP, and System QoS

Denial of service (DoS) attacks take many forms and affect both servers and infrastructure in any network environment, especially in data centers. Attacks targeted at infrastructure devices generate IP traffic streams at very high data rates. These IP data streams contain packets that are destined for processing by the control plane of the route processor (RP). Based on the high rate of rogue packets presented to the RP, the control plane is forced to spend an inordinate amount of time processing this DoS traffic. This scenario usually results in one of the following issues:

- Loss of line protocol keepalives, which cause a line to go down and lead to route flaps and major network transitions.
- Excessive packet processing because packets are being punted to the CPU.
- Loss of routing protocol updates, which leads to route flaps and major network transitions.
- Unstable Layer 2 network
- Near 100% CPU utilization that locks up the router and prevents it from completing high-priority processing (resulting in other negative side effects).
- RP at near 100% utilization, which slows the response time at the user command line (CLI) or locks out the CLI. This prevents the user from taking corrective action to respond to the attack.
- Consumption of resources such as memory, buffers, and data structures, causing negative side effects.
- Backup of packet queues, leading to indiscriminate drops of important packets.
- Router crashes

To overcome the challenges of DoS/DDoS attacks and excessive packet processing, NX-OS gives users two-stage policing:

- Rate-limiting packets in hardware on a per-module basis before sending the packets to the CPU

- Policy-based traffic policing using control plane policing (CoPP) for traffic that has passed rate-limiters

The hardware rate-limiters and CoPP policy together increase device security by protecting its CPU (Route-Processor) from unnecessary traffic or DoS attacks and gives priority to relevant traffic destined for the CPU. Note that the hardware rate limiters are available only with Nexus 7000 and Nexus 9000 series switches and are not available on other Nexus platforms.

Packets that hit the CPU or reach the control plane are classified into these categories:

- **Received packets:** These packets are destined for the router (such as keepalive messages)
- **Multicast packets:** These packets are further divided into three categories:
  - Directly connected sources
  - Multicast control packets
- **Copy packets:** For supporting features such as ACL-log, a copy of the original packet is made and sent to the supervisor. Thus, these are called copy packets.
  - ACL-log copy
  - FIB unicast copy
  - Multicast copy
  - NetFlow copy
- **Exception packets:** These packets need special handling. Hardware is unable to process them or detects an exception, so they are sent to the supervisor for further processing. Such packets fall under the exception category. Some of the following exceptions fall under this category of packets:
  - Same interface check
  - TTL expiry
  - MTU failure
  - Dynamic Host Control Protocol (DHCP) ACL redirect
  - ARP ACL redirect
  - Source MAC IP check failure
  - Unsupported rewrite
  - Stale adjacency error

HWRL, CoPP, and System QoS

- **Glean packets:** When an L2 MAC for the destination IP or next hop is not present in the FIB, the packet is sent to the supervisor. The supervisor then takes care of generating an ARP request for the destination host or next hop.

- **Broadcast, non-IP packets:** The following packets fall under this category:
    - Broadcast MAC + non-IP packet
    - Broadcast MAC + IP unicast
    - Multicast MAC + IP unicast

Remember that both the CoPP policy and rate-limiters are applied on per-module, per-forwarding engine (FE) basis.

Note On the Nexus 7000 platform, CoPP policy is supported on all line cards except F1 series cards. F1 series cards exclusively use rate-limiters to protect the CPU. HWRL is supported on Nexus 7000/7700 and Nexus 9000 series platforms.

Example 3-59 displays the output of the command **show hardware rate-limiters [module** *slot*] to view the rate-limiter configuration and statistics per each line card module present in the chassis.

Example 3-59 *Verifying Hardware Rate-Limiters on N7k and N9k Switches*

```
n7k-1# show hardware rate-limiter module 3

Units for Config: packets per second
Allowed, Dropped & Total: aggregated since last clear counters
rl-1: STP and Fabricpath-ISIS
rl-2: L3-ISIS and OTV-ISIS
rl-3: UDLD, LACP, CDP and LLDP
rl-4: Q-in-Q and ARP request
rl-5: IGMP, NTP, DHCP-Snoop, Port-Security, Mgmt and Copy traffic

Module: 3

Rate-limiter PG Multiplier: 1.00

    R-L Class          Config          Allowed          Dropped          Total
    +------------------+---------------+----------------+----------------+----------------+
    L3 mtu              500             0                0                0
    L3 ttl              500             0                0                0
    L3 control          10000           0                0                0
    L3 glean            100             0                0                0
```

```
    L3 mcast dirconn         3000              1               0               1
    L3 mcast loc-grp         3000              0               0               0
    L3 mcast rpf-leak         500              0               0               0
    L2 storm-ctrl         Disable
    access-list-log           100              0               0               0
    copy                    30000          54649               0           54649
    receive                 30000         292600               0          292600
    L2 port-sec               500              0               0               0
    L2 mcast-snoop          10000           2242               0            2242
    L2 vpc-low               4000              0               0               0
    L2 l2pt                   500              0               0               0
    L2 vpc-peer-gw           5000              0               0               0
    L2 lisp-map-cache        5000              0               0               0
    L2 dpss                   100              0               0               0
    L3 glean-fast             100              0               0               0
    L2 otv                    100              0               0               0
    L2 netflow                500              0               0               0

    Port group with configuration same as default configuration
        Eth3/1-32

N9K-1# show hardware rate-limiter module 2

Units for Config: packets per second
Allowed, Dropped & Total: aggregated since last clear counters

Module: 2
    R-L Class              Config         Allowed         Dropped           Total
    +-------------------+---------+---------------+---------------+-----------------+
    L3 glean                  100              0               0               0
    L3 mcast loc-grp         3000              0               0               0
    access-list-log           100              0               0               0
    bfd                     10000              0               0               0
    exception                  50              0               0               0
    fex                      3000              0               0               0
    span                       50              0               0               0
    dpss                     6400              0               0               0
    sflow                   40000              0               0               0
```
For verifying the rate-limiter statistics on F1 module on Nexus 7000 switches, use the command **show hardware rate-limiter [f1 rl-1 | rl-2 | rl-3 | rl-4 | rl-5]**.

The Nexus 7000 series switches also enable you to view the rate-limiters for the SUP bound traffic and its usage. Different modules determine what exceptions match each rate-limiter. These differences are viewed using the command **show hardware internal forwarding rate-limiter usage** [module *slot*]. Example 3-60 displays the output of this command, showing not only the different rate-limiters but also which packet streams or rate-limiters are handled by either CoPP or the L2 or L3 rate-limiters.

Example 3-60 *Rate-Limiter Usage*

```
N7K-1# show hardware internal forwarding rate-limiter usage module 3

Note: The rate-limiter names have been abbreviated to fit the display.

-------------------------+------+------+--------+------+--------+--------
 Packet streams          | CAP1 | CAP2 | DI     | CoPP | L3 RL  | L2 RL
-------------------------+------+------+--------+------+--------+--------
L3 control (224.0.0.0/24) Yes    x     sup-hi   x      control  copy
L2 broadcast              x      x     flood    x      x        strm-ctl
ARP request               Yes    x     sup-lo   Yes    x        copy
Mcast direct-con          Yes    x     x        Yes    m-dircon copy
ISIS                      Yes    x     sup-lo   x      x        x
L2 non-IP multicast       x      x     x        x      x        x
Access-list log           x      Yes   acl-log  x      x        acl-log
L3 unicast control        x      x     sup-hi   Yes    x        receive
L2 control                x      x     x        x      x        x
Glean                     x      x     sup-lo   x      x        glean
Port-security             x      x     port-sec x      x        port-sec
IGMP-Snoop                x      x     m-snoop  x      x        m-snoop
-------------------------+------+------+--------+------+--------+--------
 Exceptions              | CAP1 | CAP2 | DI     | CoPP | L3 RL  | L2 RL
-------------------------+------+------+--------+------+--------+--------
IPv4 header options       0      0     x        Yes             x
FIB TCAM no route         0      0     x        Yes             x
Same interface check      0      0     x        x      ttl      x
IPv6 scope check fail     0      0     drop     x               x
Unicast RPF more fail     0      0     drop     x               x
Unicast RPF fail          0      0     drop     Yes             x
Multicast RPF fail        0      0     drop     x               x
Multicast DF fail         0      0     drop     x               x
TTL expiry                0      0     x        x      ttl      x
Drop                      0      0     drop     x               x
L3 ACL deny               0      0     drop     x               x
L2 ACL deny               0      0     drop     x               x
IPv6 header options       0      0     drop     Yes             x
MTU fail                  0      0     x        x      mtu      x
DHCP ACL redirect         0      0     x        Yes    mtu      x
ARP ACL redirect          0      0     x        Yes    mtu      x
Smac IP check fail        0      0     x        x      mtu      x
Hardware drop             0      0     drop     x               x
Software drop             0      0     drop     x               x
Unsupported RW            0      0     x        x      ttl      x
Invalid packet            0      0     drop     x               x
L3 proto filter fail      0      0     drop     x               x
```

```
Netflow error              0    0    drop    x           x
Stale adjacency error      0    0    x       x    ttl    x
Result-bus drop            0    0    drop    x           x
Policer drop               0    0    x       x           x
```

Information about specific exceptions is seen using the command **show hardware internal forwarding l3 asic exceptions** *exception* **detail [module** *slot*].

The configuration settings for both l2 and l3 ASIC rate-limiters are viewed using the command **show hardware internal forwarding [l2 | l3] asic rate-limiter** *rl-name* **detail [module** *slot*], where the *rl-name* variable is the name of the rate-limiter. Example 3-61 displays the output for L3 ASIC exceptions, as well as the L2 and L3 rate-limiters. The first output shows the configuration and statistics for packets that fail the RPF check. The second and third outputs show the rate-limiter and exception configuration for packets that fail the MTU check.

Example 3-61 *L2 and L3 Rate-Limiter and Exception Configuration*

```
! L2 Rate-Limiter
N7K-1# show hardware internal forwarding l2 asic rate-limiter layer-3-glean detail
Device: 1
Device: 1
       Enabled:    0
   Packets/sec:    0

Match fields:
       Cap1 bit: 0
       Cap2 bit: 0
       DI select: 0
              DI: 0
       Flood bit: 0


Replaced result fields:
       Cap1 bit: 0
       Cap2 bit: 0
              DI: 0
! L3 Rate-Limiter
N7K-1# show hardware internal forwarding l3 asic rate-limiter layer-3-mtu detail
slot  3
=======
Dev-id: 0
Rate-limiter configuration: layer-3 mtu
       Enabled:   1
   Packets/sec:   500
  Packet burst:   325 [burst period of 1 msec]
L3 Exceptions
N7K-1# show hardware internal forwarding l3 asic exceptions mtu-fail detail
```

```
slot  3
=======
Egress exception priority table programming:
              Reserved: 0
     Disable LIF stats: 0
               Trigger: 0
               Mask RP: 0x1
         Dest info sel: 0
   Clear exception flag: 0x1
            Egress L3 : 0
   Same IF copy disable: 0x1
     Mcast copy disable: 0x1
     Ucast copy disable: 0
     Exception dest sel: 0x6
        Enable copy mask: 0
       Disable copy mask: 0x1

Unicast destination table programming:
      Reserved: 0
        L2 fwd: 0x1
      Redirect: 0x1
  Rate-limiter: 0x6
         Flood: 0
    Dest index: 0x10c7
           CCC: 0

Multicast destination table programming:
      Reserved: 0
        L2 fwd: 0
      Redirect: 0
  Rate-limiter: 0
         Flood: 0
    Dest index: 0x285f
           CCC: 0
```

CoPP in Nexus platforms is also implemented in hardware, which helps protects the supervisor from DoS attacks. It controls the rate at which the packets are allowed to reach the supervisor CPU. Remember that traffic hitting the CPU on the supervisor module comes in through four paths:

1. In-band interfaces for traffic sent by the line cards

2. Management interface

3. Control and monitoring processor (CMP) interface, which is used for the console

4. Ethernet Out of Band Channel (EOBC)

Only the traffic sent through the in-band interface is sent to the CoPP because this is the only traffic that reaches the supervisor module though different forwarding engines (FE) on the line cards. CoPP policing is implemented individually on each FE.

When any Nexus platform boots up, the NX-OS installs a default CoPP policy named *copp-system-policy*. NX-OS also comes with different profile settings for CoPP, to provide different protection levels to the system. These CoPP profiles include the following:

- **Strict:** Defines a BC value of 250 ms for regular classes and 1000 ms for the important class.
- **Moderate:** Defines a BC value of 310 ms for regular classes and 1250 ms for the important class.
- **Lenient:** Defines a BC value of 375 ms for regular classes and 1500 ms for the important class.
- **Dense:** Recommended when the chassis has more F2 line cards than other I/O modules. Introduced in release 6.0(1).

If one of the policies is not selected during initial setup, NX-OS attaches the Strict profile to the control plane. You can choose not to use one of these profiles and instead create a custom policy to be used for CoPP. The NX-OS default CoPP policy categorizes policy into various predefined classes:

- **Critical:** Routing protocol packets with IP precedence value 6
- **Important:** Redundancy protocols such as GLBP, VRRP, and HSRP
- **Management:** All management traffic, such as Telnet, SSH, FTP, NTP, and Radius
- **Monitoring:** Ping and traceroute traffic
- **Exception:** ICMP unreachables and IP options
- **Undesirable:** All unwanted traffic

Example 3-62 shows a sample strict CoPP policy when the system comes up for the first time. The CoPP configuration is viewed using the command **show run copp all**.

Example 3-62 *CoPP Strict Policy on Nexus*

```
class-map type control-plane match-any copp-system-p-class-critical
  match access-group name copp-system-p-acl-bgp
  match access-group name copp-system-p-acl-rip
  match access-group name copp-system-p-acl-vpc
  match access-group name copp-system-p-acl-bgp6
  match access-group name copp-system-p-acl-lisp
  match access-group name copp-system-p-acl-ospf
! Output omitted for brevity
class-map type control-plane match-any copp-system-p-class-exception
```

```
  match exception ip option
  match exception ip icmp unreachable
  match exception ipv6 option
  match exception ipv6 icmp unreachable
class-map type control-plane match-any copp-system-p-class-important
  match access-group name copp-system-p-acl-cts
  match access-group name copp-system-p-acl-glbp
  match access-group name copp-system-p-acl-hsrp
  match access-group name copp-system-p-acl-vrrp
  match access-group name copp-system-p-acl-wccp
! Output omitted for brevity
class-map type control-plane match-any copp-system-p-class-management
  match access-group name copp-system-p-acl-ftp
  match access-group name copp-system-p-acl-ntp
  match access-group name copp-system-p-acl-ssh
  match access-group name copp-system-p-acl-ntp6
  match access-group name copp-system-p-acl-sftp
  match access-group name copp-system-p-acl-snmp
  match access-group name copp-system-p-acl-ssh6
! Output omitted for brevity
class-map type control-plane match-any copp-system-p-class-monitoring
  match access-group name copp-system-p-acl-icmp
  match access-group name copp-system-p-acl-icmp6
  match access-group name copp-system-p-acl-mpls-oam
  match access-group name copp-system-p-acl-traceroute
  match access-group name copp-system-p-acl-http-response
! Output omitted for brevity
class-map type control-plane match-any copp-system-p-class-normal
  match access-group name copp-system-p-acl-mac-dot1x
  match exception ip multicast directly-connected-sources
  match exception ipv6 multicast directly-connected-sources
  match protocol arp
class-map type control-plane match-any copp-system-p-class-undesirable
  match access-group name copp-system-p-acl-undesirable
  match exception fcoe-fib-miss

policy-map type control-plane copp-system-p-policy-strict
  class copp-system-p-class-critical
    set cos 7
    police cir 36000 kbps bc 250 ms conform transmit violate drop
  class copp-system-p-class-important
    set cos 6
    police cir 1400 kbps bc 1500 ms conform transmit violate drop
```

```
class copp-system-p-class-management
  set cos 2
  police cir 10000 kbps bc 250 ms conform transmit violate drop
class copp-system-p-class-normal
  set cos 1
  police cir 680 kbps bc 250 ms conform transmit violate drop
class copp-system-p-class-exception
  set cos 1
  police cir 360 kbps bc 250 ms conform transmit violate drop
class copp-system-p-class-monitoring
  set cos 1
  police cir 130 kbps bc 1000 ms conform transmit violate drop
class class-default
  set cos 0
  police cir 100 kbps bc 250 ms conform transmit violate drop
```

To view the differences in the different CoPP profiles, use the command **show copp diff profile** *profile-type* **profile** *profile-type*. The command displays the policy-map configuration differences of both specified profiles.

Note Starting with NX-OS Release 6.2(2), the *copp-system-p-class-multicast-router*, *copp-system-p-class-multicast-host*, and *copp-system-p-class-normal* classes were added for multicast traffic. Before Release 6.2(2), this was achieved through custom user configuration.

Both HWRL and CoPP are done at the forwarding engine (FE) level. An aggregate amount of traffic from multiple FEs can still overwhelm the CPU. Thus, both the HWRL and CoPP are best-effort approaches. Another important point to keep in mind is that the CoPP policy should not be too aggressive; it also should be designed based on the network design and configuration. For example, if the rate at which routing protocol packets are hitting the CoPP policy is more than the policed rate, even the legitimate sessions can be dropped and protocol flaps can be seen. If the predefined CoPP policies must be modified, create a custom CoPP policy by copying a preclassified CoPP policy and then edit the new custom policy. None of the predefined CoPP profiles can be edited. Additionally, the CoPP policies are hidden from the **show running-config** output. The CoPP policies are viewed from the **show running-config all** or **show running-config copp all** commands. Example 3-63 shows how to use the CoPP policy configuration and create a custom strict policy.

Example 3-63 *Viewing a CoPP Policy and Creating a Custom CoPP Policy*

```
R1# show running-config copp
copp profile strict

R1# show running-config copp all
class-map type control-plane match-any copp-system-p-class-critical
  match access-group name copp-system-p-acl-bgp
  match access-group name copp-system-p-acl-rip
  match access-group name copp-system-p-acl-vpc
  match access-group name copp-system-p-acl-bgp6
! Output omitted for brevity

R1# copp copy profile strict ?
  prefix  Prefix for the copied policy
  suffix  Suffix for the copied policy
R1# copp copy profile strict prefix custom

R1# configure terminal
R1(config)# control-plane
R1(config-cp)# service-policy input custom-copp-policy-strict
```

The command **show policy-map interface control-plane** displays the counters of the CoPP policy. For an aggregated view, use this command with the **include "class|conform|violated"** filter to see how many packets have been conformed and how many have been violated and dropped (see Example 3-64).

Example 3-64 show policy-map interface control-plane *Output*

```
R1# show policy-map interface control-plane | include "class|conform|violated"
    class-map custom-copp-class-critical (match-any)
      conformed 123126534 bytes; action: transmit
      violated 0 bytes; action: drop
      conformed 0 bytes; action: transmit

      violated 0 bytes; action: drop
      conformed 107272597 bytes; action: transmit
      violated 0 bytes; action: drop
      conformed 0 bytes; action: transmit
      violated 0 bytes; action: drop
    class-map custom-copp-class-important (match-any)
      conformed 0 bytes; action: transmit
      violated 0 bytes; action: drop
      conformed 0 bytes; action: transmit
```

```
            violated 0 bytes; action: drop
         conformed 0 bytes; action: transmit
            violated 0 bytes; action: drop
         conformed 0 bytes; action: transmit
            violated 0 bytes; action: drop
! Output omitted for brevity
```

One problem that is faced with the access lists part of the CoPP policy is that the **statistics per-entry** command is not supported for IP and MAC access control lists (ACL); thus, it has no effect when applied under the ACLs. To view the CoPP policy-referenced IP and MAC ACL counters on an input/output (I/O) module, use the command **show system internal access-list input entries detail**. Example 3-65 displays the output of the command **show system internal access-list input entries detail**, showing the hits on the MAC ACL for the FabricPath MAC address 0180.c200.0041.

Example 3-65 *IP and MAC ACL Counters in TCAM*

```
n7k-1# show system internal access-list input entries detail | grep 0180.c200.0041
[020c:4344:020a] qos 0000.0000.0000 0000.0000.0000 0180.c200.0041 ffff.ffff.ffff
   [0]
[020c:4344:020a] qos 0000.0000.0000 0000.0000.0000 0180.c200.0041 ffff.ffff.ffff
   [20034]
[020c:4344:020a] qos 0000.0000.0000 0000.0000.0000 0180.c200.0041 ffff.ffff.ffff
   [19923]
[020c:4344:020a] qos 0000.0000.0000 0000.0000.0000 0180.c200.0041 ffff.ffff.ffff
   [0]
```

Starting with NX-OS Release 5.1, the threshold value is configured to generate a syslog message for the drops enforced by the CoPP policy on a particular class. The syslog messages are generated when the drops within a traffic class exceed the user-configured threshold value. The threshold is configured using the **logging drop threshold** *dropped-bytes-count* [level *logging-level*] command. Example 3-66 demonstrates how to configure the logging threshold value to be set for 100 drops and logging at level 7. It also demonstrates how the syslog message is generated in case the drop threshold is exceeded.

Example 3-66 *Drop Threshold for syslog Logging*

```
R1(config)# policy-map type control-plane custom-copp-policy-strict
R1(config-pmap)# class custom-copp-class-critical
R1(config-pmap-c)# logging drop threshold ?
  <1-80000000000>  Dropped byte count
```

```
R1(config-pmap-c)# logging drop threshold 100 ?
  <CR>
  level   Syslog level

R1(config-pmap-c)# logging drop threshold 100 level ?
  <1-7>   Specify the logging level between 1-7

R1(config-pmap-c)# logging drop threshold 100 level 7
%COPP-5-COPP_DROPS5: CoPP drops exceed threshold in class:
custom-copp-class-critical,
check show policy-map interface control-plane for more info.
```

Scale factor configuration was introduced in NX-OS starting with Version 6.0. The scale factor is used to scale the policer rate of the applied CoPP policy on a per-line card basis without changing the actual CoPP policy configuration. The scale factor configuration ranges from 0.10 to 2.0. To configure the scale factor, use the command **scale-factor** *value* [**module** *slot*] under the **control-plane** configuration mode. Example 3-67 illustrates how to configure the scale factor for various line cards present in the Nexus chassis. The scale factor settings are viewed using the command **show system internal copp info**. This command displays other information as well, including the last operation that was performed and its status, CoPP database information, and CoPP runtime status, which is useful while troubleshooting issues with CoPP policies.

Example 3-67 *Scale Factor Configuration*

```
n7k-1(config)# control-plane
n7k-1(config-cp)# scale-factor 0.5 module 3
n7k-1(config-cp)# scale-factor 1.0 module 4
n7k-1# show system internal copp info


Active Session Details:
---------------------
There isn't any active session

Last operation status:
--------------------
    Last operation: Show Command
    Last operation details: show policy-map interface
    Last operation Time stamp: 16:58:14 UTC May 14 2015
    Operation Status: Success

! Output omitted for brevity
```

```
Runtime Info:
--------------
    Config FSM current state: IDLE
    Modules online: 3 4 5 7

Linecard Configuration:
-----------------------
Scale Factors
Module 1: 1.00
Module 2: 1.00
Module 3: 0.50
Module 4: 1.00
Module 5: 1.00
Module 6: 1.00
Module 7: 1.00
Module 8: 1.00
Module 9: 1.00
```

Note Refer to the CCO documentation for the appropriate scale factor recommendation for the appropriate Nexus 7000 chassis.

A few best practices need to be kept in mind for NX-OS CoPP policy configuration:

- Use the strict CoPP profile.
- Use the **copp profile strict** command after each NX-OS upgrade, or at least after each major NX-OS upgrade. If a CoPP policy modification was previously done, it must be reapplied after the upgrade.
- The dense CoPP profile is recommended when the chassis is fully loaded with F2 series Modules or loaded with more F2 series modules than any other I/O modules.
- Disabling CoPP is not recommended. Tune the default CoPP, as needed.
- Monitor unintended drops, and add or modify the default CoPP policy in accordance with the expected traffic.

Because traffic patterns constantly change in a data center, customization of CoPP is a constant process.

MTU Settings

The MTU settings on a Nexus platform work differently than on other Cisco platforms. Two kinds of MTU settings exist: Layer 2 (L2) MTU and Layer 3 (L3) MTU. The L3

MTU is manually configured under the interface using the **mtu** *value* command. On the other hand, the L2 MTU is configured either through the network QoS policy or by setting the MTU on the interface itself on the Nexus switches that support per-port MTU. The L2 MTU settings are defined under the **network-qos** policy type, which is then applied under the **system qos** policy configuration. Example 3-68 displays the sample configuration to enable jumbo L2 MTU on the Nexus platforms.

Example 3-68 *Jumbo MTU System Configuration*

```
N7K-1(config)# policy-map type network-qos policy-MTU
N7K-1(config-pmap-nqos)# class type network-qos class-default
N7K-1(config-pmap-nqos-c)# mtu 9216
N7K-1(config-pmap-nqos-c)# exit
N7K-1(config-pmap-nqos)# exit
N7K-1(config)# system qos
N7K-1(config-sys-qos)# service-policy type network-qos policy-MTU
```

Having the jumbo L2 MTU enabled before applying jumbo L3 MTU on the interface is recommended.

Note Not all platforms support jumbo L2 MTU at the port level. The port-level L2 MTU configuration is supported only on the Nexus 7000, 7700, 9300, and 9500 platforms. All the other platforms (such as Nexus 3048, 3064, 3100, 3500, 5000, 5500, and 6000) support only network QoS policy-based jumbo L2 MTU settings.

The MTU settings on the Nexus 3000, 7000, 7700, and 9000 (platforms that support per-port MTU settings) can be viewed using the command **show interface** *interface-type x/y*. On the Nexus 3100, 3500, 5000, 5500, and 6000 (platforms supporting network QoS policy-based MTU settings), these are verified using the command **show queuing interface** *interface-type x/y*.

FEX Jumbo MTU Settings

The jumbo MTU on the Nexus 2000 FEXs is configured on the parent switch. If the parent switch supports setting the MTU on per-port basis, the MTU is configured on the FEX fabric port-channel interface. If the parent switch does not support per-port MTU settings, the configuration is done under the network QoS policy. Example 3-69 demonstrates that the FEX MTU settings configuration on the Nexus switch works on a per-port basis and also on the Nexus support network QoS policy.

Example 3-69 *FEX Jumbo MTU Settings*

```
! Per-Port Basis Configuration
NX-1(config)# interface port-channel101
NX-1(config-if)# switchport mode fex-fabric
NX-1(config-if)# fex associate 101
NX-1(config-if)# vpc 101
NX-1(config-if)# mtu 9216
! Network QoS based MTU Configuration
NX-1(conf)# class-map type network-qos match-any c-MTU-custom
(config-cmap-nqos)# match cos 0-7

NX-1(config)# policy-map type network-qos MTU-custom template 8e
NX-1(config-pmap-nqos)# class type network-qos c-MTU-custom
! Below command configures the congestion mechanism as tail-drop
NX-1(config-pmap-nqos-c)# congestion-control tail-drop
NX-1(config-pmap-nqos-c)# mtu 9216

NX-1(config)# system qos
NX-1(config-sys-qos)# service-policy type network-qos MTU-custom
```

Note Beginning with NX-OS Version 6.2, the per-port MTU configuration on FEX ports is not supported on Nexus 7000 switches. A custom network QoS policy is required to configure these (see Example 3-69).

Troubleshooting MTU Issues

MTU issues commonly arise because of misconfigurations or improper network design, with the MTU not set properly on the interface or at the system level. Such misconfigurations are to be rectified by updating the configuration and reviewing the network design. The challenge comes when the MTU on the interface or system level is configured properly but the software or hardware is not programmed correctly. In such cases, a few checks can confirm whether the MTU is properly programmed.

The first step for MTU troubleshooting is to verify the MTU settings on the interface using the **show interface** or the **show queuing interface** *interface-type x/y* commands. The devices supporting network QoS policy-based MTU settings use the command **show policy-map system type network-qos** to verify the MTU settings (see Example 3-70).

Example 3-70 *Network QoS Policy Verification*

```
N7K-1# show policy-map system type network-qos
  Type network-qos policy-maps
  =============================
  policy-map type network-qos policy-MTU template 8e
    class type network-qos class-default
      mtu 9216
      congestion-control tail-drop threshold burst-optimized
```

In NX-OS, the Ethernet Port Manager (ethpm) process manages the port-level MTU configuration. The MTU information under the ethpm process is verified using the command **show system internal ethpm info interface** *interface-type x/y* (see Example 3-71).

Example 3-71 *MTU Verification under the ethpm Process*

```
NX-1# show system internal ethpm info interface ethernet 2/1 | egrep MTU
  medium(broadcast), snmp trap(on), MTU(9216),
```

The MTU settings also can be verified on the Earl Lif Table Manager (ELTM) process, which maintains Ethernet state information. The ELTM process also takes care of managing the logical interfaces, such as switch virtual interfaces (SVI). To verify the MTU settings under the ELTM process on a particular interface, use the command **show system internal eltm info interface** *interface-type x/y* (see Example 3-72).

Example 3-72 *MTU Verification Under the ELTM Process*

```
NX-1# show system internal eltm info interface e2/1 | in mtu
  mtu = 9216 (0x2400), f_index = 0 (0x0)
```

Note If MTU issues arise across multiple devices or a software issue is noticed with the ethpm process or MTU settings, capture the **show tech-support ethpm** and **show tech-support eltm [detail]** output in a file and open a TAC case for further investigation.

Summary

This chapter focused on troubleshooting various hardware- and software-related problems on Nexus platforms. From the hardware troubleshooting perspective, this chapter covered the following topics:

- GOLD tests
- Line card and process crashes

- Packet loss and platform errors
- Interface errors and drops
- Troubleshooting for Fabric Extenders

This chapter detailed how VDCs work and explored how to troubleshoot any issues with the same. Various issues arise with a combination of modules within a VDC. This chapter also demonstrated how to limit the resources on a VDC and deeply covered various NX-OS components, such as Netstack, UFDM and IPFIB, EthPM, and Port-Client. Finally, the chapter addressed CoPP and how to troubleshoot for any drops in the CoPP policy, including how to fix any MTU issues on the Ethernet and FEX ports.

References

Cisco, Cisco Nexus 7000 Series: Configuring Online Diagnostics, http://www.cisco.com.

Cisco, Cisco Nexus Fabric Extenders, http://www.cisco.com.

Cisco, Cisco Nexus 7000 Series: Virtual Device Context Configuration Guide, http://www.cisco.com.

Chapter 4

Nexus Switching

This chapter covers the following topics:

- Network Layer 2 Communication Overview
- Virtual LANs
- Private VLANs
- Spanning Tree Protocol (STP)
- Detecting and Remediating Forwarding Loops
- Port Security

When Cisco launched the Nexus product line, it introduced a new category of networking devices called *data center switching*. Data center switching products provide high-density, high-speed switching capacity to serve the needs of the servers (physical and virtual) in the data center. This chapter focuses on the core components of network switching and how to verify which components are working properly to isolate and troubleshoot Layer 2 forwarding issues.

Network Layer 2 Communication Overview

The Ethernet protocol first used technologies such as Thinnet (10Base2) or Thicknet (10Base5), which connected all the network devices via the same cable. This caused problems when two devices tried to talk at the same time, because Ethernet devices use *Carrier Sense Multiple Access/Collision Detect (CSMA/CD)* to ensure that only one device talked at time in a collision domain. If a device detected that another device was transmitting data, it delayed transmitting packets until the cable was quiet.

As more devices were added to a cable, the less efficient the network became. All these devices were in the same *collision domain (CD)*. Network hubs proliferated the problem because they added port density while repeating traffic. Network hubs do not have any intelligence in them to direct network traffic.

Network switches enhance scalability and stability in a network through the creation of virtual channels. Switches maintain a table that associate a host's MAC Ethernet addresses to the port that sourced the network traffic. Instead of flooding all traffic out of every port, a switch uses the MAC address table to forward network traffic only to the destination port associated to the destination MAC address of the packet. Packets are forwarded out of all network ports for that LAN only if the destination MAC address is not known on the switch (known as unicast flooding).

Network broadcasts (MAC Address: ff:ff:ff:ff:ff:ff) cause the switch to broadcast the packet out of every LAN switch port interface. This is disruptive because it diminishes the efficiencies of a network switch to those of a hub because it causes communication between network devices to stop because of CSMA/CD. Network broadcasts do not cross Layer 3 boundaries (that is, from one subnet to another subnet). All devices that reside in the same Layer 2 (L2) segment are considered to be in the same *broadcast domain*.

Figure 4-1 displays PC-A's broadcast traffic that is being advertised to all devices on that network, which include PC-B, PC-C, and R1. R1 does not forward the broadcast traffic from one broadcast domain (192.168.1.0/24) to the other broadcast domain (192.168.2.0/24).

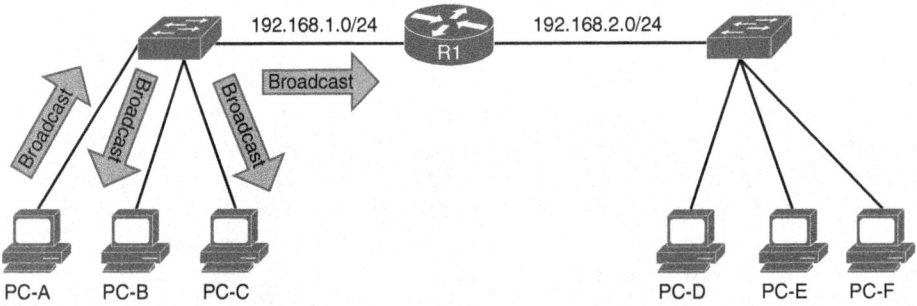

Figure 4-1 *Broadcast Domains*

The local MAC address table contains the list of MAC addressees and the ports that those MAC addresses learned. The MAC address table is displayed with the command **show mac address-table** [**address** *mac-address*]. To ensure that the switch hardware ASICS are programmed correctly, the hardware MAC address table is displayed with the command **show hardware mac address-table** *module* [**dynamic**] [**address** *mac-address*].

Example 4-1 displays the MAC address table on a Nexus switch. Locating the switch port the network device is attached to is the first step of troubleshooting L2 forwarding. If multiple MAC addresses appear on the same port, it indicates that a switch is connected to that port, and that connecting to the switch may be required as part of the troubleshooting processs to identify the port the network device is attached to.

Example 4-1 *Viewing the MAC Addresses on a Nexus Switch*

```
NX-1# show mac address-table
Legend:
        * - primary entry, G - Gateway MAC, (R) - Routed MAC, O - Overlay MAC
        age - seconds since last seen,+ - primary entry using vPC Peer-Link,
        (T) - True, (F) - False, C - ControlPlane MAC
   VLAN     MAC Address      Type      age     Secure NTFY Ports
---------+-----------------+--------+---------+------+----+------------------
*  1       0007.b35b.c420   dynamic  0          F      F   Eth1/7
*  1       0011.2122.2370   dynamic  0          F      F   Eth1/6
*  1       0027.e398.5481   dynamic  0          F      F   Eth1/1
*  1       0027.e398.54c0   dynamic  0          F      F   Eth1/1
*  1       0035.1a93.e4c2   dynamic  0          F      F   Eth1/2
*  1       286f.7fa3.e401   dynamic  0          F      F   Eth1/3
*  1       9caf.ca2e.76c1   dynamic  0          F      F   Eth1/5
*  1       9caf.ca2e.9041   dynamic  0          F      F   Eth1/4
G  -       885a.92de.617c   static   -          F      F   sup-eth1(R)
```

```
NX-1# show hardware mac address-table 1 dynamic
FE |PI| VLAN |     MAC       |Trunk|  TGID  |Mod|Port|Virt|Static|Hit|Hit|CPU|Pend
   |  |      |               |     |        |   |    |Port|      | SA| DA|   |
---+--+------+---------------+-----+--------+---+----+----+------+---+---+---+----+
0   1  1     286f.7fa3.e401 0     0        1   3         0      1   0   0   0
0   1  1     9caf.ca2e.76c1 0     0        1   5         0      1   1   0   0
0   1  1     0027.e398.5481 0     0        1   1         0      1   0   0   0
0   1  1     0035.1a93.e4c2 0     0        1   2         0      1   0   0   0
0   1  1     0027.e398.54c0 0     0        1   1         0      0   0   0   0
0   1  1     0011.2122.2370 0     0        1   6         0      1   1   0   0
0   1  1     0007.b35b.c420 0     0        1   7         0      1   1   0   0
0   1  1     9caf.ca2e.9041 0     0        1   4         0      1   1   0   0
```

Note The terms *network device* and *hosts* are considered interchangeable in this text.

Virtual LANs

Adding a router between LAN segments helps shrink broadcast domains and provides for optimal network communication. Host placement on a LAN segment varies because of network addressing. This could lead to inefficient usage of hardware because some switch ports could go unused.

Virtual LANs (VLAN) provide a logical segmentation by creating multiple broadcast domains on the same network switch. VLANs provide higher utilization of switch ports because a port could be associated to the necessary broadcast domain, and multiple broadcast domains can reside on the same switch. Network devices in one VLAN cannot communicate with devices in a different VLAN via traditional L2 or broadcast traffic.

VLANs are defined in the Institute of Electrical and Electronics Engineers (IEEE) 802.1Q standard, which states that 32 bits are added to the packet header and are composed of the following:

- **Tag protocol identifier (TPID):** 16-bit field set to 0x8100 to identify the packet as an 802.1Q.

- **Priority code point (PCP):** A 3-bit field to indicate a class of service (CoS) as part of Layer 2 quality of service (QoS) between switches.

- **Drop Eligible Indicator (DEI):** A 1-bit field that indicates if the packet can be dropped when there is bandwidth contention.

- **VLAN identifier (VID):** A 12-bit field that specifies the VLAN associated to a network packet.

Figure 4-2 displays the VLAN packet structure.

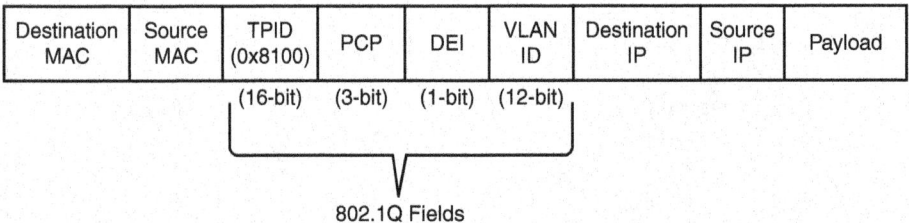

Figure 4-2 *VLAN Packet Structure*

The VLAN identifier has only 12 bits, which provide 4094 unique VLANs. NX-OS uses the following logic for VLAN identifiers:

- VLAN 0 is reserved for 802.1P traffic and cannot be modified or deleted.

- VLAN 1 is the default VLAN and cannot be modified or deleted.

- VLANs 2 to 1005 are in the normal VLAN range and can be added, deleted, or modified as necessary.

- VLANs 1006 to 3967 and 4048 to 4093 are in the extended VLAN range and can be added, deleted, or modified as necessary.
- VLANs 3968 to 4047 and 4094 are considered internal VLANs and are used internally by NX-OS. These cannot be added, deleted, or modified.
- VLANs 4095 is reserved by 802.1Q standards and cannot be used.

VLAN Creation

VLANs are created by using the global configuration command **vlan** *vlan-id*. A friendly name (32 characters) is associated to the VLAN by using the VLAN submode configuration command **name** *name*. The VLAN is not created until the CLI has been moved back to the global configuration context or a different VLAN identifier. Example 4-2 demonstrates the creation of VLAN 10 (Accounting), VLAN 20 (HR), and VLAN 30 (Security) on NX-1.

Example 4-2 *VLAN Creation*

```
NX-1(config)# vlan 10
NX-1(config-vlan)# name Accounting
NX-1(config-vlan)# vlan 20
NX-1(config-vlan)# name HR
NX-1(config-vlan)# vlan 30
NX-1(config-vlan)# name Security
```

VLANs and their port assignment are verified with the **show vlan** [**id** *vlan-id*] command, as demonstrated in Example 4-3. The output is reduced to a specific VLAN by using the optional **id** keyword. Notice that the output is broken into three separate areas: Traditional VLANs, Remote Switched Port Analyzer (RSPAN) VLANs, and Private VLANs.

Example 4-3 *Demonstration of the* **show vlan** *Command*

```
NX-1# show vlan
! Traditional and common VLANs will be listed in this section. The ports
! associated to these VLANs are displayed to the right.
VLAN Name                             Status    Ports
---- -------------------------------- --------- -------------------------------
1    default                          active    Eth1/1, Eth1/21, Eth1/22
                                                Eth1/23, Eth1/24, Eth1/25
                                                Eth1/26, Eth1/27, Eth1/28
                                                Eth1/29, Eth1/30, Eth1/31
                                                Eth1/32, Eth1/33, Eth1/34
                                                Eth1/35, Eth1/36, Eth1/37
                                                Eth1/38, Eth1/39, Eth1/40
                                                Eth1/41, Eth1/42, Eth1/43
                                                Eth1/44, Eth1/45, Eth1/46
```

```
                                            Eth1/47, Eth1/48, Eth1/49
                                            Eth1/50, Eth1/51, Eth1/52
10    Accounting                  active    Eth1/2, Eth1/3, Eth1/4, Eth1/5
                                            Eth1/6, Eth1/7, Eth1/8, Eth1/9
                                            Eth1/10, Eth1/11, Eth1/12
20    HR                          active    Eth1/13, Eth1/14, Eth1/15
                                            Eth1/16, Eth1/17, Eth1/18
                                            Eth1/19, Eth1/20
30    Security                    active

VLAN  Type     Vlan-mode
----  -----    ----------
1     enet     CE
10    enet     CE
20    enet     CE
30    enet     CE

! If a Remote SPAN VLAN is configured, it will be displayed in this section.
! Remote SPAN VLANs were explained in Chapter 2
Remote SPAN VLANs
-------------------------------------------------------------------------------

! If Private VLANs are configured, they will be displayed in this section.
! Private VLANs are covered later in this chapter.
Primary  Secondary  Type             Ports
-------  ---------  ---------------  -----------------------------------------

NX-1# show vlan id 10

VLAN Name                            Status    Ports
----  -----------------------------  --------  -------------------------------
10    Accounting                     active    Eth1/2, Eth1/3, Eth1/4, Eth1/5
                                               Eth1/6, Eth1/7, Eth1/8, Eth1/9
                                               Eth1/10, Eth1/11, Eth1/12

VLAN  Type     Vlan-mode
----  -----    ----------
10    enet     CE

Remote SPAN VLAN
----------------
Disabled

Primary  Secondary  Type             Ports
-------  ---------  ---------------  -----------------------------------------
```

Note Most engineers assume that a VLAN maintains a one-to-one ratio of subnet-to-VLAN. Multiple subnets can exist in the same VLAN by assigning a secondary IP address to a router's interface or by connecting multiple routers to the same VLAN. In situations like this, both subnets are part of the same broadcast domain.

Access Ports

Access ports are the fundamental building block of a managed switch. An access port is assigned to only one VLAN. It carries traffic from the VLAN to the device connected to it, or from the device to other devices on the same VLAN on that switch.

NX-OS places a L2 switch port as an access port by default. The port is configured as an access port with the command **switchport mode access**. A specific VLAN is associated to the port with the command **switchport access vlan** *vlan-id*. If the VLAN is not specified, it defaults to VLAN 1. The 802.1Q tags are not included on packets transmitted or received on access ports.

The **switchport mode access** command does not appear when looking at the traditional running configuration and requires the optional **all** keyword, as shown in Example 4-4.

Example 4-4 *Viewing the Access Port Configuration Command*

```
NX-1# show run interface e1/2
! Output omitted for brevity
interface Ethernet1/2
  switchport access vlan 10
```

```
NX-1# show run interface eth1/2 all | include access
  switchport mode access
  switchport access vlan 10
```

The command **show interface** *interface-id* displays the mode that the port is using. The assigned VLAN for the port is viewed with the **show vlan** command, as shown earlier in Example 4-2, or with **show interface status**. Example 4-5 demonstrates the verification of an access port and the associated VLAN. It is important to verify that both hosts must be on the same VLAN for L2 forwarding to work properly.

Example 4-5 *Verification of Access Port Mode*

```
NX-1# show interface eth1/2 | include Port
  Port mode is access
```

```
NX-1# show interface status

--------------------------------------------------------------------------------
Port            Name            Status      Vlan      Duplex   Speed     Type
--------------------------------------------------------------------------------
mgmt0           --              connected   routed    full     1000      --
Eth1/1          --              connected   trunk     full     1000      10g
Eth1/2          --              connected   10        full     1000      10g
```

Trunk Ports

Trunk ports can carry multiple VLANs across them. Trunk ports are typically used when multiple VLANs need connectivity between a switch and another switch, router, or firewall. VLANs are identified by including the 802.1Q headers in the packets as the packet is transmitted across the link. The headers are examined upon the receipt of the packet, associated to the proper VLAN, and then removed.

Trunk ports must be statically defined on Nexus switches with the interface command **switchport mode trunk**. Example 4-6 displays Eth1/1 being converted to a trunk port.

Example 4-6 *Trunk Port Configuration and Verification*

```
NX-1# config t
Enter configuration commands, one per line. End with CNTL/Z.
NX-1(config)# int eth1/1
NX-1(config-if)# switchport mode trunk
NX-1# show interface eth1/1 | include Port
  Port mode is trunk
```

The command **show interface trunk** provides a lot of valuable information into the following sections when troubleshooting connectivity between network devices:

- The first section list all the interfaces that are trunk ports, status, association to a port-channel, and native VLAN.

- The second section of the output displays the list of VLANs that are allowed on the trunk port. Traffic can be minimized on trunk ports to restrict VLANs to specific switches, thereby restricting broadcast traffic, too. Other use cases involve a form of load balancing between network links where select VLANs are allowed on one trunk link, and a different set of VLANs are allowed on a different trunk port.

- The third section displays any ports or VLANs that are in an error disabled (Err-disabled) state. Typically, these errors are related with an incomplete virtual port channel (vPC) configuration. vPCs are explained in detail in Chapter 5, "Port Channels, Virtual Port-Channels, and FabricPath."
- The fourth section displays the VLANs that are in a forwarding state on the switch. Ports that are in blocking state are not listed under this section.

Example 4-7 demonstrates the use of the **show interface trunk** command.

Example 4-7 *Output from* show interface trunk *Command*

```
NX-1# show interface trunk
! Section 1 displays the native VLAN associated on this port, the status and
! if the port is associated to a port-channel
--------------------------------------------------------------------------------
Port            Native  Status          Port
                Vlan                    Channel
--------------------------------------------------------------------------------
Eth1/1          1       trunking        --


! Section 2 displays all of the VLANs that are allowed to be transmitted across
! the trunk port
Port            Vlans Allowed on Trunk
--------------------------------------------------------------------------------
Eth1/1          1-4094


--------------------------------------------------------------------------------
! Section 3 displays ports that are disabled due to an error.
Port            Vlans Err-disabled on Trunk
--------------------------------------------------------------------------------
Eth1/1          none


--------------------------------------------------------------------------------
! Section 4 displays all of the VLANs that are allowed across the trunk and are
! in a spanning tree forwarding state
Port            STP Forwarding
--------------------------------------------------------------------------------
Eth1/1          1,10,20,30,99


--------------------------------------------------------------------------------
Port            Vlans in spanning tree forwarding state and not pruned
--------------------------------------------------------------------------------
Feature VTP is not enabled
Eth1/1          1,10,20,30,99
```

Native VLANs

Traffic on a trunk port's native VLAN does not include the 802.1Q tags. The native VLAN is a port-specific configuration and is changed with the interface command **switchport trunk native vlan** *vlan-id*.

The native VLAN should match on both ports, or traffic can change VLANs. Although connectivity between hosts is feasible (assuming that they are on the different VLAN numbers), this causes confusion for most network engineers and is not a best practice.

> **Note** All switch control-plane traffic is advertised using VLAN 1. As part of Cisco's security hardening guide, it is recommended to change the native VLAN to something other than VLAN 1. More specifically, it should be set to a VLAN that is not used at all to prevent VLAN hopping.

Allowed VLANs

As stated earlier, VLANs can be restricted from certain trunk ports as a method of traffic engineering. This can cause problems if traffic between two hosts is expected to traverse a trunk link, and the VLAN is not allowed to traverse that trunk port. The interface command **switchport trunk allowed** *vlan-ids* specifies the VLANs that are allowed to traverse the link. Example 4-8 displays sample configuration to limit the VLANs that can cross the Eth1/1 trunk link to 1, 10, 30, and 99.

Example 4-8 *Viewing the VLANs that Are Allowed on a Trunk Link*

```
NX-1# show run interface eth1/1
! Output omitted for brevity
interface Ethernet1/1
  switchport mode trunk
  switchport trunk allowed vlan 1,10,30,99
```

> **Note** The full command syntax is **switchport trunk allowed** {*vlan-ids* | **all** | **none** | **add** *vlan-ids* | **remove** *vlan-ids* | **except** *vlan-ids*} provides a lot of power in a single command.
>
> When scripting configuration changes, it is best to use the **add** or **remove** keywords because they are more prescriptive. A common mistake is using the **switchport trunk allowed** *vlan-ids* command, where only the VLAN that is being added is listed. This results in the current list being overwritten, causing traffic loss for the VLANs that were omitted.

Private VLANS

Some network designs require segmentation between network devices. This is easily accomplished by two techniques:

- Creating unique subnets for every security domain and restricting network traffic with an ACL. Using this technique can waste IP addresses when a host range falls outside of a subnet range (that is, a security zone with 65 hosts requires /25 and results in wasting 63 IP addresses; this does not take into consideration the broadcast and network addresses).

- Using private VLANs.

Private VLANs (PVLAN) provide two-tier hierarchy (primary or secondary VLAN) to restrict traffic between ports from a L2 perspective. An explicit mapping between the primary VLAN and secondary VLAN is required to allow communication outside of the PVLAN. Ports are associated into three categories:

- **Promiscuous:** Ports associated to this VLAN are a primary PVLAN (the first tier) and are allowed to communicate to all hosts. Typically, these are ports assigned to a router, firewall, or server that is providing centralized services (DHCP, DNS, and so on).

- **Isolated:** These ports are in a secondary PVLAN (in the second tier of the hierarchy) and are allowed to communicate only with ports associated to the promiscuous PVLAN. Traffic is not transmitted between ports in the same isolated VLAN.

- **Community:** These ports are in a secondary PVLAN and are allowed to communicate with other ports in this VLAN and ports associated to the promiscuous VLAN.

Figure 4-3 demonstrates the usage of PVLANs for a service provider. R1 is the router for every host in the 10.0.0.0/24 network segment and is connected with a promiscuous PVLAN. Host-2 and Host-3 are from different companies and should not be able to communicate with any host. They should only be able to communicate with R1.

Host-4 and Host-5 are from the same third company and need to talk with each other along with R1. Host-6 and Host-7 are from the same fourth company and need to talk with each other along with R1. All other communication is not allowed.

Chapter 4: Nexus Switching

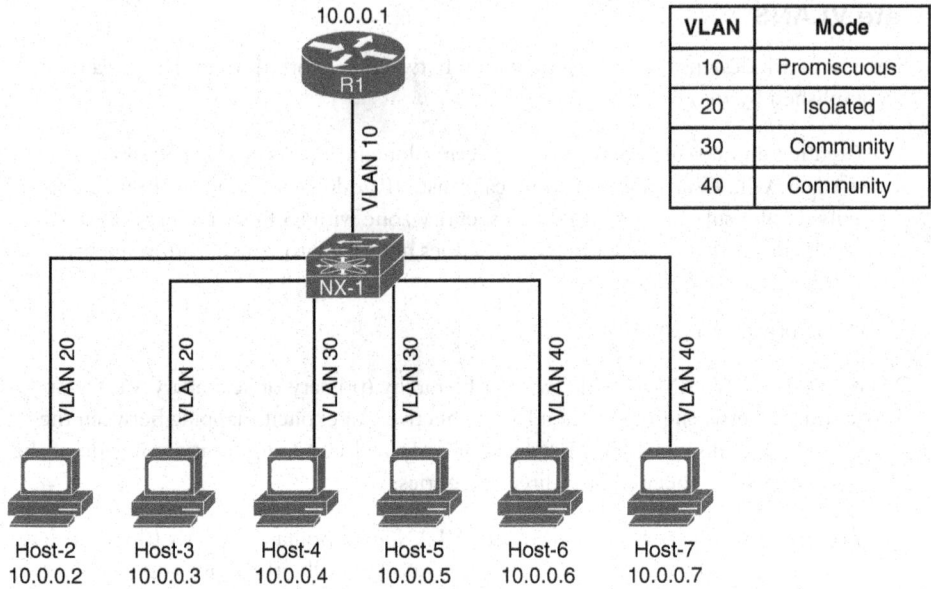

Figure 4-3 *Sample Private VLAN Topology*

Table 4-1 displays the communication capability between hosts. Notice that Host-4 and Host-5 communicate with each other; but cannot communicate with Host-2, Host-3, Host-6, and Host-7.

Table 4-1 *PVLAN Communication Capability*

	R1	Host-2	Host-3	Host-4	Host-5	Host-6	Host-7
R1	N/A	✓	✓	✓	✓	✓	✓
Host-2	✓	N/A	X	X	X	X	X
Host-3	✓	X	N/A	X	X	X	X
Host-4	✓	X	X	N/A	✓	X	X
Host-5	✓	X	X	✓	N/A	X	X
Host-6	✓	X	X	X	X	N/A	✓
Host-7	✓	X	X	X	X	✓	N/A

Isolated Private VLANs

Isolated PVLANs allow communication only with promiscuous ports; thereby, only one isolated PVLAN is needed for one L3 domain. The process for deploying isolated PVLANs on a Nexus switch is as follows:

Step 1. Enable the private VLAN feature. Enable the PVLAN feature with the command **feature private-vlan** in the global configuration mode.

Step 2. Define the isolated PVLAN. Create the isolated PVLAN with the command **vlan** *vlan-id*. Underneath the VLAN configuration context, identify the VLAN as an isolated PVLAN with the command **private-vlan isolated**.

Step 3. Define the promiscuous PVLAN. Create the promiscuous PVLAN with the command **vlan** *vlan-id*. Underneath the VLAN configuration context, identify the VLAN as a promiscuous PVLAN with the command **private-vlan primary**.

Step 4. Associate the isolated PVLAN to the promiscuous PVLAN. Underneath the promiscuous PVLAN configuration context, associate the secondary (isolated or community) PVLANs with the command **private-vlan** *secondary-pvlan-id*. If multiple secondary PVLANs are used, delineate with the use of a comma.

Step 5. Configure the switchport(s) for the promiscuous PVLAN. Change the configuration context to the switch port for the promiscuous host with the command **interface** *interface-id*. Change the switch port mode to promiscuous PVLAN with the command **switchport mode private-vlan promiscuous**.

The switch port must then be associated to the promiscuous PVLAN with the command **switchport access vlan** *promiscuous-vlan-id*. A mapping between the promiscuous PVLAN and any secondary PVLANs must be performed using the command **switchport private-vlan mapping** *promiscuous-vlan-id secondary-pvlan-vlan-id*. If multiple secondary PVLANs are used, delineate with the use of a comma.

Step 6. Configure the switchport(s) for the isolated PVLAN. Change the configuration context to the switch port for the isolated host with the command **interface** *interface-id*. Change the switch port mode to the secondary PVLAN type with the command **switchport mode private-vlan host**.

The switch port must then be associated to the promiscuous PVLAN with the command **switchport access vlan** *isolated-vlan-id*. A mapping between the promiscuous PVLAN and the isolated PVLAN must be performed using the command **switchport private-vlan mapping host-association** *promiscuous-vlan-id isolated-pvlan-vlan-id*.

Example 4-9 displays the deployment of VLAN 20 as an isolated PVLAN on NX-1, according to Figure 4-3. VLAN 10 is the promiscuous PVLAN.

Example 4-9 *Deployment of an Isolated PVLAN on NX-1*

```
NX-1(config)# feature private-vlan
Warning: Private-VLAN CLI entered...
Please disable multicast on this Private-VLAN by removing Multicast related
config(IGMP, PIM, etc.)  Please remove any VACL related config on Private-VLANs.
VLAN QOS needs to have atleast one port per ASIC instance.
NX-1(config)# vlan 20
NX-1(config-vlan)#    name PVLAN-ISOLATED
NX-1(config-vlan)#    private-vlan isolated
```

```
NX-1(config-vlan)# vlan 10
NX-1(config-vlan)#   name PVLAN-PROMISCOUS
NX-1(config-vlan)#   private-vlan primary
NX-1(config-vlan)#   private-vlan association 20
NX-1(config-vlan)# exit
NX-1(config)# interface Ethernet1/1
NX-1(config-if)#    switchport mode private-vlan promiscuous
NX-1(config-if)#    switchport access vlan 10
NX-1(config-if)#    switchport private-vlan mapping 10 20
NX-1(config-if)# interface Ethernet1/2
NX-1(config-if)#    switchport mode private-vlan host
NX-1(config-if)#    switchport access vlan 20
NX-1(config-if)#    switchport private-vlan host-association 10 20
NX-1(config-if)# interface Ethernet1/3
NX-1(config-if)#    switchport mode private-vlan host
NX-1(config-if)#    switchport access vlan 20
NX-1(config-if)#    switchport private-vlan host-association 10 20
```

After configuring a switch for PVLANs, it is recommended to verify the configuration using the command **show vlan [private-vlan]**. The optional **private-vlan** keyword only shows the output of the PVLAN section from **show vlan**.

In Example 4-10, the primary VLAN correlates to the promiscuous PVLAN, the secondary VLAN correlates to the isolated PVLAN, the PVLAN type is confirmed, and all active ports are listed off to the side. The promiscuous ports are always included. If a port is missing, recheck the interface configuration because an error probably exists in the PVLAN mapping configuration.

Example 4-10 *Verifying Isolated PVLAN Configuration*

```
NX-1# show vlan private-vlan
Primary  Secondary  Type              Ports
-------  ---------  ---------------   ------------------------------------
10       20         isolated          Eth1/1, Eth1/2, Eth1/3

NX-1# show vlan
! Output omitted for brevity

! Notice how there are not any ports listed in the regular VLAN section because
! they are all in the PVLAN section.
VLAN Name                             Status    Ports
---- -------------------------------- --------- -------------------------------
1    default                          active    Eth1/4, Eth1/5, Eth1/6, Eth1/7
10   PVLAN-PROMISCOUS                 active
20   PVLAN-ISOLATED                   active
```

```
..
Primary   Secondary   Type              Ports
-------   ---------   ---------------   ----------------------------------------
10        20          isolated          Eth1/1, Eth1/2, Eth1/3
```

Note An isolated or community VLAN can be associated with only one primary VLAN.

PVLAN ports require a different port type and are set by the **switchport mode private-vlan {promiscuous | host}** command. This setting is verified by examining the interface using the **show interface** command. Example 4-11 displays the verification of the PVLAN switch port type setting.

Example 4-11 *Verification of PVLAN Switchport Type*

```
NX-1# show interface Eth1/1 | i Port
  Port mode is Private-vlan promiscuous

NX-1# show interface Eth1/2 | i Port
  Port mode is Private-vlan host

NX-1# show interface Eth1/3 | i Port
  Port mode is Private-vlan host
```

Another technique is to verify that the isolated PVLAN host devices can reach the promiscuous host device. This is achieved with a simple **ping** test, as shown in Example 4-12.

Example 4-12 *Verification of Isolated PVLAN Communications*

```
! Verification that both hosts can ping R1
Host-2# ping 10.0.0.1
Sending 5, 100-byte ICMP Echos to 10.0.0.1, timeout is 2 seconds:
!!!!!
Success rate is 100 percent (5/5), round-trip min/avg/max = 1/5/9 ms

Host-3# ping 10.0.0.1
Sending 5, 100-byte ICMP Echos to 10.0.0.1, timeout is 2 seconds:
!!!!!
Success rate is 100 percent (5/5), round-trip min/avg/max = 1/5/9 ms

! Verification that both hosts cannot ping each other
```

```
Host-2# ping 10.0.0.3
Sending 5, 100-byte ICMP Echos to 10.0.0.3, timeout is 2 seconds:
.....
Success rate is 0 percent (0/5)

Host-3# ping 10.0.0.2
Sending 5, 100-byte ICMP Echos to 10.0.0.2, timeout is 2 seconds:
.....
Success rate is 0 percent (0/5)
```

Community Private VLANs

A *community PVLAN* allows communication only with promiscuous ports and other ports in the same community PVLAN. The process for deploying community PVLANs on a Nexus switch is as follows:

Step 1. Enable the private VLAN feature. Enable the PVLAN feature with the command **feature private-vlan** in the global configuration mode.

Step 2. Define the community PVLAN. Create the community PVLAN with the command **vlan** *vlan-id*. Underneath the VLAN configuration context, identify the VLAN as a community PVLAN with the command **private-vlan community**.

Step 3. Define the promiscuous PVLAN. Create the promiscuous PVLAN with the command **vlan** *vlan-id*. Underneath the VLAN configuration context, identify the VLAN as a promiscuous PVLAN with the command **private-vlan primary**.

Step 4. Associate the community PVLAN to the promiscuous PVLAN. Underneath the promiscuous PVLAN configuration context, associate the secondary (isolated or community) PVLANs with the command **private-vlan** *secondary-pvlan-id*. If multiple secondary PVLANs are used, delineate with the use of a comma.

Step 5. Configure the switch port(s) for the promiscuous PVLAN. Change the configuration context to the switch port for the promiscuous host with the command **interface** *interface-id*. Change the switch port mode to promiscuous PVLAN with the command **switchport mode private-vlan promiscuous**.

The switch port must then be associated to the promiscuous PVLAN with the command **switchport access vlan** *promiscuous-vlan-id*. A mapping between the promiscuous PVLAN and any secondary PVLANs needs to be performed using the command **switchport private-vlan mapping** *promiscuous-vlan-id secondary-pvlan-vlan-id*. If multiple secondary PVLANs are used, delineate with the use of a comma.

Step 6. Configure the switch port(s) for the community PVLAN. Change the configuration context to the switch port for the isolated host with the command **interface** *interface-id*. Change the switch port mode to the secondary PVLAN type with the command **switchport mode private-vlan host**.

The switch port must then be associated to the promiscuous PVLAN with the command **switchport access vlan** *isolated-vlan-id*. A mapping between the promiscuous PVLAN and the community PVLAN needs to be performed using the command **switchport private-vlan mapping host-association** *promiscuous-vlan-id community-pvlan-vlan-id*.

Example 4-13 displays the deployment of VLAN 30 as a community PVLAN for Host-4 and Host-5 along with VLAN 40 for Host-6 and Host-7, according to Figure 4-3. VLAN 10 is the promiscuous PVLAN.

Example 4-13 *Deployment of Community PVLANs on NX-1*

```
NX-1(config)# vlan 30
NX-1(config-vlan)#    name PVLAN-COMMUNITY1 10 40
NX-1(config-vlan)#    private-vlan community
NX-1(config-vlan)# vlan 40
NX-1(config-vlan)#    name PVLAN-COMMUNITY2
NX-1(config-vlan)#    private-vlan community
NX-1(config-vlan)# vlan 10
NX-1(config-vlan)#    name PVLAN-PROMISCOUS
NX-1(config-vlan)#    private-vlan primary
NX-1(config-vlan)#    private-vlan association 20,30,40
NX-1(config-vlan)# exit
NX-1(config)# interface Ethernet1/1
NX-1(config-if)#    switchport mode private-vlan promiscuous
NX-1(config-if)#    switchport access vlan 10
NX-1(config-if)#    switchport private-vlan mapping 10 20,30,40
NX-1(config-if)# interface Ethernet1/4
NX-1(config-if)#    switchport mode private-vlan host
NX-1(config-if)#    switchport access vlan 30
NX-1(config-if)#    switchport private-vlan host-association 10 30
NX-1(config-if)# interface Ethernet1/5
NX-1(config-if)#    switchport mode private-vlan host
NX-1(config-if)#    switchport access vlan 30
NX-1(config-if)#    switchport private-vlan host-association 10 30
NX-1(config-if)# interface Ethernet1/6
NX-1(config-if)#    switchport mode private-vlan host
NX-1(config-if)#    switchport access vlan 40
NX-1(config-if)#    switchport private-vlan host-association 10 40
NX-1(config-if)# interface Ethernet1/7
NX-1(config-if)#    switchport mode private-vlan host
NX-1(config-if)#    switchport access vlan 40
NX-1(config-if)#    switchport private-vlan host-association 10 40
```

Note VLAN 20 was a part of the promiscuous port configuration to demonstrate how isolated and community PVLANs co-exist as a continuation of the previous configuration to provide the solution shown in Figure 4-3.

Verification of community PVLANs is accomplished with the command **show vlan [private-vlan]**. Remember that if a port is missing in the PVLAN section, recheck the interface configuration because an error probably exists in the mapping configuration.

Example 4-14 displays all the PVLANS and associated ports. Notice how VLAN 10 is the primary VLAN for VLAN 20, 30, and 40.

Example 4-14 *Verifying Community PVLAN Configuration*

```
NX-1# show vlan
! Output omitted for brevity

VLAN Name                           Status    Ports
---- ------------------------------ --------- -------------------------------
1    default                        active
10   PVLAN-PROMISCOUS               active
20   PVLAN-ISOLATED                 active
30   PVLAN-COMMUNITY1               active
40   PVLAN-COMMUNITY2               active
..
Primary  Secondary  Type             Ports
-------  ---------  ---------------  -----------------------------------------
10       20         isolated         Eth1/1, Eth1/2, Eth1/3
10       30         community        Eth1/1, Eth1/4, Eth1/5
10       40         community        Eth1/1, Eth1/6, Eth1/7
```

Example 4-15 provides basic verification that all hosts in the isolated and community PVLANs can reach R1. All hosts are not allowed to reach any other host in the isolated PVLAN, whereas hosts in community PVLANs can only reach hosts in the same community PVLAN.

Example 4-15 *Verifying Connectivity Between PVLANs*

```
! Verification that hosts in both communities can ping R1
Host-4# ping 10.0.0.1
Sending 5, 100-byte ICMP Echos to 10.0.0.1, timeout is 2 seconds:
!!!!!
Success rate is 100 percent (5/5), round-trip min/avg/max = 1/2/9 ms

Host-6# ping 10.0.0.1
```

```
Sending 5, 100-byte ICMP Echos to 10.0.0.1, timeout is 2 seconds:
!!!!!
Success rate is 100 percent (5/5), round-trip min/avg/max = 1/2/4 ms
```

```
! Verification that both hosts can ping other hosts in the same community PVLAN
Host-4# ping 10.0.0.5
Sending 5, 100-byte ICMP Echos to 10.0.0.5, timeout is 2 seconds:
!!!!!
Success rate is 100 percent (5/5), round-trip min/avg/max = 1/5/9 ms

Host-6# ping 10.0.0.7
Type escape sequence to abort.
Sending 5, 100-byte ICMP Echos to 10.0.0.7, timeout is 2 seconds:
!!!!!
Success rate is 100 percent (5/5), round-trip min/avg/max = 1/1/1 ms
```

```
! Verification that both hosts cannot ping hosts in the other community PVLAN
Host-4# ping 10.0.0.6
Sending 5, 100-byte ICMP Echos to 10.0.0.6, timeout is 2 seconds:
.....
Success rate is 0 percent (0/5)

Host-6# ping 10.0.0.4
Sending 5, 100-byte ICMP Echos to 10.0.0.4, timeout is 2 seconds:
.....
Success rate is 0 percent (0/5)
```

```
! Verification that both hosts cannot ping hosts in the isolated PVLAN
Host-4# ping 10.0.0.2
Sending 5, 100-byte ICMP Echos to 10.0.0.2, timeout is 2 seconds:
.....
Success rate is 0 percent (0/5)

Host-6# ping 10.0.0.2
Sending 5, 100-byte ICMP Echos to 10.0.0.2, timeout is 2 seconds:
.....
Success rate is 0 percent (0/5)
```

Using a Promiscuous PVLAN Port on Switched Virtual Interface

A switched virtual interface (SVI) can be configured as a promiscuous port for a PVLAN. The primary and secondary PVLAN mappings are performed as previously explained, but the VLAN interface has the command **private-vlan mapping** *secondary-vlan-id*. Example 4-16 demonstrates NX-1 adding the SVI for VLAN 10 with the IP address of 10.0.0.10/24.

Example 4-16 *Configuring Promiscuous PVLAN SVI*

```
NX-1# conf t
NX-1(config)# interface vlan 10
NX-1(config-if)# ip address 10.0.0.10/24
NX-1(config-if)# private-vlan mapping 20,30,40
NX-1(config-if)# no shut
NX-1(config-if)# do show run vlan
! Output omitted for brevity

vlan 10
  name PVLAN-PROMISCOUS
  private-vlan primary
  private-vlan association 20,30,40
vlan 20
  name PVLAN-ISOLATED
  private-vlan isolated
vlan 30
  name PVLAN-COMMUNITY1
  private-vlan community
vlan 40
  name PVLAN-COMMUNITY2
  private-vlan community
```

The promiscuous PVLAN SVI port mapping is confirmed with the command **show interface vlan** *promiscuous-vlan-id* **private-vlan mapping**, as shown in Example 4-17.

Example 4-17 *Verification of Promiscuous PVLAN SVI Mapping*

```
NX-1# show interface vlan 10 private-vlan mapping
Interface Secondary VLAN
--------- ------------------------------------------------------------
vlan10    20   30   40
```

Example 4-18 demonstrates the connectivity between the hosts with the promiscuous PVLAN SVI. The two promiscuous devices (NX-1 and R1) can ping each other. In addition, all the hosts (demonstrated by Host-2) ping both NX-1 and R1 without impacting the PVLAN functionality assigned to isolated or community PVLAN ports.

Example 4-18 *Connectivity Verification with Promiscuous PVLAN SVI*

```
! Verification that both the promiscuous SVI can ping the other promiscuous

! host (R1)
NX-1# ping 10.0.0.1
PING 10.0.0.1 (10.0.0.1): 56 data bytes
```

```
64 bytes from 10.0.0.1: icmp_seq=0 ttl=254 time=2.608 ms
64 bytes from 10.0.0.1: icmp_seq=1 ttl=254 time=2.069 ms
64 bytes from 10.0.0.1: icmp_seq=2 ttl=254 time=2.241 ms
64 bytes from 10.0.0.1: icmp_seq=3 ttl=254 time=2.157 ms
64 bytes from 10.0.0.1: icmp_seq=4 ttl=254 time=2.283 ms

--- 10.0.0.1 ping statistics ---
5 packets transmitted, 5 packets received, 0.00% packet loss
round-trip min/avg/max = 2.069/2.271/2.608 ms
```

```
! Verification that a isolated PVLAN host can ping the physical and SVI
! promiscuous ports
Host-2# ping 10.0.0.1
Sending 5, 100-byte ICMP Echos to 10.0.0.1, timeout is 2 seconds:
!!!!!
Success rate is 100 percent (5/5), round-trip min/avg/max = 1/8/25 ms

Host-2# ping 10.0.0.10
Sending 5, 100-byte ICMP Echos to 10.0.0.10, timeout is 2 seconds:
!!!!!
Success rate is 100 percent (5/5), round-trip min/avg/max = 1/1/1 ms
```

```
! Verification that an isolated host cannot ping another host in the isolated PVLAN

Host-2# ping 10.0.0.3
Type escape sequence to abort.
Sending 5, 100-byte ICMP Echos to 10.0.0.3, timeout is 2 seconds:
.....
Success rate is 0 percent (0/5)
```

Trunking PVLANs Between Switches

Some topologies require that a PVLAN span across multiple switches. In these designs, there are three possible options depending upon the capabilities of the upstream or downstream switch. These scenarios are as follows:

- **All switches support PVLANs:** In this scenario, all the PVLANs and their primary/secondary mappings must be configured on both upstream and downstream switches. A normal 802.1Q trunk link is established between the devices. The switch with the promiscuous port is responsible for directing traffic to/from the promiscuous port. In this scenario, spanning tree maintains a separate instance for each of the PVLANs.

- **The upstream switch does not support PVLANs:** In this scenario, the PVLANs and their primary/secondary mappings must be configured on the downstream switch. Because the upstream switch does not support PVLANs, the downstream switch must merge/separate the secondary PVLANs to the primary PVLANs so that devices on the upstream switch only need to use the primary PVLAN-ID. The upstream trunk switch port is configured with the command **switchport mode private-vlan trunk promiscuous**. These trunk ports are often referred to as *promiscuous PVLAN trunk ports*.

- **The downstream switch does not support PVLANs:** In this scenario, the PVLANs and their primary/secondary mappings must be configured on the upstream switch. Because the downstream switch does not support PVLANs, the upstream switch must merge/separate the secondary PVLANs to the primary PVLANs so that devices on the downstream switch only need to use the secondary PVLAN-ID. The downstream trunk switch port is configured with the command **switchport mode private-vlan trunk secondary**. These trunk ports are often referred to as *isolated PVLAN trunk ports*.

Note In all three scenarios, regular VLANs are transmitted across the trunk link.

Note Not all Nexus platforms support the promiscuous or isolated PVLAN trunk ports. Check www.cisco.com for feature parity.

Spanning Tree Protocol Fundamentals

A good network design provides redundancy in devices and network links (paths). The simplest solution involves adding a second link between switches to overcome network link failure, or ensuring that a switch is connected to at least two switches in a topology.

However, these topologies cause problems when a switch has to forward broadcasts or unknown unicast flooding occurs. Network broadcasts forward in a continuous loop until the link becomes saturated and the switch is forced to drop packets. In addition, the MAC address table will be constantly changing ports as the packets make loops, therefore increasing CPU and memory consumption and probably crashing the switch.

The Spanning Tree Protocol is the protocol that builds a L2 loop-free topology in an environment by temporarily blocking traffic on specific ports. The Spanning Tree Protocol has multiple iterations:

- 802.1D is the original specification
- Per-VLAN Spanning Tree (PVST)
- Per-VLAN Spanning Tree Plus (PVST+)
- 802.1W Rapid Spanning Tree Protocol (RSTP)
- 802.1S Multiple Spanning Tree Protocol (MST)

Nexus switches operate as RSTP or MST mode only. Both of these are backward compatible with 802.1D standards.

IEEE 802.1D Spanning Tree Protocol

The original version of STP comes from the IEEE 802.1D standards and provides support for ensuring a loop-free topology for one VLAN. In the Spanning Tree Protocol, every port transitions through a series of the following states:

- **Disabled:** The port is in an administratively off position (that is, **shutdown**).
- **Blocking:** The switch port is enabled, but the port is not forwarding any traffic to ensure a loop is created. The switch does not modify the MAC address table. It can only receive Bridge Protocol Data Units (BPDU) from other switches.
- **Listening:** The switch port has transitioned from a blocking state and can now send or receive BPDUs. It cannot forward any other network traffic.
- **Learning:** The switch port can now modify the MAC address table with any network traffic that it receives. The switch still does not forward any other network traffic besides BPDUs. The switch port transitions into this state after the *forward delay* has expired.
- **Forwarding:** The switch port can forward all network traffic and can update the MAC address table as expected. This is the final state for a switch port to forward network traffic.
- **Broken:** The switch has detected a configuration or operational problem on a port that can have major effects. The port will discard packets for as long as the problem continues to exist.

The original Spanning Tree Protocol defined the following three port types:

- **Designated port:** A network port that receives and forwards frames to other switches. Designated ports provide connectivity to downstream devices and switches.
- **Root port:** A network port that connects to the root switch or an upstream switch in the spanning-tree topology.
- **Blocking port:** A network that is not forwarding traffic because of Spanning Tree Protocol.

Within the Spanning Tree Protocol are a couple key terms that must be understood:

- **Root bridge:** The root bridge is the most important switch in the L2 topology. All ports are in a forwarding state. This switch is considered the top of the spanning-tree for all path calculations by other switches. All ports on the root bridge are categorized as designated ports.

- **Bridge Protocol Data Unit (BPDU):** This network frame is used strictly for detecting the STP topology so that switches can identify the root bridge, root ports, designated ports, and blocking ports. The BPDU consists of the following fields: STP Type, Root Path Cost, Root Bridge Identifier, Local Bridge Identifier, Max Age, Hello Time, Forward Delay. The BPDU uses a destination MAC address of 01:80:c2:00:00:00.

- **Root Path Cost:** The combination of the cost for a specific path toward the root switch.

- **Root Bridge Identifier:** Combination of the root bridge system MAC, system-ID extension, and system priority of the root bridge.

- **Local Bridge Identifier:** Combination of the advertising switch's bridge system MAC, System ID extension, and system priority of the root bridge.

- **Max Age:** The timer the controls the maximum length of time that passes before a bridge port saves its BPDU information. On Nexus switches, this is relevant for backward compatibility with switches using traditional 802.1D STP.

- **Hello Time:** The time that a BPDU is advertised out of a port. The default value is 2 seconds and is configured to a value of 1 to 10 seconds with the command **spanning-tree vlan** *vlan-id* **hello-time** *hello-time*.

- **Forward Delay:** The amount of time that a port stays in a listening and learning state. The default value is 15 seconds and can be changed to a value of 15 to 30 seconds with the command **spanning-tree vlan** *vlan-id* **forward-time** *forward-time*.

Note A lot of STP terminology uses the term bridge, even though STP runs on switches. The term bridge and switch are interchangeable in this context.

Rapid Spanning Tree Protocol

802.1 D (the first version of Spanning Tree Protocol) created only one topology tree. For larger environments with multiple VLANs, creating different Spanning Tree Protocol topologies allowed for different VLANs to use different links. Cisco created *Per-VLAN Spanning Tree (PVST)* and *Per-VLAN Spanning Tree Plus (PVST+)* to allow for such flexibility.

PVST and PVST+ were proprietary spanning protocols. The concepts in these protocols were incorporated with other enhancements to form the IEEE 802.1W specification. The 802.1Q specification incorporated additional enhancements to provide faster convergence and is called *Rapid Spanning Tree Protocol (RSTP)*.

RSTP defines the following port roles:

- **Designated port:** A network port that receives and forwards frames to other switches. Designated ports provide connectivity to downstream devices and switches.

- **Root port:** (RP) A network port that connects to the root switch or an upstream switch in the spanning-tree topology.
- **Alternate port:** A network port that provides alternate connectivity toward the root switch via a different switch.
- **Backup port:** A network port that provides link redundancy toward the current root switch. The backup port cannot guarantee connectivity to the root bridge in the event the upstream switch fails. A backup port exists only when multiple links connect between the same switches.

With RSTP protocol, switches exchange handshakes with other switches to transition through the following Spanning Tree Protocol states faster:

- **Discarding:** The switch port is enabled, but the port is not forwarding any traffic to ensure a loop is created. This state combines the traditional Spanning Tree Protocol states of Disabled, Blocking, and Listening.
- **Learning:** The switch port now modifies the MAC address table with any network traffic that it receives. The switch still does not forward any other network traffic besides BPDUs.
- **Forwarding:** The switch port forwards all network traffic and updates the MAC address table as expected. This is the final state for a switch port to forward network traffic.

Note A switch tries to establish an RSTP handshake with the device connected to the port. If a handshake does not occur, the other device is assumed to be non-RSTP compatible, and the port defaults to regular 802.1D behavior. This means that host devices such as computers and printers still encounter a significant transmission delay (~50 seconds) after the network link is established.

Note RSTP is enabled by default for any L2 switch port with a basic configuration. Additional configuration can be applied to the switch to further tune RSTP.

Spanning-Tree Path Cost

The interface Spanning Tree Protocol cost is an essential component for root path calculation because the root path is found based upon the cumulative interface Spanning Tree Protocol cost to reach the root bridge. The interface Spanning Tree Protocol cost is associated based upon a reference value of 20 Gbps. Table 4-2 displays a list of interface speeds and the correlating interface Spanning Tree Protocol cost.

Table 4-2 *Default Interface Spanning Tree Protocol Port Costs*

Link Speed	Interface Spanning Tree Protocol Cost
10 Mbps	100
100 Mbps	19
1 Gbps	4
10 Gbps	2
20 Gbps or faster	1

Root Bridge Election

The first step with Spanning Tree Protocol is to identify the root bridge. As a switch initializes, it assumes that it is the root bridge and uses the local bridge identifier as the root bridge identifier. It then listens to its neighbor's BPDU and does the following:

- If the neighbor's BPDU is inferior to its own BPDU, the switch ignores that BPDU.

- If the neighbor's BPDU is preferred to its own BPDU, the switch updates its BPDUs to include the new root bridge identifier along with a new root path cost that correlates the total path cost to reach the new root bridge. This process continues until all switches in a topology have identified the root bridge switch.

Spanning Tree Protocol deems a switch more preferable if the priority in the bridge identifier is lower than other BPDUs. If the priority is the same, the switch prefers the BPDU with the lower system MAC.

Note Generally, older switches have a lower MAC address and are considered more preferable. Configuration changes can be made for optimizing placement of the root switch in a L2 topology.

Figure 4-4 provides a simple topology to demonstrate some important spanning-tree concepts. In this topology, NX-1, NX-2, NX-3, NX-4, and NX-5 all connect to each other. The configuration on all the switches do not include any customizations for Spanning Tree Protocol, and the focus is primarily on VLAN 1, but VLANs 10, 20, and 30 exist in the topology. NX-1 has been identified as the root bridge because its system MAC address (5e00.4000.0007) is the lowest in the topology.

The root bridge is identified with the command **show spanning-tree root**. Example 4-19 demonstrates the command being executed on NX-1. The output includes the VLAN number, root bridge identifier, root path cost, hello time, max age time, and forwarding delay. Because NX-1 is the root bridge, all ports are designated, so the Root Port field displays *This bridge is root*.

Spanning Tree Protocol Fundamentals 223

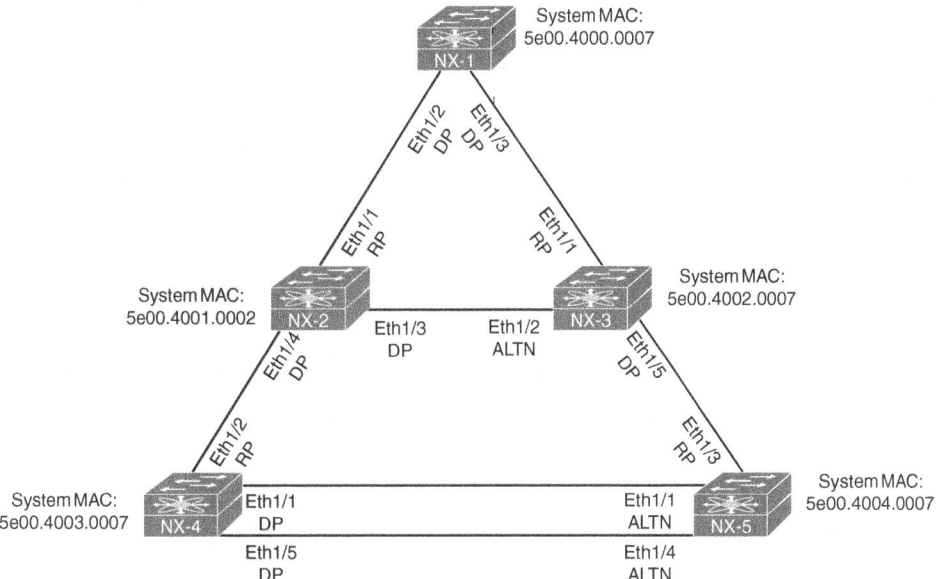

Figure 4-4 *Basic Spanning Tree Protocol Topology*

Example 4-19 *Verification of Spanning Tree Protocol Root Bridge*

```
NX-1# show spanning-tree root
                                Root  Hello Max Fwd
Vlan               Root ID      Cost  Time  Age Dly  Root Port
----------------   --------------------  -------  -----  ---  ---  ----------------
VLAN0001           32769 5e00.4000.0007     0     2    20  15   This bridge is root
VLAN0010           32778 5e00.4000.0007     0     2    20  15   This bridge is root
VLAN0020           32788 5e00.4000.0007     0     2    20  15   This bridge is root
VLAN0030           32798 5e00.4000.0007     0     2    20  15   This bridge is root
```

The same command is run on NX-2 and NX-3 with the output displayed in Example 4-20. The Root ID field is the same as NX-1; however, the root path cost has changed to 2 because both switches must use the 10 Gbps link to reach NX-1. Eth 1/1 has been identified on both of these switches as the root port.

Example 4-20 *Identification of Root Ports*

```
NX-2# show spanning-tree root
                                Root  Hello Max Fwd
Vlan               Root ID      Cost  Time  Age Dly  Root Port
----------------   --------------------  -------  -----  ---  ---  ----------------
VLAN0001           32769 5e00.4000.0007     2     2    20  15       Ethernet1/1
VLAN0010           32778 5e00.4000.0007     2     2    20  15       Ethernet1/1
```

```
VLAN0020            32788 5e00.4000.0007    2   2   20  15      Ethernet1/1
VLAN0030            32798 5e00.4000.0007    2   2   20  15      Ethernet1/1
```

```
NX-3# show spanning-tree root
                                    Root  Hello Max Fwd
Vlan                Root ID         Cost  Time  Age Dly  Root Port
---------------     --------------------  ------ ----- --- ---  ----------------
VLAN0001            32769 5e00.4000.0007    2   2   20  15      Ethernet1/1
VLAN0010            32778 5e00.4000.0007    2   2   20  15      Ethernet1/1
VLAN0020            32788 5e00.4000.0007    2   2   20  15      Ethernet1/1
VLAN0030            32798 5e00.4000.0007    2   2   20  15      Ethernet1/1
```

Locating Root Ports

After the switches have identified the root bridge, they must determine their *Root Port (RP)*. The root bridge continues to advertise BPDUs out all of its ports. The switch compares the BPDU information to identify the RP. The RP is selected using the following logic: (The next criteria is used if there is a tie.)

1. The interface associated to lowest path cost is more preferred.

2. The interface associated to the lowest system priority of the advertising switch.

3. The interface associated to the lowest system MAC address of the advertising switch.

4. When multiple links are associated to the same switch, the lowest port priority from the advertising router is preferred.

5. When multiple links are associated to the same switch, the lower port number from the advertising router is preferred.

The command **show spanning-tree root** is run on NX-4 and NX-5 with the output displayed in Example 4-21. The Root ID field is the same as NX-1 from Example 4-20; however, the root path cost has changed to 4 because both switches must traverse two 10 Gbps link to reach NX-1. Eth1/3 was identified as the RP on both switches.

Example 4-21 *Identification of Root Ports on NX-4 and NX-5*

```
NX-4# show spanning-tree root
                                    Root  Hello Max Fwd
Vlan                Root ID         Cost  Time  Age Dly  Root Port
---------------     --------------------  ------ ----- --- ---  ----------------
VLAN0001            32769 5e00.4000.0007    4   2   20  15      Ethernet1/3

NX-5# show spanning-tree root
```

```
                                  Root  Hello Max Fwd
Vlan                 Root ID      Cost  Time  Age Dly  Root Port
---------------- -------------------- ------- ----- --- ---  ----------------
VLAN0001         32769 5e00.4000.0007     4     2   20  15   Ethernet1/3
```

Locating Blocked Switch Ports

Now that the root bridge and RPs are identified, all other ports are considered designated ports. However, if two switches are connected to each other on their designated ports, one of those switch ports must be set to a blocking state to prevent a forwarding loop. The logic to calculate which ports should be blocked between the two switches is the following:

1. The interface must not be considered as a RP.

2. The system priority of the local switch is compared to the system priority of the remote switch. The local port is moved to a blocking state if the remote system priority is lower than the local switch.

3. The system MAC address of the local switch is compared to the system priority of the remote switch. The local port is moved to a blocking state if the remote system MAC address is lower than the local switch.

Note Step 3 is the last step of the selection process. If a switch has multiple links toward the root switch, the downstream switch always identifies the RP. All other ports will match the criteria for Step 2 or Step 3 and are placed into a blocking state.

The command **show spanning-tree** [**vlan** *vlan-id*] is used to provide useful information for locating a port's Spanning Tree Protocol state. Example 4-22 displays NX-1's Spanning Tree Protocol information for VLAN 1. The first portion of the output displays the relevant root bridge's information, which is then followed by the local bridge's information. The associated interface's Spanning Tree Protocol port cost, port priority, and port type are displayed as well. All of NX-1's ports are designated ports (Desg) because it is the root bridge.

There are three port types expected on NX-OS switches:

- **Point-to-Point (P2P):** This port type connects with another network device (PC or RSTP switch).

- **P2P Peer (STP):** This port type detects that it is connected to an 802.1D switch and is operating with backward compatibility.

- **Network P2P:** This port type is specifically configured to connect with another RSTP switch and to provide *bridge assurance*.

- **Edge P2P:** This port type is specifically configured to connect with another host device (PC, not a switch). Portfast is enabled on this port.

Example 4-22 *NX-1's Spanning Tree Protocol Information*

```
NX-1# show spanning-tree vlan 1

VLAN0001
  Spanning tree enabled protocol rstp
! The section displays the relevant information for the STP Root Bridge
  Root ID    Priority    32769
             Address     5e00.4000.0007
             This bridge is the root
             Hello Time  2  sec  Max Age 20 sec  Forward Delay 15 sec
! The section displays the relevant information for the Local STP Bridge
  Bridge ID  Priority    32769  (priority 32768 sys-id-ext 1)
             Address     5e00.4000.0007
             Hello Time  2  sec  Max Age 20 sec  Forward Delay 15 sec


Interface        Role Sts Cost      Prio.Nbr Type
---------------- ---- --- --------- -------- --------------------------------
Eth1/1           Desg FWD 2         128.1    P2p
Eth1/2           Desg FWD 2         128.2    P2p
Eth1/3           Desg FWD 2         128.3    P2p
```

Note If the Type field includes *TYPE_Inc –*, this indicates a port configuration mismatch between the Nexus switch and the switch to which it is connected. It is either the port type, or the port mode (access versus trunk) is misconfigured.

Example 4-23 displays the Spanning Tree Protocol topology from NX-2 and NX-3. Notice that in the first root bridge section, the output provides the total root path cost and the port on the switch that is identified as the RP.

All the ports on NX-2 are in a forwarding state, but port Eth1/2 on NX-3 is in a blocking (BLK) state. Specifically, that port has been designated as an alternate port to reach the root in the event that Eth1/1 connection fails.

The reason that NX-3's Eth1/2 port was placed into a blocking state versus NX-2's Eth1/3 port is that NX-2's system MAC address (5e00.4001.0007) is lower than NX-3's system MAC address (5e00.4002.0007). This was deduced by looking at the Figure 4-4 and the system MAC addresses in the output.

Example 4-23 *Verification of Root and Blocking Ports for a VLAN*

```
NX-2# show spanning-tree vlan 1

VLAN0001
  Spanning tree enabled protocol rstp
  Root ID    Priority    32769
```

```
                Address         5e00.4000.0007
                Cost            2
                Port            1 (Ethernet1/1)
                Hello Time  2  sec  Max Age 20 sec  Forward Delay 15 sec

  Bridge ID   Priority     32769  (priority 32768 sys-id-ext 1)
              Address      5e00.4001.0007
              Hello Time  2  sec  Max Age 20 sec  Forward Delay 15 sec


Interface         Role Sts Cost      Prio.Nbr Type
---------------- ---- --- --------- -------- --------------------------------
Eth1/1           Root FWD 2         128.1    P2p
Eth1/3           Desg FWD 2         128.3    P2p
Eth1/4           Desg FWD 2         128.4    P2p


NX-3# show spanning-tree vlan 1
! Output omitted for brevity

  Bridge ID   Priority     32769  (priority 32768 sys-id-ext 1)
              Address      5e00.4002.0007
              Hello Time  2  sec  Max Age 20 sec  Forward Delay 15 sec


Interface         Role Sts Cost      Prio.Nbr Type
---------------- ---- --- --------- -------- --------------------------------
Eth1/1           Root FWD 2         128.1    P2p
Eth1/2           Altn BLK 2         128.2    P2p
Eth1/5           Desg FWD 2         128.5    P2p
```

Verification of VLANS on Trunk Links

All the interfaces that participate in that VLAN are listed in the output of the command **show spanning-tree**. This can be a daunting task for trunk ports that carry multiple VLANs. This can quickly be checked by examining the Spanning Tree Protocol state of the interface with the command **show spanning-tree interface** *interface-id* as shown in Example 4-24. If a VLAN is missing on a trunk port, check the allowed VLANs for that trunk interface, because that VLAN is probably missing from the list.

Example 4-24 *Viewing VLANs Participating with Spanning Tree Protocol on an Interface*

```
NX-1# show spanning-tree interface e1/1
Vlan              Role Sts Cost      Prio.Nbr Type
---------------- ---- --- --------- -------- --------------------------------
VLAN0001         Desg FWD 2         128.1    P2p
VLAN0010         Desg FWD 2         128.1    P2p
VLAN0020         Desg FWD 2         128.1    P2p
VLAN0030         Desg FWD 2         128.1    P2p
```

Spanning Tree Protocol Tuning

A properly designed network strategically places the root bridge on a specific switch and modifies which ports should be designated ports (that is, forwarding state) and which ports should be alternate ports (that is, discarding/blocking state). Design considerations factor in hardware platform, resiliency, and network topology.

Root Bridge Placement

Ideally, the root bridge is placed on a core switch, and a secondary root bridge is designated to minimize changes to the overall spanning tree. Root bridge placement is accomplished by lowering the system priority on the root bridge to the lowest value possible, the secondary root bridge to a value slightly higher than the root bridge, and ideally increasing the system priority on all other switches. This ensures a consistent placement of the root bridge. The priority is set with either of the following commands:

- **spanning-tree vlan** *vlan-id* **priority** *priority*

    The priority is a value between 0–61,440 in increments of 4,096.

- **spanning-tree vlan** *vlan-id* **root {primary | secondary}**

    Selecting the **primary** keyword sets the priority to 24,576 and the **secondary** keyword sets the priority to 28,672.

Note The best way to prevent erroneous devices from taking over the root role is to set the priority to zero on the desired root bridge switch.

Example 4-25 demonstrates NX-1 being set as the root primary and NX-2 being set as the root secondary. Notice on NX-2's output that it displays the root system priority, which is different from its system priority.

Example 4-25 *Changing the Spanning Tree Protocol System Priority*

```
NX-1(config)# spanning-tree vlan 1 root primary
NX-2(config)# spanning-tree vlan 1 root secondary
```

```
NX-1(config)# do show spanning-tree vlan 1
! Output omitted for brevity
VLAN0001
  Spanning tree enabled protocol rstp
  Root ID    Priority    24577
             Address     5e00.4000.0007
             This bridge is the root

  Bridge ID  Priority    24577  (priority 24576 sys-id-ext 1)
```

```
                Address      5e00.4000.0007

NX-2# show spanning-tree vlan 1
! Output omitted for brevity
VLAN0001
  Spanning tree enabled protocol rstp
  Root ID    Priority    24577
             Address     5e00.4000.0007
             Cost        2
             Port        1 (Ethernet1/1)

  Bridge ID  Priority    28673   (priority 28672 sys-id-ext 1)
             Address     5e00.4001.0007
```

Note Notice that the priority on NX-1 is off by one. That is because the priority in the BPDU packets is the priority plus the value of the Sys-Id-Ext (which is the VLAN number). So the priority for VLAN 1 is 24,577, and the priority for VLAN 10 is 24,586.

Root Guard

Root guard is a Spanning-Tree Protocol feature that prevents a configured port from becoming a root port by placing a port in ErrDisabled state if a superior BPDU is received on a configured port. Root guard prevents a downstream switch (often misconfigured or rogue) from becoming a root bridge in a topology.

Root guard is enabled on an interface-by-interface basis with the interface command **spanning-tree guard root**. Root guard is placed on designated ports toward other switches that should never ever become a root bridge. In the sample topology, root guard should be placed on NX-2's Eth1/4 port and NX3-'s Eth1/5 port. This prevents NX-4 and NX-5 from ever becoming a root bridge, but still allows for NX-2 to maintain connectivity to NX-1 via NX-3 in the event that the NX-1 ← → NX-2 link becomes incapacitated.

Modifying Spanning Tree Protocol Root Port and Blocked Switch Port Locations

The Spanning Tree Protocol port cost is used for calculating the Spanning Tree Protocol tree. When a switch generates the BPDUs, the total path cost includes only its calculated metric to the root and does not include the port cost that the BPDU is advertised out of. The receiving router then adds the port cost on the interface the BPDU was received in conjunction with the value of the total path cost in the BPDU.

In Figure 4-4, NX-1 advertises its BPDUs to NX-3 with a total path cost of zero. NX-3 receives the BPDU and adds its Spanning Tree Protocol port cost of 2 to the total path cost in the BPDU (zero), resulting in a value of 2. NX-3 then advertises the BPDU toward NX-5 with a total path cost of 2, which NX-5 then adds to its ports cost of 2. NX-5 reports a cost of 4 to reach the root bridge via NX-3. The logic is confirmed in the output of Example 4-26. Notice that there is not a total path cost in NX-1's output.

Example 4-26 *Verification of Total Path Cost*

```
NX-1# show spanning-tree vlan 1
! Output omitted for brevity
VLAN0001
  Spanning tree enabled protocol rstp
  Root ID    Priority    32769
             Address     5e00.4000.0007
             This bridge is the root
             Hello Time   2 sec  Max Age 20 sec  Forward Delay 15 sec

  Bridge ID  Priority    32769  (priority 32768 sys-id-ext 1)
             Address     5e00.4000.0007

Interface        Role Sts Cost      Prio.Nbr Type
---------------- ---- --- --------- -------- --------------------------------
Eth1/1           Desg FWD 2         128.1    P2p
Eth1/2           Desg FWD 2         128.2    P2p
Eth1/3           Desg FWD 2         128.3    P2p

NX-3# show spanning-tree vlan 1
! Output omitted for brevity
VLAN0001
  Spanning tree enabled protocol rstp
  Root ID    Priority    32769
             Address     5e00.4000.0007
             Cost        2

  Bridge ID  Priority    32769  (priority 32768 sys-id-ext 1)
             Address     5e00.4002.0007

Interface        Role Sts Cost      Prio.Nbr Type
---------------- ---- --- --------- -------- --------------------------------
Eth1/1           Root FWD 2         128.1    P2p
Eth1/2           Altn BLK 2         128.2    P2p
Eth1/5           Desg FWD 2         128.5    P2p

NX-5# show spanning-tree vlan 1
! Output omitted for brevity
VLAN0001
  Spanning tree enabled protocol rstp
  Root ID    Priority    32769
             Address     5e00.4000.0007
             Cost        4
```

```
   Bridge ID  Priority    32769  (priority 32768 sys-id-ext 1)
             Address     5e00.4004.0007

Interface        Role Sts Cost      Prio.Nbr Type
---------------- ---- --- --------- -------- --------------------------------
Eth1/1           Altn BLK 2         128.1    P2p
Eth1/3           Root FWD 2         128.3    P2p
Eth1/4           Altn BLK 2         128.4    P2p
```

The interface path is modified to impact which ports are designated or alternate ports with the interface configuration command **spanning tree** [**vlan** *vlan-id*] **cost** *cost*. This is set up for all VLANs by omitting the optional **vlan** keyword, or for a specific VLAN.

Example 4-27 demonstrates the modification of NX-3's port cost for Eth1/1, which ultimately impacts the Spanning Tree Protocol topology because the Eth1/2 port is no longer an alternate port, but is now a designated port. NX-2's Eth1/3 port changed from a designated port to an alternate port.

Example 4-27 *Modification of Spanning Tree Protocol Port Cost*

```
NX-3(config)# interface ethernet 1/1
NX-3(config-if)# spanning-tree cost 1

NX-3# show spanning-tree vlan 1
! Output omitted for brevity
VLAN0001
  Root ID    Priority    32769
             Address     5e00.4000.0007
             Cost        1
             Port        1 (Ethernet1/1)


  Bridge ID  Priority    32769  (priority 32768 sys-id-ext 1)
             Address     5e00.4002.0007

Interface        Role Sts Cost      Prio.Nbr Type
---------------- ---- --- --------- -------- --------------------------------
Eth1/1           Root FWD 1         128.1    P2p
Eth1/2           Desg FWD 2         128.2    P2p
Eth1/5           Desg FWD 2         128.5    P2p

NX-2# show span vlan 1
! Output omitted for brevity
VLAN0001
  Root ID    Priority    32769
             Address     5e00.4000.0007
             Cost        2
             Port        1 (Ethernet1/1)
```

```
  Bridge ID  Priority    32769  (priority 32768 sys-id-ext 1)
             Address     5e00.4001.0007

Interface        Role Sts Cost      Prio.Nbr  Type
---------------- ---- --- --------- --------  ------------
Eth1/1           Root FWD 2         128.1     P2p
Eth1/3           Altn BLK 2         128.3     P2p
Eth1/4           Desg FWD 2         128.4     P2p
```

Modifying Spanning Tree Protocol Port Priority

The Spanning Tree Protocol port priority impacts which port is an alternate port when multiple links are used between switches. In Figure 4-4, there are two links between NX-4 and NX-5. The Spanning Tree Protocol port cost on Eth1/3 (which connects to NX-3) was modified to 1,234 so that one of the two links connecting to NX-4 is the RP.

Example 4-28 verifies that this change has made NX-5's Eth1/1 the RP toward NX-4. Remember that system-Id and port cost is the same, so the next check is port priority and then followed by the port number. Both the port priority and port number are controlled by the upstream switch.

Example 4-28 *Viewing a Spanning Tree Protocol Port Priority*

```
NX-5# show spanning-tree vlan 1
! Output omitted for brevity
VLAN0001

Interface        Role Sts Cost      Prio.Nbr  Type
---------------- ---- --- --------- --------  ------------
Eth1/1           Root FWD 2         128.1     P2p
Eth1/3           Altn BLK 1234      128.3     P2p
Eth1/4           Altn BLK 2         128.4     P2p
```

Modify the port priority on NX-4 with the command **spanning-tree** [**vlan** *vlan-id*] **port-priority** *priority*. The optional **vlan** keyword allows changing the priority on a VLAN-by-VLAN basis. Example 4-29 displays changing the port priority on NX-4's Eth1/5 port to 64, and the impact it has on NX-5. Notice how NX5's Eth1/4 port is now the RP.

Example 4-29 *Verification of Port Priority Impact on a Spanning Tree Protocol Topology*

```
NX-4(config)# int eth1/5
NX-4(config-if)# spanning-tree port-priority 64
```

```
NX-4# show spanning-tree vlan 1
! Output omitted for brevity
VLAN0001
```

```
Interface        Role Sts Cost      Prio.Nbr Type
---------------- ---- --- ---------- -------- --------------------------------
Eth1/1           Desg FWD 2          128.1    P2p
Eth1/2           Root FWD 2          128.2    P2p
Eth1/5           Desg FWD 2          64.5     P2p

NX-5# show spanning-tree vlan 1
! Output omitted for brevity
VLAN0001
Interface        Role Sts Cost      Prio.Nbr Type
---------------- ---- --- ---------- -------- --------------------------------
Eth1/1           Altn BLK 2          128.1    P2p
Eth1/3           Altn BLK 1234       128.3    P2p
Eth1/4           Root FWD 2          64.4     P2p
```

Topology Changes and Spanning Tree Protocol Portfast

In a Spanning-Tree Protocol topology, BPDUs traditionally flow from the root bridge toward the edge switches. Under normal operating conditions, BPDUs are not sent toward the root bridge. However, when a link becomes active or inactive, the change in topology has an impact to all the switches in the L2 topology.

The switch that detects the link status change sends a *topology change notification (TCN)* toward the root bridge. The root bridge creates a new TCN, which is then flooded toward all the switches in the L2 forwarding domain. Upon receipt of the root bridge's TCN, all switches flush their MAC address table. This results in traffic being flooded out all ports while the MAC address table is rebuilt. Remember that hosts communicate using CSMA/CD, so this behavior causes a delay in communication while the switch rebuilds its MAC address table.

TCNs are generated on a VLAN basis, so the impact of TCNs directly correlate to the number of hosts in a VLAN. As the number of hosts increase, the more likely the frequency of TCN generation occurs and the more hosts that are impacted by the broadcasts. Topology changes should be checked as part of the troubleshooting process.

Topology changes are seen with the command **show spanning-tree [vlan** *vlan-id*] **detail** on the root bridge. In the output, examine the topology change count and time since the last change has occurred. A sudden or continuous increase in TCNs indicates a potential problem and should be investigated further.

Example 4-30 displays the output of the **show spanning-tree vlan 10 detail** command. Notice that the time since the last TCN was detected in and the interface that the TCN originated from is included. The next step is to locate the switch that is connected to the port causing the TCN. This is found by looking at CDP tables or your network documentation. The **show spanning-tree [vlan** *vlan-id*] **detail** is executed again to find the last switch in the topology to identify the problematic port.

Example 4-30 *Viewing the Detailed Version of Spanning-Tree State*

```
NX-1# show spanning-tree vlan 10 detail
 VLAN0010 is executing the rstp compatible Spanning Tree protocol
  Bridge Identifier has priority 32768, sysid 10, address 5e00.4000.0007
  Configured hello time 2, max age 20, forward delay 15
  We are the root of the spanning tree
  Topology change flag set, detected flag not set
  Number of topology changes 11 last change occurred 0:00:04 ago
          from Ethernet1/2
  Times:  hold 1, topology change 35, notification 2
          hello 2, max age 20, forward delay 15
  Timers: hello 0, topology change 30, notification 0
..
```

Viewing the NX-OS event-history provides another insight to the Spanning Tree Protocol activities on a switch. The Spanning Tree Protocol event-history is displayed with the command **show spanning-tree internal event-history all** as demonstrated in Example 4-31.

Example 4-31 *Viewing Spanning Tree Protocol Event-History*

```
NX-1# show spanning-tree internal event-history all
------------------- All the active STPs -----------
VDC01 VLAN0001
0) Transition at 917636 usecs after Tue Aug 29 02:31:43 2017
      Root: 0000.0000.0000.0000 Cost: 0 Age:   0 Root Port: none Port: none
      [STP_TREE_EV_UP]

1) Transition at 703663 usecs after Tue Aug 29 02:31:44 2017
      Root: 7001.885a.92de.617c Cost: 0 Age:   0 Root Port: none Port: Ethernet1/51
      [STP_TREE_EV_MULTI_FLUSH_RCVD]

2) Transition at 723529 usecs after Tue Aug 29 02:31:44 2017
      Root: 7001.885a.92de.617c Cost: 0 Age:   0 Root Port: none Port: Ethernet1/51
      [STP_TREE_EV_MULTI_FLUSH_RCVD]

3) Transition at 609383 usecs after Tue Aug 29 02:31:45 2017
      Root: 7001.885a.92de.617c Cost: 0 Age:   0 Root Port: none Port: Ethernet1/51
      [STP_TREE_EV_MULTI_FLUSH_RCVD]

4) Transition at 601588 usecs after Tue Aug 29 02:31:47 2017
      Root: 7001.885a.92de.617c Cost: 0 Age:   0 Root Port: none Port: none
      [STP_TREE_EV_DOWN]
```

The generation of TCN for hosts does not make sense because they generally have only one connection to the network. Restricting TCN creation to only ports that connect with other switches and network devices increases the L2 network's stability and efficiency. The Spanning Tree Protocol *portfast* feature disables TCN generation for access ports.

Another benefit of the Spanning Tree Protocol portfast feature is that the access ports bypass the earlier 802.1D Spanning Tree Protocol states (learning and listening) and forward traffic immediately. This is beneficial in environments where computers use dynamic host configuration protocol (DHCP) or preboot execution environment (PXE).

The portfast feature is enabled on a specific port with the command **spanning-tree port type edge**, or globally on all access ports with the command **spanning-tree port type edge default**.

Example 4-32 demonstrates enabling portfast for NX-1's Eth1/6 port along with its verification. Notice how the portfast ports are displayed with *Edge P2P*. The last section demonstrates how portfasts are enabled globally for all access ports.

Example 4-32 *Spanning Tree Protocol Portfast Enablement*

```
NX-1(config-if)# int eth1/6
NX-1(config-if)# spanning-tree port type edge
Warning: Edge port type (portfast) should only be enabled on ports connected to
 a single host. Connecting hubs, concentrators, switches, bridges, etc... to this
 interface  when edge port type (portfast) is enabled, can cause temporary
 bridging loops.
Use with CAUTION

NX-1# show spanning-tree vlan 1
! Output omitted for brevity
VLAN0001
  Spanning tree enabled protocol rstp
  Root ID    Priority    32769
             Address     5e00.4000.0007
             This bridge is the root
             Hello Time  2  sec  Max Age 20 sec  Forward Delay 15 sec

  Bridge ID  Priority    32769  (priority 32768 sys-id-ext 1)
             Address     5e00.4000.0007

Interface        Role Sts Cost      Prio.Nbr Type
---------------- ---- --- --------- -------- --------------------------------
Eth1/1           Desg FWD 2         128.1    P2p
Eth1/2           Desg FWD 2         128.2    P2p
Eth1/3           Desg FWD 2         128.3    P2p
Eth1/4           Desg FWD 2         128.3    P2p
Eth1/5           Desg FWD 2         128.3    P2p
Eth1/6           Desg FWD 2         128.3    Edge P2p
NX-1(config)# spanning-tree port type edge default
```

Multiple Spanning-Tree Protocol (MST)

In environments with thousands of VLANs, maintaining a Spanning Tree Protocol state for all the VLANs can become a burden to the switch's processors. MST provides a blended approach by placing multiple VLANs on to a single Spanning Tree Protocol tree, called an *MST instance*. Traffic engineering is performed by modifying MST instance parameters versus modifying parameters on a VLAN-by-VLAN basis.

MST Configuration

MST is configured by the following process:

Step 1. Set the Spanning Tree Protocol mode as MST. Define MST as the spanning-tree protocol with the command **spanning-tree mode mst**.

Step 2. Define the MST instance priority (optional). The MST instance priority is set to a MST region by one of two methods:

- **spanning-tree mst** *instance-number* **priority** *priority*

    The priority is a value between 0-61,440 in increments of 4,096

- **spanning-tree mst** *instance-number* **root** {**primary** | **secondary**}

    Selecting the **primary** keyword sets the priority to 24,576 and the **secondary** keyword sets the priority to 28,672

Step 3. Associate VLANs to an MST instance. By default all VLANs are associated to the MST 0 instance. The MST configuration submode must be entered with the command **spanning-tree mst configuration**. Then the VLANs are assigned to a different MST instance with the command **instance** *instance-number* **vlan** *vlan-id*.

Step 4. Specify the MST version number. The MST version number must match for all switches in the same MST region. The MST version number is configured with the submode configuration command **revision** *version*.

Step 5. Define the MST region name (optional). MST regions are recognized by switches that share a common name. By default, a region name is an empty string. The MST region name is set with the command **name** *mst-region-name*.

Example 4-33 demonstrates the MST configuration on NX-1. MST instance 2 contains VLAN 30, MST instance 1 contains VLANs 10 and 20, and MST instance zero contains all other VLANs.

Example 4-33 *Sample MST Configuration on NX-1*

```
NX-1(config)# spanning-tree mode mst
NX-1(config)# spanning-tree mst 0 root primary
NX-1(config)# spanning-tree mst 1 root primary
NX-1(config)# spanning-tree mst 2 root primary
NX-1(config)# spanning-tree mst configuration
```

```
NX-1(config-mst)#    name NX-OS
NX-1(config-mst)#    revision 3
NX-1(config-mst)#    instance 1 vlan 10,20
NX-1(config-mst)#    instance 2 vlan 30
```

The command **show spanning-tree mst configuration** provides a quick verification of the MST configuration on a switch. Example 4-34 demonstrates the output. Notice that MST instance zero contains all VLANs, except for VLANs 10, 20, and 30, regardless of whether those VLANs are configured on the switch.

Example 4-34 *Verification of MST Configuration*

```
NX-2# show spanning-tree mst configuration
Name        [NX-OS]
Revision    3       Instances configured 3
Instance    Vlans mapped
--------    ---------------------------------------------------------------
0           1-9,11-19,21-29,31-4094
1           10,20
2           30
```

MST Verification

The relevant spanning tree information can still be obtained with the command **show spanning-tree**. The primary difference is that the VLAN numbers are not shown, but the MST instance is provided instead. As well, the priority value for a switch is the MST instance plus the switch priority. Example 4-35 displays the output of this command.

Example 4-35 *Brief Review of MST Status*

```
NX-1# show spanning-tree
! Output omitted for brevity
! Spanning Tree information for Instance 0 (All VLANs but 10,20, and 30)
MST0000
  Spanning tree enabled protocol mstp
  Root ID    Priority    0
             Address     5e00.0000.0007
             This bridge is the root
             Hello Time  2  sec  Max Age 20 sec  Forward Delay 15 sec

  Bridge ID  Priority    32768    (priority 32768 sys-id-ext 0)
             Address     5e00.0000.0007
             Hello Time  2  sec  Max Age 20 sec  Forward Delay 15 sec

Interface        Role Sts Cost      Prio.Nbr Type
---------------- ---- --- --------- -------- --------------------------------
Eth1/1           Desg FWD 2         128.1    P2p
```

```
Eth1/2           Desg FWD 2          128.2    P2p
Eth1/3           Desg FWD 2          128.3    P2p

! Spanning Tree information for Instance 1 (VLANs 10 and 20)
MST0001
  Spanning tree enabled protocol mstp
  Root ID    Priority    24577
             Address     5e00.0000.0007
             This bridge is the root

  Bridge ID  Priority    32769  (priority 32768 sys-id-ext 1)
             Address     5e00.0000.0007

Interface        Role Sts Cost       Prio.Nbr Type
---------------- ---- --- ---------  -------- --------------------------------
Eth1/1           Desg FWD 2          128.1    P2p
Eth1/2           Desg FWD 2          128.2    P2p
Eth1/3           Desg FWD 2          128.3    P2p

! Spanning Tree information for Instance 0 (VLAN 30)
MST0002
  Spanning tree enabled protocol mstp
  Root ID    Priority    24578
             Address     5e00.0000.0007
             This bridge is the root
             Hello Time  2  sec  Max Age 20 sec  Forward Delay 15 sec

  Bridge ID  Priority    32770  (priority 32768 sys-id-ext 2)
             Address     5e00.0000.0007
             Hello Time  2  sec  Max Age 20 sec  Forward Delay 15 sec

Interface        Role Sts Cost       Prio.Nbr Type
---------------- ---- --- ---------  -------- --------------------------------
Eth1/1           Desg FWD 2          128.1    P2p
Eth1/2           Desg FWD 2          128.2    P2p
Eth1/3           Desg FWD 2          128.3    P2p
```

A consolidated view of the MST topology table is displayed with the command **show spanning-tree mst** [*instance-number*]. The optional *instance-number* can be included to restrict the output to a specific instance. The command is demonstrated in Example 4-36. Notice that the VLANs are displayed next to the MST instance, simplifying any steps for troubleshooting.

Example 4-36 *Granular View of MST Topology*

```
NX-1# show spanning-tree mst
! Output omitted for brevity

##### MST0    vlans mapped:   1-9,11-19,21-29,31-4094
Bridge        address 5e00.0000.0007  priority     0      (0 sysid 0)
Root          this switch for the CIST

Regional Root this switch
Operational   hello time 2 , forward delay 15, max age 20, txholdcount 6
Configured    hello time 2 , forward delay 15, max age 20, max hops    20

Interface        Role Sts Cost      Prio.Nbr Type
---------------- ---- --- --------- -------- --------------------------------
Eth1/1           Desg FWD 2         128.1    P2p
Eth1/2           Desg FWD 2         128.2    P2p
Eth1/3           Desg FWD 2         128.3    P2p


##### MST1    vlans mapped:   10,20
Bridge        address 5e00.0000.0007  priority     24577 (24576 sysid 1)
Root          this switch for MST1

Interface        Role Sts Cost      Prio.Nbr Type
---------------- ---- --- --------- -------- --------------------------------
Eth1/1           Desg FWD 2         128.1    P2p
Eth1/2           Desg FWD 2         128.2    P2p
Eth1/3           Desg FWD 2         128.3    P2p


##### MST2    vlans mapped:   30
Bridge        address 5e00.0000.0007  priority     24578 (24576 sysid 2)
Root          this switch for MST2

Interface        Role Sts Cost      Prio.Nbr Type
---------------- ---- --- --------- -------- --------------------------------
Eth1/1           Desg FWD 2         128.1    P2p
Eth1/2           Desg FWD 2         128.2    P2p
Eth1/3           Desg FWD 2         128.3    P2p
```

The specific MST settings are viewed for a specific interface with the command **show spanning-tree mst interface** *interface-id*. Example 4-37 demonstrates the command. Notice that the output also includes additional information about optional Spanning Tree Protocol features, like BPDU Filter and BPDU Guard.

Example 4-37 *Viewing Interface Specific MST Settings*

```
NX-2# show spanning-tree mst interface ethernet 1/1

Eth1/1 of MST0 is root forwarding
Port Type: normal          (default)      port guard  : none        (default)
Link type: point-to-point (auto)          bpdu filter: disable      (default)
Boundary : internal                       bpdu guard : disable      (default)
Bpdus sent 9, received 119


Instance Role Sts Cost       Prio.Nbr Vlans mapped
-------- ---- --- ---------  -------- -------------------------------
0        Root FWD 2          128.1    1-9,11-19,21-29,31-4094
1        Root FWD 2          128.1    10,20
2        Root FWD 2          128.1    30
```

MST Tuning

MST supports the tuning of port cost and port priority. The interface configuration command **spanning-tree mst** *instance-number* **cost** *cost* sets the interface cost. Example 4-38 demonstrates the configuration of NX-3's Eth1/1 port being modified to a cost of 1, and verification of the interface cost before and after the change.

Example 4-38 *Changing the MST Interface Cost*

```
NX-3# show spanning-tree mst 0
! Output omitted for brevity
Interface        Role Sts Cost      Prio.Nbr Type
---------------- ---- --- --------- -------- --------------------------------
Eth1/1           Desg FWD 2         128.1    P2p
Eth1/2           Root FWD 2         128.2    P2p
Eth1/5           Desg FWD 2         128.5    P2p
```

```
NX-3(config)# interface eth1/1
NX-3(config-if)# spanning-tree mst 0 cost 1
```

```
NX-3# show spanning-tree mst 0
! Output omitted for brevity
Interface        Role Sts Cost      Prio.Nbr Type
---------------- ---- --- --------- -------- --------------------------------
Eth1/1           Desg FWD 1         128.1    P2p
Eth1/2           Root FWD 2         128.2    P2p
Eth1/5           Desg FWD 2         128.5    P2p
```

The interface configuration command **spanning-tree mst** *instance-number* **port-priority** *priority* sets the interface priority. Example 4-39 demonstrates the configuration of

NX-4's Eth1/5 port being modified to a priority of 64, and verification of the interface priority before and after the change.

Example 4-39 *Changing the MST Interface Priority*

```
NX-4# show spanning-tree mst 0
! Output omitted for brevity
##### MST0    vlans mapped:   1-9,11-19,21-29,31-4094
Interface        Role Sts Cost      Prio.Nbr Type
---------------- ---- --- --------- -------- --------------------------------
Eth1/1           Desg FWD 2         128.1    P2p
Eth1/2           Root FWD 2         128.2    P2p
Eth1/5           Desg FWD 2         128.5    P2p
```

```
NX-4(config)# interface eth1/5
NX-4(config-if)# spanning-tree mst 0 port-priority 64
```

```
NX-4# show spanning-tree mst 0
! Output omitted for brevity
##### MST0    vlans mapped:   1-9,11-19,21-29,31-4094
Interface        Role Sts Cost      Prio.Nbr Type
---------------- ---- --- --------- -------- --------------------------------
Eth1/1           Desg FWD 2         128.1    P2p
Eth1/2           Root FWD 2         128.2    P2p
Eth1/5           Desg FWD 2          64.5    P2p
```

Detecting and Remediating Forwarding Loops

High CPU consumption and low free-memory space are common symptoms of a L2 forwarding loop. Network packets do not decrement the Time-To-Live portion of the header as a packet is forwarded in a L2 topology. In an L2 forwarding packet, besides constantly consuming switch bandwidth, the CPU spikes as well. As the packet is received on a different interface, the switch must move the MAC address from one interface to the next. Eventually the switches in the topology crash because of exhausted CPU and memory resources.

Some common scenarios for L2 forwarding loops are the following:

- Misconfigured load-balancer that transmits traffic out multiple ports with same MAC address.
- Misconfigured virtual switch that bridges two physical ports. Virtual switches typically do not participate in Spanning Tree Protocol.
- Use of a dumb network switch or hub by end users.
- Virtual Machine migration to a different physical host. (This is not an L2 loop but does display a change of MAC address between ports.)

Fortunately, NX-OS includes a couple safeguards and protection mechanisms for L2 forwarding loops.

MAC Address Notifications

The most important option is to be able to identify which packets are being looped and the interfaces that they are being looped on. Nexus switches detect the change of MAC address and notify via syslog of the MAC address move. The NX-OS MAC address notification feature is enabled by default on newer software versions, but can be manually added with the global configuration command **mac address-table notification mac-move**.

Cisco added a protection mechanism that keeps CPU utilization from increasing during a L2 forwarding loop. When the MAC address move threshold is crossed (three times back and forth across a set of ports in a 10-second interval), the Nexus switch flushes the MAC address table and stops learning MAC addresses for a specific amount of time. Packets continue to be forwarded in a loop fashion, but the CPU does not max out, and it allows for other diagnostic commands to be executed so that the situation is remediated.

Example 4-40 displays the detection of the forwarding loop on VLAN 1 and the flushing of the MAC address table.

Example 4-40 *NX-OS Detection of Forwarding Loop*

```
07:39:56 NX-1 %$ VDC-1 %$ %L2FM-2-L2FM_MAC_FLAP_DISABLE_LEARN_N3K: Loops detected
    in the network for mac 9caf.ca2e.9040 among ports Eth1/49 and Eth1/51 vlan 1 -
    Disabling dynamic learning notifications for a period between 120 and 240 sec-
    onds on vlan 1
07:39:56 NX-1 %$ VDC-1 %$ %-SLOT1-5-BCM_L2_LEARN_DISABLE: MAC Learning Disabled
    unit=0
07:42:13 NX-1 %$ VDC-1 %$ %-SLOT1-5-BCM_L2_LEARN_ENABLE: MAC Learning Enabled
    unit=0
```

NX-OS provides an enhancement to this detection and places the port in a shutdown state when it detects a flapping MAC address. This functionality is enabled with the command **mac address-table loop-detect port-down**. Example 4-41 demonstrates the configuration of this feature, an occurrence where the feature is engaged, and how the interface is confirmed to be in a down state.

Example 4-41 *Configuration of Port Down upon MAC Move Notification*

```
NX-1(config)# mac address-table loop-detect port-down
06:27:37 NX-1 %$ VDC-1 %$ %L2FM-2-L2FM_MAC_MOVE_PORT_DOWN: Loops detected in the
    network for mac 9caf.ca2e.9040 among ports Eth1/2 and Eth1/3 vlan 1 - Port Eth1/2
    Disabled on loop detection
06:27:37 NX-1 %$ VDC-1 %$ last message repeated 9 times

NX-1# show interface status
----------------------------------------------------------------------------------
```

```
Port          Name          Status          Vlan   Duplex   Speed   Type
-------------------------------------------------------------------------------
mgmt0         --            notconnec       routed auto     auto    --
Eth1/1        --            disabled        1      full     10G     10Gbase-SR
Eth1/2        --            errDisabl       1      full     10G     10Gbase-SR
Eth1/3        --            connected       1      full     10G     10Gbase-SR
```

Note Some platforms do not display the MAC notifications by default and require the following additional configuration commands:

```
logging level spanning-tree 6
logging level fwm 6
logging monitor 6
```

BPDU Guard

BPDU guard is a safety mechanism that shuts down ports configured with Spanning Tree Protocol portfast upon receipt of a BPDU. This ensures that loops cannot accidentally be created if an unauthorized switch is added to a topology.

BPDU guard is enabled globally on all Spanning Tree Protocol portfast ports with the command **spanning-tree port type edge bpduguard default**. BPDU guard can be enabled or disabled on a specific interface with the command **spanning-tree bpduguard {enable | disable}**. Example 4-42 displays the BPDU guard configuration for a specific port or globally on all access ports. Upon examination of the spanning-tree port details the *by default* keyword indicates that the global configuration is what applied BPDU guard to that port.

Example 4-42 *BPDU Guard Configuration*

```
NX-1(config)# interface Ethernet1/6
NX-1(config-if)# spanning-tree bpduguard enable
NX-1(config)# spanning-tree port type edge bpduguard default
NX-1# show spanning-tree interface ethernet 1/1 detail
 Port 1 (Ethernet1/1) of VLAN0001 is designated forwarding
   Port path cost 4, Port priority 128, Port Identifier 128.1
   Designated root has priority 28673, address 885a.92de.617c
   Designated bridge has priority 28673, address 885a.92de.617c
   Designated port id is 128.1, designated path cost 0
   Timers: message age 0, forward delay 0, hold 0
   Number of transitions to forwarding state: 1
   The port type is edge by default
   Link type is point-to-point by default
   Bpdu guard is enabled by default
   BPDU: sent 32151, received 0
```

> **Note** BPDU guard should be configured on all host facing ports. However, do not enable BPDU guard on PVLAN promiscuous ports.

By default, ports that are put in ErrDisabled because of BPDU guard do not automatically restore themselves. The Error Recovery service can be used to reactivate ports that are shut down for a specific problem, thereby reducing administrative overhead. The Error Recovery service recovers ports shutdown from BPDU guard with the command **errdisable recovery cause bpduguard**. The period that the Error Recovery checks for ports is configured with the command **errdisable recovery interval** *time-seconds*.

Example 4-43 demonstrates the configuration of the Error Recovery service for BPDU guard and Error Recovery in action.

Example 4-43 *Error Recovery Service Configuration and Demonstration*

```
NX-1(config)# errdisable recovery cause bpduguard
NX-1(config)# errdisable recovery interval 60
11:16:17 NX-1 %$ VDC-1 %$ %STP-2-BLOCK_BPDUGUARD: Received BPDU on port Ethernet1/6
  with BPDU Guard enabled. Disabling port.
11:16:17 NX-1 %$ VDC-1 %$ %ETHPORT-5-IF_DOWN_ERROR_DISABLED: Interface Ethernet1/6
  is down (Error disabled. Reason:BPDUGuard)
11:21:17 NX-1 %$ VDC-1 %$ %ETHPORT-5-IF_ERRDIS_RECOVERY: Interface Ethernet1/6 is
  being recovered from error disabled state (Last Reason:BPDUGuard)
```

BPDU Filter

BPDU filter quite simply blocks BPDUs from being transmitted out of a port. BPDU filter can be enabled globally or on a specific interface. The behavior changes depending upon the configuration:

- If BPDU filter is enabled globally with the command **spanning-tree port type edge bpdufilter enable**, the port sends a series of at least 10 BPDUs. If the remote port has BPDU guard on it, that generally shuts down the port as a loop prevention mechanism.

- If BPDU filter is enabled on a specific interface with the command **spanning-tree bpdufilter enable**, the port does not send any BPDUs on an ongoing basis. However, the switch sends a series of at least 10 BPDUs when a port first becomes active. If the remote port has BPDU guard on it, that generally shuts down the port as a loop prevention mechanism.

> **Note** Be careful with the deployment of BPDU filter because it could cause problems. Most network designs do not require BPDU filter, and the use of BPDU filter adds an unnecessary level of complexity while introducing risk.

Example 4-44 verifies the BPDU filter was enabled globally on the Eth1/1 interface. This configuration sends the 10 BPDUs when the port first becomes active.

Example 4-44 *Verification of BPDU Filter*

```
NX-1# show spanning-tree interface ethernet 1/1 detail
 Port 1 (Ethernet1/1) of VLAN0001 is designated forwarding
   Port path cost 4, Port priority 128, Port Identifier 128.1
   Designated root has priority 28673, address 885a.92de.617c
   Designated bridge has priority 28673, address 885a.92de.617c
   Designated port id is 128.1, designated path cost 0
   Timers: message age 0, forward delay 0, hold 0
   Number of transitions to forwarding state: 1
   The port type is edge by default
   Link type is point-to-point by default
   Bpdu filter is enabled by default
   BPDU: sent 32151, received 0
```

Problems with Unidirectional Links

Network topologies that use fiber for connectivity can encounter unidirectional traffic flows because one cable transmits data from downstream to upstream switches while the other cable transmits data from upstream to downstream switches. In these scenarios, BPDUs are not able to be transmitted, so the downstream switch eventually times out the existing root port and identifies a different port as the root port. Now traffic is received on one port and forwarded out a different port, creating a forwarding loop.

There are three solutions to resolve this situation:

- Spanning Tree Protocol LoopGuard
- Unidirectional Link Detection
- Bridge Assurance

Spanning Tree Protocol Loop Guard

Loop guard prevents any alternative or root ports from becoming designated ports (ports toward downstream switches) because of a loss of BPDUs on the root port. Loop guard places the original port in an ErrDisabled state while BPDUs are not being received. When BPDU transmission starts again on that interface, the port recovers and begins to transition through the Spanning Tree Protocol states again.

Loop guard is enabled globally using the command **spanning-tree loopguard default**, or it can be enabled on an interface basis with the interface command **spanning-tree guard loop**. It is important to note that loop guard should not be enabled on portfast enabled ports (directly conflicts with the root/alternate port logic) nor should it be enabled on virtual port-channel (vPC) ports.

Example 4-45 demonstrates the configuration of loop guard on NX-2's Eth1/1 port.

Example 4-45 *Loop Guard Configuration*

```
NX-2(config)# interface Eth1/1
NX-2(config-if)# spanning-tree guard loop
```

Placing BPDU filter on NX-2's Eth1/1 port that connects to the NX-1 (the root bridge) triggers loop guard. This is demonstrated in Example 4-46.

Example 4-46 *Syslog of Triggered Loop Guard*

```
NX-2(config-if)# interface Eth1/1
NX-2(config-if)# spanning-tree bpdufilter enable
18:46:06 NX-2 %$ VDC-1 %$ %STP-2-LOOPGUARD_BLOCK: Loop guard blocking port
        Ethernet1/1 on VLAN0001.
18:46:07 NX-2 %$ VDC-1 %$ %STP-2-LOOPGUARD_BLOCK: Loop guard blocking port Ethernet1/1
        on VLAN0010.
18:46:07 NX-2 %$ VDC-1 %$ %STP-2-LOOPGUARD_BLOCK: Loop guard blocking port Ethernet1/1
        on VLAN0020.
18:46:07 NX-2 %$ VDC-1 %$ %STP-2-LOOPGUARD_BLOCK: Loop guard blocking port
  Ethernet1/1
        on VLAN0030.
```

At this point in time, the port is considered in an inconsistent state. Inconsistent ports are viewed with the command **show spanning-tree inconsistentports**, as shown in Example 4-47. Notice how an entry exists for all the VLANs carried across the Eth1/1 port.

Example 4-47 *Viewing the Inconsistent Spanning Tree Protocol Ports*

```
NX-2# show spanning-tree inconsistentports
Name                  Interface              Inconsistency
-------------------   --------------------   -----------------
VLAN0001              Eth1/1                 Loop Inconsistent
VLAN0010              Eth1/1                 Loop Inconsistent
VLAN0020              Eth1/1                 Loop Inconsistent
VLAN0030              Eth1/1                 Loop Inconsistent

Number of inconsistent ports (segments) in the system : 4
```

Unidirectional Link Detection

Unidirectional link detection (UDLD) allows for the bidirectional monitoring of fiber-optic and copper Ethernet cables. UDLD operates by transmitting UDLD packets to a neighbor device that includes the system-ID and port-ID of the interface transmitting the UDLD packet. The receiving router then repeats that information back to the originating router, which includes its system-ID and port-ID. The process continues indefinitely. If the frame is not acknowledged, the port is placed into an ErrDisabled state.

The UDLD feature must be enabled first with the command **feature udld**. UDLD is then enabled under the specific interface with the command **udld enable**. Example 4-48 demonstrates NX-1's UDLD configuration on the link to NX-2.

Example 4-48 *UDLD Configuration*

```
NX-1(config)# feature udld
NX-1(config)# interface e1/2
NX-1(config-if)# udld enable
```

UDLD must be enabled on the remote switch as well. Once configured, the status of UDLD for an interface is checked using the command **show udld** *interface-id*. Example 4-49 displays the output of UDLD status for an interface. The output contains the current state, Device-IDs (Serial Numbers), originating interface-IDs, and return interface-IDs.

Example 4-49 *Verifying UDLD Switch Port Status*

```
NX-1# show udld ethernet 1/2

Interface Ethernet1/49
--------------------------------
Port enable administrative configuration setting: enabled
Port enable operational state: enabled
Current bidirectional state: bidirectional
Current operational state:  advertisement - Single neighbor detected
Message interval: 15
Timeout interval: 5

        Entry 1
        ---------------
        Expiration time: 35
        Cache Device index: 1
        Current neighbor state: bidirectional
        Device ID: FDO1348R0VM
        Port ID: Eth1/2
        Neighbor echo 1 devices: FOC1813R0C
        Neighbor echo 1 port: Ethernet1/1

        Message interval: 15
        Timeout interval: 5
        CDP Device name: NX-2


        Last pkt send on: 291908, 19:07:51 2017
                Probe pkt send on: 291908, Sep  1 19:07:51 2017
                Echo  pkt send on: 177683, Sep  1 19:06:21 2017
                Flush pkt send on: None.
```

Chapter 4: Nexus Switching

```
          Last pkt recv on: 469579, 19:07:50 2017
              Probe pkt recv on: 469579, Sep  1 19:07:50 2017
              Echo  pkt recv on: 470536, Sep  1 19:06:21 2017
              Flush pkt recv on: None.

      Deep pkt inspections done: None.
      Mismatched if index found: None.
      Deep pkt inspection drops: None.
```

After a UDLD failure, the interface state indicates that the port is down because of UDLD failure, as shown in Example 4-50.

Example 4-50 *Interface Status Reflects UDLD Error*

```
NX-1# show interface brief
! Output omitted for brevity
Ethernet      VLAN    Type Mode   Status Reason              Speed      Port
Interface                                                                Ch #
--------------------------------------------------------------------------------
Eth1/1         --     eth  routed up     none                10G(D)     --
Eth1/2         --     eth  trunk  down   UDLD empty echo     auto(D)    --
```

The event-history provides relevant information for troubleshooting UDLD errors. The history is viewed with the command **show udld internal event-history errors**. This provides a time stamp and preliminary indication as to the cause of the problem. The history is displayed in Example 4-51.

Example 4-51 *UDLD Event-History*

```
NX-1# show udld internal event-history errors

1) Event:E_DEBUG, length:75, at 177895 usecs after NX-011 09:42:23 2014
   [102] udld_demux(646): (646): (Warning) unexpected mts msg (opcode - 61467)

2) Event:E_DEBUG, length:70, at 983485 usecs after NX-011 09:42:22 2014
   [102] udldDisablePort(3985): Ethernet1/2: Port UDLD set error disabled

3) Event:E_DEBUG, length:70, at 983415 usecs after NX-011 09:42:22 2014
   [102] udldDisablePort(3975): calling mts_msg_send_recv_ethpm() w/ f01b

4) Event:E_DEBUG, length:77, at 983387 usecs after NX-011 09:42:22 2014
   [102] udldDisablePort(3915): current bidirdetect_flag (error): udld_empty_echo

5) Event:E_DEBUG, length:73, at 983180 usecs after NX-011 09:42:22 2014
   [102] udldDisablePort(3888): calling udld_send_flush_msg for: Ethernet1/2
```

```
6) Event:E_DEBUG, length:151, at 983036 usecs after NX-011 09:42:22 2014
   [102] udld_recv_det1(5640): Ethernet1/2: UDLD error Unidirection detected
   during extended detection, sent UDLD_MAIN_EV_DETECTION_WINDOW_CONCLUSION_OTHER
```

There are two common UDLD failures, which are described in the following sections:

- Empty Echo
- Tx-Rx Loop

Empty Echo

The Empty echo UDLD problem occurs in the following circumstances:

- The UDLD session times out.
- The remote switch does not process the UDLD packets.
- The local switch does not transmit the UDLD packets.

Example 4-52 demonstrates the syslog messages that appear with a UDLD Empty Echo Detection.

Example 4-52 *UDLD Empty Echo Detection*

```
11:57:56.155 NX-1 ETHPORT-2-IF_DOWN_ERROR_DISABLED Interface Ethernet1/2 is down
  (Error disabled. Reason:UDLD empty echo)
11:57:56.186 NX-1 ETH_PORT_CHANNEL-5-PORT_INDIVIDUAL_DOWN individual port
  Ethernet1/2 is down
11:57:56.336 NX-1 ETHPORT-2-IF_DOWN_ERROR_DISABLED Interface Ethernet1/2 is down
  (Error disabled. Reason:UDLD empty echo)
```

Tx-Rx Loop

This condition occurs when a UDLD frame appears to be received on the same port that it was advertised on. This means that the system-ID and port-ID in the received UDLD packet match the system-ID and port-ID on the receiving switch (that is, what was transmitted by the other switch). The Tx-Rx loop occurs in the following circumstances:

- A misconfiguration or incorrect wiring in an intermediate device (optical transport)
- Incorrect wiring or media problem

Example 4-53 demonstrates the syslog messages that appear with a UDLD Empty Echo Detection.

Example 4-53 *TX-RX Loop Detection*

```
14:52:30 NX-1 %ETHPORT-2-IF_DOWN_ERROR_DISABLED: Interface Ethernet17/5 is down
  (Error disabled. Reason:UDLD Tx-Rx Loop)
14:52:30 NX-1 %ETHPORT-2-IF_DOWN_ERROR_DISABLED: Interface Ethernet17/5 is down
  (Error disabled. Reason:UDLD Tx-Rx Loop)
```

Bridge Assurance

Bridge assurance overcomes some of the limitations that loop guard and UDLD are affected by. Bridge assurance works on Spanning Tree Protocol designated ports (which loop guard cannot) and overcomes issues when a port starts off in a unidirectional state. Bridge assurance makes Spanning Tree Protocol operate like a routing protocol (EIGRP/OSPF, and so on) where it requires health-check packets to occur bidirectionally.

The bridge assurance process is enabled by default, but requires that the trunk ports are explicitly configured with the command **spanning-tree port type network**. Example 4-54 demonstrates bridge assurance being configured on the interfaces connecting NX-1, NX-2, and NX-3 with each other.

Example 4-54 *Bridge Assurance Configuration*

```
NX-1(config)# interface eth1/2,eth1/3
NX-1(config-if-range)# spanning-tree port type network

NX-2(config)# interface eth1/1,eth1/3
NX-2(config-if-range)# spanning-tree port type network

NX-3(config)# interface eth1/1,eth1/2
NX-3(config-if-range)# spanning-tree port type network
```

Example 4-55 displays the Spanning Tree Protocol port type after configuring bridge assurance. Notice how the Network keyword has been added to the P2P type.

Example 4-55 *Viewing the Spanning Tree Protocol Type of Ports with Bridge Assurance*

```
NX-1# show spanning-tree vlan 10 | b Interface
Interface        Role Sts Cost      Prio.Nbr Type
---------------- ---- --- --------- -------- --------------------------------
Eth1/2           Desg FWD 2         128.2    Network P2p
Eth1/3           Desg FWD 2         128.3    Network P2p

NX-2# show spanning-tree vlan 10 | b Interface
Interface        Role Sts Cost      Prio.Nbr Type
---------------- ---- --- --------- -------- --------------------------------
Eth1/1           Root FWD 2         128.1    Network P2p
Eth1/3           Desg FWD 2         128.3    Network P2p
```

```
Eth1/4           Desg FWD 2       128.4    P2p

NX-3# show spanning-tree vlan 10 | b Interface
Interface        Role Sts Cost    Prio.Nbr Type
---------------- ---- --- -------- -------- --------------------------------
Eth1/1           Root FWD 2       128.1    Network P2p
Eth1/2           Altn BLK 2       128.2    Network P2p
Eth1/5           Desg FWD 2       128.5    P2p
```

Example 4-56 demonstrates a BPDU filter being applied on NX-2's link to NX-3. Almost instantly, bridge assurance has engaged on NX-2 and NX-3 because it cannot maintain a mutual handshake of BPDU packets.

Example 4-56 *Bridge Assurance Engaging*

```
NX-2(config-if)# interface Eth1/3
NX-2(config-if)# spanning-tree bpdufilter enable
20:46:34 NX-2 %$ VDC-1 %$ %STP-2-BRIDGE_ASSURANCE_BLOCK: Bridge Assurance blocking
  port Ethernet1/3 VLAN0001.
20:46:35 NX-2 %$ VDC-1 %$ %STP-2-BRIDGE_ASSURANCE_BLOCK: Bridge Assurance blocking
  port Ethernet1/3 VLAN0002.
20:46:35 NX-2 %$ VDC-1 %$ %STP-2-BRIDGE_ASSURANCE_BLOCK: Bridge Assurance blocking
  port Ethernet1/3 VLAN0010.
20:46:35 NX-2 %$ VDC-1 %$ %STP-2-BRIDGE_ASSURANCE_BLOCK: Bridge Assurance blocking
  port Ethernet1/3 VLAN0020.
20:46:35 NX-2 %$ VDC-1 %$ %STP-2-BRIDGE_ASSURANCE_BLOCK: Bridge Assurance blocking
  port Ethernet1/3 VLAN0030.
```

The Spanning Tree Protocol port types now include the comment *BA_Inc*, which refers to the fact that those interfaces are now in an inconsistent port state for bridge assurance. Example 4-57 displays the new interface port types.

Example 4-57 *Detecting Inconsistent Port State*

```
NX-2# show spanning-tree vlan 10 | b Interface
Interface        Role Sts Cost    Prio.Nbr Type
---------------- ---- --- -------- -------- --------------------------------
Eth1/1           Root FWD 2       128.1    Network P2p
Eth1/3           Desg BKN*2       128.3    Network P2p *BA_Inc
Eth1/4           Desg FWD 2       128.4    P2p

NX-3# show spanning-tree vlan 10 | b Interface
Interface        Role Sts Cost    Prio.Nbr Type
---------------- ---- --- -------- -------- --------------------------------
Eth1/1           Root FWD 2       128.1    Network P2p
Eth1/2           Desg BKN*2       128.2    Network P2p *BA_Inc
Eth1/5           Desg FWD 2       128.5    P2p
```

The command **show spanning-tree inconsistentports** list all the interfaces and the reasons that port is identified as inconsistent. Example 4-58 demonstrates the use of the command on NX-2. This is relevant to cross-referencing the event-history as shown earlier.

Example 4-58 *Viewing Inconsistent Ports*

```
NX-2# show spanning-tree inconsistentports
Name                    Interface              Inconsistency
--------------------    --------------------   ------------------
VLAN0001                Eth1/3                 Bridge Assurance Inconsistent
VLAN0002                Eth1/3                 Bridge Assurance Inconsistent
VLAN0010                Eth1/3                 Bridge Assurance Inconsistent
VLAN0020                Eth1/3                 Bridge Assurance Inconsistent
VLAN0030                Eth1/3                 Bridge Assurance Inconsistent


Number of inconsistent ports (segments) in the system : 5
```

And upon removal of the BPDU filter, bridge assurance disengages and returns the port to a forwarding state, as shown in Example 4-59.

Example 4-59 *Restoring Connectivity by Allowing BPDUs to Process*

```
NX-2(config)# int Eth1/3
NX-2(config-if)# no spanning-tree bpdufilter
NX-2(config-if)#
20:48:30 NX-2 %$ VDC-1 %$ %STP-2-BRIDGE_ASSURANCE_UNBLOCK: Bridge Assurance
   unblocking port Ethernet1/3 VLAN0001.
20:48:31 NX-2 %$ VDC-1 %$ %STP-2-BRIDGE_ASSURANCE_UNBLOCK: Bridge Assurance
   unblocking port Ethernet1/3 VLAN0002.
20:48:31 NX-2 %$ VDC-1 %$ %STP-2-BRIDGE_ASSURANCE_UNBLOCK: Bridge Assurance
   unblocking port Ethernet1/3 VLAN0010.
20:48:32 NX-2 %$ VDC-1 %$ %STP-2-BRIDGE_ASSURANCE_UNBLOCK: Bridge Assurance
   unblocking port Ethernet1/3 VLAN0020.
20:48:32 NX-2 %$ VDC-1 %$ %STP-2-BRIDGE_ASSURANCE_UNBLOCK: Bridge Assurance
   unblocking port Ethernet1/3 VLAN0030.
```

Note Bridge assurance is the preferred method for detection of unidirectional links protection and should be used when all platforms support it.

Summary

This chapter provided a brief review of the Ethernet communication standards and the benefits that a managed switch provides to L2 topology. Troubleshooting L2 forwarding issues are composed of many components. The first step in troubleshooting L2 forwarding is to identify both the source and destination switch ports. From there it is best to follow the flowchart in Figure 4-5 for troubleshooting. Depending upon the outcome, the flowchart will redirect you back to the appropriate section in this chapter.

Figure 4-5 *Flowchart for Troubleshooting L2 Forwarding Issues*

References

Fuller, Ron, David Jansen, and Matthew McPherson. *NX-OS and Cisco Nexus Switching*. Indianapolis: Cisco Press, 2013.

Cisco. Cisco NX-OS Software Configuration Guides, www.cisco.com.

Chapter 5

Port-Channels, Virtual Port-Channels, and FabricPath

This chapter covers the following topics:

- Port-Channels
- Virtual Port-Channels (vPC)
- FabricPath
- Virtual Port-Channel Plus (vPC+)

Proper network design takes into account single points of failure by ensuring that alternate paths and devices can forward traffic in case of failure. Routing protocols make sure that redundant paths can still be consumed because of equal-cost multipath (ECMP). However, Spanning Tree Protocol (STP) stops forwarding on redundant links between switches to prevent forwarding loops.

Although STP is beneficial, it limits the amount of bandwidth to be achieved between switches. Port-channels provide a way to combine multiple physical links into a virtual link to increase bandwidth because all the member interfaces can forward network traffic. This chapter explains port-channel operations and the techniques to troubleshoot port-channels when they do not operate as intended.

Port-Channels

Port-channels are a logical link that consists of one or multiple physical member links. Port-channels are defined in the IEEE 803.3AD Link Aggregation Specification and are sometimes referred to as EtherChannels. The physical interfaces that are used to assemble the logical port-channel are called member interfaces. Port-channels are either Layer 2 (L2) switching or Layer 3 (L3) routing.

Figure 5-1 visualizes some of the key components of a port-channel (member interface and logical interface), along with the advantages it provides over individual links.

A primary advantage of using port-channels is the reduction of topology changes when a member link is added or removed for a port-channel. A change might trigger an L2 STP tree calculation or L3 SPF calculation, but forwarding still occurs between the devices in the port-channel.

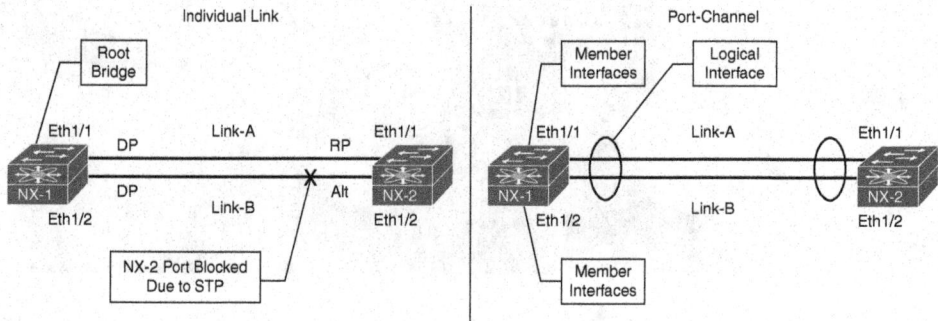

Figure 5-1 *Advantages of Port-Channels Versus Individual Links*

Nexus switches successfully form a port-channel by statically setting them to an "on" state or by using link-aggregation control packets (LACP) to detect connectivity between devices. Most network engineers prefer to use LACP because it ensures end-to-end connectivity between devices. LACP provides a method to detect failures with unidirectional links for member interfaces or identify when other devices are in the path (for example, dense wavelength-division multiplexing [DWDM] devices that do not support link propagation).

In Figure 5-2, NX-1 and NX-2 have combined their Ethernet1/1 and Ethernet1/2 interfaces into Port-Channel1. A failure on Link-A between the optical transport devices DWDM-1 and DWDM-2 is not propagated to the Eth1/1 interface on NX-1 or NX-2. The Nexus switches continue to forward traffic out the Eth1/1 interface because those ports still maintain physical state to DWDM-1 or DWDM-2. There is not a health-check mechanism with the port-channel ports being statically set to "on." However, if LACP was configured, NX-1 and NX-2 would detect that traffic cannot flow end-to-end on the upper path and would remove that link from the logical port-channel.

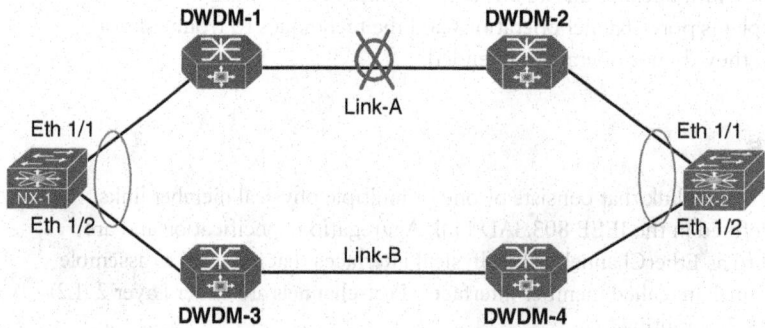

Figure 5-2 *Port-Channel Link State Propagation and Detection*

A member link becomes active within a port-channel after establishing an LACP using the following messages:

- **Sync (S):** Initial flag, indicating that the local switch includes the member interface as part of the port-channel
- **Collecting (C):** Second flag, indicating that the local switch processes network traffic that is received on this interface
- **Distributing (D):** Third flag, indicating that the local switch transmits network traffic using this member interface

When a port comes up, messages are exchanged following these steps:

Step 1. Both switches (source and destination) advertise LACP packets with the Sync, Collecting, and Distributing flags set to zero (off).

Step 2. As the source switch receives an LACP packet from the destination switch, it collects the system-ID and port-ID from the initial LACP packet. The source switch then transmits a Sync LACP packet indicating that it is willing to participate in the port-channel. The initial LACP Sync packet includes the local system-ID, port-ID, and port-priority, along with the detected remote switches' information (system-ID, port-ID, and port-priority). LACP members for the port-channel are selected at this time.

The destination switch repeats this step as well.

Step 3. Upon receipt of the Sync LACP packet, the source switch verifies that the local and remote (destination switch) system-IDs match the Sync LACP packets to ensure that the switch-ID is the same across all member links and that no multiple devices exist on a link (that is, no device is operating in the middle, providing connectivity to a third switch). The source switch then transmits a Collecting LACP packet indicating that the source switch is ready to receive traffic on that interface.

Step 4. The destination switch verifies the accuracy of the Sync LACP packet for the source switch against what was performed by the source switch. The destination switch then sends a Collecting LACP packet indicating that the destination switch is ready to receive traffic on that interface.

Step 5. The source switch receives the Collecting LACP packet from the destination switch and transmits a Distributing LACP packet to the destination switch indicating that it is transmitting data across that member link.

Step 6. The destination switch receives the Collecting LACP packet from the source switch and transmits a Distributing LACP packet to the source switch indicating that it is transmitting data across that member link.

Step 7. Both switches transmit data across the member link interface that has completed the previous steps successfully.

> **Note** The LACP packets in Step 7 happen independently of other switches, assuming that the requirements are met.

Figure 5-3 demonstrates the exchange of LACP messages between NX-1 (source switch) and NX-2 (destination switch).

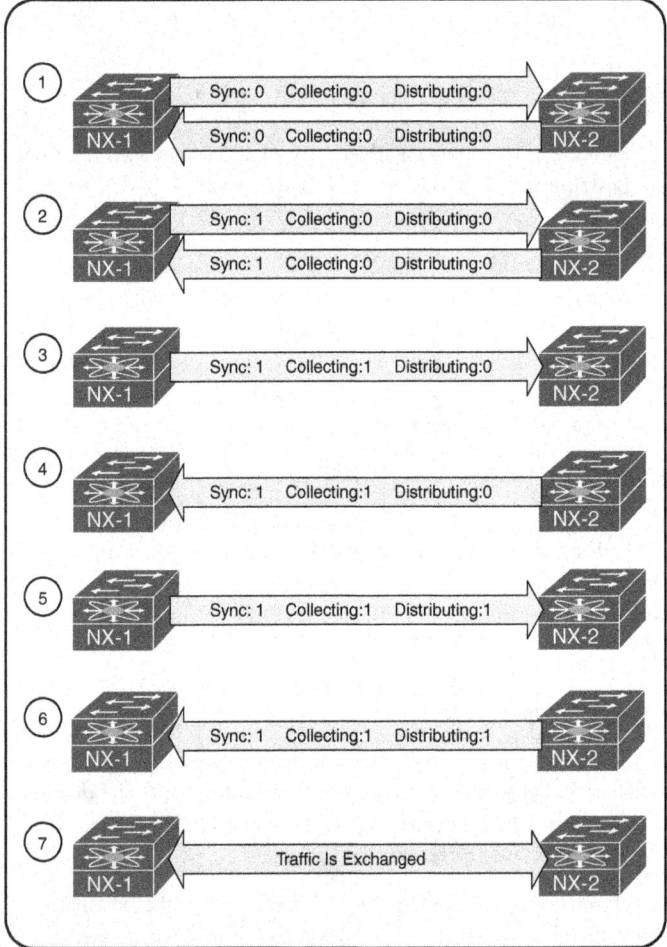

Figure 5-3 *LACP Negotiation*

> **Note** This process occurs on every member link when it joins a port-channel interface.

Basic Port-Channel Configuration

Port-channels are configured by going into interface configuration mode for the member interfaces and then assigning them to a port-channel and statically setting them to "on," or with LACP dynamic negotiation. LACP operates with two modes:

- **Passive:** An interface does not initiate a port-channel to be established and does not transmit LACP packets out of it. If the remote switch receives an LACP packet, this interface responds and then establishes an LACP adjacency. If both devices are LACP passive, no LACP adjacency forms.

- **Active:** An interface tries to initiate a port-channel establishment and transmits LACP packets out of it. Active LACP interfaces can establish an LACP adjacency only if the remote interface is configured to active or passive.

The LACP feature must first be enabled with the global command **feature lacp**. Then the interface parameter command **channel-group** *portchannel-number* **mode** {**on** | **active** | **passive**} converts a regular interface into a member interface.

Example 5-1 demonstrates the configuration port-channel 1 using the member interfaces Eth1/1 and Eth1/2. Notice that the port-channel is configured as a trunk interface, not as the individual member interfaces.

Example 5-1 *Sample Port-Channel Configuration*

```
NX-1# conf t
Enter configuration commands, one per line. End with CNTL/Z.
NX-1(config)# feature lacp
NX-1(config)# interface ethernet 1/1-2
NX-1(config-if-range)# channel-group 1 mode active
! Output omitted for brevity
03:53:14 NX-1 %$ VDC-1 %$ %ETH_PORT_CHANNEL-5-CREATED: port-channel1 created
03:53:14 NX-1 %$ VDC-1 %$ %ETHPORT-5-IF_DOWN_CHANNEL_MEMBERSHIP_UPDATE_IN_PROGRESS:
  Interface Ethernet1/2 is down (Channel membership update in progress)
03:53:14 NX-1 %$ VDC-1 %$ %ETHPORT-5-IF_DOWN_CHANNEL_MEMBERSHIP_UPDATE_IN_PROGRESS:
  Interface Ethernet1/1 is down (Channel membership update in progress)
..
03:53:16 NX-1 %$ VDC-1 %$ %ETHPORT-5-SPEED: Interface port-channel1, operational
  speed changed to 10 Gbps
03:53:16 NX-1 %$ VDC-1 %$ %ETHPORT-5-IF_DUPLEX: Interface port-channel1, operational
  duplex mode changed to Full
03:53:21 NX-1 %$ VDC-1 %$ %ETH_PORT_CHANNEL-5-PORT_UP: port-channel1: Ethernet1/1
  is up
03:53:21 NX-1 %$ VDC-1 %$ %ETH_PORT_CHANNEL-5-FOP_CHANGED: port-channel1: first
  operational port changed from none to Ethernet1/1
03:53:21 NX-1 %$ VDC-1 %$ %ETH_PORT_CHANNEL-5-PORT_UP: port-channel1: Ethernet1/2
  is up
03:53:21 NX-1 %$ VDC-1 %$ %ETHPORT-5-IF_UP: Interface Ethernet1/1 is up in mode
  access
```

```
03:53:21 NX-1 %$ VDC-1 %$ %ETHPORT-5-IF_UP: Interface port-channel1 is up in mode
  access
03:53:21 NX-1 %$ VDC-1 %$ %ETHPORT-5-IF_UP: Interface Ethernet1/2 is up in mode
  access
NX-1(config-if-range)# interface port-channel 1
NX-1(config-if)# switchport mode trunk
! Output omitted for brevity
03:53:21 NX-1 %$ VDC-1 %$ %ETHPORT-5-IF_DOWN_CFG_CHANGE: Interface port-channel1 is
  down(Config change)
03:53:21 NX-1 %$ VDC-1 %$ %ETH_PORT_CHANNEL-5-PORT_DOWN: port-channel1: Ethernet1/1
  is down
03:53:21 NX-1 %$ VDC-1 %$ %ETH_PORT_CHANNEL-5-PORT_DOWN: port-channel1: Ethernet1/2
  is down
..
03:53:29 NX-1 %$ VDC-1 %$ %ETH_PORT_CHANNEL-5-PORT_UP: port-channel1: Ethernet1/1
  is up
03:53:29 NX-1 %$ VDC-1 %$ %ETH_PORT_CHANNEL-5-FOP_CHANGED: port-channel1: first
  operational port changed from none to Ethernet1/1
03:53:29 NX-1 %$ VDC-1 %$ %ETH_PORT_CHANNEL-5-PORT_UP: port-channel1: Ethernet1/2
  is up
03:53:29 NX-1 %$ VDC-1 %$ %ETHPORT-5-IF_UP: Interface Ethernet1/1 is up in mode
  trunk
03:53:29 NX-1 %$ VDC-1 %$ %ETHPORT-5-IF_UP: Interface port-channel1 is up in mode
  trunk
03:53:29 NX-1 %$ VDC-1 %$ %ETHPORT-5-IF_UP: Interface Ethernet1/2 is up in mode
  trunk
```

Verifying Port-Channel Status

Now that the port-channel is configured, verifying that the port-channel is established is essential. The command **show port-channel summary** provides an overview of all configured port-channels and their status. Example 5-2 displays the use of this command.

Example 5-2 *Viewing Port-Channel Summary Status*

```
NX-1# show port-channel summary
Flags:  D - Down        P - Up in port-channel (members)
        I - Individual  H - Hot-standby (LACP only)
        s - Suspended   r - Module-removed
        S - Switched    R - Routed
        U - Up (port-channel)
        p - Up in delay-lacp mode (member)
        M - Not in use. Min-links not met
--------------------------------------------------------------------------------
Group Port-       Type     Protocol  Member Ports
      Channel
--------------------------------------------------------------------------------
1     Po1(SU)     Eth      LACP      Eth1/1(P)   Eth1/2(P)
```

When viewing the output of the **show port-channel summary** command, check the port-channel status, which is listed below the port-channel interface. The status should be "U," as in Example 5-2.

Examine Table 5-1 to understand the port-channel flags.

Table 5-1 *Logical Port-Channel Interface Status Fields*

Field	Description
U	The port-channel interface is working properly.
D	The port-channel interface is down.
M	The port-channel interface has successfully established at least one LACP adjacency. However, the port-channel is configured to have a minimum number of active interfaces that exceeds the number of active participating member interfaces. Traffic does not forward across this port-channel. The command **lacp min-links** *number-member-interfaces* is configured on the port-channel interface.
S	The port-channel interface is configured for Layer 2 (L2) switching.
R	The port-channel interface is configured for Layer 3 (L3) routing.

Table 5-2 briefly explains the fields related to the member interfaces.

Table 5-2 *Port-Channel Member Interface Status Fields*

Field	Description
P	The interface is actively participating and forwarding traffic for this port-channel.
H	The port-channel is configured with the maximum number of active interfaces. This interface is participating with LACP with the remote peer, but it is acting as a hot-standby and does not forward traffic. The command **lacp max-bundle** *number-member-interfaces* is configured on the port-channel interface.
I	The member interface is treated as an individual and does not detect any LACP activity on this interface.
w	This field indicates the time left to receive a packet from this neighbor to ensure that it is still alive.
s	The member interface is in a suspended state.
r	The switch module associated with this interface has been removed from the chassis.

The logical interface is viewed with the command **show interface port-channel** *port-channel-id*. The output includes data fields that are typically displayed with a traditional

Ethernet interface, with the exception of the member interfaces and the fact that the bandwidth reflects the combined throughput of all active member interfaces. As this changes, factors such as QoS policies and interface costs for routing protocols adjust accordingly.

Example 5-3 displays the use of the command on NX-1. Notice that the bandwidth is 20 Gbps and correlates to the two 10-Gbps interfaces in the port-channel interface.

Example 5-3 *Viewing Port-Channel Interface Status*

```
NX-1# show interface port-channel 1
! Output omitted for brevity
port-channel1 is up
admin state is up,
  Hardware: Port-Channel, address: 885a.92de.6158 (bia 885a.92de.6158)
  MTU 1500 bytes, BW 20000000 Kbit, DLY 10 usec
  reliability 255/255, txload 1/255, rxload 1/255
  Encapsulation ARPA, medium is broadcast
  Port mode is trunk
  full-duplex, 10 Gb/s
  Input flow-control is off, output flow-control is off
  Auto-mdix is turned off
  Switchport monitor is off
  EtherType is 0x8100
  Members in this channel: Eth1/1, Eth1/2
..
```

Verifying LACP Packets

NX-OS logging provides many relevant syslog messages to identify configuration incompatibilities. A vital step in troubleshooting the establishment of port-channels is to verify that LACP packets are being transmitted between devices. The first troubleshooting step is to verify the LACP counters using the command **show lacp counters** [**interface port-channel** *port-channel-number*].

The output includes a list of the port-channel interfaces, their associated member interfaces, counters for LACP packets sent/received, and any errors. An interface should see the Sent and Received columns increment over a time interval. If the counters do not increment, this indicates a problem. The problem could be related to the physical link or an incomplete/incompatible configuration with the remote device. Check the LACP counters on that device to see if it is transmitting LACP packets.

Example 5-4 demonstrates the command. Notice that the Received column does not increment on Ethernet1/2 for port-channel 1, but it does increment on the Sent column.

Example 5-4 *Viewing LACP Packet Counters*

```
NX-1# show lacp counters
NOTE: Clear lacp counters to get accurate statistics

--------------------------------------------------------------------------
                        LACPDUs                    Markers/Resp  LACPDUs
Port            Sent            Recv               Recv  Sent    Pkts Err
--------------------------------------------------------------------------
port-channel1
Ethernet1/1     5753            5660                0     0       0
Ethernet1/2     5319            0                   0     0       0
```

```
NX-1# show lacp counters
NOTE: Clear lacp counters to get accurate statistics

--------------------------------------------------------------------------
                        LACPDUs                    Markers/Resp  LACPDUs
Port            Sent            Recv               Recv  Sent    Pkts Err
--------------------------------------------------------------------------
port-channel1
Ethernet1/1     5755            5662                0     0       0
Ethernet1/2     5321            0                   0     0       0
```

Another method involves using the command **show lacp internal info interface** *interface-id*. This command includes a time stamp for the last time a packet was transmitted or received out of an interface. Example 5-5 demonstrates the use of this command.

Example 5-5 *Viewing Time Stamps for LACP Transmissions on an Interface*

```
NX-1# show lacp internal info interface ethernet 1/1
Interface Ethernet1/1(0x1a030000) info
--------------------------------------
  port_pr 0x8000
  rid type IF-Rid: ifidx 0x1a030000: ch_num 0
  cfg_pc_if_idx 0x16000000: oper_pc_if_idx 0x16000000
  is state_change_notif_pending  0
  lacp detected link down   0
  lag [(8000, 0-62-ec-9d-c5-0, 1, 8000, 11c), (8000, 88-5a-92-de-61-7c, 8000,
  8000, 131)]
  aggr_id 0x0
  LACP last pkt sent at     : Mon Oct 23 03:50:41 2017, 153348 usecs
        LACP PDU sent at    : Mon Oct 23 03:50:41 2017, 153348 usecs
        MARKER RESP sent at: None.
```

```
              ERROR PDU sent at    : None.
   LACP last pkt recv at           : Mon Oct 23 03:50:35 2017, 864017 usecs
         LACP PDU recv at          : Mon Oct 23 03:50:35 2017, 864017 usecs
         MARKER PDU recv at        : None.
         ERROR PDU recv at         : None.
```

The command **show lacp neighbor** [interface port-channel *port-channel-number*] displays additional information about the port-channel interface, its member interfaces, and the remote device on a link-by-link basis.

Example 5-6 demonstrates the use of this command. The output includes the neighbor's system ID, system priority, remote port number, remote port-priority, and details on whether it is using fast or slow LACP packet intervals.

Example 5-6 *Viewing LACP Neighbor Information*

```
NX-1# show lacp neighbor
Flags:  S - Device is sending Slow LACPDUs  F - Device is sending Fast LACPDUs
        A - Device is in Active mode         P - Device is in Passive mode
port-channel1 neighbors
Partner's information
! The following section provides the remote neighbors system priority, system-id,
! port number, LACP state, and fast/slow LACP interval in that order.
            Partner                 Partner                      Partner
Port        System ID               Port Number      Age         Flags
Eth1/1      32768,18-9c-5d-11-99-800x138             985         SA
! The following section includes the remote device LACP port-priority
            LACP Partner            Partner                      Partner
            Port Priority           Oper Key                     Port State
            32768                   0x1                          0x3d


Partner's information
            Partner                 Partner                      Partner
Port        System ID               Port Number      Age         Flags
Eth1/2      32768,18-9c-5d-11-99-800x139             985         SA

            LACP Partner            Partner                      Partner
            Port Priority           Oper Key                     Port State
            32768                   0x1                          0x3d
```

Note Use the LACP system identifier to verify that the member interfaces are connected to the same device and are not split between devices. The local LACP system-ID is viewed using the command **show lacp system-identifier**.

The NX-OS Ethanalyzer tool is used to view the LACP packets being transmitted and received on the local Nexus switch by capturing packets with the LACP MAC destination address. The command **ethanalyzer local interface inband capture-filter "ether host 0180.c200.0002" [detail]** captures LACP packets that are received. The optional **detail** keyword provides additional information. Example 5-7 demonstrates the technique.

Example 5-7 *Capturing LACP Packets with Ethanalyzer*

```
NX-1# ethanalyzer local interface inband capture-filter "ether host 0180.c200.0002"
Capturing on inband
2017-10-23 03:58:11.213625 88:5a:92:de:61:58 -> 01:80:c2:00:00:02 LACP Link Aggr
egation Control Protocol
2017-10-23 03:58:11.869668 88:5a:92:de:61:59 -> 01:80:c2:00:00:02 LACP Link Aggr
egation Control Protocol
2017-10-23 03:58:23.381249 00:62:ec:9d:c5:1c -> 01:80:c2:00:00:02 LACP Link Aggr
egation Control Protocol
2017-10-23 03:58:24.262746 00:62:ec:9d:c5:1b -> 01:80:c2:00:00:02 LACP Link Aggr
egation Control Protocol
2017-10-23 03:58:41.218262 88:5a:92:de:61:58 -> 01:80:c2:00:00:02 LACP Link Aggr
egation Control Protocol
```

Advanced LACP Configuration Options

The following section explains some of the advanced LACP configuration options and their behavioral impact on member interface selection for a port-channel.

Minimum Number of Port-Channel Member Interfaces

A port-channel interface becomes active and up when only one member interface successfully forms an LACP adjacency with a remote device. In some design scenarios, a minimum number of LACP adjacencies is required before a port-channel interface becomes active. This option is configured with the port-channel interface command **lacp min-links** *min-links*.

Example 5-8 demonstrates setting the minimum number of port-channel interfaces to two and then shutting down one of the member interfaces on NX-1. Notice that the port-channel status is "Not in use."

Example 5-8 *Configuring a Minimum Number of Port-Channel Member Interfaces*

```
NX-1# conf t
NX-1(config)# interface port-channel 1
NX-1(config-if)# lacp min-links 2
NX-1(config-if)# interface Eth1/1
NX-1(config-if)# shut
```

```
04:22:45 NX-1 %$ VDC-1 %$ %ETH_PORT_CHANNEL-5-PORT_DOWN: port-channel1: Ethernet1/1
  is down
04:22:45 NX-1 %$ VDC-1 %$ %ETHPORT-5-IF_DOWN_CFG_CHANGE: Interface Ethernet1/1 is
  down(Config change)
04:22:45 NX-1 %$ VDC-1 %$ %ETHPORT-5-IF_DOWN_ADMIN_DOWN: Interface Ethernet1/1 is
  down (Administratively down)
04:22:47 NX-1 %$ VDC-1 %$ %ETHPORT-5-IF_DOWN_PORT_CHANNEL_MEMBERS_DOWN: Interface
  port-channel1 is down (No operational members)
04:22:47 NX-1 %$ VDC-1 %$ %ETH_PORT_CHANNEL-5-PORT_DOWN: port-channel1: Ethernet1/2
  is down
04:22:47 NX-1 %$ VDC-1 %$ %ETH_PORT_CHANNEL-5-FOP_CHANGED: port-channel1: first
  operational port changed from Ethernet1/2 to none
04:22:47 NX-1 %$ VDC-1 %$ %ETHPORT-5-IF_DOWN_INITIALIZING: Interface Ethernet1/2 is
  down (Initializing)
04:22:47 NX-1 %$ VDC-1 %$ %ETHPORT-5-IF_DOWN_PORT_CHANNEL_MEMBERS_DOWN: Interface
  port-channel1 is down (No operational members)
04:22:47 NX-1 %$ VDC-1 %$ %ETHPORT-5-SPEED: Interface port-channel1, operational
  speed changed to 10 Gbps
04:22:47 NX-1 %$ VDC-1 %$ %ETHPORT-5-IF_DUPLEX: Interface port-channel1, operational
  duplex mode changed to Full
04:22:47 NX-1 %$ VDC-1 %$ %ETHPORT-5-IF_RX_FLOW_CONTROL: Interface port-channel1,
  operational Receive Flow Control state changed to off
04:22:47 NX-1 %$ VDC-1 %$ %ETHPORT-5-IF_TX_FLOW_CONTROL: Interface port-channel1,
  operational Transmit Flow Control state changed to off
04:22:50 NX-1 %$ VDC-1 %$ %ETH_PORT_CHANNEL-5-PORT_SUSPENDED: Ethernet1/2:
  Ethernet1/2 is suspended

NX-1# show port-channel summary
Flags:   D - Down        P - Up in port-channel (members)
         I - Individual  H - Hot-standby (LACP only)
         s - Suspended   r - Module-removed
         S - Switched    R - Routed
         U - Up (port-channel)
         p - Up in delay-lacp mode (member)
         M - Not in use. Min-links not met
--------------------------------------------------------------------------------
Group Port-       Type     Protocol  Member Ports
      Channel
--------------------------------------------------------------------------------
1     Po1(SM)     Eth      LACP      Eth1/1(D)   Eth1/2(s)
```

Note The minimum number of port-channel member interfaces does not need to be configured on both devices to work properly. However, configuring it on both switches is recommended to accelerate troubleshooting and assist operational staff.

Maximum Number of Port-Channel Member Interfaces

A port-channel can be configured to have a maximum number of member interfaces in a port-channel. This is a common design scenario to ensure that the active member interface count keeps with the power of twos (2, 4, 8, 16) to accommodate load-balancing hashes. The maximum number of member interfaces in a port-channel is configured with the port-channel interface command **lacp max-bundle** *max-links*.

Example 5-9 displays configuring the maximum number of active member interfaces for a port-channel and demonstrates that those interfaces now show as "Hot-Standby."

Example 5-9 *Configuration and Verification of Maximum Links*

```
NX-1# configure terminal
Enter configuration commands, one per line. End with CNTL/Z.
NX-1(config)# interface port-channel 2
NX-1(config-if)# lacp max-bundle 4
04:44:04 NX-1 %$ VDC-1 %$ %ETH_PORT_CHANNEL-5-PORT_DOWN: port-channel2: Ethernet1/7
  is down
04:44:04 NX-1 %$ VDC-1 %$ %ETHPORT-5-IF_DOWN_INITIALIZING: Interface Ethernet1/7 is
  down (Initializing)
04:44:04 NX-1 %$ VDC-1 %$ %ETH_PORT_CHANNEL-5-PORT_DOWN: port-channel2: Ethernet1/8
  is down
04:44:04 NX-1 %$ VDC-1 %$ %ETHPORT-5-IF_DOWN_INITIALIZING: Interface Ethernet1/8 is
  down (Initializing)
04:44:06 NX-1 %$ VDC-1 %$ %ETH_PORT_CHANNEL-5-PORT_HOT_STANDBY: port-channel2: Eth-
  ernet1/7 goes to hot-standby
04:44:06 NX-1 %$ VDC-1 %$ %ETH_PORT_CHANNEL-5-PORT_HOT_STANDBY: port-channel2: Eth-
  ernet1/8 goes to hot-standby

NX-1# show port-channel summary
Flags:  D - Down        P - Up in port-channel (members)
        I - Individual  H - Hot-standby (LACP only)
        s - Suspended   r - Module-removed
        S - Switched    R - Routed
        U - Up (port-channel)
        p - Up in delay-lacp mode (member)
        M - Not in use. Min-links not met
--------------------------------------------------------------------------------
Group Port-       Type     Protocol  Member Ports
      Channel
--------------------------------------------------------------------------------
1     Po1(SU)     Eth      LACP      Eth1/1(P)   Eth1/2(P)
2     Po2(SU)     Eth      LACP      Eth1/3(P)   Eth1/4(P)   Eth1/5(P)
                                     Eth1/6(P)   Eth1/7(H)   Eth1/8(H)
```

The maximum number of port-channel member interfaces can be configured on only one switch for that port-channel; however, configuring it on both switches is recommended to accelerate troubleshooting and assist operational staff. The interfaces show as "suspended" on the secondary switch.

The port-channel master switch controls which member interfaces (and associated links) are active by examining the LACP port priority. A lower port priority is preferred. If the port-priority is the same, the lower interface number is preferred.

LACP System Priority

The LACP system priority identifies which switch is the master switch for a port-channel. The master switch on a port-channel is responsible for choosing which member interfaces are active in a port-channel when the number of member interfaces is greater than the maximum number of member interfaces associated to a port-channel interface. The switch with the lower system priority is preferred. The LACP system priority is changed with the global command **lacp system-priority** *priority*.

Example 5-10 demonstrates how the LACP system priority is verified and changed.

Example 5-10 *Viewing and Changing the LACP System Priority*

```
NX-1# show lacp system-identifier
32768,88-5a-92-de-61-7c
```

```
NX-1# configuration t
Enter configuration commands, one per line. End with CNTL/Z.
NX-1(config)# lacp system-priority 1
```

```
NX-1# show lacp system-identifier
1,88-5a-92-de-61-7c
```

LACP Interface Priority

The LACP port interface priority enables the master switch to choose which member interfaces are active in a port-channel when the number of member interfaces is greater than the maximum number of member-interfaces for a port-channel. A port with a lower port priority is preferred. The interface configuration command **lacp port-priority** *priority* sets the interface priority.

Example 5-11 changes the port priority on NX-1 for Eth1/8 so that it is the most preferred interface. Because NX-1 is the master switch for port-channel 2, the Eth1/8 interface becomes active, and ports Eth1/6 and Eth1/7 are in Hot-Standby because of the previous configuration of maximum links set to four.

Example 5-11 *Changing the LACP Port Priority*

```
NX-1(config)# interface e1/8
NX-1(config-if)# lacp port-priority 1
05:00:08 NX-1 %$ VDC-1 %$ %ETH_PORT_CHANNEL-5-PORT_DOWN: port-channel2: Ethernet1/6
  is down
05:00:08 NX-1 %$ VDC-1 %$ %ETHPORT-5-IF_DOWN_INITIALIZING: Interface Ethernet1/6 is
  down (Initializing)
05:00:12 NX-1 %$ VDC-1 %$ %ETH_PORT_CHANNEL-5-PORT_UP: port-channel2: Ethernet1/8
  is up
05:00:12 NX-1 %$ VDC-1 %$ %ETHPORT-5-IF_UP: Interface Ethernet1/8 is up in mode
  trunk
```

```
NX-1# show port-channel summary
Flags:  D - Down        P - Up in port-channel (members)
        I - Individual  H - Hot-standby (LACP only)
        s - Suspended   r - Module-removed
        S - Switched    R - Routed
        U - Up (port-channel)
        p - Up in delay-lacp mode (member)
        M - Not in use. Min-links not met
--------------------------------------------------------------------------------
Group Port-      Type     Protocol  Member Ports
      Channel
--------------------------------------------------------------------------------
1     Po1(SU)    Eth      LACP      Eth1/1(P)   Eth1/2(P)
2     Po2(SU)    Eth      LACP      Eth1/3(P)   Eth1/4(P)   Eth1/5(P)
                                    Eth1/6(s)   Eth1/7(s)   Eth1/8(P)
```

LACP Fast

The original LACP standards sent out LACP packets every 30 seconds. A link is deemed unusable if an LACP packet is not received after three intervals. This results in potentially 90 seconds of packet loss for a link before that member interface is removed from a port-channel.

An amendment to the standards was made so that LACP packets are advertised every second. This is known as LACP fast because a link is identified and removed in 3 seconds, compared to the 90 seconds of the initial LACP standard. LACP fast is enabled on the member interfaces with the interface configuration command **lacp rate fast**.

Note All interfaces on both switches must be configured the same, either LACP fast or LACP slow, for the port-channel to successfully come up.

> **Note** When using LACP fast, check your respective platform's release notes to ensure that in-service software upgrade (ISSU) and graceful switchover are still supported.

Example 5-12 demonstrates identifying the current LACP state on the local and neighbor interface, along with converting an interface to LACP fast.

Example 5-12 *Configuring LACP Fast and Verifying LACP Speed State*

```
NX-1# show lacp interface ethernet1/1 | i Timeout|Local|Neighbor
Local Port: Eth1/1    MAC Address= 88-5a-92-de-61-7c
  LACP_Timeout=Long Timeout (30s)
  Partner information refresh timeout=Long Timeout (90s)
Neighbor: 0x11c
  LACP_Timeout=Long Timeout (30s)
```

```
NX-1# conf t
Enter configuration commands, one per line. End with CNTL/Z.
NX-1(config)# interface Eth1/1
NX-1(config-if)# lacp rate fast
```

```
NX-1# show lacp interface ethernet1/1 | i Timeout|Local|Neighbor
Local Port: Eth1/1    MAC Address= 88-5a-92-de-61-7c
  LACP_Timeout=Short Timeout (1s)
  Partner information refresh timeout=Long Timeout (90s)
Neighbor: 0x11c
  LACP_Timeout=Long Timeout (30s)
```

Graceful Convergence

Nexus switches have LACP graceful convergence enabled by default with the port-channel interface command **lacp graceful-convergence**. When a Nexus switch is connected to a non-Cisco peer device, its graceful failover defaults can delay the time to bring down a disabled port.

Another scenario involves forming LACP adjacencies with devices that do not fully support the LACP specification. For example, a non-compliant LACP device might start to transmit data upon receiving the Sync LACP message (step 2 from forming LACP adjacencies) before transmitting the Collecting LACP message to a peer. Because the local switch still has not reached a Collecting state, these packets are dropped.

The solution involves removing LACP graceful convergence on port-channel interfaces when connecting to noncompliant LACP devices with the **no lacp graceful-convergence** command. The Nexus switch then waits longer for the port to initialize before sending a

Sync LACP message to the peer. This ensures that the port receives packets upon sending the Sync LACP message.

Suspend Individual

By default, Nexus switches place an LACP port in a suspended state if it does not receive an LACP PDU from the peer. Typically, this behavior helps prevent loops that occur with a bad switch configuration. However, it can cause some issues with some servers that require LACP to logically bring up the port.

This behavior is changed by disabling the feature with the port-channel interface command **no lacp suspend-individual**.

Port-Channel Member Interface Consistency

Because a port-channel is a logical interface, all member interfaces must have the same characteristics. The following must match on the member interfaces:

- **Port Type:** All ports in the interface must be consistently configured to be an L2 switch port or an L3 routed port. The error message "port not compatible [Ethernet Layer]" indicates this failure condition.

- **Port Mode:** L2 port-channels must be configured as either an access port or a trunk port. They cannot be mixed. The error message "port not compatible [port mode]" appears in this scenario.

- **Native virtual local area network (VLAN):** The member interfaces on an L2 trunk port-channels must be configured with the same native VLAN with the command **switchport trunk native vlan** *vlan-id*. Otherwise, the error message "port not compatible [port native VLAN]" appears.

- **Allowed VLAN:** The member interfaces on an L2 trunk port-channel must be configured to support the same VLANs with the command **switchport trunk allowed** *vlan-ids*. Otherwise, the error message "port not compatible [port allowed VLAN list]' appears.

- **Speed:** All member interfaces must be the same speed. In this scenario, an interface is placed into a suspended state and the syslog message "%ETH_PORT_CHANNEL-5-IF_DOWN_SUSPENDED_BY_SPEED" appears.

- **Duplex:** The duplex must be the same for all member interfaces. Otherwise, the syslog message "command failed: port not compatible [Duplex Mode]" appears. This is applicable only for interfaces operating at 100 Mbps or slower.

- **MTU:** All L3 member interfaces must have the same maximum transmission unit (MTU) configured. The interface cannot be added to the port-channel if the MTU does not match the other member interfaces. The syslog message "command failed: port not compatible [Ethernet Layer]" appears in this scenario. This message matches the Port Type message and requires examining the member interface configuration to identify the mismatched MTU.

- **Load Interval:** The load interval must be configured on all member interfaces. Otherwise, the syslog message "command failed: port not compatible [load interval]" appears.

- **Storm Control:** The port-channel member ports must be configured with the same storm control settings. Otherwise, the syslog message "port not compatible [Storm Control]" appears.

> **Note** A full list of compatibility parameters that must match is included with the command **show port-channel compatibility-parameters**.

As a general rule, when configuring port-channels on a Nexus switch, place the member interfaces into the appropriate switch port type (L2 or L3) and then associate the interfaces with a port-channel. All other port-channel configuration is done via the port-channel interface.

If a consistency error occurs, locate member interfaces with the **show port-channel summary** command, view a member interface configuration, and apply it to the interface you want to join the port-channel group.

Troubleshooting LACP Interface Establishment

The following list summarizes areas to check when troubleshooting the establishment of a port-channel interface on Nexus switches:

- Ensure that links are between only two devices.
- Confirm that the member ports are all active.
- Determine that both end links are statically set to "on" or are LACP enabled, with at least one side set to "active."
- Ensure that all member interface ports are consistently configured (except for LACP port priority).
- Verify LACP packet transmission and receipt on both devices.

Troubleshooting Traffic Load-Balancing

Traffic that flows across a port-channel interface is not forwarded out of member links on a round-robin basis per packet. Instead, a hash is calculated and packets are consistently forwarded across a link based upon that hash that runs on the various packet header fields. The load-balancing hash is a system-wide configuration that uses the global command **port-channel load-balance ether** *hash*. The *hash* option has the following keyword choices:

- **destination-ip:** Destination IP address
- **destination-mac:** Destination MAC address

- **destination-port:** Destination TCP/UDP port
- **source-dest-ip:** Source and destination IP address (includes L2)
- **source-dest-ip-only:** Source and destination IP addresses only
- **source-dest-mac:** Source and destination MAC address
- **source-dest-port:** Source and destination TCP/UDP port (includes L2 and L3)
- **source-dest-port-only:** Source and destination TCP/UDP port only
- **source-ip:** Source IP address
- **source-mac:** Source MAC address
- **source-port:** Source TCP/UDP port

Some member links in a port-channel might have a higher utilization than other links. This scenario can occur depending on the port-channel configuration and the traffic crossing it.

The command **show port-channel traffic** [**interface port-channel** *port-channel-number*] displays all the member interfaces and the amount of traffic crossing that member interface. Example 5-13 demonstrates the command.

Example 5-13 *Viewing the Traffic Load on Member Interfaces*

```
NX-1# show port-channel traffic
NOTE: Clear the port-channel member counters to get accurate statistics

ChanId     Port  Rx-Ucst Tx-Ucst Rx-Mcst Tx-Mcst Rx-Bcst Tx-Bcst
------     ----  ------- ------- ------- ------- ------- -------
     1    Eth1/1  98.68%  66.66%   4.08%  85.12%  70.95%    0.0%
     1    Eth1/2   1.31%  33.33%  95.91%  14.87%  29.04% 100.00%
```

The load-balancing hash is seen with the command **show port-channel load-balance**, as Example 5-14 shows. The default system hash is *source-dest-ip*, which calculates the hash based upon the source and destination IP address in the packet header.

Example 5-14 *Viewing the Port-Channel Hash Algorithm*

```
NX-1# show port-channel load-balance

Port Channel Load-Balancing Configuration:
System: source-dest-ip

Port Channel Load-Balancing Addresses Used Per-Protocol:
Non-IP: source-dest-mac
IP: source-dest-ip
```

If the links are unevenly distributed, changing the hash value might provide a different distribution ratio across member-links. For example, if the port-channel is established with a router, using a MAC address as part of the hash could impact the traffic flow because the router's MAC address does not change (the MAC address for the source or destination is always the router's MAC address). A better choice is to use the source/destination IP address or base it off session ports.

> **Note:** Add member links to a port-channel in powers of 2 (2, 4, 8, 16) to ensure that the hash is calculated consistently.

In rare cases, troubleshooting is required to determine which member link a packet is traversing on a port-channel. This involves checking for further diagnostics (optic, ASIC, and so on) when dealing with random packet loss. A member link is identified with the command **show port-channel load-balance** [**forwarding-path interface port-channel** *number* { . | **vlan** *vlan_ID* } [**dst-ip** *ipv4-addr*] [**dst-ipv6** *ipv6-addr*] [**dst-mac** *dst-mac-addr*] [**l4-dst-port** *dst-port*] [**l4-src-port** *src-port*] [**src-ip** *ipv4-addr*] [**src-ipv6** *ipv6-addr*] [**src-mac** *src-mac-addr*]].

Example 5-15 demonstrates how the member link is identified on NX-1 for a packet coming from 192.168.2.2 toward 192.168.1.1 on port-channel 1.

Example 5-15 *Identifying a Member Link for Specific Network Traffic*

```
NX-1# show port-channel load-balance forwarding-path interface port-channel 1 src-
  interface ethernet 1/1 dst-ip 192.168.1.1 src-ip 192.168.2.2
Missing params will be substituted by 0's.
        Outgoing port id: Ethernet1/1
Param(s) used to calculate load-balance:
        dst-ip:     192.168.1.1
        src-ip:     192.168.2.2
        dst-mac:    0000.0000.0000
        src-mac:    0000.0000.0000
        VLAN: 0
```

Virtual Port-Channel

Port-channels lend many benefits to a design, but only two devices (one local and one remote) can be used. NX-OS includes a feature called virtual port-channel (vPC) that enables two Nexus switches to create a virtual switch in what is called a vPC domain. vPC peers then provide a logical Layer 2 (L2) port-channel to a remote device.

Figure 5-4 provides a topology to demonstrate vPCs. NX-2 and NX-3 are members of the same vPC domain and are configured with a vPC providing a logical port-channel toward NX-1. From the perspective of NX-1, it is connected to only one switch.

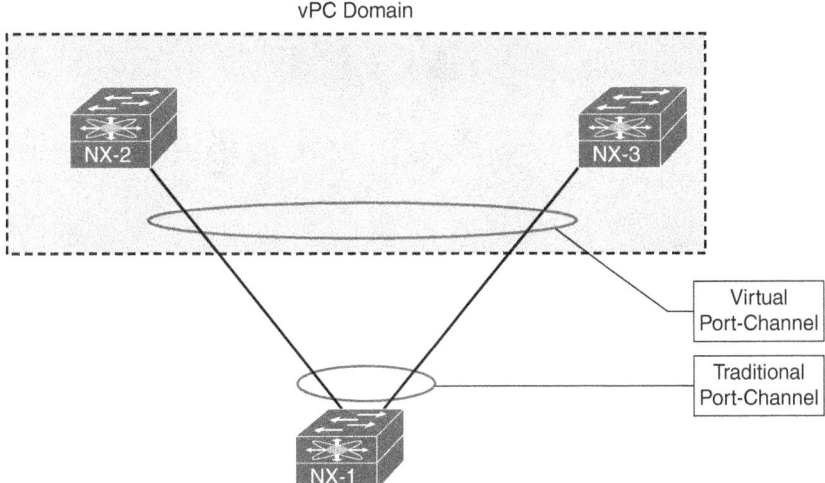

Figure 5-4 *Virtual Port-Channel*

Note Unlike switch stacking or Virtual Switching Systems (VSS) clustering technologies, the configuration of the individual switch ports remains separate. In other words, the Nexus switches are configured independently.

vPC Fundamentals

Only two Nexus switches can participate in a vPC domain. The vPC feature also includes a vPC peer-keepalive link, vPC member links, and the actual vPC interface. Figure 5-5 shows a topology with these components.

vPC Domain

A Nexus switch can have regular port-channel and vPC interfaces at the same time. A different LACP system ID is used in the LACP advertisements between the port-channel and vPC interfaces. Both Nexus peer switches use a virtual LACP system ID for the vPC member link.

One of the switches is the primary device and the other is the secondary device. The Nexus switches select the switch with the lower role priority as the primary device. If a tie occurs, the Nexus switch with the lower MAC address is preferred. No pre-emption takes place in identifying the primary device, so the concept of operational primary device and operational secondary device is introduced.

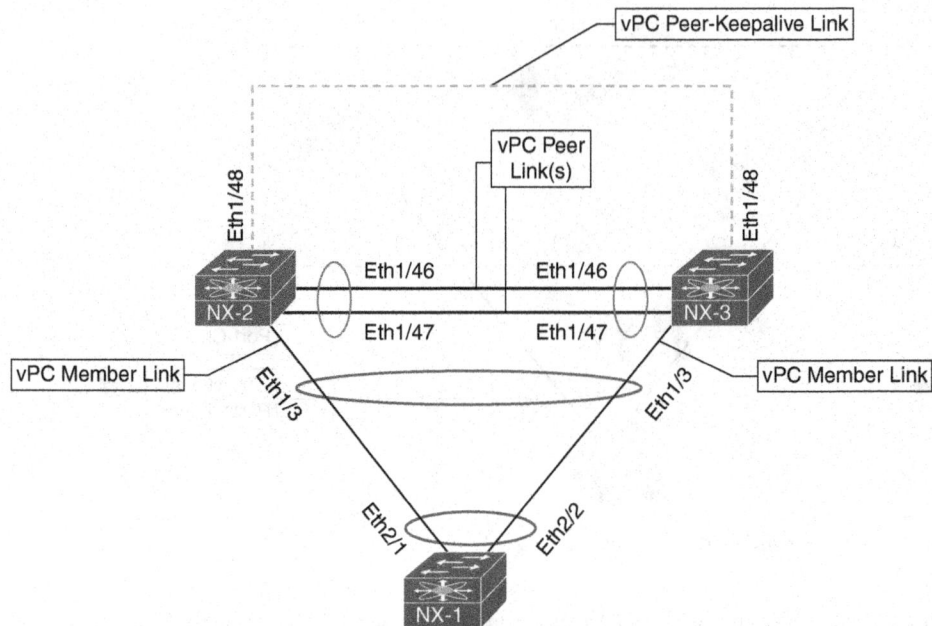

Figure 5-5 *vPC Components*

This concept is demonstrated in the following steps by imagining that NX-2 and NX-3 are in the same vPC domain, and NX-2 has a lower role priority.

Step 1. As both switches boot and initialize, neither switch has been elected as the vPC domain primary device. Then NX-2 becomes the primary device and the operational primary device, while NX-3 becomes the secondary device and the operational secondary device.

Step 2. NX-2 is reloaded. NX-3 then becomes the primary device and the operational primary device.

Step 3. When NX-2 completes its initialization, it again has the lower role priority but does not preempt NX-3. At this stage, NX-2 is the primary device and the operational secondary device, and NX-3 is the secondary device and the operational primary device. Only when NX-3 reloads or shuts down all vPC interfaces does NX-2 become the operational primary device.

vPC Peer-Keepalive

The vPC peer-keepalive link monitors the health of the peer vPC device. It sends keepalive messages on a periodic basis (system default of 1 second). The heartbeat packet is 96 bytes in length, using UDP port 3200. If the peer link fails, connectivity is checked across the vPC peer link. Not a lot of network traffic is submitted across the peer-keepalive link, so a 1-Gbps interface is used.

A vPC peer device detects a peer failure by not receiving any peer-keepalive messages. A hold-timeout timer starts as soon as the vPC peer is deemed unavailable. During the hold-timeout period (system default of 5 seconds), the secondary vPC device ignores any vPC keep-alive messages to ensure that the network can converge before action is taken against vPC interfaces. After the hold-timeout period expires, the timeout timer begins (system default of 3 seconds). If a vPC keep-alive message is not received during this interval, the vPC interfaces on the secondary vPC switch are shut down. This behavior prevents a split-blain scenario.

Note Although using a VLAN interface for the peer-keepalive interface is technically feasible, this approach is discouraged because it can cause confusion. Additionally, the link should be directly connected where possible (with the exception of the management ports).

vPC Peer Link

The vPC peer link is used to synchronize state and forward data between devices. For example, imagine that a server is attached to NX-1 and is communicating with a host attached to NX-2. Because the port-channel hash on NX-1, traffic is sent out the Ethernet2/2 link toward NX-3. NX-3 uses the vPC peer link to forward the packet toward NX-2 so that NX-2 can forward the traffic toward the directly attached host.

The vPC peer link must be on a 10-Gbps or higher Ethernet port. Typically, a port-channel is used to ensure that enough bandwidth exists for traffic sent from one vPC peer to be redirected where appropriate to the remote vPC peer. In addition, on modular Nexus switches, the links should be spread across different line cards/modules to ensure that the peer link stays up during a hardware failure.

vPC Member Links

The vPC member links are the individual links on the Nexus switches in the vPC domain. A port-channel identifier is associated with the vPC member ports.

vPC Operational Behavior

NX-OS modifies STP behavior with the three following changes:

- The vPC peer link never enters a blocking state.
- Only the operational primary Nexus switch generates and processes BPDUs. The operational secondary Nexus switch forwards BPDUs received across the peer link toward the operational primary Nexus switch.
- Traffic received on a vPC peer link is never advertised out a vPC member port. This is part of a loop-prevention mechanism.

The *Hot Standby Router Protocol (HSRP)* runs on network devices and provides a fault-tolerant virtual IP for hosts on a network segment. With HSRP, only one network device actively forwards traffic for the virtual IP. However, on some Nexus platforms that are deployed with vPC, both Nexus switches actively forward traffic for the virtual gateway. This improves bandwidth and reduces sending Layer 3 (L3) network traffic across the vPC peer link.

vPC Configuration

The vPC configuration contains the following basic steps:

Step 1. **Enable the vPC feature.** The vPC feature must be enabled with the command **feature vpc**.

Step 2. **Enable the LACP feature.** vPC port-channels require the use of LACP, so the LACP feature must be enabled with the command **feature lacp**.

Step 3. **Configure the peer-keepalive link.** The peer-keepalive link must be configured. Cisco recommends creating a dedicated virtual routing and forwarding (VRF) for the peer-keepalive link. Then an IP address must be associated with that interface using the command **ip address** *ip-address mask*.

> **Note** Using the management interface for the peer-keepalive link is possible, but this requires a management switch to provide connectivity between peer devices. If a system has multiple supervisors (as with Nexus 7000/9000), both the active and standby management ports on each vPC peer need to connect to the management switch.

Step 4. **Configure the vPC domain.** The vPC domain is the logical construct that both Nexus peers use. The vPC domain is created with the command **vpc domain** *domain-id*. The domain ID must match on both devices.

In the vPC domain context, the peer-keepalive interfaces must be identified with the command **peer-keepalive destination** *remote-nexus-ip* [**hold-timeout** *secs* | **interval** *msecs* {**timeout** *secs*} | **source** *local-nexus-ip* | **vrf** *name*]. The source interface is optional, but statically assigning it as part of the configuration is recommended. The peer-keepalive advertisement interval, hold-timeout, and timeout values are configured by using the optional keywords **hold-timeout, interval,** and **timeout**.

NX-OS automatically creates a vPC system MAC address for the LACP messaging, but the MAC address is defined with the **system-mac** *mac-address* command. The LACP system priority for vPC domain is 32768, but it can be modified with the command **system-priority** *priority* to increase or lower the virtual LACP priority.

Step 5. **Configure the vPC device priority (optional).** The vPC device priority is configured with the command **role priority** *priority*. The *priority* can be set from 1 to 65,535, with the lower value more preferred. The preferred node is the primary vPC node; the other node is the secondary.

Step 6. **Configure the vPC System priority (optional).** Regular port-channel negotiation between two switches must identify the master switch; the same concept applies to vPC interfaces. The vPC LACP system priority is configured with the domain configuration command **system-priority** *priority*.

Step 7. **Configure vPC autorecovery (optional but recommended) link.** As a safety mechanism, a vPC peer does not enable any vPC interfaces until it detects the other vPC peer. In some failure scenarios, such as power failures, both vPC devices are restarted and do not detect each other. This can cause a loss of traffic because neither device forwards traffic.

The vPC autorecovery feature provides a method for one of the vPC peers to start forwarding traffic. Upon initialization, if the vPC peer link is down and three consecutive peer-keepalive messages are not responded to, the secondary device assumes the operational primary role and initializes vPC interfaces to allow some traffic to be forwarded. vPC autorecovery is explained later in this chapter.

This feature is enabled with the vPC domain configuration command **auto-recovery** [**reload-delay** *delay*]. The default delay is 240 seconds before engaging this feature, but this can be changed using the optional **reload-delay** keyword. The delay is a value between 240 and 3600.

Step 8. **Configure the vPC.** Ports are assigned to the port-channel with the command **channel-group** *portchannel-number* **mode active** command. The port-channel interface is assigned a unique vPC identifier with the command **vpc** *vpc-id*. The *vpc-id* needs to match on the remote peer device.

Example 5-16 demonstrates the vPC configuration of NX-2 from Figure 5-5.

Example 5-16 *Demonstration of vPC Configuration*

```
NX-2# configuration t
Enter configuration commands, one per line. End with CNTL/Z.
! Enable the vPC and LACP features
NX-2(config)# feature vpc
NX-2(config)# feature lacp
! Creation of the vPC Peer-KeepAlive VRF and association of IP address
NX-2(config)# vrf context VPC-KEEPALIVE
NX-2(config-vrf)# address-family ipv4 unicast
NX-2(config-vrf-af-ipv4)# interface Ethernet1/48
NX-2(config-if)# description vPC-KeepAlive
NX-2(config-if)# no switchport
NX-2(config-if)# vrf member VPC-KEEPALIVE
```

```
NX-2(config-if)# ip address 192.168.1.1/30
NX-2(config-if)# no shutdown
! Configuration of the vPC Domain
NX-2(config-if)# vpc domain 100
NX-2(config-vpc-domain)# peer-keepalive destination 192.168.1.2 source 192.168.1.1
  vrf VPC-KEEPALIVE
! Configuration of the vPC Peer-Link
NX-2(config)# interface Ethernet1/46-47
NX-2(config-if-range)# description vPC-PeerLink
NX-2(config-if-range)# channel-group 100 mode active
NX-2(config-if-range)# interface port-channel 100
NX-2(config-if)# switchport mode trunk
NX-2(config-if)# vpc peer-link
! Creation of the vPC Port-Channel
NX-2(config)# interface ethernet 1/1
NX-2(config-if)# channel-group 1 mode active
NX-2(config-if)# interface port-channel 1
NX-2(config-if)# vpc 1
NX-2(config-if)# switchport mode trunk
```

vPC Verification

Now that both Nexus switches are configured, the health of the vPC domain must be examined.

Verifying the vPC Domain Status

The **show vpc** command verifies the operational state of the vPC domain. The output includes the peer status, the vPC keep-alive status, the consistency check status, the vPC device role (primary/secondary), the vPC port-channel interface, and supported VLANS, along with a listing of the vPC(s) configured on the local switch.

Example 5-17 demonstrates the output of the **show vpc** command for NX-2.

Example 5-17 *Viewing vPC Status*

```
NX-2# show vpc
Legend:
                (*) - local vPC is down, forwarding via vPC peer-link

vPC domain id                     : 100
Peer status                       : peer adjacency formed ok
vPC keep-alive status             : peer is alive
Per-vlan consistency status       : success
Type-2 consistency status         : success
```

Virtual Port-Channel

```
vPC role                        : primary
Number of vPCs configured       : 1
Peer Gateway                    : Disabled
Dual-active excluded VLANs      : -
Graceful Consistency Check      : Enabled
Auto-recovery status            : Disabled
Delay-restore status            : Timer is off.(timeout = 30s)
Delay-restore SVI status        : Timer is off.(timeout = 10s)
Operational Layer3 Peer-router  : Disabled


vPC Peer-link status
---------------------------------------------------------------------
id    Port     Status Active vlans
--    ----     ------ --------------------------------------------
1     Po100    up     1,10,20



vPC status
----------------------------------------------------------------------------
Id    Port          Status Consistency Reason          Active vlans
--    ------------  ------ ----------- ------          --------------
1     Po1           up     success     success         1
```

As stated earlier, the peer link should be in a forwarding state. This is verified by examining the STP state with the command **show spanning-tree**, as Example 5-18 demonstrates. Notice that the vPC interface (port-channel 100) interface is in a forwarding state and is identified as a network point-to-point port.

Example 5-18 *Viewing STP Behavior Changes with vPC*

```
NX-2# show spanning-tree vlan 1

VLAN0001
  Spanning tree enabled protocol rstp
  Root ID    Priority    28673
             Address     885a.92de.617c
             Cost        1
             Port        4096 (port-channel1)
             Hello Time  2  sec  Max Age 20 sec  Forward Delay 15 sec

  Bridge ID  Priority    32769  (priority 32768 sys-id-ext 1)
             Address     88f0.3187.3b8b
             Hello Time  2  sec  Max Age 20 sec  Forward Delay 15 sec
```

```
Interface         Role Sts Cost      Prio.Nbr Type
---------------- ---- --- ---------  -------- --------------------------------
Po1               Root FWD 1          128.4096 (vPC) P2p
Po100             Desg FWD 1          128.4195 (vPC peer-link) Network P2p
Eth1/45           Desg FWD 2          128.45   P2p

NX-3# show spanning-tree vlan 1
! Output omitted for brevity
Interface         Role Sts Cost      Prio.Nbr Type
---------------- ---- --- ---------  -------- --------------------------------
Po1               Root FWD 1          128.4096 (vPC) P2p
Po100             Root FWD 1          128.4195 (vPC peer-link) Network P2p
Eth1/45           Altn BLK 2          128.45   P2p
```

Verifying the Peer-Keepalive

If a problem is reported with the vPC keepalive, the command **show vpc peer-keepalive** provides the detailed status of the peer-keepalive link. The output includes the vPC keepalive status, the duration that the peer was active or down, the interface used for the keepalive, and the keepalive timers. Example 5-19 displays the vPC peer-keepalive status using this command.

Example 5-19 *Viewing the vPC Peer-Keepalive Status*

```
NX-2# show vpc peer-keepalive

vPC keep-alive status             : peer is alive
--Peer is alive for               : (1440) seconds, (939) msec
--Send status                     : Success
--Last send at                    : 2017.11.03 03:37:49 799 ms
--Sent on interface               : Eth1/48
--Receive status                  : Success
--Last receive at                 : 2017.11.03 03:37:49 804 ms
--Received on interface           : Eth1/48
--Last update from peer           : (0) seconds, (414) msec

vPC Keep-alive parameters
--Destination                     : 192.168.1.2
--Keepalive interval              : 1000 msec
--Keepalive timeout               : 5 seconds
--Keepalive hold timeout          : 3 seconds
--Keepalive vrf                   : VPC-KEEPALIVE
--Keepalive udp port              : 3200
--Keepalive tos                   : 192
```

If the status shows as "down," verify that each switch can ping the other switch from the VRF context that is configured. If the ping fails, troubleshooting basic connectivity between the two switches needs to be performed.

vPC Consistency-Checker

Just as with port-channel interfaces, certain parameters must match on both Nexus switches in the vPC domain. NX-OS contains a specific process called the *consistency-checker* to ensure that the settings are compatible and to prevent unpredictable packet loss. The consistency-checker has two types of errors:

- Type 1
- Type 2

Type 1

When a Type 1 vPC consistency-checker error occurs, the vPC instance and vPC member ports on the operational secondary Nexus switch enter a suspended state and stop forwarding network traffic. The operational primary Nexus switch still forwards network traffic. These settings must match to avoid a Type 1 consistency error:

- Port-channel mode: on, off, or active
- Link speed per channel
- Duplex mode per channel
- Trunk mode per channel
    - Native VLAN
    - VLANs allowed on trunk
    - Tagging of native VLAN traffic
- STP mode
- STP region configuration for Multiple Spanning Tree
- Same enable/disable state per VLAN
- STP global settings
    - Bridge Assurance setting
    - Port type setting (recommended: setting all vPC peer link ports as network ports)
    - Loop Guard settings
- STP interface settings
    - Port type setting
    - Loop Guard
    - Root Guard

- MTU
- Allowed VLAN bit set

> **Note** NX-OS version 5.2 introduced a feature called *graceful consistency checker* that changes the behavior for Type 1 inconsistencies. The graceful consistency checker enables the operational primary device to forward traffic. If this feature is disabled, the vPC is shut down completely. This feature is enabled by default.

Type 2

A Type 2 vPC consistency-checker error indicates the potential for undesired forwarding behavior, such as having a VLAN interface on one node and not another.

Identifying the vPC Consistency Checker Settings

Example 5-20 displays the output from **show vpc** when the consistency checker detects a failed consistency check status and provides the reason for the error. Depending on the error, all vPC interfaces or just one might be in a failed state.

Example 5-20 *vPC Status with Consistency Checker Error*

```
NX-2# show vpc
Legend:
                (*) - local vPC is down, forwarding via vPC peer-link

vPC domain id                     : 100
Peer status                       : peer adjacency formed ok
vPC keep-alive status             : peer is alive
Configuration consistency status  : failed
Per-vlan consistency status       : success
Configuration inconsistency reason: vPC type-1 configuration incompatible - STP
Mode inconsistent
Type-2 consistency status         : success
vPC role                          : primary
Number of vPCs configured         : 1
Peer Gateway                      : Disabled
Dual-active excluded VLANs        : -
Graceful Consistency Check        : Enabled
Auto-recovery status              : Disabled
Delay-restore status              : Timer is off.(timeout = 30s)
Delay-restore SVI status          : Timer is off.(timeout = 10s)
Operational Layer3 Peer-router    : Disabled
```

```
vPC Peer-link status
-----------------------------------------------------------------
id    Port    Status Active vlans
--    ----    ------ ------------
1     Po100   up     1,10,20


vPC status
-----------------------------------------------------------------
Id    Port         Status Consistency Reason            Active vlans
--    ------------ ------ ----------- ------            ------------
1     Po1          up     failed      Global compat check  1,10,20
                                      failed
```

The command **show vpc consistency-parameters** {**global** | **vlan** | **vpc** *vpc-id* | **port-channel** *port-channel-identifier*} provides a side-by-side comparison of the local and remote settings, along with the consistency checker error level. The command parameter executed depends on the output of the **show vpc** command.

Example 5-21 displays the output for the **show vpc consistency-parameters global** command.

Example 5-21 show vpc consistency-parameters *Command*

```
NX-3(config)# show vpc consistency-parameters global

    Legend:
        Type 1 : vPC will be suspended in case of mismatch

Name                           Type Local Value            Peer Value
-------------                  ---- ---------------------- ----------------------
QoS (Cos)                      2    ([0-7], [], [], [],    ([0-7], [], [], [],
                                    [], [])                [], [])
Network QoS (MTU)              2    (1500, 1500, 1500,     (1500, 1500, 1500,
                                    1500, 0, 0)            1500, 0, 0)
Network Qos (Pause:            2    (F, F, F, F, F, F)     (F, F, F, F, F, F)
T->Enabled, F->Disabled)
Input Queuing (Bandwidth)      2    (0, 0, 0, 0, 0, 0)     (0, 0, 0, 0, 0, 0)
Input Queuing (Absolute        2    (F, F, F, F, F, F)     (F, F, F, F, F, F)
Priority: T->Enabled,
F->Disabled)
Output Queuing (Bandwidth      2    (100, 0, 0, 0, 0, 0)   (100, 0, 0, 0, 0, 0)
Remaining)
```

```
Output Queuing (Absolute      2    (F, F, F, T, F, F)    (F, F, F, T, F, F)
Priority: T->Enabled,
F->Disabled)
Vlan to Vn-segment Map        1    No Relevant Maps      No Relevant Maps
STP Mode                      1    Rapid-PVST            Rapid-PVST
STP Disabled                  1    None                  None
STP MST Region Name           1    " "                   " "
STP MST Region Revision       1    0                     0
STP MST Region Instance to    1
  VLAN Mapping
STP Loopguard                 1    Disabled              Disabled
STP Bridge Assurance          1    Enabled               Enabled
STP Port Type, Edge           1    Normal, Disabled,     Normal, Disabled,
BPDUFilter, Edge BPDUGuard         Disabled              Disabled
STP MST Simulate PVST         1    Enabled               Enabled
Nve Admin State, Src Admin    1    None                  None
  State, Secondary IP, Host
  Reach Mode
Nve Vni Configuration         1    None                  None
Interface-vlan admin up       2
Interface-vlan routing        2    1                     1
  capability
Allowed VLANs                 -    1,10,20               1,10,20
Local suspended VLANs         -    -                     -
```

Example 5-22 displays the output for the **show vpc consistency-parameters vlan** command. Configuration inconsistencies in this output can introduce undesirable forwarding behaviors.

Example 5-22 show vpc consistency-parameters vlan *Command*

```
NX-2# show vpc consistency-parameters vlan

Name                          Type  Reason Code           Pass Vlans

------------                  ----  --------------------  --------------------
Vlan to Vn-segment Map        1     success               0-4095
STP Mode                      1     success               0-4095
STP Disabled                  1     success               0-4095
STP MST Region Name           1     success               0-4095
STP MST Region Revision       1     success               0-4095
STP MST Region Instance to    1     success               0-4095
  VLAN Mapping
STP Loopguard                 1     success               0-4095
STP Bridge Assurance          1     success               0-4095
STP Port Type, Edge           1     success               0-4095
BPDUFilter, Edge BPDUGuard
```

```
STP MST Simulate PVST          1    success            0-4095
Nve Admin State, Src Admin     1    success            0-4095
 State, Secondary IP, Host
 Reach Mode
Nve Vni Configuration          1    success            0-4095
Pass Vlans                     -                       0-4095
```

vPC consistency parameters that are directly related to a port-channel interface are displayed with the command **show vpc consistency-parameters** {**vpc** *vpc-id* | **port-channel** *port-channel-identifier*} options. The port-channel is viewed by identifying the *vpc-id* (which might be different from the port-channel interface number). The output is exactly the same for either iteration of the command. Example 5-23 displays the output for the **show vpc consistency-parameters vpc** *vpc-id* command.

Example 5-23 show vpc consistency-parameters vpc *vpc-id* Command

```
NX-2# show vpc consistency-parameters vpc 1

    Legend:
         Type 1 : vPC will be suspended in case of mismatch

Name                        Type Local Value             Peer Value
-------------               ---- ----------------------  ----------------------
STP Port Type               1    Default                 Default
STP Port Guard              1    Default                 Default
STP MST Simulate PVST       1    Default                 Default
lag-id                      1    [(1,                    [(1,
                                 88-5a-92-de-61-7c,      88-5a-92-de-61-7c,
                                 8000, 0, 0), (7f9b,     8000, 0, 0), (7f9b,
                                 0-23-4-ee-be-64, 8001,  0-23-4-ee-be-64, 8001,
                                 0, 0)]                  0, 0)]
mode                        1    active                  active
delayed-lacp                1    disabled                disabled
Speed                       1    10 Gb/s                 10 Gb/s
Duplex                      1    full                    full
Port Mode                   1    trunk                   trunk
Native Vlan                 1    1                       1
MTU                         1    1500                    1500
LACP Mode                   1    on                      on
Interface type              1    port-channel            port-channel
Admin port mode             1    trunk                   trunk
Switchport Isolated         1    0                       0
vPC card type               1    N9K TOR                 N9K TOR
Allowed VLANs               -    1,10,20                 1,10,20
Local suspended VLANs       -    -                       -
```

Advanced vPC Features

The following sections examine some of the more advanced vPC features, functions, and design scenarios.

vPC Orphan Ports

A vPC orphan port is a non-vPC port associated with a vPC peer that has a VLAN associated with it that is present on the vPC or the vPC peer link. In other words, a server is connected to Ethernet 1/1 on VLAN 10, and a vPC interface contains VLAN 10 on it; then Ethernet 1/1 is an orphan port. If the vPC interface did not contain VLAN 10, Ethernet 1/1 is a regular access port. An orphan-port is viewed with the command **show vpc orphan-ports**. Example 5-24 demonstrates how to locate vPC orphan ports.

Example 5-24 *Viewing vPC Orphan Ports*

```
NX-2# show vpc orphan-ports
Note:
--------::Going through port database. Please be patient..::--------

VLAN            Orphan Ports
-------         ------------------------
1               Eth1/44, Eth1/45
```

As a general rule, orphan ports should be avoided by following these guidelines:

- Ensure that all downstream devices are connected by vPC interfaces.
- Prune VLANS from all the vPC interfaces and vPC peer link interfaces with the **switchport trunk allowed vlan** command. Those VLANS then are associated with the interface when a device can connect to only one network link. This is more of a design change.

An orphan port can be suspended on the operational secondary switch to prevent packet loss when the secondary peer suspends its vPC ports (upon a peer link or peer-keepalive failure). The interface configuration command **vpc orphan-port suspend** accomplishes this.

Example 5-25 displays this feature being enabled on Ethernet 1/44 and 1/45 on NX-2.

Example 5-25 *Suspending a vPC Orphan Port During vPC Failure*

```
NX-2# configure terminal
Enter configuration commands, one per line. End with CNTL/Z.
NX-2(config-if)# interface Eth1/44-45
NX-2(config-if)# vpc orphan-port suspend
```

vPC Autorecovery

As a safety mechanism, a vPC peer does not enable any vPC interfaces until it detects the other vPC peer. In some failure scenarios, such as power failures, both vPC devices are restarted and do not detect each other. This can cause a loss of traffic because neither device forwards traffic.

The vPC autorecovery feature provides a method for one of the vPC peers to start forwarding traffic. Upon initialization, if the vPC peer link is down and three consecutive peer-keepalive messages were not responded to, the secondary device assumes the operational primary role and can initialize vPC interfaces to allow some traffic to forward.

This feature is enabled with the vPC domain configuration command **auto-recovery** [**reload-delay** *delay*]. The default delay is 240 seconds before engaging this feature, but this can be changed with the optional **reload-delay** keyword. The delay is a value between 240 and 3600. Example 5-26 displays the configuration and verification of vPC autorecovery.

Example 5-26 *Configuration and Verification of vPC Autorecovery*

```
NX-2# configure terminal
Enter configuration commands, one per line. End with CNTL/Z.
NX-2(config)# vpc domain 100
NX-2(config-vpc-domain)# auto-recovery

NX-2# show vpc
! Output omitted for brevity
Legend:
 ..
Auto-recovery status               : Enabled, timer is off.(timeout = 240s)
```

vPC Peer-Gateway

The vPC peer-gateway capability allows a vPC device to route packets that are addressed to the router MAC address of the vPC peer. This functionality is used to overcome scenarios with misconfigurations and issues that arise with load balancers or network attached storage (NAS) devices that try to optimize packet forwarding.

For example, Figure 5-6 demonstrates a topology in which NX-2 and NX-3 are acting as the gateway for VLAN 100 and VLAN 200. NX-2 and NX-3 have a vPC configured for the web server and NX-1, which connects to the NAS. NX-1 is only switching (not routing) packets to or from the NAS device.

290   Chapter 5: Port-Channels, Virtual Port-Channels, and FabricPath

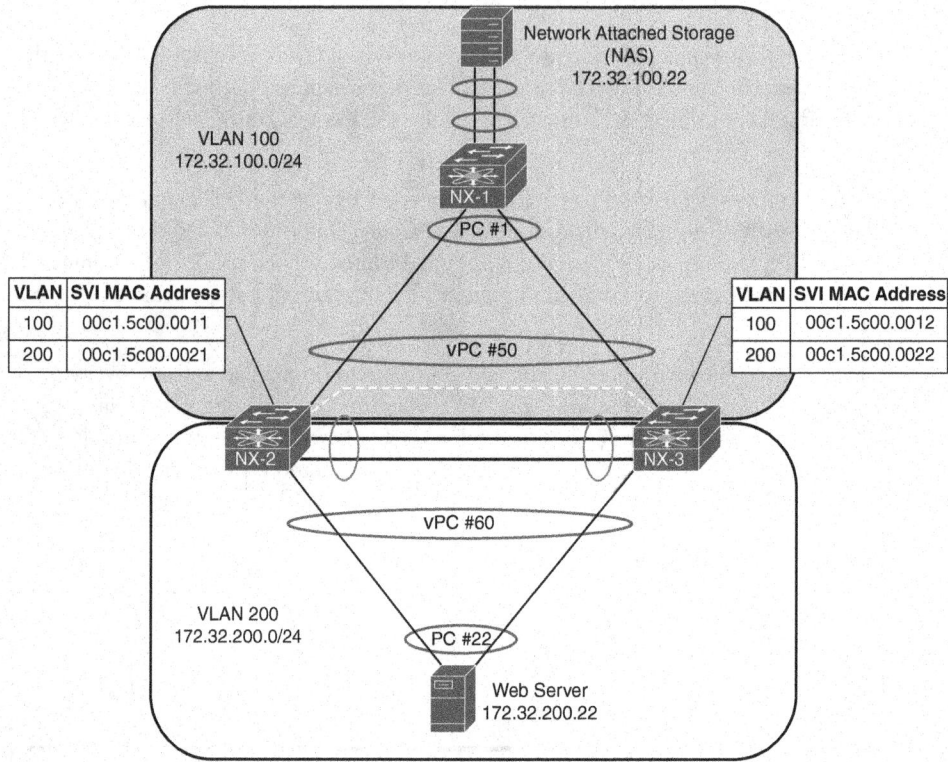

Figure 5-6 *vPC Peer-Gateway*

When the web server sends a packet to the NAS device (172.32.100.22), it computes a hash to identify which link it should send the packet on to reach the NAS device. Assume that the web server sends the packet to NX-2, which then changes the packet's source MAC address to 00c1.5c00.0011 (part of the routing process) and forwards the packet on to NX-1. NX-1 forwards (switches) the packet on to the NAS device.

Now the NAS device creates the reply packet and, when generating the packet headers, uses the destination MAC address of the HSRP gateway 00c1.1234.0001 and forwards the packet to NX-1. NX-1 computes a hash based on the source and destination IP address and forwards the packet toward NX-3. NX-2 and NX-3 both have the destination MAC address for the HSRP gateway and can then route the packet for the 172.32.200.0/24 network and forward it back to the web server. This is the correct and normal forwarding behavior.

The problem occurs when the NAS server enables a feature for optimizing packet flow. After the NAS device receives the packet from the web server and generates the reply packet headers, it just uses the source and destination MAC addresses from the packet it originally received. When NX-1 receives the reply packet, it calculates the hash and forwards the packet toward NX-3. Now NX-3 does not have the MAC address

00c1.5c00.0011 (NX-2's VLAN 100 interface) and cannot forward the packet toward NX-1. The packet is dropped because packets received on a vPC member port cannot be forwarded across the peer link, as a loop-prevention mechanism.

Enabling a vPC peer-gateway on NX-2 and NX-3 allows NX-3 to route packets destined for NX-2's MAC addresses, and vice versa. The vPC peer-gateway feature is enabled with the command **peer-gateway** under the vPC domain configuration. The vPC peer-gateway functionality is verified with the **show vpc** command. Example 5-27 demonstrates the configuration and verification of the peer-gateway feature.

Example 5-27 *Configuration and Verification of vPC Peer-Gateway*

```
NX-2(config)# vpc domain 100
NX-2(config-vpc-domain)# peer-gateway

NX-2# show vpc
! Output omitted for brevity
Legend:
                (*) - local vPC is down, forwarding via vPC peer-link

vPC domain id                   : 100
..
vPC role                        : primary
Number of Cs configured         : 1
Peer Gateway                    : Enabled
```

Note In addition, NX-OS automatically disables IP redirects on SVIs where the VLAN is enabled on a vPC trunk link.

Note Packets that are forwarded by the peer-gateway feature have their time to live (TTL) decremented. Packets carrying a TTL of 1 thus might get dropped in transit because of TTL expiration.

vPC ARP Synchronization

The previous section demonstrated how traffic becomes asymmetric depending on the hash calculated by the device with the regular port-channel interface. During normal operations, the device builds the Address Resolution Protocol (ARP) table (IP to MAC) in normal manner, but this is not fast enough when a node comes online after a reload. NX-OS includes an ARP synchronization feature that keeps the table synchronized between both vPC peers, thereby drastically speeding up the process for a vPC peer that was just restarted.

ARP synchronization is enabled with the command **ip arp synchronize** under the vPC domain configuration. Example 5-28 demonstrates enabling ARP synchronization on NX-2.

Example 5-28 *Enabling vPC ARP Synchronization*

```
NX-2# conf t
Enter configuration commands, one per line. End with CNTL/Z.
NX-2(config)# vpc domain 100
NX-2(config-vpc-domain)# ip arp synchronize
```

Backup Layer 3 Routing

Give special consideration to network designs when Nexus switches act as a gateway while providing vPC to hosts on that network segment. Certain failure scenarios can occur, or a Type 1 consistency check might trigger and shut down vPC ports.

Figure 5-7 demonstrates a simple topology in which NX-2 and NX-3 have an SVI interface for VLAN 200 that acts a gateway for the web server. NX-2, NX-3, and R4 are all running OSPF so that NX-2 and NX-3 can forward packets to R4. NX-3 is the operational primary Nexus switch.

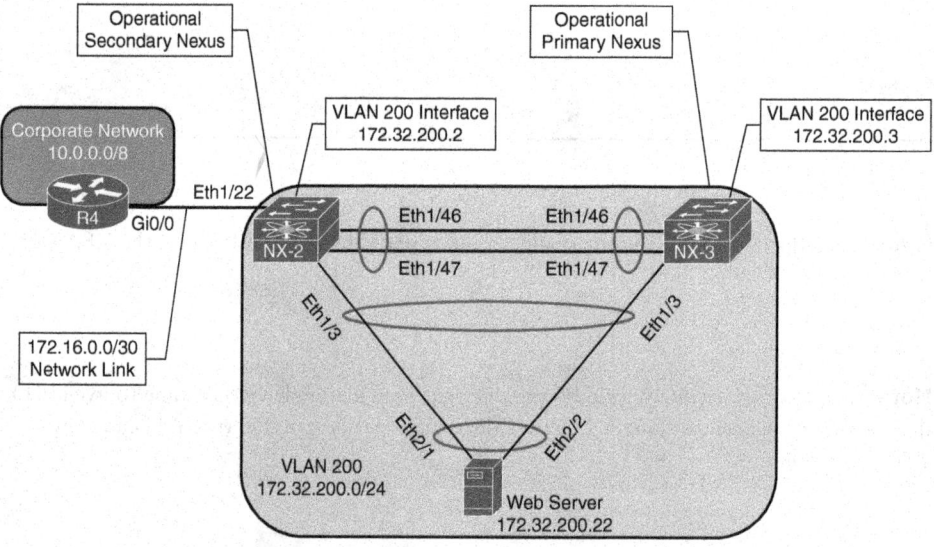

Figure 5-7 *Bad Layer 3 Routing Design*

If the vPC peer link is broken (physically or through an accidental change that triggers a Type 1 consistency checker error), NX-2 suspends activity on its vPC member port and shuts down the SVI for VLAN 200. NX-3 drops its routing protocol adjacency with NX-2 and then cannot provide connectivity to the corporate network for the web server. Any packets from the web server for the corporate network received by NX-3 are dropped.

This scenario is overcome by deploying a dedicated L3 connection between vPC peers. These are either individual links or an L3 port-channel interface.

Note Remember that the vPC peer link does not support the transmission of routing protocols as transient traffic. For example, suppose that Eth1/22 on NX-2 is a switch port that belongs to VLAN 200 and R4's Gi0/0 interface is configured with the IP address of 172.32.200.5. R4 pings NX-3, but it does not establish an OSPF adjacency with NX-3 because the OSPF packets are not transmitted across the vPC peer link. This is resolved by deploying the second solution listed previously.

Layer 3 Routing over vPC

vPC interfaces only forward traffic, from an L2 perspective. An IP address cannot be assigned directly to the vPC interface. The vPC devices provide gateway service to downstream devices by assigning IP addresses to the switched virtual interface (SVI) on the vPC devices.

However, vPC functionality was never meant to provide a logical L2 link to be used to form routing protocol adjacencies. However, the release of NX-OS version 7.3 provides the capability for the SVIs to form a routing protocol adjacency using a vPC interface with a router.

Note L3 Routing over vPC is specific only to unicast and does not include support for multicast network traffic.

Figure 5-8 demonstrates the concept in which NX-2 and NX-3 want to exchange routes using OSPF with R4 across the vPC interface. NX-2 and NX-3 enable Layer 3 routing over vPC to establish an Open Shortest Path First (OSPF) neighborship with R4. In essence, this design places NX-2, NX-3, and R4 on the same LAN segment.

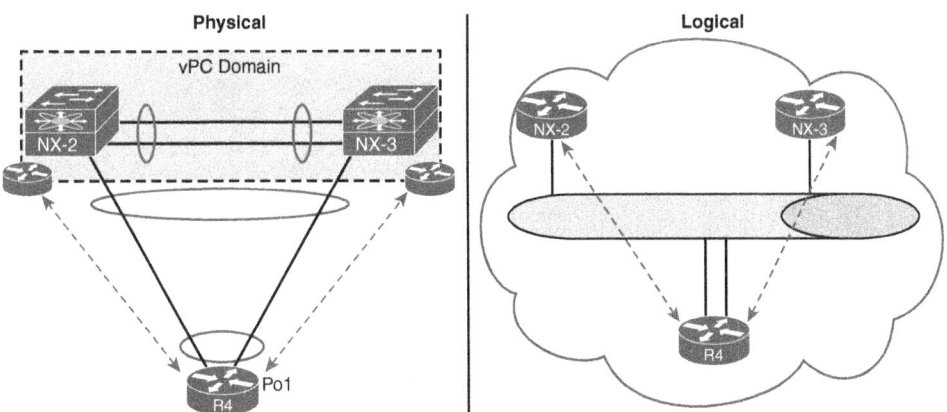

Figure 5-8 *Layer 3 Routing over vPC*

Layer 3 routing over vPC is configured under the vPC domain with the command **layer3 peer-router**. The peer-gateway is enabled when using this feature. The feature is verified with the command **show vpc**.

Example 5-29 demonstrates the configuration and verification of Layer 3 routing over vPC.

Example 5-29 *Configuration and Verification of Layer 3 Routing over vPC*

```
NX-2# configure terminal
Enter configuration commands, one per line. End with CNTL/Z.
NX-2(config)# vpc domain 100
NX-2(config-vpc-domain)# layer3 peer-router
```

```
NX-2# show vpc
! Output omitted for brevity
..
Delay-restore SVI status          : Timer is off.(timeout = 10s)
Operational Layer3 Peer-router    : Enabled
```

Note If vPC peering is not being established or vPC inconsistencies result, collect the **show tech vpc** command output and contact Cisco technical support.

FabricPath

Until recently, all L2 networks traditionally were enabled with STP to build a loop-free topology. However, the STP-based L2 network design introduces some limitations. One limitation is the inability of STP to leverage parallel forwarding paths. STP blocks additional paths, forcing the traffic to take only one path as the STP forms a forwarding tree rooted at a single device, even though redundant paths are physically available. Other limitations include the following:

- STP convergence is disruptive.
- MAC address tables don't scale.
- The tree topology provides limited bandwidth.
- The tree topology introduces suboptimal paths.
- Host flooding impacts the whole network.
- Local problems have a network-wide impact, making troubleshooting difficult.

To overcome these challenges, vPC was introduced in 2008. An Ethernet device then could connect simultaneously to two discrete Nexus switches while bundling these links into a logical port-channel. vPC provided users with active-active forwarding paths, thus overcoming the limitation of STP. Still, although vPC overcame most of the challenges, others remained. For example, no provision was made for adding third or fourth aggregation layer switches to further increase the density or bandwidth on the downstream switch. In addition, vPC doesn't overcome the traditional STP design limitation of extending the VLANs.

The Cisco FabricPath feature provides a foundation for building a simplified, scalable, and multipath-enabled L2 fabric. From the control plane perspective, FabricPath uses a shortest path first (SPF)–based routing protocol, which helps with best path selection to reach a destination within the FabricPath domain. It uses the L2 IS-IS protocol, which provides all IS-IS capabilities for handling unicast, broadcast, and multicast packets. Enabling a separate process for the L2 IS-IS is not needed; this is automatically enabled on the FabricPath-enabled interfaces.

FabricPath provides Layer 3 routing benefits to flexible L2 bridged Ethernet networks. It provides the following benefits of both routing and switching domains:

- Routing
    - Multipathing (ECMP), with up to 256 links active between any two devices
    - Fast convergence
    - High scalability
- Switching
    - Easy configuration
    - Plug and Play
    - Provision flexibility

Because the FabricPath core runs on L2 IS-IS, no STP is enabled between the spine and the leaf nodes, thus providing reliable L2 any-to-any connectivity. A single MAC address lookup at the ingress edge device identifies the exit port across the fabric. The traffic is then switched using the shortest path available.

FabricPath-based design allows hosts to leverage the benefit of multiple active Layer 3 default gateways, as Figure 5-9 shows. The hosts see a single default gateway. The fabric provides forwarding toward the active default gateways transparently and simultaneously, thus extending the multipathing from inside the fabric to the Layer 3 domain outside the fabric.

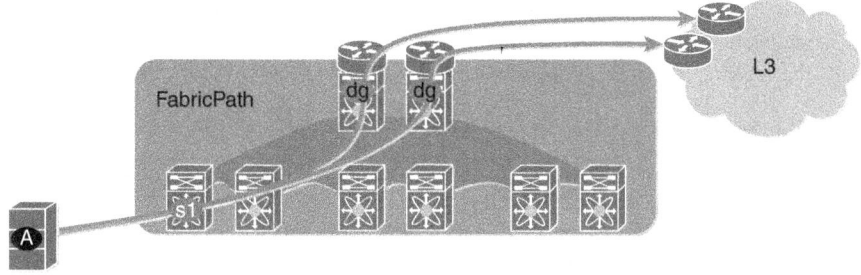

Figure 5-9 *Access to Multiple Active Default Gateways*

The fabric also is used to extend Layer 3 networks. An arbitrary number of routed interfaces can be created at the edge or within the fabric. The attached Layer 3 devices peer with those interfaces, thus providing a seamless Layer 3 network integration.

FabricPath Terminologies and Components

Before understanding the packet flow within the FabricPath (FP)–enabled network, it is important to understand the various terminologies and components that collectively form the FabricPath architecture. Figure 5-10 examines a standard FabricPath-enabled spine-leaf topology, also known as the Clos fabric. The leaf or edge switches in the topology have two different interfaces:

- FabricPath (FP) core ports
- Classical Ethernet (CE) edge ports

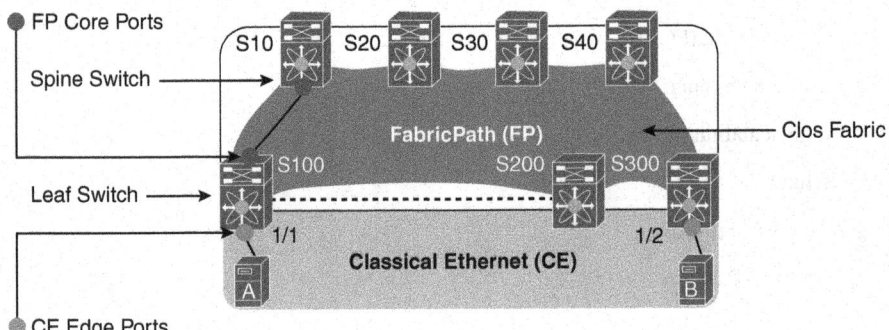

Figure 5-10 *FabricPath and Clos Fabric*

The FP core ports provide connectivity to the spine and are FabricPath-enabled interfaces. The FP core network is used to perform the following functions:

- Send and receive FP frames
- Avoid STP, require no MAC learning, and require no MAC address table maintained by FP Core ports
- Decide the best path by using a routing table computed by IS-IS

The CE edge ports are regular trunk or access ports that provide connectivity to the hosts or other classical switches. The CE ports perform the following functions:

- Send and receive regular Ethernet frames
- Run STP, perform MAC address learning, and maintain a MAC address table

The FP edge device maintains the association of MAC addresses and switch-IDs (which IS-IS automatically assigns to all switches). FP also introduces a new data plane encapsulation by adding a 16-byte FP frame on top of the classical Ethernet header. Figure 5-11 displays the FP encapsulation header, which is also called the MAC-in-MAC header. The external FP header consists of Outer Destination Address, Outer Source Address, and FP tag. Important fields of the Outer Source or Destination address fields within the FP header include the following:

- **Switch-ID (SID):** Identifies each FP switch by a unique number
- **Sub-Switch ID (sSID):** Identifies devices and hosts connected via vPC+
- **Local ID (LID):** Identifies the exact port that sourced the frame or to which the frame is destined. The egress FP switch uses LID to determine the output interface, thus removing the requirement for MAC learning on FP core ports. LID is locally significant.

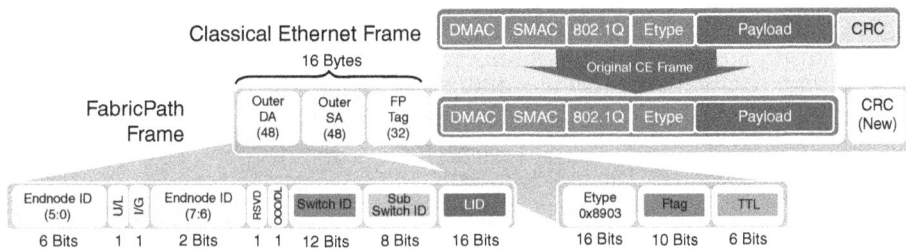

Figure 5-11 *FabricPath Packet Structure*

The FP tag primarily has three fields:

- **Etype:** The Ethernet type is set to 0x8903.
- **Ftag:** This is the forwarding tag, a unique 10-bit number identifying the topology and/or distribution tree. For unicast packets, the Ftag identifies which FP IS-IS topology to use. For multidestination packets (broadcast, unknown unicast, and multicast packets), the Ftag identifies which distribution tree to use. FTAG 1 is used for broadcast, unknown unicast, and multicast (BUM) traffic; FTAG 2 is used for multicast. FTAG is a 10-bit field, allowing support for 1024 forwarding trees or topologies.
- **TTL:** The TTL is decremented at each switch hop, to prevent frames from looping infinitely.

Note If more than 1024 topologies are required, the FTAG value is set to 0 and the VLAN is used to identify the topology for multidestination trees.

FabricPath Packet Flow

To understand packet forwarding in a FabricPath domain, examine the topology and steps shown in Figure 5-12. This figure has four spine switches (S10, S20, S30, and S40) and three leaf/edge switches (S100, S200, and S300). Each leaf switch has connectivity to each of the four spine switches. Host A with MAC address A is connected to CE port on S100, and Host B with MAC address B is connected to CE port on S300.

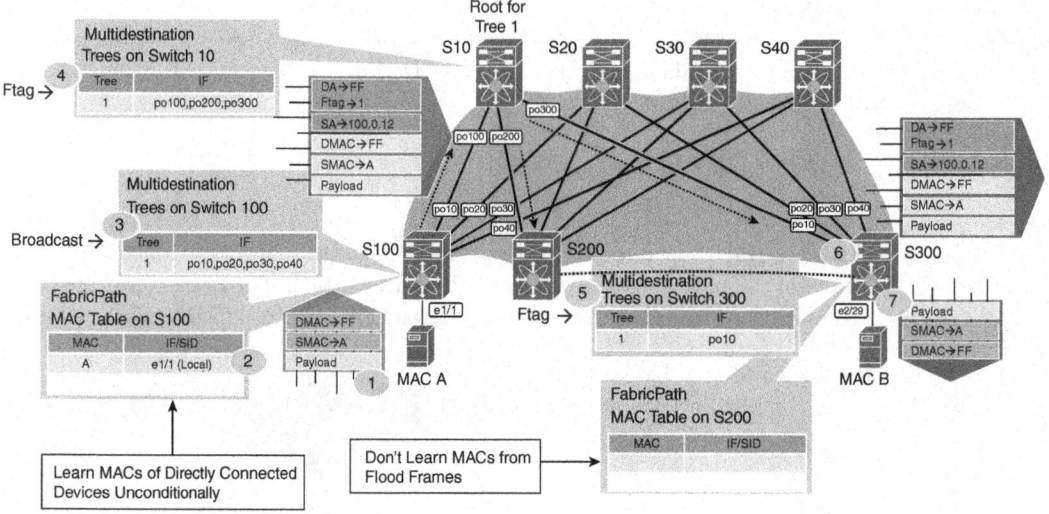

Figure 5-12 *Broadcast ARP Request Packet*

When hosts A and B do not know about each other's MAC addresses, the first packet is a broadcast ARP request. The following steps describe the packet flow for the broadcast frame from host A to host B:

Step 1. Host A sends an ARP request for host B. Because the ARP request is a broadcast packet, the source MAC is set to A and the destination MAC is set to FF (the broadcast address).

Step 2. When the packet reaches the CE edge port on leaf S100, the MAC address table of S100 is updated with MAC address A and the interface from which it is learned. In this case, it is Ethernet1/1.

Step 3. The leaf switch S100 then encapsulates the Ethernet frame with an FP header. Because the FP core ports are enabled, IS-IS has already precalculated multi-destination trees on S100. Tree 1 represents the multidestination tree and indicates that the packet must be sent over the FP core ports (po10, po20, po30, and po40). Because this is a broadcast frame, the Ftag is set to 1. Note that the broadcast graph uses Tree ID 1 (Ftag 1) and the packet is forwarded to S10.

Step 4. When the FP encapsulated frame reaches S10, it honors the Ftag 1 and does a lookup for the Tree ID.

Step 5. In this case, the Tree ID 1 represents a multidestination tree pointing to FP core interface po100, po200, and po300 toward the S100, S200, and S300 leaf switches. Node S10 also performs a reverse path forwarding (RPF) check to validate the reception of the packet over the L2 interface and sends the packet over the multidestination FP encapsulated frame to S200 and S300.

Step 6. The egress FP switch (S300) receives the packet on link po10, performs an RPF check to validate the reception of the packet, and floods the packet to its CE ports.

FabricPath   299

Step 7.   S300 then removes the FP header and floods the packet within the VLAN based on the broadcast frame. Note that the egress FP switch (S300, in this case) does not update its MAC address table with A. This is because the edge devices don't learn the MAC address from flood frames received from the FP core where the destination MAC address is set to FF. The original broadcast packet is then sent to host B.

When the ARP request reaches host B, the ARP reply is a unicast packet. Figure 5-13 depicts the packet flow for ARP reply from host B to host A.

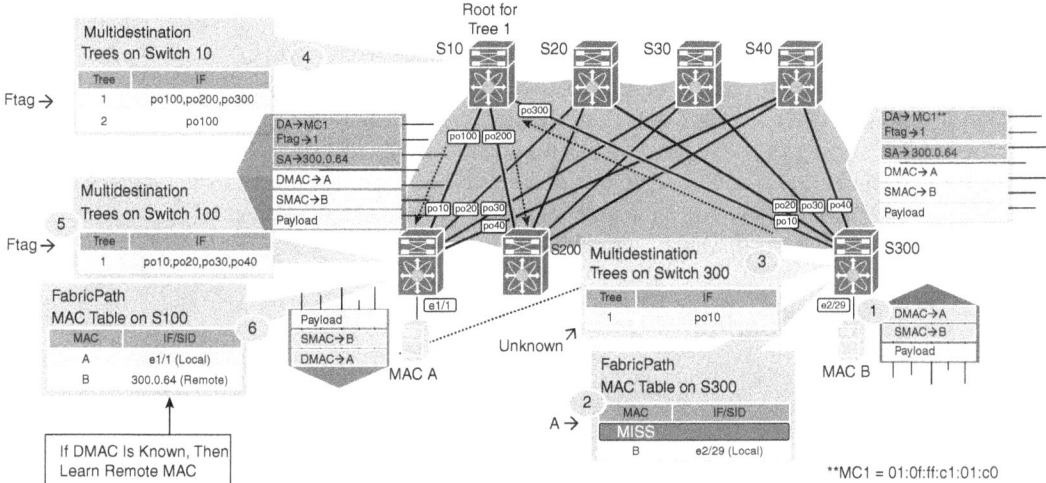

Figure 5-13 *Unicast ARP Reply Packet*

The following steps describe the packet flow for ARP reply from B to A across the fabric.

Step 1.   Host B with MAC address B sends the ARP reply back to host A. In the ARP response, the source MAC is set to B and the destination MAC is set to A.

Step 2.   When the packet reaches the leaf switch S300, it updates its MAC address table with MAC address B, but it still does not have information about MAC address A. This makes the packet an unknown unicast packet.

Step 3.   S300, the ingress FP switch, determines which tree to use. Unknown unicast typically uses the first Tree ID (Ftag 1). The Tree ID 1 points to all the FP core interfaces on switch S300 (po10, po20, po30, and po40). The ingress FP switch also sets the outer destination MAC address to the well-known "flood to fabric" multicast address represented as MC1—01:0F:FF:C1:01:C0.

Step 4.   The FP encapsulated unknown unicast packet is sent to all the spine switches. Other FP switches honor the Tree ID selected by the ingress switch (Tree 1, in this case). When the packet reaches the root for Tree 1 (S10), it uses the same Ftag 1 and forwards the packet out of interfaces po100 and po200. (It does not forward the packet on po300 because this is the interface from which the frame was received).

Step 5. When the packet reaches S100, it performs a lookup on the FP trees and uses Tree ID 1, which is set to po10. Because the packet from S10 was received on po10 on the S100 switch, the packet is not forwarded back again to the fabric.

Step 6. The FP header is then decapsulated and the ARP reply is forwarded to the host with MAC A. At this point, the MAC address table on S100 is updated with MAC address B, with the IF/SID pointing to S300. This is because the destination MAC is known inside the frame.

The next time host A sends a packet to host B, the packet from A is sent with source MAC A and destination MAC B. The switch S100 receives the packet on the CE port, and the destination MAC is already known and points to the switch S300 in an FP-enabled network. The FP routing table is looked up to find the shortest path to S300 using a flow-based hash because multiple paths to S300 exist. The packet is encapsulated with the FP header with a source switch-ID (SWID) of S100 and a destination SWID of S300, and the FTAG is set to 1. The packet is received on one of the spine switches. The spine switch then performs an FP routing lookup for S300 and sends the packet to an outgoing interface toward S300. When the packet reaches S300, the MAC address for A is updated in the MAC address table with the IF/SID pointing to S100.

FabricPath Configuration

To configure FabricPath and verify a FabricPath-enabled network, examine the topology shown in Figure 5-14. This figure has two spine nodes (NX-10 and NX-20) and three leaf nodes (NX-1, NX-2, and NX-3). The end host nodes, host A and host B, are connected to leaf nodes NX-1 and NX-3.

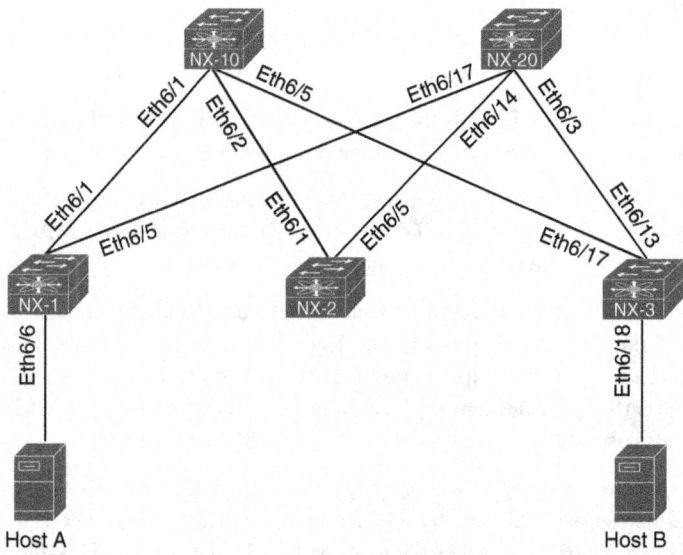

Figure 5-14 *FabricPath-Enabled Topology*

Enabling the FabricPath feature is a bit different than enabling other features. First the FabricPath feature set is installed, then the feature-set fabricpath is enabled, and then the FabricPath feature is enabled. Example 5-30 demonstrates the configuration for enabling FabricPath feature. FabricPath uses the Dynamic Resource Allocation Protocol (DRAP) for the allocation of switch-IDs. However, a switch-ID can be manually configured on a Nexus switch using the command **fabricpath switch-id [1-4094]**. Every switch in the FabricPath domain is required to be configured with the unique switch-ID.

Example 5-30 *Enabling the FabricPath Feature*

```
NX-1# configure terminal
NX-1(config)# install feature-set fabricpath
NX-1(config)# feature-set fabricpath
NX-1(config)# fabricpath switch-id 1
```

When **feature-set fabricpath** is enabled, configure the FP VLANs. Two kinds of VLANs exist:

- Classical Ethernet (CE) VLANs
- FabricPath (FP) VLANs

FP VLANs are the VLANs that are carried over the FP-enabled links; CE VLANs are regular VLANs carried over the classical Ethernet links, such as trunk or access ports. To enable a VLAN as an FP VLAN, use the command **mode fabricpath** under VLAN configuration mode. When the FP VLAN is configured, configure the FP core links using the command **switchport mode fabricpath**. Finally, configure the CE link as a trunk or access port. Example 5-31 examines the configuration of FP VLAN, FP ports, and CE ports on NX-1 as shown in topology.

Example 5-31 *Enabling FP Core Ports, FP VLAN, and CE Edge Ports*

```
NX-1(config)# vlan 100, 200, 300, 400, 500
NX-1(config-vlan)# mode fabricpath
NX-1(config)# interface eth 6/1, eth6/5
NX-1(config-if-range)# switchport
NX-1(config-if-range)# switchport mode fabricpath
NX-1(config-if-range)# no shut
NX-1(config)# interface eth6/6
NX-1(config-if)# switchport
NX-1(config-if)# switchport access vlan 100
NX-1(config-if)# no shut
```

Various timers can also be configured with FabricPath, ranging from 1 to 1200 seconds:

- **allocate-delay:** This timer is used when a new switch-ID is allocated and is required to be propagated throughout the network. The allocate-delay defines the delay before the new switch-ID is propagated and becomes available and permanent.
- **linkup-delay:** This timer configures the delay before the link is brought up, to detect any conflicts in the switch-ID.
- **transition-delay:** This command sets the delay for propagating the transitioned switch-ID value in the network. During this period, all old and new switch-ID values exist in the network.

> **Note** The default value of all these timers is 10 seconds.

FabricPath does not require a specific IS-IS configuration. Authentication and other IS-IS-related configuration settings (such as IS-IS hello timers, hello-padding, and metrics) can be configured using the command **fabricpath isis** under interface configuration mode.

Example 5-32 illustrates the configuration for enabling IS-IS MD5 authentication for FabricPath. The example also displays the various IS-IS settings defined under the interface. Ensure that the configuration matches on both ends of the interface.

Example 5-32 *Enabling Authentication on FP Ports*

```
NX-1(config)# interface ethernet6/1
NX-1(config-if)# fabricpath isis ?
  authentication               Set hello authentication keychain
  authentication-check         Check authentication on received hellos
  authentication-type          Set hello authentication type
  csnp-interval                Set CSNP interval in seconds
  hello-interval               Set Hello interval in seconds
  hello-multiplier             Set multiplier for Hello holding time
  hello-padding                Pad IS-IS hello PDUs to full MTU
  lsp-interval                 Set LSP transmission interval
  mesh-group                   Set IS-IS mesh group
  metric                       Configure the metric for interface
  mtu-check                    Check mtu on received hellos, if its padded
  retransmit-interval          Set per-LSP retransmission interval
  retransmit-throttle-interval Set interface LSP retransmission interval

NX-1(config-if)# fabricpath isis authentication key-chain cisco
NX-1(config-if)# fabricpath isis authentication-type md5
NX-1(config-if)# exit
NX-1(config)# key chain cisco
NX-1(config-keychain)# key 1
NX-1(config-keychain-key)# key-string cisco
```

FabricPath Verification and Troubleshooting

When the fabric is enabled with FabricPath, verify the switch-IDs within the network. This is done using the command **show fabricpath switch-id**. This command displays all the learned switch-IDs within the fabric and their current state. If the switch-IDs are not statically assigned, the IS-IS process dynamically allocates them. Examine the output of the command **show fabricpath switch-id** to validate all the nodes in the fabric, as in Example 5-33.

Example 5-33 show fabricpath switch-id *Command Output*

```
NX-1# show fabricpath switch-id
                  FABRICPATH SWITCH-ID TABLE
Legend: '*' - this system
        '[E]' - local Emulated Switch-id
        '[A]' - local Anycast Switch-id
Total Switch-ids: 5
================================================================================
    SWITCH-ID      SYSTEM-ID       FLAGS        STATE       STATIC   EMULATED/
                                                                     ANYCAST
    ---------------+---------------+------------+-----------+--------------------
      10          6c9c.ed4e.c141   Primary     Confirmed    Yes       No
      20          6c9c.ed4e.c143   Primary     Confirmed    Yes       No
*     100         6c9c.ed4e.4b41   Primary     Confirmed    Yes       No
      200         6c9c.ed4e.4b42   Primary     Confirmed    Yes       No
      300         6c9c.ed4e.4b43   Primary     Confirmed    Yes       No
```

In addition to verifying the FP switch-IDs, it is important to verify which interfaces are participating as part of the FP core links and which are CE-facing links. The FP core links on a leaf or spine node are easily identified using the command **show fabricpath isis interface [brief]**. The command output with the **brief** keyword displays brief information about core interfaces, such as the interfaces enabled with command **switchport mode fabricpath**, their state, the circuit-type (which is typically 0x1 or L1), MTU, Metric, Priority, Adjacency, and Adjacency Up state. More detailed information can be viewed using the same command without the **brief** keyword. The command **show fabricpath isis interface** displays information such as authentication (if enabled), adjacency information, and topology information, along with the information from the brief output. Example 5-34 displays both the brief and detailed information of FP core interfaces on leaf node NX-1.

Example 5-34 *Verifying FP Core Interfaces*

```
NX-1# show fabricpath isis interface brief
Fabricpath IS-IS domain: default
Interface   Type  Idx  State      Circuit   MTU   Metric  Priority  Adjs/AdjsUp
--------------------------------------------------------------------------------
Ethernet6/1  P2P   1   Up/Ready   0x01/L1   1500  40      64        1/1
Ethernet6/5  P2P   3   Up/Ready   0x01/L1   1500  40      64        1/1
```

```
NX-1# show fabricpath isis interface
Fabricpath IS-IS domain: default
Interface: Ethernet6/1
  Status: protocol-up/link-up/admin-up
  Index: 0x0001, Local Circuit ID: 0x01, Circuit Type: L1
  Authentication type MD5
  Authentication keychain is cisco
  Authentication check specified
  Extended Local Circuit ID: 0x1A280000, P2P Circuit ID: 0000.0000.0000.00
  Retx interval: 5, Retx throttle interval: 66 ms
  LSP interval: 33 ms, MTU: 1500
  P2P Adjs: 1, AdjsUp: 1, Priority 64
  Hello Interval: 10, Multi: 3, Next IIH: 00:00:01
  Level   Adjs    AdjsUp  Metric    CSNP   Next CSNP   Last LSP ID
  1       1       1       40        60     Inactive    ffff.ffff.ffff.ff-ff
  Topologies enabled:
    Level Topology Metric  MetricConfig Forwarding
    0     0        40      no           UP
    1     0        40      no           UP

Interface: Ethernet6/5
  Status: protocol-up/link-up/admin-up
  Index: 0x0003, Local Circuit ID: 0x01, Circuit Type: L1
  No authentication type/keychain configured
  Authentication check specified
  Extended Local Circuit ID: 0x1A284000, P2P Circuit ID: 0000.0000.0000.00
  Retx interval: 5, Retx throttle interval: 66 ms
  LSP interval: 33 ms, MTU: 1500
  P2P Adjs: 1, AdjsUp: 1, Priority 64
  Hello Interval: 10, Multi: 3, Next IIH: 00:00:03
  Level   Adjs    AdjsUp  Metric    CSNP   Next CSNP   Last LSP ID
  1       1       1       40        60     Inactive    ffff.ffff.ffff.ff-ff
  Topologies enabled:
    Level Topology Metric  MetricConfig Forwarding
    0     0        40      no           UP
    1     0        40      no           UP
```

The IS-IS adjacency between the leaf and the spine nodes is also verified using the command **show fabricpath isis adjacency [detail]**. Example 5-35 displays the adjacency on NX-1 and NX-10. The command displays the system ID, circuit type, interface participating in IS-IS adjacency for FabricPath, topology ID, and forwarding state. The command also displays the last time when the FabricPath transitioned to current state (that is, the last time the adjacency flapped).

Example 5-35 *Verifying IS-IS Adjacency*

```
NX-1# show fabricpath isis adjacency detail
Fabricpath IS-IS domain: default Fabricpath IS-IS adjacency database:
System ID        SNPA             Level  State  Hold Time  Interface
NX-10            N/A              1      UP     00:00:29   Ethernet6/1
  Up/Down transitions: 1, Last transition: 00:07:36 ago
  Circuit Type: L1
  Topo-id: 0, Forwarding-State: UP

NX-20            N/A              1      UP     00:00:22   Ethernet6/5
  Up/Down transitions: 1, Last transition: 00:12:13 ago
  Circuit Type: L1
  Topo-id: 0, Forwarding-State: UP
```

Next, validate whether the necessary FabricPath VLANs are configured on the edge/leaf switches. This is verified by using the command **show fabricpath isis vlan-range**. When the FP VLANs are configured and CE-facing interfaces are configured, the edge devices learn about the MAC addresses of the hosts attached to the edge node. This is verified using the traditional command **show mac address-table vlan** *vlan-id*. Example 5-36 verifies the FP VLAN and the MAC addresses learned from the hosts connected to the FP VLAN 100.

Example 5-36 *Verifying FabricPath VLANs and MAC Address Table*

```
NX-1# show fabricpath isis vlan-range
Fabricpath IS-IS domain: default
MT-0
Vlans configured:
100, 200, 300, 400, 500, 4040-4041
```

```
NX-1# show mac address-table vlan 100
 Note: MAC table entries displayed are getting read from software.
 Use the 'hardware-age' keyword to get information related to 'Age'

 Legend:
         * - primary entry, G - Gateway MAC, (R) - Routed MAC, O - Overlay MAC
         age - seconds since last seen,+ - primary entry using vPC Peer-Link,
         (T) - True, (F) - False , ~~~ - use 'hardware-age' keyword to retrieve
age info
    VLAN     MAC Address      Type        age     Secure NTFY Ports/SWID.SSID.LID
---------+-----------------+--------+---------+------+----+------------------
*  100      30e4.db97.e8bf   dynamic    ~~~       F     F   Eth6/6
   100      30e4.db98.0e7f   dynamic    ~~~       F     F   300.0.97
```

```
NX-3# show mac address-table vlan 100
Note: MAC table entries displayed are getting read from software.
Use the 'hardware-age' keyword to get information related to 'Age'

Legend:
        * - primary entry, G - Gateway MAC, (R) - Routed MAC, O - Overlay MAC
        age - seconds since last seen,+ - primary entry using vPC Peer-Link,
        (T) - True, (F) - False , ~~~ - use 'hardware-age' keyword to retrieve
age info
   VLAN     MAC Address      Type        age     Secure NTFY Ports/SWID.SSID.LID
---------+----------------+--------+---------+------+----+------------------
   100     30e4.db97.e8bf   dynamic    ~~~       F     F   100.0.85
*  100     30e4.db98.0e7f   dynamic    ~~~       F     F   Eth6/18
```

Similar to Layer 3 IS-IS, Layer-2 IS-IS maintains multiple topologies within the network. Each topology is represented as a tree ID in the FabricPath domain. The trees are nothing but multidestination trees within the fabric. To view the IS-IS topologies in FabricPath domain, use the command **show fabricpath isis topology [summary]**. Example 5-37 displays the different IS-IS topologies in the present topology.

Example 5-37 *FabricPath Topology Information*

```
NX-1# show fabricpath isis topology summary
FabricPath IS-IS Topology Summary
Fabricpath IS-IS domain: default
MT-0
  Configured interfaces:  Ethernet6/1  Ethernet6/5
 Max number of trees: 2   Number of trees supported: 2
    Tree id: 1, ftag: 1, root system: 6c9c.ed4e.c143, 20
    Tree id: 2, ftag: 2, root system: 6c9c.ed4e.c141, 10
Ftag Proxy Root: 6c9c.ed4e.c143

NX-1# show fabricpath isis topology
FabricPath IS-IS Topology
Fabricpath IS-IS domain: default
MT-0
Fabricpath IS-IS Graph 0 Level-1 for MT-0 IS routing table
NX-3.00, Instance 0x0000005C
    *via NX-10, Ethernet6/1, metric 80
    *via NX-20, Ethernet6/5, metric 80
NX-10.00, Instance 0x0000005C
    *via NX-10, Ethernet6/1, metric 40
NX-20.00, Instance 0x0000005C
    *via NX-20, Ethernet6/5, metric 40
! Output omitted for brevity
```

If issues arise with traffic forwarding or MAC addresses not being learned, it is important to check whether the FP IS-IS adjacency has been established and whether the FP IS-IS routes are present in the Unicast Routing Information Base (URIB). This is easily validated through the command **show fabricpath route [detail | switchid** *switch-id*]. This command displays the routes for the remote nodes (leaf or spine nodes). The route is seen in the form of ftag/switch-id/subswitch-id. In Example 5-38, the route for remote edge device NX-3 is seen with FTAG 1, switch-ID 300, and Subswitch-ID 0 (because no vPC+ configuration was enabled).

Example 5-38 *Verifying FabricPath Routes in URIB*

```
NX-1# show fabricpath route detail
FabricPath Unicast Route Table
'a/b/c' denotes ftag/switch-id/subswitch-id
'[x/y]' denotes [admin distance/metric]
ftag 0 is local ftag
subswitch-id 0 is default subswitch-id



FabricPath Unicast Route Table for Topology-Default

0/100/0, number of next-hops: 0
        via ---- , [60/0], 0 day/s 00:16:18, local
1/10/0, number of next-hops: 1
        via Eth6/1, [115/40], 0 day/s 00:16:01, isis_fabricpath-default
1/20/0, number of next-hops: 1
        via Eth6/5, [115/40], 0 day/s 00:15:52, isis_fabricpath-default
1/200/0, number of next-hops: 2
        via Eth6/1, [115/80], 0 day/s 00:16:01, isis_fabricpath-default
        via Eth6/5, [115/80], 0 day/s 00:15:52, isis_fabricpath-default
1/300/0, number of next-hops: 2
        via Eth6/1, [115/80], 0 day/s 00:09:14, isis_fabricpath-default
        via Eth6/5, [115/80], 0 day/s 00:09:14, isis_fabricpath-default
```

```
NX-1# show fabricpath route switchid 300
! Output omitted for brevity
ftag 0 is local ftag
subswitch-id 0 is default subswitch-id



FabricPath Unicast Route Table for Topology-Default

1/300/0, number of next-hops: 2
        via Eth6/1, [115/80], 0 day/s 00:34:49, isis_fabricpath-default
        via Eth6/7, [115/80], 0 day/s 00:34:49, isis_fabricpath-default
```

The previous output makes it clear that the route for NX-3 has an FTAG value of 1. When the route is verified in URIB, validate that the route is installed in the Forwarding Information Base (FIB). To verify the route present in the FIB, use the line card command **show fabricpath unicast routes vdc** *vdc-number* [**ftag** *ftag*] [**switchid** *switch-id*]. This command displays hardware route information along with its RPF interface in the software table on the line card. As part of the platform-dependent information, the command output returns the hardware table address, which is further used to verify the hardware forwarding information for the route. In the output shown in Example 5-39, the software table shows that the route is a remote route with the RPF interface of Ethernet6/5. It also returns the hardware table address of 0x18c0.

Example 5-39 *Verifying Software Table in Hardware for FP Route*

```
NX-1# attach module 6
Attaching to module 6 ...
To exit type 'exit', to abort type '$.'

module-6# show fabricpath unicast routes vdc 1 ftag 1 switchid 300
Route in VDC 1
---------------

-----------------------------------------------------------------------
 FTAG  | SwitchID  | SubSwitchID | Loc/Rem | RPF | RPF Intf | Num Paths | Merge V
-----------------------------------------------------------------------
 0001  |   0300    |    0000     | Remote  | Yes |  Eth6/5  |    2     |   1
-----------------------------------------------------------------------
PD Information for Prefix:

 FE num | ADDR TYPE   | HTBL ADDR | TCAM ADDR | SWSI
-----------------------------------------------------------------------
     0  | HASH TABLE  |  000018c0 |  000000ff | 000011c1
     1  | HASH TABLE  |  000018c0 |  000000ff | 000011c1
-----------------------------------------------------------------------
PD Information for ECMP:
      Common Info
-----------------------------------------------------------------------
AMM key : 0x24
-----------------------------------------------------------------------
Next Hop |   Interface   | LID
-----------------------------------------------------------------------
     0  |    Eth6/1     | 00000050
     1  |    Eth6/5     | 00000054
-----------------------------------------------------------------------
        Per FE Info
-----------------------------------------------------------------------
```

```
FE num   | MP_base   | ref_count
-------------------------------
       0 | 00000024  |        1
       1 | 00000024  |        1
-------------------------------------------------------------------------
```

Note The commands in Example 5-39 are relevant for F2 and F3 line card modules on Nexus 7000/7700 series switches. The verification commands vary among line cards and also platforms (for instance, Nexus 5500).

Using the hardware address in the software table, execute the command **show hardware internal forwarding instance** *instance-id* **table sw start** *hw-entry-addr* **end** *hw-entry-addr*. The *instance-id* value is achieved from the FE num field in the previous example. The *hw-entry-addr* address is the address highlighted in the previous example output. This command output displays the switch-ID (swid), the Subswitch-ID (sswid), and various other fields. One of the important fields to note is ssw_ctrl. If the ssw_ctrl field is 0x0 or 0x3, the switch does not have subswitch-IDs (available only in the case of vPC+). If vPC+ configuration is available, the value is usually 0x1. Another field to look at is the local field. If the local field is set to n, multipath is available for the route, so a multipath table is required for verification. Example 5-40 demonstrates this command.

Example 5-40 *Verifying FabricPath Routes in URIB*

```
module-6# show hardware internal forwarding inst 0 table sw start 0x18c0 end 0x18c0
-----------------------------------------------------------
---------------------- SW Table -----------------------
                      (INST# 0)
-----------------------------------------------------------
[18c0]| KEY
[18c0]| vdc                        :       0       sswid          :       0
[18c0]| swid                       :     12c       ftag           :       1

[18c0]| DATA
[18c0]| valid                      :       y       mp_mod         :       1
[18c0]| mp_base                    :      24       local          :       n
[18c0]| cp_to_sup1                 :       n       cp_to_sup2     :       n
[18c0]| drop                       :       n       dc3_si         :    11c1
[18c0]| data_tbl_ptr               :       0       ssw_ctrl       :       0
[18c0]| iic_port_idx               :      54
[18c0]| l2tunnel_remote (CR only)  :               0
```

Duplicate switch-IDs can cause forwarding issues and instability in the FabricPath-enabled network. To check whether the network has duplicate or conflicting switch-IDs, use the command **show fabricpath conflict all**. In case of any FabricPath-related errors, event-history logs for a particular switch-ID can be verified using the command **show system internal fabricpath switch-id event-history errors**. Alternatively, the **show tech-support fabricpath** command output can be collected for further investigation.

> **Note** If an issue arises with FabricPath, collect the following **show tech-support** outputs during the problematic state:
>
> ```
> show tech u2rib
> show tech pixm
> show tech eltm
> show tech l2fm
> show tech fabricpath isis
> show tech fabricpath topology
> show tech fabricpath switch-id
> ```
>
> Along with these **show tech** outputs, **show tech details** are useful in investigating issues in the FabricPath environment.

FabricPath Devices

FabricPath is supported on Nexus 7000/7700 and Nexus 5500 series switches. Check the FabricPath Configuration Guide for scalability and supported switch modules.

Emulated Switch and vPC+

In modern data center design, servers are usually connected to multiple edge devices to provide redundancy. In a FabricPath-enabled network, only the edge switches learn the L2 MAC addresses. The learning consists of mapping the MAC address to a switch-ID, which is a one-to-one association performed in a data plane. This association or mapping detects a MAC move when the host changes its location to another switch. A vPC allows links that are physically connected to two different Nexus switches to appear as single port-channel to a server or another switch. This provides a loop-free topology, eliminates the spanning tree blocked ports, and maximizes bandwidth usage.

In a FabricPath-enabled network, it is paramount to support the same configuration, with a host or Ethernet switch connected through a port-channel to two FabricPath edge switches. A dual-connected host can send a packet into the FabricPath network from both edge switches, leading to a MAC flap. Figure 5-15 illustrates the MAC flap caused by a dual-connected host. Host A is dual-connected to both edge switches S1 and S2 and is communicating with host B. When the frames are sent from switch S1, MAC-A is associated with switch S1; when frames are sent from S2, MAC-A is associated with switch S2. This results in a MAC flap. To address the problem, FabricPath implements the emulated switch.

Emulated Switch and vPC+ 311

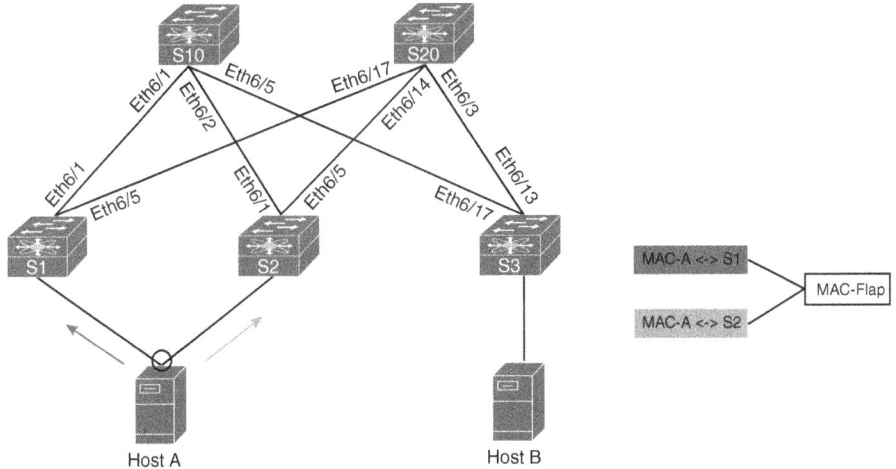

Figure 5-15 *FabricPath Topology with Dual-Connected Host*

An emulated switch construct enables two or more FabricPath switches to work as a single switch to the rest of the FabricPath network. An emulated switch-ID is assigned to the emulated switch used to map the source MAC address when the packet leaves any FabricPath switch that emulates the single switch. The emulated switch implementations in FabricPath in which two FabricPath edge switches provide a vPC to a third device are called vPC+. The two emulating switches thus must be directly connected via peer link, and a peer keepalive path should exist between the two switches.

With emulating switches, it is also important to understand the forwarding mechanism for multidestination packets. In a FabricPath network, eliminating duplication of multidestination frames is achieved by computing multidestination trees rooted at shared nodes that guarantee a loop-free path to any switch. This implies that only one of the emulating switches should announce connectivity to the emulated switch for a particular multidestination tree and should be responsible for forwarding packets to the emulated switch. Likewise, traffic from the emulated switch can ingress from one of the emulating switches into the FabricPath network along the graph path that has reachability to the emulating switch. Otherwise, the packet will be dropped by ingress interface check (IIC). For this reason, for each multidestination tree, one emulating switch is used for ingress and egress traffic.

vPC+ Configuration

To configure vPC+, two primary features must be enabled on the Nexus switch:

- FabricPath
- vPC

To understand how the vPC+ feature works, examine the topology in Figure 5-16. In this topology, NX-1 and NX-2 are forming a vPC with SW-12, and NX-3 and NX-4 are forming a vPC with SW-34. All the links among the four Nexus switches are FabricPath-enabled links, including the vPC peer link.

312   Chapter 5: Port-Channels, Virtual Port-Channels, and FabricPath

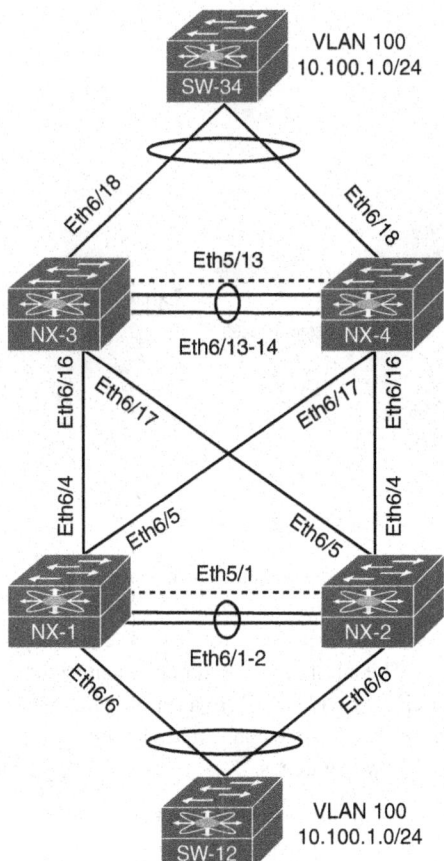

Figure 5-16 *vPC+ Topology*

Examine the vPC and FabricPath configuration for NX-1 and NX-3 in Example 5-41. Most of the configuration is similar to the configuration shown in the section on vPC and FabricPath. The main differentiating configuration is the **fabricpath switch-id** *switch-id* command configured under vPC configuration mode. The same switch-ID values are assigned on both the emulated switches NX-1 and NX-2 (assigned the switch-ID of 100) and NX-3 and NX-4 (assigned the switch-ID of 200).

Example 5-41 *vPC+ Configuration on NX-1 and NX-3*

```
NX-1
install feature-set fabricpath
feature-set fabricpath
feature vpc
vlan 100,200,300,400,500
```

```
    mode fabricpath
!
fabricpath switch-id 100
!
vpc domain 10
  peer-keepalive destination 10.12.1.2 source 10.12.1.1 vrf default
  fabricpath switch-id 100
!
interface port-channel1
  switchport mode fabricpath
  vpc peer-link
!
interface Ethernet6/4
  switchport mode fabricpath
!
interface Ethernet6/5
  switchport mode fabricpath
!
interface port-channel10
  switchport
  switchport mode trunk
  vpc 10
```

NX-3
```
install feature-set fabricpath
feature-set fabricpath
feature vpc
vlan 100,200,300,400,500
  mode fabricpath
!
fabricpath switch-id 200
!
vpc domain 20
  peer-keepalive destination 10.34.1.4 source 10.34.1.3 vrf default
  fabricpath switch-id 200
!
interface port-channel1
  switchport mode fabricpath
  vpc peer-link
!
interface Ethernet6/16
  switchport mode fabricpath
```

```
!
interface Ethernet6/17
  switchport mode fabricpath
!
interface port-channel20
  switchport
  switchport mode trunk
  vpc 20
```

vPC+ Verification and Troubleshooting

When the FabricPath and vPC configuration is complete, verify that the vPC peer adjacency is established. When vPC+ is configured, the command **show vpc** not only displays the vPC-related information: It also shows the vPC+ switch-ID, which is the emulated switch-ID; the DF Flag, which indicates whether the switch is acting as a Designated Forwarder (DF); and the FP MAC route, which is assigned by the vPC Manager. Example 5-42 displays the **show vpc** command output highlighting these fields.

Example 5-42 show vpc *Command Output*

```
NX-1# show vpc
Legend:
                (*) - local vPC is down, forwarding via vPC peer-link

vPC domain id                     : 10
vPC+ switch id                    : 100
Peer status                       : peer adjacency formed ok
vPC keep-alive status             : peer is alive
vPC fabricpath status             : peer is reachable through fabricpath
Configuration consistency status  : success
Per-vlan consistency status       : success
Type-2 consistency status         : success
vPC role                          : primary
Number of vPCs configured         : 1
Peer Gateway                      : Disabled
Dual-active excluded VLANs and BDs : -
Graceful Consistency Check        : Enabled
Auto-recovery status              : Enabled (timeout = 240 seconds)
Fabricpath load balancing         : Disabled
Operational Layer3 Peer-router    : Disabled
Port Channel Limit                : limit to 244
Self-isolation                    : Disabled
vPC Peer-link status
---------------------------------------------------------------------
```

```
id Port Status Active vlans Active BDs
-- ---- ------ --------------------------------------------------------------
1  Po1  up    100,200,300,400,500 -
vPC status
Id : 10
  Port : Po10
  Status : up
  Consistency : success
  Reason : success
  Active Vlans : 100,200,300,400,500
  VPC+ Attributes: DF: Yes, FP MAC: 100.11.65535
```

When verifying the emulated FabricPath switch-IDs, the command **show fabricpath switch-id** displays not only the static switch-IDs, but also the emulated switch-IDs. The Flag (E) is set beside the node representing the local emulated switch. Example 5-43 displays the emulated switch-IDs using the **show fabricpath switch-id** command.

Example 5-43 *Verifying Emulated Switch-IDs*

```
NX-1# show fabricpath switch-id
                      FABRICPATH SWITCH-ID TABLE
Legend: '*' - this system
        '[E]' - local Emulated Switch-id
        '[A]' - local Anycast Switch-id
Total Switch-ids: 8
================================================================================
      SWITCH-ID    SYSTEM-ID       FLAGS        STATE       STATIC   EMULATED/
                                                                     ANYCAST
     --------------+----------------+------------+-----------+--------------------
*     10          6c9c.ed4f.28c2   Primary      Confirmed   Yes      No
      20          d867.d97f.fc42   Primary      Confirmed   Yes      No
      30          6c9c.ed4f.28c3   Primary      Confirmed   Yes      No
      40          d867.d97f.fc43   Primary      Confirmed   Yes      No
[E]   100         6c9c.ed4f.28c2   Primary      Confirmed   No       Yes
      100         d867.d97f.fc42   Primary      Confirmed   No       Yes
      200         6c9c.ed4f.28c3   Primary      Confirmed   No       Yes
      200         d867.d97f.fc43   Primary      Confirmed   No       Yes
```

When both edge devices running the emulated switch learn the MAC addresses from the remote edge nodes, the address for the interfaces is shown with the MAC route assigned on the vPC interface of the remote edge node. Example 5-44 displays the MAC address table on both NX-1 and NX-3 nodes. Notice that the MAC address for the remote host connected on the NX-3/NX-4 vPC link is learned with the interface assigned with FP MAC route 200.11.65535 on NX-1. For the host connected to NX-1 and NX-2, the vPC link is learned with the interface assigned with FP MAC route 100.11.65535.

Example 5-44 *MAC Address Table*

```
NX-1# show mac address-table vlan 100
Note: MAC table entries displayed are getting read from software.
Use the 'hardware-age' keyword to get information related to 'Age'

Legend:
        * - primary entry, G - Gateway MAC, (R) - Routed MAC, O - Overlay MAC
        age - seconds since last seen,+ - primary entry using vPC Peer-Link, E -
EVPN entry
        (T) - True, (F) - False ,   ~~~ - use 'hardware-age' keyword to retrieve
age info
   VLAN/BD    MAC Address      Type      age     Secure NTFY Ports/SWID.SSID.LID
---------+-----------------+--------+---------+------+----+------------------
   100       0022.56b9.007f   dynamic   ~~~      F     F    200.11.65535
*  100       24e9.b3b1.8cff   dynamic   ~~~      F     F    Po10

NX-3# show mac address-table vlan 100
Note: MAC table entries displayed are getting read from software.
Use the 'hardware-age' keyword to get information related to 'Age'

Legend:
        * - primary entry, G - Gateway MAC, (R) - Routed MAC, O - Overlay MAC
        age - seconds since last seen,+ - primary entry using vPC Peer-Link, E -
EVPN entry
        (T) - True, (F) - False ,   ~~~ - use 'hardware-age' keyword to retrieve
age info
   VLAN/BD    MAC Address      Type      age     Secure NTFY Ports/SWID.SSID.LID
---------+-----------------+--------+---------+------+----+------------------
*  100       0022.56b9.007f   dynamic   ~~~      F     F    Po20
   100       24e9.b3b1.8cff   dynamic   ~~~      F     F    100.11.65535
```

If issues arise with MAC learning, check that an IS-IS adjacency exists between the devices. The IS-IS adjacency is established with the vPC peer device and the other spines or edge nodes based on their connectivity. After verifying the adjacency, the FP routes are learned through IS-IS. The route for the emulated switch from the vPC peer is learned through the vPC Manager (vPCM) and is seen in the URIB as learned through vpcm, as Example 5-45 shows. Looking deeper into the URIB, notice that the route learned from remote emulated switch has the Flag or Attribute set to E.

Example 5-45 *Verifying Local and Remote FP Routes in URIB*

```
NX-1# show fabricpath route detail
FabricPath Unicast Route Table
'a/b/c' denotes ftag/switch-id/subswitch-id
'[x/y]' denotes [admin distance/metric]
```

```
ftag 0 is local ftag
subswitch-id 0 is default subswitch-id


FabricPath Unicast Route Table for Topology-Default

0/10/0, number of next-hops: 0
        via ---- , [60/0], 0 day/s 02:16:33, local
0/10/3, number of next-hops: 1
        via sup-eth1, [81/0], 0 day/s 02:16:33, fpoam
0/100/1, number of next-hops: 0
0/100/3, number of next-hops: 1
        via sup-eth1, [81/0], 0 day/s 01:54:49, fpoam
0/100/11, number of next-hops: 1
        via Po10, [80/0], 0 day/s 01:47:44, vpcm
1/20/0, number of next-hops: 1
        via Po1, [115/20], 0 day/s 01:33:20, isis_fabricpath-default
1/30/0, number of next-hops: 1
        via Eth6/4, [115/40], 0 day/s 02:13:59, isis_fabricpath-default
1/40/0, number of next-hops: 1
        via Eth6/5, [115/40], 0 day/s 02:13:14, isis_fabricpath-default
1/100/0, number of next-hops: 0
        via ---- , [60/0], 0 day/s 01:54:49, local
1/100/0, number of next-hops: 1
        via Po1, [115/20], 0 day 00:00:00, isis_fabricpath-default
1/200/0, number of next-hops: 2
        via Eth6/4, [115/40], 0 day/s 01:41:01, isis_fabricpath-default
        via Eth6/5, [115/40], 0 day/s 01:41:01, isis_fabricpath-default
2/100/0, number of next-hops: 0
        via ---- , [60/0], 0 day/s 01:54:49, local
```

```
NX-1# show fabricpath isis route detail
Fabricpath IS-IS domain: default MT-0
Topology 0, Tree 0, Swid routing table
20, L1
Attribute:P* Instance 0x0000002B
 via port-channel1, metric 20*
! Output omitted for brevity
100, L1
Attribute:E* Instance 0x0000002B
 via port-channel1, metric 20*
200, L1
Attribute:E* Instance 0x0000002B
 via Ethernet6/4, metric 40*
 via Ethernet6/5, metric 40*
Legend E:Emulated, A:Anycast P:Physical, * - directly connected
```

The edge ports are usually vPC ports in a vPC+-based design, so verifying the vPCM information related to the vPC link is vital. This is verified using the command **show system internal vpcm info interface** *interface-id*. This command displays the outer FP MAC address of the port-channel interface, VLANs, vPC peer information, and also the information stored in the PSS. Note that the PSS information helps ensure restoration of the information in case of any link flaps or VDC/switch reloads. Example 5-46 displays the vPCM information for port-channel 10 on NX-1 node, highlighting the FP MAC addresses and the information from vPC peers.

Example 5-46 *Verifying FP MAC Information in vPCM*

```
NX-1# show system internal vpcm info interface po10
! Output omitted for brevity
port-channel10 - if_index: 0x16000009
--------------------------------------------------------------------

IF Elem Information:

        IF Index: 0x16000009
        MCEC NUM: 10 Is MCEC
        Allowed/Config VLANs    : 6 - [1,100,200,300,400,500]
        Allowed/Config BDs      : 0 - []

MCECM DB Information:
        IF Index        : 0x16000009
        vPC number      : 10
        Num members     : 0
        vPC state       : Up
        Internal vPC state: Up
        Compat Status   :
                Old Compat Status       : Pass
                Current Compat Status: Pass

                Reason Code             : SUCCESS
                Param compat reason code:0(SUCCESS)
        Individual mode: N
        Flags : 0x0
        Is AutoCfg Enabled : N
        Is AutoCfg Sync Complete : N
        Number of members: 0
        FEX Parameters:
                vPC is a non internal-vpc
                vPC is a non fabric-vpc
                FPC bringup: FALSE
                Parent vPC number: 0
        Card type       : F2
        Hardware prog state  : No R2 prog
```

```
        Fabricpath outer MAC address info: 100.11.65535
        Designated forwarder state: Allow
        Assoc flag: Disassociated
        Is switchport: Yes   Is shared port: FALSE


        Up VLANs                  : 5 - [100,200,300,400,500]
        Suspended VLANs           : 1 - [1]
        Compat check pass VLANs: 4096 - [0-4095]
        Compat check fail VLANs: 0 - []

        Up BDs                    : 0 - []
        Suspended BDs             : 0 - []
        Compat check pass BDs     : 0 - []
        Compat check fail BDs     : 0 - []
        Compat check pass VNIs    : 0 - []
        Compat check fail VNIs    : 0 - []


        vPC Peer Information:


        Peer Number   : 10
        Peer IF Index: 0x16000009
        Peer state    : Up
        Card type                 : F2
        Fabricpath outer MAC address info of peer: 100.11.0
        Peer configured VLANs   : 6 - [1,100,200,300,400,500]
        Peer Up VLANs           : 5 - [100,200,300,400,500]
        Peer configured VNIs    : 0 - []
        Peer Up BDs             : 0 - []
PSS Information:

        IF Index  : 0x16000009
        vPC number: 10
        vPC state: Up
        Internal vPC state: Up
        Old Compat Status: Pass
        Compat Status: Pass
        Card type     : F2
        Fabricpath outer MAC address info: 100.11.65535
        Designated forwarder state: Allow
        Up VLANs                  : 5 - [100,200,300,400,500]
        Suspended VLANs           : 1 - [1]
        Up BDs                    : 0 - []
        Suspended BDs             : 0 - []


        vPC Peer Information:
```

```
            Peer number: 10
            Peer if_index: 0x16000009
            Peer state: Up
            Card type       : F2
            Fabricpath outer MAC address info of peer: 100.11.0
            Peer configured VLANs     : 6 - [1,100,200,300,400,500]
            Peer Up VLANs             : 5 - [100,200,300,400,500]
..
```

Other platform-level verification is done as shown in the FabricPath section to validate the hardware programming on the line card for the FabricPath route.

Note The platform-dependent commands vary among platforms and also depend on the line card present on the Nexus 7000/7700 chassis. If you encounter any issues with vPC+, collect the following **show tech-support** command outputs:

```
show tech-support fabricpath
show tech-support vpc
```

Other **show tech-support** commands are collected as covered in the FabricPath section.

Summary

This chapter covered the technologies and features that provide resiliency and increased capacity between switches from an L2 forwarding perspective. Port-channels and virtual port-channels enable switches to create a logical interface with physical member ports. Consistency in port configuration for all member ports is the most common problem when troubleshooting these issues. This chapter detailed additional techniques and error messages to look for when troubleshooting these issues.

FabricPath provides a different approach for removing spanning tree while increasing link throughput and scalability and minimizing broadcast issues related to spanning tree. Quite simply, FabricPath involves routing packets in an L2 realm in an encapsulated state; the packet is later decapsulated before being forwarded to a host. Troubleshooting packet forwarding in a FabricPath topology uses some of the basic concepts from troubleshooting STP and port forwarding while combining them with concepts involved in troubleshooting an IS-IS network.

References

Fuller, Ron, David Jansen, and Matthew McPherson, Matthew. *NX-OS and Cisco Nexus Switching* (Indianapolis: Cisco Press, 2013).

Cisco NX-OS Software Configuration Guides. http://www.cisco.com.

Chapter 6

Troubleshooting IP and IPv6 Services

This chapter covers the following topics:

- IP SLA
- Object Tracking
- IPv4 Services
- IPv6 Services
- Troubleshooting for First-Hop Redundancy Protocols

IP SLA

IP Service Level Agreement (SLA) is a network performance monitoring application that enables users to do service-level monitoring, troubleshooting, and resource planning. It is an application-aware synthetic operation agent that monitors network performance by measuring response time, network reliability, resource availability, application performance, jitter, connect time, and packet loss. The statistics gained from this feature help with SLA monitoring, troubleshooting, problem analysis, and network topology design. The IP SLA feature consists of two main entities:

- **IP SLA sender:** The IP SLA sender generates active measurement traffic based on the operation type, as configured by the user and reports metrics. Apart from reporting metrics, the IP SLA sender also detects threshold violations and sends notifications. Figure 6-1 shows the various measurements for different operation types.

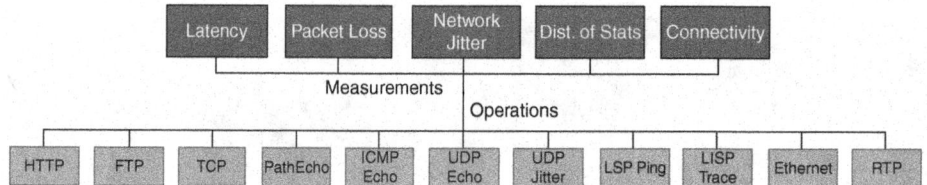

Figure 6-1 *IP SLA Measurement for Different Operation Types*

- **IP SLA responder:** The responder runs on a separate switch from the sender. It responds to the User Datagram Protocol/Transmission Control Protocol (UDP/TCP) probes and reacts to control packets. The control packets and the command-line interface (CLI) determine the TCP/UDP ports and addresses the responder checks for the packets from the sender.

The IP SLA feature is not enabled by default. To enable the IP SLA feature, use the command **feature sla [responder | sender]**. Unless the IP SLA sender device is also acting as a responder for a remote device, both SLA sender and responder features are not required to be enabled on the same device.

Different IP SLA probes can be configured on Nexus:

- ICMP Echo
- ICMP Jitter
- UDP Echo
- UDP Jitter
- TCP Connect

ICMP Echo Probe

The sender sends an Internet Control Message Protocol (ICMP) ping packet (echo packet) to a destination (responder) to measure reachability and round-trip time (RTT). The sender creates an ICMP ping packet, adds a time stamp to it, and sends it to another node (the responder). The responder receives the probe, adds its own time stamp, and responds to the ICMP ping packet. The sender receives this packet, calculates the RTT, and stores the statistics. Example 6-1 illustrates the configuration of an ICMP echo probe between two Nexus switches, NX-1 and NX-2. An IP SLA probe is configured using the command **ip sla** *number*. Further under the configuration, the command **icmp-echo** *dest-ip-address* [**source-interface** *interface-id* | **source-ip** *src-ip-address*] defines the ICMP echo probe. The command **frequency** *frequency-in-seconds* defines how frequently the probe is sent. The command option **request-data-size** *size* sends the probe with a certain data size.

After it is configured, the probe does not start on its own. It can start immediately or after a certain period of time, specified using the global configuration **ip sla schedule** *number* **start-time [now | after** *time* **|** *time*], where *time* is specified in hh:mm:ss format.

Example 6-1 *IP SLA ICMP Echo Probe Configuration*

```
feature sla sender
!
ip sla 10
  icmp-echo 192.168.2.2 source-interface loopback0
    request-data-size 1400
    frequency 5
ip sla schedule 10 start-time now
```

For ICMP echo probes, it is not required to configure the IP SLA responder on the remote device where the probe is destined to. After the probe is started, the statistics for the probe are verified using the command **show ip sla statistics** [*number*] [**aggregated** | **details**]. The **aggregated** option displays the aggregated statistics, whereas the **details** option displays the detailed statistics. Example 6-2 displays the statistics of the ICMP echo probe configured in Example 6-1. In the **show ip sla statistics** command output, carefully verify fields such as the RTT value, return code, number of successes, and number of failures. In the aggregated command output, the RTT value is shown as an aggregated value (for example, the Min/Avg/Max values of RTT for the probe).

Example 6-2 *IP SLA Statistics*

```
NX-1# show ip sla statistics 10

IPSLAs Latest Operation Statistics

IPSLA operation id: 10
        Latest RTT: 2 milliseconds
Latest operation start time: 06:16:13 UTC Sat Sep 30 2017
Latest operation return code: OK
Number of successes: 678
Number of failures: 0
Operation time to live: 213 sec
NX-1# show ip sla statistics aggregated

IPSLAs aggregated statistics

IPSLA operation id: 10
Type of operation: icmp-echo
Start Time Index: 05:19:48 UTC Sat Sep 30 2017

RTT Values:
        Number Of RTT: 694              RTT Min/Avg/Max: 2/2/7 milliseconds
Number of successes: 694
Number of failures: 0
```

Chapter 6: Troubleshooting IP and IPv6 Services

> **Note** The configuration for an IP SLA probe can be viewed using either the command **show running-config sla sender** or the command **show ip sla configuration** *number*.

UDP Echo Probe

The sender sends a single UDP packet of a user-defined size to a destination (responder) and measures the RTT. The sender creates a UDP packet, opens a socket with user-specified parameters, sends it to another node (the responder), and marks down the time. The responder receives the probe and sends back the same packet to the sender with the same socket parameters. The sender receives this packet, notes the time of receipt, calculates the RTT, and stores the statistics.

To define a UDP Echo IP SLA probe, use the command **udp-echo** [*dest-ip-address* | *dest-hostname*] *dest-port-number* **source-ip** [*src-ip-address* | *src-hostname*] **source-port** *src-port-number* [**control** [**enable** | **disable**]]. Example 6-3 illustrates a UDP Echo probe on the NX-1 switch and a responder configured on the NX-2 switch. This section of the output also displays the statistics after the probe is enabled. Note that unless the responder is configured on the remote end, the probe results in failures. To configure the IP SLA responder, use the command **ip sla responder**. To configure the UDP Echo probe responder, use the command **ip sla responder ipaddress** *ip-address* **port** *port-number*.

Example 6-3 *IP SLA UDP Echo Probe and Statistics*

```
NX-1 (Sender)
ip sla 11
  udp-echo 192.168.2.2 5000 source-ip 192.168.1.1 source-port 65000
    tos 180
    frequency 10
ip sla schedule 11 start-time now
```

```
NX-2 (Responder)
ip sla responder
ip sla responder udp-echo ipaddress 192.168.2.2 port 5000
```

```
NX-1
NX-1# show ip sla statistics 11 details

IPSLAs Latest Operation Statistics

IPSLA operation id: 11
        Latest RTT: 2 milliseconds
Latest operation start time: 04:45:38 UTC Sun Oct 01 2017
Latest operation return code: OK
Number of successes: 3
Number of failures: 6
Operation time to live: 3459 sec
Operational state of entry: Active
Last time this entry was reset: Never
```

Note When a UDP Echo probe responder is configured, the responder device continuously listens on the specified UDP port on the responder node.

UDP Jitter Probe

The UDP jitter probe sends out a series of UDP packets at regularly spaced intervals to a destination to measure packet jitter. You can also specify a codec that determines the payload size, packet interval, and number of packets to send, to simulate the given voice codec. The sender puts its send time stamp in the packet before sending it to the responder. Upon receiving the packet, the responder sends a copy of it back to the sender, with the receiver's receive time and processing time. The sender receives this copy and uses the receive time of the packet plus the previous three values (sender send time, responder receive time, and responder processing time) to calculate the RTT and update the jitter statistics.

The UDP Plus operation is a superset of the UDP echo operation. In addition to measuring UDP RTT, the UDP Plus operation measures per-direction packet loss and jitter. Jitter is interpacket delay variance. Jitter statistics are useful for analyzing traffic in a voice over IP (VoIP) network.

The UDP jitter probe is defined using the command **udp-jitter** [*dest-ip-address* | *dest-hostname*] *dest-port-number* **codec** *codec-type* [**codec-numpackets** *number-of-packets*] [**codec-size** *number-of-bytes*] [**codec-interval** *milliseconds*] [**advantage-factor** *value*] **source-ip** [*src-ip-address* | *src-hostname*] **source-port** *src-port-number* [**control** [**enable** | **disable**]]. The default request packet data size for an IP SLAs UDP jitter operation is 32 bytes. Use the **request-data-size** option under the **ip sla** command to modify this value.

Table 6-1 shows some of the options that are specified in the **udp-jitter** configuration.

Table 6-1 udp-jitter *Options*

Option	Description
control {**enable**	**disable**}	(Optional) Enables or disables the sending of IP SLA control messages to the IP SLA responder.
codec *codec-type*	Enables the generation of estimated voice-quality scores in the form of Calculated Planning Impairment Factor (ICPIF) and Mean Opinion Score (MOS) values. Three types of codes can be configured with UDP jitter probe: ■ g711alaw: G.711 A Law (64-kbps transmissions) ■ g711ulaw: G.711 U Law (64-kbps transmissions) ■ g729a: G.729 (8-kbps transmissions)
codec-numpackets *number-of-packets*	(Optional) Specifies the number of packets to be transmitted per operation. The range is from 1 to 60000. The default is 1000.

Option	Description
codec-size *number-of-bytes*	(Optional) Specifies the number of bytes in each packet transmitted. (Also called the payload size or request size.) The range is from 16 to 1500. The default varies by codec.
codec-interval *milliseconds*	Specifies the interval (delay) between packets that should be used for the operation, in milliseconds (ms). The range is from 1 to 60000. The default is 20.
advantage-factor *value*	Specifies the expectation factor to be used for ICPIF calculations. This value is subtracted from the measured impairments to yield the final ICPIF value (and corresponding MOS value).

Example 6-4 illustrates the configuration of UDP jitter probe using the g729a codec, which is set with a type of service (ToS) value of 180. Specify the life of the probe along with the **ip sla schedule** command by specifying the command option **life** [*time-in-seconds* | **forever**]. For a UDP jitter probe, more detailed information is maintained as part of the statistics. Statistical information of one-way latency, jitter time, packet loss, and voice score values is maintained for UDP jitter probe.

Example 6-4 *IP SLA UDP Jitter Probe and Statistics*

```
NX-1
ip sla 15
  udp-jitter 192.168.2.2 5000 codec g729a codec-numpackets 50 codec-interval 100
    tos 180
    verify-data
    frequency 10
ip sla schedule 15 life forever start-time now
NX-1# show ip sla statistics 15 details

IPSLAs Latest Operation Statistics

IPSLA operation id: 15
Type of operation: udp-jitter
        Latest RTT: 20 milliseconds
Latest operation start time: 06:53:31 UTC Sun Oct 01 2017
Latest operation return code: OK
RTT Values:
        Number Of RTT: 47              RTT Min/Avg/Max: 9/20/34 milliseconds
Latency one-way time:
        Number of Latency one-way Samples: 0
        Source to Destination Latency one way Min/Avg/Max: 0/0/0 milliseconds
        Destination to Source Latency one way Min/Avg/Max: 0/0/0 milliseconds
```

```
        Source to Destination Latency one way Sum/Sum2: 0/0
        Destination to Source Latency one way Sum/Sum2: 0/0
Jitter Time:
        Number of SD Jitter Samples: 0
        Number of DS Jitter Samples: 0
        Source to Destination Jitter Min/Avg/Max: 0/0/0 milliseconds
        Destination to Source Jitter Min/Avg/Max: 0/0/0 milliseconds
        Source to destination positive jitter Min/Avg/Max: 0/0/0 milliseconds
        Source to destination positive jitter Number/Sum/Sum2: 0/0/0
        Source to destination negative jitter Min/Avg/Max: 0/0/0 milliseconds
        Source to destination negative jitter Number/Sum/Sum2: 0/0/0
        Destination to Source positive jitter Min/Avg/Max: 0/0/0 milliseconds
        Destination to Source positive jitter Number/Sum/Sum2: 0/0/0
        Destination to Source negative jitter Min/Avg/Max: 0/0/0 milliseconds
        Destination to Source negative jitter Number/Sum/Sum2: 0/0/0
        Interarrival jitterout: 0      Interarrival jitterin: 0
        Jitter AVG: 0
        Over thresholds occured: FALSE
Packet Loss Values:
        Loss Source to Destination: 0
        Source to Destination Loss Periods Number: 0
        Source to Destination Loss Period Length Min/Max: 0/0
        Source to Destination Inter Loss Period Length Min/Max: 0/0
        Loss Destination to Source: 0
        Destination to Source Loss Periods Number: 0
        Destination to Source Loss Period Length Min/Max: 0/0
        Destination to Source Inter Loss Period Length Min/Max: 0/0
        Out Of Sequence: 0      Tail Drop: 50
        Packet Late Arrival: 0  Packet Skipped: 0
Voice Score Values:
        Calculated Planning Impairment Factor (ICPIF): 11
        MOS score: 4.06
Number of successes: 23
Number of failures: 1
Operation time to live: forever
Operational state of entry: Active
Last time this entry was reset: Never
```

Note To cause an IP SLA operation to check each reply packet for data corruption, use the **verify-data** command under **ip sla** configuration mode.

As the latency and jitter increases, the MOS score goes down. Such statistics help the network design and implementation team optimize the network for the applications.

TCP Connect Probe

A TCP Connect Probe makes a nonblocking TCP connection for a given source and destination IP address and port, marking the current time as the operation time. If it gets a successful response from the responder immediately, it updates the RTT using the difference between the current time and the operation time and then uses this to update its statistics components. If the sender does not get a successful response immediately, it sets a timer and waits for a callback triggered by a response from the destination IP. Upon receiving the callback, it updates the RTT and statistics as before.

The TCP connection operation is used to discover the time required to connect to the target device. This operation is used to test virtual circuit availability or application availability. If the target is a Cisco router, the IP SLA probe makes a TCP connection to any port number the user specifies. If the destination is a non-Cisco IP host, you must specify a known target port number (for example, 21 for File Transfer Protocol [FTP], 23 for Telnet, or 80 for Hypertext Transfer Protocol [HTTP] server). This operation is useful in testing Telnet or HTTP connection times.

To define a TCP connect IP SLA probe, use the command **tcp-connect** [*dest-ip-address* | *dest-hostname*] *dest-port-number* **source-ip** [*src-ip-address* | *src-hostname*] **source-port** *src-port-number* [**control** [**enable** | **disable**]]. For the TCP connect probe, the responder must be configured on the destination router/switch using the command **ip sla responder tcp-connect ipaddress** *ip-address* **port** *port-number*. Example 6-5 demonstrates the configuration of an IP SLA TCP connect probe to probe a TCP connection between NX-1 and NX-2 switches.

Example 6-5 *IP SLA TCP Connect Probe Configuration and Statistics*

```
NX-1 (Sender)
ip sla 20
  tcp-connect 192.168.2.2 10000 source-ip 192.168.1.1
ip sla schedule 20 life forever start-time now

NX-2 (Responder)
ip sla responder tcp-connect ipaddress 192.168.2.2 port 10000

NX-1
NX-1# show ip sla statistics 20 details

IPSLAs Latest Operation Statistics

IPSLA operation id: 20
        Latest RTT: 304 milliseconds
Latest operation start time: 16:23:03 UTC Sun Oct 01 2017
Latest operation return code: OK
Number of successes: 2
Number of failures: 0
Operation time to live: forever
Operational state of entry: Active
Last time this entry was reset: Never
```

> **Note** Refer to Nexus Cisco Connection Online (CCO) documentation for additional information on other command options available with IP SLA.

Object Tracking

Several IP and IPv6 services, such as First-Hop Redundancy Protocol (FHRP), are deployed in a network for reliability and high availability purposes, to ensure load balancing and failover capability. In spite of all these capabilities, network uptime is not guaranteed when, for example, the WAN link goes down, which is more likely to occur in a network than router failure. This results in considerable downtime on the link.

Object tracking offers a flexible and customizable mechanism for affecting and controlling the failovers in the network. With this feature, you can track specific objects in the network and take necessary action when any object's state change affects the network traffic. The main objective of the object tracking feature is to allow the processes and protocols in a router system to monitor the properties of other unrelated processes and protocols in the same system, to accomplish the following goals:

- Provide an optimal level of service
- Increase the availability and speed of recovery of a network
- Decrease network outages and their duration

Clients such as Hot Standby Router Protocol (HSRP), Virtual Router Redundancy Protocol (VRRP), and Gateway Load Balancing Protocol (GLBP) can register their interest in specific tracked objects and take action when the state of the object changes. Along with these protocols, other clients that use this feature include the following:

- Embedded Event Manager (EEM)
- Virtual Port-Channel (vPC)

Object tracking is configured for tracking the following objects:

- Line protocol state change
- Route reachability
- Object track list

Object tracking has the configuration syntax of **track** *number <object-type> <object-instance> <object-parameter>*, where the object-number value ranges from 1 to 1000. The object-type indicates one of the supported tracked objects (interface, ip route, or track list). Object-instance refers to an instance of a tracked object (interface-name, route prefix, mask, and so on). The object-parameter indicates the parameters related to the object-type.

Object Tracking for the Interface

The command **track** *number* **interface** *interface-id* [**line protocol** | **ip routing** | **ipv6 routing**] creates an object to track the interface status and either the line protocol status or the IP/IPv6 routing on the interface. Example 6-6 demonstrates the configuration of interface tracking for the line protocol and the IP routing status. In the first test, when the interface is shut down, the track status for both the line protocol and IP routing goes down. In the second test, if the interface is made an L2 port (that is, it is configured with the **switchport** command), only track 2, which is for IP routing, goes down because IP routing is now disabled on the port Eth2/5. Use the command **show track** to check the status of the configured tracking objects.

Example 6-6 *Object Tracking for Interface Status*

```
NX-1
NX-1(config)# track 1 interface ethernet 2/5 line-protocol
NX-1(config)# track 2 interface ethernet 2/5 ip routing
NX-1(config)# interface ethernet2/5
NX-1(config-if)# shut
```

```
NX-1# show track
Track 1
  Interface Ethernet2/5 Line Protocol
  Line Protocol is DOWN
  2 changes, last change 00:00:08

Track 2
  Interface Ethernet2/5 IP Routing
  IP Routing is DOWN
  2 changes, last change 00:00:08
```

```
NX-1(config)# interface ethernet2/5
NX-1(config-if)# no shut
NX-1(config-if)# switchport
```

```
NX-1# show track
Track 1
  Interface Ethernet2/5 Line Protocol
  Line Protocol is UP
  5 changes, last change 00:00:41

Track 2
  Interface Ethernet2/5 IP Routing
  IP Routing is DOWN
  4 changes, last change 00:00:42
```

Object Tracking for Route State

To configure the route state tracking object, use the command **track** *number* **ip route** *ip-address/mask* **reachability** for IPv4 routes and **track** *number* **ipv6 route** *ipv6-address/mask* **reachability** for IPv6 routes. This command creates a route object to track the reachability of the route. Example 6-7 demonstrates the configuration for both IPv4 and IPv6 route status tracking objects. If the reachability for the tracked route is lost for any reason (such as packet loss or routing protocol flap), the track goes down. You can also configure the delay for the up and down events. The command **delay [down | up]** *time-in-seconds* sets the track down delay and track up delay in seconds. The **delay** command option prevents transient or nonpersistent events from triggering the track to go down.

Example 6-7 *Object Tracking for Route Status*

```
NX-1
NX-1(config)# track 5 ip route 192.168.2.2/32 reachability
NX-1(config-track)# delay down 3
NX-1(config-track)# delay up 1
NX-1# show track 5
Track 5
  IP Route 192.168.2.2/32 Reachability
  Reachability is UP
  3 changes, last change 00:02:07
  Delay up 1 secs, down 3 secs
```

A tracking object is also configured for the IP SLA probe using the command **track** *number* **ip sla [reachability | status]**. Thus, the tracking object can indirectly be verifying reachability to the remote prefix. The benefit of using IP SLA probes is that network operators can use IP SLA not only to verify reachability, but also to track the status of other probes for UDP echo, UDP jitter, and TCP connection.

Example 6-8 displays the configuration for object tracking with IP SLA probes. Notice that the **show track** command output not only displays the state information, but also returns the operation code and RTT information, which is actually part of the **show ip sla statistics** command output.

Example 6-8 *Object Tracking for IP SLA Probe*

```
NX-1
ip sla 10
  icmp-echo 192.168.2.2 source-interface loopback0
    request-data-size 1400
    frequency 5
ip sla schedule 10 start-time now
!
track 10 ip sla 10 state
NX-1# show track 10
Track 10
  IP SLA 10 State
  State is UP
  1 changes, last change 00:01:01
  Latest operation return code: OK
  Latest RTT (millisecs): 3
```

Object Tracking for Track-List State

You can create conditional track objects that are based on the state of multiple objects. This is achieved using a track list. Within a track list, multiple objects are added; a Boolean expression consisting of **and** and **or** functions treats those objects to get the track list state. A track list object is configured using the command **track** *number* **list boolean [and | or]**. Under track configuration mode, multiple objects can be listed using the command **object** *object-number* **[not]**. Note that the option **not** is used when the condition for an object should not hold true.

Example 6-9 illustrates the configuration for object tracking on a track list using both **and** and **or** Boolean expressions. Note that, in the second section, the **show track** command output for track list object 20 shows the state as DOWN. This is because the object 2 state is not UP as a result of IP routing being enabled on interface Eth2/5.

Example 6-9 *Object Tracking for Track List*

```
NX-1
! Previous track configurations
NX-1# show run track
track 1 interface Ethernet2/5 line-protocol
track 2 interface Ethernet2/5 ip routing
track 5 ip route 192.168.2.2/32 reachability
 delay up 1 down 3
track 10 ip sla 10

! Track List with Boolean AND for matching track 1 and not matching track 2.
NX-1(config)# track 20 list boolean and
NX-1(config-track)# object 1
NX-1(config-track)# object 2 not

! Track List with Boolean OR for matching track 1 or matching track 5.
NX-1(config)# track 30 list boolean or
NX-1(config-track)# object 1
NX-1(config-track)# object 5
NX-1# show track 20
Track 20
  List  Boolean and
  Boolean and is DOWN
  2 changes, last change 00:03:14
  Track List Members:
    object 2 not UP
    object 1 UP

NX-1# show track 30
Track 30
```

```
List    Boolean or
Boolean or is UP
1 changes, last change 00:01:23
Track List Members:
  object 5 UP
  object 1 UP
```

You can also specify the threshold value used to maintain the state of the track list. The threshold is defined in two forms:

- Percentage
- Weight

Either of these methods can be used with a track list, using the command **track** *number* **list threshold [percentage | weight]**.

The percentage threshold is configured using the command **threshold percentage up** *value* **down** *value*. If the percentage of configured track list objects in the UP state exceeds the configured threshold value, the track state remains up; otherwise, it goes down.

Similarly, the weight-based threshold value is configured using the command **threshold weight up** *value* **down** *value*. The combined weight of the objects in the UP state must exceed the configured threshold weight for the track to remain in the UP state.

Example 6-10 displays the sample configuration for the percentage- and weight-based threshold for track list objects. In the first configuration, with the percentage threshold, at least two objects should be in the UP state because the UP percentage is configured to be 60. In the second example, with a weight-based threshold, the track remains in the UP state only if object 1 and either of the other two objects (object 2 or object 5) are in the UP state because the weight for UP state is configured to be 45.

Example 6-10 *Threshold for Track List Object*

```
NX-1(config)# track 100 list threshold percentage
NX-1(config-track)# threshold percentage up 60 down 40
NX-1(config-track)# object 1
NX-1(config-track)# object 2
NX-1(config-track)# object 5
NX-1(config)# track 200 list threshold weight
NX-1(config-track)# threshold weight up 45 down 30
NX-1(config-track)# object 1 weight 30
NX-1(config-track)# object 2 weight 15
NX-1(config-track)# object 5 weight 15
```

Using Track Objects with Static Routes

Object tracking can be integrated with static routes, which influence traffic forwarding in case the track goes down. A tracking object is associated with a static route, which installs the route in the routing table (i.e., the Unicast Routing Information Base [URIB]) as long as the track state is UP. The Netstack/IP component continuously listens to messages, which are exchanged with Message and Transactional Services (MTS), from the object tracking component. If the track state goes down, the track component on NX-OS sends an MTS message to the Netstack component and removes the route associated with the track object from URIB. To switch over the traffic in case the track state goes down, preconfigure another static route toward the same destination, but with a higher administrative distance (AD) value and a different next hop. Example 6-11 illustrates the use of track object with static routes to deliver faster recovery in case of a failure event. In the following example, the route for 192.168.2.2/32 with next-hop 10.12.1.2 is installed in the routing table as long as the track 1 status is UP.

Example 6-11 *Track Object with Static Routes*

```
NX-1
NX-1(config)# ip route 192.168.2.2/32 10.12.1.2 track 1
NX-1(config)# ip route 192.168.2.2/32 10.13.1.3 254
NX-1# show ip route 192.168.2.2/32
192.168.2.2/32, ubest/mbest: 1/0
    *via 10.12.1.2, [1/0], 00:00:48, static

! Shutting down the interface E2/5 having subnet 10.12.1.0/24

NX-1(config)# interface e2/5
NX-1(config-if)# shutdown

NX-1# show track 1
Track 1
  Interface Ethernet2/5 Line Protocol
  Line Protocol is DOWN
  8 changes, last change 00:00:03

! Change in track status leading to failover of traffic to different next-hop
NX-1# show ip route 192.168.2.2/32
192.168.2.2/32, ubest/mbest: 1/0
    *via 10.13.1.3, [254/0], 00:00:40, static
```

Note If any issues with object tracking arise, collect the **show tech track** command output and share it with the Cisco Technical Assistance Center (TAC).

IPv4 Services

NX-OS contains a wide array of critical network services that provide flexibility, scalability, reliability, and security in the network and solve critical problems that enterprise or data centers face. This section discusses the following IP services:

- DHCP relay
- DHCP snooping
- Dynamic ARP inspection
- IP source guard
- Unicast RPF

DHCP Relay

Unlike traditional Cisco IOS or Cisco IOS XE software, NX-OS does not support the Dynamic Host Configuration Protocol (DHCP) server feature. However, you can enable the NX-OS device to function as a DHCP relay agent. A DHCP relay agent is a device that helps in relaying DHCP requests/replies between the DHCP client and the DHCP server when they are on different subnets. The relay agent listens for the client's request and adds vital data such as the client's link information, which the server needs to allocate address for the client. When the server replies, the relay agent forwards the information back to the client.

The DHCP relay agent is a useful feature, but some security concerns do arise:

- A host on one port cannot see other hosts traffic on other ports.
- Hosts connected to the metro port can no longer be trusted. Therefore, a mechanism is needed to identify them more securely.
- Protection from network spoofing attacks by malicious hosts (IP exhaustion, IP spoofing, denial of service [DoS] attacks, and so on).

DHCP option 82 helps overcome these issues. Defined in RFC 3046, DHCP option 82 is a new type of container option that contains suboption information gathered by the relay agent. Figure 6-2 shows the format of the DHCP relay agent information option.

```
    Code      Length     Agent    Information    Field
 +---------+---------+---------+---------+---------+
 |   82    |    N    |    i1   |   ...   |    iN   |
 +---------+---------+---------+---------+---------+
```

Figure 6-2 *Relay Agent Packet Format*

The length *N* gives the total number of bytes in the Agent Information Field, which consists of a sequence of SubOpt/Length/Value tuples for each suboption.

Following is a sample sequence of a DHCP message flow when the DHCP option 82 feature is enabled on the access switch:

- The client broadcasts a DHCPDISCOVER message with UDP destination port 67 and UDP source port 68 from switch port.

- The relay agent on the switch intercepts the broadcast request and inserts the option 82 data (circuit ID and remote ID). It places the relay agent IP address in the DHCP packet giaddr field, replaces UDP source port 68 with relay agent server port 67, and then unicasts the client request to the DHCP server on the same UDP destination port. The DHCP server IP address is configured as an IP helper address when option 82 feature is enabled on the relay agent interface.

- The DHCP server receives and processes the relayed DHCP client request. A DHCP server that is capable of handling option 82 data responds with a DHCPOFFER message that includes an available network address in the message yiaddr field, along with all the option 82 data. The response is a UDP unicast message directly routed to the relay agent with the UDP destination port as 67.

- The relay agent receives the server reply. It removes the option 82 data and either unicasts or broadcasts the DHCPOFFER message back to the client.

- The client might receive multiple DHCPOFFERs from multiple DHCP servers. When it decides to accept an offer from a particular DHCP server, it broadcasts a DHCPREQUEST message to the server with a UDP destination port of 67. It uses the server identifier option in the message to indicate which server it has selected.

- Similarly, the relay agent intercepts the broadcast request, inserts the option 82 data, and relays the request to the DHCP server.

- The selected DHCP server acknowledges the request by committing the assigned IP address and it unicasts a DHCPACK message to the relay agent with the UDP destination port as 67.

- The relay agent receives the reply, removes the option 82 data from the message, and relays the message back to the client.

- When the client receives the DHCPACK message with the configuration parameter, it performs an Address Resolution Protocol (ARP) check for allocated IP addresses to make sure it is not being used by another host. If it detects the same IP address already in use, it sends a DHCPDECLINE message to the server and restarts the configuration process. Similarly, the relay agent intercepts the message and relays it.

- When the client chooses to relinquish its lease on the IP address, it sends a DHCPRELEASE message to the server. The DHCPRELEASE message is always a unicast message to the server, so no relay agent is used here.

- Upon receipt of DHCPRELEASE message, the server marks the IP address as not allocated.

To enable the DHCP relay agent on NX-OS, the DHCP feature must be enabled on the system using the command **feature dhcp**. To enable the device to act as a DHCP relay agent, configure the global command **ip dhcp relay**. The DHCP relay is configured on the interface using the command **ip dhcp relay address** *ip-address*, where the *ip-address* variable is the address of the DHCP server. To enable the DHCP option 82, configure the global command option **ip dhcp relay information option**.

To further understand the DHCP Relay feature, examine the topology in Figure 6-3. In this topology, NX-1 is acting as the relay agent.

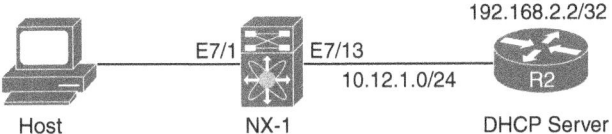

Figure 6-3 *Topology with DHCP Relay Agent*

Example 6-12 displays the configuration of the DHCP relay agent on NX-1. Note that there should be reachability to the DHCP server sourcing the interface on which the DHCP relay is configured.

Example 6-12 *DHCP Relay Configuration*

```
NX-1
NX-1(config)# feature dhcp
NX-1(config)# ip dhcp relay
NX-1(config)# interface e7/1
NX-1(config-if)# ip dhcp relay address 192.168.2.2
```

When the configuration is done and the client tries to request an IP address, the DHCP relay agent helps exchange the messages between the client and the server. Use the command **show ip dhcp relay** to verify that the interface is enabled with DHCP relay. After the messages are exchanged, verify the statistics of all the messages received and forwarded by the relay agent in both directions (between server and client) using the command **show ip dhcp relay statistics**. Example 6-13 examines the DHCP relay configuration and statistics on NX-1. The **show ip dhcp relay statistics** command output displays the statistics for all the different kinds of DHCP packets received, forwarded, and dropped by the relay agent. Along with this information, the command output displays the various reasons why a relay agent drops the packet, along with its statistics.

Example 6-13 *Verifying DHCP Relay Information and Statistics*

```
NX-1# show ip dhcp relay
DHCP relay service is enabled
Insertion of option 82 is disabled
Insertion of VPN suboptions is disabled
Insertion of cisco suboptions is disabled
Global smart-relay is disabled
Relay Trusted functionality is disabled
```

Chapter 6: Troubleshooting IP and IPv6 Services

```
Relay Trusted Port is Globally disabled
V4 Relay Source Address HSRP is Globally disabled
! Output omitted for brevity
Helper addresses are configured on the following interfaces:
 Interface        Relay Address    VRF Name
 ------------     -------------    --------
 Ethernet7/1      192.168.2.2
NX-1# show ip dhcp relay statistics
-----------------------------------------------------------------
Message Type             Rx              Tx             Drops
-----------------------------------------------------------------
Discover                 22              22              0
Offer                    1               1               0
Request(*)               1               1               0
Ack                      1               1               0
Release(*)               0               0               0
Decline                  0               0               0
Inform(*)                0               0               0
Nack                     0               0               0
-----------------------------------------------------------------
Total                    25              25              0
-----------------------------------------------------------------

DHCP L3 FWD:
Total Packets Received                      :        0
Total Packets Forwarded                     :        0
Total Packets Dropped                       :        0
Non DHCP:
Total Packets Received                      :        0
Total Packets Forwarded                     :        0
Total Packets Dropped                       :        0
DROP:
DHCP Relay not enabled                      :        0
Invalid DHCP message type                   :        0
Interface error                             :        0
Tx failure towards server                   :        0
Tx failure towards client                   :        0
Unknown output interface                    :        0
Unknown vrf or interface for server         :        0
Max hops exceeded                           :        0
Option 82 validation failed                 :        0
Packet Malformed                            :        0
Relay Trusted port not configured           :        0
* - These counters will show correct value when switch
receives DHCP request packet with destination ip as broadcast
address. If request is unicast it will be HW switched
```

When DHCP relay address is configured, access control list (ACL) programming happens on the Nexus switch:

- If the L3 interface is a physical/subinterface, router ACL (RACL) is programmed to redirect all DHCP packets to the DHCP snoop process on the supervisor.
- If the L3 interface is Switched Virtual Interface (SVI), the VLAN ACL (VACL) is programmed on the hardware.
- If the L3 interface is a port-channel, the RACL is programmed on all the port-channel members.

The programmed RACL or VACL has two primary specifications:

- Filter
    - Permit source ports 67 and 68 to any destination port
    - Permit any port to destination ports 67 and 68
- Action
    - Redirect to DHCP Snoop on supervisor

The DHCP process registers with Netstack for this particular exception cause. As a result, all DHCP requests/replies captured by the LC come to the DHCP snooping process via Netstack fast MTS queue.

When the DHCP relay is configured on the interface, the command **show system internal access-list interface** *interface-id* [**module** *slot*] checks that the ACL is programmed in hardware (see Example 6-14). Notice that, in the output, the policy type is DHCP and the policy name is Relay. The command output displays the number of ternary content-addressable memory (TCAM) entries held by the ACL and the number of adjacencies.

Example 6-14 *Verifying ACL on the Line Card for DHCP Relay*

```
NX-1# show system internal access-list interface ethernet 7/1 module 7
Policies in ingress direction:
        Policy type            Policy Id      Policy name
    -----------------------------------------------------------
      DHCP                         4            Relay

No Netflow profiles in ingress direction




INSTANCE 0x0
---------------

  Tcam 1 resource usage:
  ---------------------
```

Chapter 6: Troubleshooting IP and IPv6 Services

```
      Label_b = 0x201
      Bank 0
      ------
        IPv4 Class
          Policies: DHCP(Relay)    [Merged]
          Netflow profile: 0
          Netflow deny profile: 0
          5 tcam entries

      0 l4 protocol cam entries
      0 mac etype/proto cam entries
      0 lous
      0 tcp flags table entries
      1 adjacency entries

No egress policies
No Netflow profiles in egress direction
```

When the ACL is programmed on the line card, view the hardware statistics for the ACL using the command **show system internal access-list input statistics [module** *slot*]. Example 6-15 displays the statistics for the DHCP relay ACL, where five hits match the traffic coming from source port 67. If during regular operation DHCP is not functioning properly, use the command **show system internal access-list input statistics [module** *slot*] and the command in the previous example to ensure that both the DHCP relay ACL is programmed in hardware and the statistics counters are incrementing.

Example 6-15 *Verifying ACL Statistics on the Line Card for DHCP Relay*

```
NX-1# show system internal access-list input statistics module 7
              VDC-2 Ethernet7/1 :
              ====================


INSTANCE 0x0
---------------

  Tcam 1 resource usage:
  ----------------------
  Label_b = 0x201
  Bank 0
  ------
    IPv4 Class
      Policies: DHCP(Relay)    [Merged]
      Netflow profile: 0
      Netflow deny profile: 0
```

```
        Entries:
           [Index] Entry [Stats]
           --------------------
   [0058:000e:000e] prec 1 redirect(0x0) udp 0.0.0.0/0 255.255.255.255/32 eq 68 f
 low-label 68   [0]
   [0059:000f:000f] prec 1 redirect(0x0) udp 0.0.0.0/0 255.255.255.255/32 eq 67 f
 low-label 67   [5]
   [005a:0010:0010] prec 1 redirect(0x0) udp 0.0.0.0/0 eq 68 255.255.255.255/32 f
 low-label 262144   [0]
   [005b:0011:0011] prec 1 redirect(0x0) udp 0.0.0.0/0 eq 67 255.255.255.255/32 f
 low-label 196608   [0]
   [005c:0012:0012] prec 1 permit ip 0.0.0.0/0 0.0.0.0/0   [0]
```

DHCP Snooping

DHCP snooping is an L2 security feature. It resolves some types of DoS attacks that can be engineered by DHCP messages and helps avoid IP spoofing, in which a malicious host tries to use the IP address of another host. DHCP snooping works at two levels:

- Discovery
- Enforcement

Discovery includes the functions of intercepting DHCP messages and building a database of {IP address, MAC address, Port, VLAN} records. This database is called the binding table. Enforcement includes the functions of DHCP message validation, rate limiting, and conversion of DHCP broadcasts to unicasts.

DHCP snooping provides the following security features:

- Prevention of DoS attacks through DHCP messages
- DHCP message validation
- Creation of a DHCP binding table that helps validate DHCP messages
- Option 82 insertion/removal
- Rate limiting on the number of DHCP messages on an interface

Note DHCP snooping is associated with the DHCP relay agent, which helps extend the same security features when the DHCP client and server are in different subnets.

To understand how DHCP snooping works, examine the same topology in Figure 6-4. In this topology, both the DHCP server and the client are part of same VLAN 100. Nexus switch NX-1 is providing Layer 2 connectivity between the DHCP server and the client host.

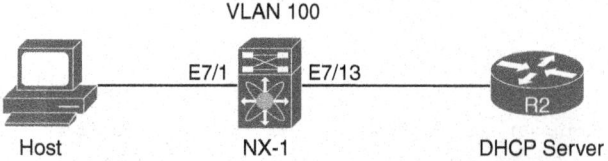

Figure 6-4 *Topology with DHCP Server and Client*

To enable DHCP snooping, configure the command **ip dhcp snooping** *globally* on the Nexus switch and then enable the DHCP snooping for the VLAN using the command **ip dhcp snooping vlan** *vlan-id*. Usually, the ports connected to the DHCP server are configured as trusted ports and the ports connecting the clients are untrusted ports. To configure the port connecting the server as a trusted port, enable the interface configuration command **ip dhcp snooping trust**. Example 6-16 illustrates the configuration of DHCP snooping on NX-1. When DHCP snooping is enabled, use the command **show ip dhcp snooping** to validate the status of DHCP snooping on the switch. Notice that, in the output of the command **show ip dhcp snooping**, NX-1 shows the DHCP snooping feature being enabled and operational for VLAN 100.

Example 6-16 *DHCP Snooping Configuration and Validation*

```
NX-1
NX-1(config)# ip dhcp snooping
NX-1(config)# ip dhcp snooping vlan 100
NX-1(config)# interface e7/13
NX-1(config-if)# ip dhcp snooping trust
NX-1# show ip dhcp snooping
Switch DHCP snooping is enabled
DHCP snooping is configured on the following VLANs:
100
DHCP snooping is operational on the following VLANs:
100
Insertion of Option 82 is disabled
Verification of MAC address is enabled
DHCP snooping trust is configured on the following interfaces:
Interface              Trusted
------------           -------
Ethernet7/13           Yes
```

After the requests/replies are exchanged between the client and the server, a binding entry is built on the device with DHCP snooping configuration for the untrusted port. The binding table is also used by IP source guard (IPSG) and the Dynamic ARP Inspection (DAI) feature. To view the binding table, use the command **show ip dhcp snooping binding** (see Example 6-17). In this example, notice that the entry is built for the untrusted port Eth7/1 and also shows the IP address assigned to the host with the listed MAC address.

Example 6-17 *DHCP Snooping Binding Database*

```
NX-1# show ip dhcp snooping binding
MacAddress         IpAddress       Lease(Sec)   Type         VLAN   Interface
-----------------  --------------  ----------   ----------   ----   -------------
d4:2c:44:fa:cf:47  10.12.1.2       84741        dhcp-snoop   100    Ethernet7/1
```

For packets received on untrusted ports, the following validation is performed:

- Allow request (BOOTREQUEST) from client (source port 68) to server (destination port 67).

- DHCPRELEASE/DHCPDECLINE messages are verified against the binding table entries to prevent a host from releasing or declining addresses for another host.

For packets received on trusted ports, the following validation is performed:

- For server (src port 67) to client (dst port 68) response (BOOTREPLY), perform binding table updates, strip off option 82, and forward the packet.

- For client (src port 68) to server (dst port 67), just forward the request without any validation.

Thus, for performing the previously mentioned validations, an ACL gets installed on the line card for the DHCP snooping feature and you can view the statistics for the different entries' part of the programmed ACL. Example 6-18 displays the DHCP snooping ACL programmed in hardware and the statistics for the same.

Example 6-18 *DHCP Snooping ACL Programming*

```
NX-1# show system internal access-list module 7
              VLAN 100 :
              =========
Policies in ingress direction:
         Policy type              Policy Id      Policy name
--------------------------------------------------------------
    DHCP                              4            Snooping

No Netflow profiles in ingress direction

INSTANCE 0x0
---------------

  Tcam 1 resource usage:
  ----------------------
   Label_b = 0x201
   Bank 0
   ------
```

```
      IPv4 Class
        Policies: DHCP(Snooping)   [Merged]
        Netflow profile: 0
        Netflow deny profile: 0
        5 tcam entries

  0 l4 protocol cam entries
  0 mac etype/proto cam entries
  0 lous
  0 tcp flags table entries
  1 adjacency entries
! Output omitted for brevity
NX-1# show system internal access-list input statistics module 7
              VLAN 100  :
              =========


INSTANCE 0x0
---------------


  Tcam 1 resource usage:
  ----------------------
  Label_b = 0x201
   Bank 0
   ------
     IPv4 Class
       Policies: DHCP(Snooping)   [Merged]
       Netflow profile: 0
       Netflow deny profile: 0
       Entries:
         [Index] Entry [Stats]
         ---------------------
 [0058:000e:000e] prec 1 redirect(0x0) udp 0.0.0.0/0 0.0.0.0/0 eq 68 flow-label
 68   [0]
 [0059:000f:000f] prec 1 redirect(0x0) udp 0.0.0.0/0 0.0.0.0/0 eq 67 flow-label
 67   [5]
 [005a:0010:0010] prec 1 redirect(0x0) udp 0.0.0.0/0 eq 68 0.0.0.0/0 flow-label
 262144  [0]
 [005b:0011:0011] prec 1 redirect(0x0) udp 0.0.0.0/0 eq 67 0.0.0.0/0 flow-label
 196608  [0]
 [005c:0012:0012] prec 1 permit ip 0.0.0.0/0 0.0.0.0/0   [0]
```

```
INSTANCE 0x3
---------------

  Tcam 1 resource usage:
  ---------------------
  Label_b = 0x201
   Bank 0
   ------
     IPv4 Class
        Policies: DHCP(Snooping)    [Merged]
        Netflow profile: 0
        Netflow deny profile: 0
        Entries:
           [Index] Entry [Stats]
           ---------------------
  [0058:000e:000e] prec 1 redirect(0x0) udp 0.0.0.0/0 0.0.0.0/0 eq 68 flow-label
68   [2]
  [0059:000f:000f] prec 1 redirect(0x0) udp 0.0.0.0/0 0.0.0.0/0 eq 67 flow-label
67   [0]
  [005a:0010:0010] prec 1 redirect(0x0) udp 0.0.0.0/0 eq 68 0.0.0.0/0 flow-label
262144   [0]
  [005b:0011:0011] prec 1 redirect(0x0) udp 0.0.0.0/0 eq 67 0.0.0.0/0 flow-label
196608   [0]
  [005c:0012:0012] prec 1 permit ip 0.0.0.0/0 0.0.0.0/0   [0]
```

Dynamic ARP Inspection

Security in any network environment is the biggest concern. Malicious hosts can poison the ARP cache of hosts as well as routers and switches. The Dynamic ARP Inspection feature helps protect hosts and other network devices from ARP cache poisoning. DAI verifies the sanity of the ARP requests and responses sent by hosts connected to the switch. DAI checks each ARP packet for correct MAC-IP binding with respect to the binding table created by DHCP snooping. If the check fails, the ARP packet is not forwarded.

DAI is enabled on a per-VLAN basis and supports enabling src-MAC, dst-MAC, and IP address validation. The [Source, Destination] and [MAC, IP] addresses of the ARP packets are validated against the snooping binding entry for valid unicast IP addresses. If a device has no binding entry, a DAI trust port needs to be configured for that ingress interface before ARP inspection works on that device.

Example 6-19 displays the configuration for DAI on VLAN 100 and the use of the command **show ip arp inspection statistics vlan** *vlan-id* to display the statistics of the ARP requests/responses and the number of packets forwarded. DAI is configured for a

VLAN using the command **ip arp inspection vlan** *vlan-id*. The port toward the server is configured as the trusted port, so it is enabled using the interface-level command **ip arp inspection trust**. On a DAI trusted port, no checks are placed for the rx and tx packets.

Example 6-19 *Dynamic ARP Inspection Configuration and Verification*

```
NX-1(config)# ip arp inspection vlan 100
NX-1(config)# interface e7/13
NX-1(config-if)# ip arp inspection trust
NX-1# show ip arp inspection statistics vlan 100


Vlan : 100
-----------
ARP Req Forwarded    = 2
ARP Res Forwarded    = 3
ARP Req Dropped      = 0
ARP Res Dropped      = 0
DHCP Drops           = 0
DHCP Permits         = 5
SMAC Fails-ARP Req   = 0
SMAC Fails-ARP Res   = 0
DMAC Fails-ARP Res   = 0
IP Fails-ARP Req     = 0
IP Fails-ARP Res     = 0
```

For DAI, an ARP snooping ACL (VACL) is programmed on the line card. Note that because the DAI feature is enabled along with the DHCP snooping feature, both the ACLs are seen on the line card. Example 6-20 displays the ACL programmed on the line card and the relevant statistics for the same.

Example 6-20 *ACL Programming and Statistics for DAI*

```
NX-1# show system internal access-list vlan 100 module 7
Policies in ingress direction:
         Policy type              Policy Id      Policy name
  -----------------------------------------------------------
         DHCP                         4          Snooping
         ARP                          5          Snooping

No Netflow profiles in ingress direction



INSTANCE 0x0
--------------
```

```
  Tcam 1 resource usage:
  ----------------------
   Label_b = 0x202
   Bank 0
   ------
     IPv4 Class
       Policies: DHCP(Snooping)   [Merged]
       Netflow profile: 0
       Netflow deny profile: 0
       5 tcam entries
     ARP Class
       Policies: ARP(Snooping)   [Merged]
       Netflow profile: 0
       Netflow deny profile: 0
       3 tcam entries

   0 l4 protocol cam entries
   0 mac etype/proto cam entries
   0 lous
   0 tcp flags table entries
   2 adjacency entries

! Output omitted for brevity
NX-1# show system internal access-list input statistics module 7
              VLAN 100  :
              =========

INSTANCE 0x0
---------------

  Tcam 1 resource usage:
  ----------------------
   Label_b = 0x202
   Bank 0
   ------
     IPv4 Class
       Policies: DHCP(Snooping)   [Merged]

! Output omitted for brevity

     ARP Class
       Policies: ARP(Snooping)   [Merged]
```

```
            Netflow profile: 0
            Netflow deny profile: 0
            Entries:
              [Index] Entry [Stats]
              --------------------
    [0062:0018:0018] prec 1 redirect(0x0) arp/response ip 0.0.0.0/0 0.0.0.0/0 0000
.0000.0000 0000.0000.0000     [2]
    [0063:0019:0019] prec 1 redirect(0x0) arp/request ip 0.0.0.0/0 0.0.0.0/0 0000.
0000.0000 0000.0000.0000      [1]
    [0064:001a:001a] prec 1 permit arp-rarp/all ip 0.0.0.0/0 0.0.0.0/0 0000.0000.0
000 0000.0000.0000     [0]
```

ARP ACLs

In non-DHCP (no DHCP snooping enabled) scenarios, you can define ARP ACLs to filter out malicious ARP requests and responses. No packets are redirected to the supervisor. ARP packets coming on the line card get forwarded and dropped in the line card based on the ACL list by user config for the ARP inspection filter. The ARP ACL filters are configured on a per-VLAN basis. An ARP ACL is configured using the command **arp access-list** *acl-name*. It accepts the entries in the format of [**permit** | **deny**] [**request** | **response**] **ip** *ip-address subnet-mask* **mac** [*mac-address mac-address-range*]. Example 6-21 demonstrates an ARP ACL that is applied as an ARP inspection filter for VLAN 100. After it is configured, the ARP ACL gets programmed in the hardware and you can verify the statistics in hardware using the same command of **show system internal access-list input statistics** [**module** *slot*].

Example 6-21 *ARP ACLs Configuration and Verification*

```
NX-1(config)# arp access-list ARP-ACL
NX-1(config-arp-acl)# permit request ip 10.12.1.0 255.255.255.0 mac d42c.44fa.cf47
  d42c.44fa.efff log
NX-1(config-arp-acl)# deny ip any mac any log
NX-1(config-arp-acl)# exit
NX-1(config)# ip arp inspection filter ARP-ACL vlan 100
NX-1# show arp access-lists ARP-ACL

ARP access list ARP-ACL
10 permit request ip 10.12.1.0 255.255.255.0 mac d42c.44fa.cf47 d42c.44fa.efff log
20 deny ip any mac any log
NX-1# show system internal access-list input statistics module 7
                VLAN 100   :
                =========
```

```
INSTANCE 0x0
---------------

  Tcam 1 resource usage:
  ----------------------
  Label_b = 0x202
   Bank 0
   ------
    ARP Class
       Policies: VACL(ARP-ACL) ARP(Snooping)    [Merged]
       Netflow profile: 0
       Netflow deny profile: 0
       Entries:
          [Index] Entry [Stats]
          ---------------------
  [005d:0013:0013] prec 1 redirect(0x0) arp/request ip 10.12.1.0/24 0.0.0.0/0 d4
2c.44fa.cf47 d42c.44fa.efff    [1]
  [005e:0014:0014] prec 2 deny arp-rarp/all ip 0.0.0.0/0 0.0.0.0/0 0000.0000.000
0 0000.0000.0000  log  [2]
! Output omitted for brevity
```

IP Source Guard

IP Source Guard (IPSG) provides IP and MAC filters to restrict IP traffic on DHCP snooping untrusted ports. IP traffic with source IP and MAC addresses that correspond to a valid IP source binding (both static IP and DHCP binding) is permitted; all other IP traffic except DHCP is dropped. Traditionally, this prevents IP spoofing by allowing only IP addresses obtained through DHCP snooping on a particular port.

The IPSG feature is enabled on a DHCP snooping untrusted Layer 2 port. Initially, all IP traffic on the port is blocked except for DHCP packets that are captured by the DHCP snooping process. When a client receives a valid IP address from the DHCP server, IP traffic from hosts connected to the switch are allowed only if the MAC–IP address matches with what is programmed by the IPSG module. The IPSG feature picks up the MAC–IP bindings from the binding table and programs the source MAC (SMAC)–IP binding check in the reverse path forwarding (RPF) table on the line card, thus providing a per-port IP traffic filter in hardware.

IPSG is enabled on the L2 port on the switch connecting the host using the command **ip verify source dhcp-snooping-vlan**. Verify the IPSG table after the host has been assigned an IP address using the command **show ip verify source interface** *interface-id*. Example 6-22 demonstrates IPSG being enabled on port Ethernet 7/1, which is the port facing the host (untrusted port) and the IPSG table, after the DHCP server has assigned a DHCP address.

Example 6-22 *IP Source Guard Configuration*

```
NX-1(config)# interface e7/1
NX-1(config-if)# ip verify source dhcp-snooping-vlan
NX-1# show ip verify source interface e7/1
IP source guard is  enabled on this interface.

Interface        Filter-mode      IP-address      Mac-address        Vlan
-----------      -----------      ----------      --------------     ----
Ethernet7/1      active           10.12.1.3       d4:2c:44:fa:cf:47  100
```

When IPSG is enabled and IP–MAC entries have been programmed through the Forwarding Information Base (FIB), all the traffic is checked for IP–MAC binding. For instance, PING from that client (with a valid IP–MAC binding) should work. When the IPSG Binding entry is removed, the PING fails and the FIB drops any such invalid traffic. The SMAC–IP binding in the RPF table is programmed through Security Abstraction Layer (SAL), a virtual device context (VDC) local and conditional compulsory process running on a Nexus system. It uses the NX-OS infrastructure for system startup, restart, and high availability (HA) capability and interprocess communication. SAL is thus treated as a hardware abstraction layer in the supervisor for programming the IPSG bindings database in FIB, which ensures security in the packet forwarding stage.

The SAL database information is viewed using the command **show system internal sal info database vlan** *vlan-id*. This command provides the IPv4 and IPv6 table IDs, which are further used to verify the information in the FIB using the command **show system internal forwarding table** *table-id* **route** *ip-address/mask* [**module** *slot*] (here, *table-id* is the field received from the SAL database output). Example 6-23 demonstrates how to verify the IPSG FIB programming using SAL database info.

Example 6-23 *SAL Database Info and FIB Verification for IPSG*

```
NX-1# show system internal sal info database vlan   100

VLAN ID: 100
Security Features Enabled: IP Source
Table-id Information:
    V4 Table-id: 17
    V6 Table-id: 0x80000011
! Table 17 in hex is 0x11
NX-1# show  system internal forwarding table 0x11 route 10.12.1.3/32 mod 7


Routes for table 17



----+--------------------+----------+----------+-----------
Dev | Prefix             | PfxIndex | AdjIndex | LIF
----+--------------------+----------+----------+-----------
  0    10.12.1.3/32          0x406      0x4d      0xfff
```

Unicast RPF

Unicast Reverse Path Forwarding (URPF) is a technique that matches on source IP addresses to drop the traffic at the edge of the network. In other words, URPF prevents the network from source IP spoofing attacks. This allows other legitimate sources to send their traffic towards the destination server. URPF is implemented in two different modes:

- **Loose mode:** A loose mode check is successful when a lookup of a packet source address in the FIB returns a match and the FIB result indicates that the source is reachable through at least one real interface. The ingress interface through which the packet is received is not required to match any of the interfaces in the FIB result.

- **Strict mode:** A strict mode check is successful when Unicast RFP finds a match in the FIB for the packet source address and *the ingress interface through which the packet is received matches one of the Unicast RPF interfaces in the FIB match*. If this check fails, the packet is discarded. Use this type of Unicast RPF check when packet flows are expected to be symmetrical.

Strict mode URPF is used on up to eight ECMP interfaces; if more than eight are in use, it reverts to loose mode. Loose mode URPF is used on up to 16 ECMP interfaces. URPF is applied on L3 interfaces, SVI, L3 port-channels, and subinterfaces. One caveat of URPF strict mode is that /32 ECMP routes are incompatible. Thus, using URPF strict mode on the uplink to the core is not recommended because the /32 route could be dropped.

URPF is configured using the command **ip verify unicast source reachable-via [any [allow-default] | rx]**. The **rx** option enables strict mode; the **any** option enables loose mode URPF. The **allow-default** option is used with loose mode to include IP addresses that are not specifically contained in the routing table. Example 6-24 demonstrates the configuration for enabling URPF strict mode on an L3 interface. After configuration, use the command **show ip interface** *interface-id* to check whether URPF has been enabled on the interface. In the following example, the URPF mode enabled on interface Eth7/1 is strict mode.

Example 6-24 *Unicast RPF Configuration and Verification*

```
NX-1(config)# interface e7/1
NX-1(config-if)# ip verify unicast source reachable-via rx
NX-1# show ip interface e7/1
IP Interface Status for VRF "default"(1)
Ethernet7/1, Interface status: protocol-up/link-up/admin-up, iod: 175,
  IP address: 10.13.1.1, IP subnet: 10.13.1.0/24 route-preference: 0, tag: 0
  IP broadcast address: 255.255.255.255
  IP multicast groups locally joined: none
  IP MTU: 1500 bytes (using link MTU)
  IP primary address route-preference: 0, tag: 0
  IP proxy ARP : disabled
  IP Local Proxy ARP : disabled
```

```
IP multicast routing: disabled
IP icmp redirects: enabled
IP directed-broadcast: disabled
IP Forwarding: disabled
IP icmp unreachables (except port): disabled
IP icmp port-unreachable: enabled
IP unicast reverse path forwarding: strict
IP load sharing: none
! Output omitted for brevity
```

IPv6 Services

With data centers growing so rapidly, IPv6 has become more relevant in the network to overcome addressing as well as security challenges. NX-OS provides various IPv6 services that provide reliability as well as security in a scaled data center environment. This section discusses the following IPv6 services:

- Neighbor discovery
- IPv6 address assignment
- IPv6 first-hop security

This section details those features and shows how to troubleshoot them on NX-OS switches.

Neighbor Discovery

Defined in RFC 4861, IPv6 Neighbor Discovery (ND) is a set of messages and processes that determine the relationships between two IPv6 neighboring nodes. The IPv6 ND is built on top of ICMPv6, which is defined in RFC 2463. IPv6 ND replaces protocols such as ARP, ICMP redirect, and ICMP router discovery messages, used in IPv4. Both IPv6 ND and ICMPv6 are critical for operations of IPv6.

IPv6 ND defines five ICMPv6 packets to provide the nodes with the information they must and should know before establishing a communication:

- Router Solicitation (ICMPv6 Type 133, code 0)
- Router Advertisement (ICMPv6 Type 134, code 0)
- Neighbor Solicitation (ICMPv6 Type 135, code 0)
- Neighbor Advertisement (ICMPv6 Type 136, code 0)
- Redirect Message (ICMPv6 Type 137, code 0)

When an interface is enabled, hosts can send out a Router Solicitation (RS) that requests routers to generate Router Advertisements immediately instead of at their next scheduled time. When an RS message is sent, the source address field is set to the MAC address of the sending network interface card (NIC). The destination address field is set to 33:33:00:00:00:02 in the Ethernet header. In the IPv6 header, the source address field is set to either the link-local IPv6 address assigned to the sending interface or the IPv6 unspecified address (::). The destination address is set to All Router multicast address with link local scope (FF02:2) and the hop limit is set to 255.

Routers advertise their presence together with various link and Internet parameters either periodically or in response to a Router Solicitation message. Router Advertisements (RAs) contain prefixes that are used for on-link determination and/or address configuration, a suggested hop limit value, maximum transmission unit (MTU), and so on. In the Ethernet header of the RA message, the source address field is set to the sending NIC; the destination address field is set to 33:33:00:00:00:01 or the unicast MAC address of the host that sent a RS message from a unicast address. Similar to the RS message, the source address field is set to the link-local address assigned to the sending interface; the destination address is set to either the all-nodes multicast address with link-local scope (FF02:1) or the unicast IPv6 address of the host that sent the RS message. The hop limit field is set to 255.

A Neighbor Solicitation (NS) is sent by a node to determine the link-layer address of a neighbor or to verify that a neighbor is still reachable via a cached link-layer address. Neighbor Solicitations are also used for duplicate address detection (DAD). In the Ethernet header of the NS message, the destination MAC address corresponds to the solicited-node address of the target. In a unicast NS message, the destination address field is set to the unicast MAC address of the neighbor. In the IPv6 header, the source address is set to IPv6 address of the sending interface or, during DAD, the unspecified address (::). For a multicast NS, the destination address is set to target the solicited node address. For unicast NS, the destination is set to the IPv6 unicast address of the target.

A Neighbor Advertisement (NA) is a response to a Neighbor Solicitation message. A node can also send unsolicited Neighbor Advertisements to announce a link-layer address change. In the Ethernet header of a solicited NA, the destination MAC is set to the unicast MAC address of the initial NS sender. For an unsolicited NA, the destination MAC is set to 33:33:00:00:00:01, which is the link-local scope all-nodes multicast address. In the IPv6 header, the source address is set to an IPv6 unicast address assigned on the sending interface. The destination IPv6 address for a solicited NA is set to the IPv6 unicast address of the sender of initial NS message. For an unsolicited NA, the destination field is set to the link-local scope all-nodes multicast address (FF02::1).

A Redirect Message (RM) is used by routers to inform hosts of a better first hop for a destination. In the Ethernet header, the destination MAC is set to the unicast MAC of the originating sender. In the IPv6 header, the source address field is set to the unicast IPv6 address of the sending interface and the destination address is set to the unicast address of the originating host.

To enable neighbor discovery, the first step is to enable IPv6 or configure an IPv6 address on an interface. An IPv6 address is configured using either the command **ipv6 address** *ipv6-address* [**eui64**] or the command **ipv6 address use-link-local-only**. The command option **eui64** configures the IPv6 address in EUI64 format. The command option **use-link-local-only** manually configures a link-local address on the interface instead of using the automatically assigned link-local address. Examine an IPv6-enabled link between two switches NX-1 and NX-2, as in Figure 6-5. In this topology, the link is configured with the IPv6 address of subnet 2002:10:12:1::/64.

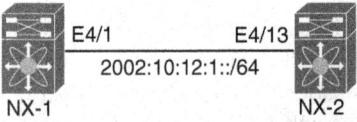

Figure 6-5 *IPv6-Enabled Topology*

When the IPv6 address is configured on both sides of the link and one of the sides initiates a ping, the ND process starts and an IPv6 neighborship is established. An IPv6 neighbor is viewed using the command **show ipv6 neighbor [detail]**. Example 6-25 demonstrates an IPv6 neighborship between two switches. Notice that when the IPv6 address is configured and the user initiates a ping to either the IPv6 unicast address or the link-local address of the remote peer, the IPv6 ND process is initiated, messages are exchanged, and an IPv6 neighborship is formed.

Example 6-25 *IPv6 Neighbor Discovery*

```
NX-1
NX-1(config)# interface Eth4/1
NX-1(config-if)# ipv6 address 2002:10:12:1::1/64
```

```
NX-2
NX-2(config)# interface Eth4/13
NX-2(config-if)# ipv6 address 2002:10:12:1::2/64
```

```
NX-1
! IPv6 neighbor output after initiating ipv6 ping
NX-1# show ipv6 neighbor

Flags: # - Adjacencies Throttled for Glean
       G - Adjacencies of vPC peer with G/W bit

IPv6 Adjacency Table for VRF default
Total number of entries: 2
Address          Age       MAC Address     Pref Source    Interface
2002:10:12:1::2  00:11:51  0002.0002.0012  50   icmpv6    Ethernet4/1
fe80::202:ff:fe02:12
                 00:00:04  0002.0002.0012  50   icmpv6    Ethernet4/1
```

To understand the whole process of neighbor discovery, use the Ethanalyzer tool. Ethanalyzer is used not only to identify the process of IPv6 ND, but also to assist with any ND issues. Example 6-26 displays the Ethanalyzer output when an ICMPv6 ping is initiated to the peer device from NX-1. When the ping is initiated from NX-1, an NS message is sent toward NX-2. The reply packet is an NA message received from NX-2 on NX-1. Notice that, as part of the NA message, the Router (rtr), Solicited (sol), and Override (ovr) flags are set; the target address is set to 2002:10:12:1::2 and is reached at MAC address 0002.0002.0012.

Example 6-26 *IPv6 Neighbor Discovery: Ethanalyzer Capture*

```
NX-1
NX-1# ethanalyzer local interface inband display-filter "ipv6" limit-captured-frames 0
Capturing on inband
2017-10-14 21:25:51.314297 2002:10:12:1::1 -> ff02::1:ff00:2 ICMPv6 86 Neighbor
  Solicitation for 2002:10:12:1::2 from 00:01:00:01:00:12
4 2017-10-14 21:25:51.315476 2002:10:12:1::2 -> 2002:10:12:1::1 ICMPv6 86 Neighbor
  Advertisement 2002:10:12:1::2 (rtr, sol, ovr) is at 00:02:00:02:00:12
2017-10-14 21:25:53.319291 2002:10:12:1::1 -> 2002:10:12:1::2 ICMPv6 118 Echo (ping)
  request id=0x1eaf, seq=1, hop limit=255
2017-10-14 21:25:53.319620 2002:10:12:1::2 -> 2002:10:12:1::1 ICMPv6 118 Echo (ping)
  reply id=0x1eaf, seq=1, hop limit=2 (request in 2580)
! Output omitted for brevity
```

While troubleshooting IPv6 ND issues, it is worth checking global as well as interface-level IPv6 ND information. The command **show ipv6 nd** [**global traffic** | **interface** *interface-id*] helps with this (see Example 6-27). In this example, notice that the interface-level information displays details on when different ICMPv6 messages were sent for ND and the parameters for different ND messages. The global traffic command displays the global statistics on the switch, which is cumulative statistics for all the interfaces enabled for IPv6 and participating in IPv6 ND.

Example 6-27 *IPv6 ND Interface Information*

```
NX-1
NX-1# show ipv6 nd interface ethernet 4/1
ICMPv6 ND Interfaces for VRF "default"
Ethernet4/1, Interface status: protocol-up/link-up/admin-up
  IPv6 address:
    2002:10:12:1::1/64 [VALID]
  IPv6 link-local address: fe80::201:ff:fe01:12 [VALID]
  ND mac-extract : Disabled
  ICMPv6 active timers:
      Last Neighbor-Solicitation sent: 00:07:38
      Last Neighbor-Advertisement sent: 00:06:26
      Last Router-Advertisement sent: 00:01:34
      Next Router-Advertisement sent in: 00:06:50
  Router-Advertisement parameters:
      Periodic interval: 200 to 600 seconds
```

```
            Send "Managed Address Configuration" flag: false
            Send "Other Stateful Configuration" flag: false
            Send "Current Hop Limit" field: 2
            Send "MTU" option value: 1500
            Send "Router Lifetime" field: 1800 secs
            Send "Reachable Time" field: 0 ms
            Send "Retrans Timer" field: 0 ms
            Suppress RA: Disabled
            Suppress MTU in RA: Disabled
    Neighbor-Solicitation parameters:
            NS retransmit interval: 1000 ms
            ND NUD retry base: 1
            ND NUD retry interval: 1000
            ND NUD retry attempts: 3
    ICMPv6 error message parameters:
            Send redirects: true (0)
            Send unreachables: false
    ICMPv6 DAD parameters:
            Maximum DAD attempts: 1
            Current DAD attempt : 1
NX-1# show ipv6 nd global traffic
    ICMPv6 packet Statisitcs (sent/received):
    Total Messages             :         260/274
    Error Messages             :         0/0
    Interface down drop count  :         0/0
    Adjacency not recovered from AM aft HA:        0/0
! Output omitted for brevity
    Echo Request               :         10/4
    Echo Replies               :         4/21
    Redirects                  :         0/0
    Packet Too Big             :         0/0
    Router Advertisements      :         115/125
    Router Solicitations       :         0/0
    Neighbor Advertisements    :         65/65
    Neighbor Solicitations     :         66/59
    Fastpath Packets           :         0
    Ignored Fastpath Packets   :         0
    Duplicate router RA received:        0/0
    ICMPv6 MLD Statistics (sent/received):
    V1 Queries:          0/0
    V2 Queries:          0/0
    V1 Reports:          0/0
    V2 Reports:          0/0
    V1 Leaves :          0/0
```

IPv6 Address Assignment

In an IPv6 network, hosts get IPv6 addresses using one of the following address allocation methods:

- **Manual:** An IPv6 address can be manually configured using CLI or a graphical user interface (GUI).

- **Stateless auto-address configuration (SLAAC):** SLAAC automates the process of IPv6 address allocation. IPv6 hosts use a combination of the IPv6 prefix received in the RA message from the router and its link-local address to form a unique IPv6 address. With SLAAC, addresses are not selectively assigned and policies are not enforced on clients' allowed addresses. With SLAAC, the DHCP server is needed only to get other configuration information, such as DNS servers and the domain search list. Currently, this method is not supported on NX-OS.

- **Stateful configuration:** In stateful configuration, the DHCPv6 server assigns the IPv6 addresses. The DHCP server entity is required to have an on-link presence because the DHCPv6 basic operation between client and server uses link-local communication. This entity can either be a DHCPv6 server or, if a server is not present, a DHCPv6 relay agent. You can use a predefined link-scoped multicast address called All_DHCP_Relay_Agents_and_Servers (FF02:: 1:2) to communicate with neighboring relay agents and servers. All servers and relay agents are members of this multicast group. In many situations, the DHCPv6 server is not always directly connected to every link due, for practical and network management reasons. Thus, a relay agent is used. A relay agent intercepts the link-local DHCPv6 messages and forwards these to DHCPv6 server(s), configured by the administrator. A relay agent can be configured with a list of destination addresses, which can include unicast addresses, the All_DHCP_Servers multicast address, or other addresses that the network administrator selects.

DHCPv6 Relay Agent

The DHCPv6 relay agent is similar to the IPv4 DHCP relay agent. The DHCPv6 relay agent intercepts DHCPv6 request packets from clients, performs basic validations, constructs DHCPv6 RELAY-FORWARD messages, and then forwards to all the DHCPv6 servers configured on the given relay agent. Similarly, the DHCPv6 relay agent intercepts all DHCPv6 RELAY-REPLY packets from the servers, performs basic validations, and then constructs the actual DHCPv6 RELAY-REPLY message from the relay message option of the received packet and forwards it to the intended client. NX-OS also supports relay chaining functionality, in which the DHCPv6 relay agent gets RELAY-FORWARD messages from another relay agent and forwards them to relevant DHCPv6 servers. It also inserts Remote-ID and Interface-ID options in the RELAY-FORWARD messages and removes them from the RELAY-REPLY message before forwarding them to the client/relay agent.

To enable the DHCPv6 relay agent, configure the global command **ipv6 dhcp relay**. After enabling the DHCPv6 relay agent globally, it must be enabled on the client-facing interface, which is either an L3 interface, SVI, an L3 port-channel, or a subinterface, using the command **ipv6 dhcp relay address** *ipv6-address* [**use-vrf** *vrf-name* **interface** *interface-id*] (the **use-vrf** option is used when the DHCP server is reachable via a different VRF). The DHCPv6 relay is enabled across VRFs by using the global configuration **ipv6 dhcp relay option vpn.** The DHCPv6 relay agent on NX-OS also provides an option to specify the source interface using the global configuration **ipv6 dhcp relay source-interface** *interface-id*.

When the DHCPv6 relay agent is configured and messages are exchanged between the client and the server, view the statistics for the relay agent using the command **show ipv6 dhcp relay statistics.** Example 6-28 displays the DHCPv6 relay statistics on module 7, where the client is connected. Remember that when the client sends a DHCPv6 request, it sends a DHCPv6 solicit message to the router or switch connected to it. When received by the first hop or the relay agent, these solicit messages are then relayed to the DHCPv6 server as a relay-forward message. The server sends a RELAY-REPLY message to return a response to the client if the original message from the client was relayed to the server in a relay-forward message. If any DHCPv6 packets are dropped, the output also shows those drop counters.

Example 6-28 *DHCPv6 Relay Statistics*

```
NX-1# show ipv6 dhcp relay statistics interface Eth7/1
-----------------------------------------------------------------
Message Type                    Rx              Tx              Drops
-----------------------------------------------------------------
SOLICIT                         5               0               0
ADVERTISE                       0               2               0
REQUEST                         1               0               0
CONFIRM                         0               0               0
RENEW                           0               0               0
REBIND                          0               0               0
REPLY                           0               2               0
RELEASE                         1               0               0
DECLINE                         0               0               0
RECONFIGURE                     0               0               0
INFORMATION_REQUEST             0               0               0
RELAY_FWD                       0               7               0
RELAY_REPLY                     4               0               0
UNKNOWN                         0               0               0
-----------------------------------------------------------------
Total                           11              11              0
-----------------------------------------------------------------
DHCPv6 Server stats:
```

```
-------------------------------------------------------------------------------
Relay Address            VRF name           Dest. Interface     Request    Response
-------------------------------------------------------------------------------
2001:10:12:1::1            ---                   ---               7          4
DROPS:
------
DHCPv6 Relay is disabled                      :  0
Max hops exceeded                             :  0
Packet validation fails                       :  0
Unknown output interface                      :  0
Invalid VRF                                   :  0
Option insertion failed                       :  0
Direct Replies (Recnfg/Adv/Reply) from server:  0
IPv6 addr not configured                      :  0
Interface error                               :  0
VPN Option Disabled                           :  0
IPv6 extn headers present                     :  0
```

Similar to the IPv4 DHCP relay agent, an ACL gets programmed in hardware for the DHCPv6 relay. View the statistics using the command **show system internal access-list input statistics** [**module** *slot*] (see Example 6-29).

Example 6-29 *DHCPv6 Relay ACL Line Card Statistics*

```
NX-1# show system internal access-list input statistics module 7
              VDC-4 Ethernet7/1 :
              ====================

INSTANCE 0x0
---------------

  Tcam 1 resource usage:
  ----------------------
  Label_b = 0x201
   Bank 0
   ------
     IPv6 Class
       Policies: DHCP(DHCPV6 Relay)   [Merged]
       Netflow profile: 0
       Netflow deny profile: 0
       Entries:
         [Index] Entry [Stats]
         --------------------
  [0058:000e:000e] prec 1 redirect(0x0) udp 0x0/0 0xffffffb8/32 eq 547
flow-label 547  [6]
  [0059:000f:000f] prec 1 permit ip 0x0/0 0x0/0   [8]
```

DHCPv6 Relay LDRA

DHCPv6 operates primarily at Layer 2, using link-scope multicast, because the clients do not have an IPv6 address or do not know the location of DHCPv6 servers until they complete the DHCPv6 transaction. In networks where DHCPv6 servers and clients are not located in the same link, the use of DHCPv6 relay agents allows the DHCPv6 servers to handle clients from beyond its local link.

A DHCPv6 relay agent adds an interface identifier option in the upstream DHCPv6 message (from client to server) to identify the interface on which the client is connected. The DHCPv6 relay agent uses this information while forwarding the downstream DHCPv6 message to the DHCPv6 client.

This works fine when end hosts are directly connected to DHCPv6 relay agents. In some network configurations, however, one or more Layer 2 devices reside between DHCPv6 clients and the relay agent. In these network scenarios, using the DHCPv6 relay agent Interface-ID option for client identification is difficult. A Layer 2 device thus needs to append an Interface-ID option in DHCPv6 messages because they are close to the end hosts. Such devices are typically known as a Lightweight DHCPv6 Relay Agent (LDRA).

When clients do not have an IPv6 address or do not know the location of DHCPv6 servers, DHCPv6 sends an Information-Request message to a reserved, link-scoped multicast address ff02::1:2. The clients listen for DHCPv6 messages on UDP port 546. Servers and relay agents listen for DHCPv6 messages on UDP port 547. LDRA checks whether the incoming interface is L3 or L2. If it is L3, the packet is sent to the DHCPv6 Relay Agent; if it is L2, the following checks are performed:

- The LDRA feature checks whether LDRA is enabled or disabled on the incoming interface or VLAN. If it is disabled, the packet is switched normally.

- The incoming interface on which LDRA is enabled needs to be classified among the following categories; if it is not one of these, LDRA drops the packet.

    - Client-facing trusted

    - Client-facing untrusted

    - Server-facing untrusted

- If a RELAY-FORWARD message is received on a client-untrusted interface, the packet is dropped.

- The packet is dropped if it is of one of the following message types:

    - ADVERTISE

    - REPLY

    - RECONFIGURE RELAY-REPLY

- If hop count is greater than the maximum allowed value, the packet is dropped.
- If the packet passes all the validation checks, a new frame is created and relayed to the server.
  - msg-type: RELAY-FORWARD
  - hop-count:
    - If the received message is not RELAY-FORWARD, hop-count is set to 0.
    - Otherwise, hop-count increases by 1.
  - link-address: Unspecified (::)
  - peer-address: Client's link-local address (source IP address received in the incoming frame's IP header)
  - Interface-ID option: Fill in the Interface-ID details to identify the interface on which the packet was received.
  - Relay-Message option: Original received message

As previously shown, the link-address parameter must be set to 0. LDRA includes the Interface-ID option and the Relay-Message option in Relay-Forward messages. All other options are optional. LDRA uses the Interface-ID to denote both the switch and the interface on which the packet is received. Interface-ID is an opaque value; the server does not try to parse the contents of the Interface-ID option. LDRA creates a String with the switch MAC address, along with the interface ifindex, and uses it as Interface-ID. If the incoming message is a RELAY-FORWARD message and is received on a client-trusted interface, then a Layer 2 or Layer 3 agent is already available in the network and precedes the local relay agent.

When the LDRA-enabled device receives a response from the server, the device performs the following actions:

- If the RELAY-REPLY message is not received on a server-facing trusted interface, the packet is dropped. If other DHCP message types, the packet also is dropped.
- If a packet does not have Interface-ID Option, the packet is dropped.
- LDRA checks whether the packet is intended for it.
- While forwarding the request, LDRA added the interface-id option, which contains both switch and interface details. The L2 relay agent extracts this information.
- If switch-related information is available in the interface-id option, the L2 relay agent's identification is not matched. In that case, the packet is simply forwarded without making any changes because this message is intended for some other relay agent in network.

To enable LDRA globally, configure the command **ipv6 dhcp-ldra**. Then enable LDRA on the L2 interface using the command **ipv6 dhcp-ldra**. LDRA also enables you to specify the interface policy using the command **ipv6 dhcp-ldra attach-policy [client-facing-untrusted | client-facing-trusted | client-facing-disabled | server-facing-trusted]**. The policy options perform different actions:

- **Client-facing-untrusted:** A regular client is connected on this interface.

- **Client-facing-trusted:** Any other L2 or L3 relay agent that precedes this box in the network is connected on this interface. The relay agent connected on this interface should be between the actual client and this L2 relay agent (that is, on the upstream network).

- **Server-facing-trusted:** Any DHCP server or L3 relay agent that follows this box toward the server end should be connected on this interface. If a relay agent is connected on this interface, it should reside on the network path from this box toward the actual DHCP server.

Note If any issues arise with DHCPv6 relay agents, collect the **show tech dhcp** command output to be further analyzed by Cisco TAC.

IPv6 First-Hop Security

IPv4 First-Hop Security (FHS) has been deployed in the data center for many years, particularly with Cisco gear such as Catalyst switches and, more recently on Nexus switches. The vulnerabilities the FHS features are resolving are comparable to what is seen on the campus. In the data center, the hosts are typically applications dedicated to a physical server, or virtual machines (VM) sharing the same physical server. Unlike other environments in which FHS is deployed, the main reason for the servers and VMs to be untrusted is that they might be victims of malware installed by attackers over one of the allowed protocols (such as HTTP).

Some of the IPv6 First Hop Security features are just as applicable as in IPv4. For instance, some malware installed on a VM could send Router Advertisements to pretend to be the default gateway for other VMs on the link. Note that although this scenario is plausible, rogue Router Advertisements in the enterprise and the campus networks mainly come from careless users. This problem is much less critical in the data center because the VMs and servers are usually managed. Still, some VMs might be unmanaged, so the careless user issue then becomes relevant. Table 6-2 lists common attacks in IPv6 networks and the associated FHS mitigation technique.

Table 6-2 *IPv6 Attacks and Mitigation Techniques*

Attack	Mitigating Feature	Capability
MAC spoofing by a rogue virtual machine	Port Security	Restricts MAC addresses on a port.
IPv6 address spoofing by an infected virtual machine	IPv6 Source Guard	Validates the IP source on a port/MAC/VLAN basis.
ND cache poisoning on other virtual machines, hosts, and network devices	IPv6 snooping	Monitors ND and DHCP traffic and gleans the address assignment. Feeds the Source and Destination guard with a list of valid source and destination addresses.
Rogue DHCP server	DHCPv6 guard	Prevents untrusted entities from acting as DHCP servers.
Rogue routers	RA Guard	Prevents untrusted entities from acting as routers.

This section covers RA Guard, IPv6 Snooping, and DHCPv6 Guard.

Note Other FHS techniques exist, but this chapter does not address them. Refer to the Cisco.com documentation for more details.

RA Guard

RA Guard is a feature that enables the user of the Layer 2 switch to configure which switch ports face routers. Router Advertisements received on any other port are dropped, so they never reach the end hosts of the link. RA Guard performs further deep packet inspection to validate the source of the RA, the prefix list, the preference, and any other information carried. RA Guard is specified in RFC 6105. The goal of this feature is to inspect Router Neighbor Discovery (ND) traffic (such as Router Solicitations [RS], Router Advertisements [RA], and redirects) and to drop bogus messages. The feature introduces the capability to block unauthorized messages based on policy configuration (for example, RAs are not allowed on a Host port).

To enable IPv6 RA Guard, first an RA Guard policy is defined and then the policy is applied on an interface. The RA Guard policy is defined using the command **ipv6 nd raguard policy** *policy-name*. Table 6-3 displays all the options available as part of the RA Guard policy.

Table 6-3 *RA Guard Policy Subconfiguration Options*

Option	Description
device-role [host | router | monitor | switch]	Defines the role of the device attached to the port, which can be a host, router, monitor, or switch.
hop-limit [maximum | minimum limit]	Verifies the specified hop-count limit. If this is not configured, the check is bypassed.
managed-config-flag [on | off]	Checks whether the advertised managed-config flag is on or off. If this is not configured, the check is bypassed.
other-config-flag [on | off]	Verifies the advertised "other" configuration parameters.
router-preference maximum [high | low | medium]	Checks that the advertised default router preference parameter value is lower than or equal to a specified limit.
trusted-port	Specifies that the policy is being applied to trusted ports.

When the policy is defined, it is applied to the interface using the interface-level configuration command **ipv6 nd raguard attach-policy** *policy-name*. Example 6-30 displays the sample RA Guard configuration. The command **show ipv6 nd raguard policy** *policy-name* shows the RA Guard policy attached on different interfaces.

Example 6-30 *IPv6 RA Guard Configuration*

```
NX-1(config)# ipv6 nd raguard policy RAGUARD
NX-1(config-raguard-policy)# device-role router
NX-1(config-raguard-policy)# trusted-port
NX-1(config-raguard-policy)# exit
NX-1(config)# interface e7/1
NX-1(config-if)# ipv6 nd raguard attach-policy RAGUARD
NX-1# show ipv6 nd raguard policy RAGUARD

Policy RAGUARD configuration:
  trusted-port
  device-role router
Policy RAGUARD is applied on the following targets:
Target            Type    Policy          Feature         Target range
Eth7/1            PORT    RAGUARD         RA guard        vlan all
```

Note To debug any issues with IPv6 RA Guard, use the debug command **debug ipv6 snooping raguard**, which is captured in a **debug logfile**.

IPv6 Snooping

IPV6 Snooping is a combination of two features: ND Snooping and DHCPv6 Snooping. IPv6 ND Snooping analyzes IPv6 neighbor discovery traffic and determines whether it is harmless for nodes on the link. During this inspection, it gleans address bindings (IP, MAC, port) when available and stores them in a binding table. The binding entry is then used to determine address ownership, in case of contention between two clients. IPv6 DHCP Snooping traps DHCPv6 packets between the client and the server. From the packets snooped, assigned addresses are learned and stored in the binding table. The IPv6 Snooping feature can also limit the number of addresses that any node on the link can claim. This helps protect the switch binding table against DoS flooding attacks. Figure 6-6 explains the role of IPv6 snooping and shows how it prevents the device from invalid or unwanted hosts.

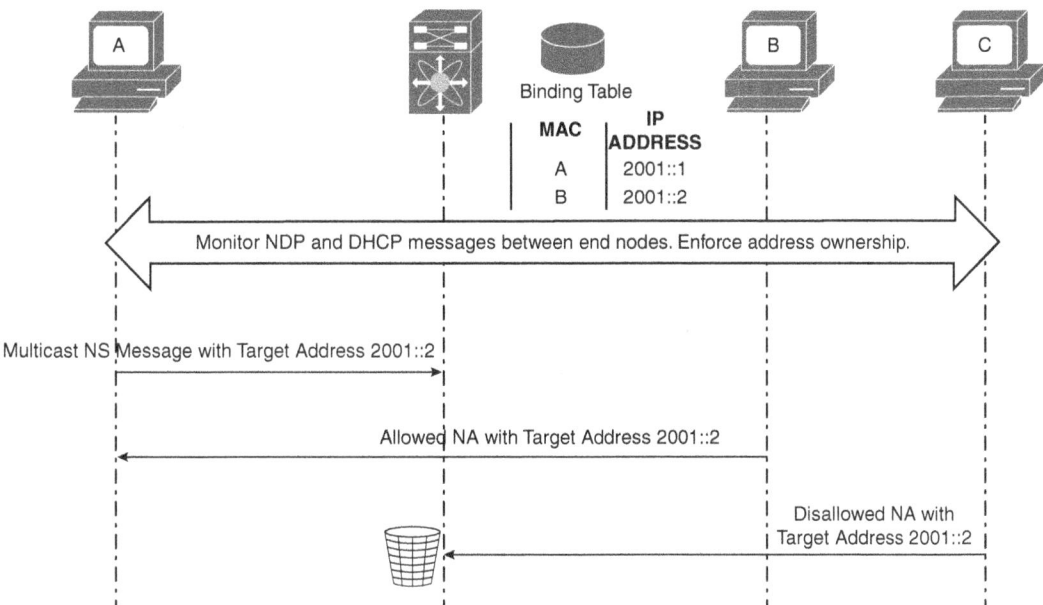

Figure 6-6 *IPv6 Snooping*

IPv6 snooping is configured in two simple steps:

- Define the snooping policy.
- Attach the snooping policy to VLAN(s).

The IPv6 snooping policy is configured using the command **ipv6 snooping policy** *policy-name*. Within the IPv6 snooping policy, you can specify various options, as in Table 6-4.

Table 6-4 *IPv6 Snooping Policy Suboptions*

Suboption	Description
device-role [node | switch]	Specifies the device role of the device attached to the port. By default, the device role is "node." The device role (combined with the **trusted-port** command) has a direct influence on the preference level of an entry learned from the interface where this policy applies.
	The **device-role** node has an inherent preference of access port and the **device-role switch** has a preference of trunk port.
tracking [enable [reachable-lifetime *value*] | disable [stale-lifetime *value*]]	Override the default tracking policy on the port where this policy applies.
	This is especially useful on trusted ports for which tracking entries is not desired the entry should be present in the binding table to prevent stealing. In this case, configure the command **tracking disable stale-lifetime** *infinite*.
trusted port	When receiving messages on ports with this policy, limited to no verification is performed. Nevertheless, to protect against address spoofing, messages still are analyzed so that the binding information they carry can be used to maintain the binding table. Bindings discovered from these ports are considered more trustable than bindings received from untrusted ports.
validate source-mac	When receiving Neighbor Discovery Protocol (NDP) messages that contain a link-layer address option, the source MAC address is checked against the link-layer address option. The packet is dropped if they are different.
protocol [dhcp | ndp]	Specifies which protocol should be redirected to the snooping component for analysis.
security-level [glean | inspect | guard]	Specifies the security level enforced by the IPv6 snooping feature. The default is guard.
	glean: Learns bindings but does not drop the packets.
	inspect: Learns bindings and drops packets if it detects an issue.
	guard: Works like inspect, but also drops IPv6, ND, RA, and IPv6 DHCP server packets in case of a threat.

When the policy is defined, it can be attached using the command **ipv6 snooping attach-policy** *policy-name* under the **vlan configuration** *vlan-id* subconfiguration mode. Example 6-31 displays the configuration of IPv6 snooping policy for VLAN 100.

Example 6-31 *IPv6 Snooping Configuration*

```
NX-1(config)# ipv6 snooping policy V6-SNOOP-VLAN-100
NX-1(config-snoop-policy)# device-role switch
NX-1(config-snoop-policy)# protocol ndp
NX-1(config-snoop-policy)# trusted-port
NX-1(config-snoop-policy)# exit
NX-1(config)# vlan configuration 100
NX-1(config-vlan-config)# ipv6 snooping attach-policy V6-SNOOP-VLAN-100
NX-1# show ipv6 snooping policy

Policy V6-SNOOP-VLAN-100 configuration:
  trusted-port
  security-level guard
  device-role switch
  gleaning from Neighbor Discovery
  gleaning from DHCP
  NOT gleaning from protocol unkn
Policy V6-SNOOP-VLAN-100 is applied on the following targets:
Target              Type  Policy              Feature       Target range
vlan 100            VLAN  V6-SNOOP-VLAN-100   Snooping      vlan all
```

Similar to other FHS features, IPv6 snooping programs an ACL in the hardware, which is verified using the command **show system internal access-list interface** *interface-id* [**module** *slot*]. The command **show system internal access-list input statistics** [**module** *slot*] shows the statistics (see Example 6-32).

Example 6-32 *Verification of Hardware Statistics for IPv6 Snooping*

```
NX-1# show system internal access-list input statistics module 7
               VLAN 100  :
               =========

INSTANCE 0x0
---------------


  Tcam 1 resource usage:
  ----------------------
  Label_b = 0x201
   Bank 0
   ------
     IPv6 Class
       Policies: DHCP_FHS(DHCP SISF)  [Merged]
       Netflow profile: 0
       Netflow deny profile: 0
```

```
        Entries:
          [Index] Entry [Stats]
          --------------------
[0058:000e:000e] prec 1 redirect(0x0)  icmp 0x0/0 0x0/0 137 0 flow-label 35072   [0]
[0059:000f:000f] prec 1 redirect(0x0)  icmp 0x0/0 0x0/0 136 0 flow-label 34816   [0]
[005a:0010:0010] prec 1 redirect(0x0)  icmp 0x0/0 0x0/0 135 0 flow-label 34560   [0]
[005b:0011:0011] prec 1 redirect(0x0)  icmp 0x0/0 0x0/0 134 0 flow-label 34304   [0]
[005c:0012:0012] prec 1 redirect(0x0)  icmp 0x0/0 0x0/0 133 0 flow-label 34048   [0]
[005d:0013:0013] prec 1 redirect(0x0)  udp 0x0/0 0x0/0 eq 547 flow-label 547     [0]
[005e:0014:0014] prec 1 redirect(0x0)  udp 0x0/0 0x0/0 eq 546 flow-label 546     [0]
[005f:0015:0015] prec 1 redirect(0x0)  udp 0x0/0 eq 547 0x0/0 flow-label 196608
[0]
[0060:0016:0016] prec 1 permit ip 0x0/0 0x0/0   [0]
```

DHCPv6 Guard

The main purpose of the DHCPv6 Guard feature is to block DHCP replies or advertisements that do not come from a legitimate DHCP server or relay agents. Based on what configuration is deployed, it decides whether to bridge, switch, or block them. It also verifies information found in the message, such as whether the addresses and prefixes in the message are in the specified range. The device can be configured in a client or server mode, which protects the clients from receiving replies from rogue DHCP servers.

The default mode of the box is to guard, so by default, all ports configured with DHCPv6 Guard are in client mode. Thus, all ports drop any DHCPv6 server messages by default. For a meaningful DHCPv6 deployment, at least one port should be assigned to the dhcp-server role, which then permits DHCPv6 server messages. This is the simplest configuration for a reasonable level of security.

When DHCP Guard is enabled on an interface or VLAN, ACLs are programmed in the hardware with ACL action to punt DHCP packets to the Supervisor. The ACL has the following filter:

- Match on UDP protocol
- The source port should be either the DHCP client port (port 546) or the server port (port 547).
- The destination port should be either the DHCP client port (port 546) or the server port (port 547).

The ACL can be verified on the line card or hardware using the command **show system internal access-list input interface** *interface-id* **module** *slot*.

When both DHCPv6 Guard and DHCPv6 relay features are configured on the same device, DHCPv6 request packets received by FHS are first handled by the DHCPv6

Guard feature. After all processing is done by the DHCPv6 Guard process, the packet is given to DHCPv6 Relay feature, which relays it to the specified server.

Similarly, the DHCP relay agent first processes DHCP reply packets from another relay agent or DHCP server. If the enclosed packet is not a relay packet (Relay forward or Relay reply), it is passed on to DHCP Guard feature.

Note DHCP Guard and the DHCP relay agent essentially work together only at the first hop. In later hops, DHCP relay agent is given priority over DHCP Guard. Statistics are maintained separately for both features.

To configure DHCPv6 Guard policy, use the command **ipv6 dhcp guard policy** *policy-name*. Under the policy, the first step is to define the device role, which is client, server, or monitor. Then you define the advertised minimum and maximum allowed server preference. You can also specify whether the device is connected on a trusted port using the **trusted port** command option. After configuring the policy, use the command **ipv6 dhcp guard attach-policy** *policy-name* command to attach the policy to a port or a VLAN. Example 6-33 shows the configuration of DHCPv6 Guard. To check the policy configuration, use the command **show ipv6 dhcp guard policy** or use the command **show ipv6 snooping policies** to verify both the IPv6 snooping and the DHCPv6 guard policies; DHCPv6 Guard works in conjunction with IPv6 snooping.

Example 6-33 *DHCPv6 Guard Configuration and Policy Verification*

```
NX-1(config)# ipv6 dhcp guard policy DHCPv6-Guard
NX-1(config-dhcpg-policy)# device-role ?
  client   Attached device is a client (default)
  monitor  Attached device is a monitor/sniffer
  server   Attached device is a dhcp server

NX-1(config-dhcpg-policy)# device-role server
NX-1(config-dhcpg-policy)# preference max 255
NX-1(config-dhcpg-policy)# preference min 0
NX-1(config-dhcpg-policy)# trusted port
NX-1(config-dhcpg-policy)# exit
NX-1(config-if)# interface e7/13
NX-1(config-if)# switchport
NX-1(config-if)# switchport access vlan 200
NX-1(config-if)# ipv6 dhcp guard attach-policy DHCPv6-Guard
NX-1(config-if)# exit
NX-1(config)# vlan configuration 200
NX-1(config-vlan-config)# ipv6 dhcp guard attach-policy DHCPv6-Guard
NX-1(config-vlan-config)# end
NX-1# show ipv6 dhcp guard policy
```

```
  Dhcp guard policy: DHCPv6-Guard
          Trusted Port
          Target: Eth7/13 vlan 200
NX-1# show ipv6 snooping policies


Target              Type   Policy              Feature          Target range
Eth7/13             PORT   DHCPv6-Guard        DHCP Guard       vlan all
vlan 100            VLAN   V6-SNOOP-VLAN-100   Snooping         vlan all
vlan 200            VLAN   DHCPv6-Guard        DHCP Guard       vlan all
```

First-Hop Redundancy Protocol

First-Hop Redundancy Protocol (FHRP) provides routing redundancy for a network. FHRP was designed to provide transparent failover of the first-hop IP gateway in a network. FHRP can be implemented using the following features on the switch or a router:

- Hot Standby Routing Protocol (HSRP)
- Virtual Router Redundancy Protocol (VRRP)
- Gateway Load-Balancing Protocol (GLBP)

This section explains how those FHRP protocols work and details how to troubleshoot them.

HSRP

Defined in RFC 2281, Hot Standby Routing Protocol (HSRP) provides transparent failover of the first-hop device, which typically acts as a gateway to the hosts. HSRP provides routing redundancy for IP hosts on Ethernet networks configured with a default gateway IP address. It requires a minimum of two devices to enable HSRP; one device acts as the active device and takes care of forwarding the packets, and the other acts as a standby, ready to take over the role of active device in case of any failure.

On a network segment, a virtual IP is configured on each HSRP-enabled interface that belongs to the same HSRP group. HSRP selects one of the interfaces to act as the HSRP active router. Along with the virtual IP, a virtual MAC address is assigned for the group. The active router receives and routes the packets destined for the virtual MAC address of the group. When the HSRP active device fails, the HSRP standby device assumes control of the virtual IP and MAC address of the group. If more than two devices are part of the HSRP group, a new HSRP standby device is selected. Network operators control which device should act as the HSRP active device by defining interface priority (the default is 100). The higher priority determines which device will act as an HSRP active device.

HSRP-enabled interfaces send and receive multicast UDP-based hello messages to detect any failure and designate active and standby routers. If the standby device does not receive a hello message or the active device fails to send a hello message, the standby device with the second-highest priority becomes HSRP active. The transition of HSRP active between the devices is transparent to all hosts on the segment.

HSRP supports two versions: version 1 and version 2. Table 6-5 includes some of the differences between HSRP versions.

Table 6-5 *HSRP Version 1 Versus Version 2*

	HSRP Version 1	**HSRP Version 2**
Timers	Does not support millisecond timer	Supports millisecond timer values
Group Range	0–255	0–4095
Multicast Address	224.0.0.2	224.0.0.102
MAC Address Range	0000.0C07.ACxy, where xy is a hex value representing an HSRP group number	0000.0C9F.F000 to 0000.0C9F.FFFF
Authentication	Does not support authentication	Supports MD5 authentication

Note Transitioning from HSRP version 1 to version 2 can be disruptive, given the change in MAC address between both versions.

When the HSRP is configured on the segment and both the active and standby devices are chosen, the HSRP control packets contain the following fields:

- Source MAC: Virtual MAC of the active device or the interface MAC of the standby or listener device
- Destination MAC: 0100.5e00.0002 for version 1 and 0100.5e00.0066 for version 2
- Source IP: Interface IP
- Destination IP: 224.0.0.2 for version 1 and 224.0.0.102 for version 2
- UDP port 1985

To understand the functioning of HSRP, examine the topology in Figure 6-7. Here, HSRP is running on VLAN 10.

372 Chapter 6: Troubleshooting IP and IPv6 Services

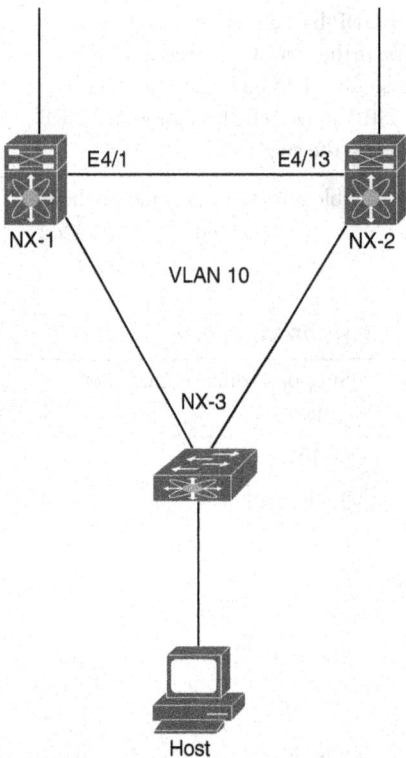

Figure 6-7 *HSRP Topology*

To enable HSRP, use the command **feature hsrp**. When configured, HSRP runs on default HSRP version 1. To manually change the HSRP version, use the command **hsrp version [1 | 2]** under the interface where HSRP is configured.

Example 6-34 illustrates the configuration of HSRP for VLAN 10. In this example, HSRP is configured with the group number 10 and a VIP of 10.12.1.1. NX-1 is set to a priority of 110, which means that NX-1 acts as the active HSRP gateway. HSRP is also configured with preemption; in case of a failure on NX-1 and the HSRP active gateway failover to NX-2, the NX-1 regains the active role when NX-1 becomes active and available.

Example 6-34 *HSRP Configuration*

```
NX-1
interface Vlan10
  no shutdown
  no ip redirects
  ip address 10.12.1.2/24
  hsrp version 2
  hsrp 10
   preempt
    priority 110
```

```
    ip 10.12.1.1
NX-2
interface Vlan10
  no shutdown
  no ip redirects
  ip address 10.12.1.3/24
  hsrp version 2
  hsrp 10
    ip 10.12.1.1
```

To view the status of HSRP groups and determine which device is acting as an active or standby HSRP device, use the command **show hsrp brief**. This command displays the group information, the priority of the local device, the active and standby HSRP interface address, and also the group address, which is the HSRP VIP. You can also use the command **show hsrp [detail]** to view more details about the HSRP groups. This command not only details information about the HSRP group, but it also lists the timeline of the state machine a group goes through. This command is useful when troubleshooting any HSRP finite state machine issues. The **show hsrp [detail]** command also displays any authentication configured for the group, along with the virtual IP (VIP) and virtual MAC address for the group. Example 6-35 displays both the **show hsrp brief** and **show hsrp detail** command outputs. One important point to note in the following output is that if no authentication is configured, the **show hsrp detail** command displays it as *Authentication text "cisco"*.

Example 6-35 *HSRP Verification and Detailed Information*

```
NX-1
NX-1# show hsrp brief
*:IPv6 group   #:group belongs to a bundle
                    P indicates configured to preempt.
                    |
 Interface   Grp  Prio  P State    Active addr    Standby addr    Group addr
 Vlan10      10   110   P Active   local          10.12.1.3       10.12.1.1
    (conf)
NX-1# show hsrp detail
Vlan10 - Group 10 (HSRP-V2) (IPv4)
  Local state is Active, priority 110 (Cfged 110), may preempt
    Forwarding threshold(for vPC), lower: 1 upper: 110
  Hellotime 3 sec, holdtime 10 sec
  Next hello sent in 0.951000 sec(s)
  Virtual IP address is 10.12.1.1 (Cfged)
 Active router is local
  Standby router is 10.12.1.3 , priority 100 expires in 9.721000 sec(s)
  Authentication text "cisco"
  Virtual mac address is 0000.0c9f.f00a (Default MAC)
```

```
   2 state changes, last state change 00:03:07
   IP redundancy name is hsrp-Vlan10-10 (default)


  ----- Detailed information -----
  State History
  ------------------------------------------------------------
    Time            Prev State      State         Event
  ------------------------------------------------------------
    (20)-20:04:55 Active            Active        Sby Timer Expired

    (20)-19:38:58 Standby           Active        Act Timer Expired.

    (20)-19:38:47 Speak             Standby       Sby Timer Expired.

    (20)-19:38:47 Listen            Speak         Act Timer Expired.

    (20)-19:38:37 Initial           Listen        If Enabled-VIP.
```

When HSRP is configured on an interface, the interface automatically joins the HSRP multicast group based on the HSRP version. This information is viewed using the command **show ip interface** *interface-id*. This command does not provide information on the HSRP virtual IP on the interface. To view the virtual IP along with the HSRP multicast group, use the command **show ip interface** *interface-id* **vaddr**. Example 6-36 displays the output of both commands.

Example 6-36 *HSRP Multicast Group and VIP*

```
NX-1# show ip interface vlan 10
IP Interface Status for VRF "default"(1)
Vlan10, Interface status: protocol-up/link-up/admin-up, iod: 148,
  IP address: 10.12.1.2, IP subnet: 10.12.1.0/24 route-preference: 0, tag: 0
  IP broadcast address: 255.255.255.255
  IP multicast groups locally joined:
      224.0.0.102
  IP MTU: 1500 bytes (using link MTU)
! Output omitted for brevity
NX-1# show ip interface vlan 10 vaddr
IP Interface Status for VRF "default"(1)
Vlan10, Interface status: protocol-up/link-up/admin-up, iod: 148,
  IP address: 10.12.1.2, IP subnet: 10.12.1.0/24 route-preference: 0, tag: 0
  Virtual IP address(406): 10.12.1.1, IP subnet: 10.12.1.1/32
  IP broadcast address: 255.255.255.255
  IP multicast groups locally joined:
      224.0.0.102
  IP MTU: 1500 bytes (using link MTU)
```

The active HSRP gateway device also populates the ARP table with the virtual IP and the virtual MAC address, as in Example 6-37. Notice that the virtual IP 10.12.1.1 maps to MAC address 0000.0c9f.f00a, which is the virtual MAC of group 10.

Example 6-37 *HSRP Virtual MAC and Virtual IP Address in ARP Table*

```
NX-1# show ip arp vlan 10

Flags: * - Adjacencies learnt on non-active FHRP router
       + - Adjacencies synced via CFSoE
       # - Adjacencies Throttled for Glean
       D - Static Adjacencies attached to down interface

IP ARP Table
Total number of entries: 1
Address         Age       MAC Address      Interface
10.12.1.1       -         0000.0c9f.f00a   Vlan10
```

If the HSRP is down or flapping between the two devices, or if the HSRP has not established the proper states between the two devices (for example, both devices are showing in Active/Active state), it might be worth enabling packet capture or running a debug to investigate whether the HSRP hello packets are making it to the other end or whether they are being generated locally on the switch. Because the HSRP control packets are destined for the CPU, use Ethanalyzer to capture those packets. The display-filter of **hsrp** helps capture HSRP control packets and determine whether any are not being received.

Along with Ethanalyzer, you can enable HSRP debug to see whether the hello packet is being received. The HSRP debug for the hello packet is enabled using the command **debug hsrp engine packet hello interface** *interface-id* **group** *group-number*. The command displays the hello packet from and to the peer, along with other information such as authentication, hello, and the hold timer.

Example 6-38 displays the Ethanalyzer and HSRP debug for capturing hello packets. Note that HSRP version 2 assigns a 6-byte ID to identify the sender of the HSRP hello packet, which is usually the interface MAC address.

Example 6-38 *Ethanalyzer and HSRP Hello Debug*

```
NX-2
NX-2# ethanalyzer local interface inband display-filter hsrp limit-captured-frames 0
Capturing on inband
1 2017-10-21 07:45:18.646334    10.12.1.2 -> 224.0.0.102  HSRPv2 94 Hello (state
   Active)
2 2017-10-21 07:45:18.915261    10.12.1.3 -> 224.0.0.102  HSRPv2 94 Hello (state
   Standby)
2 2017-10-21 07:45:21.503535    10.12.1.2 -> 224.0.0.102  HSRPv2 94 Hello (state
   Active)
```

Chapter 6: Troubleshooting IP and IPv6 Services

```
   4 2017-10-21 07:45:21.602261       10.12.1.3 -> 224.0.0.102   HSRPv2 94 Hello (state
     Standby)
NX-1
NX-1# debug logfile hsrp
NX-1# debug hsrp engine packet hello interface vlan 10 group 10
NX-1#
NX-1# show debug logfile hsrp
! Below hello packet is received by remote peer
2017 Oct 20 19:49:45.351470 hsrp: Vlan10[10/V4]: Hello in from 10.12.1.3 Peer/My
  State Standby/Active pri 100 ip 10.12.1.1
2017 Oct 20 19:49:45.351516 hsrp: Vlan10[10/V4]: hel 3000 hol 10000 auth cisco
2017 Oct 20 19:49:46.739041 hsrp: Vlan10[10/V4]: Hello out Active pri 110 ip
  10.12.1.1

! Below packet is the hello packet generated locally by the switch

2017 Oct 20 19:49:46.739063 hsrp: Vlan10[10/V4]: hel 3000 hol 10000 id
  5087.8940.2042

2017 Oct 20 19:49:48.039809 hsrp: Vlan10[10/V4]: Hello in from 10.12.1.3 Peer/My
  State Standby/Active pri 100 ip 10.12.1.1
2017 Oct 20 19:49:48.039829 hsrp: Vlan10[10/V4]: hel 3000 hol 10000 auth cisco
2017 Oct 20 19:49:49.595505 hsrp: Vlan10[10/V4]: Hello out Active pri 110 ip
  10.12.1.1
2017 Oct 20 19:49:49.595526 hsrp: Vlan10[10/V4]: hel 3000 hol 10000 id
  5087.8940.2042
```

One of the most common problems with HSRP is the group remaining in down state. This can happen for the following reasons:

- The virtual IP is not configured.
- The interface is down.
- The interface IP is not configured.

Thus, while troubleshooting any HSRP group down-state issues, these points should all be checked.

HSRPv6

HSRP for IPv6 (HSRPv6) provides the same functionality to IPv6 hosts as HSRP for IPv4. An HSRP IPv6 group has a virtual MAC address that is derived from the HSRP group number and has a virtual IPv6 link-local address that is, by default, derived from the HSRP virtual MAC address. When the HSRPv6 group is active, periodic RA messages are sent for the HSRP virtual IPv6 link-local address. These RA messages stop after a final RA is sent, when the group leaves the active state (moves to standby state).

HSRPv6 has a different MAC address range and UDP port than HSRP for IPv4. Consider some of these values:

- HSRP version 2
- UDP port: 2029
- MAC address range: 0005.73A0.0000 to 0005.73A0.0FFF
- Hellos Multicast Address: FF02::66 (link-local scope multicast address)
- Hop limit: 255

No separate feature is required to enable HSRPv6. **Feature hsrp** enables HSRP for both IPv4 and IPv6 address families. Example 6-39 illustrates the configuration of HSRPv6 between NX-1 and NX-2 on VLAN 10. In this example, NX-2 is set with a priority of 110, which means NX-2 acts as the active switch and NX-1 acts as the standby. In this example, a virtual IPv6 address is defined using the command **ip** *ipv6-address*, but this virtual IPv6 address is a secondary virtual IP address. The primary virtual IPv6 address is automatically assigned for the group.

Example 6-39 *HSRPv6 Configuration*

```
NX-1
interface Vlan10
  no shutdown
  no ipv6 redirects
  ipv6 address 2001:db8::2/48
  hsrp version 2
  hsrp 20 ipv6
    ip 2001:db8::1
NX-2
interface Vlan10
  no shutdown
  no ipv6 redirects
  ipv6 address 2001:db8::3/48
  hsrp version 2
  hsrp 20 ipv6
    preempt
    priority 110
    ip 2001:db8::1
```

Similar to IPv4, HSRPv6 group information is viewed using the command **show hsrp** [**group** *group-number*] [**detail**]. The command displays information related to the current state of the device, priority, the primary and secondary virtual IPv6 address, the virtual MAC address, and the state history for the group. Example 6-40 displays the detailed output of HSRP group 20 configured on VLAN 10. Notice that the virtual IPv6 address is calculated based on the virtual MAC address assigned for the group. The configured virtual IPv6 address is under the secondary VIP list.

Example 6-40   *HSRPv6 Group Detail*

```
NX-2
NX-2# show hsrp group 20 detail
Vlan10 - Group 20 (HSRP-V2) (IPv6)
  Local state is Active, priority 110 (Cfged 110), may preempt
    Forwarding threshold(for vPC), lower: 1 upper: 110
  Hellotime 3 sec, holdtime 10 sec
  Next hello sent in 1.621000 sec(s)
  Virtual IP address is fe80::5:73ff:fea0:14 (Implicit)
  Active router is local
  Standby router is fe80::5287:89ff:fe40:2042 , priority 100 expires in 9.060000
sec(s)
  Authentication text "cisco"
  Virtual mac address is 0005.73a0.0014 (Default MAC)
  2 state changes, last state change 00:02:40
  IP redundancy name is hsrp-Vlan10-20-V6 (default)
  Secondary VIP(s):
                  2001:db8::1

----- Detailed information -----
State History
------------------------------------------------------------
  Time              Prev State       State           Event
------------------------------------------------------------
  (21)-20:22:39 Standby          Active          Act Timer Expired.

  (21)-20:22:28 Speak            Standby         Sby Timer Expired.

  (21)-20:22:28 Listen           Speak           Act Timer Expired.

  (21)-20:22:18 Initial          Listen          If Enabled-VIP.

  (21)-20:22:18 No Trans         Initial         N/A.
```

HSRPv6 does not come up if the virtual IPv6 address is configured and assigned on the interface. This information is verified using the command **show ipv6 interface** *interface-id*. In addition, the virtual IPv6 address and virtual MAC addresses must be added to ICMPv6. This information is validated using the command **show ipv6 icmp vaddr [link-local | global]**. The keyword **link-local** displays the primary virtual IPv6 address, which is automatically calculated using the virtual MAC. The keyword **global** displays the manually configured virtual IPv6 address. Example 6-41 examines the output of both these commands.

Example 6-41 *HSRPv6 Virtual Address Verification*

```
NX-2
NX-2# show ipv6 interface vlan 10
IPv6 Interface Status for VRF "default"(1)
Vlan10, Interface status: protocol-up/link-up/admin-up, iod: 121
  IPv6 address:
    2001:db8::3/48 [VALID]
  IPv6 subnet:  2001:db8::/48
  IPv6 link-local address: fe80::e6c7:22ff:fe1e:9642 (default) [VALID]
  IPv6 virtual addresses configured:
      fe80::5:73ff:fea0:14  2001:db8::1
  IPv6 multicast routing: disabled
! Output omitted for brevity
NX-2# show ipv6 icmp vaddr link-local
  Virtual IPv6 addresses exists:
  Interface: Vlan10, context_name: default (1)
    Group id: 20, Protocol: HSRP, Client UUID: 0x196, Active: Yes (1) client_state:1
      Virtual IPv6 address: fe80::5:73ff:fea0:14
      Virtual MAC: 0005.73a0.0014, context_name: default (1)

NX-2# show ipv6 icmp vaddr global
    Group id: 20, Protocol: HSRP, Client UUID: 0x196, Active: Yes
      Interface: Vlan10, Virtual IPv6 address: 2001:db8::1
      Virtual MAC: 0005.73a0.0014, context_name: default (1) flags:3
```

For flapping HSRPv6 neighbors, the same Ethanalyzer trigger can be used as for IPv4. Example 6-42 displays the Ethanalyzer output for HSRPv6 control packets, showing packets from both HSRP active and standby switches.

Example 6-42 *Ethanalyzer for HSRPv6*

```
NX-2
NX-2# ethanalyzer local interface inband display-filter hsrp limit-captured-frames 0
Capturing on inband
20:32:29.596977 fe80::5287:89ff:fe40:2042 -> ff02::66    HSRPv2 114 Hello (state
  Standby)
20:32:29.673860 fe80::e6c7:22ff:fe1e:9642 -> ff02::66    HSRPv2 114 Hello (state
  Active)
20:32:32.307507 fe80::5287:89ff:fe40:2042 -> ff02::66    HSRPv2 114 Hello (state
  Standby)
20:32:32.333125 fe80::e6c7:22ff:fe1e:9642 -> ff02::66    HSRPv2 114 Hello (state
  Active)
```

Note For any failure or problem with HSRP or HSRPv6, collect the **show tech hsrp** output in problematic state.

VRRP

Virtual Router Redundancy Protocol (VRRP) was initially defined in RFC 2338, which defines version 1. RFC 3768 and RFC 5798 define version 2 and version 3, respectively. NX-OS supports only VRRP version 2 and version 3. VRRP works in a similar concept as HSRP. VRRP provides box-to-box redundancy by enabling multiple devices to elect a member as a VRRP master that assumes the role of default gateway, thus eliminating a single point of failure. The nonmaster VRRP member forms a VRRP group and takes the role of backup. If the VRRP master fails, the VRRP backup assumes the role of VRRP master and acts as the default gateway.

VRRP is enabled using the command **feature vrrp**. VRRP has a similar configuration as HSRP. VRRP is configured using the command **vrrp** *group-number*. Under the interface VRRP configuration mode, network operators can define the virtual IP, priority, authentication, and so on. A **no shutdown** is necessary under the vrrp configuration to enable the vrrp group. Example 6-43 displays the VRRP configuration between NX-1 and NX-2.

Example 6-43 *VRRP Configuration*

```
NX-1
interface Vlan10
  no shutdown
  no ip redirects
  ip address 10.12.1.2/24
  vrrp 10
    priority 110
    authentication text cisco
    address 10.12.1.1
    no shutdown
NX-2
interface Vlan10
  no shutdown
  no ip redirects
  ip address 10.12.1.3/24
  vrrp 10
    authentication text cisco
    address 10.12.1.1
    no shutdown
```

To verify the VRRP state, use the command **show vrrp [master | backup]**. The master and backup options display information on the respective nodes. The **show vrrp [detail]** command output is used to gather more details about the VRRP. Example 6-44 displays the detailed VRRP output, as well as VRRP state information. Notice that, in this example, the command **show vrrp detail** output displays the virtual IP as well as the virtual MAC address. The VRRP virtual MAC address is of the format 0000.5e00.01xy, where xy is the hex representation of the group number.

Example 6-44 *VRRP State and Detail Information*

```
NX-1
NX-1# show vrrp master
      Interface  VR IpVersion Pri   Time Pre State    VR IP addr
   --------------------------------------------------------------
         Vlan10  10    IPV4    110   1 s  Y  Master   10.12.1.1

NX-1# show vrrp detail

Vlan10 - Group 10 (IPV4)
    State is Master
    Virtual IP address is 10.12.1.1
    Priority 110, Configured 110
    Forwarding threshold(for VPC), lower: 1 upper: 110
    Advertisement interval 1
    Preemption enabled
    Authentication text "cisco"
    Virtual MAC address is 0000.5e00.010a
    Master router is Local
NX-2
NX-2# show vrrp backup
      Interface  VR IpVersion Pri   Time Pre State    VR IP addr
   --------------------------------------------------------------
         Vlan10  10    IPV4    100   1 s  Y  Backup   10.12.1.1
```

For any VRRP flapping issues, use the command **show vrrp statistics** to determine whether the flapping is the result of some kind of error or a packet being wrongly received. The command displays the number of times the device has become a master, along with other error statistics such as TTL errors, invalid packet length, and a mismatch in address list. Example 6-45 displays the output of the **show vrrp statistics.** Notice that NX-1 received five authentication failure statistics for group 10.

Example 6-45 *VRRP Statistics*

```
NX-1
NX-1# show vrrp statistics

Vlan10 - Group 10 (IPV4) statistics

Number of times we have become Master : 1
Number of advertisement packets received : 0
Number of advertisement interval mismatch : 0
Authentication failure cases : 5
TTL Errors : 0
```

```
Zero priority advertisements received : 0
Zero priotiy advertisements sent : 0
Invalid type field received : 0
Mismatch in address list between ours & received packets : 0
Invalid packet length : 0
```

VRRP version 2 has support only for the IPv4 address family, but VRRP version 3 (VRRP3) has support for both IPv4 and IPv6 address families. On NX-OS, both VRRP and VRRPv3 cannot be enabled on the same device. If the feature VRRP is already enabled on the Nexus switch, enabling the feature VRRPv3 displays an error stating that VRRPv2 is already enabled. Thus, a migration must be performed from VRRP to VRRPv3, which has minimal impact on the services. Refer to the following steps to perform the migration from VRRP version 2 to version 3.

Step 1. Disable the feature VRRP using the command **no feature vrrp**.

Step 2. Enable the feature VRRPv3 using the command **feature vrrpv3**.

Step 3. Under the interface, configure the VRRPv3 group using the command **vrrpv3** *group-number* **address-family** [**ipv4** | **ipv6**].

Step 4. Use the address command to define the VRRPv3 primary and secondary virtual IP.

Step 5. Use the command **vrrpv2** to enable backward compatibility with VRRP version 2. This helps in exchanging state information with other VRRP version 2 devices.

Step 6. Perform a **no shutdown** on the VRRPv3 group.

Example 6-46 illustrates a migration configuration from VRRPv2 to VRRPv3 on the NX-1 switch.

Example 6-46 *VRRPv3 Migration Configuration*

```
NX-1
NX-1(config)# feature vrrpv3
Cannot enable VRRPv3: VRRPv2 is already enabled

NX-1(config)# no feature vrrp
NX-1(config)# feature vrrpv3
NX-1(config)# interface vlan 10
NX-1(config-if)# vrrpv3 10 address-family ipv4
NX-1(config-if-vrrpv3-group)# address 10.12.1.1 primary
NX-1(config-if-vrrpv3-group)# address 10.12.1.5 secondary
NX-1(config-if-vrrpv3-group)# vrrpv2
NX-1(config-if-vrrpv3-group)# preempt
NX-1(config-if-vrrpv3-group)# no shutdown
NX-1(config-if-vrrpv3-group)# end
```

The command **show vrrpv3 [brief | detail]** verifies the information of the VRRPv3 groups. The **show vrrpv3 brief** command option displays the brief information related to the group, such as group number, address family, priority, preemption, state, master address, and group address (which is the virtual group IP). The **show vrrpv3 detail** command displays additional information, such as advertisements sent and received for both VRRPv2 and VRRPv3, virtual MAC address, and other statistics related to errors and transition states. Example 6-47 displays both the brief and detailed command output of **show vrrpv3**.

Example 6-47 show vrrpv3 *Command Output*

```
NX-1
NX-1# show vrrpv3 brief

  Interface        Grp  A-F Pri  Time Own Pre State   Master addr/Group addr
  Vlan10           10   IPv4 100    0  N   Y  MASTER  10.12.1.2(local) 10.12.1.1

NX-1# show vrrpv3 detail

Vlan10 - Group 10 - Address-Family IPv4
  State is MASTER
  State duration 1 mins 3.400 secs
  Virtual IP address is 10.12.1.1
  Virtual secondary IP addresses:
    10.12.1.5
  Virtual MAC address is 0000.5e00.010a
  Advertisement interval is 1000 msec
  Preemption enabled
  Priority is 100
  Master Router is 10.12.1.2 (local), priority is 100
  Master Advertisement interval is 1000 msec (expires in 594 msec)
  Master Down interval is unknown
  VRRPv3 Advertisements: sent 72 (errors 0) - rcvd 0
  VRRPv2 Advertisements: sent 32 (errors 0) - rcvd 15
  Group Discarded Packets: 0
    VRRPv2 incompatibility: 0
    IP Address Owner conflicts: 0
    Invalid address count: 0
    IP address configuration mismatch : 0
    Invalid Advert Interval: 0
    Adverts received in Init state: 0
    Invalid group other reason: 0
  Group State transition:
    Init to master: 0
    Init to backup: 1 (Last change Sat Oct 21 16:16:39.737 UTC)
```

```
      Backup to master: 1 (Last change Sat Oct 21 16:16:43.347 UTC)
      Master to backup: 0
      Master to init: 0
      Backup to init: 0
```

You can also use the **show vrrpv3 statistics** command output to view the error statistics. This command displays the counters for dropped packets and packets dropped for various reasons, such as invalid TTL, invalid checksum, or invalid message type. The second half of the output is similar to the **show vrrpv3 detail** output. Example 6-48 displays the output of the command **show vrrpv3 statistics**.

Example 6-48 show vrrpv3 statistics *Command Output*

```
NX-1
NX-1# show vrrpv3 statistics

VRRP Global Statistics:
  Dropped Packets : 0
VRRP Statistics for Vlan10
  Header Discarded Packets: 0
    Invalid TTL/Hop Limit: 0
    Invalid Checksum: 0
    Invalid Version: 0
    Invalid Msg Type: 0
    Invalid length/Incomplete packet: 0
    Invalid group no: 0
    Invalid packet other reason: 0

VRRP Statistics for Vlan10 - Group 10 - Address-Family IPv4
  State is MASTER
  State duration 40.332 secs
  VRRPv3 Advertisements: sent 560 (errors 0) - rcvd 0
  VRRPv2 Advertisements: sent 520 (errors 0) - rcvd 89
  Group Discarded Packets: 0
    VRRPv2 incompatibility: 0
    IP Address Owner conflicts: 0
    Invalid address count: 0
    IP address configuration mismatch : 89
    Invalid Advert Interval: 0
    Adverts received in Init state: 0
    Invalid group other reason: 0
  Group State transition:
    Init to master: 0
```

```
Init to backup: 1 (Last change Sat Oct 21 16:16:39.737 UTC)
Backup to master: 2 (Last change Sat Oct 21 16:25:56.905 UTC)
Master to backup: 1 (Last change Sat Oct 21 16:24:28.198 UTC)
Master to init: 0
Backup to init: 0
```

Note For any failure or issues with VRRP, collect the output from the commands **show tech vrrp [brief]** or **show tech vrrpv3 [detail]** during problematic state for further investigation by Cisco TAC.

GLBP

As the name suggests, Gateway Load-Balancing Protocol (GLBP) provides gateway redundancy and load balancing to the network segment. It provides redundancy with an active/standby gateway and supplies load balancing by ensuring that each member of the GLBP group takes care of forwarding the traffic to the appropriate gateway. GLBP is enabled on NX-OS using the command **feature glbp**. When defining a GLBP group, the following parameters can be configured:

- Group number, primary and secondary IP addresses
- Priority value for selecting the Active Virtual Gateway (AVG)
- Preemption time and preemption delay time
- Priority value and preemption delay time for virtual forwarders
- Initial weighting value, upper and lower threshold values for a secondary gateway to become AVG
- Gateway load-balancing method
- MD5 and clear-text authentication attributes
- GLBP timer values
- Interface tracking

GLBP provides three load-balancing mechanisms:

- **None:** Functionality is similar to HSRP.
- **Host-dependent:** The host MAC address is used to decide which virtual forwarder MAC the packet is redirected to. This method ensures that the host uses the same virtual MAC address, as long as the number of virtual forwarders does not change within the group.

- **Round-robin:** Each virtual forwarder MAC address is used to sequentially reply for the virtual IP address.
- **Weighted:** Weights are determined for each device in the GLBP group, to define the ratio of load balancing between the devices.

Example 6-49 displays the GLBP configuration between NX-1 and NX-2.

Example 6-49 *GLBP Configuration*

```
NX-1
NX-1(config)# interface vlan 10
NX-1(config-if)# glbp 10
NX-1(config-if-glbp)# timers 1 4
NX-1(config-if-glbp)# priority 110
NX-1(config-if-glbp)# preempt
NX-1(config-if-glbp)# load-balancing ?
  host-dependent  Load balance equally, source MAC determines forwarder choice
  round-robin     Load balance equally using each forwarder in turn
  weighted        Load balance in proportion to forwarder weighting

NX-1(config-if-glbp)# load-balancing host-dependent
NX-1(config-if-glbp)# forwarder preempt ?
  <CR>
  delay  Wait before preempting

NX-1(config-if-glbp)# forwarder preempt
NX-1(config-if-glbp)# ip 10.12.1.1
NX-1(config-if-glbp)# end
NX-2
NX-2(config-if-glbp)# interface vlan 10
NX-2(config-if)# glbp 10
NX-2(config-if-glbp)# ip 10.12.1.1
NX-2(config-if-glbp)# timers 1 4
NX-2(config-if-glbp)# load-balancing host-dependent
NX-2(config-if-glbp)# forwarder preempt
NX-2(config-if-glbp)# end
```

Similar to HSRP version 2, GLBP communicates its hello packets over the multicast address 224.0.0.102. However, it uses the UDP source and destination port number of 3222.

To view the details of the GLBP group, use the command **show glbp [brief]**. The command displays the configured virtual IP, the group state, and all the other information related to the group. The command output also displays information regarding the forwarders, their MAC address, and their IP addresses. Example 6-50 examines the output of both the command **show glbp** and the command **show glbp brief**, displaying the information of the GLBP group 10 along with its forwarder information and their states.

Example 6-50 show glbp *and* show glbp brief *Command Output*

```
NX-1
NX-1# show glbp

Extended-hold (NSF) is Disabled

Vlan10 - Group 10
  State is Active
    4 state change(s), last state change(s) 00:01:54
  Virtual IP address is 10.12.1.1
  Hello time 1 sec, hold time 4 sec
    Next hello sent in 990 msec
  Redirect time 600 sec, forwarder time-out 14400 sec
  Preemption enabled, min delay 0 sec
  Active is local
  Standby is 10.12.1.3, priority 100 (expires in 3.905 sec)
  Priority 110 (configured)
  Weighting 100 (default 100), thresholds: lower 1, upper 100
  Load balancing: host-dependent
  Group members:
    5087.8940.2042 (10.12.1.2) local
    E4C7.221E.9642 (10.12.1.3)
  There are 2 forwarders (1 active)
  Forwarder 1
   State is Active
     2 state change(s), last state change 00:01:50
   MAC address is 0007.B400.0A01 (default)
   Owner ID is 5087.8940.2042
   Preemption enabled, min delay 30 sec
   Active is local, weighting 100

  Forwarder 2
   State is Listen
     1 state change(s), last state change 00:00:40
   MAC address is 0007.B400.0A02 (learnt)
   Owner ID is E4C7.221E.9642
   Redirection enabled, 599.905 sec remaining (maximum 600 sec)
   Time to live: 14399.905 sec (maximum 14400 sec)
   Preemption enabled, min delay 30 sec
   Active is 10.12.1.3 (primary), weighting 100 (expires in 3.905 sec)
NX-1# show glbp brief
```

```
Interface        Grp Fwd Pri State   Address       Active rtr    Standby rtr
Vlan10           10  -   110 Active  10.12.1.1     local         10.12.1.3

! Below is the list of forwarders
Vlan10           10  1   7   Active  0007.B400.0A01 local         -
Vlan10           10  2   7   Listen  0007.B400.0A02 10.12.1.3     -
```

For troubleshooting GLBP issues, use tools such as Ethanalyzer to capture GLBP control packeks. The detailed command output of Ethanalyzer supplies what information is being received or sent as part of the GLBP control packet. Example 6-51 displays the output of Ethanalyzer for GLBP packets.

Example 6-51 *Ethanalyzer for GLBP Packets*

```
NX-2
NX-2# ethanalyzer local interface inband display-filter glbp limit-captured-frames 0
Capturing on inband
2017-10-22 20:33:43.857524    10.12.1.2 -> 224.0.0.102   GLBP 102 G: 10, Hello, I
Pv4, Request/Response?
2017-10-22 20:33:43.857934    10.12.1.3 -> 224.0.0.102   GLBP 102 G: 10, Hello, I
Pv4, Request/Response?
2 2017-10-22 20:33:44.858861  10.12.1.2 -> 224.0.0.102   GLBP 102 G: 10, Hello, I
Pv4, Request/Response?
4 2017-10-22 20:33:44.859474  10.12.1.3 -> 224.0.0.102   GLBP 102 G: 10, Hello, I
Pv4, Request/Response?
NX-2# ethanalyzer local interface inband display-filter glbp limit-captured-frames 1
   detail
Capturing on inband
1
Frame 1: 102 bytes on wire (816 bits), 102 bytes captured (816 bits) on interfac
e 0
    Interface id: 0
    Encapsulation type: Ethernet (1)
    Arrival Time: Oct 22, 2017 20:33:54.873326000 UTC
    [Time shift for this packet: 0.000000000 seconds]
    Epoch Time: 1508704434.873326000 seconds
    [Time delta from previous captured frame: 0.000000000 seconds]
    [Time delta from previous displayed frame: 0.000000000 seconds]
    [Time since reference or first frame: 0.000000000 seconds]
    Frame Number: 1
    Frame Length: 102 bytes (816 bits)
    Capture Length: 102 bytes (816 bits)
    [Frame is marked: False]
    [Frame is ignored: False]
    [Protocols in frame: eth:ip:udp:glbp]
```

```
Ethernet II, Src: Cisco_00:0a:02 (00:07:b4:00:0a:02), Dst: IPv4mcast_00:00:66
(01:00:5e:00:00:66)
    Destination: IPv4mcast_00:00:66 (01:00:5e:00:00:66)
        Address: IPv4mcast_00:00:66 (01:00:5e:00:00:66)
            .... ..0. .... .... .... .... = LG bit: Globally unique address (factory
 default)
            .... ...1 .... .... .... .... = IG bit: Group address (multicast/
broadcast)
    Source: Cisco_00:0a:02 (00:07:b4:00:0a:02)
        Address: Cisco_00:0a:02 (00:07:b4:00:0a:02)
            .... ..0. .... .... .... .... = LG bit: Globally unique address (factory
 default)
            .... ...0 .... .... .... .... = IG bit: Individual address (unicast)
    Type: IP (0x0800)
Internet Protocol Version 4, Src: 10.12.1.3 (10.12.1.3), Dst: 224.0.0.102
(224.0.0.102)
    Version: 4
    Header length: 20 bytes
    Differentiated Services Field: 0xc0 (DSCP 0x30: Class Selector 6; ECN: 0x00:
 Not-ECT (Not ECN-Capable Transport))
        1100 00.. = Differentiated Services Codepoint: Class Selector 6 (0x30)
        .... ..00 = Explicit Congestion Notification: Not-ECT (Not ECN-Capable
Transport) (0x00)
    Total Length: 88
    Identification: 0xbd59 (48473)
    Flags: 0x00
        0... .... = Reserved bit: Not set
        .0.. .... = Don't fragment: Not set
        ..0. .... = More fragments: Not set
    Fragment offset: 0
    Time to live: 255
    Protocol: UDP (17)
    Header checksum: 0x1206 [correct]
        [Good: True]
        [Bad: False]
    Source: 10.12.1.3 (10.12.1.3)
    Destination: 224.0.0.102 (224.0.0.102)
User Datagram Protocol, Src Port: glbp (3222), Dst Port: glbp (3222)
    Source port: glbp (3222)
    Destination port: glbp (3222)
    Length: 68
    Checksum: 0x9f53 [validation disabled]
        [Good Checksum: False]
        [Bad Checksum: False]
```

```
Gateway Load Balancing Protocol
    Version?: 1
    Unknown1: 0
    Group: 10
    Unknown2: 0000
    Owner ID: e4:c7:22:1e:96:42 (e4:c7:22:1e:96:42)
    TLV l=28, t=Hello
        Type: Hello (1)
        Length: 28
        Unknown1-0: 00
        VG state?: Standby (16)
        Unknown1-1: 00
        Priority: 100
        Unknown1-2: 0000
        Helloint: 1000
        Holdint: 4000
        Redirect: 600
        Timeout: 14400
        Unknown1-3: 0000
        Address type: IPv4 (1)
        Address length: 4
        Virtual IPv4: 10.12.1.1 (10.12.1.1)
    TLV l=20, t=Request/Response?
        Type: Request/Response? (2)
        Length: 20
        Forwarder?: 2
        VF state?: Active (32)
        Unknown2-1: 00
        Priority: 167
        Weight: 100
        Unknown2-2: 00384002580000
        Virtualmac: Cisco_00:0a:02 (00:07:b4:00:0a:02)
```

Note In case of an issue with GLBP, collect the **show tech glbp** command output for further investigation by Cisco TAC.

Summary

NX-OS supports multiple IP and IPv6 services that complement the Nexus platforms, along with their routing and switching capabilities within the data center and position the Nexus switches at different layers. This chapter detailed how IP SLA is leveraged to maintain track reachability, limit jitter between a specified source and destination, and support both UDP- and TCP-based probes. Along with IP SLA, the object tracking feature is leveraged to perform conditional actions in the system. The object tracking feature supports tracking an interface, an IP or IPv6 route, and a track list, as well as using them with static routes.

A part of the IPv4 services, NX-OS provides support for DHCP relay, snooping, and other IPv4 security–related features. This chapter covered in detail how DHCP Relay and DHCP Snooping can be used in data center environments to extend the capability of DHCP server and, at the same time, protect the network from attacks. The DHCP Relay feature can be used when the DHCP server and the host are extended across different VLANs or subnets. This chapter also showed how to use security features such as DAI, IP Source Guard, and URPF. When enabling all these services, NX-OS configures ACLs in the hardware to permit relevant traffic.

For IPv6 services, this chapter covered the IPv6 neighbor discovery process and IPv6 first-hop security features such as RA Guard, IPv6 snooping, and DHCPv6 Guard. Additionally, the chapter looked at FHRP protocols such as HSRP for both IPv4 and IPv6, VRRP, and GLBP. The FHRP protocols provide hosts with gateway redundancy. Finally, the chapter looked at how different FHRP protocols work and how to configure and troubleshoot them.

Chapter 7

Troubleshooting Enhanced Interior Gateway Routing Protocol (EIGRP)

This chapter covers the following topics:

- EIGRP Fundamentals
- Troubleshooting EIGRP Neighbor Adjacencies
- Troubleshooting EIGRP Path Selection and Missing Routes
- Problems with Convergence

Enhanced Interior Gateway Routing Protocol (EIGRP) is an enhanced distance vector routing protocol commonly implemented in enterprise networks. Initially, EIGRP was a Cisco proprietary protocol, but in 2013, Cisco released EIGRP to the Internet Engineering Task Force (IETF) through an informational Request for Comment (RFC), which has now become a standard under RFC 7868.

This chapter focuses on identifying and troubleshooting issues that are caused with forming EIGRP neighbor adjacency, path selection, missing routes, and problems with convergence.

EIGRP Fundamentals

A Nexus switch can run multiple EIGRP processes. Each process forms adjacencies with other routers or NX-OS switches under the same common routing domain—otherwise known as an *autonomous system (AS)*. EIGRP devices within the same AS exchange routes only with members of the same AS and use the same metric calculation formula.

EIGRP uses factors outside of hop-count and adds logic to the route-selection algorithm. EIGRP uses a Diffusing Update Algorithm (DUAL) to identify network paths and provides for fast convergence using pre-calculated loop-free backup paths.

Figure 7-1 is used as a reference topology for NX-1 calculating the best path to the 10.4.4.0/24 network.

Chapter 7: Troubleshooting Enhanced Interior Gateway Routing Protocol (EIGRP)

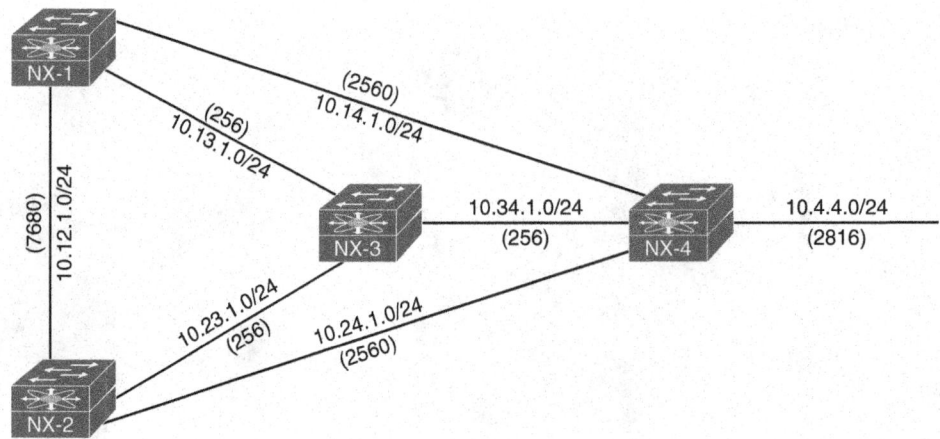

Figure 7-1 *EIGRP Reference Topology*

Table 7-1 contains key terms, definitions, and their correlation to Figure 7-1.

Table 7-1 *EIGRP Terminology*

Term	Definition
Successor Route	The route with the lowest path metric to reach a destination. The successor route for NX-1 to reach 10.4.4.0/24 on NX-4 is NX-1→NX-3→NX-4.
Successor	The first next-hop router for the successor route. The successor for 10.4.4.0/24 is NX-3.
Feasible Distance (FD)	The metric value for the lowest-metric path to reach a destination. The feasible distance is calculated locally using the formula shown in the Path Metric Calculation section later in this chapter. The FD calculated by NX-1 for the 10.4.4.0/24 network is 3,328. (256+256+2,816).
Reported Distance (RD)	Distance reported by a router to reach a prefix. The reported distance value is the feasible distance for the advertising router. NX-3 advertises the 10.4.4.0/24 prefix with a RD of 3,072 (256+2,816). NX-4 advertises the 10.4.4.0/24 to NX-1 and NX-2 with a RD of 2,816.
Feasibility Condition	For a route to be considered a backup route, the reported distance received for that route must be less than the feasible distance calculated locally. This logic guarantees a loop-free path.
Feasible Successor	A route that satisfies the feasibility condition is maintained as a backup route (feasible successor route). The feasibility condition ensures that the backup route is loop free. The route NX-1→NX-4 is the feasible successor because the RD of 2,816 is lower than the FD 3,328 for the NX-1→NX-3→NX-4 path.

Topology Table

EIGRP contains a topology table that is a vital component to DUAL and contains information to identify loop-free backup routes. The topology table contains all the network prefixes advertised within an EIGRP AS. Each entry in the table contains the following:

- Network prefix
- Nearby EIGRP neighbors that have advertised that prefix
- Metrics from each neighbor (reported distance, hop-count)
- Values used for calculating the metric (load, reliability, total delay, minimum bandwidth)

The command **show ip eigrp topology** [*network-prefix/prefix-length*] [**active** | **all-links**] displays the EIGRP topology table. Using the optional active keyword displays prefixes that are in an active state, and the **all-links** keyword displays all paths (including those that are not successors or feasible successors). Figure 7-2 displays the topology table for NX-1 from Figure 7-1.

```
NX01# show ip eigrp topology
! Output omitted for brevity
IPv4-EIGRP Topology Table for AS(100) /
ID(192.168.1.1)

Codes: P - Passive, A - Active, U - Update, Q -
Query, R - Reply,
       r - reply Status, s - sia Status

P 10.12.1.0/24, 1 successors, FD is 2816
        via Connected, Ethernet1/1
P 10.13.1.0/24, 1 successors, FD is 2816
        via Connected, Ethernet2/2
P 10.14.1.0/24, 1 successors, FD is 5120
        via Connected, Ethernet1/3
P 10.23.1.0/24, 2 successors, FD is 3072
        via 10.12.1.2 (3072/2816), Ethernet1/1
        via 10.13.1.3 (3072/2816), Ethernet1/2
P 10.24.1.0/24, 2 successors, FD is 3072
        via 10.12.1.2 (3072/2816), Ethernet1/1
        via 10.14.1.4 (3072/2816), Ethernet1/3
P 10.4.4.0/24, 1 successors, FD is 3328
        via 10.13.1.3 (3328/3072), Ethernet1/2
        via 10.14.1.4 (5376/2816), Ethernet1/3
```

Annotations:
- 3328 → Feasible Distance
- via 10.13.1.3 (3328/3072), Ethernet1/2 → Successor Route
- Path Metric, Reported Distance
- Feasible Successor — Passes Feasibility Condition 2816<3328

Figure 7-2 *EIGRP Topology Table*

Upon examining the network 10.4.4.0/24, notice that NX-1 calculates a FD of 3,328 for the successor route. The successor (upstream router) advertises the successor route with a reported distance (RD) of 3,072. The second path entry has a metric of 5,376 and has an RD of 2,816. Because 2,816 is less than 3,072, the second entry passes the feasibility condition and classifies the second entry as the feasible successor for prefix.

The 10.4.4.0/24 route is *Passive (P)*, which means that the topology is stable. During a topology change, routes go into an *Active (A)* state when computing a new path.

Path Metric Calculation

Metric calculation is a critical component for any routing protocol. EIGRP uses multiple factors to calculate the metric for a path. Metric calculation uses *bandwidth* and *delay* by default, but can include interface load and reliability too.

The path metric formula shown in Figure 7-3 is described in RFC 7868, which explains EIGRP.

$$\text{Metric} = \left[\left(K_1 * BW + \frac{K_2 * BW}{256 - \text{Load}} + K_3 * \text{Delay}\right) * \frac{K_5}{K_4 + \text{Reliability}}\right]$$

Figure 7-3 *EIGRP Metric Formula*

EIGRP uses *K values* to define which coefficients the formula uses and the associated impact with that coefficient when calculating the metric. A common misconception is that the K values directly apply to bandwidth, load, delay, or reliability; this is not accurate. For example, K_1 and K_2 both reference *bandwidth (BW)*.

BW represents the slowest link in the path scaled to a 10 Gigabit per second link (10^7). Link speed is collected from the configured interface bandwidth on an interface. Delay is the total measure of delay in the path measured in tenths of microseconds (μs).

The EIGRP formula is based off the IGRP metric formula, except the output is multiplied by 256 to change the metric from 24 bits to 32 bits. Taking these definitions into consideration, the formula for EIGRP is shown in Figure 7-4.

$$\text{Metric} = 256 * \left[\left(K_1 * \frac{10^7}{\text{Min. Bandwidth}} + \frac{K_2 * \text{Min. Bandwidth}}{256 - \text{Load}} + \frac{K_3 * \text{Total Delay}}{10}\right) * \frac{K_5}{K_4 + \text{Reliability}}\right]$$

Figure 7-4 *EIGRP RFC Formula with Definitions*

By default, K_1 and K_3 have a value of 1, and K_2, K_4, and K_5 are set to 0. Figure 7-5 places default K values into the formula and then shows a streamlined version of the formula.

$$\text{Metric} = 256 * [(1 * \frac{10^7}{\text{Min. Bandwidth}} + \frac{0 * \text{Min. Bandwidth}}{256 - \text{Load}} + \frac{1 * \text{Total Delay}}{10}) * \frac{0}{0 + \text{Reliability}}]$$

Equals

$$\text{Metric} = 256 * (\frac{10^7}{\text{Min. Bandwidth}} + \frac{\text{Total Delay}}{10})$$

Figure 7-5 *EIGRP Formula with Default K Values*

Note EIGRP includes a second formula to address high-speed interfaces called EIGRP wide metrics, which add a sixth K value. EIGRP wide metrics is explained later in the chapter.

The EIGRP update packet includes path attributes associated with each prefix. The EIGRP path attributes can include hop count, cumulative delay, minimum bandwidth link speed, and reported distance. The attributes are updated at each hop along the way, allowing each router to independently identify the shortest path.

Table 7-2 shows some of the common network types, link speeds, delays, and EIGRP metrics using the streamlined formula from Figure 7-5.

Table 7-2 *Default EIGRP Interface Metrics*

Interface Type	Link Speed (Kbps)	Delay	Metric
Serial	64	20,000 μs	40,512,000
T1	1,544	20,000 μs	2,170,031
Ethernet	10,000	1,000 μs	281,600
FastEthernet	100,000	100 μs	28,160
GigabitEthernet	1,000,000	10 μs	2,816
10 GigabitEthernet	10,000,000	10 μs	512

Note Notice how the delay is the same between Serial and T1 interfaces, so the only granularity is the link speed. In addition, there is not a differentiation of delay between the Gigabit Ethernet and 10 Gigabit Ethernet interfaces.

Using the topology from Figure 7-1, the metric from NX-1 for the 10.4.4.0/24 network is calculated using the formula in Figure 7-5. The link speed for both Nexus switches is 1 Gbps, and the total delay is 30 μs (10 μs for the 10.4.4.0/24 link, 10 μs for the 10.34.1.0/24 link, and 10 μs for the 10.13.1.0/24 link to NX-3).

The EIGRP metric for a specific prefix is queried directly from EIGRP's topology table with the command **show ip eigrp topology** *network/prefix-length*. Example 7-1 shows NX-1's topology table output for the 10.4.4.0/24 network. Notice that the output includes the successor route, any feasible successor paths, and the EIGRP state for the prefix. Each path contains the EIGRP attributes minimum bandwidth, total delay, interface reliability, load, and hop count.

Example 7-1 *EIGRP Topology for a Specific Prefix*

```
NX-1# show ip eigrp topology 10.4.4.0/24
IP-EIGRP (AS 1): Topology entry for 10.4.4.0/24
  State is Passive, Query origin flag is 1, 1 Successor(s), FD is 3328
  Routing Descriptor Blocks:
  10.13.1.3 (Ethernet1/2), from 10.13.1.3, Send flag is 0x0
      Composite metric is (3328/3072), Route is Internal
      Vector metric:
      Minimum bandwidth is 1000000 Kbit
      Total delay is 30 microseconds
        Reliability is 255/255
        Load is 1/255
        Minimum MTU is 1500
        Hop count is 2
        Internal tag is 0
  10.14.1.4 (Ethernet1/3), from 10.14.1.4, Send flag is 0x0
      Composite metric is (5376/2816), Route is Internal
      Vector metric:
      Minimum bandwidth is 1000000 Kbit
      Total delay is 110 microseconds
        Reliability is 255/255
        Load is 1/255
        Minimum MTU is 1500
        Hop count is 1
        Internal tag is 0
```

Note The EIGRP topology table maintains other paths besides the successor and feasible successor. The command **show ip eigrp topology all-links** displays the other ones.

EIGRP Communication

EIGRP uses five packet types to communicate with other routers, as shown in Table 7-3. EIGRP uses its own IP protocol number (88), and uses multicast packets where possible and unicast packets when necessary. Communication between EIGRP devices is accomplished using the multicast group address of 224.0.0.10 or MAC address of 01:00:5e:00:00:0a when possible.

Table 7-3 *EIGRP Packet Types*

Type	Packet Name	Function
1	Hello	Used for discovery of EIGRP neighbors, and for detection of when a neighbor is no longer available
2	Acknowledgement (ACK)	Packets sent to the originating router for any other EIGRP packet containing a nonzero sequence number
3	Update	Packets used to transmit routing and reachability information with other EIGRP routers
4	Query	Packets sent out searching for another path during convergence
5	Reply	Packets that are sent in response of a query packet

EIGRP uses the Reliable Transport Protocol (RTP) to ensure that packets are delivered in order and that routers receive specific packets. A sequence number is included in all of the EIGRP packets. A sequence value of zero does not require a response from the receiving EIGRP router; all other values require an Acknowledgement packet that includes the original sequence number.

Ensuring that packets are received makes the transport method reliable. All Updates, Queries, and Reply packets are deemed reliable, whereas Hello and Acknowledgement packets do not require acknowledgement and could be unreliable.

If the originating router does not receive an acknowledgement packet from the neighbor before the retransmit timeout expires, it notifies the nonresponsive router to stop processing its multicast packets. The originating router sends all traffic via unicast, until the neighbor is fully synchronized. Upon complete synchronization, the originating router notifies the destination router to start processing multicast packets again. All unicast packets require acknowledgement. EIGRP will retry up to 16 times for each packet that requires confirmation and will reset the neighbor relationship when the neighbor reaches the retry limit of 16.

Baseline EIGRP Configuration

The EIGRP configuration process on a NX-OS switch requires configuration under the EIGRP process and under the interface configuration submode. The following steps explain the process for configuring EIGRP on a NX-OS device.

Step 1. Enable the EIGRP feature. The EIGRP feature must be enabled with the global configuration command **feature eigrp**.

Step 2. Define an EIGRP process tag. The EIGRP process must be defined with the global configuration command **router eigrp** *process-tag*. The *process-tag* can be up to 20 alphanumeric characters in length.

Step 3. Define the Router-ID (optional). The *Router-ID (RID)* is a 32-bit unique number that identifies an EIGRP router. EIGRP uses the RID as a loop prevention mechanism. The RID can be set manually or dynamically, but should be unique for each EIGRP process. The command **router-id** *router-id* is used to statically set the RID.

If a RID is not manually configured, the Loopback 0 IP address is always preferred. If the Loopback 0 does not exist, NX-OS selects the IP address for the first loopback interface in the configuration. If no loopback interfaces exist, NX-OS selects the IP address for the first physical interface in the configuration.

Step 4. Define the address family. EIGRP supports IPv4 and IPv6 address-families under the same EIGRP process. Therefore, the address-family should be defined with the command **address-family [ipv4 | ipv6] unicast**.

This step is optional for exchanging IPv4 addresses on Nexus switches.

Step 5. Define the Autonomous System Number (ASN) for the EIGRP process. The autonomous system must be defined for the EIGRP process with the command **autonomous-system** *as-number*.

This step is optional if the EIGRP process tag is only numeric and matches the ASN used by the EIGRP process.

Step 6. Enable EIGRP on interfaces. The interface that EIGRP is enabled on is selected with the command **interface** *interface-id*. The EIGRP process is then enabled on that interface with the command **ip router eigrp** *process-tag*.

Note Unlike IOS devices, enabling EIGRP on an interface advertises any secondary connected network into the topology table.

The configuration in Example 7-2 enables EIGRP only on interfaces Ethernet1/1, VLAN 10, and Loopback 0.

Example 7-2 *Baseline EIGRP Configuration*

```
NX-1# configure terminal
NX-1(config)# feature eigrp
NX-1(config)# router eigrp NXOS
17:10:19 NX-1 %$ VDC-1 %$ eigrp[27525]: EIGRP-5-HA_INFO: EIGRP HA info msg -
  SYSMGR_SUPSTATE_ACTIVE
NX-1(config-router)# autonomous-system 12
NX-1(config-router)# address-family ipv4 unicast
NX-1(config-router-af)# interface Ethernet1/1
NX-1(config-if)# ip router eigrp NXOS
NX-1(config-if)# interface vlan10
NX-1(config-if)# ip router eigrp NXOS
NX-1(config-if)# interface loopback0
NX-1(config-if)# ip router eigrp NXOS
17:10:19 NX-1 %$ VDC-1 %$ %EIGRP-5-NBRCHANGE_DUAL: eigrp-NXOS [27525] (default-
  base) IP-EIGRP(0) 123: Neighbor 10.12.1.2 (Ethernet1/2) is up: new adjacency
```

Troubleshooting EIGRP Neighbor Adjacency

EIGRP requires a neighbor relationship to form before routes are processed and added to the *Routing Information Base (RIB)* (a.k.a. routing table). The neighbor adjacency table is vital for tracking neighbor status and the updates sent to each neighbor. This section explains the process for troubleshooting EIGRP neighbor adjacencies on NX-OS switches.

Figure 7-6 provides a simple topology with two Nexus switches that are used to explain how to troubleshoot EIGRP adjacency problems.

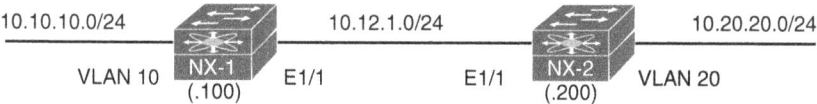

Figure 7-6 *Topology with Two NX-OS Switches*

The first step is to verify devices that have successfully established an EIGRP adjacency with the command **show ip eigrp neighbors** [**detail**] [*interface-id* | *neighbor-ip-address* | **vrf** {*vrf-name* | **all**}]. Example 7-3 demonstrates the command being run on NX-1.

Example 7-3 *Display of EIGRP Neighbors*

```
NX-1# show ip eigrp neighbors
IP-EIGRP neighbors for process 12 VRF default
H   Address                 Interface       Hold  Uptime    SRTT   RTO   Q    Seq
                                            (sec)           (ms)         Cnt  Num
0   10.12.1.200             Eth1/1          14    00:09:45  1      50    0    17
```

Table 7-4 provides a brief explanation to the key fields shown in Example 7-3.

Table 7-4 *EIGRP Neighbor Columns*

Field	Description
Address	IP address of the EIGRP neighbor
Interface	Interface the neighbor was detected on
Holdtime	Time left to receive a packet from this neighbor to ensure it is still alive
SRTT	Time for a packet to be sent to a neighbor, and a reply from that neighbor received in milliseconds
RTO	Timeout for retransmission (Waiting for ACK)
Q Cnt	Number of packets (update/query/reply) in queue for sending
Seq Num	Sequence number that was last received from this router

Besides enabling EIGRP on the network interfaces of an NX-OS device, the following parameters must match for the two routers to become neighbors:

- Interfaces must be *Active*
- Connectivity between devices must exist using the primary subnet
- Autonomous system numbers (ASN) matches
- Metric formula K values
- Hello and Hold timers support timely communication
- Authentication parameters

Verification of Active Interfaces

Upon configuring EIGRP, it is a good practice to verify that only the intended interfaces are running EIGRP. The command **show ip eigrp interface** [**brief** | *interface-id*] [**vrf** {*vrf-name* | **all**}] displays the active EIGRP interfaces. Appending the optional **brief** keyword shrinks the amount of content shown to what is displayed in Example 7-4.

Example 7-4 *Display of Active EIGRP Interfaces*

```
NX-1# show ip eigrp interfaces brief
IP-EIGRP interfaces for process 123 VRF default

                    Xmit Queue   Mean   Pacing Time   Multicast    Pending
Interface   Peers   Un/Reliable  SRTT   Un/Reliable   Flow Timer   Routes
Eth1/1      1       0/0          6      0/0           50           0
Lo0         0       0/0          0      0/0           0            0
Vlan10      0       0/0          0      0/0           0            0
```

Table 7-5 provides a brief explanation of the key fields shown with the EIGRP interfaces.

Table 7-5 *EIGRP Interface Fields*

Field	Description
Interface	Interfaces running EIGRP.
Peers	Number of peers detected on that interface.
Xmt Queue Un/Reliable	Number of unreliable/reliable packets remaining in the transmit queue. A value of zero is an indication of a stable network.
Mean SRTT	Average time for a packet to be sent to a neighbor, and a reply from that neighbor received in milliseconds.
Pacing Time Un/Reliable	Used to determine when EIGRP packets should be sent out of the interface (for unreliable and reliable packets).
Multicast Flow Timer	Maximum time (seconds) that the router sent multicast packets.
Pending Routes	Number of routes in the transmit queue that need to be sent.

Passive Interface

Some network topologies require advertising a network segment into EIGRP, but need to prevent neighbors from forming adjacencies on that segment. Example scenarios involve advertising access layer networks in a campus topology.

To illustrate how this can cause problems, NX-1 and NX-2 cannot establish an EIGRP adjacency. Viewing the EIGRP interfaces on both switches and the peering link E1/1 is not displayed as expected in Example 7-5.

Example 7-5 *Identification of Active EIGRP Interfaces*

```
NX-1# show ip eigrp interfaces brief
IP-EIGRP interfaces for process 12 VRF default

                    Xmit Queue   Mean   Pacing Time   Multicast    Pending
Interface    Peers  Un/Reliable  SRTT   Un/Reliable   Flow Timer   Routes
Vlan10       0      0/0          0      0/0           0            0

NX-2# show ip eigrp interfaces brief
IP-EIGRP interfaces for process 12 VRF default

                    Xmit Queue   Mean   Pacing Time   Multicast    Pending
Interface    Peers  Un/Reliable  SRTT   Un/Reliable   Flow Timer   Routes
Lo0          0      0/0          0      0/0           0            0
Vlan20       0      0/0          0      0/0           0            0
```

A passive interface is not displayed when displaying the EIGRP interfaces as explained in the previous section. Examining the EIGRP process with the command **show ip eigrp** [*process-tag*] provides a count of active and passive interfaces as seen in Example 7-6.

Example 7-6 *Viewing EIGRP Passive Interfaces*

```
NX-1# show ip eigrp
! Output omitted for brevity
IP-EIGRP AS 12 ID 192.168.100.100 VRF default
  Number of EIGRP interfaces: 1 (0 loopbacks)
  Number of EIGRP passive interfaces: 2
  Number of EIGRP peers: 0
```

The configuration must then be examined for the following:

- The interface parameter command **ip passive-interface eigrp** *process-tag*, which makes only that interface passive.

- The global EIGRP configuration command **passive-interface default**, which makes all interfaces under that EIGRP process passive. The interface parameter command **no ip passive-interface eigrp** *process-tag* takes precedence over the global command and makes that interface active.

Example 7-7 displays the configuration on NX-1 and NX-2 that prevents the two Nexus switches from forming an EIGRP adjacency. The Ethernet1/1 interfaces must be active on both switches for an adjacency to form. The command **no ip passive-interface eigrp NXOS** should be moved to Interface E1/1 on NX-1, and the command **ip passive-interface eigrp NXOS** should be moved from E1/1 to Vlan20 on NX-2.

Example 7-7 *EIGRP Configuration with Passive Interfaces*

```
NX-1# show run eigrp
! Output omitted for brevity
router eigrp NXOS
  autonomous-system 12
  passive-interface default
  address-family ipv4 unicast

interface Vlan10
  ip router eigrp NXOS
  no ip passive-interface eigrp NXOS

interface loopback0
  ip router eigrp NXOS

interface Ethernet1/1
  ip router eigrp NXOS

NX-2# show run eigrp
```

```
! Output omitted for brevity
router eigrp NXOS
  autonomous-system 12
  address-family ipv4 unicast

interface Vlan20
  ip router eigrp NXOS

interface loopback0
  ip router eigrp NXOS

interface Ethernet1/1
  ip router eigrp NXOS
  ip passive-interface eigrp NXOS
```

Note In addition to placing an interface into a passive state, an interface can have EIGRP temporarily shut down with the command **ip eigrp** *process-tag* **shutdown**. This disables EIGRP on that interface while leaving EIGRP configuration on that interface.

Verification of EIGRP Packets

A vital step in troubleshooting EIGRP adjacency issues is to ensure that a device is transmitting or receiving EIGRP network traffic. The command **show ip eigrp traffic** displays a high-level summary of packet types that have been sent or received from a device. Example 7-8 shows the use of this command.

Example 7-8 *EIGRP Traffic Statistics*

```
NX-1# show ip eigrp traffic
IP-EIGRP Traffic Statistics for AS 12 VRF default
  Hellos sent/received: 1486/623
  Updates sent/received: 13/8
  Queries sent/received: 0/0
  Replies sent/received: 0/0
  Acks sent/received: 6/8
  Input queue high water mark 1, 0 drops
  SIA-Queries sent/received: 0/0
  SIA-Replies sent/received: 0/0
  Hello Process ID: (no process)
  PDM Process ID: (no process)
```

Debug functionality is used to acquire granularity on the receipt or transmission of a packet. The command **debug ip eigrp packets** [siaquery | siareply | hello | query | reply |

request | update | verbose] enables debug functionality for the type of packet that is selected. Example 7-9 displays the use of the EIGRP packet debugs.

Example 7-9 *EIGRP Packet Debugs*

```
NX-1# debug ip eigrp packets hello
! Output omitted for brevity
03:58:18.813041 eigrp: NXOS [26942] EIGRP: Received HELLO on Vlan10
03:58:18.814582 eigrp: NXOS [26942] nbr 10.10.10.10
03:58:18.814613 eigrp: NXOS [26942]   AS 12, Flags 0x0, Seq 0/0idbQ 0/0
03:58:18.814618 eigrp: NXOS [26942] iidbQ un/rely 0/0
03:58:18.814623 eigrp: NXOS [26942] peerQ un/rely 0/0
03:58:18.965326 eigrp: NXOS [26942] EIGRP: Received HELLO on Ethernet1/1
03:58:18.965415 eigrp: NXOS [26942] nbr 10.12.1.200
03:58:18.965424 eigrp: NXOS [26942]   AS 12, Flags 0x0, Seq 0/0idbQ 0/0
03:58:18.965430 eigrp: NXOS [26942] iidbQ un/rely 0/0
03:58:18.965435 eigrp: NXOS [26942] peerQ un/rely 0/0
03:58:20.244286 eigrp: NXOS [26942] EIGRP: Sending HELLO on Vlan10
03:58:20.244304 eigrp: NXOS [26942]   AS 12, Flags 0x0, Seq 0/0idbQ 0/0
03:58:20.244310 eigrp: NXOS [26942] iidbQ un/rely 0/0
03:58:21.273574 eigrp: NXOS [26942] EIGRP: Sending HELLO on Ethernet1/1
03:58:21.273651 eigrp: NXOS [26942]   AS 12, Flags 0x0, Seq 0/0idbQ 0/0
03:58:21.273660 eigrp: NXOS [26942] iidbQ un/rely 0/0
```

Performing EIGRP debugs shows only the packets that have reached the supervisor CPU. If packets are not displayed in the debugs, further troubleshooting must be taken by examining quality of service (QoS) policies, access control list (ACL), control plane policing (CoPP), or just verification of the packet leaving or entering an interface.

QoS policies may or may not be deployed on an interface. If they are deployed, the policy-map must be examined for any dropped packets, which must then be referenced to a class-map that matches the EIGRP routing protocol. The same logic applies to CoPP policies because they are based on QoS settings.

Example 7-10 displays the process for checking the CoPP policy with the following logic:

- Examine the CoPP policy with the command **show running-config copp all**. This displays the relevant policy-map name, classes defined, and the police rate for each class.

- Investigate the class-maps to identify the conditional matches for that class-map.

- After the class-map has been verified, examine the policy-map drops for that class with the command **show policy-map interface control-plane**.

Example 7-10 *Verification of CoPP for EIGRP*

```
NX-1# show run copp all
! Output omitted for brevity
class-map type control-plane match-any copp-system-p-class-critical
  match access-group name copp-system-p-acl-bgp
  match access-group name copp-system-p-acl-rip
  match access-group name copp-system-p-acl-vpc
  match access-group name copp-system-p-acl-bgp6
  match access-group name copp-system-p-acl-lisp
  match access-group name copp-system-p-acl-ospf
  match access-group name copp-system-p-acl-rip6
  match access-group name copp-system-p-acl-rise
  match access-group name copp-system-p-acl-eigrp
  match access-group name copp-system-p-acl-lisp6
  match access-group name copp-system-p-acl-ospf6
  match access-group name copp-system-p-acl-rise6
  match access-group name copp-system-p-acl-eigrp6
  match access-group name copp-system-p-acl-otv-as
  match access-group name copp-system-p-acl-mac-l2pt
  match access-group name copp-system-p-acl-mpls-ldp
  match access-group name copp-system-p-acl-mpls-rsvp
  match access-group name copp-system-p-acl-mac-l3-isis
  match access-group name copp-system-p-acl-mac-otv-isis
  match access-group name copp-system-p-acl-mac-fabricpath-isis
..
policy-map type control-plane copp-system-p-policy-strict
  class copp-system-p-class-critical
    set cos 7
    police cir 36000 kbps bc 250 ms conform transmit violate drop

NX-1# show run aclmgr all | section copp-system-p-acl-eigrp
ip access-list copp-system-p-acl-eigrp
  10 permit eigrp any any

NX-1# show policy-map interface control-plane class copp-system-p-class-critical
! Output omitted for brevity
Control Plane
  service-policy input copp-system-p-policy-strict

    class-map copp-system-p-class-critical (match-any)
      ..
      module 1:
        conformed 1623702 bytes,
          5-min offered rate 995 bytes/sec
```

```
                peak rate 1008 bytes/sec at Tues 16:08:39 2018
          violated 0 bytes,
            5-min violate rate 0 bytes/sec
            peak rate 0 bytes/sec
```

> **Note** This CoPP policy was taken from a Nexus 7000 switch; the policy-name and class-maps may vary depending on the platform.

The next phase is to identify if packets were transmitted or received on an interface. This technique involves creating a specific access control entity (ACE) for the EIGRP protocol. The ACE for EIGRP should appear before any other ambiguous ACE entries to ensure a proper count. The ACL configuration command **statistics per-entry** is required to display the specific hits that are encountered per ACE.

Example 7-11 demonstrates the configuration of an ACL to detect EIGRP traffic on the Ethernet1/1 interface. Notice that the ACL includes a **permit ip any any** command to allow all traffic to pass through this interface. Failing to do so could result in the loss of traffic.

Example 7-11 *Verification of EIGRP Packets with ACL*

```
NX-1# configure terminal
NX-1(config)# ip access-list EIGRP
NX-1(config-acl)# permit eigrp any any
NX-1(config-acl)# permit icmp any any
NX-1(config-acl)# permit ip any any
NX-1(config-acl)# statistics per-entry
NX-1(config-acl)# interface e1/1
NX-1(config-if)# ip access-group EIGRP in
```

```
NX-1# show ip access-list
IP access list EIGRP
        statistics per-entry
        10 permit eigrp any any [match=108]
        20 permit icmp any any [match=5]
        30 permit ip any any [match=1055]
```

Example 7-11 uses an Ethernet interface, which generally indicates a one-to-one relationship, but on multi-access interfaces like Switched Virtual Interfaces (SVI) (a.k.a. *Interface VLANs*) the neighbor may need to be specified in a specific ACE.

Example 7-12 displays the configuration for an ACL that is placed on a SVI with an ACE entry for the neighbor 10.12.100.200. EIGRP packets from other neighbors are collected with the second entry, line 20.

Example 7-12 *Granular Verification of EIGRP Packets with ACL*

```
ip access-list EIGRP
  statistics per-entry
    permit eigrp 10.12.100.200/32 any any
    permit eigrp any any
    permit icmp any any
    permit ip any any
interface vlan 10
  ip access-group EIGRP in
```

```
NX-1# show ip access-list
IP access list EIGRP
        statistics per-entry
        10 permit eigrp 10.12.100.200/32 any log [match=100]
        20 permit eigrp any any [match=200]
        30 permit icmp any any [match=0]
        40 permit ip any any [match=5]
```

An alternative to using an ACL is to use the built-in NX-OS Ethanalyzer to capture the EIGRP packets. Example 7-13 demonstrates the command syntax. The optional **detail** keyword is used to view the contents of the packets.

Example 7-13 *Verification of EIGRP Packets Using Ethanalyzer*

```
NX-1# ethanalyzer local interface inband capture-filter "proto eigrp"
Capturing on inband
2017-09-03 04:21:12.688751    10.12.1.2 -> 224.0.0.10    EIGRP Hello
2017-09-03 04:21:12.690573    10.12.1.1 -> 224.0.0.10    EIGRP Hello
2017-09-03 04:21:12.701393    10.12.1.2 -> 224.0.0.10    EIGRP Hello
2017-09-03 04:21:12.705344    10.12.1.2 -> 10.12.1.1     EIGRP Update
2017-09-03 04:21:12.705344    10.12.1.2 -> 10.12.1.1     EIGRP Update
```

Connectivity Must Exist Using the Primary Subnet

EIGRP routers must be able to communicate with their peer routers by using the network associated to the primary IP address. EIGRP adjacency is formed only using primary IP addresses; it cannot form an adjacency using secondary IP addresses. The subnet mask was changed on NX-2 from 10.12.1.200/24 to 10.12.1.200/25 for this section. This places NX-2 in the 10.12.1.128/25 network from NX-1 (10.12.1.100).

Example 7-14 demonstrates that NX-1 detects NX-2 and registers it as a neighbor, whereas NX-2 does not detect NX-1.

Example 7-14 *NX-1 Detects NX-2 as Neighbor*

```
NX-1# show ip eigrp neighbor
IP-EIGRP neighbors for process 12 VRF default
H   Address               Interface       Hold   Uptime    SRTT   RTO    Q     Seq
                                          (sec)            (ms)          Cnt   Num
0   10.12.1.200           Eth1/1          13     00:00:10  1      5000   1     0

NX-2# show ip eigrp neighbor
IP-EIGRP neighbors for process 12 VRF default
```

In addition, NX-1 keeps changing the neighbor state for NX-2 (10.12.1.200) after a retry limit was exceeded, as shown in Example 7-15.

Example 7-15 *EIGRP Adjacency Dropping due to Retry Limit*

```
NX-1
13:28:06 NX-1 %$ VDC-1 %$ %EIGRP-5-NBRCHANGE_DUAL: eigrp-NXOS [26809] (default-base)
    IP-EIGRP(0) 12: Neighbor 10.12.1.200 (Ethernet1/1) is down: retry limit exceeded
13:28:09 NX-1 %$ VDC-1 %$ %EIGRP-5-NBRCHANGE_DUAL: eigrp-NXOS [26809] (default-base)
    IP-EIGRP(0) 12: Neighbor 10.12.1.200 (Ethernet1/1) is up: new adjacency
21:19:00 NX-1 %$ VDC-1 %$ %EIGRP-5-NBRCHANGE_DUAL: eigrp-NXOS [26809] (default-base)
    IP-EIGRP(0) 123: Neighbor 10.12.1.200 (Ethernet1/1) is down: retry limit exceeded
21:19:00 NX-1 %$ VDC-1 %$ %EIGRP-5-NBRCHANGE_DUAL: eigrp-NXOS [26809] (default-base)
    IP-EIGRP(0) 123: Neighbor 10.12.1.200 (Ethernet1/1) is up: new adjacency
```

Note NX-OS does not provide the syslog message "is blocked: not on common subnet" that is included with IOS routers.

Remember that EIGRP will retry up to 16 times for each packet that requires confirmation, and it will reset the neighbor relationship when the neighbor reaches the retry limit of 16. The actual retry values are examined on NX-OS by using the command **show ip eigrp neighbor detail**, as demonstrated in Example 7-16.

Example 7-16 *Viewing EIGRP Retry Values for Neighbors*

```
NX-1# show ip eigrp neighbors detail
IP-EIGRP neighbors for process 12 VRF default
H   Address               Interface       Hold   Uptime    SRTT   RTO    Q     Seq
                                          (sec)            (ms)          Cnt   Num
0   10.12.1.200           Eth1/1          14     00:01:12  1      5000   1     0
    Version 8.0/1.2, Retrans: 15, Retries: 15, BFD state: N/A, Waiting for Init,
    Waiting for Init Ack
       UPDATE seq 13 ser 0-0 Sent 78084 Init Sequenced

NX-1# show ip eigrp neighbors detail
```

```
IP-EIGRP neighbors for process 12 VRF default
H   Address                 Interface       Hold  Uptime    SRTT  RTO   Q    Seq
                                            (sec)           (ms)        Cnt  Num
0   10.12.1.200             Eth1/1          13    00:01:19  1     5000  1    0
    Version 8.0/1.2, Retrans: 16, Retries: 16, BFD state: N/A, Waiting for Init,
    Waiting for Init Ack
      UPDATE seq 13 ser 0-0 Sent 79295 Init Sequenced
```

The next step is to try to ping the primary IP address between nodes, as shown in Example 7-17.

Example 7-17 *Verify Connectivity Between Primary Subnets*

```
NX-1# ping 10.12.1.200
PING 10.12.1.200 (10.12.1.200): 56 data bytes
Request 0 timed out
Request 1 timed out
Request 2 timed out
Request 3 timed out
Request 4 timed out

--- 10.12.1.200 ping statistics ---
5 packets transmitted, 0 packets received, 100.00% packet loss
```
```
NX-2# ping 10.12.1.100
PING 10.12.1.100 (10.12.1.100): 56 data bytes
ping: sendto 10.12.1.100 64 chars, No route to host
Request 0 timed out
ping: sendto 10.12.1.100 64 chars, No route to host
Request 1 timed out
ping: sendto 10.12.1.100 64 chars, No route to host
Request 2 timed out
ping: sendto 10.12.1.100 64 chars, No route to host
Request 3 timed out
ping: sendto 10.12.1.100 64 chars, No route to host
Request 4 timed out
```

NX-1 cannot ping NX-2, and NX-2 cannot ping NX-1 because it does not have a route to the host. This also means that NX-1 might have been able to send the packets to NX-2, but NX-2 did not have a route to send the ICMP response.

Example 7-18 displays the routing table on NX-1 and NX-2 to help locate the reason.

Example 7-18 *NX-1 and NX-2 Routing Table for Adjacency*

```
NX-1# show ip route 10.12.1.200
IP Route Table for VRF "default"
'*' denotes best ucast next-hop
'**' denotes best mcast next-hop
'[x/y]' denotes [preference/metric]
'%<string>' in via output denotes VRF <string>

10.12.1.200/32, ubest/mbest: 1/0, attached
    *via 10.12.1.200, Eth1/1, [250/0], 00:30:29, am
```

```
NX-2# show ip route 10.12.1.100
IP Route Table for VRF "default"
'*' denotes best ucast next-hop
'**' denotes best mcast next-hop
'[x/y]' denotes [preference/metric]
'%<string>' in via output denotes VRF <string>

Route not found
```

At this point, check the IP address configuration on both devices. This should result in the mismatch of prefix-length for the subnet mask. Correcting this allows for the EIGRP devices to communicate properly.

EIGRP ASN Mismatch

EIGRP requires that the ASN match in the EIGRP Hello packets to form an adjacency. Problems can occur on Nexus switches because EIGRP uses the number specified in the process tag as the ASN by default. This mentality aligns with the Classic mode configuration of EIGRP on IOS routers.

If an ASN is specified within the EIGRP configuration, that value is used in lieu of the number used to identify the EIGRP process. If the EIGRP process tag is alphanumeric, and an ASN is not specified, it assumes an ASN of 0, which indicates that instance is in a shutdown state.

Example 7-19 displays a configuration that might be confusing to junior network engineers. Is the EIGRP ASN 12 or 1234?

Example 7-19 *Confusing EIGRP ASN Configuration*

```
NX-1# show run eigrp
! Output omitted for brevity

router eigrp 12
  autonomous-system 1234

interface Ethernet1/1
  ip router eigrp 12
```

Unfortunately, no debugs or log messages are provided if the EIGRP ASNs are mismatched. Check the EIGRP ASN on both sides to verify that it is the same.

The ASN for an EIGRP instance is found by examining the EIGRP protocol with the command **show ip eigrp**, which is listed beside the router-id. The ASN is also displayed when viewing the EIGRP interfaces with the command **show ip eigrp interfaces brief**.

Example 7-20 displays how the AS is viewed on a Nexus switch.

Example 7-20 *Identifying the EIGRP AS*

```
NX-1# show ip eigrp
! Output omitted for brevity
IP-EIGRP AS 1234 ID 192.168.100.100 VRF default
  Process-tag: 12
  Instance Number: 1
  Status: running
```

```
NX-1# show ip eigrp interfaces brief
IP-EIGRP interfaces for process 1234 VRF default

                    Xmit Queue    Mean    Pacing Time    Multicast    Pending
Interface    Peers  Un/Reliable   SRTT    Un/Reliable    Flow Timer   Routes
Eth1/1       0      0/0           0       0/0            0            0
Lo0          0      0/0           0       0/0            0            0
Vlan10       0      0/0           0       0/0            0            0
```

Note Specifying the AS in the EIGRP configuration removes any potential for confusion by network engineers of all skill level. This is considered a best practice.

Mismatch K Values

EIGRP uses *K values* to define which factors that the best path formula uses. To ensure a consistent routing logic and prevent routing loops from forming, all EIGRP neighbors must use the same K values. The K values are included as part of the EIGRP Hello packets.

Example 7-21 displays the syslog message that indicates a mismatch of K values. The K values are identified on the local router by looking at the EIGRP process with the command **show ip eigrp**.

Example 7-21 *Indication of EIGRP K Values Mismatch*

```
04:11:19 NX-1 %$ VDC-1 %$ %EIGRP-5-NBRCHANGE_DUAL: eigrp-NXOS [30489] (default-
  base) IP-EIGRP(0) 12: Neighbor 10.12.1.200 (Ethernet1/1) is down: K-value mismatch
04:11:37 NX-1 %$ VDC-1 %$ last message repeated 3 times
04:11:37 NX-1 %$ VDC-1 %$ %EIGRP-5-NBRCHANGE_DUAL: eigrp-NXOS [30489]
  (default-base) IP-EIGRP(0) 12: Neighbor 10.12.1.200 (Ethernet1/1) is down:
  Interface Goodbye received
```

```
NX-1# show ip eigrp
! Output omitted for brevity
IP-EIGRP AS 12 ID 192.168.100.100 VRF default
  Process-tag: NXOS
  Instance Number: 1
  Status: running
  none
  Metric weights: K1=1 K2=1 K3=1 K4=1 K5=1
```

The K values on Nexus switches are configured with the command **metric weights** *TOS K_1 K_2 K_3 K_4 K_5 [K_6]* under the EIGRP process. The K_6 value is optional unless EIGRP wide metrics are configured. TOS is not used and should be set to zero. Example 7-22 displays an EIGRP configuration with custom K values.

Example 7-22 *EIGRP Configuration with Custom K Values*

```
NX-1# show run eigrp
! Output omitted for brevity
router eigrp NXOS
  autonomous-system 12
  metric weights 0 1 1 1 1
  address-family ipv4 unicast
```

Problems with Hello and Hold Timers

A secondary function to the EIGRP Hello packets is to ensure that EIGRP neighbors are still healthy and available. EIGRP Hello packets are sent out in intervals referred to as the Hello Timer. The default EIGRP Hello timer is 5 seconds by default on Nexus switches.

EIGRP uses a second timer called the hold time, which is the amount of time EIGRP deems the router reachable and functioning. The hold time value defaults to three times the Hello interval. The default value is 15 seconds, and 180 seconds for slow-speed interfaces. The hold time decrements, and upon receipt of a Hello packet, the hold time resets and restarts the countdown. If the hold time reaches zero, EIGRP declares the neighbor unreachable and notifies the DUAL algorithm of a topology change.

If the EIGRP Hello timer is greater than the Hold timer on the other EIGRP neighbor, the session will continuously flap. Example 7-23 demonstrates NX-1 periodically resetting the adjacency with NX-2 because of the holding time expiring on NX-1.

Example 7-23 *EIGRP Adjacency Failure due to Holding Timer*

```
NX-1
03:11:35 NX-1 %$ VDC-1 %$ %EIGRP-5-NBRCHANGE_DUAL: eigrp-NXOS [30489] (default-
  base) IP-EIGRP(0) 12: Neighbor 10.12.1.200 (Ethernet1/1) is down: holding time
  expired
03:11:39 NX-1 %$ VDC-1 %$ %EIGRP-5-NBRCHANGE_DUAL: eigrp-NXOS [30489] (default-
  base) IP-EIGRP(0) 12: Neighbor 10.12.1.200 (Ethernet1/1) is up: new adjacency
03:11:54 NX-1 %$ VDC-1 %$ %EIGRP-5-NBRCHANGE_DUAL: eigrp-NXOS [30489] (default-
  base) IP-EIGRP(0) 12: Neighbor 10.12.1.200 (Ethernet1/1) is down: holding time
  expired
03:11:59 NX-1 %$ VDC-1 %$ %EIGRP-5-NBRCHANGE_DUAL: eigrp-NXOS [30489] (default-
  base) IP-EIGRP(0) 12: Neighbor 10.12.1.200 (Ethernet1/1) is up: new adjacency
```

```
NX-2
03:11:35 NX-2 %$ VDC-1 %$ %EIGRP-5-NBRCHANGE_DUAL: eigrp-NXOS [26807] (default-
  base) IP-EIGRP(0) 12: Neighbor 10.12.1.100 (Ethernet1/1) is down: Interface
  Goodbye received
03:11:39 NX-2 %$ VDC-1 %$ %EIGRP-5-NBRCHANGE_DUAL: eigrp-NXOS [26807] (default-
  base) IP-EIGRP(0) 12: Neighbor 10.12.1.100 (Ethernet1/1) is up: new adjacency
03:11:54 NX-2 %$ VDC-1 %$ %EIGRP-5-NBRCHANGE_DUAL: eigrp-NXOS [26807] (default-
  base) IP-EIGRP(0) 12: Neighbor 10.12.1.100 (Ethernet1/1) is down: Interface
  Goodbye received
03:11:59 NX-2 %$ VDC-1 %$ %EIGRP-5-NBRCHANGE_DUAL: eigrp-NXOS [26807] (default-
  base) IP-EIGRP(0) 12: Neighbor 10.12.1.100 (Ethernet1/1) is up: new adjacency
```

The EIGRP Hello and Hold timers for an interface are seen with the command **show ip eigrp interface** [*interface-id*] [**vrf** {*vrf-name* | **all**}]. The optional **brief** keyword cannot be used to view the timers. Example 7-24 displays sample output for NX-1 and NX-2.

Example 7-24 *Verification of EIGRP Hello and Hold Timers*

```
NX-1# show ip eigrp interfaces
! Output omitted for brevity
IP-EIGRP interfaces for process 12 VRF default

                Xmit Queue    Mean   Pacing Time   Multicast    Pending
Interface  Peers Un/Reliable  SRTT   Un/Reliable   Flow Timer   Routes
Eth1/1       1     0/0         1        0/0           50           0
  Hello interval is 5 sec
  Holdtime interval is 15 sec
  Next xmit serial <none>

NX-2# show ip eigrp interfaces
! Output omitted for brevity
IP-EIGRP interfaces for process 12 VRF default
```

```
                   Xmit Queue   Mean   Pacing Time   Multicast    Pending
Interface    Peers Un/Reliable  SRTT   Un/Reliable   Flow Timer   Routes
Eth1/1         1      0/0        3        0/0            50         0
  Hello interval is 120 sec
  Holdtime interval is 15 sec
  Next xmit serial <none>
```

NX-2 is displaying a Hello timer of 120 seconds which exceeds NX-1's Hold timer of 15 seconds which is the reason that NX-1 keeps tearing down the EIGRP adjacency.

Example 7-25 verifies that the Hello interval was modified with the interface command **ip hello-interval eigrp** *process-tag hello-time*. Changing the Hello time back to the default value or a value less than 15 seconds (NX-1's Hold timer) allows the switches to form an adjacency.

Example 7-25 *EIGRP Configuration with Modified Hello Timer*

```
NX-2# show run eigrp
! Output omitted for brevity
router eigrp NXOS
  autonomous-system 12
  address-family ipv4 unicast

interface Ethernet1/1
  ip router eigrp NXOS
  ip hello-interval eigrp NXOS 120
```

Note The EIGRP interface Hold timer is modified with the command **ip hold-time eigrp** *process-tag hold-time*.

EIGRP Authentication Issues

Authentication is a mechanism for ensuring that only authorized EIGRP devices are eligible to become EIGRP neighbors. A precomputed password hash is included with all EIGRP packets, and the receiving router decrypts the hash. If the passwords do not match, the router discards the packet; thereby preventing an adjacency from forming.

Unfortunately, no debugs or log messages are provided if there is a mismatch in authentication enablement or password inconsistency. The EIGRP authentication needs to be verified on both devices to ensure that it is enabled on both sides and the parameters are the same.

If authentication is explicitly configured on an interface, the status is displayed underneath the EIGRP interfaces as shown in Example 7-26. Notice that authentication only appears to be enabled on Ethernet1/1.

Example 7-26 *Viewing EIGRP Authentication on Interfaces*

```
NX-2# show ip eigrp interfaces
! Output omitted for brevity
Eth1/1            1        0/0       2       0/0         50          0
  Hello interval is 5 sec
  Holdtime interval is 15 sec
  Next xmit serial <none>
  Un/reliable mcasts: 0/55  Un/reliable ucasts: 85/65
  Mcast exceptions: 0  CR packets: 0  ACKs suppressed: 20
  Retransmissions sent: 8  Out-of-sequence rcvd: 0
  Authentication mode is md5,  key-chain is "EIGRP"
Lo0               0        0/0       0       0/0          0          0
  ..
  Authentication mode is not set
Vlan20            0        0/0       0       0/0          0          0
  ..
  Authentication mode is not set
```

EIGRP encrypts the password using an MD5 using the keychain function. Keychains allow the configuration of multiple passwords and sequences that can have the validity period set so that passwords could be rotated. When using time-based keychains, it is important that the Nexus switches time is synchronized with NTP and that some overlap of time is provided between key iterations.

The hash is composed of the key number and a password. EIGRP authentication does not encrypt the entire EIGRP packet, just the password. The password is seen with the command **show key chain [mode decrypt]**. The optional keywords **mode decrypt** display the password in plain text between a pair of quotation marks, which is helpful to detect unwanted characters such as spaces. Example 7-27 displays how the keychain password is verified.

Example 7-27 *Verification of Keychains*

```
NX-1# show key chain
Key-Chain EIGRP
  Key 1 -- text 7 "0802657d2a36"
    accept lifetime (always valid) [active]
    send lifetime (always valid) [active]
```

```
NX-1# show key chain mode decrypt
Key-Chain EIGRP
  Key 1 -- text 0 "CISCO"
    accept lifetime (always valid) [active]
    send lifetime (always valid) [active]
```

> **Note** The hash does not match between EIGRP devices if the key number is different, even if the password is identical. So the key number and password must match.

Interface-Based EIGRP Authentication

Remediation of authentication-related issues requires that authentication is enabled on both neighbors' interfaces and that the password is the same. The process for enabling EIGRP authentication on Nexus switches consist of the following steps:

Step 1. Create the keychain. The command **key chain** *key-chain-name* creates the local keychain.

Step 2. Identify the key sequence. The key sequence is specified with the command **key** *key-number*, where the key number can be anything from 0 to 2147483647.

Step 3. Specify the password. The pre-shared password is entered with the command **key-string** *text*. Steps 2 and 3 could be repeated as needed to accommodate multiple key strings.

Step 4. Identify the keychain for an interface. The keychain used by the interface must be specified with the command **ip authentication key-chain eigrp** *process-tag key-chain-name*.

Step 5. Enable authentication for an interface. Authentication is then enabled on the interface with the command **ip authentication mode eigrp** *process-tag* **md5**.

Example 7-28 demonstrates a sample configuration for EIGRP authentication on Ethernet1/1.

Example 7-28 *EIGRP Interface Level Authentication*

```
key chain EIGRP
  key 1
    key-string CISCO

router eigrp NXOS
  autonomous-system 12
  authentication mode md5

interface Ethernet1/1
  ip router eigrp NXOS
  ip authentication key-chain eigrp NXOS EIGRP
  ip authentication key-chain eigrp mode eigrp NXOS md5
```

Global EIGRP Authentication

At the time of this writing, if the EIGRP authentication is enabled globally, the authentication does not appear under all the interfaces with the command **show ip eigrp interfaces**.

Troubleshooting globally enabled authentication requires examination of the configuration. The main difference is that after the keychain is created, authentication is enabled with the following commands under the EIGRP process:

- **authentication mode md5**
- **authentication key-chain** *key-chain-name*

Example 7-29 displays the configuration for enabling authentication globally.

Example 7-29 *EIGRP Process Level Authentication*

```
key chain EIGRP
  key 1
    key-string CISCO

router eigrp NXOS
  autonomous-system 12
  authentication mode md5
  authentication key-chain EIGRP
  address-family ipv4 unicast
```

Note Interface-based authentication settings override any global EIGRP authentication settings.

Troubleshooting Path Selection and Missing Routes

Figure 7-7 provides a sample topology used to demonstrate how to troubleshoot various problems within the EIGRP protocol. All routers are connected with each other using 10 Gb links. NX-1 is advertising two networks, 10.1.1.0/24 and 10.11.11.0/24, while NX-6 is advertising the 10.6.6.0/24 network.

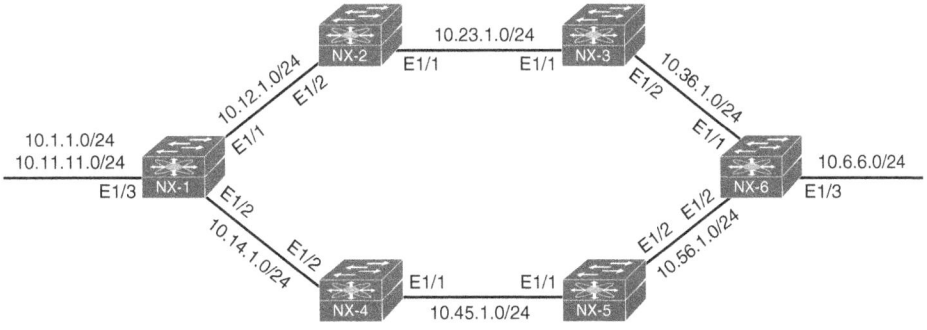

Figure 7-7 *Topology to Demonstrate Path Selection*

Example 7-30 displays a portion of NX-1 and NX-6's routing table. Notice that two paths exist between NX-1 and NX-6 in both directions for the corresponding advertised network prefixes.

Example 7-30 *NX-1's Routing Table*

```
NX-1# show ip route
! Output omitted for brevity
10.6.6.0/24, ubest/mbest: 2/0
    *via 10.12.1.2, Eth1/1, [90/129088], 00:00:02, eigrp-NXOS, internal
    *via 10.14.1.4, Eth1/2, [90/129088], 00:11:27, eigrp-NXOS, internal

NX-6# show ip route
! Output omitted for brevity
10.1.1.0/24, ubest/mbest: 2/0
    *via 10.36.1.3, Eth1/1, [90/1280], 00:00:07, eigrp-NXOS, internal
    *via 10.56.1.5, Eth1/2, [90/1280], 00:00:07, eigrp-NXOS, internal
10.11.11.0/24, ubest/mbest: 2/0
    *via 10.36.1.3, Eth1/1, [90/1280], 00:00:07, eigrp-NXOS, internal
    *via 10.56.1.5, Eth1/2, [90/1280], 00:00:07, eigrp-NXOS, internal
```

EIGRP routes that are installed into the RIB are seen with the command **show ip route [eigrp]**. The optional **eigrp** keyword only shows EIGRP learned routes. EIGRP routes are indicated by the **eigrp**-*process-tag*.

EIGRP routes originating within the autonomous system have an *administrative distance (AD)* of 90 and have the *internal* flag listed after the process-tag. Routes that originate from outside of the AS are external EIGRP routes. External EIGRP routes have an AD of 170, and have the *external* flag listed after the process-tag. Placing external EIGRP routes into the RIB with a higher AD acts as a loop prevention mechanism.

Example 7-31 displays the EIGRP routes from the sample topology in Figure 7-7. The metric for the selected route is the second number in brackets.

Example 7-31 *Viewing EIGRP Routes on NX-1*

```
NXOS6# show ip route
! Output omitted for brevity
IP Route Table for VRF "default"
'*' denotes best ucast next-hop
'**' denotes best mcast next-hop
'[x/y]' denotes [preference/metric]
10.1.1.0/24, ubest/mbest: 2/0
    *via 10.36.1.3, Eth1/1, [90/1280], 00:00:07, eigrp-NXOS, internal
    *via 10.56.1.5, Eth1/2, [90/1280], 00:00:07, eigrp-NXOS, internal
```

```
10.11.11.0/24, ubest/mbest: 2/0
    *via 10.36.1.3, Eth1/1, [90/1280], 00:00:07, eigrp-NXOS, internal
    *via 10.56.1.5, Eth1/2, [90/1280], 00:00:07, eigrp-NXOS, internal
..
10.36.1.0/24, ubest/mbest: 1/0, attached
    *via 10.36.1.6, Eth1/1, [0/0], 06:08:04, direct
10.56.1.1/32, ubest/mbest: 1/0, attached
    *via 10.56.1.6, Eth1/2, [0/0], 06:08:04, local
172.16.0.0/16, ubest/mbest: 1/0
    *via 10.56.1.5, Eth1/2, [170/3072], 00:00:02, eigrp-NXOS, external
192.168.2.2/32, ubest/mbest: 1/0
    *via 10.56.1.5, Eth1/2, [90/130816], 00:01:43, eigrp-NXOS, internal
```

Load Balancing

EIGRP allows multiple successor routes (same metric) to be installed into the RIB. Installing multiple paths into the RIB for the same prefix is called *equal- cost multipath (ECMP)* routing. At the time of this writing, the default maximum ECMP paths value for Nexus nodes is eight.

The default ECMP setting are changed with the command **maximum-paths** *maximum-paths* under the EIGRP process to increase the default value to 16.

NXOS does not support EIGRP unequal-cost load balancing, which allows installation of both successor routes and feasible successors into the EIGRP RIB. Unequal-cost load balancing is supported in other Cisco operating systems with the **variance** command.

Stub

EIGRP stub functionality allows an EIGRP router to conserve router resources. An EIGRP stub router announces itself as a stub within the EIGRP Hello packet. Neighboring routers detect the stub field and update the EIGRP neighbor table to reflect the router's stub status.

If a route goes active, EIGRP does not send EIGRP Queries to an EIGRP stub router. This provides faster convergence within an EIGRP AS because it decreases the size of the Query domain for that prefix.

EIGRP stubs do not advertise routes that they learn from other EIGRP peers. By default, EIGRP stubs advertise only connected and summary routes, but can be configured so that they only receive routes or advertise any combination of redistributed routes, connected routes, or summary routes.

The routing tables in Example 7-32 look different on NX-1 and NX-6 from the baseline routing table that was displayed in Example 7-30.

Example 7-32 *Routing Tables with Impact*

```
NX-1# show ip route eigrp-NXOS
! Output omitted for brevity
10.6.6.0/24, ubest/mbest: 1/0
    *via 10.14.1.4, Eth1/2, [90/129088], 00:14:42, eigrp-NXOS, internal
```

```
NX-6# show ip route eigrp-NXOS
! Output omitted for brevity
10.1.1.0/24, ubest/mbest: 1/0
    *via 10.56.1.5, Eth1/2, [90/1280], 00:15:24, eigrp-NXOS, internal
10.11.11.0/24, ubest/mbest: 1/0
    *via 10.56.1.5, Eth1/2, [90/1280], 00:15:24, eigrp-NXOS, internal
```

The routes from NX-1 and NX-2 seem to be available only on the lower path (NX-1 → NX-4 → NX-5 → NX-6). Has a problem occurred on the upper path (NX-1 → NX2 → NX-3 → NX-6)? The first step is to check the EIGRP adjacency, which is shown in Example 7-33.

Example 7-33 *Verification of EIGRP Neighbor Adjacency as Troubleshooting*

```
NX-1# show ip eigrp neighbors
IP-EIGRP neighbors for process 100 VRF default
H   Address           Interface       Hold  Uptime    SRTT  RTO  Q    Seq
                                      (sec)           (ms)       Cnt  Num
0   10.12.1.2         Eth1/1          14    00:01:15  1     50   0    72
1   10.14.1.4         Eth1/2          14    00:24:07  1     50   0    70

NX-2# show ip eigrp neighbors
IP-EIGRP neighbors for process 100 VRF default
H   Address           Interface       Hold  Uptime    SRTT  RTO  Q    Seq
                                      (sec)           (ms)       Cnt  Num
1   10.12.1.1         Eth1/2          13    00:01:39  1     50   0    75
0   10.23.1.3         Eth1/1          13    00:01:43  1     50   0    62

NX-3# show ip eigrp neighbors
IP-EIGRP neighbors for process 100 VRF default
H   Address           Interface       Hold  Uptime    SRTT  RTO  Q    Seq
                                      (sec)           (ms)       Cnt  Num
0   10.23.1.2         Eth1/1          13    00:02:07  1     50   0    73
1   10.36.1.6         Eth1/2          12    00:19:42  1     50   0    86

NX-6# show ip eigrp neighbors
IP-EIGRP neighbors for process 100 VRF default
```

H	Address	Interface	Hold (sec)	Uptime	SRTT (ms)	RTO	Q Cnt	Seq Num
1	10.36.1.3	Eth1/1	11	00:19:03	1	50	0	61
0	10.56.1.5	Eth1/2	13	00:19:03	1	50	0	34

All the routers have established adjacency. Using the optional **detail** keyword may provide more insight to the problem. Example 7-34 displays the command **show ip eigrp neighbors detail**.

Example 7-34 *Advanced Verification of EIGRP Neighbors*

```
NX-1# show ip eigrp neighbors detail
IP-EIGRP neighbors for process 100 VRF default
H   Address              Interface      Hold  Uptime    SRTT   RTO  Q   Seq
                                        (sec)           (ms)        Cnt Num
0   10.12.1.2            Eth1/1         14    00:00:10  1      50   0   89
   Version 8.0/1.2, Retrans: 0, Retries: 0, BFD state: N/A, Prefixes: 1
   Stub Peer Advertising ( CONNECTED/DIRECT SUMMARY ) Routes
   Suppressing queries
1   10.14.1.4            Eth1/2         14    00:28:26  1      50   0   86
   Version 8.0/1.2, Retrans: 1, Retries: 0, BFD state: N/A, Prefixes: 4
```

```
NX-6# show ip eigrp neighbors detail
IP-EIGRP neighbors for process 100 VRF default
H   Address              Interface      Hold  Uptime    SRTT   RTO  Q   Seq
                                        (sec)           (ms)        Cnt Num
1   10.36.1.3            Eth1/1         13    00:23:18  1      50   0   76
   Version 8.0/1.2, Retrans: 0, Retries: 0, BFD state: N/A, Prefixes: 2
0   10.56.1.5            Eth1/2         13    00:23:18  1      50   0   38
   Version 8.0/1.2, Retrans: 0, Retries: 0, BFD state: N/A, Prefixes: 5
```

NX-1 was able to detect that the 10.12.1.2 peer (NX-2) has the EIGRP stub feature configured. The stub feature prevented NX-2 from advertising routes learned on the E1/2 interface toward the E1/1 interface and vice versa.

The next step is to verify and remove the EIGRP configuration. The EIGRP command **eigrp stub** {**direct** | **leak-map** *leak-map-name* |**receive-only** | **redistributed** | **static** | **summary**} configures stub functionality on a switch and is displayed in Example 7-35. Removing the stub configuration allows for the routes to transit across NX-2.

Note The **receive-only** option cannot be combined with other EIGRP stub options. Give the network design special consideration to ensure bidirectional connectivity for any networks connected to an EIGRP router with the receive-only stub option to ensure that routers know how to send return traffic.

Example 7-35 *EIGRP Stub Configuration*

```
NX-2# show run eigrp
router eigrp NXOS
  autonomous-system 100
  stub

interface Ethernet1/1
  ip router eigrp NXOS

interface Ethernet1/2
  ip router eigrp NXOS
```

Note At the time of this writing, full EIGRP support is available only in Enterprise Services, whereas only EIGRP Stub functionality is included in LAN Base licensing for specific platforms. Please check current licensing options, because this could cause issues.

Maximum-Hops

EIGRP is a hybrid distance vector routing protocol and does keep track of hop counts.

In addition to filtering by prefixes, EIGRP supports filtering by hop counts. By default, an EIGRP router allows only routes up to 100 hops away to be installed into the EIGRP topology table. Routes with the EIGRP hop count path attribute higher than 100 do not install into the EIGRP topology table. The hop count is changed with the EIGRP configuration command **metric maximum-hops** *hop-count*.

Just as before, a change is notated in the routing table of NX-1 where paths appear to have disappeared. The routing table for NX-1 and NX-6 is provided in Example 7-36.

Example 7-36 *Routing Table of NX-1 and NX-6*

```
NX-1# show ip route eigrp
! Output omitted for brevity
10.6.6.0/24, ubest/mbest: 1/0
    *via 10.14.1.4, Eth1/2, [90/1280], 00:29:28, eigrp-NXOS, internal
10.23.1.0/24, ubest/mbest: 1/0
    *via 10.12.1.2, Eth1/1, [90/768], 00:00:50, eigrp-NXOS, internal
10.36.1.0/24, ubest/mbest: 1/0
    *via 10.12.1.2, Eth1/1, [90/1024], 00:00:50, eigrp-NXOS, internal
```

```
                10.45.1.0/24, ubest/mbest: 1/0
                   *via 10.14.1.4, Eth1/2, [90/768], 00:34:40, eigrp-NXOS, internal
                10.56.1.0/24, ubest/mbest: 1/0
                   *via 10.14.1.4, Eth1/2, [90/1024], 00:34:37, eigrp-NXOS, internal

                NX-6# show ip route eigrp
                10.1.1.0/24, ubest/mbest: 2/0
                   *via 10.36.1.3, Eth1/1, [90/1280], 00:01:20, eigrp-NXOS, internal
                   *via 10.56.1.5, Eth1/2, [90/1280], 00:29:59, eigrp-NXOS, internal
                10.11.11.0/24, ubest/mbest: 2/0
                   *via 10.36.1.3, Eth1/1, [90/1280], 00:01:20, eigrp-NXOS, internal
                   *via 10.56.1.5, Eth1/2, [90/1280], 00:29:59, eigrp-NXOS, internal
                10.12.1.0/24, ubest/mbest: 1/0
                   *via 10.36.1.3, Eth1/1, [90/1024], 00:01:20, eigrp-NXOS, internal
                10.14.1.0/24, ubest/mbest: 1/0
                   *via 10.56.1.5, Eth1/2, [90/1024], 00:29:59, eigrp-NXOS, internal
                10.23.1.0/24, ubest/mbest: 1/0
                   *via 10.36.1.3, Eth1/1, [90/768], 00:29:59, eigrp-NXOS, internal
                10.45.1.0/24, ubest/mbest: 1/0
                   *via 10.56.1.5, Eth1/2, [90/768], 00:29:59, eigrp-NXOS, internal
```

NX-1 is missing the upper (NX-1 → NX-2 → NX-3 → NX-6) path for the 10.6.6.0/24 network, whereas NX-6 maintains full paths to the 10.1.1.0/24 and 10.11.11.0/24 network. This means that there is connectivity in both directions and that EIGRP stub functionality has not been deployed. It also states that there is EIGRP adjacency along all paths, so some form of filtering or path manipulation was performed.

Examining the EIGRP configuration on NX-1, NX-2, NX-3, and NX-6 identifies the cause of the problem. NX-2 has configured the maximum-hops feature and set it to 1, as shown in Example 7-37. This allows for the relevant routes (from NX-6's perspective) to be seen equally. Removing the **metric maximum-hops** command or changing the value to a normal value returns the routing table to normal.

Example 7-37 *Configuration with Maximum Hops Configured*

```
NX-2# show run eigrp
! Output omitted for brevity
router eigrp NXOS
  autonomous-system 100
  metric maximum-hops 1

interface Ethernet1/1
  ip router eigrp NXOS

interface Ethernet1/2
  ip router eigrp NXOS
```

Distribute List

EIGRP supports filtering of routes with a distribute list that is placed on an individual interface. The distribute list uses the command **ip distribute-list eigrp** *process-tag* {**route-map** *route-map-name* | **prefix-list** *prefix-list-name* {**in** | **out**}. The following rules apply:

- If the direction is set to **in**, inbound filtering drops routes prior to the DUAL processing; therefore, the routes are not installed into the RIB.

- If the direction is set to **out**, the filtering occurs during outbound route advertisement; the routes are processed by DUAL and install into the local RIB of the receiving router.

- Any routes that pass the prefix-list are advertised or received. Routes that do not pass the prefix-list are filtered.

- In lieu of specifying a prefix-list, a route-map can specified to modify path attributes, in addition to filtering.

A network engineer has identified that a path for the 10.1.1.0/24 route has disappeared on NX-6 while the 10.11.11.0/24 route has both paths in it. Example 7-38 displays the current routing table of NX-6, which is different from the original routing table displayed in Example 7-30.

Example 7-38 *Missing Path for Only One Route*

```
NX-6# show ip route eigrp-NXOS
IP Route Table for VRF "default"
! Output omitted for brevity
10.1.1.0/24, ubest/mbest: 1/0
    *via 10.56.1.5, Eth1/2, [90/1280], 00:05:41, eigrp-NXOS, internal
10.11.11.0/24, ubest/mbest: 2/0
    *via 10.36.1.3, Eth1/1, [90/1280], 00:41:15, eigrp-NXOS, internal
    *via 10.56.1.5, Eth1/2, [90/1280], 00:05:41, eigrp-NXOS, internal
..
10.45.1.0/24, ubest/mbest: 1/0
    *via 10.56.1.5, Eth1/2, [90/768], 00:05:43, eigrp-NXOS, internal
```

Because the 10.11.11.0/24 network has two paths and it is connected to the same Nexus switch (NX-1), some form of path manipulation is enabled. Checking the routing table along the missing path should identify the router causing this behavior.

Example 7-39 displays NX-2's routing table that shows the path for 10.1.1.0/24 coming from NX-3 when the path from NX-1 appears to be more optimal.

Example 7-39 *Path Changed for the 10.1.1.0/24 Route*

```
NX-2# show ip rout eigrp-NXOS
! Output omitted for brevity

10.1.1.0/24, ubest/mbest: 1/0
    *via 10.23.1.3, Eth1/1, [90/1792], 00:00:03, eigrp-NXOS, internal
10.11.11.0/24, ubest/mbest: 1/0
    *via 10.12.1.1, Eth1/2, [90/768], 00:40:28, eigrp-NXOS, internal
..
10.56.1.0/24, ubest/mbest: 1/0
    *via 10.23.1.3, Eth1/1, [90/1024], 23:45:07, eigrp-NXOS, internal
```

This means that the filtering is happening either on NX-1 (outbound) or on NX-2 (inbound). Example 7-40 displays the configuration on NX-2 that filters the path for the 10.1.1.0/24 inbound. Notice that sequence 5 blocks the 10.1.1.0/24 route, while sequence 10 allows all other routes to pass.

Example 7-40 *Sample Distribute List Configuration*

```
NX-2
interface Ethernet1/2
  description To NX-1
  ip router eigrp NXOS
  ip distribute-list eigrp NXOS prefix-list DISTRIBUTE out

ip prefix-list DISTRIBUTE seq 5 deny 10.1.1.0/24
ip prefix-list DISTRIBUTE seq 10 permit 0.0.0.0/0 le 32
```

Offset Lists

Modifying the EIGRP path metric provides traffic engineering in EIGRP. Modifying the delay setting for an interface modifies all routes that are received and advertised from that router's interface. *Offset lists* allow for the modification of route attributes based upon direction of the update, specific prefix, or combination of direction and prefix. The offset list is applied under the interface with the command **ip offset-list eigrp** *process-tag* {**route-map** *route-map-name* | **prefix-list** *prefix-list-name* {**in** | **out** } *off-set value*. The following rules apply:

- If the direction is set to **in**, the offset value is added as routes are added to the EIGRP topology table.

- If the direction is set to **out**, the path metric increases by the offset value specified in the offset list as advertised to the EIGRP neighbor.

- Any routes that pass the route-map or the prefix-list will have the metric added to the path attributes.

428 Chapter 7: Troubleshooting Enhanced Interior Gateway Routing Protocol (EIGRP)

The *offset-value* is calculated from an additional delay value that is added to the existing delay in the EIGRP path attribute. Figure 7-8 shows the modified path metric formula when an offset delay is included.

$$\text{Metric + Offset Value} = 256 * \left(\left(\frac{10^7}{\text{Min. Bandwidth}} + \frac{\text{Total Delay}}{10}\right) + \text{Offset Delay}\right)$$

Equals

$$\text{Offset Value} = 256 * \text{Offset Delay}$$

Figure 7-8 *EIGRP Offset Value Calculation*

Example 7-41 displays an offset list configuration on NX-2 that adds 256 to the path metric to only the 10.1.1.0/24 prefix received from NX-1.

Example 7-41 *Sample Offset List Configuration*

```
NX-2
interface Ethernet1/2
  description To NX-1
  ip router eigrp NXOS
  ip offset-list eigrp NXOS prefix-list OFFSET in 256

ip prefix-list OFFSET seq 5 permit 10.1.1.0/24
```

Example 7-42 displays the topology for the 10.1.1.0/24 prefix that is advertised from NX-1 toward NX-2 from Figure 7-8. Notice that the path metric has increased from 768 to 1,024 and that the delay increased by 10 microseconds.

Example 7-42 *EIGRP Path Attributes for 10.1.1.0/24*

```
Before Offset List is Applied on NX-2
NX-2# show ip eigrp topology 10.1.1.0/24
! Output omitted for brevity
IP-EIGRP (AS 100): Topology entry for 10.1.1.0/24
  10.12.1.1 (Ethernet1/2), from 10.12.1.1, Send flag is 0x0
      Composite metric is (768/512), Route is Internal
      Vector metric:
        Minimum bandwidth is 10000000 Kbit
        Total delay is 20 microseconds
        Reliability is 255/255

After Offset List is Applied on NX-2
NX-2# show ip eigrp topology 10.1.1.0/24
```

```
! Output omitted for brevity
IP-EIGRP (AS 100): Topology entry for 10.1.1.0/24
  10.12.1.1 (Ethernet1/2), from 10.12.1.1, Send flag is 0x0
      Composite metric is (1024/768), Route is Internal
      Vector metric:
        Minimum bandwidth is 10000000 Kbit
        Total delay is 30 microseconds
```

The metric value added in Example 7-41 was explicitly calculated using the EIGRP path metric formula so that a delay value of 10 was added. Adding a metric value at one point in the path may not be the same metric increase later on, depending on whether the bandwidth changes further downstream on that path.

Example 7-43 displays how the increase of the metric (256) has impacted only the path from 10.1.1.0/24 and not the path from 10.11.11.0/24.

Example 7-43 *Path Modification on NX-6*

```
NX-6# show ip route
! Output omitted for brevity
10.1.1.0/24, ubest/mbest: 1/0
    *via 10.56.1.5, Eth1/2, [90/1280], 00:11:15, eigrp-NXOS, internal
10.11.11.0/24, ubest/mbest: 2/0
    *via 10.36.1.3, Eth1/1, [90/1280], 00:11:12, eigrp-NXOS, internal
    *via 10.56.1.5, Eth1/2, [90/1280], 00:11:15, eigrp-NXOS, internal

NX-6# show ip eigrp topology 10.1.1.0/24
! Output omitted for brevity
 IP-EIGRP (AS 100): Topology entry for 10.1.1.0/24
  10.56.1.5 (Ethernet1/2), from 10.56.1.5, Send flag is 0x0
      Composite metric is (1280/1024), Route is Internal
      Vector metric:
        Minimum bandwidth is 10000000 Kbit
        Total delay is 40 microseconds
        ..
  10.36.1.3 (Ethernet1/1), from 10.36.1.3, Send flag is 0x0
      Composite metric is (1536/1280), Route is Internal
      Vector metric:
        Minimum bandwidth is 10000000 Kbit
        Total delay is 50 microseconds

NX-6# show ip eigrp topology 10.11.11.0/24
! Output omitted for brevity
```

```
IP-EIGRP (AS 100): Topology entry for 10.11.11.0/24
  10.36.1.3 (Ethernet1/1), from 10.36.1.3, Send flag is 0x0
      Composite metric is (1280/1024), Route is Internal
      Vector metric:
        Minimum bandwidth is 10000000 Kbit
        Total delay is 40 microseconds
  10.56.1.5 (Ethernet1/2), from 10.56.1.5, Send flag is 0x0
      Composite metric is (1280/1024), Route is Internal
      Vector metric:
        Minimum bandwidth is 10000000 Kbit
        Total delay is 40 microseconds
```

Interface-Based Settings

EIGRP assigns the delay and bandwidth to an interface automatically based on the interface's negotiated connection speed. In some instances these values are modified for traffic engineering. If the traffic flow is not as expected, check the EIGRP configuration for the following commands:

- **ip bandwidth eigrp** *process-tag bandwidth* changes the value used by the EIGRP process when calculating the minimum bandwidth path attribute.

- **ip delay eigrp** *process-tag delay-value* [picoseconds] changes the interface delay used by the EIGRP process when adding delay to the total delay path attribute.

The usage of these commands affects all prefixes that are received or advertised from the associated interface, whereas with an offset list, the prefixes can be selectively chosen.

Note As stated earlier, the path metric can be manipulated with an EIGRP offset list or the use of a distribute-list when a route-map is used. In both scenarios, EIGRP modifies the metric through the total delay path attribute. When small values are scaled for EIGRP, the potential to lose precision can occur on IOS-based routers because they use integer math. These devices may not be able to register a difference between the value of 4007 and 4008, whereas a Nexus switch can.

In general, use larger values where the rounding does not have an effect on the path decision. Be sure to accommodate decisions that could be impacted further away from where the change is being made.

Redistribution

Every routing protocol has a different methodology for calculating the best path for a route. For example, EIGRP can use bandwidth, delay, load, and reliability for calculating its best path, whereas OSPF primarily uses the path metric for calculating the shortest path first (SPF) tree (SPT). OSPF cannot calculate the SPF tree using EIGRP path attributes, and EIGRP cannot run Diffusing Update Algorithm (DUAL) using only the total path metric. The destination protocol must provide relevant metrics to the destination protocols so that the destination protocol can calculate the best path for the redistributed routes.

Redistributing into EIGRP uses the command **redistribute** [**bgp** *asn* | **direct** | **eigrp** *process-tag* | **isis** *process-tag* | **ospf** *process-tag* | **rip** *process-tag* | **static**] **route-map** *route-map-name*. A route-map is required as part of the redistribution process on Nexus switches.

Every protocol provides a seed metric at the time of redistribution that allows the destination protocol to calculate a best path. EIGRP uses the following logic when setting the seed metric:

- The default seed metric on Nexus switches is 100,000 Kbps for minimum bandwidth, 1000 μs of delay, reliability of 255, load of 1, and MTU of 1492.

- The default seed metric is not needed, and path attributes are preserved when redistributing between EIGRP processes.

Note The default seed metric behavior on Nexus switches is different from IOS and IOS XR routers that use a default seed value of infinity. Setting the seed metric to infinity prevents routes from being installed into the topology table.

The default seed metrics can be changed to different values for bandwidth, load, delay, reliability, and maximum transmission unit (MTU) if desired. The EIGRP process command **metric weights** *tos bandwidth delay reliability load mtu* changes the value for all routes that are redistributed into that process, or the command **set metric weights** *bandwidth delay reliability load mtu* can be used for selective manipulation within a route-map.

Example 7-44 provides the necessary configuration to demonstrate the process of redistribution. NX-1 redistributes the connected routes for 10.1.1.0/24 and 10.11.11.0/24 in lieu of them being advertised with the EIGRP routing protocol. Notice that the route-map can be a simple permit statement without any conditional matches.

Example 7-44 *NX-1 Redistribution Configuration*

```
router eigrp NXOS
  autonomous-system 100
  redistribute direct route-map REDIST
!
route-map REDIST permit 10
```

Example 7-45 displays the routing table on NX-2. The 10.1.1.0/24 and 10.11.11.0/24 routes are tagged as external, and the AD is set to 170. The topology table is shown to display the EIGRP path metrics. Notice that EIGRP contains an attribute for the source protocol (*Connected*) as part of the route advertisement from NX-1.

Example 7-45 *External Routes on NX-2*

```
NX-2# show ip route eigrp-NXOS
! Output omitted for brevity
10.1.1.0/24, ubest/mbest: 1/0
    *via 10.12.1.1, Eth1/2, [170/51456], 00:00:07, eigrp-NXOS, external
10.11.11.0/24, ubest/mbest: 1/0
    *via 10.12.1.1, Eth1/2, [170/51456], 00:00:07, eigrp-NXOS, external
10.14.1.0/24, ubest/mbest: 1/0
    *via 10.12.1.1, Eth1/2, [90/768], 00:33:45, eigrp-NXOS, internal
```

```
NX-2# show ip eigrp topology 10.1.1.0/24
IP-EIGRP (AS 100): Topology entry for 10.1.1.0/24
  State is Passive, Query origin flag is 1, 1 Successor(s), FD is 51456
  Routing Descriptor Blocks:
  10.12.1.1 (Ethernet1/2), from 10.12.1.1, Send flag is 0x0
      Composite metric is (51456/51200), Route is External
      Vector metric:
        Minimum bandwidth is 100000 Kbit
        Total delay is 1010 microseconds
        Reliability is 255/255
        Load is 1/255
        Minimum MTU is 1492
        Hop count is 1
        Internal tag is 0
      External data:
        Originating router is 10.1.1.1
        AS number of route is 0
        External protocol is Connected, external metric is 0
        Administrator tag is 0 (0x00000000)
```

Note EIGRP router-ids are used as a loop prevention mechanism for external routes. An EIGRP router does not install an external route that contains the router-id that matches itself. Ensuring unique router-ids on all devices in an EIGRP AS prevents problems with external EIGRP routes.

Classic Metrics vs. Wide Metrics

The original EIGRP specifications measured delay in 10 microsecond (μs) units and bandwidth in kilobytes per second, which did not scale well with higher-speed interfaces. Earlier in Table 7-2, notice that the delay is the same for the Gigabit Ethernet and 10-Gigabit Ethernet interfaces.

Example 7-46 provides some metric calculations for common LAN interface speeds. Notice how there is no a differentiation between an 11 Gbps interface and a 20 Gbps interface. The composite metric stays at 256 despite having different bandwidth rates.

Example 7-46 *Metric Calculation for Common LAN Interface Speeds*

```
GigabitEthernet:
Scaled Bandwidth = 10,000,000 / 1000000
Scaled Delay = 10 / 10
Composite Metric = 10 + 1 * 256 = 2816
```

```
10 GigabitEthernet:
Scaled Bandwidth = 10,000,000 / 10000000
Scaled Delay = 10 / 10
Composite Metric = 1 + 1 * 256 = 512
```

```
11 GigabitEthernet:
Scaled Bandwidth = 10,000,000 / 11000000
Scaled Delay = 10 / 10
Composite Metric = 0 + 1 * 256 = 256
```

```
20 GigabitEthernet:
Scaled Bandwidth = 10,000,000 / 20000000
Scaled Delay = 10 / 10
Composite Metric = 0 + 1 * 256 = 256
```

EIGRP includes support for a second set of metrics known as *wide metrics* that addresses the issue of scalability with higher-capacity interfaces. EIGRP wide metric support is supported and must be configured to be enabled on NX-OS.

Note IOS routers support EIGRP wide metrics only in named configuration mode, and IOS-XR routers use wide metrics by default.

Figure 7-9 shows the explicit EIGRP wide metric formula. Notice that an additional K value (K_6) is included that adds an extended attribute to measure jitter, energy, or other future attributes.

$$\text{Wide Metric} = [(K_1 * BW + \frac{K_2 * BW}{256 - \text{Load}} + K_3 * \text{Latency} + K_6 * \text{Extended}) * \frac{K_5}{K_4 + \text{Reliability}}]$$

Figure 7-9 *EIGRP Wide Metric Formula*

Just as EIGRP scaled by 256 to accommodate IGRP, EIGRP wide metrics scale by 65,535 to accommodate higher-speed links. This provides support for interface speeds up to 655 terabits per second (65,535 * 10^7) without encountering any scalability issues. Latency is the total interface delay measured in picoseconds (10^{-12}) instead of measuring in microseconds (10^{-6}), which scales as well with higher speed interfaces. Figure 7-10 displays the updated formula that takes into account the conversions in latency and scalability.

$$\text{Wide Metric} = 65{,}535 * [(\frac{K_1 * 10^7}{\text{Min. Bandwidth}} + \frac{\frac{K_2 * 10^7}{\text{Min. Bandwidth}}}{256 - \text{Load}} + \frac{K_3 * \text{Latency}}{10^{-6}} + K_6 * \text{Extended}) * \frac{K_5}{K_4 + \text{Reliability}}]$$

Figure 7-10 *EIGRP Wide Metric Formula with Definitions*

EIGRP wide metrics were designed with backward compatibility in mind. EIGRP wide metrics set K_1 and K_3 to a value of 1, and K_2, K_4, K_5, and K_6 are set to 0, which allows backward compatibility because the K value metrics match with Classic metrics. As long as K_1–K_5 are the same and K_6 is not set, the two metric styles allow an adjacency between routers.

> **Note** The metric style used by a Nexus switch is identified with the command **show ip eigrp**. If a K_6 metric is present, the router is using wide style metrics.

EIGRP can detect when peering with a router is using classic metrics, and *unscales* the metric to the formula in Figure 7-11.

$$\text{Unscaled Bandwidth} = (\frac{\text{EIGRP Bandwidth} * \text{EIGRP Classic Scale}}{\text{Scaled Bandwidth}})$$

Figure 7-11 *Formula for Calculating Unscaled EIGRP Metrics*

This conversion results in loss of clarity if routes pass through a mixture of classic metric and wide metric devices. An end result of this intended behavior is that paths learned via wide metric peers always look better than paths learned via classic paths. This could lead to suboptimal routing.

Revisiting the topology from Figure 7-7, let's revisit the effects of changing the Nexus switches to EIGRP wide metrics. Example 7-47 displays how the path metrics have changed for the 10.1.1.0/24 network that is advertised (Ethernet1/3). Notice that minimum bandwidth has not changed, but the delay is now measured in picoseconds.

Example 7-47 *Classic Versus Wide Metrics on NX-1*

```
Classic Metrics on all other Nexus switches
! Output omitted for brevity
NX-1# show ip eigrp topology 10.1.1.0/24
IP-EIGRP (AS 100): Topology entry for 10.1.1.0/24
  State is Passive, Query origin flag is 1, 1 Successor(s), FD is 512
  Routing Descriptor Blocks:
  0.0.0.0 (loopback0), from Connected, Send flag is 0x0
      Composite metric is (512/0), Route is Internal
      Vector metric:
        Minimum bandwidth is 10000000 Kbit
        Total delay is 10 microseconds
        Reliability is 255/255
        Load is 1/255
        Minimum MTU is 1500
```

```
Wide Metrics on NX-1. Classic Metrics on all other Nexus switches
NX-1# show ip eigrp topology 10.1.1.0/24
! Output omitted for brevity
IP-EIGRP (AS 100): Topology entry for 10.1.1.0/24
  State is Passive, Query origin flag is 1, 1 Successor(s), FD is 131072
  Routing Descriptor Blocks:
  0.0.0.0 (loopback0), from Connected, Send flag is 0x0
      Composite metric is (131072/0), Route is Internal
      Vector metric:
        Minimum bandwidth is 10000000
        Total delay is 1000000
        Reliability is 255/255
        Load is 1/255
        Minimum MTU is 1500
        Hop count is 0
        Internal tag is 0
```

Note It is important to note the microseconds (10^{-6}) to picoseconds (10^{-12}). A value of 10 microseconds is equal to 10,000,000. If you recheck the delay value for NX-1 metric, that decimal place has been removed (that is, a zero was removed).

Example 7-48 displays the EIGRP topology table for the 10.1.1.0/24 network on NX-6 while classic metric values are configured on the entire network. Notice that both paths have the same FD of 1,280.

Example 7-48 *Classic Metric on All Nexus Switches*

```
NX-6# show ip eigrp topology 10.1.1.0/24
! Output omitted for brevity
IP-EIGRP (AS 100): Topology entry for 10.1.1.0/24
  State is Passive, Query origin flag is 1, 2 Successor(s), FD is 1280
  Routing Descriptor Blocks:
  10.36.1.3 (Ethernet1/1), from 10.36.1.3, Send flag is 0x0
      Composite metric is (1280/1024), Route is Internal
      Vector metric:
        Minimum bandwidth is 10000000 Kbit
        Total delay is 40 microseconds
        ..
        Hop count is 3
  10.56.1.5 (Ethernet1/2), from 10.56.1.5, Send flag is 0x0
      Composite metric is (1280/1024), Route is Internal
      Vector metric:
        Minimum bandwidth is 10000000 Kbit
        Total delay is 40 microseconds
        ..
        Hop count is 3
```

Example 7-49 displays the EIGRP topology table for the 10.1.1.0/24 network on NX-6, and wide metrics have been enabled on NX-1 and NX-2. EIGRP classic metric values are configured on the remaining switches network. Notice that the total delay has changed on the path from NX-1 → NX-2 → NX-3 → NX-6 to 30 µs. This is because the first two hops of this path were calculated using picoseconds instead of microseconds, resulting in a 10 µs reduction. NX-6 uses this path only for forwarding traffic.

Example 7-49 *Wide Metrics on NX-1 and NX-2*

```
NX-6# show ip eigrp topology 10.1.1.0/24
! Output omitted for brevity
IP-EIGRP (AS 100): Topology entry for 10.1.1.0/24
  State is Passive, Query origin flag is 1, 1 Successor(s), FD is 1024
  Routing Descriptor Blocks:
  10.36.1.3 (Ethernet1/1), from 10.36.1.3, Send flag is 0x0
      Composite metric is (1024/768), Route is Internal
      Vector metric:
        Minimum bandwidth is 10000000 Kbit
        Total delay is 30 microseconds
        ..
        Hop count is 3
  10.56.1.5 (Ethernet1/2), from 10.56.1.5, Send flag is 0x0
      Composite metric is (1280/1024), Route is Internal
```

```
    Vector metric:
      Minimum bandwidth is 10000000 Kbit
      Total delay is 40 microseconds
      ..
      Hop count is 3
```

Example 7-50 displays the EIGRP topology table for the 10.1.1.0/24 network on NX-5 and NX-6, whereas wide metrics have been enabled on NX-1, NX-2, and NX-3. The delay is now reduced to 20 μs along the NX-1 → NX-2 → NX-3 → NX-6 path. The path NX-1 → NX-4 → NX-5 → NX-6 no longer passes the feasible successor condition on NX-6 and does not show up in the topology table.

Notice that NX-5 has now calculated the path NX-1 → NX-2 → NX-3 → NX-6 → NX-5 the same amount of delay as NX-1 → NX-4 → NX-5. When load balanced, a portion of the traffic is forwarded suboptimally along the longer path.

Example 7-50 *Wide Metrics on NX-1, NX-2, and NX-3*

```
NX-6# show ip eigrp topology 10.1.1.0/24
! Output omitted for brevity
IP-EIGRP (AS 100): Topology entry for 10.1.1.0/24
  State is Passive, Query origin flag is 1, 1 Successor(s), FD is 768
  Routing Descriptor Blocks:
  10.36.1.3 (Ethernet1/1), from 10.36.1.3, Send flag is 0x0
      Composite metric is (768/512), Route is Internal
      Vector metric:
        Minimum bandwidth is 10000000 Kbit
        Total delay is 20 microseconds
        ..
        Hop count is 3

NX-5# show ip eigrp topology 10.1.1.0/24
! Output omitted for brevity
IP-EIGRP (AS 100): Topology entry for 10.1.1.0/24
  State is Passive, Query origin flag is 1, 2 Successor(s), FD is 1024
  Routing Descriptor Blocks:
  10.45.1.4 (Ethernet1/1), from 10.45.1.4, Send flag is 0x0
      Composite metric is (1024/768), Route is Internal
      Vector metric:
        Minimum bandwidth is 10000000 Kbit
        Total delay is 30 microseconds
        ..
        Hop count is 2
  10.56.1.6 (Ethernet1/2), from 10.56.1.6, Send flag is 0x0
```

```
    Composite metric is (1024/768), Route is Internal
    Vector metric:
      Minimum bandwidth is 10000000 Kbit
      Total delay is 30 microseconds
      ..
      Hop count is 4
```

The number of classic or wide metric EIGRP neighbors is identified by looking at the EIGRP interfaces in nonbrief format. Example 7-51 displays the command and relevant output on NX-6.

Example 7-51 *Viewing Number of Classic and Wide EIGRP Neighbors*

```
NX-6# show ip eigrp interfaces
! Output omitted for brevity
IP-EIGRP interfaces for process 100 VRF default

                   Xmit Queue   Mean   Pacing Time   Multicast    Pending
Interface   Peers  Un/Reliable  SRTT   Un/Reliable   Flow Timer   Routes
Eth1/1       1     0/0          1      0/0           50           0
  Hello interval is 5 sec
  ..
  Classic/wide metric peers: 0/1
Eth1/2       1     0/0          1      0/0           50           0
  Hello interval is 5 sec
  ..
  Classic/wide metric peers: 1/0
```

Example 7-52 displays the EIGRP topology table for the 10.1.1.0/24 network on NX-6 and NX-5, whereas wide metrics were enabled on NX-1, NX-2, NX-3 and NX-6. NX-6 contains only the wide metric path, and the delay is shown only in picoseconds.

NX-5 has now calculated the path NX-1 → NX-2 → NX-3 → NX-6 → NX-5 as the best path due to the unscaling formula. All traffic to the 10.1.1.0/24 network takes the longer path.

Example 7-52 *Wide Metrics on NX-1, NX-2, NX-3, and NX-6*

```
NX-6# show ip eigrp topology 10.1.1.0/24
! Output omitted for brevity
IP-EIGRP (AS 100): Topology entry for 10.1.1.0/24
  State is Passive, Query origin flag is 1, 1 Successor(s), FD is 327680
  Routing Descriptor Blocks:
  10.36.1.3 (Ethernet1/1), from 10.36.1.3, Send flag is 0x0
      Composite metric is (327680/262144), Route is Internal
      Vector metric:
```

```
              Minimum bandwidth is 10000000
              Total delay is 4000000
              ..
              Hop count is 3
```

```
NX-5# show ip eigrp topology 10.1.1.0/24
! Output omitted for brevity
IP-EIGRP (AS 100): Topology entry for 10.1.1.0/24
  State is Passive, Query origin flag is 1, 1 Successor(s), FD is 768
  Routing Descriptor Blocks:
  10.56.1.6 (Ethernet1/2), from 10.56.1.6, Send flag is 0x0
      Composite metric is (768/512), Route is Internal
      Vector metric:
        Minimum bandwidth is 10000000 Kbit
        Total delay is 20 microseconds
        ..
        Hop count is 4
  10.45.1.4 (Ethernet1/1), from 10.45.1.4, Send flag is 0x0
      Composite metric is (1024/768), Route is Internal
      Vector metric:
        Minimum bandwidth is 10000000 Kbit
        Total delay is 30 microseconds
        ..
        Hop count is 2
```

Careful planning is needed when enabling EIGRP wide metrics. When enabling wide metrics, it is best to enable all the devices in an area or along the same path to a destination to ensure optimal routing.

Problems with Convergence

When a link fails and the interface protocol moves to a down state, any neighbor attached to that interface moves to a down state too. When an EIGRP neighbor moves to a down state, path recomputation must occur for any prefix where that EIGRP neighbor was a successor (upstream router).

When EIGRP detects that it has lost its successor for a path, the feasible successor instantly becomes the successor route providing a backup route. The Nexus switch sends out an Update packet for that path because of the new EIGRP path metrics. Downstream switches run their own DUAL algorithm for any impacted prefixes to account for the new EIGRP metrics. It is possible that a change of the successor route or feasible successor to occur upon receipt of new EIGRP metrics from a successor switch for a prefix.

Figure 7-12 demonstrates such a scenario when the link between NX-1 and NX-3 fails.

440 Chapter 7: Troubleshooting Enhanced Interior Gateway Routing Protocol (EIGRP)

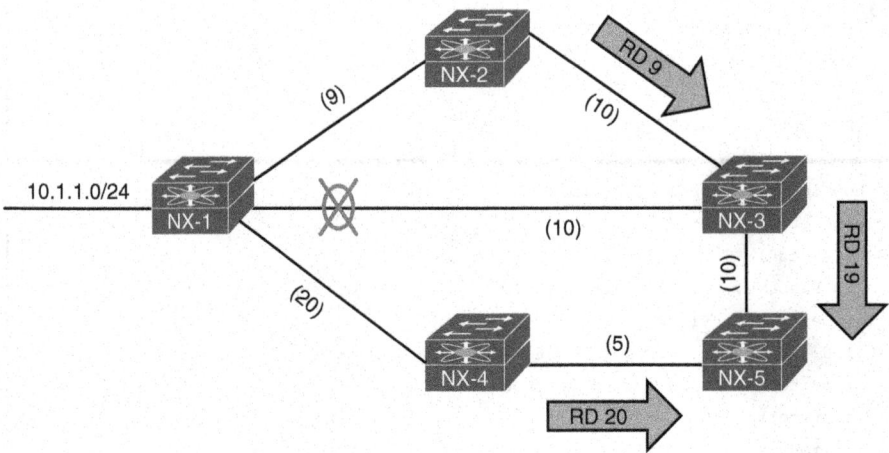

Figure 7-12 *EIGRP Topology with Link Failure*

The following actions then occur:

- NX-3 installs the feasible successor path advertised from NX-2 as the successor route.
- NX-3 sends an Update packet with a new RD of 19 for the 10.1.1.0/24 prefix to NX-5.
- NX-5 receives the Update packet from NX-3 and calculates a FD of 29 for the NX-3 →NX-2 →NX-1 path to 10.1.1.0/24.
- NX-5 compares that path to the one received from NX-4, which has a path metric of 25.
- NX-5 chooses the path via NX-4 as the successor route.

Example 7-53 provides simulated output of the NX-5's EIGRP topology for the 10.1.1.0/24 prefix after the NX-1-NX-3 link fails.

Example 7-53 *EIGRP Topology for the 10.1.1.0/24 Network*

```
NX-5# show ip eigrp topology 10.1.1.0/24
IP-EIGRP (AS 100): Topology entry for 10.1.1.0/24
  State is Passive, Query origin flag is 1, 1 Successor(s), FD is 25
  Routing Descriptor Blocks:
  10.45.1.4 (Ethernet1/2), from 10.45.1.4, Send flag is 0x0
      Composite metric is (25/20), Route is Internal
      Vector metric:
        ..
        Hop count is 2
        Originating router is 192.168.1.1
  10.35.1.3 (Ethernet1/1), from 10.35.1.3, Send flag is 0x0
      Composite metric is (29/19), Route is Internal
```

```
Vector metric:
 ..
 Hop count is 3
 Originating router is 192.168.1.1
```

If a feasible successor is not available for the prefix, DUAL must compute a new route calculation. The route state changes from *Passive (P)* to *Active (A)* in the EIGRP topology table.

Active Query

The router detecting the topology change sends out Query packets to EIGRP neighbors for the route. The Query packet includes the network prefix with the delay set to infinity so that other routers are aware that it has gone Active. When the router sends the EIGRP Query packets, it sets the Reply status flag set for each neighbor on a prefix basis.

Upon receipt of a Query packet, an EIGRP router does one of the following:

- Reply to the Query that the router does not have a route to the prefix.
- If the Query did not come from the successor for that route, it detects the delay set for infinity but ignores it because it did not come from the successor. The receiving router replies with the EIGRP attributes for that route.
- If the Query came from the successor for the route, the receiving router detects the delay set for infinity, sets the prefix as Active in the EIGRP topology, and sends out a Query packet to all downstream EIGRP neighbors for that route.

The Query process continues from router to router until a router establishes the Query boundary. A Query boundary is established when a router does not mark the prefix as Active, meaning that it responds to a query with the following:

- Not having a route to the prefix
- Replying with EIGRP attributes because the query did not come from the successor

When a router receives a Reply for all its downstream queries, it completes the DUAL algorithm, changes the route to Passive, and sends a Reply packet to any upstream routers that sent a Query packet to it. Upon receiving the Reply packet for a prefix, the reply packet is notated for that neighbor and prefix. The reply process continues upstream for the Queries until the first router's Queries are received.

Figure 7-13 represents a topology where the link between NX-1 and NX-2 has failed.

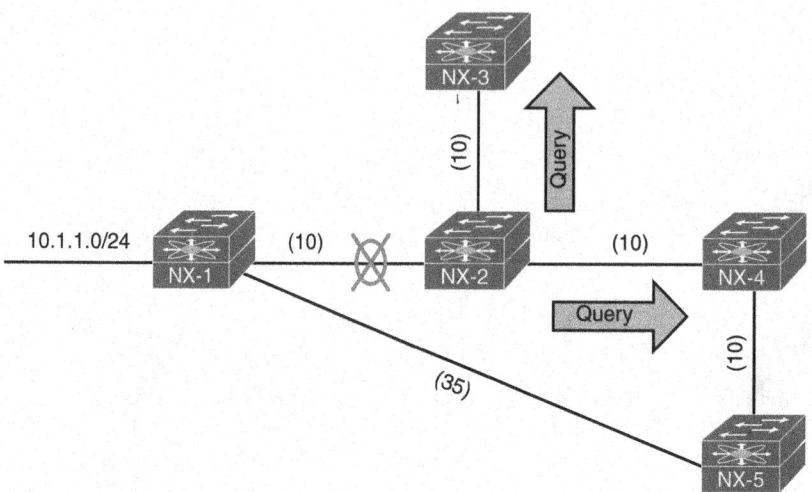

Figure 7-13 *EIGRP Convergence Topology*

The following steps are processed in order from the perspective of NX-2 calculating a new route to the 10.1.1.0/24 network.

Step 1. NX-2 detects the link failure. NX-2 did not have a feasible successor for the route, set the 10.1.1.0/24 prefix as active, and sent Queries to NX-3 and NX-4.

Step 2. NX-3 receives the Query from NX-2, and processes the delay field that is set to infinity. NX-3 does not have any other EIGRP neighbors and sends a Reply to NX-2 that a route does not exists. NX-4 receives the Query from NX-2 and processes the delay field that is set to infinity. Because the Query was received by the successor, and a feasible successor for the prefix does not exist, NX-4 marks the route as active and sends a Query to NX-5.

Step 3. NX-5 receives the Query from NX-4 and detects that the delay field is set to infinity. Because the Query was received by a nonsuccessor, and a successor exists on a different interface, a REPLY for the 10.4.4.0/24 network is sent back to NX-4 with the appropriate EIGRP attributes.

Step 4. NX-4 receives NX-5's Reply, acknowledges the packet, and computes a new path. Because this is the last outstanding Query packet on NX-4, NX-4 sets the prefix as passive. With all Queries satisfied, NX-4 responds to NX-2's query with the new EIGRP metrics.

Step 5. NX-2 receives NX-4's Reply, acknowledges the packet, and computes a new path. Because this is the last outstanding Query packet on NX-4, NX-4 sets the prefix as passive.

Stuck in Active

DUAL is very efficient at finding loop-free paths quickly, and normally finds a backup path in seconds. Occasionally an EIGRP Query is delayed because of packet loss, slow neighbors, or a large hop count. EIGRP waits half of the active timer (90 seconds default) for a Reply. If the router does not receive a response within 90 seconds, the originating router sends a *Stuck In Active (SIA) Query* to EIGRP neighbors that have not responded.

Upon receipt of a *SIA-Query*, the router should respond within 90 seconds with a *SIA-REPLY*. A SIA-Reply contains the route information, or provides information on the Query process itself. If a router fails to respond to a SIA-Query by the time the active timer expires, EIGRP deems the router as *Stuck In Active (SIA)*. If the SIA state is declared for a neighbor, DUAL deletes all routes from that neighbor and treats the situation as if the neighbor responded with unreachable messages for all routes. Active Queries are shown with the command **show ip eigrp topology active**.

Figure 7-14 shows a topology where the link between NX-1 and NX-2 has failed. NX-2 sends out Queries to NX-4 and NX-3 for the 10.1.1.0/24 and 10.12.1.0/24 networks. NX-4 sends a Reply back to NX-2, and NX-3 sends a Query onto R5, which then sends a query on to R6.

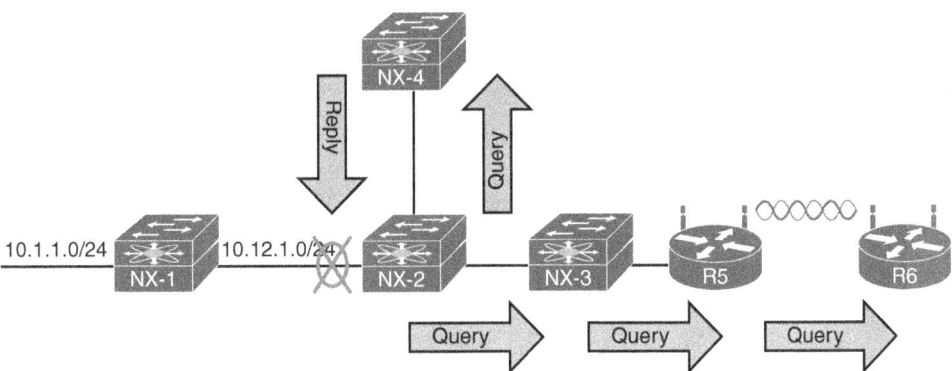

Figure 7-14 *EIGRP SIA Topology*

A network engineer sees the syslog message for the down link and immediately runs the **show ip eigrp topology active** command on NX-2 and sees output the output from Example 7-54.

The "r" next to the 10.23.1.3 indicates that NX-2 is still waiting on the reply from NX-3. NX-1 is registered as down, and the path is set to infinity. The **show ip eigrp topology** command can then be executed on NX-3, which indicates it is waiting on a response from NX-5. Then the command can be run again on R5, which indicates it is waiting on R6. Executing the command on R6 does not show any active prefixes, inferring that R6 never received a Query from R5. R5's Query could have been dropped on the wireless connection.

Example 7-54 *Output for SIA Timers*

```
NX-2# show ip eigrp topology active
IP-EIGRP Topology Table for AS(100)/ID(10.23.1.2) VRF default

Codes: P - Passive, A - Active, U - Update, Q - Query, R - Reply,
       r - reply Status, s - sia Status

A 10.1.1.0/24, 0 successors, FD is 768
    1 replies, active 00:00:08, query-origin: Local origin
        via 10.12.1.1 (Infinity/Infinity), Ethernet1/2
      Remaining replies:
        via 10.23.1.3, r, Ethernet1/1
A 10.12.1.0/24, 1 successors, FD is Inaccessible
    1 replies, active 00:00:08, query-origin: Local origin
        via Connected (Infinity/Infinity), Ethernet1/2
      Remaining replies:
        via 10.23.1.3, r, Ethernet1/1
```

After the 90-second window has passed, the switch sends out a SIQ Query, which is seen by examining the EIGRP traffic counters. Example 7-55 displays the traffic counters before and after the 90-second window.

Example 7-55 *EIGRP Traffic Counters with SIA Queries and Replies*

```
Before 90 second window
NX-2# show ip eigrp traffic
IP-EIGRP Traffic Statistics for AS 100 VRF default
  Hellos sent/received: 65/64
  Updates sent/received: 0/0
  Queries sent/received: 2/0
  Replies sent/received: 0/1
  Acks sent/received: 1/2
  Input queue high water mark 3, 0 drops
  SIA-Queries sent/received: 0/0
  SIA-Replies sent/received: 0/0
  Hello Process ID: (no process)
  PDM Process ID: (no process)

After 90 second window
NX-2# show ip eigrp traffic
IP-EIGRP Traffic Statistics for AS 100 VRF default
  Hellos sent/received: 115/115
  Updates sent/received: 7/6
  Queries sent/received: 2/0
  Replies sent/received: 0/1
```

```
    Acks sent/received: 7/9
    Input queue high water mark 3, 0 drops
    SIA-Queries sent/received: 2/0
    SIA-Replies sent/received: 0/2
    Hello Process ID: (no process)
    PDM Process ID: (no process)
```

Example 7-56 displays the EIGRP topology table after the SIA Replies are received. And just after that, the SIA message appears in the syslog, and the EIGRP peering is reset.

Example 7-56 *Topology Table After SIA Replies*

```
NX-2# show ip eigrp topology active
IP-EIGRP Topology Table for AS(100)/ID(10.23.1.2) VRF default

Codes: P - Passive, A - Active, U - Update, Q - Query, R - Reply,
       r - reply Status, s - sia Status

A 10.1.1.0/24, 0 successors, FD is 768
    1 replies, active 00:04:40, query-origin: Local origin, retries(3)
        via 10.12.1.1 (Infinity/Infinity), Ethernet1/2
        via 10.23.1.3 (Infinity/Infinity), r, Ethernet1/1, serno 112
A 10.12.1. 0/24, 1 successors, FD is Inaccessible
    1 replies, active 00:04:40, query-origin: Local origin, retries(3)
        via Connected (Infinity/Infinity), Ethernet1/2
        via 10.23.1.3 (Infinity/Infinity), r, Ethernet1/1, serno 111
```

```
NX-2
03:57:41 NX-2 %EIGRP-3-SIA_DUAL:  eigrp-NXOS [8394] (default-base) Route
    10.12.1.0/24 stuck-in-active state in IP-EIGRP(0) 100. Cleaning up
03:57:41 NX-2 %EIGRP-5-NBRCHANGE_DUAL:  eigrp-NXOS [8394] (default-base) IP-EIGRP(0)
    100: Neighbor 10.23.1.3 (Ethernet1/1) is down: stuck in active
03:57:42 NX-2 %EIGRP-5-NBRCHANGE_DUAL:  eigrp-NXOS [8394] (default-base) IP-EIGRP(0)
    100: Neighbor 10.23.1.3 (Ethernet1/1) is up: new adjacency
```

Having an invalid route stuck in the routing table because of a busy router can be frustrating. There are two possible solutions:

- Change the active timer to a different value with the command **timers active-time** {*disabled | 1-65535_minutes*} under the EIGRP process.

- Use network summarization within the network design. EIGRP summarization is useful for creating query boundaries to reduce the realm that a query will be executed in.

The active timer is shown by examining the EIGRP process with the **show ip eigrp** command. The SIA timer is displayed in the Active Timer field. Example 7-57 displays the active timer value of three minutes.

Example 7-57 *Output for SIA Timers*

```
NX-2# show ip eigrp
! Output omitted for brevity
IP-EIGRP AS 100 ID 10.23.1.2 VRF default
..
  Max paths: 8
  Active Interval: 3 minute(s)
```

Summary

This chapter provided a logical overview of how the most common issues with EIGRP can be identified so that any issue can be remediated.

The following parameters must match when troubleshooting EIGRP adjacency with other devices:

- Interfaces must be *Active*.
- Connectivity between devices must exist using the primary subnet.
- Autonomous system number (ASN) matches.
- Metric formula K values.
- Authentication parameters.

EIGRP is a distance vector routing protocol, which creates a topology map based on the information it has received from downstream neighbors. When troubleshooting suboptimal path selection or missing routes, it is best to start at the destination and work toward the source of the route. Along each hop, the following items should be checked to see if there is explicit modification of path information:

- EIGRP adjacency with another device that is toward the source.
- Enablement of the EIGRP stub feature.
- Filtering by hop-count or distribute-list.
- Manipulation of metrics. This can be an offset list to increase the metric for that path, or the explicit configuration of bandwidth or delay for an interface.
- A router that is using two different processes to contain the upstream and downstream routing interface. In these instances the routes need to be mutually redistributed between the processes.
- Poorly planned implementation of EIGRP wide metrics that does not take into account the scale factor on higher speed interfaces.

EIGRP's DUAL algorithm is extremely intelligent and overcomes barriers that apply to most vector-based routing protocols. DUAL provides fast convergence, but occasionally has difficulties during convergence when remote routers become unresponsive. The convergence time period can be reduced by implementing lower SIA timers, or through the deployment of route summarization.

References

RFC 7868, Cisco's Enhanced Interior Gateway Routing Protocol (EIGRP). Savage, D., J. Ng, S. Moore, et al. IETF, https://tools.ietf.org/html/rfc7868, May 2016.

Edgeworth, Brad, Aaron Foss, and Ramiro Garza Rios. *IP Routing on Cisco IOS, IOS XE and IOS XR*. Indianapolis: Cisco Press, 2014.

Cisco. Cisco NX-OS Software Configuration Guides, http://www.cisco.com.

Chapter 8

Troubleshooting Open Shortest Path First (OSPF)

This chapter covers the following topics:

- OSPF Fundamentals
- Troubleshooting OSPF Neighbor Adjacency
- Troubleshooting Missing Routes
- Troubleshooting OSPF Path Selection

Open Shortest Path First (OSPF) is a link-state routing protocol that provides every router with a complete map for all destination networks. Every router in the network calculates the best, shortest, loop-free paths using this complete map of the network.

This chapter focuses on identifying and troubleshooting issues that are caused with forming OSPF neighbor adjacency, path selection, and missing routes.

OSPF Fundamentals

OSPF advertises *link-state advertisements (LSA)* that contain the link state and metric to neighboring routers. Received LSAs are stored in a local database called the *link-state database (LSDB)*, which are then advertised to neighboring routers exactly as the LSAs were received. The same LSA is flooded throughout the OSPF area just as the advertising router advertised it. The LSDB provides the topology of the network, in essence providing the router a complete map of the network.

All routers run the *Dijkstra Shortest Path First (SPF)* algorithm to construct a loop-free topology of shortest paths. Each router sees itself as the top of the tree, and the tree contains all network destinations within the OSPF domain. The *SPF Tree (SPT)* is different for each OSPF router, but the LSDB used to calculate the SPT is identical for all OSPF routers in that area.

Inter-Router Communication

OSPF runs on its own protocol (89) and multicast where possible to reduce unnecessary traffic. The two OSPF multicast addresses are as follows:

- **AllSPFRouters:** IPv4 Address 224.0.0.5 or MAC 01:00:5E:00:00:05

  All routers running OSPF should be able to receive these packets.

- **AllDRouters:** IPv4 Address 224.0.0.6 or MAC 01:00:5E:00:00:06

  Communication with Designated Routers uses this address.

Within the OSPF protocol are five types of packets. Table 8-1 provides an overview of the OSPF packet types and a brief description for each type.

Table 8-1 *OSPF Packet Types*

Type	Packet Name	Functional Overview
1	Hello	**Discover & Maintain neighbors** Packets are sent out periodically on all OSPF interfaces to discover new neighbors while ensuring other neighbors are still online.
2	Database Description (DBD) or (DDP)	**Summarize Database Contents** Packets are exchanged when an OSPF adjacency is first being formed. These packets are used to describe the contents of the LSDB.
3	Link State Request (LSR)	**Database Download** When a router thinks that part of its LSDB is stale, it may request a portion of a neighbor's database using this packet type.
4	Link State Update (LSU)	**Database Update** This is an explicit LSA for a specific network link and normally is sent in direct response to a LSR.
5	Link State Ack	**Flooding Acknowledgement** These packets are sent in response to the flooding of LSAs, therefore making the flooding a reliable transport feature.

OSPF Hello Packets

OSPF Hello packets are responsible for discovering and maintaining neighbors. In most instances, the router sends Hello packets to the AllSPFRouters address (224.0.0.5). Table 8-2 provides a listing of some of the data contained within an OSPF Hello packet.

Table 8-2 *OSPF Hello Fields*

Data Field	Description
Router-ID (RID)	A unique 32-bit ID within an OSPF domain.
Authentication Options	Allows secure communication between OSPF routers to prevent malicious activity. Options are None, Clear Text, or MD5.
Area-ID	OSPF area that the OSPF interface belongs to. It is a 32-bit number that can be written in dotted decimal format (0.0.1.0) or decimal (256).
Interface Address Mask	The network mask for the primary IP for the interface that the Hello is sent out.
Interface Priority	Router Interface priority for Designated Router elections.
Hello Interval	Time span, in seconds, that a router sends out Hello packets on the interface.
Dead Interval	Time span, in seconds, that a router will wait to hear a Hello from a neighbor router before it declares that router Down.
Designated Router & Backup Designated Router	IP address of the Designated Router & Backup Designated Router for that network link.
Active Neighbor	A list of OSPF neighbors seen on that network segment. Must have received a Hello from the neighbor within the Dead Interval.

Neighbor States

An OSPF neighbor is a router that shares a common OSPF-enabled network link. OSPF routers discover other neighbors via the OSPF Hello packets. An adjacent OSPF neighbor is an OSPF neighbor that shares a synchronized OSPF database between the two neighbors.

Each OSPF process maintains a table for adjacent OSPF neighbors and the state of each router. Table 8-3 provides an overview of the OSPF neighbor states.

Table 8-3 *OSPF Neighbor States*

State	Description
Down	Initial state of a neighbor relationship. It indicates that it has not received any LSAs from that router.
Attempt	This state is relevant to nonbroadcast multiple access (NBMA) networks that do not support broadcast and require explicit neighbor configuration. This state indicates that no recent information has been received, but the router is still attempting communication.

State	Description
Init	A Hello packet has been received from another a router, but bidirectional communication has not been established.
2-Way	Bidirectional communication has been established. If a Designated Router or Backup Designated Router is needed, the election occurs during this state.
ExStart	This is the first state of forming an adjacency. Routers identify which router will be the master or slave for the LSDB synchronization.
Exchange	During this state, routers are exchanging link-states and via DBD packets.
Loading	LSR packets are sent to the neighbor asking for the more recent LSAs that have been discovered (but not received) in the Exchange state.
Full	Neighboring routers are fully adjacent.

Designated Routers

Multi-access networks such as Ethernet (LANs) allow more than two routers to exist on a network segment. This could cause scalability problems with OSPF as the number of routers on a segment increases. Additional routers flood more LSAs on the segment, and OSPF traffic becomes excessive as OSPF neighbor adjacencies increase. If 6 routers share the same multi-access network, 15 OSPF adjacencies would form along with 15 occurrences of database flooding on that one network.

Multi-access networks overcome this inefficiency by using a *Designated Router (DR)*. DRs reduce the number of OSPF adjacencies on a multi-access network segment because routers only form a full OSPF adjacency with the DR and not each other. The DR is then responsible for flooding the update to all OSPF routers on that segment as updates occur.

If the DR fails, OSPF must form new adjacencies invoking all new LSAs and could potentially cause a temporary loss of routes. In the event of DR failure, a *Backup Designated Router (BDR)* becomes the new DR; then an election occurs to replace the BDR. To minimize transition time, the BDR also forms a full OSPF adjacency with all OSPF routers on that segment.

The DROther is a router on the DR-enabled segment that is not the DR or the BDR; it is simply the other router.

Note Neighbors are selected as the DR and BDR based on the highest OSPF priority, followed by higher Router ID (RID) when the priority is a tie. The OSPF priority is set on an interface with the command **ip ospf priority** *0-255*. Setting the value to zero prevents that router from becoming a DR for that segment.

Areas

OSPF provides scalability for the routing table by using multiple OSPF areas with the routing domain. Each OSPF area provides a collection of connected networks and hosts that are grouped together. OSPF uses a two-tier hierarchical architecture where Area 0 is a special area known as the *backbone*, and all other OSPF areas must connect to Area 0. In other words, Area 0 provides transit connectivity between nonbackbone areas. Nonbackbone areas advertise routes into the backbone, and the backbone then advertises routes into other nonbackbone areas.

The exact topology of the area is invisible from outside of the area while still providing connectivity to routers outside of the area. This means that routers outside the area do not have a complete topological map for that area, which reduces OSPF network traffic in that area. By segmenting an OSPF routing domain into multiple areas, it is no longer true that all OSPF routers will have identical LSDBs; however, all routers *within the same area* will have identical area LSDBs. The reduction in routing traffic uses less router memory and resources providing scalability.

Area Border Routers (ABR) are OSPF routers connected to Area 0 and another OSPF area. ABRs are responsible for advertising routes from one area and injecting them into a different OSPF area. Every ABR needs to participate in Area 0; otherwise, routes do not advertise into another area.

When a router redistributes external routes into an OSPF domain, the router is called an *Autonomous System Boundary Router (ASBR)*. An ASBR can be any OSPF router, and the ASBR function is independent of the ABR function.

Link State Advertisements

Understanding how OSPF builds a topology table and the how various link state advertisement (LSA) types function helps with troubleshooting missing routes. Table 8-4 provides a summary of the OSPF LSAs discussed.

Table 8-4 *OSPF LSA Types*

LSA Type	Description
1	**Router Link**—Every OSPF router advertises a Type-1 LSA. Type-1 LSAs are the most basic LSA within the LSDB. A Type-1 LSA entry exists for all OSPF enabled links (that is, interfaces) and reflects an actual network. Router links are classified either as either stub or transit. A stub router link includes a netmask, whereas a transit link does not.
2	**Network Link**—Type-2 LSAs represent multi-access network segments that use a DR. The DR always advertises the Type-2 LSA, and connects the Type-1 transit link type LSAs together. Type-2 LSAs also provide the network mask for the Type-1 transit link types.

LSA Type	Description
	If a DR has not been elected, a Type-2 LSA is not present in the LSDB because the corresponding Type-1 transit link type LSA will be a stub. Type-2 LSAs are not flooded outside of the originating OSPF area in an identical fashion to Type-1 LSAs.
3	**Summary Link**—The role of the ABRs is to participate in multiple OSPF areas and ensure that the networks associated with Type-1 LSAs are reachable in the non-originating OSPF area. ABRs do not forward Type-1 or Type-2 LSAs into other areas. When an ABR receives a Type-1 LSA, it creates a Type-3 LSA referencing the network in the original Type-1 LSA. A Type-2 LSA is used to determine the network mask of a multi-access network. The ABR then advertises the Type-3 LSA into other areas. If an ABR receives a Type-3 LSA from Area 0 (backbone), it generates a new Type-3 LSA for the nonbackbone area, but lists itself as the advertising router.
4	**ASBR Summary**—Type-4 LSAs locate the ASBR for Type-5 LSAs. A Type-5 LSA is flooded through the OSPF domain unmodified, and the only mechanism to identify the ASBR is the RID. Routers examine the Type-5 LSA, check to see if the RID is in the local area, and if it is not, they require a mechanism to locate the ASBR. Only Type-1 or Type-2 LSAs provide a method to locate the RID within an area. The Type-4 LSA provides a way for routers to locate the ASBR when the router is in a different area from the ASBR.
5	**AS External**—When a route is redistributed into OSPF on the ASBR, the external route is flooded throughout the entire OSPF domain as a Type-5 LSA. Type-5 LSAs are not associated to a specific area and are flooded across all ABRs. Only the LSA age is modified during flooding.
7	**NSSA External**—Not So Stubby Areas (NSSA) areas are a method to reduce the LSDB within an area by preventing Type-4 and Type-5 LSAs while allowing redistribution of networks into the area. A Type-7 LSA exists only in NSSA areas where the route redistribution is occurring. An ASBR injects external routes as Type-7 LSAs into an NSSA area. The ABR does not advertise Type-7 LSAs outside of the originating NSSA area, but advertises a Type-5 LSA for the other OSPF areas. If the Type-5 LSA crosses Area 0, then the second ABR creates a Type-4 LSA for the Type-5 LSA.

OSPF Fundamentals 455

Note Every LSA contains the advertising router's RID. The router RID represents the router and is how links are connected to each other.

Figure 8-1 displays a multi-area OSPF topology with an external route redistributed into Area 56. On the left of the figure is the network prefix for the topology, and the appropriate LSA type is displayed underneath the segment it is advertised. This demonstrates where each LSA is located. Notice that Area 1234 is a broadcast area and contains a DR, which generates a Type-2 LSA. NX-6 is redistributing the 100.65.0.0/16 network into OSPF, whereas NX-5 advertises the first Type-4 LSA for the ASBR (NX-6).

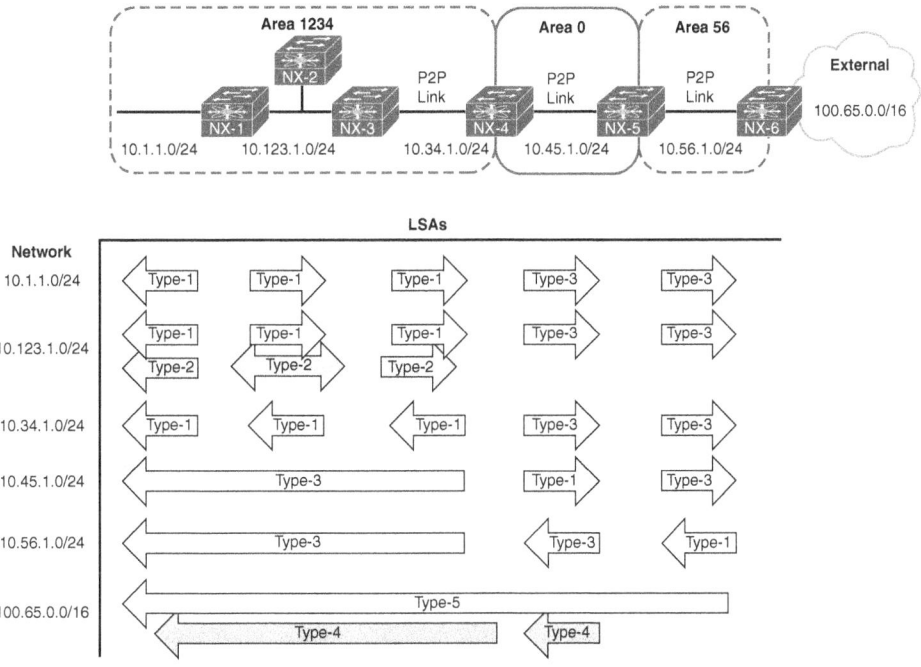

Figure 8-1 *Topology to Demonstrate OSPF LSAs*

Note The Cisco Press book *IP Routing on Cisco IOS, IOS XE and IOS XR* describes OSPF LSAs and how a router builds the actual topology table using LSAs in a visual manner.

OSPF classifies routes into the following three categories:

- **Intra-area routes:** Routes for networks that exist in that OSPF area and contain *intra* beside them in the routing table.
- **Inter-area routes:** Routes for networks that exist in the OSPF domain from a different OSPF area and contain *inter* beside them in the routing table.
- **External routes:** Routes that were redistributed into the OSPF domain and contain a *type-1* or *type-2* beside them in the routing table.

Example 8-1 displays the routing table from NX-1 from Figure 8-1 that includes intra-area, inter-area, and external OSPF routes.

Example 8-1 *Sample OSPF Routing Table*

```
NX-1# show ip route ospf
IP Route Table for VRF "default"
'*' denotes best ucast next-hop
'**' denotes best mcast next-hop
'[x/y]' denotes [preference/metric]
'%<string>' in via output denotes VRF <string>

10.34.1.0/24, ubest/mbest: 1/0
    *via 10.123.1.3, Eth1/1, [110/80], 00:10:30, ospf-NXOS, intra
10.45.1.0/24, ubest/mbest: 1/0
    *via 10.123.1.3, Eth1/1, [110/120], 00:10:15, ospf-NXOS, inter
10.56.1.0/24, ubest/mbest: 1/0
    *via 10.123.1.3, Eth1/1, [110/160], 00:10:15, ospf-NXOS, inter
10.65.0.0/16, ubest/mbest: 1/0
    *via 10.123.1.3, Eth1/1, [110/20], 00:08:02, ospf-NXOS, type-2
```

Troubleshooting OSPF Neighbor Adjacency

Now that an overview of the OSPF protocol has been provided, let's review how OSPF is configured and how to troubleshoot OSPF neighbor adjacencies for NX-OS.

Baseline OSPF Configuration

The OSPF configuration process on a NX-OS switch requires configuration under the OSPF process and under the interface configuration submode. The following steps explain the process for configuring OSPF on a NX-OS device:

Step 1. Enable the OSPF feature. The OSPF feature must be enabled with the global configuration command **feature ospf**.

Step 2. Define an OSPF process tag. The OSPF process must be defined with the global configuration command **router ospf** *process-tag*. The process-tag can be up to 20 alphanumeric characters in length.

Step 3. Enable OSPF neighbor logging (recommended). NX-OS does not log OSPF neighbor adjacencies forming or dissolving by default. The OSPF configuration command **log-adjacency-changes [detail]** enables logging and is recommended. The optional **detail** keyword lists out the OSPF neighbor states from Table 8-3 as they are entered.

Step 4. Define the Router-ID (recommended). The *OSPF Router-ID (RID)* is a 32-bit unique number that identifies an OSPF router and is synonymous with the term *Neighbor ID*. The RID must be unique for each OSPF process in an OSPF domain as it is used to build the topology table. The command **router-id** *router-id* is used to statically set the RID.

If the RID is not manually configured, the Loopback 0 IP address is always preferred. If the Loopback 0 does not exist, NX-OS selects the IP address for the first loopback interface in the configuration. If no loopback interfaces exist, NX-OS selects the IP address for the first physical interface in the configuration.

Step 5. Enable OSPF on interfaces. The interface that OSPF is enabled on is selected with the command **interface** *interface-id*. The OSPF process is then enabled on that interface with the command **ip router ospf** *process-tag* **area** *area-id*. The area-id can be entered in decimal format (1-65,536) or dotted-decimal format, but it is always stored in dotted decimal format.

Secondary networks are advertised by default after OSPF is enabled on that interface. This behavior is disabled with the command **ip router ospf** *process-tag* **area** *area-id* **secondaries none**.

Loopback interfaces are advertised as a /32 regardless of the actual subnet mask. The command **ip ospf advertise-subnet** changes the behavior so that the subnet mask is advertised with the LSA.

Note Typically, an interface can exist in only one area at a time. However, recent changes allow an interface to exist in multiple areas across only point-to-point OSPF links with the command **ip router ospf** *process-tag* **multi-area** *area-id*.

The configuration in Example 8-2 enables OSPF only on interfaces Ethernet1/1, VLAN 10, and Loopback 0.

Example 8-2 *Baseline OSPF Configuration*

```
NX-1# configure terminal
Enter configuration commands, one per line. End with CNTL/Z.
NX-1(config)# feature ospf
NX-1(config)# router ospf NXOS
NX-1(config-router)# log-adjacency-changes detail
NX-1(config-router)# router-id 192.168.100.100
NX-1(config-if)# ip router ospf NXOS area 0
NX-1(config-if)# interface vlan 10
NX-1(config-if)# ip router ospf NXOS area 0
NX-1(config-if)# interface e1/1
NX-1(config-if)# ip router ospf NXOS area 0
12:58:33 NX-1 %$ VDC-1 %$ %OSPF-5-NBRSTATE: ospf-NXOS [13016]   Process NXOS, Nbr
   10.12.1.200 on Ethernet1/1 from DOWN to INIT, HELLORCVD
12:58:42 NX-1 %$ VDC-1 %$ %OSPF-5-NBRSTATE: ospf-NXOS [13016]   Process NXOS, Nbr
   10.12.1.200 on Ethernet1/1 from INIT to EXSTART, ADJOK
12:58:42 NX-1 %$ VDC-1 %$ %OSPF-5-NBRSTATE: ospf-NXOS [13016]   Process NXOS, Nbr
   10.12.1.200 on Ethernet1/1 from EXSTART to EXCHANGE, NEGDONE
12:58:42 NX-1 %$ VDC-1 %$ %OSPF-5-NBRSTATE: ospf-NXOS [13016]   Process NXOS, Nbr
   10.12.1.200 on Ethernet1/1 from EXCHANGE to LOADING, EXCHDONE
12:58:42 NX-1 %$ VDC-1 %$ %OSPF-5-NBRSTATE: ospf-NXOS [13016]   Process NXOS, Nbr
   10.12.1.200 on Ethernet1/1 from LOADING to FULL, LDDONE
```

OSPF requires a neighbor relationship to form before routes are processed and added to the RIB. The neighbor adjacency table is vital for tracking neighbor status and the updates sent to each neighbor. This section explains the process for troubleshooting OSPF neighbor adjacencies on NX-OS switches.

Figure 8-2 provides a simple topology with two Nexus switches that are used to explain how to troubleshoot OSPF adjacency problems.

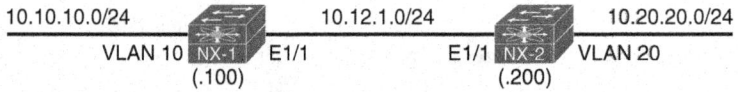

Figure 8-2 *Simple Topology with Two NX-OS Switches*

OSPF Neighbor Verification

First, verify devices that have successfully established an OSPF adjacency with the command **show ip ospf neighbors** [*interface-id* [**detail** | **summary**] | *neighbor-id* [**detail**] | **vrf** {*vrf-name* | **all**}] [**summary**]. The **summary** keyword displays the count of OSPF neighbors and the interface that those neighbors are associated with.

Example 8-3 demonstrates a couple iterations of the command being run on NX-1. Notice the additional information like *Dead timer* and *last change* that is included with the **detail** keyword.

Example 8-3 *Display of OSPF Neighbors*

```
NX-1# show ip ospf neighbors
 OSPF Process ID NXOS VRF default
 Total number of neighbors: 2
 Neighbor ID     Pri State           Up Time  Address        Interface
 192.168.200.200   1 FULL/DR         00:02:04 10.12.1.200    Eth1/1

NX-1# show ip ospf neighbors summary
 OSPF Process ID NXOS VRF default, Neighbor Summary
 Interface Down Attempt Init TwoWay ExStart Exchange Loading Full  Total
    Total    0      0    0     0      0       0       0      1     1
    Eth1/1   0      0    0     0      0       0       0      1     1

NX-1# show ip ospf neighbors 192.168.200.200 detail
 Neighbor 192.168.200.200, interface address 10.12.1.200
    Process ID NXOS VRF default, in area 0.0.0.0 via interface Ethernet1/1
    State is FULL, 6 state changes, last change 00:03:21
    Neighbor priority is 1
    DR is 10.12.1.200 BDR is 10.12.1.100
    Hello options 0x2, dbd options 0x42
    Last non-hello packet received never
      Dead timer due in 00:00:34
```

Table 8-5 provides a brief overview of the fields that appear in Example 8-3.

Table 8-5 *OSPF Neighbor State Fields*

Field	Description
Neighbor ID	Router-ID (RID) of neighboring router.
PRI	Priority for the neighbor's interface. This is used for DR/BDR elections.
State	The first field is the neighbor state as described in Table 8-3.
	The second field is the DR, BDR, or DROther role if the interface requires a DR. For non-DR network links, the second field will show '-'.
	Looking at an OSPF neighbor's state is helpful when troubleshooting adjacency issues. Depending on the LSDB size, the state may transition faster than you can see.
Dead Time	Dead time left until the router is declared unreachable.
Address	Primary IP address for the OSPF neighbor.
Interface	Local interface that the OSPF neighbor is attached to.

Besides enabling OSPF on the network interfaces of an NX-OS device, the following parameters must match for the two routers to become neighbors:

- Interfaces must be *Active*.
- Connectivity between devices must exist using the primary subnet.
- Maximum transmission unit (MTU) matches between devices.
- Router-IDs are unique.
- Interface area must match.
- OSPF stub area flags match.
- Need for DR matches based on OSPF network types.
- OSPF Hello and Dead Timers match.
- Authentication parameters.

Confirmation of OSPF Interfaces

If a neighbor adjacency is missing, it is important to verify that the correct interfaces are running OSPF. The command **show ip ospf interface [brief]** shows the OSPF-enabled interfaces. Example 8-4 provides output for the brief version of the commands.

Example 8-4 *OSPF Interface Output in Brief Format*

```
NX-1# show ip ospf interface brief
OSPF Process ID NXOS VRF default
Total number of interface: 3
Interface          ID      Area           Cost     State      Neighbors  Status
Eth1/1             2       0.0.0.0        4        BDR        1          up
VLAN10             3       0.0.0.0        4        DR         0          up
Lo0                1       0.0.0.0        1        LOOPBACK   0          up
```

Table 8-6 provides an overview of the fields in the output from Example 8-3.

Table 8-6 *OSPF Interface Columns*

Field	Description
Interface	Interfaces with OSPF enabled.
Area	The Area that this interface is associated with. Area is always displayed in dotted-decimal format.
Cost	Cost is used to calculate a metric for a path by the SPF algorithm.
State	Current interface state DR, BDR, DROTHER, LOOP, or Down.
Neighbor	Number of neighbor OSPF routers for a segment that have established an adjacency.
Status	The protocol line status for that interface. A down value reflects an interface that is not reachable.

Example 8-5 displays the output of the **show ip ospf interface** command in non-brief format. It is important to note that the primary IP address, interface network type, DR, BDR, and OSPF interface timers are included as part of the information provided.

Example 8-5 *OSPF Interface Output*

```
NX-1# show ip ospf interface
! Output omitted for brevity
Ethernet1/1 is up, line protocol is up
    IP address 10.12.1.100/24
    Process ID NXOS VRF default, area 0.0.0.0
    Enabled by interface configuration
    State BDR, Network type BROADCAST, cost 4
    Index 2, Transmit delay 1 sec, Router Priority 1
    Designated Router ID: 192.168.200.200, address: 10.12.1.200
    Backup Designated Router ID: 192.168.100.100, address: 10.12.1.100
    1 Neighbors, flooding to 1, adjacent with 1
    Timer intervals: Hello 10, Dead 40, Wait 40, Retransmit 5
      Hello timer due in 00:00:00
    No authentication
    Number of opaque link LSAs: 0, checksum sum 0
```

Passive Interface

Some network topologies require advertising a network segment into OSPF, but need to prevent neighbors from forming adjacencies on that segment. A passive interface is displayed when displaying the OSPF interfaces, so the quickest method is to check the OSPF process with the command **show ip ospf** [*process-tag*] to see whether any passive interfaces are configured. Example 8-6 displays the command and where the passive interface count is provided.

Example 8-6 *Identification if Passive OSPF Interfaces Are Configured*

```
NX-1# show ip ospf
 Routing Process NXOS with ID 192.168.100.100 VRF default
 ..
   Area BACKBONE(0.0.0.0)
        Area has existed for 00:22:02
        Interfaces in this area: 3 Active interfaces: 3
        Passive interfaces: 1  Loopback interfaces: 1
```

Now that a passive interface has been identified, the configuration must be examined for the following:

- The interface parameter command **ip ospf passive-interface**, which makes only that interface passive.

- The global OSPF configuration command **passive-interface default**, which makes all interfaces under that OSPF process passive. The interface parameter command **no ip ospf passive-interface** takes precedence over the global command and makes that interface active.

Example 8-7 displays the configuration on NX-1 and NX-2 that prevents the two Nexus switches from forming an OSPF adjacency. The Ethernet1/1 interfaces must be active on both switches for an adjacency to form. Move the command **ip ospf passive-interface** from Eth1/1 to VLAN10 on NX-1, and the command **no ip ospf passive-interface** from VLAN20 to Interface Eth1/1 on NX-2 to allow an adjacency to form.

Example 8-7 *OSPF Configuration with Passive Interfaces*

```
NX-1# show run ospf
! Output omitted for brevity
feature ospf

router ospf NXOS
  router-id 192.168.100.100
  log-adjacency-changes detail

interface loopback0
  ip router ospf NXOS area 0.0.0.0

interface Ethernet1/1
  ip ospf passive-interface
  ip router ospf NXOS area 0.0.0.0

interface VLAN10
  ip router ospf NXOS area 0.0.0.0

NX-2# show run ospf
! Output omitted for brevity
router ospf NXOS
  router-id 192.168.200.200
  log-adjacency-changes detail
  passive-interface default

interface loopback0
  ip router ospf NXOS area 0.0.0.0
```

```
interface Ethernet1/1
  ip router ospf NXOS area 0.0.0.0

interface VLAN20
  no ip ospf passive-interface
  ip router ospf NXOS area 0.0.0.0
```

Verification of OSPF Packets

A vital step in troubleshooting OSPF adjacency issues is to ensure that a device is transmitting or receiving OSPF network traffic. The command **show ip ospf traffic** [*interface-id*] [**detail**] displays a high-level summary of packet types that were sent or received from a device.

Example 8-8 displays the use of this command. Notice that there is a separation of errors and valid packets in the output. Executing the command while specifying an interface provides more granular visibility to the packets received or transmitted for an interface.

Example 8-8 *OSPF Traffic Statistics*

```
NX-1# show ip ospf traffic
 OSPF Process ID NXOS VRF default, Packet Counters (cleared 00:32:34 ago)
  Total: 319 in, 342 out
  LSU transmissions: first 23, rxmit 4, for req 5 nbr xmit 0
  Flooding packets output throttled (IP/tokens): 0 (0/0)
  Ignored LSAs: 0, LSAs dropped during SPF: 0
  LSAs dropped during graceful restart: 0
  Errors: drops in         0, drops out        0, errors in       0,
          errors out       0, hellos in        0, dbds in         0,
          lsreq in         0, lsu in           0, lsacks in       0,
          unknown in       0, unknown out      0, no ospf         0,
          bad version      0, bad crc          0, dup rid         0,
          dup src          0, invalid src      0, invalid dst     0,
          no nbr           0, passive          1, wrong area     14,
          pkt length       0, nbr changed rid/ip addr             0
          bad auth         0, no vrf           0
          bad reserved     0, no vrf           0

                 hellos      dbds      lsreqs      lsus       acks
       In:        253          18         5         25         18
       Out:       275          19         5         32         11
```

Debug functionality is used to acquire granularity on various processes on the router. Specifically, the command **debug ip ospf {adjacency | hello | packets]** displays the processing of packets that have reached the supervisor on the switch. This allows for users to verify if packets were received or advertised from a router.

Example 8-9 displays the use of the OSPF hello and packet debugs.

Example 8-9 *OSPF Hello and Packet Debugs*

```
NX-1# debug ip ospf packet
NX-1# debug ip ospf hello
13:59:28.140175 ospf: NXOS [16748] (default) LAN hello out, ivl 10/40, options 0x02,
   mask /24, prio 1, dr 0.0.0.0, bdr 0.0.0.0 nbrs 0 on Ethernet1/1 (area 0.0.0.0)
13:59:28.140631 ospf: NXOS [16748] (default) sent: prty:6 HELLO to 224.0.0.5/
   Ethernet1/1
13:59:29.165361 ospf: NXOS [16748] (default) rcvd: prty:0 ver:2 t:HELLO len:44
   rid:192.168.200.200 area:0.0.0.0 crc:0x732d aut:0 aukid:0 from 10.12.1.200/
   Ethernet1/1
13:59:29.165460 ospf: NXOS [16748] (default) LAN hello in, ivl 10/40, options 0x02,
   mask /24, prio 1, dr 0.0.0.0, bdr 0.0.0.0 on Ethernet1/1 from 10.12.1.200
```

Note Debug output can also be redirected to a logfile, as shown earlier in Chapter 2, "NX-OS Troubleshooting Tools."

Table 8-7 provides a brief description of the fields that are provided in the debug output from Example 8-9.

Table 8-7 *Relevant Fields for OSPF Debug*

Field	Description
ivl	Provides the OSPF Hello and Dead Timers in the Hello packet.
options	Identifies the area associated to that interface as a regular OSPF area, OSPF Stub, or OSPF NSSA area. These values are shown in HEX, and this chapter explains later how to verify them.
mask	The subnet mask of primary IP address on that interface.
priority	The interface priority for DR/BDR elections.
dr	The router-id of the DR.
bdr	The router-id of the BDR.
nbrs	The number of neighbors detected on that network segment.

Debug commands are generally the least preferred method for finding root cause because of the amount of data that could be generated while the debug is enabled. NX-OS provides event-history that runs in the background without performance hits that provides another method of troubleshooting. The command **show ip ospf event-history [hello | adjacency | event]** provides helpful information when troubleshooting OSPF adjacency problems. The **hello** keyword provides the same information as the debug command in Example 8-9.

Example 8-10 displays the **show ip ospf event-history hello** command. Examine the difference in the sample output on NX-1.

Example 8-10 *Hello Packet Visibility from OSPF Event History*

```
NX-1# show ip ospf event-history hello
OSPF HELLO events for Process "ospf-NXOS"
18:20:03.890150 ospf NXOS [16748]: LAN hello out, ivl 10/40, options 0x02, mask /24,
   prio 1, dr 10.12.1.200, bdr 0.0.0.0 nbrs 1 on Ethernet1/1 (area 0.0.0.0)
18:19:59.777890 ospf NXOS [16748]: LAN hello in, ivl 10/40, options 0x02, mask /24,
   prio 1, dr 10.12.1.200, bdr 0.0.0.0 on Ethernet1/1 from 10.12.1.200
18:19:56.320192 ospf NXOS [16748]: LAN hello out, ivl 10/40, options 0x02, mask /24,
   prio 1, dr 10.12.1.200, bdr 0.0.0.0 nbrs 1 on Ethernet1/1 (area 0.0.0.0)
18:19:52.101250 ospf NXOS [16748]: LAN hello in, ivl 10/40, options 0x02, mask /24,
   prio 1, dr 10.12.1.200, bdr 0.0.0.0 on Ethernet1/1 from 10.12.1.200
```

Performing OSPF debugs on a switch only shows the packets that have reached the supervisor. If packets are not displayed in the debugs or event-history, further troubleshooting must be taken by examining *quality of service (QoS)* policies, control plane policing (CoPP), or just verification of the packet leaving or entering an interface.

QoS policies may or may not be deployed on an interface. If they are deployed, the policy-map must be examined for any drop packets, which must then be referenced to a class-map that matches the OSPF routing protocol. The same process applies to CoPP policies because they are based on QoS settings as well.

Example 8-11 displays the process for checking a switch's CoPP policy with the following logic:

1. Examine the CoPP policy with the command **show running-config copp all**. This displays the relevant policy-map name, classes defined, and the police rate.

2. Investigate the class-maps to identify the conditional matches for that class-map.

3. After the class-map has been verified, examine the policy-map drops for that class with the command **show policy-map interface control-plane**.

Example 8-11 *Verification of CoPP for OSPF*

```
NX-1# show run copp all
! Output omitted for brevity

class-map type control-plane match-any copp-system-p-class-critical
  match access-group name copp-system-p-acl-bgp
  match access-group name copp-system-p-acl-rip
```

Chapter 8: Troubleshooting Open Shortest Path First (OSPF)

```
    match access-group name copp-system-p-acl-vpc
    match access-group name copp-system-p-acl-bgp6
    match access-group name copp-system-p-acl-lisp
    match access-group name copp-system-p-acl-ospf
  ..
policy-map type control-plane copp-system-p-policy-strict
  class copp-system-p-class-critical
    set cos 7
    police cir 36000 kbps bc 250 ms conform transmit violate drop
  ..
```

```
NX-1# show run aclmgr all | section copp-system-p-acl-ospf
ip access-list copp-system-p-acl-ospf
  10 permit ospf any any
NX-1# show policy-map interface control-plane class copp-system-p-class-critical
! Output omitted for brevity
Control Plane
  service-policy input copp-system-p-policy-strict

    class-map copp-system-p-class-critical (match-any)
      ..
      module 1:
        conformed 1429554 bytes,
          5-min offered rate 1008 bytes/sec
          peak rate 1008 bytes/sec at Mon 19:03:31
        violated 0 bytes,
          5-min violate rate 0 bytes/sec
          peak rate 0 bytes/sec
```

> **Note** This CoPP policy was taken from a Nexus 7000 switch, and the policy-name and class-maps may vary depending on the platform.

Because CoPP operates at the RP level, it is possible that the packets were received on an interface and did not forward to the RP. The next phase is to identify whether packets were transmitted or received on an interface. This technique involves creating a specific *access control entity (ACE)* for the OSPF protocol. The ACE for OSPF should appear before any other ambiguous ACE entries to ensure a proper count. The ACL configuration command **statistics per-entry** is required to display the specific hits that are encountered per ACE.

Example 8-12 demonstrates the configuration of an ACL to detect OSPF traffic on the Ethernet1/1 interface. Notice that the ACL includes a **permit ip any any** command to allow all traffic to pass through this interface. Failing to do so could result in the loss of traffic.

Example 8-12 *Verification of OSPF Packets with ACL*

```
NX-1# configure terminal
Enter configuration commands, one per line. End with CNTL/Z.
NX-1(config)# ip access-list OSPF
NX-1(config-acl)# permit ospf any 224.0.0.5/32
NX-1(config-acl)# permit ospf any 224.0.0.6/32
NX-1(config-acl)# permit ospf any any
NX-1(config-acl)# permit ip any any
NX-1(config-acl)# statistics per-entry
NX-1(config-acl)# int Eth1/1
NX-1(config-if)# ip access-group OSPF in
```

```
NX-1# show ip access-list
IP access list OSPF
        statistics per-entry
        10 permit ospf any 224.0.0.5/32 [match=12]
        20 permit ospf any 224.0.0.6/32 [match=2]
        30 permit ospf any any [match=7]
        40 permit ip any any [match=5]
```

Note There are three ACE entries for OSPF. The first two are tied to the multicast groups for DR and BDR communication. The third ACE applies to the initial Hello packets.

Note Example 8-12 uses an Ethernet interface, which generally indicates a one-to-one relationship, but on multi-access interfaces like switched virtual interfaces (SVI), also known as interface VLANs, the neighbor may need to be specified in a specific ACE.

An alternative to using an ACL is to use the built-in NX-OS Ethanalyzer to capture the OSPF packets. Example 8-13 demonstrates the command syntax. The optional **detail** keyword can be used to view the contents of the packets.

Example 8-13 *Verification of OSPF Packets Using Ethanalyzer*

```
NX-1# ethanalyzer local interface inband capture-filter "proto ospf"
Capturing on inband
2017-09-09 18:45:59.419456    10.12.1.1 -> 224.0.0.5    OSPF Hello Packet
2017-09-09 18:46:01.826241    10.12.1.2 -> 224.0.0.5    OSPF Hello Packet
2017-09-09 18:46:08.566112    10.12.1.1 -> 224.0.0.5    OSPF Hello Packet
2017-09-09 18:46:11.119443    10.12.1.2 -> 224.0.0.5    OSPF Hello Packet
2017-09-09 18:46:16.456222    10.12.1.1 -> 224.0.0.5    OSPF Hello Packet
```

Connectivity Must Exist Using the Primary Subnet

OSPF routers must be able to communicate with their peer routers by using the network associated to the primary IP address. Adjacency is not formed using secondary IP addresses. OSPF Hello packets include the subnet mask from the advertising interface, which is then checked with the source IP of the packet to verify that the routers are on the same subnet.

The subnet mask was changed on NX-2 from 10.12.1.200/24 to 10.12.1.200/25 for this section. This places NX-2 on the 10.12.1.128/25 network, which is different from NX-1's (10.12.1.100) network.

Examining the OSPF neighbor table does not reflect any entries on either switch. Now examine the OSPF Hello packets with the command **show ip ospf event-history**, as shown in Example 8-14. Notice that OSPF was able to detect the wrong subnet mask between the routers.

Example 8-14 *NX-1 and NX-2 Detect Bad Subnet Mask*

```
NX-1# show ip ospf event-history hello
OSPF HELLO events for Process "ospf-NXOS"
00:28:57.260176 ospf NXOS [16748]: LAN hello out, ivl 10/40, options 0x02, mask /24,
   prio 0, dr 0.0.0.0, bdr 0.0.0.0 nbrs 0 on Ethernet1/1 (area 0.0.0.0)
00:28:50.465118 ospf NXOS [16748]:  Bad mask
00:28:49.620142 ospf NXOS [16748]: LAN hello out, ivl 10/40, options 0x02, mask /24,
   prio 0, dr 0.0.0.0, bdr 0.0.0.0 nbrs 0 on Ethernet1/1 (area 0.0.0.0)
00:28:42.178993 ospf NXOS [16748]:  Bad mask

NX-2# show ip ospf event-history hello
OSPF HELLO events for Process "ospf-NXOS"
00:28:03.330191 ospf NXOS [7223]: LAN hello out, ivl 10/40, options 0x02, mask /25,
   prio 1, dr 10.12.1.200, bdr 0.0.0.0 nbrs 0 on Ethernet1/1 (area 0.0.0.0)
00:27:58.216842 ospf NXOS [7223]:  Bad mask
00:27:54.860129 ospf NXOS [7223]: LAN hello out, ivl 10/40, options 0x02, mask /25,
   prio 1, dr 10.12.1.200, bdr 0.0.0.0 nbrs 0 on Ethernet1/1 (area 0.0.0.0)
00:27:31.491788 ospf NXOS [16748]:  Bad mask
```

In the event that the problem was due to a blatant subnet mismatch, the Hello packets are not recognized in OSPF debug or event-history. Verifying connectivity by the **ping** *neighbor-ipaddress* or **show ip route** *neighbor-ipaddress* will reflect that the networks are not on matching networks. Ensuring that the OSPF routers' primary interfaces are on a common subnet ensures proper communication.

Note OSPF RFC 2328 allows neighbors to form an adjacency using disjointed networks only when using the **ip unnumbered** command on point-to-point OSPF network types. NX-OS does not support IP unnumbered addressing, so this use case is not applicable.

MTU Requirements

The OSPF header of the DBD packets includes the interface MTU. OSPF DBDs are exchanged in the EXSTART and EXCHANGE Neighbor State. Routers check the interface's MTU that is included in the DBD packets to ensure that they match. If the MTUs do not match, the OSPF devices do not form an adjacency.

Example 8-15 displays that NX-1 and NX-2 have started to form a neighbor adjacency over 3 minutes ago and are stuck in the EXSTART state.

Example 8-15 *OSPF Neighbors Stuck in EXSTART Neighbor State*

```
NX-1# show ip ospf neighbors
 OSPF Process ID NXOS VRF default
 Total number of neighbors: 1
 Neighbor ID     Pri State         Up Time  Address        Interface
 192.168.200.200   1 EXSTART/DR    00:03:47 10.12.1.200    Eth1/1

NX-2# show ip ospf neighbors
 OSPF Process ID NXOS VRF default
 Total number of neighbors: 1
 Neighbor ID     Pri State             Up Time  Address        Interface
 192.168.100.100   0 EXSTART/DROTHER   00:03:49 10.12.1.100    Eth1/1
```

Examine the OSPF event-history to identify the reason the switches are stuck in the EXSTART state. Example 8-16 displays the OSPF adjacency event-history on NX-1, in which the MTU from NX-2 has been detected as larger than the MTU on NX-1's interface.

Example 8-16 *NX-1 OSPF Adjacency Event-History with MTU Mismatch*

```
NX-1# show ip ospf event-history adjacency
Adjacency events for OSPF Process "ospf-NXOS"
07:04:01.681927 ospf NXOS [16748]:   DBD from 10.12.1.200, mtu too large
07:04:01.681925 ospf NXOS [16748]: seqnr 0x40196423, dbdbits 0x7, mtu 9216, options
   0x42
07:04:01.681923 ospf NXOS [16748]: Got DBD from 10.12.1.200 with 0 entries
07:04:01.680135 ospf NXOS [16748]: mtu 1500, opts: 0x42, ddbits: 0x7, seq:
   0x11f2da90
07:04:01.680133 ospf NXOS [16748]: Sent DBD with 0 entries to 10.12.1.200 on
   Ethernet1/1
07:04:01.680131 ospf NXOS [16748]: Sending DBD to 10.12.1.200 on Ethernet1/1
07:04:01.381284 ospf NXOS [16748]:   DBD from 10.12.1.200, mtu too large
07:04:01.381282 ospf NXOS [16748]: seqnr 0x40196423, dbdbits 0x7, mtu 9216, options
   0x42
07:04:01.381280 ospf NXOS [16748]: Got DBD from 10.12.1.200 with 0 entries
07:04:01.201829 ospf NXOS [16748]: Nbr 10.12.1.200: EXSTART --> EXSTART, event
   TWOWAYRCVD
```

Note The MTU messages appear only on the device with the smaller MTU.

MTU is examined on both switches by using the command **show interface** *interface-id* and looking for the MTU value as shown in Example 8-17. The MTU on NX-2 is larger than NX-1.

Example 8-17 *Examination of Interface's MTU*

```
NX-1# show interface E1/1 | i MTU
  MTU 1500 bytes, BW 10000000 Kbit, DLY 10 usec

NX-2# show int E1/1 | i MTU
  MTU 9216 bytes, BW 1000000 Kbit, DLY 10 usec
```

The OSPF protocol itself does not know how to handle fragmentation. It relies on IP fragmentation when packets are larger than the interface. It is possible to ignore the MTU safety check by placing the interface parameter command **ip ospf mtu-ignore** on the switch with the smaller MTU. Example 8-18 displays the configuration command on NX-1 that allows it to ignore the larger MTU from NX-2.

Example 8-18 *Configuration for OSPF to Ignore Interface MTU*

```
NX-1# show run ospf
! Output omitted for brevity
router ospf NXOS
  router-id 192.168.100.100
  log-adjacency-changes

interface Ethernet1/1
  ip ospf mtu-ignore
  ip router ospf NXOS area 0.0.0.0

interface VLAN10
  ip ospf passive-interface
  ip router ospf NXOS area 0.0.0.0
```

This technique allows for adjacencies to form, but may cause problems later. The simplest solution is to change the MTU to match on all devices.

Note If the OSPF interface is a VLAN interface (SVI), make sure that all the Layer 2 (L2) ports support the MTU configured on the SVI. For example, if VLAN 10 has an MTU of 9000, configure all the trunk ports to support an MTU of 9000 as well.

Unique Router-ID

The RID provides a unique identifier for an OSPF router. A Nexus switch drops packets that have the same RID as itself as part of a safety mechanism. The syslog message *using our routerid, packet dropped* is displayed along with the interface and RID of the other device. Example 8-19 displays what the syslog message looks like on NX-1.

Example 8-19 *Duplicate Router-ID*

```
07:15:51 NX-1 %OSPF-4-DUPRID: ospf-NXOS [16748] (default) Router 10.12.1.200 on
  interface Ethernet1/1 is using our routerid, packet dropped
07:16:01 NX-1 %OSPF-4-SYSLOG_SL_MSG_WARNING: OSPF-4-DUPRID: message repeated 1 times
  in last 16 sec
```

The RID is checked by viewing the OSPF process with the command **show ip ospf**, as displayed in Example 8-20.

Example 8-20 *Viewing the OSPF RID*

```
NX-1# show ip ospf
! Output omitted for brevity
 Routing Process NXOS with ID 192.168.12.12 VRF default
 Routing Process Instance Number 1
```

Using the command **router-id** *router-id* in the OSPF process sets the RID statically and is considered a best practice. After changing the RID on one of the Nexus switches, an adjacency should form.

Note The RID is a key component of the OSPF topology table that is built from the LSDB. All OSPF devices should maintain a unique RID.

More information on how to interpret the OSPF topology table is found in Chapter 7, "Advanced OSPF" of the Cisco Press book *IP Routing on Cisco IOS, IOS-XE, and IOS XR*.

Interface Area Numbers Must Match

OSPF requires that the area-id match in the OSPF Hello packets to form an adjacency. The syslog message *received for wrong area* is displayed along with the interface and area-id of the other device.

Example 8-21 displays what the syslog message looks like on NX-1 and NX-2.

Example 8-21 *Syslog Message with Neighbors Configured with Different Areas*

```
06:47:52 NX-1 %OSPF-4-AREA_ERR: ospf-NXOS [16748] (default) Packet from 10.12.1.200
  on Ethernet1/1 received for wrong area 0.0.0.1
06:48:02 NX-1 %OSPF-4-SYSLOG_SL_MSG_WARNING: OSPF-4-AREA_ERR: message repeated 1
  times in last 151289 sec
06:48:10 NX-1 %OSPF-4-AREA_ERR: ospf-NXOS [16748] (default) Packet from 10.12.1.200
  on Ethernet1/1 received for wrong area 0.0.0.1
06:48:20 NX-1 %OSPF-4-SYSLOG_SL_MSG_WARNING: OSPF-4-AREA_ERR: message repeated 1
  times in last 17 sec
06:49:19 NX-2 %OSPF-4-AREA_ERR: ospf-NXOS [7223] (default) Packet from 10.12.1.100
  on Ethernet1/1 received for wrong area 0.0.0.0
06:49:29 NX-2 %OSPF-4-SYSLOG_SL_MSG_WARNING: OSPF-4-AREA_ERR: message repeated 1
  times in last 18 sec
06:49:35 NX-2 %OSPF-4-AREA_ERR: ospf-NXOS [7223] (default) Packet from 10.12.1.100
  on Ethernet1/1 received for wrong area 0.0.0.0
06:49:45 NX-2 %OSPF-4-SYSLOG_SL_MSG_WARNING: OSPF-4-AREA_ERR: message repeated 1
  times in last 16 sec
```

When this happens, check the OSPF interfaces to detect which area-ids are configured by using the command **show ip ospf interface brief**. Example 8-22 shows the output from NX-1 and NX-2. Notice that the area is different on NX-1 and NX-2 for the Ethernet1/1 interface.

Example 8-22 *Different OSPF Areas on Ethernet1/1 Interfaces*

```
NX-1# show ip ospf interface brief
OSPF Process ID NXOS VRF default
Total number of interface: 3
Interface            ID    Area         Cost    State      Neighbors Status
Eth1/1               2     0.0.0.0      4       DROTHER    0         up
VLAN10               3     0.0.0.0      4       DR         0         up
Lo0                  1     0.0.0.0      1       LOOPBACK   0         up

NX-2# show ip ospf interface brief
OSPF Process ID NXOS VRF default
Total number of interface: 3
Interface            ID    Area         Cost    State      Neighbors Status
Eth1/1               2     0.0.0.1      40      DR         0         up
VLAN20               3     0.0.0.0      40      DR         0         up
Lo0                  1     0.0.0.0      1       LOOPBACK   0         up
```

Changing the interface areas to the same value on NX-1 and NX-2 allows for an adjacency to form between them.

> **Note** The area-id is always stored in dot-decimal format on Nexus switches. This may cause confusion when working with other devices that store the area-id in decimal format. To convert decimal to dot-decimal, follow these steps:
>
> **Step 1.** Convert the decimal value to binary.
>
> **Step 2.** Split the binary value into four octets starting with the furthest right number.
>
> **Step 3.** Add zeroes as required to complete each octet.
>
> **Step 4.** Convert each octet to decimal format, which provides dot-decimal format.

OSPF Stub (Area Flags) Settings Must Match

The OSPF Hello packet contains an Options field, specifically the E-bit, which reflects the area's ability to contain Type-5 LSAs (Stub capability) settings. The interfaces in an area must be in the following types to form an adjacency:

- **Normal:** External routes (Type-5 LSAs) are allowed in this area.

- **Stubby/Totally Stubby:** External LSAs (Type-5 LSAs) are not allowed in this area. No redistribution is allowed in this area.

- **Not So Stubby Area (NSSA)/Totally NSSA:** External LSAs (Type-5 LSAs) are not allowed in this area. Redistribution is allowed in this area.

The OSPF Hello event-history detects a mismatched OSPF area setting. Example 8-23 displays the concept where NX-1 has detected a different area flag from what is configured on its interface.

Example 8-23 *OSPF Event-History with Mismatched Area Flags*

```
NX-1# show ip ospf event-history hello
OSPF HELLO events for Process "ospf-NXOS"
07:27:01.940673 ospf NXOS [10809]: LAN hello out, ivl 10/40, options 0x00, mask /24,
  prio 1, dr 10.12.1.100, bdr 0.0.0.0 nbrs 0 on Ethernet1/1 (area 0.0.0.1)
07:27:00.422461 ospf NXOS [10809]:  Hello packet options mismatch ours: 0, theirs
  0x2
07:26:52.750167 ospf NXOS [10809]: LAN hello out, ivl 10/40, options 0x00, mask /24,
  prio 1, dr 10.12.1.100, bdr 0.0.0.0 nbrs 0 on Ethernet1/1 (area 0.0.0.1)
07:26:51.446550 ospf NXOS [10809]:  Hello packet options mismatch ours: 0, theirs
  0x2
```

Verify the area settings on the two routers that cannot form an adjacency. Example 8-24 displays that NX-1 has Area 1 configured as a stub, whereas NX-2 does not.

Example 8-24 *Verification of OSPF Area Settings*

```
NX-1# show running-config ospf
! Output omitted for brevity
router ospf NXOS
  router-id 192.168.100.100
  area 0.0.0.1 stub
  log-adjacency-changes

NX-2(config-if)# show running-config ospf
! Output omitted for brevity
  router-id 192.168.200.200
  log-adjacency-changes
```

Setting the area to the same stub setting on both routers allows for the area flag check to pass and the routers to form an adjacency.

DR Requirements

Different media types can provide different characteristics or might limit the number of nodes allowed on a segment. Table 8-8 defines the five OSPF network types—which ones are configurable on NX-OS and which network types can peer with other network types.

Table 8-8 *OSPF Network Types on NX-OS*

Interface Type	Configurable on NX-OS	DR/BDR Field in OSPF Hellos	Can Establish Peering With
Broadcast	Yes	Yes	Broadcast, no changes necessary Non-Broadcast, OSPF timers need modification
Non-Broadcast	No	Yes	Non-Broadcast, no changes necessary Broadcast, OSPF timers need modification
Point-to-Point	Yes	No	Point-to-Point, no changes necessary Point-to-Multipoint, OSPF timers need modification
Point-to-Multipoint	No	No	Point-to-Multipoint, no changes necessary Point-to-Point, OSPF timers need modification
Loopback	No	N/A	N/A

Ethernet provides connectivity to more than two OSPF devices on a network segment, therefore requiring a DR. The default OSPF network type for Nexus switches is the Broadcast OSPF network type because all its interfaces are Ethernet, and the Broadcast network type provides a DR.

Note On OSPF network segments that require a DR (Broadcast/Non-Broadcast), an adjacency does not form if a router cannot be elected a DR because the OSPF priority has been set to zero for all interfaces. Neighbors are stuck in a 2WAY state in this scenario.

There are times when a Nexus switch forms only one OSPF adjacency for that interface. An example is two Ethernet ports configured as Layer 3 (L3) with a direct cable. In scenarios like this, setting the OSPF network type to *point-to-point (P2P)* provides advantages of faster adjacency (no DR Election) and not wasting CPU cycles for DR functionality.

OSPF can form an adjacency only if the DR and BDR Hello options match. Example 8-25 displays NX-1 stuck in INIT state with NX-2. NX-2 does not consider NX-1 an OSPF neighbor. Scenarios like this indicate incompatibility in OSPF network types.

Example 8-25 *OSPF Adjacency Failure*

```
NX-1# show ip ospf neighbors
 OSPF Process ID NXOS VRF default
 Total number of neighbors: 4
 Neighbor ID      Pri State         Up Time    Address       Interface
 192.168.200.200    1 INIT/DROTHER  00:03:47   10.12.1.200   Eth1/1

NX-2# show ip ospf neighbors
```

The Ethernet1/1 OSPF interface network type is confirmed with the command **show ip ospf interface**. NX-1 is configured for Broadcast (DR required), whereas NX-2 is configured as a point-to-point (DR not required). The mismatch of DR requirements is the reason that the adjacency failed. Example 8-26 displays the discrepancy in OSPF network types.

Example 8-26 *Verification of Interface's OSPF Network Type*

```
NX-1# show ip ospf interface | i line|Network
 Ethernet1/1 is up, line protocol is up
    State DR, Network type BROADCAST, cost 4
 VLAN10 is up, line protocol is up
    State DR, Network type BROADCAST, cost 4
```

```
  loopback0 is up, line protocol is up
    State LOOPBACK, Network type LOOPBACK, cost 1
```

```
NX-2# show ip ospf interface | i line|Network
Ethernet1/1 is up, line protocol is up
    State P2P, Network type P2P, cost 40
VLAN20 is down, line protocol is down
    State DOWN, Network type BROADCAST, cost 40
loopback0 is up, line protocol is up
    State LOOPBACK, Network type LOOPBACK, cost 1
```

The OSPF network type needs to be changed on one of the devices, because both Nexus switches are using L3 Ethernet ports. Configuring both switches to use an OSPF point-to-point network type is recommended. The command **ip ospf network point-to-point** configures NX-1's Ethernet1/1 interface as an OSPF point-to-point network type. This allows for both switches to form an adjacency. Example 8-27 displays the configuration for NX-1 and NX-2 that allows them to form an adjacency.

Example 8-27 *Configuration of OSPF Network Types*

```
NX-1# show running-config ospf
! Output omitted for brevity
interface Ethernet1/1
  ip ospf network point-to-point
  ip router ospf NXOS area 0.0.0.0

NX-2# show running-config ospf
! Output omitted for brevity
interface Ethernet1/1
  ip ospf network point-to-point
  ip router ospf NXOS area 0.0.0.0
```

Timers

A secondary function to the OSPF Hello packets is to ensure that adjacent OSPF neighbors are still healthy and available. OSPF sends Hello packets at set intervals called the Hello Timer. OSPF uses a second timer called the *OSPF Dead Interval Timer*, which defaults to four times (4x) the Hello Timer. Upon receipt of the Hello packet from a neighboring router, the OSPF Dead Timer resets to the initial value and starts to decrement again.

Note The default OSPF Hello Timer interval varies upon the OSPF network type. Changing the Hello Timer interval modifies the default Dead Interval, too.

If a router does not receive a Hello before the OSPF Dead Interval Timer reaches zero, the neighbor state changes to Down. The OSPF router immediately sends out the appropriate LSA reflecting the topology change, and the SPF algorithm processes on all routers within the area.

The OSPF Hello Time and OSPF Dead Interval Time must match when forming an adjacency. In the event the timers do not match, timers are displayed in the OSPF Hello packet event history. Example 8-28 shows that NX-1 is receiving a Hello packet with different OSPF timers.

Example 8-28 *Incompatible OSPF Timers*

```
NX-1# show ip ospf event-history hello
OSPF HELLO events for Process "ospf-NXOS"
14:09:47.542331 ospf NXOS [12469]: : LAN hello out, ivl 10/40, options 0x02, mask
    /24, prio 1, dr 10.10.10.12, bdr 10.10.10.11 nbrs 3 on VLAN10 (area 0.0.0.0)
14:09:45.881230 ospf NXOS [12469]: : LAN hello in, ivl 10/40, options 0x12, mask
    /24, prio 1, dr 10.10.10.12, bdr 10.10.10.11 on VLAN10 from 10.10.10.11
14:09:45.873642 ospf NXOS [12469]: : LAN hello in, ivl 10/40, options 0x12, mask
    /24, prio 1, dr 10.10.10.12, bdr 10.10.10.11 on VLAN10 from 10.10.10.12
14:09:45.140175 ospf NXOS [12469]: : LAN hello out, ivl 10/40, options 0x02, mask
    /24, prio 1, dr 10.12.1.100, bdr 0.0.0.0 nbrs 0 on Ethernet1/1 (area 0.0.0.0)
14:09:42.522692 ospf NXOS [12469]: :     Mismatch in configured hello interval
14:09:39.910300 ospf NXOS [12469]: : LAN hello out, ivl 10/40, options 0x02, mask
    /24, prio 1, dr 10.10.10.12, bdr 10.10.10.11 nbrs 3 on VLAN10 (area 0.0.0.0)
14:09:39.725303 ospf NXOS [12469]: : LAN hello in, ivl 10/40, options 0x12, mask
    /24, prio 1, dr 10.10.10.12, bdr 10.10.10.11 on VLAN10 from 1
0.10.10.10
```

The OSPF interfaces of both switches need to be examined with the command **show ip ospf interface** to view the Hello and Dead Timers. Example 8-29 displays NX-1 and NX-2 OSPF timers for Ethernet1/1. Notice that the Hello and Dead Timers are different between the two switches.

Example 8-29 *Different OSPF Hello Timers*

```
NX-1# show ip ospf interface | i line|Timer
 Ethernet1/1 is up, line protocol is up
    Timer intervals: Hello 10, Dead 40, Wait 40, Retransmit 5
 VLAN10 is up, line protocol is up
    Timer intervals: Hello 10, Dead 40, Wait 40, Retransmit 5
 loopback0 is up, line protocol is up

NX-2# show ip ospf interface | i line|Timer
 Ethernet1/1 is up, line protocol is up
    Timer intervals: Hello 15, Dead 60, Wait 60, Retransmit 5
 VLAN20 is down, line protocol is down
    Timer intervals: Hello 10, Dead 40, Wait 40, Retransmit 5
 loopback0 is up, line protocol is up
```

Example 8-30 displays the configuration on both switches for examination to identify a fix. NX-2 has the command **ip ospf hello-interval 15** on the Ethernet1/1 interface to modify the Hello interval. Removing the **ip ospf hello-interval** command on NX-2 or setting the same timers on NX-1 allows the switches to form an adjacency.

Example 8-30 *Mismatched OSPF Hello Timers*

```
NX-1# show run ospf
! Output omitted for brevity
interface Ethernet1/1
  ip router ospf NXOS area 0.0.0.0
```

```
NX-2# show run ospf
interface Ethernet1/1
  ip ospf hello-interval 15
  ip router ospf NXOS area 0.0.0.0
```

Note IOS routers support OSPF fast-packet Hellos for subsecond detection of neighbors with issues. Nexus and IOS XR do not support OSPF fast-packet Hellos. The use of *bidirectional forwarding detection (BFD)* provides fast convergence across IOS, IOS XR, and Nexus devices and is the preferred method of subsecond failure detection.

Authentication

OSPF supports two types of authentication: plaintext and a MD5 cryptographic hash. Plaintext mode provides little security, because anyone with access to the link can see the password with a network sniffer. MD5 crytographic hash uses a hash instead, so the password is never sent out the wire, and this technique is widely accepted as being the more secure mode.

OSPF authentication operates on an interface-by-interface basis or all interfaces in an area. The password is set only as an interface parameter and must be set for every interface. Missing an interface sets the default password to a null value.

Plaintext authentication is enabled for an OSPF area with the command **area** *area-id* **authentication**, and the interface parameter command **ip ospf authentication** sets plaintext authentication only on that interface. The plaintext password is configured with the interface parameter command **ip ospf authentication-key** *password*.

Example 8-31 displays plaintext authentication on NX-1's Ethernet1/1 interface and all Area 0 interfaces on NX-2 using both commands explained previously.

Example 8-31 *OSPF Plaintext Authentication*

```
NX-1# conf t
Enter configuration commands, one per line. End with CNTL/Z.
NX-1(config)# int eth1/1
NX-1(config-if)# ip ospf authentication
NX-1(config-if)# ip ospf authentication-key CISCO
NX-1 %OSPF-4-AUTH_ERR:  ospf-NXOS [8792] (default) Received packet from 10.12.1.200
  on Ethernet1/1 with bad authentication 0
```

```
NX-2# conf t
Enter configuration commands, one per line. End with CNTL/Z.
NX-2(config)# router ospf NXOS
NX-2(config-router)# area 0 authentication
NX-2(config-router)# int eth1/1
NX-2(config-if)# ip ospf authentication-key CISCO
```

Notice the authentication error that NX-1 produced upon enabling authentication. When there is a mismatch of OSPF authentication parameters, the Nexus switch produces the syslog message that contains *bad authentication*, which requires verification of the authentication settings.

Authentication is verified by looking at the OSPF interface and looking for the authentication option. Example 8-32 verifies the use of OSPF plaintext passwords on NX-1 and NX-2 interfaces.

Example 8-32 *Verification of OSPF Plaintext Authentication*

```
NX-1# show ip ospf interface
 Ethernet1/1 is up, line protocol is up
    IP address 10.12.1.100/24
    Process ID NXOS VRF default, area 0.0.0.0
    Enabled by interface configuration
    State P2P, Network type P2P, cost 4
    Index 2, Transmit delay 1 sec
    0 Neighbors, flooding to 0, adjacent with 0
    Timer intervals: Hello 10, Dead 40, Wait 40, Retransmit 5
      Hello timer due in 00:00:06
    Simple authentication
    Number of opaque link LSAs: 0, checksum sum 0
```

```
NX-2# show ip ospf interface | i protocol|authent
 Ethernet1/1 is up, line protocol is up
    Simple authentication
 VLAN20 is down, line protocol is down
    Simple authentication
 loopback0 is up, line protocol is up
```

It is important to note that the password is stored in encrypted format. It may be easier to reconfigure the password when explicitly configured on an interface. Example 8-33 displays how the password can be viewed.

Example 8-33 *Viewing OSPF Password for Simple Authentication*

```
NX-2# sho run ospf
! Output omitted for brevity
router ospf NXOS
  router-id 192.168.200.200
  area 0.0.0.0 authentication

interface loopback0
  ip router ospf NXOS area 0.0.0.0

interface Ethernet1/1
  ip ospf authentication-key 3 bdd0c1a345e1c285
  ip router ospf NXOS area 0.0.0.0
```

MD5 authentication is enabled for an OSPF area with the command **area** *area-id* **authentication message-digest**, and the interface parameter command **ip ospf authentication message-digest** sets MD5 authentication for that interface. The MD5 password is configured with the interface parameter command **ip ospf message-digest-key** *key#* **md5** *password* or set by using a key-chain with the command **ip ospf authentication key-chain** *key-chain-name*. The MD5 authentication is a hash of the key number and password combined. If the keys do not match, the hash is different between the nodes.

> **Note** Detailed instruction on key chain creation was provided in Chapter 7, "Troubleshooting Enhanced Interior Gateway Routing Protocol (EIGRP)."

Example 8-34 displays encrypted OSPF authentication on NX-1's Ethernet1/1 interface and all Area 0 interfaces on NX-2 using both commands previously explained. NX-2 is using a key chain to maintain the password.

Example 8-34 *OSPF Encrypted Authentication*

```
NX-1# conf t
Enter configuration commands, one per line. End with CNTL/Z.
NX-1(config)# int eth1/1
NX-1(config-if)# ip ospf authentication message-digest
NX-1(config-if)# ip ospf message-digest-key 2 md5 CISCO

NX-2# conf t
NX-2(config)# key chain OSPF-AUTH
```

```
NX-2(config-keychain)# key 2
NX-2(config-keychain-key)# key-string CISCO
NX-2(config-keychain-key)# router ospf NXOS
NX-2(config-router)# area 0 authentication message-digest
NX-2(config-router)# int eth1/1
NX-2(config-if)# ip ospf authentication key-chain OSPF-AUTH
```

Example 8-35 provides verification that encrypted password authentication is enabled. NX-2 directly states the key-chain name used for authentication. Notice how VLAN20 on NX-2 has encrypted authentication enabled, but a password is not identified. This is because it is still using the default key id of zero.

Example 8-35 *Verification of OSPF Encrypted Authentication*

```
NX-1# show ip ospf interface | i protocol|auth
Ethernet1/1 is up, line protocol is up
   Message-digest authentication, using key id 2
VLAN10 is up, line protocol is up
   No authentication
loopback0 is up, line protocol is up
```

```
NX-2# show ip ospf interface | i protocol|auth
Ethernet1/1 is up, line protocol is up
   Message-digest authentication, using keychain OSPF-AUTH (ready)
VLAN20 is down, line protocol is down
   Message-digest authentication, using default key id 0
loopback0 is up, line protocol is up
```

A benefit to using keychains is that passwords are verified as shown in Example 8-36. This allows for network engineers to examine a password, versus forcing them to reenter the password.

Example 8-36 *Viewing Keychain Passwords*

```
NX-2# show key chain OSPF-AUTH
Key-Chain OSPF-AUTH
  Key 2 -- text 7 "072c087f6d26"
    accept lifetime (always valid) [active]
    send lifetime (always valid) [active]
```

```
NX-2# show key chain OSPF-AUTH mode decrypt
Key-Chain OSPF-AUTH
  Key 2 -- text 0 "CISCO"
    accept lifetime (always valid) [active]
    send lifetime (always valid) [active]
```

Upon enabling authentication, it is important to check the syslog for error messages that indicate *bad authentication*. For those that do, the authentication options and password need to be verified on all peers for that network link.

Troubleshooting Missing Routes

After explaining how to troubleshoot OSPF adjacencies, this chapter explains how to troubleshoot missing routes.

Discontiguous Network

Network engineers who do not fully understand OSPF design may create a topology such as the one illustrated in Figure 8-3. Although NX-2 and NX-3 have OSPF interfaces in Area 0, traffic from Area 12 must cross Area 23 to reach Area 34. An OSPF network with this design is discontiguous because interarea traffic is trying to cross a nonbackbone area.

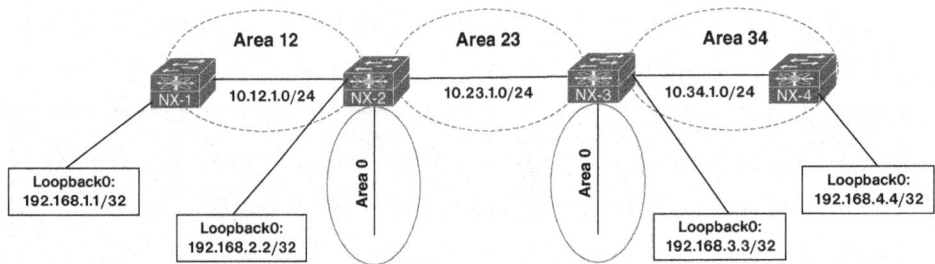

Figure 8-3 *Discontiguous Network*

Example 8-37 shows that NX-2 and NX-3 appear to have full connectivity to all networks in the OSPF domain. NX-2 maintains connectivity to the 10.34.1.0/24 network and 192.168.4.4/32 network, and NX-3 maintains connectivity to the 10.12.1.0/24 network and 192.168.1.1/32 network.

Example 8-37 *Verification of Remote Area Routes on NX-2 and NX-3*

```
NX-2# show ip route ospf-NXOS
! Output omitted for brevity

10.34.1.0/24, ubest/mbest: 1/0
    *via 10.23.1.3, Eth1/2, [110/80], 00:02:56, ospf-NXOS, inter
192.168.1.1/32, ubest/mbest: 1/0
    *via 10.12.1.1, Eth1/1, [110/41], 00:04:37, ospf-NXOS, intra
192.168.3.3/32, ubest/mbest: 1/0
    *via 10.23.1.3, Eth1/2, [110/41], 00:06:14, ospf-NXOS, inter
```

```
    192.168.4.4/32, ubest/mbest: 1/0
        *via 10.23.1.3, Eth1/2, [110/81], 00:02:35, ospf-NXOS, inter

NX-3# show ip route ospf
! Output omitted for brevity

10.12.1.0/24, ubest/mbest: 1/0
    *via 10.23.1.2, Eth1/2, [110/80], 00:07:29, ospf-NXOS, inter
192.168.1.1/32, ubest/mbest: 1/0
    *via 10.23.1.2, Eth1/2, [110/81], 00:06:10, ospf-NXOS, inter
192.168.2.2/32, ubest/mbest: 1/0
    *via 10.23.1.2, Eth1/2, [110/41], 00:07:29, ospf-NXOS, inter
192.168.4.4/32, ubest/mbest: 1/0
    *via 10.34.1.4, Eth1/1, [110/41], 00:04:14, ospf-NXOS, intra
```

Example 8-38 shows the route tables for NX-1 and NX-4. NX-1 is missing route entries for Area 34, and NX-4 is missing route entries for Area 12. When Area 12's Type-1 LSAs reach NX-2, NX-2 generates a Type-3 LSA into Area 0 and Area 23. NX-3 receives the Type-3 LSA and inserts it into the LSDB for Area 23. NX-3 does not create a new Type-3 LSA for Area 0 or Area 34.

Example 8-38 *Verification of Remote Area Routes on NX-1 and NX-4*

```
NX-1# show ip route ospf
! Output omitted for brevity

10.23.1.0/24, ubest/mbest: 1/0
    *via 10.12.1.2, Eth1/1, [110/80], 00:13:12, ospf-NXOS, inter
192.168.2.2/32, ubest/mbest: 1/0
    *via 10.12.1.2, Eth1/1, [110/41], 00:13:12, ospf-NXOS, inter

NX-4# show ip route ospf
! Output omitted for brevity

10.23.1.0/24, ubest/mbest: 1/0
    *via 10.34.1.3, Eth1/1, [110/80], 00:11:54, ospf-NXOS, inter
192.168.3.3/32, ubest/mbest: 1/0
    *via 10.34.1.3, Eth1/1, [110/41], 00:11:54, ospf-NXOS, inter
```

OSPF ABRs use the following logic for Type-3 LSAs when entering another OSPF Area:

- Type-1 LSAs received from a nonbackbone area create Type-3 LSAs into backbone area and nonbackbone areas.
- Type-3 LSAs received from Area 0 are created for the nonbackbone area.

484   Chapter 8: Troubleshooting Open Shortest Path First (OSPF)

- Type-3 LSAs received from a nonbackbone area only insert into the LSDB for the source area. ABRs do not create a Type-3 LSA for the other nonbackbone areas.

The simplest fix for a discontiguous network is to install a virtual link between NX-2 and NX-3. Virtual links overcome the ABR limitations by extending Area 0 into a nonbackbone area. It is similar to running a virtual tunnel for OSPF between an ABR and another multi-area OSPF router. The virtual link extends Area 0 across Area 23, making Area 0 a contiguous OSPF area.

The virtual link configuration is applied to the OSPF routing process with the command **area** *area-id* **virtual-link** *endpoint-rid*. The configuration is applied on both end devices as shown in Example 8-39.

Example 8-39 *Virtual Link Configuration*

```
NX-2
router ospf NXOS
  area 0.0.0.23 virtual-link 192.168.3.3

NX-3
router ospf NXOS
  area 0.0.0.23 virtual-link 192.168.2.2
```

Example 8-40 displays the routing table of NX-1 after the virtual link is configured between NX-2 and NX-3. Notice that the 192.168.4.4 network is present. In addition, the virtual link appears as an OSPF interface.

Example 8-40 *Verification of Connectivity After Virtual Link*

```
NX-1# show ip route ospf
! Output omitted for brevity

10.23.1.0/24, ubest/mbest: 1/0
    *via 10.12.1.2, Eth1/1, [110/80], 00:22:47, ospf-NXOS, inter
10.34.1.0/24, ubest/mbest: 1/0
    *via 10.12.1.2, Eth1/1, [110/120], 00:00:13, ospf-NXOS, inter
192.168.2.2/32, ubest/mbest: 1/0
    *via 10.12.1.2, Eth1/1, [110/41], 00:22:47, ospf-NXOS, inter
192.168.3.3/32, ubest/mbest: 1/0
    *via 10.12.1.2, Eth1/1, [110/81], 00:00:13, ospf-NXOS, inter
192.168.4.4/32, ubest/mbest: 1/0
    *via 10.12.1.2, Eth1/1, [110/121], 00:00:13, ospf-NXOS, inter

NX-2# show ip ospf interface brief
 OSPF Process ID NXOS VRF default
```

```
Total number of interface: 4
Interface              ID     Area         Cost    State       Neighbors  Status
VL1                    4      0.0.0.0      40      P2P         1          up
Eth1/1                 1      0.0.0.12     40      P2P         1          up
Eth1/2                 2      0.0.0.23     40      P2P         1          up
Lo0                    3      0.0.0.0      1       LOOPBACK    0          up
```

Duplicate Router ID

Router IDs (RID) play a critical role for the creation of the topology. If two adjacent routers have the same RID, an adjacency does not form as shown earlier. However, if two routers have the same RID and have an intermediary router, it prevents those routes from being installed in the topology.

The RID act as a unique identifier in the OSPF LSAs. When two different routers advertise LSAs with the same RID, it causes confusion in the OSPF topology, which can result in routes not populating or packets being forwarded toward the wrong router. It also prevent LSA propagation because the receiving router may assume that a loop exists.

Figure 8-4 provides a sample topology in which all Nexus switches are advertising their peering network and their loopback addresses in the 192.168.0.0/16 network space. NX-2 and NX-4 have been configured with the same RID of 192.168.4.4. NX-3 sits between NX-2 and NX-4 and has a different RID, therefore allowing NX-2 and NX-4 to establish full neighbor adjacencies with their peers.

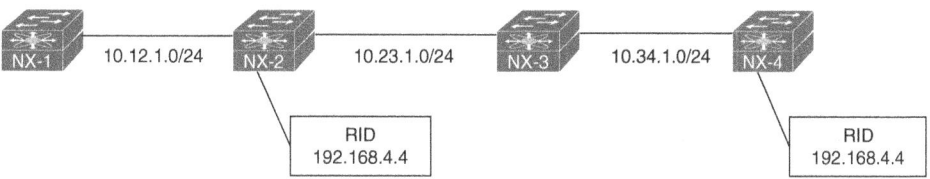

Figure 8-4 *Duplicate Router ID Topology*

From NX-1's perspective, the first apparent issue is that NX-4's loopback interface (192.168.4.4/32) is missing. Example 8-41 displays NX-1's routing table.

Example 8-41 *NX-1's Routing Table with Missing NX-4's Loopback Interface*

```
NX-1# show ip route ospf
! Output omitted for brevity

10.23.1.0/24, ubest/mbest: 1/0
    *via 10.12.1.2, Eth1/1, [110/80], 2d08h, ospf-NXOS, intra
10.34.1.0/24, ubest/mbest: 1/0
    *via 10.12.1.2, Eth1/1, [110/120], 2d08h, ospf-NXOS, intra
```

```
192.168.2.2/32, ubest/mbest: 1/0
    *via 10.12.1.2, Eth1/1, [110/41], 2d08h, ospf-NXOS, intra
192.168.3.3/32, ubest/mbest: 1/0
    *via 10.12.1.2, Eth1/1, [110/81], 2d08h, ospf-NXOS, intra
```

On NX-2 and NX-4, there are complaints about LSAs and *Possible router-id collision* syslog messages, as shown in Example 8-42.

Example 8-42 *Syslog Messages with LSAs with Duplicate RIDs*

```
05:15:23 NX-2 %OSPF-4-SELF_LSA:  ospf-NXOS [9225]   context default: Received updated
  self-originated router LSA. Possible router-id collision
05:16:55 NX-4 %OSPF-4-SELF_LSA:  ospf-NXOS [8486]   context default: Received updated
  self-originated router LSA. Possible router-id collision
```

Example 8-43 displays the routing table of the two Nexus switches with the *Possible router-id collision* syslog messages. Notice that NX-2 is missing NX-1's loopback interface (192.168.1.1/32) and NX-4's loopback interface (192.168.4.4/32); whereas NX-4 is missing the 10.12.1.0/24 and NX-2's loopback interface (192.168.2.2/32) network interface.

Example 8-43 *Routing Tables of NX-2 and NX-4*

```
NX-2# show ip route ospf
! Output omitted for brevity

10.34.1.0/24, ubest/mbest: 1/0
    *via 10.23.1.3, Eth1/2, [110/80], 2d08h, ospf-NXOS, intra
192.168.1.1/32, ubest/mbest: 1/0
    *via 10.12.1.1, Eth1/1, [110/41], 2d08h, ospf-NXOS, intra
192.168.3.3/32, ubest/mbest: 1/0
    *via 10.23.1.3, Eth1/2, [110/41], 2d08h, ospf-NXOS, intra

NX-4# show ip route ospf
! Output omitted for brevity

10.23.1.0/24, ubest/mbest: 1/0
    *via 10.34.1.3, Eth1/1, [110/80], 2d08h, ospf-NXOS, intra
192.168.3.3/32, ubest/mbest: 1/0
    *via 10.34.1.3, Eth1/1, [110/41], 2d08h, ospf-NXOS, intra
```

A quick check of the RIDs is done by examining the OSPF processes on both Nexus switches that reported the *Possible router-id collision* using the **show ip ospf** command. Notice that in Example 8-44, NX-2 and NX-4 have the same RID.

Example 8-44 *Syslog Messages with LSAs with Duplicate RIDs*

```
NX-2# show ip ospf | i ID
 Routing Process NXOS with ID 192.168.4.4 VRF default
```

```
NX-4# show ip ospf | i ID
 Routing Process NXOS with ID 192.168.4.4 VRF default
```

Remember that the RID can be dynamically set or statically set. Generally, this problem is a result of a configuration being copied from one router to another and not changing the RID. The RID is changed using the command **router-id** *router-id* under the OSPF process. The OSPF process restarts upon changing the RID on a Nexus switch.

Filtering Routes

NX-OS provides multiple methods of filtering networks after they are entered into the OSPF database. Filtering of routes occurs on ABRs for internal OSPF networks and ASBRs for external OSPF networks. The following includes some configurations that should be examined when routes are present in one area but not present in a different area.

- **Area Filtration:** Routes are filtered upon receipt or advertisement to an ABR with the process level configuration command **area** *area-id* **filter-list route-map** *route-map-name* {**in**|**out**}.

- **Route Summarization:** Internal routes are summarized on ABRs using the command **area** *area-id* **range** *summary-network* [**not-advertise**]. If the not-advertise keyword is configured, a Type-3 LSA is not generated for any of the component routes; thereby hiding them to only the area of origination.

External routes are summarized on ASBRs using the command **summary-address** *summary-network* [**not-advertise**]. The not-advertise keyword stops the generation of any Type-5/Type-7 LSAs for component routes within the summary network.

Note ABRs for NSSA areas act as an ASBR when the Type 7 LSAs are converted to Type 5 LSA. External summarization is performed only on ABRs when they match this scenario.

Redistribution

Redistributing into OSPF uses the command **redistribute** [**bgp** *asn* | **direct** | **eigrp** *process-tag* | **isis** *process-tag* | **ospf** *process-tag* | **rip** *process-tag* | **static**] **route-map** *route-map-name*. A route-map is required as part of the redistribution process on Nexus switches.

Every protocol provides a seed metric at the time of redistribution that allows the destination protocol to calculate a best path. OSPF uses the following default settings for seed metrics:

- The network is configured as an OSPF Type-2 external network.
- The default redistribution metric is set to 20 unless the source protocol is BGP which provides a default seed metric of 1.

The default seed metrics can be changed to different values for OSPF external network type (1 versus 2), redistribution metric, and a route-tag if desired.

Example 8-45 provides the necessary configuration to demonstrate the process of redistribution. NX-1 redistributes the connected routes for 10.1.1.0/24 and 10.11.11.0/24 in lieu of them being advertised with the OSPF routing protocol. Notice that the route-map can be a simple permit statement without any conditional matches.

Example 8-45 *NX-1 Redistribution Configuration*

```
router ospf NXOS
  redistribute direct route-map REDIST
!
route-map REDIST permit 10
```

OSPF Forwarding Address

OSPF Type-5 LSAs include a field known as the *forwarding address* that optimizes forwarding traffic when the source uses a shared network segment. The forwarding address scenario defined in RFC 2328 is not common, but Figure 8-5 provides a sample topology. The following is included in this topology:

- OSPF is enabled on all the links in Area 0 (10.13.1.0/24, 10.24.1.0/24, and 10.34.1.0/24).
- Users are trying to connect to the proxy server that is located in a DMZ (172.16.1.1) off of the firewall.
- NX-1 has a static route for the 172.16.1.0/24 network pointing toward the firewall (10.120.1.10).
- NX-1 is redistributing the route into OSPF as a Type-1 External route.
- NX-1 and NX-2 have direct connectivity using VLAN 120 (10.120.1.0/24) to the firewall.

Example 8-46 displays NX-1's configuration for advertising the 172.16.1.0/24 network into the OSPF domain. In addition, NX-1's static route is verified for installation into the OSPF database and is then checked on NX-3.

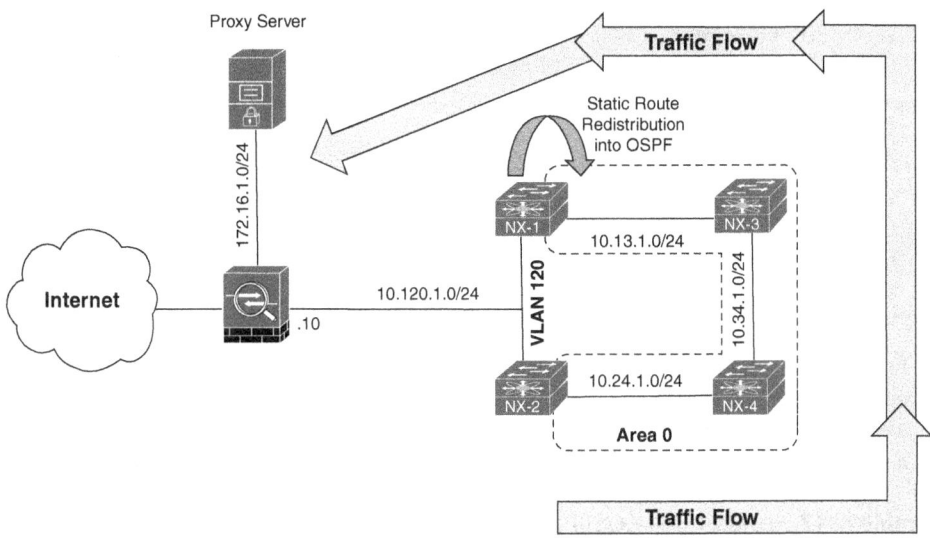

Figure 8-5 *Default OSPF Forwarding Address*

Example 8-46 *NX-1 Configuration to Redistribute 172.16.1.0/24 into OSPF*

```
NX-1
ip route 172.16.1.0/24 10.120.1.10
!
route-map REDIST permit 10
  set metric-type type-1
!
router ospf NXOS
  redistribute static route-map REDIST
  log-adjacency-changes
!
 interface Ethernet1/1
   ip router ospf NXOS area 0.0.0.0

NX-1# show ip route
! Output omitted for brevity
10.13.1.0/24, ubest/mbest: 1/0, attached
    *via 10.13.1.1, Eth2/1, [0/0], 00:09:19, direct
..
10.120.1.0/24, ubest/mbest: 1/0, attached
    *via 10.120.1.1, Eth2/9, [0/0], 00:09:15, direct
..
```

```
172.16.1.0/24, ubest/mbest: 1/0
    *via 10.120.1.10, [1/0], 00:09:15, static
```

```
NX-3# show ip route ospf-NXOS
! Output omitted for brevity
10.24.1.0/24, ubest/mbest: 1/0
    *via 10.34.1.4, Eth2/2, [110/80], 00:09:57, ospf-NXOS, intra
172.16.1.0/24, ubest/mbest: 1/0
    *via 10.13.1.1, Eth2/1, [110/60], 00:02:30, ospf-NXOS, type-1
```

Example 8-47 displays the Type-5 LSA for the external route for the 172.16.1.0/24 network to the proxy server. The ASBR is identified as NX-1 (192.168.1.1), which is the device that all Nexus switches forward packets to in order to reach the 172.16.1.0/24 network. Notice that the forwarding address is the default value of 0.0.0.0.

Example 8-47 *Default FA in OSPF Type-5 LSA*

```
NX-4# show ip ospf database external detail
        OSPF Router with ID (192.168.4.4) (Process ID NXOS VRF default)

            Type-5 AS External Link States

   LS age: 199
   Options: 0x2 (No TOS-capability, No DC)
   LS Type: Type-5 AS-External
   Link State ID: 172.16.1.0 (Network address)
   Advertising Router: 192.168.1.1
   LS Seq Number: 0x80000002
   Checksum: 0x7c98
   Length: 36
   Network Mask: /24
        Metric Type: 1 (Same units as link state path)
        TOS: 0
        Metric: 20
        Forward Address: 0.0.0.0
        External Route Tag: 0
```

```
NX-1# show ip ospf | i ID
 Routing Process NXOS with ID 192.168.1.1 VRF default
```

Traffic from NX-2 (and NX-4) takes the non-optimal route (NX-2→NX-4→NX-3→ NX-1→FW), as shown in Example 8-48. The optimal route would allow NX-2 to use the directly connected 10.120.1.0/24 network toward the firewall.

Example 8-48 *Verification of Suboptimal Routing*

```
NX-2# trace 172.16.1.1
traceroute to 172.16.1.1 (172.16.1.1), 30 hops max, 40 byte packets
 1  10.24.1.4 (10.24.1.4)  1.402 ms  1.369 ms  1.104 ms
 2  10.34.1.3 (10.34.1.3)  2.886 ms  2.846 ms
 3  10.13.1.1 (10.13.1.1)  4.052 ms  3.527 ms  3.659 ms
 4  10.120.1.10 (10.120.1.10)  5.221 ms *
```

```
NX-4# trace 172.16.1.1
traceroute to 172.16.1.1 (172.16.1.1), 30 hops max, 40 byte packets
 1  10.34.1.3 (10.34.1.3)  1.485 ms  1.29 ms  1.18 ms
 2  10.13.1.1 (10.13.1.1)  2.385 ms  2.34 ms  2.478 ms
 3  10.120.1.10 (10.120.1.10)  3.856 ms * *
```

The forwarding address in OSPF Type-5 LSAs is specified in RFC 2328 for scenarios such as this. When the forwarding address is 0.0.0.0, all routers forward packets to the ASBR, introducing the potential for suboptimal routing.

The OSPF forwarding address changes from 0.0.0.0 to the next-hop IP address in the source routing protocol when the following occurs:

- OSPF is enabled on the ASBR's interface that points to the next-hop IP address. In this scenario, NX-1's VLAN120 interface has OSPF enabled, which correlates to the 172.16.1.0/24 static route's next-hop address of 10.120.1.10.

- That interface is not set to passive.

- That interface is a broadcast or nonbroadcast OSPF network type.

Now OSPF is enabled on the NX-1's and NX-2's VLAN120 interface, which has been associated to area 120. Figure 8-6 illustrates the current topology. VLAN interfaces default to the broadcast OSPF network type, and all conditions were met to set the FA to an explicit IP address.

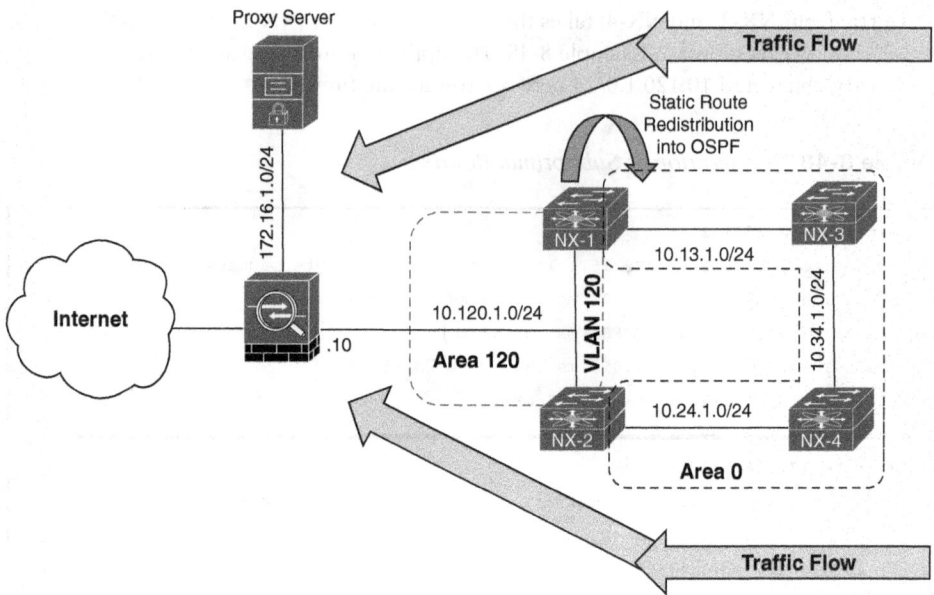

Figure 8-6 *OSPF Forwarding Address Nondefault*

Example 8-49 displays the Type-5 LSA for the 172.16.1.0/24 network. Now that OSPF is enabled on NX-1's 10.120.1.1 interface and the interface is a broadcast network type, the forwarding address changed from 0.0.0.0 to 10.120.1.10.

Example 8-49 *Viewing the Nondefault OSPF Forwarding Address*

```
NX-2# show ip ospf database external detail
! Output omitted for brevity

        OSPF Router with ID (192.168.2.2) (Process ID NXOS VRF default)

            Type-5 AS External Link States

LS Type: Type-5 AS-External
Link State ID: 172.16.1.0 (Network address)
Advertising Router: 192.168.1.1
Network Mask: /24
      Metric Type: 1 (Same units as link state path)
      TOS: 0
      Metric: 20
      Forward Address: 10.120.1.10
      External Route Tag: 0
```

Example 8-50 verifies that connectivity from NX-2 and NX-4 now takes the optimal path because the forwarding address changed to 10.120.1.10.

Example 8-50 *Verification of Optimal Routing*

```
NX-2# traceroute 172.16.1.1
traceroute to 172.16.1.1 (172.16.1.1), 30 hops max, 40 byte packets
 1  10.120.1.10 (10.120.1.10)  2.845 ms  *  3.618 ms
```

```
NX-4# traceroute 172.16.1.1
traceroute to 172.16.1.1 (172.16.1.1), 30 hops max, 40 byte packets
 1  10.24.1.2 (10.24.1.2)  1.539 ms  1.288 ms  1.071 ms
 2  10.120.1.10 (10.120.1.10)  3.4 ms  *  3.727 ms
```

A junior network engineer identified that the 10.120.1.0/24 network is no longer needed. The engineer implemented filtering on Area 120 LSAs from being advertised into Area 0, as shown in Example 8-51.

Example 8-51 *Configuration to Filter 10.120.1.10 Network in OSPF*

```
NX-1
router ospf NXOS
  redistribute static route-map REDIST
  area 0.0.0.120 range 10.0.0.0/8 not-advertise
  log-adjacency-changes
```

```
NX-2
router ospf NXOS
  area 0.0.0.120 range 10.0.0.0/8 not-advertise
  log-adjacency-changes
```

After the junior network engineer made the change, the 172.16.1.0/24 network disappeared on all the routers in Area 0. Only the other peering network is present, as shown in Example 8-52.

Example 8-52 *Verification of Missing 172.16.1.0/24 Network*

```
NX-3# show ip route ospf
! Output omitted for brevity

10.24.1.0/24, ubest/mbest: 1/0
    *via 10.34.1.4, Eth1/2, [110/80], 00:23:31, ospf-NXOS, intra
```

```
NX-4# show ip route ospf
```

```
! Output omitted for brevity

10.13.1.0/24, ubest/mbest: 1/0
    *via 10.34.1.3, Eth1/2, [110/80], 00:23:42, ospf-NXOS, intra
```

If the Type-5 LSA forwarding address is not a default value, the address must be an intra-area or inter-area OSPF route. If the FA is not resolved, the LSA is ignored and does not install into the RIB. The FA provides a mechanism to introduce multiple paths to the external next-hop address. Otherwise, there is not a reason to include the FA in the LSA. Removing the filtering on NX-1 and NX-2 restores connectivity.

Note In the scenario provided, there was not any redundancy to provide connectivity in the event that NX-1 failed. Typically, the configuration is repeated on other routers, which provides resiliency. Be considerate of the external networks when applying filtering of routes on ABRs.

Troubleshooting OSPF Path Selection

OSPF executes *Dijkstra's Shortest Path First (SPF)* algorithm to create a loop-free topology of shortest paths. All routers use the same logic to calculate the shortest path for each network. Path selection prioritizes paths by using the following order of path selection:

- Intra-Area
- Inter-Area
- External Type-1
- External Type-2

The following sections explain each component in detail.

Intra-Area Routes

Routes advertised via a Type-1 LSA for an Area are always preferred over Type-3 and Type-5 LSAs. If multiple intra-area routes exist, the path with the lowest total path metric is installed in the RIB. If there is a tie in metric, both routes install into the RIB.

Note Even if the path metric from an intra-area route is higher than an inter-area path metric; the intra-area path is selected.

Inter-Area Routes

Inter-area routes take the lowest total path metric to the destination. If there is a tie in metric, both routes install into the RIB. All inter-area paths for a route must go through Area 0.

In Figure 8-7, NX-1 is computing the path to NX-6. NX-1 uses the path NX-1→NX-3→NX-5→NX-6 because its total path metric is 35 versus the NX-1→NX-2→NX-4→NX-6 path with a metric of 40.

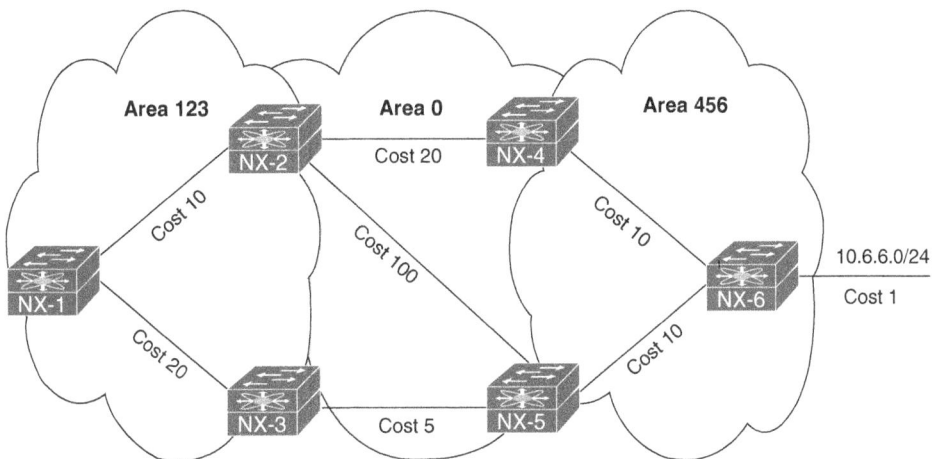

Figure 8-7 *Inter-Area Route Selection*

External Route Selection

Earlier in this chapter, OSPF external routes were briefly explained as Type-1 or Type-2. The main differences between Type-1 and Type-2 external OSPF routes include the following:

- Type-1 routes are preferred over Type-2.
- The Type-1 path metric equals the following: redistribution metric + total path metric to reach the ASBR.
- The Type-2 path metrics equals only the redistribution metric.

Another critical factor to identify is whether the devices are operating in RFC 1583 or RFC 2328 mode. Cisco NX-OS switches operate in 2328 mode by default, whereas Cisco IOS, IOS XE, and IOS XR operate only in 1583 mode. The following subsection explains the path selection logic depending on whether the device is operating in RFC 1583 or RFC 2328 mode.

E1 and N1 External Routes

The following are the differences in path selection for OSPF External Type-1 routes:

- **RFC 1583 Mode:** External OSPF Type-1 route calculation uses the redistribution metric + the lowest path metric to reach the ASBR that advertised the network. Type-1 path metrics are lower for routers closer to the originating ASBR, whereas generally the path metric is higher for a router 10 hops away from the ASBR.

  If there is a tie in the path metric, both routes install into the RIB. If the ASBR is in a different area, the path of the traffic must go through Area 0. An ABR router does not install an O E1 and O N1 route into the RIB at the same time. O N1 is given preference for a typical NSSA area and prevents the O E1 from installing on the ABR.

- **RFC 2328 Mode:** Preference first goes to the ASBR in the same area as the calculating router. In the event that the ASBR is not in the same area as the calculating router, the rules for calculating the best path follow those as RFC 1583 Mode.

Note There is an option with NSSA areas that prevents the redistributed routes from being advertised outside of the NSSA area (setting the P-bit to zero), which may change the behavior. This concept is outside of the scope of this book; it is explained in depth in RFC 2328 and 3101.

Figure 8-8 shows the topology for NX-1 and NX-3 computing a path to the external network (100.65.0.0/16) that is being redistributed on NX-6 and NX7.

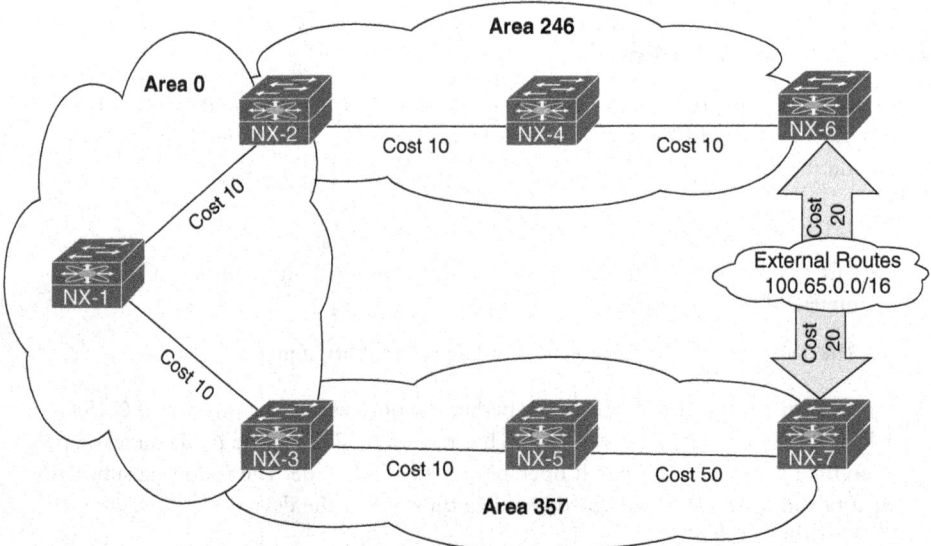

Figure 8-8 *External Type-2 Route Selection Topology*

The path NX-1→NX-2→NX-4→NX-6 has a metric of 50, which is less than the path NX-1→NX-3→NX-5→NX-7, which has a path metric of 90. NX-1 selects the NX-1→NX-2→NX-4→NX-6 path to reach the 100.65.0.0/16 network, whereas NX-3 selects the NX-3→NX-5→NX-7 path that has a higher metric.

The decisions were made based upon RFC 2328 logic because NX-1 is not in an area with an ASBR, whereas NX-3 is in the same area as NX-7. Example 8-53 displays the routing tables and path metrics from NX-1 and NX-3's perspective.

Example 8-53 *External OSPF Path Selection for Type-1 Networks*

```
NX-1# show ip route ospf | b 100.65
100.65.0.0/16, ubest/mbest: 1/0
    *via 10.12.1.2, Eth1/1, [110/50], 00:33:55, ospf-NXOS, type-1

NX-3# show ip route ospf | b 100.65
100.65.0.0/16, ubest/mbest: 1/0
    *via 10.35.1.5, Eth1/1, [110/80], 00:00:15, ospf-NXOS, type-1
```

E2 and N2 External Routes

Here are the differences in path selection for OSPF External Type-2 routes:

- **RFC 1583 Mode:** External OSPF Type-2 routes do not increment in metric respective of the path metric to the ASBR. If there is a tie in the redistribution metric, the router compares the forwarding cost. The forwarding cost is the metric to the ASBR that advertised the network, and the lower forwarding cost is preferred. If there is a tie in forwarding cost, both routes install into the routing table. An ABR router does not install an O E2 and O N2 route into the RIB at the same time. O N2 is given preference for a typical NSSA area and prevents the O E2 from installing on the ABR.

- **RFC 2328 Mode:** Preference first goes to the ASBR in the same area as the calculating router. In the event that the ASBR is not in the same area as the calculating router, the rules for calculating the best path follow those as RFC 1583 Mode.

Reusing the topology from Figure 8-6, all paths reflect a metric of 20. The first deciding step is to check to see if the ASBR for the 100.65.0.0/16 network is in the same area as the ASBR. NX-1 is not, so it selects the path based on forwarding cost. Forwarding cost is calculated on NX-OS.

Example 8-54 walks through the steps for calculating the forwarding cost.

Step 1. The ASBRs must be identified by looking at the OSPF LSDB with the command **show ip ospf database external** *network*.

Step 2. The metric reported by the ABR for the ASBR address (Type-4 LSA) is examined with the command **show ip ospf database asbr-summary detail**. (This provides the path metric from the ASBR to the area's ABR.)

498   Chapter 8: Troubleshooting Open Shortest Path First (OSPF)

Step 3. Find the metric to the ABR of the Type-4 LSA with the command **show ip ospf database router** *abr-ip-address* **detail**.

Step 4. Combine the two metrics to calculate a forwarding cost of 30 from NX-1 to NX-6, and a forwarding cost of 70 from NX-1 to NX-7. The path to NX-6 is the lowest and is selected by NX-1.

Example 8-54 *NX-1 External OSPF Path Selection for Type-2 Network*

```
NX-1# show ip route ospf | b 100.65
100.65.0.0/16, ubest/mbest: 1/0
    *via 10.12.1.2, Eth1/1, [110/20], 00:04:33, ospf-NXOS, type-2
```

```
NX-1# show ip ospf database external 100.65.0.0
        OSPF Router with ID (192.168.1.1) (Process ID NXOS VRF default)

                Type-5 AS External Link States

Link ID         ADV Router      Age     Seq#        Checksum Tag
100.65.0.0      192.168.6.6     31      0x80000002  0x277b    0
100.65.0.0      192.168.7.7     375     0x80000002  0x1a86    0
```

```
NX-1# show ip ospf database asbr-summary detail | i ID|Metric
        OSPF Router with ID (192.168.1.1) (Process ID NXOS VRF default)
    Link State ID: 192.168.6.6 (AS Boundary Router address)
      TOS:   0 Metric: 20
    Link State ID: 192.168.7.7 (AS Boundary Router address)
      TOS:   0 Metric: 60
```

```
NX-1# show ip ospf database router 192.168.2.2 detail | i Router|Metric
        OSPF Router with ID (192.168.1.1) (Process ID NXOS VRF default)
                Router Link States (Area 0.0.0.0)
    LS Type: Router Links
    Advertising Router: 192.168.2.2
      Link connected to: a Router (point-to-point)
     (Link ID) Neighboring Router ID: 192.168.1.1
     (Link Data) Router Interface address: 10.12.1.2
        TOS   0 Metric: 10
        TOS   0 Metric: 10
```

```
NX-1# show ip ospf database router 192.168.3.3 detail | i Router|Metric
        OSPF Router with ID (192.168.1.1) (Process ID NXOS VRF default)
                Router Link States (Area 0.0.0.0)
    LS Type: Router Links
    Advertising Router: 192.168.3.3
      Link connected to: a Router (point-to-point)
```

```
(Link ID) Neighboring Router ID: 192.168.1.1
(Link Data) Router Interface address: 10.13.1.3
    TOS   0 Metric: 10
    TOS   0 Metric: 10
```

NX-3's path is selected based on RFC 2328's guidelines because NX-3 is in the same area as NX-7. Example 8-55 confirms the path from NX-3 → NX-5 → NX-7.

Example 8-55 *NX-3 External OSPF Path Selection for Type-2 Network*

```
NX-3# show ip route ospf | b 100.65
100.65.0.0/16, ubest/mbest: 1/0
    *via 10.35.1.5, Eth1/1, [110/80], 00:00:15, ospf-NXOS, type-1
```

Problems with Intermixed RFC 1583 and RFC 2328 Devices

RFC 2328 logic is generally sufficient for finding the next-hop for external routes, but it could lead to suboptimal paths (as shown in the previous section) or cause routing loops when combined with devices that do not use RFC 2328 logic. Figure 8-9 displays a sample topology that creates a routing loop because IOS routers operate with RFC 1583 logic.

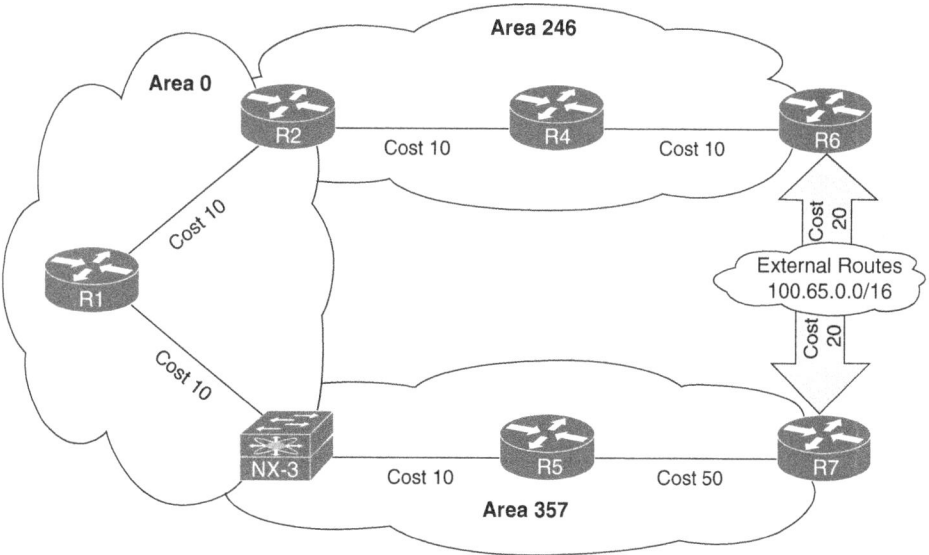

Figure 8-9 *External Type-2 Route Selection with Nexus and IOS Devices*

NX-3 selects R7 as the ASBR for the 100.65.0.0/16 network using RFC 2328 standards and forwards packets toward R5. R5 uses RFC 1583 standards and forwards packets back to NX-3, causing a loop. Example 8-56 verifies that the loop exists using a simple traceroute from NX-3 toward the 100.65.0.0/16 network.

Example 8-56 *Routing Loop Because of Intermixed OSPF Devices*

```
NX-3# trace 100.65.1.1
traceroute to 100.65.1.1 (100.65.1.1), 30 hops max, 40 byte packets
 1  10.35.1.5 (10.35.1.5)  1.819 ms  1.124 ms  0.982 ms
 2  10.35.1.3 (10.35.1.3)  1.9 ms  1.459 ms  1.534 ms
 3  10.35.1.5 (10.35.1.5)  2.427 ms  2.214 ms  2.111 ms
```

The solution involves placing the Nexus switches into RFC 1583 mode with the OSPF command **rfc1583compatibility**. Example 8-57 displays the configuration to remove the routing loop.

Example 8-57 *Verification of RFC1583 Compatibility*

```
NX-3# show run ospf
! Output omitted for brevity
router ospf NXOS
  rfc1583compatibility
```

Note Another significant change between RFC 1583 and RFC 2328 is the summarization metric. With RFC 1583, an ABR uses the lowest metric from any of the component routes for the metric of the summarized network. RFC 2328 uses the highest metric from any of the component routes for the metric of the summarized route. Deploying **rfc1583compatibility** on the ABR changes the behavior.

Interface Link Costs

Interface cost is essential component for Dijkstra's SPF calculation because the shortest path metric is based on the cumulative interface cost (metric) from the router to the destination. OSPF assigns the OSPF link cost (metric) for an interface using the following formula:

Cost = Interface Bandwidth/Reference Bandwidth

The default reference bandwidth for NX-OS is 40 Gbps, whereas for other Cisco OSs (IOS and IOS XR) it is 100 Mbps. Table 8-9 provides the OSPF cost for common network interface types using the default reference bandwidth.

Troubleshooting OSPF Path Selection

Table 8-9 *OSPF Interface Costs Using Default Settings*

Interface Type	Default NX-OS OSPF Cost	Default IOS OSPF Cost
T1	N/A	64
Ethernet	4000	10
FastEthernet	400	1
GigabitEthernet	40	1
10-GigabitEthernet	4	1
40-GigabitEthernet	1	1
100-GigabitEthernet	1	1

Notice in Table 8-9 that there is no differentiation in the link cost associated to a FastEthernet interface and a 100-Gigabit Ethernet interface on IOS routers. This can result in suboptimal path selection and is magnified when a NX-OS switch is inserted into a path.

Figure 8-10 displays a topology that introduces problems because of the reference bandwidth not being set properly. Connectivity between the two WAN service providers should take the 10 Gigabit Path (R1→NX-3→NX-4→R2) and use the 1 Gigabit link between R1 and R2 only as a backup path, because traffic is likely be dropped by the QoS policy to support only business-critical traffic.

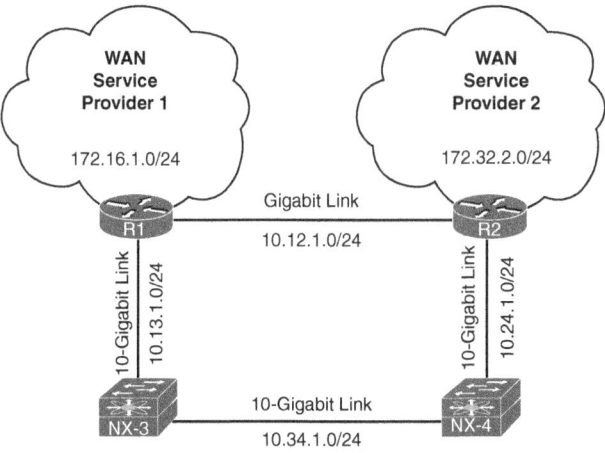

Figure 8-10 *Topology to Demonstrate Problems with Reference Bandwidth*

Example 8-58 displays the routing table of R1 with the default reference bandwidth. Traffic between 172.16.1.0/24 and 172.32.2.0/24 flows across the backup 1 Gigabit link (10.12.1.0/24), which does not follow the intended traffic patterns. Notice that the OSPF path metric is 2 to the 172.32.2.0/24 network using the 1 Gigabit link.

Example 8-58 *R1's Routing Table with Default OSPF Auto-Cost Bandwidth*

```
R1# show ip route ospf | b Gate
Gateway of last resort is not set

      10.0.0.0/8 is variably subnetted, 6 subnets, 2 masks
O        10.24.1.0/24 [110/2] via 10.12.1.2, 00:10:24, GigabitEthernet0/1
O        10.34.1.0/24 [110/5] via 10.13.1.3, 00:10:09, TenGigabitEthernet1/2
      172.32.0.0/24 is subnetted, 1 subnets
O        172.32.2.0 [110/2] via 10.12.1.2, 00:03:20, GigabitEthernet0/1
```

Now let's shut down the 1 Gigabit link and examine the OSPF metrics using the 10 Gigabit path. Example 8-59 displays the process. Notice that R1's path metric is 10 to the 172.32.2.0/24 network using the 10 Gigabit link path.

Example 8-59 *R1's Routing Table with 1 Gigabit Link Shutdown*

```
R1# conf t
Enter configuration commands, one per line. End with CNTL/Z.
R1(config)# int gi0/1
R1(config-if)# shut
16:04:43.107: %OSPF-5-ADJCHG: Process 1, Nbr 192.168.2.2 on GigabitEthernet0/1 from
  FULL to DOWN, Neighbor Down: Interface down or detached
16:04:45.077: %LINK-5-CHANGED: Interface GigabitEthernet0/1, changed state to
  administratively down
16:04:46.077: %LINEPROTO-5-UPDOWN: Line protocol on Interface GigabitEthernet0/1,
  changed state to down
R1(config-if)# do show ip route ospf | b Gatewa
Gateway of last resort is not set

      10.0.0.0/8 is variably subnetted, 5 subnets, 2 masks
O        10.12.1.0/24 [110/10] via 10.13.1.3, 00:00:09, TenGigabitEthernet1/2
O        10.24.1.0/24 [110/9] via 10.13.1.3, 00:00:09, TenGigabitEthernet1/2
O        10.34.1.0/24 [110/5] via 10.13.1.3, 00:11:40, TenGigabitEthernet1/2
      172.32.0.0/24 is subnetted, 1 subnets
O        172.32.2.0 [110/10] via 10.13.1.3, 00:00:09, TenGigabitEthernet1/2
```

R1 and R2 are taking the suboptimal path because of the differences in reference bandwidth. Change the reference bandwidth to match the NX-OS's default setting of 40 Gbps. The reference bandwidth on IOS and NX-OS devices is set with the command **auto-cost reference-bandwidth** *speed-in-megabits*. Example 8-60 displays the reference bandwidth being changed on R1 and R2.

Troubleshooting OSPF Path Selection   503

Example 8-60 *Changing of OSPF Reference Bandwidth on R1 and R2*

```
R1(config-if)# router ospf 1
R1(config-router)# auto-cost reference-bandwidth ?
  <1-4294967>  The reference bandwidth in terms of Mbits per second

R1(config-router)# auto-cost reference-bandwidth 40000
% OSPF: Reference bandwidth is changed.
        Please ensure reference bandwidth is consistent across all routers.
```

```
R2# conf t
Enter configuration commands, one per line. End with CNTL/Z.
R2(config)# router ospf 1
R2(config-router)# auto-cost reference-bandwidth 40000
% OSPF: Reference bandwidth is changed.
        Please ensure reference bandwidth is consistent across all routers.
```

Now let's examine the new OSPF metric cost using the 10 Gigabit path, and then reactivate the 1 Gigabit link on R1. Example 8-61 demonstrates this change and then verifies which path is now used to connect the 172.16.1.0/24 and 172.32.2.0/24 networks.

Example 8-61 *Verification of New Path After New Reference OSPF Bandwidth Is Configured on R1 and R2*

```
R1(config-router)# do show ip route ospf | b Gate
Gateway of last resort is not set

      10.0.0.0/8 is variably subnetted, 5 subnets, 2 masks
O        10.12.1.0/24 [110/13] via 10.13.1.3, 00:01:55, TenGigabitEthernet1/2
O        10.24.1.0/24 [110/12] via 10.13.1.3, 00:01:55, TenGigabitEthernet1/2
O        10.34.1.0/24 [110/8] via 10.13.1.3, 00:01:55, TenGigabitEthernet1/2
      172.32.0.0/24 is subnetted, 1 subnets
O        172.32.2.0 [110/13] via 10.13.1.3, 00:01:55, TenGigabitEthernet1/2
```

```
R1# conf t
Enter configuration commands, one per line. End with CNTL/Z.
R1(config)# int gi0/1
R1(config-if)# no shut
16:09:10.887: %LINK-3-UPDOWN: Interface GigabitEthernet0/1, changed state to up
16:09:11.887: %LINEPROTO-5-UPDOWN: Line protocol on Interface GigabitEthernet0/1,
  changed state to up
16:09:16.623: %OSPF-5-ADJCHG: Process 1, Nbr 192.168.2.2 on GigabitEthernet0/1 from
  LOADING to FULL, Loading Done
R1(config-if)# do show ip route ospf | b Gate
Gateway of last resort is not set
```

```
      10.0.0.0/8 is variably subnetted, 6 subnets, 2 masks
         10.24.1.0/24 [110/12] via 10.13.1.3, 00:02:46, TenGigabitEthernet1/2
         10.34.1.0/24 [110/8] via 10.13.1.3, 00:02:46, TenGigabitEthernet1/2
      172.32.0.0/24 is subnetted, 1 subnets
         172.32.2.0 [110/13] via 10.13.1.3, 00:02:46, TenGigabitEthernet1/2
```

The path between 172.16.1.0/24 and 172.32.2.0/24 continues to use the 10 Gigabit path because the path metric cost using the 1 Gigabit path would be 41 ((1,000/40,000) + 1 (for loopback).

Note Another solution involves statically setting the OSPF cost on an interface with the command **ip ospf cost** *1-65535* for NX-OS and IOS devices.

Summary

This chapter provided a brief review of the OSPF routing protocols, and then explored the methods for troubleshooting adjacency issues between devices, missing routes, and path selection.

The following parameters must be compatible for the two routers to become neighbors:

- Interfaces must be *Active*.
- Connectivity between devices must exist using the primary subnet.
- MTU matches between devices.
- Router-IDs are unique.
- Interface Area must match.
- Need for Designated Router matches based on OSPF network types.
- OSPF stub area flags match.

OSPF is a link state routing protocol that builds a complete map based on LSAs. Routes are missing from the OSPF routing domain typically because of bad network design or through filtering of routes as they are advertised across area boundaries. This chapter provided some common bad OSPF designs that cause loss of path information.

OSPF builds a loop-free topology from the computing router to all destination networks. All routers use the same logic to calculate the shortest-path for each network. Path selection prioritizes paths by using the following logic:

- Intra-Area
- Inter-Area
- External Type-1
- External Type-2

When the redistribution metric is the same, Nexus switches select external paths using RFC 2328 by default, which states to prefer intra-area connectivity over inter-area connectivity when multiple ABSRs are present. Cisco IOS and IOS XR routers use RFC 1583 external path selection, which selects an ABSR by the lowest forwarding cost. This can cause routing loops when Nexus switches are intermixed with IOS or IOS XR routers, but the Nexus switches can be placed in RFC 1583 compatibility mode.

References

RFC 1583, OSPF Version 2. IETF, http://www.ietf.org/rfc/rfc1583.txt, March 1997.

RFC 2328, OSPF Version 2. IETF, http://www.ietf.org/rfc/rfc2328.txt, April 1998.

Edgeworth, Brad, Aaron Foss, Ramiro Garza Rios. *IP Routing on Cisco IOS, IOS XE and IOS XR*. Indianapolis: Cisco Press, 2014.

Cisco. Cisco NX-OS Software Configuration Guides, http://www.cisco.com.

Chapter 9

Troubleshooting Intermediate System-Intermediate System (IS-IS)

This chapter covers the following topics:

- IS-IS Fundamentals
- Troubleshooting IS-IS Adjacency Issues
- Troubleshooting Missing Routes
- Troubleshooting IS-IS Path Selection

Intermediate System-to-Intermediate System (IS-IS) is a link-state routing protocol that is commonly found in service providers and some enterprise networks. IS-IS provides fast convergence, supports a large number of networks, and can support multiple protocols. Cisco uses IS-IS in a lot of underlying technologies, such as Overlay Transport Virtualization (OTV), Application Centric Infrastructure (ACI), and Software Defined Access (SD-Access).

This chapter focuses on identifying and troubleshooting issues that are caused with forming IS-IS neighbor adjacency, path selection, missing routes, and problems with convergence.

IS-IS Fundamentals

IS-IS uses a two-level hierarchy consisting of Level 1 (L1) and Level 2 (L2) connections. IS-IS communication occurs at L1, L2, or both (L1-L2). L2 routers communicate only with other L2 routers, and L1 routers communicate only with other L1 routers. L1-L2 routers provide connectivity between the L1 and L2 levels. An L2 router can communicate with L2 routers in the same or a different area, whereas an L1 router communicates only with other L1 routers within the same area. The following list indicates the type of adjacencies that are formed between IS-IS routers:

- L1 ←→ L1
- L2 ←→ L2

- L1-L2 ←→ L1
- L1-L2 ←→ L2
- L1-L2 ←→ L1-L2

Note The terms L1 and L2 are used frequently in this chapter, and refer only to the IS-IS levels. They should not be confused with the OSI model.

IS-IS uses the link-state packets (LSP) for building a link-state packet database (LSPDB) similar to OSPF's link-state database (LSDB). IS-IS then runs the Dijkstra Shortest Path First (SPF) algorithm to construct a loop-free topology of shortest paths.

Areas

OSPF and IS-IS use a two-level hierarchy but work differently between the protocols. OSPF provides connectivity between areas by allowing a router to participate in multiple areas, whereas IS-IS places the entire router and all its interfaces in a specific area. OSPF's hierarchy is based on areas advertising prefixes into the backbone, which then are advertised into nonbackbone areas. Level 2 is the IS-IS backbone and can cross multiple areas, unlike OSPF, as long as the L2 adjacencies are contiguous.

Figure 9-1 demonstrates these basic differences between OSPF and IS-IS. Notice that the IS-IS backbone extends across four areas, unlike OSPF's backbone, which is limited to Area 0.

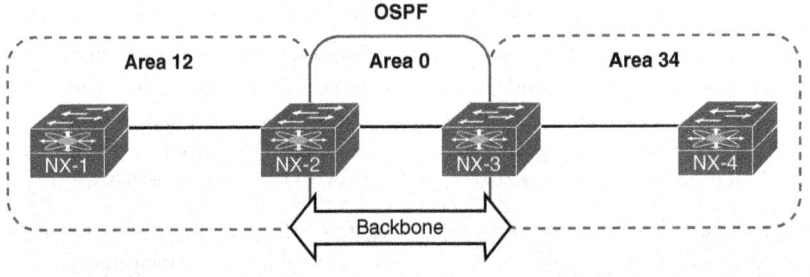

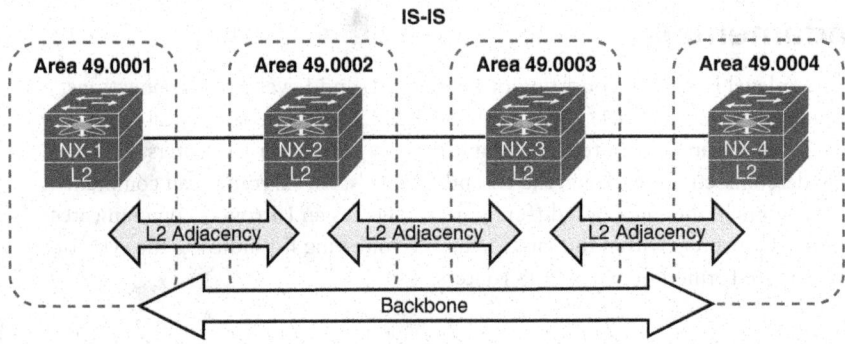

Figure 9-1 *Comparison of Areas Between OSPF and IS-IS*

In Figure 9-2, NX-1 and NX-2 form an L1 adjacency with each other, and NX-4 and NX-5 form an L1 adjacency with each other. Although NX-2 and NX-4 are L1-L2 routers, NX-1 and NX-5 support only an L1 connection. The area address must be the same to establish an L1 adjacency. NX-2 establishes an L2 adjacency with NX-3, and NX-3 establishes an L2 adjacency with NX-4. NX-2 and NX-4 are L1-L2 routers and can form an L1 and L2 adjacency on them.

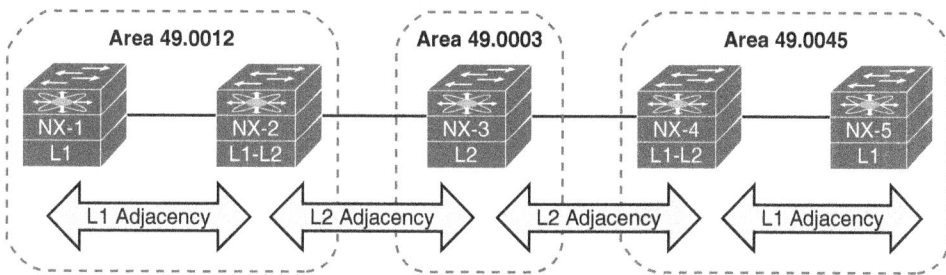

Figure 9-2 *IS-IS Adjacencies*

All L1 IS-IS routers in the same level maintain an identical copy of the LSPDB, and all L1 routers do not know about any routers or networks outside of their level (area). In a similar fashion, L2 routers maintain a separate LSPDB that is identical with other L2 routers. L2 routers are aware only of other L2 routers and networks in the L2 LSPDB.

L1-L2 routers inject L1 prefixes into the L2 topology. L1-L2 routers do not advertise L2 routes into the L1 area, but they set the attached bit in their L1 LSP, indicating that the router has connectivity to the IS-IS backbone network. If an L1 router does not have a route for a network, it searches the LSPDB for the closest router with the attached bit, which acts as a route of last resort.

NET Addressing

IS-IS routers share an area topology through link-state packets (LSP) that allows them to build the LSPDB. IS-IS uses NET addresses to build the LSPDB topology. The NET address is included in the IS header for all the LSPs. Ensuring that a router is unique in an IS-IS routing domain is essential for properly building the LSPDB. NET addressing is based off the OSI model's *Network Service Access Point (NSAP)* address structure that is between 8 to 20 bytes in length. NSAP addressing is variable based on the logic for addressing domains.

The dynamic length in the *Inter-Domain Part (IDP)* portion of the NET address causes unnecessary confusion. Instead of reading the NET address left to right, most network engineers read the NET address from right to left. In the most simplistic form, the first byte is always the selector (SEL) (with a value of 00), with the next 6 bytes as the system ID, and the remaining 1 to 13 bytes are the Area Address, as shown in Figure 9-3.

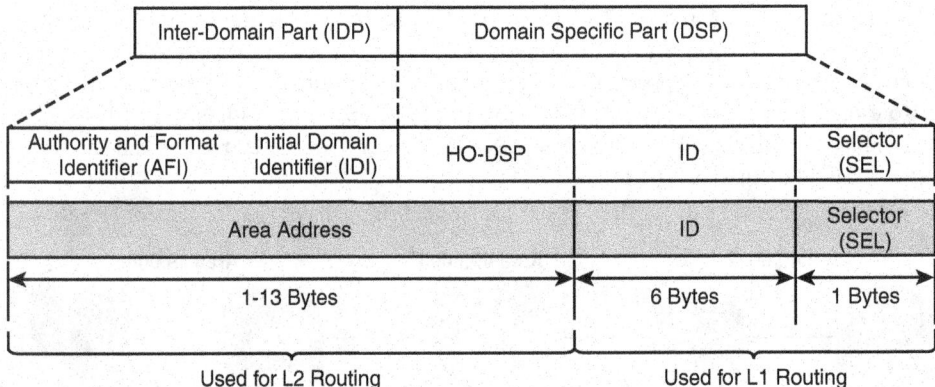

Figure 9-3 *Expanded NSAP Address Structure*

Figure 9-4 demonstrates three variations of NET addressing:

- A simple 8-byte NET address structure. The Authority and Format Identifier (AFI) is not needed because the length does not enter into the Inter-Domain Part (IDP) portion of the NSAP address. Notice that the Area Address is 1-byte, which provides up to 256 unique areas.

- A common 10-byte NET address structure. The private AFI (49) is used, and the area uses 2 bytes, providing up to 65,535 unique areas. Notice that the Area Address is 49.1234.

- Typical Open System Interconnection (OSI) NSAP address that includes the domain address. Notice that the Area Address is 49.0456.1234 and that the private AFI (49) is used.

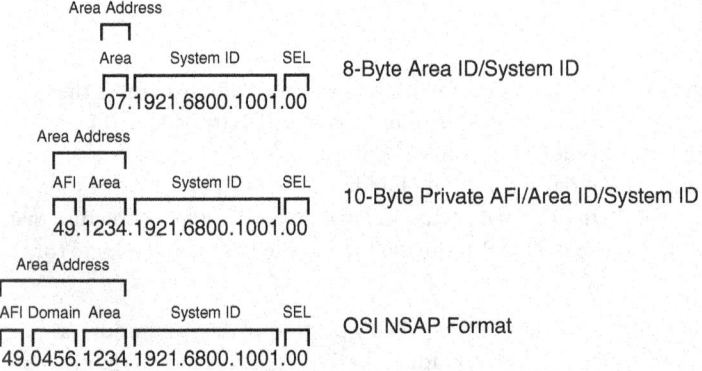

Figure 9-4 *Example NET Address Structures*

> **Note** In essence, the router's System ID is equivalent to EIGRP, or OSPF's router-id. The NET address is used to construct the network topology and must be unique.

Inter-Router Communication

Unlike other routing protocols, intermediate system (IS) communication is protocol independent because inter-router communication is not encapsulated in the third layer (network) of the OSI model. IS communication uses the second layer of the OSI model. IP, IPv6, and other protocols all use the third layer addressing in the OSI model.

IS protocol data units (PDU) (packets) follow a common header structure that identifies the type of the PDU. Data specific to each PDU type follows the header, and the last fields use optional variable-length fields that contain information specific to the IS PDU type.

IS packets are categorized into three PDU types, with each type differentiating between L1 and L2 routing information:

- **IS-IS Hello (IIH) Packets:** IIH packets are responsible for discovering and maintaining neighbors.
- **Link State Packets (LSP):** LSPs provide information about a router and associated networks. Similar to an OSPF LSA, except OSPF uses multiple LSAs.
- **Sequence Number Packets (SNP):** *Sequence number packets (SNP)* control the synchronization process of LSPs between routers.
  - *Complete sequence number packets (CSNP)* provide the LSP headers for the LSPDB of the advertising router to ensure the LSPDB is synchronized.
  - *Partial sequence number packets (PSNP)* acknowledge receipt of a LSP on point-to-point networks and request missing link state information when the LSPDB is identified as being out of sync.

IS Protocol Header

Every IS packet includes a common header that describes the PDU. All eight fields are 1-byte long and are in all packets.

Table 9-1 provides an explanation for the fields listed in the IS Protocol Header.

Table 9-1 *IS-IS Packet Types*

Field	Description
Intra Domain Routing Protocol Discriminator (Protocol Identifier)	Network Layer identifier assigned by ISO.
	IS-IS communication uses 0×83.
	ES-IS communication uses 0×81.
PDU Header Length	Length of PDU Header because it is dynamic in nature.
Version	Protocol Version Identifier.
System ID Length	The system ID can be between 1–8 bytes; network vendors have standardized on 6 bytes. This field indicates the length of the system ID. A value of 0 infers the default length of 6 bytes.

Field	Description
PDU Type	1-byte representation of the PDU type. Indicates whether it is a Hello, LSP, or SNP.
Reserved	Indicates the level of the packet. A value of 1 indicates Level 1 only; 2 indicates L2 with manual mode.
Max Areas	Value between 1 and 254 to represent the number of areas that a router will support. Default value is 3.

ISO 10589 states that a value of *0* in the IS packet header is treated in a special way in for the IS Type, LSPF Database Overload Bit, and Maximum Area Addresses field. A value of zero infers the default setting indicated in Table 9-1.

TLVs

A portion of IS PDUs uses variable modules that contain routing information. Each module specifies the type of information, length of data, and the value itself, and are commonly referred to as *type, length, and value (TLV)* tuples. Every TLV maintains a 1-byte numeric label to identify the type (function) and length of the data. TLVs support the capability of nesting, so a sub-TLV can exist inside another TLV.

TLVs provide functionality and scalability to the IS protocol. Developing new features for the IS protocol involves the addition of TLVs to the existing structure. For example, IPv6 support was added to the IS protocol by adding TLV #232 (IPv6 Interface Address) and #236 (IPv6 Reachability).

IS PDU Addressing

Communication between IS devices uses Layer 2 addresses. The source address is always the network interface's Layer 2 address, and the destination address varies depending upon the network type. Nexus switches are Ethernet based and therefore use Layer 2 MAC addresses for IS-IS communication.

ISO standards classify network media into two categories: broadcast and general topology.

Broadcast networks provide communication to multiple devices with a single packet. Broadcast interfaces communicate in a multicast fashion using well-known Layer 2 addresses so that only the nodes running IS-IS process the traffic. IS-IS does not send unicast traffic on broadcast network types, because all routers on the segment should be aware of what is happening with the network.

Table 9-2 provides a list of destination MAC addresses used for IS communication.

Table 9-2 *IS-IS Destination MAC Addresses*

Name	Destination MAC Address
All L1 ISs	0180.c200.0014
All L2 ISs	0180.c200.0015
All Intermediate Systems	0900.2b00.0005
All End Systems	0900.2b00.0004

General topology networks are based off network media that allows communication only with another device if a single packet is sent out. General topology networks are often referred to in IS-IS documentation as *point-to-point networks*. Point-to-point networks communicate with a directed destination address that matches the Layer 2 address for the remote device. NBMA technologies such as Frame Relay may not guarantee communication to all devices with a single packet. A common best practice is to use point-to-point subinterfaces on NMBA technologies to ensure proper communication between IS-IS nodes.

IS-IS Hello (IIH) Packets

IS-IS Hello (IIH) packets are responsible for discovering and maintaining neighbors. IS-IS communication has five types of hellos listed in Table 9-3. Only the first three are involved with IS-IS neighbor adjacencies; the other two are related to ES-IS communication.

Routers that form an L1-L2 adjacency with another IS-IS router send both L1 and L2 IIHs on broadcast links. To save bandwidth on WAN links, point-to-point links use the Point-to-Point Hello, which services both L1 and L2 adjacencies.

Table 9-3 provides a brief overview of the five IS Hello packet types.

Table 9-3 *IS-IS Hello Types*

Type	Description
L1 IS-IS Hello (IIH) PDU Type 15	Discovers, forms, and maintains Level 1 IS-IS neighbors
L2 IS-IS Hello (IIH) PDU Type 16	Discovers, forms, and maintains Level 2 IS-IS neighbors
Point-to-Point Hello (IIH) IS-IS PDU Type 17	Discovers, forms, and maintains point-to-point IS-IS neighbors
End System Hello (ESH)	Used for end systems (ES) to discover intermediate systems (IS) and vice versa; similar to ICMP
Intermediate System Hello (ISH)	Used for end systems (ES) to discover intermediate systems (IS) and vice versa for router selection

Table 9-4 provides a brief list of information included in the IIH Hello Packet.

Table 9-4 *Fields in IIH Packets*

Type	Description
Circuit Type	0×1 Level 1 only
	0×2 Level 2 only
	0×3 Level 1 and Level 2
System-ID	System ID of router sending the IIH
Holding Timer	Holding Timer to be used for this Intermediate System
PDU Length	Entire Length of the PDU
Priority	Router interface priority for Designated Intermediate System (DIS) elections
	(This is not included on point-to-point IIHs.)
System-ID of DIS	System ID of DIS for the Broadcast Segment
	(This is not included on point-to-point IIHs.)

Table 9-5 provides a list of common TLVs found in IIH PDUs.

Table 9-5 *Common TLVs Found in IIH PDUs*

TLV Number	Name	Description
1	Area Addresses	List of Area Addresses from advertising router.
6	IS Neighbors	List of subnetwork point of addresses (SNPA) from a neighboring IS router. SNPA is the Layer 2 hardware addresses for IS-IS routers.
		(Not included on point-to-point hellos)
8	Padding	TLVs used to inflate the packet to full maximum transmission unit (MTU). Data within this TLV is ignored.
10	Authentication	Identifies the type of authentication and includes the plain-text password or the MD5 hash.
132	IP Interface Addresses	List of IP Addresses from the transmitting interface that includes secondary IP addresses.
240	Adjacency State	Used by point-to-point links to ensure three-way IS-IS handshakes.

Link-State Packets

Link-state packets (LSP) are similar to OSPF LSAs where they advertise neighbors and attached networks, except that IS-IS uses only two types of LSPs. IS-IS defines a LSP type for each level. L1 LSPs are flooded throughout the area they originate, and L2 LSPs are flooded throughout the Level 2 network.

LSP ID

The LSP ID is a fixed 8-byte field that provides a unique identification of the LSP originator. The LSP ID is composed of the following:

- **System ID (6 bytes):** The system ID is extracted from the NET address configured on the router.

- **Pseudonode ID (1 byte):** The pseudonode ID identifies the LSP for a specific pseudonode (virtual router) or for the physical router. LSPs with a pseudonode ID of zero describe the links from the system and can be called non-pseudonode LSPs.

    LSPs with a nonzero number indicate that the LSP is a pseudonode LSP. The pseudonode ID correlates to the router's circuit ID for the interface performing the *designated intermediate system (DIS)* function. The pseudonode ID is unique among any other broadcast segments for which the same router is the DIS on that level. Pseudonodes and DIS are explained later in this chapter.

- **Fragment ID (1 byte):** If an LSP is larger than the max MTU value of the interface it needs to be sent out of, that LSP must be fragmented. IS-IS fragments the LSP as it is created, and the fragment-ID allows the receiving router to process fragmented LSPs.

Figure 9-5 shows two LSP IDs. The LSP ID on the left indicates that it is for a specific IS router, and the LSP ID on the right indicates that it is for the DIS because the pseudonode ID is not zero.

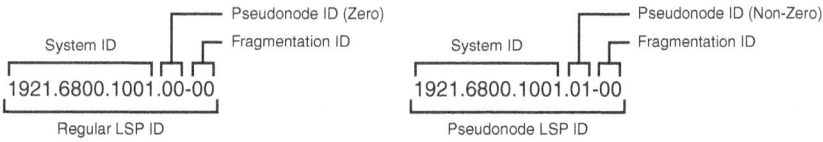

Figure 9-5 *LSP ID Structure*

Attribute Fields

The last portion of the LSP header is an 8-bit section that references four components of the IS-IS specification:

- **Partition Bit:** The partition bit identifies whether a router supports the capability for partition repair. Partition repair allows a broken L1 area to be repaired by L2 routers that belong to the same area as the L1 routers. Cisco and most other network vendors do not support partition repair.

- **Attached Bit:** The next four bits reflect the attached bit set by a L1-L2 router connected to other areas via the L2 backbone. The attached bit is in L1 LSPs.

- **Overload Bit:** The overload bit indicates when a router is in an overloaded condition. During SPF calculation, routers should avoid sending traffic through this router. Upon recovery, the router advertises a new LSP without the overload bit, and the SPF calculation occurs normally without avoiding routes through the previously overloaded node.

- **Router Type:** The last two bits indicate whether the LSP is from a L1 or L2 router.

LSP Packet and TLVs

Table 9-6 provides a list of common TLVs found in LSPs, which are used to build the topology table and for placing routes into the routing information base (RIB).

Table 9-6 *Common TLVs Found in LSP PDUs*

TLV Number	Name	Description
1	Area Addresses	List of Area Addresses on the configured router.
2	IS Neighbors	List of subnetwork point of addresses (SNPA) from a neighboring IS router and associated interface metric. SNPA is the Layer 2 hardware addresses for IS-IS routers.
10	Authentication	Identifies the type of authentication and includes the plain-text password or the MD5 hash.
128	IP Internal Reachability Information	List of internal IS-IS network and interface metric for the advertising router.
130	IP External Reachability Information	List of external (redistributed) networks and metrics associated when redistributed into IS-IS. Metrics can be internal or external.
132	IP Interface Addresses	List of IP addresses from the transmitting interface, which includes secondary IP addresses. (Limited to 63 IP addresses within the TLV.)
137	Hostname	Router hostname so that it can be used to identify the router in lieu of the system ID.

Designated Intermediate System

Broadcast networks allow more than two routers to exist on a network segment. This could cause scalability problems with IS-IS as the number of routers on a segment increase. Additional routers flood more LSPs on the segment, and ensuring that the databases are synchronized can be resource intensive.

IS-IS overcomes this inefficiency by creating a *pseudonode* (virtual router) to manage the synchronization issues that arise on the broadcast network segment. A router on the broadcast segment, known as the *Designated Intermediate System (DIS)*, assumes the role of the pseudonode. If the acting DIS router fails, another router becomes the new DIS and assumes the responsibilities. A pseudonode and DIS exist for each IS-IS level (L1 and L2) which means that a broadcast segment can have two pseudonodes and two DISs.

By inserting the logical pseudonode into a broadcast segment, the multi-access network segment is converted into multiple point-to-point networks in the LSPDB.

Note There is a natural tendency to associate IS-IS DIS behavior with OSPF's designated router (DR) behavior, but they operate in a different nature. All IS-IS routers form a full neighbor adjacency with each other. Any router can advertise non-pseudonode LSPs to all other IS-IS routers on that segment, whereas OSPF specifies that LSAs are sent to the DR to be advertised to the network segment.

The DIS advertises a pseudonode LSP that indicates the routers that attach to the pseudonode. The pseudonode LSP acts like an OSPF Type-2 LSA because it indicates the attached neighbors and informs the nodes which router is acting as the DIS. The system IDs of the routers connected to the pseudonode are listed in the IS Reachability TLV with an interface metric set to zero because SPF uses the metric for the non-pseudonode LSPs for calculating the SPF tree.

The pseudonode advertises the *complete sequence number packets (CSNP)* every 10 seconds. IS-IS routers check their LSPDBs to verify that all LSPs listed in the CSNP exist, and that the sequence number matches the version in the CSNP.

- If an LSP is missing or the router has an outdated (lower sequence number) LSP than what is contained in the CSNP, the router advertises a *partial sequence number packet (PSNP)* requesting the correct or missing LSP. All IS-IS routers receive the PSNP, but only the DIS sends out the correct LSP, thereby reducing traffic on that network segment.

- If a router detects that the sequence number in the CSNP is lower than the sequence number for any LSP that is stored locally in its LSPDB, it advertises the local LSP with the higher sequence number. All IS-IS routers receive the LSP and process it accordingly. The DIS should send out an updated CSNP with the updated sequence number for the advertised LSP.

Path Selection

Note that the IS-IS path selection is quite straightforward after reviewing the following key definitions:

- *Intra-area routes* are routes that are learned from another router within the same level and area address.

- *Inter-area routes* are routes that are learned from another L2 router that came from a L1 router or from a L2 router from a different area address.
- *External routes* are routes that are redistributed into the IS-IS domain. External routes can choose between two metric types:
  - *Internal metrics* are directly comparable with IS-IS path metrics and are selected by default by Nexus switches. IS-IS treats these routes with the same preferences as those advertised normally via TLV #128.
  - *External metrics* cannot be comparable with internal path metrics.

IS-IS best-path selection follows the processing order shown in the following steps to identify the route with the lowest path metric for each stage.

Step 1. L1 intra-area routes

L1 external routes with internal metrics

Step 2. L2 intra-area routes

L2 external routes with internal metric

L1→L2 inter-area routes

L1→L2 inter-area external routes with internal metrics

Step 3. Leaked routes (L2→L1) with internal metrics

Step 4. L1 external routes with external metrics

Step 5. L2 external routes with external metrics

L1→L2 inter-area external routes with external metrics

Step 6. Leaked routes (L2→L1) with external metrics

Note Under normal IS-IS configuration, only the first three steps are used. External routes with external metrics require the external metric-type to be explicitly specified in the route-map at the time of redistribution.

Troubleshooting IS-IS Neighbor Adjacency

Now that an overview of the IS-IS protocol has been provided, let's review the IS-IS configuration for NX-OS and begin troubleshooting neighbor adjacency issues.

Baseline IS-IS Configuration

The IS-IS configuration process on a NX-OS switch requires configuration under the IS-IS process and under the interface configuration submode. The following steps explain the process for configuring IS-IS on a Nexus switch.

Step 1. Enable the IS-IS feature. The IS-IS feature must be enabled with the global configuration command **feature isis**.

Step 2. Define an IS-IS process tag. The IS-IS process must be defined with the global configuration command **router isis** *instance-tag*. The instance-tag can be up to 20 alphanumeric characters in length.

Step 3. Define the IS-IS NET address. The NET address must be configured with the command **net** *net-address*.

Step 4. Define the IS-IS type (optional). By default, Nexus switches operate at L1-L2 IS-IS types. This means that an L1 adjacency is formed with L1 neighbors, a L2 adjacency is formed with L2 neighbors, and two sessions (L1 and L2) are formed with another L1-L2 IS-IS peer.

The IS-IS router type is changed with the command **is-type** {**level-1** | **level-1-2** | **level-2**}.

Step 5. Enable L1 route propagation to L2 networks (optional). Nexus switches do not propagate L1 networks to L2 networks automatically. The command **distribute level-1 into level-2** {**all** | **route-map** *route-map-name*}.

Step 6. Enable IS-IS on interfaces. The interface that IS-IS is enabled on is selected with the command **interface** *interface-id*. The IS-IS process is then enabled on that interface with the command **ip router isis** *instance-tag*.

The configuration in Example 9-1 enables IS-IS only on interfaces Ethernet1/1, VLAN 10, and Loopback 0.

Example 9-1 *Baseline IS-IS Configuration*

```
NX-1# configure terminal
Enter configuration commands, one per line. End with CNTL/Z.
NX-1(config)# feature isis
NX-1(config)# router isis NXOS
13:27:13 NX-1 isis[11140]: ISIS-6-START: Process start. Reason - configuration
NX-1(config-router)# net 49.0012.0000.0000.0001.00
NX-1(config-router)# interface lo0
NX-1(config-if)# ip router isis NXOS
NX-1(config-if)# interface ethernet1/1
NX-1(config-if)# ip router isis NXOS
NX-1(config-if)# interface VLAN10
NX-1(config-if)# ip router isis NXOS

NX-2# conf t
Enter configuration commands, one per line. End with CNTL/Z.
NX-2(config)# feature isis
NX-2(config)# router isis NXOS
```

```
13:32:22 NX-1 isis[11140]: ISIS-6-START: Process start. Reason - configuration
NX-2(config-router)# net 49.0012.0000.0000.0002.00
NX-2(config-router)# interface lo0
NX-2(config-if)# ip router isis NXOS
NX-2(config-if)# interface ethernet1/1
NX-2(config-if)# ip router isis NXOS
NX-2(config-if)# interface VLAN20
NX-2(config-if)# ip router isis NXOS
13:33:11 NX-2 %ISIS-5-ADJCHANGE:  isis-NXOS [24168]  LAN adj L2 0000.0000.0001
    over Ethernet1/1 - INIT (New) on MT--1
13:33:11 NX-2 %ISIS-5-ADJCHANGE:  isis-NXOS [24168]  LAN adj L2 0000.0000.0001
    over Ethernet1/1 - UP on MT-0
13:33:11 NX-2 %ISIS-5-ADJCHANGE:  isis-NXOS [24168]  LAN adj L1 0000.0000.0001
    over Ethernet1/1 - INIT (New) on MT--1
13:33:11 NX-2 %ISIS-5-ADJCHANGE:  isis-NXOS [24168]  LAN adj L1 0000.0000.0001
    over Ethernet1/1 - UP on MT-0
```

IS-IS requires that neighboring routers form an adjacency before LSPs are processed. The IS-IS neighbor adjacency process consists of three states: down, initializing, and up. This section explains the process for troubleshooting IS-IS neighbor adjacencies on Nexus switches.

Figure 9-6 provides a simple topology with two Nexus switches that are used to explain how to troubleshoot IS-IS adjacency problems.

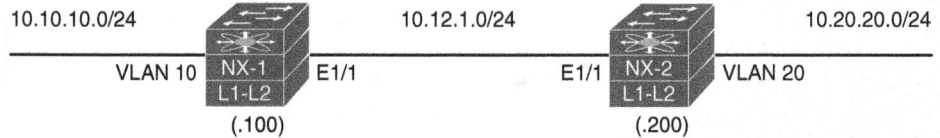

Figure 9-6 *Simple Topology with Two NX-OS Switches*

IS-IS Neighbor Verification

The first step is to verify devices that have successfully established an IS-IS adjacency with the command **show isis adjacency** [**interface** *interface-id*] [**detail** | **summary**] [**vrf** *{vrf-name}*]. The **detail** keyword parameter provides the neighbor's uptime and any secondary IP addresses configured on the neighboring nodes.

Example 9-2 displays the output of the nondetailed command on NX-1. Notice that there is an entry for the L1 adjacency and a separate entry for the L2 adjacency. This is expected behavior for L1-L2 adjacencies with other routers.

Example 9-2 *Display of IS-IS Neighbors*

```
NX-1# show isis adjacency
IS-IS process: NXOS VRF: default
IS-IS adjacency database:
Legend: '!': No AF level connectivity in given topology
System ID       SNPA             Level State Hold Time Interface
NX-2            0021.21ae.c123   1     UP    00:00:07  Ethernet1/1
NX-2            0021.21ae.c123   2     UP    00:00:07  Ethernet1/1
```

Table 9-7 provides a brief overview of the fields used in Example 9-2. Notice that the Holdtime for NX-2 is relatively low because NX-2 is the DIS for the 10.12.1.0/24 network.

Table 9-7 *IS-IS Neighbor State Fields*

Field	Description
System ID	The system ID (SEL) abstracted from the NET address.
Subnetwork Point of Addresses (SNPA)	Layer 2 hardware addresses for IS-IS routers. Nexus switches will always show the MAC address because of Ethernet.
Level	Type of adjacency formed with a neighbor: L1, L2, or L1-L2.
State	Displays whether the neighbor is up or down.
Holdtime	Time required to receive another IIH to maintain the IS-IS adjacency.
Interface	Interface used to peer with neighbor router.

Note Notice that the system ID actually references the router's hostname instead of the 6-byte system ID. IS-IS provides a name to system ID mapping under the optional TLV #137 that is found as part of the LSP. This feature is disabled under the IS-IS router configuration with the command **no hostname dynamic**.

Example 9-3 displays the **show isis adjacency** command using the **summary** and **detail** keywords. Notice that the optional **detail** keyword provides accurate timers for transition states for a particular neighbor.

Example 9-3 *Display of IS-IS Neighbors with* **summary** *and* **detail** *Keywords*

```
NX-1# show isis adjacency summary
IS-IS process: NXOS VRF: default
IS-IS adjacency database summary:
Legend: '!': No AF level connectivity in given topology
P2P            UP      INIT    DOWN    All
   L1          0       0       0       0
   L2          0       0       0       0
```

```
     L1-2              0        0        0       0
     SubTotal          0        0        0       0

LAN                    UP       INIT     DOWN    All
     L1                1        0        0       1
     L2                1        0        0       1
     SubTotal          2        0        0       2

Total                  2        0        0       2
```

```
NX-1# show isis adjacency detail
IS-IS process: NXOS VRF: default
IS-IS adjacency database:
Legend: '!': No AF level connectivity in given topology
System ID         SNPA              Level  State  Hold Time  Interface
NX-2              0021.21ae.c123    1      UP     00:00:06   Ethernet1/1
  Up/Down transitions: 1, Last transition: 00:38:30 ago
  Circuit Type: L1-2
  IPv4 Address: 10.12.1.200
  IPv6 Address: 0::
  Circuit ID: NX-2.01, Priority: 64
  BFD session for IPv4 not requested
  BFD session for IPv6 not requested
  Restart capable: 1; ack 0;
  Restart mode: 0; seen(ra 0; csnp(0; l1 0; l2 0)); suppress 0

NX-2              0021.21ae.c123    2      UP     00:00:08   Ethernet1/1
  Up/Down transitions: 1, Last transition: 00:38:30 ago
  Circuit Type: L1-2
  IPv4 Address: 10.12.1.200
  IPv6 Address: 0::
  Circuit ID: NX-2.01, Priority: 64
  BFD session for IPv4 not requested
  BFD session for IPv6 not requested
  Restart capable: 1; ack 0;
  Restart mode: 0; seen(ra 0; csnp(0; l1 0; l2 0)); suppress 0
```

Besides enabling IS-IS on the network interfaces on Nexus switches, the following parameters must match for the two switches to become neighbors:

- IS-IS interfaces must be *Active*.
- Connectivity between devices must exist using the primary subnet.
- MTU matches.

- L1 adjacencies require the area address to match the peering L1 router, and the system ID must be unique between neighbors.
- L1 routers can form adjacencies with L1 or L1-L2 routers, but not L2.
- L2 routers can form adjacencies with L2 or L1-L2 routers, but not L1.
- DIS requirements match.
- IIH Authentication Type & Credentials (if any).

Confirmation of IS-IS Interfaces

If a neighbor adjacency is missing for a specific IS-IS level, it is important to verify that the correct interfaces are running IS-IS for that level. The command **show isis interface** [*interface-id* | **brief**] [**level-1** | **level-2**] [**vrf** *vrf-name*] lists all the interfaces and any relevant information for IS-IS enabled interfaces. Providing a specific interface limits the output to the specified interface.

Some of the output in Example 9-4 has been omitted for brevity, but the following relevant information is shown in the output:

- The IS-IS interface is operating as a L1-L2 interface (Cisco default).
- The Default MTU is 1500 for Ethernet.
- The LAN ID (pseudonode ID) is NX-1.01.
- L1 and L2 metrics are set to 10 (Cisco default).
- Two IS-IS adjacencies have formed at the L1 and L2 level.
- The priority for the interface is 64 for L1 and L2 (Cisco default).
- The IS-IS interface is operating as a L1-L2 interface (Cisco default).
- The Default MTU is 1500 for Ethernet.
- The LAN ID (pseudonode ID) is NX-1.01.
- L1 and L2 metrics are set to 10 (Cisco default).
- Two IS-IS adjacencies have formed at the L1 and L2 level.
- The priority for the interface is 64 for L1 and L2 (Cisco default).

Example 9-4 *IS-IS Interface Verification*

```
NX-1# show isis interface
! Output omitted for brevity
IS-IS process: NXOS VRF: default
Ethernet1/1, Interface status: protocol-up/link-up/admin-up
  IP address: 10.12.1.100, IP subnet: 10.12.1.0/24
```

```
  IPv6 routing is disabled
  Level1
    No auth type and keychain
    Auth check set
  Level2
    No auth type and keychain
    Auth check set
  Index: 0x0002, Local Circuit ID: 0x01, Circuit Type: L1-2
  BFD IPv4 is locally disabled for Interface Ethernet1/1
  BFD IPv6 is locally disabled for Interface Ethernet1/1
  MTR is disabled
  LSP interval: 33 ms, MTU: 1500
  Level   Metric-0   Metric-2    CSNP  Next CSNP   Hello   Multi   Next IIH
  1         4          0         10    00:00:07    10       3      00:00:04
  2         4          0         10    00:00:08    10       3      0.384739
  Level  Adjs   AdjsUp Pri  Circuit ID       Since
  1       1       0    64   NX-1.01          00:57:39
  2       1       0    64   NX-1.01          00:57:39
  Topologies enabled:
    L  MT  Metric  MetricCfg  Fwdng  IPV4-MT  IPV4Cfg  IPV6-MT  IPV6Cfg
    1  0     4        no        UP     UP       yes      DN       no
    2  0     4        no        UP     UP       yes      DN       no      Metric (L1/L2): 10/10

loopback0, Interface status: protocol-up/link-up/admin-up
  IP address: 192.168.100.100, IP subnet: 192.168.100.100/32
  IPv6 routing is disabled
  Level1
    No auth type and keychain
    Auth check set
  Level2
    No auth type and keychain
    Auth check set
  Index: 0x0001, Local Circuit ID: 0x01, Circuit Type: L1-2
  BFD IPv4 is locally disabled for Interface loopback0
  BFD IPv6 is locally disabled for Interface loopback0
  MTR is disabled
  Level      Metric
  1            1
  2            1
  Topologies enabled:
    L  MT  Metric  MetricCfg  Fwdng  IPV4-MT  IPV4Cfg  IPV6-MT  IPV6Cfg
    1  0     1        no        UP     UP       yes      DN       no
    2  0     1        no        UP     UP       yes      DN       no
```

```
NX-1# show isis interface brief
IS-IS process: NXOS VRF: default
Interface     Type  Idx State       Circuit       MTU  Metric   Priority  Adjs/AdjsUp

                                                       L1 L2    L1  L2    L1   L2
--------------------------------------------------------------------------------
Topology: TopoID: 0
Vlan10        Bcast 3   Down/Ready  0x02/L1-2 1500 4  4     64  64    0/0  0/0
Topology: TopoID: 0
loopback0     Loop  1   Up/Ready    0x01/L1-2 1500 1  1     64  64    0/0  0/0
Topology: TopoID: 0
VLAN10        Bcast 2   Up/Ready    0x01/L1-2 1500 4  4     64  64    1/0  1/0
Topology: TopoID: 0
VLAN10        Bcast 4   Up/Ready    0x03/L1-2 1500 4  4     64  64    0/0  0/0
```

The command **show isis** lists the IS-IS interfaces and provides an overview of the IS-IS configuration for the router that might seem more efficient. Example 9-5 displays the command. Notice that the System ID, MTU, metric styles, area address, and topology mode are provided.

Example 9-5 *IS-IS Protocol Verification*

```
NX-1# show isis
! Output omitted for brevity
ISIS process : NXOS
 Instance number :  1
VRF: default
  System ID : 0000.0000.0001  IS-Type : L1-L2
  SAP : 412  Queue Handle : 15
  Maximum LSP MTU: 1492
  Stateful HA enabled
  Graceful Restart enabled. State: Inactive
  Last graceful restart status : none
  Start-Mode Complete
  BFD IPv4 is globally disabled for ISIS process: NXOS
  BFD IPv6 is globally disabled for ISIS process: NXOS
  Topology-mode is base
  Metric-style : advertise(wide), accept(narrow, wide)
 Area address(es) :
    49.0012
  Process is up and running
  VRF ID: 1
  Stale routes during non-graceful controlled restart
```

```
       Interfaces supported by IS-IS :
         loopback0
         Ethernet1/1
         Vlan10
       Topology : 0
       Address family IPv4 unicast :
         Number of interface : 3
         Distance : 115
       Address family IPv6 unicast :
         Number of interface : 0
         Distance : 115
       Topology : 2
       Address family IPv4 unicast :
         Number of interface : 0
         Distance : 115
       Address family IPv6 unicast :
         Number of interface : 0
         Distance : 115
       Level1
       No auth type and keychain
       Auth check set
       Level2
       No auth type and keychain
       Auth check set
```

Passive Interface

Some network topologies require advertising a network segment into IS-IS, but need to prevent routers in that segment from forming neighbor adjacencies on that segment. A passive interface is displayed as *Inactive* when displaying the IS-IS interfaces. The command **show isis interface** displays all IS-IS interfaces and the current status. Example 9-6 displays the use of this command. Notice that the Ethernet1/1 interface is passive for L1 only, whereas it is active for L2.

Example 9-6 *Identification if Passive IS-IS Is Configured for a Level*

```
NX-1# show isis interface
! Output omitted for brevity

Ethernet1/1, Interface status: protocol-up/link-up/admin-up
  IP address: 10.12.1.100, IP subnet: 10.12.1.0/24
  IPv6 routing is disabled
```

```
Level1
  No auth type and keychain
  Auth check set
Level2
  No auth type and keychain
  Auth check set
Index: 0x0002, Local Circuit ID: 0x01, Circuit Type: L1-2
BFD IPv4 is locally disabled for Interface Ethernet1/1
BFD IPv6 is locally disabled for Interface Ethernet1/1
MTR is disabled
Passive level: level-1
LSP interval: 33 ms, MTU: 1500
Level-2 Designated IS: NX-2
Level    Metric-0   Metric-2   CSNP   Next CSNP   Hello   Multi   Next IIH
1            4         0        10    Inactive     10      3      Inactive
2            4         0        10    00:00:06     10      3      00:00:03
Level  Adjs   AdjsUp  Pri  Circuit ID        Since
1       0       0      64   0000.0000.0000.00  00:01:55
2       1       1      64   NX-2.01            00:01:57
Topologies enabled:
  L   MT   Metric   MetricCfg   Fwdng   IPV4-MT   IPV4Cfg   IPV6-MT   IPV6Cfg
  1   0      4         no        UP       DN        yes       DN        no
  2   0      4         no        UP       UP        yes       DN        no
```

Now that a passive interface has been identified, the configuration must be examined for the following:

- The interface parameter command **isis passive-interface** {level-1 | level-2 | level-1-2}, which makes only that interface passive for the specified IS-IS level.

- The global IS-IS configuration command **passive-interface default** {level-1 | level-2 | level-1-2}, which makes all interfaces under that IS-IS process passive. The interface parameter command **no isis passive-interface** {level-1 | level-2 | level-1-2} takes precedence over the global command and makes that interface active.

Example 9-7 displays the configuration on NX-1 and NX-2 that prevents the two Nexus switches from forming an IS-IS adjacency on L1 or L2. The Ethernet1/1 interfaces must be active on both switches per IS-IS level for an adjacency to form. The interfaces can be made active by removing the command **isis passive-interface level-1** from Ethernet1/1 on NX-1 and setting the command **no isis passive-interface level-1-2** to Interface Ethernet1/1 on NX-2 to allow an adjacency to form on L1 and L2.

Example 9-7 *IS-IS Configuration with Passive Interfaces*

```
NX-1# show run isis
! Output omitted for brevity
router isis NXOS
  net 49.0012.0000.0000.0001.00

interface loopback0
  ip router isis NXOS

interface Ethernet1/1
  ip router isis NXOS
  isis passive-interface level-1

interface VLAN10
  ip router isis NXOS

NX-2# show run isis
! Output omitted for brevity
router isis NXOS
  net 49.0012.0000.0000.0002.00
  passive-interface default level-1-2

interface loopback0
  ip router isis NXOS

interface Ethernet1/1
  ip router isis NXOS
  no isis passive-interface level-1

interface VLAN20
  ip router isis NXOS
```

Verification of IS-IS Packets

A vital step in troubleshooting IS-IS adjacency issues is to ensure that a device is transmitting or receiving IS-IS network traffic. The command **show isis traffic** [**interface** *interface-id*] displays a high-level summary of packet types that have been sent or received from a device.

Example 9-8 displays the use of this command. Notice that there is a separation of authentication errors from other errors. Executing the command while specifying an interface provides more granular visibility to the packets received or transmitted for an interface.

Example 9-8 *IS-IS Traffic Statistics*

```
NX-1# show isis traffic
IS-IS process: NXOS
VRF: default
IS-IS Traffic:
PDU         Received        Sent   RcvAuthErr  OtherRcvErr  ReTransmit
LAN-IIH       30087        11023       0           506         n/a
P2P-IIH           0            0       0             0         n/a
CSNP           4387         4630       0             0         n/a
PSNP              0            0       0             0         n/a
LSP             353          187       0             0           0
```

Debug functionality is used to acquire granularity on various processes on the router. Specifically, the command **debug isis {adjacency | iih | lsp {flooding | generation}}** displays the processing of packets that have reached the supervisor on the switch. This allows for users to verify whether packets were received or advertised from a router.

Example 9-9 displays the transmission and receipt of L1 and L2 IIH packets.

Example 9-9 *IS-IS Hello Debugs*

```
NX-1# debug isis iih
NX-1# conf t
Enter configuration commands, one per line. End with CNTL/Z.
NX-1(config)# int Ethernet1/1
NX-1(config-if)# no shut
03:25:37 NX-1 %ETHPORT-5-SPEED: Interface Ethernet1/1, operational speed changed to
  1 Gbps
03:25:37 NX-1 %ETHPORT-5-IF_DUPLEX: Interface Ethernet1/1, operational duplex mode
  changed to Full
03:25:37 NX-1 %ETHPORT-5-IF_RX_FLOW_CONTROL: Interface Ethernet1/1, operational
  Receive Flow Control state changed to off
03:25:37 NX-1 %ETHPORT-5-IF_TX_FLOW_CONTROL: Interface Ethernet1/1, operational
  Transmit Flow Control state changed to off
03:25:37 NX-1 %ETHPORT-5-IF_UP: Interface Ethernet1/1 is up in Layer3
03:25:37.567524 isis: NXOS L2 IIH timer expired for interface Ethernet1/1
03:25:37.567620 isis: NXOS Sending normal restart tlv
03:25:37.567642 isis: NXOS Build L2 LAN IIH for Ethernet1/1 len 1497
03:25:37.567664 isis: NXOS Send L2 LAN IIH over Ethernet1/1 len 1497 prio 6,dmac
  0180.c200.0015
03:25:37.580195 isis: NXOS L1 IIH timer expired for interface Ethernet1/1
03:25:37.580286 isis: NXOS Sending normal restart tlv
03:25:37.580303 isis: NXOS Build L1 LAN IIH for Ethernet1/1 len 1497
03:25:37.580324 isis: NXOS Send L1 LAN IIH over Ethernet1/1 len 1497 prio 6,dmac
  0180.c200.0014
```

```
03:25:37.583037 isis: NXOS Receive L1 LAN IIH over Ethernet1/1 from NX-2 (0021.21ae.
    c123) len 1497 prio 0
03:25:37.583102 isis: NXOS Failed to find IPv6 address TLV MT-0
03:25:37 NX-1 %ISIS-5-ADJCHANGE:  isis-NXOS  LAN adj L1 NX-2 over Ethernet1/1 - INIT
    (New) on MT--1
03:25:37.583158 isis: NXOS isis_iih_find_bfd_enable: MT 0 : isis_topo_bfd_required =
    FALSE
03:25:37.583176 isis: NXOS isis_iih_find_bfd_enable: MT 0 : isis_topo_usable = TRUE
03:25:37.583193 isis: NXOS isis_receive_lan_iih: isis_bfd_required = 0, isis_
    neighbor_useable 1
03:25:37.583229 isis: NXOS Set adjacency NX-2 over Ethernet1/1 IPv4 address to
    10.12.1.200
03:25:37.583271 isis: NXOS isis_receive_lan_iih BFD TLV: Bring UP adjacency
03:25:37.583295 isis: NXOS 2Way Advt pseudo-lsp : LAN adj L1 NX-2 over Ethernet1/1
03:25:37 NX-1 %ISIS-5-ADJCHANGE:  isis-NXOS  LAN adj L1 NX-2 over Ethernet1/1 - UP
    on MT-0
03:25:37.583365 isis: NXOS Obtained Restart TLV RR=0, RA=0, SA=0
03:25:37.583383 isis: NXOS Process restart tlv for adjacency NX-2 over Ethernet1/1
    address 10.12.1.200
03:25:37.583397 isis: NXOS Process restart info for NX-2 on Ethernet1/1: RR=no,
    RA=no SA=no
03:25:37.583410 isis: NXOS Restart TLV present SA did not change SA state unsuppress
    adj changed
03:25:37.583467 isis: NXOS     Timer started with holding time 30 sec
03:25:37.583484 isis: NXOS Sending triggered LAN IIH on Ethernet1/1
03:25:37.583501 isis: NXOS Sending triggered LAN IIH on Ethernet1/1
03:25:37.583516 isis: NXOS isis_receive_lan_iih: Triggering DIS election
03:25:37.583571 isis: NXOS LAN IIH parse complete
03:25:37.604100 isis: NXOS Receive L2 LAN IIH over Ethernet1/1 from NX-2 (0021.21ae.
    c123) len 1497 prio 0
```

Debug commands are generally the least preferred method for finding root cause because of the amount of data that could be generated while the debug is enabled. NX-OS provides event-history that runs in the background without performance hits that provides another method of troubleshooting. The command **show isis event-history [adjacency | dis | iih | lsp-flood | lsp-gen]** provides helpful information when troubleshooting IS-IS. The **iih** keyword provides the same information as the debug command in Example 9-9.

Example 9-10 displays the **show isis even-history iih** command. Examine the difference in the sample output on NX-1 with the previous debug output. There is not much difference of information.

Example 9-10 *Hello Packet Visibility from IS-IS Event-History*

```
NX-1# show isis event-history iih
ISIS NXOS process

 iih Events for ISIS process
```

```
03:33:27.593010 isis NXOS [11140]: [11145]: 2Way Advt pseudo-lsp : LAN adj L1 NX-2
  over Ethernet1/1
03:33:27.592977 isis NXOS [11140]: [11145]: Set adjacency NX-2 over Ethernet1/1 IPv4
  address to 10.12.1.200
03:33:27.592957 isis NXOS [11140]: [11145]: isis_receive_lan_iih: isis_bfd_required
  = 0, isis_neighbor_useable 1
03:33:27.592904 isis NXOS [11140]: [11145]: Failed to find IPv6 address TLV MT-0
03:33:27.592869 isis NXOS [11140]: [11145]: Receive L1 LAN IIH over Ethernet1/1 from
  NX-2 (0021.21ae.c123) len 1497 prio 0
03:33:27.590316 isis NXOS [11140]: [11141]: isis_elect_dis(): Sending triggered LAN
  IIH on Ethernet1/1
03:33:27.590253 isis NXOS [11140]: [11141]: Advertising MT-0 adj 0000.0000.0000.00
  for if Ethernet1/1
03:33:27.590241 isis NXOS [11140]: [11141]: Advertising MT-0 adj NX-2.01 for if
  Ethernet1/1
03:33:27.590181 isis NXOS [11140]: [11141]: Send L1 LAN IIH over Ethernet1/1 len
  1497 prio 6,dmac 0180.c200.0014
03:33:27.582343 isis NXOS [11140]: [11145]: Sending triggered LAN IIH on Ethernet1/1
03:33:27.582339 isis NXOS [11140]: [11145]: Sending triggered LAN IIH on Ethernet1/1
03:33:27.582307 isis NXOS [11140]: [11145]: Process restart tlv for adjacency NX-2
  over Ethernet1/1 address 10.12.1.200
03:33:27.582242 isis NXOS [11140]: [11145]: 2Way Advt pseudo-lsp : LAN adj L2 NX-2
  over Ethernet1/1
03:33:27.582207 isis NXOS [11140]: [11145]: Set adjacency NX-2 over Ethernet1/1 IPv4
  address to 10.12.1.200
03:33:27.582154 isis NXOS [11140]: [11145]: isis_receive_lan_iih: isis_bfd_required
  = 0, isis_neighbor_useable 1
03:33:27.582101 isis NXOS [11140]: [11145]: Failed to find IPv6 addr
ess TLV MT-0
03:33:27.582066 isis NXOS [11140]: [11145]: Receive L2 LAN IIH over Ethernet1/1 from
  NX-2 (0021.21ae.c123) len 1497 prio 0
03:33:27.579283 isis NXOS [11140]: [11141]: Send L2 LAN IIH over Ethernet1/1 len
  1497
prio 6,dmac 0180.c200.0015
```

Performing IS-IS debugs shows only the packets that have reached the supervisor CPU. If packets are not displayed in the debugs or event-history, further troubleshooting must be taken by examining quality of service (QoS) policies, control plane policing (CoPP), or just verification of the packet leaving or entering an interface.

QoS policies may or may not be deployed on an interface. If they are deployed, the policy-map must be examined for any drop packets, which must then be referenced to a class-map that matches the IS-IS routing protocol. The same process applies to CoPP policies because they are based on QoS settings as well.

Example 9-11 displays the process for checking a switch's CoPP policy with the following logic:

1. Examine the CoPP policy with the command **show running-config copp all**. This displays the relevant policy-map name, classes defined, and the police rate.

532 Chapter 9: Troubleshooting Intermediate System-Intermediate System (IS-IS)

2. Investigate the class-maps to identify the conditional matches for that class-map.

3. After the class-map has been verified, examine the policy-map drops for that class with the command **show policy-map interface control-plane**. If drops are found, the CoPP policy needs to be modified to accommodate a higher IS-IS packet flow.

Example 9-11 *Verification of CoPP for IS-IS*

```
NX-1# show run copp all
! Output omitted for brevity

class-map type control-plane match-any copp-system-p-class-critical
  ..
  match access-group name copp-system-p-acl-mac-l2pt
  match access-group name copp-system-p-acl-mpls-ldp
  match access-group name copp-system-p-acl-mpls-rsvp
  match access-group name copp-system-p-acl-mac-l3-isis
  match access-group name copp-system-p-acl-mac-otv-isis
  match access-group name copp-system-p-acl-mac-fabricpath-isis
  ..
policy-map type control-plane copp-system-p-policy-strict
  class copp-system-p-class-critical
    set cos 7
    police cir 36000 kbps bc 250 ms conform transmit violate drop
```

```
NX-1# show run aclmgr all | section copp-system-p-acl-mac-l3-isis
mac access-list copp-system-p-acl-mac-l3-isis
  10 permit any 0180.c200.0015 0000.0000.0000
  20 permit any 0180.c200.0014 0000.0000.0000
  30 permit any 0900.2b00.0005 0000.0000.0000
```

```
NX-1# show policy-map interface control-plane class copp-system-p-class-critical
! Output omitted for brevity
Control Plane
  service-policy input copp-system-p-policy-strict

    class-map copp-system-p-class-critical (match-any)
      ..
      module 1:
        conformed 816984 bytes,
          5-min offered rate 999 bytes/sec
          peak rate 1008 bytes/sec at Wed 16:08:39
        violated 0 bytes,
          5-min violate rate 0 bytes/sec
          peak rate 0 bytes/sec
```

Troubleshooting IS-IS Neighbor Adjacency 533

> **Note** This CoPP policy was taken from a Nexus 7000 switch, and the policy-name and class-maps may vary depending on the platform.

Another technique to see if the packets are reaching the Nexus switch is to use the built in Ethanalyzer. The Ethanalyzer is used because IS-IS uses Layer 2 addressing, which restricts packet captures on Layer 3 ports. The command **ethanalyzer local interface inband** [capture-filter "ether host *isis-mac-address*"] [detail] is used. The capture-filter restricts traffic to specific types of traffic, and the filter **ether host** *isis-mac-address* restricts traffic to IS-IS based on the values from Table 9-2. The optional **detail** provides a packet-level view of any matching traffic. The use of Ethanalyzer is shown in Example 9-12 to identify L2 IIH packets.

Example 9-12 *Verification of IS-IS Packets Using Ethanalyzer*

```
NX-1# ethanalyzer local interface inband capture-filter "ether host
  01:80:c2:00:00:15"

Capturing on inband
09:08:42.979127 88:5a:92:de:61:7c -> 01:80:c2:00:00:15 ISIS L2 HELLO,
 System-ID: 0000.0000.0001
09:08:46.055807 88:5a:92:de:61:7c -> 01:80:c2:00:00:15 ISIS L2 HELLO,
 System-ID: 0000.0000.0001
09:08:47.489024 88:5a:92:de:61:7c -> 01:80:c2:00:00:15 ISIS L2 CSNP,
 Source-ID: 0000.0000.0001.00, Start LSP-ID: 0000.0000.0000.00-00, End LSP-ID: ff
 ff.ffff.ffff.ff-ff
09:08:48.570401 00:2a:10:03:f2:80 -> 01:80:c2:00:00:15 ISIS L2 HELLO,
 System-ID: 0000.0000.0002
09:08:49.215861 88:5a:92:de:61:7c -> 01:80:c2:00:00:15 ISIS L2 HELLO,
 System-ID: 0000.0000.0001
09:08:52.219001 88:5a:92:de:61:7c -> 01:80:c2:00:00:15 ISIS L2 HELLO,
 System-ID: 0000.0000.0001
```

```
NX-1# ethanalyzer local interface inband capture-filter "ether host
  01:80:c2:00:00:15" detail

Capturing on inband
Frame 1 (1014 bytes on wire, 1014 bytes captured)
    Arrival Time: May 22, 2017 09:07:16.082561000
    [Time delta from previous captured frame: 0.000000000 seconds]
    [Time delta from previous displayed frame: 0.000000000 seconds]
    [Time since reference or first frame: 0.000000000 seconds]
    Frame Number: 1
    Frame Length: 1014 bytes
    Capture Length: 1014 bytes
    [Frame is marked: False]
```

```
    [Protocols in frame: eth:llc:osi:isis]
IEEE 802.3 Ethernet
    Destination: 01:80:c2:00:00:15 (01:80:c2:00:00:15)
        Address: 01:80:c2:00:00:15 (01:80:c2:00:00:15)
            .... ...1 .... .... .... .... = IG bit: Group address (multicast/broadcast)
            .... ..0. .... .... .... .... = LG bit: Globally unique address (factory
 default)
    Source: 88:5a:92:de:61:7c (88:5a:92:de:61:7c)
        Address: 88:5a:92:de:61:7c (88:5a:92:de:61:7c)
            .... ...0 .... .... .... .... = IG bit: Individual address (unicast)
            .... ..0. .... .... .... .... = LG bit: Globally unique address (factory
 default)
    Length: 1000
Logical-Link Control
    DSAP: ISO Network Layer (0xfe)
    IG Bit: Individual
    SSAP: ISO Network Layer (0xfe)
    CR Bit: Command
    Control field: U, func=UI (0x03)
        000. 00.. = Command: Unnumbered Information (0x00)
        .... ..11 = Frame type: Unnumbered frame (0x03)
ISO 10589 ISIS InTRA Domain Routeing Information Exchange Protocol
    Intra Domain Routing Protocol Discriminator: ISIS (0x83)
    PDU Header Length  : 27
    Version (==1)       : 1
    System ID Length    : 0
    PDU Type            : L2 HELLO (R:000)
    Version2 (==1)      : 1
    Reserved (==0)      : 0
    Max.AREAs: (0==3)   : 0
    ISIS HELLO
        Circuit type              : Level 2 only, reserved(0x00 == 0)
        System-ID {Sender of PDU} : 0000.0000.0001
        Holding timer             : 9
        PDU length                : 997
        Priority                  : 64, reserved(0x00 == 0)
        System-ID {Designated IS} : 0000.0000.0001.01
        Area address(es) (4)
            Area address (3): 49.0012
        Protocols Supported (1)
            NLPID(s): IP (0xcc)
        IP Interface address(es) (4)
            IPv4 interface address    : 10.12.1.100 (10.12.1.100)
        IS Neighbor(s) (6)
```

```
            IS Neighbor: 00:2a:10:03:f2:80
    Restart Signaling (1)
        Restart Signaling Flags      : 0x00
            .... .0.. = Suppress Adjacency: False
            .... ..0. = Restart Acknowledgment: False
            .... ...0 = Restart Request: False
    Padding (255)
    Padding (255)
    Padding (255)
    Padding (171)
```

Connectivity Must Exist Using the Primary Subnet

Although IS-IS operates at Layer 2 of the OSI model, the primary IP address must be on the same network as the peer IS-IS router. The IS-IS IIH packets include the interface IP address, and the receiving router must be able to resolve a connected route to the interface that IIH was received on in order to add that entry to the IIH IS Neighbors entry. If a router does not see itself in the IIH IS Neighbors entry, the session stays in an INIT state and does not progress to an UP state.

The subnet mask was changed on NX-2 from 10.12.1.200/24 to 10.12.1.200/25 for this section. This places NX-2 in the 10.12.1.128/25 network, which is different from NX-1 (10.12.1.100).

When examining the IS-IS neighbor table, note that NX-1 is in INIT state with NX-2, but NX-2 does not detect NX-1. This is shown in Example 9-13.

Example 9-13 *NX-1 Stuck in INIT State with NX-2*

```
NX-1# show isis adjacency
IS-IS process: NXOS VRF: default
IS-IS adjacency database:
Legend: '!': No AF level connectivity in given topology
System ID        SNPA            Level   State   Hold Time   Interface
NX-2             0021.21ae.c123  1       INIT    00:00:29    Ethernet1/1
NX-2             0021.21ae.c123  2       INIT    00:00:23    Ethernet1/1

NX-2# show isis adjacency
IS-IS process: NXOS VRF: default
IS-IS adjacency database:
Legend: '!': No AF level connectivity in given topology
System ID        SNPA            Level   State   Hold Time   Interface
```

The next plan of action is to check the IS-IS event-history for adjacency and IIH on NX-1 and NX-2. NX-1 has adjacency entries for NX-2, whereas NX-2 does not have any adjacency entries. After checking the IIH event-history, NX-2 displays that it cannot find a usable IP address, as shown in Example 9-14.

Example 9-14 *NX-1 and NX-2 Event-History*

```
NX-1# show isis event-history adjacency
ISIS NXOS process

 adjacency Events for ISIS process
04:33:36.052173 isis NXOS [11140]: : Set adjacency NX-2 over Ethernet1/1 IPv4
   address to 10.12.1.200
04:33:36.052112 isis NXOS [11140]: : LAN adj L2 NX-2 over Ethernet1/1 - INIT (New)
   T -1
04:33:36.052105 isis NXOS [11140]: : isis_init_topo_adj LAN adj 2 NX-2 over
   Ethernet1/1 - LAN MT-0
04:33:30.612053 isis NXOS [11140]: : Set adjacency NX-2 over Ethernet1/1 IPv4
   address to 10.12.1.200
04:33:30.611992 isis NXOS [11140]: : LAN adj L1 NX-2 over Ethernet1/1 - INIT (New)
   T -1
04:33:30.611986 isis NXOS [11140]: : isis_init_topo_adj LAN adj 1 NX-2 over
   Ethernet1/1 - LAN MT-0
```

```
NX-1# show isis event-history iih
ISIS NXOS process

 iih Events for ISIS process
04:40:30.890260 isis NXOS [11140]: [11141]: Send L1 LAN IIH over Ethernet1/1 len
   1497 prio 6,dmac 0180.c200.0014
04:40:28.712993 isis NXOS [11140]: [11145]: Process restart tlv for adjacency
   0000.0000.0002 over Ethernet1/1 address 10.12.1.200
04:40:28.712988 isis NXOS [11140]: [11145]:  Neighbor TLV missing in hello from
   0000.0000.0002 , hence adjacency in INIT state
04:40:28.712986 isis NXOS [11140]: [11145]: Fail to find iih nbr tlv
04:40:28.712946 isis NXOS [11140]: [11145]: isis_receive_lan_iih: isis_bfd_required
   = 0, isis_neighbor_useable 1
04:40:28.712941 isis NXOS [11140]: [11145]: Failed to find IPv6 address TLV MT-0
04:40:28.712896 isis NXOS [11140]: [11145]: Receive L2 LAN IIH over Ethernet1/1 from
   0000.0000.0002 (0021.21ae.c123) len 1497 prio 0
04:40:27.023004 isis NXOS [11140]: [11145]: Process restart tlv for adjacency
   0000.0000.0002 over Ethernet1/1 address 10.12.1.200
04:40:27.022997 isis NXOS [11140]: [11145]:  Neighbor TLV missing in  hello from
   0000.0000.0002 , hence adjacency in INIT state
```

```
NX-2# show isis event-history adjacency
ISIS NXOS process

 adjacency Events for ISIS process
```

```
NX-2# show isis event-history iih
```

```
ISIS NXOS process

 iih Events for ISIS process
04:39:22.419356 isis NXOS [24168]: [24185]: Receive L1 LAN IIH over
Ethernet1/1 from 0000.0000.0001 (0012.34ed.82a8) len 1497 prio 0
04:39:18.419396 isis NXOS [24168]: [24185]: Failed to find IPv6 address TLV MT-0
04:39:18.419394 isis NXOS [24168]: [24185]: isis_iih_find_ipv4_addr: Unable to find
  IPv4 address for Ethernet1/1
04:39:18.419385 isis NXOS [24168]: [24185]: Fail to find usable IPv4 address
04:39:18.419356 isis NXOS [24168]: [24185]: Receive L2 LAN IIH over
Ethernet1/1 from 0000.0000.0001 (0012.34ed.82a8) len 1497 prio 0
04:39:15.939106 isis NXOS [24168]: [24185]: Failed to find IPv6 address TLV MT-0
04:39:15.939104 isis NXOS [24168]: [24185]: isis_iih_find_ipv4_addr: Unable to find
  IPv4 address for Ethernet1/1
04:39:15.939095 isis NXOS [24168]: [24185]: Fail to find usable IPv4 address
```

The next step is to check and correct IP addressing/subnet masks on the two IS-IS router's interfaces so that connectivity is established.

MTU Requirements

IS-IS hellos (IIH) are padded with TLV #8 to reach the maximum transmission unit (MTU) size of the network interface. Padding IIHs provides the benefit of detecting errors with large frames or mismatched MTU on remote interfaces. Broadcast interfaces transmit L1 and L2 IIHs wasting bandwidth if both interfaces use the same MTU.

To demonstrate the troubleshooting process for mismatch MTU, the MTU on NX-1 is set to 1000, whereas the MTU remains at 1500 for NX-2.

The first step is to check the IS-IS adjacency state as shown in Example 9-15. NX-1 does not detect NX-2, whereas NX-2 detects NX-1.

Example 9-15 *NX-1 Does Not Detect NX-2*

```
NX-1# show isis adjacency
! Output omitted for brevity
System ID      SNPA            Level  State  Hold Time  Interface


NX-2# show isis adjacency
! Output omitted for brevity
System ID      SNPA            Level  State  Hold Time  Interface
NX-1           0012.34ed.82a8  1      INIT   00:00:29   Ethernet1/1
NX-1           0012.34ed.82a8  2      INIT   00:00:29   Ethernet1/1
```

The next step is to examine the IS-IS IIH event-history to identify the problem. In Example 9-16, NX-1 is sending IIH packets with a length of 997, and they are received on NX-2. NX-2 is sending IIH packets with a length of 1497 to NX-1, which are received. The length of the IIH packets indicates an MTU problem.

Example 9-16 *NX-1 IS-IS Adjacency Event-History with MTU Mismatch*

```
NX-3# show isis event-history iih
ISIS NXOS process


 iih Events for ISIS process
15:25:30.583389 isis NXOS [13932]: [13933]: Send L1 LAN IIH over Ethernet1/1 len 997
   prio 6,dmac 0180.c200.0014
15:25:29.536721 isis NXOS [13932]: [13933]: Send L2 LAN IIH over Ethernet1/1 len 997
   prio 6,dmac 0180.c200.0015
15:25:25.824258 isis NXOS [13932]: [13937]: Process restart tlv for adjacency NX-2
   over Ethernet1/1 address 10.12.1.200
15:25:25.824168 isis NXOS [13932]: [13937]: Failed to find IPv6 address TLV MT-0
15:25:25.824094 isis NXOS [13932]: [13937]: Receive L1 LAN IIH over Ethernet1/1 from
   NX-2 (002a.1003.f280) len 1497 prio 0
15:25:25.281611 isis NXOS [13932]: [13937]: Process restart tlv for adjacency NX-2
   over Ethernet1/1 address 10.12.1.200
15:25:25.281521 isis NXOS [13932]: [13937]: Failed to find IPv6 address TLV MT-0
15:25:25.281446 isis NXOS [13932]: [13937]: Receive L2 LAN IIH over Ethernet1/1 from
   NX-2 (002a.1003.f280) len 1497 prio 0
15:25:18.019441 isis NXOS [13932]: [13937]: Receive L1 LAN IIH over Ethernet1/1 from
   NX-2 (002a.1003.f280) len 1497 prio 0
15:25:17.456734 isis NXOS [13932]: [13933]: Send L2 LAN IIH over Ethernet1/1 len 997
   prio 6,dmac 0180.c200.0015
15:25:15.166714 isis NXOS [13932]: [13933]: Send L1 LAN IIH over Ethernet1/1 len 997
   prio 6,dmac 0180.c200.0014
```

MTU is examined on both switches by examining the MTU values with the command **show interface** *interface-id* and looking for the MTU value, as shown in Example 9-17. The MTU on NX-2 is larger than NX-1.

Example 9-17 *Examination of Interface's MTU*

```
NX-1# show interface e1/1 | i MTU
  MTU 1000 bytes, BW 10000000 Kbit, DLY 10 usec
```

```
NX-2# show interface e1/1 | i MTU
  MTU 1500 bytes, BW 1000000 Kbit, DLY 10 usec
```

Cisco introduced a feature that disables the MTU padding after the router sends the first five IIHs out of an interface. This eliminates wasted bandwidth while still providing a mechanism for checking the MTU between routers. Nexus switches disable the IIH padding with the interface parameter command **no isis hello padding [always]**. The **always** keyword does not pad any IIH packets, which allows NX-1 to form an adjacency but could result in problems later. The best solution is to modify the interface MTU to the highest MTU that is acceptable between the two device's interfaces.

Note If the IS-IS interface is a VLAN interface (SVI), make sure that all the L2 ports support the MTU configured on the SVI. For example, if VLAN 10 has an MTU of 9000, all the trunk ports should be configured to support an MTU of 9000 as well.

Unique System-ID

The System-ID provides a unique identifier for an IS-IS router in the same area. A Nexus switch drops packets that have the same System-ID as itself as part of a safety mechanism. The syslog message *Duplicate system ID* is displayed along with the interface and System-ID of the other device. Example 9-18 displays what the syslog message looks like on NX-2.

Example 9-18 *Duplicate System-ID*

```
05:48:56 NX-2 %ISIS-4-LAN_DUP_SYSID:  isis-NXOS [24168]  L1 LAN IIH - Duplicate
  system ID 0000.0000.0001 detected over Ethernet1/1 from 0012.34ed.82
05:48:57 NX-2 %ISIS-4-SYSLOG_SL_MSG_WARNING: ISIS-4-LAN_DUP_SYSID: message repeated
  12 times in last 237176 sec
```

Typically, a duplicate System-ID occurs when the IS-IS configuration from another switch is copied. The System-ID portion of the NET address needs to be changed for an adjacency to form.

Area Must Match Between L1 Adjacencies

Earlier in this chapter, it was explained that IS-IS routers can operate at L1, L2, or L1-L2. L1 adjacencies are intra-area and from only between other L1 or L1-L2 routers. L1 adjacencies require that the area id matches the router it will establish a L1 adjacency with.

Example 9-19 displays NX-1 and NX-2's IS-IS adjacency tables. Notice that both Nexus switches have established an L2 adjacency, but there is not an L1 adjacency like those shown previously in this chapter.

Example 9-19 *Only an L2 IS-IS Adjacency*

```
NX-1# show isis adjacency
! Output omitted for brevity
System ID        SNPA            Level  State  Hold Time  Interface
```

Chapter 9: Troubleshooting Intermediate System-Intermediate System (IS-IS)

| NX-2 | 002a.1003.f280 | 2 | UP | 00:00:28 | Ethernet1/1 |

```
NX-2# show isis adjacency
| Output omitted for brevity
System ID        SNPA            Level  State  Hold Time  Interface
NX-1             885a.92de.617c  2      UP     00:00:09   Ethernet1/1
```

Through logical deduction, NX-1 and NX-2 can establish and maintain bidirectional transmission of IS-IS packets because the L2 adjacency is established. This indicates incorrect authentication parameters, invalid timers, or that the area numbers do not match.

Example 9-20 displays the IS-IS event-history for NX-1 and NX-2. Notice that the error message *No common area* is displayed before the message indicating that the L1 IIH is received.

Example 9-20 *IS-IS Event-History Indicates Different Areas*

```
NX-1# show isis event-history iih
ISIS NXOS process


 iih Events for ISIS process
 03:30:01.385298 isis NXOS [27230]: [27235]: Failed to find IPv6 address TLV MT-0
 03:30:01.385260 isis NXOS [27230]: [27235]: Receive L2 LAN IIH over Ethernet1/1 from
   NX-2 (002a.1003.f280) len 1497 prio 0
 03:30:00.470215 isis NXOS [27230]: [27231]: Send L2 LAN IIH over Ethernet1/1 len
   1497 prio 6,dmac 0180.c200.0015
 03:29:57.250206 isis NXOS [27230]: [27231]: Send L2 LAN IIH over Ethernet1/1 len
   1497 prio 6,dmac 0180.c200.0015
 03:29:57.095233 isis NXOS [27230]: [27235]: No common area
 03:29:57.095231 isis NXOS [27230]: [27235]: Failed to find IPv6 address TLV MT-0
 03:29:57.095199 isis NXOS [27230]: [27235]: Receive L1 LAN IIH over Ethernet1/1 from
   NX-2 (002a.1003.f280) len 1497 prio 0

NX-2# show isis event-history iih
ISIS NXOS process


 iih Events for ISIS process
 03:29:52.986467 isis NXOS [12392]: [12442]: Receive L2 LAN IIH over Ethernet1/1 from
   NX-1 (885a.92de.617c) len 1497 prio 0
 03:29:520.780227 isis NXOS [12392]: [12404]: Send L2 LAN IIH over Ethernet1/1 len
   1497 prio 6,dmac 0180.c200.0015

 03:29:51.966543 isis NXOS [12392]: [12442]: No common area
 03:29:51.966542 isis NXOS [12392]: [12442]: Failed to find IPv6 address TLV MT-0
 03:29:51.966510 isis NXOS [12392]: [12442]: Receive L1 LAN IIH over Ethernet1/1 from
   NX-1 (885a.92de.617c) len 1497 prio 0
```

The final step is to verify the configuration and check the NET Addressing. Example 9-21 displays the NET entries for NX-1 and NX-2. NX-1 has an area of 49.0012 and NX-2 has an area of 49.0002.

Example 9-21 *Verification of NET Addressing*

```
NX-1# show run isis
! Output omitted for brevity
router isis NXOS
  net 49.0012.0000.0000.0001.00
```

```
NX-2# show run isis
! Output omitted for brevity
router isis NXOS
  net 49.0002.0000.0000.0002.00
```

Changing the area portion of the NET address to match on either Nexus switch allows for the L1 adjacency to form.

Checking IS-IS Adjacency Capabilities

IS-IS routers do not have a mechanism to detect if their area is at the end (edge) or middle (transit) of the L2 backbone. Only humans can identify an area as transit, so Cisco defaults to making all routers L1-L2. The default behavior guarantees that all routers are able to route transit traffic, but also limits scalability of the protocol.

The IS-IS level that a Nexus switch operates at is set with the IS-IS configuration command **is-type {level-1 | level-1-2 | level-2-only)**.

The setting is verified by looking at the IS-IS process as shown in Example 9-22.

Example 9-22 *Verification of IS-IS Process Level Type*

```
NX-1# show isis
ISIS process : NXOS
 Instance number :  1
 UUID: 1090519320
 Process ID 27230
VRF: default
  System ID : 0000.0000.0001   IS-Type : L2
```

```
NX-1# show run isis
! Output omitted for brevity
router isis NXOS
  net 49.0012.0000.0000.0001.00
   is-type level-2
```

Other topology designs may specify that a specific interface should establish only a specific IS-IS level adjacency. This is accomplished with the interface parameter command **isis circuit-type {level-1 | level-1-2 | level-2-only}**.

This setting is verified by looking at the IS-IS process as shown in Example 9-23. Notice that Ethernet1/1 is set to allow only L1 connections.

Example 9-23 *Verification of IS-IS Interface Level Type*

```
NX-1# show isis interface | i protocol|Type
loopback0, Interface status: protocol-up/link-up/admin-up
  Index: 0x0001, Local Circuit ID: 0x01, Circuit Type: L1-2
Ethernet1/1, Interface status: protocol-up/link-up/admin-up
  Index: 0x0002, Local Circuit ID: 0x01, Circuit Type: L1
EthernetVlan10, Interface status: protocol-down/link-down/admin-down
  Index: 0x0003, Local Circuit ID: 0x02, Circuit Type: L1-2

NX-1# show run isis
! Output omitted for brevity
router isis NXOS
  net 49.0012.0000.0000.0001.00
  is-type level-1-2

interface loopback0
  ip router isis NXOS

interface Ethernet1/1
  isis circuit-type level-1
  ip router isis NXOS

interface EthernetVlan10
  ip router isis NXOS
```

It is possible to set the Nexus switch to a specific IS-IS level functionality with a different setting for a circuit from the global IS-IS setting. When the settings are combined, the Nexus switch uses the most restrictive level when forming an adjacency. Table 9-8 displays the capable adjacencies for a router based solely on the IS-IS router type, and IS-IS circuit-type.

Table 9-8 *IS-IS Neighbor Adjacency Capability Chart*

	Router Set IS-Type L1	**Router Set IS-Type L2**	**Router Set IS-Type L1-L2**
Circuit-Type L1	Level-1	Not Configured (default value)	Level-1
Circuit-Type L2	Not Configured (default value)	Level-2	Level-2
Circuit-Type L1-L2	Level-1	Level-2	Level-1 and Level-2

If IIH packets are missing from the event-history, the IS-IS Router and Interface-level settings need to be verified on both routers.

DIS Requirements

The default IS-IS interface on Nexus switches is a *broadcast interface* and requires a DIS. Broadcast interface IS-IS interfaces that are directly connected with only two IS-IS routers do not benefit from the use of a pseudonode. Resources are wasted on electing a DIS. CSNPs are continuously flooded into a segment, and an unnecessary pseudonode LSP is included in the LSPDB of all routers in that level. IS-IS allows general topology interfaces to behave like a point-to-point interface with the interface command **isis network point-to-point.**

An adjacency will not form between IS-IS Nexus switches that have one broadcast interface and an IS-IS point-to-point interface. Neither device shows an IS-IS adjacency, but the general topology switch reports the message *Fail: Receiving P2P IIH over LAN interface xx* in the IS-IS IIH event-history. IS-IS event-history indicates which neighbor has advertised the P2P interface. When those messages are detected, the interface type needs to be changed on one node to ensure that they are consistent.

Example 9-24 displays NX-2's IS-IS event-history and the relevant configurations for NX-1 and NX-2.

Example 9-24 *IS-IS Mismatch of Interface Types*

```
NX-2# show isis event-history iih
ISIS NXOS process


 iih Events for ISIS process
02:50:33.000228 isis NXOS [24168]: [24169]: Send L2 LAN IIH over Ethernet1/1 len
   1497 prio 6,dmac 0180.c200.0015
02:50:30.200875 isis NXOS [24168]: [24185]: P2P IIH parse failed!
02:50:30.200873 isis NXOS [24168]: [24185]: Fail: Receiving P2P IIH over LAN
   interface Ethernet1/1
02:50:30.200870 isis NXOS [24168]: [24185]: Receive P2P IIH over Ethernet1/1 from
   NX-1 len 1497 prio 0
02:50:25.390172 isis NXOS [24168]: [24169]: Send L1 LAN IIH over Ethernet1/1 len
   1497 prio 6,dmac 0180.c200.0014
```

```
NX-1# show run isis
! Output omitted for brevity
router isis NXOS
  net 49.0012.0000.0000.0001.00

interface loopback0
  ip router isis NXOS
```

```
interface Ethernet1/1
  isis network point-to-point
  ip router isis NXOS

interface EthernetVlan10
  ip router isis NXOS
```

```
NX-2# show run isis
! Output omitted for brevity
router isis NXOS
  net 49.0012.0000.0000.0002.00

interface loopback0
  ip router isis NXOS

interface Ethernet1/1
  ip router isis NXOS

interface EthernetVlan20
  ip router isis NXOS
```

Adding the command **isis network point-to-point** to NX-2's Ethernet1/1 interface sets both interfaces to the same type, and then an adjacency forms.

IIH Authentication

IS-IS allows for the authentication of IIH packets that are required to form an adjacency. IIH authentication is configured on an interface by interface perspective. IIH authentication uses different settings for each IS-IS level. Authenticating on one PDU type is sufficient for most designs.

IS-IS provides two types of authentication: plaintext and a MD5 cryptographic hash. Plaintext mode provides little security, because anyone with access to the link can see the password with a network sniffer. MD5 cryptographic hash uses a hash instead, so the password is never included in the PDUs, and this technique is widely accepted as being the more secure mode. All IS-IS authentication is stored in TLV#10 that is part of the IIH.

Nexus switches enable IIH authentication with the interface parameter command **isis authentication key-chain** *key-chain-name* {**level-1** | **level-2**}. The authentication type is identified with the command **isis authentication-type** {**md5** | **cleartext**} {**level-1** | **level-2**}.

Example 9-25 displays MD5 authentication on NX-1's Ethernet1/1 interface.

Example 9-25 *L1 IIH Authentication on NX-1*

```
NX-1# conf t
Enter configuration commands, one per line. End with CNTL/Z.
NX-1(config)# key chain IIH-AUTH
NX-1(config-keychain)# key 2
NX-1(config-keychain-key)# key-string CISCO
NX-1(config-keychain-key)# interface Ethernet1/1
NX-1(config-if)# isis authentication key-chain CISCO level-1
NX-1(config-if)# isis authentication-type md5 level-1
```

After configuring L1 IIH authentication on NX-1's Ethernet1/1 interface, the L1 adjacency is dropped between NX-1 and NX-2. NX-2 is actually trying to bring up the NX-1 session, but is stuck in an INIT state, as shown in Example 9-26. The L2 adjacency is maintained because no changes were made to the L2 authentication.

Example 9-26 *L1 Adjacency Is Affected by L1 IIH Authentication on NX-1*

```
NX-1# show isis adjacency
! Output omitted for brevity
System ID       SNPA            Level   State   Hold Time   Interface
NX-2            002a.1003.f280  2       UP      00:00:29    Ethernet1/1

NX-2# show isis adjacency
! Output omitted for brevity
System ID       SNPA            Level   State   Hold Time   Interface
NX-1            885a.92de.617c  1       INIT    00:00:29    Ethernet1/1
NX-1            885a.92de.617c  2       UP      00:00:07    Ethernet1/1
```

In lieu of checking configuration, the authentication parameters are displayed for an interface with the command **show isis interface** [*interface-id*]. Example 9-27 displays the output for NX-1. Notice that the L1 portion has authentication, whereas the L2 portion does not have authentication enabled.

Example 9-27 *Viewing of IIH Authentication*

```
NX-1# show isis interface Ethernet1/1
! Output omitted for brevity
IS-IS process: NXOS VRF: default
Ethernet1/1, Interface status: protocol-up/link-up/admin-up
  IP address: 10.12.1.100, IP subnet: 10.12.1.0/24
    IPv6 routing is disabled
  Level1
    Auth type:MD5
    Auth keychain: IIH-AUTH
```

```
      Auth check set
Level2
  No auth type and keychain
      Auth check set
```

The password in the keychain is viewed with the command **show key chain key-chain-name [mode decrypt]**. The optional **mode decrypt** keywords display the password in plaintext as displayed in Example 9-28.

Example 9-28 *Viewing Keychain Passwords*

```
NX-1# show key chain IIH-AUTH
Key-Chain IIH-AUTH
  Key 2 -- text 7 "072c087f6d26"
    accept lifetime (always valid) [active]
    send lifetime (always valid) [active]

NX-1# show key chain IIH-AUTH mode decrypt
Key-Chain IIH-AUTH
  Key 2 -- text 0 "CISCO"
    accept lifetime (always valid) [active]
    send lifetime (always valid) [active]
```

Upon enabling authentication, it is important to check the syslog for error messages that indicate *bad authentication*. For those that do, verify the authentication options and password on all peers for that network link.

Troubleshooting Missing Routes

After explaining how to troubleshoot IS-IS neighbor adjacencies, this chapter explains how to troubleshoot missing routes and identify issues that arise when intermixing different device types (IOS, IOS XR, for instance) with Nexus switches running IS-IS.

Duplicate System ID

The IS-IS system ID plays a critical role for the creation of the topology. If two adjacent routers have the same system ID in the same L1 area, an adjacency does not form as shown earlier. However, if two routers have the same system ID in the same L1 area and have an intermediary router, it prevents those routes from being installed in the topology.

Figure 9-7 provides a sample topology in which all Nexus switches are in the same area with only L1 adjacencies. NX-2 and NX-4 have been configured with the same system

ID of 0000.0000.0002. NX-3 sits between NX-2 and NX-4 and has a different system ID, therefore allowing NX-2 and NX-4 to establish full neighbor adjacencies.

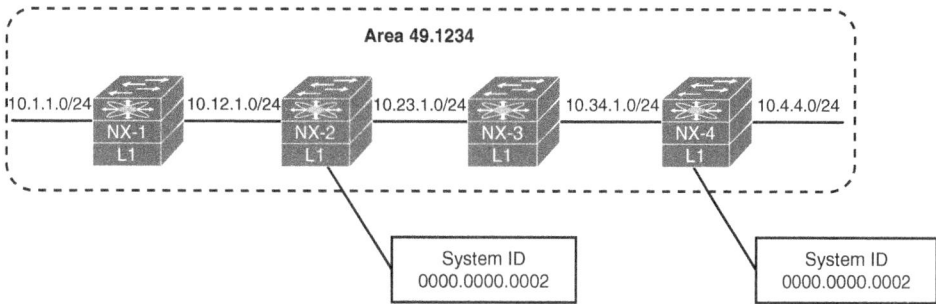

Figure 9-7 *Duplicate System ID Topology*

From NX-1's perspective, the first apparent issue is that NX-4's 10.4.4.0/24 network is missing, as shown in Example 9-29.

Example 9-29 *NX-1's Routing Table with Missing NX-4's 10.4.4.0/24 Network*

```
NX-1# show ip route isis
! Output omitted for brevity

10.23.1.0/24, ubest/mbest: 1/0
    *via 10.12.1.2, Eth1/1, [115/8], 00:16:56, isis-NXOS, L1
10.34.1.0/24, ubest/mbest: 1/0
    *via 10.12.1.2, Eth1/1, [115/12], 00:16:49, isis-NXOS, L1
```

On NX-2 and NX-4, there are complaints about LSPs with duplicate system IDs: *L1 LSP—Possible duplicate system ID*, as shown in Example 9-30.

Example 9-30 *Syslog Messages with LSPs with Duplicate System IDs*

```
15:45:26 NX-2 %ISIS-4-LSP_DUP_SYSID:   isis-NXOS [15772]   L1 LSP - Possible duplicate
  system ID 0000.0000.0002 detected
15:41:47 NX-4 %ISIS-4-LSP_DUP_SYSID:   isis-NXOS [23550]   L1 LSP - Possible duplicate
  system ID 0000.0000.0002 detected
```

Example 9-31 displays the routing table of the two Nexus switches with the *Possible duplicate system ID* syslog messages. Notice that NX-2 is missing only NX-4's interface (10.4.4.0/24), whereas NX-4 is missing the 10.12.1.0/24 and NX-1's Ethernet interface (10.1.1.0/24). Examining the IS-IS database displays a flag (*) that indicates a problem with NX-2.

Example 9-31 *Routing Tables of NX-2 and NX-4*

```
NX-2# show ip route is-is
! Output omitted for brevity
10.1.1.1/32, ubest/mbest: 1/0
    *via 10.12.1.1, Eth2/1, [115/8], 00:04:00, isis-NXOS, L1
10.34.1.0/24, ubest/mbest: 1/0
    *via 10.23.1.3, Eth2/2, [115/8], 00:04:03, isis-NXOS, L1
```

```
NX-2(config-router)# do show isis database
IS-IS Process: NXOS LSP database VRF: default
IS-IS Level-1 Link State Database
  LSPID              Seq Number    Checksum   Lifetime   A/P/O/T
  NX-1.00-00         0x00000004    0x42EC     939        0/0/0/1
  NX-1.01-00         0x00000003    0x804A     960        0/0/0/1
  NX-2.00-00       * 0x00000134    0xDC3E     1199       0/0/0/1
  NX-2.01-00       ? 0x00000003    0xA027     974        0/0/0/1
  NX-3.00-00         0x00000021    0x9D74     1196       0/0/0/1
  NX-3.02-00         0x0000001D    0x5D4E     1110       0/0/0/1
```

```
NX-4# show ip route is-is
! Output omitted for brevity
10.23.1.0/24, ubest/mbest: 1/0
    *via 10.34.1.3, Eth2/1, [115/8], 00:04:02, isis-NXOS, L1
```

```
NX-4(config-router)# do show isis database
IS-IS Process: NXOS LSP database VRF: default
IS-IS Level-1 Link State Database
  LSPID              Seq Number    Checksum   Lifetime   A/P/O/T
  NX-1.00-00         0x00000004    0x42EC     914        0/0/0/1
  NX-1.01-00         0x00000003    0x804A     936        0/0/0/1
  NX-4.00-00       * 0x00000139    0xAC16     1194       0/0/0/1
  NX-4.01-00       * 0x00000003    0xA027     954        0/0/0/1
  NX-3.00-00         0x00000021    0x9D74     1173       0/0/0/1
  NX-3.02-00         0x0000001D    0x5D4E     1087       0/0/0/1
```

A quick check of the router's system ID is done by examining the IS-IS processes on both Nexus switches that reported the *Possible duplicate system ID* using the **show isis | i system** command. Notice that in Example 9-32, NX-2 and NX-4 have the same system ID.

Example 9-32 *Verification of IS-IS System IDs*

```
NX-2# show isis | i System
  System ID : 0000.0000.0002  IS-Type : L1
```

```
NX-4# show isis | i System
  System ID : 0000.0000.0002  IS-Type : L1
```

Interface Link Costs

The IS-IS interface metric is an essential component for Dijkstra's SPF calculation because the shortest path metric is the cumulative interface metric from the source router to the destination router. Nexus switches assign the IS-IS interface metric based on the following formula:

Interface Metric = Interface Bandwidth/Reference Bandwidth

The default reference bandwidth for NX-OS is 40 Gbps, whereas other Cisco OSs (IOS and IOS XR) statically set the interface link metric to 10 regardless of interface speed. Table 9-9 provides the default IS-IS metric for common network interface types using the default reference bandwidth.

Table 9-9 *IS-IS Interface Costs Using Default Settings*

Interface Type	Default NX-OS IS-IS Cost	Default IOS IS-IS Cost
FastEthernet	400	10
GigabitEthernet	40	10
10-GigabitEthernet	4	10
40-GigabitEthernet	1	10

Notice in Table 9-9 that there is no differentiation in the link cost associated to a Fast Ethernet Interface and a 40-Gigabit Ethernet interface on IOS routers. In essence, suboptimal routing can exist when Nexus switches interact with IOS-based devices in an IS-IS topology. For example, Figure 9-8 displays a topology in which connectivity between R1 and R2 should take the 10 Gigabit Path (R1→NX-3→NX-4→R2) because the 1 Gigabit link between R1 and R2 should be used only as a backup path.

Chapter 9: Troubleshooting Intermediate System-Intermediate System (IS-IS)

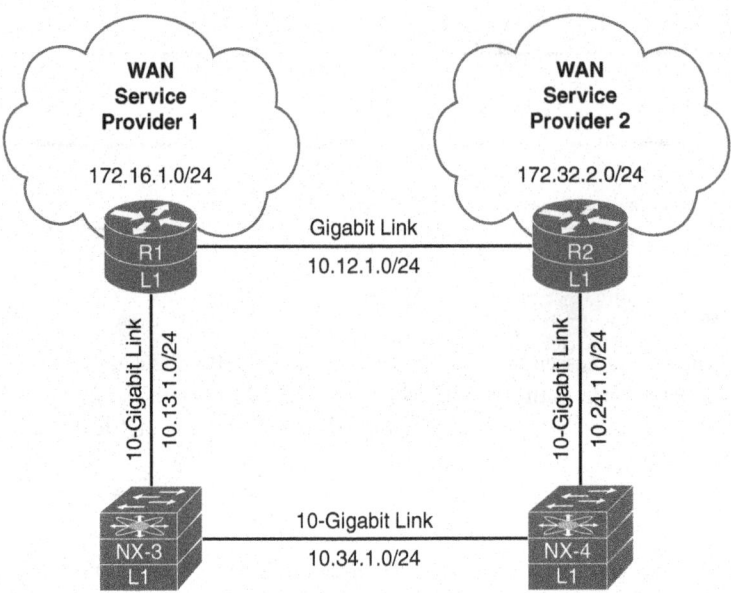

Figure 9-8 *Topology to Demonstrate Problems with Interface Metrics*

Example 9-33 displays the routing table of R1 with the default interface metrics on all the devices. Traffic between 172.16.1.0/24 and 172.32.2.0/24 flows across the backup 1 Gigabit link (10.12.1.0/24), which does not follow the intended traffic patterns. Notice that the IS-IS path metric is 20 to the 172.32.2.0/24 network using the 1 Gigabit link.

Example 9-33 *R1's Routing Table with Default Interface Metrics Bandwidth*

```
R1# show ip route isis | begin Gateway
Gateway of last resort is not set

      10.0.0.0/8 is variably subnetted, 6 subnets, 2 masks
i L1    10.24.1.0/24 [115/18] via 10.13.1.3, 00:04:51, TenGigabitEthernet2/2
i L1    10.34.1.0/24 [115/14] via 10.13.1.3, 00:04:51, TenGigabitEthernet2/2
      172.16.0.0/16 is variably subnetted, 3 subnets, 2 masks
i L1    172.32.2.0/24 [115/20] via 10.12.1.2, 00:00:08, GigabitEthernet0/1
```

Now one of the beautiful things about IS-IS is how it structures networks as objects that exist on top of the routers themselves. Instead of viewing the routing table, the IS-IS topology table is viewed with the command **show isis topology**. The IS-IS topology table lists the total path metric to reach the destination router, next-hop node, and outbound interface. Example 9-34 displays the topology table from R1 and NX-3's perspective. R1 is selecting the path to R2 via the direct link on Gi0/1.

Example 9-34 *R1's and NX-3's IS-IS Topology Table with Default Metric*

```
R1# show isis topology

IS-IS TID 0 paths to level-1 routers
System Id            Metric     Next-Hop           Interface    SNPA
R1                   --
R2                   10         R2                 Gi0/1        fa16.3e10.00b6
NX-3                 10         NX-3               Te2/2        0012.1298.1231
NX-4                 14         NX-3               Te2/2        0012.1298.1231
```

```
NX-3# show isis topology
IS-IS process: NXOS
VRF: default
IS-IS Level-1 IS routing table
R1.00, Instance 0x0000001D
   *via R1, Ethernet1/2, metric 4
R1.03, Instance 0x0000001D
   *via R1, Ethernet1/2, metric 14
R2.00, Instance 0x0000001D
   *via NX-4, Ethernet1/1, metric 8
R2.02, Instance 0x0000001D
   *via NX-4, Ethernet1/1, metric 8
NX-4.00, Instance 0x0000001D
   *via NX-4, Ethernet1/1, metric 4

IS-IS Level-2 IS routing table
```

Notice how R1 and NX-3 have conflicting metric values when they point to each other. To ensure that routing takes the optimal path, three options ensure optimal routing:

- Statically set the IS-IS metric on IS-IS devices that are not Nexus switches. IOS-based devices use the interface parameter command **isis metric** *metric-value*.

- Statically set the IS-IS metric on a Nexus interface to reflect network links that are more preferred with the interface parameter command **isis metric** *metric-value* {**level-1** | **level-2**}.

- Change the reference bandwidth on Nexus switches to a higher value to make those links more preferred. The reference bandwidth is set with the IS-IS process configuration command **reference-bandwidth** *reference-bw* {**gbps** | **mbps**}.

There are not any intermediary routers between R1 and R2, so the only option that makes sense is to modify the IS-IS metrics on R1 and R2. Example 9-35 displays the metric for the 10.12.1.0/24 link being statically set to 40, and the metric being set to 4 for the 10 Gbps interface. The value correlates to a reference bandwidth of 40 Gbps.

Example 9-35 *Setting Static IS-IS Metric on R1 and R2*

```
R1# conf t
Enter configuration commands, one per line.  End with CNTL/Z.
R1(config)# interface GigabitEthernet0/1
R1(config-if)# isis metric ?
  <1-16777214>  Default metric
  maximum       Maximum metric. All routers will exclude this link from their
                SPF

R1(config-if)# isis metric 40
R1(config-if)# interface TenGigabitEthernet2/2
R1(config-if)# isis metric 4
```

```
R2(config)# int GigabitEthernet0/1
R2(config-if)# isis metric 40
R2(config)# int TenGigabitEthernet2/2
R2(config-if)# isis metric 4
```

Now that the change has been made, let's examine the IS-IS routing table and topology table on R1 and NX-3, as shown in Example 9-36. Now the interface metrics match for the 10.13.1.0/24 and 10.24.1.0/24 networks. In addition, R1 is now selecting the 10 Gbps path as the preferred path to reach R2.

Example 9-36 *IS-IS Routing and Topology Table After Static Metric Configuration*

```
R1# show ip route isis | beg Gate
Gateway of last resort is not set

      10.0.0.0/8 is variably subnetted, 6 subnets, 2 masks
i L1     10.24.1.0/24 [115/12] via 10.13.1.3, 00:01:08, TenGigabitEthernet2/2
i L1     10.34.1.0/24 [115/8] via 10.13.1.3, 00:01:08, TenGigabitEthernet2/2
      172.16.0.0/16 is variably subnetted, 3 subnets, 2 masks
i L1     172.32.2.0/24 [115/22] via 10.13.1.3, 00:01:08, TenGigabitEthernet2/2
```

```
R1# show isis topology

IS-IS TID 0 paths to level-1 routers
System Id         Metric    Next-Hop         Interface    SNPA
R1                --
R2                12        NX-3             Gi0/2        0012.1298.1231
NX-3              4         NX-3             Te2/2        0012.1298.1231
NX-4              8         NX-3             Te2/2        0012.1298.1231
```

```
NX-3# show isis topology
IS-IS process: NXOS
```

```
VRF: default
IS-IS Level-1 IS routing table
R1.00, Instance 0x00000023
   *via R1, Ethernet1/2, metric 4
R2.00, Instance 0x00000023
   *via NX-4, Ethernet1/1, metric 8
R2.02, Instance 0x00000023
   *via NX-4, Ethernet1/1, metric 8
NX-4.00, Instance 0x00000023
   *via NX-4, Ethernet1/1, metric 4
```

Mismatch of Metric Modes

The IS-IS interface metric is a vital component within the LSP. RFC 1195 specified the interface metric as a 6-bit field that supports a value between 1 and 63 and is included in the IS Neighbors TLV (2) and IP Reachability TLVs (128 and 130). Limiting the interface metric to 63 introduces other issues dependent on the variance of network bandwidth in an IS-IS topology, considering links can range between 10 Mbps and 100 Gbps. These metrics are commonly referred to as *narrow metrics*.

RFC 3784 provided a method for the interface metric to use a 24-bit number that allows for the metric to be set between 1 and 16,777,214. The 24-bit metrics are available in the Extended IS Reachability TLV (22) and the Extended IP Reachability TLV (135), and are commonly referred to as *wide metrics*.

Nexus switches accept narrow or wide metrics and advertise only wide metrics by default. IOS and IOS XR accept and advertise only narrow metrics by default, which causes problems when integrating non-Nexus switches in a topology. Figure 9-9 displays a simple L1 topology with multiple device types. All devices and interfaces have IS-IS enabled on them.

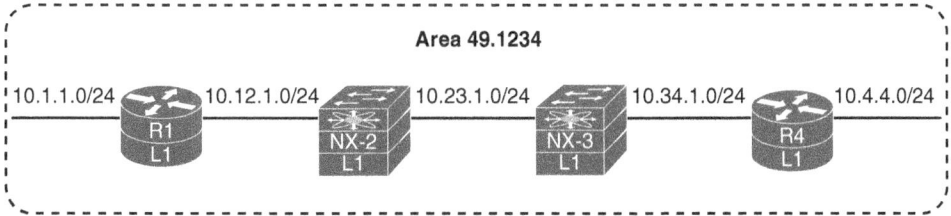

Figure 9-9 *Simple IS-IS L1 Topology with Multiple Device Types*

Example 9-37 displays R1's and NX-2's IS-IS routing entries. R1 does not have any IS-IS routes in the routing table, whereas NX-2 has routes to all the networks in the topology.

Example 9-37 *R1's and NX-2's IS-IS Routing Table Entries*

```
R1# show ip route isis
Codes: L - local, C - connected, S - static, R - RIP, M - mobile, B - BGP
       D - EIGRP, EX - EIGRP external, O - OSPF, IA - OSPF inter area
       N1 - OSPF NSSA external type 1, N2 - OSPF NSSA external type 2
       E1 - OSPF external type 1, E2 - OSPF external type 2
       i - IS-IS, su - IS-IS summary, L1 - IS-IS level-1, L2 - IS-IS level-2
       ia - IS-IS inter area, * - candidate default, U - per-user static route
       o - ODR, P - periodic downloaded static route, H - NHRP, l - LISP
       a - application route
       + - replicated route, % - next hop override, p - overrides from PfR

Gateway of last resort is not set

NX-2# show ip route isis
! Output omitted for brevity

10.1.1.0/24, ubest/mbest: 1/0
    *via 10.12.1.1, Eth1/1, [115/14], 00:02:30, isis-NXOS, L1
10.4.4.0/24, ubest/mbest: 1/0
    *via 10.23.1.3, Eth1/2, [115/18], 00:02:14, isis-NXOS, L1
10.34.1.0/24, ubest/mbest: 1/0
    *via 10.23.1.3, Eth1/2, [115/8], 00:17:28, isis-NXOS, L1
```

The first step to identify missing routes is to verify neighbor adjacencies and then check the IS-IS topology table. Example 9-38 displays the topology table on R1 and NX-2. R1 displays double asterisks (**) for all the metrics to the other routers, whereas NX-2 has populated metrics. This is because R1 is configured only for narrow metrics, which use different TLVs than the wide metric TLVs that are advertised from NX-2.

Example 9-38 *IS-IS Topology Table with Mismatched Metric Types*

```
R1# show isis topology

IS-IS TID 0 paths to level-1 routers
System Id           Metric     Next-Hop             Interface    SNPA
R1                  --
NX-2                **
NX-3                **
R4                  **

NX-2# show isis topology
IS-IS process: NXOS
VRF: default
```

```
IS-IS Level-1 IS routing table
R1.00, Instance 0x0000000C
    *via R1, Ethernet1/1, metric 4
NX-3.00, Instance 0x0000000C
    *via NX-3, Ethernet1/2, metric 4
R4.00, Instance 0x0000000C
    *via NX-3, Ethernet1/2, metric 8
R4.01, Instance 0x0000000C
    *via NX-3, Ethernet1/2, metric 8
```

To confirm the theory, the metric types are checked on R1 and NX-2 by looking at the IS-IS protocol, as shown in Example 9-39. R1 is set to accept and generate only narrow metrics, whereas NX-OS accepts both narrow and wide metrics while advertising only wide metrics.

Example 9-39 *Checking IS-IS Metric Configuration*

```
R1# show isis protocol | i metric
  Generate narrow metrics:  level-1-2
  Accept narrow metrics:    level-1-2
  Generate wide metrics:    none
  Accept wide metrics:      none

NX-2# show isis | i Metric
  Metric-style : advertise(wide), accept(narrow, wide)
```

The Nexus switches are placed in metric transition mode using the command **metric-style transition**, which makes the Nexus switch populate the LSP with narrow and wide metric TLVs. This allows other routers that operate in narrow metric mode to compute a total path metric for a topology.

Example 9-40 displays the configuration and verification on NX-2 for IS-IS metric transition mode.

Example 9-40 *IS-IS Metric Transition Mode Configuration and Verification*

```
NX-2# show run isis
! Output omitted for brevity

router isis NXOS
  net 49.1234.0000.0000.0002.00
  is-type level-1
  metric-style transition

NX-2# show isis | i Metric
  Metric-style : advertise(narrow, wide), accept(narrow, wide)
```

Example 9-41 displays the IS-IS topology table and routing table for the IOS routers now that the Nexus switches are placed in IS-IS metric transition mode.

Example 9-41 *Verification of IOS Devices After NX-OS Metric Transition Mode*

```
R1# show isis topology

IS-IS TID 0 paths to level-1 routers
System Id              Metric        Next-Hop         Interface      SNPA
R1                     --
NX-2                   10            NX-2             Gi0/1          0022.2222.2222
NX-3                   14            NX-2             Gi0/1          0023.3333.3333
R4                     18            NX-2             Gi0/1          0022.2222.2222
```

```
R1# show ip route isis
! Output omitted for brevity

Gateway of last resort is not set

      10.0.0.0/8 is variably subnetted, 7 subnets, 2 masks
i L1     10.4.4.0/24 [115/28] via 10.12.1.2, 00:01:30, GigabitEthernet0/1
i L1     10.23.1.0/24 [115/14] via 10.12.1.2, 00:02:55, GigabitEthernet0/1
i L1     10.34.1.0/24 [115/18] via 10.12.1.2, 00:01:30, GigabitEthernet0/1
```

```
R4# show ip route isis
! Output omitted for brevity

Gateway of last resort is not set

      10.0.0.0/8 is variably subnetted, 7 subnets, 2 masks
i L1     10.1.1.0/24 [115/28] via 10.34.1.3, 00:01:54, GigabitEthernet0/1
i L1     10.12.1.0/24 [115/18] via 10.34.1.3, 00:01:54, GigabitEthernet0/1
i L1     10.23.1.0/24 [115/14] via 10.34.1.3, 00:01:54, GigabitEthernet0/1
```

L1 to L2 Route Propagations

IS-IS operates on a two-level hierarchy. A primary function of the L1-L2 routers is to act as a gateway for L1 routers to the L2 IS-IS backbone. Figure 9-10 displays a simple topology with NX-1 and NX-2 in Area 49.0012 while NX-3 and NX-4 are in Area 49.0034. NX-1's 10.1.1.0/24 network should be advertised to Area 49.0034 by NX-2, and NX-4's 10.4.4.0/24 network is advertised to Area 49.0012 by NX-3.

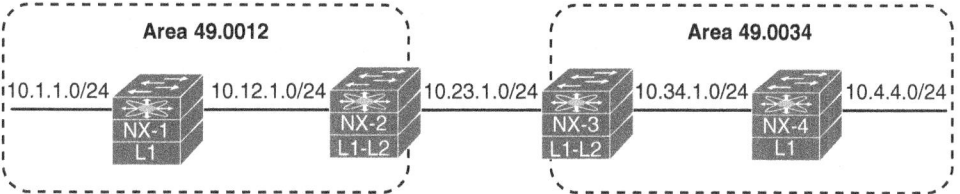

Figure 9-10 *IS-IS Topology to Demonstrate IS-IS L1 to L2 Route Propagation*

Example 9-42 displays all four Nexus switches' routing tables. Notice that NX-3 is missing the 10.1.1.0/24 network. This network exists in NX-2's routing table as an IS-IS L1 route. The same behavior exists for NX-4's 10.4.4.0/24 network, which appears on NX-3.

Example 9-42 *Routing Table of NX-1, NX-2, NX-3, and NX-4*

```
NX-1# show ip route isis
! Output omitted for brevity


0.0.0.0/0, ubest/mbest: 1/0
    *via 10.12.1.2, Eth1/1, [115/4], 00:02:43, isis-NXOS, L1
10.23.1.0/24, ubest/mbest: 1/0
    *via 10.12.1.2, Eth1/1, [115/8], 00:02:33, isis-NXOS, L1
```

```
NX-2# show ip route isis
! Output omitted for brevity


10.1.1.1/32, ubest/mbest: 1/0
    *via 10.12.1.1, Eth1/1, [115/8], 00:01:42, isis-NXOS, L1
10.34.1.0/24, ubest/mbest: 1/0
    *via 10.23.1.3, Eth1/2, [115/8], 00:01:38, isis-NXOS, L2
```

```
NX-3# show ip route isis
! Output omitted for brevity


10.4.4.4/32, ubest/mbest: 1/0
    *via 10.34.1.4, Eth1/1, [115/8], 00:02:45, isis-NXOS, L1
10.12.1.0/24, ubest/mbest: 1/0
    *via 10.23.1.2, Eth1/2, [115/8], 00:02:45, isis-NXOS, L2
```

```
NX-4# show ip route isis
! Output omitted for brevity


0.0.0.0/0, ubest/mbest: 1/0
    *via 10.34.1.3, Eth1/1, [115/4], 00:00:28, isis-NXOS, L1
10.23.1.0/24, ubest/mbest: 1/0
    *via 10.34.1.3, Eth1/1, [115/8], 00:03:48, isis-NXOS, L1
```

The next step is to examine the IS-IS database with the command **show isis database [level-1 | level-2] [detail]** [*lsp-id*] to make sure that the appropriate LSPs are in the LSPDB. LSPs are restricted by specifying an IS-IS level or the specific LSPID for an advertising router.

Example 9-43 displays all the LSPs for L1 and L2 in NX-2's LSPDB. From the output, NX-2 has received NX-1's L1 LSP and has received NX-3's L2 LSP.

Example 9-43 *NX-2's LSPDB*

```
NX-2# show isis database
IS-IS Process: NXOS LSP database VRF: default
IS-IS Level-1 Link State Database
  LSPID                 Seq Number     Checksum   Lifetime   A/P/O/T
  NX-1.00-00            0x00000006     0x9FC1     743        0/0/0/1
  NX-1.01-00            0x00000002     0x8249     1137       0/0/0/1
  NX-2.00-00          * 0x0000000A     0x9AE9     1179       1/0/0/3

IS-IS Level-2 Link State Database
  LSPID                 Seq Number     Checksum   Lifetime   A/P/O/T
  NX-2.00-00          * 0x00000003     0x0E82     1179       0/0/0/3
  NX-3.00-00            0x00000003     0x5CF5     1153       0/0/0/3
  NX-3.02-00            0x00000002     0x952F     1152       0/0/0/3
```

```
NX-2# show isis database level-2
IS-IS Process: NXOS LSP database VRF: default
IS-IS Level-2 Link State Database
  LSPID                 Seq Number     Checksum   Lifetime   A/P/O/T
  NX-2.00-00          * 0x00000003     0x0E82     1155       0/0/0/3
  NX-3.00-00            0x00000003     0x5CF5     1130       0/0/0/3
  NX-3.02-00            0x00000002     0x952F     1129       0/0/0/3
```

Table 9-10 explains some of the key fields in the output from Example 9-43.

Table 9-10 *General IS-IS Database Fields*

Field	Description
LSPID	The LSP ID is a fixed 8-byte field that provides a unique identification of the LSP originator. The system ID portion of the LSPID includes the switch's hostname instead of the numeric representation. IS-IS provides a name to system ID mapping under the optional TLV #137 that is found as part of the LSP to simplify troubleshooting. Ensuring all devices have unique hostnames helps when examining the LSPDB.
Lifetime	The time that the advertised LSP remains valid before it is timed out and purged.
Attached Bit (A)	Identifies whether this router is an L1-L2 router and provides connectivity to the IS-IS L2 backbone.

Field	Description
Partition Bit (P)	Indicates whether the partition repair bit is set on this LSP.
Overload Bit (O)f	Indicates whether the overload bit is set on the advertising router. The overload bit indicates that system maintenance is being performed or the router has just started up and is waiting to fully converge. The overload bit acts as a form of traffic engineering and directs traffic via other paths where possible, and in essence provides the same effect as costing out (placing high interface costs) on all links.
	Nexus switches set the overload bit with the command **set-overload-bit**.
Topology Bit (T)	Indicates the function of the router. A value of 1 indicates that the router is an IS-IS L1 router. The value of 3 indicates that the router could be an L1 or L1-L2, depending on whether the LSPID exists in both IS-IS levels.

Using the optional **detail** keyword provides a list of all the networks, metrics, and TLV types when viewing the LSPDB. Example 9-44 displays all of NX-2's L2 IS-IS LSP information in detail. The output includes every network that NX-2 advertises to other L2 neighbors. Notice that the 10.1.1.0/24 network entry is not present on NX-2's LSP, nor is the 10.4.4.0/24 network entry on NX-3's LSP.

Example 9-44 *Examination of NX-2's L2 Detailed LSPDB*

```
NX-2# show isis database level-2 detail
IS-IS Process: NXOS LSP database VRF: default
IS-IS Level-2 Link State Database
  LSPID                 Seq Number    Checksum  Lifetime   A/P/O/T
  NX-2.00-00          * 0x00000003    0x0E82    1135       0/0/0/3
    Instance        : 0x00000003
    Area Address    : 49.0012
    NLPID           : 0xCC
    Router ID       : 192.168.2.2
    IP Address      : 192.168.2.2
    Hostname        : NX-2              Length : 4
    Extended IS     : NX-3.02           Metric : 4
    Extended IP     :     10.23.1.0/24  Metric : 4            (U)
    Extended IP     :     10.12.1.0/24  Metric : 4            (U)
    Digest Offset   : 0
  NX-3.00-00            0x00000003    0x5CF5    1109       0/0/0/3
    Instance        : 0x00000001
    Area Address    : 49.0034
    NLPID           : 0xCC
    Router ID       : 192.168.3.3
    IP Address      : 192.168.3.3
    Hostname        : NX-3              Length : 4
    Extended IS     : NX-3.02           Metric : 4
```

```
    Extended IP    :       10.23.1.0/24   Metric : 4          (U)
    Extended IP    :       10.34.1.0/24   Metric : 4          (U)
    Digest Offset :    0
NX-3.02-00                 0x00000002   0x952F     1108      0/0/0/3
    Instance       :   0x00000001
    Extended IS    :   NX-2.00            Metric : 0
    Extended IS    :   NX-3.00            Metric : 0
    Digest Offset :    0
```

Note Remember that the pseudonode portion of the LSP ID is zero for the actual router and contains all its links. If the pseudonode portion of the LSP ID is nonzero, it reflects the DIS for the segment and lists the LSP IDs for the routers connected to it. The LSP ID NX-3.02-00 is the DIS for the NX-2 to NX-3 network link.

The IS-IS LSPDB indicates that NX-1's L1 routes are not propagating to NX-2's L2 database, and the same behavior is occurring between NX-4 and NX-3. This is caused by a difference in operational behavior between NX-OS and other Cisco operating systems (IOS, IOS XR, etc.). Nexus switches require explicit configuration with the command **distribute level-1 into level-2** {**all** | **route-map** *route-map-name*} on L1-L2 routers to insert L1 routes into the L2 topology.

Example 9-45 displays the relevant IS-IS configuration on NX-2 and NX-3 to enable L1 route propagation into the L2 LSPDB.

Example 9-45 *Configuration for L1 Route Propagation*

```
NX-2# show run isis
! Output omitted for brevity
router isis NXOS
  net 49.0012.0000.0000.0002.00
  distribute level-1 into level-2 all
  log-adjacency-changes

NX-3# show run isis
! Output omitted for brevity
router isis NXOS
  net 49.0034.0000.0000.0003.00
  distribute level-1 into level-2 all
  log-adjacency-changes
```

Example 9-46 displays NX-3's LSP that was advertised to NX-2, now that L1 route propagation has been configured on NX-2 and NX-3. Notice that it now includes the L1 route 10.4.4.0/24.

Example 9-46 *NX-3's LSP After Enabling Route Propagation*

```
NX-2# show isis database level-2 detail NX-3.00-00
IS-IS Process: NXOS LSP database VRF: default
IS-IS Level-2 Link State Database
  LSPID                 Seq Number   Checksum  Lifetime  A/P/O/T
  NX-3.00-00            0x00000004   0x7495    1069      0/0/0/3
    Instance       :  0x00000002
    Area Address   :  49.0034
    NLPID          :  0xCC
    Router ID      :  192.168.3.3
    IP Address     :  192.168.3.3
    Hostname       :  NX-3             Length : 4
    Extended IS    :  NX-3.02          Metric : 4
    Extended IP    :      10.4.4.0/24  Metric : 8      (U)
    Extended IP    :      10.23.1.0/24 Metric : 4      (U)
    Extended IP    :      10.34.1.0/24 Metric : 4      (U)
    Digest Offset  :  0
```

Example 9-47 displays NX-2's and NX-4's routing table after the L1 route propagation was configured on NX-2 and NX-3. Now the 10.1.1.0/24 and 10.4.4.0/24 network are reachable on both the L1-L2 switches.

Example 9-47 *NX-2 and NX-4's Routing Table After L1 Route Propagation*

```
NX-2# show ip route isis
! Output omitted for brevity

10.1.1.0/24, ubest/mbest: 1/0
    *via 10.12.1.1, Eth1/1, [115/8], 00:11:52, isis-NXOS, L1
10.4.4.0/24, ubest/mbest: 1/0
    *via 10.23.1.3, Eth1/2, [115/12], 00:00:40, isis-NXOS, L2
10.34.1.0/24, ubest/mbest: 1/0
    *via 10.23.1.3, Eth1/2, [115/8], 00:11:48, isis-NXOS, L2
```

```
NX-3# show ip route isis
! Output omitted for brevity

10.1.1.0/24, ubest/mbest: 1/0
    *via 10.23.1.2, Eth1/2, [115/12], 00:01:44, isis-NXOS, L2
10.4.4.0/24, ubest/mbest: 1/0
    *via 10.34.1.4, Eth1/1, [115/8], 00:12:13, isis-NXOS, L1
10.12.1.0/24, ubest/mbest: 1/0
    *via 10.23.1.2, Eth1/2, [115/8], 00:05:12, isis-NXOS, L2
```

Suboptimal Routing

As mentioned in the previous section, L1-L2 routers act as a gateway for L1 routers to the L2 IS-IS backbone. L1-L2 routers do not advertise L2 routes into the L1 area, but they set the attached bit in their L1 LSP indicating that the router has connectivity to the IS-IS backbone network. If an L1 router does not have a route for a network, it searches the LSPDB for the closest router with the attached bit, which acts as a route of last resort.

In Figure 9-11, Area 49.1234 connects to Area 49.0005 and Area 49.0006. NX-1 and NX-3 are L1 routers, and NX-2 and NX-4 are L1-L2 routers.

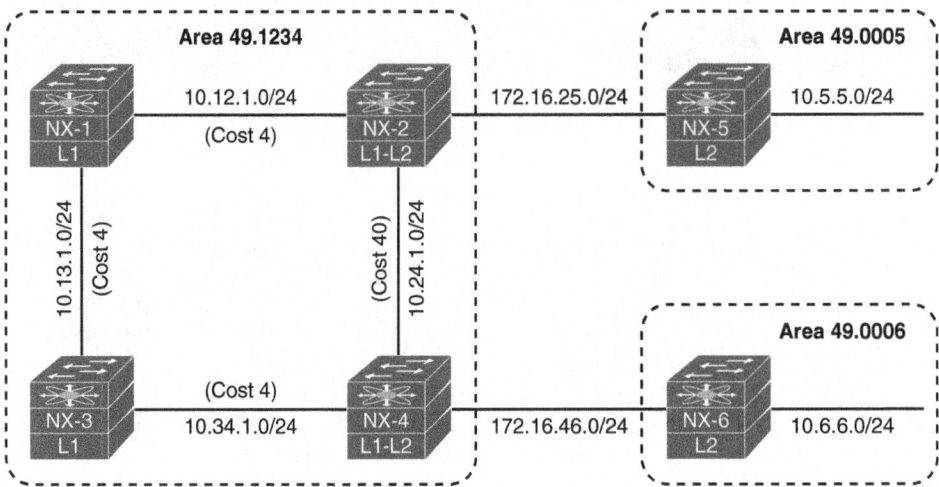

Figure 9-11 *IS-IS InterArea Topology*

The problem comes from the suboptimal routing that occurs when NX-1 tries to connect with 10.6.6.0/24 network, as it crosses the higher cost 10.24.1.0/24 network link. The same problem occurs for NX-3 connecting with the 10.5.5.0/24 network. Example 9-48 displays the suboptimal path taken by both NX-1 and NX-3.

Example 9-48 *Suboptimal Path Selection*

```
NX-1# trace 10.6.6.6 so lo0
traceroute to 10.6.6.6 (10.6.6.6) from 192.168.1.1 (192.168.1.1), 30 hops max, 40
  byte packets
 1  10.12.1.2 (10.12.1.2)  1.95 ms  1.36 ms  1.397 ms
 2  10.24.1.4 (10.24.1.4)  2.758 ms  2.498 ms  2.423 ms
 3  172.16.46.6 (172.16.46.6)  4.037 ms *  4.103 ms
```

```
NX-3# trace 10.5.5.5 so lo0
traceroute to 10.5.5.5 (10.5.5.5) from 192.168.3.3 (192.168.3.3), 30 hops max, 40
  byte packets
 1  10.34.1.4 (10.34.1.4)  1.826 ms  1.127 ms  1.249 ms
 2  10.24.1.2 (10.24.1.2)  2.434 ms  2.461 ms  2.19 ms
 3  172.16.25.5 (172.16.25.5)  5.262 ms
```

Example 9-49 displays the IS-IS database on NX-1 and NX-3. The attached bit 'A' is detected for NX-2 and NX-4. In essence, the attached bit provides a L1 default route toward the advertising L1-L2 router.

Example 9-49 *IS-IS Database for Area 49.1234*

```
NX-1# show isis database
IS-IS Process: NXOS LSP database VRF: default
IS-IS Level-1 Link State Database
  LSPID               Seq Number    Checksum   Lifetime   A/P/O/T
  NX-1.00-00        * 0x0000001D    0xC67A     1038       0/0/0/1
  NX-2.00-00          0x00000021    0xAF03     1120       1/0/0/3
  NX-3.00-00          0x0000001F    0xD222     1055       0/0/0/1
  NX-4.00-00          0x00000021    0x94B5     1154       1/0/0/3
```

Now NX-1 and NX-2 must identify the closest router with the attached bit. Normally this is a manual process of cross-referencing the IS-IS database with the IS-IS topology table, but NX-OS does this for you automatically. The IS-IS topology table for NX-1 and NX-3 is displayed in Example 9-50.

Example 9-50 *IS-IS Topology for Area 49.1234*

```
NX-1# show isis topology
IS-IS process: NXOS
VRF: default
IS-IS Level-1 IS routing table
NX-2.00, Instance 0x00000022
    *via NX-2, Ethernet1/2, metric 4
NX-3.00, Instance 0x00000022
    *via NX-3, Ethernet1/1, metric 4
NX-4.00, Instance 0x00000022
    *via NX-3, Ethernet1/1, metric 8
0000.0000.0000.00, Instance 0x00000022, Default
    *via NX-2, Ethernet1/2, metric 4

NX-3# show isis topology
IS-IS process: NXOS
VRF: default
IS-IS Level-1 IS routing table
NX-1.00, Instance 0x0000001F
    *via NX-1, Ethernet1/1, metric 4
NX-2.00, Instance 0x0000001F
    *via NX-1, Ethernet1/1, metric 8
NX-4.00, Instance 0x0000001F
    *via NX-4, Ethernet1/2, metric 4
0000.0000.0000.00, Instance 0x0000001F, Default
    *via NX-4, Ethernet1/2, metric 4
```

Example 9-51 displays the routing table of NX-1 and NX-3. Notice that an entry does not exist for the 10.5.5.0/24 or 10.6.6.0/24 networks, so the default network is used instead. Notice that the default route correlates with the IS-IS topology table entry from Example 9-50.

Example 9-51 *NX-1 and NX-3's Routing Table*

```
NX-1# show ip route isis
! Output omitted for brevity

0.0.0.0/0, ubest/mbest: 1/0
    *via 10.12.1.2, Eth1/2, [115/4], 00:07:05, isis-NXOS, L1
10.24.1.0/24, ubest/mbest: 1/0
    *via 10.12.1.2, Eth1/2, [115/44], 00:07:05, isis-NXOS, L1
10.34.1.0/24, ubest/mbest: 1/0
    *via 10.13.1.3, Eth1/1, [115/8], 00:04:39, isis-NXOS, L1
172.16.25.0/24, ubest/mbest: 1/0
    *via 10.12.1.2, Eth1/2, [115/8], 00:07:05, isis-NXOS, L1
172.16.46.0/24, ubest/mbest: 1/0
    *via 10.13.1.3, Eth1/1, [115/12], 00:04:39, isis-NXOS, L1
```

```
NX-3# show ip route isis
! Output omitted for brevity

0.0.0.0/0, ubest/mbest: 1/0
    *via 10.34.1.4, Eth1/2, [115/4], 00:07:32, isis-NXOS, L1
10.12.1.0/24, ubest/mbest: 1/0
    *via 10.13.1.1, Eth1/1, [115/8], 00:05:11, isis-NXOS, L1
10.24.1.0/24, ubest/mbest: 1/0
    *via 10.34.1.4, Eth1/2, [115/44], 00:07:32, isis-NXOS, L1
172.16.25.0/24, ubest/mbest: 1/0
    *via 10.13.1.1, Eth1/1, [115/12], 00:05:11, isis-NXOS, L1
172.16.46.0/24, ubest/mbest: 1/0
    *via 10.34.1.4, Eth1/2, [115/8], 00:07:32, isis-NXOS, L1
```

Suboptimal routing is corrected by route leaking, a technique that redistributes the L2 level routes into the L1 level. IS-IS route leaking is configured with the command **distribute level-2 into level-1 {all | route-policy** *route-policy-name*}. Example 9-52 displays the highlighted L2 route-leaking configuration.

Example 9-52 *IS-IS L2 Route-Leaking Configuration*

```
NX-2# show run isis
! Output omitted for brevity

router isis NXOS
 net 49.1234.0000.0000.0002.00
```

```
   distribute level-1 into level-2 all
   distribute level-2 into level-1 all
   metric-style transition
```

```
NX-3# show run isis
! Output omitted for brevity

router isis NXOS
  net 49.1234.0000.0000.0003.00
  distribute level-1 into level-2 all
  distribute level-2 into level-1 all
  metric-style transition
```

Note Route leaking normally uses a restrictive route map to control which routes are leaked; otherwise, running all the area routers in L2 mode makes more sense.

Let's verify the change by checking the IS-IS database to see if the 10.5.5.0/24 and 10.6.6.0/24 networks are being advertised by NX-2 and NX-4 into IS-IS L1 for Area 49.1234. After that is verified, check the routing table to verify that those entries are added to the RIB. Example 9-53 displays the IS-IS Database with L2 Route Leaking.

Example 9-53 *IS-IS Database with L2 Route Leaking*

```
NX-1# show isis database detail NX-2.00-00
! Output omitted for brevity
IS-IS Level-1 Link State Database
    Extended IP    :    10.6.6.0/24      Metric : 54          (D)
    Extended IP    :    10.5.5.0.24      Metric : 14          (D)
..
    Extended IP    :    172.16.25.0/24   Metric : 4           (U)
```

```
NX-1# show isis database detail NX-4.00-00
! Output omitted for brevity
IS-IS Level-1 Link State Database
    Extended IP    :    10.6.6.0/24      Metric : 14          (D)
    Extended IP    :    10.5.5.0/24      Metric : 54          (D)
..
    Extended IP    :    172.16.46.0/24   Metric : 4           (U)
```

```
NX-1# show ip route isis
```

```
! Output omitted for brevity

0.0.0.0/0, ubest/mbest: 1/0
    *via 10.12.1.2, Eth1/2, [115/4], 06:41:03, isis-NXOS, L1
10.5.5.0/24, ubest/mbest: 1/0
    *via 10.12.1.2, Eth1/2, [115/18], 00:01:02, isis-NXOS, L1
10.6.6.0/24, ubest/mbest: 1/0
    *via 10.13.1.3, Eth1/1, [115/22], 00:01:20, isis-NXOS, L1
10.24.1.0/24, ubest/mbest: 1/0
    *via 10.12.1.2, Eth1/2, [115/44], 06:41:03, isis-NXOS, L1
10.34.1.0/24, ubest/mbest: 1/0
    *via 10.13.1.3, Eth1/1, [115/8], 06:38:37, isis-NXOS, L1
172.16.25.0/24, ubest/mbest: 1/0
    *via 10.12.1.2, Eth1/2, [115/8], 06:41:03, isis-NXOS, L1
172.16.46.0/24, ubest/mbest: 1/0
    *via 10.13.1.3, Eth1/1, [115/12], 06:38:37, isis-NXOS, L1
```

Example 9-54 verifies that NX-1 and NX-3 are forwarding traffic using the optimal path.

Example 9-54 *Path Check After L2 Route Leaking*

```
NX-1# trace 10.6.6.6
traceroute to 10.6.6.6 (10.6.6.6), 30 hops max, 40 byte packets
 1  10.13.1.3 (10.13.1.3)  1.41 ms  1.202 ms  1.223 ms
 2  10.34.1.4 (10.34.1.4)  2.454 ms  2.46 ms  2.588 ms
 3  172.16.46.6 (172.16.46.6)  4.368 ms
```

```
NX-3# trace 10.5.5.5
traceroute to 10.5.5.5 (10.5.5.5), 30 hops max, 40 byte packets
 1  10.13.1.1 (10.13.1.1)  1.73 ms  1.387 ms  1.409 ms
 2  10.12.1.2 (10.12.1.2)  2.376 ms  2.814 ms  2.48 ms
 3  172.16.25.5 (172.16.25.5)  4.38 ms *  4.702 ms
```

Redistribution

Redistributing into IS-IS uses the command **redistribute [bgp** *asn* | **direct** | **eigrp** *process-tag* | **isis** *process-tag* | **ospf** *process-tag* | **rip** *process-tag* | **static] route-map** *route-map-name*. A route-map is required as part of the redistribution process on Nexus switches. Every protocol provides a seed metric at the time of redistribution that allows the destination protocol to calculate a best path. IS-IS provides a default redistribution metric of 10.

Example 9-55 provides the necessary configuration to demonstrate the process of redistribution. NX-1 redistributes the connected routes for 10.1.1.0/24 and 10.11.11.0/24 in lieu of them being advertised with the IS-IS routing protocol. Notice that the route-map is a simple permit statement without any conditional matches.

Example 9-55 *NX-1 Redistribution Configuration*

```
router isis NXOS
  redistribute direct route-map REDIST
!
route-map REDIST permit 10
```

The route is redistributed on NX-1 and is injected into the IS-IS database with the 10.1.1.0/24 and 10.11.11.0/24 prefix. The redistribution of prefixes is verified by looking at the LSPDB on other devices, such as NX-2, as shown in Example 9-56.

Example 9-56 *Verification of Redistributed Networks*

```
NX-2# show isis database detail NX-1.00-00
! Output omitted for brevity
IS-IS Process: NXOS LSP database VRF: default
IS-IS Level-1 Link State Database
  LSPID                 Seq Number   Checksum  Lifetime   A/P/O/T
  NX-1.00-00            0x00000008   0x2064    1161       0/0/0/3
    Instance      :  0x00000005
    Area Address  :  49.0012
    NLPID         :  0xCC
    Router ID     :  10.12.1.100
    IP Address    :  10.12.1.100
    Hostname      :  NX-1            Length : 4
    Extended IS   :  NX-1.01         Metric : 4
    Extended IP   :       10.1.1.0/24  Metric : 10       (U)
    Extended IP   :     10.11.11.0/24  Metric : 10       (U)
    Extended IP   :      10.12.1.0/24  Metric : 4        (U)
    Digest Offset :  0
```

Summary

This chapter provided a brief review of the IS-IS routing protocols and then explored the methods for troubleshooting adjacency issues between devices, missing routes, and path selection.

The following parameters must match for the two routers to become neighbors:

- IS-IS interfaces must be *Active*.
- Connectivity between devices must exist using the primary subnet.
- MTU matches.
- L1 adjacencies require the area address to match, and the system ID must be unique between neighbors.
- L1 routers can form adjacencies with L1 or L1-L2 routers, but not L2.
- L2 routers can form adjacencies with L2 or L1-L2 routers, but not L1.
- DIS requirements match.
- IIH Authentication Type & Credentials (if any)

IS-IS is a link-state routing protocol that creates a complete map based on LSPs. Routes are missing from the routing database typically because of bad network design, mismatch of metric types, or through configurations that do not support L1-to-L2 route propagation. This chapter provided some common bad IS-IS designs and their solutions to prevent the loss of path information.

References

RFC 1195, Use of OSI IS-IS for Routing in TCP/IP and Dual Environments.

R. Callon. IETF, http://tools.ietf.org/html/rfc1195, December 1990.

RFC 3784, Intermediate System to Intermediate System (IS-IS) Extensions for Traffic Engineering (TE). Tony Li, Henk Smit. IETF, https://tools.ietf.org/html/rfc3784, June 2004.

Edgeworth, Brad, Aaron Foss, Ramiro Garza Rios. *IP Routing on Cisco IOS, IOS XE and IOS XR*. Indianapolis: Cisco Press, 2014.

Cisco. Cisco NX-OS Software Configuration Guides, http://www.cisco.com.

Chapter 10

Troubleshooting Nexus Route-Maps

This chapter covers the following topics:

- Conditional matching with ACLs, Prefix Lists, and Regular Expression
- Route-Maps
- Troubleshooting RPM
- Redistribution
- Policy-Based Routing

Nexus Operating System (NX-OS) *route-maps* provide the capability to filter routes and modify route attributes and routing behavior. These technologies use conditional match criteria to allow actions to occur based upon route characteristics.

Before route-maps are explained, the concepts involved with conditional matching using *access control lists (ACL)*, prefix lists, and conditional matching of BGP communities must be explained.

Conditional Matching

Route-maps typically use some form of conditional matching so that only certain prefixes are blocked, accepted, or modified. Network prefixes are conditionally matched by a variety of routing protocol attributes, but the following sections explain the most common techniques for conditionally matching a prefix.

Access Control Lists

Originally, *access control lists (ACL)* were intended to provide filtering of packets flowing into or out of a network interface, similar to the functionality of a basic firewall.

Today, ACLs provide a method of identifying networks within routing protocols. ACLs are also useful to isolate the direction of the problem or identify where the packet is getting dropped while troubleshooting a complex network environment.

ACLs in NX-OS are generic expressions for filtering traffic based on Layer 2, Layer 3, or Layer 4 information. ACLs are composed of *access control entries (ACE)*, which are entries in the ACL that identify the action to be taken (**permit** or **deny**) and the relevant packet classification. Packet classification starts at the top (lowest sequence) and proceeds down (higher sequence) until a matching pattern is identified. After a match is found, the appropriate action (**permit** or **deny**) is taken and processing stops. At the end of every ACL is an implicit **deny** ACE, which denies all packets that did not match earlier in the ACL.

ACLs are classified into two categories:

- **Standard ACLs:** Define the packets based solely on the source network.

- **Extended ACLs:** Define the packet based upon source, destination, protocol, port or combination of other packet attributes. Standard ACLs use the numbered entry 1–99, 1300–1999, or a named ACL. Extended ACLs use the numbered entry 100–199, 2000–2699, or a named ACL. Named ACLs provide relevance to the functionality of the ACL, are used with standard or extended ACLs, and are generally preferred.

The behavior for selecting a network prefix with an extended ACL varies depending on whether the protocol is an IGP such as Enhanced Interior Gateway Protocol (EIGRP), Open Shortest Path First (OSPF), Intermediate System-to-Intermediate System (IS-IS) or Border Gateway Protocol (BGP).

ACLs and ACL Manager Component

In NX-OS, ACLs are managed by a component named ACL Manager (ACLMGR). The ACLMGR is a platform-independent module that serves as a central location for managing ACL definitions for IP, IPv6, and MAC ACLs, as well as for policy objects. The ACLMGR is responsible for processing the configuration received from the user and associating the security ACLs and the enabled interfaces.

Using ACLMGR, the following functionalities are available with ACL:

- Object-Groups (Matching IP Addresses, TCP or UDP ports)

- Time ranges

- IPv6 wildcard matching

- Packet length based matching

- Stateful restarts

- Per-entry statistics

Along with applying ACLs on the interface or using ACLs along with route-maps, which is then used by routing protocols for route filtering purposes, ACLs have the following applications:

- Control Plane Policing (CoPP)
- Dynamic Host Configuration Protocol (DHCP)
- Policy-Based Routing (PBR)
- Web Cache Communication Protocol (WCCP)

NX-OS supports the following ACL formats:

- IPv4/IPv6 ACLs
- Media access control (MAC) ACL
- Address resolution protocol (ARP) ACL
- Virtual LAN (VLAN) access-map

In NX-OS, when an ACL is applied to a target, a policy is created. NX-OS supports the following types of ACL policies:

- Router ACL (RACL)
- Port ACL (PACL)
- VLAN ACL (VACL)
- Virtual terminal line (VTY) ACL

Note PACL can be applied only on ingress packets for L2/L3 physical Ethernet interfaces (including L2 port-channel interfaces).

Example 10-1 illustrates the various ACL configurations supported on NX-OS. In the following example, the command **statistics per-entry** is configured to enable the statistics for the ACEs configured under the ACLs. If the command **statistics per-entry** is not configured, the command **show ip access-list** does not display any statistics for the packets hitting a particular ACE.

Example 10-1 *ACL Formats*

```
IP ACL
NX-1(config)# ip access-list TEST
NX-1(config-acl)# permit ip host 192.168.33.33 host 192.168.3.3
NX-1(config-acl)# permit ip any any
NX-1(config-acl)# statistics per-entry
```

Chapter 10: Troubleshooting Nexus Route-Maps

```
IPv6 ACL
NX-1(config)# ipv6 access-list TESTv6
NX-1(config-ipv6-acl)# permit icmp host 2001::33 host 2001::3
NX-1(config-ipv6-acl)# permit ipv6 any any
NX-1(config-ipv6-acl)# statistics per-entry
```

```
MAC ACL
NX-1(config)# mac access-list TEST-MAC
NX-1(config-mac-acl)# permit 00c0.cf00.0000 0000.00ff.ffff any
NX-1(config-mac-acl)# permit any any
NX-1(config-mac-acl)# statistics per-entry
```

```
ARP ACL
NX-1(config)# arp access-list TEST-ARP
NX-1(config-arp-acl)# deny ip host 192.168.10.11 mac 00c0.cf00.0000 ffff.ff00.0000
NX-1(config-arp-acl)# permit ip any mac any
```

```
VLAN Access-map
NX-1(config)# vlan access-map TEST-VLAN-MAP
NX-1(config-access-map)# match ip address TEST
NX-1(config-access-map)# action drop
NX-1(config-access-map)# statistics per-entry
```

Note Validate the ACL-related configuration using the command **show run aclmgr**. This command displays both the ACL configuration and the ACL attach points.

Example 10-2 illustrates the difference between the output of the **show ip access-list** command when the **statistics per-entry** command is configured, compared to when it is not configured. In the following example, the ACL configuration that has the **statistics per-entry** command configured displays the statistics for the confirmed hits.

Example 10-2 *ACL Statistics*

```
Output when statistics per-entry command is configured
NX-1# show ip access-list TEST
IP access list TEST
        statistics per-entry
        10 permit ip 192.168.33.33/32 192.168.3.3/32 [match=5]
        20 permit ip any any [match=1]
```

```
Output when statistics per-entry command is not configured
NX-1# show ip access-list TEST
```

```
IP access list TEST
        10 permit ip 192.168.33.33/32 192.168.3.3/32
        20 permit ip any any
```

When an ACL is attached to an interface or any other component, the ACL gets programmed in the ternary content addressable memory (TCAM). The TCAM programming for the access-list is verified using the command **show system internal access-list interface** *interface-id* **input statistics [module** *slot*]. This command displays under which bank the ACL is programmed and what kind of policy is created when the ACL is attached to an attach point. Along with this, the command displays the statistics of each ACE entry in the ACL.

If the **statistics per-entry** command is not configured, the counters in the TCAM increment only for the entry for all traffic; that is, **permit ip 0.0.0.0/0 0.0.0.0/0**. Example 10-3 demonstrates the ACL entry on TCAM and the TCAM statistics when statistics per-entry command is not configured.

Example 10-3 *Verifying Access-List Counters in TCAM*

```
Per-Entry Statistics is Configured
NX-1# show system internal access-list interface e4/2 input statistics module 4
INSTANCE 0x0
---------------
  Tcam 1 resource usage:
  ----------------------
  Label_b = 0x2
   Bank 0
   ------
     IPv4 Class
       Policies: RACL(TEST)
       Netflow profile: 0
       Netflow deny profile: 0
       Entries:
          [Index] Entry [Stats]
          ---------------------
  [0018:14242:0004] prec 1 permit-routed ip 192.168.33.33/32 192.168.3.3/32   [5]
  [0019:14c42:0005] prec 1 permit-routed ip 0.0.0.0/0 0.0.0.0/0   [2]
  [001a:15442:0006] prec 1 deny-routed ip 0.0.0.0/0 0.0.0.0/0   [0]

Per-Entry Statistics is Not Configured
NX-1# show system internal access-list interface e4/2 input statistics module 4
INSTANCE 0x0
---------------
  Tcam 1 resource usage:
  ----------------------
```

```
   Label_b = 0x3
     Bank 0
     ------
       IPv4 Class
         Policies: RACL(TEST)    [Merged]
         Netflow profile: 0
         Netflow deny profile: 0
         Entries:
           [Index] Entry [Stats]
           --------------------
   [001b:15262:0007] prec 1 permit-routed ip 0.0.0.0/0 0.0.0.0/0   [33]
! Output after 5 packets are sent between the host 192.168.3.3 and 192.168.33.33
NX-1# show system internal access-list interface e4/2 input statistics module 4
INSTANCE 0x0
---------------
   Tcam 1 resource usage:
   ----------------------
   Label_b = 0x3
     Bank 0
     ------
       IPv4 Class
         Policies: RACL(TEST)    [Merged]
         Netflow profile: 0
         Netflow deny profile: 0
         Entries:
           [Index] Entry [Stats]
           --------------------
   [001b:15262:0007] prec 1 permit-routed ip 0.0.0.0/0 0.0.0.0/0   [38]
```

As stated before, the ACLMGR takes care of creating the policies when an ACL is attached to an attach point. The policies created by the ACLMGR are verified using the command **show system internal aclmgr access-lists policies interface** *interface-id*. This command displays the policy type and interface index, which points to the interface where the ACL is attached, as shown in Example 10-4.

Example 10-4 *Verifying Access-List Counters in Hardware*

```
NX-1# show system internal aclmgr access-lists policies ethernet 4/2
{
    0x11498cfc
    type = SC_TYPE_PORT; mode = SC_MODE_L3;
    flags =
    ifindex = 0x1a181000 (Ethernet4/2); vdc = 0; vlan = 0;
```

```
    2 policies: {
        ACLMGR_POLICY_INBOUND_IPV4_GHOST_RACL: 0x4400282
        ACLMGR_POLICY_INBOUND_IPV4_RACL: 0x4400283
    }
    no links
}

Policy node 0x04400282, name TEST, policy type 0x00400004
Destination: vdc = 1; vlan = 0; ifindex = 0x1a181000;
Effective destinations: no-destination
  Ifelse node 0x04400265
    TRUE action node 0x04400266, action type 0x00200002
    FALSE action node 0x04400267, action type 0x00200001
    NOMATCH action node 0x04400267, action type 0x00200001

Policy node 0x04400283, name TEST, policy type 0x00400010
Destination: vdc = 1; vlan = 0; ifindex = 0x1a181000;
Effective destinations: no-destination
  Ifelse node 0x04400265
    TRUE action node 0x04400266, action type 0x00200002
    FALSE action node 0x04400267, action type 0x00200001
    NOMATCH action node 0x04400267, action type 0x00200001
```

NX-OS has a packet processing filter (PPF) API, which is used to filter the security rules received and processed by the ACLMGR to the relevant clients. The clients can be an interface, a port-channel, a VLAN manager, VSH, and so on. It is important to remember that the ACLMGR stores all the data in the form of a PPF database, where each element is a node. Based on the node ID received from the previous command, more details about the policy can be verified by performing a lookup in the PPF database on that node.

Example 10-5 illustrates the use of the command **show system internal aclmgr ppf node** *node-id* to perform a lookup on the PPF database of the ACLMGR for the policy node created when the policy is attached to an attach point. This command is useful when troubleshooting ACL/filtering-related issues, such as ACL not filtering the traffic properly or not matching the ACL entry at all on NX-OS platform.

Example 10-5 *Verifying the PPF Database*

```
NX-1# show system internal aclmgr ppf node 0x04400283
 ACLMGR PRIVATE DATA VERSION IN USE : 1
========= PPF Node: 0x4400283 ========
   .nlinks = 1
       0x4400265
   .noptlinks = 0
```

```
.nrefs = 0
.id = 0x4400283
.group = 0x0
.flags = 0x0
.priv_data_size = 0
.type = Policy Instance
.dest.vdc = 1
.dest.vrf = 0
.dest.vlan = 0
.dest.ifindex = 0x1a181000
.dir = IN
.u.pinst.type = 0x400010 (racl_ipv4)
.u.pinst.policy.head = 0x4400265
.u.pinst.policy.tail = 0x0
.u.pinst.policy.size = 0x0
.u.pinst.policy.el_field = 0
.u.pinst.policy.el_field = 0
```

Note When troubleshooting any ACL related issues, it is recommended that you collect the command **show tech aclmgr [detail]** or **show tech aclqos [detail]** during a problem. The ACLQOS component on the line card provides statistics for ACLs on a per-line card basis and are important when you are troubleshooting ACL-related issues.

Interior Gateway Protocol (IGP) Network Selection

When ACLs are used for the IGP network selection during redistribution, the source fields of the ACL are used to identify the network, and the destination fields identify the smallest prefix length allowed in the network range. Table 10-1 provides sample ACL entries from within the ACL configuration mode and specifies the networks that match with the extended ACL. Notice that the subtle difference for the destination wildcard for the 172.16.0.0 network affects the actual network ranges that are permitted in the second and third rows of the table.

Table 10-1 *Extended ACL for IGP Route Selection*

ACE Entry	Networks
permit ip any any	Permits all networks
permit ip host 172.16.0.0 host 255.240.0.0	Permits all networks in the 172.16.0.0/12 range
permit ip host 172.16.0.0 host 255.255.0.0	Permits all networks in the 172.16.0.0/16 range
permit host 192.168.1.1	Permits only the 192.168.1.1/32 network

Note Extended ACLs that are used for distribute-list use the source fields to identify the source of the network advertisement, and the destination fields identify the network prefix.

BGP Network Selection

Extended ACLs react differently when matching BGP routes than when matching IGP routes. The source fields match against the network portion of the route, and the destination fields match against the network mask, as shown in Figure 10-1. Extended ACLs were originally the only match criteria used by IOS with BGP before the introduction of prefix-lists.

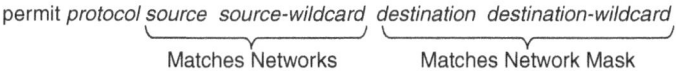

Figure 10-1 *BGP Extended ACL Matches*

Table 10-2 demonstrates the concept of the wildcard for the network and subnet mask.

Table 10-2 *Extended ACL for BGP Route Selection*

Extended ACL	Matches These Networks
permit ip 10.0.0.0 0.0.0.0 255.255.0.0 0.0.0.0	Permits only the 10.0.0.0/16 network
permit ip 10.0.0.0 0.0.255.0 255.255.255.0 0.0.0.0	Permits any 10.0.x.0 network with a /24 prefix length
permit ip 172.16.0.0 0.0.255.255 255.255.255.0 0.0.0.255	Permits any 172.16.x.x network with a /24 to /32 prefix length
permit ip 172.16.0.0 0.0.255.255 255.255.255.128 0.0.0.127	Permits any 172.16.x.x network with a /25 to /32 prefix length

Prefix Matching and Prefix-Lists

Prefix lists provide another method of identifying networks in a routing protocol. They identify a specific IP address, network, or network range, and allow for the selection of multiple networks with a variety of prefix lengths (subnet masks) by using a *prefix match specification*. This technique is preferred over the ACL's network selection method because most network engineers find it easier to understand.

Prefix Matching

The structure for a prefix match specification contains two parts: high-order bit pattern and high-order bit count, which determine the high-order bits in the bit pattern that are to be matched. Some documentation refers to the *high-order bit pattern* as the *address* or *network*, and the *high-order bit count* as *length* or *mask length*.

In Figure 10-2, the prefix match specification has the high-order bit pattern of 192.168.0.0 and a high-order bit count of 16. The high-order bit pattern has been converted to binary to demonstrate where the high-order bit count lays. Because no additional matching length parameters are included, the high-order bit count is an exact match.

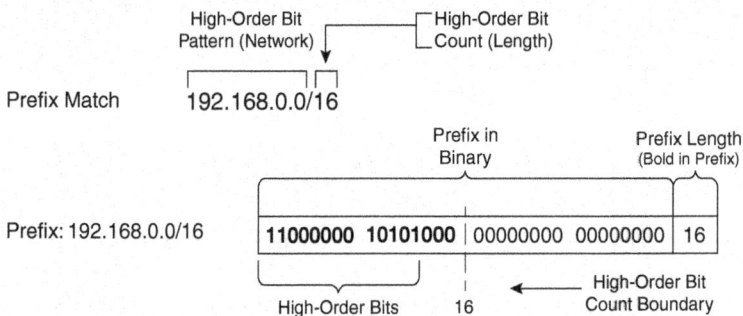

Figure 10-2 *Basic Prefix Match Pattern*

The prefix match specification logic might look identical to the functionality of an access-list. The true power and flexibility comes by using matching length parameters to identify multiple networks with specific prefix lengths with one statement. The matching length parameter options are as follows:

- **le** (less than or equal to <=)
- **ge** (greater than or equal to >=), or both.

Figure 10-3 demonstrates the prefix match specification with a high-order bit pattern of 10.168.0.0, high-order bit count of 13, and the matching length of the prefix must be greater than or equal to 24.

The 10.168.0.0/13 prefix does not qualify because the prefix length is less than the minimum of 24 bits, whereas the 10.168.0.0/24 prefix does meet the matching length parameter. The 10.173.1.0/28 prefix qualifies because the first 13 bits match the high-order bit pattern, and the prefix length is within the matching length parameter. The 10.104.0.0/24 prefix does not qualify because the high-order bit-pattern does not match within the high-order bit count.

Conditional Matching 579

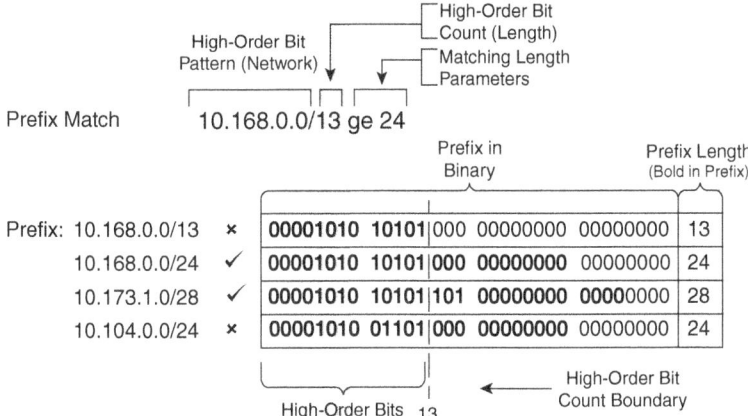

Figure 10-3 *Prefix Match Pattern with Matching Length Parameters*

Figure 10-4 demonstrates a prefix match specification with a high-order bit pattern of 10.0.0.0, high-order bit count of 8, and the matching length must be between 22 and 26.

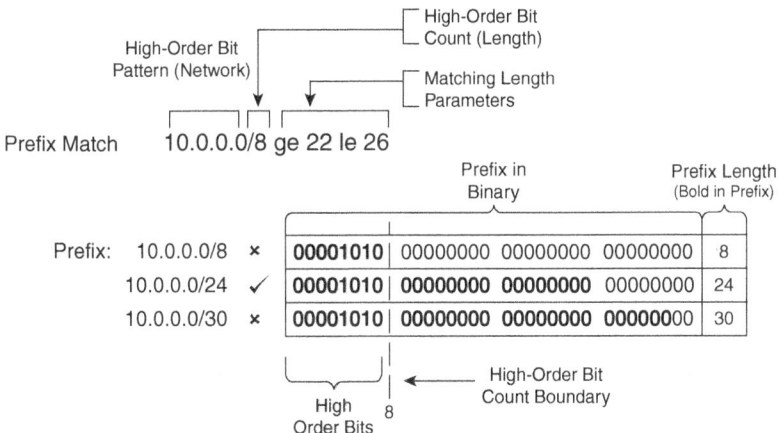

Figure 10-4 *Prefix Match with Ineligible Matched Prefixes*

The 10.0.0.0/8 prefix does not match because the prefix length is too short. The 10.0.0.0/24 qualifies because the bit pattern matches and the prefix length is between 22 and 26. The 10.0.0.0/30 prefix does not match because the bit pattern is too long. Any prefix that starts with 10 in the first octet and has a prefix length between 22 and 26 will match the prefix match specification.

Prefix Lists

Prefix lists contain multiple prefix matching specification entries that contain a **permit** or **deny** action. Prefix lists process in sequential order in a top-down fashion, and the first prefix match processes with the appropriate permit or deny action.

NX-OS prefix lists are configured with the global configuration command **ip prefix-list** *prefix-list-name* [**seq** *sequence-number*] {**permit** | **deny**} *high-order-bit-pattern/high-order-bit-count* [{**eq** *match-length-value* | **le** *le-value* | **ge** *ge-value* [**le** *le-value*]}].

If a sequence is not provided, the sequence number auto-increments by 5 based off the highest sequence number. The first entry is 5. Sequencing allows the deletion of a specific entry. Because prefix lists cannot be resequenced, it is advisable to leave enough space for insertion of sequence numbers at a later time.

Example 10-6 provides a sample prefix list named RFC 1918 for all the networks in the RFC 1918 address range. The prefix list only allows /32 prefixes to exist in the 192.168.0.0 network range and not exist in any other network range in the prefix list.

Example 10-6 *Sample Prefix List*

```
NX-1(config)# ip prefix-list RFC1918 seq 5 permit 192.168.0.0/13 ge 32
NX-1(config)# ip prefix-list RFC1918 seq 10 deny 0.0.0.0/0 ge 32
NX-1(config)# ip prefix-list RFC1918 seq 15 permit 10.0.0.0/7 ge 8
NX-1(config)# ip prefix-list RFC1918 seq 20 permit 172.16.0.0/11 ge 12
NX-1(config)# ip prefix-list RFC1918 seq 25 permit 192.168.0.0/15 ge 16
```

Notice that sequence 5 permits all /32 prefixes in the 192.168.0.0/13 bit pattern, then sequence 10 denies all /32 prefixes in any bit pattern, and then sequence 15, 20, 25 permit routes in the appropriate network ranges. The sequence order is important for the first two entries to ensure that only /32 prefixes exist in the 192.168.0.0 in the prefix list.

The command **show ip prefix-list** *prefix-list-name high-order-bit-pattern/high-order-bit-count* **first-match** provides the capability for a specific network prefix to be checked against a prefix-list to identify the matching sequence, if any.

Example 10-7 displays the command being executed against three network prefix patterns based upon the RFC1918 prefix-list created earlier. The first command uses a high-order bit count of 32, which matches against sequence 5, whereas the second command uses a high-order bit count of 16, which matches against sequence 25. The last command matches against sequence 10, which has a **deny** action.

Example 10-7 *Identification of Matching Sequence for a Specific Prefix Pattern*

```
NX-1# show ip prefix-list RFC1918 192.168.1.1/32 first-match
   seq 5 permit 192.168.0.0/13 ge 32
```

```
NX-1# show ip prefix-list RFC1918 192.168.1.1/16 first-match
   seq 25 permit 192.168.0.0/15 ge 16
```

```
NX-1# show ip prefix-list RFC1918 172.16.1.1/32 first-match
   seq 10 deny 0.0.0.0/0 ge 32
```

Note This command demonstrated in Example 10-7 is useful for verifying that the network prefix matches the intended sequence in a prefix-list.

Route-Maps

Route-maps provide many features to a variety of routing protocols. At the simplest level, route-maps filter networks similar to an ACL, but also provide additional capability by adding or modifying a network attribute. Route-maps must be referenced within a routing-protocol to influence it. Route-maps are a critical to BGP because it is the main component of modifying a unique routing policy on a neighbor-by-neighbor basis.

Route-maps are composed of four components:

- **Sequence Number:** Dictates the processing order of the route-map.
- **Conditional Matching Criteria:** Identifies prefix characteristics (network, BGP path attribute, next-hop, and so on) for a specific sequence.
- **Processing Action:** Permits or denies the prefix.
- **Optional Action:** Allows for manipulations dependent upon how the route-map is referenced on the router. Actions include modification, addition, or removal of route characteristics.

Route-maps use the following command syntax **route-map** *route-map-name* [**permit** | **deny**] [*sequence-number*]. The following rules apply to route-map statements:

- If a processing action is not provided, the default value of **permit** is used.
- If a sequence number is not provided, the sequence number defaults to 10.
- If a conditional matching statement is not included, an implied *all prefixes* is associated to the statement.
- Processing within a route-map stops after all optional actions have processed (if configured) after matching a conditional matching criteria.
- If a route is not conditionally matched, there is an implicit deny for that route.

Example 10-8 provides a sample route-map to demonstrate the four components of a route-map shown earlier. The conditional matching criteria is based upon network ranges specified in an ACL. Comments have been added to explain the behavior of the route-map in each sequence.

Example 10-8 *Sample Route-Map*

```
route-map EXAMPLE permit 10
 match ip address ACL-ONE
 ! Prefixes that match ACL-ONE are permitted. Route-map completes processing upon
   a match

route-map EXAMPLE deny 20
 match ip address ACL-TWO
 ! Prefixes that match ACL-TWO are denied. Route-map completes processing upon a match

route-map EXAMPLE permit 30
 match ip address ACL-THREE
 set metric 20
 ! Prefixes that match ACL-THREE are permitted and modify the metric. Route-map
   completes
 ! processing upon a match

route-map EXAMPLE permit 40
 ! Because a matching criteria was not specified, all other prefixes are permitted
 ! If this sequence was not configured, all other prefixes would drop because of the
 ! implicit deny for all route-maps
```

Note When deleting a specific route-map statement, include the sequence number to prevent deleting the entire route-map.

Conditional Matching

Now that the components and processing order of a route-map were explained, this section expands upon the aspect of how to match a route. Example 10-9 shows the various options available within NX-OS.

Example 10-9 *Sample Route-Map*

```
NX-1(config)# route-map TEST permit 10
NX-1(config-route-map)# match ?
  as-number       Match BGP peer AS number
  as-path         Match BGP AS path list
```

```
  community         Match BGP community list
  extcommunity      Match BGP community list
  interface         Match first hop interface of route
  ip                Configure IP features
  ipv6              Configure IPv6 features
  length            Packet length
  mac-list          Match entries of mac-lists
  metric            Match metric of route
  route-type        Match route-type of route
  source-protocol   Match source protocol
  tag               Match tag of route
  vlan              Vlan ID
```

As you can see, a number of conditional matching options are available. Some of the options, like **vlan** and **mac-list**, are applicable only for policy-based routing. Table 10-3 provides the command syntax for the most common methods for matching prefixes and describes their usage.

Table 10-3 *Conditional Match Options*

Match Command	Description
**match as-number { *number* [, *number* ...]	as-path-access-list name *acl-name* }**	Matches routes that come from peers with the matching ASNs
match as-path *acl-number*	Selects prefixes based on regex query to isolate the ASN in the BGP *path attribute (PA)* AS-Path
	Allows for multiple match variables
match community *community-list-name*	Selects prefixes based on BGP communities
	Allows for multiple match variables
match extcommunity *extcommunity-list-name*	Selects prefixes based on extended BGP communities
match interface *interface-id*	Select prefixes based on the interface that they are associated to
	Allows for multiple match variables
match ip address {*acl-number*	*acl-name*}	Selects prefixes based on network selection criteria defined in the ACL
	Allows for multiple match variables
match ip address prefix-list *prefix-list-name*	Selects prefixes based on prefix selection criteria
	Allows for multiple match variables

Match Command	Description
match ip route-source prefix-list *prefix-list-name*	Selects prefixes based on prefix selection criteria *Allows for multiple match variables*
match local-preference	Selects prefixes based on the BGP attribute *Local Preference* *Allows for multiple match variables*
match metric {*1-4294967295* | **external** *1-4294967295*} [*+- deviation*]	Selects prefixes based on the metric that can be exact, a range, or within acceptable deviation
match route-type *protocol-specific-flag*	Selects prefixes based on the source protocol or sub-classification of routes in the source routing protocol. *Allows for multiple match variables*
match tag *tag-value*	Selects prefixes based on a numeric tag (0-4294967295) which was set by another router *Allows for multiple match variables*

Multiple Conditional Match Conditions

If there are multiple variables (ACLs, prefix-lists, tags, and the like) of the same type configured for a specific route-map sequence, only one variable must match for the prefix to qualify. The Boolean logic uses an *or* operator for this configuration.

In Example 10-10, sequence 10 requires that a prefix pass ACL-ONE or ACL-TWO. Notice that sequence 20 does not have a match statement, so all prefixes that are not passed in sequence 10 qualify and are denied.

Example 10-10 *Multiple Match Variables Example Route-Map*

```
route-map EXAMPLE permit 10
 match ip address ACL-ONE ACL-TWO
!
route-map EXAMPLE deny 20
```

Note Sequence 20 is redundant because of the implicit deny for any prefixes that are not matched in sequence 10. However it provides clarity for junior network engineers.

If multiple match options are configured for a specific route-map sequence, both match options must be met for the prefix to qualify for that sequence. The Boolean logic uses an *and* operator for this configuration.

In Example 10-11, sequence 10 requires that the prefix match ACL ACL-ONE and that the metric be a value between 500 and 600. If the prefix does not qualify for both match options, the prefix does not qualify for sequence 10 and is denied because another sequence does not exist with a permit action.

Example 10-11 *Multiple Match Options Example Route-Map*

```
route-map EXAMPLE permit 10
 match ip address ACL-ONE
 match metric 550 +- 50
```

Complex Matching

Some network engineers find route-maps too complex if the conditional matching criteria uses an ACL, AS-Path ACL, or prefix list that contains a **deny** statement in it. Example 10-12 demonstrates a configuration where the ACL uses a deny statement for the 172.16.1.0/24 network range.

Example 10-12 *Complex Matching Route-Maps*

```
ip access-list standard ACL-ONE
 deny   172.16.1.0 0.0.0.255
 permit 172.16.0.0 0.0.255.255
!
route-map EXAMPLE permit 10
 match ip address ACL-ONE
!
route-map EXAMPLE deny 20
 match ip address ACL-ONE
!
route-map EXAMPLE permit 30
 set metric 20
```

Reading configurations like this must follow the sequence order first, conditional matching criteria second, and only after a match occurs should the processing action and optional action be used. Matching a **deny** statement in the conditional match criteria excludes the route from that sequence in the route-map.

The prefix 172.16.1.0/24 is denied by ACL-ONE, so that infers that there is not a match in sequence 10 and 20; therefore, the processing action (**permit** or **deny**) is not needed. Sequence 30 does not contain a match clause, so any remaining routes are permitted, The prefix 172.16.1.0/24 passes on sequence 30 with the metric set to 20. The prefix 172.16.2.0/24 matches ACL-ONE and passes in sequence 10.

> **Note** Route-maps process in the order of evaluation of the sequence, conditional match criteria, processing action, and optional action, in that order. Any deny statements in the match component are isolated from the route-map sequence action.

Optional Actions

In addition to permitting the prefix to pass, route-maps modify route attributes. Table 10-4 provides a brief overview of the most popular attribute modifications.

Table 10-4 *Route-Map Set Actions*

Set Action	Description
set as-path prepend {*as-number-pattern* | last-as *1-10*}	Prepends the AS-Path for the network prefix with the pattern specified, or from multiple iterations from neighboring AS.
set ip next-hop { *ip-address* | peer-address | self }	Sets the next-hop IP address for any matching prefix. BGP dynamic manipulation uses the peer-address or self keywords.
set local-preference *0-4294967295*	Sets the BGP PA *Local Preference*.
set metric {+*value* | -*value* | *value*} *Value parameters are 0-4294967295	Modifies the existing metric or sets the metric for a route.
set origin {igp | incomplete}	Sets the BGP PA *Origin*.
set tag *tag-value*	Sets a numeric tag (0-4294967295) for identification of networks by other routers.
set weight *0-65535*	Sets the BGP path attribute *Weight*.

Incomplete Configuration of Routing Policies

Another common issue with route policies is the partial configuration of route-maps—specifically, the conditional matching that refers to an ACL, prefix-list, AS-Path ACL, BGP community list, and so on, and that entity is not defined. In some instances, all paths are accepted, and in other instances, no paths are accepted. This problem exists regardless of whether the route-map is used directly with a BGP neighbor, or during route redistribution.

Verifying that all components of a route-map are defined is a vital component of troubleshooting.

Diagnosing Route Policy Manger

NX-OS includes a process called Route Policy Manager (RPM) that provides the route-map functionality with the following properties:

- Operates as a stateful, restartable, and multithreaded process

- Maintains state in a database that exists in private memory
- Supports IPv4 and IPv6 address families
- Provides API interaction for other processes like BGP or OSPF
- Interacts with the unicast RIB (URIB), ARP table

NX-OS's RPM provides additional methods to verify route-map interaction on a Nexus switch. Figure 10-5 provides a sample topology where NX-2 is redistributing OSPF learned routes into EIGRP.

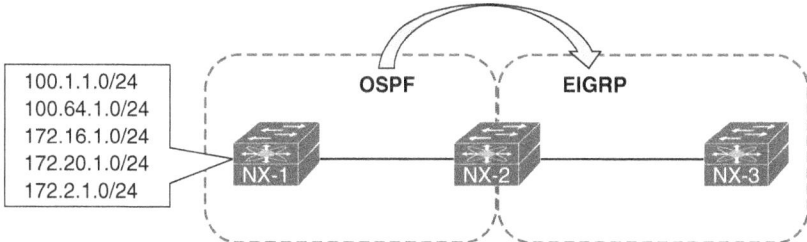

Figure 10-5 *Sample Topology Displaying Redistribution*

Example 10-13 displays the relevant EIGRP configuration that redistributes OSPF and directly connected routes into EIGRP. The route-map is selective with the routes that are being redistributed into EIGRP.

Example 10-13 *NX-2 Redistribution Configuration*

```
NX-2
ip prefix-list PRE1 seq 5 permit 100.1.1.0/24
ip prefix-list PRE2 seq 5 permit 100.64.1.0/24
!
route-map REDIST-CONNECTED-2-EIGRP permit 10
  match interface Vlan10
route-map REDIST-OSPF-2-EIGRP permit 10
  match ip address prefix-list PRE1 PRE2
  set metric 10000 1 255 1 1500
!
router eigrp NXOS
  router-id 192.168.2.2
  address-family ipv4 unicast
    autonomous-system 100
    redistribute direct route-map REDIST-CONNECTED-2-EIGRP
    redistribute ospf NXOS route-map REDIST-OSPF-2-EIGRP
```

Chapter 10: Troubleshooting Nexus Route-Maps

When routes are not installed in EIGRP as anticipated, the first step is to check to make sure that any relevant policies were bound to the destination routing protocol. The command **show system internal rpm event-history rsw** displays low-level events that are handled by RPM.

Example 10-14 displays the command. Notice that two different route-maps were applied to EIGRP: one was for OSPF and the other for directly connected interfaces as the source redistribution protocols.

Example 10-14 *Viewing RPM Event-History*

```
NX-2# show system internal rpm event-history rsw

Routing software interaction logs of RPM
1) Event:E_DEBUG, length:98, at 211881 usecs after 02:01:35 [120] [4933]:
    Bind ack sent - client eigrp-NXOS uuid 0x41000130 for policy
    REDIST-CONNECTED-2-EIGRP
2) Event:E_DEBUG, length:93, at 211857 usecs after 02:01:35 [120] [4933]:
    Bind request - client eigrp-NXOS uuid 0x41000130 policy
    REDIST-CONNECTED-2-EIGRP
3) Event:E_DEBUG, length:114, at 17980 usecs after 02:01:21 [120] [4933]:
    Notify of clients aborted for policy REDIST-CONNECTED-2-EIGRP - change
    status: 0 - config refcount: 0
4) Event:E_DEBUG, length:85, at 95007 usecs after 02:01:06 [120] [4933]:
    Trying to notify for policy REDIST-CONNECTED-2-EIGRP - config refcount 1
5) Event:E_DEBUG, length:85, at 815063 usecs after 02:01:02 [120] [4933]:
    Trying to notify for policy REDIST-CONNECTED-2-EIGRP - config refcount 1
6) Event:E_DEBUG, length:93, at 381829 usecs after 01:59:30 [120] [4933]:
    Bind ack sent - client eigrp-NXOS uuid 0x41000130 for policy
    REDIST-OSPF-2-EIGRP
7) Event:E_DEBUG, length:88, at 381614 usecs after 01:59:30 [120] [4933]:
    Bind request - client eigrp-NXOS uuid 0x41000130 policy REDIST-OSPF-2-EIGRP
```

It might be simpler to get a count of the number of RPM processes that have attached to a protocol using the command **show system internal rpm clients**, as demonstrated in Example 10-15. If the *Bind-count* did not match the anticipated number of route-maps used by that protocol, viewing the RPM event-history will indicate the error.

Example 10-15 *Viewing the Number of RPM Clients per Protocol*

```
NX-2# show system internal rpm clients
PBR: policy based routing    RF/RD: route filtering/redistribution

Client      Bind-count    Client-name         [VRF-name/Status/Id]
 RF/RD       0            bgp-100
 RF/RD       2            eigrp-NXOS
```

```
RF/RD        0              ospf-NXOS
RF/RD        0              icmpv6
RF/RD        0              igmp
RF/RD        0              u6rib
RF/RD        0              tcp
RF/RD        0              urib
```

In addition to viewing the accuracy of a prefix-list as shown in Example 10-2, the capability to view the internal programming for a prefix-list is beneficial. The command **show system internal rpm ip-prefix-list** displays all the prefix-lists configured on the Nexus switch for the route-map from Example 10-13. Notice that the clients show you the route-map referencing the prefix list. In addition, each prefix-list entry displays the number of sequences and version history for that prefix-list. Example 10-16 displays the use of the **show system internal rpm ip-prefix-list** command for NX-2.

Example 10-16 *Viewing Prefix-Lists from RPM Perspective*

```
NX-2# show system internal rpm ip-prefix-list
Policy name: PRE1               Type: ip prefix-list
Version: 2                      State: Ready
Ref. count: 1                   PBR refcount: 0
Stmt count: 1                   Last stmt seq: 5
Set nhop cmd count: 0           Set vrf cmd count: 0
Set intf cmd count: 0           Flags: 0x00000003
PPF nodeid: 0x00000000          Config refcount: 0
PBR Stats: No
Clients:
    REDIST-OSPF-2-EIGRP (internal - route-map)

Policy name: PRE2               Type: ip prefix-list
Version: 2                      State: Ready
Ref. count: 1                   PBR refcount: 0
Stmt count: 1                   Last stmt seq: 5
Set nhop cmd count: 0           Set vrf cmd count: 0
Set intf cmd count: 0           Flags: 0x00000003
PPF nodeid: 0x00000000          Config refcount: 0
PBR Stats: No
Clients:
    REDIST-OSPF-2-EIGRP (internal - route-map)
```

The last method is to view relevant changes from a debug perspective. Traditionally, the route-map option needs to be enabled from the destination protocol. Example 10-17 displays the debugs for the route-maps associated to the redistribution into EIGRP.

Example 10-17 *Viewing Debug Information for Redistribution*

```
NX-2# debug ip eigrp route-map
NX-2# config t
NX-2(config)# router eigrp NXOS
NX-2(config-router)# address-family ipv4 unicast
NX-2(config-router-af)# redistribute ospf NXOS route-map REDIST-OSPF-2-EIGRP
! Output omitted for brevity
02:59:50.071881 eigrp: librpm NXOS [9600] Setting up referee policy PRE1 -
    referer handle 0x820d5e4 referee_plcy 0x5f835614
02:59:50.071917 eigrp: librpm NXOS [9600] rpm_build_prefix_trie_pfl() - List:
    PRE1, No. of entries: 1
02:59:50.071954 eigrp: librpm NXOS [9600] rpm_create_prefix_in_trie()
    - ip addr: 100.1.1.0 mask_len: 24
02:59:50.071973 eigrp: librpm NXOS [9600] Successfully cloned the policy PRE1
    with version 2 rules_flag 0x00000001
02:59:50.071987 eigrp: librpm NXOS [9600] Stats AVL initialized with keysize 12
    and offset 16
02:59:50.072001 eigrp: librpm NXOS [9600] Setting up referee policy PRE2 -
    referer handle 0x820d5e4 referee_plcy 0x5f83556c
02:59:50.072016 eigrp: librpm NXOS [9600] rpm_build_prefix_trie_pfl() - List:
    PRE2, No. of entries: 1
02:59:50.072030 eigrp: librpm NXOS [9600] rpm_create_prefix_in_trie() - ip addr:
    100.64.1.0 mask_len: 24
02:59:50.072043 eigrp: librpm NXOS [9600] Successfully cloned the policy PRE2
    with version 2 rules_flag 0x00000001
02:59:50.072055 eigrp: librpm NXOS [9600] Stats AVL initialized with keysize 12
    and offset 16
02:59:50.072070 eigrp: librpm NXOS [9600] Successfully cloned the policy
    REDIST-OSPF-2-EIGRP with version 5 rules_flag 0x00000409
02:59:50.072086 eigrp: librpm NXOS [9600] Stats AVL initialized with keysize 12
    and offset 16
02:59:50.072099 eigrp: librpm NXOS [9600] Stats successfully init for policy
    REDIST-OSPF-2-EIGRP and context 0x0820d894
02:59:50.072125 eigrp: librpm NXOS [9600] rpm_bind request sent with uuid
    0x41000130 client name eigrp-NXOS policy <REDIST-OSPF-2-EIGRP> type <route-map>
02:59:50.072688 eigrp: librpm NXOS [9600] Recvd msg-type <BIND_ACK> pname
    <REDIST-OSPF-2-EIGRP> ptype <route-map> pversion <0> data <0x0820d894>
02:59:50.076902 eigrp: librpm NXOS [9600] ========== RPM Evaluation starting for
    policy REDIST-OSPF-2-EIGRP ==========
..
```

Policy-Based Routing

A router makes forwarding decisions based upon the destination address of the IP packet. Some scenarios accommodate other factors, such as packet length or source address, when deciding where the router should forward a packet.

Policy-based routing (PBR) allows for conditional forwarding of packets based on the following packet characteristics:

- Routing by protocol type (Internet Control Message Protocol [ICMP], Transmission Control Protocol [TCP], User Datagram Protocol [UDP] and so on)
- Routing by source IP address, destination IP address, or both
- Manually assigning different network paths to the same destination based upon tolerance for latency, link-speed, or utilization for specific transient traffic

Packets are examined for PBR processing as they are received on the router interface. PBR verifies the existence of the next-hop IP address and then forwards packets using the specified next-hop address. Additional next-hop addresses are configured so that in the event that the first next-hop address is not in the RIB, the secondary next-hop addresses are used. If none of the specified next-hop addresses exist in the routing table, the packets are not conditionally forwarded.

Note PBR policies do not modify the RIB because the policies are not universal for all packets. This often complicates troubleshooting because the routing table displays the next-hop address learned from the routing protocol, but does not accommodate for a different next-hop address for the conditional traffic.

NX-OS PBR configuration use a route-map with **match** and **set** statements that are then attached to the inbound interface. The following steps are used:

Step 1. Enable the PBR feature. The PBR feature is enabled with the global configuration command **feature pbr**.

Step 2. Define a route-map. The route-map is configured with the global configuration command **route-map** *route-map-name* [**permit** | **deny**] [*sequence-number*].

Step 3. Identify the conditional match criteria. The conditional match criteria is based upon packet length with the command **match length** *minimum-length maximum-length*, or by using the packet ip address fields with an ACL using the command **match ip address** {*access-list-number* | *acl-name*}.

Step 4. Specify the next-hop. The route-map configuration command **set ip [default] next-hop** *ip-address* [... *ip-address*] is used to specify one or more next-hops for packets that match the criteria. The optional default keyword changes the behavior so that the next-hop address specified by the route-map is used only if the destination address does not exist in the RIB. If a viable route exists in the RIB, that is the next-hop address that is used for forwarding the packet.

Step 5. Apply the route-map to the inbound interface. The route-map is applied with the interface parameter command **ip policy route-map** *route-map-name*.

Step 6. Enable PBR statistics (optional). Statistics of PBR forwarding are enabled with the command **route-map** *route-map-name* **pbr-statistics**.

Figure 10-6 displays a topology to demonstrate how PBR operates. The default path between NX-1 and NX-6 is NX-1 → NX-2 → NX-3 → NX-5 → NX-6 because the link cost of 10.23.1.0/24 is lower than 10.24.1.0/24 link. However, specific traffic sourced from NX-1's Loopback 0 (192.168.1.1) to NX-6's Loopback 0 (192.168.6.6) must not forward through NX-3. These packets must forward through NX-4 even though it has a higher path cost.

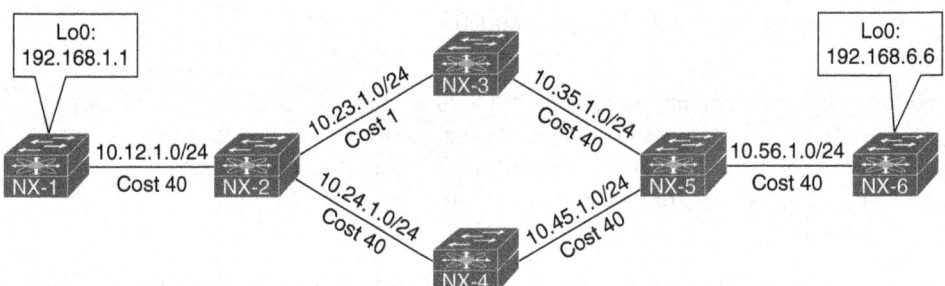

Figure 10-6 *Policy-Based Routing Topology*

Example 10-18 displays NX-2's PBR configuration.

Example 10-18 *NX-2's PBR Configuration*

```
NX-2
feature pbr
!
ip access-list R1-TO-R6
  10 permit ip 192.168.1.1/32 192.168.6.6/32
!
route-map PBR pbr-statistics
route-map PBR permit 10
  match ip address R1-TO-R6
```

```
   set ip next-hop 10.24.1.4
!
interface Ethernet2/1
  description to NX-1
  ip address 10.12.1.2/24
  ip router ospf NXOS area 0.0.0.0
  ip policy route-map PBR
```

Example 10-19 displays a traceroute from NX-1, which displays traffic flowing through NX-3. A source interface was not specified, so traffic is sourced from the 10.12.1.1 IP address. This is confirmed based upon the routing table on NX-2 for the 192.168.6.6 network prefix.

Example 10-19 *Normal Traffic Flow to NX-6's Loopback 0 Interface*

```
NX-1# traceroute 192.168.6.6
traceroute to 192.168.6.6 (192.168.6.6), 30 hops max, 40 byte packets
 1  10.12.1.2 (10.12.1.2)   2.016 ms  1.382 ms  1.251 ms
 2  10.23.1.3 (10.23.1.3)   3.24 ms   3.372 ms  3.364 ms
 3  10.35.1.5 (10.35.1.5)   5.819 ms  5.497 ms  3.844 ms
 4  10.56.1.6 (10.56.1.6)   5.577 ms  *  5.359 ms

NX-2# show ip route 192.168.6.6
! Output omitted for brevity

192.168.6.6/32, ubest/mbest: 1/0
    *via 10.23.1.3, Eth2/2, [110/82], 3d01h, ospf-NXOS, intra
```

Example 10-20 displays a traceroute from NX-1's Loopback 0 interface to be redirected on NX-2 toward NX-4. The traceroute displays that PBR is working as intended.

Example 10-20 *Verification of PBR-Based Traffic*

```
NX-1# traceroute 192.168.6.6 source 192.168.1.1
traceroute to 192.168.6.6 (192.168.6.6) from 192.168.1.1 (192.168.1.1), 30 hops max,
  40 byte packets
 1  10.12.1.2 (10.12.1.2)   1.33 ms   1.199 ms  1.064 ms
 2  10.24.1.4 (10.24.1.4)   3.354 ms  2.978 ms  2.825 ms
 3  10.45.1.5 (10.45.1.5)   3.818 ms  3.707 ms  3.487 ms
 4  10.56.1.6 (10.56.1.6)   4.542 ms  *  4.907 ms
```

PBR statistics were enabled on NX-2 that allows for network engineers to see how much traffic was forwarded by PBR. Example 10-21 displays output for PBR statistics before and after traffic was conditionally forwarded.

Example 10-21 *Sample Output of PBR Statistics*

```
PBR Statistics after Example 10-32
NX-2# show route-map PBR pbr-statistics
route-map PBR, permit, sequence 10
  Policy routing matches: 0 packets

Default routing: 12 packets
```

```
PBR Statistics after Example 10-33
NX-2# show route-map PBR pbr-statistics
route-map PBR, permit, sequence 10
  Policy routing matches: 12 packets

Default routing: 12 packets
```

Note The PBR configuration shown is for transient traffic. For PBR on locally generated traffic, use the command **ip local policy route-map** *route-map-name*.

Summary

This chapter covered several important building block features that are necessary for understanding the conditional matching process used within NX-OS route-maps:

- Access control lists provide a method of identifying networks. Extended ACLS provide the capability to select the network and advertising router for IGP protocols and provide the capability to use wildcards for the network and subnet mask for BGP routes.

- Prefix lists identify networks based upon the high-order bit pattern, high-order bit count, and required prefix length requirements.

- Regular expressions (regex) provide a method of parsing output in a systematic way. Regex is commonly used for BGP filtering, but it is also used in the CLI for parsing output, too.

Route-maps filter routes similar to an ACL and provide the capability to modify route attributes. Route-maps are composed of sequence numbers, matching criteria, processing action, and optional modifying actions. They use the following logic:

- If matching criteria is not specified, all routes qualify for that route-map sequence.

- Multiple conditional matching requirements of the same type are a Boolean *or*, and multiple conditional matching requirements of different type are a Boolean *and*.

- NX-OS uses RPM that operate as a separate process and memory space from the actual protocols. This provides an additional method for diagnosing unintentional behaviors in a protocol.

The default packet-forwarding decisions bypass routing protocols altogether through the use of policy-based routing to place specific network traffic onto a different path that was selected by the routing protocol.

References

Edgeworth, Brad, Aaron Foss, and Ramiro Garza Rios. *IP Routing on Cisco IOS, IOS XE and IOS XR*. Indianapolis: Cisco Press, 2014.

Cisco. Cisco NX-OS Software Configuration Guides, www.cisco.com.

Chapter 11

Troubleshooting BGP

This chapter covers the following topics:

- BGP Fundamentals
- Troubleshooting BGP peering issues
- BGP Route Updates and Route Propagation
- BGP Route Filtering

BGP Fundamentals

Defined in RFC 1654, Border Gateway Protocol (BGP) is a path-vector routing protocol that provides scalability, flexibility, and network stability. When BGP was first developed, the primary design consideration was for IPv4 inter-organizational routing information exchange across the public networks, such as the Internet, or for private dedicated networks. BGP is often referred to as the protocol for the Internet, because it is the only protocol capable of holding the Internet routing table, which has more than 600,000 IPv4 routes and over 42,000 IPv6 routes, both of which continue to grow.

From the perspective of BGP, an *autonomous system (AS)* is a collection of routers under a single organization's control. Organizations requiring connectivity to the Internet must obtain an *autonomous system number (ASN)*. ASNs were originally 2 bytes (16-bit) providing 65,535 ASNs. Due to exhaustion, RFC 4893 expands the ASN field to accommodate 4 bytes (32-bit). This allows for 4,294,967,295 unique ASNs, providing quite a leap from the original 65,535 ASNs. The *Internet Assigned Numbers Authority (IANA)* is responsible for assigning all public ASNs to ensure that they are globally unique.

Two blocks of private ASNs are available for any organization to use as long as they are never exchanged publicly on the Internet. ASNs 64,512 to 65,535 are private ASNs within the 16-bit ASN range, and 4,200,000,000 to 4,294,967,294 are private ASNs within the extended 32-bit range.

> **Note** It is imperative that you use only the ASN assigned by IANA, the ASN assigned by your service provider, or private ASNs. Not only that, the public prefixes are mapped with the relevant ASN numbers of the organizations. Thus, mistakenly or maliciously advertising a prefix using the wrong ASN could result in traffic loss and causing havoc on the Internet.

Address Families

Originally, BGP was intended for routing of IPv4 prefixes between organizations, but RFC 2858 added *Multi-Protocol BGP (MP-BGP)* capability by adding extensions called *address-family identifier (AFI)*. An address-family correlates to a specific network protocol, such as IPv4, IPv6, and so on, and additional granularity through *subsequent address-family identifier (SAFI)*, such as unicast and multicast. MBGP achieves this separation by using the BGP *path attributes (PA)* MP_REACH_NLRI and MP_UNREACH_NLRI. These attributes are carried inside BGP update messages and are used to carry network reachability information for different address families.

> **Note** Some network engineers refer to Multi-Protocol BGP as MP-BGP and other network engineers use the term MBGP. Both terms are the same thing.

Network engineers and vendors continue to add functionality and feature enhancements to BGP. BGP now provides a scalable control plane for signaling for overlay technologies like Multiprotocol Label Switching (MPLS) Virtual Private Networks (VPN), IPsec Security Associations, and *Virtual Extensible Lan (VXLAN)*. These overlays provide Layer 3 connectivity via MPLS L3VPNs, or Layer 2 connectivity via *Ethernet VPNs (eVPN)*.

Every address-family maintains a separate database and configuration for each protocol (address-family + subaddress-family) in BGP. This allows for a routing policy in one address-family to be different from a routing policy in a different address-family, even though the router uses the same BGP session to the other router. BGP includes an AFI and SAFI with every route advertisement to differentiate between the AFI and SAFI databases. Table 11-1 provides a small list of common AFI and SAFIs used with BGP.

Table 11-1 *BGP AFI/SAFI*

AFI	SAFI	Network Layer Information
1	1	IPv4 Unicast
1	2	IPv4 Multicast
1	4	MPLS Label
1	128	MPLS L3VPN IPv4
2	1	IPv6 Unicast
2	4	MPLS Label
2	128	MPLS L3VPN IPv6
25	65	Virtual Private Lan Service (VPLS)
25	70	Ethernet VPN (EVPN)

Path Attributes

BGP attaches *path attributes (PA)* associated with each network path. The PAs provide BGP with granularity and control of routing policies within BGP. The BGP prefix PAs are classified as follows:

- Well-known mandatory
- Well-known discretionary
- Optional transitive
- Optional nontransitive

Per RFC 4271, well-known attributes must be recognized by all BGP implementations. Well-known mandatory attributes must be included with every prefix advertisement, whereas well-known discretionary attributes may or may not be included with the prefix advertisement.

Optional attributes do not have to be recognized by all BGP implementations. Optional attributes can be set so that they are transitive and stay with the route advertisement from AS to AS. Other PAs are *nontransitive* and cannot be shared from AS to AS. In BGP, the *Network Layer Reachability Information (NLRI)* is the routing update that consists of the network prefix, prefix-length, and any BGP PAs for that specific route.

Loop Prevention

BGP is a path vector routing protocol and does not contain a complete topology of the network like link state routing protocols. BGP behaves similar to distance vector protocols to ensure a path is a loop-free path.

The BGP attribute AS_PATH is a well-known mandatory attribute and includes a complete listing of all the ASNs that the prefix advertisement has traversed from its source AS. The AS_PATH is used as a loop-prevention mechanism in the BGP protocol. If a BGP router receives a prefix advertisement with its AS listed in the AS_PATH, it discards the prefix because the router thinks the advertisement forms a loop.

Note The other IBGP-related loop-prevention mechanism are discussed later in this chapter.

BGP Sessions

A BGP session refers to the established adjacency between two BGP routers. BGP sessions are always point-to-point and are categorized into two types:

- **Internal BGP (iBGP):** Sessions established with an iBGP router that are in the same AS or participate in the same BGP confederation. iBGP sessions are considered more secure, and some of BGP's security measures are lowered in comparison to EBGP sessions. iBGP prefixes are assigned an *administrative distance (AD)* of 200 upon installing into the router's Routing Information Base (RIB).

- **External BPG (EBGP):** Sessions established with a BGP router that are in a different AS. EBGP prefixes are assigned an AD of 20 upon installing into the router's RIB.

Note Administrative distance (AD) is a rating of the trustworthiness of a routing information source. If a router learns about a route to a destination from more than one routing protocol and they all have the same prefix length, AD is compared. The preference is given to the route with the lower AD.

BGP uses TCP port 179 to communicate with other routers. Transmission Control Protocol (TCP) allows for handling of fragmentation, sequencing, and reliability (acknowledgement and retransmission) of communication (control plane) packets. Although BGP can form neighbor adjacencies that are directly connected, it can also form adjacencies that are multiple hops away. Multihop sessions require that the router use an underlying route installed in the RIB (static or from any routing protocol) to establish the TCP session with the remote endpoint.

Note BGP neighbors connected via the same network use the ARP table to locate the IP address of the peer. Multihop BGP sessions require route table information for finding the IP address of the peer. It is common to have a static route or Interior Gateway Protocol (IGP) running between iBGP peers for providing the topology path information for establishing the BGP TCP session. A default route is not sufficient to establish a multihop BGP session.

BGP can be thought of as a control plane routing protocol or as an application, because it allows for the exchanging of routes with peers multiple hops away. BGP routers do not have to be in the data plane (path) to exchange prefixes, but all routers in the data path need to know all the routes that will be forwarded through them.

BGP Identifier

The *BGP Router-ID (RID)* is a 32-bit unique number that identifies the BGP router in the advertised prefixes as the BGP Identifier. The RID is also used as a loop prevention mechanism for routers advertised within an autonomous system. The RID can be set manually or dynamically for BGP. A nonzero value must be set for routers to become neighbors. NX-OS nodes use the IP address of the lowest *up* loopback interface. If there are no *up* loopback interfaces, then the IP address of the lowest active *up* interface becomes the RID when the BGP process initializes.

Router-IDs typically represent an IPv4 address that resides on the router, such as a loopback address. Any IPv4 address can be used, including IP addresses not configured on the router. NX-OS uses the command **router-id** *router-id* under the BGP router configuration to statically assign the BGP RID. Upon changing the router-id, all BGP sessions reset and need to reestablish.

Note It is a best practice to statically assign the BGP Router-ID.

BGP Messages

BGP communication uses four message types as shown in Table 11-2.

Table 11-2 *BGP Packet Types*

Type	Name	Functional Overview
1	OPEN	Sets up and establishes BGP adjacency
2	UPDATE	Advertises, updates, or withdraws routes
3	NOTIFICATION	Indicates an error condition to a BGP neighbor
4	KEEPALIVE	Ensures that BGP neighbors are still alive

OPEN

The OPEN message is used to establish a BGP adjacency. Both sides negotiate session capabilities before a BGP peering establishes. The OPEN message contains the BGP version number, ASN of the originating router, *Hold Time*, *BGP Identifier*, and other optional parameters that establish the session capabilities.

The *Hold Time* attribute sets the *Hold Timer* in seconds for each BGP neighbor. Upon receipt of an UPDATE or KEEPALIVE, the Hold Timer resets to the initial value. If the Hold Timer reaches zero, the BGP session is torn down, routes from that neighbor are removed, and an appropriate update route withdraw message is sent to other BGP neighbors for the impacted prefixes. The Hold Time is a heartbeat mechanism for BGP neighbors to ensure that the neighbor is healthy and alive.

When establishing a BGP session, the routers use the smaller Hold Time value contained in the two router's OPEN messages. The Hold Time value must be set to at least 3 seconds, or zero. For Cisco routers the default hold timer is 180 seconds.

UPDATE

The UPDATE message advertises any feasible routes, withdraws previously advertised routes, or can do both. The UPDATE message includes the *Network Layer Reachability Information (NLRI)* that includes the prefix and associated BGP PAs when advertising prefixes. Withdrawn NLRIs include only the prefix. An UPDATE message can act as a KEEPALIVE message to reduce unnecessary traffic.

NOTIFICATION

A NOTIFICATION message is sent when an error is detected with the BGP session, such as a Hold Timer expiring, a neighbor capabilities change, or a BGP session reset is requested. This causes the BGP connection to close.

Note More details on the BGP messages are discussed during troubleshooting sections.

KEEPALIVE

BGP does not rely upon the TCP connection state to ensure that the neighbors are still alive. KEEPALIVE messages are exchanged every 1/3 of the Hold Timer agreed upon between the two BGP routers. Cisco devices have a default Hold Time of 180 seconds, so the default KEEPALIVE interval is 60 seconds. If the Hold Time is set for zero, no KEEPALIVE messages are sent between the BGP neighbors.

BGP Neighbor States

BGP forms a TCP session with neighbor routers called *peers*. BGP uses the *Finite State Machine (FSM)* to maintain a table of all BGP peers and their operational status. The BGP session may report in the following state:

- Idle
- Connect
- Active
- OpenSent
- OpenConfirm
- Established

Figure 11-1 displays the BGP FSM and the states in order of establishing a BGP session.

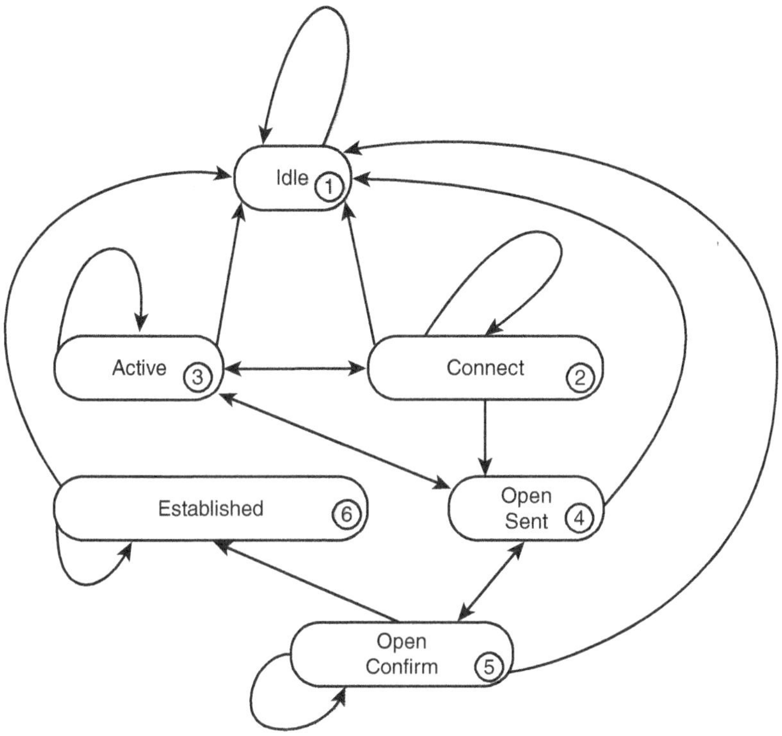

Figure 11-1 *BGP Finite State Machine*

Idle

This is the first stage of the BGP FSM. BGP detects a start event and tries to initiate a TCP connection to the BGP peer and also listens for a new connect from a peer router.

If an error causes BGP to go back to the Idle state for a second time, the ConnectRetryTimer is set to 60 seconds and must decrement to zero before the connection is initiated again. Further failures to leave the Idle state result in the ConnectRetryTimer doubling in length from the previous time.

Connect

In this state, BGP initiates the TCP connection. If the 3-way TCP handshake completes, the established BGP Session BGP process resets the ConnectRetryTimer and sends the Open message to the neighbor, and changes to the OpenSent State.

If the ConnectRetry timer depletes before this stage is complete, a new TCP connection is attempted, the ConnectRetry timer is reset, and the state is moved to Active. If any other input is received, the state is changed to Idle.

During this stage, the neighbor with the higher IP address manages the connection. The router initiating the request uses a dynamic source port, but the destination port is always 179.

> **Note** Service providers consistently assign their customers the higher or lower IP address for their networks. This helps the service provider create proper instructions for ACLs or firewall rules, or for troubleshooting them.

Active

In this state, BGP starts a new 3-way TCP handshake. If a connection is established, an Open message is sent, the Hold Timer is set to 4 minutes, and the state moves to OpenSent. If this attempt for TCP connection fails, the state moves back to the Connect state and resets the ConnectRetryTimer.

OpenSent

In this state, an Open message has been sent from the originating router and is awaiting an Open message from the other router. After the originating router receives the OPEN message from the other router, both OPEN messages are checked for errors. The following items are being compared:

- BGP versions must match.
- The source IP Address of the OPEN message must match the IP address that is configured for the neighbor.
- The AS number in the OPEN message must match what is configured for the neighbor.
- BGP Identifiers (RID) must be unique. If a RID does not exist, this condition is not met.
- Security Parameters (Password, Time to Live [TTL], and so on)

If the Open messages do not have any errors, the Hold Time is negotiated (using the lower value), and a KEEPALIVE message is sent (assuming the value is not set to zero). The connection state is then moved to OpenConfirm. If an error is found in the OPEN message, a Notification message is sent, and the state is moved back to Idle.

If TCP receives a disconnect message, BGP closes the connection, resets the ConnectRetryTimer, and sets the state to Active. Any other input in this process results in the state moving to Idle.

OpenConfirm

In this state, BGP waits for a Keepalive or Notification message. Upon receipt of a neighbor's Keepalive, the state is moved to Established. If the Hold Timer expires, a stop event occurs, or a Notification message is received, the state is moved to Idle.

Established

In this state, the BGP session is established. BGP neighbors exchange routes via Update messages. As Update and Keepalive messages are received, the Hold Timer is reset. If the Hold Timer expires, an error is detected, and BGP moves the neighbor back to the Idle state.

BGP Configuration and Verification

BGP configuration on NX-OS can be laid out in few simple steps, but the BGP command line is available only after enabling the BGP feature. Use the command **feature bgp** to enable the BGP feature on Nexus platforms. The steps for configuring BGP on an NX-OS device are as follows:

Step 1. Create the BGP routing process. Initialize the BGP process with the global configuration command **router bgp** *as-number*.

Step 2. Assign a BGP router-id. Assign a unique BGP router-id under the BGP router process. The router-id can be an IP address assigned to a physical interface or a Loopback interface.

Step 3. Initialize the address-family. Initialize the address-family with the BGP router configuration command **address-family** *afi safi* so it can be associated to a BGP neighbor.

Step 4. Identify the BGP neighbor's IP address and autonomous system number. Identify the BGP neighbor's IP address and autonomous system number with the BGP router configuration command **neighbor** *ip-address* **remote-as** *as-number*.

Step 5. Activate the address-family for the BGP neighbor. Activate the address-family for the BGP neighbor with the BGP neighbor configuration command **address-family** *afi safi*.

Examine the topology shown in Figure 11-2. This topology is used as reference for the next section as well. In this topology, Nexus devices NX-1, NX-2, and NX-4 are part of AS 65000, whereas router NX-6 belongs to AS 65001.

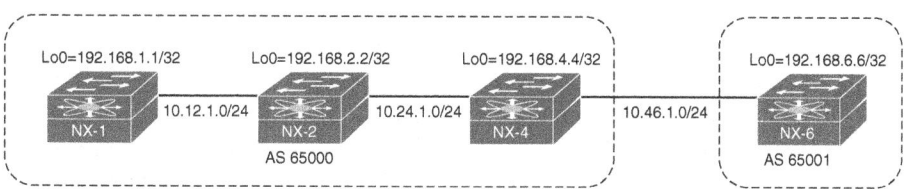

Figure 11-2 *Reference Topology*

Example 1-4 displays the BGP configuration for router NX-4 demonstrating both IBGP and EBGP peering. For this example, NX-4 is trying to establish an IBGP peering with

NX-1 and an EBGP peering with NX-6. While configuring a BGP peering, it is important to ensure the following information is correct:

- Local and remote ASN
- Source peering IP
- Remote peering IP
- Authentication passwords (optional)
- EBGP-multihop (EBGP only)

In Example 11-1, NX-4 is forming an IBGP peering with NX-1 and an EBGP peering with NX-6 router. The NX-4 device is also advertising its loopback address under the IPv4 address family using the **network** command.

Example 11-1 *NX-OS BGP Configuration*

```
NX-4
feature bgp
router bgp 65000
  router-id 192.168.4.4
  address-family ipv4 unicast
    network 192.168.4.4/32
    redistribute direct route-map conn
  neighbor 10.46.1.6
    remote-as 65001
    address-family ipv4 unicast
  neighbor 192.168.1.1
    remote-as 65000
    update-source loopback0
    address-family ipv4 unicast
      next-hop-self
!
ip prefix-list connected-routes seq 5 permit 10.46.1.0/24
!
route-map conn permit 10
  match ip address prefix-list connected-routes
```

After the configuration is performed on NX-4, peering should be established between NX-1 and NX-4 as well as between NX-4 and NX-6. The BGP peerings are verified using the command **show bgp** *afi safi* **summary**, where *afi* and *safi* are used for different address families. In this case, IPv4 unicast address family is used. Examine the verification of BGP peering between the NX-1, NX-4, and NX-6, as shown in Example 11-2. Notice that both the IBGP and EBGP peering is established on the NX-4 switch, and a prefix is being learned from each neighbor.

Example 11-2 *NX-OS BGP Peering Verification*

```
NX-4# show bgp ipv4 unicast summary
BGP summary information for VRF default, address family IPv4 Unicast
BGP router identifier 192.168.4.4, local AS number 65000
BGP table version is 8, IPv4 Unicast config peers 2, capable peers 2
4 network entries and 4 paths using 576 bytes of memory
BGP attribute entries [3/432], BGP AS path entries [1/6]
BGP community entries [0/0], BGP clusterlist entries [0/0]

Neighbor        V       AS MsgRcvd MsgSent   TblVer  InQ OutQ Up/Down   State/PfxRcd
10.46.1.6       4    65001      24      27        8    0    0 00:16:01 1
192.168.1.1     4    65000      23      24        8    0    0 00:16:24 1
```

After the BGP peering is established, the BGP prefixes are verified using the command **show bgp** *afi safi*. This command lists all the BGP prefixes in the respective address families. Example 11-3 displays the output of the BGP prefixes on NX-4. In the output, the BGP table holds locally advertised prefixes with the next-hop value of 0.0.0.0, the next-hop IP address, and a flag to indicate whether the prefix was learned from an IBGP (i) or EBGP (e) peer.

Example 11-3 *NX-OS BGP Table Output*

```
NX-4# show bgp ipv4 unicast
BGP routing table information for VRF default, address family IPv4 Unicast
BGP table version is 20, local router ID is 192.168.4.4
Status: s-suppressed, x-deleted, S-stale, d-dampened, h-history, *-valid, >-best
Path type: i-internal, e-external, c-confed, l-local, a-aggregate, r-redist,
I-injected
Origin codes: i - IGP, e - EGP, ? - incomplete, | - multipath, & - backup

   Network              Next Hop            Metric     LocPrf     Weight Path
*>r10.46.1.0/24         0.0.0.0                  0        100      32768 ?
*>i192.168.1.1/32       192.168.1.1                       100          0 i
*>l192.168.4.4/32       0.0.0.0                           100      32768 i
*>e192.168.6.6/32       10.46.1.6                                      0 65001 i
```

On NX-OS, the BGP process is instantiated the moment the **router bgp** *asn* command is configured. The details of the BGP process and the summarized configuration are viewed using the command **show bgp process**. This command displays the BGP process ID, state, number of configured and active BGP peers, BGP attributes, VRF information, redistribution and relevant route-maps used with various redistribute statements, and so on. If there is a problem with the BGP process, this command can be viewed to verify the state of BGP along with the memory information of the BGP process. Example 11-4 displays the output of the command **show bgp process**, highlighting some of the important fields in the output in Example 11-3.

Example 11-4 *NX-OS BGP Process*

```
NX-4# show bgp process

BGP Process Information
BGP Process ID                    : 9618
BGP Protocol Started, reason:     : configuration
BGP Protocol Tag                  : 65000
BGP Protocol State                : Running
BGP MMODE                         : Not Initialized
BGP Memory State                  : OK
BGP asformat                      : asplain

BGP attributes information
Number of attribute entries       : 4
HWM of attribute entries          : 4
Bytes used by entries             : 400
Entries pending delete            : 0
HWM of entries pending delete     : 0
BGP paths per attribute HWM       : 3
BGP AS path entries               : 1
Bytes used by AS path entries     : 26

Information regarding configured VRFs:

BGP Information for VRF default
VRF Id                            : 1
VRF state                         : UP
Router-ID                         : 192.168.4.4
Configured Router-ID              : 192.168.4.4
Confed-ID                         : 0
Cluster-ID                        : 0.0.0.0
No. of configured peers           : 2
No. of pending config peers       : 0
No. of established peers          : 2
VRF RD                            : Not configured

    Information for address family IPv4 Unicast in VRF default
    Table Id                      : 1
    Table state                   : UP
    Peers      Active-peers    Routes    Paths    Networks    Aggregates
    2          2               4         4        1           0

    Redistribution
        direct, route-map conn
```

```
    Wait for IGP convergence is not configured

    Nexthop trigger-delay
        critical 3000 ms
        non-critical 10000 ms

    Information for address family IPv6 Unicast in VRF default
    Table Id                       : 80000001
    Table state                    : UP
    Peers       Active-peers       Routes      Paths       Networks    Aggregates
    0           0                  0           0           0           0

    Redistribution
        None

    Wait for IGP convergence is not configured

    Nexthop trigger-delay
        critical 3000 ms
        non-critical 10000 ms
```

Troubleshooting BGP Peering Issues

BGP peering issues fall primarily into two categories:

- BGP peering down
- Flapping BGP peer

BGP peering issues are one of the most common issues that are experienced by network operators in the production environment. Though one of the common issues, the impact of down peer or a flapping BGP peer can be from very minimal (if there is redundancy in the network) to huge (where the peering to the Internet provider is completely down). This section focuses on troubleshooting both issues.

Troubleshooting BGP Peering Down Issues

When a configured BGP session is not in an established state, network engineers refer to this scenario as *BGP peering down*. A BGP peering down is one of the most common issues seen in most BGP environments. The peering down issue is detected when the following occurs:

- During establishment of BGP sessions because of misconfiguration
- Triggered by network migration or event, software or hardware upgrades
- Failure to maintain BGP keepalives due to transmission problems

A down BGP peer state is in either an Idle or Active state. From the peer state standpoint, these states would mean the following possible problems:

- Idle State
  - No connected route to peer
- Active State
  - No route to peer address (IP connectivity not present)
  - Configuration error, such as update-source missing or wrongly configured
- Idle/Active State
  - TCP establishes but BGP negotiation fails; for example, misconfigured AS
  - Router did not agree on the peering parameters

The following subsections list the various steps involved in troubleshooting BGP peering down issues.

Verifying Configuration

The very first step in troubleshooting BGP peering issues is verifying the configuration and understanding the design. Many times, a basic configuration mistake causes a BGP peering not to establish. The following items should be checked when a new BGP session is configured:

- Local AS number
- Remote AS number
- Verifying the network topology and other documentations

It is important to understand the traffic flow of BGP packets between peers. The source IP address of the BGP packets still reflects the IP address of the outbound interface. When a BGP packet is received, the router correlates the source IP address of the packet to the BGP neighbor table. If the BGP packet source does not match an entry in the neighbor table, the packet cannot be associated to a neighbor and is discarded.

In most of the deployments, the iBGP peering is established over loopback interface, and if the update-source interface is not specified, the session does not come up. The explicit sourcing of BGP packets from an interface is verified by ensuring that the **update-source** *interface-id* command under the **neighbor** *ip-address* configuration section is correctly configured for the peer.

If there are multiple hops between the EBGP peers, then proper hop count is required. Ensure the **ebgp-multihop** [*hop-count*] is configured with the correct hop count. If the *hop-count* is not specified, the default value is set to 255. Note that the default TTL value for IBGP sessions is 255 whereas the default value of EBGP session is 1. If an EBGP peering is established between two directly connected devices but over the loopback address, users can also use the **disable-connected-check** command instead of using the **ebgp-multihop 2** command.

This command disables the connection verification mechanism, which by default, prevents the session from getting established when the EBGP peer is not in the directly connected segment.

Another configuration that is important, although optional, for successful establishment of a BGP session is peer authentication. Misconfiguration or typo errors in authentication passwords will cause the BGP session to fail.

Verifying Reachability and Packet Loss

After the configuration has been verified, the connectivity between the peering IPs needs to be verified. If the peering is being established between loopback interfaces, a loopback-to-loopback ping test should be performed. If a ping test is performed without specifying the source interface, the outgoing interface IP address is used for a packet's source IP address that does not correlate with the peering IP address. Example 11-5 displays a loopback-to-loopback ping test between NX-1 and NX-4 as they are peering loopback addresses.

Example 11-5 *Ping with Source Interface as Loopback*

```
NX-4# ping 192.168.1.1 source 192.168.4.4
PING 192.168.1.1 (192.168.1.1) from 192.168.4.4: 56 data bytes
64 bytes from 192.168.1.1: icmp_seq=0 ttl=253 time=4.555 ms
64 bytes from 192.168.1.1: icmp_seq=1 ttl=253 time=2.72 ms
64 bytes from 192.168.1.1: icmp_seq=2 ttl=253 time=2.587 ms
64 bytes from 192.168.1.1: icmp_seq=3 ttl=253 time=2.559 ms
64 bytes from 192.168.1.1: icmp_seq=4 ttl=253 time=2.695 ms

--- 192.168.1.1 ping statistics ---
5 packets transmitted, 5 packets received, 0.00% packet loss
round-trip min/avg/max = 2.559/3.023/4.555 ms
```

Note At times, users may experience packet loss when performing a ping test. If there is a pattern seen in the ping test, it is most likely be due to CoPP policy, which is dropping those packets.

Using the preceding ping methods, reachability is verified for both the IBGP and EBGP peers. But if there is a problem with the reachability, use the following procedure to isolate the problem or direction of the problem.

Identify the direction of packet loss. The **show ip traffic** command on NX-OS is used to identify the packet loss or direction of the packet loss. If there is a complete or random packet loss of the ping (ICMP) packets from source to destination, use this method. The command output has the section of *ICMP Software Processed Traffic Statistics*, which consists of two subsections: *Transmission and Reception*. Both the sections consist of statistics for echo request and echo reply packets. To perform this test, first ensure that the sent and receive counters are stable (not incrementing) on both the source and the destination devices. Then initiate the ping test toward the destination by specifying the source interface or IP address. After the ping is completed, verify the **show ip traffic** command to validate the increase in counters on both sides to understand the direction of the packet loss. Example 11-6 demonstrates the method for isolating the direction of packet loss. In this example, the ping is initiated from NX-1 to NX-4 loopback. The first output displays that the echo request packets received at 10 and the echo reply sent are 10 as well. After the ping test from NX-1 to NX-4 loopback, the counters increase to 15 for both echo request and echo reply.

Example 11-6 *Ping Test and* **show ip traffic** *Command Output*

```
NX-4
NX-4# show ip traffic | in Transmission:|Reception:|echo
Transmission:
  Redirect: 0, unreachable: 0, echo request: 33, echo reply: 10,
Reception:
  Redirect: 0, unreachable: 0, echo request: 10, echo reply: 29,
```

```
NX-1
NX-1# ping 192.168.4.4 source 192.168.1.1
PING 192.168.4.4 (192.168.4.4) from 192.168.1.1: 56 data bytes
64 bytes from 192.168.4.4: icmp_seq=0 ttl=253 time=3.901 ms
64 bytes from 192.168.4.4: icmp_seq=1 ttl=253 time=2.913 ms
64 bytes from 192.168.4.4: icmp_seq=2 ttl=253 time=2.561 ms
64 bytes from 192.168.4.4: icmp_seq=3 ttl=253 time=2.502 ms
64 bytes from 192.168.4.4: icmp_seq=4 ttl=253 time=2.571 ms

--- 192.168.4.4 ping statistics ---
5 packets transmitted, 5 packets received, 0.00% packet loss
round-trip min/avg/max = 2.502/2.889/3.901 ms
```

```
NX-4
NX-4# show ip traffic | in Transmission:|Reception:|echo
Transmission:
  Redirect: 0, unreachable: 0, echo request: 33, echo reply: 15,
Reception:
  Redirect: 0, unreachable: 0, echo request: 15, echo reply: 29,
```

Similarly, the outputs are verified on NX-1 as well for echo reply received counters. In the previous example, the ping test is successful, and thus both the echo request received and echo reply sent counters incremented, but in situations when the ping test is failing, it is worth checking these counters closely and with multiple iterations of test. If the ping to the destination device is failing but still both the counters increment on the destination device, the problem could be with the return path, and the users may have to check the path for the return traffic.

ACLs prove to be really useful when troubleshooting packet loss or reachability issues. Configuring an ACL matching the source and the destination IP helps to confirm whether the packet has actually reached the destination router. The only caution that needs to be taken is that while configuring ACL, **permit ip any any** should be configured at the end, or else it could cause the other packets to get dropped and thus cause a service impact.

Verifying ACLs and Firewalls in the Path

In most of the deployments, the edge routers or Internet Gateway (IGW) routers are configured with ACLs to limit the traffic allowed in the network. If the BGP session is being established across those links where the ACL is configured, ensure that BGP packets (TCP port 179) are not getting dropped due to those ACLs.

Example 11-7 shows how the ACL configuration should look if BGP is passing through that link. The example shows the configuration for both IPv4 as well as **ipv6 access-list** in case of IPv6 BGP sessions. For applying IPv4 ACL on interface, **ip access-group** *access-list-name* {in|out} command is used on all platforms. For IPv6 ACL, **ipv6 traffic-filter** *access-list-name* {in|out} interface command is used on NX-OS.

Example 11-7 *ACL for Permitting BGP Traffic*

```
NX-4(config)# ip access-list v4_BGP_ACL
NX-4(config-acl)# permit tcp any eq bgp any
NX-4(config-acl)# permit tcp any any eq bgp
! Output omitted for brevity
NX-4(config)# ipv6 access-list v6_BGP_ACL
NX-4(config-ipv6-acl)# permit tcp any eq bgp any
NX-4(config-ipv6-acl)# permit tcp any any eq bgp
! Output omitted for brevity
NX-4(config)# interface Ethernet2/1
NX-4(config-if)# ip access-group v4_BGP_ACL in
NX-4(config-if)# ipv6 traffic-filter v6_BGP_ACL in
```

Other than having ACLs configured on the edge devices, lot of deployments have firewalls to protect the network from unwanted and malicious traffic. It is a better option to have a firewall installed than to have a huge ACL configured on the routers and switches. Firewalls can be configured in two modes:

- Routed mode
- Transparent mode

In routed mode, the firewall has routing capabilities and is considered to be a routed hop in the network. In transparent mode, the firewall is not considered as a router hop to the connected device but merely acts like a *bump in the wire*. Thus, if an EBGP session is being established across a transparent firewall, **ebgp-multihop** might not be required, and even if it is required to configure ebgp-multihop due to multiple devices in the path, the firewall is not counted as another routed hop.

Firewalls implement various security levels for the interfaces. For example, the ASA Inside interface is assigned a security level of 100 and the Outside interface is assigned security level 0. An ACL needs to be configured to permit the relevant traffic from the least secure interface going toward the higher security interface. This rule applies for both routed as well as transparent mode firewalls, and ACL is required in both cases.

Bridge groups are configured in transparent mode firewall for each network to help minimize the overhead on security contexts. The interfaces are made part of a bridge group and a Bridge Virtual Interface (BVI) interface is configured with a management IP address.

Example 11-8 displays an ASA ACL configuration that allows ICMP as well as BGP packets to traverse across the firewall and shows how to assign the ACL to the interface. Any traffic that is not part of the ACL is dropped.

Example 11-8 *Configuration on Transparent Firewall*

```
interface GigabitEthernet0/0
  nameif Inside
  bridge-group 200
  security-level 100
!
interface GigabitEthernet0/1
  nameif Outside
  bridge-group 200
  security-level 0
!
! Creating BVI with Management IP and should be the same subnet
! as the connected interface subnet
interface BVI200
  ip address 10.1.13.10 255.255.255.0
!
access-list Out extended permit icmp any any
access-list Out extended permit tcp any eq bgp any
access-list Out extended permit tcp any any eq bgp
!
access-group Out in interface Outside
```

In the access-list named Out, though, both the statements permitting the BGP packets are not required, but it is good practice to have both.

Another problem users might run into with a firewall in middle is with a couple of features on an ASA firewall:

- Sequence number randomization
- Enabling TCP Option 19 for MD5 authentication

ASA firewalls by default perform sequence number randomization and thus can cause BGP sessions to flap. Also, if the BGP peering is secured using MD5 authentication, enable TCP option 19 on the firewall's policy.

Verifying TCP Sessions

Before a BGP peering comes up, establish a TCP session. Thus, it is vital to ensure that TCP sessions are getting established and not being blocked anywhere in the path between the two BGP peering devices. TCP connections on NX-OS are verified using the command **show sockets connection tcp**. Example 11-9 shows the TCP in Listening state for port 179 and also the TCP connections that are established on NX-4 for both IBGP and EBGP peerings.

Example 11-9 *TCP Socket Connections*

```
NX-4# show sockets connection tcp
! Output omitted for brevity
 Total number of tcp sockets: 6
 Active connections (including servers)
 Protocol State/         Recv-Q/   Local Address(port)/
          Context        Send-Q    Remote Address(port)
 tcp      LISTEN         0         *(179)
          Wildcard       0         *(*)


 tcp6     LISTEN         0         *(179)
          Wildcard       0         *(*)


 [host]: tcp     ESTABLISHED  0         10.46.1.4(53879)
                 default      0         10.46.1.6(179)


 [host]: tcp     ESTABLISHED  0         192.168.4.4(179)
                 default      0         192.168.1.1(21051)
```

If BGP peering is not getting established, it may be possible that there is a stale entry in the TCP table. The stale entry may show the TCP session to be in established state and thus prevent the router from initiating another TCP connection, thus preventing the router from establishing a BGP peering.

A good troubleshooting technique for down BGP peers is using Telnet on TCP port 179 toward the destination peer IP and using local peering IP as the source. This technique helps ensure that the TCP is not getting blocked or dropped between the two BGP peering devices. This test is useful for verifying any TCP issues on the destination router and also helps verify any ACL that could possibly block the BGP packets.

Example 11-10 shows the use of Telnet on port 179 from NX-1 (192.168.1.1) to NX-4 (192.168.4.4) to verify BGP session. When this test is performed, the BGP TCP session gets established but is closed/disconnected immediately.

Example 11-10 *Using Telnet to Port 179*

```
NX-4# show sockets connection tcp foreign 192.168.1.1 detail

Total number of tcp sockets: 4
Active connections (including servers)
```

```
NX-1# telnet 192.168.4.4 179 source 192.168.1.1
Trying 192.168.4.4...
Connected to 192.168.4.4.
Escape character is '^]'.
Connection closed by foreign host.
```

```
NX-4# show sockets connection tcp foreign 192.168.1.1 detail

Total number of tcp sockets: 5
Active connections (including servers)
[host]: Local host: 192.168.4.4 (179), Foreign host: 192.168.1.1 (40944)
  Protocol: tcp, type: stream, ttl: 64, tos: 0xc0, Id: 18
  Options: REUSEADR, pcb flags none, state: | ISDISCONNECTED
! Output omittied for brevity
```

If the **telnet** is not sourced from the interface or IP that the remote device is configured to form a BGP neighborship with, the Telnet request is refused. This is another way to confirm that the peering device configuration is as per the documentation or not.

When troubleshooting TCP connection issues, it is also important to check the event-history logs for a netstack process as well. Netstack is an implementation of a Layer-2 to Layer-4 stack on NX-OS. It is one of the critical components involved in the control plane on NX-OS. If there is a problem with establishing a TCP session on a Nexus device, it could be a problem with the netstack process. The **show sockets internal event-history events** command helps understand what TCP state transitions happened for the BGP peer IP.

Example 11-11 demonstrates the use of the **show sockets internal event-history events** command to see the TCP session getting closed for BGP peer IP 192.168.2.2, but it does not show any request coming in.

Example 11-11 show sockets internal event-history events *Command*

```
NX-4# show sockets internal event-history event
1) Event:E_DEBUG, length:67, at 192101 usecs after Fri Sep  1 05:21:38 2017
    [138] [4226]: Marking desc 22 in mts_open for client 25394, sotype 2
! Output omitted for brevity
4) Event:E_DEBUG, length:91, at 810192 usecs after Fri Sep  1 05:17:09 2017
    [138] [4137]: PCB: Removing pcb from hash list L: 192.168.4.4.179, F: 192.16
8.1.1.21051 C: 1
5) Event:E_DEBUG, length:62, at 810184 usecs after Fri Sep  1 05:17:09 2017
    [138] [4137]: PCB: Detach L 192.168.4.4.179 F 192.168.1.1.21051
6) Event:E_DEBUG, length:77, at 810164 usecs after Fri Sep  1 05:17:09 2017
    [138] [4137]: TCP: Closing connection L: 192.168.4.4.179, F: 192.168.1.1.21051
```

Note For any problems encountered with TCP-related protocol such as BGP, capture **show tech netstack [detail]** and share the information with Cisco TAC.

OPEN Message Errors

If the information within the OPEN message is wrong, BGP peering does not get established. Rather, a BGP notification is sent to the peer by the BGP speaker, which receives the wrong information than what is configured on the router. A few such reasons for a BGP OPEN message error are the following:

- Unsupported version number
- Wrong Peer AS
- Bad or wrong BGP router ID
- Unsupported optional parameters

Out of the reasons listed, wrong peer AS or bad BGP Identifier are the most common OPEN message errors and are usually caused due to documentation or human error. The notification messages are also self-explanatory for the two errors and clearly indicate the wrong value and the expected value in the notification message, as shown in Example 11-12. In this example, the router is expecting the peer AS to be in AS 65001 but it's receiving the AS 65002.

Example 11-12 *BGP Wrong Peer AS Notification Message*

```
04:51:33 NX-4 %BGP-3-BADPEERAS:  bgp-100 [9544]   VRF default, Peer 10.46.1.6 - bad
remote-as, expecting 65001 received 65002.
```

During the initial BGP negotiation between the BGP speakers, certain capabilities are exchanged. If any of the BGP speakers are receiving a capability that they do not support,

BGP detects an OPEN message error for unsupported capability (or unsupported optional parameter). For instance, one of the BGP speakers is having the capability of enhanced route refresh, but the BGP speaker on the receiving end is running an old software that does not have the capability, then it detects this as an OPEN message error. The following optional capabilities are negotiated between the BGP speakers:

- Route Refresh capability
- 4-byte AS capability
- Multiprotocol capability
- Single/Multisession capability

To overcome the challenges of unsupported capability, use the command **dont-capability-negotiate** under the BGP neighbor configuration mode. This command disables the capability negotiations between the BGP peers and allows the BGP peer to come up.

BGP Debugs

Running debugs should always be the last resort for troubleshooting any network problem because debugs can sometimes cause an impact in the network if not used carefully. But sometimes they are the only option when other troubleshooting techniques don't help understand the problem. Using the NX-OS debug logfile, users can mitigate any kind of impact due to chatty debug outputs. Along with using debug logfile, network operators can put a filter on the debugs using the debug-filter and filtering the output for specific neighbor, prefix, and even the address-family, thus removing any possibility of an impact on the Nexus switch.

When a BGP peer is down, and all the other troubleshooting steps are not helping figure out where the problem is, enable debugs enabled to see if the router is generating and sending the necessary BGP packets, and if it's receiving the relevant packets or not. However, debug is not required on NX-OS because the traces in BGP have sufficient information to debug the problem. There are several debugs that are available for BGP. Depending on the state in which BGP is stuck, certain debug commands are helpful.

For a BGP peering down situation, one of the key debugs used is for BGP keepalives. The BGP keepalive debug is enabled using the command **debug bgp keepalives**. In the debug output, the two important factors to consider for ensuring a successful BGP peering are as follows:

- If the BGP keepalive is being generated at regular intervals
- If the BGP keepalive is being received at regular intervals

If the BGP keepalive is being generated at regular intervals but the BGP peering still remains down, it may be possible that the BGP keepalive couldn't make it to the other end, or it reached the peering router but was not processed or dropped. In such cases, BGP keepalive debugs are useful. Enable the debug command **debug bgp keepalives** to verify whether the BGP keepalives are being sent and received. Example 11-13 illustrates the use of BGP keepalive debug. The first output helps the user verify that the BGP keepalive is being generated every 60 seconds. The second output shows the keepalive being received from the remote peer 192.168.1.1.

Example 11-13 *BGP Keepalive Debugs*

```
NX-4# debug logfile bgp
NX-4# debug bgp keepalives

NX-4# show debug logfile bgp | grep "192.168.1.1 sending"
05:37:13.870261 bgp: 100 [9544] (default) ADJ: 192.168.1.1 sending KEEPALIVE
05:38:13.890290 bgp: 100 [9544] (default) ADJ: 192.168.1.1 sending KEEPALIVE
05:39:13.900376 bgp: 100 [9544] (default) ADJ: 192.168.1.1 sending KEEPALIVE
05:40:13.920290 bgp: 100 [9544] (default) ADJ: 192.168.1.1 sending KEEPALIVE
05:41:13.940395 bgp: 100 [9544] (default) ADJ: 192.168.1.1 sending KEEPALIVE
05:42:13.960350 bgp: 100 [9544] (default) ADJ: 192.168.1.1 sending KEEPALIVE
05:43:13.980363 bgp: 100 [9544] (default) ADJ: 192.168.1.1 sending KEEPALIVE

NX-4# show debug logfile bgp | grep 192.168.1.1
05:37:13.870160 bgp: 100 [9544] (default) ADJ: 192.168.1.1 keepalive timer fired
05:37:13.870236 bgp: 100 [9544] (default) ADJ: 192.168.1.1 keepalive
 timer fired for peer
05:37:13.870261 bgp: 100 [9544] (default) ADJ: 192.168.1.1 sending KEEPALIVE
05:37:13.870368 bgp: 100 [9544] (default) ADJ: 192.168.1.1 next keep
alive expiry due in 00:00:59
05:37:13.946248 bgp: 100 [9544] (default) ADJ: Peer 192.168.1.1 has
pending data on socket during recv, extending expiry timer
05:37:13.946387 bgp: 100 [9544] (default) ADJ: 192.168.1.1 KEEPALIVE rcvd
```

Demystifying BGP Notifications

BGP notifications play a crucial role in understanding and troubleshooting failed BGP peering or flapping peer issues. A BGP notification is sent from a BGP speaker to a peer when an error is detected. The notification can be sent either before the BGP session has been established or after it is established, based on the type of error. Each message has a fixed-size header. There may or may not be a data portion following the header, depending on the message type. The layout of these fields is shown in Figure 11-3.

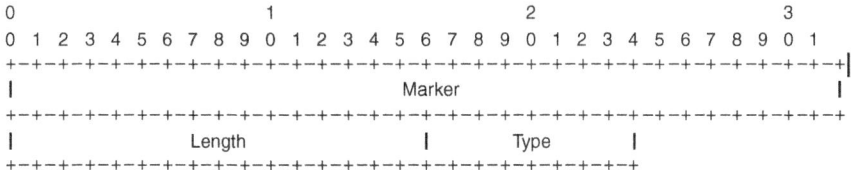

Figure 11-3 *BGP Notification Header*

In addition to the fixed-size BGP message header, a notification contains the following, as shown in Figure 11-4.

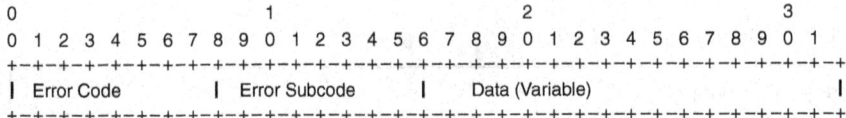

Figure 11-4 *Notification Section Information in BGP Header*

The Error code and Error-Subcode values are defined in RFC 4271. Table 11-3 shows all the Error codes, Error-Subcode and their interpretation.

Table 11-3 *BGP Notification Error and Error-Subcode*

Error Code	Subcode	Description
01	00	Message Header Error
01	01	Message Header Error—Connection Not Synchronized
01	02	Message Header Error—Bad Message Length
01	03	Message Header Error—Bad Message Type
02	00	OPEN Message Error
02	01	OPEN Message Error—Unsupported Version Number
02	02	OPEN Message Error—Bad Peer AS
02	03	OPEN Message Error—Bad BGP Identifier
02	04	OPEN Message Error—Unsupported Optional Parameter
02	05	OPEN Message Error—Deprecated
02	06	OPEN Message Error—Unacceptable Hold Time
03	00	Update Message Error
03	01	Update Message Error—Malformed Attribute List
03	02	Update Message Error—Unrecognized Well-Known Attribute
03	03	Update Message Error—Missing Well-Known Attribute
03	04	Update Message Error—Attribute Flags Error
03	05	Update Message Error—Attribute Length Error
03	06	Update Message Error—Invalid Origin Attribute
03	07	(Deprecated)
03	08	Update Message Error—Invalid NEXT_HOP Attribute
03	09	Update Message Error—Optional Attribute Error

Error Code	Subcode	Description
03	0A	Update Message Error—Invalid Network Field
03	0B	Update Message Error—Malformed AS_PATH
04	00	Hold Timer Expired
05	00	Finite State Machine Error
06	00	Cease
06	01	Cease—Maximum Number of Prefixes Reached
06	02	Cease—Administrative Shutdown
06	03	Cease—Peer Deconfigured
06	04	Cease—Administrative Reset
06	05	Cease—Connection Rejected
06	06	Cease—Other Configuration Change
06	07	Cease—Connection Collision Resolution
06	08	Cease—Out of Resources

Whenever a notification is generated, the error code and the subcode are always printed in the message. These notification messages are really helpful when troubleshooting down peering issues or flapping peer issues.

Troubleshooting IPv6 Peers

With the depletion of IPv4 routes, the IPv6 addresses have caught up pace. Most of the service providers have already upgraded or are planning to upgrade their infrastructure to dual stack for supporting both IPv4 and IPv6 traffic and offering IPv6 ready services to the Enterprise customers. Even the new applications are being developed with IPv6 compatibility or completely running on IPv6. With such a pace, there is also a need to have appropriate techniques for troubleshooting IPv6 BGP neighbors.

The methodology for troubleshooting IPv6 BGP peers is same as that of IPv4 BGP peers. Here are a few steps you can use to troubleshoot down peering issues for IPv6 BGP neighbors:

Step 1. Verify the configuration for correct peering IPv6 addresses, AS numbers, update-source interface, authentication passwords, EBGP multihop configuration.

Step 2. Verify reachability using the **ping ipv6** *ipv6-neighbor-address* [**source** *interface-id* | *ipv6-address*].

Step 3. Verify the TCP connections using the command **show socket connection tcp** on NX-OS. In case of IPv6, check for TCP connections for source and destination IPv6 addresses and one of the ports as port 179.

Step 4. Verify any IPv6 ACL's in path. Like IPv4, the IPv6 ACLs in the path should permit for TCP connections on port 179 and ICMPv6 packets that can help in verifying reachability.

Step 5. Debugs. On NX-OS switches, use the **debug bgp ipv6 unicast neighbors** *ipv6-neighbor-address* debug command to capture IPv6 BGP packets. Before enabling the debugs, enable the **debug logfile** for BGP debug. For filtering the debugs for a particular IPv6 neighbor, use the IPv6 ACL to filtering the debug output for that particular neighbor.

BGP Peer Flapping Issues

When the BGP session is down, the state never goes to Established state. The session keeps flapping between Idle and Active. But when the BGP peer is flapping, it means it is changing state after the session is established. In this case the BGP state keeps flapping between Idle and Established states. Following are the two flapping states in BGP:

- **Idle/Active:** Discussed in previous section
- **Idle/Established:** Bad update, TCP problem (MSS size in multihop deployment)

Flapping BGP peers could be due to one of several reasons:

- Bad BGP update
- Hold Timer expired
- MTU mismatch
- High CPU
- Improper control-plane policing

Bad BGP Update

A bad BGP update refers to a corrupted update packet received from a peer. This condition is not a normal condition. It is usually caused because of one of these reasons:

- Bad link carrying the update or bad hardware
- Problem with BGP update packaging
- Malicious update generated or the UPDATE packet modified by an attacker (hacker)

Whenever a BGP update is corrupted, a BGP notification is generated with the error code of 3, as shown in Table 11-3. When an error is noticed in the BGP update, BGP generates a hex-dump of the bad update message, which can be further decoded to understand which section of the update was corrupted. Along with the hex-dump, BGP also generates a log message that explains what kind of update error has occurred, as shown in Example 11-14.

Example 11-14 *Corrupt BGP Update Message*

```
22:10:13.366354 bgp: 65000 [14982] Hexdump at 0xd5893430, 19 bytes:
22:10:13.366362 bgp: 65000 [14982]     FFFFFFFF FFFFFFFF FFFFFFFF FFFFFFFF
22:10:13.366368 bgp: 65000 [14982]     001302
22:10:13.366379 bgp: 65000 [14982] (default) UPD: Badly formatted UPDATE message
  from peer 10.46.1.4, illegal length for withdrawn routes 65001 [afi/safi: 1/1]
22:10:13.366393 bgp: 65000 [14982] (default) UPD: Sending NOTIFY bad msg length
  error of length 2 to peer 10.46.1.4
22:10:13.366403 bgp: 65000 [14982] Hexdump at 0xd7eaa5fc, 23 bytes:
22:10:13.366413 bgp: 65000 [14982]     FFFFFFFF FFFFFFFF FFFFFFFF FFFFFFFF
22:10:13.366426 bgp: 65000 [14982]     00170301 02FFFF
22:10:13 %BGP-5-ADJCHANGE:  bgp-65000 [14982] (default) neighbor 10.46.1.4 Down -
  bad msg length error
```

Use the command **debug bgp packets** to view the BGP messages in hexdump, which can be further decoded. If too many BGP updates and messages are being exchanged on the NX-OS devices, a better option is to perform an Ethanalyzer or SPAN to capture a malformed BGP update packet to further analyze it.

Note The hexdump in the BGP message can be further analyzed using some online tools, such as http://bgpaste.convergence.cx.

Hold Timer Expired

Hold Timer expiry is a very common cause for flapping BGP peers. It simply means that the router didn't receive or process a Keepalive message or an Update message. Thus, it sends a notification message 4/0 (Hold Timer Expired) and closes the session. BGP flaps due to Hold Timer expiry are caused by one of the following reasons:

- Interface/platform drops
- MTS queue stuck
- Control-plane policy drops
- BGP Keepalive generation
- MTU issues

One reason may be Interface/platform drops. Various Interface issues like a physical layer issue or drops on the interface can lead to the BGP session getting flapped due to Hold Timer expiry. If the interface is carrying excessive traffic or even the line card itself is overloaded or busy, the packets may get dropped on the interface level or on the line card ASIC. If the BGP keepalive or update packets are dropped in such instances, BGP may notify the peer of Hold Timer expiry.

Another possibility is that the MTS queue is stuck. Sometimes, BGP Keepalives have arrived at the TCP receiving queue but are not being processed and moved to the BGP InQ. This is noticed when the BGP InQ queues are empty and a BGP neighbor goes down due to Hold Timer expiry. The most common reason for such a scenario on Nexus switches is because the MTS queue is stuck on either the BGP or TCP process. MTS is the main component that takes care of carrying information from one component to another component within NX-OS. In such scenarios, it may be possible that multiple BGP peers may get impacted on the system. To recover, a supervisor switchover or a reload may be required.

In addition, CoPP policy drops can also be a cause. The CoPP policy is designed to prevent the CPU from excessive and unwanted traffic. But a poorly designed CoPP policy causes control-plane protocol flaps. If the CoPP policy has not been accommodated to take care of all the BGP control-plane packets and the number of BGP peers on the router, there might be instances where those packets get dropped. In such situations, users might experience random BGP flaps due to CoPP policy dropping certain packets.

Note MTS, CoPP, and other platform troubleshooting is covered in detail in Chapter 3, "Troubleshooting Nexus Platform Issues."

BGP Keepalive Generation

In networks, there are instances when a BGP peering might flap randomly. Apart from the scenarios such as packet loss or control-plane policy drops, there might be other reasons that the BGP peering flaps and the reason is still seen as hold timer expiry. One such reason may be due to the BGP keepalives not being generated in a timely manner. For troubleshooting such instances, the first step is to understand if there is any pattern to the BGP flaps. This information is gathered by getting answers to the following questions:

- At what time of the day is the BGP flap happening?
- How frequently is the flap happening?
- How is the traffic load on the interface/system when the flap occurs?
- Is the CPU high during the time of the flap? If yes, is it due to traffic or a particular process?

These questions help lay out a pattern for the BGP flaps, and relevant troubleshooting can be performed around the same time. To further troubleshoot the problem, understand that the BGP flap is due to two reasons:

- Either keepalives getting generated at regular intervals but not leaving the router or not making it to the other end.
- Keepalives are not getting generated at regular intervals.

If the keepalives are getting generated at regular intervals but not leaving the router, then notice that the OutQ for the BGP peer keeps piling up. The OutQ keeps incrementing due to keepalive generation, but the MsgSent does not increase, which may be an indication that the messages are stuck in the OutQ. Example 11-15 illustrates such a scenario where the BGP keepalives are generated at regular intervals but do not leave the router, leading to a BGP flap due to hold timer expiry. Notice that in this example, the OutQ value increases from 10 to 12, but the MsgSent counter is stagnant at 3938. In this scenario, the peering may flap every BGP hold timer.

Example 11-15 *BGP Message Sent and OutQ*

```
NX-4# show bgp ipv4 unicast summary
BGP summary information for VRF default, address family IPv4 Unicast
BGP router identifier 192.168.4.4, local AS number 65000
BGP table version is 19, IPv4 Unicast config peers 2, capable peers 2
4 network entries and 4 paths using 576 bytes of memory
BGP attribute entries [4/576], BGP AS path entries [1/6]
BGP community entries [0/0], BGP clusterlist entries [0/0]

Neighbor        V     AS MsgRcvd MsgSent   TblVer  InQ OutQ Up/Down  State/PfxRcd
10.46.1.6       4  65001    3933    3938       19    0   10 14:30:46 1
192.168.1.1     4  65000     997    1009       19    0    0 15:02:52 1
```
```
NX-4# show bgp ipv4 unicast summary
! Output omitted for brevity

Neighbor        V     AS MsgRcvd MsgSent   TblVer  InQ OutQ Up/Down  State/PfxRcd
10.46.1.6       4  65001    3933    3938       19    0   12 14:30:46 1
192.168.1.1     4  65000     997    1009       19    0    0 15:02:52 1
```

But if the device experiences random BGP flaps and at irregular intervals, it is possible that the BGP keepalives are getting generated at regular intervals, although the flaps may still happen frequently. For instance, a BGP peering flaps between 4 to 10 minutes. These issues are hard to troubleshoot and may require a different technique than just running **show** commands. The reason is that it is not easy to isolate which device is not generating the keepalive in a timely manner, or if the keepalive is generated in a timely manner but there is a delay that occurs when the keepalive makes it to the remote peer. To troubleshoot, follow the two-step process between the two ends of the BGP connection.

Step 1. Enable BGP keepalive debug on both routers along with the debug logfile.

Step 2. Enable Ethanalyzer on both routers.

The purpose of enabling Ethanalyzer or any other packet capture tool (based on the underlying platform) is that it is possible that the BGP keepalives reach the other end in a timely manner, but those keepalives may be delayed before reaching BGP process itself. Based on the outputs of the BGP keepalive debug and the Ethanalyzer from the far end device, the timelines could be matched to conclude where exactly the delay might be happening that is causing the BGP to flap. It may be the BGP process that is delaying the keepalive generation, or it may be the other components that interact with BGP to delay the keepalive processing.

MTU Mismatch Issues

Generally, maximum transmission unit (MTU) is not a big concern when bringing up a BGP neighborship, but MTU mismatch issues can cause BGP sessions to flap. MTU settings vary in different devices in the network because of various factors, such as

- Improper planning and network design
- Device not supporting Jumbo MTU or certain MTU values
- Change due to application requirement
- Change due to end customer requirement

BGP sends updates based on the Maximum Segment Size (MSS) value calculated by TCP. If *Path-MTU-Discovery (PMTUD)* is not enabled, the BGP MSS value defaults to 536 bytes as defined in RFC 879. The problem with that is, if a huge number of updates are getting exchanged between the two routers at the MSS value of 536 bytes, convergence issues will be noticed and thus an inefficient use of the network. The reason is that the interface with an MTU size of 1500 is capable of sending nearly three times the MSS value and can be much higher if the interface supports jumbo MTU, but it has to break down the updates in chunks of 536 bytes.

Defined in RFC 1191, PMTUD is introduced to reduce the chances of IP packets getting fragmented along the path and thus helping with faster convergence. Using PMTUD, the source identifies the lowest MTU along the path to the destination and thus decides what packet size should be sent.

How does PMTUD work? When the source generates a packet, it sets the MTU size equal to the outgoing interface with a DF (Do-Not-Fragment) bit set. For any intermediate device that receives the packet and has an MTU value of its egress interface lower than the packet it received, the device drops the packet and sends an ICMP error message with Type 3 (Destination Unreachable) and Code 4 (Fragmentation needed and DF bit set) along with the MTU information of the outgoing interface in the Next-Hop MTU field back toward the source. When the source receives the ICMP unreachable error message, it modifies the MTU size of the outgoing packet to the value specified in the Next-Hop MTU field above. This process continues until the packet successfully reaches the final destination.

BGP also supports PMTUD. PMTUD allows a BGP router to discover the best MTU size along the path to a neighbor to ensure efficient usage of exchanging packets. With Path

MTU discovery enabled, the initial TCP negotiation between two neighbors has MSS value equal to (IP MTU – 20 byte IP Header – 20 byte TCP Header) and DF bit set. Thus, if the IP MTU value is 1500 (equal to the interface MTU) then the MSS value is 1460. If the device in the path has a lower MTU or even if the destination router has a lower MTU—for example, 1400, then the MSS value is negotiated based on 1400–40 bytes = 1360 bytes. To derive MSS calculation, use the following formulas:

- **MSS without MPLS** = MTU – IP Header (20 bytes) – TCP Header (20 bytes)

- **MSS over MPLS** = MTU – IP Header – TCP Header – n*4 bytes (where n is the number of labels in the label stack)

- **MSS across GRE Tunnel** = MTU – IP Header (Inner) – TCP Header – [IP Header (Outer) + GRE Header (4 bytes)]

Note MPLS VPN providers should increase the MPLS MTU to at least 1508 (assuming a minimum of 2 labels) or MPLS MTU of 1516 (to accommodate up to 4 labels)

Now the question is why the MTU mismatch causes BGP sessions to flap? When the BGP connection is established, the MSS value is negotiated over the TCP session. When the BGP update is generated, BGP updates are packaged in the BGP update message, which can hold prefixes and header information to the maximum capacity of the MSS bytes. These BGP update messages are then sent to the remote peer with the do-not-fragment (df-bit) set. If a device in path or even the destination is not able to accept the packets with a higher MTU, it sends an ICMP error message back to BGP speaker. The destination router either waits for the BGP Keepalive or BGP Update packet to update its hold down timer. After 180 seconds, the destination router sends a Notification back to Source with a *Hold Time expired* error message.

Note When a BGP router sends an update to a BGP neighbor, it does not send a BGP Keepalive separately. But rather it updates the Keepalive timer for that neighbor. During the BGP update process, the update message is treated as a keepalive by the BGP speakers.

Example 11-16 illustrates a BGP peer flapping problem when there is a MTU mismatch in the path. Consider the same set of devices NX-1, NX-2, NX-4, and NX-6 from the topology shown in Figure 11-2. In this topology, assume the devices have ICMP unreachable disabled on its interfaces. The NX-6 device is advertising 10,000 prefixes to NX-4, which is being further advertised toward NX-1. The interface MTU on NX-1 and NX-4 is set to 9100, whereas the MTU on the interface on NX-2 facing NX-1 is still set to the default; that is, 1500. Because the path MTU discovery (PMTUD) is enabled, the MSS is negotiated to value 9060. The ICMP unreachable message is denied because the lower MTU setting on the NX-2 interface is not received by NX-1.

Example 11-16 *BGP Flaps due to MSS Issue*

```
NX-4
NX-4# show bgp ipv4 unicast summary
! Output omitted for brevity

Neighbor        V    AS    MsgRcvd  MsgSent  TblVer  InQ OutQ Up/Down   State/PfxRcd
10.46.1.6       4  65001   10475    10482    26      0   0    1d17h     10000
192.168.1.1     4  65000   2643     2659     26      0   0    00:01:59  1
```

```
NX-1
NX-1# show bgp ipv4 unicast summary
BGP summary information for VRF default, address family IPv4 Unicast
BGP router identifier 192.168.1.1, local AS number 65000
BGP table version is 37, IPv4 Unicast config peers 1, capable peers 1
4 network entries and 4 paths using 576 bytes of memory
BGP attribute entries [4/576], BGP AS path entries [1/6]
BGP community entries [0/0], BGP clusterlist entries [0/0]

Neighbor        V    AS    MsgRcvd  MsgSent  TblVer  InQ OutQ Up/Down   State/PfxRcd
192.168.4.4     4  65000   2579     2566     37      0   0    00:02:49  0

NX-1# show sockets connection tcp foreign 192.168.4.4 detail
Total number of tcp sockets: 4
[host]: Local host: 192.168.1.1 (22543), Foreign host: 192.168.4.4 (179)
  Protocol: tcp, type: stream, ttl: 64, tos: 0xc0, Id: 19
  Options: none, pcb flags  unknown, state:  | NBIO
  MTS: sap 10486
  Receive buffer:
    cc: 0, hiwat: 17184, lowat: 1, flags: none
  Send buffer:
    cc: 0, hiwat: 17184, lowat: 2048, flags: none
  Sequence number state:
    iss: 987705410, snduna: 987705603, sndnxt: 987705603, sndwnd: 17184
    irs: 82840884, rcvnxt: 82841199, rcvwnd: 17184, sndcwnd: 4296
  Timing parameters:
    srtt: 3200 ms, rtt: 0 ms, rttv: 0 ms, krtt: 1000 ms
    rttmin: 1000 ms, mss: 9060, duration: 43800 ms
  State: ESTABLISHED
  Flags:  | SENDCCNEW
No MD5 peers  Context: default
```

```
NX-1
! Logs showing BGP flap after hold timer expiry
00:56:27.873 NX-1 %BGP-5-ADJCHANGE:  bgp-65000 [6884] (default) neighbor 192.168.4.4
 Down - holdtimer expired error
00:57:26.627 NX-1 %BGP-5-ADJCHANGE:  bgp-65000 [6884] (default) neighbor 192.168.4.4 Up
```

The BGP flap does not occur when a small amount of prefixes are exchanged between the peers because the BGP packet size is under 1460 bytes. One symptom of BGP flaps due to MSS/MTU issues is a repetitive BGP flap that occurs because the Hold Timer expires.

The following are the few possible causes of BGP session flapping due to MTU mismatch:

- The interface MTU on both the peering routers do not match.
- The Layer 2 path between the two peering routers does not have consistent MTU settings.
- PMTUD didn't calculate correct MSS for the TCP BGP session.
- BGP PMTUD could be failing due to blocked ICMP messages by a router or a firewall in path.

To verify there are MTU mismatch issues in the path, perform an extended **ping** test by setting the size of the packet as the outgoing interface MTU value along with DF bit set. Also, ensure that ICMP messages are not being blocked in the path to have PMTUD function properly. Ensure that the MTU values are consistent throughout the network with a proper review of the configuration.

Perform a ping test to remote peer with the packet size as the MTU of the interface and do not fragment (df-bit) set as shown in Example 11-17.

Example 11-17 *PING with DF-Bit Set*

```
NX-1# ping 192.168.4.4 source 192.168.1.1 packet-size 1500 df-bit
PING 192.168.4.4 (192.168.4.4) from 192.168.1.1: 1500 data bytes
Request 0 timed out
Request 1 timed out
Request 1 timed out
--- 192.168.4.4 ping statistics ---
3 packets transmitted, 0 packets received, 100.00% packet loss

NX-1# ping 192.168.4.4 source 192.168.1.1 packet-size 1472 df-bit
PING 192.168.4.4 (192.168.4.4) from 192.168.1.1: 1472 data bytes
1480 bytes from 192.168.4.4: icmp_seq=0 ttl=253 time=5.298 ms
1480 bytes from 192.168.4.4: icmp_seq=1 ttl=253 time=3.494 ms
1480 bytes from 192.168.4.4: icmp_seq=2 ttl=253 time=4.298 ms
1480 bytes from 192.168.4.4: icmp_seq=3 ttl=253 time=4.528 ms
1480 bytes from 192.168.4.4: icmp_seq=4 ttl=253 time=3.606 ms


--- 192.168.4.4 ping statistics ---
5 packets transmitted, 5 packets received, 0.00% packet loss
round-trip min/avg/max = 3.494/4.244/5.298 ms
```

> **Note** Nexus platform adds 28 bytes (20 bytes IP header + 8 bytes ICMP header) when performing the ping with MTU size. Thus, when the ping test is performed with DF-bit set, the ping with 1500 size fails. To successfully test the ping with the interface MTU packet size and df-bit set, subtract 28 bytes from the MTU value on the interface. In this case, 1500 − 28 = 1472.

BGP Route Processing and Route Propagation

After the BGP peering is established, exchange network prefixes and path attributes for BGP peers. Unlike IGP, BGP allows a routing policy to be different for each peer within an AS. BGP route processing for inbound and outbound exchange of network prefixes can be understood in a simple way, as shown in Figure 11-5. When a BGP router receives a route from peer, the BGP installs those routes in the BGP table by filtering those routes through an inbound policy if configured. If the BGP table contains multiple paths for the same prefix, a best path is selected, and then the best path is installed in the routing table. Similarly, when advertising a prefix, only the best route is advertised to the peer device. If there is an outbound policy, the prefixes are filtered before being advertised to the remote peer.

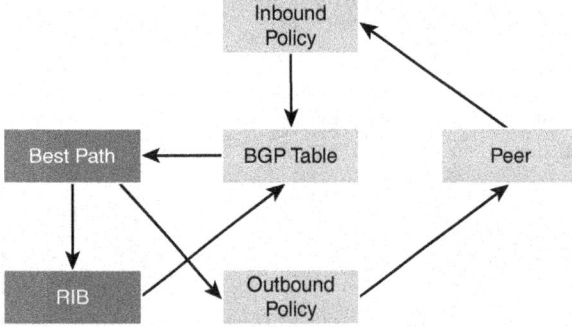

Figure 11-5 *BGP Route Processing*

Let's now understand the various fundamentals of route advertisement in the sections that follow. For this section, examine the topology shown in Figure 11-6.

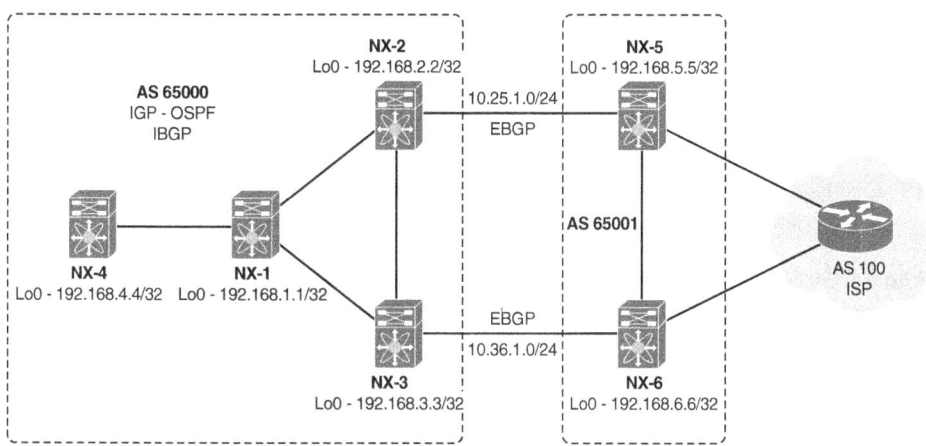

Figure 11-6 *BGP Route Propagation Topology*

BGP Route Advertisement

BGP prefixes are injected into the BGP table for advertisement by explicit configuration. The four methods that are used to inject the BGP prefixes into the BGP table are the following:

- **Network statement:** Using **network** *ip-address/length* command.

- **Redistribution:** Redistribute directly connected links, static routes, and IGP, such as Routing Information Protocol (RIP), Open Shortest Path First (OSPF), Enhanced Interior Gateway Routing Protocol (EIGRP), Intermediate System to Intermediate System (IS-IS), and Locator ID Separation Protocol (LISP). A route-map is required when a prefix is being redistributed from another routing protocol including directly connected links.

- **Aggregate Route:** Summarizing a route, though the component route must exist in the BGP table.

- **Default Route:** Using the **default-information originate** command.

Network Statement

A BGP prefix is advertised via BGP using a network statement. For the network statement to function properly, the route must be present in the routing table. If the route is not present in the routing table, the network statement neither installs the route in the BGP table nor advertises it to the BGP peers. Example 11-18 illustrates the use of network statements to advertise two prefixes. One of the prefixes has the loopback configured locally on the router, and the other prefix does not have the route present in the routing table. It is clear from the output of the command **show bgp ipv4 unicast neighbors** *ip-address* **advertised-routes** that the prefix 192.168.4.4/32 gets advertised to the BGP peer 192.168.1.1 but not the prefix 192.168.44.44/32. When looking at the BGP table for any address-family, it is important to verify the status flags, which would indicate how the prefix is learned on the router. These status flags and their meaning are highlighted before the prefixes in the BGP table are listed. In Example 11-18, the prefix is a local prefix and thus has the status flag as *L* along with the flag *>, which indicates the route is selected as the best route.

Example 11-18 *Prefix Advertisement Using* **network** *Command*

```
NX-4
router bgp 65000
  router-id 192.168.4.4
  log-neighbor-changes
  address-family ipv4 unicast
    network 192.168.4.4/32
    network 192.168.44.44/32
  neighbor 192.168.1.1
    remote-as 65000
    update-source loopback0
    address-family ipv4 unicast
      next-hop-self
```

```
NX-4# show ip route 192.168.4.4/32
IP Route Table for VRF "default"
'*' denotes best ucast next-hop
'**' denotes best mcast next-hop
'[x/y]' denotes [preference/metric]
'%<string>' in via output denotes VRF <string>

192.168.4.4/32, ubest/mbest: 2/0, attached
    *via 192.168.4.4, Lo0, [0/0], 1w1d, local
    *via 192.168.4.4, Lo0, [0/0], 1w1d, direct
NX-4# show ip route 192.168.44.44/32

Route not found
```

```
NX-4# show bgp ipv4 unicast
BGP routing table information for VRF default, address family IPv4 Unicast
BGP table version is 27, local router ID is 192.168.4.4
Status: s-suppressed, x-deleted, S-stale, d-dampened, h-history, *-valid, >-best
Path type: i-internal, e-external, c-confed, l-local, a-aggregate, r-redist,
I-injected
Origin codes: i - IGP, e - EGP, ? - incomplete, | - multipath, & - backup
```

```
    Network              Next Hop          Metric    LocPrf    Weight Path
*>i192.168.1.1/32        192.168.1.1                 100            0 i
*>l192.168.4.4/32        0.0.0.0                     100        32768 i
   l192.168.44.44/32     0.0.0.0                     100        32768 i


NX-4# show bgp ipv4 unicast neighbors 192.168.1.1 advertised-routes
! Output omitted for brevity

    Network              Next Hop          Metric    LocPrf    Weight Path
*>l192.168.4.4/32        0.0.0.0                     100        32768 i
```

Redistribution

Redistributing routes into BGP is a common method of populating the BGP table. Examine the same topology shown in Figure 11-6. On router NX-1, OSPF is being redistributed into BGP. While redistributing the routes from OSPF to BGP, the route-map permits for prefixes 192.168.4.4/32 and 192.168.44.44/32, although the routing table only learns 192.168.4.4/32 from NX-4. Example 11-19 demonstrates the redistribution process into BGP. Notice in the output, the prefix 192.168.4.4/32 has an *r* flag, which indicates redistributed prefix. Also, the redistributed prefix has a question mark (?) in the AS path list.

Example 11-19 *BGP and IGP Redistribution*

```
NX-1
router bgp 65000
  address-family ipv4 unicast
    redistribute ospf 100 route-map OSPF-BGP
!
ip prefix-list OSPF-BGP seq 5 permit 192.168.4.4/32
ip prefix-list OSPF-BGP seq 10 permit 192.168.44.44/32
!
route-map OSPF-BGP permit 10
  match ip address prefix-list OSPF-BGP
    redistribute ospf 100 route-map OSPF-BGP
```
```
NX-1# show ip route ospf
192.168.4.4/32, ubest/mbest: 1/0
    *via 10.14.1.4, Eth2/1, [110/41], 00:30:27, ospf-100, intra

NX-1# show bgp ipv4 unicast
BGP routing table information for VRF default, address family IPv4 Unicast
BGP table version is 6, local router ID is 192.168.1.1
Status: s-suppressed, x-deleted, S-stale, d-dampened, h-history, *-valid, >-best
```

```
Path type: i-internal, e-external, c-confed, l-local, a-aggregate, r-redist,
I-injected
Origin codes: i - IGP, e - EGP, ? - incomplete, | - multipath, & - backup

   Network            Next Hop           Metric      LocPrf     Weight Path
*>i192.168.2.2/32    192.168.2.2                       100          0 i
*>r192.168.4.4/32    0.0.0.0               41          100      32768 ?
```

> **Note** The redistribution process is the same for other routing protocols, static routes, and directly connected links, as shown in Example 11-19.

There are a few caveats when performing redistribution for OSPF and IS-IS as listed:

- **OSPF:** When redistributing OSPF into BGP, the default behavior includes only routes that are internal to OSPF. The redistribution of external OSPF routes requires a conditional match on route-type under route-map.

- **IS-IS:** IS-IS does not include directly connected subnets for any destination routing protocol. This behavior is overcome by redistributing the connected networks into BGP.

Example 11-20 displays the various match route-type options available under the route-map. The route-type options are available for both OSPF and IS-IS route types.

Example 11-20 match route-map *Command Options*

```
NX-1(config-route-map)# match route-type ?
  external       External route (BGP, EIGRP and OSPF type 1/2)
  inter-area     OSPF inter area route
  internal       Internal route (including OSPF intra/inter area)
  intra-area     OSPF intra area route
  level-1        IS-IS level-1 route
  level-2        IS-IS level-2 route
  local          Locally generated route
  nssa-external  Nssa-external route (OSPF type 1/2)
  type-1         OSPF external type 1 route
  type-2         OSPF external type 2 route
```

Route Aggregation

Not all devices in the network are powerful enough to hold all the routes learned via BGP or other routing protocols. Also, having multiple paths in the network leads to consumption of more CPU and memory resources. To overcome this challenge, route aggregation or summarization can be performed. Route aggregation in BGP is performed using the command **aggregate-address** *aggregate-prefix/length* [**advertise-map** | **as-set** | **attribute-map** | **summary-only** | **suppress-map**]. Table 11-4 describes all the optional command options available with the **aggregate-address** command.

Table 11-4 aggregate-address *Command Options*

Option	Description
advertise-map *map-name*	Used to select attribute information from specific routes.
as-set	Generates an AS_SET path information and community information from the contributing paths.
attribute-map *map-name*	Used to set the attribute information for specific routes. Allows the attributes of the aggregate route to be changed.
summary-only	Filters all more specific routes from the updates and only advertises summary route.
suppress-map *map-name*	Conditionally filters more specific routes specified in the route-map.

Example 11-21 demonstrates the use of the **summary-only** attribute with the **aggregate-address** command. Notice that NX-2 has 3 prefixes but only a single aggregate prefix gets advertised to NX-5. Notice that on NX-2, when the summary-only command is configured, the more specific routes are suppressed.

Example 11-21 *Route Aggregation*

```
NX-2
router bgp 65000
   address-family ipv4 unicast
    network 192.168.2.2/32
    aggregate-address 192.168.0.0/16 summary-only


NX-2# show bgp ipv4 unicast
BGP routing table information for VRF default, address family IPv4 Unicast
BGP table version is 19, local router ID is 192.168.2.2
Status: s-suppressed, x-deleted, S-stale, d-dampened, h-history, *-valid, >-best
Path type: i-internal, e-external, c-confed, l-local, a-aggregate, r-redist,
I-injected
Origin codes: i - IGP, e - EGP, ? - incomplete, | - multipath, & - backup

   Network            Next Hop         Metric     LocPrf     Weight Path
*>a192.168.0.0/16     0.0.0.0                     100         32768 i
s>i192.168.1.1/32     192.168.1.1                 100             0 i
s>l192.168.2.2/32     0.0.0.0                     100         32768 i
s>i192.168.4.4/32     192.168.4.4                 100             0 i

NX-5# show bgp ipv4 unicast

   Network            Next Hop         Metric     LocPrf     Weight Path
*>e192.168.0.0/16     10.25.1.2                                   0 65000 i
```

Default-Information Originate

Not every external route can be redistributed and advertised within the network. In such instances, the gateway or edge device advertises a default route to other parts of the network using a routing protocol. To advertise a default route using BGP, use the command **default-information originate** under the neighbor configuration mode. It is important to note that the command only advertises the default route if the default route is present in the routing table. If there is no default route present, create a default route pointing to null0 interface.

BGP Best Path Calculation

In BGP, route advertisements consist of the *Network Layer Reachability Information (NLRI)* and the path attributes (PA). The NLRI comprises the network prefix and prefix-length, and the BGP attributes, such as AS-Path, Origin, and so on, are stored in the path attributes.

BGP uses three tables for maintaining the network prefix and path attributes (PA)s for a route. The following BGP tables are briefly explained:

- **Adj-RIB-in:** Contains the NLRIs in original form before inbound route policies are processed. The table is purged after all route-policies are processed to save memory.

- **Loc-RIB:** Contains all the NLRIs that originated locally or were received from other BGP peers. After NLRIs pass the validity and next-hop reachability check, the BGP best path algorithm selects the best NLRI for a specific prefix. The Loc-RIB table is the table used for presenting routes to the ip routing table.

- **Adj-RIB-out:** Contains the NLRIs after outbound route-policies have processed. A BGP route may contain multiple paths to the same destination network. Every path's attributes impact the desirability of the route when a router selects the best path. A BGP router advertises only the best path to the neighboring routers.

Inside the BGP Loc-RIB table, all the routes and their path attributes are maintained with the best path calculated. The best path is then installed in the RIB of the router. In the event the best path is no longer available, the router can use the existing paths to quickly identify a new best path. BGP recalculates the best path for a prefix upon four possible events:

- BGP next-hop reachability change
- Failure of an interface connected to an EBGP peer
- Redistribution change
- Reception of new paths for a route

The BGP best path selection algorithm influences how traffic enters or leaves an *autonomous system (AS)*. BGP does not use metrics to identify the best path in a network. BGP uses path attributes to identify its best path. But even before BGP influences the best path selection using PAs, the router looks for the longest prefix match for the routes present in the RIB and prefers that route to be installed in the forwarding information base (FIB).

BGP path attributes are modified upon receipt or advertisement to influence routing in the local AS or neighboring AS. A basic rule for traffic engineering with BGP is that modifications in outbound routing policies influence inbound traffic, and modifications to inbound routing policies influence outbound traffic.

BGP installs the first received path as the best path automatically. When additional paths are received, the newer paths are compared against the current best path. If there is a tie, processing continues onto the next step, until a best path winner is identified.

The following list provides the attributes that the BGP best path algorithm uses for the best route selection process. These attributes are processed in the order listed in Table 11-5.

Table 11-5 *BGP Attributes*

BGP Attribute	Scope
Weight	Router only. Highest value wins.
Local Preference	Within AS boundary. Highest value wins.
Locally Originated	Network or redistribute command preferred over local aggregates (aggregate-address command).
Accumulated Interior Gateway Protocol (AIGP)	AIGP Path Attribute.
AS_PATH	Shortest AS_PATH wins: ■ Skipped if **bgp bestpath as-path ignore** configured. ■ AS_SET counts as 1. ■ CONFED parts do not count.
Origin Type	IGP < EGP < Incomplete. Lowest wins.
Mutual Exclusive Discriminator (MED)	Compare only if the first AS in AS_SEQUENCE is same for multiple paths.
EBGP over IBGP	External BGP path preferred over Internal BGP path.
Metric to Next Hop	Cost of IGP to reach BGP next-hop. Lowest metric wins.
Oldest External	When both paths are external, prefer the first (oldest).
BGP Router ID (RID)	Path with lowest BGP RID is preferred.
CLUSTER_LIST	Prefer the route with minimum CLUSTER_LIST length.
Neighbor Address	Prefer path that is received form the lowest neighbor address (neighbor configured using **neighbor** *ip-address* command).

The best path algorithm is used to manipulate network traffic patterns for a specific route by modifying various path attributes on BGP routers. Changing of BGP PA influences traffic flow into, out of, and around an *autonomous system (AS)*. The BGP routing policy varies from organization to organization based upon the manipulation of the BGP PAs. Because some PAs are transitive and carry from one AS to another AS, those changes could impact downstream routing for other SPs, too. Other PAs are nontransitive and influence only the routing policy within the organization. Network prefixes are conditionally matched on a variety of factors, such as AS-Path length, specific ASN, BGP communities, or other attributes.

Examining the topology shown in Figure 11-6, NX-5 and NX-6 advertise their loopback toward AS 65000. When NX-1 receives the loopbacks, it receives it via NX-2 and NX-3 but only one of them is chosen as the best. The command **show bgp** *afi safi ip-address/length* displays both the received paths but also displays one of the paths that was not chosen as the best path, as shown in Example 11-22. In this example, initially the path for 192.168.5.5/32 is chosen via NX-2 due to the lowest RID, but when an inbound policy on NX-3 is defined to set a higher local preference, the path via NX-3 is chosen as the best.

Example 11-22 *BGP Best Path Selection*

```
NX-1# show bgp ipv4 unicast 192.168.5.5/32
BGP routing table information for VRF default, address family IPv4 Unicast
BGP routing table entry for 192.168.5.5/32, version 32
Paths: (2 available, best #1)
Flags: (0x08001a) on xmit-list, is in urib, is best urib route, is in HW,

  Advertised path-id 1
  Path type: internal, path is valid, is best path
  AS-Path: 65001 , path sourced external to AS
    192.168.2.2 (metric 41) from 192.168.2.2 (192.168.2.2)
      Origin IGP, MED not set, localpref 100, weight 0

  Path type: internal, path is valid, not best reason: Router Id
  AS-Path: 65001 , path sourced external to AS
    192.168.3.3 (metric 41) from 192.168.3.3 (192.168.3.3)
      Origin IGP, MED not set, localpref 100, weight 0

  Path-id 1 advertised to peers:
    192.168.3.3         192.168.4.4

NX-3(config)# route-map LP permit 10
NX-3(config-route-map)# set local-preference 200
NX-3(config-route-map)# exit
NX-3(config)# router bgp 65000
NX-3(config-router)# neighbor 10.36.1.6
NX-3(config-router-neighbor)# address-family ipv4 unicast
```

```
NX-3(config-router-neighbor-af)# route-map LP in
NX-3(config-router-neighbor-af)# end
```

```
NX-1# show bgp ipv4 unicast 192.168.5.5/32
BGP routing table information for VRF default, address family IPv4 Unicast
BGP routing table entry for 192.168.5.5/32, version 38
Paths: (2 available, best #2)
Flags: (0x08001a) on xmit-list, is in urib, is best urib route, is in HW,

  Path type: internal, path is invalid, not best reason: Local Preference, is de
leted, no labeled nexthop
  AS-Path: 65001 , path sourced external to AS
    192.168.2.2 (metric 41) from 192.168.2.2 (192.168.2.2)
      Origin IGP, MED not set, localpref 100, weight 0

  Advertised path-id 1
  Path type: internal, path is valid, is best path
  AS-Path: 65001 , path sourced external to AS
    192.168.3.3 (metric 41) from 192.168.3.3 (192.168.3.3)
      Origin IGP, MED not set, localpref 200, weight 0

  Path-id 1 advertised to peers:
    192.168.2.2         192.168.4.4
```

```
NX-1# show bgp ipv4 unicast 192.168.5.5/32
BGP routing table information for VRF default, address family IPv4 Unicast
BGP routing table entry for 192.168.5.5/32, version 38
Paths: (1 available, best #1)
Flags: (0x08001a) on xmit-list, is in urib, is best urib route, is in HW,

  Advertised path-id 1
  Path type: internal, path is valid, is best path
  AS-Path: 65001 , path sourced external to AS
    192.168.3.3 (metric 41) from 192.168.3.3 (192.168.3.3)
      Origin IGP, MED not set, localpref 200, weight 0

  Path-id 1 advertised to peers:
    192.168.2.2         192.168.4.4
```

Note While a prefix is being removed from the BGP RIB (BRIB), the prefix is marked as deleted and the path is never used for forwarding. After the update is complete, the BRIB does not show the path/prefix that was removed.

BGP Multipath

BGP's default behavior is to advertise only the best path to the RIB, which means that only one path for a network prefix is used when forwarding network traffic to a destination. BGP *multipath* allows for multiple paths to be presented to the RIB, so that both paths can forward traffic to a network prefix at the same time. BGP multipath is an enhanced form of BGP multihoming.

Note It is vital to understand that the primary difference between BGP multihoming and BGP multipath is how *load balancing* works. BGP multipath attempts to distribute the load of the traffic dynamically. BGP multihoming is distributed somewhat by the nature of the BGP best path algorithm, but manipulation to the inbound/outbound routing policies is required to reach a more equally distributed load among the links.

BGP supports three types of *equal cost multipath (ECMP)*: EBGP multipath, IBGP multipath, or eiBGP multipath. In all three types of BGP multipath, the following BGP *path attributes (PA)* must match for multipath to be eligible:

- Weight
- Local Preference
- AS-Path length and content (confederations can contain a different AS_CONFED_SEQ path)
- Origin
- MED
- Advertisement method must match (IBGP or EBGP); if the prefix is learned via an IBGP advertisement, the IGP cost must match to be considered equal

Note NX-OS does not support the eiBGP multipath feature at the time of writing.

EBGP and IBGP Multipath

EBGP multipath is enabled on NX-OS with the BGP configuration command **maximum-paths** *number-paths*. The number of paths indicates the allowed number of EBGP paths to install in the RIB. Note that the EBGP multipath configuration only allows for external path type to be selected as multipath best path. For internal path types, the IBGP multipath feature is required. The command **maximum-paths ibgp** *number-paths* sets the number of IBGP routes to install in the RIB. The commands are placed under the appropriate address-family.

Examine the topology shown in Figure 11-6. In this topology, NX-1 learns same prefixes from both NX-2 and NX-3. Because there is an IBGP peering between NX-1, NX-2, and NX-3, the paths learned via NX-1 are internal. To have multiple BGP paths installed in the RIB and BRIB, multipath IBGP is configured on NX-1. Example 11-23 demonstrates the IBGP multipath functionality as explained.

Example 11-23 *IBGP Multipath*

```
NX-1# show bgp ipv4 unicast 192.168.5.5/32
BGP routing table information for VRF default, address family IPv4 Unicast
BGP routing table entry for 192.168.5.5/32, version 32
Paths: (2 available, best #1)
Flags: (0x08001a) on xmit-list, is in urib, is best urib route, is in HW,

  Advertised path-id 1
  Path type: internal, path is valid, is best path
  AS-Path: 65001 , path sourced external to AS
    192.168.2.2 (metric 41) from 192.168.2.2 (192.168.2.2)
      Origin IGP, MED not set, localpref 100, weight 0

  Path type: internal, path is valid, not best reason: Router Id
  AS-Path: 65001 , path sourced external to AS
    192.168.3.3 (metric 41) from 192.168.3.3 (192.168.3.3)
      Origin IGP, MED not set, localpref 100, weight 0

  Path-id 1 advertised to peers:
    192.168.3.3        192.168.4.4
```

```
NX-1(config)# router bgp 65000
NX-1(config-router)# address-family ipv4 unicast
NX-1(config-router-af)# maximum-paths ibgp 2
```

```
NX-1# show bgp ipv4 unicast
BGP routing table information for VRF default, address family IPv4 Unicast
BGP table version is 65, local router ID is 192.168.1.1
Status: s-suppressed, x-deleted, S-stale, d-dampened, h-history, *-valid, >-best
Path type: i-internal, e-external, c-confed, l-local, a-aggregate, r-redist,
  I-injected
Origin codes: i - IGP, e - EGP, ? - incomplete, | - multipath, & - backup

   Network            Next Hop         Metric     LocPrf     Weight Path
*>l192.168.1.1/32     0.0.0.0                     100        32768 i
*>i192.168.2.2/32     192.168.2.2                 100            0 i
*>i192.168.3.3/32     192.168.3.3                 100            0 i
*>i192.168.4.4/32     192.168.4.4                 100            0 i
*>i192.168.5.5/32     192.168.2.2                 100            0 65001 i
*|i                   192.168.3.3                 100            0 65001 i
*>i192.168.6.6/32     192.168.2.2                 100            0 65001 i
*|i                   192.168.3.3                 100            0 65001 i
```

```
NX-1# show bgp ipv4 unicast 192.168.5.5
BGP routing table information for VRF default, address family IPv4 Unicast
BGP routing table entry for 192.168.5.5/32, version 59
Paths: (2 available, best #1)
Flags: (0x08001a) on xmit-list, is in urib, is best urib route, is in HW,
Multipath: iBGP

  Advertised path-id 1
  Path type: internal, path is valid, is best path
  AS-Path: 65001 , path sourced external to AS
    192.168.2.2 (metric 41) from 192.168.2.2 (192.168.2.2)
      Origin IGP, MED not set, localpref 100, weight 0

  Path type: internal, path is valid, not best reason: Router Id, multipath
  AS-Path: 65001 , path sourced external to AS
    192.168.3.3 (metric 41) from 192.168.3.3 (192.168.3.3)
      Origin IGP, MED not set, localpref 100, weight 0

  Path-id 1 advertised to peers:
    192.168.3.3         192.168.4.4

NX-1# show ip route 192.168.5.5/32 detail

192.168.5.5/32, ubest/mbest: 2/0
    *via 192.168.2.2, [200/0], 00:45:02, bgp-65000, internal, tag 65001,
        client-specific data: a
        recursive next hop: 192.168.2.2/32
        extended route information: BGP origin AS 65001 BGP peer AS 65001
    *via 192.168.3.3, [200/0], 00:02:22, bgp-65000, internal, tag 65001,
        client-specific data: a
        recursive next hop: 192.168.3.3/32
        extended route information: BGP origin AS 65001 BGP peer AS 65001
```

The BGP event-history logs are used to verify the second-best path being added to the Unicast Routing Information Base (URIB). Use the command **show bgp event-history detail** to view the details for both the best path and the second-best path of a prefix being added to URIB, as shown in Example 11-24. In Example 11-24, first the best path is selected, which is via 192.168.2.2, and then another path is added to the URIB, which is learned via nexthop 192.168.3.3.

Example 11-24 *Event-History Logs for BGP Multipath*

```
NX-1# show bgp event-history detail | in 192.168.5.5
16:48:55.864118: (default) RIB: [IPv4 Unicast] Adding path (0x18) to
 192.168.5.5/32 via 192.168.3.3 in URIB (table-id 0x1, flags 0x10, nh 192.168.3.
3) extcomm-len=0, preference=200
16:48:55.864112: (default) RIB: [IPv4 Unicast]: adding route 192.168.5.5/32 via
   192.168.3.3
16:48:55.864108: (default) RIB: [IPv4 Unicast] Sending route 192.168.5.5/32 to URIB
16:48:55.864101: (default) RIB: [IPv4 Unicast] No change (0x80038) in best path
 for 192.168.5.5/32 , resync with RIB, backup/multipath changed
16:48:55.864093: (default) RIB: [IPv4 Unicast] Begin select bestpath for
 192.168.5.5/32, adv_all=0, cal_nth=0, install_to_rib=0, flags=0x80038
16:48:55.863833: (default) RIB: [IPv4 Unicast] Triggering bestpath s
election for 192.168.5.5/32 , flags=0x8003a

! Output omitted for brevity

16:06:15.704376: (default) BRIB: [IPv4 Unicast] 192.168.5.5/32, no Label AF
16:06:15.704373: (default) RIB: [IPv4 Unicast] 192.168.5.5/32 path#1
: set to rid=192.168.2.2 nh=192.168.2.2, flags=0x12, changed=1
16:06:15.704369: (default) RIB: [IPv4 Unicast] Selected new bestpath
 192.168.5.5/32 flags=0x880018 rid=192.168.2.2 nh=192.168.2.2
```

BGP Update Generation Process

The update generation process on NX-OS is a bit different than both Cisco IOS and IOS XR based platforms. Unlike IOS and IOS XR, NX-OS does not have any concept of update-groups. BGP processes route update messages received from its peers, runs prefixes and attributes through any configured inbound policy, and installs the new paths in the BGP RIB (BRIB). After the route has been updated in the BRIB, BGP then marks the route for further update generation. Before the prefixes are packaged, they are processed through any configured outbound policies. The BGP puts the marked routes into the update message and sends them to peers. Example 11-25 illustrates the BGP update generation on NX-OS. For understanding the update generation process, debug commands **debug ip bgp update** and **debug ip bgp brib** can be enabled. From the debug output in Example 11-25, notice that the update received from NX-4 (192.168.4.4) includes the advertisement for prefix 192.168.44.44/32, which is then updated in the BRIB. Then NX-4, and then further updates are generated for the peers NX-2 and NX-3. Notice that the updates are generated separately for NX-2 (192.168.2.2) and NX-3 (192.168.3.3).

Example 11-25 *Debugs for BGP Update and Route Installation in BRIB*

```
NX-1# debug logfile bgp
NX-1# debug ip bgp update
NX-1# debug ip bgp brib
NX-1# show debug logfile bgp

! Receiving an update from peer for 192.168.44.44/32

22:40:31.707254 bgp: 65000 [10739] (default) UPD: Received UPDATE message from
 192.168.4.4
22:40:31.707422 bgp: 65000 [10739] (default) UPD: 192.168.4.4 parsed UPDATE
 message from peer, len 55 , withdraw len 0, attr len 32, nlri len 0
22:40:31.707499 bgp: 65000 [10739] (default) UPD: Attr code 1, length 1,
 Origin: IGP
22:40:31.707544 bgp: 65000 [10739] (default) UPD: Attr code 5, length 4,
 Local-pref: 100
22:40:31.707601 bgp: 65000 [10739] (default) UPD: Peer 192.168.4.4 nexthop
 length in MP reach: 4
22:40:31.707672 bgp: 65000 [10739] (default) UPD: Recvd NEXTHOP 192.168.4.4
22:40:31.707716 bgp: 65000 [10739] (default) UPD: Attr code 14, length 14,
 Mp-reach
22:40:31.707787 bgp: 65000 [10739] (default) UPD: [IPv4 Unicast] Received prefix
 192.168.44.44/32 from peer 192.168.4.4, origin 0, next hop 192.168.4.4,
 localpref 100, med 0
22:40:31.707859 bgp: 65000 [10739] (default) BRIB: [IPv4 Unicast] Installing
 prefix 192.168.44.44/32 (192.168.4.4) via 192.168.4.4  into BRIB with extcomm
22:40:31.707915 bgp: 65000 [10739] (default) BRIB: [IPv4 Unicast] Created new
 path to 192.168.44.44/32 via 0.0.0.0 (pflags=0x0)
22:40:31.707962 bgp: 65000 [10739] (default) BRIB: [IPv4 Unicast]
 (192.168.44.44/32 (192.168.4.4)): bgp_brib_add: handling nexthop
22:40:31.708054 bgp: 65000 [10739] (default) BRIB: [IPv4 Unicast]
 (192.168.44.44/32 (192.168.4.4)): returning from bgp_brib_add, new_path: 1,
 change : 1, undelete: 0, history: 0, force: 0, (pflags=0x2010), reeval=0
22:40:31.708292 bgp: 65000 [10739] (default) BRIB: [IPv4 Unicast]
 192.168.44.44/32, no Label AF

! Generating update for peer 192.168.2.2

22:40:31.709476 bgp: 65000 [10739] (default) UPD: [IPv4 Unicast] Starting
 update run for peer 192.168.2.2 (#65)
22:40:31.709514 bgp: 65000 [10739] (default) UPD: [IPv4 Unicast] consider
 sending 192.168.44.44/32 to peer 192.168.2.2, path-id 1, best-ext is off
22:40:31.709553 bgp: 65000 [10739] (default) UPD: 192.168.2.2 Sending attr
 code 1, length 1, Origin: IGP
```

```
22:40:31.709581 bgp: 65000 [10739] (default) UPD: 192.168.2.2 Sending attr
 code 5, length 4, Local-pref: 100
22:40:31.709613 bgp: 65000 [10739] (default) UPD: 192.168.2.2 Sending attr
 code 9, length 4, Originator: 192.168.4.4
22:40:31.709654 bgp: 65000 [10739] (default) UPD: 192.168.2.2 Sending attr
 code 10, length 4, Cluster-list
22:40:31.709700 bgp: 65000 [10739] (default) UPD: 192.168.2.2 Sending attr
 code 14, length 14, Mp-reach
22:40:31.709744 bgp: 65000 [10739] (default) UPD: 192.168.2.2 Sending nexthop
 address 192.168.4.4 length 4
22:40:31.709789 bgp: 65000 [10739] (default) UPD: [IPv4 Unicast] 192.168.2.2
 Created UPD msg (len 69) with prefix 192.168.44.44/32 ( Installed in HW
 ) path-id 1 for peer
22:40:31.709820 bgp: 65000 [10739] (default) UPD: [IPv4 Unicast] 192.168.2.2:
 walked 0 nodes and packed 0/0 prefixes
22:40:31.709859 bgp: 65000 [10739] (default) UPD: [IPv4 Unicast] (#66) Finished
 update run for peer 192.168.2.2 (#66)

! Generating update for peer 192.168.3.3

22:40:31.709891 bgp: 65000 [10739] (default) UPD: [IPv4 Unicast] Starting update
 run for peer 192.168.3.3 (#65)
22:40:31.709917 bgp: 65000 [10739] (default) UPD: [IPv4 Unicast] consider
 sending 192.168.44.44/32 to peer 192.168.3.3, path-id 1, best-ext is off
22:40:31.709948 bgp: 65000 [10739] (default) UPD: 192.168.3.3 Sending attr
 code 1, length 1, Origin: IGP
22:40:31.709974 bgp: 65000 [10739] (default) UPD: 192.168.3.3 Sending attr
 code 5, length 4, Local-pref: 100
22:40:31.709998 bgp: 65000 [10739] (default) UPD: 192.168.3.3 Sending attr
 code 9, length 4, Originator: 192.168.4.4
22:40:31.710149 bgp: 65000 [10739] (default) UPD: 192.168.3.3 Sending attr
 code 10, length 4, Cluster-list
22:40:31.710180 bgp: 65000 [10739] (default) UPD: 192.168.3.3 Sending attr
 code 14, length 14, Mp-reach
22:40:31.710204 bgp: 65000 [10739] (default) UPD: 192.168.3.3 Sending nexthop
 address 192.168.4.4 length 4
22:40:31.710231 bgp: 65000 [10739] (default) UPD: [IPv4 Unicast] 192.168.3.3
 Created UPD msg (len 69) with prefix 192.168.44.44/32 ( Installed in HW)
 path-id 1 for peer
22:40:31.710261 bgp: 65000 [10739] (default) UPD: [IPv4 Unicast] 192.168.3.3:
 walked 0 nodes and packed 0/0 prefixes
22:40:31.710286 bgp: 65000 [10739] (default) UPD: [IPv4 Unicast] (#66)
 Finished update run for peer 192.168.3.3 (#66)
```

On NX-OS, debugs are not necessarily required to understand the update generation process. Use the command **show bgp event-history detail** to view the detailed event logs. The detail option is not available by default and thus is required to be configured under the **router bgp** configuration using the command **event-history detail** [*size large* | *medium* | *small*]. Example 11-26 displays the detailed output of the BGP event-history logs showing the same update process. In this example, the update is being generated for NX-3. If the event-history logs are rolled over and the issue still keeps occurring again and again, in such situations debugs can be enabled, as demonstrated in Example 11-25.

Example 11-26 *Event-History Logs for BGP Update Generation*

```
NX-1# show bgp event-history detail
BGP event-history detail
22:40:31.710283: (default) UPD: [IPv4 Unicast] (#66) Finished update
 run for peer 192.168.3.3 (#66)
22:40:31.710258: (default) UPD: [IPv4 Unicast] 192.168.3.3: walked 0 nodes and
 packed 0/0 prefixes
22:40:31.710226: (default) UPD: [IPv4 Unicast] 192.168.3.3 Created UPD msg
 (len 69) with prefix 192.168.44.44/32 ( Installed in HW) path-id 1 for peer
22:40:31.710201: (default) UPD: 192.168.3.3 Sending nexthop address
 192.168.4.4 length 4
22:40:31.710177: (default) UPD: 192.168.3.3 Sending attr code 14, length 14,
 Mp-reach
22:40:31.710145: (default) UPD: 192.168.3.3 Sending attr code 10, length 4,
 Cluster-list
22:40:31.709995: (default) UPD: 192.168.3.3 Sending attr code 9, length 4,
 Originator: 192.168.4.4
22:40:31.709971: (default) UPD: 192.168.3.3 Sending attr code 5, length 4,
 Local-pref: 100
22:40:31.709945: (default) UPD: 192.168.3.3 Sending attr code 1, length 1,
 Origin: IGP
22:40:31.709913: (default) UPD: [IPv4 Unicast] consider sending 192.
 168.44.44/32 to peer 192.168.3.3, path-id 1, best-ext is off
22:40:31.709887: (default) UPD: [IPv4 Unicast] Starting update run for peer
 192.168.3.3 (#65)
! Output omitted for brevity
```

BGP Convergence

BGP convergence depends on various factors. BGP convergence is all about the speed of the following:

- Establishing sessions with a number of peers.

- Locally generate all the BGP paths (either via network statement, redistribution of static/connected/IGP routes), and/or from other component for other address-family (for example, Multicast VPN (MVPN) from multicast, L2VPN from l2vpn manager, and so on).

- Send and receive multiple BGP tables; that is, different BGP address-families to/from each peer.

- Upon receiving all the paths from peers, perform best path calculation to find the best path and/or multipath, additional-path, backup path.

- Installing the best path into multiple routing tables like default or VRF routing table.

- Import and export mechanism.

- For other address-family like L2VPN or multicast, pass the path calculation result to different lower layer components.

BGP uses a lot of CPU cycles when processing BGP updates and requires memory for maintaining BGP peers and routes in BGP tables. Based on the role of the BGP router in the network, appropriate hardware should be chosen. The more memory a router has, the more routes it can support, much like how a router with a faster CPU supports larger number of peers.

Note BGP updates rely on TCP, optimization of router resources, like memory, and TCP session parameters, like *maximum segment size (MSS)*, path MTU discovery, interface input queues, TCP window size, and so on to help improve convergence.

There are various steps that should be followed to verify whether the BGP has converged and the routes are installed in the BRIB.

If there is a traffic loss, before BGP has completed its convergence for a given address-family, verify the routing information in the URIB and the forwarding information in the FIB. Example 11-27 demonstrates a BGP route getting refreshed. The command **show bgp event-history [event | detail]** is used to validate that the prefix is installed in BRIB table and that the command **show routing event-history [add-route | modify-route | delete-route]** used to check the route has been installed in the URIB. In the URIB, verify the timestamp of when the route was downloaded to the URIB. If the prefix was recently downloaded to the URIB, there might have been an event that caused the route to get refreshed. Also, the difference in the time between when the prefix was installing in BRIB and when it was further downloaded to URIB will help understand the convergence time.

Example 11-27 *BRIB and URIB Route Installation*

```
NX-1# show bgp event-history detail
BGP event-history detail
! Output omitted for brevity
22:40:31.707849: (default) BRIB: [IPv4 Unicast] Installing prefix 19
2.168.44.44/32 (192.168.4.4) via 192.168.4.4  into BRIB with extcomm
```

```
NX-1# show routing internal event-history add-route | grep 192.168.44.44
22:40:31.708531 urib: "bgp-65000": 192.168.44.44/32 xri info for rnh
 192.168.4.4/32: origin AS fde8 peer AS fde8
22:40:31.708530 urib: "bgp-65000": 192.168.44.44/32, new rnh 192.168
.4.4/32, metric [200/0] route-type internal tag 0x0000fde8 flags 0x0000080e
22:40:31.708496 urib: "bgp-65000": 192.168.44.44/32 add rnh 192.168.
4.4/32 epoch 1 recursive
22:40:31.708495 urib: "bgp-65000": 192.168.44.44/32, adding rnh 192.
168.4.4/32, metric [200/0] route-type internal tag 0x0000fde8 flags 0x00000010
```

BGP convergence for relevant address-family is checked using the command **show bgp convergence detail vrf all**. Example 11-28 shows the output of the **show bgp convergence details vrf all** command. This command shows when the best-path selection process was started and the time to complete it. Not only that, the command also displays the time taken to converge the prefix to URIB, which can be used to understand how the device is performing from BGP and URIB convergence perspective.

Example 11-28 show bgp convergence detail *Command Output*

```
NX-1# show bgp convergence detail vrf all
Global settings:
BGP start time 1 day(s), 04:38:39 ago
Config processing completed 0.068404 after start
BGP out of wait mode 0.068493 after start
LDP convergence not required
Convergence to ULIB not required

Information for VRF default
Initial-bestpath timeout: 300 sec, configured 0 sec
BGP update-delay-always is not enabled
First peer up 00:06:14 after start
Bestpath timer not running

   IPv4 Unicast:
    First bestpath signalled 0.068443 after start
    First bestpath completed 0.069397 after start
    Convergence to URIB sent 0.082041 after start
```

```
    Peer convergence after start:
    192.168.2.2          (EOR after bestpath)
    192.168.3.3          (EOR after bestpath)
    192.168.4.4          (EOR after bestpath)

    IPv6 Unicast:
    First bestpath signalled 0.068467 after start
    First bestpath completed 0.069574 after start
```

Note If the BGP best-path has not run yet, the problem is likely not related to BGP on that node.

If the best-path runs before EOR is received, or if a peer fails to send EOR marker, it can lead to traffic loss. In such situations, enable debug for BGP updates with relevant debug-filters for VRF, address-family, and peer, as shown in Example 11-29.

Example 11-29 *Debug Commands with Filter*

```
debug logfile bgp
debug bgp events updates rib brib import
debug-filter bgp address-family ipv4 unicast
debug-filter bgp neighbor 192.168.4.4
debug-filter bgp prefix 192.168.44.44/32
```

From the debug output, check the event log to look at the timestamp to see when the most recent EOR was sent to the peer. This also shows how many routes were advertised to the peer before the sending of the EOR. A premature EOR sent to the peer can also lead to traffic loss if the peer flushes stale routes early.

If the route in URIB has not been downloaded, it needs to be further investigated because it may not be a problem with BGP. The following commands can be run to check the activity in URIB that could explain the loss:

- **show routing internal event-history ufdm**
- **show routing internal event-history ufdm-summary**
- **show routing internal event-history recursive**

Scaling BGP

BGP is one of the most feature-rich protocols ever developed that provides ease of routing and control using policies. Although BGP has many inbuilt features that scale the protocol very well, these enhancements were never utilized properly. This poses various challenges when BGP is deployed in a scaled environment.

BGP is a heavy protocol because it uses the most CPU and memory resources on a router. Many factors explain why it keeps utilizing more and more resources. The three major factors for BGP memory consumption are as follows:

- Prefixes
- Paths
- Attributes

BGP can hold many prefixes, and each prefix consumes some amount of memory. But when the same prefix is learned via multiple paths, that information is also maintained in the BGP table. Each path adds to more memory. Because BGP was designed to give control to each AS to manage the flow of traffic through various attributes, each prefix can have various attributes per path. This is put down as a mathematical function, where N represents the number of prefixes, M represents the number of paths for a given prefix, and L represents the attributes attached to given prefix:

- **Prefixes:** $(O(N))$
- **Paths:** $(O(M \times N))$
- **Attributes:** $(O(L \times M \times N))$

Tuning BGP Memory

To reduce or tune the BGP memory consumption, make adjustments to the three major factors leading to most BGP memory consumption, as discussed. The next sections examine the various adjustments that can be made for each factor.

Prefixes

BGP memory consumption becomes huge when BGP is holding a large number of prefixes or holding the Internet routing table. In most cases, not all the BGP prefixes are required to be maintained by all the routers running BGP in the network. To reduce the number of prefixes, take the following actions:

- Aggregation
- Filtering
- Partial routing table instead of full routing table

With the use of aggregation, multiple specific routes can be aggregated into one route. But aggregation is challenging when tried on a fully deployed running network. After the network is up and running, the complete IP addressing scheme has to be looked at to perform aggregation. Aggregation is a good option for *green field* deployments. The green field deployments give more control on the IP addressing scheme, which makes it easier to apply aggregation.

Filtering provides control over the number of prefixes maintained in the BGP table or advertised to BGP peers. BGP provides filtering based on prefix, BGP attributes, and communities. One important point to remember is that complex route filtering, or route filtering applied for a large number of prefixes, helps reduce the memory, but the router takes a hit on the CPU.

Many deployments do not require all the BGP speakers to maintain a full BGP routing table. Especially in an enterprise and data center deployments, there is no real need to having the full Internet routing table. The BGP speakers can maintain even a partial routing table containing the most relevant and required prefixes or just a default route toward the Internet gateway. Such designs greatly reduce the resources being used throughout the network and increase scalability.

Paths

Sometimes the BGP table carries fewer prefixes but still holds more memory because of multiple paths. A prefix can be learned via multiple paths, but only the best or multiple best paths are installed in the routing table. To reduce the memory consumption by BGP due to multiple paths, the following solutions should be adopted:

- Reduce the number of peerings.
- Use RRs instead of IBGP full mesh.

Multiple BGP paths are a direct effect of the multiple BGP peerings. Especially in an IBGP full-mesh environment, the number of BGP sessions increases exponentially and thus the number of paths. A lot of customers increase the number of IBGP neighbors to have more redundant paths, but two paths are sufficient to maintain redundancy. Increasing the number of peerings can cause scaling issues both from the perspective of the number of sessions and from the perspective of BGP memory utilization.

It is a well-known fact that IBGP needs to be in full mesh. Figure 11-7 illustrates an IBGP full-mesh topology. In an IBGP full-mesh deployment of n nodes, there are a total of $n*(n-1)/2$ IBGP sessions and $(n-1)$ sessions per BGP speaker.

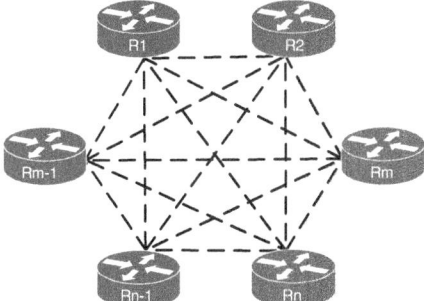

Figure 11-7 *IBGP Full Mesh*

This not only affects the scalability of an individual node or router but the whole network. To increase the scalability of IBGP network, two design approaches can be used:

- Confederations
- Route Reflectors

> **Note** BGP Confederations and Route Reflectors are discussed in another section later in this chapter.

Attributes

A BGP route is a "bag" of attributes. Every BGP prefix has certain default or mandatory attributes that are assigned automatically, such as next-hop or AS-PATH, or attributes that are configured manually, such as *Multi-Exit Discriminator (MED)* and the like, assigned by customers. Each attribute attached to the prefix adds up some memory utilization. Along with attributes, communities—both standard and extended—add to increased memory consumption. To reduce the BGP memory consumption due to various attributes and communities, the following solutions can be adopted:

- Reduce the number of attributes.
- Filter standard or extended communities.
- Limit local communities.

On NX-OS, use the command **show bgp private attr detail** to view the various attributes attached to the BGP prefixes. Example 11-30 displays the various global BGP attributes on NX-1. These attributes were learned across various prefixes, including the community attached to the prefix learned from NX-4.

Example 11-30 *BGP Attributes Detail*

```
NX-1# show bgp private attr detail
BGP Global attributes vxlan-enable:0  nve-api-init:0 nve-up:0 mac:0000.0000.0000

BGP attributes information
Number of attribute entries     : 4
HWM of attribute entries        : 5
Bytes used by entries           : 400
Entries pending delete          : 0
HWM of entries pending delete   : 0
BGP paths per attribute HWM     : 4
BGP AS path entries             : 1
Bytes used by AS path entries   : 26

BGP as-path traversal count     : 20

Attribute 0x64c1b8bc : Hash: 191, Refcount: 1, Attr ID 10
  origin        : IGP
  as-path       : 65001
                : 0 (path hash)
                : 1 (path refcount)
                : 20 (path marker)
```

```
    localpref     : 100
    weight        : 0
        Extcommunity presence mask: (nil)

Attribute 0x64c1b7dc : Hash: 2649, Refcount: 1, Attr ID 5
    origin        : IGP
    as-path       :
    localpref     : 100
    weight        : 32768
        Extcommunity presence mask: (nil)

Attribute 0x64c1b84c : Hash: 2651, Refcount: 1, Attr ID 2
    origin        : IGP
    as-path       :
    localpref     : 100
    weight        : 0
        Extcommunity presence mask: (nil)

Attribute 0x64c1b6fc : Hash: 3027, Refcount: 1, Attr ID 12
    origin        : IGP
    as-path       :
    localpref     : 100
    weight        : 0
        Community: 65000:44
        Extcommunity presence mask: (nil)
```

There is no method to get rid of the default BGP attributes, but the use of other attributes can be controlled. Using attributes that make things more complex is of no use. For example, using MED and various MED-related commands, such as the command **bgp always-compare-med** or **bgp deterministic-med**, can have an adverse impact on the network and can lead to route instability or routing loop conditions. At the same time, the user-assigned attributes will consume more BGP memory, which can easily be avoided.

Scaling BGP Configuration

BGP templates are used to assign common policies and attributes, such as AS number or source-interface, and so on for multiple neighbors. This saves on a lot of typing when there are multiple neighbors having the same policy. The NX-OS implementation of peer templates consists of three template types: **peer-policy**, **peer-session**, and **peer** template.

A **peer-policy** defines the address-family dependent policy aspects for a peer, including inbound and outbound policy, filter-list and prefix-lists, soft-reconfiguration, and so on. A **peer-session** template defines session attributes, such as transport details and session timers. Both the **peer-policy** and **peer-session** templates are inheritable; that is, a **peer-policy** or **peer-session** can inherit attributes from another **peer-policy** or **peer-session**, respectively. A peer template pulls the peer-session and peer-policy sections together to allow cookie-cutter neighbor definitions. Example 11-31 illustrates the configuration of BGP templates on NX-1.

Example 11-31 *BGP Template Configuration*

```
NX-1(config)# router bgp 65000
! Configure peer-policy template
NX-1(config-router)# template peer-policy PEERS-V4
NX-1(config-router-ptmp)# route-reflector-client
NX-1(config-router-ptmp)# exit
! Configure peer-session template
NX-1(config-router)# template peer-session PEER-DEFAULT
NX-1(config-router-stmp)# remote-as 65530
NX-1(config-router-stmp)# update-source loopback0
NX-1(config-router-stmp)# password cisco
NX-1(config-router-stmp)# exit
! Configure peer template
NX-1(config-router)# template peer IBGP-RRC
NX-1(config-router-neighbor)# inherit peer-session PEER-DEFAULT
NX-1(config-router-neighbor)# address-family ipv4 unicast
NX-1(config-router-neighbor-af)# inherit peer-policy PEERS-V4 10
! Applying Peer Template to BGP peers
NX-1(config-router)# neighbor 192.168.4.4
NX-1(config-router-neighbor)# inherit peer IBGP-RRC
NX-1(config-router-neighbor)# exit
NX-1(config-router)# neighbor 192.168.3.3
NX-1(config-router-neighbor)# inherit peer IBGP-RRC
NX-1(config-router-neighbor)# exit
NX-1(config-router)# neighbor 192.168.2.2
NX-1(config-router-neighbor)# inherit peer IBGP-RRC
NX-1(config-router-neighbor)# exit
```

Soft Reconfiguration Inbound Versus Route Refresh

BGP updates are requested for resend from peers when making adjustments to inbound BGP policies. BGP updates are incremental; that is, after the initial update is completed, only the changes are received. Thus, the BGP sessions are required to be reset, to request our peers to send us a BGP UPDATE message with all the NLRIs, so that those updates could be rerun via the new filter. There are two methods to perform the session reset:

- **Hard Reset:** Dropping and reestablishing BGP session. Performed by the command **clear bgp** *afi safi* [* | *ip-address*].

- **Soft Reset:** A soft reset uses filtered prefixes stored in the memory to reconfigure and activate BGP routing tables without tearing down the BGP session. Performed using the command **clear bgp** *afi safi* [* | *ip address*] **soft** [**in** | **out**].

Hard reset of a BGP session is disruptive to an operational network. If a BGP session is reset repeatedly over a short period of time due to multiple changes in BGP policy, it can result in other routers in the network dampening prefixes, causing destinations to be unreachable and traffic to be black-holed.

Soft reconfiguration is a traditional way to allow route-policy to be applied on the inbound BGP route update. BGP soft reconfiguration is enabled using the command **soft-reconfiguration inbound** under the neighbor configuration mode. When configured, the BGP stores an unmodified copy of all routes received from that peer at all times, even when the routing policies did not change frequently. Enabling soft reconfiguration means that the router also stores prefixes/attributes received prior to any policy application. This causes an extra overhead on memory and CPU on the router.

To manually perform a soft reset, use the command **clear bgp ipv4 unicast** [* | *ip-address*] **soft** [**in** | **out**]. The soft-reconfiguration feature is useful when the operator wants to know which prefixes have been sent to a router prior to the application of any inbound policy.

To overcome the challenges of **soft-reconfiguration inbound** configuration, *BGP route refresh capability* was introduced and is defined in RFC 2918. The BGP route refresh capability has a capability code of 2 and the capability length of 0. Using the route refresh capability, the router sends out a route refresh request to peer to get the full table from the peer again. The good part of route refresh capability is there is no preconfiguration needed to enable this capability. The ROUTE-REFRESH message is a new BGP message type described in Figure 11-8.

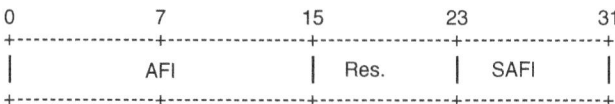

Figure 11-8 *BGP Route Refresh Message*

The AFI and SAFI in the ROUTE-REFRESH message points to the address-family where the configured peer is negotiating the route refresh capability. The Reserved bits are unused and are set to 0 by the sender and ignored by the receiver.

A BGP speaker sends a ROUTE-REFRESH message only if it has negotiated the route refresh capability with its peer. This implies that all the participating routes should support the route refresh capability. The router sends a route refresh request (*REFRESH_REQ*) to the peer. After the speaker receives a route refresh request, the BGP speaker readvertises to the peer the Adj-RIB-Out of the AFI and SAFI carried in the message, to its peer. If the BGP speaker has an outbound route filtering policy, the updates are filtered accordingly. The route refresh requesting peer receives the filtered routes.

The **clear ip bgp** *ip-address* **in** or **clear bgp** *afi safi ip-address* **in** command tells the peer to resend the full BGP announcement by sending a route-refresh request. Whereas the **clear bgp** *afi safi ip-address* **out** command resends the full BGP announcement to the peer, it does not initiates a route refresh request. The route refresh capability is verified using the **show bgp** *afi safi* **neighbor** *ip-address* command. Example 11-32 displays the route refresh capability negotiated between the two BGP peers.

Example 11-32 *BGP Route Refresh Capability*

```
NX-1
NX-1# show bgp ipv4 unicast neighbors 192.168.2.2
BGP neighbor is 192.168.2.2, remote AS 65000, ibgp link, Peer index 1
  Inherits peer configuration from peer-template IBGP-RRC
  BGP version 4, remote router ID 192.168.2.2
  BGP state = Established, up for 01:10:46
  Using loopback0 as update source for this peer
  Last read 00:00:43, hold time = 180, keepalive interval is 60 seconds
  Last written 00:00:31, keepalive timer expiry due 00:00:28
  Received 77 messages, 0 notifications, 0 bytes in queue
  Sent 80 messages, 0 notifications, 0 bytes in queue
  Connections established 1, dropped 0
  Last reset by us never, due to No error
  Last reset by peer never, due to No error

Neighbor capabilities:
  Dynamic capability: advertised (mp, refresh, gr) received (mp, refresh, gr)
  Dynamic capability (old): advertised received
  Route refresh capability (new): advertised received
  Route refresh capability (old): advertised received
  4-Byte AS capability: advertised received
  Address family IPv4 Unicast: advertised received
  Graceful Restart capability: advertised received
! Output omitted for brevity
```

Note When the soft-reconfiguration feature is configured, BGP route refresh capability is not used, even though the capability is negotiated. The soft-reconfiguration configuration controls the processing or initiating route refresh.

The BGP refresh request (REFRESH_REQ) is sent in one of the following cases:

- **clear bgp** *afi safi* [* | *ip-address*] **in** command is issued.
- **clear bgp** *afi safi* [* | *ip-address*] **soft in** command is issued.
- Adding or changing inbound filtering on the BGP neighbor via route-map.

- When configuring **allowas-in** for the BGP neighbor.
- Configuring **soft-reconfiguration inbound** for the BGP neighbor.
- Adding a **route-target import** to a VRF in MPLS VPN (for AFI/SAFI value 1/128 or 2/128).

Note It is recommended to use **soft-reconfiguration inbound** only on EBGP peering whenever it is required to know what the original prefix attributes are before being filtered or modified by the inbound route-map. It is not recommended on routers that receive a large number of prefixes being exchanged, such as the Internet routing table.

Scaling BGP with Route-Reflectors

The inability for BGP to advertise a prefix learned from one iBGP peer to another iBGP peer can lead to scalability issues within an AS. The formula $n(n-1)/2$ provides the number of sessions required, where n represents the number of routers. A full mesh topology of 5 routers requires 10 sessions, and a topology of 10 routers requires 45 sessions. IBGP scalability becomes an issue for large networks.

RFC 1966 introduces the concept that an iBGP peering can be configured so that it reflects routes to another iBGP peer. The router reflecting routes is known as a *route reflector (RR)*, and the router receiving reflected routes is a *route reflector client*. The RR design turns an IBGP mesh into a hub-and-spoke design where the RR is the hub router. The RR clients are either regular IBGP peers—that is, they are not directly connected to each other—or the other design could have RR clients that are interconnected. Three basic rules involve route reflectors and route reflection:

- **Rule #1:** If an RR receives an NLRI from a non-RR client, the RR advertises the NLRI to a RR client. It will not advertise the NLRI to a non-RR client.
- **Rule #2:** If an RR receives an NLRI from an RR client, it advertises the NLRI to RR client(s) and non-RR client(s). Even the RR client that sent the advertisement receives a copy of the route, but it discards the NLRI because it sees itself as the route originator.
- **Rule #3:** If an RR receives a route from an EBGP peer, it advertises the route to RR client(s) and non-RR client(s). Only route-reflectors are aware of this change in behavior because no additional BGP configuration is performed on route-reflector clients. BGP route reflection is specific to each address-family. The command **route-reflector-client** is used on NX-OS devices under the neighbor address-family configuration.

Examine the two RR design scenarios shown in Figure 11-9. The topology in (a) has R1 acting as the RR, whereas R2, R3, and R4 are the RR clients. The topology shown in (b) has a similar setup to that of (a) with a difference that the RR clients are fully meshed with each other.

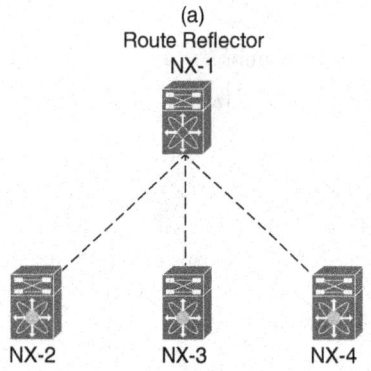 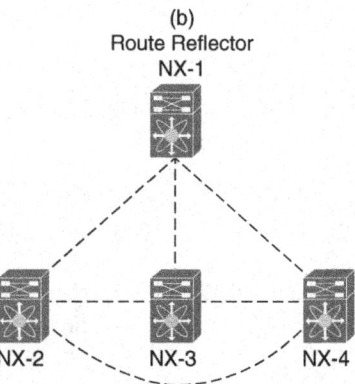

Figure 11-9 *Topology*

The RR and the client peers form a cluster and are not required to be fully meshed. Because the topology in (b) has an RR along with fully meshed IBGP client peers, which actually defies the purpose of having RR, the BGP RR reflection behavior should be disabled. The BGP RR client-to-client reflection is disabled using the command **no bgp client-to-client reflection**. This command is required only on the RR and not on the RR clients. Example 11-33 displays the configuration for disabling BGP client-to-client reflection.

Example 11-33 *Disabling BGP Client-to-Client Reflection*

```
NX-1(config)# router bgp 65000
NX-1(config-router)# address-family ipv4 unicast
NX-1(config-router-af)# no client-to-client reflection
```

Loop Prevention in Route Reflectors

Removing the full mesh requirements in an iBGP topology introduces the potential for routing loops. When RFC 1966 was drafted, two other BGP route reflector specific attributes were added to prevent loops.

ORIGINATOR_ID

This optional nontransitive BGP attribute is created by the first route-reflector and sets the value to the RID of the router that injected/advertised the route into the AS. If the ORIGINATOR_ID is already populated on an NLRI, it should not be overwritten.

If a router receives an NLRI with its RID in the Originator attribute, the NLRI is discarded.

CLUSTER_LIST

This nontransitive BGP attribute is updated by the route-reflector. This attribute is appended (not overwritten) by the route-reflector with its cluster-id. By default, this is the BGP identifier. The cluster-id is set with the BGP configuration command **cluster-id**.

If a route reflector receives an NLRI with its cluster-id in the Cluster List attribute, the NLRI is discarded.

Example 11-34 provides a sample prefix output from a route that was reflected by the route reflector NX-1, as shown in Figure 11-9. Notice that the originator ID is the advertising router and that the cluster list contains the route-reflector ID. The cluster list contains the route-reflectors that the prefix traversed in the order of the last route-reflector that advertised the route.

Example 11-34 *Output of an RR Reflected Prefix*

```
NX-4# show bgp ipv4 unicast 192.168.5.5/32
BGP routing table information for VRF default, address family IPv4 Unicast
BGP routing table entry for 192.168.5.5/32, version 52
Paths: (1 available, best #1)
Flags: (0x08001a) on xmit-list, is in urib, is best urib route, is in HW,

  Advertised path-id 1
  Path type: internal, path is valid, is best path
  AS-Path: 65001 , path sourced external to AS
    192.168.2.2 (metric 81) from 192.168.1.1 (192.168.1.1)
        Origin IGP, MED not set, localpref 100, weight 0
        Originator: 192.168.2.2 Cluster list: 192.168.1.1

  Path-id 1 not advertised to any peer
```

If a topology contains more than one RR and both the RRs are configured with different cluster IDs, the second RR holds the path from the first RR and hence consumes more memory and CPU resources. Having either single cluster-id or multiple cluster-id has its own disadvantages.

- **Different cluster-id:** Additional memory and CPU overhead on RR
- **Same cluster-id:** Less redundant paths

If the RR clients are fully meshed within the cluster, **no bgp client-to-client reflection** command can be enabled on the RR.

Maximum Prefixes

By default, a BGP peer holds all the routes advertised by the peering router. The number of routes are filtered either on the inbound of the local router or on the outbound of the peering router. But there can still be instances where the number of routes are more than what a router needs or a router can handle.

NX-OS supports the BGP maximum-prefix feature that allows you to limit the number of prefixes on a per-peer basis. Generally, this feature is enabled for EBGP sessions, but it is also used for IBGP sessions. Although this feature helps scale and prevent the network from an excess number of routes, it is very important to understand when to use this feature. The BGP maximum-prefix feature is enabled in the following situations:

- Know how many BGP routes are anticipated from the peer.
- What actions need to be taken if the number of routes are exceeded. Should the BGP connection be reset or should a warning message be logged?

To limit the number of prefixes, use the command **maximum-prefix** *maximum* [*threshold*] [**restart** *restart-interval* | **warning-only**] for each neighbor. Table 11-6 elaborates each of the fields in the command.

Table 11-6 *BGP* **maximum-prefix** *Command Options*

maximum	Defines the maximum prefix limit.
threshold	Defines the threshold percentage at which a warning is generated.
restart *restart-interval*	Default behavior. Resets the BGP connection after the specified prefix limit is exceeded. The restart-interval is configured in minutes. BGP tries to reestablish the peering after the specified time interval is passed. When the **restart** option is set, a cease notification is sent to the neighbor, and the BGP connection is terminated.
warning-only	Only gives a warning message when the specified limit is exceeded.

An important point to remember is that when the **restart** option is configured with the **maximum-prefix** command, the only other way apart from waiting for the restart-interval timer to expire, to reestablish the BGP connection, is to perform a manual reset of the peer using the **clear bgp** *afi safi ip-address* command.

Example 11-35 illustrates the use of the maximum-prefix command. NX-2 is receiving over 10 prefixes from neighbor 10.25.1.5, but the device has set the maximum-prefix limit to 10 prefixes. In such an instance, the BGP peering is shut on the device where maximum-prefix is set, but the remote end peer remains in Idle state. While troubleshooting BGP peering issues, validate the **show bgp** *afi safi* **neighbors** *ip-address* command to verify the reason for last reset.

Example 11-35 *Maximum-Prefixes*

```
NX-2(config)# router bgp 65000
NX-2(config-router)# neighbor 10.25.1.5
NX-2(config-router-neighbor)# address-family ipv4 unicast
NX-2(config-router-neighbor-af)# maximum-prefix 10
```

```
NX-2# show bgp ipv4 unicast summary
BGP summary information for VRF default, address family IPv4 Unicast
BGP router identifier 192.168.2.2, local AS number 65000
BGP table version is 257, IPv4 Unicast config peers 2, capable peers 1
106 network entries and 108 paths using 15424 bytes of memory
BGP attribute entries [16/2304], BGP AS path entries [11/360]
BGP community entries [0/0], BGP clusterlist entries [2/8]

Neighbor        V    AS MsgRcvd MsgSent   TblVer  InQ OutQ Up/Down  State/PfxRcd
10.25.1.5       4 65001    7349    7354        0    0    0 00:00:08 Shut (PfxCt)
192.168.1.1     4 65000    7781    7778      257    0    0 3d05h    5
```

```
NX-5# show bgp ipv4 unicast neighbors 10.25.1.2
BGP neighbor is 10.25.1.2,  remote AS 65000, ebgp link,  Peer index 1
  BGP version 4, remote router ID 0.0.0.0
  BGP state = Idle, down for 00:32:34, retry in 00:00:01
  Last read never, hold time = 180, keepalive interval is 60 seconds
  Last written never, keepalive timer not running
  Received 7354 messages, 1 notifications, 0 bytes in queue
  Sent 7379 messages, 0 notifications, 0 bytes in queue
  Connections established 1, dropped 1
  Connection attempts 28
  Last reset by us 00:01:27, due to session closed
  Last reset by peer 00:32:34, due to maximum prefix count error
 Message statistics:
                         Sent               Rcvd
    Opens:                 31                  1
    Notifications:          0                  1
    Updates:               13                 20
    Keepalives:          7333               7330
    Route Refresh:          0                  0
    Capability:             2                  2
    Total:               7379               7354
    Total bytes:       140687             140306
    Bytes in queue:         0                  0
! Output omitted for brevity
```

BGP Max AS

Various attributes are, by default, assigned to every BGP prefix. The length of attributes that can be attached to a single prefix can grow up to size of 64 KB, which can cause scaling as well as convergence issues for BGP.

A lot of times, the as-path prepend option is used to increase the AS-PATH list to make a path with lower AS-PATH list preferred. This operation does not have much of an impact. But from the perspective of the Internet, a longer AS-PATH list cannot only cause convergence issues but can also cause security loopholes. The AS-PATH list actually signifies a router's position on the Internet.

To limit the maximum number of AS-PATH length supported in the network, the **maxas-limit** command was introduced. Using the command **maxas-limit** *1-512* in NX-OS, any route with AS-PATH length higher than the specified number is discarded.

BGP Route Filtering and Route Policies

BGP, along with being scalable, also has the capability to provide route filtering, traffic engineering, and traffic load-sharing capabilities. BGP provides all these functionalities by defining route policies and route filters. This route filtering is defined using three methods:

- Prefix-lists
- Filter-lists
- Route-maps

The BGP route-maps provide more dynamic capability as compared to prefix-lists and filter-lists, because it not only allows you to perform route filtering but also allows the network operators to define policies and set attributes that can be further used to control traffic flow within the network. All these route filtering and route policy methods are discussed in future sections.

Example 11-36 displays the BGP table of Nexus switch NX-2 in the topology shown in Figure 11-9. The NX-2 switch is used as the base to demonstrate all the filtering techniques shown further in this chapter.

Example 11-36 *BGP Table on NX-2*

```
NX-2# show bgp ipv4 unicast | b Network
   Network              Next Hop         Metric   LocPrf   Weight Path
*>e100.1.1.0/24         10.25.1.5                          0 65001 100 {220} e
*>e100.1.2.0/24         10.25.1.5                          0 65001 100 {220} e
*>e100.1.3.0/24         10.25.1.5                          0 65001 100 {220} e
*>e100.1.4.0/24         10.25.1.5                          0 65001 100 {220} e
*>e100.1.5.0/24         10.25.1.5                          0 65001 100 {220} e
```

```
*>e100.1.6.0/24       10.25.1.5                        0 65001 100 {220} e
*>e100.1.7.0/24       10.25.1.5                        0 65001 100 {220} e
*>e100.1.8.0/24       10.25.1.5                        0 65001 100 {220} e
*>e100.1.9.0/24       10.25.1.5                        0 65001 100 {220} e
*>e100.1.10.0/24      10.25.1.5                        0 65001 100 {220} e
*>e100.1.11.0/24      10.25.1.5                        0 65001 100 292 {218 230}
*>e100.1.12.0/24      10.25.1.5                        0 65001 100 292 {218 230}
*>e100.1.13.0/24      10.25.1.5                        0 65001 100 292 {218 230}
*>e100.1.14.0/24      10.25.1.5                        0 65001 100 292 {218 230}
*>e100.1.15.0/24      10.25.1.5                        0 65001 100 292 {218 230}
*>e100.1.16.0/24      10.25.1.5                        0 65001 100 292 {218 230}
*>e100.1.17.0/24      10.25.1.5                        0 65001 100 292 {218 230}
*>e100.1.18.0/24      10.25.1.5                        0 65001 100 292 {218 230}
*>e100.1.19.0/24      10.25.1.5                        0 65001 100 292 {218 230}
*>e100.1.20.0/24      10.25.1.5                        0 65001 100 292 {218 230}
*>e100.1.21.0/24      10.25.1.5                        0 65001 100 228 274 {300 243}
*>e100.1.22.0/24      10.25.1.5                        0 65001 100 228 274 {300 243}
*>e100.1.23.0/24      10.25.1.5                        0 65001 100 228 274 {300 243}
*>e100.1.24.0/24      10.25.1.5                        0 65001 100 228 274 {300 243}
*>e100.1.25.0/24      10.25.1.5                        0 65001 100 228 274 {300 243}
*>e100.1.26.0/24      10.25.1.5                        0 65001 100 228 274 {300 243}
*>e100.1.27.0/24      10.25.1.5                        0 65001 100 228 274 {300 243}
*>e100.1.28.0/24      10.25.1.5                        0 65001 100 228 274 {300 243}
*>e100.1.29.0/24      10.25.1.5                        0 65001 100 228 274 {300 243}
*>e100.1.30.0/24      10.25.1.5                        0 65001 100 228 274 {300 243}
*>i192.168.1.1/32     192.168.1.1         100          0 i
*>l192.168.2.2/32     0.0.0.0             100      32768 i
*>i192.168.3.3/32     192.168.3.3         100          0 i
*>i192.168.4.4/32     192.168.4.4         100          0 i
*>e192.168.5.5/32     10.25.1.5                        0 65001 i
*>e192.168.6.6/32     10.25.1.5                        0 65001 i
*>i192.168.44.0/24    192.168.4.4         100          0 i
```

Prefix-List-Based Filtering

As explained in Chapter 10, "Troubleshooting Nexus Route-Maps," prefix lists provide another method of identifying networks in a routing protocol. They identify a specific IP address, network, or network range, and allow for the selection of multiple networks with a variety of prefix lengths (subnet masks) by using a *prefix match specification*.

The prefix-list can be applied directly to a BGP peer and also as a match statement within the route-map. A prefix-list is configured using the command **ip prefix-list** *name* [**seq** *sequence-number*] [**permit** *ip-address/length* | **deny** *ip-address/length*] [**le** *length* | **ge** *length* | **eq** *length*]. Examine the same topology as shown in Figure 11-6.

Example 11-37 illustrates the configuration of BGP inbound and outbound route filtering using prefix-lists on NX-2. The inbound prefix-list permits for 5 networks, whereas the outbound prefix-list permits for host network entries is /32 prefixes matching in subnet 192.168.0.0/16. When the prefix-lists are configured, use the command **show bgp** *afi safi* **neighbor** *ip-address* to ensure that the prefix-lists have been attached to the neighbor.

Example 11-37 *Prefix-List-Based Route Filtering*

```
NX-2(config)# ip prefix-list Inbound permit 100.1.1.0/24
NX-2(config)# ip prefix-list Inbound permit 100.1.2.0/24
NX-2(config)# ip prefix-list Inbound permit 100.1.3.0/24
NX-2(config)# ip prefix-list Inbound permit 100.1.4.0/24
NX-2(config)# ip prefix-list Inbound permit 100.1.5.0/24
NX-2(config)#
NX-2(config)# ip prefix-list Outbound permit 192.168.0.0/16 eq 32
NX-2(config)# router bgp 65000
NX-2(config-router)# neighbor 10.25.1.5
NX-2(config-router-neighbor)# address-family ipv4 unicast
NX-2(config-router-neighbor-af)# prefix-list Inbound in
NX-2(config-router-neighbor-af)# prefix-list Outbound out
NX-2(config-router-neighbor-af)# end

NX-2# show bgp ipv4 unicast neighbors 10.25.1.5
BGP neighbor is 10.25.1.5,   remote AS 65001, ebgp link, Peer index 2
  BGP version 4, remote router ID 192.168.5.5
  BGP state = Established, up for 2d00h
! output omitted for brevity
  For address family: IPv4 Unicast
  BGP table version 1085, neighbor version 1085
  5 accepted paths consume 400 bytes of memory
  4 sent paths
  Inbound ip prefix-list configured is Inbound, handle obtained
  Outbound ip prefix-list configured is Outbound, handle obtained
  Last End-of-RIB received 1d23h after session start

  Local host: 10.25.1.2, Local port: 58236
  Foreign host: 10.25.1.5, Foreign port: 179
  fd = 74
```

Example 11-38 displays the output of the BGP table after the prefix-lists have been configured and attached to BGP neighbor 10.25.1.5. Notice that in this example, on the NX-2 switch, only 5 prefixes are seen from neighbor 10.25.1.5. On NX-5, all the loopback addresses of the nodes in AS 65000 are advertised apart from 192.168.44.0/24.

Example 11-38 *BGP Table Output After Prefix-List Configuration*

```
NX-2# show bgp ipv4 unicast
BGP routing table information for VRF default, address family IPv4 Unicast
BGP table version is 1085, local router ID is 192.168.2.2
Status: s-suppressed, x-deleted, S-stale, d-dampened, h-history, *-valid, >-best
Path type: i-internal, e-external, c-confed, l-local, a-aggregate, r-redist,
  I-injected
Origin codes: i - IGP, e - EGP, ? - incomplete, | - multipath, & - backup

   Network            Next Hop         Metric     LocPrf     Weight Path
*>e100.1.1.0/24       10.25.1.5                   0 65001    100 220
*>e100.1.2.0/24       10.25.1.5                   0 65001    100 220
*>e100.1.3.0/24       10.25.1.5                   0 65001    100 220
*>e100.1.4.0/24       10.25.1.5                   0 65001    100 220
*>e100.1.5.0/24       10.25.1.5                   0 65001    100 220
*>i192.168.1.1/32     192.168.1.1                 100           0 i
*>l192.168.2.2/32     0.0.0.0                     100       32768 i
*>i192.168.3.3/32     192.168.3.3                 100           0 i
*>i192.168.4.4/32     192.168.4.4                 100           0 i

NX-5# show bgp ipv4 unicast neighbors 10.25.1.2 routes
Peer 10.25.1.2 routes for address family IPv4 Unicast:
BGP table version is 1209, local router ID is 192.168.5.5
Status: s-suppressed, x-deleted, S-stale, d-dampened, h-history, *-valid, >-best
Path type: i-internal, e-external, c-confed, l-local, a-aggregate, r-redist,
  I-injected
Origin codes: i - IGP, e - EGP, ? - incomplete, | - multipath, & - backup

   Network            Next Hop         Metric     LocPrf     Weight Path
*>e192.168.1.1/32     10.25.1.2                              0 65000 i
*>e192.168.2.2/32     10.25.1.2                              0 65000 i
*>e192.168.3.3/32     10.25.1.2                              0 65000 i
*>e192.168.4.4/32     10.25.1.2                              0 65000 i
```

On the inbound direction on NX-2, use the command **show bgp event-history detail** to view the details of the prefixes being matched against the prefix-list *Inbound*. Based on the match, the prefixes are either permitted or denied. If no entry exists for the prefix in the prefix-list, it is dropped by BGP and will not be part of the BGP table. Example 11-39 displays the event-history detail output demonstrating how a prefix 100.1.30.0/24 is rejected or dropped by BGP prefix-list and the prefix 100.1.5.0/24 being permitted at the same time.

Example 11-39 *BGP Event-History for Inbound Prefixes*

```
! Event-History output for incoming prefixes
NX-2# show bgp event-history detail
14:54:41.278141: (default) UPD: [IPv4 Unicast] 10.25.1.5 processing EOR update from
  peer
14:54:41.278138: (default) UPD: 10.25.1.5 parsed UPDATE message from peer, len 29 ,
  withdraw len 0, attr len 6, nlri len 0
14:54:41.278135: (default) UPD: Received UPDATE message from 10.25.1.5
14:54:41.278131: (default) UPD: [IPv4 Unicast] Dropping prefix 100.1.30.0/24 from
  peer 10.25.1.5, due to prefix policy rejected
14:54:41.278129: (default) UPD: [IPv4 Unicast] Prefix 100.1.30.0/24 from peer
  10.25.1.5 rejected by inbound policy
14:54:41.278126: (default) UPD: [IPv4 Unicast] 10.25.1.5 Inbound ip prefix-list
  Inbound, action deny
14:54:41.278124: (default) UPD: [IPv4 Unicast] Received prefix 100.1.30.0/24 from
  peer 10.25.1.5, origin 1, next hop 10.25.1.5, localpref
0, med 0
14:54:41.278119: (default) UPD: [IPv4 Unicast] Dropping prefix 100.1.29.0/24 from
  peer 10.25.1.5, due to prefix policy rejected
14:54:41.278116: (default) UPD: [IPv4 Unicast] Prefix 100.1.29.0/24 from peer
  10.25.1.5 rejected by inbound policy

! output omittied for brevity

14:54:41.277740: (default) BRIB: [IPv4 Unicast] (100.1.5.0/24 (10.25.1.5)):
  returning from bgp_brib_add, new_path: 0, change: 0, undelete:
 0, history: 0, force: 0, (pflags=0x28), reeval=0
14:54:41.277737: (default) BRIB: [IPv4 Unicast] 100.1.5.0/24 from 10.25.1.5 was
  already in BRIB with same attributes
14:54:41.277734: (default) BRIB: [IPv4 Unicast] (100.1.5.0/24 (10.25.1.5)): bgp_
  brib_add: handling nexthop
14:54:41.277731: (default) BRIB: [IPv4 Unicast] Path to 100.1.5.0/24 via 192.168.5.5
  already exists, dflags=0x8001a
14:54:41.277728: (default) BRIB: [IPv4 Unicast] Installing prefix 100.1.5.0/24
  (10.25.1.5) via 10.25.1.5  into BRIB with extcomm
14:54:41.277723: (default) UPD: [IPv4 Unicast] 10.25.1.5 Inbound ip prefix-list
  Inbound, action permit
14:54:41.277720: (default) UPD: [IPv4 Unicast] Received prefix 100.1.5.0/24 from
  peer 10.25.1.5, origin 1, next hop 10.25.1.5, localpref 0 , med 0
```

For the outbound direction, the **show bgp event-history detail** command output displays the prefixes in the BGP table being permitted and denied based on the matching entries in the outbound prefix-list named *Outbound*. After the filtering is performed, the prefixes are then advertised to the BGP peer along with relevant attributes, as shown in Example 11-40.

Example 11-40 *BGP Event-History for Outbound Prefixes*

```
NX-2# show bgp event-history detail
BGP event-history detail

17:53:22.110665: (default) UPD: [IPv4 Unicast] 10.25.1.5 192.168.44.0/24 path-id 1
  not sent to peer due to: outbound policy
17:53:22.110659: (default) UPD: [IPv4 Unicast] 10.25.1.5 Outbound ip prefix-list
  Outbound, action deny
17:53:22.110649: (default) UPD: [IPv4 Unicast] 10.25.1.5 Created UPD msg (len 54)
  with prefix 192.168.4.4/32 ( Installed in HW) path-id 1 for peer
17:53:22.110643: (default) UPD: 10.25.1.5 Sending nexthop address 10.25.1.2 length 4
17:53:22.110638: (default) UPD: 10.25.1.5 Sending attr code 14, length 14, Mp-reach
17:53:22.110631: (default) UPD: 10.25.1.5 Sending attr code 2, length 6, AS-Path:
  <65000 >
17:53:22.110624: (default) UPD: 10.25.1.5 Sending attr code 1, length 1, Origin: IGP
17:53:22.110614: (default) UPD: [IPv4 Unicast] 10.25.1.5 Outbound ip prefix-list
  Outbound, action permit
17:53:22.110605: (default) UPD: [IPv4 Unicast] consider sending 192.168.4.4/32 to
  peer 10.25.1.5, path-id 1, best-ext is off
```

NX-OS also has CLI to verify policy-based statistics for prefix-lists. The statistics are verified for the policy implied in both inbound and outbound directions and shows the number of prefixes permitted and denied in either direction. Use the command **show bgp** *afi safi* **policy statistics neighbor** *ip-address* **prefix-list [in | out]** to view the policy statistics for prefix-list applied on a BGP neighbor. The counters of the policy statistics command increment every time a BGP neighbor flaps or a soft clear is performed on the neighbor. Example 11-41 demonstrates the use of a policy statistics command for BGP peer 10.25.1.5 in both inbound and outbound directions to understand how many prefixes are being permitted and dropped in both inbound and outbound directions. In this example, a soft clear is performed on the outbound direction, and it is seen that the counters increment for the outbound prefix-list policy statistics by 4 for permitted prefixes and 1 for a dropped prefix.

Example 11-41 *BGP Policy Statistics for Prefix-List*

```
NX-2# show bgp ipv4 unicast policy statistics neighbor 10.25.1.5 prefix-list in
Total count for neighbor rpm handles: 1

C: No. of comparisons, M: No. of matches

ip prefix-list Inbound seq 5 permit 100.1.1.0/24           M: 3
ip prefix-list Inbound seq 10 permit 100.1.2.0/24          M: 3
ip prefix-list Inbound seq 15 permit 100.1.3.0/24          M: 3
ip prefix-list Inbound seq 20 permit 100.1.4.0/24          M: 3
ip prefix-list Inbound seq 25 permit 100.1.5.0/24          M: 3
```

```
Total accept count for policy: 15
Total reject count for policy: 81
```

```
NX-2# show bgp ipv4 unicast policy statistics neighbor 10.25.1.5 prefix-list out
Total count for neighbor rpm handles: 1

C: No. of comparisions, M: No. of matches

ip prefix-list Outbound seq 5 permit 192.168.0.0/16 eq 32      M: 17

Total accept count for policy: 17
Total reject count for policy: 3
```

```
! Perform soft clear out on neighbor 10.25.1.5
NX-2# clear bgp ipv4 unicast 10.25.1.5 soft out
NX-2# show bgp ipv4 unicast policy statistics neighbor 10.25.1.5 prefix-list out
Total count for neighbor rpm handles: 1

C: No. of comparisons, M: No. of matches

ip prefix-list Outbound seq 5 permit 192.168.0.0/16 eq 32      M: 21

Total accept count for policy: 21
Total reject count for policy: 4
```

If at any point there is a problem noticed with an inbound or outbound prefix-list on a BGP neighbor, verify the route policy manager (RPM) NX-OS component. The first step of verification is to ensure that the prefix-list is attached to the BGP process or not. This is verified using the command **show system internal rpm ip-prefix-list**. This command displays the name of the prefix-list and its client information. This command also displays the number of entries present in the prefix-list.

After verifying the prefix-list and its clients, use the command **show system internal rpm event-history rsw** to ensure the correct prefix-list has been bound to the BGP process. An incorrect binding or a missing binding event-history log can indicate that the prefix-list is not properly associated with the BGP process or the BGP neighbor.

Example 11-42 shows the output of both the preceding commands.

Example 11-42   *RPM Client Info and Event-History for Prefix-Lists*

```
NX-2# show system internal rpm ip-prefix-list
Policy name: Inbound          Type: ip prefix-list
Version: 6                    State: Ready
Ref. count: 1                 PBR refcount: 0
```

```
Stmt count: 5                    Last stmt seq: 25
Set nhop cmd count: 0            Set vrf cmd count: 0
Set intf cmd count: 0            Flags: 0x00000003
PPF nodeid: 0x00000000           Config refcount: 0
PBR Stats: No
Clients:
    bgp-65000 (Route filtering/redistribution)    ACN version: 0

Policy name: Outbound            Type: ip prefix-list
Version: 2                       State: Ready
Ref. count: 1                    PBR refcount: 0
Stmt count: 1                    Last stmt seq: 5
Set nhop cmd count: 0            Set vrf cmd count: 0
Set intf cmd count: 0            Flags: 0x00000003
PPF nodeid: 0x00000000           Config refcount: 0
PBR Stats: No
Clients:
    bgp-65000 (Route filtering/redistribution)    ACN version: 0

NX-2# show system internal rpm event-history rsw

Routing software interaction logs of RPM
1) Event:E_DEBUG, length:81, at 104214 usecs after Sun Sep 17 06:01:47 2017
    [120] [5736]: Bind ack sent - client bgp-65000 uuid 0x0000011b for policy
Outbound
2) Event:E_DEBUG, length:76, at 104179 usecs after Sun Sep 17 06:01:47 2017
    [120] [5736]: Bind request - client bgp-65000 uuid 0x0000011b policy Outbound
3) Event:E_DEBUG, length:80, at 169619 usecs after Sun Sep 17 06:01:42 2017
    [120] [5736]: Bind ack sent - client bgp-65000 uuid 0x0000011b for policy
Inbound
4) Event:E_DEBUG, length:75, at 169469 usecs after Sun Sep 17 06:01:42 2017
    [120] [5736]: Bind request - client bgp-65000 uuid 0x0000011b policy Inbound
```

Filter-Lists

BGP filter-lists allow for filtering of prefixes based on AS-Path lists. A BGP filter-list can be applied in both inbound and outbound directions. A BGP filter-list is configured using the command **filter-list** *as-path-list-name* [**in** | **out**] under the neighbor address-family configuration mode. Example 11-43 illustrates a sample configuration of filter-list on NX-2 switch in the topology referenced in Figure 11-6. In this example, an inbound filter-list is configured to allow the prefixes that have AS 274 in the AS_PATH list. The second output of the example shows that the filter-list is applied on the inbound direction.

Example 11-43 *BGP Filter-Lists*

```
NX-2(config)# ip as-path access-list ALLOW_274 permit 274
NX-2(config)# router bgp 65000
NX-2(config-router)# neighbor 10.25.1.5
NX-2(config-router-neighbor)# address-family ipv4 unicast
NX-2(config-router-neighbor-af)# filter-list ALLOW_274 in
NX-2(config-router-neighbor-af)# end
```

```
NX-2# show bgp ipv4 unicast neighbors 10.25.1.5
BGP neighbor is 10.25.1.5,  remote AS 65001, ebgp link, Peer index 2
  BGP version 4, remote router ID 192.168.5.5
  BGP state = Established, up for 2d00h
! output omitted for brevity
  For address family: IPv4 Unicast
  BGP table version 1085, neighbor version 1085
  5 accepted paths consume 400 bytes of memory
  4 sent paths
  Inbound as-path-list configured is ALLOW_274, handle obtained
  Outbound ip prefix-list configured is Outbound, handle obtained
  Last End-of-RIB received 1d23h after session start

  Local host: 10.25.1.2, Local port: 58236
  Foreign host: 10.25.1.5, Foreign port: 179
  fd = 74
```

Note AS-Path access-list is discussed later in this chapter.

Example 11-44 displays the prefixes in the BGP table received from peer 10.25.1.5 after being filtered by the filter-list. Notice that all the prefixes shown in the BGP table have AS 274 in their AS_PATH list.

Example 11-44 *BGP Table with Filter-List Applied*

```
! Output after configuring filter-list
NX-2# show bgp ipv4 unicast neighbor 10.25.1.5 routes
! Output omitted for brevity
   Network          Next Hop         Metric  LocPrf  Weight Path
*>e100.1.21.0/24    10.25.1.5                          0 65001 100 228 274 {300
   243}
*>e100.1.22.0/24    10.25.1.5                          0 65001 100 228 274 {300
   243}
*>e100.1.23.0/24    10.25.1.5                          0 65001 100 228 274 {300
   243}
```

BGP Route Filtering and Route Policies 671

```
*>e100.1.24.0/24        10.25.1.5                       0 65001 100 228 274 {300
   243}
*>e100.1.25.0/24        10.25.1.5                       0 65001 100 228 274 {300
   243}
*>e100.1.26.0/24        10.25.1.5                       0 65001 100 228 274 {300
   243}
*>e100.1.27.0/24        10.25.1.5                       0 65001 100 228 274 {300
   243}
*>e100.1.28.0/24        10.25.1.5                       0 65001 100 228 274 {300
   243}
*>e100.1.29.0/24        10.25.1.5                       0 65001 100 228 274 {300
   243}
*>e100.1.30.0/24        10.25.1.5                       0 65001 100 228 274 {300
   243}
```

Note If a BGP peer is configured with the **soft-reconfiguration inbound** command, you can also use the command **show bgp** *afi safi* **neighbor** *ip-address* **received-routes** to view the received BGP prefixes.

The easiest way to verify which prefixes are being permitted and denied is to use the **show bgp event-history** detail command output, but if the **event-history detail** command is not enabled under the **router bgp** configuration, you can enable debugs to verify the updates. The **debug bgp updates** command can be used to verify both the inbound and the outbound updates. Example 11-45 demonstrates the use of **debug bgp updates** to verify which prefixes are being permitted and which are being denied. The action of permit or deny is always based on the entries present in the AS-path list.

Example 11-45 debug bgp updates *Output*

```
NX-2# debug logfile bgp
NX-2# debug bgp updates
NX-2# clear bgp ipv4 unicast 10.25.1.5 soft in
NX-2# show debug logfile bgp
21:39:01.721587 bgp: 65000 [10743] (default) UPD: [IPv4 Unicast] 10.25.1.5 Inbound
  as-path-list ALLOW_274, action deny
21:39:01.721622 bgp: 65000 [10743] (default) UPD: [IPv4 Unicast] Received prefix
  100.1.1.0/24 from peer 10.25.1.5, origin 1, next hop 10.25.1.5, localpref 0, med 0
21:39:01.721649 bgp: 65000 [10743] (default) UPD: [IPv4 Unicast] Dropping prefix
  100.1.1.0/24 from peer 10.25.1.5, due to attribute policy rejected
21:39:01.721678 bgp: 65000 [10743] (default) UPD: [IPv4 Unicast] Received prefix
  100.1.2.0/24 from peer 10.25.1.5, origin 1, next hop 10.25.1.5, localpref 0, med 0
21:39:01.721702 bgp: 65000 [10743] (default) UPD: [IPv4 Unicast] Dropping prefix
  100.1.2.0/24 from peer 10.25.1.5, due to attribute policy rejected
! Output omittied for brevity
```

672 Chapter 11: Troubleshooting BGP

```
21:39:01.723538 bgp: 65000 [10743] (default) UPD: [IPv4 Unicast] 10.25.1.5 Inbound
  as-path-list ALLOW_274, action permit
21:39:01.723592 bgp: 65000 [10743] (default) UPD: [IPv4 Unicast] Received prefix
  100.1.21.0/24 from peer 10.25.1.5, origin 1, next hop 10.25.1.5, localpref 0, med 0
21:39:01.723687 bgp: 65000 [10743] (default) UPD: [IPv4 Unicast] Received prefix
  100.1.22.0/24 from peer 10.25.1.5, origin 1, next hop 10.25.1.5, localpref 0, med 0
```

Similar to policy statistics for prefix-lists, the statistics are also available for filter-list entries. When executing the command **show bgp** *afi safi* **policy statistics neighbor** *ip-address* **filter-list [in | out]**, notice the relevant AS-path access list referenced as part of the filter-list command and the number of matches per each entry. The output also displays the number of accepted and rejected prefixes by the filter-list, as displayed in Example 11-46.

Example 11-46 *BGP Filter-Lists*

```
NX-2# show bgp ipv4 unicast policy statistics neighbor 10.25.1.5 filter-list in
Total count for neighbor rpm handles: 1

C: No. of comparisons, M: No. of matches

ip as-path access-list ALLOW_274 permit "274"              C: 5        M: 1

Total accept count for policy: 1
Total reject count for policy: 4
```

Because the filter-list uses AS-path access-list, RPM information can be verified for as-path-access-list using the command **show system internal rpm as-path-access-list** *as-path-acl-name*. This command confirms if the AS-path access-list is associated with the BGP process. The command **show system internal rpm event-history rsw** is used to validate if the AS-path access-list is bound to the BGP process. Example 11-47 displays both the command outputs.

Example 11-47 *BGP Filter-Lists*

```
NX-2# show system internal rpm as-path-access-list ALLOW_274
Policy name: ALLOW_274           Type: as-path-list
Version: 2                       State: Ready
Ref. count: 1                    PBR refcount: 0
Stmt count: 1                    Last stmt seq: 1
Set nhop cmd count: 0            Set vrf cmd count: 0
Set intf cmd count: 0            Flags: 0x00000003
PPF nodeid: 0x00000000           Config refcount: 0
PBR Stats: No
```

```
Clients:
    bgp-65000 (Route filtering/redistribution)    ACN version: 0
```

```
! RPM Event-History
NX-2# show system internal rpm event-history rsw

Routing software interaction logs of RPM
1) Event:E_DEBUG, length:82, at 684846 usecs after Sun Sep 17 19:46:46 2017
    [120] [5736]: Bind ack sent - client bgp-65000 uuid 0x0000011b for policy
  ALLOW_274
2) Event:E_DEBUG, length:77, at 684797 usecs after Sun Sep 17 19:46:46 2017
    [120] [5736]: Bind request - client bgp-65000 uuid 0x0000011b policy ALLOW_274
```

BGP Route-Maps

BGP uses route-maps to provide route filtering capability and traffic engineering by setting various attributes to the prefixes that help control the inbound and outbound traffic. Route-maps typically use some form of conditional matching so that only certain prefixes are blocked or accepted. At the simplest level, route-maps can filter networks similar to an AS-Path filter/prefix-list, but also provide additional capability by adding or modifying a network attribute. Route-maps are referenced to a specific route-advertisement or BGP neighbor and require specifying the direction of the advertisement (inbound/outbound). Route-maps are a critical component of BGP because they allow for a unique routing policy on a neighbor-by-neighbor basis.

Example 11-48 illustrates a sample configuration of a multisequence route-map that is applied to a neighbor. Notice that in this example, the route-map sequence 10 is matching on prefix-list to match certain set of prefixes and on sequence 20 matches AS-Path access-list. Note that there is no sequence 30. Absence of any other entry in the route-map acts as an implicit deny statement and denies all prefixes.

Example 11-48 *BGP Route-Map Configuration*

```
NX-2(config)# route-map Inbound-RM permit 10
NX-2(config-route-map)# match ip address prefix-list Inbound
NX-2(config-route-map)# set local-preference 200
NX-2(config-route-map)# exit
NX-2(config)# route-map Inbound-RM permit 20
NX-2(config-route-map)# match as-path AlLOW_274
NX-2(config-route-map)# set local-preference 300
NX-2(config-route-map)# exit
! The above referenced Prefix-list and AS-Path Access-list were shown in previous
! examples
NX-2(config)# router bgp 65000
```

```
NX-2(config-router)# neighbor 10.25.1.5
NX-2(config-router-neighbor)# address-family ipv4 unicast
NX-2(config-router-neighbor-af)# route-map Inbound-RM in
NX-2(config-router-neighbor-af)# end
```

Example 11-49 shows the BGP table after inbound route-map filtering. Notice that the prefixes 100.1.1.0/24 to 100.1.5.0/24 are set with the local preference of 200, whereas the prefixes that match AS 274 in the AS-path list are set with the local preference of 300. Because there is no route-map entry matching sequence 30, all the other prefixes are denied by the inbound route-map filtering.

Example 11-49 *BGP Table Output with Route-Map Filtering*

```
NX-2# show bgp ipv4 unicast neighbor 10.25.1.5 routes
BGP routing table information for VRF default, address family IPv4 Unicast
BGP table version is 1141, local router ID is 192.168.2.2
Status: s-suppressed, x-deleted, S-stale, d-dampened, h-history, *-valid, >-best
Path type: i-internal, e-external, c-confed, l-local, a-aggregate, r-redist, I-injected
Origin codes: i - IGP, e - EGP, ? - incomplete, | - multipath, & - backup

   Network            Next Hop        Metric    LocPrf   Weight Path
*>e100.1.1.0/24       10.25.1.5                 200           0 65001 100 {220} e
*>e100.1.2.0/24       10.25.1.5                 200           0 65001 100 {220} e
*>e100.1.3.0/24       10.25.1.5                 200           0 65001 100 {220} e
*>e100.1.4.0/24       10.25.1.5                 200           0 65001 100 {220} e
*>e100.1.5.0/24       10.25.1.5                 200           0 65001 100 {220} e
*>e100.1.21.0/24      10.25.1.5                 300           0 65001 100 228 274 {300 243}
*>e100.1.25.0/24      10.25.1.5                 300           0 65001 100 228 274 {300 243}
*>e100.1.26.0/24      10.25.1.5                 300           0 65001 100 228 274 {300 243}
*>e100.1.27.0/24      10.25.1.5                 300           0 65001 100 228 274 {300 243}
*>e100.1.28.0/24      10.25.1.5                 300           0 65001 100 228 274 {300 243}
*>e100.1.29.0/24      10.25.1.5                 300           0 65001 100 228 274 {300 243}
*>e100.1.30.0/24      10.25.1.5                 300           0 65001 100 228 274 {300 243}
```

The **show bgp event-history detail** command can be used again to verify which prefixes are being permitted or denied based on the route-map policy. Based on the underlying match statements, relevant set actions are taken (if any). Example 11-50 displays the event-history detail output demonstrating prefixes being permitted and denied by route-map.

Example 11-50 *BGP Event-History*

```
NX-2# show bgp event-history detail
04:36:32.954809: (default) BRIB: [IPv4 Unicast] Installing prefix 100.1.21.0/24
  (10.25.1.5) via 10.25.1.5 into BRIB with extcomm
04:36:32.954796: (default) UPD: [IPv4 Unicast] 10.25.1.5 Inbound route-map Inbound-
  RM, action permit
```

BGP Route-Maps 675

```
04:36:32.954763: (default) UPD: [IPv4 Unicast] Received prefix 100.1.21.0/24 from
  peer 10.25.1.5, origin 1, next hop 10.25.1.5, localpref 0, med 0
! Output omitted for brevity
04:36:32.954690: (default) UPD: [IPv4 Unicast] Dropping prefix 100.1.20.0/24 from
  peer 10.25.1.5, due to prefix policy rejected
04:36:32.954684: (default) UPD: [IPv4 Unicast] Prefix 100.1.20.0/24 from peer
  10.25.1.5 rejected by inbound policy
04:36:32.954679: (default) UPD: [IPv4 Unicast] 10.25.1.5 Inbound route-map Inbound-
  RM, action deny
04:36:32.954647: (default) UPD: [IPv4 Unicast] Received prefix 100.1.20.0/24 from
  peer 10.25.1.5, origin 1, next hop 10.25.1.5, localpref 0, med 0
```

You can also validate the policy statistics for the route-map similar to prefix-list and filter-list. The command **show bgp ipv4 unicast policy statistics neighbor** *ip-address* **route-map [in | out]** displays the matching prefix-list or AS-path access-list or any other attributes under each route-map sequence and its matching statistics, as shown in Example 11-51.

Example 11-51 *BGP Policy Statistics for Route-Map*

```
NX-2# show bgp ipv4 unicast policy statistics neighbor 10.25.1.5 route-map in
Total count for neighbor rpm handles: 1

C: No. of comparisons, M: No. of matches

route-map Inbound-RM permit 10
  match ip address prefix-list Inbound                  C: 52      M: 5
route-map Inbound-RM permit 20
  match as-path ALLOW_274                               C: 47      M: 30


Total accept count for policy: 35
Total reject count for policy: 17
```

Within route-maps, various conditional matching features are used, such as prefix-lists, *regular expressions (regex)*, AS-Path access-list, BGP communities, and community-lists. When multiple filtering mechanisms are configured under the same neighbor, the following order of preference is used for both inbound and outbound filtering:

- Inbound Filtering
  - Route-map
  - Filter-list
  - Prefix-list, distribute-list

- Outbound Filtering
    - Filter-list
    - Route-map
    - Advertise-map (conditional advertisement)
    - Prefix-list, distribute-list

Network prefixes are conditionally matched by a variety of routing protocol attributes, but the following sections explain the most common techniques for conditionally matching a prefix.

Regular Expressions (RegEx)

There may be times when conditionally matching network prefixes is too complicated, and identifying all routes from a specific organization is preferred. In this manner, path selection is made off of the BGP AS-Path.

To parse through the large amount of available ASNs (4,294,967,295), *regular expressions (regex)* are used. Regular expressions are based upon query modifiers to select the appropriate content. The BGP table is parsed with regex using the command **show bgp afi safi regexp** *"regex-pattern"* on Nexus switches.

> **Note** NX-OS devices require the regex-pattern to be placed within a pair of double-quotes "".

Table 11-7 provides a brief list and description of the common regex query modifiers.

Table 11-7 *RegEx Query Modifiers*

Modifier	Description
_ (Underscore)	Matches a space
^ (Caret)	Indicates the start of the string
$ (Dollar Sign)	Indicates the end of the string
[] (Brackets)	Matches a single character or nesting within a range
- (Hyphen)	Indicates a range of numbers in brackets
[^] (Caret in Brackets)	Excludes the characters listed in brackets
() (Parentheses)	Used for nesting of search patterns
| (Pipe)	Provides *or* functionality to the query
. (Period)	Matches a single character, including a space
* (Asterisk)	Matches zero or more characters or patterns
+ (Plus Sign)	One or more instances of the character or pattern
? (Question Mark)	Matches one or no instances of the character or pattern

Note The .^$*+()[]? characters are special control characters that cannot be used without using the backslash \ escape character. For example, to match on the * in the output use the * syntax.

The following section provides a variety of common tasks to help demonstrate each of the regex modifiers. Example 11-52 provides a reference BGP table for displaying scenarios of each regex query modifier for querying the prefixes learned via Figure 11-10.

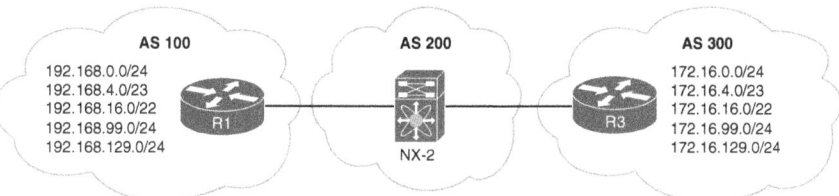

Figure 11-10 *BGP Regex Reference Topology*

Example 11-52 *BGP Table for Regex Queries*

```
NX-2# show bgp ipv4 unicast
! Output omitted for brevity
   Network          Next Hop        Metric LocPrf Weight Path
*>e172.16.0.0/24    172.32.23.3     0                 0 300 80 90 21003 2100 i
*>e172.16.4.0/23    172.32.23.3     0                 0 300 878 1190 1100 1010 i
*>e172.16.16.0/22   172.32.23.3     0                 0 300 779 21234 45 i
*>e172.16.99.0/24   172.32.23.3     0                 0 300 145 40 i
*>e172.16.129.0/24  172.32.23.3     0                 0 300 10010 300 1010 40 50 i
*>e192.168.0.0/16   172.16.12.1     0                 0 100 80 90 21003 2100 i
*>e192.168.4.0/23   172.16.12.1     0                 0 100 878 1190 1100 1010 i
*>e192.168.16.0/22  172.16.12.1     0                 0 100 779 21234 45 i
*>e192.168.99.0/24  172.16.12.1     0                 0 100 145 40 i
*>e192.168.129.0/24 172.16.12.1     0                 0 100 10010 300 1010 40 50 i
```

Note The AS-Path for the prefix 172.16.129.0/24 has the AS 300 twice nonconsecutively for a specific purpose. This is not seen in real life, because it indicates a routing loop.

_ Underscore

    Query Modifier Function: Matches a space

    Scenario: Only display ASs that passed through AS 100. The first assumption is that the syntax **show bgp ipv4 unicast regex "100"** as shown in Example 11-53 is ideal.

Chapter 11: Troubleshooting BGP

The regex query includes the following unwanted ASNs: 1100, 2100, 21003, and 10010.

Example 11-53 *BGP Regex Query for AS 100*

```
NX-2# show bgp ipv4 unicast regex "100"
! Output omitted for brevity
    Network             Next Hop        Metric LocPrf Weight Path
*>e172.16.0.0/24        172.32.23.3          0              0 300 80 90 21003 2100 i
*>e172.16.4.0/23        172.32.23.3          0              0 300 878 1190 1100 1010 i
*>e172.16.129.0/24      172.32.23.3          0              0 300 10010 300 1010 40 50 i
*>e192.168.0.0/16       172.16.12.1          0              0 100 80 90 21003 2100 i
*>e192.168.4.0/23       172.16.12.1          0              0 100 878 1190 1100 1010 i
*>e192.168.16.0/22      172.16.12.1          0              0 100 779 21234 45 i
*>e192.168.99.0/24      172.16.12.1          0              0 100 145 40 i
*>e192.168.129.0/24     172.16.12.1          0              0 100 10010 300 1010 40 50 i
```

Example 11-54 uses the underscore (_) to imply a space left of the 100 to remove the unwanted ASNs. The regex query includes the following unwanted ASNs: 10010.

Example 11-54 *BGP Regex Query for AS _100*

```
NX-2# show bgp ipv4 unicast regexp "_100"
! Output omitted for brevity
    Network             Next Hop        Metric LocPrf Weight Path
    Network             Next Hop        Metric LocPrf Weight Path
*>e172.16.129.0/24      172.32.23.3          0              0 300 10010 300 1010 40 50 i
*>e192.168.0.0/16       172.16.12.1          0              0 100 80 90 21003 2100 i
*>e192.168.4.0/23       172.16.12.1          0              0 100 878 1190 1100 1010 i
*>e192.168.16.0/22      172.16.12.1          0              0 100 779 21234 45 i
*>e192.168.99.0/24      172.16.12.1          0              0 100 145 40 i
*>e192.168.129.0/24     172.16.12.1          0              0 100 10010 300 1010 40 i
```

Example 11-55 provides the final query by using the underscore (_) before and after the ASN (100) to finalize the query for the route that passes through AS 100.

Example 11-55 *BGP Regex Query for AS _100_*

```
NX-2# show bgp ipv4 unicast regexp "_100_"
! Output omitted for brevity
    Network             Next Hop        Metric LocPrf Weight Path
*>e192.168.0.0/16       172.16.12.1          0              0 100 80 90 21003 2100 i
*>e192.168.4.0/23       172.16.12.1          0              0 100 878 1190 1100 1010 i
*>e192.168.16.0/22      172.16.12.1          0              0 100 779 21234 45 i
*>e192.168.99.0/24      172.16.12.1          0              0 100 145 40 i
*>e192.168.129.0/24     172.16.12.1          0              0 100 10010 300 1010 40 50 i
```

^ Caret

Query Modifier Function: Indicates the start of the string.

Scenario: Only display routes that were advertised from AS 300. At first glance, the command **show bgp ipv4 unicast regex "_300_"** might be acceptable for use, but in Example 11-56 the route 192.168.129.0/24 is also included.

Example 11-56 *BGP Regex Query for AS 300*

```
NX-2# show bgp ipv4 unicast regexp "_300_"
! Output omitted for brevity
    Network          Next Hop        Metric  LocPrf  Weight  Path
*>e172.16.0.0/24    172.32.23.3      0                0  300 80 90 21003 2100 i
*>e172.16.4.0/23    172.32.23.3      0                0  300 878 1190 1100 1010 i
*>e172.16.16.0/22   172.32.23.3      0                0  300 779 21234 45 i
*>e172.16.99.0/24   172.32.23.3      0                0  300 145 40 i
*>e172.16.129.0/24  172.32.23.3      0                0  300 10010 300 1010 40 50 i
*>e192.168.129.0/24 172.16.12.1      0                0  100 10010 300 1010 40 50 i
```

Because AS 300 is directly connected, it is more efficient to ensure that AS 300 was the first AS listed. Example 11-57 shows the caret (^) in the regex pattern.

Example 11-57 *BGP Regex Query with Caret*

```
NX-2# show bgp ipv4 unicast regexp "^300_"
! Output omitted for brevity
    Network          Next Hop        Metric  LocPrf  Weight  Path
*>e172.16.0.0/24    172.32.23.3      0                0  300 80 90 21003 2100 i
*>e172.16.4.0/23    172.32.23.3      0                0  300 878 1190 1100 1010 i
*>e172.16.16.0/22   172.32.23.3      0                0  300 779 21234 45 i
*>e172.16.99.0/24   172.32.23.3      0                0  300 145 40 i
*>e172.16.129.0/24  172.32.23.3      0                0  300 10010 300 1010 40 50 i
```

$ Dollar Sign

Query Modifier Function: Indicates the end of the string.

Scenario: Only display routes that originated in AS 40. In Example 11-58 the regex pattern "_40_" was used. Unfortunately, this also includes routes that originated in AS 50.

Example 11-58 *BGP Regex Query with AS 40*

```
NX-2# show bgp ipv4 unicast regexp "_40_"
! Output omitted for brevity
   Network              Next Hop         Metric   LocPrf Weight Path
*>e172.16.99.0/24       172.32.23.3      0                 0 300 145 40 i
*>e172.16.129.0/24      172.32.23.3      0                 0 300 10010 300 1010 40 50 i
*>e192.168.99.0         172.16.12.1      0                 0 100 145 40 i
*>e192.168.129.0        172.16.12.1      0                 0 100 10010 300 1010 40 50 i
```

Example 11-59 provides the solution using the dollar sign ($) for the regex the pattern "_40$".

Example 11-59 *BGP Regex Query with Dollar Sign*

```
NX-2# show bgp ipv4 unicast regexp "_40$"
! Output omitted for brevity
   Network              Next Hop         Metric   LocPrf Weight Path
*>e172.16.99.0/24       172.32.23.3      0                 0 300 145 40 i
*>e192.168.99.0         172.16.12.1      0        100      0 100 145 40 i
```

[ ] Brackets

Query Modifier Function: Matches a single character or nesting within a range.

Scenario: Only display routes with an AS that contains 11 or 14 in it. The regex filter "1[14]" can be used as shown in Example 11-60.

Example 11-60 *BGP Regex Query with Brackets*

```
NX-2# show bgp ipv4 unicast regexp "1[14]"
! Output omitted for brevity
   Network              Next Hop         Metric LocPrf Weight Path
*>e172.16.4.0/23        172.32.23.3      0               0 300 878 1190 1100 1010 i
*>e172.16.99.0/24       172.32.23.3      0               0 300 145 40 i
*>e192.168.4.0/23       172.16.12.1      0               0 100 878 1190 1100 1010 i
*>e192.168.99.0         172.16.12.1      0               0 100 145 40 i
```

- Hyphen

Query Modifier Function: Indicates a range of numbers in brackets.

Scenario: Only display routes with the last two digits of the AS of 40, 50, 60, 70, or 80. Example 11-61 uses the regex query "[5-8]0_". See the output in Example 11-60.

Example 11-61 *BGP Regex Query with Hyphen*

```
NX-2# show bgp ipv4 unicast regexp "[4-8]0_"
! Output omitted for brevity
    Network          Next Hop    Metric LocPrf Weight Path
*>e172.16.0.0/24    172.32.23.3      0              0 300 80 90 21003 2100 i
*>e172.16.99.0/24   172.32.23.3      0              0 300 145 40 i
*>e172.16.129.0/24  172.32.23.3      0              0 300 10010 300 1010 40 50 i
*>e192.168.0.0      172.16.12.1      0              0 100 80 90 21003 2100 i
*>e192.168.99.0     172.16.12.1      0              0 100 145 40 i
*>e192.168.129.0    172.16.12.1      0              0 100 10010 300 1010 40 50 i
```

[^] Caret in Brackets

Query Modifier Function: Excludes the character listed in brackets.

Scenario: Only display routes where the second AS from AS 100 or AS 300 does not start with 3, 4, 5, 6, 7, or 8. The first component of the regex query is to restrict the AS to the AS 100 or 300 with the regex query "^[13]00_", and the second component is to filter out AS starting with 3-8 with the regex filter "_[^3-8]". The complete regex query is "^[13]00_[^3-8]" as shown in Example 11-62.

Example 11-62 *BGP Regex Query with Caret in Brackets*

```
NX-2# show bgp ipv4 unicast regexp "^[13]00_[^3-8]"
! Output omitted for brevity
    Network          Next Hop    Metric LocPrf Weight Path
*>e172.16.99.0/24   172.32.23.3      0              0 300 145 40 i
*>e172.16.129.0/24  172.32.23.3      0              0 300 10010 300 1010 40 50 i
*>e192.168.99.0     172.16.12.1      0              0 100 145 40 i
*>e192.168.129.0    172.16.12.1      0              0 100 10010 300 1010 40 50 i
```

( ) Parentheses and | Pipe

Query Modifier Function: Nesting of search patterns and provides *or* functionality.

Scenario: Only display routes where the AS_PATH ends with AS 40 or 45 in it. The regex filter "_4(5|0)$" is shown in Example 11-63.

Example 11-63 *BGP Regex Query with Parentheses*

```
NX-2# show bgp ipv4 unicast regexp "_4(5|0)$"
! Output omitted for brevity
     Network          Next Hop      Metric LocPrf Weight Path
*>e172.16.16.0/22    172.32.23.3        0               0 300 779 21234 45 i
*>e172.16.99.0/24    172.32.23.3        0               0 300 145 40 i
*>e192.168.16.0/22   172.16.12.1        0               0 100 779 21234 45 i
*>e192.168.99.0      172.16.12.1        0               0 100 145 40 i
```

. Period

Query Modifier Function: Matches a single character, including a space.

Scenario: Only display routes with an originating AS of 1–99. In Example 11-64, the regex query "_..$" requires a space, and then any character after that (including other spaces).

Example 11-64 *BGP Regex Query with Period*

```
NX-2# show bgp ipv4 unicast regexp "_..$"
! Output omitted for brevity
     Network          Next Hop      Metric LocPrf Weight Path
*>e172.16.16.0/22    172.32.23.3        0               0 300 779 21234 45 i
*>e172.16.99.0/24    172.32.23.3        0               0 300 145 40 i
*>e172.16.129.0/24   172.32.23.3        0               0 300 10010 300 1010 40 50 i
*>e192.168.16.0/22   172.16.12.1        0    100        0 100 779 21234 45 i
*>e192.168.99.0      172.16.12.1        0    100        0 100 145 40 i
*>e192.168.129.0     172.16.12.1        0    100        0 100 10010 300 1010 40 50 i
```

+ Plus Sign

Query Modifier Function: One or more instances of the character or pattern.

Scenario: Only display routes where they contain at least one or more '11' in the AS path. The regex pattern is "(11)+" as shown in Example 11-65.

Example 11-65 *BGP Regex Query with Plus Sign*

```
NX-2# show bgp ipv4 unicast regexp "(10)+[^(100)]"
! Output omitted for brevity
     Network          Next Hop      Metric LocPrf Weight Path
*>e172.16.4.0/23     172.32.23.3        0               0 300 878 1190 1100 1010 i
*>e192.168.4.0/23    172.16.12.1        0               0 100 878 1190 1100 1010 i
```

? Question Mark

Query Modifier Function: Matches one or no instances of the character or pattern.

Scenario: Only display routes from the neighboring AS or its directly connected AS (that is, restrict to two ASs away). This query is more complicated and requires you to define an initial query for identifying the AS, which is "[0-9]+". The second component includes the space and an optional second AS. The "?" limits the AS match to one or two ASs as shown in Example 11-66.

Note The CTRL+V escape sequence must be used before entering the ?.

Example 11-66 *BGP Regex Query with Dollar Sign*

```
NX-2# show bgp ipv4 unicast regexp "^[0-9]+ ([0-9]+)?$"
! Output omitted for brevity
   Network          Next Hop       Metric LocPrf Weight Path
*>e172.16.99.0/24   172.32.23.3         0            0 300 40 i
*>e192.168.99.0     172.16.12.1         0    100     0 100 40 i
```

* Asterisk

Query Modifier Function: Matches zero or more characters or patterns.

Scenario: Display all routes from any AS. This may seem like a useless task, but may be a valid requirement when using AS-Path access lists, which are explained later in this chapter. Example 11-67 shows the regex query.

Example 11-67 *BGP Regex Query with Asterisk*

```
NX-2# show bgp ipv4 unicast regexp ".*"
! Output omitted for brevity
   Network          Next Hop       Metric LocPrf Weight Path
*>e172.16.0.0/24    172.32.23.3         0            0 300 80 90 21003 2100 i
*>e172.16.4.0/23    172.32.23.3         0            0 300 1080 1090 1100 1110 i
*>e172.16.16.0/22   172.32.23.3         0            0 300 11234 21234 31234 i
*>e172.16.99.0/24   172.32.23.3         0            0 300 40 i
*>  172.16.129.0/24 172.32.23.3         0            0 300 10010 300 30010 30050 i
*>e192.168.0.0      172.16.12.1         0    100     0 100 80 90 21003 2100 i
*>e192.168.4.0/23   172.16.12.1         0    100     0 100 1080 1090 1100 1110 i
*>e192.168.16.0/22  172.16.12.1         0    100     0 100 11234 21234 31234 i
*>e192.168.99.0     172.16.12.1         0    100     0 100 40 i
*>e192.168.129.0    172.16.12.1         0    100     0 100 10010 300 30010 30050 i
```

AS-Path Access List

Selecting routes by using the AS_Path in a route-map requires the definition of an *AS-path access-list (AS-path ACL)*. Processing is peformed in a sequential top-down order, and the first qualifying match processes against the appropriate **permit** or **deny** action. An implicit deny exists at the end of the AS-Path ACL. IOS supports up to 500 AS-path ACLs and uses the command **ip as-path access-list** *acl-number* {**deny** | **permit**} *regex-query* for creating the as-path access-list.

Example 11-68 provides two sample AS-Path access lists. AS-Path access-list 1 matches against any local IBGP prefix, or any prefix that passes through AS 300 where as AS-Path access-list 2 provides a more complicated AS-Path access list that matches the 16-bit private ASN range (64,512 – 65,536).

Example 11-68 *AS-Path Access List Configuration*

```
ip as-path access-list 1 permit _300_
ip as-path access-list 1 permit ^$
ip as-path access-list 2 permit _(6451[2-9])_
ip as-path access-list 2 permit _(645[2-9][0-9])_
ip as-path access-list 2 permit _(64[6-9][0-9][0-9])_
ip as-path access-list 2 permit _(65[0-4][0-9][0-9])_
ip as-path access-list 2 permit _(655[0-2][0-9])_
ip as-path access-list 2 permit _(6553[0-6])_
```

BGP Communities

BGP communities provide additional capability for tagging routes and are considered either *well-known* or *private* BGP communities. Private BGP communities are used for conditional matching for a router's route-policy, which could influence routes during inbound or outbound route-policy processing. There are four well-known communities that affect only outbound route-advertisement:

- **No-Advertise:** The No_Advertise community (0xFFFFFF02 or 4,294,967,042) specifies that routes with this community should not be advertised to any BGP peer. The No-Advertise BGP community can be advertised from an upstream BGP peer or locally with an inbound BGP policy. In either method, the No-Advertise community is set in the BGP Loc-RIB table that affects outbound route advertisement.

- **No-Export:** The No_Export community (0xFFFFFF01 or 4,294,967,041) specifies that when a route is received with this community, the route is not advertised to any EBGP peer. If the router receiving the No-Export route is a confederation member, the route is advertised to other sub ASs in the confederation.

- **Local-AS:** The No_Export_SubConfed community (0xFFFFFF03 or 4,294,967,043) known as the Local-AS community specifies that a route with this community is not advertised outside of the local AS. If the router receiving a route with the Local-AS community is a confederation member, the route is advertised only within the sub-AS (Member-AS) and is not advertised between Member-ASs.

- **Internet:** Advertise this route to the Internet community and all the routers that belong to it.

The private community value is of the format (*as-number:16-bit-number*). Conditionally matching BGP communities allows for selection of routes based upon the BGP communities within the route's path attributes so that selective processing occurs in a route-map.

NX-OS devices do not advertise BGP communities to peers by default. Communities are enabled on a neighbor-by-neighbor basis with the BGP address-family configuration command **send-community** [**standard** | **extended** | **both**] under the neighbor's address family configuration. Standard communities are sent by default, unless the optional **extended** or **both** keywords are used.

Conditionally matching on NX-OS devices requires the creation of a community list. A community list shares a similar structure to an ACL, is standard or expanded, and is referenced via number or name. Standard community lists match either well-known communities or a private community number (*as-number:16-bit-number*), whereas Expanded community lists use regex patterns.

Examining the same topology as shown in Figure 11-6. In this topology, NX-5 assigns a community value of 65001:274 for the prefixes that have AS 274 in their AS_Path list. Example 11-69 illustrates the configuration on NX-5 to a community value attached to prefixes.

Example 11-69 *Advertising Community Value*

```
NX-5(config)# ip as-path access-list ASN_274 permit 274
NX-5(config)# route-map set-Comm
NX-5(config-route-map)# match as-path ASN_274
NX-5(config-route-map)# set community 65001:274
NX-5(config-route-map)# route-map set-Comm per 20
NX-5(config-route-map)# exit
NX-5(config)# router bgp 65001
NX-5(config-router)# neighbor 10.25.1.2
NX-5(config-router-neighbor)# address-family ipv4 unicast
NX-5(config-router-neighbor-af)# route-map set-Comm out
NX-5(config-router-neighbor-af)# send-community
NX-5(config-router-neighbor-af)# end
```

```
NX-2# show bgp ipv4 unicast 100.1.25.0/24
BGP routing table information for VRF default, address family IPv4 Unicast
BGP routing table entry for 100.1.25.0/24, version 1195
Paths: (1 available, best #1)
Flags: (0x08001a) on xmit-list, is in urib, is best urib route, is in HW,

  Advertised path-id 1
  Path type: external, path is valid, is best path
```

```
   AS-Path: 65001 100 228 274 {300 243} , path sourced external to AS
      10.25.1.5 (metric 0) from 10.25.1.5 (192.168.5.5)

        Origin EGP, MED not set, localpref 100, weight 0
        Community: 65001:274


   Path-id 1 advertised to peers:
     192.168.1.1
```

On NX-2, if an operator wants to set a BGP attribute based on the matching community value, community-list is used in the matching statement under route-map. Example 11-70 illustrates the configuration for using BGP community values for influencing route policy.

Example 11-70 *Influencing Route Policy Using BGP Community*

```
NX-2(config)# ip community-list standard Comm-65001:274 permit 65001:274
NX-2(config)# route-map Match-Comm per 10
NX-2(config-route-map)# match community Comm-65001:274
NX-2(config-route-map)# set local-preference 200
NX-2(config-route-map)# route-map Match-Comm per 20
NX-2(config-route-map)# exit
NX-2(config)# router bgp 65000
NX-2(config-router)# neighbor 10.25.1.5
NX-2(config-router-neighbor)# address-family ipv4 unicast
NX-2(config-router-neighbor-af)# route-map Match-Comm in
NX-2(config-router-neighbor-af)# end
```

```
NX-2# show bgp ipv4 unicast neighbor 10.25.1.5 routes
BGP routing table information for VRF default, address family IPv4 Unicast
BGP table version is 1141, local router ID is 192.168.2.2
Status: s-suppressed, x-deleted, S-stale, d-dampened, h-history, *-valid, >-best
Path type: i-internal, e-external, c-confed, l-local, a-aggregate, r-redist, I-injected
Origin codes: i - IGP, e - EGP, ? - incomplete, | - multipath, & - backup
   Network            Next Hop         Metric  LocPrf  Weight Path
! Output omittied for brevity
*>e100.1.21.0/24      10.25.1.5        200             0 65001 100 228 274 {300 243}
*>e100.1.22.0/24      10.25.1.5        200             0 65001 100 228 274 {300 243}
*>e100.1.23.0/24      10.25.1.5        200             0 65001 100 228 274 {300 243}
*>e100.1.24.0/24      10.25.1.5        200             0 65001 100 228 274 {300 243}
*>e100.1.25.0/24      10.25.1.5        200             0 65001 100 228 274 {300 243}
*>e100.1.26.0/24      10.25.1.5        200             0 65001 100 228 274 {300 243}
*>e100.1.27.0/24      10.25.1.5        200             0 65001 100 228 274 {300 243}
*>e100.1.28.0/24      10.25.1.5        200             0 65001 100 228 274 {300 243}
*>e100.1.29.0/24      10.25.1.5        200             0 65001 100 228 274 {300 243}
*>e100.1.30.0/24      10.25.1.5        200             0 65001 100 228 274 {300 243}
```

Looking Glass and Route Servers

Hands-on experience is helpful when learning technologies such as regex. There are public devices called *looking glass* or *route servers* that allow users to log in and view BGP tables. Most of these devices are Cisco routers, but there are other vendors as well. These servers allow network engineers to see if they are advertising their routes to the Internet, as they had intended, and provide a great method to try out regular expressions on the Internet BGP table. A quick search on the Internet provides website listings of looking glass and route servers.

Logs Collection

In event of BGP failure, the following show tech logs can be collected:

- show tech bgp
- show tech netstack

If there is some issue seen with BGP route policies, collect the following logs along with **show tech bgp:**

- show tech rpm

In case the routes are not being installed in the routing table but are present in the BGP table, you can also collect the following show tech output:

- Show tech routing ipv4 unicast [brief]

Collect and share these logs with Cisco TAC for a root-cause analysis of the problem.

Summary

BGP is a powerful path vector routing protocol that provides scalability and flexibility that cannot be compared to any other routing protocol. BGP uses TCP port 179 for establishing neighbors, which allows for BGP to establish sessions with directly attached routers or with routers that are multiple hops away.

Originally BGP was intended for routing of IPv4 prefixes between organizations, but over the years has had significant increase in functionality and feature enhancements. BGP has expanded from being an Internet routing protocol to other aspects of the network, including the data center.

BGP provides a scalable control plane signaling for overlay topologies, including MPLS VPNs, IPsec SAs, and VXLAN. These overlays provide Layer 3 services, such as L3VPNs, or Layer 2 services, such as eVPNs, across a widely used scalable control plane for everything from provider-based services to data center overlays. Every AFI/SAFI combination maintains an independent BGP table and routing policy, which makes BGP the perfect control plane application.

This chapter focused on various techniques for troubleshooting BGP peering issues and flapping peering issues related to MTU mismatch or due to bad BGP updates. Then the chapter dives deep into BGP route processing and convergence issues. The route processing concepts such as BGP update generation, route advertisement, best path calculation, and multipath are covered as part of the BGP route processing. This chapter then covers various scaling techniques for BGP, including BGP route reflectors.

The chapter then focuses on route filtering concepts using prefix-lists, filter-lists, and route-maps and goes over various matching criteria available with route-maps, such as prefix-lists, community-lists, and regular expressions.

Further Reading

Some of the topics involving validity checks and next-hop resolution are explained further in the following books:

Halabi, Sam. *Internet Routing Architectures*. Indianapolis: Cisco Press, 2000.

Zhang, Randy, and Micah Bartell. *BGP Design and Implementation*. Indianapolis: Cisco Press 2003.

White, Russ, Alvaro Retana, and Don Slice. *Optimal Routing Design*. Indianapolis: Cisco Press, 2005.

Jain, Vinit, and Brad Edgeworth. *Troubleshooting BGP*. Indianapolis: Cisco Press, 2016.

References

Jain, Vinit, and Brad Edgeworth. *Troubleshooting BGP*. Indianapolis: Cisco Press, 2016.

Edgeworth, Brad, Aaron Foss, and Ramiro Garza Rios. *IP Routing on Cisco IOS, IOS XE and IOS XR*. Indianapolis: Cisco Press, 2014.

Cisco. Cisco NX-OS Software Configuration Guides, www.cisco.com.

Chapter 12

High Availability

This chapter covers the following topics:

- Bidirectional Forwarding Detection (BFD)
- Nexus High Availability
- Graceful Insertion and Removal

Nexus OS (NX-OS) is a resilient OS that has been designed on the paradigms of high availability not just at the system level, but at both the network and process levels as well. Some of the Nexus switches provide high availability by redundancy hardware such as redundant fabric, supervisor cards, and power supplies. Network-level high availability is provided by features such as virtual port-channels (vPC) and First Hop Redundancy Protocol (FHRP), which give users backup paths to failover in case the primary path fails. NX-OS leverages various system components to provide process restartability and virtualization capability, thus providing process-level high availability. This chapter covers some of the important features and components within NX-OS that provide high availability in the network.

Bidirectional Forwarding Detection

Bidirectional forwarding detection (BFD) is a simple, fixed-length hello protocol that is used for faster detection of failures. BFD provides a low-overhead, short-duration mechanism for detecting failures in the path between adjacent forwarding engines. Defined in RFC 5880 through RFC 5884, BFD supports adaptive detection times and a three-way handshake ensuring that both systems are aware of any changes. BFD control packets contain the desired tx and rx intervals by the sender. For example, if a node cannot handle a high rate of BFD packets, it can specify a large desired rx interval. In this way, its neighbor(s) cannot send packets at a smaller interval. The following features of BFD make it a most desirable protocol for failure detection:

- Subsecond failure detection
- Media independence (Ethernet, POS, Serial, and so on)
- Capability to run over User Data Protocol (UDP), data protocol independence (IPv4, IPv6, Label Switched Path [LSP])
- Application Independent Interior Gateway Protocol (IGP), tunnel liveliness, Fast Reroute (FRR) trigger

When an application (Border Gateway Protocol [BGP], Open Shortest Path First [OSPF], and so on) creates or modifies a BFD session, it provides the following information:

- Interface handle (single-hop session)
- Address of the neighbor
- Local address
- Desired interval
- Multiplier

The product of the desired interval and the multiplier indicates the *desired failure detection interval*. The operational workflow of BFD for a given protocol *P* is as follows:

- User-configured BFD for *P* on the physical interface
- *P* initiates creation of BFD session.
- After the BFD session is created, timers are negotiated.
- BFD sends periodic control packets to its peer.
- If a link failure occurs, BFD detects the failure in the desired failure detection interval (desired interval × multiplier) and informs both the peer and the local BFD client (such as BGP) of the failure.
- The session for *P* goes down immediately instead of waiting for the Hold Timer to expire.

BFD runs on two modes:

- Asynchronous mode
- Demand mode

Note Demand mode is not supported on Cisco platforms. In demand mode, no hello packets are exchanged after the session is established. In this mode, BFD assumes there is another way to verify connectivity between the two endpoints. Either host may still send hello packets if needed, but they are not generally exchanged.

Asynchronous Mode

Asynchronous mode is the primary mode of operation and is mandatory for BFD to function. In this mode, each system periodically sends BFD control packets to one another. For example, packets sent by router R1 have a source address of NX-1 and a destination address of router NX-2, as Figure 12-1 shows.

Figure 12-1 *BFD Asynchronous Mode*

Each stream of BFD control packets is independent and does not follow a request-response cycle. If the other system does not receive the configured number of packets in a row (based on the BFD timer and multiplier), the session is declared down. An adaptive failure detection time is used to avoid false failures if a neighbor is sending packets slower than what it is advertising.

BFD async packets are sent on UDP port 3784. The BFD source port must be in the range of 49152 through 65535. The BFD control packets contain the fields in Table 12-1.

Table 12-1 *BFD Control Packet Fields*

Control Packet Fields	Description
Version	Version of the BFD control header.
Diag	A diagnostic code specifying the local system's reason for the last change in session state, detection time expired, echo failed, and so on.
State	The current BFD session state, as seen by the transmitting system.
P (Poll Bit)	Poll bit. If set, the transmitting system is requesting verification of connectivity or a parameter change and is expecting a packet with the Final (F) bit in reply.
F (Final Bit)	Final bit. If set, the transmitting system is responding to a received BFD control packet that has the Poll (P) bit set.

Control Packet Fields	Description
Detect Multiplier	Detection time multiplier. The negotiated transmit interval, multiplied by this value, provides the detection time for the transmitting system in asynchronous mode.
My Discriminator	A unique, nonzero discriminator value generated by the transmitting system, used to demultiplex multiple BFD sessions between the same pair of systems.
Your Discriminator	The discriminator received from the corresponding remote system. This field reflects back the received value of My Discriminator; if that value is unknown, this field is zero.
Desired Min TX Interval	The minimum interval, in microseconds, that the local system wants to use when transmitting BFD control packets.
Desired Min RX Interval:	The minimum interval, in microseconds, between received BFD control packets that this system is capable of supporting.
Required Min Echo RX Interval	The minimum interval, in microseconds, between received BFD echo packets that this system is capable of supporting.

Figure 12-2 shows the BFD control packets defined by the IETF.

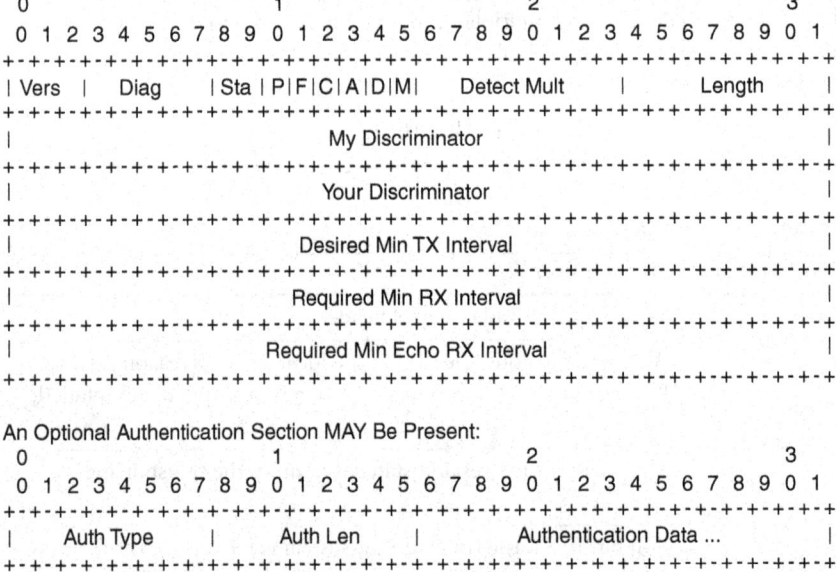

```
 0                   1                   2                   3
 0 1 2 3 4 5 6 7 8 9 0 1 2 3 4 5 6 7 8 9 0 1 2 3 4 5 6 7 8 9 0 1
+-+-+-+-+-+-+-+-+-+-+-+-+-+-+-+-+-+-+-+-+-+-+-+-+-+-+-+-+-+-+-+-+
| Vers  |  Diag   |Sta|P|F|C|A|D|M|  Detect Mult  |    Length     |
+-+-+-+-+-+-+-+-+-+-+-+-+-+-+-+-+-+-+-+-+-+-+-+-+-+-+-+-+-+-+-+-+
|                       My Discriminator                        |
+-+-+-+-+-+-+-+-+-+-+-+-+-+-+-+-+-+-+-+-+-+-+-+-+-+-+-+-+-+-+-+-+
|                      Your Discriminator                       |
+-+-+-+-+-+-+-+-+-+-+-+-+-+-+-+-+-+-+-+-+-+-+-+-+-+-+-+-+-+-+-+-+
|                    Desired Min TX Interval                    |
+-+-+-+-+-+-+-+-+-+-+-+-+-+-+-+-+-+-+-+-+-+-+-+-+-+-+-+-+-+-+-+-+
|                   Required Min RX Interval                    |
+-+-+-+-+-+-+-+-+-+-+-+-+-+-+-+-+-+-+-+-+-+-+-+-+-+-+-+-+-+-+-+-+
|                 Required Min Echo RX Interval                 |
+-+-+-+-+-+-+-+-+-+-+-+-+-+-+-+-+-+-+-+-+-+-+-+-+-+-+-+-+-+-+-+-+

An Optional Authentication Section MAY Be Present:
 0                   1                   2                   3
 0 1 2 3 4 5 6 7 8 9 0 1 2 3 4 5 6 7 8 9 0 1 2 3 4 5 6 7 8 9 0 1
+-+-+-+-+-+-+-+-+-+-+-+-+-+-+-+-+-+-+-+-+-+-+-+-+-+-+-+-+-+-+-+-+
|   Auth Type   |   Auth Len    |    Authentication Data ...    |
+-+-+-+-+-+-+-+-+-+-+-+-+-+-+-+-+-+-+-+-+-+-+-+-+-+-+-+-+-+-+-+-+
```

Figure 12-2 *BFD Control Plane Packet Format*

Note BFD supports keyed SHA-1 authentication on NX-OS beginning with Release 5.2.

Asynchronous Mode with Echo Function

Asynchronous mode with echo function is designed to test only the forwarding path, not the host stack on the remote system. It is enabled only after the session is enabled. BFD echo packets are sent in such a way that the other end just loops them back through its forwarding path. For example, a packet sent by router NX-1 is sent with both the source and destination address belonging to NX-1 (see Figure 12-3).

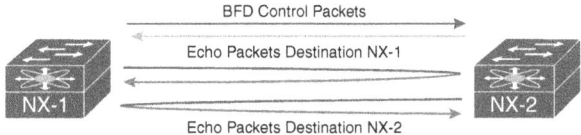

Figure 12-3 *BFD Asynchronous Mode with Echo Function*

Because echo packets do not require application or host stack processing on the remote end, this function can be used for aggressive detections timers. Another benefit of using echo function is that the sender has complete control of the response time. For the echo function to work, the remote node should also be capable of echo function. The BFD control packets with echo function enabled are sent as UDP packets with the source and destination port 3785.

Configuring and Verifying BFD Sessions

To enable BFD on the Nexus device, configure the command **feature bfd**. When enabling the **feature bfd** command on the Nexus switch, the device prints a notification message to disable Internet Control Message Protocol (ICMP) and ICMPv6 redirects on all IPv4- and IPv6 BFD–enabled interfaces. Example 12-1 displays the terminal message that gets printed when the BFD feature is enabled.

Example 12-1 *Enabling BFD Feature*

```
NX-1(config)# feature bfd
Please disable the ICMP / ICMPv6 redirects on all IPv4 and IPv6 interfaces
running BFD sessions using the command below

'no ip redirects '
'no ipv6 redirects '
```

BFD configuration must be enabled under the routing protocol configuration and also under the interface that will be participating in BFD. To enable configuration under the routing protocol (for instance, OSPF), use the command **bfd** under the **router ospf** configuration. Under the interface, two important BFD commands are defined:

- BFD interval
- BFD echo function

The BFD interval can be defined both under the interface and in global configuration mode. It is defined using the command **bfd interval** *tx-interval* **min_rx** *rx-interval* **multiplier** *number*. The BFD echo function is enabled by default. To disable or enable the BFD echo function, use the command [**no**] **bfd echo**. Example 12-2 illustrates the configuration for enabling BFD for OSPF.

Example 12-2 *Configuring BFD for OSPF*

```
NX-1
NX-1(config)# int e4/1
NX-1(config-if)# no ip redirects
NX-1(config-if)# no ipv6 redirects
NX-2(config)# bfd interval 300 min_rx 300 multiplier 3
NX-1(config-if)# ip ospf bfd
NX-1(config-if)# no bfd echo
NX-1(config-if)# exit
NX-1(config)# router ospf 100
NX-1(config-router)# bfd
```

Note To enable BFD for other routing protocols, refer to the Cisco documentation for the configuration on different Nexus devices.

When BFD is enabled, a BFD session gets established. Use the command **show bfd neighbors** [**detail**] to verify the status of BFD. The **show bfd neighbors** command displays the state of the BFD neighbor, along with the interface, local and remote discriminator, and Virtual Routing and Forwarding (VRF) details. The output with the **detail** keyword displays all the fields that are part of the BFD control packet, which is useful for debugging purposes to see whether a mismatch could cause the BFD session to flap. Ensure that the State bit is set to *Up* instead of *AdminDown*. The output also shows that the echo function is enabled or disabled. Example 12-3 displays the output of the command **show bfd neighbors** [**detail**].

Example 12-3 *Verifying BFD Neighbors*

```
NX-1# show bfd neighbors detail

OurAddr     NeighAddr   LD/RD                    RH/RS   Holdown(mult)  State   Int
  Vrf
10.1.12.1   10.1.12.2   1090519044/1107296259    Up      667(3)         Up      Eth4/1
  default

Session state is Up and not using echo function
Local Diag: 0, Demand mode: 0, Poll bit: 0, Authentication: None
MinTxInt: 300000 us, MinRxInt: 300000 us, Multiplier: 3
```

```
Received MinRxInt: 300000 us, Received Multiplier: 3
Holdown (hits): 900 ms (0), Hello (hits): 300 ms (47)
Rx Count: 47, Rx Interval (ms) min/max/avg: 0/1600/260 last: 134 ms ago
Tx Count: 47, Tx Interval (ms) min/max/avg: 236/236/236 last: 136 ms ago
Registered protocols:  ospf
Uptime: 0 days 0 hrs 36 mins 9 secs
Last packet: Version: 1              - Diagnostic: 0
             State bit: Up            - Demand bit: 0
             Poll bit: 0              - Final bit: 0
             Multiplier: 3            - Length: 24
             My Discr.: 1107296259    - Your Discr.: 1090519044
             Min tx interval: 300000  - Min rx interval: 300000
             Min Echo interval: 50000 - Authentication bit: 0
Hosting LC: 4, Down reason: None, Reason not-hosted: None
```

Before troubleshooting any BFD-related issue, it is important to verify the state of the feature. This is done by using the command **show system internal feature-mgr feature** *feature-name* **current status**. If a problem arises with the process (for instance, a process is not running or has crashed), the state of the process does not show as Running. Example 12-4 displays the state of BFD feature. Here, the BFD is currently in the Running state.

Example 12-4 *BFD Feature Status*

```
NX-1# show system internal feature-mgr feature bfd current status
Feature Name     State      Feature   ID UUID   SAP    PID    Service State
----------------  --------   -------   -------   -----  -----  --------------
bfd              enabled    87        706       121    2574   Running
```

As with other features, BFD also maintains internal event-history logs that are useful in debugging any state machine-related or BFD flaps. The event-history for BFD provides various command-line options. To view the BFD event-history, use the command **show system internal bfd event-history** [**all** | **errors** | **logs** | **msgs** | **session** [*discriminator*]]. The **all** option shows all the event-history (that is, all the events and error event-history logs). The **errors** option shows only the BFD-related errors. The **logs** options shows all the events for BFD. The **msgs** option shows BFD-related messages, and the **session** option helps view the logs related to errors, log messages, and app-events for a particular session.

Example 12-5 displays the BFD event-history logs for a BFD session hosted on an interface on module 4 with the discriminator *0x41000004*. This example also helps you understand the information exchange and steps the system goes through in bringing up a BFD session. These are the steps, listed in sequence:

Step 1.   The session begins with an Admin Down state.

Step 2.   The BFD client (BFDC) adds a BFD session with the interface and IP addresses of the devices between which the session will be established.

Step 3. The BFD component sends an MTS message to the BFDC component on the line card.

Step 4. BFD sends a received session notification to its clients.

> **Note** The BFD process runs on the supervisor, whereas the BFDC runs on the line card.

Example 12-5 *BFD Event-History Logs*

```
NX-1# show system internal bfd event-history logs

1) Event:E_DEBUG, length:95, at 686796 usecs after Sat Oct 28 14:07:10 2017
    [102] bfd_mts_send_msg_to_bfdc(4848): opc 116747 length 36 sent to host_module 4
rrtok 0x27de77d


2) Event:E_DEBUG, length:95, at 676629 usecs after Sat Oct 28 13:14:38 2017
    [102] bfd_mts_send_msg_to_bfdc(4848): opc 116747 length 36 sent to host_module 4
rrtok 0x27ceb4e


3) Event:E_DEBUG, length:95, at 506685 usecs after Sat Oct 28 13:14:11 2017
    [102] bfd_mts_send_msg_to_bfdc(4848): opc 116747 length 36 sent to host_module 4
rrtok 0x27ce825


4) Event:E_DEBUG, length:106, at 92550 usecs after Sat Oct 28 13:14:08 2017
    [102] bfd_mts_sess_change_state_notif_cb(2379): Received sess 0x41000004 notif 3
reason_code No Diagnostic


5) Event:E_DEBUG, length:151, at 92524 usecs after Sat Oct 28 13:14:08 2017
    [102] bfd_mts_sess_change_state_notif_cb(2366): notif 0x41000004 3: [1 if Eth4/1
0x1a180000 iod 0x26 10c010a:0:0:0=10.1.12.1 -> 20c010a:0:0:0=10.1
.12.2]


6) Event:E_DEBUG, length:96, at 315822 usecs after Sat Oct 28 13:14:06 2017
    [102] bfd_mts_send_msg_to_bfdc(4848): opc 116745 length 396 sent to host_module 4
rrtok 0x27ce7ef


7) Event:E_DEBUG, length:81, at 315599 usecs after Sat Oct 28 13:14:06 2017
    [102] bfd_fu_timer_cancel_app_client_expiry(244): disc 0x41000004 app
1090519321:1
```

Bidirectional Forwarding Detection 697

```
8) Event:E_DEBUG, length:167, at 315560 usecs after Sat Oct 28 13:14:06 2017
    [102] bfd_sess_create_session(1713): Client Add 1:1090519321 to session
0x41000004  [1 if Eth4/1 0x1a180000 iod 0x26 10c010a:0:0:0=10.1.12.1 -> 20
c010a:0:0:0=10.1.12.2]


9) Event:E_DEBUG, length:114, at 399344 usecs after Sat Oct 28 13:14:02 2017
    [102] bfd_mts_sess_change_state_notif_cb(2379): Received sess 0x41000004 notif 1
reason_code Administratively Down
```

Example 12-6 displays the detailed information about the session using the command **show system internal bfd event-history session** *discriminator*. The discriminator value is calculated from the *LD* or *your discriminator* value from the **show bfd neighbor detail** output. This value is calculated in hex, as shown in Example 12-6, and is used with the **event-history** command output. The **event-history session** command views the errors, logs such as parameters exchanged and state changes, and app events related to a given BFD session.

Example 12-6 *BFD Session-Based Event-History*

```
NX-1# hex 1090519044
0x41000004


NX-1# show system internal bfd event-history session 0x41000004

Start of errors for session 0x41000004
1:1365  292509 usecs after Sat Oct 28 13:13:15 2017
        : Code 0x1 0x0 0x0 0x0


End of errors for session 0x41000004

Start of Logs for session 0x41000004
1:2455  612556 usecs after Sat Oct 28 13:14:08 2017
        : Session active params changed: State 3(Up), TX(300000), RX(300000),
Mult(3)
2:2455  332770 usecs after Sat Oct 28 13:14:08 2017
        : Session active params changed: State 3(Up), TX(300000), RX(300000),
Mult(3)
3:649   92566 usecs after Sat Oct 28 13:14:08 2017
        : Session Up
4:628   92526 usecs after Sat Oct 28 13:14:08 2017
        : Session state changed: 1(Down) -> 3(Up), New diag: 0(No Diagnostic),
After: 6 secs
5:2523  92282 usecs after Sat Oct 28 13:14:08 2017
        : Session remote disc changed: 0(0x0) -> 1107296261(0x42000005)
```

```
6:2523    732472 usecs after Sat Oct 28 13:14:02 2017
          : Session remote disc changed: 1107296260(0x42000004) -> 0(0x0)
7:2523    732438 usecs after Sat Oct 28 13:14:02 2017
          : Session remote disc changed: 0(0x0) -> 1107296260(0x42000004)
8:2523    452189 usecs after Sat Oct 28 13:14:02 2017
          : Session remote disc changed: 1107296260(0x42000004) -> 0(0x0)
9:2523    452163 usecs after Sat Oct 28 13:14:02 2017
          : Session remote disc changed: 0(0x0) -> 1107296260(0x42000004)
10:707    399365 usecs after Sat Oct 28 13:14:02 2017
          : Session Down Diag 7(Administratively Down)
11:628    399285 usecs after Sat Oct 28 13:14:02 2017
          : Session state changed: 3(Up) -> 1(Down), New diag: 7(Administratively
Down), After: 44 secs
12:2523   398654 usecs after Sat Oct 28 13:14:02 2017
          : Session remote disc changed: 1107296260(0x42000004) -> 0(0x0)
13:2455   49895 usecs after Sat Oct 28 13:13:19 2017
          : Session active params changed: State 3(Up), TX(300000), RX(300000),
Mult(3)
14:2455   49490 usecs after Sat Oct 28 13:13:19 2017
          : Session active params changed: State 3(Up), TX(300000), RX(300000),
Mult(3)
15:2455   770894 usecs after Sat Oct 28 13:13:18 2017
          : Session active params changed: State 3(Up), TX(300000), RX(300000),
Mult(3)
16:649    769776 usecs after Sat Oct 28 13:13:18 2017
          : Session Up
17:628    769732 usecs after Sat Oct 28 13:13:18 2017
          : Session state changed: 1(Down) -> 3(Up), New diag: 0(No Diagnostic),
After: 3 secs
18:2523   59514 usecs after Sat Oct 28 13:13:17 2017
          : Session remote disc changed: 0(0x0) -> 1107296260(0x42000004)
19:1396   347952 usecs after Sat Oct 28 13:13:15 2017
          : ACL installed
20:602    293945 usecs after Sat Oct 28 13:13:15 2017
          : Session installed on LC 4
21:112    292529 usecs after Sat Oct 28 13:13:15 2017
          : Session Created if 0x1a180000 iod 38 (Eth4/1) src 10.1.12.1, dst 10.1.12.2
22:1364   292508 usecs after Sat Oct 28 13:13:15 2017
          : Code 0x1 0x0 0x0 0x0

End of Logs for session 0x41000004

Start of app-events for session 0x41000004
1:958     315615 usecs after Sat Oct 28 13:14:06 2017
          : Client Add type 1, 1090519321 in state 14
```

```
2:1709   292536 usecs after Sat Oct 28 13:13:15 2017
        : Client Add type 1, 1090519321 in state 10
3:1363   292507 usecs after Sat Oct 28 13:13:15 2017
        : Code 0x1 0x0 0x0 0x0

End of app-events for session 0x41000004
```

The command **show system internal bfd transition-history** shows the different internal state machine-related events that the BFD session goes through (see Example 12-7). Note that the final state a BFD session should be in *BFD_SESS_ST_SESSION_UP*. If the BFD session is stuck in one of the other states, this command can identify where the session is stuck.

Example 12-7 *BFD Transition History Logs*

```
NX-1# show system internal bfd transition-history

>>>>FSM: <Proto  Sess 0x41000004> has 8 logged transitions<<<<<

1) FSM:<Proto  Sess 0x41000004> Transition at 292788 usecs after Sat Oct 28 13:13:15
2017
    Previous state: [BFD_SESS_ST_INIT]
    Triggered event: [BFD_SESS_EV_INTERFACE]
    Next state: [BFD_SESS_ST_INSTALLING_SESSION]

2) FSM:<Proto  Sess 0x41000004> Transition at 293898 usecs after Sat Oct 28 13:13:15
2017
    Previous state: [BFD_SESS_ST_INSTALLING_SESSION]
    Triggered event: [BFD_SESS_EV_SESSION_INSTALL_SUCCESS]
    Next state: [BFD_SESS_ST_INSTALLING_ACL]

3) FSM:<Proto  Sess 0x41000004> Transition at 347878 usecs after Sat Oct 28 13:13:15
2017
    Previous state: [BFD_SESS_ST_INSTALLING_ACL]
    Triggered event: [BFD_SESS_EV_ACL_RESPONSE]
    Next state: [FSM_ST_NO_CHANGE]

4) FSM:<Proto  Sess 0x41000004> Transition at 347948 usecs after Sat Oct 28 13:13:15
2017
    Previous state: [BFD_SESS_ST_INSTALLING_ACL]
    Triggered event: [BFD_SESS_EV_ACL_INSTALL_SUCCESS]
    Next state: [BFD_SESS_ST_SESSION_DOWN]
```

```
5) FSM:<Proto  Sess 0x41000004> Transition at 769773 usecs after Sat Oct 28 13:13:18
2017
    Previous state: [BFD_SESS_ST_SESSION_DOWN]
    Triggered event: [BFD_SESS_EV_SESSION_UP]
    Next state: [BFD_SESS_ST_SESSION_UP]

6) FSM:<Proto  Sess 0x41000004> Transition at 399361 usecs after Sat Oct 28 13:14:02
2017
    Previous state: [BFD_SESS_ST_SESSION_UP]
    Triggered event: [BFD_SESS_EV_SESSION_DOWN]
    Next state: [BFD_SESS_ST_SESSION_DOWN]

7) FSM:<Proto  Sess 0x41000004> Transition at 315593 usecs after Sat Oct 28 13:14:06
2017
    Previous state: [BFD_SESS_ST_SESSION_DOWN]
    Triggered event: [BFD_SESS_EV_CLIENT_ADD]
    Next state: [FSM_ST_NO_CHANGE]

8) FSM:<Proto  Sess 0x41000004> Transition at 92563 usecs after Sat Oct 28 13:14:08
2017
    Previous state: [BFD_SESS_ST_SESSION_DOWN]
    Triggered event: [BFD_SESS_EV_SESSION_UP]
    Next state: [BFD_SESS_ST_SESSION_UP]

    Curr state: [BFD_SESS_ST_SESSION_UP]
```

When a BFD session is configured, an access list is installed in the hardware; it is verified using the command **show system internal access-list interface** *interface-id* **module** *slot*. The relevant statistics for the hardware Access Control List (ACL) can be viewed using the command **show system internal access-list input statistics module** *slot*. Note that when the BFD is enabled on an interface, the ACL gets installed for both IPv4 and IPv6 in the hardware. Example 12-8 illustrates ACL programmed in the hardware for BFD on the Nexus 7000 switch.

Example 12-8 *ACL for BFD in Hardware*

```
NX-1# show system internal access-list interface ethernet 4/1 module 4
Policies in ingress direction:
        Policy type                  Policy Id     Policy name
-----------------------------------------------------------------
        QoS                              3
        BFD                              6

No Netflow profiles in ingress direction
```

```
  INSTANCE 0x0
  ---------------

    Tcam 1 resource usage:
    ----------------------
     Label_b = 0x2
     Bank 0
     ------
       IPv4 Class
         Policies: BFD()  [Merged]
         Netflow profile: 0
         Netflow deny profile: 0
         4 tcam entries
       IPv6 Class
         Policies: BFD()  [Merged]
         Netflow profile: 0
         Netflow deny profile: 0
         2 tcam entries

     0 l4 protocol cam entries
     0 mac etype/proto cam entries
     2 lous
     0 tcp flags table entries
     1 adjacency entries

! Output omitted for brevity
```
NX-1# **show system internal access-list input statistics module 4**
```
                  VDC-1 Ethernet4/1 :
                  ====================

  INSTANCE 0x0
  ---------------

    Tcam 1 resource usage:
    ----------------------
     Label_b = 0x2
     Bank 0
     ------
       IPv4 Class
         Policies: BFD()  [Merged]
         Netflow profile: 0
         Netflow deny profile: 0
         Entries:
           [Index] Entry [Stats]
           ----------------------
```

Chapter 12: High Availability

```
     [0008:0408:0006] prec 1 redirect(0x40001)-routed udp 0.0.0.0/0 0.0.0.0/0 eq 3785
ttl eq 254  flow-label 3785  [0]
     [0009:0508:0007] prec 1 redirect(0x40001)-routed udp 0.0.0.0/0 0.0.0.0/0 eq 3784
ttl eq 255  flow-label 3784  [26874]
     [000a:0608:0008] prec 1 permit-routed ip 0.0.0.0/0 0.0.0.0/0        [1641]
     [000b:0488:0009] prec 1 permit-routed ip 0.0.0.0/0 0.0.0.0/0 fragment    [0]
  IPv6 Class
    Policies: BFD()   [Merged]
    Netflow profile: 0
    Netflow deny profile: 0
    Entries:
      [Index] Entry [Stats]
      --------------------
     [000c:0509:000a] prec 1 redirect(0x40001)-routed udp 0x0/0 0x0/0 eq 3784 ttl eq
255  flow-label 3784  [0]
     [000d:0409:000b] prec 1 redirect(0x40001)-routed udp 0x0/0 0x0/0 eq 3785 ttl eq
254  flow-label 3785  [0]
```

Note The ACL programming on the hardware is dependent on the underlying line card hardware and the Nexus platform. The behavior might differ among Nexus hardware platforms.

To enable the BFD echo function, configure the command **bfd echo** under the interface. When the session is configured with the echo function, the BFD session starts in asynchronous mode using a slow interval of 2 seconds. When the session is up, and if the interval specified by the client is less than 2 seconds, the echo function gets activated (assuming that the echo function is enabled on the remote peer as well).

Example 12-9 illustrates the configuration of the BFD echo function between NX-1 and NX-2 and the changes in the **show bfd neighbors detail** command output after the BFD session is established.

Example 12-9 *BFD with Echo Function Configuration and Verification*

```
NX-1(config)# interface Ethernet4/1
NX-1(config-if)# bfd echo
NX-1(config-if)# bfd interval 50 min_rx 50 multiplier 3
NX-1# show bfd neighbors detail

OurAddr    NeighAddr    LD/RD                RH/RS   Holdown(mult)  State  Int
  Vrf
10.1.12.1  10.1.12.2    1090519047/1107296265  Up     667(3)         Up     Eth4/1
  default

Session state is Up and using echo function with 50 ms interval
Local Diag: 0, Demand mode: 0, Poll bit: 0, Authentication: None
```

```
MinTxInt: 50000 us, MinRxInt: 2000000 us, Multiplier: 3
Received MinRxInt: 2000000 us, Received Multiplier: 3
Holdown (hits): 6000 ms (0), Hello (hits): 2000 ms (1690)
Rx Count: 1690, Rx Interval (ms) min/max/avg: 0/1880/1807 last: 268 ms ago
Tx Count: 1690, Tx Interval (ms) min/max/avg: 1806/1806/1806 last: 269 ms ago
Registered protocols:  ospf
Uptime: 0 days 0 hrs 50 mins 52 secs
Last packet: Version: 1              - Diagnostic: 0
             State bit: Up            - Demand bit: 0
             Poll bit: 0              - Final bit: 0
             Multiplier: 3            - Length: 24
             My Discr.: 1107296265    - Your Discr.: 1090519047
             Min tx interval: 50000   - Min rx interval: 2000000
             Min Echo interval: 50000 - Authentication bit: 0
Hosting LC: 4, Down reason: None, Reason not-hosted: None
```

If a failure occurs, NX-OS logs a syslog message for BFD failure along with a reason code for the failure and the session discriminator value. Example 12-10 displays the syslog message of a BFD failure on NX-1. Notice that, in this case, the reason is 0x2, which indicates "Echo Function Failed."

Example 12-10   *BFD Failure Log*

```
02:42:01 NX-1  BFD-5-SESSION_STATE_DOWN  BFD session  1107296259  to neighbor
   10.1.12.2 on interface Eth4/1 has gone down. Reason: 0x2.
02:44:01 NX-1  BFD-5-SESSION_STATE_DOWN  BFD session  1090519047  to neighbor
   10.1.12.2 on interface Eth4/1 has gone down. Reason: 0x2.
```

Table 12-2 lists all the BFD failure reason codes, along with their description.

Table 12-2   *BFD Failure Reason Codes and Description*

Reason Code	Description
0	No Diag
1	Control packet detection timer expired
2	Echo function failed
3	Neighbor signaled session down
4	Forwarding plane reset
5	Path down
6	Concatenated path down
7	Administratively down
8	Reverse concatenated path down

> **Note** In case of any BFD failure event, capturing **show tech bfd** soon after the BFD flap event is recommended. It is also necessary to capture the **show tech** *feature* output for the relevant feature with which BFD is associated; for instance, in case of OSPF, this is **show tech ospf**.

Nexus also supports BFD over L3 port-channels or BFD on SVI interfaces over L2 port-channel. In both cases, Link Aggregation Control Protocol (LACP) must be enabled for the port-channel interface. BFD is enabled on L3 port-channel interfaces for two methods:

- BFD per-link
- Micro BFD session

To enable BFD per-link, use the command **bfd per-link** under the port-channel interface along with the **no ip redirects** command. That enables the BFD for the client protocol enabled on that L3 port-channel interface. When BFD per-link mode is used, BFD creates a session for each link in the port-channel and provides accumulated or aggregated results to the client protocol. Example 12-11 demonstrates the configuration of per-link BFD configuration on port-channel interface and its verification using the **show bfd neighbors [detail]** command output. Use the command **show port-channel summary** to verify the member ports of the port-channel interface.

Example 12-11 *BFD over Port-Channel per-Link Configuration*

```
NX-1
NX-1(config)# interface port-channel1
NX-1(config-if)# no ip redirects
NX-1(config-if)# bfd per-link
NX-1(config-if)# ip router ospf 100 area 0.0.0.0
NX-1(config-if)# ip ospf network point-to-point
NX-1(config-if)# exit
NX-1(config)# router ospf 100
NX-1(config-router)# bfd

NX-1# show port-channel summary
! Output omitted for brevity
--------------------------------------------------------------------------
Group Port-        Type     Protocol  Member Ports
      Channel
--------------------------------------------------------------------------
1     Po1(RU)      Eth      LACP      Eth4/1(P)

NX-1# show bfd neighbors details

OurAddr      NeighAddr    LD/RD              RH/RS  Holdown(mult)  State   Int
  Vrf
```

```
10.1.12.1   10.1.12.2  1090519048/0              Up    N/A(3)           Up    Po1
  default

Session state is Up
Local Diag: 0
Registered protocols:  ospf
Uptime: 0 days 0 hrs 0 mins 9 secs
Hosting LC: 0, Down reason: None, Reason not-hosted: None
Parent session, please check port channel config for member info


OurAddr     NeighAddr   LD/RD                    RH/RS  Holdown(mult)   State  Int
  Vrf
10.1.12.1   10.1.12.2  1090519049/1107296267    Up     148(3)           Up     Eth4/1
  default

Session state is Up and not using echo function
Local Diag: 0, Demand mode: 0, Poll bit: 0, Authentication: None
MinTxInt: 50000 us, MinRxInt: 50000 us, Multiplier: 3
Received MinRxInt: 50000 us, Received Multiplier: 3
Holdown (hits): 150 ms (0), Hello (hits): 50 ms (176)
Rx Count: 176, Rx Interval (ms) min/max/avg: 0/2133/72 last: 1 ms ago
Tx Count: 176, Tx Interval (ms) min/max/avg: 48/48/48 last: 2 ms ago
Registered protocols:
Uptime: 0 days 0 hrs 0 mins 9 secs
Last packet: Version: 1              - Diagnostic: 0
             State bit: Up            - Demand bit: 0
             Poll bit: 0              - Final bit: 0
             Multiplier: 3            - Length: 24
             My Discr.: 1107296267    - Your Discr.: 1090519049
             Min tx interval: 50000   - Min rx interval: 50000
             Min Echo interval: 50000 - Authentication bit: 0
Hosting LC: 4, Down reason: None, Reason not-hosted: None
Member session under parent interface Po1
```

Nexus 9000 also supports BFD on every link aggregation group (LAG) member interfaces, as defined in RFC 7130. This method is called IETF Micro BFD session. The echo function is not supported on micro BFD sessions. The benefit of using micro BFD sessions is that if any member port goes down, the port is removed from the forwarding table and traffic disruption is prevented on that member link.

Micro BFD sessions are configured using the commands **port-channel bfd track-member-link** and **port-channel bfd destination** *ip-address* on an active L3 port-channel interface. Example 12-12 demonstrates the configuration of micro BFD session configuration on Nexus 9000 switches N9k-1 and N9k-2.

Example 12-12 *BFD over Port-Channel (Micro BFD Session Configuration)*

```
N9k-1
N9k-1(config)# interface port-channel2
N9k-1(config-if)# port-channel bfd track-member-link
N9k-1(config-if)# port-channel bfd destination 172.16.0.1
```

```
N9k-2
N9k-2(config)# interface port-channel2
N9k-2(config-if)# port-channel bfd track-member-link
N9k-2(config-if)# port-channel bfd destination 172.16.0.0
```

During verification, it is noticed that the BFD session is established on each member port of the port-channel. In this method, the BFD client is the port-channel itself. Example 12-13 verifies the BFD session on the port-channel interface configured with the micro BFD session. Notice that the client is Ethernet port-channel.

Example 12-13 *BFD over Port-Channel*

```
N9k-1
N9k-1# show bfd neighbors

OurAddr       NeighAddr     LD/RD                    RH/RS   Holdown(mult)   State   Int
  Vrf
172.16.0.0    172.16.0.1    1090519044/0             Up      N/A(3)          Up      Po2
  default
172.16.0.0    172.16.0.1    1090519045/1090519045    Up      121(3)          Up      Eth1/3
  default
N9k-1# show bfd neighbors details

OurAddr       NeighAddr     LD/RD                    RH/RS   Holdown(mult)   State   Int
  Vrf
172.16.0.1    172.16.0.0    1090519044/0             Up      N/A(3)          Up      Po2
  default

Session state is Up
Local Diag: 0
Registered protocols:  eth_port_channel
Uptime: 0 days 0 hrs 9 mins 56 secs
Hosting LC: 0, Down reason: None, Reason not-hosted: None
Parent session, please check port channel config for member info


172.16.0.1    172.16.0.0    1090519045/1090519045    Up      121(3)          Up      Eth1/3
  default


Session state is Up and not using echo function
Local Diag: 0, Demand mode: 0, Poll bit: 0, Authentication: None
```

```
MinTxInt: 50000 us, MinRxInt: 50000 us, Multiplier: 3
Received MinRxInt: 50000 us, Received Multiplier: 3
Holdown (hits): 150 ms (0), Hello (hits): 50 ms (12619)
Rx Count: 12357, Rx Interval (ms) min/max/avg: 1/1987/48 last: 25 ms ago
Tx Count: 12619, Tx Interval (ms) min/max/avg: 47/47/47 last: 32 ms ago
Registered protocols:   eth_port_channel
Uptime: 0 days 0 hrs 9 mins 56 secs
Last packet: Version: 1              - Diagnostic: 0
             State bit: Up            - Demand bit: 0
             Poll bit: 0              - Final bit: 0
             Multiplier: 3            - Length: 24
             My Discr.: 1090519045    - Your Discr.: 1090519045
             Min tx interval: 50000   - Min rx interval: 50000
             Min Echo interval: 50000 - Authentication bit: 0
Hosting LC: 1, Down reason: None, Reason not-hosted: None
Member session under parent interface Po2
```

Note In case of any issues with a per-link BFD or micro BFD session, collect the **show tech bfd** and **show tech lacp all** output and share the captured logs with Cisco Technical Assistance Center (TAC) for investigation purposes.

Nexus High Availability

NX-OS was built around the pillars of high availability (HA) and virtualization. With Nexus devices being designed for data centers and enterprises, the NX-OS architecture adds a huge benefit in maintaining high availability in such environments with various features and capabilities. These features help reduce downtime:

- Stateful switchover (SSO)
- In-service software upgrade (ISSU)
- Graceful insertion and removal

This section discusses in detail these features and shows how they provide HA capability to Nexus devices.

Stateful Switchover

Various Nexus platforms (including the Nexus 7000, Nexus 7700, and Nexus 9500) have support for fabric as well as supervisor redundancy. The benefit of the hardware-based redundancy is that if the active hardware (fabric or supervisor card) fails, the standby hardware takes over the role of active and prevents any kind of traffic and service disruption. In addition, some of the software-based HA features, such as nonstop routing (NSR), nonstop forwarding (NSF), and graceful restart (GR), are leveraged only when a redundant supervisor card is available to synchronize the state to the standby supervisor and seamlessly take over the role of active supervisor when the old active supervisor fails.

With redundant hardware, the supervisor cards must stay in active/ha-standby mode. The supervisor states are verified using the command **show module**. This command displays all the supervisor cards, line cards, and fabric cards present in the chassis. Example 12-14 displays the **show module** output on the Nexus 7000 switch. Notice that, in the output, the supervisor card in slot 1 is in ha-standby state and the one in slot 2 is in active state.

Example 12-14 show module *Command Output*

```
NX-1# show module
Mod  Ports  Module-Type                            Model            Status
---  -----  -------------------------------------- ---------------- ----------
1    0      Supervisor Module-2                    N7K-SUP2E        ha-standby
2    0      Supervisor Module-2                    N7K-SUP2E        active *
3    32     10 Gbps Ethernet XL Module             N7K-M132XP-12L   ok
4    32     1/10 Gbps Ethernet Module              N7K-F132XP-15    powered-dn
5    48     10/100/1000 Mbps Ethernet XL Module    N7K-M148GT-11L   ok
6    48     1/10 Gbps Ethernet Module              N7K-F248XP-25E   ok
7    32     10 Gbps Ethernet XL Module             N7K-M132XP-12L   ok
8    48     1/10 Gbps Ethernet Module              N7K-F248XP-25    ok
! Output omitted for brevity
```

The HA state is also verified using the command **show system redundancy status**. When the standby supervisor is booting up, or after a switchover event when the active supervisor moves to a standby role, the ha-standby state is not achieved immediately. The standby supervisor requires synchronizing the state with that of the active supervisor. This is achieved with the *system manager (sysmgr)* component on the active supervisor. The sysmgr component initiates a global sync (gsync) of active supervisor state to standby supervisor. During the synchronization process, the state is seen as *HA synchronization in progress*. Note that the standby should not be in this state for too long because it can indicate failure and other issues.

When all the components and states are synchronized between the active and standby supervisor, the Module-Manager is informed that the standby supervisor is up. The Module-Manager then informs all the software components on active supervisor about the availability of the standby supervisor and configures them. This event is known as the Standby Sup Insertion Sequence. Any error faced during this sequence results in a reboot of the standby supervisor.

Example 12-15 displays the system redundancy status. An ideal state for redundancy is active/standby state. In this example, the standby supervisor is currently synchronizing its states with the active supervisor in slot 2.

Example 12-15 *System Redundancy State*

```
NX-1# show system redundancy status
Redundancy mode
---------------
       administrative:   HA
          operational:   HA

This supervisor (sup-2)
-----------------------
    Redundancy state:    Active
    Supervisor state:    Active
      Internal state:    Active with HA standby

Other supervisor (sup-1)
------------------------
    Redundancy state:    Standby
    Supervisor state:    HA standby
      Internal state:    HA synchronization in progress
```

Note In case of failure during Standby Sup Insertion Sequence, collect the following commands to help identify where the failure has occurred:

- **show logging [nvram]**
- **show module internal exception-log**
- **show system reset-reason**
- **show module internal event-history module** *slot*

On the Nexus 7000 or Nexus 7700 series platform, where virtual device context (VDC) is supported, the HA state should also be maintained across all VDCs configured on the system. This is verified using the command **show system redundancy ha status**. Example 12-16 verifies the system redundancy state across all VDCs.

Example 12-16 *System Redundancy HA Status*

```
NX-1# show system redundancy ha status
VDC No    This supervisor            Other supervisor
------    ---------------            ----------------
vdc 1     Active with HA standby     HA standby
vdc 2     Active with HA standby     HA standby
```

Synchronization is achieved using the sysmgr component, so the state information can also be verified using the sysmgr state command **show system internal sysmgr state**. In this command, verify that the sysmgr state is set to Active/HotStandby, as shown in Example 12-17. This command also shows the current state of the active supervisor card, which is set to Active (*SYSMGR_CARDSTATE_ACTIVE*) here.

Example 12-17 *System Manager State Information*

```
NX-1# show system internal sysmgr state

The master System Manager has PID 4967 and UUID 0x1.
Last time System Manager was gracefully shutdown.
The state is SRV_STATE_MASTER_ACTIVE_HOTSTDBY entered at time Thu Oct 26 13:20:5
4 2017.

The '-b' option (disable heartbeat) is currently disabled.

The '-n' (don't use rlimit) option is currently disabled.

Hap-reset is currently enabled.

Process restart capability is currently disabled.

Watchdog checking is currently enabled.

Watchdog kgdb setting is currently disabled.


        Debugging info:

The trace mask is 0x00000000, the syslog priority enabled is 3.
The '-d' option is currently disabled.
The statistics generation is currently enabled.


        HA info:

slotid = 2    supid = 0
cardstate = SYSMGR_CARDSTATE_ACTIVE .
cardstate = SYSMGR_CARDSTATE_ACTIVE (hot switchover is configured enabled).
Configured to use the real platform manager.
Configured to use the real redundancy driver.
Redundancy register: this_sup = RDN_ST_AC, other_sup = RDN_ST_SB.
EOBC device name: veobc.
Remote addresses:   MTS - 0x00000101/3      IP - 127.1.1.1
MSYNC done.
```

```
Remote MSYNC not done.
Module online notification received.
Local super-state is: SYSMGR_SUPERSTATE_STABLE
Standby super-state is: SYSMGR_SUPERSTATE_STABLE
Swover Reason : SYSMGR_UNKNOWN_SWOVER
Total number of Switchovers: 0
Swover threshold settings: 5 switchovers within 4800 seconds
Switchovers within threshold interval: 0
Last switchover time: 0 seconds after system start time
Cumulative time between last 0 switchovers: 0
Start done received for 1 plugins, Total number of plugins = 1



       Statistics:

Message count:          0
Total latency:          0              Max latency:           0
Total exec:             0              Max exec:              0
```

When the system is in HA or redundancy state, performing a switchover from active to standby supervisor card does not have much impact on the services. Switchovers are usually performed when an upgrade needs to be performed, the Message and Transaction Service (MTS) queue is stuck, when misprogramming has occurred on the supervisor card, and so on. A manual switchover is performed using the command **system switchover**. When the command is executed, the standby supervisor takes over the role of active and the initial active supervisor is rebooted. Note that when the supervisor switchover happens, some protocols (stateless protocols) might experience flaps, but this does not affect the forwarding. Example 12-18 demonstrates a manual switchover of the system and, at the same time, availability of the system via the redundant supervisor module present in the system.

Example 12-18 *Redundancy Switchover*

```
NX-1 SUP-1
NX-1# system switchover
NX-1#
User Access Verification
NX-1 login:
User Access Verification
NX-1 login:
>>>
>>>
>>>
NX7k SUP BIOS version ( 2.12 ) : Build - 05/29/2013 11:58:20
```

```
PM FPGA Version : 0x00000025
Power sequence microcode revision - 0x00000009 : card type - 10156EEA0
Booting Spi Flash : Primary
  CPU Signature - 0x000106e4: Version - 0x000106e0
  CPU - 2 : Cores - 4 : HTEn - 1 : HT - 2 : Features - 0xbfebfbff
  FSB Clk - 532 Mhz :  Freq - 2140 Mhz - 2128 Mhz
  MicroCode Version : 0x00000002
  Memory - 32768 MB : Frequency - 1067 MHZ
  Loading Bootloader: Done
  IO FPGA Version   : 0x1000d
  PLX Version       : 861910b5
Bios digital signature verification - Passed
USB bootflash status : [1-1:1-1]


Reset Reason Registers: 0x1 0x0
 Filesystem type is ext2fs, partition type 0x83



            GNU GRUB   version 0.97

Autobooting bootflash:/n7000-s2-kickstart.7.3.2.D1.1.bin bootflash:/n7000-s2-dk
9.7.3.2.D1.1.bin...
 Filesystem type is ext2fs, partition type 0x83
! Output omitted for brevity
NX-1 SUP-2
NX-1 login: admin
Password:


Cisco Nexus Operating System (NX-OS) Software
TAC support: http://www.cisco.com/tac
! Output omitted for brevity
NX-1#
```

Note During manual switchover, while the initial active supervisor is being rebooted to take over the role as standby, if the newly active supervisor crashes or reloads, it can lead to a whole system reload and cause major outages. Thus, a manual switchover should always take place during a planned maintenance window.

ISSU

Performing upgrades in any network deployment, especially in a huge data center and enterprise, is unpleasant. In most cases, when a device needs to be upgraded, services and traffic are shifted to the backup or redundant devices, boot variables are set, and then the device is brought down using **reload** command to perform the upgrade. This becomes more challenging on devices such as the Nexus 7000, with multiple VDCs running on a single box, acting as individual devices and playing different roles. To overcome the challenges of upgrades in the network, leverage the ISSU feature.

ISSU is not a new concept. It is available on multiple Cisco catalyst platforms, including 4500 and 6500 switches. ISSU follows the same concept on Nexus 7000 series devices. The whole ISSU process takes place in a few simple steps:

Step 1. Upgrade the Basic Input and Output System (BIOS) on supervisors and line card modules.

Step 2. Bring up the standby supervisor card with a new image.

Step 3. Switch over from the active to the standby supervisor, which is running on the new image.

Step 4. Bring up old active supervisor card with the new image.

Step 5. Perform a hitless line card upgrade (one at a time).

Step 6. Upgrade the Connectivity Management Processor (CMP).

Note Starting with NX-OS Release 5.2(1), simultaneous multiple line card upgrades happen on Nexus switches, thus reducing the upgrade time using ISSU.

Before ISSU is performed, especially when the software is being downgraded, perform a sanity check for the configuration compatibility between the existing software version running on the system and the old image to which the system is being downgraded. This check helps inform the network administrators about the features and configurations that are available in the new release but not in the old release, and those configurations then are removed. The incompatibilities are verified using the command **show incompatibility-all system** *nx-os-file-name*, as in Example 12-19.

Example 12-19 *Verifying Configuration Incompatibilities*

```
NX-1# show incompatibility-all system bootflash:n7000-s2-dk9.7.3.2.D1.1.bin

Checking incompatible configuration(s) for vdc 'NX-1':
-----------------------------------------------------
No incompatible configurations
```

```
Checking dynamic incompatibilities for vdc 'NX-1':
-------------------------------------------------
No incompatible configurations

Checking incompatible configuration(s) for vdc 'TEST':
------------------------------------------------------
No incompatible configurations

Checking dynamic incompatibilities for vdc 'TEST2':
---------------------------------------------------
No incompatible configurations

Checking incompatible configuration(s) for vdc 'TEST3':
-------------------------------------------------------
No incompatible configurations

Checking dynamic incompatibilities for vdc 'TEST4':
---------------------------------------------------
No incompatible configurations
```

An ISSU upgrade is performed using the command **install all kickstart** *kickstart-image* **system** *system-image* **[parallel]**. The **parallel** keyword is used to perform parallel upgrade with I/O modules. ISSU is supposed to perform a nondisruptive software upgrade, which upgrades the software on the Nexus switch without affecting the data plane. For a nondisruptive upgrade, the software must be compatible across releases. If the image is not compatible, the upgrade can be disruptive. Example 12-20 illustrates an example of a disruptive software upgrade from the 6.2(16) image to the 7.3(2)D1(1) image. The output shows that the image is incompatible, so the impact of the upgrade is thus disruptive.

Example 12-20 *ISSU Upgrade*

```
NX-1# install all kickstart bootflash:n7000-s2-kickstart.7.3.2.D1.1.bin system
  bootflash:n7000-s2-dk9.7.3.2.D1.1.bin
Installer will perform compatibility check first. Please wait.

Verifying image bootflash:/n7000-s2-kickstart.7.3.2.D1.1.bin for boot variable
 "kickstart".
[####################] 100% -- SUCCESS

Verifying image bootflash:/n7000-s2-dk9.7.3.2.D1.1.bin for boot variable "system".
[####################] 100% -- SUCCESS

Performing module support checks.
[####################] 100% -- SUCCESS
```

```
Verifying image type.
[####################] 100% -- SUCCESS

Extracting "system" version from image bootflash:/n7000-s2-dk9.7.3.2.D1.1.bin.
[####################] 100% -- SUCCESS

Extracting "kickstart" version from image bootflash:/n7000-s2-
  kickstart.7.3.2.D1.1.bin.
[####################] 100% -- SUCCESS

Extracting "bios" version from image bootflash:/n7000-s2-dk9.7.3.2.D1.1.bin.
[####################] 100% -- SUCCESS

Extracting "lcflnn7k" version from image bootflash:/n7000-s2-dk9.7.3.2.D1.1.bin.
[####################] 100% -- SUCCESS

Notifying services about system upgrade.
[####################] 100% -- SUCCESS




Compatibility check is done:
Module  bootable        Impact  Install-type  Reason
------  --------  --------------  ------------  ------------------
     1       yes       disruptive         reset  Incompatible image
     2       yes       disruptive         reset  Incompatible image
     3       yes       disruptive         reset  Incompatible image
     4       yes       disruptive         reset  Incompatible image




Images will be upgraded according to following table:
Module     Image            Running-Version(pri:alt)           New-Version  Upg-Required
------  ----------  ---------------------------------------  -----------  ------------
     1      system                                              6.2(16)    7.3(2)D1(1)       yes
     1   kickstart                                              6.2(16)    7.3(2)D1(1)       yes
     1        bios  v2.12.0(05/29/2013):v2.12.0(05/29/2013)  v2.12.0(05/29/2013)     no
     2      system                                              6.2(16)    7.3(2)D1(1)       yes
     2   kickstart                                              6.2(16)    7.3(2)D1(1)       yes
     2        bios  v2.12.0(05/29/2013):v2.12.0(05/29/2013)  v2.12.0(05/29/2013)     no
     3    lcflnn7k                                              6.2(16)    7.3(2)D1(1)       yes
     3        bios  v3.0.29(12/15/2015):v3.0.29(12/15/2015)  v3.0.29(12/15/2015)     no
```

```
          4     lcflnn7k                       6.2(16)     7.3(2)D1(1)           yes
          4        bios   v3.0.29(12/15/2015):v3.0.29(12/15/2015)   v3.0.29(12/15/2015)   no


Switch will be reloaded for disruptive upgrade.
Do you want to continue with the installation (y/n)?  [n] y

Install is in progress, please wait.

Performing runtime checks.
[####################] 100% -- SUCCESS

Syncing image bootflash:/n7000-s2-kickstart.7.3.2.D1.1.bin to standby.
[####################] 100% -- SUCCESS

Syncing image bootflash:/n7000-s2-dk9.7.3.2.D1.1.bin to standby.
[####################] 100% -- SUCCESS

Setting boot variables.
[####################] 100% -- SUCCESS

Performing configuration copy.
[####################] 100% -- SUCCESS

Module 1:  Upgrading bios/loader/bootrom.
Warning: please do not remove or power off the module at this time.
[####################] 100% -- SUCCESS

Module 2:  Upgrading bios/loader/bootrom.
Warning: please do not remove or power off the module at this time.
[####################] 100% -- SUCCESS

Module 3:  Upgrading bios/loader/bootrom.
Warning: please do not remove or power off the module at this time.
[####################] 100% -- SUCCESS

Module 4:  Upgrading bios/loader/bootrom.
Warning: please do not remove or power off the module at this time.
[####################] 100% -- SUCCESS

Finishing the upgrade, switch will reboot in 10 seconds.
```

```
NX-1#
>>>
>>>
>>>
NX7k SUP BIOS version ( 2.12 ) : Build - 05/29/2013 11:58:20
PM FPGA Version : 0x00000025
Power sequence microcode revision - 0x00000009 : card type - 10156EEA0
Booting Spi Flash : Primary
  CPU Signature - 0x000106e4: Version - 0x000106e0
  CPU - 2 : Cores - 4 : HTEn - 1 : HT - 2 : Features - 0xbfebfbff
  FSB Clk - 532 Mhz :  Freq - 2144 Mhz - 2128 Mhz
  MicroCode Version : 0x00000002
  Memory - 32768 MB : Frequency - 1067 MHZ
  Loading Bootloader: Done
  IO FPGA Version   : 0x1000d
  PLX Version       : 861910b5
Bios digital signature verification - Passed
USB bootflash status : [1-1:1-1]


Reset Reason Registers: 0x10 0x0
 Filesystem type is ext2fs, partition type 0x83



             GNU GRUB   version 0.97

Autobooting bootflash:/n7000-s2-kickstart.7.3.2.D1.1.bin bootflash:/n7000-s2-dk
9.7.3.2.D1.1.bin...
 Filesystem type is ext2fs, partition type 0x83
Booting kickstart image: bootflash:/n7000-s2-kickstart.7.3.2.D1.1.bin....
................................................................
................................................................
Kickstart digital signature verification Successful
Image verification OK

INIT: version 2boot device node /dev/sda
Bootflash firmware upgrade not required
boot device node /dev/sda
boot mirror device node /dev/sdb
Bootflash mirror firmware upgrade not required
boot mirror device node /dev/sdb
obfl device node /dev/sdc
OBFL firmware upgrade not required
```

```
obfl device node /dev/sdc
slot0 flash device node /dev/sdd
Checking obfl filesystem.
Checking all filesystems..r.r.r.retval=[1]
r done.
Starting mcelog daemon
Creating logflash directories
Loading system software
/bootflash//n7000-s2-dk9.7.3.2.D1.1.bin read done
System image digital signature verification successful.
Uncompressing system image: bootflash:/n7000-s2-dk9.7.3.2.D1.1.bin Sun Mar 5
  09:19:07 UTC 2017
blogger: nothing to do.
C
..done Sun Mar 5 09:19:12 UTC 2017
INIT: Entering runlevel: 3
Starting portmap daemon...
creating NFS state directory: done

System is coming up ... Please wait ...
System is coming up ... Please wait ...
System is coming up ... Please wait ...
System is coming up ... Please wait ...
```

Failures in ISSU can happen at different stages:

- Pre-upgrade and BIOS upgrade
- Standby bootup and switchover
- Line card upgrade

When an ISSU upgrade fails, it is important to determine which component caused the failure. At this point, the first step is to collect the following logs:

- Installer log

    show system internal log install [details]

- Sysmgr and HA-related event-history logs

    show system internal log sysmgr state

    show system internal log sysmgr event-history errors

- Module Manager log

    show module internal event module *slot*

- Upgrade log on line card

    show system internal log sysmgr rtdbctrl

After capturing the relevant logs, it is important to restore the services from ISSU failure. This is done using the command **install all**. This command ensures that the system normalizes with running image and that all the modules are running the same image.

It is important to remember that an ISSU upgrade might not be compatible with all scenarios, such as OTV (in certain releases), LACP Fast rate, and continuous TCNs in the network. Reviewing the ISSU caveats on CCO is thus recommended before performing an upgrade.

Note In case of ISSU failure, it is also important to collect **show tech-support issu** and **show tech-support ha** outputs before the services are recovered.

Graceful Insertion and Removal

In any network deployment, network engineers must perform hardware replacements, hardware and software replacements, or even an intrusive debugging session to identify a root cause of a problem. In any of these instances, engineers do not want to impact any services running on the network. Usually a maintenance window is scheduled and traffic is diverted to a backup path or redundant device to minimize the impact on any services, but this is a tedious task. NX-OS provides the Graceful Insertion and Removal (GIR) feature, which enables you to put devices in maintenance mode and perform any of the previously stated activities without impacting any services. The intent of GIR is to simplify the isolation of a switch from the network using a single set of commands instead of having to manually shut interfaces or alter metrics. In other words, GIR can essentially be called a macro that automates all manual steps to isolate the switch from the network.

GIR has two modes:

- Maintenance mode
- Normal mode

In maintenance mode (also known as the Graceful Removal phase), all data traffic bypasses the node. A parallel path should be available for the GIR to function properly. If no available parallel path exists, service disruptions to the network can arise. Maintenance mode is used to perform maintenance-related activities such as software/hardware upgrades, swaps for bad hardware, or other disruptive activities on the node. The node then can go back to normal mode (also known as Graceful Insertion phase).

To understand the functioning of GIR, examine the topology in Figure 12-4. This topology is a typical spine-leaf topology with two spine nodes and six leaf nodes. The connectivity between spine and leaf is via OSPF.

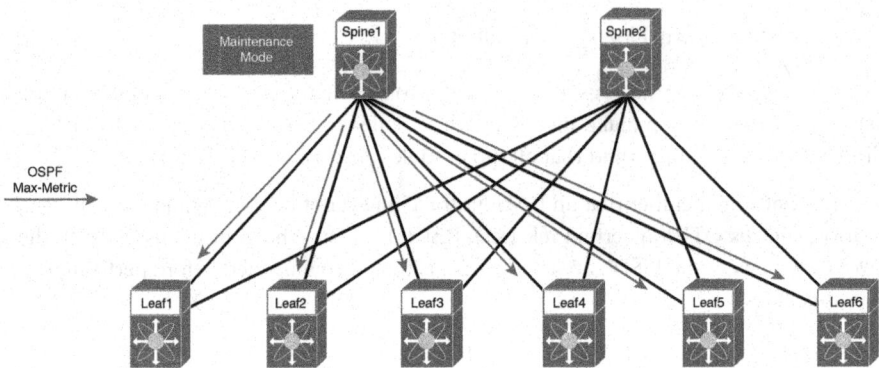

Figure 12-4 *Typical Spine-Leaf Topology*

In this topology, suppose that the spine node Spine1 is set to maintenance mode for performing a software upgrade. The first step in GIR is to advertise costly metrics within the routing protocols. Thus, Spine1 advertises the OSPF max-metric to all its OSPF neighbors. When the leaf nodes receive the max-metric, they alter their forwarding path to push all the traffic through Spine2. At this point, the OSPF neighborship is still up between Spine1 and all six leaf nodes (assuming the default Isolate mode, to be discussed), but no data forwarding is happening via Spine1.

Maintenance mode is supported on Nexus 7000 and 7700 series platforms starting with Release 7.2.0 and on Nexus 5500/5600 platforms starting with Release 7.1.0. Maintenance mode is configured using the command **system mode maintenance [shutdown]**. When the command **system mode maintenance** is configured, GIR is enabled in default mode, also known as Isolate mode. In this mode, the protocol neighborship is maintained and traffic is diverted to the backup or parallel path. When the command **system mode maintenance shutdown** is configured, the GIR is enabled in shutdown mode; the protocols go into shutdown state, links are shut down, and traffic loss can occur. Isolate mode for GIR is recommended over shutdown mode.

Example 12-21 demonstrates the differences in feature-level configuration when the device is configured for isolate mode versus shutdown maintenance mode. In both modes, the command **show system mode** shows that the system mode is *Maintenance*. Before the system goes into maintenance mode, NX-OS takes a snapshot of the current state of the device and saves it as the *before_maintenance* snapshot.

Example 12-21 *Isolate and Shutdown Maintenance Mode*

```
N7k-1(config)# system mode maintenance

Following configuration will be applied:

router bgp 100
  isolate
router eigrp 100
  isolate
router ospf 100
  isolate
router isis IS-IS
  isolate


Do you want to continue (yes/no)? [no] yes

Generating a snapshot before going into maintenance mode

Starting to apply commands...

Applying : router bgp 100
Applying :   isolate
Applying : router eigrp 100
Applying :   isolate
Applying : router ospf 100
Applying :   isolate
Applying : router isis IS-IS
Applying :   isolate

Maintenance mode operation successful.
N7k-1(config)#
2017 Mar  5 20:40:45 N7k-1 %$ VDC-2 %$ %MMODE-2-MODE_CHANGED: System changed to
   "maintenance" mode.

N7k-1# show system mode
System Mode: Maintenance
Maintenance Mode Timer: not running
N7k-1(config)# system mode maintenance shutdown

Following configuration will be applied:

router bgp 100
  shutdown
router eigrp 100
```

Chapter 12: High Availability

```
      shutdown
    address-family ipv6 unicast
      shutdown
router ospf 100
    shutdown
router isis IS-IS
    shutdown
system interface shutdown

NOTE: 'system interface shutdown' will shutdown all interfaces excluding mgmt 0
Do you want to continue (yes/no)? [no] yes

Generating a snapshot before going into maintenance mode

Starting to apply commands...

Applying : router bgp 100
Applying :    shutdown
Applying : router eigrp 100
Applying :    shutdown
Applying :    address-family ipv6 unicast
Applying :       shutdown
Applying : router ospf 100
Applying :    shutdown
Applying : router isis IS-IS
Applying :    shutdown
Applying : system interface shutdown

Maintenance mode operation successful.
```

When the system goes into maintenance mode, the processes that were influenced by maintenance mode change their running state to *Isolate* or *Shutdown*. Example 12-22 displays the different routing protocol processes and their current state on the system.

Example 12-22 *Routing Protocol States during Maintenance Mode*

```
N7k-1# show bgp process

BGP Process Information
BGP Process ID                 : 20105
BGP Protocol Started, reason:  : configuration
BGP Protocol Tag               : 100
BGP Protocol State             : Running (Isolate)
BGP MMODE                      : Initialized
BGP Memory State               : OK
BGP asformat                   : asplain
```

```
! Output omitted for brevity
N7k-1# show ip eigrp
IP-EIGRP AS 100 ID 0.0.0.0 VRF default
  Process-tag: 100
  Instance Number: 1
  Status: running (isolate)
  Authentication mode: none
  Authentication key-chain: none
! Output omitted for brevity
  Redistributed max-prefix: Disabled
  MMODE: Initialized
  Suppress-FIB-Pending Configured
N7k-1# show isis protocol

ISIS process : IS-IS
 Instance number :  1
 UUID: 1090519320
 Process ID 20143
VRF: default
  System ID : 0000.0000.0001  IS-Type : L1-L2
  SAP : 412  Queue Handle : 15
  Maximum LSP MTU: 1492
  Stateful HA enabled
  Graceful Restart enabled. State: Inactive
  Last graceful restart status : none
  Start-Mode Complete
  BFD IPv4 is globally disabled for ISIS process: IS-IS
  BFD IPv6 is globally disabled for ISIS process: IS-IS
  Topology-mode is base
  Metric-style : advertise(wide), accept(narrow, wide)
  Area address(es) :
    49.0001
  Process is up and running (isolate)
! Output omitted for brevity
N7k-1# show ip ospf internal

ospf 100 VRF default
ospf process tag 100
ospf process instance number 1
ospf process uuid 1090519321
ospf process linux pid 20064
ospf process state running(isolate)
System uptime 05:18:06
SUP uptime 2 05:18:06
```

```
Server up           : L3VM|IFMGR|RPM|AM|CLIS|URIB|U6RIB|IP|IPv6|SNMP|BGP|MMODE
Server required    : L3VM|IFMGR|RPM|AM|CLIS|URIB|IP|SNMP
Server registered: L3VM|IFMGR|RPM|AM|CLIS|URIB|IP|SNMP|BGP|MMODE
Server optional    : BGP|MMODE
Early hello : OFF
Force write PSS: FALSE
OSPF mts pkt sap 324
OSPF mts base sap 320
```

After the maintenance activity is performed, the **no system mode maintenance** configuration command brings the system out of maintenance mode. When this command is configured, the system is rolled back to normal mode and all the configuration changes made during the isolate or shutdown maintenance mode are rolled back. Example 12-23 illustrates moving the system from maintenance mode to normal mode. Another snapshot then is taken, with the name *after_maintenance*.

Example 12-23 *Switching from Maintenance Mode to Normal Mode*

```
N7k-1(config)# no system mode maintenance

Following configuration will be applied:

router isis IS-IS
  no isolate
router ospf 100
  no isolate
router eigrp 100
  no isolate
router bgp 100
  no isolate


Do you want to continue (yes/no)? [no] yes


Starting to apply commands...

Applying : router isis IS-IS
Applying :   no isolate
Applying : router ospf 100
Applying :   no isolate
Applying : router eigrp 100
Applying :   no isolate
Applying : router bgp 100
Applying :   no isolate
```

```
Maintenance mode operation successful.

The after_maintenance snapshot will be generated in 120 seconds
After that time, please use 'show snapshots compare before_maintenance after_
  maintenance' to check the health of the system
```

When the system is back to normal mode, verify that the services are normalized, with routes in the Routing Information Base (RIB), VLANs, and so on. The snapshots taken before and after maintenance help verify the same with just a single command. The current available snapshots are verified using the command **show snapshots**. When both the before and after maintenance snapshots are available, use the command **show snapshots compare** *before_maintenance after_maintenance* [**summary**] to compare the system for any differences. Example 12-24 demonstrates the comparison of before and after maintenance snapshots.

Example 12-24 *Comparing Before and After Maintenance Snapshots*

```
N7k-1# show snapshots
Snapshot Name          Time                       Description
--------------------------------------------------------------------------------
after_maintenance      Wed Nov  1 02:42:07 2017   system-internal-snapshot
before_maintenance     Wed Nov  1 02:38:01 2017   system-internal-snapshot
N7k-1# show snapshots compare before_maintenance after_maintenance summary


================================================================================
Feature                           before_maintenance after_maintenance changed
================================================================================
basic summary
  # of interfaces                         63              63
  # of vlans                               1               1
  # of ipv4 routes vrf default            43              43
  # of ipv4 paths  vrf default            46              46
  # of ipv4 routes vrf management          9               9
  # of ipv4 paths  vrf management          9               9
  # of ipv6 routes vrf default             3               3
  # of ipv6 paths  vrf default             3               3

interfaces
  # of eth interfaces                     60              60
  # of eth interfaces up                   7               7
  # of eth interfaces down                53              53
  # of eth interfaces other                0               0
```

```
# of vlan interfaces                  1          1
# of vlan interfaces up               0          0
# of vlan interfaces down             1          1
# of vlan interfaces other            0          0
```

Most production environments have a limit on the duration of the maintenance window. To set the time limit of the system for the maintenance window, configure the timeout value for the maintenance mode using the command **system mode maintenance timeout** *time-in-minutes*. When the timeout value is reached, the system automatically rolls back to normal mode from maintenance mode. Example 12-25 examines configuring the maintenance timeout to 30 minutes and verifying the timeout value using the command **show maintenance timeout**.

Example 12-25 *Maintenance Mode Timeout Settings*

```
N7k-1(config)# system mode maintenance timeout 30

Timer will be started for 30 minutes when the system switches to maintenance mode.
N7k-1# show maintenance timeout
Maintenance mode timeout value: 30 minutes
```

Not all maintenance windows are supposed to be nondisruptive. Some maintenance windows require a system reload, and some are automatically rebooted because of an expected problem on the switch that you are trying to replicate. Thus, before getting into maintenance mode, define the reset-reason for the reload. The command **system mode maintenance on-reload reset-reason** *options* enables you to set the options for different kinds of reloads that are expected during the maintenance window. Multiple options can be set for the reset-reason. Example 12-26 displays all the available reset-reason options and also demonstrates how to set multiple reset-reason options for maintenance mode. The command **show maintenance on-reload reset-reasons** validates the reset-reasons set for a reload event during the maintenance window.

Example 12-26 *On-Reload Reset-Reason Configuration and Verification*

```
Spine2(config)# system mode maintenance on-reload reset-reason ?
  HW_ERROR        Hardware Error
  SVC_FAILURE     Critical service failure
  KERN_FAILURE    Kernel panic
  WDOG_TIMEOUT    Watchdog reset
  FATAL_ERROR     Fatal errors
  LC_FAILURE      LC failure
  MANUAL_RELOAD   Manual reload
  MAINTENANCE     Maintenance mode
  ANY_OTHER       Any other reset
  MATCH_ANY       Any of the above listed reasons
```

```
Spine2(config)# system mode maintenance on-reload reset-reason MANUAL_RELOAD
Spine2(config)# system mode maintenance on-reload reset-reason MAINTENANCE
Spine2# show maintenance on-reload reset-reasons
Reset reasons for on-reload maintenance mode:
---------------------------------------------
MANUAL_RELOAD
MAINTENANCE

bitmap = 0xc0
```

Note If any issues arise with maintenance mode, collect the command **show tech-support mmode** output during or just after the problem is seen.

Custom Maintenance Profile

Both Isolate and Shutdown mode GIR have their respective benefits, but this is not always useful. For instance, if a Nexus switch is acting as a BGP route reflector and is not in the data path, the best approach might be not to shut down BGP on that device or isolate the device from BGP. In such cases, shutdown or isolate maintenance mode could impact services. For such instances, a custom maintenance profile can be created.

Two primary maintenance profiles exist:

- Maintenance-mode
- Normal-mode

Configuration for these profiles first gets generated after the system has been put in maintenance mode and switched back to normal mode. While creating custom profiles, the profile names remain the same, but the configuration inside the profiles can be modified. When you create custom profiles, it appends the commands to the existing maintenance profile. Hence, the first step is to check whether a maintenance profile has been defined. This is verified using the command **show maintenance profile**, as in Example 12-27.

Example 12-27 *Verifying Maintenance and Normal Profile Configurations*

```
N7k-1# show maintenance profile
[Normal Mode]
router isis IS-IS
  no isolate
router ospf 100
  no isolate
router eigrp 100
  no isolate
```

```
router bgp 100
  no isolate

[Maintenance Mode]
router bgp 100
  isolate
router eigrp 100
  isolate
router ospf 100
  isolate
router isis IS-IS
  isolate
```

If the maintenance-mode and normal-mode profiles are not empty, it is better to remove the existing maintenance profiles content and then create the custom profile from scratch. To remove the maintenance profiles, use the command **no configure maintenance profile [maintenance-mode | normal-mode]**. These commands are executed from the exec mode. After removing the existing profile configuration, the command **configure maintenance profile [maintenance-mode | normal-mode]** configures custom profiles from configuration mode. When both the customer maintenance and normal profiles are configured, it is important to also configure the command **system maintenance mode always-use-custom-profile** so that the system-generated custom profile configuration is not generated and used. Example 12-28 demonstrates all the steps to configure the custom profiles for both maintenance and normal modes. In this example, the maintenance-mode profile is configured to isolate BGP and Intermediate System-to-Intermediate System (ISIS) protocols but shut down OSPF, Enhanced Interior Gateway Routing Protocol (EIGRP), and interface Ethernet 3/1. Along with configuring custom maintenance profiles, it is important to save the configuration so that the customer profiles are retained even after the reloads.

Example 12-28 *Configuring Custom Maintenance Profiles*

```
N7k-1# no configure maintenance profile maintenance-mode
Maintenance mode profile maintenance-mode successfully deleted
Enter configuration commands, one per line.  End with CNTL/Z.
Exit maintenance profile mode.
N7k-1# no configure maintenance profile normal-mode
Maintenance mode profile normal-mode successfully deleted
Enter configuration commands, one per line.  End with CNTL/Z.
Exit maintenance profile mode.
N7k-1(config)# configure maintenance profile maintenance-mode
Please configure 'system mode maintenance always-use-custom-profile' if you want to
  use custom profile always for maintenance mode.
```

```
N7k-1(config-mm-profile)#
N7k-1(config-mm-profile)# router bgp 100
N7k-1(config-mm-profile-router)# isolate
N7k-1(config-mm-profile-router)# router ospf 100
N7k-1(config-mm-profile-router)# shutdown
N7k-1(config-mm-profile-router)# router eigrp 100
N7k-1(config-mm-profile-router)# shutdown
N7k-1(config-mm-profile-router)# router isis IS-IS
N7k-1(config-mm-profile-router)# isolate
N7k-1(config-mm-profile-router)# interface e3/1
N7k-1(config-mm-profile-if-verify)# shutdown
N7k-1(config-mm-profile-if-verify)# end

N7k-1(config)# configure maintenance profile normal-mode
Please configure 'system mode maintenance always-use-custom-profile' if you want to
  use custom profile always for maintenance mode.
N7k-1(config-mm-profile)# router ospf 100
N7k-1(config-mm-profile-router)# no shutdown
N7k-1(config-mm-profile-router)# router eigrp 100
N7k-1(config-mm-profile-router)# no shutdown
N7k-1(config-mm-profile-router)# router isis IS-IS
N7k-1(config-mm-profile-router)# no isolate
N7k-1(config-mm-profile-router)# router bgp 100
N7k-1(config-mm-profile-router)# no isolate
N7k-1(config-mm-profile-router)# interface ethernet 3/1
N7k-1(config-mm-profile-if-verify)# no shutdown
N7k-1(config-mm-profile-if-verify)# exit
N7k-1(config-mm-profile)# exit
N7k-1(config)# system mode maintenance always-use-custom-profile

N7k-1# copy running-config startup-config
[########################################] 100%
N7k-1# show maintenance profile
[Normal Mode]
router ospf 100
  no shutdown
router eigrp 100
  no shutdown
router isis IS-IS
  no isolate
router bgp 100
  no isolate
interface Ethernet3/1
  no shutdown
```

```
[Maintenance Mode]
router bgp 100
  isolate
router ospf 100
  shutdown
router eigrp 100
  shutdown
router isis IS-IS
  isolate
interface Ethernet3/1
  shutdown
```

> **Note** Use the command **show running-config mmode** to validate all the configuration settings related to maintenance mode.

To activate maintenance mode with custom profiles, configure the command **system mode maintenance dont-generate-profile**. This command uses the configuration from the custom profile created on the Nexus switch to get into maintenance mode. Example 12-29 illustrates activating maintenance mode using custom profile configurations.

Example 12-29 *Activating Maintenance Mode with Custom Profiles*

```
N7k-1(config)# system mode maintenance dont-generate-profile

Following configuration will be applied:

router bgp 100
  isolate
router ospf 100
  shutdown
router eigrp 100
  shutdown
router isis IS-IS
  isolate
interface Ethernet3/1
  shutdown

Do you want to continue (yes/no)? [no] yes

Generating a snapshot before going into maintenance mode
```

```
Starting to apply commands...

Applying : router bgp 100
Applying :   isolate
Applying : router ospf 100
Applying :   shutdown
Applying : router eigrp 100
Applying :   shutdown
Applying : router isis IS-IS
Applying :   isolate
Applying : interface Ethernet3/1
Applying :   shutdown

Maintenance mode operation successful.
```

Note To debug maintenance mode, use the command **debug mmode logfile**. Enabling this debug also enables logging of the debug logs into a logfile that is viewed using the command **show system internal mmode logfile**. Collecting **show tech-support mmode** command output is also recommended, in case of any failures with GIR.

Summary

NX-OS being the OS for data center switches was built on paradigms of high availability (HA). This chapter focused on some of the high availability features that are commonly used on Nexus switches, including achieving high availability using BFD, which is used with various routing protocols and features. This chapter detailed verifying the hardware programming and using event-history logs to troubleshoot any BFD issues. The following areas should be verified while troubleshooting BFD session issues:

- Ensure that the **no ip redirects** or **no ipv6 redirects** command is enabled on the interface.
- Verify the Error code, explains the reason for the BFD failure:
    - No Diag
    - 1: Control packet detection timer expired
    - 2: Echo function failed
    - 3: Neighbor signaled session down
    - 4: Forwarding plane reset
    - 5: Path down

- 6: Concatenated path down
- 7: Administratively down
- 8: Reverse concatenated path down

In addition, this chapter covered the system high availability features, such as SSO and ISSU, which are critical in a production environment. Performing incremental ISSU upgrades that are nondisruptive is better than performing upgrades using the **reload** command.

The chapter also examined Graceful Insertion and Removal (GIR) and looked at how GIR is used to perform maintenance activities in the network without requiring too many changes. With GIR, maintenance mode is enabled in two modes:

- Isolate mode
- Shutdown mode

Isolate mode is recommended for use with GIR. Finally, this chapter elaborated on how to create and use custom profiles for maintenance windows instead of using system-generated profiles.

References

RFC 5880, Bidirectional Forwarding Detection. D. Katz and D. Ward. IETF, http://tools.ietf.org/html/rfc5880, June 2010.

RFC 5881, Bidirectional Forwarding Detection for IPv4 and IPv6 (Single Hop). D. Katz and D. Ward. IETF, http://tools.ietf.org/html/rfc5881, June 2010.

RFC 5882, Generic Application of Bidirectional Forwarding Detection. D. Katz and D. Ward. IETF, http://tools.ietf.org/html/rfc5882, June 2010.

RFC 5883, Bidirectional Forwarding Detection for Multihop Paths. D. Katz and D. Ward. IETF, http://tools.ietf.org/html/rfc5883, June 2010.

RFC 5884, Bidirectional Forwarding Detection for MPLS Label Switched Paths. R. Aggarwal, K. Kompella, T. Nadeau, and G. Swallow. IETF, http://tools.ietf.org/html/rfc5884, June 2010.

Cisco.com Cisco NX-OS Software Configuration Guides. http://www.cisco.com.

Chapter 13

Troubleshooting Multicast

This chapter covers the following topics:

- Multicast Fundamentals
- NX-OS Multicast Architecture
- IGMP Protocol Operation
- IGMP Configuration and Verification
- PIM Protocol Operation
- PIM Configuration and Verification
- Multicast and Virtual Port-channels (vPC)
- Ethanalyzer Examples For Multicast

Multicast traffic is found in nearly every network deployed today. The concept of multicast communication is easy to understand. A host transmits a message that is intended for multiple recipients. Those recipients are enabled to listen specifically for the multicast traffic of interest and ignore the rest, which supports the efficient use of system resources. However, bringing this simple concept to life in a modern network can be confusing and misunderstood. This chapter introduces multicast communication using Cisco NX-OS. After discussing the fundamental concepts, it presents examples to demonstrate how to verify that the control plane and data plane are functioning as intended. Multicast is a broad topic, and including an example for every feature is not possible. The chapter primarily focuses on the most common deployment options for IPv4; it does not cover multicast communication with IPv6.

Multicast Fundamentals

Network communication is often described as being one of the following types:

- Unicast (one-to-one)
- Broadcast (one-to-all)
- Anycast (one-to-nearest-one)
- Multicast (one-to-many)

The concept of unicast traffic is simply a single source host sending packets to a single destination host. Anycast is another type of unicast traffic, with multiple destination devices sharing the same network layer address. The traffic originates from a single host with a destination anycast address. Packets follow unicast routing to reach the nearest anycast host, where routing metrics determine the nearest device.

Broadcast and multicast both provide a method of one-to-many communication on a network. What makes multicast communication different from broadcast communication is that broadcast traffic must be received and processed by each host that receives it. This typically results in using system resources to process frames that end up being discarded. Multicast traffic, in contrast, is processed only by devices that are interested in receiving the traffic. Multicast traffic is also routable across Layer 3 (L3) subnet boundaries, whereas broadcast traffic is typically constrained to the local subnet. Figure 13-1 demonstrates the difference between broadcast and multicast communication behavior.

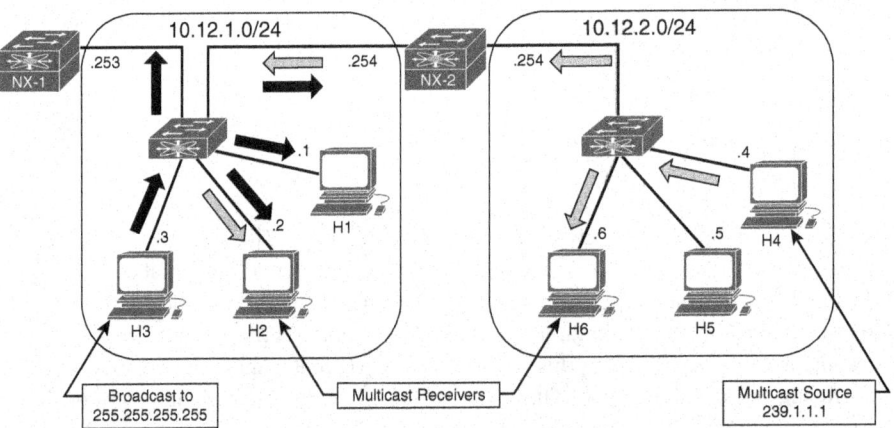

Figure 13-1 *Multicast and Broadcast Communication*

NX-2 is configured to route between the two L3 subnets in Figure 13-1. Host 3 sent a broadcast packet with a destination IP address 255.255.255.255 and destination MAC address of ff:ff:ff:ff:ff:ff. The broadcast traffic is represented by the black arrows. The broadcast packet is flooded from all ports in the L2 switch and received by each device in the 10.12.1.0/24 subnet. Host 1 is the only device running an application that needs to receive this broadcast. Receiving the packets on every other device results in wasted bandwidth and packet processing. NX-2 receives the broadcast but does not forward the packet to the 10.12.2.0/24 subnet. This behavior limits the scope of communication to only devices that are within the same broadcast domain or L3 subnet. Figure 13-1 demonstrates the potential inefficiency of using broadcasts when certain hosts do not need to receive those packets.

Host 4 is sending multicast traffic represented by the white arrows to a group address of 239.1.1.1. These multicast packets are handled differently by the L2 switch and flooded only to Host 6 and NX-2, which is acting as an L3 multicast router (mrouter). NX-2 performs multicast routing and forwards the traffic to the L2 switch, which finally forwards the packets to Host 2. Because NX-1 is not receiving multicast traffic, the L2 switch does not consider it to be an mrouter. If NX-1 is reconfigured to be a multicast router with interested receivers attached, the packet is received and again multicast routed by NX-1 toward its receivers on other subnets. This theoretical behavior of NX-1 is mentioned to demonstrate that the scope of a multicast packet is limited by the time to live (TTL) value set in the IP header by the multicast source, not by an L3 subnet boundary as with broadcasts. Scope is also limited by administrative boundaries, access lists (ACL), or protocol-specific filtering techniques.

Multicast Terminology

The terminology used to describe the state and behaviors of multicast must be defined before diving further into concepts. Table 13-1 lists the multicast terms with their corresponding definition used throughout this chapter.

Table 13-1 *Multicast Terminology*

Term	Definition
mroute	An entry in the Multicast Routing Information Base (MRIB). Different types of mroute entries are associated with the source tree or the shared tree.
Incoming interface (IIF)	The interface of a device that multicast traffic is expected to be received on.
Outgoing interface (OIF)	The interface of a device that multicast traffic is expected to be transmitted out of, toward receivers.
Outgoing interface list (OIL)	The OIFs on which traffic is sent out of the device, toward interested receivers for a particular mroute entry.
Group address	Destination IP address for a multicast group.
Source address	The unicast address of a multicast source. Also referred to as a sender address.

Term	Definition
L2 replication	The act of duplicating a multicast packet at the branch points along a multicast distribution tree. Replication for multicast traffic at L2 is done without rewriting the source MAC address or decrementing the TTL, and the packets stay inside the same broadcast domain.
L3 replication	The act of duplicating a multicast packet at the branch points along a multicast distribution tree. Replication for multicast traffic at L3 requires PIM state and multicast routing. The source MAC address is updated and the TTL is decremented by the multicast router.
Reverse Path Forwarding (RPF) check	Compares the IIF for multicast group traffic to the routing table entry for the source IP address or the RP address. Ensures that multicast traffic flows only away from the source.
Multicast distribution tree (MDT)	Multicast traffic flows from the source to all receivers over the MDT. This tree can be shared by all sources (a shared tree), or a separate distribution tree can be built for each source (a source tree). The shared tree can be one-way or bidirectional.
Protocol Independent Multicast (PIM)	Multicast routing protocol that is used to create MDTs.
RP Tree (RPT)	The MDT between the last-hop router (LHR) and the PIM RP. Also referred to as the shared tree.
Shortest-path tree (SPT)	The MDT between the LHR and the first-hop router (FHR) to the source. Typically follows the shortest path as determined by unicast routing metrics. Also known as the source tree.
Divergence point	The point where the RPT and the SPT diverge toward different upstream devices.
Upstream	A device that is relatively closer to the source along the MDT.
Downstream	A device that is relatively closer to the receiver along the MDT.
Sparse mode	Protocol Independent Multicast Sparse mode (PIM SM) relies on explicit joins from a PIM neighbor before sending traffic toward the receiver.
Dense mode	PIM dense mode (PIM DM) relies on flood-and-prune forwarding behavior. All possible receivers are sent the traffic until a prune is received from uninterested downstream PIM neighbors. NX-OS does not support PIM DM.
rendezvous point (RP)	The multicast router that is the root of the PIM SM shared multicast distribution tree.

Term	Definition
Join	A type of PIM message, but more generically, the act of a downstream device requesting traffic for a particular group or source. This can result in an interface being added to the OIL.
Prune	A type of PIM message, but more generically, the act of a downstream device indicating that traffic for the group or source is no longer requested by a receiver. This can result in the interface being removed from the OIL if no other downstream PIM neighbors are present.
First-hop router (FHR)	The L3 router that is directly adjacent to the multicast source. The FHR performs registration of the source with the PIM RP.
Last-hop router (LHR)	The L3 router that is directly adjacent to the multicast receiver. The LHR initiates a join to the PIM RP and initiates switchover from the RPT to the SPT.
Intermediate router	An L3 multicast-enabled router that forwards packets for the MDT.

The example multicast topology in Figure 13-2 illustrates the terminology in Table 13-1.

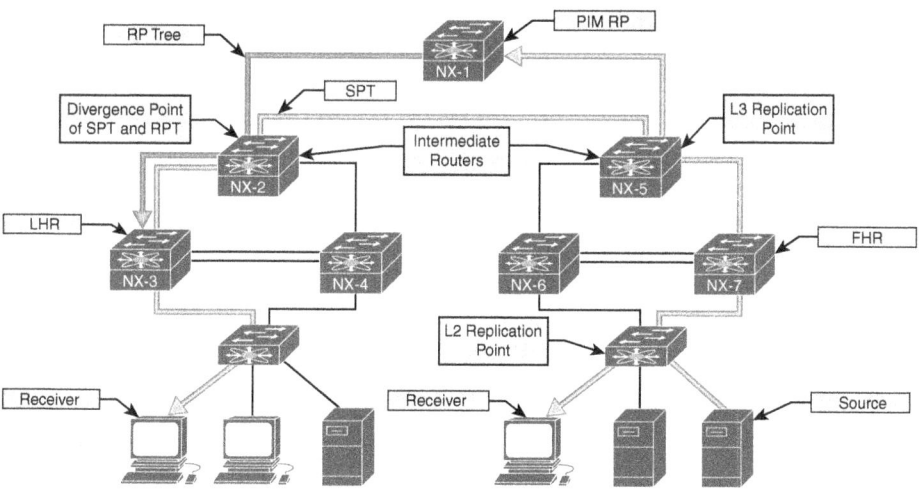

Figure 13-2 *Visualizing Multicast Terminology*

Figure 13-2 illustrates a typical deployment of PIM Sparse mode any-source multicast (ASM). The end-to-end traffic flow from the source to the receiver is made possible through several intermediate steps to build the MDT:

Step 1. Register the source with the PIM RP.

Step 2. Establish the RPT from the RP to the receiver.

Step 3. Establish the SPT from the source to the receiver.

When troubleshooting a multicast problem, determining which of these intermediate steps are completed guides the investigation based on the current state of the network. Each intermediate step consists of different checks, conditions, and protocol state machines that this chapter explores in depth.

Note Figure 13-2 shows both the RP tree and the source tree in the diagram, for demonstration purposes. This state does not persist in reality because NX-3 prunes itself from the RP tree and receives the group traffic from the source tree.

Layer 2 Multicast Addresses

At L2, hosts communicate using Media Access Control Addresses (MAC addresses). A MAC address is 48-bits in length and is a unique identifier for a Network Interface Card (NIC) on the LAN Segment. MAC addresses are represented by a 12-digit hexadecimal number in the format 0012.3456.7890, or 00:12:34:56:78:90.

The MAC address used by a host is typically assigned by the manufacturer and is referred to as the Burned-In-Address (BIA). When two hosts in the same IP subnet communicate, the destination address of the L2 frame is set to the target device's MAC address. As frames are received, if the target MAC address matches the BIA of the host, the frame is accepted and handed to higher layers for further processing.

Broadcast messages between hosts are sent to the reserved address of FF:FF:FF:FF:FF:FF. A host receiving a broadcast message must process the frame and pass its contents to a higher layer for additional processing where the frame is either discarded or acted upon by an application. As mentioned previously, for applications that do not need to be received by each host on the network the inefficiencies of broadcast communication can be improved upon by utilizing multicast.

Multicast communication requires a way of identifying frames at Layer 2 that are not broadcasts but can still be processed by one or more hosts on the LAN segment. This allows hosts that are interested in this traffic to process the frames and permits hosts that are not interested to throw away the frames and save processing and buffer resources.

The multicast MAC address differentiates multicast from unicast or broadcast frames at Layer 2. The reserved range of multicast MAC addresses designated in RFC 1112 are from 01:00:5E:00:00:00 to 01:00:5E:7F:FF:FF. The first 24 bits are always 01:00:5E. The first byte contains the individual/group (I/G) bit, which is set to 1 to indicate a multicast MAC address. The 25th bit is always 0, which leaves 23 bits of the address remaining. The Layer 3 group address is mapped to the remaining 23 bits to form the complete multicast MAC address (see Figure 13-3).

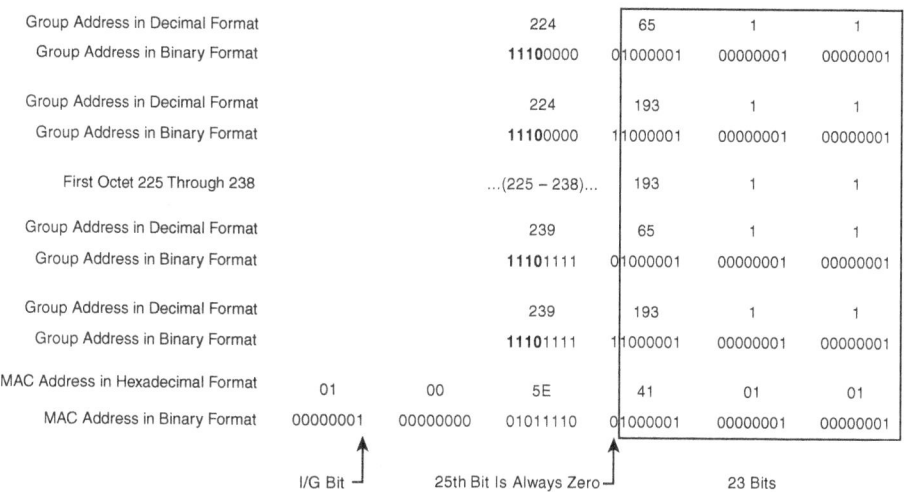

Figure 13-3 *Mapping Layer 3 Group Address to Multicast MAC Address*

When expanded in binary format, it is clear that multiple L3 group addresses must map to the same multicast MAC address. In fact, 32 L3 multicast group addresses map to each multicast MAC address. This is because 9 bits from the L3 group address do not get mapped to the multicast MAC address. The 4 high-order bits of the first octet are always 1110, and the remaining 4 bits of the first octet are variable. Remember that the multicast group IP address has the first octet in the range of 224 to 239. The first high-order bit of the third octet is ignored when the L3 group address is mapped to the multicast MAC address. This is the 25th bit of the multicast MAC address that is always set to zero. Combined, the potential variability of those 5 bits is 32 (2^5), which explains why 32 multicast groups map to each multicast MAC address.

For a host, this overlap means that if its NIC is programmed to listen to a particular multicast MAC address, it could receive frames for multiple multicast groups. For example, imagine that a source is active on a LAN segment and is generating multicast group traffic to 233.65.1.1, 239.65.1.1 and 239.193.1.1. All these groups are mapped to the same multicast MAC address. If the host is interested only in packets for 239.65.1.1, it cannot differentiate the different groups at L2. All the frames are passed to a higher layer where the uninteresting frames get discarded, while the interesting frames are sent to the application for processing. The 32:1 overlap must be considered when deciding on a multicast group addressing scheme. It is also advisable to avoid using groups X.0.0.Y and X.128.0.Y because the multicast MAC overlaps with 224.0.0.X. These frames are flooded by switches on all ports in the same VLAN.

Layer 3 Multicast Addresses

IPv4 multicast addresses are identified by the value of the first octet. A multicast address has the first octet of the address fall in the range of 224.0.0.0 to 239.255.255.255, which is also referred to as the Class D range. Viewed in binary format, a multicast address always has the first 4 bits in the first octet set to a value of *1110*. The concept of subnetting does not exist with multicast because each address identifies an individual multicast group address. However, various address blocks within the 224.0.0.0/4 multicast range signify a specific purpose based on their address. The Internet Assigned Numbers Authority (IANA) lists the multicast address ranges provided in Table 13-2.

Table 13-2 *IPv4 Multicast Address Space Registry*

Designation	Multicast Address Range
Local Network Control Block	224.0.0.0 to 224.0.0.255
Internetwork Control Block	224.0.1.0 to 224.0.1.255
AD-HOC Block I	224.0.2.0 to 224.0.255.255
Reserved	224.1.0.0 to 224.1.255.255
SDP/SAP Block	224.2.0.0 to 224.2.255.255
AD-HOC Block II	224.3.0.0 to 224.4.255.255
Reserved	224.5.0.0 to 224.251.255.255
DIS Transient Groups	224.252.0.0 to 224.255.255.255
Reserved	225.0.0.0 to 231.255.255.255
Source-Specific Multicast Block	232.0.0.0 to 232.255.255.255
GLOP Block	233.0.0.0 to 233.251.255.255
AD-HOC Block III	233.252.0.0 to 233.255.255.255
Unicast Prefix-based IPv4 Multicast Addresses	234.0.0.0 to 234.255.255.255
Reserved	235.0.0.0 to 238.255.255.255
Organization-Local Scope	239.0.0.0 to 239.255.255.255

The Local Network Control Block is used for protocol communication traffic. Examples are the *All routers in this subnet* address of 224.0.0.2 and the *All OSPF routers* address of 224.0.0.5. Addresses in this range should not be forwarded by any multicast router, regardless of the TTL value carried in the packet header. In practice, protocol packets that utilize the Local Network Control Block are almost always sent with a TTL of 1.

The Internetwork Control Block is used for protocol communication traffic that is forwarded by a multicast router between subnets or to the Internet. Examples include Cisco-RP-Announce 224.0.1.39, Cisco-RP-Discovery 224.0.1.40, and NTP 224.0.1.1.

Table 13-3 provides the well-known multicast addresses used by control plane protocols from the Local Network Control Block and from the Internetwork Control Block. It is important to become familiar with these specific reserved addresses so they are easily identifiable while troubleshooting a control plane problem.

Table 13-3 *Well-Known Reserved Multicast Addresses*

Description	Multicast Address
All Hosts in this subnet (all-hosts group)	224.0.0.1
All Routers in this subnet (all-routers)	224.0.0.2
All OSPF routers (AllSPFRouters)	224.0.0.5
All OSPF DRs (AllDRouters)	224.0.0.6
All RIPv2 routers	224.0.0.9
All EIGRP routers	224.0.0.10
All PIM routers	224.0.0.13
VRRP	224.0.0.18
IGMPv3	224.0.0.22
HSRPv2 and GLBP	224.0.0.102
NTP	224.0.1.1
Cisco-RP-Announce (Auto-RP)	224.0.1.39
Cisco-RP-Discovery (Auto-RP)	224.0.1.40
PTPv1	224.0.1.129 to 224.0.1.132
PTPv2	224.0.1.129

The Source-Specific Multicast Block is used by SSM, an extension of PIM Sparse mode that is described later in this chapter. It is optimized for one-to-many applications when the host application is aware of the specific source IP address of a multicast group. Knowing the source address eliminates the need for a PIM RP and does not require any multicast routers to maintain state on the shared tree.

The Organization-Local Scope is also known as the Administratively Scoped Block. These addresses are the multicast equivalent to RFC1918 unicast IP addresses, in which an organization assigns addresses from this range as needed. These addresses are not publicly routed or administered by IANA.

NX-OS Multicast Architecture

The multicast architecture of NX-OS inherits the same design principals as the operating system itself. Each component process is fully modular, creating the foundation for high availability (HA), reliability, and scalability.

The NX-OS HA architecture allows for stateful process restart and in-service software upgrades (ISSU) with minimal disruption to the data plane. As Figure 13-4 shows, the architecture is distributed with platform-independent (PI) components running on the supervisor module and hardware-specific components that forward traffic running on the I/O modules or system application-specific integrated circuits (ASIC).

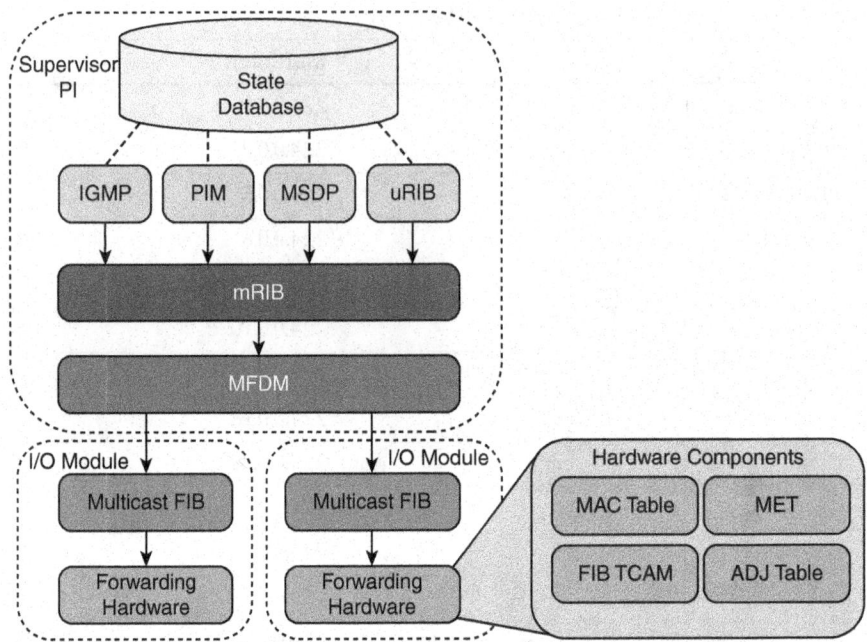

Figure 13-4 *NX-OS Multicast Architecture*

This common architecture is used across all NX-OS platforms. However, each platform can implement the forwarding components differently, depending on the capabilities of the specific hardware ASICs.

Each protocol, such as Internet Group Management Protocol (IGMP), Protocol Independent Multicast (PIM), and Multicast Source Discovery Protocol (MSDP), operates independently with its own process state, which is stored using the NX-OS Persistent Storage Services (PSS). Message and Transactional Services (MTS) is used to communicate and exchange protocol state messages with other services, such as the Multicast Routing Information Base (MRIB).

The MRIB is populated by client protocols such as PIM, IGMP, and MSDP to create multicast routing state entries. These mroute states describe the relationship of the router to a particular MDT and are populated by the various MRIB client protocols, such as IGMP, PIM, and IP. After MRIB creates the mroute state, it pushes this state to the Multicast Forwarding Distribution Manager (MFDM).

The MRIB interacts with the Unicast Routing Information Base (URIB) to obtain routing protocol metrics and next-hop information used during Reverse Path Forwarding (RPF) lookups. Any multicast packets that are routed by the supervisor in the *software forwarding* path are also handled by the MRIB.

MFDM is an intermediary between the MRIB and the platform-forwarding components. It is responsible for taking the mroute state from the MRIB and allocating platform resources for each entry. MFDM translates the MRIB into data structures that the platform components understand. The data structures are then pushed from MFDM to each I/O module, in the case of a distributed platform such as the Nexus 7000 series. In a nonmodular platform, MFDM distributes its information to the platform-forwarding components.

The Multicast Forwarding Information Base (MFIB) programs the (*, G) and (S, G) and RPF entries it receives from MFDM into hardware forwarding tables known as FIB (ternary content-addressable memory) TCAM. The TCAM is a high-speed memory space that is used to store a pointer to the adjacency. The adjacency is then used to obtain the Multicast Expansion Table (MET) index. The MET index contains information about the OIFs and how to replicate and forward the packet to each downstream interface. Many platforms and I/O modules have dedicated replication ASICs. The steps described here vary based on the type of hardware a platform uses, and troubleshooting at this depth typically involves working with Cisco TAC Support. Table 13-4 provides a mapping of multicast components to show commands used to verify the state of each component process.

Table 13-4 *CLI Commands for Each Multicast Component*

Component	CLI Command
IGMP	show ip igmp route
	show ip igmp groups
	show ip igmp snooping groups
PIM	show ip pim route
MSDP	show ip msdp route
	show ip msdp sa-cache
URIB	show ip route
MRIB	show routing ip multicast [group] [source]
	show ip mroute
MFDM	show forwarding distribution ip multicast route
	show forwarding distribution ip igmp snooping
Multicast FIB	show forwarding ip multicast route module [module number]
Forwarding Hardware	show system internal forwarding ip multicast route
	show system internal ip igmp snooping
TCAM, MET, ADJ Table	Varies by platform and hardware type

When Virtual Device Contexts (VDC) are used with the Nexus 7000 series, all of the previously mentioned PI components are unique to the VDC. Each VDC has its own PIM, IGMP, MRIB, and MFDM processes. However, in each I/O module, the system resources are shared among the different VDCs.

Replication

Multicast communication is efficient because a single packet from the source can be replicated many times as it traverses the MDT toward receivers located along different branches of the tree. Replication can occur at L2 when multiple receivers are in the same VLAN on different interfaces, or at L3 when multiple downstream PIM neighbors have joined the MDT from different OIFs.

Replication of multicast traffic is handled by specialized hardware, which is different on each Nexus platform. In the case of a distributed platform with different I/O modules, *egress replication* is used (see Figure 13-5).

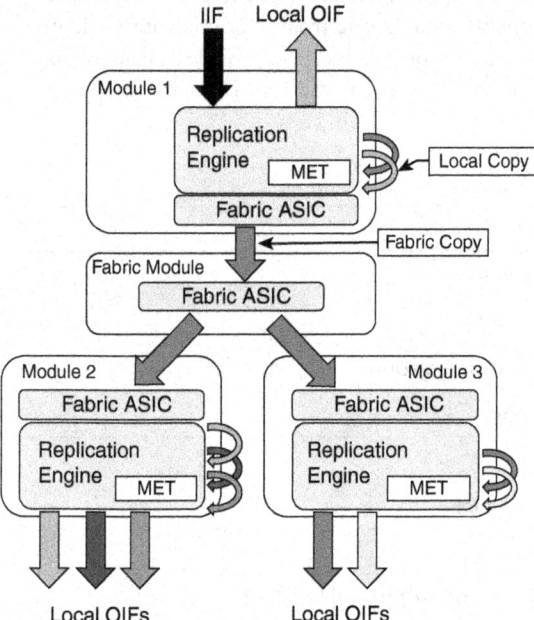

Figure 13-5 *Egress Multicast Replication*

The benefit of egress replication is that it allows all modules of the system to share the load of packet replication, which increases the forwarding capacity and scalability of the platform. As traffic arrives from the IIF, the following happens:

- The packet is replicated for any receivers on the local module.
- A copy of the packet is sent to the fabric module.
- The fabric module replicates additional copies of the packet, one for each module that has an OIF.
- At each egress module, additional packet copies are made for each local receiver based on the contents of the MET table.

The MET tables on each module contain a list of local OIFs. For improved scalability, each module maintains its own MET tables. In addition, multicast forwarding entries that share the same OIFs can share the same MET entries, which further improves scalability.

Protecting the Central Processing Unit

Multicast traffic can be directed to the Supervisor CPU for a number of reasons. A few possibilities include these:

- Non-RPF traffic used to generate a PIM Assert message
- A packet in which the TTL has expired in transit
- The initial packet from a new source used to create a PIM register message
- IGMP membership reports used to create entries in the snooping table
- Multicast control plane packets for PIM or IGMP

NX-OS uses control plane policing (CoPP) policies to protect the supervisor CPU from excessive traffic. The individual CoPP classes used for multicast traffic vary from platform to platform, but they all serve an important role: to protect the device. Leaving CoPP enabled is always recommended, although exceptional cases require modifying some of the classes or policer rates. The currently applied CoPP policy is viewed with the **show policy-map interface control-plane** command. Table 13-5 provides additional detail about the default CoPP classes related to multicast traffic.

Table 13-5 *CoPP Classes for Multicast*

CoPP Class	Description
copp-system-p-class-multicast-router	Matches multicast control plane protocols such as MSDP, PIM messages to ALL-PIM-ROUTERs (224.0.0.13) and PIM register messages (unicast)
copp-system-p-class-multicast-host	Matches IGMP packets
copp-system-p-class-normal	Matches traffic from directly connected multicast sources that is used to build PIM register messages
Class-default	Catchall class any packets that do not match another CoPP class

In addition to CoPP, which polices traffic arriving at the supervisor, the Nexus 7000 series uses a set of hardware rate limiters (HWRL). The hardware rate limiters exist on each I/O module and control the amount of traffic that can be directed toward the supervisor. The status of the HWRL is viewed with the **show hardware rate-limiter** (see Example 13-1).

Example 13-1 *Nexus 7000 Hardware Rate Limiters*

```
NX-1# show hardware rate-limiter
! Output omitted for brevity

Units for Config: packets per second
Allowed, Dropped & Total: aggregated since last clear counters
rl-1: STP and Fabricpath-ISIS
rl-2: L3-ISIS and OTV-ISIS
rl-3: UDLD, LACP, CDP and LLDP
rl-4: Q-in-Q and ARP request
rl-5: IGMP, NTP, DHCP-Snoop, Port-Security, Mgmt and Copy traffic


Module: 3

Rate-limiter PG Multiplier: 1.00


    R-L Class           Config          Allowed         Dropped           Total
+-------------------+-----------+-----------------+---------------+-----------------+
    L3 mtu               500              0                0                0
    L3 ttl               500              12               0                12
    L3 control           10000            0                0                0
    L3 glean             100              1                0                1
    L3 mcast dirconn     3000             13               0                13
    L3 mcast loc-grp     3000             2                0                2
    L3 mcast rpf-leak    500              0                0                0
    L2 storm-ctrl        Disable
    access-list-log      100              0                0                0
    copy                 30000            7182002          0                7182002
    receive              30000            27874374         0                27874374
    L2 port-sec          500              0                0                0
    L2 mcast-snoop       10000            34318            0                34318
    L2 vpc-low           4000             0                0                0
    L2 l2pt              500              0                0                0
    L2 vpc-peer-gw       5000             0                0                0
    L2 lisp-map-cache    5000             0                0                0
    L2 dpss              100              0                0                0
    L3 glean-fast        100              0                0                0
    L2 otv               100              0                0                0
    L2 netflow           48000            0                0                0
    L3 auto-config       200              0                0                0
    Vxlan-peer-learn     100              0                0                0
```

Table 13-6 describes each multicast HWRL.

Table 13-6 *Hardware Rate Limiters for Multicast*

R-L Class	Description
L3 mcast dirconn	Packets for which the source is directly connected. These packets are sent to the CPU to generate PIM register messages.
L3 mcast loc-grp	Packets sent to the CPU at the LHR to trigger SPT switchover.
L3 mcast rpf-leak	Packets sent to the CPU to create a PIM assert message.
L2 mcast-snoop	IGMP membership reports, queries, and PIM hello packets punted to the CPU for IGMP snooping.

As with the CoPP policy, disabling any of the HWRLs that are enabled by default is not advised. In most deployments, no modification to the default CoPP or HWRL configuration is necessary.

If excessive traffic to the CPU is suspected, incrementing matches or drops in a particular CoPP class or HWRL provide a hint about what traffic is arriving. For additional detail, an Ethanalyzer capture can look at the CPU-bound traffic for troubleshooting purposes.

NX-OS Multicast Implementation

Many network environments consist of a mix of Cisco NX-OS devices and other platforms. It is therefore important to understand the differences in default behavior between NX-OS and Cisco IOS devices. NX-OS has the following differences:

- Multicast does not have to be enabled globally.
- Certain features (PIM, MSDP) must be enabled before they are configurable. IGMP is automatically enabled when PIM is enabled.
- Removing a feature removes all related configuration.
- PIM dense mode is not supported.
- Multipath support is enabled by default. This allows multicast traffic to be load-balanced across equal-cost multipath (ECMP) routes.
- Punted multicast data packets are not replicated by default (this is enabled by configuring **ip routing multicast software-replicate** only if needed).
- PIM IPsec AH-MD5 neighbor authentication is supported.
- PIM snooping is not supported.
- IGMP snooping uses an IP-based forwarding table by default. IGMP snooping based on MAC address table lookup is a configurable option.
- NX-OS platforms might require the allocation of TCAM space for multicast routes.

Static Joins

In general, static joins should not be required when multicast has been correctly configured. However, this is a useful option for troubleshooting in certain situations. For example, if a receiver is not available, a static join is used to build multicast state in the network.

NX-OS offers the **ip igmp join-group** [*group*] [*source*] interface command, which configures the NX-OS device as a multicast receiver for the group. Providing the source address is not required unless the join is for IGMPv3. This command forces NX-OS to issue an IGMP membership report and join the group as a host. All packets received for the group address are processed in the control plane of the device. This command can prevent packets from being replicated to other OIFs and should be used with caution.

The second option is the **ip igmp static-oif** [*group*] [*source*] interface command, which statically adds an OIF to an existing mroute entry and forwards packets to the OIF in hardware. The source option is used only with IGMPv3. It is important to note that if this command is being added to a VLAN interface, you must also configure a static IGMP snooping table entry with the **ip igmp snooping static-group** [*group*] [*source*] **interface** [*interface name*] VLAN configuration command to actually forward packets.

Clearing an MROUTE Entry

A common way to clear the data structures associated with a multicast routing entry is to use the **clear ip mroute** command. In Cisco IOS platforms, this command is effective in clearing the entry. However, in NX-OS, the data structures associated with a particular mroute entry might have come from any MRIB client protocol. NX-OS provides the commands necessary to clear the individual MRIB client entries. In NX-OS 7.3, the **clear ip mroute *** command was enhanced to automatically clear the individual client protocols as well as the MRIB entry. In older releases of NX-OS, it is necessary to issue additional commands to completely clear an mroute entry from the MRIB and all associated client protocols:

- **clear ip mroute *** clears entries from the MRIB.
- **clear ip pim route *** clears PIM entries created by PIM join messages.
- **clear ip igmp route *** clears IGMP entries created by IGMP membership reports.
- **clear ip mroute data-created *** clears MRIB entries created by receiving multicast data packets.

Multicast Boundary and Filtering

The Cisco IOS equivalent of a multicast boundary does not exist in NX-OS. In Cisco IOS, the multicast boundary command is a filter applied to an interface to create an administratively scoped boundary where multicast traffic can be filtered on the interface. The following control plane and data plane filtering techniques are used to create an administrative boundary in NX-OS:

- Filter PIM join messages: **ip pim jp-policy** [*route-map*] [*in* | *out*]
- Filter IGMP membership reports: **ip igmp report-policy** [*route-map*]
- Data traffic filter: **ip access-group** [*ACL*] [*in* | *out*]

In addition, the **ip pim border** command can be configured on an interface to prevent the forwarding of any Auto-RP, bootstrap, or candidate-RP messages.

Event-Histories and Show Techs

NX-OS provides event-histories, which are an always-on log of significant process events for enabled features. In many cases, the event-history log is sufficient for troubleshooting in detail without additional debugging. The various event-history logs for multicast protocols and processes are referenced throughout this chapter for troubleshooting purposes. Certain troubleshooting situations call for an increase in the default event-history size because of the large volume of protocol messages. Each event-history type can be increased in size, independent of the other types. For PIM, the event-history size is increased with the **ip pim event-history** [*event type*] **size** [*small* | *medium* | *large*] configuration command. IGMP is increased with the **ip igmp event-history** [*event type*] **size** [*small* | *medium* | *large*] configuration command.

Each feature or service related to forwarding multicast traffic in NX-OS has its own **show tech-support** [*feature*] output. These commands are typically used to collect the majority of data for a problem in a single output that can be analyzed offline or after the fact. The tech support file contains configurations, data structures, and event-history output for each specific feature. If a problem is encountered and the time to collect information is limited, the following list of NX-OS tech support commands can be captured and redirected to individual files in bootflash for later review:

- show tech-support ip multicast
- show tech-support forwarding l2 multicast vdc-all
- show tech-support forwarding l3 multicast vdc-all
- show tech-support pixm
- show tech-support pixmc-all
- show tech-support module all

Knowing what time the problem might have occurred is critical so that the various system messages and protocol events can be correlated in the event-history output. If the problem occurred in the past, some or all of the event-history buffers might have wrapped and the events related to the problem condition could be gone. In such situations, increasing the size of certain event-history buffers might be useful for when the problem occurs again.

After collecting all the data, the files can be combined into a single archive and compressed for Cisco support to investigate the problem.

Providing an exhaustive list of commands for every possible situation is impossible. However, the provided list will supply enough information to narrow the scope of the problem, if not point to a root cause. Also remember that multicast problems are rarely isolated to a single device, which means it could be necessary to collect the data set from a peer device or PIM neighbor as well.

IGMP

Hosts use the IGMP protocol to dynamically join and leave a multicast group through the LHR. With IGMP, a host can join or leave a group at any time. Without IGMP, a multicast router has no way of knowing when interested receivers reside on one of its interfaces or when those receivers are no longer interested in the traffic. It should be obvious that, without IGMP, the efficiencies in bandwidth and resource utilization in a multicast network would be severely diminished. Imagine if every multicast router sent traffic for each group on every interface! For that reason, hosts and routers must support IGMP if they are configured to support multicast communication. In the NX-OS implementation of IGMP, a single IGMP process serves all virtual routing and forwarding (VRF) instances. If Virtual Device Contexts (VDC) are being used, an IGMP process runs on each VDC.

IGMPv1 was defined in RFC 1112 and provided a state machine and the messaging required for hosts to join and leave multicast groups by sending membership reports to the local router. Finding a device using IGMPv1 in a modern network is uncommon, but an overview of its operation is provided for historical purposes so that the differences and evolution in IGMPv2 and IGMPv3 are easier to understand.

A multicast router configured for IGMPv1 periodically sends query messages to the *All-Hosts* address of 224.0.0.1. The host then waits for a random time interval, within the bounds of a report delay timer, to send a membership report using the group address as the destination address for the membership report. The multicast router receives the message indicating that traffic for a specific group should be sent. When the router receives the membership report, it knows that a host on the segment is a current member of the multicast group and starts forwarding the group traffic onto the segment. A functional reason for using the group address as the destination of the membership report is so that hosts are aware of the presence of other receivers for the group on the same network. This allows a host to suppress its own report message, to reduce the volume of IGMP traffic on a segment. A multicast router needs to receive only a single membership report to begin sending traffic onto the segment.

When a host wants to join a new multicast group, it can immediately send a membership report for the group; it does not have to wait for a query message from a multicast router. However, when a host wants to leave a group, IGMPv1 does not provide a way to indicate this to the local multicast router. The host simply stops responding to queries. If the router receives no further membership reports, it sends three queries before pruning off the interface from the OIL and determining that interested receivers are no longer present.

IGMPv2

Defined in RFC 2236, IGMPv2 provides additional functionality over IGMPv1. It required an additional message to be defined to implement the new functionality. Figure 13-6 shows the IGMP message format.

8 Bits	8 Bits	16 Bits
Type	Max Resp Time	Checksum
Group Address		

Figure 13-6 *IGMP Message Format*

The IGMPv2 message fields are defined in the following list:

- **Type:**
    - 0x11 Membership query (general query or group specific query)
    - 0x12 Version 1 membership report (used for backward compatibility)
    - 0x16 Version 2 membership report
    - 0x17 Leave group
- **Max Response Time:** Used only in membership query messages and is set to zero in all other message types. This is used to tune the response time of hosts and the leave latency observed when the last member decides to leave the group.
- **Checksum:** Used to ensure the integrity of the IGMP message.
- **Group Address:** Set to zero in a general query and set to the group address when sending a group specific query. In a membership report or leave group message, the group address is set to the group being reported or left.

Note IP packets carrying IGMP messages have the TTL set to 1 and the router alert option set in the IP header, to force routers to examine the packet contents.

In IGMPv2, an election to determine the IGMP querier is specified whenever more than one multicast router is present on the network segment. Upon startup, a multicast router sends an IGMP general query message to the All-Hosts group 224.0.0.1. When a router receives a general query message from another multicast router, a check is performed and the router with the lowest IP address assumes the role of the querier. The querier is then responsible for sending query messages on the network segment.

The process of joining a multicast group is similar in IGMPv2 to IGMPv1. A host responds to general queries as well as group-specific queries with a membership report message. A host implementation chooses a random time to respond, between zero seconds and the max-response-interval sent in the query message. A host can also send an unsolicited membership report when a new group is joined to initiate the flow of multicast traffic on the segment.

The leave group message was defined to address the IGMPv1 problem in which a host could not explicitly inform the network after deciding to leave a group. This message type is used to inform a router when the multicast group is no longer needed on the segment and all members have left the group. If a host is the last member to send a membership report on the segment, it should send a leave group message when the host no longer wants to receive the group traffic. This leave group message is sent to the All-Routers multicast address 224.0.0.2. When the querier receives this message, it sends a group-specific query in response, which is also a new functionality enhancement over IGMPv1. The group-specific query message uses the multicast group's destination IP address, to ensure that any host listening on the group receives the query. These messages are sent based on the last member query interval. If a membership report is not received, the router prunes the interface from the OIL.

IGMPv3

IGMPv3 was specified in RFC 3376. It allows a host to support the functionality required for Source Specific Multicast (SSM). SSM multicast allows a receiver to specifically join not only the multicast group address, but also the source address for a particular group. Applications running on a multicast receiver host can now request specific sources.

In IGMPv3, the interface state of the host includes a filter mode and source list. The filter mode can be include or exclude. When the filter mode is include, traffic is requested only from the sources in the source list. If the filter mode is exclude, traffic is requested for any source except the ones present in the source list. The source list is an unordered list of IP unicast source addresses, which can be combined with the filter mode to implement source-specific logic. This allows IGMPv3 to signal only the sources of interest to the receiver in the protocol messages.

Figure 13-7 provides the IGMPv3 membership query message format, which includes several new fields when compared to the IGMPv2 membership query message, although the message type remains the same (0x11).

8 Bits	8 Bits	16 Bits
Type = 0x11	Max Resp Code	Checksum
Group Address		
Resv / S / QRV	QQIC	Number of Sources (N)
Source Address [1]		
Source Address [2]		
.		
Source Address [N]		

Figure 13-7 *IGMPv3 Membership Query Message Format*

The IGMPv3 membership query message fields are defined as follows:

- **Type 0x11:** Membership query (general query, group specific query, or group and source specific query). These messages are differentiated by the contents of the group address and source address fields.
- **Max Resp Code:** The maximum time allowed for a host to send a responding report. It enables the operator to tune the burstiness of IGMP traffic and the leave latency.
- **Checksum:** Ensures the integrity of the IGMP message. It is calculated over the entire IGMP message.
- **Group Address:** Set to zero for general query and is equal to the group address for group specific or source and group specific queries.
- **Resv:** Set to zero and ignored on receipt.
- **S Flag:** When set to 1, suppresses normal timer updates that routers perform when receiving a query.
- **QRV:** Querier's robustness variable. Used to overcome a potential packet loss. It allows a host to send multiple membership report messages to ensure that the querier receives them.
- **QQIC:** Querier's query interval code. Provides the querier's query interval (QQI).
- **Number of Sources:** Specifies how many sources are present in the query.
- **Source Address:** Specific source unicast IP addresses.

Several differences appear when compared to IGMPv2. The most significant is the capability to have group and source specific queries, enabling query messages to be sent for specific sources of a multicast group.

The membership report message type for IGMPv3 is identified by the message type 0x22 and involves several changes when compared to the membership report message used in IGMPv2. Receiver hosts use this message type to report the current membership state of their interfaces, as well as any change in the membership state to the local multicast router. Hosts send this message to multicast routers using the group IP destination address of 224.0.0.22. Figure 13-8 shows the format of the membership report for IGMPv3.

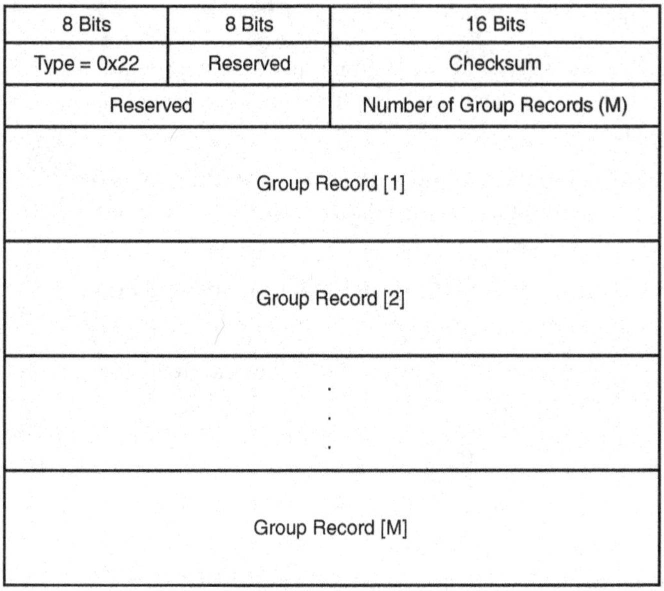

754   Chapter 13: Troubleshooting Multicast

8 Bits	8 Bits	16 Bits
Type = 0x22	Reserved	Checksum
Reserved		Number of Group Records (M)
Group Record [1]		
Group Record [2]		
. . .		
Group Record [M]		

Figure 13-8 *IGMPv3 Membership Report Message Format*

Each group record in the membership report uses the format shown in Figure 13-9.

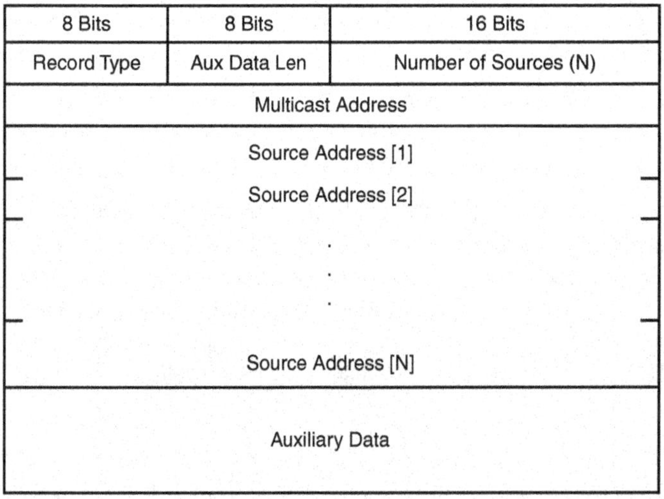

8 Bits	8 Bits	16 Bits
Record Type	Aux Data Len	Number of Sources (N)
Multicast Address		
Source Address [1]		
Source Address [2]		
. . .		
Source Address [N]		
Auxiliary Data		

Figure 13-9 *IGMPv3 Membership Report Group Record Format*

The IGMPv3 membership report message fields are defined in the following list:

- **Type 0x22:** IGMPv3 membership report
- **Reserved:** Set to zero on transmit and ignored on receipt

- **Checksum:** Verifies the integrity of the message
- **Number of Group Records:** Provides the number of group records present in this membership report
- **Group Record:** A block of fields that provides the sender's membership in a single multicast group on the interface from which the report was sent

The fields in each group record are defined here:

- **Record Type:** The type of group record.
    - **Current-State Record:** The current reception state of the interface
        - **Mode_is_include:** Filter mode is include
        - **Mode_is_exclude:** Filter mode is exclude
    - **Filter-Mode-Change Record:** Indication that the filter mode has changed
        - **Change_to_Include_Mode:** Filter mode change to include
        - **Change_to_Exclude_Mode:** Filer mode change to exclude
    - **Source-List-Change Record:** Indication that the source list has changed, not the filter mode
        - **Allow_New_Sources:** List new sources being requested
        - **Block_Old_Sources:** List sources no longer being requested
- **Aux Data Len:** Length of auxiliary data in the group record.
- **Number of Sources:** How many sources are present in this group record.
- **Multicast Address:** The multicast group this record pertains to.
- **Source Address:** The unicast IP address of a source for the group.
- **Auxiliary Data:** Indication that auxiliary data is not defined for IGMPv3. The Aux Data Len should be set to zero and the auxiliary data should be ignored.
- **Additional Data:** Accounted for in the IGMP checksum, but any data beyond the last group record is ignored.

The most significant difference in the IGMPv3 membership report when compared to the IGMPv2 membership report is the inclusion of the group record block data. This is where the IGMPv3-specific functionality for the filter mode and source list is implemented.

IGMPv3 is backward compatible with previous versions of IGMP and still follows the same general state machine mechanics. When a host or router running an older version of IGMP is detected, the queries and report messages are translated from IGMPv2 into their IGMPv3 equivalent. For example, an IGMPv3-compatible representation of an IGMPv2 membership report for 239.1.1.1 includes all sources in IGMPv3.

As in IGMPv2, general queries are still sent to the All-Hosts group 224.0.0.1 from the querier. Hosts respond with a membership report message, which now includes specific sources in a source list and includes or excludes logic in the record type field. Hosts that want to join a new multicast group or source use unsolicited membership reports. When leaving a group or specific source, a host sends an updated current state group record message to indicate the change in state. The leave group message found in IGMPv2 is not used in IGMPv3. If no other members are in the group or source, the querier sends a group or group and source-specific query message before pruning off the source tree. The multicast router keeps an interface state table for each group and source and updates it as needed when an include or exclude update is received in a group record.

IGMP Snooping

Without IGMP snooping, a switch must flood multicast packets to each port in a VLAN to ensure that every potential group member receives the traffic. Obviously, bandwidth and processing efficiency are reduced if ports on the switch do not have an interested receiver attached. IGMP snooping inspects (or "snoops on") the higher-layer protocol communication traversing the switch. Looking into the contents of IGMP messages allows the switch to learn where multicast routers and interested receivers for a group are attached. IGMP snooping operates in the control plane by optimizing and suppressing IGMP messages from hosts, and operates in the data plane by installing multicast MAC address and port-mapping entries into the local multicast MAC address table of the switch. The entries created by IGMP snooping are installed in the same MAC address table as unicast entries. Despite the fact that different commands are used for viewing the entries installed by normal unicast learning and IGMP snooping, they share the same hardware resources provided by the MAC address table.

An IGMP snooping switch listens for IGMP query messages and PIM hello messages to determine which ports are connected to mrouters. When a port is determined to be an mrouter port, it receives all multicast traffic in the VLAN so that appropriate control plane state on the mrouter is created and sources are registered with the PIM RP, if applicable. The snooping switch also forwards IGMP membership reports to the mrouter to initiate the flow of multicast traffic to group members.

Host ports are discovered by listening for IGMP membership report messages. The membership reports are evaluated to determine which groups and sources are being requested, and the appropriate forwarding entries are added to the multicast MAC address table or IP-based forwarding table. An IGMP snooping switch should not forward membership reports to hosts because it results in hosts suppressing their own membership reports for IGMPv1 and IGMPv2.

If a multicast packet for the Network Control Block 224.0.0.0/24 arrives, it might need to be flooded on all ports. This is because devices can listen for groups in this range without sending a membership report for the group, and suppressing those packets could interrupt control plane protocols.

IGMP snooping is a separate process from the IGMP control plane process and is enabled by default in NX-OS. No user configuration is required to have the basic functionality running on the device. NX-OS builds its IGMP snooping table based on the group IP address instead of the multicast MAC address for the group. This behavior allows for optimal forwarding even if the L3 group addresses of multiple groups overlap to the same multicast group MAC address. The output in Example 13-2 demonstrates how to verify the IGMP snooping state and lookup mode for a VLAN.

Example 13-2 *Verify IGMP Snooping*

```
NX-2# show ip igmp snooping vlan 115
Global IGMP Snooping Information:
  IGMP Snooping enabled
  Optimised Multicast Flood (OMF) enabled
  IGMPv1/v2 Report Suppression enabled
  IGMPv3 Report Suppression disabled
  Link Local Groups Suppression enabled

IGMP Snooping information for vlan 115
  IGMP snooping enabled
  Lookup mode: IP
  Optimised Multicast Flood (OMF) enabled
  IGMP querier present, address: 10.115.1.254, version: 2, i/f Po1
  Switch-querier disabled
  IGMPv3 Explicit tracking enabled
  IGMPv2 Fast leave disabled
  IGMPv1/v2 Report suppression enabled
  IGMPv3 Report suppression disabled
  Link Local Groups suppression enabled
  Router port detection using PIM Hellos, IGMP Queries
  Number of router-ports: 1
  Number of groups: 1
  VLAN vPC function disabled
  Active ports:
    Po1 Po2     Eth3/19
```

It is possible to configure the device to use a MAC address–based forwarding mechanism on a per-VLAN basis, although it can lead to suboptimal forwarding because of address overlap. This option is configured in the VLAN configuration submode in Example 13-3.

Example 13-3 *Enable MAC Address Lookup Mode*

```
NX-2(config)# vlan configuration 115
NX-2(config-vlan-config)# layer-2 multicast lookup mac
```

If multicast traffic arrives for a group that a host has not requested via a membership report message, those packets are forwarded to the mrouter ports only, by default. This is called optimized multicast flooding in NX-OS and is shown as enabled by default in Example 13-2. If this feature is disabled, traffic for an unknown group is flooded to all ports in the VLAN.

> **Note** Optimized multicast flooding should be disabled in IPv6 networks to avoid problems related to neighbor discovery (ND) that rely specifically on multicast communication. This feature is disabled with the **no ip igmp snooping optimised-multicast-flood** command in VLAN configuration mode.

IGMP membership reports are suppressed by default to reduce the number of messages the mrouter receives. Recall that the mrouter needs to receive a membership report from only one host for the interface to be added to the OIL for a group.

NX-OS has several options available when configuring IGMP snooping. Most of the configuration is applied per VLAN, but certain parameters can be configured only globally. Global values apply to all VLANs. Table 13-7 provides the default configuration parameters for IGMP snooping that apply globally on the switch.

Table 13-7 *IGMP Snooping Global Configuration Parameters*

Parameter	CLI Command	Description
IGMP snooping	**ip igmp snooping**	Enables IGMP snooping on the active VDC. The default is enabled. **Note:** If the global setting is disabled, all VLANs are treated as disabled, whether they are enabled or not.
Event-history	**ip igmp snooping event-history** { vpc | igmp-snoop-internal | mfdm | mfdm-sum | vlan | vlan-events } size *buffer-size*	Configures the size of the IGMP snooping history buffers. The default is small.
Group timeout	**ip igmp snooping group-timeout** { *minutes* | never }	Configures the group membership timeout for all VLANs on the device.
Link-local groups suppression	**ip igmp snooping link-local-groups-suppression**	Configures link-local groups suppression on the device. The default is enabled.
Optimise-multicast-flood (OMF)	**ip igmp optimise-multicast-flood**	Configures OMF on all VLANs. The default is enabled.

Parameter	CLI Command	Description
Proxy	ip igmp snooping proxy general-inquiries [mrt *seconds*]	Enables the snooping function to proxy reply to general queries from the multicast router while also sending round-robin general queries on each switchport with the specified MRT value. The default is 5 seconds.
Report suppression	ip igmp snooping report-suppression	Limits the membership report traffic sent to multicast-capable routers on the device. When you disable report suppression, all IGMP reports are sent as is to multicast-capable routers. The default is enabled.
IGMPv3 report suppression	ip igmp snooping v3-report-suppression	Configures IGMPv3 report suppression and proxy reporting on the device. The default is disabled.

Table 13-8 provides the IGMP snooping configuration parameters, which are configured per VLAN. The per-VLAN configuration is applied in the **vlan configuration** [*vlan-id*] submode.

Table 13-8 *IGMP Snooping per-VLAN Configuration Parameters*

Parameter	CLI Command	Description
IGMP snooping	ip igmp snooping	Enables IGMP snooping on a per-VLAN basis. The default is enabled.
Explicit tracking	ip igmp snooping explicit-tracking	Tracks IGMPv3 membership reports from individual hosts for each port on a per-VLAN basis. The default is enabled.
Fast leave	ip igmp snooping fast-leave	Enables the software to remove the group state when it receives an IGMP leave report without sending an IGMP query message. This parameter is used for IGMPv2 hosts when no more than one host is present on each VLAN port. The default is disabled.
Group timeout	ip igmp snooping group-timeout { *minutes*	**never** }	Modifies or disables the default behavior of expiring IGMP snooping group membership after three missed general queries.

Parameter	CLI Command	Description
Last member query interval	**ip igmp snooping last-member-query-interval** *seconds*	Sets the interval that the software waits after sending an IGMP query to verify that a network segment no longer has hosts that want to receive a particular multicast group. If no hosts respond before the last member query interval expires, the software removes the group from the associated VLAN port. Values range from 1 to 25 seconds. The default is 1 second.
Optimize-multicast-flood	**ip igmp optimised-multicast-flood**	Configures OMF on the specified VLAN. The default is enabled.
Proxy	**ip igmp snooping proxy general-queries [mrt** *seconds* **]**	Enables the snooping function to proxy reply to general queries from the multicast router while also sending round-robin general queries on each switchport with the specified MRT value. The default is 5 seconds.
Snooping querier	**ip igmp snooping querier** *ip-address*	Configures a snooping querier on an interface when you do not enable PIM because multicast traffic does not need to be routed.
Query timeout	**ip igmp snooping querier-timeout** *seconds*	Query timeout value for IGMPv2. The default is 255 seconds.
Query interval	**ip igmp snooping query-interval** *seconds*	Time between query transmissions. The default is 125 seconds.
Query max response time	**ip igmp snooping query-max-response-time** *seconds*	Max response time for query messages. The default is 10 seconds.
Startup count	**ip igmp snooping startup-query-count** *value*	Number of queries sent at startup. The default is 2.
Startup interval	**ip igmp snooping startup-query-interval** *seconds*	Interval between queries at startup. The default is 31 seconds.
Robustness variable	**ip igmp snooping robustness-variable** *value*	Configures the robustness value for the specified VLANs. The default is 2.

Parameter	CLI Command	Description
Report suppression	**ip igmp snooping report-suppression**	Limits the membership report traffic sent to multicast-capable routers on a per-VLAN basis. When you disable report suppression, all IGMP reports are sent as is to multicast-capable routers. The default is enabled.
Static mrouter port	**ip igmp snooping mrouter interface** *interface*	Configures a static connection to a multicast router. The interface to the router must be in the selected VLAN.
Layer 2 static group	**ip igmp snooping static-group** *group-ip-addr* [**source** *source-ip-addr*] **interface** *interface*	Configures a Layer 2 port of a VLAN as a static member of a multicast group.
Link-local groups suppression	**ip igmp snooping link-local-groups-suppression**	Configures link-local groups suppression on a per-VLAN basis. The default is enabled.
IGMPv3 report suppression	**ip igmp snooping v3-report-suppression**	Configures IGMPv3 report suppression and proxy reporting on a per-VLAN basis. The default is enabled per VLAN.
Version	**ip igmp snooping version** *value*	Configures the IGMP version number for the specified VLANs.

In a pure L2 deployment of multicast, a snooping querier *must* be configured. This applies to situations in which PIM is not enabled on any interfaces, no mrouter is present, and no multicast traffic is being routed between VLANs.

Note When vPC is configured with IGMP snooping, configuring the same IGMP parameters on both vPC peers is recommended. IGMP state is synchronized between vPC peers with Cisco Fabric Services (CFS).

IGMP Verification

IGMP is enabled by default when PIM is enabled on an interface. Troubleshooting IGMP problems typically involves scenarios in which the LHR does not have an mroute entry populated by IGMP and the problem needs to be isolated to the LHR, the L2 infrastructure, or the host itself. Often IGMP snooping must be verified during this process because it is enabled by default and therefore plays an important role in delivering the queries to hosts and delivering the membership report messages to the mrouter.

In the topology in Figure 13-10, NX-1 is acting as the LHR for receivers in VLAN 115 and VLAN 116. NX-1 is also the IGMP querier for both VLANs. NX-2 is an IGMP snooping switch that is not performing any multicast routing. All L3 devices are configured for PIM ASM, with an anycast RP address shared between NX-3 and NX-4.

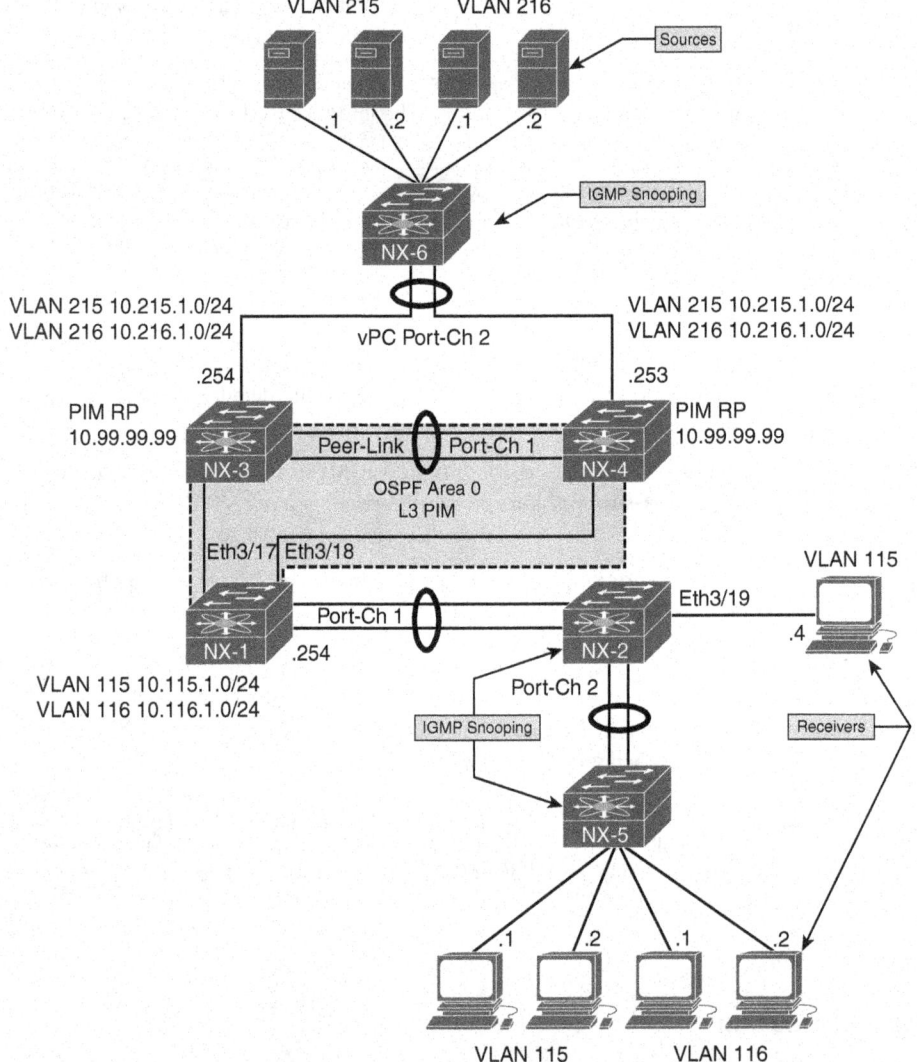

Figure 13-10 *IGMP Verification Example Topology*

If a receiver is not getting multicast traffic for a group, verify IGMP for correct state and operation. To begin the investigation, the following information is required:

- Multicast Group Address: 239.215.215.1
- IP address of the source: 10.215.1.1

- IP address of the receiver: 10.115.1.4
- LHR: NX-1
- Scope of the problem: The groups, sources, and receivers that are not functioning

The purpose of IGMP is to inform the LHR that a receiver is interested in group traffic. At the most basic level, this is communicated through a membership report message from the receiver and should create a (*, G) state at the LHR. In most circumstances, checking the mroute at the LHR for the presence of the (*, G) is enough to verify that at least one membership report was received. The OIL for the mroute should contain the interface on which the membership report was received. If this check passes, typically the troubleshooting follows the MDT to the PIM RP or source to determine why traffic is not arriving at the receiver.

In the following examples, no actual IGMP problem condition is present because the (*, G) state exists on NX-1. Instead of troubleshooting a specific problem, this section reviews the IGMP protocol state and demonstrates the command output, process events, and methodology used to verify functionality.

Verification begins from NX-2, which is the IGMP snooping switch connected to the receiver 10.115.1.4, and works across the L2 network toward the mrouter NX-1. Example 13-4 contains the output of **show ip igmp snooping vlan 115**, which is where the receiver is connected to NX-2. This output is used to verify that IGMP snooping is enabled and that the mrouter port is detected.

Example 13-4 *IGMP Snooping Status for VLAN 115*

```
NX-2# show ip igmp snooping vlan 115
Global IGMP Snooping Information:
  IGMP Snooping enabled
  Optimised Multicast Flood (OMF) enabled
  IGMPv1/v2 Report Suppression enabled
  IGMPv3 Report Suppression disabled
  Link Local Groups Suppression enabled

IGMP Snooping information for vlan 115
  IGMP snooping enabled
  Lookup mode: IP
  Optimised Multicast Flood (OMF) enabled
  IGMP querier present, address: 10.115.1.254, version: 2, i/f Po1
  Switch-querier disabled
  IGMPv3 Explicit tracking enabled
  IGMPv2 Fast leave disabled
  IGMPv1/v2 Report suppression enabled
  IGMPv3 Report suppression disabled
```

```
Link Local Groups suppression enabled
Router port detection using PIM Hellos, IGMP Queries
Number of router-ports: 1
Number of groups: 1
VLAN vPC function disabled
Active ports:
  Po1 Po2    Eth3/19
```

The Number of Groups field indicates that one group is present. The **show ip igmp snooping groups vlan 115** command is used to obtain additional detail about the group, as in Example 13-5.

Example 13-5 *VLAN 115 IGMP Snooping Group Membership*

```
NX-2# show ip igmp snooping groups vlan 115
Type: S - Static, D - Dynamic, R - Router port, F - Fabricpath core port

Vlan  Group Address      Ver  Type  Port list
115   */*                -    R     Po1
115   239.215.215.1      v2   D     Eth3/19
```

The last reporter is seen using the detail keyword, shown in Example 13-6.

Example 13-6 *Detailed VLAN 115 IGMP Snooping Group Membership*

```
NX-2# show ip igmp snooping groups vlan 115 detail
IGMP Snooping group membership for vlan 115
  Group addr: 239.215.215.1
    Group ver: v2 [old-host-timer: not running]
    Last reporter: 10.115.1.4
    Group Report Timer: 0.000000
    IGMPv2 member ports:
    IGMPv1/v2 memb ports:
      Eth3/19 [0 GQ missed], cfs:false, native:true
    vPC grp peer-link flag: include
    M2RIB vPC grp peer-link flag: include
```

Note If MAC-based multicast forwarding was configured for VLAN 115, the multicast MAC table entry can be confirmed with the **show hardware mac address-table** [*module*] [*VLAN identifier*] command. There is no software MAC table entry in the output of **show mac address-table multicast** [*VLAN identifier*], which is expected.

NX-2 is configured to use IP-based lookup for IGMP snooping. The **show forwarding distribution ip igmp snooping vlan** [*VLAN identifier*] command in Example 13-7 is used to find the platform index, which is used to direct the frames to the correct output interfaces. The platform index is also known as the Local Target Logic (LTL) index. This command provides the Multicast Forwarding Distribution Manager (MFDM) entry, which was discussed in the NX-OS "NX-OS Multicast Architecture" section of this chapter.

Example 13-7 *IGMP Snooping MFDM Entry*

```
NX-2# show forwarding distribution ip igmp snooping vlan 115 group 239.215.215.1
  detail
Vlan: 115, Group: 239.215.215.1, Source: 0.0.0.0
  Route Flags: 0
  Outgoing Interface List Index: 13
  Reference Count: 2
  Platform Index: 0x7fe8
  Vpc peer link exclude flag clear
  Number of Outgoing Interfaces: 2
    port-channel1
    Ethernet3/19
```

The Ethernet3/19 interface is populated by the membership report from the receiver. The Port-channel 1 interface is included as an outgoing interface because it is the mrouter port. Verify the platform index as shown in Example 13-8 to ensure that the correct interfaces are present and match the previous MFDM output. The **show system internal pixm info ltl** [*index*] command obtains the output from the Port Index Manager (PIXM). The IFIDX/RID is 0xd, which matches the Outgoing Interface List Index of 13.

Example 13-8 *Verify the Platform LTL Index*

```
NX-2# show system internal pixm info ltl 0x7fe8
MCAST LTLs allocated for VDC:1
=============================================
LTL     IFIDX/RID   LTL_FLAG CB_FLAG
0x7fe8 0x0000000d 0x00       0x0002

mi | v5_f3_fpoe | v4_fpoe | v5_fpoe | clp_v4_l2 | clp_v5_l2 | clp20_v4_l3
 | clp_cr_v4_l3 | flag | proxy_if_index
0x3 | 0x3 | 0x0 | 0x3 | 0x0 | 0x3 | 0x3 | 0x3 | 0x0 | none


Member info
------------------
IFIDX           LTL
-------------------------------
Eth3/19         0x0012
Po1             0x0404
```

Note If the IFIDX of interest is a port-channel, the physical interface is found by examining the LTL index of the port-channel. Chapter 5, "Port-Channels, Virtual Port-Channels, and FabricPath," demonstrates the port-channel load balance hash and how to find the port-channel member link that will be used to transmit the packet.

At this point, the IGMP snooping control plane was verified in addition to the forwarding plane state for the group with the available **show** commands. NX-OS also provides several useful event-history records for IGMP, as well as other multicast protocols. The event-history output collects significant events from the process and stores them in a circular buffer. In most situations, for multicast protocols, the event-history records provide the same level of detail that is available with process debugs.

The **show ip igmp snooping internal event-history vlan** command provides a sequence of IGMP snooping events for VLAN 115 and the group of interest, 239.215.215.1. Example 13-9 shows the reception of a general query message from Port-channel 1, as well as the membership report message received from 10.115.1.4 on Eth3/19.

Example 13-9 *IGMP Snooping VLAN Event-History*

```
NX-2# show ip igmp snooping internal event-history vlan | inc
239.215.215.1|General
! Output omitted for brevity
02:19:33.729983 igmp [7177]: [7314]: SN: <115> Forwarding report for
(*, 239.215.215.1) came on Eth3/19
02:19:33.729973 igmp [7177]: [7314]: SN: <115> Updated oif Eth3/19 for
(*, 239.215.215.1) entry
02:19:33.729962 igmp [7177]: [7314]: SN: <115> Received v2 report:
group 239.215.215.1 from 10.115.1.4 on Eth3/19
02:19:33.721639 igmp [7177]: [7314]: SN: <115> Report timer not running.
..starting with MRT expiry 10 for group: 239.215.215.1
02:19:33.721623 igmp [7177]: [7314]: SN: <115> Received v2 General query
from 10.115.1.254 on Po1
```

The Ethanalyzer tool provides a way to capture packets at the netstack component level in NX-OS. This is an extremely useful tool for troubleshooting any control plane protocol exchange. In Example 13-10, an Ethanalyzer capture filtered for IGMP packets clearly shows the receipt of the general query messages, as well as the membership report from 10.115.1.4. Ethanalyzer output is directed to local storage with the *write* option. The file can then be copied off the device for a detailed protocol examination, if needed.

Example 13-10 *Ethanalyzer Capture of IGMP Messages on NX-2*

```
NX-2# ethanalyzer local interface inband-in capture-filter "igmp"
! Output omitted for brevity
Capturing on inband
1 02:29:24.420135 10.115.1.254 -> 224.0.0.1    IGMPv2 Membership Query, general
2 02:29:24.421061 10.115.1.254 -> 224.0.0.1    IGMPv2 Membership Query, general
3 02:29:24.430482 10.115.1.4 -> 239.215.215.1 IGMPv2 Membership Report group
  239.215.215.1
```

NX-OS maintains statistics for IGMP snooping at both the global and interface level. These statistics are viewed with either the **show ip igmp snooping statistics global** command or the **show ip igmp snooping statistics vlan** [*VLAN identifier*] command. Example 13-11 shows the statistics for VLAN 115 on NX-2. The VLAN statistics also include global statistics, which are useful for confirming how many and what type of IGMP and PIM messages are being received on a VLAN. If additional packet-level details are needed, using Ethanalyzer with an appropriate filter is recommended.

Example 13-11 *NX-2 VLAN 115 IGMP Snooping Statistics*

```
NX-2# show ip igmp snooping statistics vlan 115
Global IGMP snooping statistics: (only non-zero values displayed)
  Packets received: 3783
  Packets flooded: 1882
  vPC PIM DR queries fail: 2
  vPC PIM DR updates sent: 6
  vPC CFS message response sent: 19
  vPC CFS message response rcvd: 16
  vPC CFS unreliable message sent: 403
  vPC CFS unreliable message rcvd: 1632
  vPC CFS reliable message sent: 16
  vPC CFS reliable message rcvd: 19
  STP TCN messages rcvd: 391
  IM api failed: 1
VLAN 115 IGMP snooping statistics, last reset: never (only non-zero values
  displayed)
  Packets received: 666
  IGMPv2 reports received: 242
  IGMPv2 queries received: 267
  IGMPv2 leaves received: 4
  PIM Hellos received: 1065
  IGMPv2 reports suppressed: 1
  IGMPv2 leaves suppressed: 2
  Queries originated: 2
```

```
    IGMPv2 proxy-leaves originated: 1
    Packets sent to routers: 242
    STP TCN received: 18
    vPC Peer Link CFS packet statistics:
        IGMP packets (sent/recv/fail): 300/150/0
IGMP Filtering Statistics:
Router Guard Filtering Statistics:
```

With NX-2 verified, the examination moves to the LHR, NX-1. NX-1 is the mrouter for VLAN 115 and the IGMP querier. The IGMP state on NX-1 is verified with the **show ip igmp interface vlan 115** command, as in Example 13-12.

Example 13-12 *NX-1 IGMP Interface VLAN 115 State*

```
NX-1# show ip igmp interface vlan 115
IGMP Interfaces for VRF "default"
Vlan115, Interface status: protocol-up/link-up/admin-up
  IP address: 10.115.1.254, IP subnet: 10.115.1.0/24
  Active querier: 10.115.1.254, version: 2, next query sent in: 00:00:06
  Membership count: 1
  Old Membership count 0
  IGMP version: 2, host version: 2
  IGMP query interval: 125 secs, configured value: 125 secs
  IGMP max response time: 10 secs, configured value: 10 secs
  IGMP startup query interval: 31 secs, configured value: 31 secs
  IGMP startup query count: 2
  IGMP last member mrt: 1 secs
  IGMP last member query count: 2
  IGMP group timeout: 260 secs, configured value: 260 secs
  IGMP querier timeout: 255 secs, configured value: 255 secs
  IGMP unsolicited report interval: 10 secs
  IGMP robustness variable: 2, configured value: 2
  IGMP reporting for link-local groups: disabled
  IGMP interface enable refcount: 1
  IGMP interface immediate leave: disabled
  IGMP VRF name default (id 1)
  IGMP Report Policy: None
  IGMP State Limit: None
  IGMP interface statistics: (only non-zero values displayed)
    General (sent/received):
      v2-queries: 999/1082, v2-reports: 0/1266, v2-leaves: 0/15
    Errors:
  Interface PIM DR: Yes
  Interface vPC SVI: No
```

```
    Interface vPC CFS statistics:
      DR queries sent: 1
      DR queries rcvd: 1
      DR updates sent: 1
      DR updates rcvd: 3
```

The membership report NX-2 forwarded from the host is received on Port-channel 1. The query messages and membership reports are viewed in the **show ip igmp internal event-history debugs** output in Example 13-13. When the membership report message is received, NX-1 determines that state needs to be created.

Example 13-13 *NX-1 IGMP Debugs Event-History*

```
NX-1# show ip igmp internal event-history debugs
! Output omitted for brevity

debugs events for IGMP process
04:39:34.349013 igmp [7011]: : Processing report for (*, 239.215.215.1)
[i/f Vlan115], entry not found, creating
 04:39:34.348973 igmp [7011]: : Received v2 Report for 239.215.215.1 from
10.115.1.4 (Vlan115)
 04:39:34.336092 igmp [7011]: : Received General v2 Query from 10.115.1.254
(Vlan115), mrt: 10 sec
 04:39:34.335543 igmp [7011]: : Sending SVI query packet to IGMP-snooping module
 04:39:34.335541 igmp [7011]: : Send General v2 Query on Vlan115 (mrt:10 sec)
```

IGMP creates a route entry based on the received membership report in VLAN 115. The IGMP route entry is shown in the output of Example 13-14.

Example 13-14 *IGMP Route Entry on NX-1*

```
NX-1# show ip igmp route
IGMP Connected Group Membership for VRF "default" - 1 total entries
Type: S - Static, D - Dynamic, L - Local, T - SSM Translated
Group Address      Type Interface      Uptime    Expires   Last Reporter
239.215.215.1       D    Vlan115       01:59:49  00:03:49  10.115.1.4
```

IGMP must also inform the MRIB so that an appropriate mroute entry is created. This is seen in the **show ip igmp internal event-history igmp-internal** output in Example 13-15. An IGMP update is sent to the MRIB process buffer through Message and Transactional Services (MTS). Note that IGMP receives notification from MRIB that the message was processed and the message buffer gets reclaimed.

Example 13-15 *IGMP Event-History of Internal Events*

```
NX-1# show ip igmp internal event-history igmp-internal
! Output omitted for brevity

igmp-internal events for IGMP process
04:39:34.354419 igmp [7011]: [7564]: MRIB: Processing ack: reclaiming buffer
0x0x967cbe4, xid 0xffff000c, count 1
04:39:34.354416 igmp [7011]: [7564]: Received Message from MRIB minor 16
04:39:34.353742 igmp [7011]: [7566]: default: Sending IGMP update-route buffer
0x0x967cbe4, xid 0xffff000c, count 1 to MRIB
04:39:34.353738 igmp [7011]: [7566]: default: Moving MRIB txlist member marker
to version 12
04:39:34.353706 igmp [7011]: [7566]: Inserting IGMP update-update for
(*, 239.215.215.1) (context 1) into MRIB buffer
```

The message identifier 0xffff000c is used to track this message in the MRIB process events. Example 13-16 shows the MRIB processing of this message from the **show routing ip multicast event-history rib** output.

Example 13-16 *MRIB Creating (*, G) State*

```
NX-1# show routing ip multicast event-history rib
! Output omitted for brevity

04:39:34.355736 mrib [7170]::RPF change for (*, 239.215.215.1/32) (10.99.99.99)
, iif: Ethernet3/18 (iod 64), RPF nbr: 10.1.13.3
04:39:34.355730 mrib [7170]::RPF lookup for route (*, 239.215.215.1/32)
RPF Source 10.99.99.99 is iif: Ethernet3/18 (iod 64), RPF nbr: 10.1.13.3,  pa
04:39:34.354481 mrib [7170]::Inserting add-op-update for (*, 239.215.215.1/32)
 (context 1) from txlist into MFDM route buffer
04:39:34.354251 mrib [7170]::Copy oifs to all (Si,G)s for "igmp"
04:39:34.354246 mrib [7170]::Doing multi-route add for "igmp"
04:39:34.354126 mrib [7170]::    OIF : Vlan115
04:39:34.354099 mrib [7170]::"igmp" add route (*, 239.215.215.1/32)
(list-00000000)[1],rpf Null 0.0.0.0(0.0.0.0), iod 0, mdt_encap_index 0, bidir: 0
, multi-route
04:39:34.353994 mrib [7170]::update IPC message (type:mts) from "igmp", 1 routes
 present: [xid: 0xffff000c]
```

When the MRIB process receives the MTS message from IGMP, an mroute is created for (*, 239.215.215.1/32) and the MFDM is informed. The RPF toward the PIM RP (10.99.99.99) is then confirmed and added to the entry.

The output of **show ip mroute** in Example 13-17 confirms that a (*, G) entry has been created by IGMP and the OIF was also populated by IGMP.

Example 13-17 *IGMP Created MROUTE Entry on NX-1*

```
NX-1# show ip mroute
IP Multicast Routing Table for VRF "default"

(*, 232.0.0.0/8), uptime: 10:08:39, pim ip
  Incoming interface: Null, RPF nbr: 0.0.0.0
  Outgoing interface list: (count: 0)

(*, 239.215.215.1/32), uptime: 01:59:08, igmp ip pim
  Incoming interface: Ethernet3/18, RPF nbr: 10.1.13.3
  Outgoing interface list: (count: 1)
    Vlan115, uptime: 01:59:08, igmp

(10.215.1.1/32, 239.215.215.1/32), uptime: 02:14:30, pim mrib ip
  Incoming interface: Ethernet3/17, RPF nbr: 10.2.13.3
  Outgoing interface list: (count: 1)
    Vlan115, uptime: 01:59:08, mrib
```

Note Additional events occur after this point when traffic arrives from the source, 10.215.1.1. The arrival of data traffic from the RP triggers a PIM join toward the source and creation of the (S, G) mroute. This is explained in the "PIM Any Source Multicast" section later in this chapter.

PIM Multicast

PIM is the multicast routing protocol used to build shared trees and shortest-path trees that facilitates the distribution of multicast traffic in an L3 network. As the name suggests, PIM was designed to be protocol independent. PIM essentially creates a multicast overlay network built upon the information available from the underlying unicast routing topology. The term *protocol independent* is based on the fact that PIM can use the unicast routing information in the Routing Information Base (RIB) from any source protocol, such as EIGRP, OSPF, or BGP. The unicast routing table provides PIM with the relative location of sources, rendezvous points, and receivers, which is essential to building a loop-free MDT.

PIM is designed to operate in one of two modes, dense mode or sparse mode. Dense mode (DM) operates under the assumption that receivers are densely dispersed through the network. In dense mode, the assumption is that all PIM neighbors should receive the traffic. In this mode of operation, multicast traffic is flooded to all downstream neighbors. If the group traffic is not required, the neighbor prunes itself from the tree. This is referred to as a push model because traffic is pushed from the root of the tree toward the leaves, with the assumption that there are many leaves and they are all interested in receiving the traffic. NX-OS does not support PIM dense mode because PIM sparse mode offers several advantages and is the most popular mode deployed in modern data centers.

PIM sparse mode (SM) is based on a pull model. The pull model assumes that receivers are sparsely dispersed through the network and that it is therefore more efficient to have traffic forward to only the PIM neighbors that are explicitly requesting the traffic. PIM sparse mode works well for the distribution of multicast when receivers are sparsely or densely populated in the topology. Because of its explicit join behavior, it has become the preferred mode of deploying multicast.

The role of PIM in the process of distributing multicast traffic from a source to a receiver is described by the following responsibilities:

- Registering multicast sources with the PIM RP (ASM)
- Joining an interested receiver to the MDT
- Deciding which tree should be joined on behalf of the receiver
- If multiple PIM routers exist on the same L3 network, determining which PIM router will forward traffic

This section of the chapter introduces the PIM protocol and messages PIM uses to build MDTs and create forwarding state. The different operating models of PIM SM are examined, including ASM, SSM, and Bi-Directional PIM (Bidir).

Note RFC 2362 initially defined PIM as an experimental protocol that was later made obsolete by RFC 4601. Recently, RFC 4601 was updated by RFC 7761. The NX-OS implementation of PIM is based on RFC 4601.

PIM Protocol State and Trees

Before diving into the PIM protocol mechanics and message types, it is important to understand the different types of multicast trees. PIM uses both RPT and SPT to build loop-free forwarding paths for the purpose of delivering multicast traffic to the receiver. The RPT is rooted at the PIM RP, and the SPT is rooted at the source. Both tree types in PIM SM are unidirectional. Traffic flows from the root toward the leaves, where receivers are attached. If at any point the traffic diverges toward different branches to reach leaves, replication must occur.

The mroute state is often referred to when discussing multicast forwarding. With PIM multicast, the (*, G) state is created by the receiver at the LHR and represents the RPT's relationship to the receiver. The (S, G) state is created by the receipt of multicast data traffic and represents the SPT's relationship to the source.

As packets arrive on a multicast router, they are checked against the unicast route to the root of the tree. This is known as the Reverse Path Forwarding (RPF) check. The RPF check ensures that the MDT remains loop-free. When a router sends a PIM join-prune message to create state, it is sent toward the root of the tree from the RPF interface that is determined by the best unicast route to the root of the tree. Figure 13-11 illustrates the concepts of mroute state and PIM MDTs.

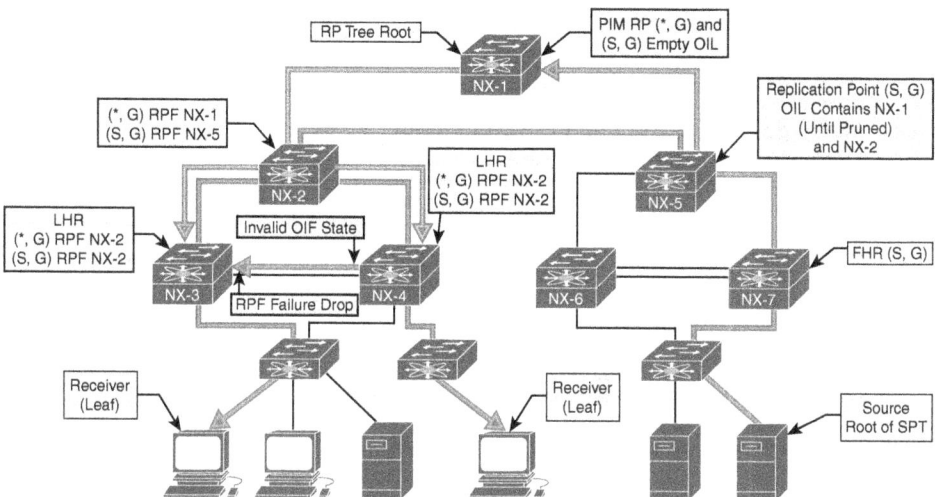

Figure 13-11 *PIM MDTs and MROUTE State*

PIM Message Types

PIM defines several message types that enable the protocol to discover neighbors and build MDTs. All PIM messages are carried in an IP packet and use IP protocol 103. Some messages, such as register and register-stop, use a unicast destination address and might traverse multiple L3 hops from source to destination. However, other messages, such as hello and join-prune, are delivered through multicast communication and rely on the ALL-PIM-ROUTERS well-known multicast address of 224.0.0.13 with a TTL value of 1. All PIM messages use the same common message format, regardless of whether they are delivered through multicast or unicast packets. Figure 13-12 shows the PIM control message header format.

4 Bits	4 Bits	8 Bits	16 Bits
PIM Ver	Type	Reserved	Checksum

Figure 13-12 *PIM Control Message Header Format*

The PIM control message header format fields are defined in the following list:

- **PIM Version:** The PIM version number is 2.
- **Type:** This is the PIM message type (refer to Table 13-9).

- **Reserved:** This field is set to zero on transmit and is ignored upon receipt.
- **Checksum:** The checksum is calculated on the entire PIM message, except for the multicast data packet portion of a register message.

The type field of the control message header identifies the type of PIM message being sent. Table 13-9 describes the various PIM message types listed in RFC 6166.

Table 13-9 *PIM Control Message Types*

Type	Message Type	Destination Address	Description
0	Hello	224.0.0.13	Used for neighbor discovery.
1	Register	RP Address (Unicast)	Sent by FHR to RP to register a source. PIM SM only.
2	Register-stop	FHR (Unicast)	Sent by RP to FHR in response to a register message. PIM SM only.
3	Join-Prune	224.0.0.13	Join or Prune from an MDT. Not used in PIM DM.
4	Bootstrap	224.0.0.13	Sent hop by hop from the bootstrap router to disperse RP mapping in the domain. Used in PIM SM and BiDIR.
5	Assert	224.0.0.13	Used to elect a single forwarder when multiple forwarders are detected on a LAN segment.
6	Graft	Unicast to the RPF neighbor	Rejoins a previously pruned branch to the MDT
7	Graft-Ack	Unicast to the graft originator	Acknowledges a graft message to a downstream neighbor.
8	Candidate RP Advertisement	BSR address (Unicast)	Sent to the BSR to announce an RP's candidacy.
9	State refresh	224.0.0.13	Sent hop by hop from the FHR to refresh prune state. Used only in PIM DM.
10	DF Election	224.0.0.13	Used in PIM BiDIR to elect a forwarder. Subtypes are offer, winner, backoff, and pass.
11–14	Unassigned	—	—
15	Reserved	—	RFC 6166, future expansion of the type field

Note This chapter does not cover the PIM messages specific to PIM DM because NX-OS does not support PIM DM. Interested readers should review RFC 3973 to learn about the various PIM DM messages.

PIM Hello Message

The PIM hello message is periodically sent on all PIM-enabled interfaces to discover neighbors and form PIM neighbor adjacencies. The PIM hello message is identified by a PIM message type of zero.

The value of the DR priority option is used in the Designated Router (DR) election process. The default value is one, and the neighbor with the numerically higher priority is elected as the PIM DR. If the DR priority is equal, then the higher IP address wins the election. The PIM DR is responsible for registering multicast sources with the PIM RP and for joining the MDT on behalf of the multicast receivers on the interface.

The hello message carries different option types in a Type, Length, Value (TLV) format. The various hello message option types follow:

- **Option Type 1:** Holdtime is the amount of time to keep the neighbor reachable. A value of 0xffff indicates that the neighbor should never be timed out, and a value of zero indicates that the neighbor is about to go down or has changed its IP address.

- **Option Type 2:** LAN prune delay is used to tune prune propagation delay on multiaccess LAN networks. It is used only if all routers on the LAN support this option, and it is used by upstream routers to figure out how long they should wait for a join override message before pruning an interface.

- **Option 3 to 16:** Reserved for future use.

- **Option 18:** Deprecated and should not be used.

- **Option 19:** DR priority is used during the DR election.

- **Option 20:** Generation ID (GENID) is a random 32-bit value on the interface where the hello message is sent. The value remains the same until PIM is restarted on the interface.

- **Option 24:** Address list is used to inform neighbors about secondary IP addresses on an interface.

PIM Register Message

The PIM register message is sent in a unicast packet by the PIM DR to the PIM RP. The purpose of the register message is to inform the PIM RP that a source is actively sending multicast traffic to a group address. This is achieved by sending encapsulated multicast packets from the source in the register message to the RP. When data traffic is received from a source, the PIM DR performs the following:

1. The multicast data packet arrives from the source and is sent to the supervisor.

2. The supervisor creates hardware forwarding state for the group, builds the register message, and then sends the register message to the PIM RP.

3. Subsequent packets that the router receives from the source after the hardware forwarding state is built are not sent to the supervisor to create register messages. This is done to limit the amount of traffic sent to the supervisor control plane.

In contrast, a Cisco IOS PIM DR continues to send register messages until it receives a register-stop message from the PIM RP. NX-OS provides the **ip pim register-until-stop** global configuration command that modifies the default NX-OS behavior to behave like Cisco IOS. In most cases, the default behavior of NX-OS does not need to be modified.

The PIM register message contains the following fields:

- **Type:** The value is 1 for a register message.
- **The Border Bit (B - Bit):** This is set to zero on transmit and ignored on receipt (RFC 7761). RFC 4601 described PIM Multicast Border Router (PMBR) functionality that used this bit to designate a local source when set to 0, or set to 1 for a source in a directly connected cloud on a PMBR.
- **The Null-Register Bit:** This is set to 1 if the packet is a null register message. The null register message encapsulates a dummy IP header from the source, not the full encapsulated packet that is present in a register message.
- **Multicast Data Packet:** In a register message, this is the original packet sent by the source. The TTL of the original packet is decremented before encapsulation into the register message. If the packet is a null register, this portion of the register message contains a dummy IP header containing the source and group address.

PIM Register-Stop Message

The PIM register-stop message is a unicast packet that the PIM RP sends to a PIM DR in response to receiving a register message. The destination address of the register-stop is the source address used by the PIM DR that sent the register message. The purpose of the register-stop message is to inform the DR to cease sending the encapsulated multicast data packets to the PIM RP and to acknowledge the receipt of the register message. The register-stop message has the following encoded fields:

- **Type:** The value is 2 for a register-stop message.
- **Group Address:** This is the group address of the multicast packet encapsulated in the register message.
- **Source Address:** This is the IP address of the source in the encapsulated multicast data packet from the register message.

PIM Join-Prune Message

The PIM join-prune message is sent by PIM routers to an upstream neighbor toward the source or the PIM RP using the ALL-PIM-ROUTERS multicast address of 224.0.0.13. A join is sent to build RP trees (RPT) to the PIM RP (shared trees) or to build shortest-path trees (SPT) to the source (source trees). The join-prune message contains an encoded list of groups and sources to be joined, as well as list of sources to be pruned. These are referred to as group sets and source lists.

Two types of group sets exist, and both types have a join source list and a prune source list. The wildcard group set represents the entire multicast group range (224.0.0.0/4), and the group-specific set represents a valid multicast group address. A single join-prune message can contain multiple group-specific sets but may contain only a single instance of the wildcard group set. A combination of a single wildcard group set and one or more group-specific sets is also valid in the same join-prune message. The join-prune message contains the following fields:

- **Type:** Value is 3 for a join-prune message.
- **Unicast Neighbor Upstream Address:** The address of the upstream neighbor that is the target of the message.
- **Holdtime:** The amount of time to keep the join-prune state alive.
- **Number of Groups:** The number of multicast group sets contained in the message.
- **Multicast Group Address:** The multicast group address identifies the group set. This can be wildcard or group specific.
- **Number of Joined Sources:** The number of joined sources for the group.
- **Joined Source Address 1 .. n:** The source list that provides the sources being joined for the group. Three flags are encoded in this field:
    - **S: Sparse bit.** This is set to a value of 1 for PIM SM.
    - **W: Wildcard bit.** This is set to 1 to indicate that the encoded source address represents the wildcard in a (*, G) entry. When set to 0, it indicates that the encoded source address represents the source address of an (S, G) entry.
    - **R: RP Bit.** When set to 1, the join is sent to the PIM RP. When set to 0, the join is sent toward the source.
- **Number of Pruned Sources:** The number of pruned sources for the group.
- **Pruned Source Address 1 .. n:** The source list that provides the sources being pruned for the group. The same three flags are found here as in the joined source address field (S, W, R).

Note In theory, it is possible that the number of group sets exceeds the maximum IP packet size of 65535. In this case, multiple join-prune messages are used. It is important to ensure that PIM neighbors have a matching L3 MTU size because a neighbor could sent a join-prune message that is too large for the receiving interface to accommodate. This results in missing multicast state on the receiving PIM neighbor and a broken MDT.

PIM Bootstrap Message

The PIM bootstrap message is originated by the Bootstrap Router (BSR) and provides an RP set that contains group-to-RP mapping information. The bootstrap message is sent to the ALL-PIM-ROUTERS address of 224.0.0.13 and is forwarded hop by hop throughout the multicast domain. Upon receiving a bootstrap message, a PIM router processes its contents and builds a new packet to forward the bootstrap message to all PIM neighbors per interface. It is possible for a bootstrap message to be fragmented into multiple Bootstrap Message Fragments (BSMF). Each fragment uses the same format as the bootstrap message. The PIM bootstrap message contains the following fields:

- **Type:** The value is 4 for a bootstrap message.
- **No-Forward Bit:** Instruction that the bootstrap message should not be forwarded.
- **Fragment Tag:** Randomly generated number used to distinguish BSMFs that belong to the same bootstrap message. Each fragment carries the same value.
- **Hash Mask Length:** The length, in bits, of the mask to use in the hash function.
- **BSR Priority:** The priority value of the originating BSR. The value can be 0 to 255 (higher is preferred).
- **BSR Address:** The address of the bootstrap router for the domain.
- **Group Address 1 .. n:** The group ranges associated with the candidate-RPs.
- **RP Count 1 .. n:** The number of candidate-RP addresses included in the entire bootstrap message for the corresponding group range.
- **Frag RP Count 1 .. m:** The number of candidate-RP addresses included in this fragment of the bootstrap message for the corresponding group range.
- **RP Address 1 .. m:** The address of the candidate-RP for the corresponding group range.
- **RP1 .. m Holdtime:** The holdtime, in seconds, for the corresponding RP.
- **RP1 .. m Priority:** The priority of the corresponding RP and group address. This field is copied from the candidate-RP advertisement message. The highest priority is zero and is per RP and per group address.

PIM Assert Message

A PIM assert message is used to resolve forwarder conflicts between multiple routers on a common network segment and is sent to the ALL-PIM-ROUTERS address of 224.0.0.13. The assert message is sent when a router receives a multicast data packet on an interface on which the router itself should have normally sent that packet out. This condition occurs when two or more routers are both sending traffic onto the same network segment. An assert message is also sent in response to receiving an assert message from another router. The assert message allows both sending routers to determine which router should continue forwarding and which router should cease forwarding, based on the metric value and administrative distance to the source or RP address. Assert messages are sent as group specific (*, G) or as source specific (S, G), which represents traffic from all sources to a group or for a specific source for a group. The assert message contains the following fields:

- **Type:** The value is 5 for a PIM assert message.
- **Group Address:** The group address for which the forwarder conflict needs to be resolved.

- **Source Address:** The source address for which the forwarder conflict needs to be resolved. A value of zero indicates a (*, G) assert.
- **RPT-Bit:** This value is set to 1 for (*, G) assert messages and 0 for (S, G) assert messages.
- **Metric Preference:** The preference value assigned to the unicast routing protocol that provided the route to the source or PIM RP. This value refers to the administrative distance of the unicast routing protocol.
- **Metric:** The unicast routing table metric for the route to the source or PIM RP.

PIM Candidate RP Advertisement Message

When the PIM domain is configured to use the BSR method of RP advertisement, each candidate PIM RP (C-RP) periodically unicasts a PIM candidate RP advertisement message to the BSR. The purpose of this message is to inform the BSR that the C-RP is willing to function as an RP for the included groups. The PIM candidate RP advertisement message has the following fields:

- **Type:** The value is 8 for a candidate RP advertisement message.
- **Prefix Count:** The number of group addresses included in the message. Must not be zero.
- **Priority:** The priority of the included RP for the corresponding group addresses. The highest priority is zero.
- **Holdtime:** The amount of time, in seconds, for which the advertisement is valid.
- **RP Address:** The address of the interface to advertise as a candidate-RP.
- **Group Address 1 .. n:** The group ranges associated with the candidate-RP.

PIM DF Election Message

In PIM BiDIR, the Designated Forwarder (DF) election chooses the best router on a network segment to forward traffic traveling down the tree from the Rendezvous Point Link (RPL) to the network segment. The DF is also responsible for sending packets traveling upstream from the local network segment toward the RPL. The DF is elected based on its unicast routing metrics to reach the Rendezvous Point Address (RPA). Routers on a common network segment use the PIM DF election message to determine which router is the DF, per RPA. The routers advertise their metrics in offer, winner, backoff, and pass messages, which are distinct submessage types of the DF election message. The PIM DF election message contains the following fields:

- **Type:** The value is 10 for the PIM DF election message and has four subtypes.
  - **Offer:** Subtype 1. Sent by routers that believe they have a better metric to the RPA than the metric that has been seen in offers so far.
  - **Winner:** Subtype 2. Sent by a router when assuming the role of the DF or when reasserting in response to worse offers.

- **Backoff:** Subtype 3. Used by the DF to acknowledge better offers. It instructs other routers with equal or worse offers to wait until the DF passes responsibility to the sender of the offer.
- **Pass:** Subtype 4. Used by the old DF to pass forwarding responsibility to a router that has previously made an offer. The Old-DF-Metric is the current metric of the DF at the time the pass is sent.
- **RP Address:** The RPA for which the election is taking place.
- **Sender Metric Preference:** The preference value assigned to the unicast routing protocol that provided the route to the RPA. This value refers to the administrative distance of the unicast routing protocol.
- **Sender Metric:** The unicast routing table metric that the message sender used to reach the RPA.

The Backoff message adds the following fields to the common election message format:

- **Offering Address:** The address of the router that made the last (best) offer.
- **Offering Metric Preference:** The preference value assigned to the unicast routing protocol that the offering router used for the route to the RPA.
- **Offering Metric:** The unicast routing table metric that the offering router used to reach the RPA.
- **Interval:** The backoff interval, in milliseconds, to be used by routers with worse metrics than the offering router.

The Pass message adds the following fields to the common election message format:

- **New Winner Address:** The address of the router that made the last (best) offer.
- **New Winner Metric Preference:** The preference value assigned to the unicast routing protocol that the offering router used for the route to the RPA.
- **New Winner Metric:** The unicast routing table metric that the offering router used to reach the RPA.

PIM Interface and Neighbor Verification

NX-OS requires installation of the LAN_ENTERPRISE_SERVICES_PKG license to enable **feature pim**. The various PIM configuration commands are not available to the user until the license is installed and the feature is enabled.

PIM is enabled on an interface with the **ip pim sparse-mode** command, as in Example 13-18.

Example 13-18 *Configuring PIM Sparse Mode on an Interface*

```
NX-1# show run pim
! Output omitted for brevity
!Command: show running-config pim

version 7.2(2)D1(2)
feature pim

interface Vlan115
  ip pim sparse-mode

interface Vlan116
  ip pim sparse-mode

interface Ethernet3/17
  ip pim sparse-mode

interface Ethernet3/18
  ip pim sparse-mode
```

After PIM is enabled on an interface, hello packets are sent and PIM neighbors form if there is another router on the link that is also PIM enabled.

Note The hello interval for PIM is configured in milliseconds. The minimum accepted value is 1000 ms, which is equal to 1 second. If an interval lower than the default is needed to detect a failed PIM neighbor, use BFD for PIM instead of a reduced hello interval.

In the output of Example 13-19, NX-1 has formed PIM neighbors with NX-3 and NX-4. The output shows whether the neighbor is BiDIR capable and also provides the priority value of each neighbor which is used for DR election.

Example 13-19 *PIM Neighbors on NX-1*

```
NX-1# show ip pim neighbor

PIM Neighbor Status for VRF "default"
Neighbor         Interface       Uptime   Expires   DR        Bidir-  BFD
                                                    Priority  Capable State
10.2.13.3        Ethernet3/17    4d21h    00:01:34  1         yes     n/a
10.1.13.3        Ethernet3/18    4d21h    00:01:19  1         yes     n/a
```

PIM has several interface-specific parameters that determine how the protocol operates. The specific details are viewed for each PIM enabled interface with the **show ip pim interface** [*interface identifier*] command (see Example 13-20). The most interesting aspects of this output for troubleshooting purposes are the per-interface statistics, which provide useful counters for the different PIM message types and the fields related to the hello packets. The DR election state is also useful for determining which device registers sources on the segment for PIM sparse mode and which device forwards traffic to receivers known through IGMP membership reports.

Example 13-20 *PIM Interface Parameters on NX-1*

```
NX-1# show ip pim interface e3/18

PIM Interface Status for VRF "default"
Ethernet3/18, Interface status: protocol-up/link-up/admin-up
  IP address: 10.1.13.1, IP subnet: 10.1.13.0/24
  PIM DR: 10.1.13.3, DR's priority: 1
  PIM neighbor count: 1
  PIM hello interval: 30 secs, next hello sent in: 00:00:10
  PIM neighbor holdtime: 105 secs
  PIM configured DR priority: 1
  PIM configured DR delay: 3 secs
  PIM border interface: no
  PIM GenID sent in Hellos: 0x2cc432ed
  PIM Hello MD5-AH Authentication: disabled
  PIM Neighbor policy: none configured
  PIM Join-Prune inbound policy: none configured
  PIM Join-Prune outbound policy: none configured
  PIM Join-Prune interval: 1 minutes
  PIM Join-Prune next sending: 1 minutes
  PIM BFD enabled: no
  PIM passive interface: no
  PIM VPC SVI: no
  PIM Auto Enabled: no
  PIM Interface Statistics, last reset: never
    General (sent/received):
      Hellos: 19246/19245 (early: 0), JPs: 8246/8, Asserts: 0/0
      Grafts: 0/0, Graft-Acks: 0/0
      DF-Offers: 0/0, DF-Winners: 0/0, DF-Backoffs: 0/0, DF-Passes: 0/0
    Errors:
      Checksum errors: 0, Invalid packet types/DF subtypes: 0/0
      Authentication failed: 0
```

```
      Packet length errors: 0, Bad version packets: 0, Packets from self: 0
      Packets from non-neighbors: 0
          Packets received on passiveinterface: 0
      JPs received on RPF-interface: 0
      (*,G) Joins received with no/wrong RP: 0/0
      (*,G)/(S,G) JPs received for SSM/Bidir groups: 0/0
      JPs filtered by inbound policy: 0
      JPs filtered by outbound policy: 0
```

In addition to the per-interface statistics, NX-OS provides statistics aggregated for the entire PIM router process (global statistics). This output is viewed with the **show ip pim statistics** command (see Example 13-21). These statistics are useful when troubleshooting PIM RP-related message activity.

Example 13-21 *PIM Global Statistics*

```
NX-1# show ip pim statistics

PIM Global Counter Statistics for VRF:default, last reset: never
  Register processing (sent/received):
    Registers: 1/3, Null registers: 1/293, Register-Stops: 4/2
    Registers received and not RP: 1
    Registers received for SSM/Bidir groups: 0/0
  BSR processing (sent/received):
    Bootstraps: 0/0, Candidate-RPs: 0/0
    BSs from non-neighbors: 0, BSs from border interfaces: 0
    BS length errors: 0, BSs which RPF failed: 0
    BSs received but not listen configured: 0
    Cand-RPs from border interfaces: 0
    Cand-RPs received but not listen configured: 0
  Auto-RP processing (sent/received):
    Auto-RP Announces: 0/0, Auto-RP Discoveries: 0/0
    Auto-RP RPF failed: 0, Auto-RP from border interfaces: 0
    Auto-RP invalid type: 0, Auto-RP TTL expired: 0
    Auto-RP received but not listen configured: 0
  General errors:
    Control-plane RPF failure due to no route found: 2
    Data-plane RPF failure due to no route found: 0
    Data-plane no multicast state found: 0
    Data-plane create route state count: 5
```

If a specific PIM neighbor is not forming on an interface, investigate the problem using the event-history or Ethanalyzer facilities available in NX-OS. The **show ip pim internal event-history hello** output in Example 13-22 confirms that PIM hello messages are being sent from NX-1 and that hello messages are being received on Ethernet 3/18 from NX-3.

Example 13-22 *PIM Event-History for Hello Messages*

```
NX-1# show ip pim internal event-history hello
! Output omitted for brevity
02:19:48.277885 pim [31641]: :   GenID Option: 0x2da27857
02:19:48.277882 pim [31641]: :   Bidir Option present
02:19:48.277881 pim [31641]: :   DR Priority Option: 1
02:19:48.277878 pim [31641]: :   Holdtime Option: 105 secs
02:19:48.277875 pim [31641]: : Received Hello from 10.1.13.3 on Ethernet3/18,
length: 30
02:19:42.688032 pim [31641]: : iod = 64 - Send Hello on Ethernet3/18 from
10.1.13.1, holdtime: 105 secs, genID: 0x2cc432ed, dr-priority: 1, vpc: 0
02:19:41.714660 pim [31641]: : iod = 259 - Send Hello on Vlan116 from
10.116.1.254, holdtime: 105 secs, genID: 0xfb8dc7c, dr-priority: 1, vpc: 0
02:19:38.268071 pim [31641]: : iod = 258 - Send Hello on Vlan115 from
10.115.1.254, holdtime: 105 secs, genID: 0x2fd1ac5d, dr-priority: 1, vpc: 0
```

If additional detail about the PIM message contents is desired, the packets can be captured using the Ethanalyzer tool (see Example 13-23). The packet detail is examined locally using the *detail* option, or the capture may be saved for offline analysis with the *write* option.

Example 13-23 *PIM Ethanalyzer Capture of a PIM Hello Message*

```
NX-1# ethanalyzer local interface inband-in capture-filter "pim" detail
! Output omitted for brevity

Capturing on inband
Frame 1: 64 bytes on wire (512 bits), 64 bytes captured (512 bits)
    Encapsulation type: Ethernet (1)
    Arrival Time: Oct 29, 2017 00:48:35.186687000 UTC
    [Time shift for this packet: 0.000000000 seconds]
    Epoch Time: 1509238115.186687000 seconds
    [Time delta from previous captured frame: 0.029364000 seconds]
    [Time delta from previous displayed frame: 0.029364000 seconds]
    [Time since reference or first frame: 3.751505000 seconds]
    Frame Number: 5
    Frame Length: 64 bytes (512 bits)
    Capture Length: 64 bytes (512 bits)
    [Frame is marked: False]
    [Frame is ignored: False]
    [Protocols in frame: eth:ip:pim]
```

```
<>
Internet Protocol Version 4, Src: 10.1.13.3 (10.1.13.3), Dst: 224.0.0.13
  (224.0.0.13)
<>
Protocol Independent Multicast
    0010 .... = Version: 2
    .... 0000 = Type: Hello (0)
    Reserved byte(s): 00
    Checksum: 0x3954 [correct]
    PIM options: 4
        Option 1: Hold Time: 105s
            Type: 1
            Length: 2
            Holdtime: 105s
        Option 19: DR Priority: 1
            Type: 19
            Length: 4
            DR Priority: 1
        Option 22: Bidir Capable
            Type: 22
            Length: 0
        Option 20: Generation ID: 765622359
            Type: 20
            Length: 4
            Generation ID: 765622359
```

Note NX-OS supports PIM neighbor authentication, as well as BFD for PIM neighbors. Refer to the NX-OS configuration guides for information on these features.

PIM Any Source Multicast

The most commonly deployed form of PIM sparse mode is referred to as any source multicast (ASM). ASM uses both RP Trees (RPT) rooted at the PIM RP and shortest-path trees (SPT) rooted at the source to distribute multicast traffic to receivers. The *any source* designation means that when a receiver joins a group, it is joining *any sources* that might send traffic to the group. That might sound intuitive, but it's an important distinction to make between ASM and Source Specific Multicast (SSM).

With PIM ASM, all sources are registered to the PIM RP by their local FHR. This makes the PIM RP the device in the topology with knowledge of all sources. When a receiver joins a group, its local router (LHR) joins the RPT. When multicast traffic arrives at the LHR from the RPT, the source address for the group is known and a PIM join message is sent toward the source to join the SPT. This is referred to as the SPT switchover. After receiving traffic on the SPT, the RPT is pruned from the LHR so that traffic is arriving only from the SPT. Each of these events has corresponding state in the mroute table, which is used to determine the current state of the MDT for the receiver. Figure 13-13 shows an example topology configured with PIM ASM, to better visualize the events that have occurred.

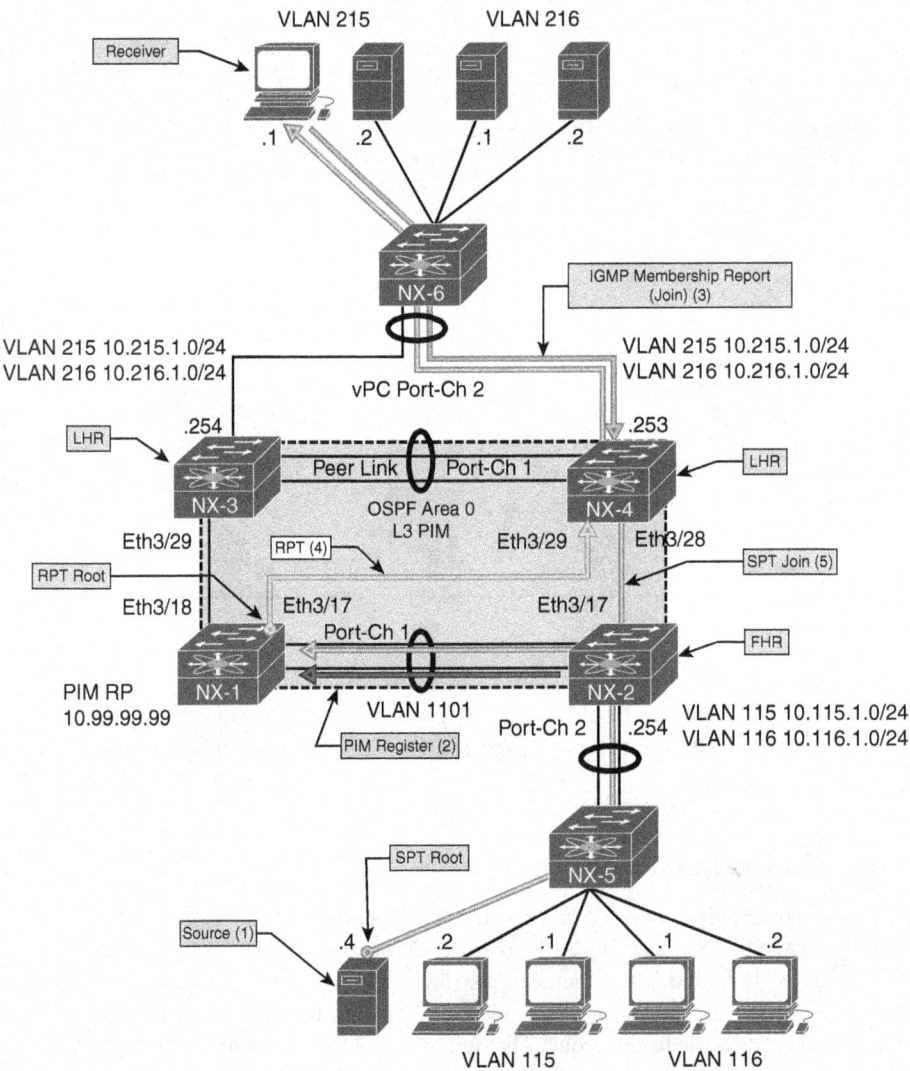

Figure 13-13 *PIM ASM Topology*

Figure 13-13 illustrates the following steps:

Step 1. Source 10.115.1.4 starts sending traffic to group 239.115.115.1. NX-2 receives the traffic and creates an (S,G) mroute entry for (10.115.1.4, 239.115.115.1).

Step 2. NX-2 registers the source with PIM RP NX-1 (10.99.99.1). The PIM RP creates an (S, G) mroute and sends a register-stop message in response. NX-2 continues to periodically send null register messages to the PIM RP as long as data traffic is arriving from the source.

Step 3. Receiver 10.215.1.1 sends an IGMP membership report to join 239.115.115.1. NX-4 receives the report. This results in a (*, G) mroute entry for (*, 239.115.115.1).

Step 4. NX-4 sends a PIM join to the PIM RP NX-1 and traffic arrives on the RPT.

Step 5. NX-4 receives traffic from the RPT and then switches to the SPT by sending a PIM join to NX-2. When NX-2 receives this PIM join message, an OIF for Eth3/17 is added to the (S,G) mroute entry.

Step 6. Although Figure 13-13 does not explicitly show it, NX-4 prunes itself from the RPT and traffic continues to flow from NX-2 on the SPT.

The order of these steps can vary if the receiver joins the RPT before the source is active, but the mentioned steps are required and still occur. Knowledge of these mandatory events can be combined with the mroute state on the FHR, LHR, PIM RP, and intermediate routers to determine exactly where the MDT is broken when a receiver is not getting traffic. It is important to remember that multicast state is created by control plane events in IGMP and PIM, as well as the receipt of multicast traffic in the data plane.

Note The SPT switchover is optional in PIM ASM. The **ip pim spt-threshold infinity** command is used to force a device to remain on the RPT.

PIM ASM Configuration

The configuration for PIM ASM is straightforward. Each interface that is part of the multicast domain is configured with **ip pim sparse-mode.** This includes L3 interfaces between routers and any interface where receivers are connected. It is also considered a best practice to enable the PIM RP Loopback interface with **ip pim sparse-mode** for simplicity and consistency, although this might not be required on some platforms. The PIM RP address must be configured on every PIM router and must have a consistent mapping of groups to a particular RP address. NX-OS supports BSR and Auto-RP for automatically configuring the PIM RP address in the domain; this is covered in the "PIM RP Configuration" section of this chapter. Example 13-24 contains the PIM configuration for NX-1, which is currently acting as the PIM RP. The other PIM routers have a similar configuration but do not have a Loopback99 interface. Loopback99 is the interface where the PIM RP address is configured on NX-1. It is possible to configure multiple PIM RPs in the network and restrict which groups are mapped to a particular RP with the *group-list* or a *prefix-list* option.

Example 13-24 *PIM ASM Configuration on NX-1*

```
NX-1# show run pim
!Command: show running-config pim

feature pim

ip pim rp-address 10.99.99.99 group-list 224.0.0.0/4
ip pim ssm range 232.0.0.0/8


interface Vlan1101
  ip pim sparse-mode

interface loopback99
  ip pim sparse-mode

interface Ethernet3/17
  ip pim sparse-mode

interface Ethernet3/18
  ip pim sparse-mode
```

Depending on the scale of the network environment, it might be necessary to increase the size of the PIM event-history logs when troubleshooting a problem. The size is increased per event-history with the **ip pim event-history** [*event type*] **size** [*event-history size*] configuration command.

PIM ASM Verification

When troubleshooting a multicast routing problem with PIM ASM, it is generally best to start by verifying the multicast state at the LHR where the problematic receiver is attached. This is because determining the LHR has knowledge of the receiver from IGMP is critical. This step determines whether the problem is with L2 (IGMP) or L3 multicast routing (PIM). It also guides the next troubleshooting step to either the RPT or the SPT.

The presence of a (*, G) state at the LHR indicates that a receiver sent a valid membership report and the LHR sent an RPT join toward the PIM RP using the unicast route for the PIM RP to choose the interface. Note that the presence of a (*, G) indicates only *a receiver* sent a membership report, which might mean that the problematic receiver did not. Verify IGMP snooping forwarding tables for each switch that carries the VLAN to be sure that the receivers port is programmed for receiving the traffic. A receiver host or L2 forwarding problem can be confirmed if other receivers in the same VLAN can get the group traffic.

If the LHR has only a (*, G), it typically indicates that traffic is not arriving from the RPT. In that case, verify the mroute state between the LHR and the PIM RP and on any intermediate PIM routers along the tree. If the PIM RP has a valid OIF toward the LHR and packet counts are incrementing, a data plane problem might be keeping traffic from arriving at the LHR on the RPT, or the TTL of the packets might be expiring in transit. Tools such as Switch Port Analyzer (SPAN) capture, the ACL hit counter, or even the Embedded Logic Analyzer Module (ELAM) can isolate the problem to a specific device along the RPT.

After traffic arrives at the LHR on the RPT, it attempts to switch to the SPT. This step involves a routing table lookup for the source address to determine which PIM interface to send the SPT join message on. The LHR has (S, G) state for the SPT at this point with an OIL that contains the interface toward the receiver. The IIF for the SPT can be different than the IIF for the RPT, but it does not have to be.

The LHR sends a PIM SPT join toward the source. Each intermediate router along the path also has an (S, G) state with an OIF toward the LHR and an IIF toward the source for the SPT. At the FHR, the IIF is the interface where the source is attached and the OIF contains the interface on which the PIM SPT join was received, pointing in the direction of the LHR.

The same methodology can be used to troubleshoot multicast forwarding along the SPT. Determine whether any receivers, perhaps on another branch of the SPT, can receive traffic. Determine which device in the SPT is the merge point where the problem branch and working branch converge. The mroute state on that device should indicate that the interfaces for both branches are in the OIL. If they are not, verify PIM to determine why the SPT join was not received. If the OIL does contain both OIFs, the problem could be related to a data plane packet drop issue. In that case, SPAN, ACL, or ELAM is the best option to isolate the problem further. When the problem is isolated to a specific device along the tree, verify the control plane and platform-specific hardware forwarding entries to determine the root cause of the problem.

PIM ASM Event-History and MROUTE State Verification

The primary way to verify which PIM messages have been sent and received is to use the NX-OS event-history for PIM. This output adds debug-level visibility to the PIM process and messaging without any impact to the system resources. Figure 13-13 shows the topology used to examine the PIM messages and mroute state on each device when a new source becomes active and then when a receiver joins the group.

Source 10.115.1.4 begins sending traffic to 239.115.115.1, which arrives at NX-2 on VLAN 115. The receipt of this traffic causes an (S, G) mroute to be created (see Example 13-25). The *ip* flag on the mroute indicates that this state was created by receiving traffic.

Example 13-25 *MROUTE State on NX-2 with Active Source*

```
NX-2# show ip mroute 239.115.115.1
! Output omitted for brevity
IP Multicast Routing Table for VRF "default"

(10.115.1.4/32, 239.115.115.1/32), uptime: 00:00:04, ip pim
  Incoming interface: Vlan115, RPF nbr: 10.115.1.4
  Outgoing interface list: (count: 0)
```

NX-2 then registers this source with the PIM RP NX-1 (10.99.99.99) by sending a PIM register message with an encapsulated data packet from the source. NX-1 receives this register message, as the output of **show ip pim internal event-history null-register** in Example 13-26 shows. The first register message has pktlen 84, which creates the mroute state at the PIM RP. Subsequent null-register messages that do not have the encapsulated source packet are only 20 bytes. NX-1 responds to each register message with a register-stop.

Example 13-26 *Register Message Received on NX-1*

```
NX-1# show ip pim internal event-history null-register
! Output omitted for brevity
null-register events for PIM process
16:36:33.724154 pim [31641]::Send Register-Stop to 10.115.1.254 for
(10.115.1.4/32, 239.115.115.1/32)
16:36:33.724133 pim [31641]::Received NULL Register from 10.115.1.254
for (10.115.1.4/32, 239.115.115.1/32) (pktlen 20)
16:34:35.177572 pim [31641]::Send Register-Stop to 10.115.1.254
for (10.115.1.4/32, 239.115.115.1/32)
16:34:35.177543 pim [31641]::Add new route (10.115.1.4/32, 239.115.115.1/32)
to MRIB, multi-route TRUE
16:34:35.177508 pim [31641]::Create route for (10.115.1.4/32, 239.115.115.1/32)
16:34:35.177398 pim [31641]::Received  Register from 10.115.1.254 for
(10.115.1.4/32, 239.115.115.1/32) (pktlen 84)
```

Note NX-OS can have a separate event-history for receiving encapsulated data register messages, depending on the version. The command is **show ip pim internal event-history data-register-receive**. In older NX-OS releases, **debug ip pim data-register send** and **debug ip pim data-register receive** are used to debug the PIM registration process.

Because no receivers currently exist in the PIM domain, NX-1 adds an (S, G) mroute with an empty OIL (see Example 13-27). The IIF is the L3 interface between NX-1 and NX-2 Vlan1101, which is carried over Port-channel 1. The mroute has the PIM flag to indicate that PIM created this mroute state.

Example 13-27 *MROUTE State on NX-1 with No Receivers*

```
NX-1# show ip mroute 239.115.115.1
! Output omitted for brevity
IP Multicast Routing Table for VRF "default"

(10.115.1.4/32, 239.115.115.1/32), uptime: 00:00:09, pim ip
  Incoming interface: Vlan1101, RPF nbr: 10.1.11.2, internal
  Outgoing interface list: (count: 0)
```

After adding the mroute entry, NX-1 sends a register-stop message back to NX-2 (see Example 13-28). NX-2 suppresses its first null register message because it has just received a register-stop for a recent encapsulated data register message. After the register-stop, NX-2 starts its Register-Suppression timer. Just before expiring the timer, another null-register is sent. If the timer expires without a register stop from the RP, the DR resumes sending full encapsulated packets.

Example 13-28 *Register-stop Message Received from NX-1*

```
NX-2# show ip pim internal event-history null-register
! Output omitted for brevity

null-register events for PIM process
16:36:29.667674 pim [10076]::Received Register-Stop from 10.99.99.99 for
(10.115.1.4/32, 239.115.115.1/32)
16:36:29.666010 pim [10076]::Send Null Register to RP 10.99.99.99 for
(10.115.1.4/32, 239.115.115.1/32)
16:35:29.466161 pim [10076]::Suppress Null Register for
(10.115.1.4/32, 239.115.115.1/32) due to recent data Register sent
16:34:31.121180 pim [10076]::Received Register-Stop from 10.99.99.99 for
(10.115.1.4/32, 239.115.115.1/32)
```

The source has been successfully registered with the PIM RP. This state persists until a receiver joins the group, with NX-2 periodically informing NX-1 via null register messages that the source is still actively sending to the group address.

A receiver in VLAN 215 connected to NX-4 sends a membership report to initiate the flow of multicast for the 239.115.115.1 group. When this message arrives at NX-4, it triggers the creation of a (*, G) mroute entry by IGMP with an OIL containing VLAN 215 (see Example 13-29). The IIF Ethernet 3/29 is the interface used to reach the PIM RP address on NX-1.

Example 13-29 *MROUTE State on NX-4 with a Receiver*

```
NX-4# show ip mroute 239.115.115.1
! Output omitted for brevity
IP Multicast Routing Table for VRF "default"

(*, 239.115.115.1/32), uptime: 00:01:12, igmp ip pim
  Incoming interface: Ethernet3/29, RPF nbr: 10.2.13.1
  Outgoing interface list: (count: 1)
    Vlan215, uptime: 00:01:12, igmp
```

The mroute entry corresponds to a PIM RPT join being sent from NX-4 toward NX-1 (see Example 13-30).

Example 13-30 *PIM RPT Join from NX-4 to NX-1*

```
NX-4# show ip pim internal event-history join-prune
! Output omitted for brevity
16:36:32.630520 pim [13449]::Send Join-Prune on Ethernet3/29, length: 34
16:36:32.630489 pim [13449]::Put (*, 239.115.115.1/32), WRS in join-list for
nbr 10.2.13.1
16:36:32.630483 pim [13449]::wc_bit = TRUE, rp_bit = TRUE
```

When NX-1 receives this RPT Join from NX-4, the OIF Ethernet 3/17 is added to the OIL of the mroute (see Example 13-31).

Example 13-31 *PIM RPT Join Received on NX-1*

```
NX-1# show ip pim internal event-history join-prune
! Output omitted for brevity
16:36:36.688773 pim [31641]::Add Ethernet3/17 to all (S,G)s for group
239.115.115.1
16:36:36.688652 pim [31641]::No (*, 239.115.115.1/32) route exists, to us
16:36:36.688643 pim [31641]::pim_receive_join: We are target comparing with iod
16:36:36.688604 pim [31641]::pim_receive_join: route: (*, 239.115.115.1/32),
wc_bit: TRUE, rp_bit: TRUE
16:36:36.688593 pim [31641]::Received Join-Prune from 10.2.13.3 on Ethernet3/17
length: 34, MTU: 9216, ht: 210
```

The receipt of the join triggers the creation of a (*, G) mroute state on NX-1 and also triggers a join from NX-1 to NX-2 over VLAN 1101 for the source (see Example 13-32).

Example 13-32 *PIM Join Sent from NX-1 to NX-2*

```
NX-1# show ip pim internal event-history join-prune
! Output omitted for brevity
16:36:36.690787 pim [31641]::Send Join-Prune on loopback99, length: 34
16:36:36.690481 pim [31641]::Send Join-Prune on Vlan1101, length: 34
16:36:36.690227 pim [31641]::Put (10.115.1.4/32, 239.115.115.1/32),
S in join-list for nbr 10.1.11.2
16:36:36.690220 pim [31641]::wc_bit = FALSE, rp_bit = FALSE
16:36:36.690158 pim [31641]::Put (10.115.1.4/32, 239.115.115.1/32),
RS in prune-list for nbr 10.99.99.99
16:36:36.690150 pim [31641]::wc_bit = FALSE, rp_bit = TRUE
16:36:36.690078 pim [31641]::(*, 239.115.115.1/32) we are RPF nbr
```

The result of this join from NX-1 to NX-2 is that NX-2 adds an OIF of VLAN 1101 (see Example 13-33).

Example 13-33 *PIM Join Received from NX-1 on NX-2*

```
NX-2# show ip pim internal event-history join-prune
! Output omitted for brevity
16:36:32.634207 pim [10076]::(10.115.1.4/32, 239.115.115.1/32) route exists,
RPF if Vlan115, to us
16:36:32.634186 pim [10076]::pim_receive_join: We are target comparing with iod
16:36:32.634142 pim [10076]::pim_receive_join: route:
(10.115.1.4/32, 239.115.115.1/32), wc_bit: FALSE, rp_bit: FALSE
16:36:32.634125 pim [10076]::Received Join-Prune from 10.1.11.1 on Vlan1101,
length: 34, MTU: 9216, ht: 210
```

Traffic now flows from the source, through NX-2 toward NX-1. NX-1 receives the traffic and forwards it through the RPT to NX-4. At NX-4, traffic is now received on the RPT and the SPT switchover occurs, as seen in the PIM event-history output in Example 13-34. NX-4 first sends the SPT join to NX-2 (10.2.23.2) and then prunes itself from the RPT to NX-1 (10.2.13.1).

Example 13-34 *SPT Switchover on NX-4*

```
NX-4# show ip pim internal event-history join-prune
! Output omitted for brevity
16:36:33.256859 pim [13449]:: Send Join-Prune on Ethernet3/29, length: 34 in context 1
16:36:33.256735 pim [13449]::Put (10.115.1.4/32, 239.115.115.1/32), RS in prune-list
   for nbr 10.2.13.1
16:36:33.256729 pim [13449]::wc_bit = FALSE, rp_bit = TRUE
16:36:33.255153 pim [13449]::Send Join-Prune on Ethernet3/28, length: 34 in context 1
16:36:33.253999 pim [13449]::Put (10.115.1.4/32, 239.115.115.1/32), S in join-list
   for nbr 10.2.23.2
16:36:33.253991 pim [13449]::wc_bit = FALSE, rp_bit = FALSE
```

The resulting mroute state on NX-4 is that the (S, G) was created and the OIL contains VLAN215. The IIF for the (S, G) points toward NX-2, while the IIF for the (*, G) points to the PIM RP at NX-1. Example 13-35 shows the **show ip mroute** output from NX-4.

Example 13-35 *MROUTE State on NX-4 after SPT Switchover*

```
NX-4# show ip mroute 239.115.115.1
! Output omitted for brevity
IP Multicast Routing Table for VRF "default"

(*, 239.115.115.1/32), uptime: 00:01:12, igmp ip pim
  Incoming interface: Ethernet3/29, RPF nbr: 10.2.13.1
  Outgoing interface list: (count: 1)
    Vlan215, uptime: 00:01:12, igmp

(10.115.1.4/32, 239.115.115.1/32), uptime: 00:01:11, ip mrib pim
  Incoming interface: Ethernet3/28, RPF nbr: 10.2.23.2
  Outgoing interface list: (count: 1)
    Vlan215, uptime: 00:01:11, mrib
```

NX-2 has an (S, G) mroute with the IIF of VLAN 115 and the OIF of Ethernet 3/17 that is connected to NX-4. Example 13-36 shows the mroute state of NX-2.

Example 13-36 *MROUTE State on NX-2 after SPT Switchover*

```
NX-2# show ip mroute 239.115.115.1
! Output omitted for brevity
IP Multicast Routing Table for VRF "default"

(10.115.1.4/32, 239.115.115.1/32), uptime: 00:03:09, ip pim
  Incoming interface: Vlan115, RPF nbr: 10.115.1.4
  Outgoing interface list: (count: 1)
    Ethernet3/17, uptime: 00:01:07, pim
```

NX-1 has (*, G) state from NX-4 but no OIF for the (S, G) state. Example 13-37 contains the mroute table of NX-1 after the SPT switchover. The IIF of the (*, G) is the RP interface of Loopback99, which is the root of the RPT.

Example 13-37 *MROUTE State on NX-1 after SPT Switchover*

```
NX-1# show ip mroute 239.115.115.1
! Output omitted for brevity
IP Multicast Routing Table for VRF "default"
 (*, 239.115.115.1/32), uptime: 03:34:42, pim ip
  Incoming interface: loopback99, RPF nbr: 10.99.99.99
```

```
    Outgoing interface list: (count: 1)
      Ethernet3/17, uptime: 03:34:42, pim

(10.115.1.4/32, 239.115.115.1/32), uptime: 03:36:44, pim ip
  Incoming interface: Vlan1101, RPF nbr: 10.1.11.2, internal
  Outgoing interface list: (count: 0)
```

As the previous section demonstrates, the mroute state and the event-history in NX-OS make it possible to determine whether the problem involves the RPT or the SPT and to determine which device along the tree is causing trouble.

PIM ASM Platform Verification

During troubleshooting, verifying the hardware programming of a multicast routing entry might be necessary. This is required when the control plane PIM messages and the mroute table indicate that packets should be leaving an interface, but the downstream PIM neighbor is not receiving the traffic.

An example verification is provided here for reference using NX-2, which is a Nexus 7700 with an F3 module. The verification steps provided here are similar on other NX-OS platforms until the Input/Output (I/O) module is reached. When troubleshooting reaches that level, the verification commands vary significantly, depending on the platform.

The platform-independent (PI) components, such as the mroute table, the mroute table clients (PIM, IGMP, and MSDP), and the Multicast Forwarding Distribution Manager (MFDM), are similar across NX-OS platforms. The way that those entries get programmed into the forwarding and replication ASICs varies. Troubleshooting to the ASIC programming level is best left to Cisco TAC because it is easy to misinterpret the information presented in the output without a firm grasp on the platform-dependent (PD) architecture.

Verify the current mroute state as shown in Example 13-38.

Example 13-38 *MROUTE Verification on NX-2*

```
NX-2# show ip mroute 239.115.115.1
! Output omitted for brevity
IP Multicast Routing Table for VRF "default"

(10.115.1.4/32, 239.115.115.1/32), uptime: 00:00:31, ip pim
  Incoming interface: Vlan115, RPF nbr: 10.115.1.4
  Outgoing interface list: (count: 1)
    Ethernet3/17, uptime: 00:00:31, pim
```

The mroute provides the IIF and OIF, dictating which modules need to be verified. Knowing which modules are involved is important because the Nexus 7000 series performs egress replication for multicast traffic. With egress replication, packets arrive on the ingress module and a copy of the packet is sent to any local receivers on the same I/O module. Another copy of the packet is directed to the fabric toward the I/O module of the interfaces in the OIL of the mroute. When the packet arrives at the egress module, another lookup is done to replicate the packet to the egress interfaces.

The OIL contains L3 interface Ethernet 3/17, and the IIF is VLAN 115. To confirm which physical interface the traffic is arriving on in VLAN 115, the ARP cache and MAC address table entries are checked for the multicast source. The **show ip arp** command provides the MAC address of the source (see Example 13-39).

Example 13-39 *ARP Entry for the Multicast Source*

```
NX-2# show ip arp 10.115.1.4
! Output omitted for brevity


Flags: * - Adjacencies learnt on non-active FHRP router
       + - Adjacencies synced via CFSoE
       # - Adjacencies Throttled for Glean
       D - Static Adjacencies attached to down interface

IP ARP Table
Total number of entries: 1
Address         Age        MAC Address     Interface
10.115.1.4      00:10:53   64a0.e73e.12c2  Vlan115
```

Now check the MAC address table to confirm which interface packets should be arriving on from 10.115.1.4. Example 13-40 shows the output of the MAC address table.

Example 13-40 *MAC Address Table Entry for the Multicast Source*

```
NX-2# show mac address-table dynamic vlan 115
! Output omitted for brevity

Note: MAC table entries displayed are getting read from software.
 Use the 'hardware-age' keyword to get information related to 'Age'

Legend:
        * - primary entry, G - Gateway MAC, (R) - Routed MAC, O - Overlay MAC
        age - seconds since last seen,+ - primary entry using vPC Peer-Link, E -
 EVPN entry
          (T) - True, (F) - False , ~~~ - use 'hardware-age' keyword to retrieve
 age info
   VLAN/BD   MAC Address     Type       age     Secure NTFY Ports/SWID.SSID.LID
---------+-----------------+--------+---------+------+----+------------------
*  115      64a0.e73e.12c2  dynamic     ~~~     F     F    Eth3/19
```

It has now been confirmed that packets are coming into NX-2 on Ethernet 3/19 and egressing on Ethernet 3/17 toward NX-4. The next step in the verification is to check the MFDM entry for the group to ensure that it is present with the correct IIF and OIL (see Example 13-41).

Example 13-41 *MFDM Verification on NX-2*

```
NX-2# show forwarding distribution ip multicast route group 239.115.115.1
! Output omitted for brevity
show forwarding distribution ip multicast route group 239.115.115.1

  (10.115.1.4/32, 239.115.115.1/32), RPF Interface: Vlan115, flags:
    Received Packets: 18 Bytes: 1862
   Number of Outgoing Interfaces: 1
    Outgoing Interface List Index: 30
      Ethernet3/17
```

The MFDM entry looks correct. The remaining steps are performed from the LC console, which is accessed with the **attach module** [*module number*] command. If the verification is being done in a nondefault VDC, it is important to use the **vdc** [*vdc number*] command to enter the correct context after logging into the module. After logging into the correct ingress module, confirm the correct L3LKP ASIC.

Note Verification can be completed without logging into the I/O module by using the **slot** [*module number*] **quoted** [*LC CLI command*] to obtain output from the module.

The F3 module uses a switch-on-chip (SOC) architecture, where groups of front panel ports are serviced by a single SOC. Example 13-42 demonstrates this mapping with the **show hardware internal dev-port-map** command.

Example 13-42 *Determining the SoC Instances on Module 3 of NX-2*

```
NX-2# attach mod 3
! Output omitted for brevity
Attaching to module 3 ...
To exit type 'exit', to abort type '$.'
module-3# show hardware internal dev-port-map
--------------------------------------------------------------
CARD_TYPE:       48 port 10G
>Front Panel ports:48
--------------------------------------------------------------
 Device name           Dev role              Abbr num_inst:
--------------------------------------------------------------
```

```
>  Flanker Eth Mac Driver   DEV_ETHERNET_MAC         MAC_0       6
>  Flanker Fwd Driver       DEV_LAYER_2_LOOKUP       L2LKP       6
>  Flanker Xbar Driver      DEV_XBAR_INTF            XBAR_INTF   6
>  Flanker Queue Driver     DEV_QUEUEING             QUEUE       6
>  Sacramento Xbar ASIC     DEV_SWITCH_FABRIC        SWICHF      1
>  Flanker L3 Driver        DEV_LAYER_3_LOOKUP       L3LKP       6
>  EDC                      DEV_PHY                  PHYS        7
+-------------------------------------------------------------------+
+-----------------+++FRONT PANEL PORT TO ASIC INSTANCE MAP+++-------+
+-------------------------------------------------------------------+
FP port |  PHYS  |  MAC_0  |  L2LKP  |  L3LKP  |  QUEUE  | SWICHF
   17        2        2         2         2         2         0
   18        2        2         2         2         2         0
   19        2        2         2         2         2         0
   20        2        2         2         2         2         0
   21        2        2         2         2         2         0
```

In this particular scenario, the ingress port and egress port are using the same SOC instance (2), and are on the same module. If the module or SOC instance were different, each SOC on each module would need to be verified to ensure that the correct information is present.

With the SOC numbers confirmed for the ingress and egress interfaces, now check the forwarding entry on the I/O module. This entry has the correct incoming interface of Vlan115 and the correct OIL, which contains Ethernet 3/17 (see Example 13-43). Verify the outgoing packets counter to ensure that it is incrementing periodically.

Example 13-43 *I/O Module MFIB Verification on Module 3*

```
Module-3# show forwarding ip multicast route group 239.115.115.1
! Output omitted for brevity

(10.115.1.4/32, 239.115.115.1/32), RPF Interface: Vlan115, flags:
  Received Packets: 1149 Bytes: 117224
  Number of Outgoing Interfaces: 2
  Outgoing Interface List Index: 31
    Vlan1101    Outgoing Packets:0 Bytes:0
    Ethernet3/17   Outgoing Packets:1148 Bytes:117096
```

All information so far has the correct IIF and OIF, so the final step is to check the programming from the SOC (see Example 13-44).

Example 13-44 *Hardware Forwarding Verification on Module 3*

```
Module-3# show system internal forwarding multicast route source 10.115.1.4
group 239.115.115.1 detail
! Output omitted for brevity
Hardware Multicast FIB Entries:
 Flags Legend:
  * - s_star_priority
  S - sg_entry
  D - Non-RPF Drop
  B - Bi-dir route  W - Wildcard route

(10.115.1.4/32, 239.115.115.1/32), Flags: *S
  Dev: 2, HWIndex: 0x6222 Priority: 0x4788, VPN/Mask: 0x1/0x1fff
  RPF Interface: Vlan115, LIF: 0x15
  MD Adj Idx: 0x5c, MDT Idx: 0x1, MTU Idx: 0x0, Dest Idx: 0x2865
  PD oiflist Idx: 0x1, EB MET Ptr: 0x1
  Dev: 2 Index: 0x70      Type: OIF     elif: 0x5      Ethernet3/17
                          Dest Idx: 0x10       SMAC: 64a0.e73e.12c1
module-3#
```

Cisco TAC should interpret the various fields present. These fields represent the pointers to the various table lookups required to replicate the multicast packet locally, or to the fabric if the egress interface is on a different module or SOC. Verification of these indexes requires multiple ELAM captures at the various stages of forwarding lookup and replication.

PIM Bidirectional

PIM BiDIR is another version of PIM SM in which several modifications to traditional ASM behavior have been made. The differences between PIM ASM and PIM BiDIR follow:

- BiDIR uses bidirectional shared trees, whereas ASM relies on unidirectional shared and source trees.

- BiDIR does not use any (S, G) state. ASM must maintain (S, G) state for every source sending traffic to a group address.

- BiDIR does not need any source registration process, which reduces processing overhead.

- Both ASM and BiDIR must have every group mapped to a rendezvous point (RP). The RP in BiDIR does not actually do any packet processing. In BiDIR, the RP address (RPA) is just a route vector that is used as a reference point for forwarding up or down the shared tree.

- BiDIR uses the concept of a Designated Forwarder (DF) that is elected on every link in the PIM domain.

Because BiDIR does not require any (S, G) state, only a single (*, G) mroute entry is required to represent a group. This can dramatically reduce the number of mroute entries in a network with many sources, compared to ASM. With a reduction of mroute entries, the potential scalability of the network is higher because any router platform has a finite number of table entries that can be stored before resources become exhausted. The increase in scale does come with a trade-off of losing visibility into the traffic of individual sources because there is no (S, G) state to track them. However, in very large, many-to-many environments, this downside is outweighed by the reduction in state and the elimination of the registration process.

BiDIR has important terminology that must be defined before looking further into how it operates. Table 13-10 provides these definitions.

Table 13-10 *PIM BiDIR Terminology*

Term	Definition
Rendezvous point address (RPA)	An address that is used as the root of the MDT for all groups mapped to it. The RPA must be reachable from all routers in the PIM domain. The address used for the RPA does not need to be configured on the interface of any router in the PIM domain.
Rendezvous point link (RPL)	The physical link used to reach the RPA. All packets for groups mapped to the RPA are forwarded out of the RPL. The RPL is the only interface where a DF election does not occur.
Designated forwarder (DF)	A single DF is elected on every link for each RPA. The DF is elected based on its unicast routing metric to the RPA. The DF is responsible for sending traffic down the tree to its link and is also responsible for sending traffic from its link upstream toward the RPA. In addition, the DF is responsible for sending PIM Join-Prune messages upstream toward the RPA, based on the state of local receivers or PIM neighbors.
RPF interface	The interface used to reach an address, based on unicast routing protocol metrics.
RPF neighbor	The PIM neighbor used to reach an address, based on the unicast routing protocol metrics. With BiDIR, the RPF neighbor might not be the router that should receive Join-Prune messages. All Join-Prune messages should be directed to the elected DF.

PIM neighbors that can understand BiDIR set the BiDIR capable bit in their PIM hello messages. This is a foundational requirement for BiDIR to become operational. As the PIM process becomes operational on each router, the group-to-RP mapping table is populated by either static configuration or through Auto-RP or BSR. When the RPA(s) are known, the router determines its unicast routing metric for the RPA(s) and moves to the next phase, to elect the DF on each interface.

Initially, all routers begin sending PIM DF election messages that carry the *offer* subtype. The offer message contains the sending router's unicast routing metric to reach the RPA. As these messages are exchanged, all routers on the link become aware of each other and what each router's metric is to the RPA. If a router receives an offer message with a better metric, it stops sending offer messages, to allow the router with the better metric to become elected as the DF. However, if the DF election does not occur, the election process restarts. The result of this initial DF election should be that all routers except for the one with the best metric stop sending offer messages. This allows the router with the best metric to assume the DF role after sending three offers and not receiving additional offers from any other neighbor. After assuming the DF role, the router transmits a DF election message with the *winner* subtype, which tells all routers on the link which device is the DF and informs them of the winning metric.

During normal operation, a new router might come online or metrics toward the RPA could change. This essentially results in offer messages sent to the current DF. If the current DF still has the best metric to the RPA, it responds with a winner message. If the received metric is better than the current DF, the current DF sends a backoff message. The backoff message tells the challenging router to wait before assuming the DF role so that all routers on the link have an opportunity to send an offer message. During this time, the original DF is still acting as the DF. After the new DF is elected, the old DF transmits a DF election message with the *pass* subcode, which hands over the DF responsibility to the new winner. After the DF is elected, the PIM BiDIR network is ready to begin forwarding multicast packets bidirectionally using shared trees rooted at the RPA.

Packets arriving from a downstream link are forwarded upstream until they reach the router with the RPL, which contains the RPA. Because no registration process occurs and no switchover to an SPT takes place, the RPA does not need to be on a router. This is initially confusing, but it works because packets are forwarded out the RPL toward the RPA, and (*, G) state is built from every FHR connected to a source and from every LHR with an interested receiver toward the RPA. In other words, with BiDIR, packets do not have to actually *traverse* the RP as they do in ASM. The intersecting branches of the bidirectional (*, G) tree can distribute multicast directly between source and receiver.

In NX-OS, up to eight BiDIR RPAs are supported per VRF. Redundancy for the RPA is achieved using a concept referred to as a phantom RP. The term is used because the RPA is not assigned to any router in the PIM domain. For example, assume an RPA address of 10.1.1.1. NX-1 could have 10.1.1.0/30 configured on its Loopback10 interface and NX-3 could have 10.1.1.0/29 configured on its Loopback10 interface. All routers in the PIM domain follow the longest-prefix-match rule in their routing table to prefer NX-1. If NX-1 failed, NX-3 would then become the preferred path to the RPL and thus the RP as soon as the unicast routing protocol converges.

The topology in Figure 13-14 demonstrates the configuration and troubleshooting of PIM BiDIR.

802 Chapter 13: Troubleshooting Multicast

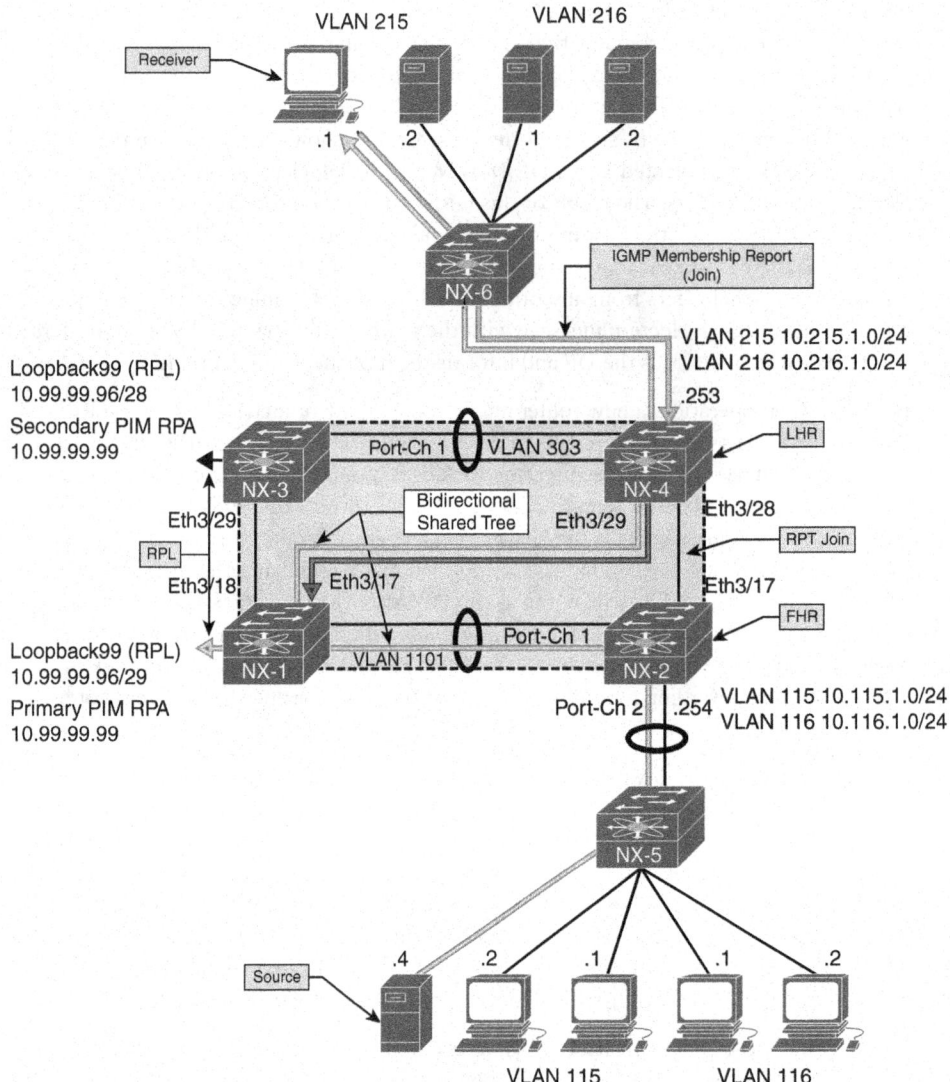

Figure 13-14 *PIM BiDIR Topology*

When a receiver attached to VLAN 215 on NX-4 joins 239.115.115.1, a (*, G) mroute entry is created on NX-4. On the link between NX-4 and NX-1, NX-1 is the elected DF because it has a better unicast metric to the RPA. Therefore the (*, G) join from NX-4 is sent to NX-1 upstream toward the primary RPA.

NX-1 and NX-3 are both configured with a link (Loopback99) to the phantom RP 10.99.99.99. However, NX-1 has a *more specific* route to the RPA through its RPL and is used by all routers in the topology to reach the RPA.

When 10.115.1.4 begins sending multicast traffic to 239.115.115.1, the traffic arrives on VLAN 115 on NX-2. Because NX-2 is the elected DF on VLAN 115, the traffic is forwarded upstream toward the RPA on its RPF interface, VLAN 1101. NX-1 is the elected DF for VLAN 1101 between NX-2 and NX-1 because it has a better metric to the RPA. NX-1 receives the traffic from NX-2 and forwards it based on the current OIL for its (*, G) mroute entry. The OIL contains both the Ethernet 3/17 link to NX-4 and also the Loopback99 interface with is the RPL. As traffic flows from the source to the receiver, the shared tree is used end to end, and NX-4 never uses the direct link it has to NX-2 because no SPT switchover takes place with BiDIR. No source needs to be registered with a PIM RP and no (S, G) state needs to be created because all traffic for the group flows along the shared tree.

BiDIR Configuration

The configuration for PIM BiDIR is similar to the configuration of PIM ASM. PIM sparse mode must be enabled on all interfaces. The *BiDIR capable* bit is set in PIM hello messages by default, so no interface-level command is required to specifically enable PIM BiDIR. An RP is designated as a BiDIR RPA when it is configured with the *bidir* keyword in the **ip pim rp-address** [*RP address*] **group-range** [*groups*] **bidir** command.

Example 13-45 shows the phantom RPA configuration that was previously described. Loopback99 is the RPL, which is configured with a subnet that contains the RPA. The RPA is not actually configured on any router in the topology, which is a major difference between PIM BiDIR and PIM ASM. This RPA is advertised to the PIM domain with OSPF; because you want OSPF to advertise the link as 10.99.99.96/29, the **ip ospf network point-to-point** command is used. This forces OSPF on NX-1 to advertise this as a *stub-link* in the type 1 router link-state advertisement (LSA).

Example 13-45 *PIM BiDIR Configuration on NX-1*

```
NX-1# show run pim
! Output omitted for brevity
!Command: show running-config pim

feature pim

ip pim rp-address 10.99.99.99 group-list 224.0.0.0/4 bidir
ip pim ssm range 232.0.0.0/8

interface Vlan1101
  ip pim sparse-mode

interface loopback0
  ip pim sparse-mode

interface loopback99
 ip pim sparse-mode
```

```
interface Ethernet3/17
  ip pim sparse-mode

interface Ethernet3/18
  ip pim sparse-mode
NX-1# show run interface loopback99
! Output omitted for brevity

!Command: show running-config interface loopback99

interface loopback99
  ip address 10.99.99.98/29
  ip ospf network point-to-point
  ip router ospf 1 area 0.0.0.0
  ip pim sparse-mode
NX-1# show ip pim group-range 239.115.115.1
PIM Group-Range Configuration for VRF "default"
Group-range        Action Mode  RP-address      Shrd-tree-range   Origin

224.0.0.0/4        -      Bidir 10.99.99.99     -                 Static
NX-1# show ip pim rp
PIM RP Status Information for VRF "default"
BSR disabled
Auto-RP disabled
BSR RP Candidate policy: None
BSR RP policy: None
Auto-RP Announce policy: None
Auto-RP Discovery policy: None

RP: 10.99.99.99, (1),
 uptime: 22:29:39   priority: 0,
 RP-source: (local),
 group ranges:
 224.0.0.0/4  (bidir)
```

Note All other routers in the topology have the same BiDIR-specific configuration, which is the static RPA with the **BiDIR** keyword. NX-1 and NX-3 are the only routers configured with an RPL to the RPA.

BiDIR Verification

To understand the mroute state and BiDIR events, verification begins from NX-4, where a receiver is connected in VLAN 215. Example 13-46 gives the output of **show ip mroute** from NX-4, which is the LHR. The (*, G) mroute was created as a result of the IGMP membership report from the receiver. Because this is a bidirectional shared tree, notice that the RPF interface Ethernet 3/29 used to reach the RPA is also included in the OIL for the mroute.

Example 13-46 *PIM BiDIR MROUTE Entry on NX-4*

```
NX-4# show ip mroute
! Output omitted for brevity
IP Multicast Routing Table for VRF "default"

(*, 224.0.0.0/4), bidir, uptime: 00:06:39, pim ip
  Incoming interface: Ethernet3/29, RPF nbr: 10.2.13.1
  Outgoing interface list: (count: 1)
    Ethernet3/29, uptime: 00:06:39, pim, (RPF)

(*, 239.115.115.1/32), bidir, uptime: 00:04:08, igmp ip pim
  Incoming interface: Ethernet3/29, RPF nbr: 10.2.13.1
  Outgoing interface list: (count: 2)
    Ethernet3/29, uptime: 00:04:08, pim, (RPF)
    Vlan215, uptime: 00:04:08, igmp
```

The DF election process in BiDIR determines which PIM router on each interface is responsible for sending join-prune messages and routing packets from upstream to downstream and vice versa on the bidirectional shared tree. The output of **show ip pim df** provides a concise view of the current DF state on each PIM-enabled interface (see Example 13-47). On VLAN 215, this router is the DF; on the RPF interface toward the RPA, this router is not the DF because the peer has a better metric to the RPA.

Example 13-47 *PIM BiDIR DF Status on NX-4*

```
NX-4# show ip pim df
! Output omitted for brevity
Bidir-PIM Designated Forwarder Information for VRF "default"

RP Address (ordinal)    RP Metric       Group Range
10.99.99.99 (1)         [110/5]         224.0.0.0/4

  Interface             DF Address      DF State    DF Metric    DF Uptime
  Vlan303               10.2.33.2       Winner      [110/5]      00:22:28
  Vlan216               10.216.1.254    Loser       [110/5]      00:22:29
```

Vlan215	10.215.1.253	Winner	[110/5]	00:19:58	
Lo0	10.2.2.3	Winner	[110/5]	00:22:29	
Eth3/28	10.2.23.2	Loser	[110/2]	00:22:29	
Eth3/29	10.2.13.1	Loser	[0/0]	00:22:29	(RPF)

If additional detail is needed about the BiDIR DF election process, the output of **show ip pim internal event-history bidir** provides information on the interface state machine and its reaction to the received PIM DF election messages. Example 13-48 shows the event-history output from NX-4. The DF election is seen for VLAN 215; no other offers are received and NX-4 becomes the winner. On Ethernet 3/29, NX-4 (10.2.13.3) has a worse metric (-1/-1) than the current DF (10.2.13.1) and does not reply with an offer message. This allows NX-1 to become the DF on this interface.

Example 13-48 *PIM BiDIR Event-History on NX-4*

```
NX-4# show ip pim internal event-history bidir
! Output omitted for brevity

bidir events for PIM process
20:32:46.269627 pim [10572]:: pim_update_df_state: vrf: default: rp:
10.99.99.99 iod Ethernet3/29 prev_state 2 Notify IGMP
20:32:46.269623 pim [10572]:: Entering Lose state on Ethernet3/29
20:32:46.269439 pim [10572]:: pim_update_df_state: vrf: default: rp:
10.99.99.99 iod Ethernet3/29 prev_state 2 Notify IGMP
20:32:46.269433 pim [10572]:: Our metric: -1/-1 is worse than received
metric: 0/0 RPF Ethernet3/29 old_winner 10.2.13.1
20:32:46.269419 pim [10572]:: Received DF-Winner from 10.2.13.1 on Ethernet3/29
RP 10.99.99.99, metric 0/0
20:32:40.205960 pim [10572]:: Add RP-route for RP 10.99.99.99,
Bidir-RP Ordinal:1, DF-interfaces: 00000000
20:32:40.205947 pim [10572]:: pim_df_expire_timer: Entering Winner state
on Vlan215
20:32:40.205910 pim [10572]:: Expiration timer fired in Offer state for RP
10.99.99.99 on Vlan215
```

Because NX-4 is the DF election winner on VLAN 215, it sends a PIM join for the shared tree to the DF on the RPF interface Ethernet 3/29. The **show ip pim internal event-history join-prune** command is used to view these events (see Example 13-49 for the output).

PIM Multicast

Example 13-49 *PIM BiDIR Join-prune Event-History on NX-4*

```
NX-4# show ip pim internal event-history join-prune
! Output omitted for brevity

join-prune events for PIM process
20:34:34.286181 pim [10572]:: Keep bidir (*, 239.115.115.1/32) entry alive due
to joined oifs exist
20:33:40.056128 pim [10572]: [10739]: skip sending periodic join not having
any oif
20:33:40.056116 pim [10572]:: Keep bidir (*, 224.0.0.0/4) prefix-entry alive
20:33:34.016224 pim [10572]:: Send Join-Prune on Ethernet3/29, length:
34 in context 1
20:33:34.016186 pim [10572]:: Put (*, 239.115.115.1/32), WRS in join-list for
nbr 10.2.13.1
20:33:34.016179 pim [10572]:: wc_bit = TRUE, rp_bit = TRUE
```

In addition to the detailed information in the event-history output, the interface statistics can be checked to view the total number of BiDIR messages that were exchanged (see Example 13-50).

Example 13-50 *PIM BiDIR Interface Counters on NX-4*

```
NX-4# show ip mroute
! Output omitted for brevity
show ip pim interface ethernet 3/29
PIM Interface Status for VRF "default"
Ethernet3/29, Interface status: protocol-up/link-up/admin-up
  IP address: 10.2.13.3, IP subnet: 10.2.13.0/24
  PIM DR: 10.2.13.3, DR's priority: 1
  PIM neighbor count: 1
  PIM hello interval: 30 secs, next hello sent in: 00:00:22
  PIM neighbor holdtime: 105 secs
  PIM configured DR priority: 1
  PIM configured DR delay: 3 secs
  PIM border interface: no
  PIM GenID sent in Hellos: 0x140c2403
  PIM Hello MD5-AH Authentication: disabled
  PIM Neighbor policy: none configured
  PIM Join-Prune inbound policy: none configured
  PIM Join-Prune outbound policy: none configured
  PIM Join-Prune interval: 1 minutes
  PIM Join-Prune next sending: 0 minutes
  PIM BFD enabled: no
  PIM passive interface: no
```

```
    PIM VPC SVI: no
    PIM Auto Enabled: no
    PIM Interface Statistics, last reset: never
      General (sent/received):
        Hellos: 4880/2121 (early: 0), JPs: 378/0, Asserts: 0/0
        Grafts: 0/0, Graft-Acks: 0/0
        DF-Offers: 1/3, DF-Winners: 0/381, DF-Backoffs: 0/0, DF-Passes: 0/0
      Errors:
        Checksum errors: 0, Invalid packet types/DF subtypes: 0/0
        Authentication failed: 0
        Packet length errors: 0, Bad version packets: 0, Packets from self: 0
        Packets from non-neighbors: 0
            Packets received on passiveinterface: 0
        JPs received on RPF-interface: 0
        (*,G) Joins received with no/wrong RP: 0/0
        (*,G)/(S,G) JPs received for SSM/Bidir groups: 0/0
        JPs filtered by inbound policy: 0
        JPs filtered by outbound policy: 0
```

The next hop in the bidirectional shared tree is NX-1, which is NX-4's RPF neighbor to the RPA. The join-prune event-history confirms that the (*, G) join was received from NX-4 (see Example 13-51).

Example 13-51 *PIM BiDIR Join-Prune Event-History on NX-1*

```
NX-1# show ip pim internal event-history join-prune
! Output omitted for brevity

bidir events for PIM process
20:33:34.020037 pim [7851]:: -----
20:33:34.020020 pim [7851]:: (*, 239.115.115.1/32) route exists, RPF if
loopback99, to us
20:33:34.020008 pim [7851]:: pim_receive_join: We are target comparing with iod
20:33:34.019968 pim [7851]:: pim_receive_join: route: (*, 239.115.115.1/32),
wc_bit: TRUE, rp_bit: TRUE
20:33:34.019341  pim [7851]:: Received Join-Prune from 10.2.13.3 on
Ethernet3/17, length: 34, MTU: 9216, ht: 210
```

The mroute state for NX-1 contains Ethernet3/17 as well as Loopback99, which is the RPL in Example 13-52. All groups that map to the RPA are forwarded on the RPL toward the RPA.

Example 13-52 *PIM BiDIR MROUTE Entry on NX-1*

```
NX-1# show ip mroute
! Output omitted for brevity


IP Multicast Routing Table for VRF "default"

(*, 224.0.0.0/4), bidir, uptime: 00:13:22, pim ip
  Incoming interface: loopback99, RPF nbr: 10.99.99.99
  Outgoing interface list: (count: 1)
    loopback99, uptime: 00:13:22, pim, (RPF)

(*, 239.115.115.1/32), bidir, uptime: 00:14:13, pim ip
  Incoming interface: loopback99, RPF nbr: 10.99.99.99
  Outgoing interface list: (count: 2)
    Ethernet3/17, uptime: 00:08:47, pim
    loopback99, uptime: 00:13:22, pim, (RPF)
```

Example 13-53 gives the output of **show ip pim df**. Because the RPL is local to this device, it is the DF winner on all interfaces except for the RPL. No DF is elected on the RPL in PIM BiDIR.

Example 13-53 *PIM DF Status on NX-1*

```
NX-1# show ip pim df
! Output omitted for brevity
Bidir-PIM Designated Forwarder Information for VRF "default"

RP Address (ordinal)    RP Metric      Group Range
10.99.99.99 (1)         [0/0]          224.0.0.0/4

  Interface             DF Address     DF State    DF Metric    DF Uptime
  Vlan1101              10.1.11.1      Winner      [0/0]        00:14:43
  Po3                   10.1.12.2      Winner      [0/0]        00:14:43
  Lo0                   10.1.1.1       Winner      [0/0]        00:14:43
  Lo99                  0.0.0.0        Loser       [0/0]        00:14:43     (RPF)
  Eth3/17               10.2.13.1      Winner      [0/0]        00:14:43
  Eth3/18               10.1.13.1      Winner      [0/0]        00:14:43
```

No (S, G) join exists from the RPA toward the source as there would have been in PIM ASM. In BiDIR, all traffic from the source is forwarded from NX-2, which is the FHR toward the RPA. Therefore, a join from NX-1 to NX-2 is not required to pull the traffic to NX-1 across VLAN1101. This fact highlights one troubleshooting disadvantage of BiDIR.

No visibility from the RPA to the FHR is available about this particular source because the (S, G) state does not exist.

An ELAM capture can be used on NX-1 to verify that traffic is arriving from NX-2. Another useful technique is to configure a permit line in an ACL to match the traffic. Configure the ACL with **statistics per-entry**, which provides a counter to verify that traffic has arrived. In the output of Example 13-54, the ACL named *verify* was configured to match the source connected on NX-2. The ACL is applied ingress on VLAN 1101, which is the interface traffic should be arriving on.

Example 13-54 *ACL to Match Traffic on NX-1*

```
NX-1# show run | sec verify
! Output omitted for brevity
ip access-list verify
  statistics per-entry
  10 permit ip 10.115.1.4/32 239.115.115.1/32
  20 permit ip any any
NX-1# show running-config interface Vlan1101
! Output omitted for brevity

interface Vlan1101
  description L3 to 7009-B-NX-2
  no shutdown
  mtu 9216
  ip access-group verify in
  no ip redirects
  ip address 10.1.11.1/30
  no ipv6 redirects
  ip ospf cost 1
  ip router ospf 1 area 0.0.0.0
  ip pim sparse-mode
NX-1# show access-list verify

IP access list verify
        statistics per-entry
        10 permit ip 10.115.1.4/32 239.115.115.1/32 [match=448]
        20 permit ip any any [match=108]
```

In this exercise, the source is connected to NX-2, so the mroute entry can be verified to ensure that VLAN 1101 to NX-1 is included in the OIL. Example 13-55 shows the mroute from NX-2. The mroute entry covers all groups mapped to the RPA.

Example 13-55 *PIM BiDIR MROUTE Entry on NX-2*

```
NX-2# show ip pim df
! Output omitted for brevity
Bidir-PIM Designated Forwarder Information for VRF "default"

RP Address (ordinal)    RP Metric       Group Range
10.99.99.99 (1)         [110/2]         224.0.0.0/4

  Interface             DF Address      DF State    DF Metric   DF Uptime
  Vlan1101              10.1.11.1       Loser       [0/0]       00:08:49    (RPF)
  Vlan116               10.116.1.254    Winner      [110/2]     00:08:49
  Vlan115               10.115.1.254    Winner      [110/2]     00:08:49
  Eth3/17               10.2.23.2       Winner      [110/2]     00:08:49
  Eth3/18               10.1.23.2       Winner      [110/2]     00:08:48


NX-2# show ip mroute
IP Multicast Routing Table for VRF "default"

(*, 224.0.0.0/4), bidir, uptime: 2d12h, pim ip
  Incoming interface: Vlan1101, RPF nbr: 10.1.11.1
  Outgoing interface list: (count: 1)
    Vlan1101, uptime: 2d12h, pim, (RPF)
```

Because NX-2 is the DF winner on VLAN 115, it is responsible for forwarding multicast traffic from VLAN 115 toward the RPF interface for the RPA that is on VLAN 1101. With BiDIR, NX-2 has no need to register its source with the RPA; it simply forwards traffic from VLAN 115 up the bidirectional shared tree.

This section explained PIM BiDIR and detailed how to confirm the DF and mroute entries at each multicast router participating in the bidirectional shared tree. BiDIR and ASM have several differences with respect to multicast state and forwarding behavior. When faced with troubleshooting a BiDIR problem, it is important to know which RPA should be used for the group and which devices along the tree are functioning as the DR. It should then be possible to trace from the receiver toward the source and isolate the problem to a particular device along the path.

PIM RP Configuration

When PIM SM is configured for ASM or BiDIR, each multicast group must map to a PIM RP address. This mapping must be consistent in the network, and each router in the PIM domain must know the RP address–to–group mapping. Three options are available for configuring the PIM RP address in a multicast network:

1. **Static PIM RP:** The RP-to-group mapping is configured on each router statically.

2. **Auto-RP:** PIM RPs announce themselves to a mapping agent. The mapping agent advertises the RP to group mapping to all routers in the PIM domain. Cisco created Auto-RP before the PIM BSR mechanism was standardized.

3. **BSR:** Candidate RPs announce themselves to the bootstrap router. The bootstrap router advertises the group to RP mapping in a bootstrap message to all routers in the PIM domain.

Static RP Configuration

Static RP is the simplest mechanism to implement. Each router in the domain is configured with a PIM RP address, as shown in Example 13-56.

Example 13-56 *PIM Static RP on NX-3 Configuration Example*

```
NX-3# show run pim
! Output omitted for brevity

!Command: show running-config pim

feature pim

ip pim rp-address 10.99.99.99 group-list 224.0.0.0/4
ip pim ssm range 232.0.0.0/8

interface Vlan215
  ip pim sparse-mode

interface Vlan216
  ip pim sparse-mode

interface Vlan303
  ip pim sparse-mode

interface Ethernet3/28
  ip pim sparse-mode

interface Ethernet3/29
  ip pim sparse-mode
```

The simplicity has drawbacks, however. Any change to the group mapping requires the network operator to update the configuration on each router. In addition, a single static PIM RP could become a scalability bottleneck as hundreds or thousands of sources are being registered. If the network is small in scale, or if a single PIM RP address is being used for all groups, a static RP could be a good option.

Note If a static RP is configured and dynamic RP–to–group mapping is received, the router uses the dynamic learned address if it is more specific. If the group mask length is equal, the higher IP address is used. The *override* keyword forces a static RP to win over Auto-RP or BSR.

Auto-RP Configuration and Verification

Auto-RP uses the concept of candidate RPs and candidate mapping agents. Candidate RPs send their configured multicast group ranges in RP-announce messages that are multicast to 224.0.1.39. Mapping agents listen for the RP-announce messages and collect the RP-to-group mapping data into a local table. After resolving any conflict in the mapping, the list is passed to the network using RP-discovery messages that are sent to multicast address 224.0.1.40. Routers in the network are configured to listen for the RP-discovery messages sent by the elected mapping agent. Upon receiving the RP-discovery message, each router in the PIM domain updates its local RP-to-group mapping table.

Multiple mapping agents could exist in the network, so a deterministic method is needed to determine which mapping agent routers should listen to. Routers in the network use the mapping agent with the highest IP address to populate their group-to-RP mapping tables. See Figure 13-15 for the topology used here to discuss the operation and verification of Auto-RP.

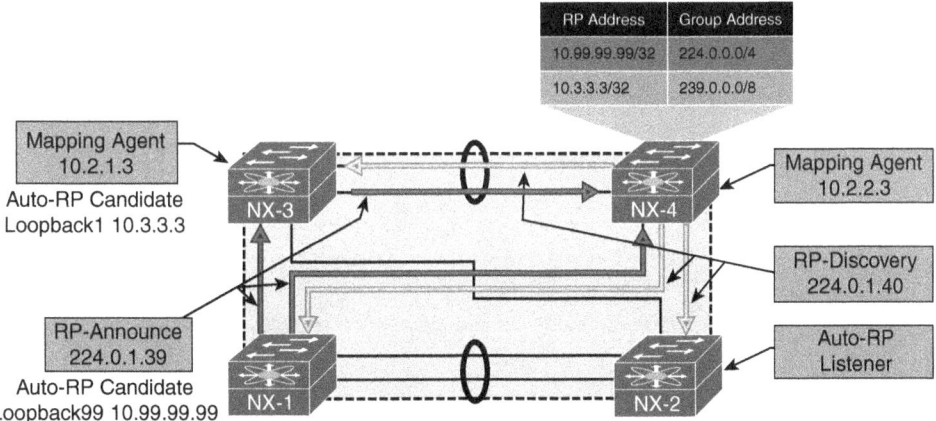

Figure 13-15 *PIM Auto-RP Topology*

In the topology in Figure 13-15, NX-1 is configured to send RP-announce messages for 224.0.0.0/4 with RP address 10.99.99.99. NX-3 is configured to send RP-announce messages for 239.0.0.0/8 with RP address 10.3.3.3. NX-3 is also configured as an Auto-RP mapping agent with address 10.2.1.3. NX-4 is configured as an Auto-RP mapping agent with address 10.2.2.3, and NX-2 is simply listening for Auto-RP discovery messages to populate the local RP-to-group mapping information. This example was built to illustrate the fact that multiple candidate RPs (and multiple mapping agents) can coexist.

When the PIM domain has overlapping or conflicting information, such as two candidate RPs announcing the same group, the mapping agent must decide which RP is advertised in the RP-discovery messages. The tie-breaking rule is as follows:

1. Choose the RP announcing the more specific group address.

2. If the groups are announced with an equal number of mask bits, choose the RP with the higher IP address.

In the example here, NX-3 is announcing a more specific advertisement of 239.0.0.0/8 versus the NX-1 advertisement of 224.0.0.0/4. The resulting behavior is that NX-3 is chosen as the RP for 239.0.0.0/8 groups, and NX-1 is chosen for all other groups. If multiple Auto-RP mapping agents are configured, NX-OS will choose to listen to RP-discovery messages from the mapping agent with the higher IP address.

Example 13-57 shows the PIM configuration for NX-1. The **ip pim auto-rp rp-candidate** command configures NX-1 to send Auto-RP RP-announce messages with a TTL of 16 for all multicast groups. NX-OS does not listen to or forward Auto-RP messages by default. The **ip pim auto-rp forward listen** command instructs the device to listen for and forward the Auto-RP groups 224.0.1.39 and 224.0.1.40. The local PIM RP-to-group mapping is shown with the **show ip pim rp** command. It displays the current group mapping for each RP, along with the RP-source, which is the mapping agent NX-4 (10.2.2.3).

Example 13-57 *PIM Auto-RP Candidate-RP Configuration on NX-1*

```
NX-1# show run pim
! Output omitted for brevity

!Command: show running-config pim

feature pim

ip pim rp-address 10.99.99.99 group-list 224.0.0.0/4
ip pim auto-rp rp-candidate 10.99.99.99 group-list 224.0.0.0/4 scope 16
ip pim ssm range 232.0.0.0/8
ip pim auto-rp forward listen

interface Vlan1101
  ip pim sparse-mode

interface loopback99
  ip pim sparse-mode

interface Ethernet3/17
  ip pim sparse-mode
```

```
  interface Ethernet3/18
    ip pim sparse-mode

NX-1# show ip pim rp
PIM RP Status Information for VRF "default"
BSR disabled
Auto-RP RPA: 10.2.2.3, uptime: 00:55:41, expires: 00:02:28
BSR RP Candidate policy: None
BSR RP policy: None
Auto-RP Announce policy: None
Auto-RP Discovery policy: None

RP: 10.3.3.3, (0), uptime: 00:48:46, expires: 00:02:28,
  priority: 0, RP-source: 10.2.2.3 (A), group ranges:
      239.0.0.0/8
RP: 10.99.99.99*, (0), uptime: 1w5d, expires: 00:02:28 (A),
  priority: 0, RP-source: 10.2.2.3 (A), (local), group ranges:
      224.0.0.0/4
```

The group range can be configured for additional granularity using the *group-list*, *prefix-list*, or *route-map* options.

Note The interface used as an Auto-RP candidate-RP or mapping agent must be configured with **ip pim sparse-mode**.

Example 13-58 shows the Auto-RP mapping agent configuration from NX-4. This configuration results in NX-4 sending RP-discovery messages with a TTL of 16. In the output of **show ip pim rp**, because NX-4 is the current mapping agent, a timer is displayed to indicate when the next RP-discovery message will be sent.

Example 13-58 *Auto-RP Mapping Agent Configuration on NX-4*

```
NX-4# show run pim
! Output omitted for brevity

!Command: show running-config pim

feature pim

ip pim auto-rp mapping-agent loopback0 scope 16
ip pim ssm range 232.0.0.0/8
ip pim auto-rp listen forward
```

Chapter 13: Troubleshooting Multicast

```
interface Vlan215
  ip pim sparse-mode

interface Vlan216
  ip pim sparse-mode

interface Vlan303
  ip pim sparse-mode

interface loopback0
  ip pim sparse-mode

interface Ethernet3/28
  ip pim sparse-mode

interface Ethernet3/29
  ip pim sparse-mode
NX-4# show ip pim rp
PIM RP Status Information for VRF "default"
BSR disabled
Auto-RP RPA: 10.2.2.3*, next Discovery message in: 00:00:29
BSR RP Candidate policy: None
BSR RP policy: None
Auto-RP Announce policy: None
Auto-RP Discovery policy: None

RP: 10.3.3.3, (0),
 uptime: 01:18:01   priority: 0,
 RP-source: 10.3.3.3 (A),
 group ranges:
 239.0.0.0/8    , expires: 00:02:37 (A)
RP: 10.99.99.99, (0),
 uptime: 01:20:27   priority: 0,
 RP-source: 10.99.99.99 (A),
 group ranges:
 224.0.0.0/4    , expires: 00:02:36 (A)
```

Note Do not use an anycast IP address for the mapping agent address. This could result in frequent refreshing of the RP mapping in the network.

NX-3 is configured to act as both an Auto-RP candidate RP and a mapping agent. Example 13-59 shows the configuration for NX-3. Note that the interface Loopback0 is being used as the mapping agent address, and Loopback1 is being used as the candidate-rp address; both are configured with **ip pim sparse-mode**.

Example 13-59 *Auto-RP Configuration on NX-3*

```
NX-3# show run pim
! Output omitted for brevity

!Command: show running-config pim

feature pim

ip pim rp-address 10.3.3.3 group-list 239.0.0.0/8
ip pim auto-rp rp-candidate 10.3.3.3 group-list 239.0.0.0/8 scope 16
ip pim auto-rp mapping-agent loopback0 scope 16
ip pim ssm range 232.0.0.0/8
ip pim auto-rp listen forward

interface Vlan215
  ip pim sparse-mode

interface Vlan216
  ip pim sparse-mode

interface Vlan303
  ip pim sparse-mode

interface loopback0
  ip pim sparse-mode

interface loopback1
  ip pim sparse-mode

interface Ethernet3/28
  ip pim sparse-mode

interface Ethernet3/29
  ip pim sparse-mode
NX-3# show ip pim rp
PIM RP Status Information for VRF "default"
BSR disabled
Auto-RP RPA: 10.2.2.3, uptime: 01:21:50, expires: 00:02:49
BSR RP Candidate policy: None
BSR RP policy: None
Auto-RP Announce policy: None
Auto-RP Discovery policy: None
```

```
RP: 10.3.3.3*, (0), uptime: 01:16:28, expires: 00:02:49 (A),
  priority: 0, RP-source: 10.2.2.3 (A), (local), group ranges:
      239.0.0.0/8
RP: 10.99.99.99, (0), uptime: 01:18:18, expires: 00:02:49,
  priority: 0, RP-source: 10.2.2.3 (A), group ranges:
      224.0.0.0/4
```

Finally, the configuration of NX-2 is to simply act as an Auto-RP listener and forwarder. Example 13-60 shows the configuration, which allows NX-4 to receive the Auto-RP RP-discovery messages from NX-4 and NX-3.

Example 13-60 *Auto-RP Listener Configuration on NX-2*

```
NX-2# show run pim
! Output omitted for brevity

!Command: show running-config pim

feature pim

ip pim ssm range 232.0.0.0/8
ip pim auto-rp listen forward

interface Vlan115
  ip pim sparse-mode

interface Vlan116
  ip pim sparse-mode

interface Vlan1101
  ip pim sparse-mode

interface Ethernet3/17
  ip pim sparse-mode

interface Ethernet3/18
  ip pim sparse-mode
NX-2# show run pim
PIM RP Status Information for VRF "default"
BSR disabled
Auto-RP RPA: 10.2.2.3, uptime: 00:07:29, expires: 00:02:25
BSR RP Candidate policy: None
BSR RP policy: None
```

```
Auto-RP Announce policy: None
Auto-RP Discovery policy: None

RP: 10.3.3.3, (0),
 uptime: 00:00:34   priority: 0,
 RP-source: 10.2.2.3 (A),
 group ranges:
  239.0.0.0/8   , expires: 00:02:25 (A)
RP: 10.99.99.99, (0),
 uptime: 00:02:59   priority: 0,
 RP-source: 10.2.2.3 (A),
 group ranges:
  224.0.0.0/4   , expires: 00:02:25 (A)
```

Because the Auto-RP messages are bound by their configured TTL scope, care must be taken to ensure that all RP-announce messages can reach all mapping agents in the network. It is also important to ensure that the scope of the RP-discovery messages is large enough for all routers in the PIM domain to receive the messages. If multiple mapping agents exist and the TTL is misconfigured, it is possible to have inconsistent RP-to-group mapping throughout the PIM domain, depending on the proximity to the mapping agent.

NX-OS provides a useful event-history for troubleshooting Auto-RP message problems. The **show ip pim internal event-history rp** output is provided from NX-4 in Example 13-61. The output is verbose, but it shows that NX-4 elects itself as the mapping agent. An Auto-RP discovery message is then sent out of each PIM-enabled interface. This output also shows that Auto-RP messages are subject to passing an RPF check. If the check fails, the message is discarded. Finally, an RP-announce message is received from NX-3, resulting in the installation of a new PIM RP-to-group mapping.

Example 13-61 *Auto-RP Event-history on NX-4*

```
NX-4# show ip pim internal event-history rp
! Output omitted for brevity
02:34:30.112521 pim [13449]::Scan MRIB to process RP change event
02:34:30.112255 pim [13449]::RP 10.1.1.1, group range 239.0.0.0/8 cached
02:34:30.112248 pim [13449]::(default) pim_add_rp: RP:10.1.1.1 rp_change:yes
change_flag: yes bidir:no, group:239.0.0.0/8 rp_priority: -1,
static: no, action: Permit, prot_souce: 4 hash_len: 181
02:34:30.112138 pim [13449]::(default) pim_add_rp: Added the following in pt_rp_
   cache_by_group: group: 239.0.0.0/8, pcib->pim_rp_change: yes
02:34:30.112133 pim [13449]::Added group range: 239.0.0.0/8 from
pim_rp_cache_by_group
02:34:30.112127 pim [13449]::(default) pim_add_rp: Added the following in pt_rp_
   cache_by_rp: RP: 10.1.1.1, rp_priority: 0, prot_souce: 4, pcib->pim_
rp_change: yes
```

```
02:34:30.112070 pim [13449]::(default) pim_add_rp: Received rp_entry from
caller: RP: 10.1.1.1 bidir:no, group:239.0.0.0/8 rp_priority: -1, static:
no, prot_souce: 4 override: no hash_len: 181 holdtime: 180
02:34:30.112030 pim [13449]::RPF interface is Ethernet3/29, RPF check passed
02:34:30.111913 pim [13449]::Received Auto-RP v1 Announce from
10.1.1.1 on Ethernet3/29, length: 20, ttl: 15, ht: 180
02:34:30.110112 pim [13449]::10.2.2.3 elected new RP-mapping Agent,
 old RPA: 10.2.2.3
02:34:30.110087 pim [13449]::RPF interface is loopback0, RPF check passed
02:34:30.110064 pim [13449]::Received Auto-RP v1 Discovery from
10.2.2.3 on loopback0, length: 8, ttl: 16, ht: 180
02:34:30.109856 pim [13449]::Send Auto-RP Discovery message on Vlan216,
02:34:30.109696 pim [13449]::Send Auto-RP Discovery message on Vlan215,
02:34:30.109496 pim [13449]::Send Auto-RP Discovery message on Vlan303,
02:34:30.109342 pim [13449]::Send Auto-RP Discovery message on Ethernet3/29,
02:34:30.107940 pim [13449]::Send Auto-RP Discovery message on Ethernet3/28,
02:34:30.107933 pim [13449]::Build Auto-RP Discovery message, holdtime: 180
02:34:30.107900 pim [13449]::Elect ourself as new RP-mapping Agent
```

Auto-RP state is dynamic and must be refreshed periodically by sending and receiving RP-announce and RP-discovery messages in the network. If RP state is lost on a device or is incorrect, the investigation should follow the appropriate Auto-RP message back to its source to identify any misconfiguration. The NX-OS event-history and Ethanalyzer utilities are the primary tools for finding the root cause of the problem.

BSR Configuration and Verification

The BSR method of dynamic RP configuration came after Cisco created Auto-RP. It is currently described by RFC 4601 and RFC 5059. Both BSR and Auto-RP provide a method of automatically distributing PIM RP information throughout the PIM domain; however, BSR is an IETF standard and Auto-RP is Cisco proprietary.

BSR relies on candidate-RPs (C-RPs) and a bootstrap router (BSR), which is elected based on the highest priority. If priority is equal, the highest IP address is used as a tie breaker to elect a single BSR. When a router is configured as a candidate-BSR (C-BSR), it begins sending bootstrap messages that allow all the C-BSRs to hear each other and determine which should become the elected BSR. After the BSR is elected, it should be the only router sending bootstrap messages in the PIM domain.

C-RPs listen for bootstrap messages from the elected BSR to discover the unicast address the BSR is using. This allows the C-RPs to announce themselves to the elected BSR by sending unicast candidate-RP messages. The messages from the C-RP include the RP address and groups for which it is willing to become an RP, along with other details, such as the RP priority. The BSR receives RP information from all C-RPs and then builds a PIM bootstrap message to advertise this information to the rest of the network. The same bootstrap message that is used to advertise the list of group-to-RP mappings in the network is also used by C-BSRs to determine the elected BSR, offering a streamlined approach. This approach also allows another C-BSR to assume the role of the elected BSR in case the active BSR stops sending bootstrap messages for some reason.

Until now, the process sounds similar to Auto-RP. However, unlike the Auto-RP mapping agent, the BSR does not attempt to perform any selection of RP-to-group mappings to include in the bootstrap message. Instead, the BSR includes the data received from all C-RPs in the bootstrap message.

The bootstrap message is sent to the ALL-PIM-ROUTERS multicast address of 224.0.0.13 on each PIM-enabled interface. When a router is configured to listen for and forward BSR, it examines the received bootstrap message contents and then builds a new packet to send the *same* BSR message out each PIM-enabled interface. The BSR message travels in this manner throughout the PIM domain hop by hop so that each router has a consistent list of C-RPs–to–multicast group mapping data. Each router in the network applies the same algorithm to the data in the BSR message to determine the group-to-RP mapping, resulting in network-wide consistency.

When a router receives the bootstrap message from the BSR, it must determine which RP address will be used for each group range. This process is summarized as follows:

1. Perform a longest match on the group range and mask length to obtain a list of RPs.

2. Find the RP with the highest priority from the list.

3. If only one RP remains, the RP selection process is finished for that group range.

4. If multiple RPs are in the list, use the PIM hash function to choose the RP.

The hash function is applied when multiple RPs for a group range have the same longest match mask length and priority. The hash function on each router in the domain returns the same result so that a consistent group-to-RP mapping is applied in the network. Section 4.7.2 of RFC 4601 describes the hash function as follows:

Value(G,M,C(i))=

(1103515245 * ((1103515245 * (G&M) + 12345) XOR C(i)) + 12345) mod 2^31

The variable inputs in this calculation follow:

- G = The multicast group address
- M = The hash length provided by the bootstrap message from the BSR
- C(i) = The address of the candidate-RP

The calculation is done for each C-RP matching the group range, and it returns the RP address to be used. The RP with the highest resulting hash calculated value is chosen for the group. If two C-RPs happen to have the same hash result, the RP with the higher IP address is used. The default hash length of 30 results in four consecutive multicast group addresses being mapped to the same RP address.

The topology in Figure 13-16 is used here in reviewing the configuration and verification steps for BSR.

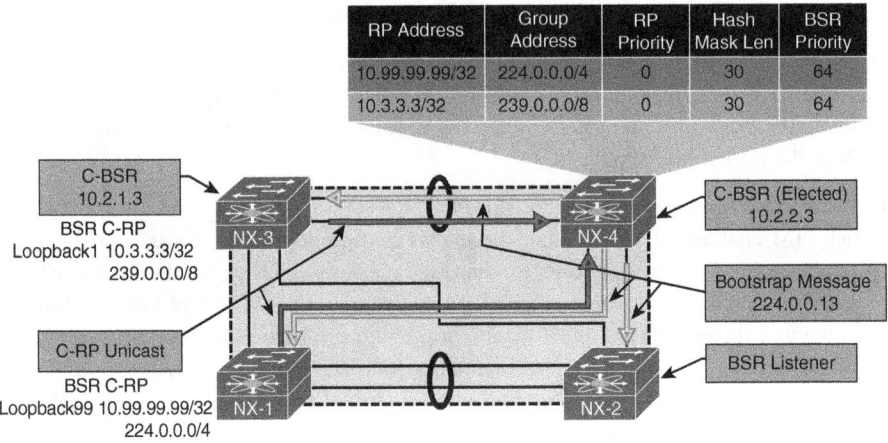

Figure 13-16 *PIM BSR Topology*

NX-1 is configured to be a C-RP for the 224.0.0.0/4 multicast group range (see Example 13-62). Because routers do not listen for or forward BSR messages by default, the device is configured with the **ip pim bsr listen forward** command. After NX-1 learns of the BSR address through a received bootstrap message, it begins sending unicast C-RP messages advertising the willingness to be an RP for 224.0.0.0/4.

The output of **show ip pim rp** provides the RP-to-group mapping selection being used, based on the information received from the bootstrap message originated by the elected BSR.

Example 13-62 *BSR Configuration on NX-1*

```
NX-1# show run pim
! Output omitted for brevity

!Command: show running-config pim

feature pim

ip pim bsr rp-candidate loopback99 group-list 224.0.0.0/4 priority 0
ip pim ssm range 232.0.0.0/8
ip pim bsr listen forward
```

```
interface Vlan1101
  ip pim sparse-mode

interface loopback0
  ip pim sparse-mode

interface loopback99
  ip pim sparse-mode

interface Ethernet3/17
  ip pim sparse-mode

interface Ethernet3/18
  ip pim sparse-mode

NX-1# show ip pim rp

PIM RP Status Information for VRF "default"
BSR: 10.2.2.3, uptime: 06:36:03, expires: 00:02:00,
     priority: 64, hash-length: 30
Auto-RP disabled
BSR RP Candidate policy: None
BSR RP policy: None
Auto-RP Announce policy: None
Auto-RP Discovery policy: None

RP: 10.3.3.3, (0), uptime: 06:30:44, expires: 00:02:20,
  priority: 0, RP-source: 10.2.2.3 (B), group ranges:
      239.0.0.0/8
RP: 10.99.99.99*, (0), uptime: 06:30:15, expires: 00:02:20,
  priority: 0, RP-source: 10.2.2.3 (B), group ranges:
      224.0.0.0/4
```

The elected BSR is NX-4 because its BSR IP address is higher than that of NX-3 (10.2.2.3 vs. 10.2.1.3); both C-BSRs have equal default priority of 64. The **ip pim bsr-candidate loopback0** command configures NX-4 to be a C-BSR and allows it to begin sending periodic bootstrap messages. The output of **show ip pim rp** confirms that the local device is the current BSR and provides a timer value that indicates when the next bootstrap message is sent. The hash length is the default value of 30, but it is configurable in the range of 0 to 32. Example 13-63 shows the configuration and RP mapping information for NX-4.

Example 13-63 *BSR Configuration on NX-4*

```
NX-4# show run pim
! Output omitted for brevity

!Command: show running-config pim

feature pim

ip pim bsr-candidate loopback0
ip pim ssm range 232.0.0.0/8
ip pim bsr listen forward

interface Vlan215
  ip pim sparse-mode

interface Vlan216
  ip pim sparse-mode

interface Vlan303
  ip pim sparse-mode

interface loopback0
  ip pim sparse-mode

interface Ethernet3/28
  ip pim sparse-mode

interface Ethernet3/29
  ip pim sparse-mode
NX-4# show ip pim rp
PIM RP Status Information for VRF "default"
BSR: 10.2.2.3*, next Bootstrap message in: 00:00:53,
     priority: 64, hash-length: 30
Auto-RP disabled
BSR RP Candidate policy: None
BSR RP policy: None
Auto-RP Announce policy: None
Auto-RP Discovery policy: None

RP: 10.3.3.3, (0),
 uptime: 06:30:36   priority: 0,
 RP-source: 10.3.3.3 (B),
 group ranges:
 239.0.0.0/8    , expires: 00:02:11 (B)
```

```
RP: 10.99.99.99, (0),
 uptime: 06:30:07   priority: 0,
 RP-source: 10.99.99.99 (B),
 group ranges:
 224.0.0.0/4    , expires: 00:02:28 (B)
```

Example 13-64 shows the configuration of NX-3, which is configured to be both a C-RP for 239.0.0.0/8 and a C-BSR. NX-3 has a lower C-BSR address than NX-4, so it does not send any bootstrap messages after losing the BSR election.

Example 13-64 *BSR Configuration on NX-3*

```
NX-3# show run pim
! Output omitted for brevity
feature pim

ip pim bsr-candidate loopback0
ip pim bsr rp-candidate loopback1 group-list 239.0.0.0/8 priority 0
ip pim ssm range 232.0.0.0/8
ip pim bsr listen forward

interface Vlan215
  ip pim sparse-mode

interface Vlan216
  ip pim sparse-mode

interface Vlan303
  ip pim sparse-mode

interface loopback0
  ip pim sparse-mode

interface loopback1
  ip pim sparse-mode

interface Ethernet3/28
  ip pim sparse-mode

interface Ethernet3/29
  ip pim sparse-mode
NX-3# show ip pim rp
```

```
PIM RP Status Information for VRF "default"
BSR: 10.2.2.3, uptime: 07:05:30, expires: 00:02:05,
    priority: 64, hash-length: 30
Auto-RP disabled
BSR RP Candidate policy: None
BSR RP policy: None
Auto-RP Announce policy: None
Auto-RP Discovery policy: None

RP: 10.3.3.3*, (0), uptime: 00:00:04, expires: 00:02:25,
  priority: 0, RP-source: 10.2.2.3 (B), group ranges:
      239.0.0.0/8
RP: 10.99.99.99, (0), uptime: 06:59:41, expires: 00:02:25,
  priority: 0, RP-source: 10.2.2.3 (B), group ranges:
      224.0.0.0/4
```

The final router to review is NX-2, which is acting only as a BSR listener and forwarder. In this configuration, NX-2 receives the bootstrap message from NX-4 and inspects its contents. It then selects the RP-to-group mapping for each group range and installs the entry in the local RP cache. Note that NX-4, NX-3, and NX-1 are BSR clients as well, but they are also acting as C-RPs or C-BSRs. Example 13-65 shows the configuration and RP mapping from NX-2.

Example 13-65 *BSR Configuration on NX-2*

```
NX-2# show run pim
! Output omitted for brevity
!Command: show running-config pim

feature pim

ip pim ssm range 232.0.0.0/8
ip pim bsr listen forward

interface Vlan115
  ip pim sparse-mode

interface Vlan116
  ip pim sparse-mode

interface Vlan1101
  ip pim sparse-mode
```

```
interface Ethernet3/17
  ip pim sparse-mode

interface Ethernet3/18
  ip pim sparse-mode
NX-2# show ip pim rp
PIM RP Status Information for VRF "default"
BSR: 10.2.2.3, uptime: 07:11:35, expires: 00:01:39,
    priority: 64, hash-length: 30
Auto-RP disabled
BSR RP Candidate policy: None
BSR RP policy: None
Auto-RP Announce policy: None
Auto-RP Discovery policy: None

RP: 10.3.3.3, (0),
 uptime: 07:06:15   priority: 0,
 RP-source: 10.2.2.3 (B),
 group ranges:
 239.0.0.0/8    , expires: 00:01:59 (B)
RP: 10.99.99.99, (0),
 uptime: 07:05:47   priority: 0,
 RP-source: 10.2.2.3 (B),
 group ranges:
 224.0.0.0/4    , expires: 00:01:59 (B)
```

Unlike Auto-RP, BSR messages are not constrained by a configured TTL scope. In a complex BSR design, defining which C-RPs are allowed to communicate with a particular BSR might be desirable. This is achieved by filtering the bootstrap messages and the RP-Candidate messages using the **ip pim bsr** [*bsr-policy* | *rp-candidate-policy*] commands and using a route map for filtering purposes.

Similar to Auto-RP, the **show ip pim internal event-history rp** command is used to monitor C-BSR, C-RP, and bootstrap message activity on a router. Example 13-66 gives a sample of this event-history.

Example 13-66 *PIM Event-History for RP from NX-4 with BSR*

```
NX-4# show ip pim internal event-history rp
! Output omitted for brevity

 rp events for PIM process
02:50:51.766388 pim [13449]::Group range 239.0.0.0/8 cached
02:50:51.766385 pim [13449]::(default) pim_add_rp: RP:10.3.3.3
```

```
rp_change:no change_flag: yes
 bidir:no, group:239.0.0.0/8 rp_priority: 0, static: no, action: Permit,
prot_souce: 2 hash_len: 30
02:50:51.766325 pim [13449]::(default) pim_add_rp: Received rp_entry from
caller: RP: 10.3.3.3 bidir:no, group:239.0.0.0/8 rp_priority: 0, static:
no, prot_souce: 2 override: no hash_len: 30 holdtime: 150
02:50:51.766304 pim [13449]::RP 10.3.3.3, prefix count: 1, priority: 0,
holdtime: 150
02:50:51.766297 pim [13449]::Received Candidate-RP from 10.3.3.3, length: 76
02:50:09.705668 pim [13449]::Group range 224.0.0.0/4 cached
02:50:09.705664 pim [13449]::(default) pim_add_rp: RP:10.99.99.99 rp_change:no
   change_flag:
yes bidir:no, group:224.0.0.0/4 rp_priority: 0, static: no, action: Permit,
prot_souce: 2 hash_len: 30
02:50:09.705603 pim [13449]::(default) pim_add_rp: Received rp_entry from
caller: RP: 10.99.99.99 bidir:no, group:224.0.0.0/4 rp_priority: 0, static:
no, prot_souce: 2 override: no hash_len: 30 hold time: 150
02:50:09.705581 pim [13449]::RP 10.99.99.99, prefix count: 1, priority: 0,
holdtime: 150
02:50:09.705574 pim [13449]::Received Candidate-RP from 10.99.99.99, length: 76
02:50:03.996080 pim [13449]::Send Bootstrap message on Vlan216
02:50:03.996039 pim [13449]::Send Bootstrap message on Vlan215
02:50:03.995995 pim [13449]::Send Bootstrap message on Vlan303
02:50:03.995940 pim [13449]::Send Bootstrap message on Ethernet3/29
02:50:03.995894 pim [13449]::Send Bootstrap message on Ethernet3/28
02:50:03.995863 pim [13449]::  RP 10.3.3.3, priority: 0, holdtime 150
02:50:03.995860 pim [13449]::Group range 239.0.0.0/8, RPs:
02:50:03.995857 pim [13449]::  RP 10.99.99.99, priority: 0, holdtime 150
02:50:03.995853 pim [13449]::Group range 224.0.0.0/4, RPs:
02:50:03.995847 pim [13449]::Build Bootstrap message, priority: 64, hash-len: 30
```

In addition to the event-history output, the **show ip pim statistics** command is useful for viewing device-level aggregate counters for the various messages associated with BSR and for troubleshooting. Example 13-67 shows the output from NX-4.

Example 13-67 *PIM Statistics on NX-4 with BSR*

```
NX-4# show ip pim statistics
! Output omitted for brevity
PIM Global Counter Statistics for VRF:default, last reset: never
  Register processing (sent/received):
    Registers: 0/0, Null registers: 0/0, Register-Stops: 0/0
    Registers received and not RP: 0
    Registers received for SSM/Bidir groups: 0/0
```

```
    BSR processing (sent/received):
      Bootstraps: 2025/1215, Candidate-RPs: 0/796
      BSs from non-neighbors: 0, BSs from border interfaces: 0
      BS length errors: 0, BSs which RPF failed: 0
      BSs received but not listen configured: 0
      Cand-RPs from border interfaces: 0
      Cand-RPs received but not listen configured: 0
    Auto-RP processing (sent/received):
      Auto-RP Announces: 0/0, Auto-RP Discoveries: 0/0
      Auto-RP RPF failed: 0, Auto-RP from border interfaces: 0
      Auto-RP invalid type: 0, Auto-RP TTL expired: 0
      Auto-RP received but not listen configured: 0
    General errors:
      Control-plane RPF failure due to no route found: 9
      Data-plane RPF failure due to no route found: 0
      Data-plane no multicast state found: 0
      Data-plane create route state count: 10
    vPC packet stats:
      rpf-source metric requests sent: 11
      rpf-source metric requests received: 483
      rpf-source metric request send error: 0
      rpf-source metric response sent: 483
      rpf-source metric response received: 11
      rpf-source metric response send error: 0
      rpf-source metric rpf change trigger sent: 2
      rpf-source metric rpf change trigger received: 13
      rpf-source metric rpf change trigger send error: 0
```

When multiple C-RPs exist for a particular group range, determining which group range is mapped to which RP can be challenging. NX-OS provides two commands to assist the user (see Example 13-68).

The first command is the **show ip pim group-range** [*group address*] command, which provides the current PIM mode used for the group, the RP address, and the method used to obtain the RP address. The second command is the **show ip pim rp-hash** [*group address*] command, which runs the PIM hash function on demand and provides the hash result and selected RP among all the C-RPs for the group range.

Example 13-68 *PIM Group–to–RP Mapping Information from NX-2*

```
NX-2# show ip pim group-range 239.1.1.1

PIM Group-Range Configuration for VRF "default"
Group-range          Action Mode  RP-address      Shrd-tree-range   Origin
239.0.0.0/8          -     ASM    10.3.3.3        -                 BSR
NX-2# show ip pim rp-hash 239.1.1.1

PIM Hash Information for VRF "default"
PIM RPs for group 239.1.1.1, using hash-length: 30 from BSR: 10.2.2.3
  RP 10.99.99.99, hash: 645916811
  RP 10.3.3.3, hash: 1118649067 (selected)
```

Running both Auto-RP and BSR in the same PIM domain is not supported. Auto-RP and BSR both are capable of providing dynamic and redundant RP mapping to the network. If third-party vendor devices are also participating in the PIM domain, BSR is the IETF standard choice and allows for multivendor interoperability.

Anycast-RP Configuration and Verification

Redundancy is always a factor in modern network design. In a multicast network, no single device is more important to the network overall than the PIM RP. The previous section discussed Auto-RP and BSR, which provide redundancy in exchange for additional complexity in the election processes and the distribution of multicast group–to–RP mapping information in the network.

Fortunately, another approach is available for administrators who favor the simplicity of a static PIM RP but also desire RP redundancy. Anycast RP configuration involves multiple PIM routers sharing a single common IP address. The IP address is configured on a Loopback interface using a /32 mask. Each router that is configured with the anycast address advertises the connected host address into the network's chosen routing protocol. Each router in the PIM domain is configured to use the anycast address as the RP. When an FHR needs to register a source, the network's unicast routing protocol automatically routes the PIM message to the closest device configured with the anycast address. This allows many devices to share the load of PIM register messages and provides redundancy in the case of an RP failure.

Obviously, intentionally configuring the same IP address on multiple devices should be done with care. For example, any routing protocol or management functions that could mistakenly use the anycast Loopback address as a router-id or source address should be configured to always use a different interface. With those caveats addressed, using an anycast address is perfectly safe, and this is a popular option in large and multiregional multicast networks.

Two methods are available for configuring anycast RP functionality:

1. Anycast RP with Multicast Source Discovery Protocol (MSDP)
2. PIM Anycast RP as specified in RFC 4610

This section examines both options.

Anycast RP with MSDP

The MSDP protocol defines a way for PIM RPs to advertise the knowledge of registered, active sources to each other. Initially, MSDP was designed to connect multiple independent PIM domains that each use their own PIM RP together. However, the protocol was also chosen as an integral part of the Anycast RP specification in RFC 3446.

MSDP allows each PIM RP configured with the Anycast RP address to act independently, while still sharing active source information with all other Anycast RPs in the domain. For example, in the topology in Figure 13-17, an FHR can register a source for a multicast group with Anycast RP NX-3, and then a receiver can join that group through Anycast RP NX-4. After traffic is received through the RPT, normal PIM SPT switchover behavior occurs on the LHR.

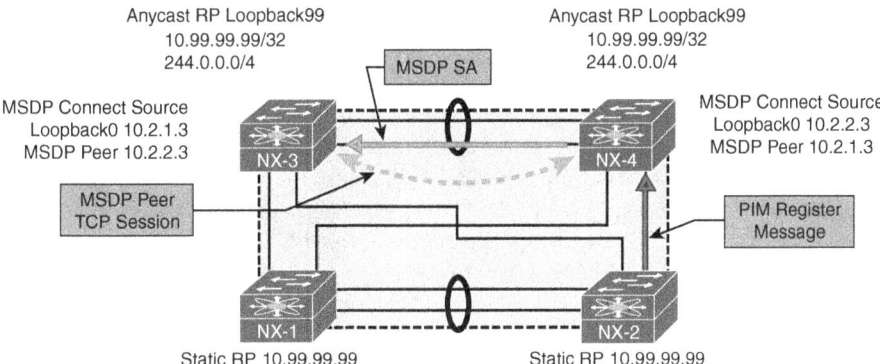

Figure 13-17 *Anycast RP with MSDP*

Anycast RP with MSDP requires that each Anycast RP have an MSDP peer with every other Anycast RP. The MSDP peer session is established over Transmission Control Protocol (TCP) port 639. When the TCP session is established, MSDP can send keepalive and source-active (SA) messages between peers, encoded in a TLV format.

When an Anycast RP learns of a new source, it uses the SA message to inform all its MSDP peers about that source. The SA message contains the following information:

- Unicast address of the multicast source
- Multicast group address
- IP address of the PIM RP (originator-id)

When the peer receives the MSDP SA, it subjects the message to an RPF check, which compares the IP address of the PIM RP in the SA message to the MSDP peer address. This address must be a unique IP address on each MSDP peer and cannot be an anycast address. NX-OS provides the **ip msdp originator-id** [*address*] command to configure the originating RP address that gets used in the SA message.

> **Note** Other considerations for the MSDP SA message RPF check are not relevant to the MSDP example used in this chapter. Section 10 of RFC 3618 gives the full explanation of the MSDP SA message RPF check.

If the SA message is accepted, it is sent to all other MSDP peers except the one from which the SA message was received. A concept called a mesh group can be configured to reduce the SA message flooding when many anycast RPs are configured with MSDP peering. The mesh group is a group of MSDP peers that have an MSDP neighbor with every other mesh group peer. Therefore, any SA message received from a mesh group peer does not need to be forwarded to any peers in the mesh group because all peers should have received the same message from the originator.

MSDP supports the use of SA filters, which can be used to enforce specific design parameters through message filtering. SA filters are configured with the **ip msdp sa-policy** [*peer address*] [*route-map* | *prefix-list*] command. It is also possible to limit the total number of SA messages from a peer with the **ip msdp sa-limit** [*peer address*] [*number of SAs*] command.

The example network in Figure 13-17 was configured with anycast RPs and MSDP between NX-3 and NX-4. NX-3 and NX-4 are both configured with the Anycast RP address of 10.99.99.99 on their Loopback99 interfaces. The Loopback0 interface on NX-3 and NX-4 is used to establish the MSDP peering. NX-1 and NX-2 are statically configured to use the anycast RP address of 10.99.99.99.

The output of Example 13-69 shows the configuration for anycast RP with MSDP from NX-3. As with PIM, before MSDP can be configured, the feature must be enabled with the **feature msdp** command. The originator-id and the MSDP connect source are both using the unique IP address configured on interface Loopback0, while the PIM RP is configured to use the anycast IP address of Loopback99. The MSDP peer address is the Loopback0 interface of NX-4.

Example 13-69 *NX-3 Anycast RP with MSDP Configuration*

```
NX-3# show run pim
! Output omitted for brevity

!Command: show running-config pim

feature pim

ip pim rp-address 10.99.99.99 group-list 224.0.0.0/4
```

```
ip pim ssm range 232.0.0.0/8

interface Vlan215
  ip pim sparse-mode

interface Vlan216
  ip pim sparse-mode

interface Vlan303
  ip pim sparse-mode

interface loopback0
  ip pim sparse-mode

interface loopback99
  ip pim sparse-mode

interface Ethernet3/28
  ip pim sparse-mode

interface Ethernet3/29
  ip pim sparse-mode
NX-3# show run msdp
! Output omitted for brevity
!Command: show running-config msdp

feature msdp

ip msdp originator-id loopback0
ip msdp peer 10.2.2.3 connect-source loopback0
NX-3# show run interface lo0 ; show run interface lo99
! Output omitted for brevity

show running-config interface lo0

interface loopback0
  ip address 10.2.1.3/32
  ip router ospf 1 area 0.0.0.0
  ip pim sparse-mode

!Command: show running-config interface loopback99

interface loopback99
  ip address 10.99.99.99/32
  ip router ospf 1 area 0.0.0.0
  ip pim sparse-mode
```

834　Chapter 13: Troubleshooting Multicast

The configuration of NX-4 is similar to that of NX-3; the only difference is the Loopback0 IP address and the IP address of the MSDP peer, which is NX-3's Loopback0 address. Example 13-70 contains the anycast RP with MSDP configuration for NX-4.

Example 13-70　*NX-4 Anycast RP with MSDP Configuration*

```
NX-4# show run pim
! Output omitted for brevity

!Command: show running-config pim

feature pim

ip pim rp-address 10.99.99.99 group-list 224.0.0.0/4
ip pim ssm range 232.0.0.0/8

interface Vlan215
  ip pim sparse-mode

interface Vlan216
  ip pim sparse-mode

interface Vlan303
  ip pim sparse-mode

interface loopback0
  ip pim sparse-mode

interface loopback99
  ip pim sparse-mode

interface Ethernet3/28
  ip pim sparse-mode

interface Ethernet3/29
  ip pim sparse-mode
NX-3# show run msdp
! Output omitted for brevity
!Command: show running-config msdp

feature msdp

ip msdp originator-id loopback0
ip msdp peer 10.2.1.3 connect-source loopback0
NX-3# show run interface lo0 ; show run interface lo99
```

```
! Output omitted for brevity

show running-config interface lo0

interface loopback0
  ip address 10.2.2.3/32
  ip router ospf 1 area 0.0.0.0
  ip pim sparse-mode
!Command: show running-config interface loopback99

interface loopback99
  ip address 10.99.99.99/32
  ip router ospf 1 area 0.0.0.0
  ip pim sparse-mode
```

After the configuration is applied, NX-3 and NX-4 establish the MSDP peering session between their Loopback0 interfaces using TCP port 639. The MSDP peering status can be confirmed with the **show ip msdp peer** command (see Example 13-71). The output provides an overview of the MSDP peer status and how long the peer has been established. It also lists any configured SA policy filters or limits and provides counters for the number of MSDP messages exchanged with the peer.

Example 13-71 *MSDP Peer Status on NX-4*

```
NX-4# show ip msdp peer

MSDP peer 10.2.1.3 for VRF "default"
AS 0, local address: 10.2.2.3 (loopback0)
  Description: none
  Connection status: Established
    Uptime(Downtime): 00:13:34
    Password: not set
  Keepalive Interval: 60 sec
  Keepalive Timeout: 90 sec
  Reconnection Interval: 10 sec
  Policies:
    SA in: none, SA out: none
    SA limit: unlimited
  Member of mesh-group: no
  Statistics (in/out):
    Last messaged received: 00:00:55
    SAs: 0/13, SA-Requests: 0/0, SA-Responses: 0/0
    In/Out Ctrl Msgs: 0/12, In/Out Data Msgs: 0/1
    Remote/Local Port 14/13
```

```
        Keepalives: 0/0, Notifications: 0/0
    Remote/Local Port 65205/639
    RPF check failures: 0
    Cache Lifetime: 00:03:30
    Established Transitions: 1
    Connection Attempts: 0
    Discontinuity Time: 00:13:34
```

As in previous examples in this chapter, multicast source 10.115.1.4 is attached to NX-2 on its VLAN 115 interface. When 10.115.1.4 starts sending traffic for group 239.115.115.1, NX-2 sends a PIM register message to its RP address of 10.99.99.99. Both NX-3 and NX-4 own this address because it is the anycast address. In this example, NX-2 sends the register message to NX-4. When the register message arrives, NX-4 replies with a register-stop and creates an (S, G) mroute entry. NX-4 also creates an MSDP SA message that is sent to NX-3 with the source IP address, group, and configured originator-id in the RP field. NX-3 receives the message and evaluates it for the RPF check and any filters that are applied. If all checks pass, the entry is added to the SA cache and an MSDP created mroute (S, G) state is added to the SA cache and an MSDP created mroute (S, G) state is added to the mroute table (see Example 13-72).

Example 13-72 *MSDP SA State and MROUTE Status on NX-3*

```
NX-3# show ip msdp count

SA State per ASN, VRF "default" - 1 total entries
 note: only asn below   65536
  <asn>: <(S,G) count>/<group count>
       0:     1/1
NX-3# show ip msdp sa-cache

MSDP SA Route Cache for VRF "default" - 1 entries
Source           Group          RP              ASN          Uptime
10.115.1.4       239.115.115.1  10.2.2.3        0            01:21:30
NX-3# show ip mroute
! Output omitted for brevity

IP Multicast Routing Table for VRF "default"

(*, 239.115.115.1/32), uptime: 16:41:50, igmp ip pim
  Incoming interface: loopback99, RPF nbr: 10.99.99.99
  Outgoing interface list: (count: 1)
    Vlan215, uptime: 16:41:50, igmp

(10.115.1.4/32, 239.115.115.1/32), uptime: 01:23:25, ip mrib msdp pim
  Incoming interface: Ethernet3/28, RPF nbr: 10.1.23.2
  Outgoing interface list: (count: 1)
```

The most common anycast RP problems relate to missing state or no synchronization between the configured RPs for active sources. The first step in troubleshooting this type of problem is to identify which of the possibly many anycast RPs are being sent the register message from the FHR for the problematic source and group. Next, ensure that the MSDP peer session is established between all anycast RPs. If the (S, G) mroute entry exists on the originating RP, the problem could result from MSDP not advertising the source and group through an SA message. The NX-OS event-history logs or the Ethanalyzer can help determine which messages are being sent from one MSDP peer to the next.

When 10.115.1.4 starts sending traffic to 239.115.115.1, NX-2 sends a PIM register message to NX-4. When the source is registered, the output in Example 13-73 is stored in the **show ip msdp internal event-history route** and **show ip msdp internal event-history tcp** commands. This event-history has the following interesting elements:

- SA messages were added to the SA Buffer at 04:06:14 and 04:13:27.
- The MSDP TCP event-history can be correlated to those time stamps.
  - The 104-byte message was an encapsulated data packet SA message.
  - The 20-byte message was a null register data packet SA message.
  - The 3-byte messages are keepalives to and from the peer.

Example 13-73 *MSDP Event-History on NX-4*

```
NX-4# show ip msdp internal event-history routes
! Output omitted for brevity

 routes events for MSDP process
2017 Nov  1 04:13:27.815880 msdp [1621]: : Add (10.115.1.4, 239.115.115.1, RP:
  10.99.99.99) to SA buffer
2017 Nov  1 04:12:47.969879 msdp [1621]: : Processing for (*, 239.115.115.1/32)
2017 Nov  1 04:12:47.967291 msdp [1621]: : Processing for (10.115.1.4/32,
  239.115.115.1/32)
2017 Nov  1 04:12:47.967286 msdp [1621]: : Processing for (*, 239.115.115.1/32)
2017 Nov  1 04:06:14.875895 msdp [1621]: : Add (10.115.1.4, 239.115.115.1, RP:
  10.99.99.99) to SA buffer
2017 Nov  1 04:06:04.758524 msdp [1621]: : Processing for (10.115.1.4/32,
  239.115.115.1/32)
NX-4# show ip msdp internal event-history tcp
! Output omitted for brevity

 tcp events for MSDP process
04:13:27.816367 msdp [1621]: : TCP at peer 10.2.1.3 accepted 20 bytes,
0 bytes left to send from buffer, total send bytes: 0
04:13:27.815998 msdp [1621]: : 20 bytes enqueued for send (20 bytes in buffer)
to peer 10.2.1.3
```

```
04:06:04.659887 msdp [1621]: : TCP at peer 10.2.1.3 accepted 104 bytes, 0 bytes
 left to send from buffer, total send bytes: 0
04:06:04.659484 msdp [1621]: : 104 bytes enqueued for send (104 bytes in buffer)
to peer 10.2.1.3
04:05:17.778269 msdp [1621]: : Read 3 bytes from TCP with peer 10.2.1.3 ,
buffer offset 0
04:05:17.736188 msdp [1621]: : TCP at peer 10.2.1.3 accepted 3 bytes, 0 bytes
left to send from buffer, total send bytes: 0
04:04:20.111337 msdp [1621]: : Connection established on passive side
04:04:13.085442 msdp [1621]: : We are listen (passive) side of connection, using
local address 10.2.2.3
```

Even if the MSDP SA message is correctly generated and advertised to the peer, it can still be discarded because of an RPF failure, an SA failure, or an SA limit. The same event-history output on the peer is used to determine why MSDP is discarding the message upon receipt. Remember that the PIM RP is the root of the RPT. If an LHR has an (S, G) state for a problematic source and group, the problem is likely to be on the SPT rooted at the source.

All examples in the "Anycast RP with MSDP" section of this chapter used a static PIM RP configuration. Using the anycast RP with MSDP functionality in combination with Auto-RP or BSR is fully supported, for dynamic group-to-RP mapping and provides the additional benefits of an anycast RP.

PIM Anycast RP

RFC 4610 specifies PIM anycast RP. The design goal of PIM anycast RP is to remove the dependency on MSDP and to achieve anycast RP functionality using only the PIM protocol. The benefit of this approach is that the end-to-end process has one fewer control plane protocol and one less point of failure or misconfiguration.

PIM anycast RP relies on the PIM register and register-stop messages between the anycast RPs to achieve the same functionality that MSDP provided previously. PIM anycast is designed around the following requirements:

- Each anycast RP is configured with the same anycast RP address.
- Each anycast RP also has a unique address to use for PIM messages between the anycast RPs.
- Every anycast RP is configured with the addresses of all the other anycast RPs.

The example network in Figure 13-18 helps in understanding PIM anycast RP configuration and troubleshooting.

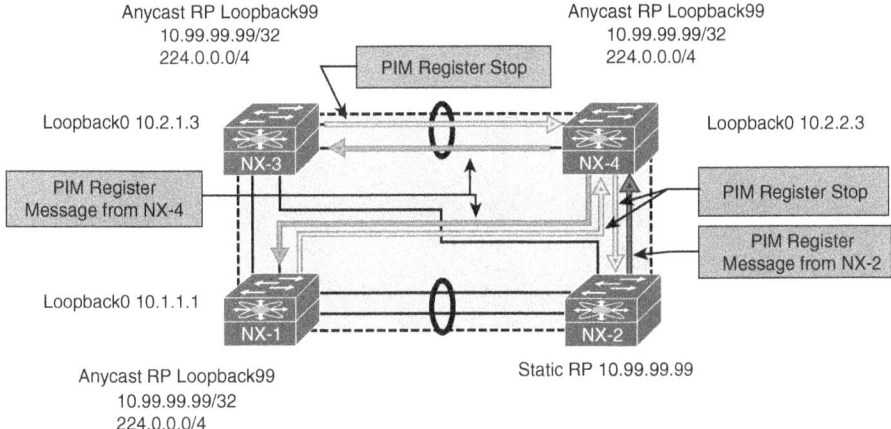

Figure 13-18 *PIM Anycast RP*

As with the previous examples in this chapter, a multicast source 10.115.1.4 is attached to NX-2 on VLAN 115 and begins sending to group 239.115.115.4. This is not illustrated in Figure 13-18, for clarity. NX-2 is the FHR and is responsible for registering the source with the RP. When NX-2 builds the register message, it performs a lookup in the unicast routing table to find the anycast RP address 10.99.99.99. The anycast address 10.99.99.99 is configured on NX-1, NX-3, and NX-4, which are all members of the same anycast RP set. The register message is sent to NX-4 following the best routing in the routing table.

When the register message arrives at NX-4, the PIM anycast RP functionality implements additional checks and processing on the received message. NX-4 builds its (S, G) state just as any PIM RP would. However, NX-4 looks at the source of the register message and determines that because the address is *not* part of the anycast RP set, it must be an FHR. NX-4 must then build a register message originated from its own Loopback0 address and send it to all other anycast RPs that are in the configured anycast RP set. NX-4 then sends a register-stop message to the FHR, NX-2. When NX-1 and NX-3 receive the register message from NX-4, they also build an (S, G) state in the mroute table and reply back to NX-4 with a register stop. Because NX-4 is part of the anycast RP set on NX-1 and NX-3, they recognize NX-4 as a member of the anycast RP set and no additional register messages are required to be built on NX-1 and NX-3.

The PIM anycast RP configuration uses the standard PIM messaging of register and register-stop that happens between FHRs and RPs and applies it to the members of the anycast RP set. The action of building a register message to inform the other anycast RPs is based on the source address of the register. If it is not a member of the anycast RP set, then the sender of the message must an FHR, so a register message is sent to the other members of the anycast RP set. The approach is elegant and straightforward.

Example 13-74 shows the configuration for NX-4. The static RP of 10.99.99.99 for groups 224.0.0.0/4 is configured on every PIM router in the domain. The anycast RP set is exactly the same on NX-1, NX-3, and NX-4 and includes all anycast RP Loopback0 interface addresses, including the local device's own IP.

Example 13-74 *PIM Anycast RP Configuration on NX-4*

```
NX-4# show run pim
! Output omitted for brevity

!Command: show running-config pim

feature pim

ip pim rp-address 10.99.99.99 group-list 224.0.0.0/4
ip pim ssm range 232.0.0.0/8
ip pim anycast-rp 10.99.99.99 10.1.1.1
ip pim anycast-rp 10.99.99.99 10.2.1.3
ip pim anycast-rp 10.99.99.99 10.2.2.3

interface Vlan215
  ip pim sparse-mode

interface Vlan216
  ip pim sparse-mode

interface Vlan303
  ip pim sparse-mode

interface loopback0
  ip pim sparse-mode

interface loopback99
  ip pim sparse-mode

interface Ethernet3/28
  ip pim sparse-mode

interface Ethernet3/29
  ip pim sparse-mode
```

The same debugging methodology used for the PIM source registration process can be applied to the PIM Anycast RP set. The **show ip pim internal event-history null-register** and **show ip pim internal event-history data-header-register** outputs provide a record of the messages being exchanged between the Anycast-RP set and any FHRs that are sending register messages to the device.

Example 13-75 shows the event-history output from NX-4. The null register message from 10.115.1.254 is from NX-2, which is the FHR. After adding the mroute entry, NX-4 forwards the register message to the other members of the anycast RP set and then receives a register stop message in response.

Example 13-75 *PIM Null Register Event-History on NX-4*

```
NX-4# show ip pim internal event-history null-register
! Output omitted for brevity

04:26:04.289082 pim [31641]:: Received Register-Stop from 10.2.1.3 for
(10.115.1.4/32, 239.115.115.1/32)
04:26:02.289082 pim [31641]:: Received Register-Stop from 10.1.1.1 for
(10.115.1.4/32, 239.115.115.1/32)
04:25:02.126926 pim [31641]:: Send Register-Stop to 10.115.1.254 for
(10.115.1.4/32, 239.115.115.1/32)
04:25:02.126909 pim [31641]:: Forward Register to Anycast-RP member 10.2.1.3
04:25:02.126885 pim [31641]:: Forward Register to Anycast-RP member 10.1.1.1
04:25:02.126874 pim [31641]:: RP 10.99.99.99 is an Anycast-RP
04:25:02.126866 pim [31641]:: Add new route (10.115.1.4/32, 239.115.115.1/32)
to MRIB, multi-route TRUE
04:25:02.126715 pim [31641]:: Create route for (10.115.1.4/32, 239.115.115.1/32)
04:25:02.126600 pim [31641]:: Received NULL Register from 10.115.1.254 for
  (10.115.1.4/32, 239.115.115.1/32) (pktlen 20)
```

All examples in the PIM anycast RP section of this book used a static PIM RP configuration. Using the PIM anycast RP functionality in combination with Auto-RP or BSR is fully supported, for dynamic group-to-RP mapping and to benefit from the advantages of anycast RP.

PIM Source Specific Multicast

The PIM SSM service model, defined in RFC 4607, allows a receiver to be joined directly to the source tree without the need for a PIM RP. This type of multicast delivery is optimized for one-to-many communication and is used extensively for streaming video applications such as IPTV. SSM is also popular for the provider multicast groups used to deliver IP Multicast over L3 VPN (MVPN).

SSM functions without a PIM RP because the receiver has knowledge of each source and group address that it will join. This knowledge can be preconfigured in the application, resolved through a Domain Name System (DNS) query, or mapped at the LHR. Because no PIM RP exists in SSM, the entire concept of the RPT or shared tree is eliminated along with the SPT switchover. The process of registering a source with the RP is also no longer required, which results in greater efficiency and less protocol overhead, compared to PIM ASM.

PIM SSM refers to a (source, group) combination as a uniquely identifiable channel. In PIM ASM mode, any source may send traffic to a group. In addition, the receiver implicitly joins any source that is sending traffic to the group address. In SSM, the receiver requests each source explicitly through an IGMPv3 membership report. This allows different applications to share the same multicast group address by using a unique source address. Because NX-OS implements an IP-based IGMP snooping table by default, it is possible for hosts to receive traffic for only the sources requested. A MAC-based IGMP snooping table has no way to distinguish different source addresses sending traffic to the same group.

> **Note** SSM can natively join a source in another PIM domain because the source address is known to the receiver. PIM ASM and BiDIR require the use of additional protocols and configuration to enable interdomain multicast to function.

The topology in Figure 13-19 applies to the discussion on the configuration and verification of PIM SSM.

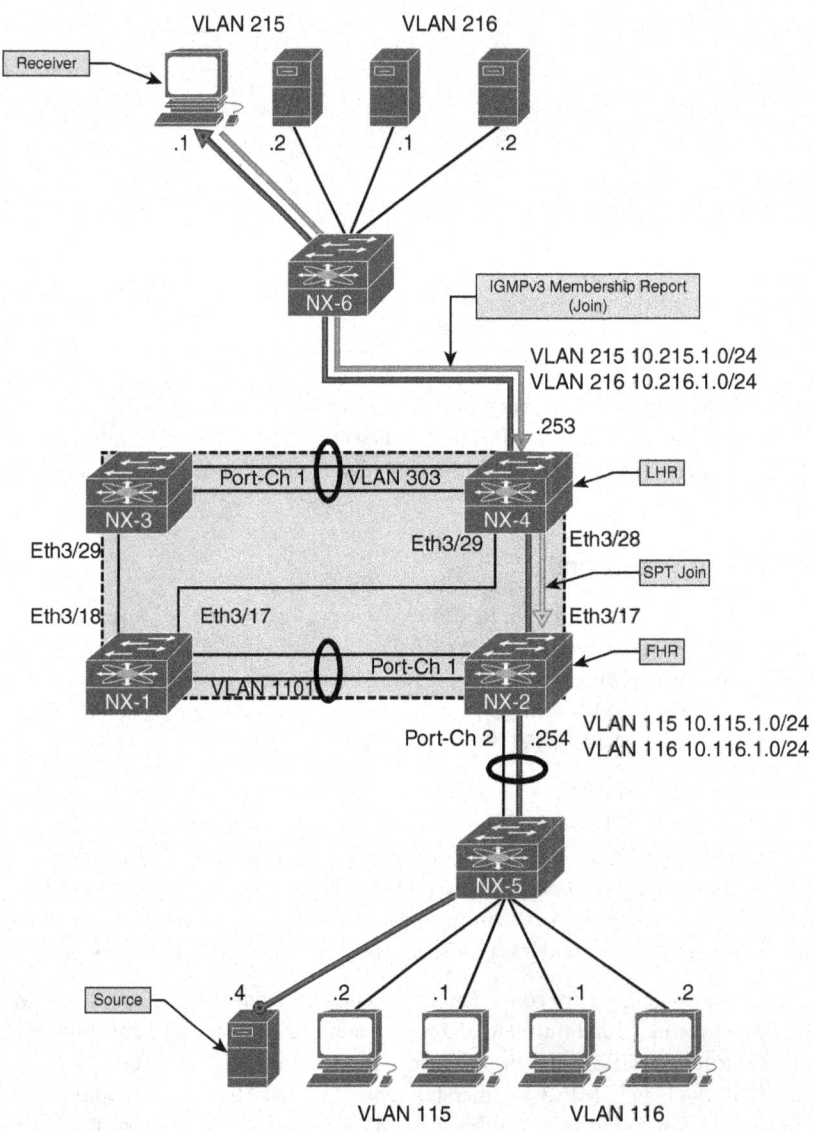

Figure 13-19 *PIM SSM Topology*

When a receiver in VLAN 215 joins (10.115.1.4, 232.115.115.1), it generates an IGMPv3 membership report. This join message includes the group and source address for the channel the receiver is interested in. The LHR (NX-4) builds an (S, G) mroute entry after it receives this join message and looks up the RPF interface toward the source. An SPT PIM join is sent to NX-2, which will also create an (S, G) state.

The (S, G) on NX-2 is created by either receiving the PIM join from NX-4 or receiving data traffic from the source, depending on which event occurs first. If no receiver exists for an SSM group, the FHR silently discards the traffic and the OIL of the mroute becomes empty. When the (S, G) SPT state is built, traffic flows downstream from the source 10.115.1.4 directly to the receiver on the SSM group 232.115.115.1.

SSM Configuration

The configuration for PIM SSM requires **ip pim sparse-mode** to be configured on each interface participating in multicast forwarding. There is no PIM RP to be defined, but any interface connected to a receiver must be configured with **ip igmp version 3**. The **ip pim ssm-range** command is configured by default to the IANA reserved range of 232.0.0.0/8. Configuring a different range of addresses is supported, but care must be taken to ensure that this is consistent throughout the PIM domain. Otherwise, forwarding is broken because the misconfigured router assumes that this is an ASM group and it does not have a valid PIM RP-to-group mapping.

The **ip igmp ssm-translate** [*group*] [*source*] command is used to translate an IGMPv1 or IGMPv2 membership report that does not contain a source address to an IGMPv3-compatible state entry. This is not required if all hosts attached to the interface support IGMPv3.

Example 13-76 shows the output of the complete SSM configuration for NX-2.

Example 13-76 *PIM SSM Configuration on NX-2*

```
NX-2# show run pim ; show run | inc translate
! Output omitted for brevity

!Command: show running-config pim

feature pim

ip pim ssm range 232.0.0.0/8

interface Vlan115
  ip pim sparse-mode

interface Vlan116
  ip pim sparse-mode
```

```
interface Vlan1101
  ip pim sparse-mode

interface Ethernet3/17
  ip pim sparse-mode

interface Ethernet3/18
  ip pim sparse-mode

ip igmp ssm-translate 232.1.1.1/32 10.215.1.1
NX-2# show run interface vlan115

!Command: show running-config interface Vlan115

interface Vlan115
  no shutdown
  no ip redirects
  ip address 10.115.1.254/24
  ip ospf passive-interface
  ip router ospf 1 area 0.0.0.0
  ip pim sparse-mode
  ip igmp version 3
```

The configuration for NX-4 is similar to NX-2 (see Example 13-77).

Example 13-77 *PIM SSM Configuration on NX-4*

```
NX-4# show run pim
! Output omitted for brevity

!Command: show running-config pim

feature pim

ip pim ssm range 232.0.0.0/8

interface Vlan215
  ip pim sparse-mode

interface Vlan216
  ip pim sparse-mode
interface Vlan303
  ip pim sparse-mode
```

PIM Multicast

```
interface loopback0
  ip pim sparse-mode

interface Ethernet3/28
  ip pim sparse-mode

interface Ethernet3/29
  ip pim sparse-mode

NX-4# show run interface vlan215

!Command: show running-config interface Vlan215

interface Vlan215
  no shutdown
  no ip redirects
  ip address 10.215.1.253/24
  ip ospf passive-interface
  ip router ospf 1 area 0.0.0.0
  ip pim sparse-mode
  ip igmp version 3
```

NX-1 and NX-3 are configured in a similar way. Because they do not play a role in forwarding traffic in this example, the configuration is not shown.

SSM Verification

To verify the SPT used in SSM, it is best to begin at the LHR where the receiver is attached. If the receiver sent an IGMPv3 membership report, an (S, G) state is present on the LHR. If this entry is missing, check the host for the proper configuration. SSM requires that the host have knowledge of the source address, and it works correctly only when the host knows which source to join, or when a correct translation is configured when the receiver is not using IGMPv3.

If any doubt arises that the host is sending a correct membership report, perform an Ethanalyzer capture on the LHR. In addition, the output of **show ip igmp groups** and **show ip igmp snooping groups** can be used to confirm that the interface has received a valid membership report. Example 13-78 shows this output from NX-4. Because this is IGMPv3 and NX-OS uses an IP-based table, both the source and group information is present.

Example 13-78 *IGMPv3 Verification on NX-4*

```
NX-4# show ip igmp groups
IGMP Connected Group Membership for VRF "default" - 1 total entries
Type: S - Static, D - Dynamic, L - Local, T - SSM Translated
Group Address     Type Interface            Uptime    Expires   Last Reporter
232.115.115.1
  10.115.1.4      D    Vlan215              01:26:41  00:02:06  10.215.1.1
NX-4# show ip igmp snooping groups
Type: S - Static, D - Dynamic, R - Router port, F - Fabricpath core port

Vlan  Group Address     Ver   Type  Port list
215   */*               -     R     Vlan215 Po2
215   232.115.115.1     v3
        10.115.1.4            D     Po2
216   */*               -     R     Vlan216
303   */*               -     R     Vlan303 Po1
```

When NX-4 receives the membership report, an (S, G) mroute entry is created. The (S, G) mroute state is created because the receiver is already aware of the precise source address it wants to join for the group. In contrast, PIM ASM builds a (*, G) state because the LHR does not yet know the source. Example 13-79 shows the mroute table for NX-4.

Example 13-79 *PIM SSM MROUTE Entry on NX-4*

```
NX-4# show ip mroute
IP Multicast Routing Table for VRF "default"

(*, 232.0.0.0/8), uptime: 00:02:07, pim ip
  Incoming interface: Null, RPF nbr: 0.0.0.0
  Outgoing interface list: (count: 0)

(10.115.1.4/32, 232.115.115.1/32), uptime: 00:00:33, igmp ip pim
  Incoming interface: Ethernet3/28, RPF nbr: 10.2.23.2
  Outgoing interface list: (count: 1)
    Vlan215, uptime: 00:00:33, igmp
```

The RPF interface to 10.115.1.4 is Ethernet 3/28, which connects directly to NX-2. The **show ip pim internal event-history join-prune** command can be checked to confirm that the SPT join has been sent from NX-4. Example 13-80 shows the output of this command.

Example 13-80 *PIM SSM Event-History Join-Prune on NX-4*

```
NX-4# show ip pim internal event-history join-prune
! Output omitted for brevity

03:44:55.372584 pim [10572]:: Send Join-Prune on Ethernet3/28, length: 34
03:44:55.372553 pim [10572]:: Put (10.115.1.4/32, 239.115.115.1/32),
S in join-list for nbr 10.2.23.2
03:44:55.372548 pim [10572]:: wc_bit = FALSE, rp_bit = FALSE
```

The PIM Join is received on NX-2, and the OIL of the mroute entry is updated to include Ethernet 3/17, which is directly connected with NX-4. Example 13-81 gives the event-history for PIM join-prune and the mroute entry from NX-2.

Example 13-81 *PIM SSM Event-History Join-Prune on NX-2*

```
NX-2# show ip pim internal event-history join-prune
! Output omitted for brevity

join-prune events for PIM process

03:44:55.429867 pim [7192]: : (10.115.1.4/32, 232.115.115.1/32) route exists
, RPF if Vlan115, to us
03:44:13.429837 pim [7192]: : pim_receive_join: We are target comparing with iod
03:44:13.429794 pim [7192]: : pim_receive_join: route:
(10.115.1.4/32, 232.115.115.1/32), wc_bit: FALSE, rp_bit: FALSE
03:44:13.429780 pim [7192]: : Received Join-Prune from 10.2.23.3 on Ethernet3/17
, length: 34, MTU: 9216, ht: 210
NX-2# show ip mroute

IP Multicast Routing Table for VRF "default"

(*, 232.0.0.0/8), uptime: 00:00:47, pim ip
  Incoming interface: Null, RPF nbr: 0.0.0.0
  Outgoing interface list: (count: 0)

(10.115.1.4/32, 232.115.115.1/32), uptime: 00:00:46, ip pim
  Incoming interface: Vlan115, RPF nbr: 10.115.1.4
  Outgoing interface list: (count: 1)
    Ethernet3/17, uptime: 00:00:15, pim
```

Troubleshooting SSM is more straightforward than troubleshooting PIM ASM or BiDIR. No PIM RP is required, which eliminates configuration errors and protocol complexity associated with dynamic RP configuration, anycast RP, and incorrect group-to-RP mapping. Additionally, there is no source registration process, RPT, or SPT switchover, which further simplifies troubleshooting.

Most problems with SSM result from a misconfigured SSM group range on a subset of devices or stem from a receiver host that is misconfigured or that is attempting to join the wrong source address. The troubleshooting methodology is similar to the one to address problems with the SPT in PIM ASM: Start at the receiver and work through the network hop by hop until the FHR connected to the source is reached. Packet capture tools such as ELAM, ACLs, or SPAN can be used to isolate any packet forwarding problems on a router along the tree.

Multicast and Virtual Port-Channel

A port-channel is a logical bundle of multiple physical member link interfaces. This configuration allows multiple physical interfaces to behave as a single interface to upper-layer protocols. Virtual port-channels (vPC) are a special type of port-channel that allow a pair of peer switches to connect to another device and appear as a single switch.

This architecture provides loop-free redundancy at L2 by synchronizing forwarding state and L2 control plane information between the vPC peers. Strict forwarding rules are implemented for traffic that is to be sent on a vPC interface, to avoid loops and duplicated packets.

Although L2 state is synchronized between the vPC peers through Cisco Fabric Services (CFS), both peers have an independent L3 control plane. As with standard port-channels, a hash table is used to determine which member link is chosen to forward packets of a particular flow. Traffic arriving from a vPC-connected host is received on either vPC peer, depending on the hash result. Because of this, both peers must be capable of forwarding traffic to or from a vPC-connected host. NX-OS supports both multicast sources and receivers connected behind vPC. Support for multicast traffic over vPC requires the following:

- IGMP is synchronized between peers with the CFS protocol. This populates the IGMP snooping forwarding tables on both vPC peers with the same information. PIM and mroutes are not synchronized with CFS.

- The vPC peer link is an mrouter port in the IGMP snooping table, which means that all multicast packets received on a vPC VLAN are forwarded across the peer link to the vPC peer.

- Packets received from a vPC member port and sent across the peer link are not sent out of any vPC member port on the receiving vPC peer.

- With vPC-connected multicast sources, both vPC peers can forward multicast traffic to an L3 OIF.

- With vPC-connected receivers, the vPC peer with the best unicast metric to the source will forward packets. If the metrics are the same, the vPC operational primary forwards the packets. This vPC assert mechanism is implemented through CFS.

- PIM SSM and PIM BiDIR are not supported with vPC because of the possibility of incorrect forwarding behavior.

Multicast and Virtual Port-Channel 849

Note Although multicast source and receiver traffic is supported over vPC, an L3 PIM neighbor from the vPC peers to a vPC-connected multicast router is not yet supported.

vPC-Connected Source

The example network topology in Figure 13-20 illustrates the configuration and verification of a vPC-connected multicast source.

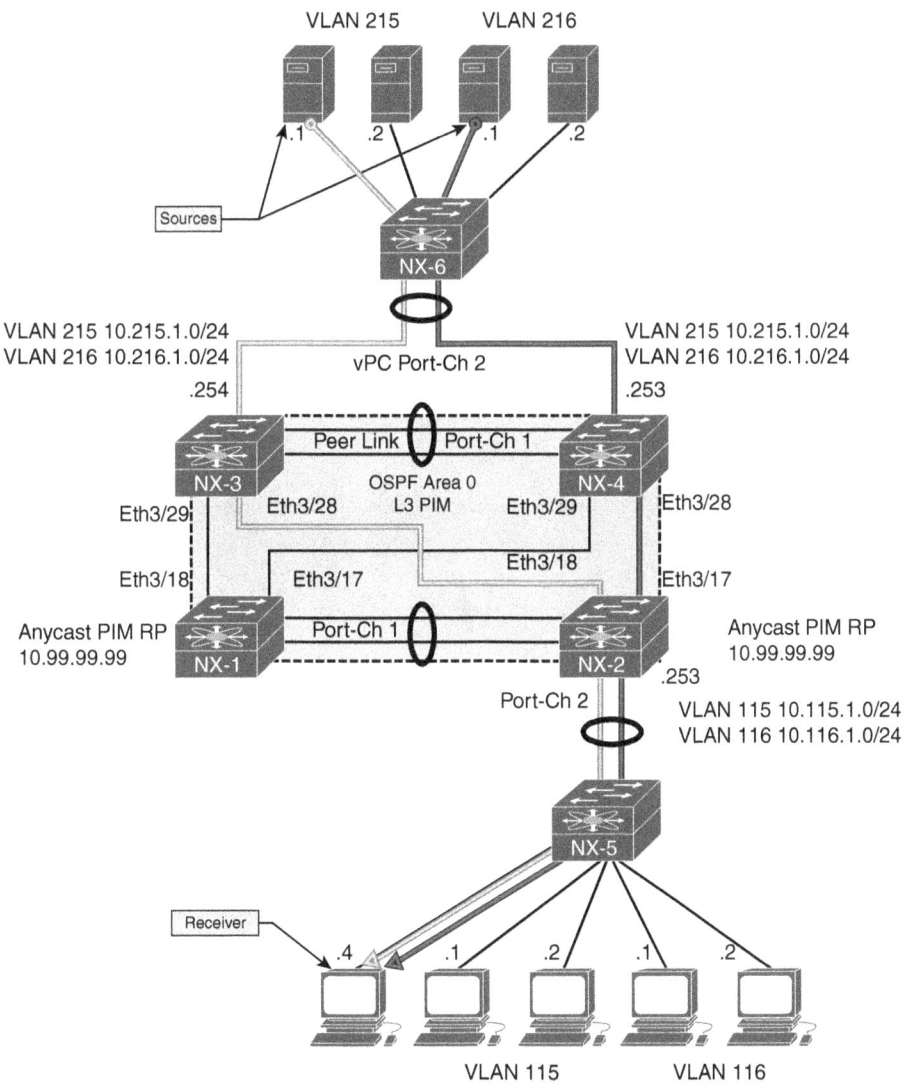

Figure 13-20 *vPC-Connected Source Topology*

Chapter 13: Troubleshooting Multicast

In Figure 13-20, the multicast sources are 10.215.1.1 in VLAN 215 and 10.216.1.1 in VLAN 216 for group 239.215.215.1. Both sources are attached to L2 switch NX-6, which uses its local hash algorithm to choose a member link to forward the traffic to. NX-3 and NX-4 are vPC peers and act as FHRs for VLAN 215 and VLAN 216, which are trunked across the vPC with NX-6.

The receiver is attached to VLAN 115 on NX-2, which is acting as the LHR. The network was configured with a static PIM anycast RP of 10.99.99.99, which is Loopback 99 on NX-1 and NX-2.

When vPC is configured, no special configuration commands are required for vPC and multicast to work together. Multicast forwarding is integrated into the operation of vPC by default and is enabled automatically. CFS handles IGMP synchronization, and PIM does not require the user to enable any vPC-specific configuration beyond enabling **ip pim sparse-mode** on the vPC VLAN interfaces.

Example 13-82 shows the PIM and vPC configuration for NX-4.

Example 13-82 *Multicast vPC Configuration on NX-4*

```
NX-4# show run pim
! Output omitted for brevity

!Command: show running-config pim

feature pim

ip pim rp-address 10.99.99.99 group-list 224.0.0.0/4
ip pim ssm range 232.0.0.0/8

interface Vlan215
  ip pim sparse-mode

interface Vlan216
  ip pim sparse-mode

interface Vlan303
  ip pim sparse-mode

interface loopback0
  ip pim sparse-mode

interface Ethernet3/28
  ip pim sparse-mode

interface Ethernet3/29
  ip pim sparse-mode
```

```
NX-4# show run vpc

!Command: show running-config vpc

feature vpc

vpc domain 2
  peer-switch
  peer-keepalive destination 10.33.33.1 source 10.33.33.2 vrf peerKA
  peer-gateway

interface port-channel1
  vpc peer-link

interface port-channel2
  vpc 2
```

Example 13-83 shows the PIM and vPC configuration on the vPC peer NX-3.

Example 13-83 *Multicast vPC Configuration on NX-3*

```
NX-3# show run pim
! Output omitted for brevity
!Command: show running-config pim

feature pim

ip pim rp-address 10.99.99.99 group-list 224.0.0.0/4
ip pim ssm range 232.0.0.0/8

interface Vlan215
  ip pim sparse-mode

interface Vlan216
  ip pim sparse-mode

interface Vlan303
  ip pim sparse-mode

interface loopback0
  ip pim sparse-mode

interface Ethernet3/28
  ip pim sparse-mode
```

```
interface Ethernet3/29
  ip pim sparse-mode

NX-3# show run vpc

!Command: show running-config vpc

feature vpc

vpc domain 2
  peer-switch
  peer-keepalive destination 10.33.33.2 source 10.33.33.1 vrf peerKA
  peer-gateway

interface port-channel1
  vpc peer-link

interface port-channel2
  vpc 2
```

After implementing the configuration, the next step is to verify that PIM and IGMP are operational on the vPC peers. The output of **show ip pim interface** from NX-4 indicates that VLAN 215 is a vPC VLAN (see Example 13-84). Note that NX-3 (10.215.1.254) is the PIM DR and handles registration of the source with the PIM RP. PIM neighbor verification on NX-3 and NX-4 for the non-vPC interfaces and for NX-1 and NX-2 is identical to the previous examples shown in the PIM ASM section of this chapter.

Example 13-84 *Multicast vPC PIM Interface on NX-4*

```
NX-4# show ip pim interface vlan215
! Output omitted for brevity
PIM Interface Status for VRF "default"
Vlan215, Interface status: protocol-up/link-up/admin-up
  IP address: 10.215.1.253, IP subnet: 10.215.1.0/24
  PIM DR: 10.215.1.254, DR's priority: 1
  PIM neighbor count: 2
  PIM hello interval: 30 secs, next hello sent in: 00:00:12
  PIM neighbor holdtime: 105 secs
  PIM configured DR priority: 1
  PIM configured DR delay: 3 secs
  PIM border interface: no
  PIM GenID sent in Hellos: 0x29002074
  PIM Hello MD5-AH Authentication: disabled
```

```
    PIM Neighbor policy: none configured
    PIM Join-Prune inbound policy: none configured
    PIM Join-Prune outbound policy: none configured
    PIM Join-Prune interval: 1 minutes
    PIM Join-Prune next sending: 0 minutes
    PIM BFD enabled: no
    PIM passive interface: no
    PIM VPC SVI: yes
    PIM Auto Enabled: no
    PIM vPC-peer neighbor: 10.215.1.254
    PIM Interface Statistics, last reset: never
      General (sent/received):
        Hellos: 14849/4299 (early: 0), JPs: 0/13, Asserts: 0/0
        Grafts: 0/0, Graft-Acks: 0/0
        DF-Offers: 1/3, DF-Winners: 2/13, DF-Backoffs: 0/0, DF-Passes: 0/0
      Errors:
        Checksum errors: 0, Invalid packet types/DF subtypes: 0/0
        Authentication failed: 0
        Packet length errors: 0, Bad version packets: 0, Packets from self: 0
        Packets from non-neighbors: 0
            Packets received on passiveinterface: 0
        JPs received on RPF-interface: 13
        (*,G) Joins received with no/wrong RP: 0/0
        (*,G)/(S,G) JPs received for SSM/Bidir groups: 0/0
        JPs filtered by inbound policy: 0
        JPs filtered by outbound policy: 0
```

The **show ip igmp interface** command in Example 13-85 indicates that VLAN 215 is a vPC VLAN. The output also identifies the PIM DR as the vPC peer, not the local interface.

Example 13-85 *Multicast vPC IGMP Interface on NX-4*

```
NX-4# show ip igmp interface vlan215
! Output omitted for brevity
IGMP Interfaces for VRF "default"
Vlan215, Interface status: protocol-up/link-up/admin-up
  IP address: 10.215.1.253, IP subnet: 10.215.1.0/24
  Active querier: 10.215.1.1, expires: 00:04:10, querier version: 2
  Membership count: 0
  Old Membership count 0
  IGMP version: 2, host version: 2
  IGMP query interval: 125 secs, configured value: 125 secs
  IGMP max response time: 10 secs, configured value: 10 secs
  IGMP startup query interval: 31 secs, configured value: 31 secs
```

```
    IGMP startup query count: 2
    IGMP last member mrt: 1 secs
    IGMP last member query count: 2
    IGMP group timeout: 260 secs, configured value: 260 secs
    IGMP querier timeout: 255 secs, configured value: 255 secs
    IGMP unsolicited report interval: 10 secs
    IGMP robustness variable: 2, configured value: 2
    IGMP reporting for link-local groups: disabled
    IGMP interface enable refcount: 1
    IGMP interface immediate leave: disabled
    IGMP VRF name default (id 1)
    IGMP Report Policy: None
    IGMP State Limit: None
    IGMP interface statistics: (only non-zero values displayed)
      General (sent/received):
        v2-queries: 2867/2908, v2-reports: 0/2898, v2-leaves: 0/31
        v3-queries: 15/1397, v3-reports: 0/1393
      Errors:
        Packets with Local IP as source: 0, Source subnet check failures: 0
        Query from non-querier:1
        Report version mismatch: 4, Query version mismatch: 0
        Unknown IGMP message type: 0
Interface PIM DR: vPC Peer
Interface vPC SVI: Yes
Interface vPC CFS statistics:
    DR queries rcvd: 1
    DR updates rcvd: 4
```

Identifying which device is acting as the PIM DR for the VLAN of interest is important because this device is responsible for registering the source with the RP, as with traditional PIM ASM. What differs in vPC for source registration is the interface on which the DR receives the packets from the source. Packets can arrive either directly on the vPC member link or from the peer link. Packets are forwarded on the peer link because it is programmed in IGMP snooping as an mrouter port (see Example 13-86).

Example 13-86 *vPC IGMP Snooping State on NX-4*

```
NX-4# show ip igmp snooping mrouter
! Output omitted for brevity
Type: S - Static, D - Dynamic, V - vPC Peer Link
      I - Internal, F - Fabricpath core port
      C - Co-learned, U - User Configured
      P - learnt by Peer
```

```
Vlan   Router-port   Type   Uptime      Expires
215    Vlan215       I      21:52:05    never
215    Po1           SV     00:43:00    never
215    Po2           D      00:36:25    00:04:59
216    Vlan216       ID     3d06h       00:04:33
216    Po1           SV     00:43:00    never
303    Vlan303       I      4d21h       never
303    Po1           SVD    3d13h       00:04:28
```

When the multicast source in VLAN 216 begins sending traffic to 239.215.215.1, the traffic arrives on NX-4. NX4 creates an (S, G) mroute entry and forwards the packet across the peer link to NX-3. NX-3 receives the packet and also creates an (S, G) mroute entry and registers the source with the RP. Traffic from 10.215.1.1 in VLAN 215 arrives at NX-3 on the vPC member link. NX-3 creates an (S, G) mroute and then forwards a copy of the packets to NX-4 over the peer link. In response to receiving the traffic on the peer link, NX-4 also creates an (S, G) mroute entry.

Example 13-87 shows the mroute entries on NX-3 and NX-4. Even though traffic from 10.216.1.1 for group 239.215.215.1 is hashing only to NX-4, notice that both vPC peers created (S, G) state. This state is created because of the packets received over the peer link.

Example 13-87 *Multicast vPC Source MROUTE Entry on NX-3 and NX-4*

```
NX-4# show ip mroute
! Output omitted for brevity

IP Multicast Routing Table for VRF "default"

 (10.215.1.1/32, 239.215.215.1/32), uptime: 00:00:14, ip pim
  Incoming interface: Vlan215, RPF nbr: 10.215.1.1
  Outgoing interface list: (count: 0)


 (10.216.1.1/32, 239.215.215.1/32), uptime: 00:00:14, ip pim
  Incoming interface: Vlan216, RPF nbr: 10.216.1.1
  Outgoing interface list: (count: 0)
NX-3# show ip mroute
! Output omitted for brevity
IP Multicast Routing Table for VRF "default"

 (10.215.1.1/32, 239.215.215.1/32), uptime: 00:00:51, ip pim
  Incoming interface: Vlan215, RPF nbr: 10.215.1.1
  Outgoing interface list: (count: 0)

(10.216.1.1/32, 239.215.215.1/32), uptime: 00:00:51, ip pim
  Incoming interface: Vlan216, RPF nbr: 10.216.1.1
  Outgoing interface list: (count: 0)
```

When the (S, G) mroutes are created on NX-3 and NX-4, both devices realize that the sources are directly connected. Both devices then determine the forwarder for each source. In this example, the sources are vPC connected, which makes the forwarding state for both sources *Win-force (forwarding)*. The result of the forwarding election is found in the output of **show ip pim internal vpc rpf-source** (see Example 13-88). This output indicates which vPC peer is responsible for forwarding packets from a particular source address. In this case, both are equal; because the source is directly attached through vPC, both NX-3 and NX-4 are allowed to forward packets in response to receiving a PIM join or IGMP membership report message.

Example 13-88 *PIM vPC RPF-Source Cache Table on NX-3 and NX-4*

```
NX-4# show ip pim internal vpc rpf-source
! Output omitted for brevity

PIM vPC RPF-Source Cache for Context "default" - Chassis Role Primary

Source: 10.215.1.1
  Pref/Metric: 0/0
  Ref count: 1
  In MRIB: yes
  Is (*,G) rpf: no
  Source role: primary
  Forwarding state: Win-force (forwarding)
  MRIB Forwarding state: forwarding

Source: 10.216.1.1
  Pref/Metric: 0/0
  Ref count: 1
  In MRIB: yes
  Is (*,G) rpf: no
  Source role: primary
  Forwarding state: Win-force (forwarding)
  MRIB Forwarding state: forwarding
NX-3# show ip pim internal vpc rpf-source
! Output omitted for brevity
PIM vPC RPF-Source Cache for Context "default" - Chassis Role Secondary

Source: 10.215.1.1
  Pref/Metric: 0/0
  Ref count: 1
  In MRIB: yes
  Is (*,G) rpf: no
  Source role: secondary
```

```
    Forwarding state: Win-force (forwarding)
    MRIB Forwarding state: forwarding

Source: 10.216.1.1
  Pref/Metric: 0/0
  Ref count: 1
  In MRIB: yes
  Is (*,G) rpf: no
  Source role: secondary
  Forwarding state: Win-force (forwarding)
  MRIB Forwarding state: forwarding
```

Note The historical vPC RPF-Source Cache creation events are viewed in the output of **show ip pim internal event-history vpc.**

NX-3 is the PIM DR for both VLAN 215 and VLAN 216 and is responsible for registering the sources with the PIM RP (NX-1 and NX-2). NX-3 sends PIM register messages to NX-1, as shown in the output of **show ip pim internal event-history null-register** in Example 13-89. Because NX-1 is part of an anycast RP set, it then forwards the register message to NX-2 and sends a register-stop message to NX-3. At this point, both vPC peers have an (S, G) for both sources, and both anycast RPs have an (S, G) state.

Example 13-89 *Multicast vPC Source Registration from NX-3*

```
NX-3# show ip pim internal event-history null-register
! Output omitted for brevity
04:18:55.957833 pim [10975]:: Received Register-Stop from
10.99.99.99 for (10.216.1.1/32, 239.215.215.1/32)
04:18:55.956223 pim [10975]:: Send Null Register to RP 10.99.99.99
for (10.216.1.1/32, 239.215.215.1/32)
04:17:55.687544 pim [10975]:: Received Register-Stop from
10.99.99.99 for (10.215.1.1/32, 239.215.215.1/32)
04:17:55.686261 pim [10975]:: Send Null Register to RP 10.99.99.99
for (10.216.1.1/32, 239.215.215.1/32)
```

After the source has been registered with the RP, the receiver in VLAN 115 sends an IGMP membership report requesting all sources for group 239.215.215.1, which arrives at NX-2. NX-2 joins the RPT and then initiates switchover to the SPT after the first packet arrives. NX-2 has two equal-cost routes to reach the sources (see Example 13-90), and it choses to join 10.215.1.1 through NX-3 and 10.216.1.1 through NX-4. NX-OS is enabled for multipath multicast by default, which means it could send a PIM join on either valid RPF interface toward the source when joining the SPT.

Example 13-90 *Unicast Routes from NX-2 for VLAN 215 and VLAN 216*

```
NX-2# show ip route 10.215.1.0
IP Route Table for VRF "default"
'*' denotes best ucast next-hop
'**' denotes best mcast next-hop
'[x/y]' denotes [preference/metric]
'%<string>' in via output denotes VRF <string>

10.215.1.0/24, ubest/mbest: 2/0
    *via 10.1.23.3, Eth3/18, [110/44], 02:49:13, ospf-1, intra
    *via 10.2.23.3, Eth3/17, [110/44], 02:49:13, ospf-1, intra
NX-2# show ip route 10.216.1.0
IP Route Table for VRF "default"
'*' denotes best ucast next-hop
'**' denotes best mcast next-hop
'[x/y]' denotes [preference/metric]
'%<string>' in via output denotes VRF <string>

10.216.1.0/24, ubest/mbest: 2/0
    *via 10.1.23.3, Eth3/18, [110/44], 02:49:18, ospf-1, intra
    *via 10.2.23.3, Eth3/17, [110/44], 02:49:18, ospf-1, intra
```

The output of **show ip pim internal event-history join-prune** confirms that NX-2 has joined the VLAN 215 source through NX-3 and has joined the VLAN 216 source through NX-4 (see Example 13-91).

Example 13-91 *PIM SPT Joins from NX-2 for vPC-Connected Sources*

```
NX-2# show ip pim internal event-history join-prune
! Output omitted for brevity

03:29:44.703690 pim [7192]:: Send Join-Prune on Ethernet3/18, length: 34
03:29:44.703666 pim [7192]:: Put (10.215.1.1/32, 239.215.215.1/32), S in
join-list for nbr 10.1.23.3
03:29:44.703661 pim [7192]:: wc_bit = FALSE, rp_bit = FALSE
03:29:44.702673 pim [7192]:: Send Join-Prune on Ethernet3/17, length: 34
03:29:44.702648 pim [7192]:: Put (10.216.1.1/32, 239.215.215.1/32), S in
join-list for nbr 10.2.23.3
03:29:44.702641 pim [7192]:: wc_bit = FALSE, rp_bit = FALSE
```

When these PIM joins arrive at NX-3 and NX-4, both are capable of forwarding packets from VLAN 215 and VLAN 216 to the receiver on the SPT. Because NX-2 chose to join (10.216.1.1, 239.215.215.1) through NX-4, its OIL is populated with Ethernet 3/28 and NX-3 forwards (10.215.1.1, 239.215.215.1) in response to the PIM join from NX-2. Example 13-92 shows the mroute entries from NX-3 and NX-4 after receiving the SPT joins from NX-2.

Example 13-92 *MROUTE Entries from NX-3 and NX-4 after SPT Join*

```
NX-3# show ip mroute
! Output omitted for brevity
IP Multicast Routing Table for VRF "default"

(10.215.1.1/32, 239.215.215.1/32), uptime: 00:01:14, ip pim
  Incoming interface: Vlan215, RPF nbr: 10.215.1.1
  Outgoing interface list: (count: 1)
    Ethernet3/28, uptime: 00:01:14, pim

(10.216.1.1/32, 239.215.215.1/32), uptime: 00:01:14, ip pim
  Incoming interface: Vlan216, RPF nbr: 10.216.1.1
  Outgoing interface list: (count: 0)

NX-4# show ip mroute
! Output omitted for brevity
IP Multicast Routing Table for VRF "default"

(10.215.1.1/32, 239.215.215.1/32), uptime: 00:01:21, ip pim
  Incoming interface: Vlan215, RPF nbr: 10.215.1.1
  Outgoing interface list: (count: 0)

(10.216.1.1/32, 239.215.215.1/32), uptime: 00:01:21, ip pim
  Incoming interface: Vlan216, RPF nbr: 10.216.1.1
  Outgoing interface list: (count: 1)
    Ethernet3/28, uptime: 00:01:21, pim
```

The final example for a vPC-connected source is to demonstrate what occurs when a vPC-connected receiver joins the group. To create this state on the vPC pair, 10.216.1.1 initiates an IGMP membership report to join group 239.215.215.1. This membership report message is sent to either NX-3 or to NX-4 by the L2 switch NX-6. When the IGMP membership report arrives on vPC port-channel 2 at NX-3 or NX-4, two events occur:

1. The IGMP membership report message is forwarded across the vPC peer link because the vPC peer is an mrouter.

2. A CFS message is sent to the peer. The CFS message informs the vPC peer to program vPC port-channel 2 with an IGMP OIF. vPC port-channel 2 is the interface on which the original IGMP membership report was received.

These events create a synchronized (*, G) mroute with an IGMP OIF on both NX-3 and NX-4 (see Example 13-93). The OIF is also added to the (S, G) mroutes that existed previously.

Example 13-93 *MROUTE Entries from NX-3 and NX-4 after IGMP Join*

```
NX-3# show ip mroute
! Output omitted for brevity
 (*, 239.215.215.1/32), uptime: 00:00:05, igmp pim ip
  Incoming interface: Ethernet3/29, RPF nbr: 10.1.13.1
  Outgoing interface list: (count: 1)
    Vlan216, uptime: 00:00:05, igmp

 (10.215.1.1/32, 239.215.215.1/32), uptime: 00:57:01, ip pim mrib
  Incoming interface: Vlan215, RPF nbr: 10.215.1.1
  Outgoing interface list: (count: 2)
    Ethernet3/28, uptime: 00:00:05, pim
    Vlan216, uptime: 00:00:05, mrib

 (10.216.1.1/32, 239.215.215.1/32), uptime: 00:57:01, ip pim mrib
  Incoming interface: Vlan216, RPF nbr: 10.216.1.1
  Outgoing interface list: (count: 2)
    Ethernet3/29, uptime: 00:00:05, pim
    Vlan216, uptime: 00:00:05, mrib, (RPF)
NX-4# show ip mroute
! Output omitted for brevity
 (*, 239.215.215.1/32), uptime: 00:00:11, igmp ip pim
  Incoming interface: Ethernet3/28, RPF nbr: 10.2.23.2
  Outgoing interface list: (count: 1)
    Vlan216, uptime: 00:00:11, igmp

 (10.215.1.1/32, 239.215.215.1/32), uptime: 00:57:11, ip pim mrib
  Incoming interface: Vlan215, RPF nbr: 10.215.1.1
  Outgoing interface list: (count: 2)
    Vlan216, uptime: 00:00:11, mrib
    Ethernet3/29, uptime: 00:00:12, pim

 (10.216.1.1/32, 239.215.215.1/32), uptime: 00:57:11, ip pim mrib
  Incoming interface: Vlan216, RPF nbr: 10.216.1.1
  Outgoing interface list: (count: 1)
    Vlan216, uptime: 00:00:11, mrib, (RPF)
```

We now have a (*, G) entry because the IGMP membership report was received, and both (S, G) mroutes now contain VLAN 216 in the OIL. In this scenario, packets are hashed by NX-6 from the source 10.215.1.1 to NX-3. While the traffic is being received at NX-3, the following events occur:

- NX-3 forwards the packets across the peer link in VLAN 215.

- NX-3 replicates the traffic and multicast-routes the packets from VLAN 215 to VLAN 216, based on its mroute entry.

- NX-3 sends packets toward the receiver in VLAN 216 on Port-channel 2 (vPC).

- NX-4 receives the packets from NX-3 in VLAN 215 from the peer link. NX-4 forwards the packets to any non-vPC receivers but does not forward the packets out a vPC VLAN.

The (RPF) flag on the (10.216.1.1, 239.215.215.1) mroute entry signifies that a source and receiver are in the same VLAN.

vPC-Connected Receiver

The same topology used to verify a vPC-connected source is reused to understand how a vPC-connected receiver works. Although the location of the source and receivers changed, the rest of the topology remains the same (see Figure 13-21).

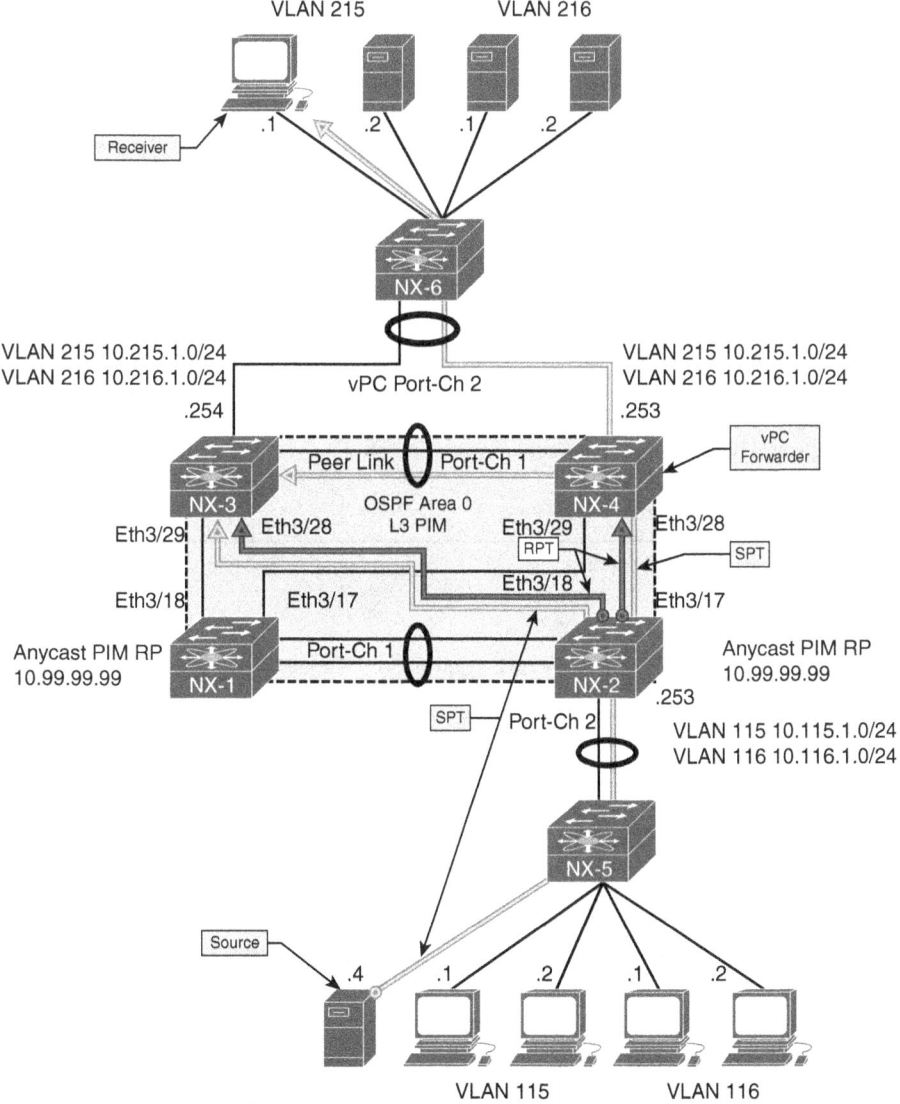

Figure 13-21 *vPC-Connected Receiver Topology*

The configuration is not modified in any way from the vPC-connected source example, with the exception of one command. The **ip pim pre-build-spt** command was configured on both NX-4 and NX-3. When configured, both vPC peers initiate an SPT join for each source, but only the elected forwarder forwards traffic toward vPC-connected receivers. The purpose of this command is to allow for faster failover in case the current vPC forwarder suddenly stops sending traffic as the result of a failure condition.

This configuration consumes additional bandwidth and additional replication of traffic in the network because the non-forwarder does not prune itself from the SPT. It continues to receive and discard the traffic until it detects the failure of the current forwarder. If this occurs, no delay is imposed by having to join the SPT. The traffic is there already waiting for the failure event to occur. In most environments, the benefits outweigh the cost, so using **ip pim pre-build-spt** is recommended for vPC environments.

When the multicast source 10.115.1.4 begins sending traffic to the group 239.115.115.1, the traffic is forwarded by L2 switch NX-5 to NX-2. Upon receiving the traffic, NX-2 creates an (S, G) entry for the traffic. Because no receivers exist yet, the OIL is empty at this time. However, NX-2 informs NX-1 about the source using a PIM register message because NX-1 and NX-2 are configured as PIM anycast RPs in the same RP set.

The receiver is 10.215.1.1 and is attached to the network in vPC VLAN 215. NX-6 forwards the IGMP membership report message to its mrouter port on Port-channel 2. This message can hash to either NX-3 or NX-4. When NX-4 receives the message, IGMP creates a (*, G) mroute entry. The membership report from the receiver is then sent across the peer link to NX-3, along with a corresponding CFS message. Upon receiving the message, NX-3 also creates a (*, G) mroute entry. Example 13-94 shows the IGMP snooping state, IGMP group state, and mroute on NX-4.

Example 13-94 *IGMP State on NX-4*

```
NX-4# show ip igmp snooping groups
! Output omitted for brevity

Type: S - Static, D - Dynamic, R - Router port, F - Fabricpath core port

Vlan   Group Address      Ver  Type  Port list
215    */*                -    R     Vlan215 Po1 Po2
215    239.115.115.1      v2   D     Po2
NX-4# show ip igmp groups

IGMP Connected Group Membership for VRF "default" - 1 total entries
Type: S - Static, D - Dynamic, L - Local, T - SSM Translated
Group Address      Type  Interface        Uptime   Expires    Last Reporter
239.115.115.1      D     Vlan215          2d18h    00:04:19   10.215.1.1
NX-4# show ip igmp internal vpc
IGMP vPC operational state UP
```

```
IGMP ES operational state DOWN
IGMP is registered with vPC library
IGMP is registered with MCEC_TL/CFS
VPC peer link is configured on port-channel1 (Up)
IGMP vPC Operating Version: 3 (mcecm ver:100)
IGMP chassis role is known
IGMP chassis role: Primary (cached Primary)
IGMP vPC Domain ID: 2
IGMP vPC Domain ID Configured: TRUE
IGMP vPC Peer-link Exclude feature enabled
IGMP emulated-switch id not configured
VPC Incremental type: no vpc incr upd, no proxy reporting, just sync (2)
    Configured type: none (0)
VPC Incremental Once download: False
IGMP Vinci Fabric Forwarding DOWN
Implicit adding router for Vinci: Enabled
IGMP single DR: FALSE
NX-4# show ip mroute


IP Multicast Routing Table for VRF "default"

(*, 239.115.115.1/32), uptime: 00:00:04, igmp ip pim
  Incoming interface: Ethernet3/28, RPF nbr: 10.2.23.2
  Outgoing interface list: (count: 1)
    Vlan215, uptime: 00:00:04, igmp
```

Example 13-95 shows the output from NX-3 after receiving the CFS messages from NX-4. Both vPC peers are synchronized to the same IGMP state, and IGMP is correctly registered with the vPC manager process.

Example 13-95 *IGMP State on NX-3*

```
NX-3# show ip igmp snooping groups
! Output omitted for brevity

Type: S - Static, D - Dynamic, R - Router port, F - Fabricpath core port

Vlan   Group Address    Ver   Type  Port list
215    */*              -     R     Vlan215 Po1 Po2
215    224.0.1.40       v2    D     Po2
215    239.115.115.1    v2    D     Po2
NX-3# show ip igmp groups
```

```
IGMP Connected Group Membership for VRF "default" - 1 total entries
Type: S - Static, D - Dynamic, L - Local, T - SSM Translated
Group Address      Type Interface            Uptime    Expires   Last Reporter
239.115.115.1      D    Vlan215              2d18h     00:04:13  10.215.1.1
NX-3# show ip igmp internal vpc
IGMP vPC operational state UP
IGMP ES operational state DOWN
IGMP is registered with vPC library
IGMP is registered with MCEC_TL/CFS
VPC peer link is configured on port-channel1 (Up)
IGMP vPC Operating Version: 3 (mcecm ver:100)
IGMP chassis role is known
IGMP chassis role: Secondary (cached Secondary)
IGMP vPC Domain ID: 2
IGMP vPC Domain ID Configured: TRUE
IGMP vPC Peer-link Exclude feature enabled
IGMP emulated-switch id not configured
VPC Incremental type: no vpc incr upd, no proxy reporting, just sync (2)
    Configured type: none (0)
VPC Incremental Once download: False
IGMP Vinci Fabric Forwarding DOWN
Implicit adding router for Vinci: Enabled
IGMP single DR: FALSE
NX-3# show ip mroute

IP Multicast Routing Table for VRF "default"

(*, 239.115.115.1/32), uptime: 00:00:09, igmp ip pim
  Incoming interface: Ethernet3/28, RPF nbr: 10.1.23.2
  Outgoing interface list: (count: 1)
    Vlan215, uptime: 00:00:09, igmp
```

The number of CFS messages sent between NX-3 and NX-4 can be seen in the output of **show ip igmp snooping statistics** (see Example 13-96). CFS is used to synchronize IGMP state and allows each vPC peer to communicate and elect a forwarder for each source.

Example 13-96 *IGMP Snooping Statistics on NX-4*

```
NX-4# show ip igmp snooping statistics
! Output omitted for brevity

Global IGMP snooping statistics: (only non-zero values displayed)
  Packets received: 43815
  Packets flooded: 21828
```

```
vPC PIM DR queries fail: 3
vPC PIM DR updates sent: 6
vPC CFS message response sent: 15
vPC CFS message response rcvd: 11
vPC CFS unreliable message sent: 3688
vPC CFS unreliable message rcvd: 28114
vPC CFS reliable message sent: 11
vPC CFS reliable message rcvd: 15
STP TCN messages rcvd: 588
```

Note IGMP control plane packet activity is seen in the output of **show ip igmp snooping internal event-history vpc**.

PIM joins are sent toward the RP from both NX-3 and NX-4, which can be seen in the **show ip pim internal event-history join-prune** output of Example 13-97.

Example 13-97 *(*, G) Join from NX-4 and NX-3*

```
NX-4# show ip pim internal event-history join-prune
! Output omitted for brevity

21:31:32.075044 pim [10572]:: Send Join-Prune on Ethernet3/28, length: 34
21:31:32.075016 pim [10572]:: Put (*, 239.115.115.1/32), WRS in join-list
for nbr 10.2.23.2
21:31:32.075010 pim [10572]:: wc_bit = TRUE, rp_bit = TRUE
NX-3# show ip pim internal event-history join-prune
! Output omitted for brevity
21:31:32.193623 pim [10975]:: Send Join-Prune on Ethernet3/28, length: 34
21:31:32.193593 pim [10975]:: Put (*, 239.115.115.1/32), WRS in join-list
for nbr 10.1.23.2
21:31:32.193586 pim [10975]:: wc_bit = TRUE, rp_bit = TRUE
```

Upon receiving the (*, G) join messages from NX-3 and NX-4, the mroute entry on NX-2 is updated to include the Ethernet 3/17 and Ethernet 3/18 interfaces to NX-3 and NX-4 in the OIL. Traffic then is sent out on the RPT.

As the traffic arrives on the RPT at NX-3 and NX-4, the source address of the group traffic becomes known, which triggers the creation of the (S, G) mroute entry. NX-3 and NX-4 then determine which device will act as the forwarder for this source using CFS. The communication for the forwarder election is viewed in the output of **show ip pim internal event-history vpc**. Because both NX-3 and NX-4 have equal metrics and route preference to the source, a tie occurs. However, because NX-4 is the vPC primary, it wins over NX-3 and acts as the forwarder for 10.115.1.4.

After the election results are obtained, an entry is created in the vPC RPF-Source cache, which is seen with the **show ip pim internal vpc rpf-source** command. Example 13-98 contains the PIM vPC forwarding election output from NX-4 and NX-3.

Example 13-98 *PIM vPC Forwarder Election on NX-3 and NX-4*

```
NX-4# show ip pim internal event-history vpc
! Output omitted for brevity
21:31:33.795807 pim [10572]: Sending RPF source updates for 1 entries to MRIB
21:31:33.795803 pim [10572]: RPF-source 10.115.1.4 state changed to
forwarding, our pref/metric: 110/44, peer's pref/metric: 110/44, updating MRIB
21:31:33.744941 pim [10572]: Updated RPF-source for local pref/metric: 110/44
for source 10.115.1.4, rpf-interface Ethernet3/28
21:31:33.743829 pim [10572]: Trigger handshake for rpf-source metrices for VRF
default upon MRIB notification
21:31:33.743646 pim [10572]: Ref count increased to 1 for vPC rpf-source
10.115.1.4
21:31:33.743639 pim [10572]: Created vPC RPF-source entry for 10.115.1.4 upon
creation of new (S,G) or (*,G) route in PIM

NX-3# show ip pim internal event-history vpc
! Output omitted for brevity
21:31:33.913558 pim [10975]: RPF-source 10.115.1.4 state changed to
not forwarding, our pref/metric: 110/44, updating MRIB
21:31:33.913554 pim [10975]: Updated RPF-source for local pref/metric: 110/44
for source 10.115.1.4, rpf-interface Ethernet3/28
21:31:33.912607 pim [10975]: Trigger handshake for rpf-source metrices for VRF
default upon MRIB notification
21:31:33.912508 pim [10975]: Ref count increased to 1 for vPC rpf-source
10.115.1.4
21:31:33.912501 pim [10975]: Created vPC RPF-source entry for 10.115.1.4 upon
creation of new (S,G) or (*,G) route in PIM
NX-4# show ip pim internal vpc rpf-source
! Output omitted for brevity
PIM vPC RPF-Source Cache for Context "default" - Chassis Role Primary

Source: 10.115.1.4
  Pref/Metric: 110/44
  Ref count: 1
  In MRIB: yes
  Is (*,G) rpf: no
  Source role: primary
  Forwarding state: Tie (forwarding)
  MRIB Forwarding state: forwarding
```

```
NX-3# show ip pim internal vpc rpf-source
PIM vPC RPF-Source Cache for Context "default" - Chassis Role Secondary

Source: 10.115.1.4
  Pref/Metric: 110/44
  Ref count: 1
  In MRIB: yes
  Is (*,G) rpf: no
  Source role: secondary
  Forwarding state: Tie (not forwarding)
  MRIB Forwarding state: not forwarding
```

For this election process to work correctly, PIM must be registered with the vPC manager process. This is indicated in the highlighted output of Example 13-99.

Example 13-99 *PIM vPC Status on NX-4*

```
NX-4# show ip pim internal vpc
! Output omitted for brevity

PIM vPC operational state UP
PIM emulated-switch operational state DOWN
PIM's view of VPC manager state: up
PIM is registered with VPC manager
PIM is registered with MCEC_TL/CFS
PIM VPC peer CFS state: up
PIM VPC CFS reliable send: no
PIM CFS sync start: yes
VPC peer link is up on port-channel1
PIM vPC Operating Version: 2
PIM chassis role is known
PIM chassis role: Primary (cached Primary)
PIM vPC Domain ID: 2
PIM emulated-switch id not configured
PIM vPC Domain Id Configured: yes
```

With **ip pim pre-build-spt**, both NX-3 and NX-4 initiate (S, G) joins toward NX-2 following the RPF path toward the source. However, because NX-3 is not the forwarder, it simply discards the packets it receives on the SPT. NX-4 forwards packets toward the vPC receiver and across the peer link to NX-3.

Example 13-100 shows the (S, G) mroute state and resulting PIM SPT joins from NX-3 and NX-4. Only NX-4 has an OIL containing VLAN 215 for the (S, G) mroute entry.

Example 13-100 *PIM (S, G) Join Events and MROUTE State*

```
NX-4# show ip pim internal event-history join-prune
! Output omitted for brevity
21:31:33.745236 pim [10572]:: Send Join-Prune on Ethernet3/28, length: 34
21:31:33.743825 pim [10572]:: Put (10.115.1.4/32, 239.115.115.1/32), S in
join-list for nbr 10.2.23.2
21:31:33.743818 pim [10572]:: wc_bit = FALSE, rp_bit = FALSE
NX-3# show ip pim internal event-history join-prune
! Output omitted for brevity
21:31:33.913795 pim [10975]:: Send Join-Prune on Ethernet3/28, length: 34
21:31:33.912603 pim [10975]:: Put (10.115.1.4/32, 239.115.115.1/32), S in
join-list for nbr 10.1.23.2
21:31:33.912597 pim [10975]:: wc_bit = FALSE, rp_bit = FALSE
NX-4# show ip mroute
! Output omitted for brevity
IP Multicast Routing Table for VRF "default"

(*, 239.115.115.1/32), uptime: 00:07:08, igmp ip pim
  Incoming interface: Ethernet3/28, RPF nbr: 10.2.23.2
  Outgoing interface list: (count: 1)
    Vlan215, uptime: 00:07:08, igmp

(10.115.1.4/32, 239.115.115.1/32), uptime: 00:07:06, ip mrib pim
  Incoming interface: Ethernet3/28, RPF nbr: 10.2.23.2
  Outgoing interface list: (count: 1)
    Vlan215, uptime: 00:07:06, mrib
NX-3# show ip mroute
! Output omitted for brevity
IP Multicast Routing Table for VRF "default"

(*, 239.115.115.1/32), uptime: 00:06:05, igmp ip pim
  Incoming interface: Ethernet3/28, RPF nbr: 10.1.23.2
  Outgoing interface list: (count: 1)
    Vlan215, uptime: 00:06:05, igmp

(10.115.1.4/32, 239.115.115.1/32), uptime: 00:06:03, ip mrib pim
  Incoming interface: Ethernet3/28, RPF nbr: 10.1.23.2
  Outgoing interface list: (count: 1)
```

More detail about the mroute state is seen in the output of the **show routing ip multicast source-tree detail** command. This command provides additional information that can be used for verification. The output confirms that NX-4 is the RPF-Source Forwarder for this (S, G) entry (see Example 13-101). NX-3 has the same OIL, but its status is set to *inactive*, which indicates that it is not forwarding.

Example 13-101 *Multicast Source Tree Detail on NX-4 and NX-3*

```
NX-4# show routing ip multicast source-tree detail
! Output omitted for brevity
IP Multicast Routing Table for VRF "default"

Total number of routes: 3
Total number of (*,G) routes: 1
Total number of (S,G) routes: 1
Total number of (*,G-prefix) routes: 1

(10.115.1.4/32, 239.115.115.1/32) Route ptr: 0x5ced35b4 , uptime: 00:14:50,
ip(0) mrib(1) pim(0)
  RPF-Source: 10.115.1.4 [44/110]
  Data Created: Yes
  VPC Flags
    RPF-Source Forwarder
  Stats: 422/37162 [Packets/Bytes], 352.000 bps
  Stats: 422/37162 [Packets/Bytes], 352.000 bps
  Incoming interface: Ethernet3/28, RPF nbr: 10.2.23.2
  Outgoing interface list: (count: 1)
    Vlan215, uptime: 00:14:50, mrib (vpc-svi)
NX-3# show routing ip multicast source-tree detail
IP Multicast Routing Table for VRF "default"

Total number of routes: 3
Total number of (*,G) routes: 1
Total number of (S,G) routes: 1
Total number of (*,G-prefix) routes: 1

(10.115.1.4/32, 239.115.115.1/32) Route ptr: 0x5cfd46b0 , uptime: 00:15:14,
ip(0) mrib(1) pim(0)
  RPF-Source: 10.115.1.4 [44/110]
  Data Created: Yes
  Stats: 440/38746 [Packets/Bytes], 352.000 bps
  Stats: 440/38746 [Packets/Bytes], 352.000 bps
  Incoming interface: Ethernet3/28, RPF nbr: 10.1.23.2
  Outgoing interface list: (count: 1) (inactive: 1)
    Vlan215, uptime: 00:15:14, mrib (vpc-svi)
```

The behavioral differences from traditional multicast must be understood to troubleshoot multicast in a vPC environment effectively. The use of (*, G) and (S, G) mroute state and knowledge on how the IIF and OIL are populated are key to determining which vPC peer to focus on when troubleshooting.

vPC Considerations for Multicast Traffic

Additional considerations with multicast traffic in a vPC environment should be understood. The considerations mentioned here might not apply to every network, but they are common enough that they should be considered when implementing vPC and multicast together.

Duplicate Multicast Packets

In some network environments, it may be possible to observe duplicate frames momentarily when multicast traffic is combined with vPC. These duplicate frames are generally seen only during the initial state transitions, such as when switching to the SPT tree. If the network applications are extremely sensitive to this and cannot deal with any duplicate frames, the following actions are recommended:

- Increase the PIM SG-Expiry timer with the **ip pim sg-expiry-timer** command. The value should be sufficiently large so that the (S, G) state does not time out during business hours.

- Configure **ip pim pre-build-spt**.

- Use multicast source-generated probe packets to populate the (S, G) state in the network before each business day.

The purpose of these steps is to have the SPT trees built before any business-critical data is sent each day. The increased (S, G) expiry timer allows the state to remain in place during critical times and avoid state timeout and re-creation for intermittent multicast senders. This avoids state transitions and the potential for duplicate traffic.

Reserved VLAN

The Nexus 5500 and Nexus 6000 series platforms utilize a reserved VLAN for the purposes of multicast routing when vPC is configured. When traffic arrives from a vPC-connected source, the following events occur:

- The traffic is replicated to any receivers in the same VLAN, including the peer link.

- The traffic is routed to any receivers in different vPC VLANs.

- A copy is sent across the peer link using the reserved VLAN.

As packets arrive from the peer link at the vPC peer, if the traffic is received from any VLAN *except for* the reserved VLAN, it will not be multicast routed. If the **vpc bind-vrf** [*vrf name*] **vlan** [*VLAN ID*] is not configured on both vPC peers, orphan ports or L3-connected receivers will not receive traffic. This command must be configured for each VRF participating in multicast routing.

Ethanalyzer Examples

Various troubleshooting steps in this chapter have relied on the NX-OS Ethanalyzer facility to capture control plane protocol messages. Table 13-11 provides examples of Ethanalyzer protocol message captures for the purposes of troubleshooting. In general, when performing an Ethanalyzer capture, you must decide whether the packets should be displayed in the session, decoded in the session, or written to a local file for offline analysis. The basic syntax of the command is **ethanalyzer local interface** [*inband*] **capture-filter** [*filter-string in quotes*] **write** [*location:filename*]. Many variations of the command exist, depending on which options are desired.

Table 13-11 *Example Ethanalyzer Captures*

What Is Being Captured	Ethanalyzer Capture Filter
Packets that are PIM *and* to/from host 10.2.23.3.	"pim && host 10.2.23.3"
Unicast PIM packets such as register or candidate RP advertisement	"pim && not host 224.0.0.13"
MSDP messages from 10.1.1.1	"src host 10.1.1.1 && tcp port 639"
IGMP general query	"igmp && host 224.0.0.1"
IGMP group specific query or report message	"igmp && host 239.115.115.1"
IGMP leave message	"igmp && host 224.0.0.2"
Multcast data packets sent to the supervisor from 10.115.1.4	"src host 10.115.1.4 && dst host 239.115.115.1"

Ethanalyzer syntax might vary slightly, depending on the platform. For example, some NX-OS platforms such as Nexus 3000 have inband-hi and inband-lo interfaces. For most control plane protocols, the packets are captured on the inband-hi interface. However, if the capture fails to collect any packets, the user might need to try a different interface option.

Summary

Multicast communication using NX-OS was covered in detail throughout this chapter. The fundamental concepts of multicast forwarding were introduced before delving into the NX-OS multicast architecture. The IGMP and PIM protocols were examined in detail to build a foundation for the detailed verification examples. The supported PIM operating modes (ASM, BiDIR, and SSM) were explored, including the various message types used for each and the process for verifying each type of multicast distribution tree. Finally, multicast and vPC were reviewed and explained, along with the differences in protocol behavior that are required when operating in a vPC environment. The goal of this chapter was not to cover every possible multicast forwarding scenario, but instead to provide you with a toolbox of fundamental concepts that can be adapted to a variety of troubleshooting situations in a complex multicast environment.

References

RFC 1112, Host Extensions for IP Multicasting, S. Deering. IETF, https://tools.ietf.org/html/rfc1112, August 1989.

RFC 2236, Internet Group Management Protocol, Version 2, W. Fenner. IETF, https://tools.ietf.org/html/rfc2236, November 1997.

RFC 3376, Internet Group Management Protocol, Version 3, B. Cain, S. Deering, I. Kouvelas, et al. IETF, https://www.ietf.org/rfc/rfc3376.txt, October 2002.

RFC 3446, Anycast Rendezvous Point (RP) Mechanism Using Protocol Independent Multicast (PIM) and Multicast Source Discovery Protocol (MSDP). D. Kim, D. Meyer, H. Kilmer, D. Farinacci. IETF, https://www.ietf.org/rfc/rfc3446.txt, January 2003.

RFC 3618, Multicast Source Discovery Protocol (MSDP). B. Fenner, D. Meyer. IETF, https://www.ietf.org/rfc/rfc3618.txt, October 2003.

RFC 4541, Considerations for Internet Group Management Protocol (IGMP) and Multicast Listener Discovery (MLD) Snooping Switches. M. Christensen, K. Kimball, F. Solensky. IETF, https://www.ietf.org/rfc/rfc4541.txt, May 2006.

RFC 4601, Protocol Independent Multicast–Sparse Mode (PIM-SM): Protocol Specification (Revised). B. Fenner, M. Handley, H. Holbrook, I. Kouvelas. IETF, https://www.ietf.org/rfc/rfc4601.txt, August 2006.

RFC 4607, Source-Specific Multicast for IP. H. Holbrook, B. Cain. IETF, https://www.ietf.org/rfc/rfc4607.txt, August 2006.

RFC 4610, Anycast-RP Using Protocol Independent Multicast (PIM). D. Farinacci, Y. Cai. IETF, https://www.ietf.org/rfc/rfc4610.txt, August 2006.

RFC 5015, Bidirectional Protocol Independent Multicast (BIDIR-PIM). M. Handley, I. Kouvelas, T. Speakman, L. Vicisano. IETF, https://www.ietf.org/rfc/rfc5015.txt, October 2007.

RFC 5059, Bootstrap Router (BSR) Mechanism for Protocol Independent Multicast (PIM). N. Bhaskar, A. Gall, J. Lingard, S. Venaas. IETF, https://www.ietf.org/rfc/rfc5059.txt, January 2008.

RFC 5771, IANA Guidelines for IPv4 Multicast Address Assignments. M. Cotton, L. Vegoda, D. Meyer. IETF, https://tools.ietf.org/rfc/rfc5771.txt, March 2010.

RFC 6166, A Registry for PIM Message Types. S. Venaas. IETF, https://tools.ietf.org/rfc/rfc6166.txt, April 2011.

Cisco NX-OS Software Configuration Guides. http://www.cisco.com.

Doyle, Jeff, and Jennifer DeHaven Carroll. *Routing TCP/IP, Volume II* (Indianapolis: Cisco Press, 2001).

Edgeworth, Brad, Aaron Foss, and Ramiro Garza Rios. *IP Routing on Cisco IOS, IOS XE and IOS XR* (Indianapolis: Cisco Press, 2014).

Esau, Matt. "Troubleshooting NXOS Multicast" (Cisco Live: San Francisco, 2014.)

Fuller, Ron, David Jansen, and Matthew McPherson. *NX-OS and Cisco Nexus Switching* (Indianapolis: Cisco Press, 2013).

IPv4 Multicast Address Space Registry, Stig Venaas, http://www.iana.org/assignments/multicast-addresses/multicast-addressess.xhtml, October 2017.

Loveless, Josh, Ray Blair, and Arvind Durai. *IP Multicast, Volume I: Cisco IP Multicast Networking* (Indianapolis: Cisco Press, 2016).

Chapter 14

Troubleshooting Overlay Transport Virtualization (OTV)

This chapter covers the following topics:

- OTV Fundamentals
- Understanding and Troubleshooting the OTV Control Plane
- Understanding and Troubleshooting the OTV Data Plane
- Advanced OTV Features

Overlay Transport Virtualization (OTV) is a MAC-in-IP overlay encapsulation that allows Layer 2 (L2) communication between sites that are separated by a Layer 3 (L3) routed network. OTV revolutionized network connectivity by extending L2 applications across multiple data centers without changing the existing network design. This chapter focuses on providing an overview of OTV, the processes for the OTV control and data plane and how to troubleshoot OTV.

OTV Fundamentals

The desire to connect data center sites at L2 is driven by the need for Virtual Machine (VM) and workload mobility, or for creating geographically diverse redundancy. Critical networks may even choose to have a fully mirrored disaster recovery site that synchronizes data and services between sites. Having the capability to put services from multiple locations into the same VLAN allows mobility between data centers without reconfiguring the network layer addressing of the host or server when it is moved.

The challenges and considerations associated with connecting two or more data centers at L2 are the following:

- Transport network types available
- Multihoming sites for redundancy
- Allowing each site to be independent from the others
- Creating fault isolation boundaries
- Ensuring the network can be expanded to future locations without disruption to existing sites

Before OTV, L2 data center interconnect (DCI) was achieved with the use of direct fiber links configured as L2 trunks, IEEE 802.1Q Tunneling (Q-in-Q), Ethernet over MPLS (EoMPLS), or Virtual Private LAN Service (VPLS). These options rely on potentially complex configuration by a transport service provider to become operational. Adding a site with those solutions means the service provider needs to be involved to complete the necessary provisioning.

OTV, however, can provide an L2 overlay network between sites using only an L3 routed underlay. Because OTV is encapsulated inside an IP packet for transport, it can take advantage of the strengths of L3 routing; for example, IP Equal Cost Multipath (ECMP) routing for load sharing and redundancy as well as optimal packet paths between OTV edge devices (ED) based on routing protocol metrics. Troubleshooting is simplified as well because traffic in the transport network is traditional IP with established and familiar troubleshooting techniques.

Solutions for L2 DCI such as Q-in-Q, EoMPLS, and VPLS all require the service provider to perform some form of encapsulation and decapsulation on the traffic for a site. With OTV, the overlay encapsulation boundary is moved from the service provider to the OTV site, which provides greater visibility and control for the network operator. The overlay configuration can be modified at will and does not require any interaction with or dependence on the underlay service provider. Modifications to the overlay include actions like adding new OTV sites or changing which VLANs are extended across the OTV overlay.

The previously mentioned transport protocols rely on static or stateful tunneling. With OTV, encapsulation of the overlay traffic happens dynamically based on MAC address to IP next-hop information supplied by OTV's Intermediate System to Intermediate System (IS-IS) control plane. This concept is referred to as *MAC address routing*, and it is explored in detail throughout this chapter. The important point to understand is that OTV maps a MAC address to a remote IP next-hop dynamically using a control plane protocol.

Multihoming is desirable for redundancy purposes, but could be inefficient if those redundant links and devices never get used. With traditional L2 switching, multihoming had to be planned and configured carefully to avoid L2 loops and Spanning-Tree Protocol (STP) blocking ports. OTV has considerations for multihoming built in to the protocol. For example, multiple OTV edge devices can be deployed in a single site, and each can actively forward traffic for different VLANs. Between data centers, multiple L3 routed links exist and provide L3 ECMP redundancy and load sharing between the OTV edge devices in each data center site.

Having redundant data centers is useful only if they exist in different fault domains, and problems from one data center do not affect the other. This implies that each data center must be isolated in terms of STP, and traffic forwarding loops between sites must be avoided. OTV allows each data center site to contain an independent STP Root Bridge for the VLANs extended across OTV. This is possible because OTV does not forward STP Bridge Protocol Data Units (BPDU) across the overlay, allowing each site to function independently.

Flood Control and Broadcast Optimization

Traditional L2 switches learn MAC addresses when frames arrive on a port. The source MAC address and associated interface mapping are kept until the MAC address is aged out or learned on a new interface. If the destination MAC address is not yet known, a switch performs unicast flooding. When this occurs, the unknown unicast traffic is flooded on all ports of the VLAN in an effort to reach the correct destination. In contrast, OTV learns MAC addresses from the remote data center through the IS-IS control plane protocol and will not flood any unknown unicast traffic across the overlay. Address Resolution Protocol (ARP) traffic is another source of flooded traffic in traditional switched networks. With OTV enabled, ARP is flooded in a controlled manner, and ARP responses are snooped and stored in a local ARP *Neighbor Discovery (ND)* cache by the OTV edge device. Any subsequent ARP requests for the host are answered by the OTV edge device on behalf of the host, which reduces the amount of broadcast traffic crossing the overlay.

Broadcast and multicast traffic in a VLAN must reach all remote data center locations. OTV relies on IP multicast in the underlay transport network to deliver this type of traffic in an efficient and scalable manner. By utilizing IP multicast transport, OTV eliminates the need for an edge device to perform head-end replication for each remote edge device. Head-end replication means that the originating OTV edge device creates a copy of the frame for each remote edge device. This can become a burden if there are many OTV sites and the packet rate is high. By using IP multicast transport, the OTV edge device needs to create only a single packet. Replication happens automatically by the multicast-enabled routers in the underlay transport network as the packets traverse the multicast tree to the receivers (Remote OTV edge devices).

Supported OTV Platforms

OTV is supported on the Nexus 7000 series and requires the Transport Service license (TRS) to be installed. Most deployments take advantage of Virtual Device Contexts (VDC) to logically separate the routing and OTV responsibilities in a single chassis.

Note OTV is also supported on Cisco ASR1000 series routers. The protocol functionality is similar but there may be implementation differences. This chapter focuses only on OTV on the Nexus 7000 series switches.

VLANs are aggregated into a distribution switch and then fed into a dedicated OTV VDC through a L2 trunk. Any traffic in a VLAN that needs to reach the remote data center is switched to the OTV VDC where it gets encapsulated by the edge device. The packet then traverses the routed VDC as an L3 IP packet and gets routed toward the remote OTV edge device for decapsulation. Traffic that requires L3 routing is fed from the L2 distribution to a routing VDC. The routing VDC typically has a First Hop Redundancy Protocol (FHRP) like Hot Standby Router Protocol (HSRP) or Virtual Router Redundancy Protocol (VRRP) to provide a default-gateway address to the hosts in the attached VLANs and to perform Inter VLAN routing.

Note Configuring multiple VDCs may require the installation of additional licenses, depending on the requirements of the deployment and the number of VDCs.

OTV Terminology

An OTV network topology example is shown in Figure 14-1. There are two data center sites connected by an L3 routed network that is enabled for IP multicast. The L3 routed network must provide IP connectivity between the OTV edge devices for OTV to function correctly. The placement of the ED is flexible as long as the OTV ED receives L2 frames for the VLANs that require extension across OTV. Usually the OTV ED is connected at the L2 and L3 boundary.

Data center 1 contains redundant OTV VDCs NX-2 and NX-4, which are the edge devices. NX-1 and NX-3 perform the routing and L2 VLAN aggregation and connect the access switch to the OTV VDC internal interface. The OTV join interface is a Layer 3 interface connected to the routing VDC. Data center 2 is configured as a mirror of Data center 1; however, the port-channel 3 interface is used as the OTV internal interface instead of the OTV join interface as in Data center 1. VLANs 100–110 are being *extended* with OTV between the data centers across the overlay.

OTV Fundamentals

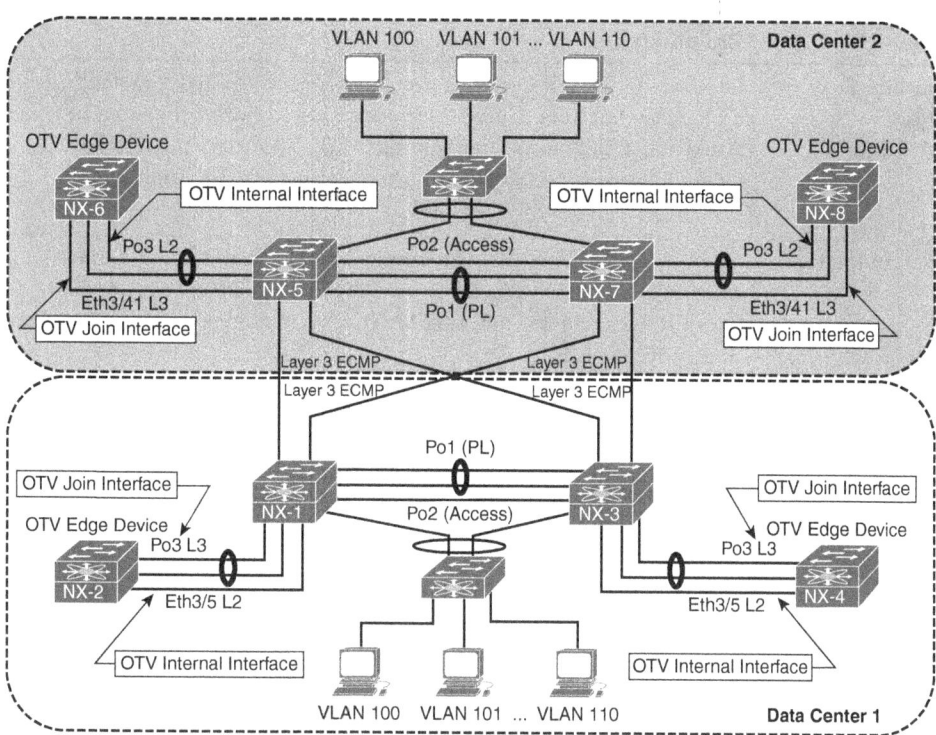

Figure 14-1 *OTV Topology Example*

The OTV terminology introduced in Figure 14-1 is explained in Table 14-1.

Table 14-1 *OTV Terminology*

Term	Definition
Edge Device (ED)	Responsible for dynamically encapsulating Ethernet frames into L3 IP packets for VLANs that are extended with OTV.
Authoritative Edge Device (AED)	Forwards traffic for an extended VLAN across OTV. Advertises MAC-address reachability for the VLANs it is active for to remote sites through the OTV IS-IS control plane. The Authoritative Edge Device (AED) is determined based on an ordinal value of 0 (zero) or 1 (one). The edge device with ordinal zero is AED for all even VLANs, and the edge device with ordinal one is AED for all odd VLANs. This ordinal is determined when the adjacency is formed between two edge devices at a site and is not configurable.
Internal Interface	Interface on the OTV edge device that connects to the local site. This interface provides a traditional L2 interface from the ED to the internal network, and MAC addresses are learned as traffic is received. The internal interface is an L2 trunk that carries the VLANs being extended by OTV.

Term	Definition
Join Interface	Interface on the OTV edge device that connects to the L3 routed network and used to source OTV encapsulated traffic. It can be a Loopback, L3 point-to-point interface, or L3 Port-channel interface. Subinterfaces may also be used. Multiple overlays can use the same join interface.
Overlay Interface	Interface on the OTV ED. The overlay interface is used to dynamically encapsulate the L2 traffic for an extended VLAN in an IP packet for transport to a remote OTV site. Multiple overlay interfaces are supported on an edge device.
Site VLAN	A VLAN that exists in the local site that connects the OTV edge devices at L2. The site VLAN is used to discover other edge devices in the local site and allows them to form an adjacency. After the adjacency is formed, the Authoritative Edge Device (AED) for each VLAN is elected. The site VLAN should be dedicated for OTV and not extended across the overlay. The site VLAN should be the same VLAN number at all OTV sites.
Site Identifier	The site-id must be the same for all edge devices that are part of the same site. Value ranges from 0x1 to 0xffffffff. The site-id is advertised in IS-IS packets, and it allows edge devices to identify which edge devices belong to the same site. Edge devices form an adjacency on the overlay as well as on the site VLAN (Dual adjacency). This allows the adjacency between edge devices in a site to be maintained even if the site VLAN adjacency gets broken due to a connectivity problem. The overlay interface will not come up until a site identifier is configured.
Site Adjacency	Formed across the site VLAN between OTV edge devices that are part of the same site. If an IS-IS Hello is received from an OTV ED on the site VLAN with a different site-id than the local router, the overlay is disabled. This is done to prevent a loop between the OTV internal interface and the overlay. This behavior is why it is recommended to make the OTV internal VLAN the same at each site.
Overlay Adjacency	OTV adjacency established on the OTV join interface. Adjacencies on the overlay interface are formed between sites, as well as for edge devices that are part of the same site. Edge devices form dual adjacency (site and overlay) for resiliency purposes. For devices in the same site to form an overlay adjacency, the site-id must match.

Deploying OTV

The configuration of the OTV edge device consists of the OTV internal interface, the join interface, and the overlay virtual interface. Before attempting to configure OTV, the capabilities of the transport network must be understood, and it must be correctly configured to support the OTV deployment model.

OTV Deployment Models

There are two OTV deployment models available, depending on the capabilities of the transport network.

- **Multicast Enabled Transport:** The control plane is encapsulated in IP multicast packets. Allows for dynamic neighbor discovery by having each OTV ED join the multicast control-group through the transport. A single multicast packet is sent by the OTV ED, which gets replicated along the multicast tree in the transport to each remote OTV ED.

- **Adjacency Server Mode:** Neighbors must be manually configured for the overlay interface. Unicast control plane packets are created for each individual neighbor and routed through the transport.

The OTV deployment model that is deployed should be decided during the planning phase after verifying the capabilities of the transport network. If multicast is supported in the transport, it is recommended to use the multicast deployment model. If there is no multicast support available in the transport network, use the adjacency server model.

The transport network must provide IP routed connectivity for unicast and multicast communication between the OTV EDs. The unicast connectivity requirements are achieved with any L3 routing protocol. If the OTV ED does not form a dynamic routing adjacency with the data center, it must be configured with static routes to reach the join interfaces of the other OTV EDs.

Multicast routing in the transport must be configured to support Protocol Independent Multicast (PIM). An Any Source Multicast (ASM) group is used for the OTV control-group, and a range of PIM Source Specific Multicast (SSM) groups are used for OTV data-groups. IGMPv3 should be enabled on the join interface of the OTV ED.

Note It is recommended to deploy PIM Rendezvous Point (RP) redundancy in the transport network for resiliency.

OTV Site VLAN

Each OTV site should be configured with an OTV site VLAN. The site VLAN should be trunked from the data center L2 switched network to the OTV internal interface of each OTV ED. Although not required, it is recommended to use the same VLAN at each OTV site in case the site VLAN is accidentally leaked between OTV sites.

With the deployment model determined and the OTV VDC created with the *TRANSPORT_SERVICES_PKG* license installed, the following steps are used to enable OTV functionality. The following examples are based upon a multicast enabled transport.

OTV Configuration

Before any OTV configuration is entered, the feature must be enabled with the **feature otv** command. Example 14-1 shows the configuration associated with the OTV internal interface, which is the L2 trunk port that participates in traditional switching with the existing data center network. The VLANs to be extended over OTV are VLAN 100–110. The site VLAN for both data centers is VLAN 10, which is being trunked over the OTV internal interface, along with VLANs 100–110.

Example 14-1 *OTV Internal Interface Configuration*

```
NX-2# show run | no-more
! Output omitted for brevity
feature otv

vlan 1,10,100-110

interface Ethernet3/5
  description To NX-1 3/19, OTV internal interface
  switchport
  switchport mode trunk
  mtu 9216
  no shutdown
```

The OTV internal interface should be considered as an access switch in the design of the data center's STP domain.

After the OTV internal interface is configured, the OTV join interface can be configured. The OTV join interface can be configured on M1, M2, M3, or F3 modules and can be a Loopback interface or an L3 point-to-point link. It is also possible to use an L3 port-channel, or a subinterface, depending on the deployment requirements. Example 14-2 shows the relevant configuration for the OTV join interface.

Example 14-2 *OTV Join Interface Configuration*

```
NX-2# show run | no-more
! Output omitted for brevity
feature otv

interface port-channel3
 description To NX-1 Po3, OTV Join interface
 mtu 9216
 ip address 10.1.12.1/24
 ip router ospf 1 area 0.0.0.0
 ip igmp version 3

interface Ethernet3/7
 description To NX-1 Eth3/22, OTV Join interface
 mtu 9216
 channel-group 3 mode active
 no shutdown

interface Ethernet3/8
 description To NX-1 Eth3/23, OTV Join interface
 mtu 9216
 channel-group 3 mode active
 no shutdown
```

The OTV join interface is an Layer 3 point-to-point interface and is configured for IGMP version 3. IGMPv3 is required so the OTV ED can join the control-group and data-groups required for OTV functionality.

Open Shortest Path First (OSPF) is the routing protocol in this topology and is used in both data centers. The OTV ED learns the unicast routes to reach all other OTV EDs through OSPF. The entire data center was configured with MTU 9216 on all infrastructure links to allow full 1500 byte frames to pass between applications without the need for fragmentation.

Beginning in NX-OS Release 8.0(1), a loopback interface can be used as the OTV join interface. If this option is used, the configuration will differ from this example, which utilizes an L3 point-to-point interface. At least one L3 routed interface must connect the OTV ED to the data center network. A PIM neighbor needs to be established over this L3 interface, and the OTV ED needs to be configured with the correct PIM Rendezvous Point (RP) and SSM-range that matches the routed data center devices and the transport network. Finally, the loopback interface used as the join interface must be configured with **ip pim sparse-mode** so that it can act as both a source and receiver for the OTV control-group and data-groups. The loopback also needs to be included in the dynamic routing protocol used for Layer 3 connectivity in the data center so that reachability exists to other OTV EDs.

> **Note** OTV encapsulation increases the size of L2 frames as they are transported across the IP transport network. The considerations for OTV MTU are further discussed later in this chapter.

With the OTV internal interface and join interface configured; the logical interface referred to as the *overlay interface* can now be configured and bound to the join interface. The overlay interface is used to dynamically encapsulate VLAN traffic between OTV sites. The number assigned to the overlay interface must be the same on all OTV EDs participating in the overlay. It is possible for multiple overlay interfaces to exist on the same OTV ED, but the VLANs extended on each overlay must not overlap.

The OTV site VLAN is used to form a site adjacency with any other OTV EDs located in the same site. Even for a single OTV ED site, the site VLAN must be configured for the overlay interface to come up. Although not required, it is recommended that the same site VLAN be configured at each OTV site. This is to allow OTV to detect if OTV sites become merged, either on purpose or in error. The site VLAN should *not* be included in the OTV extended VLAN list. The site identifier should be configured to the same value for all OTV EDs that belong to the same site. The **otv join-interface** [*interface*] command is used to bind the overlay interface to the join interface. The join interface is used to send and receive the OTV multicast control plane messaging used to form adjacencies and learn MAC addresses from other OTV EDs.

Because this configuration is utilizing a multicast capable transport network, the **otv control-group** [*group number*] is used to declare which IP PIM ASM group will be used for the OTV control plane group. The control plane group will carry OTV control plane traffic such as IS-IS hellos across the transport and allow the OTV EDs to communicate. The group number should match on all OTV EDs and must be multicast routed in the transport network. Each OTV ED acts as both a source and receiver for this multicast group.

The **otv data-group** [*group number*] is used to configure which Source Specific Multicast (SSM) groups are used to carry multicast data traffic across the overlay. This group is used to transport multicast traffic within a VLAN across the OTV overlay between sites. The number of multicast groups included in the data-group is a balance between optimization and scalability. If a single group is used, all OTV EDs receive all multicast traffic on the overlay, even if there is no receiver at the site. If a large number of groups is defined, multicast traffic can be forwarded optimally, but the number of groups present in the transport network could become a scalability concern. Presently, 256 multicast data groups are supported for OTV.

After the configuration is completed, the Overlay0 interface must be *no shutdown*. OTV adjacencies will then form between the OTV EDs, provided the underlay network has been properly configured for both unicast and multicast routing. Example 14-3 contains the configuration for *interface Overlay0* on NX-2 as well as the *site-VLAN* and *site-identifier* configurations.

Example 14-3 *OTV Overlay Interface Configuration*

```
NX-2# show running-config | no-more
! Output omitted for brevity
feature otv

otv site-vlan 10

interface Overlay0
 description Site A
 otv join-interface port-channel3
 otv control-group 239.12.12.12
 otv data-group 232.1.1.0/24
 otv extend-vlan 100-110
 no shutdown

otv site-identifier 0x1
```

Note If multihoming is planned for the deployment, it is recommended to first enable a single OTV ED at each site. After the OTV functionality has been verified, the second OTV ED can be enabled. This phased approach is recommended to allow for simplified troubleshooting if a problem occurs.

Understanding and Verifying the OTV Control Plane

Instead of relying on packet flooding and data plane MAC learning, which is implemented by traditional L2 switches, OTV takes advantage of an IS-IS control plane to exchange MAC address reachability information between sites. The benefit of this approach is that flooding of packets for an unknown unicast address can be eliminated with the assumption that there are no silent hosts.

OTV uses the existing functionality of IS-IS as much as possible. This includes the formation of neighbors and the use of LSPs and PDUs to exchange reachability information. OTV EDs discover each other with IS-IS hello packets and form adjacencies on the site VLAN as well as on the overlay, as shown in Figure 14-2.

886   Chapter 14: Troubleshooting Overlay Transport Virtualization (OTV)

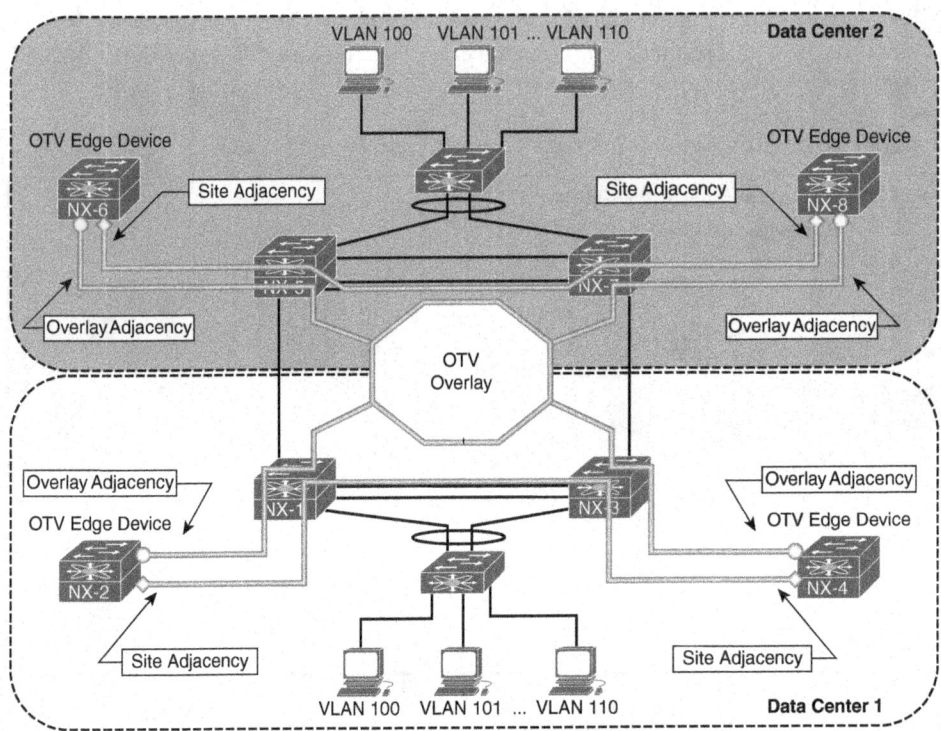

Figure 14-2 *OTV IS-IS Adjacencies*

IS-IS uses a Type-Length-Value (TLV) method to encode messages between neighbors, which allows flexibility and extendibility. Through various functionality enhancements over time, IS-IS has been extended to carry reachability information for multiple protocols by defining new corresponding TLVs. OTV uses IS-IS TLV type 147 called the *MAC-Reachability TLV* to carry MAC address reachability. This TLV contains a Topology-ID, a VLAN-ID, and a MAC address, which allows an OTV ED to learn MAC addresses from other OTV EDs and form the *MAC routing table*.

OTV is an overlay protocol, which means its operation is dependent upon the underlying transport protocols and the reachability they provide. As the control plane is examined in this chapter, it will become apparent that to troubleshoot OTV, the network operator must be able to segment the different protocol layers and understand the interaction between them. The OTV control plane consists of L2 switching, L3 routing, IP multicast, and IS-IS. If troubleshooting is being performed in the transport network, the OTV control plane packets must now be thought of as data plane packets, where the source and destination *hosts* are actually the OTV EDs. The transport network has control plane protocols that may also need investigation to solve an OTV problem.

OTV Multicast Mode

IS-IS packets on the overlay interface are encapsulated with the OTV IP multicast header and sent from each OTV ED to the transport network. For clarity, this process is depicted for a single OTV ED, NX-2 as shown in Figure 14-3. In actuality, each OTV ED is both a *source* and a *receiver* for the OTV control-group on the OTV join interface. The transport network performs multicast routing on these packets, which use a source address of the OTV ED's join interface, and a group address of the OTV control-group. Replication of the traffic across the transport happens as needed along the multicast tree so that each OTV ED that has joined the OTV control-group receives a copy of the packet. When the packet arrives at the remote OTV ED, the outer IP Multicast header encapsulation is removed, and the IS-IS packet is delivered to OTV for processing.

The transport network's multicast capability allows OTV to form IS-IS adjacencies as if each OTV ED were connected to a common LAN segment. In other words, think of the control-group as a logical multipoint connection from one OTV ED to all other OTV EDs. The site adjacency is formed over the site VLAN, which connects both OTV EDs in a site across the internal interface using direct L2 communication.

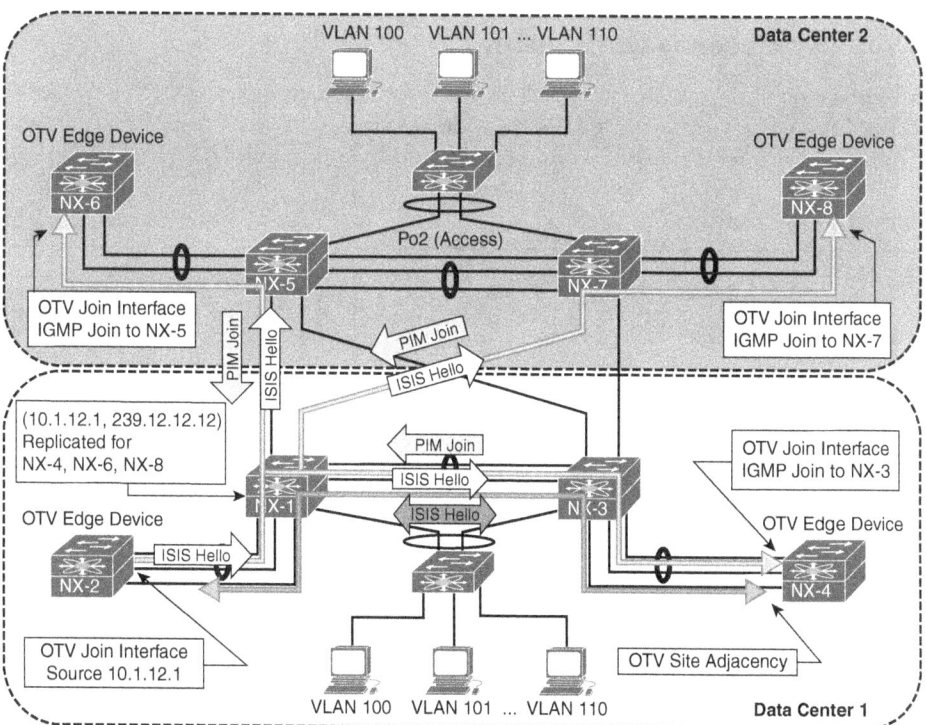

Figure 14-3 *OTV Control Plane with Multicast Transport*

> **Note** The behavior of forming Dual Adjacencies on the site VLAN and the overlay began with NX-OS release 5.2(1). Prior to this, OTV EDs in a site only formed site adjacencies.

The IS-IS protocol used by OTV does not require any user configuration for basic functionality. When OTV is configured the IS-IS process gets enabled and configured automatically. Adjacencies form provided that the underlying transport is functional and the configured parameters for the overlay are compatible between OTV EDs.

The IS-IS control plane is fundamental to the operation of OTV. It provides the mechanism to discover both local and remote OTV EDs, form adjacencies, and exchange MAC address reachability between sites. MAC address advertisements are learned through the IS-IS control plane. An SPF calculation is performed, and then the OTV MAC routing table is populated based on the result. When investigating a MAC address reachability issue, the advertisement is tracked through the OTV control plane to ensure that the ED has the correct information from all IS-IS neighbors. If a host-to-host reachability problem exists across the overlay, it is recommended to begin the investigation with a validation of the control plane configuration and operational state before moving into the data plane.

OTV IS-IS Adjacency Verification

Verification of the overlay interface is the first step to investigating any OTV adjacency problem. As shown in example 14-4, the **show otv overlay** [*overlay-identifier*] command provides key information that is required to begin investigating an OTV problem.

Example 14-4 *Status of the Overlay*

```
NX-2# show otv overlay 0

show otv overlay 0

OTV Overlay Information
Site Identifier 0000.0000.0001
Encapsulation-Format ip - gre

Overlay interface Overlay0

 VPN name            : Overlay0
 VPN state           : UP
 Extended vlans      : 100-110 (Total:11)
 Control group       : 239.12.12.12
 Data group range(s) : 232.1.1.0/24
 Broadcast group     : 239.12.12.12
 Join interface(s)   : Po3 (10.1.12.1)
 Site vlan           : 10 (up)
 AED-Capable         : Yes
 Capability          : Multicast-Reachable
```

The output of Example 14-4 verifies the Overlay0 interface is operational, which VLANs are being extended, the transport multicast groups for the OTV control-group and data-groups, the join interface, site VLAN, and AED capability. This information should match what has been configured in the overlay interface on the local and remote site OTV EDs.

Example 14-5 demonstrates how to verify that the IS-IS adjacencies are properly formed for OTV on the overlay interface.

Example 14-5 *OTV IS-IS Adjacencies on the Overlay*

```
NX-2# show otv adjacency
Overlay Adjacency database

Overlay-Interface Overlay0 :

Hostname              System-ID    Dest Addr     Up Time    State
NX-4                  64a0.e73e.12c2 10.1.22.1    03:51:57   UP
NX-8                  64a0.e73e.12c4 10.2.43.1    03:05:24   UP
NX-6                  6c9c.ed4d.d944 10.2.34.1    03:05:29   UP
```

The output of the **show otv site** command, as shown in Example 14-6, is used to verify the site adjacency. The adjacency with NX-4 is in the *Full* state, which indicates that both the overlay and site adjacencies are functional (Dual Adjacency).

Example 14-6 *OTV IS-IS Site Adjacency*

```
NX-2# show otv site

Dual Adjacency State Description
  Full    - Both site and overlay adjacency up
  Partial - Either site/overlay adjacency down
  Down    - Both adjacencies are down (Neighbor is down/unreachable)
  (!)     - Site-ID mismatch detected

Local Edge Device Information:
  Hostname NX-2
  System-ID 6c9c.ed4d.d942
  Site-Identifier 0000.0000.0001
  Site-VLAN 10 State is Up

Site Information for Overlay0:
Local device is AED-Capable
Neighbor Edge Devices in Site: 1
```

```
Hostname          System-ID        Adjacency-     Adjacency-     AED-

                                   State          Uptime         Capable

-------------------------------------------------------------------------

NX-4              64a0.e73e.12c2   Full           13:50:52       Yes
```

Examples 14-5 and 14-6 show a different adjacency uptime for the site and overlay adjacencies because these are independent IS-IS interfaces, and the adjacencies form independently of each other. The site-id for an IS-IS neighbor is found in the output of **show otv internal adjacency**, as shown in Example 14-7. This provides information about which OTV EDs are part of the same site.

Example 14-7 *Verify the Site-ID of an OTV IS-IS Neighbor*

```
NX-2# show otv internal adjacency
Overlay Adjacency database

Overlay-Interface Overlay0 :
System-ID       Dest Addr   Adj-State TM_State Adj-State inAS Site-ID
  Version
64a0.e73e.12c2 10.1.22.1   default   default   UP       UP   0000.0000.0001*
HW-St: Default N backup (null)

64a0.e73e.12c4 10.2.43.1   default   default   UP       UP   0000.0000.0002*
HW-St: Default N backup (null)

6c9c.ed4d.d944 10.2.34.1   default   default   UP       UP   0000.0000.0002*
HW-St: Default N backup (null)
```

Note OTV has several event-history logs that are useful for troubleshooting. The **show otv isis internal event-history adjacency** command is used to review recent adjacency changes.

A point-to-point tunnel is created for each OTV ED that has an adjacency. These tunnels are used to transport OTV unicast packets between OTV EDs. The output of **show tunnel internal implicit otv brief** should have a tunnel present for each OTV ED reachable on the transport network. The output from NX-2 is shown in Example 14-8.

Example 14-8 *OTV Dynamic Unicast Tunnels*

```
NX-2# show tunnel internal implicit otv brief

--------------------------------------------------------------------------------
Interface          Status     IP Address    Encap type     MTU
--------------------------------------------------------------------------------
Tunnel16384        up         --            GRE/IP         9178
Tunnel16385        up         --            GRE/IP         9178
Tunnel16386        up         --            GRE/IP         9178
```

Additional details about a specific tunnel is viewed with **show tunnel internal implicit otv tunnel_num** [*number*]. Example 14-9 shows detailed output for tunnel 16384. The MTU, transport protocol source, and destination address are shown, which allows a tunnel to be mapped to a particular neighbor. This output should be verified if a specific OTV ED is having a problem.

Example 14-9 *Verify Detailed Dynamic Tunnel Parameters*

```
NX-2# show tunnel internal implicit otv tunnel_num 16384
Tunnel16384 is up
  Admin State: up
  MTU 9178 bytes, BW 9 Kbit
  Tunnel protocol/transport GRE/IP
  Tunnel source 10.1.12.1, destination 10.2.43.1
  Transport protocol is in VRF "default"
  Rx
  0 packets input, 1 minute input rate 0 packets/sec
  Tx
  0 packets output, 1 minute output rate 0 packets/sec
  Last clearing of "show interface" counters never
```

When the OTV Adjacencies are established, the AED role is determined for each VLAN that is extended across the overlay using a hash function. The OTV IS-IS system-id is used along with the VLAN identifier to determine the AED role for each VLAN based on an *ordinal* value. The device with the lower system-id becomes AED for the even-numbered VLANs, and the device with the higher system-id becomes AED for the odd numbered VLANs.

The **show otv vlan** command from NX-2 is shown in Example 14-10. The VLAN state column lists the current state as Active or Inactive. An Active state indicates this OTV ED is the AED for that VLAN and is responsible for forwarding packets across the overlay and advertising MAC address reachability for the VLAN. This is an important piece of information to know when troubleshooting to ensure the correct device is being investigated for a particular VLAN.

Example 14-10 *Verify Which OTV ED Is the AED*

```
NX-2# show otv vlan

OTV Extended VLANs and Edge Device State Information (* - AED)

Legend:
 (NA) - Non AED, (VD) - Vlan Disabled, (OD) - Overlay Down
 (DH) - Delete Holddown, (HW) - HW: State Down
 (NFC) - Not Forward Capable


VLAN  Auth. Edge Device         Vlan State            Overlay
----  ----------------------    ---------------       -------

 100   NX-4                     inactive(NA)          Overlay0
 101*  NX-2                     active                Overlay0
 102   NX-4                     inactive(NA)          Overlay0
 103*  NX-2                     active                Overlay0
 104   NX-4                     inactive(NA)          Overlay0
 105*  NX-2                     active                Overlay0
 106   NX-4                     inactive(NA)          Overlay0
 107*  NX-2                     active                Overlay0
 108   NX-4                     inactive(NA)          Overlay0
 109*  NX-2                     active                Overlay0
 110   NX-4                     inactive(NA)          Overlay0
```

Adjacency problems are typically caused by configuration error, a packet delivery problem for the OTV control-group in the transport network, or a problem with the site VLAN for the site adjacency.

For problems with an overlay adjacency, check the IP multicast state on the multicast router connected to the OTV ED's join interface. Each OTV ED should have a corresponding (S,G) mroute for the control-group. The L3 interface that connects the multicast router to the OTV ED should be populated in the Outgoing Interface List (OIL) for the (*, G) and all active sources (S,G) of the OTV control-group because of the IGMP join from the OTV ED.

The **show ip mroute** [*group*] command from NX-1 is shown in Example 14-11. The (*, 239.12.12.12) entry has Port-channel 3 populated in the OIL by IGMP. For all active sources sending to 239.12.12.12, the OIL is populated with Port-channel 3 as well, which allows NX-2 to receive IS-IS hello and LSP packets from NX-4, NX-6, and NX-8. The source address for each Source, Group pair (S,G) are the other OTV ED's join interfaces sending multicast packets to the group.

Example 14-11 *Verify Multicast Routing for the OTV Control-Group*

```
NX-1# show ip mroute 239.12.12.12
IP Multicast Routing Table for VRF "default"

(*, 239.12.12.12/32), uptime: 1w1d, pim ip igmp
 Incoming interface: loopback99, RPF nbr: 10.99.99.99
 Outgoing interface list: (count: 1)
  port-channel3, uptime: 16:17:45, igmp

(10.1.12.1/32, 239.12.12.12/32), uptime: 1w1d, ip mrib pim
 Incoming interface: port-channel3, RPF nbr: 10.1.12.1, internal
 Outgoing interface list: (count: 4)
  port-channel3, uptime: 16:17:45, mrib, (RPF)
  Vlan1101, uptime: 16:48:24, pim
  Ethernet3/17, uptime: 6d05h, pim
  Ethernet3/18, uptime: 1w1d, pim

(10.1.22.1/32, 239.12.12.12/32), uptime: 1w1d, pim mrib ip
 Incoming interface: Vlan1101, RPF nbr: 10.1.11.2, internal
 Outgoing interface list: (count: 1)
  port-channel3, uptime: 16:17:45, mrib

(10.2.34.1/32, 239.12.12.12/32), uptime: 1w1d, pim mrib ip
 Incoming interface: Ethernet3/18, RPF nbr: 10.1.13.3, internal
 Outgoing interface list: (count: 1)
  port-channel3, uptime: 16:17:45, mrib

(10.2.43.1/32, 239.12.12.12/32), uptime: 1w1d, pim mrib ip
 Incoming interface: Ethernet3/17, RPF nbr: 10.2.13.3, internal
 Outgoing interface list: (count: 1)
  port-channel3, uptime: 16:17:45, mrib
```

The presence of a (*, G) from IGMP for a group indicates that at minimum an IGMP join message was received by the router, and there is at least one interested receiver on that interface. A PIM join message is sent toward the PIM RP from the last hop router, and the (*, G) join state should be present along the multicast tree to the PIM RP. When a data packet for the group is received on the *shared tree* by the last hop router, in this case NX-1, a PIM (S, G) join message is sent toward the source. This messaging forms what is called the *source tree*, which is built to the first-hop router connected to the source. The source tree remains in place as long as the receiver is still interested in the group.

Example 14-12 shows how to verify the receipt of traffic with the **show ip mroute summary** command, which provides packet counters and bit-rate values for each source.

Example 14-12 *Verify the Current Bit-Rate of the OTV Control-Group*

```
NX-1# show ip mroute 239.12.12.12 summary
IP Multicast Routing Table for VRF "default"

Total number of routes: 6
Total number of (*,G) routes: 1
Total number of (S,G) routes: 4
Total number of (*,G-prefix) routes: 1
Group count: 1, rough average sources per group: 4.0

Group: 239.12.12.12/32, Source count: 4
Source         packets   bytes       aps  pps   bit-rate    oifs
(*,G)          3         4326        1442 0     0.000  bps  1
10.1.12.1      927464    193003108   208  2     3.154  kbps 4
10.1.22.1      872869    173599251   198  3     3.844  kbps 1
10.2.34.1      1060046   203853603   192  3     3.261  kbps 1
10.2.43.1      1000183   203775760   203  3     3.466  kbps 1
```

Because IS-IS adjacency failures for the overlay are often caused by multicast packet delivery problems in the transport, it is important to understand what the multicast state on each router is indicating. The multicast role of each transport router must also be understood to provide context to the multicast routing table state. For example, is the device a first-hop router (FHR), PIM RP, transit router, or last-hop router (LHR)? In the network example, NX-1 is a PIM LHR, FHR, and RP for the control-group.

If NX-1 had no multicast state for the OTV control-group, it indicates that the IGMP join has not been received from NX-2. Because NX-1 is also a PIM RP for this group, it also indicates that none of the sources have been registered. If a (*, G) was present, but no (S, G), it indicates that the IGMP join was received from NX-2, but multicast data traffic from NX-4, NX-6, or NX-8 was not received by NX-1; therefore, the switchover to the source tree did not happen. At that point, troubleshooting moves toward the source and first-hop routers until the cause of the multicast problem is identified.

Note Multicast troubleshooting is covered in Chapter 13, "Troubleshooting Multicast."

The site adjacency is formed across the site VLAN. There must be connectivity between the OTV ED's internal interface across the data center network for the IS-IS adjacency to form successfully. Example 14-13 contains the output of **show otv site** where the site adjacency is down, as indicated by the *Partial* state because the overlay adjacency with NX-4 is UP.

Example 14-13 *OTV Partial Adjacency*

```
NX-2# show otv site

Dual Adjacency State Description
  Full    - Both site and overlay adjacency up
  Partial - Either site/overlay adjacency down
  Down    - Both adjacencies are down (Neighbor is down/unreachable)
  (!)     - Site-ID mismatch detected

Local Edge Device Information:
  Hostname NX-2
  System-ID 6c9c.ed4d.d942
  Site-Identifier 0000.0000.0001
  Site-VLAN 10 State is Up

Site Information for Overlay0:

Local device is AED-Capable
Neighbor Edge Devices in Site: 1

Hostname          System-ID       Adjacency-    Adjacency-   AED-
                                  State         Uptime       Capable
-------------------------------------------------------------------------------
NX-4              64a0.e73e.12c2  Partial (!)   00:12:32     Yes

NX-2# show otv adjacency
Overlay Adjacency database

Overlay-Interface Overlay0 :
Hostname          System-ID      Dest Addr     Up Time    State
NX-4              64a0.e73e.12c2 10.1.22.1     00:01:57   UP
NX-8              64a0.e73e.12c4 10.2.43.1     00:01:57   UP
NX-6              6c9c.ed4d.d944 10.2.34.1     00:02:09   UP
```

The **show otv isis site** output confirms that the adjacency was lost on the site VLAN as shown in Example 14-14.

Example 14-14 *Verify the OTV Site Adjacency*

```
NX-2# show otv isis site

OTV-ISIS site-information for: default

 BFD: Disabled

OTV-IS-IS site adjacency local database:

 SNPA          State Last Chg Hold     Fwd-state Site-ID        Version BFD
 64a0.e73e.12c2 LOST 00:01:52 00:03:34 DOWN      0000.0000.0001 3       Disabled

OTV-IS-IS Site Group Information (as in OTV SDB):

 SystemID: 6c9c.ed4d.d942, Interface: site-vlan, VLAN Id: 10, Cib: Up VLAN: Up

 Overlay    State   Next IIH   Int    Multi
 Overlay0   Up      00:00:01   3      20

 Overlay   Active SG     Last CSNP          CSNP Int Next CSNP
 Overlay0  239.12.12.12  ffff.ffff.ffff.ff-ff 2w1d    Inactive

 Neighbor SystemID: 64a0.e73e.12c2
```

The IS-IS adjacency being down indicates that IS-IS hellos (IIH Packets) are not being exchanged properly on the site VLAN. The transmit and receipt of IIH packets is recorded in the output of **show otv isis internal event-history iih**. Example 14-15 confirms that IIH packets are being sent, but none are being received across the site VLAN.

Example 14-15 *NX-2 OTV IS-IS IIH Event-History*

```
NX-2# show otv isis internal event-history iih | inc site
03:51:17.663263 isis_otv default [13901]: [13906]: Send L1 LAN IIH over site-vlan
  len 1497 prio 6,dmac 0100.0cdf.dfdf
03:51:14.910759 isis_otv default [13901]: [13906]: Send L1 LAN IIH over site-vlan
  len 1497 prio 6,dmac 0100.0cdf.dfdf
03:51:11.940991 isis_otv default [13901]: [13906]: Send L1 LAN IIH over site-vlan
  len 1497 prio 6,dmac 0100.0cdf.dfdf
03:51:08.939666 isis_otv default [13901]: [13906]: Send L1 LAN IIH over site-vlan
  len 1497 prio 6,dmac 0100.0cdf.dfdf
03:51:06.353274 isis_otv default [13901]: [13906]: Send L1 LAN IIH over site-vlan
  len 1497 prio 6,dmac 0100.0cdf.dfdf
03:51:03.584122 isis_otv default [13901]: [13906]: Send L1 LAN IIH over site-vlan
  len 1497 prio 6,dmac 0100.0cdf.dfdf
```

This event-history log confirms that the IIH packets are created, and the process is sending them out to the site VLAN. The same event-history can be checked on NX-4 to verify if the IIH packets are received. The output from NX-4 is shown in Example 14-16, which indicates the IIH packets are being sent, but none are received from NX-2.

Example 14-16 *NX-4 OTV IS-IS IIH Event-History*

```
NX-4# show otv isis internal event-history iih | inc site
03:51:19.013078 isis_otv default [24209]: [24210]: Send L1 LAN IIH over site-vlan
  len 1497 prio 6,dmac 0100.0cdf.dfdf
03:51:16.293081 isis_otv default [24209]: [24210]: Send L1 LAN IIH over site-vlan
  len 1497 prio 6,dmac 0100.0cdf.dfdf
03:51:13.723065 isis_otv default [24209]: [24210]: Send L1 LAN IIH over site-vlan
  len 1497 prio 6,dmac 0100.0cdf.dfdf
03:51:10.813105 isis_otv default [24209]: [24210]: Send L1 LAN IIH over site-vlan
  len 1497 prio 6,dmac 0100.0cdf.dfdf
03:51:07.843102 isis_otv default [24209]: [24210]: Send L1 LAN IIH over site-vlan
  len 1497 prio 6,dmac 0100.0cdf.dfdf
```

The output in Example 14-15 and Example 14-16 confirms that both NX-2 and NX-4 are sending IS-IS IIH hellos to the site VLAN, but neither side is receiving packets from the other OTV ED. At this point of the investigation, troubleshooting should follow the VLAN across the L2 data center infrastructure to confirm the VLAN is properly configured and trunked between NX-2 and NX-4. In this case, a problem was identified on NX-3 where the site VLAN, VLAN 10, was not being trunked across the vPC peer-link. This resulted in a Bridge Assurance inconsistency problem over the peer-link, as shown in the output of Example 14-17.

Example 14-17 *Verify Site-VLAN Spanning-Tree*

```
NX-1# show spanning-tree vlan 10 detail

 VLAN0010 is executing the rstp compatible Spanning Tree protocol
  Bridge Identifier has priority 24576, sysid 10, address 0023.04ee.be01
  Configured hello time 2, max age 20, forward delay 15
  We are the root of the spanning tree
  Topology change flag not set, detected flag not set
  Number of topology changes 2 last change occurred 0:05:26 ago
        from port-channel2
  Times:  hold 1, topology change 35, notification 2
          hello 2, max age 20, forward delay 15
  Timers: hello 0, topology change 0, notification 0
```

```
Port 4096 (port-channel1, vPC Peer-link) of VLAN0010 is broken (Bridge Assurance
Inconsistent, VPC Peer-link Inconsistent)
  Port path cost 1, Port priority 128, Port Identifier 128.4096
  Designated root has priority 32778, address 0023.04ee.be01
  Designated bridge has priority 0, address 6c9c.ed4d.d941
  Designated port id is 128.4096, designated path cost 0
  Timers: message age 0, forward delay 0, hold 0
  Number of transitions to forwarding state: 0
  The port type is network
  Link type is point-to-point by default
  BPDU: sent 1534, received 0
```

After correcting the trunked VLAN configuration of the vPC peer-link, the OTV site adjacency came up on the site VLAN, and the dual adjacency state was returned to *FULL*. The adjacency transitions are viewed in the output of **show otv isis internal event-history adjacency** as shown in Example 14-18.

Example 14-18 *OTV IS-IS Adjacency Event-History*

```
NX-2# show otv isis internal event-history adjacency
03:52:58.909967 isis_otv default [13901]:: LAN adj L1 64a0.e73e.12c2
over site-vlan - UP T 0
03:52:58.909785 isis_otv default [13901]:: LAN adj L1 64a0.e73e.12c2
over site-vlan - INIT (New) T -1
03:52:58.909776 isis_otv default [13901]:: isis_init_topo_adj LAN
adj 1 64a0.e73e.12c2 over site-vlan - LAN MT-0
```

The first troubleshooting step for an adjacency problem is to ensure that both neighbors are generating and transmitting IS-IS hellos properly. If they are, start stepping through the transport or underlay network until the connectivity problem is isolated.

If the site VLAN was verified to be functional across the data center, the next step in troubleshooting an adjacency problem is to perform packet captures to determine which device is not forwarding the frames correctly. Chapter 2, "NX-OS Troubleshooting Tools," covers the use of various packet capture tools available on NX-OS platforms that can be utilized to isolate the problem. An important concept to grasp is that even though these are control plane packets for OTV IS-IS on NX-2 and NX-4, as they are traversing the L3 transport network, they are handled as ordinary data plane packets.

OTV IS-IS Topology Table

After IS-IS adjacencies are formed on the overlay and site VLAN, IS-IS transmits and receives Protocol Data Units (PDU) including LSPs for the purpose of creating the OTV MAC routing table. Each OTV ED floods its LSP database so that all neighbors have a consistent view of the topology. After LSPs are exchanged, the Shortest Path First (SPF) algorithm runs and constructs the topology with MAC addresses as leafs. Entries are then installed into the OTV MAC routing table for the purpose of traffic forwarding.

An example of the OTV IS-IS database is shown in Example 14-19. This output shows the LSP for NX-4 from the IS-IS database on NX-2.

Example 14-19 *The OTV IS-IS Database*

```
NX-2# show otv isis database
OTV-IS-IS Process: default LSP database VPN: Overlay0

OTV-IS-IS Level-1 Link State Database
 LSPID           Seq Number  Checksum Lifetime   A/P/O/T
 64a0.e73e.12c2.00-00 0x0000069F  0x643C   1198     0/0/0/1
 64a0.e73e.12c4.00-00 0x00027EBC  0x13EA   1198     0/0/0/1
 6c9c.ed4d.d942.00-00* 0x00000619 0x463D   1196     0/0/0/1
 6c9c.ed4d.d942.01-00* 0x00000003 0x2278   0 (1198) 0/0/0/1
 6c9c.ed4d.d944.00-00 0x0002AA3A  0x209E   1197     0/0/0/1
 6c9c.ed4d.d944.01-00 0x0002790A  0xD43A   1199     0/0/0/1
```

The LSP lifetime shows that LSPs are only a few seconds old because the *Lifetime* counts from 1200 to zero. Issuing the command a few times may also show the *Seq Number* field incrementing, which indicates that the LSP is being updated by the originating IS-IS neighbor with changed information. This could cause OTV MAC routes to be refreshed and reinstalled as the SPF algorithm executes constantly. LSPs may refresh and get updated as part of normal IS-IS operation, but in this case the updates are happening constantly, which is abnormal in a steady-state.

To investigate the problem, check the LSP contents for changes over time. To understand which OTV ED is advertising which LSP, check the hostname to system-id mapping. The Hostname TLV provides a way to dynamically learn the system-id to hostname mapping for a neighbor. To identify which IS-IS database entries belong to which neighbors, use the **show otv isis hostname** command, as shown in Example 14-20. The asterisk (*) indicates the local system-id.

Example 14-20 *OTV IS-IS Dynamic Hostname*

```
NX-2# show otv isis hostname
OTV-IS-IS Process: default dynamic hostname table VPN: Overlay0
 Level System ID     Dynamic hostname
 1     64a0.e73e.12c2 NX-4
 1     64a0.e73e.12c4 NX-8
 1     6c9c.ed4d.d942* NX-2
 1     6c9c.ed4d.d944 NX-6
```

The contents of an individual LSP are verified with the **show otv isis database detail** [*lsp-id*]. Example 14-21 contains the LSP received from NX-4 at NX-2 and contains several important pieces of information, such as neighbor and MAC address reachability, the site-id, and which device is the AED for a particular VLAN.

Example 14-21 *OTV IS-IS Database Detail*

```
NX-2# show otv isis database detail 64a0.e73e.12c2.00-00
OTV-IS-IS Process: default LSP database VPN: Overlay0

OTV-IS-IS Level-1 Link State Database
LSPID              Seq Number  Checksum Lifetime  A/P/O/T
64a0.e73e.12c2.00-00 0x000006BB  0xAFD6   1194     0/0/0/1
  Instance   : 0x000005D0
  Area Address : 00
  NLPID      : 0xCC 0x8E
  Hostname   : NX-4        Length : 4
  Extended IS : 6c9c.ed4d.d944.01 Metric : 40
  Vlan       : 100 : Metric   : 0
   MAC Address    : 0000.0c07.ac64
  Vlan       : 102 : Metric   : 0
   MAC Address    : 0000.0c07.ac66
  Vlan       : 104 : Metric   : 0
   MAC Address    : 0000.0c07.ac68
  Vlan       : 108 : Metric   : 0
   MAC Address    : 0000.0c07.ac6c
  Vlan       : 110 : Metric   : 1
   MAC Address    : 0000.0c07.ac6e
  Vlan       : 106 : Metric   : 1
   MAC Address    : 0000.0c07.ac6a
  Vlan       : 110 : Metric   : 1
   MAC Address    : 64a0.e73e.12c1
  Vlan       : 108 : Metric   : 1
   MAC Address    : 64a0.e73e.12c1
  Vlan       : 100 : Metric   : 1
   MAC Address    : 64a0.e73e.12c1
  Vlan       : 104 : Metric   : 1
   MAC Address    : c464.135c.6600
   MAC Address    : 64a0.e73e.12c1
  Vlan       : 106 : Metric   : 1
   MAC Address    : 64a0.e73e.12c1
  Vlan       : 102 : Metric   : 1
   MAC Address    : 6c9c.ed4d.d941
   MAC Address    : 64a0.e73e.12c1
  Site ID    : 0000.0000.0001
```

Understanding and Verifying the OTV Control Plane

```
    AED-Server-ID : 64a0.e73e.12c2
Version 57
  ED Summary   :    Device ID : 6c9c.ed4d.d942 : fwd_ready : 1
  ED Summary   :    Device ID : 64a0.e73e.12c2 : fwd_ready : 1
  Site ID      : 0000.0000.0001 : Partition ID   : ffff.ffff.ffff
  Device ID : 64a0.e73e.12c2 Cluster-ID  : 0
  Vlan Status  :    AED : 0 Back-up AED  : 1 Fwd ready : 1  Priority : 0 Delete    : 0
  Local     : 1 Remote     : 1 Range    : 1 Version  : 9
Start-vlan  : 101 End-vlan    : 109 Step     : 2
  AED : 1 Back-up AED  : 0 Fwd ready : 1  Priority : 0 Delete    : 0 Local   : 1
  Remote     : 1 Range    : 1 Version  : 9
Start-vlan  : 100 End-vlan    : 110 Step     : 2
  Site ID      : 0000.0000.0001 : Partition ID   : ffff.ffff.ffff
  Device ID : 64a0.e73e.12c2 Cluster-ID  : 0
  AED SVR status :     Old-AED : 64a0.e73e.12c2 New-AED : 6c9c.ed4d.d942
  old-backup-aed : 0000.0000.0000 new-backup-aed  : 64a0.e73e.12c2
  Delete-flag   : 0 No-of-range   : 1 Version    : 9
Start-vlan  : 101 End-vlan    : 109 Step     : 2
  Old-AED : 64a0.e73e.12c2 New-AED : 64a0.e73e.12c2
  old-backup-aed : 0000.0000.0000 new-backup-aed  : 6c9c.ed4d.d942
  Delete-flag   : 0 No-of-range   : 1 Version    : 9
Start-vlan  : 100 End-vlan    : 110 Step     : 2
  Digest Offset : 0
```

To determine what information is changing in the LSP, use the NX-OS *diff* utility. As shown in Example 14-22, the *diff* utility reveals that the Sequence Number is updated, and the LSP Lifetime has refreshed again to 1198. The changing LSP contents are related to HSRP MAC addresses in several VLANs extended by OTV.

Example 14-22 *OTV IS-IS LSP Updating Frequently*

```
NX-2# show otv isis database detail 64a0.e73e.12c2.00-00 | diff
5,6c5,6
<   64a0.e73e.12c2.00-00  0x0001CD0E   0x0FF1   1196    0/0/0/1
<     Instance    : 0x0001CC23
---
>   64a0.e73e.12c2.00-00  0x0001CD11   0x193C   1198    0/0/0/1
>     Instance    : 0x0001CC26
10a11,12
>     Vlan      : 110 : Metric    : 0
>     MAC Address    : 0000.0c07.ac6e
13,16d14
<     Vlan      : 108 : Metric    : 0
<     MAC Address    : 0000.0c07.ac6c
<     Vlan      : 106 : Metric    : 0
```

```
<    MAC Address   : 0000.0c07.ac6a
19,22c17,18
<    Vlan         : 110 : Metric    : 1
<    MAC Address   : 0000.0c07.ac6e
<    Vlan         : 102 : Metric    : 1
<    MAC Address   : 0000.0c07.ac66
---
>    Vlan         : 106 : Metric    : 1
>    MAC Address   : 0000.0c07.ac6a
```

The MAC reachability information from the LSP is installed into the OTV MAC routing table. Each MAC address is installed with a next-hop known either via the site VLAN or from an OTV ED reachable across the overlay interface. The OTV MAC routing table in Example 14-23 confirms that MAC address entries are unstable and are refreshing. The *Uptime* for several entries is less than 1 minute and some were dampened with the *(D)* flag.

Example 14-23 *Instability in the OTV MAC Routing Table*

```
NX-2# show otv route | inc 00:00
! Output omitted for brevity
OTV Unicast MAC Routing Table For Overlay0

VLAN MAC-Address     Metric Uptime   Owner     Next-hop(s)
---- --------------- ------ -------- --------- -----------
 100 0000.0c07.ac64  41     00:00:18 overlay   NX-8 (D)
 101 0000.0c07.ac65  1      00:00:07 site      Ethernet3/5
 102 0000.0c07.ac66  41     00:00:12 overlay   NX-8 (D)
 103 0000.0c07.ac67  1      00:00:07 site      Ethernet3/5
 104 0000.0c07.ac68  41     00:00:12 overlay   NX-8
 105 0000.0c07.ac69  1      00:00:07 site      Ethernet3/5
 106 0000.0c07.ac6a  41     00:00:30 overlay   NX-8
 107 0000.0c07.ac6b  41     00:00:03 overlay   NX-6
 108 0000.0c07.ac6c  41     00:00:18 overlay   NX-8 (D)
 109 0000.0c07.ac6d  1      00:00:07 site      Ethernet3/5
 110 0000.0c07.ac6e  41     00:00:12 overlay   NX-8 (D)
```

Additional information is obtained from the OTV event-traces. Because you are interested in the changes being received in the IS-IS LSP from a remote OTV ED, the **show otv isis internal event-history spf-leaf** is used to view what is changing and causing the routes to be refreshed in the OTV route table. This output is provided in Example 14-24.

Example 14-24 *OTV IS-IS SPF Event-History*

```
NX-2# show otv isis internal event-history spf-leaf | egrep "Process 0103-0000.0c07.
  ac67"
20:12:48.699301 isis_otv default [13901]: [13911]: Process 0103-0000.0c07.ac67
contained in 6c9c.ed4d.d944.00-00 with metric 0
20:12:45.060622 isis_otv default [13901]: [13911]: Process 0103-0000.0c07.ac67
contained in 6c9c.ed4d.d944.00-00 with metric 0
20:12:32.909267 isis_otv default [13901]: [13911]: Process 0103-0000.0c07.ac67
contained in 6c9c.ed4d.d944.00-00 with metric 1
20:12:30.743478 isis_otv default [13901]: [13911]: Process 0103-0000.0c07.ac67
contained in 6c9c.ed4d.d944.00-00 with metric 1
20:12:28.652719 isis_otv default [13901]: [13911]: Process 0103-0000.0c07.ac67
contained in 6c9c.ed4d.d944.00-00 with metric 0
20:12:26.470400 isis_otv default [13901]: [13911]: Process 0103-0000.0c07.ac67
contained in 6c9c.ed4d.d944.00-00 with metric 0
20:12:25.978913 isis_otv default [13901]: [13911]: Process 0103-0000.0c07.ac67
contained in 6c9c.ed4d.d944.00-00 with metric 0
20:12:13.239379 isis_otv default [13901]: [13911]: Process 0103-0000.0c07.ac67
  contained in 6c9c.ed4d.d944.00-00 with metric 0
```

It is now apparent what is changing in the LSPs and why the lifetime is continually resetting to 1200. The metric is changing from zero to one.

The next step is to further investigate the problem at the remote AED that is originating the MAC advertisements across the overlay. In this particular case, the problem is caused by an incorrect configuration. The HSRP MAC addresses are being advertised across the overlay through OTV incorrectly. The HSRP MAC should be blocked using the First Hop Routing Protocol (FHRP) localization filter, as described later in this chapter, but instead it was advertised across the overlay resulting in the observed instability.

The previous example demonstrated a problem with the receipt of a MAC advertisement from a remote OTV ED. If a problem existed with MAC addresses not being advertised out to other OTV EDs from the local AED, the first step is to verify that OTV is passing the MAC addresses into IS-IS for advertisement. The **show otv isis mac redistribute route** command shown in Example 14-25 is used to verify that MAC addresses were passed to IS-IS for advertisement to other OTV EDs.

Example 14-25 *MAC Address Redistribution into OTV IS-IS*

```
NX-2# show otv isis mac redistribute route
OTV-IS-IS process: default VPN: Overlay0
OTV-IS-IS MAC redistribute route

0101-64a0.e73e.12c1, all
 Advertised into L1, metric 1 LSP-ID 6c9c.ed4d.d942.00-00
```

```
0101-6c9c.ed4d.d941, all
 Advertised into L1, metric 1 LSP-ID 6c9c.ed4d.d942.00-00
0101-c464.135c.6600, all
 Advertised into L1, metric 1 LSP-ID 6c9c.ed4d.d942.00-00
0103-64a0.e73e.12c1, all
 Advertised into L1, metric 1 LSP-ID 6c9c.ed4d.d942.00-00
0103-6c9c.ed4d.d941, all
 Advertised into L1, metric 1 LSP-ID 6c9c.ed4d.d942.00-00
0105-64a0.e73e.12c1, all
 Advertised into L1, metric 1 LSP-ID 6c9c.ed4d.d942.00-00
0105-6c9c.ed4d.d941, all
 Advertised into L1, metric 1 LSP-ID 6c9c.ed4d.d942.00-00
0107-64a0.e73e.12c1, all
 Advertised into L1, metric 1 LSP-ID 6c9c.ed4d.d942.00-00
0109-64a0.e73e.12c1, all
 Advertised into L1, metric 1 LSP-ID 6c9c.ed4d.d942.00-00
0109-6c9c.ed4d.d941, all
 Advertised into L1, metric 1 LSP-ID 6c9c.ed4d.d942.00-00
```

The integrity of the IS-IS LSP is a critical requirement for the reliability and stability of the OTV control plane. Packet corruption problems or loss in the transport can affect both OTV IS-IS adjacencies as well as the advertisement of LSPs. Separate IS-IS statistics are available for the overlay and site VLAN, as shown in Examples 14-26 and 14-27, which provide valuable clues when troubleshooting an adjacency or LSP issue.

Example 14-26 *OTV IS-IS Overlay Traffic Statistics*

```
NX-2# show otv isis traffic overlay0
OTV-IS-IS process: default
VPN: Overlay0
OTV-IS-IS Traffic for Overlay0:
PDU      Received    Sent   RcvAuthErr  OtherRcvErr  ReTransmit
LAN-IIH  112327      37520  525         11           n/a
CSNP     100939      16964  0           0            n/a
PSNP     71186       19862  0           0            n/a
LSP      817782      280896 0           0            0
```

Example 14-27 *OTV IS-IS Site-VLAN Statistics*

```
NX-2# show otv isis site statistics

OTV-ISIS site-information for: default

OTV-IS-IS Broadcast Traffic statistics for site-vlan:
```

```
OTV-IS-IS PDU statistics for site-vlan:

PDU      Received    Sent   RcvAuthErr  OtherRcvErr  ReTransmit
LAN-IIH  290557      432344    0            1           n/a
CSNP     68605       34324     0            0           n/a
PSNP     1           1         0            0           n/a
LSP      7           122       0            0           0

OTV-IS-IS Global statistics for site-vlan:

 SPF calculations:   0
 LSPs sourced:       2
 LSPs refreshed:     13
 LSPs purged:        0
```

Incrementing receive errors or retransmits indicate a problem with IS-IS PDUs, which may result in MAC address reachability problems. Incrementing *RcvAuthErr* indicates an authentication mismatch between OTV EDs.

OTV IS-IS Authentication

In some networks, using authentication for IS-IS may be desired. This is supported for OTV adjacencies built across the overlay by configuring IS-IS authentication on the overlay interface. Example 14-28 provides a sample configuration for IS-IS authentication on the overlay interface.

Example 14-28 *Configure OTV IS-IS Authentication*

```
NX-2# show running-config
! Output omitted for brevity
feature otv

otv site-vlan 10
key chain OTV-CHAIN
 key 0
  key-string 7 073c046f7c2c2d
interface Overlay0
 description Site A
 otv isis authentication-type md5
 otv isis authentication key-chain OTV-CHAIN
 otv join-interface port-channel3
 otv control-group 239.12.12.12
 otv data-group 232.1.1.0/24
 otv extend-vlan 100-110
 no shutdown
otv-isis default
otv site-identifier 0x1
```

OTV IS-IS authentication is enabled as verified with the **show otv isis interface overlay** [*overlay-number*] output in Example 14-29.

Example 14-29 *OTV IS-IS Authentication Parameters*

```
NX-2# show otv isis interface overlay 0
OTV-IS-IS process: default VPN: Overlay0
Overlay0, Interface status: protocol-up/link-up/admin-up
 IP address: none
 IPv6 address: none
 IPv6 link-local address: none
 Index: 0x0001, Local Circuit ID: 0x01, Circuit Type: L1
 Level1
  Adjacency server (local/remote) : disabled / none
  Adjacency server capability : multicast
 Authentication type is MD5
 Authentication keychain is OTV-CHAIN
 Authentication check specified
  LSP interval: 33 ms, MTU: 1400
  Level   Metric  CSNP Next CSNP Hello  Multi  Next IIH
  1       40      10   Inactive 20     3      00:00:15


  Level Adjs  AdjsUp Pri Circuit ID      Since
  1     0     0      64  6c9c.ed4d.d942.01 23:40:21
```

All OTV sites need to be configured with the same authentication commands for the overlay adjacency to form. Incrementing *RcvAuthErr* for LAN-IIH frames, as shown in the output of Example 14-30, indicates the presence of an authentication mismatch.

Example 14-30 *OTV IS-IS Authentication Error Statistics*

```
NX-2# show otv isis traffic overlay 0
OTV-IS-IS process: default
VPN: Overlay0
OTV-IS-IS Traffic for Overlay0:
PDU       Received   Sent   RcvAuthErr OtherRcvErr ReTransmit
LAN-IIH   111899     37370  260        11          n/a
CSNP      100792     16937  0          0           n/a
PSNP      71058      19832  0          0           n/a
LSP       816541     280383 0          0           0
```

The output of **show otv adjacency** and **show otv site** varies depending on which adjacencies are down. The authentication configuration is applied only to the overlay interface, so it is possible the site adjacency is up even if one OTV ED at a site has authentication misconfigured for the overlay.

Example 14-31 shows that the overlay adjacency is down, but the site adjacency is still valid. In this scenario, the state is shown as *Partial*.

Example 14-31 *OTV Overlay IS-IS Adjacency Down*

```
NX-2# show otv adjacency
Overlay Adjacency database


NX-2# show otv site

Dual Adjacency State Description
  Full    - Both site and overlay adjacency up
  Partial - Either site/overlay adjacency down
  Down    - Both adjacencies are down (Neighbor is down/unreachable)
  (!)     - Site-ID mismatch detected

Local Edge Device Information:
  Hostname NX-2
  System-ID 6c9c.ed4d.d942
  Site-Identifier 0000.0000.0001
  Site-VLAN 10 State is Up


Site Information for Overlay0:

Local device is not AED-Capable (No Overlay Remote Adjacency up)
Neighbor Edge Devices in Site: 1

Hostname         System-ID       Adjacency-    Adjacency-   AED-
                                 State         Uptime       Capable
-------------------------------------------------------------------------------
(null)           64a0.e73e.12c2  Partial       1w0d         Yes
```

Adjacency Server Mode

Starting in NX-OS release 5.2(1), *adjacency server mode* allows OTV to function over a unicast transport. Because a multicast capable transport is not used, an OTV ED in adjacency server mode must replicate IS-IS messages to each neighbor. This is less efficient because it requires each OTV ED to perform additional packet replications and transmit updates for each remote OTV ED.

A multicast transport allows the ED to generate only a single multicast packet, which is then replicated by the transport network. Therefore, it is preferred to use multicast mode whenever possible because of the increase in efficiency. However, in deployments where only two sites exist, or where multicast is not possible in the transport, adjacency server mode allows for a completely functional OTV deployment over IP unicast.

The OTV overlay configuration for each ED is configured to use the adjacency server unicast IP address as shown in Example 14-32. The role of the adjacency server is handled by a user-designated OTV ED. Each OTV ED *registers* itself with the adjacency server by sending OTV IS-IS hellos, which are transmitted from the OTV join interface as OTV encapsulated IP unicast packets. When the adjacency server forms an adjacency with a remote OTV ED, a list of OTV EDs is created dynamically. The adjacency server takes the list of known EDs and advertises it to each neighbor. All EDs then have a mechanism to dynamically learn about all other OTV EDs so that update messages are created and replicated to each remote ED.

Example 14-32 *OTV ED Adjacency Server Mode Configuration on NX-4*

```
NX-4# show run otv
! Output omitted for brevity
otv site-vlan 10

interface Overlay0
  otv join-interface port-channel3
  otv extend-vlan 100-110
  otv use-adjacency-server 10.1.12.1 unicast-only
  no shutdown
otv site-identifier 0x1
```

Example 14-33 shows the configuration for NX-2, which is now acting as the adjacency server. When configuring an OTV ED in adjacency server mode, the **otv control-group** [*multicast group*] and **otv data-group** [*multicast-group*] configuration on each OTV ED shown in the previous examples must be removed. The **otv use-adjacency-server** [*IP address*] is then configured to enable OTV adjacency server mode and the **otv adjacency-server unicast-only** command specifies that NX-2 will be the adjacency server. The join interface and internal interface configurations remain unchanged from the previous examples in this chapter.

Example 14-33 *OTV Adjacency Server Configuration on NX-2*

```
NX-2# show run otv
! Output omitted for brevity
otv site-vlan 10

interface port-channel3
  description 7009A-Main-OTV Join
  mtu 9216
  ip address 10.1.12.1/24
  ip router ospf 1 area 0.0.0.0
  ip igmp version 3
```

```
interface Overlay0
 description Site A
 otv join-interface port-channel3
 otv extend-vlan 100-110
 otv use-adjacency-server 10.1.12.1 unicast-only
 otv adjacency-server unicast-only
 no shutdown
otv site-identifier 0x1
```

Dynamically advertising a list of known OTV EDs saves the user from having to configure every OTV ED with all other OTV ED addresses to establish adjacencies. The process of registration with the adjacency server and advertisement of the OTV Neighbor List is shown in Figure 14-4. The site adjacency is still present but not shown in the figure for clarity.

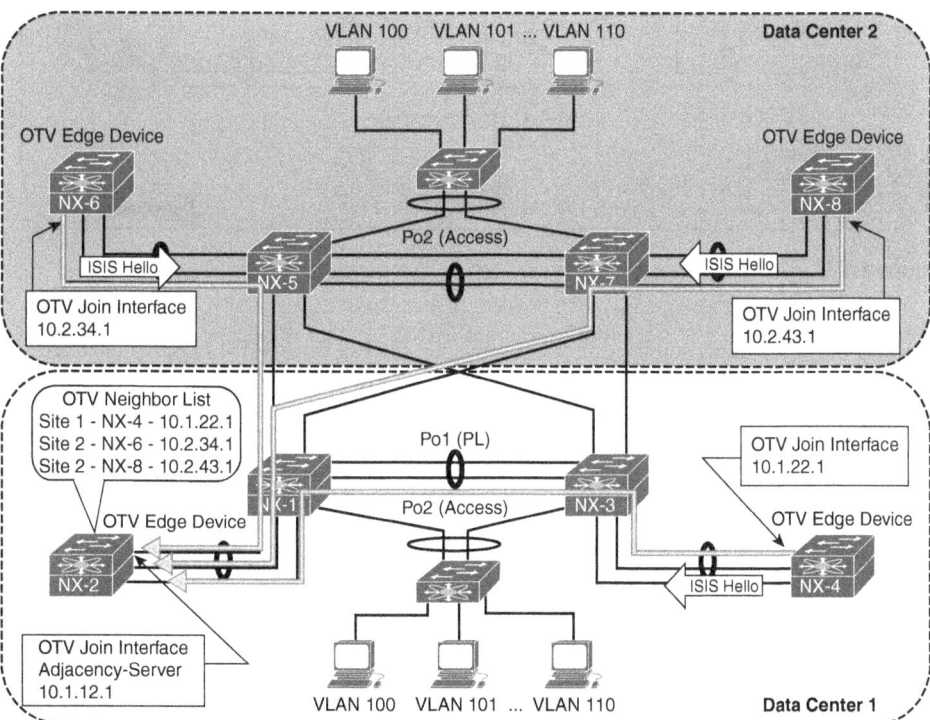

Figure 14-4 *OTV EDs Register with the Adjacency Server*

After the OTV Neighbor List (oNL) is built, it is advertised to each OTV ED from the adjacency server as shown in Figure 14-5.

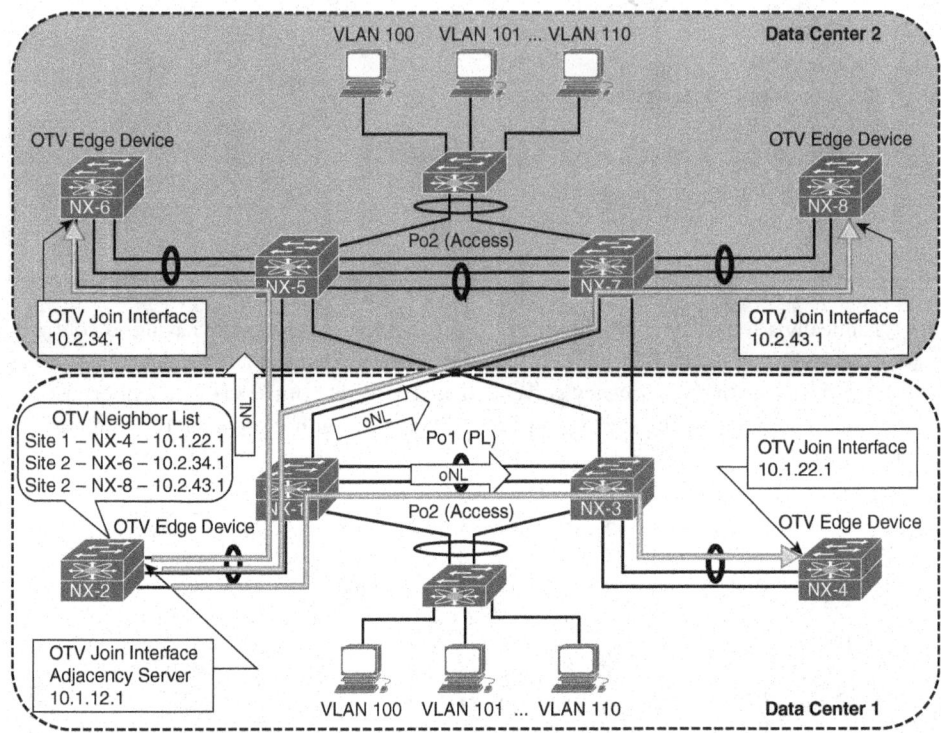

Figure 14-5 *OTV Adjacency Server Advertises the Neighbor List*

Each OTV ED then establishes IS-IS adjacencies with all other OTV EDs. Updates are sent with OTV encapsulation in IP unicast packets from each OTV ED. Each OTV ED must replicate its message to all other neighbors. This step is shown in Figure 14-6.

Example 14-34 contains the output of **show otv adjacency** from NX-4. After receiving the OTV Neighbor List from the adjacency Server, IS-IS adjacencies are formed with all other OTV EDs.

Example 14-34 *OTV Adjacency Server Mode IS-IS Neighbors*

```
NX-4# show otv adjacency
Overlay Adjacency database

Overlay-Interface Overlay0 :
Hostname            System-ID       Dest Addr     Up Time    State
NX-8                64a0.e73e.12c4  10.2.43.1     00:20:35   UP
NX-2                6c9c.ed4d.d942  10.1.12.1     00:20:35   UP
NX-6                6c9c.ed4d.d944  10.2.34.1     00:20:35   UP
```

Understanding and Verifying the OTV Control Plane   911

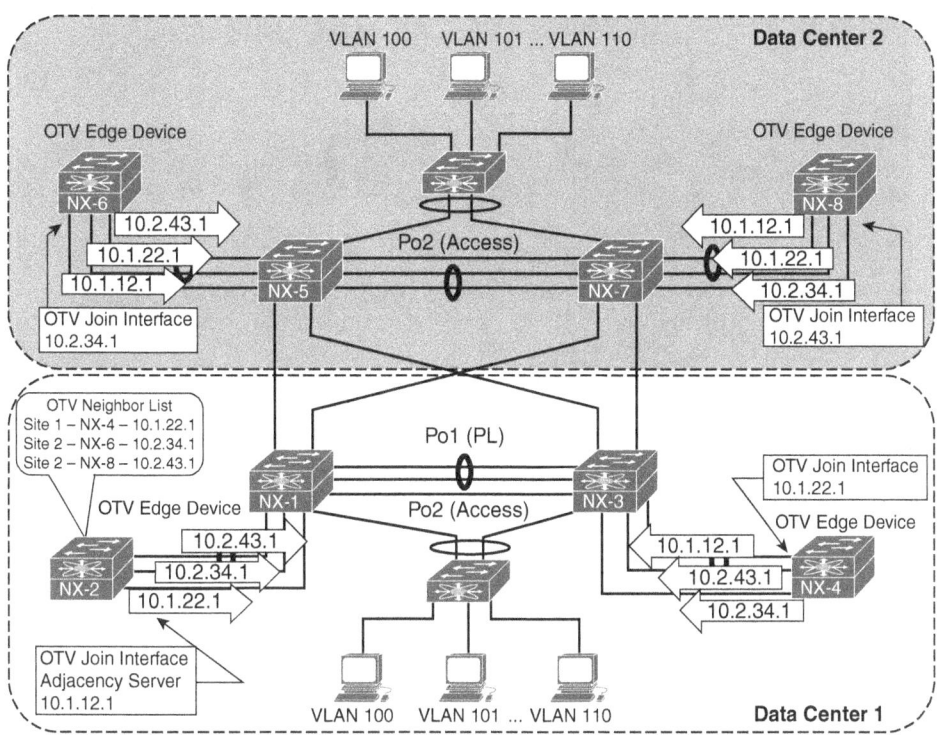

Figure 14-6 *OTV IS-IS Hellos in Adjacency Server Mode*

An OTV IS-IS site adjacency is still formed across the site VLAN, as shown in the output of **show otv site** in Example 14-35.

Example 14-35 *OTV Adjacency Server Mode Dual Adjacency*

```
NX-4# show otv site

Dual Adjacency State Description
  Full    - Both site and overlay adjacency up
  Partial - Either site/overlay adjacency down
  Down    - Both adjacencies are down (Neighbor is down/unreachable)
  (!)     - Site-ID mismatch detected

Local Edge Device Information:
  Hostname NX-4
  System-ID 64a0.e73e.12c2
  Site-Identifier 0000.0000.0001
  Site-VLAN 10 State is Up
```

```
Site Information for Overlay0:

Local device is AED-Capable
Neighbor Edge Devices in Site: 1

Hostname          System-ID       Adjacency-   Adjacency-   AED-
                                  State        Uptime       Capable
-----------------------------------------------------------------
NX-2              6c9c.ed4d.d942  Full         00:42:04     Yes
```

Troubleshooting IS-IS adjacency and LSP advertisement problems in OTV adjacency server mode follows similar methodology as with OTV Multicast mode. The difference is that the packets are sent encapsulated in IP Unicast instead of multicast across the transport network.

Redundant OTV adjacency servers are supported for resiliency purposes. However, the two adjacency servers operate independently, and they do not synchronize state with each other. If multiple adjacency servers are present, each OTV ED registers with each adjacency server. An OTV ED uses the replication list from the primary adjacency server until it is no longer available. If the adjacency with the primary adjacency server goes down, the OTV ED starts using the replication list received from the secondary adjacency server. If the primary OTV ED comes back up before a 10-minute timeout, the OTV EDs revert back to the primary replication list. If more than 10 minutes pass, a new replication-list is pushed by the primary when it finally becomes active again.

OTV Control Plane Policing (CoPP)

OTV control plane packets are subject to rate-limiting to protect the resources of the switch, just like any other packet sent to the supervisor. Excessive ARP traffic or OTV control plane traffic could impact the stability of the switch, causing high CPU or protocol adjacency flaps, so protection with CoPP is recommended.

The importance of CoPP is realized when the OTV ARP-ND-Cache is enabled. ARP Reply messages are snooped and added to the local cache so the OTV AED can answer ARP requests on behalf of the target host. These packets must be handled by the control plane and could cause policing drops or high CPU utilization if the volume of ARP traffic is excessive. The OTV ARP-ND-Cache is discussed in more detail later in this chapter.

The **show policy-map interface control-plane** command from the default VDC provides statistics for each control plane traffic class. If CoPP drops are present and ARP resolution failure is occurring, the solution is typically not to adjust the control plane policy to allow more traffic, but to instead track down the source of excessive ARP traffic. Ethanalyzer is a good tool for this type of problem along with the event histories for OTV.

Understanding and Verifying the OTV Data Plane

OTV was designed to transport L2 frames between sites in an efficient and reliable manner. Frames arriving at an OTV ED are Unicast, Multicast, or Broadcast, and each type of frame must be encapsulated for transport to the destination OTV ED with information provided by the OTV control plane.

The default overlay encapsulation for OTV is GRE, shown in Figure 14-7. This is also referred to as OTV 1.0 encapsulation.

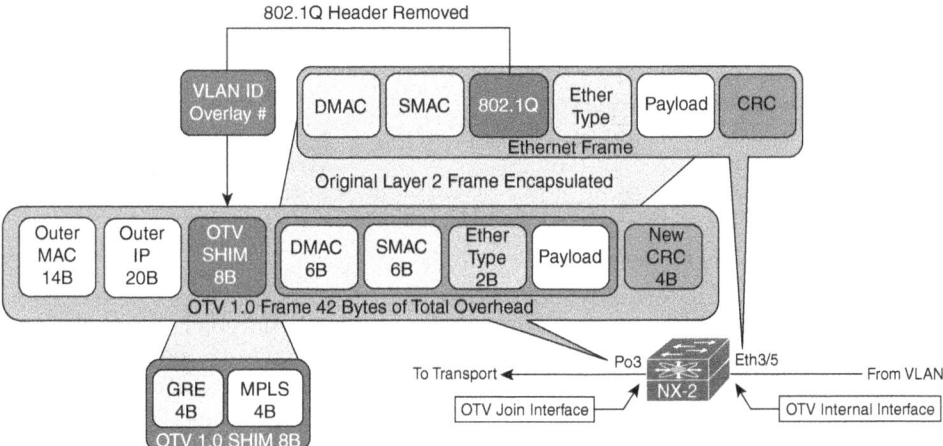

Figure 14-7 *OTV 1.0 Encapsulation*

When a frame arrives on the internal interface, a series of lookups are used to determine how to rewrite the packet for transport across the overlay. The original payload, ethertype, source MAC address, and destination MAC address are copied into the new OTV Encapsulated frame. The 802.1Q header is removed, and an OTV SHIM header is inserted. The SHIM header contains information about the VLAN and the overlay it belongs to. This field in OTV 1.0 is actually an MPLS-in-GRE encapsulation, where the MPLS label is used to derive the VLAN. The value of the MPLS label is equal to 32 + VLAN identifier. For this example, VLAN 101 is encapsulated as MPLS label 133. The outer IP header is added, which contains the source IP address of the local OTV ED and the destination IP address of the remote OTV ED.

Control plane IS-IS frames are encapsulated in a similar manner between OTV EDs across the overlay and also carry the same 42 bytes of OTV Overhead. The MPLS label used for IS-IS control plane frames is the reserved label 1, which is the *Router Alert* label.

> **Note** If a packet capture is taken in the transport, OTV 1.0 encapsulation is decoded as MPLS Pseudowire with no control-word using analysis tools, such as Wireshark. Unfortunately, at the time of this writing, Wireshark is not able to decode all the IS-IS PDUs used by OTV.

NX-OS release 7.2(0)D1(1) introduced the option of UDP encapsulation for OTV when using F3 or M3 series modules in the Nexus 7000 series switches. The OTV 2.5 UDP encapsulation is shown in Figure 14-8.

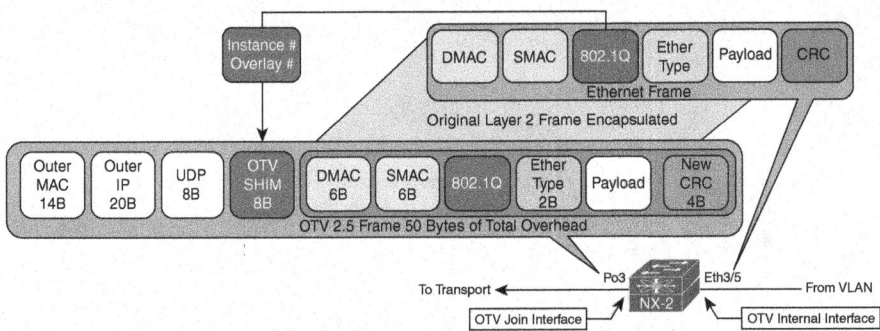

Figure 14-8 *OTV 2.5 Encapsulation*

Ethernet Frames arriving from the OTV internal interface have the original payload, ethertype, 802.1Q header, source MAC address, and destination MAC address copied into the new OTV 2.5 Encapsulated frame. The OTV 2.5 encapsulation uses the same packet format as Virtual Extensible LAN (VxLAN), which is detailed in RFC 7348.

The OTV SHIM header contains information about the Instance and Overlay. The instance is the table identifier that should be used at the destination OTV ED to lookup the destination, and the overlay identifier is used by the control plane packets to identify packets belonging to a specific overlay. A control plane packet has the VxLAN Network ID (VNI) bit set to False (zero), while an encapsulated data frame has this value set to True (one). The UDP header contains a variable source port and destination port of 8472.

Fragmentation of OTV frames containing data packets becomes a concern if the transport MTU is not at least 1550 bytes with OTV 2.5, or 1542 bytes with OTV 1.0. This is based on the assumption that a host in the data center has an interface MTU of 1500 bytes and attempts to send full MTU sized frames. When the OTV encapsulation is added, the packet no longer fits into the available MTU size.

The minimum transport MTU requirement for control plane packets is either 1442 for multicast transport, or 1450 for unicast transport in adjacency server mode. OTV sets the *Don't Fragment* bit in the outer IP header to ensure that no OTV control plane or data plane packets become fragmented in the transport network. If MTU restrictions exist, it could result in OTV IS-IS adjacencies not forming, or the loss of frames for data traffic when the encapsulated frame size exceeds the transport MTU.

Note The OTV encapsulation format must be the same between all sites (GRE or UDP) and is configured with the global configuration command **otv encapsulation-format ip** [*gre | udp*].

OTV ARP Resolution and ARP-ND-Cache

When a host communicates with another host in the same IP subnet, the communication begins with the source host resolving the MAC address of the destination host with ARP. ARP messages are shown between Host A and Host C, which are part of the same 10.101.0.0/16 subnet in Figure 14-9.

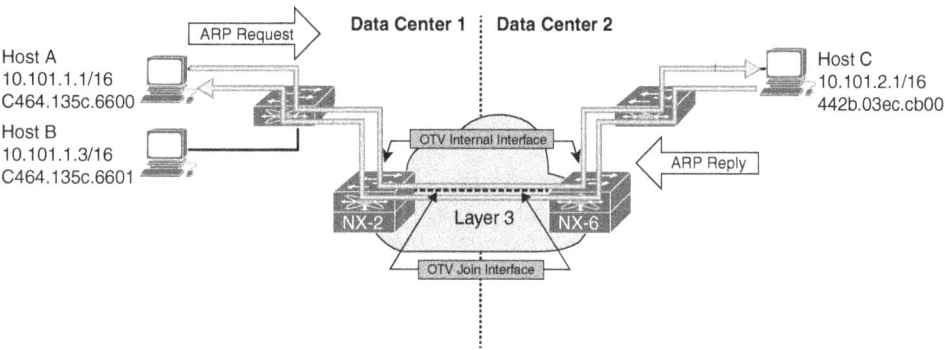

Figure 14-9 *ARP Request and Reply*

Host A broadcasts an ARP request message to the destination MAC address ff:ff:ff:ff:ff:ff with a target IP address of 10.101.2.1. This frame is sent out of all ports that belong to the same VLAN in the L2 switch, including the OTV internal interface of NX-2 and the port connected to Host B. Because NX-2 is an OTV ED for Data Center 1, it receives the frame and encapsulates it using the OTV control-group of 239.12.12.12. NX-2 also creates a MAC address table entry for Host A, known via the internal interface. Host A's MAC is advertised from NX-2 across the overlay through the IS-IS control plane, providing reachability information to all other OTV EDs.

The control-group multicast frame from NX-2 traverses the transport underlay network until it reaches NX-6 where the multicast OTV encapsulation is removed and the frame is sent out of the OTV internal interface toward Host C. Host C processes the broadcast frame and recognizes the IP address as its own. Host C then issues the ARP reply to Host A, which is sent to NX-6. NX-6 at this point has an entry in the OTV MAC routing table for Host A with an IP next-hop of NX-2 since the IS-IS update was received. There is also a MAC address table entry for Host A in VLAN101 pointing to the overlay interface.

As the ARP reply from Host C is received at NX-6, a local MAC address table entry is created pointing to the OTV internal interface. This MAC address entry is then advertised to all remote OTV EDs through IS-IS, just as NX-2 did for Host A.

NX-6 then encapsulates the ARP reply and sends it across the overlay to NX-2 in Data Center 1. NX-2 removes the OTV encapsulation from the frame and sends it out of the internal interface where it reaches Host A, following the MAC address table of the VLAN.

The *OTV ARP-ND-Cache* is populated by listening to ARP reply messages. The initial ARP request is sent to all OTV EDs via the OTV control-group. When the ARP reply comes back using the OTV control-group, each OTV ED snoops the reply and builds an entry in the cache. If Host B were to send an ARP request for Host C, NX-2 replies to the ARP request on behalf of Host C, using the cached entry created previously, which reduces unnecessary traffic across the overlay.

> **Note** If multiple OTV EDs exist at a site, only the AED forwards packets onto the overlay, including ARP request and replies. The AED is also responsible for advertising MAC address reachability to other OTV EDs through the IS-IS control plane.

The ARP-ND-Cache is populated in the same way for multicast mode or adjacency server mode. With adjacency server mode, the ARP request and response are encapsulated as OTV Unicast packets and replicated for the remote OTV EDs.

If hosts are unable to communicate with other hosts across the overlay, verify the ARP-ND-Cache to ensure it does not contain any stale information. Example 14-36 demonstrates how to check the local ARP-ND-Cache on NX-2.

Example 14-36 *Verify the ARP ND-Cache*

```
NX-2# show otv arp-nd-cache
OTV ARP/ND L3->L2 Address Mapping Cache

Overlay Interface Overlay0
VLAN MAC Address       Layer-3 Address    Age       Expires In
101  442b.03ec.cb00    10.101.2.1         00:02:29  00:06:07
```

OTV also keeps an event-history for ARP-ND cache activity, which is viewed with **show otv internal event-history arp-nd**. Example 14-37 shows this output from the AED for the VLAN 100.

Example 14-37 *ARP ND-Cache Event-History*

```
NX-4# show otv internal event-history arp-nd
ARP-ND events for OTV Process
02:33:17.816397 otv [9790]: [9810]: Updating arp nd cache entry in PSS TLVU.
Overlay:249 Mac Info: 0100-442b.03ec.cb00 L3 addr: 10.100.2.1
```

```
02:33:17.816388 otv [9790]: [9810]: Caching 10.100.2.1 -> 0100-442b.03ec.cb00 ARP
  mapping
02:33:17.816345 otv [9790]: [9810]: Caching ARP Response from overlay : Overlay0
02:33:17.816337 otv [9790]: [9810]: IPv4 ARP Response packet received from source
  10.100.2.1 on interface Overlay0
02:33:17.806853 otv [9790]: [9810]: IPv4 ARP Request packet received from source
  10.100.1.1 on interface Ethernet3/5
```

The OTV ARP-ND cache timer is configurable from 60 to 86400 seconds. The default value is 480 seconds or 8 minutes, plus an additional 2-minute grace-period. During the grace-period an AED forwards ARP requests across the overlay so that the reply refreshes the entry in the cache. It is recommended to have the ARP-ND cache time value lower than the MAC aging timer. By default, the MAC aging timer is 30 minutes.

It is possible to disable the OTV ARP-ND-Cache by configuring **no otv suppress-arp-nd** under the overlay interface. The result of this configuration is that all ARP requests are forwarded across the overlay and no ARP reply messages are cached.

Note The ARP-ND-Cache is enabled by default. In some environments with a lot of ARP activity, it may cause the CPU of the OTV ED to become high or experience CoPP drops because the supervisor CPU must handle the ARP traffic to create the cache entries.

Broadcasts

Broadcast frames received by an OTV ED on the internal interface are forwarded across the overlay by the AED for the extended VLAN. Broadcast frames, such as *ARP request*, are encapsulated into an L3 multicast packet where the source address is the local OTV EDs join interface, and the group is the OTV *Control-group* address. The multicast packet is sent to the transport where it gets replicated to each remote OTV ED that has joined the control-group.

When using a multicast enabled transport, OTV allows for the configuration of a dedicated *otv broadcast-group*, as shown in Example 14-38. This allows the operator to separate the OTV control-group from the broadcast group for easier troubleshooting and to allow different handling of the packets based on group address. For example, a different PIM rendezvous point could be defined for each group, or a different Quality of Service (QoS) treatment could be applied to the control-group and broadcast-group in the transport.

Example 14-38 *Dedicated OTV Broadcast Group*

```
NX-2# show run otv
! Output omitted for brevity
interface Overlay0
 description Site A
```

```
otv join-interface port-channel3
otv broadcast-group 239.1.1.1
otv control-group 239.12.12.12
otv data-group 232.1.1.0/24
otv extend-vlan 100-110
no shutdown
```

OTV EDs operating in adjacency server mode without a multicast-enabled transport encapsulate broadcast packets with an OTV unicast packet and replicate a copy to each remote OTV ED using head-end replication.

With either multicast or unicast transport, when the packet is received by the remote OTV ED, the outer L3 packet encapsulation is removed. The broadcast frame is then forwarded to all internal facing L2 ports in the VLAN by the AED.

Unknown Unicast Frames

The default behavior for OTV is to only flood frames to an unknown unicast MAC address on the internal interface. These packets are not forwarded across the overlay. This optimization is allowed because OTV operates under the assumption that there are no silent hosts, and an OTV ED sees traffic from all hosts eventually on the internal interface. After that traffic is received, it populates the MAC address table in the VLAN, and the MAC address is advertised by IS-IS to all OTV EDs.

There are situations where a silent host is unavoidable. To allow these hosts to function, OTV provides a configuration option to allow selective unicast flooding beginning in NX-OS 6.2(2). Example 14-39 provides a configuration example to allow flooding of packets to a specific destination MAC address in VLAN 101 across the overlay.

Example 14-39 *Selective Unicast Flooding*

```
NX-2# show run otv
! Output omitted for brevity

feature otv
otv site-identifier 0x1
otv flood mac C464.135C.6600 vlan 101
```

The result of adding this command is a static OTV route entry for the VLAN, which causes traffic to flow across the overlay, as shown in Example 14-40.

Example 14-40 *OTV Routing Table with Selective Unicast Flooding*

```
NX-2# show otv route vlan 101

OTV Unicast MAC Routing Table For Overlay0
```

```
VLAN MAC-Address      Metric Uptime    Owner    Next-hop(s)
---- ---------------- ------ -------- --------- -----------
 101 c464.135c.6600 0        00:02:38 static    Overlay0
```

OTV Unicast Traffic with a Multicast Enabled Transport

Host-to-host communication begins with an ARP request for the destination, as shown previously in Figure 14-9. After this ARP request and reply exchange is finished, the OTV ED at each site has a correctly populated OTV MAC routing table and MAC address table for both hosts.

Figure 14-10 depicts the traffic flow in VLAN 103 between Host A in Data Center 1 and Host C in Data Center 2.

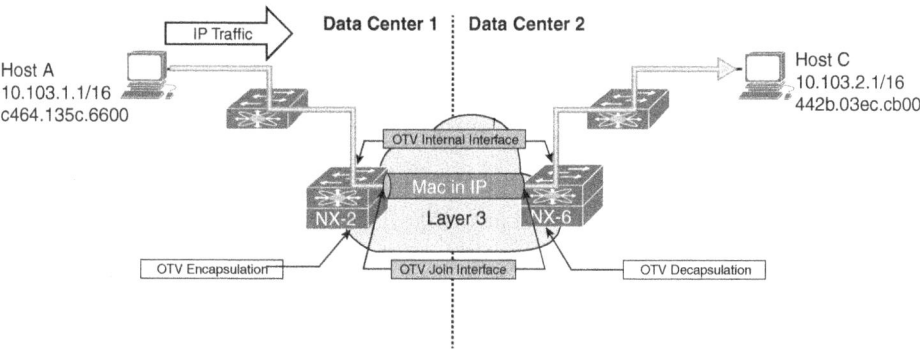

Figure 14-10 *Unicast Host-to-Host Traffic Across OTV*

Traffic from Host A is first sent to the L2 switch where it has an 802.1Q VLAN tag added for VLAN 103. The frames follow the MAC address table entries at the L2 switch across the trunk port to reach NX-2 on the OTV internal interface Ethernet3/5. When the packets arrive at NX-2, it performs a MAC address table lookup in the VLAN to determine how to reach Host C's MAC address 442b.03ec.cb00. The MAC address table of NX-2 is shown in Example 14-41.

Example 14-41 *MAC Address Table Entry for Host C*

```
NX-2# show mac address-table dynamic vlan 103
Note: MAC table entries displayed are getting read from software.
Use the 'hardware-age' keyword to get information related to 'Age'

Legend:
    * - primary entry, G - Gateway MAC, (R) - Routed MAC, O - Overlay MAC
    age - seconds since last seen,+ - primary entry using vPC Peer-Link, E - EVPN
       entry
```

```
         (T) - True, (F) - False , ~~~ - use 'hardware-age' keyword to retrieve age info
VLAN/BD     MAC Address     Type        age       Secure NTFY Ports/SWID.SSID.LID
---------+-----------------+---------+---------+------+----+------------------
* 103       0000.0c07.ac67  dynamic     ~~~       F    F   Eth3/5
O 103       442b.03ec.cb00  dynamic     -         F    F   Overlay0
* 103       64a0.e73e.12c1  dynamic     ~~~       F    F   Eth3/5
O 103       64a0.e73e.12c3  dynamic     -         F    F   Overlay0
O 103       6c9c.ed4d.d943  dynamic     -         F    F   Overlay0
* 103       c464.135c.6600  dynamic     ~~~       F    F   Eth3/5
```

The MAC address table indicates that Host C's MAC is reachable across the overlay, which means that the OTV MAC Routing table (ORIB) should be used to obtain the IP next-hop and encapsulation details. The ORIB indicates how to reach the remote OTV ED that advertised the MAC address to NX-2 via IS-IS, which is NX-6 in this example.

> **Note** If multiple OTV EDs exist at a site, ensure the data path is being followed to the AED for the VLAN. This is verified with the **show otv vlan** command. Under normal conditions the MAC forwarding entries across the L2 network should lead to the AED's internal interface.

NX-2 is the AED for VLAN103 as shown in Example 14-42.

Example 14-42 *Verify the AED for VLAN 103*

```
NX-2# show otv vlan
OTV Extended VLANs and Edge Device State Information (* - AED)

Legend:
(NA) - Non AED, (VD) - Vlan Disabled, (OD) - Overlay Down
(DH) - Delete Holddown, (HW) - HW: State Down
 (NFC) - Not Forward Capable
VLAN  Auth. Edge Device            Vlan State            Overlay
----  ---------------------------  --------------------  -------

 100  NX-4                         inactive(NA)          Overlay0
 101* NX-2                         active                Overlay0
 102  NX-4                         inactive(NA)          Overlay0
 103* NX-2                         active                Overlay0
```

After verifying the AED state for VLAN 103 to ensure you are looking at the correct device, check the ORIB to determine which remote OTV ED will receive the encapsulated frame from NX-2. The ORIB for NX-2 is shown in Example 14-43.

Example 14-43 *Verify the ORIB Entry for Host C*

```
NX-2# show otv route vlan 103

OTV Unicast MAC Routing Table For Overlay0

VLAN MAC-Address      Metric Uptime    Owner     Next-hop(s)
---- ---------------  ------ --------  --------  -----------
 103 0000.0c07.ac67   1      00:13:43  site      Ethernet3/5
 103 442b.03ec.cb00   42     00:02:44  overlay   NX-6
 103 64a0.e73e.12c1   1      00:13:43  site      Ethernet3/5
 103 64a0.e73e.12c3   42     00:13:28  overlay   NX-6
 103 6c9c.ed4d.d943   42     00:02:56  overlay   NX-6
 103 c464.135c.6600   1      00:02:56  site      Ethernet3/5
```

Recall that the ORIB data is populated by the IS-IS LSP received from NX-6, which indicates MAC address 442b.03ec.cb00 is an attached host. This is confirmed by obtaining the system-id of NX-6 in **show otv adjacency**, and then finding the correct LSP in the output of **show otv isis database detail**.

At the AED originating the advertisement, the redistribution from the local MAC table into OTV IS-IS is verified on NX-6 using the **show otv isis redistribute route** command, which is shown in Example 14-44.

At this point, it has been confirmed that NX-6 is the correct remote OTV ED to receive frames with a destination MAC address of 442b.03ec.cb00 in VLAN 103. The next step in delivering the packet to Host C is for NX-2 to rewrite the packet to impose the OTV header and send the encapsulated frame into the transport network from the join interface.

OTV uses either UDP or GRE encapsulation, and in this example the default GRE encapsulation is being used. There is a point-to-point tunnel created dynamically for each remote OTV ED that has formed an adjacency with the local OTV ED. These tunnels are viewed with **show tunnel internal implicit otv detail**, as shown in Example 14-45.

Example 14-44 *MAC Table Redistribution into OTV IS-IS*

```
NX-6# show otv isis redistribute route
! Output omitted for brevity
OTV-IS-IS process: default VPN: Overlay0
OTV-IS-IS MAC redistribute route
```

```
 0103-442b.03ec.cb00, all
  Advertised into L1, metric 1 LSP-ID 6c9c.ed4d.d944.00-00
 0103-64a0.e73e.12c3, all
  Advertised into L1, metric 1 LSP-ID 6c9c.ed4d.d944.00-00
 0103-6c9c.ed4d.d943, all
  Advertised into L1, metric 1 LSP-ID 6c9c.ed4d.d944.00-00
```

Example 14-45 *Dynamic Tunnel Encapsulation for NX-6*

```
NX-2# show tunnel internal implicit otv detail
! Output omitted for brevity
Tunnel16389 is up
  Admin State: up
  MTU 9178 bytes, BW 9 Kbit
  Tunnel protocol/transport GRE/IP
  Tunnel source 10.1.12.1, destination 10.2.34.1
  Transport protocol is in VRF "default"
  Rx
  720357 packets input, 1 minute input rate 1024 packets/sec
  Tx
  715177 packets output, 1 minute output rate 1027 packets/sec
  Last clearing of "show interface" counters never
```

The dynamic tunnels represent the software forwarding component of the OTV encapsulation. The hardware forwarding component for the OTV encapsulation is handled by performing multiple passes through the line card forwarding engine to derive the correct packet rewrite that includes the OTV encapsulation header.

Note The verification of the packet rewrite details in hardware varies depending on the type of forwarding engine present in the line card. Verify the adjacencies, MAC address table, ORIB, and tunnel state before suspecting a hardware programming problem. If connectivity fails despite correct control plane programming, and MAC addresses are learned, engage the Cisco TAC for support.

After the OTV MAC-in-IP encapsulation is performed by NX-2, the packet traverses the Layer 3 transport network with a unicast OTV header appended. The source IP address is the join interface of NX-2 and the destination IP address is the join interface of NX-6. The Layer 3 packet arrives on the OTV join interface of NX-6, which must remove the OTV encapsulation and look up the destination.

The destination IP address of the outer packet header is the OTV join interface address of NX-6, 10.2.34.1. In a similar manner to the encapsulation of OTV, removing the OTV encapsulation also requires multiple forwarding engine passes on the receiving line card.

Because the outer destination IP address belongs to NX-6, it will strip the outer IP header and look into the OTV shim header where the VLAN ID is found. The information from this lookup is originated from the ORIB, which contains the VLAN, MAC address, and destination interface, as shown in Example 14-46.

Example 14-46 *ORIB Entry for Host C on NX-6*

```
NX-6# show otv route
! Output omitted for brevity


OTV Unicast MAC Routing Table For Overlay0

VLAN MAC-Address      Metric Uptime    Owner     Next-hop(s)
---- ---------------  ------ --------  --------  -----------
 103 0000.0c07.ac67   1      4d00h     site      port-channel3
 103 442b.03ec.cb00   1      00:44:32  site      port-channel3
 103 64a0.e73e.12c1   42     4d00h     overlay   NX-2
 103 64a0.e73e.12c3   1      4d00h     site      port-channel3
 103 6c9c.ed4d.d943   1      4d00h     site      port-channel3
 103 c464.135c.6600   42     4d00h     overlay   NX-2
```

The next-pass through the forwarding engine performs a lookup on the VLAN MAC address table to find the correct outgoing interface and physical port. The MAC address table of NX-6 is shown in Example 14-47.

Example 14-47 *MAC Address Table Entry for Host C on NX6*

```
NX-6# show mac address-table dynamic vlan 103
Note: MAC table entries displayed are getting read from software.
Use the 'hardware-age' keyword to get information related to 'Age'

Legend:
     * - primary entry, G - Gateway MAC, (R) - Routed MAC, O - Overlay MAC
    age - seconds since last seen,+ - primary entry using vPC Peer-Link, E - EVPN
       entry
     (T) - True, (F) - False , ~~~ - use 'hardware-age' keyword to retrieve age info
  VLAN/BD  MAC Address    Type      age     Secure NTFY Ports/SWID.SSID.LID
---------+-----------------+--------+---------+------+----+------------------
* 103     0000.0c07.ac67  dynamic   ~~~       F    F   Po3
* 103     442b.03ec.cb00  dynamic   ~~~       F    F   Po3
O 103     64a0.e73e.12c1  dynamic    -        F    F   Overlay0
* 103     64a0.e73e.12c3  dynamic   ~~~       F    F   Po3
* 103     6c9c.ed4d.d943  dynamic   ~~~       F    F   Po3
O 103     c464.135c.6600  dynamic    -        F    F   Overlay0
```

The frame exits Port-channel 3 on the L2 trunk with a VLAN tag of 103. The L2 switch in data center 2 receives the frame and performs a MAC address table lookup to find the port where Host C is connected and delivers the frame to its destination.

> **Note** Troubleshooting unicast data traffic when using the adjacency server mode follows the same methodology used for a multicast enabled transport. The difference is that any control plane messages are exchanged between OTV EDs using a unicast encapsulation method and replicated by the advertising OTV ED to all adjacent OTV EDs. The host-to-host data traffic is still MAC-in-IP unicast encapsulated from source OTV ED to the destination OTV ED.

OTV Multicast Traffic with a Multicast Enabled Transport

OTV provides support for multicast traffic to be forwarded across the overlay in a seamless manner. The source and receiver hosts do not need to modify their behavior to exchange L2 multicast traffic across an OTV network between sites.

In a traditional L2 switched network, the receiver host sends an Internet Group Management Protocol (IGMP) membership report to indicate interest in receiving the traffic. The L2 switch is typically enabled for IGMP snooping, which listens for these membership reports to optimize flooding of multicast traffic to only the ports where there are interested receivers.

IGMP snooping must also learn where multicast routers (mrouters) are connected. Any multicast traffic must be forwarded to an mrouter so that interested receivers on other L3 networks can receive it. The mrouter is also responsible for registering the source with a rendezvous point if PIM ASM is being used. IGMP snooping discovers mrouters by listening for Protocol Independent Multicast (PIM) hello messages, which indicate an L3 capable mrouter is present on that port. The L2 forwarding table is then updated to send all multicast group traffic to the mrouter, as well as any interested receivers. OTV EDs use a dummy PIM Hello message to draw multicast traffic and IGMP membership reports to the OTV ED's internal interface.

OTV maintains its own mroute table for multicast forwarding just as it maintains an OTV routing table for unicast forwarding. There are three types of OTV mroute entries, which are described as VLAN, Source, and Group. The purpose of each type is detailed in Table 14-2.

Table 14-2 *OTV MROUTE Types*

Type	Definition
(V, *, *)	Created when a local mrouter is present in the VLAN, discovered by IGMP snooping. Used to forward traffic to the mrouter for all sources, and all groups.
(V, *, G)	Created when an IGMP membership report is received for group G. The interface on which the membership report was received is added to the Outgoing Interface (OIF) of the mroute.
(V, S, G)	Created when source S sends multicast traffic to group G, or as a result of receiving an IS-IS Group Membership Active Source (GMAS-TLV) with (S, G).

The OTV IS-IS control plane protocol is utilized to allow hosts to send and receive multicast traffic within an extended VLAN between sites without the need to send IGMP messages across the overlay. Figure 14-11 shows a simple OTV topology where Host A is a multicast source for group 239.100.100.100, and Host C is a multicast receiver. Both Host A and Host C belong to VLAN 103.

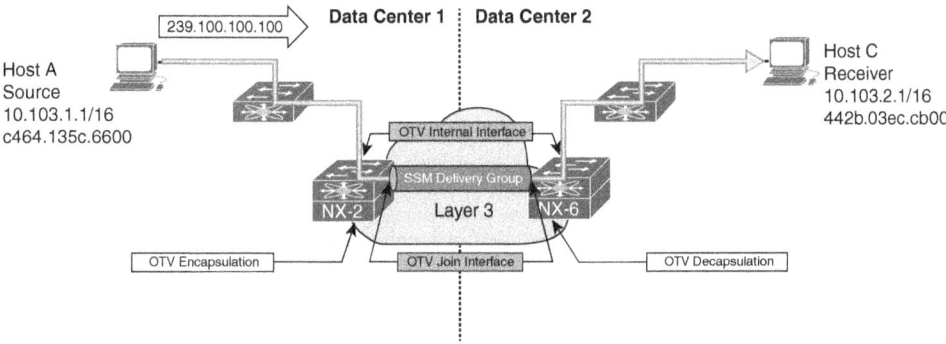

Figure 14-11 *Multicast Traffic Across OTV with Multicast Transport*

In this example, the L3 transport network is enabled for IP multicast. Each OTV ED is configured with a range of Source Specific Multicast (SSM) groups, referred to as the *Delivery Group* or *data-group*, which may be used interchangeably. The delivery group configuration of NX-6 is highlighted in the configuration sample provided in Example 14-48.

Example 14-48 *OTV SSM Data-Groups*

```
NX-6# show running-config interface overlay 0
interface Overlay0
 description Site B
 otv join-interface Ethernet3/41
 otv control-group 239.12.12.12
 otv data-group 232.1.1.0/24
 otv extend-vlan 100-110
 no shutdown
```

The delivery group must be coordinated with the L3 transport to ensure that PIM SSM is supported and that the correct range of groups are defined for use as SSM groups. Each OTV ED is configured with the same range of *otv data-groups*, and each OTV ED can be a source for the SSM group. Remote OTV EDs join the SSM group in the transport to receive multicast frames from a particular OTV ED acting as source. The signaling of which SSM group to use is accomplished with IS-IS advertisements between OTV EDs to allow for discovery of active sources and receivers at each site.

The *site group* is the multicast group that is being transported across the overlay using the delivery group. In Figure 14-11, the site group is 239.100.100.100 sourced by Host A and received by Host C. Essentially, OTV is using a *multicast-in-multicast* OTV encapsulation scheme to send the site group across the overlay using the delivery group in the transport network.

Troubleshooting is simplified by splitting the end-to-end packet delivery mechanism into two distinct layers of focus: the site group and the delivery group. At the source end, the site group troubleshooting is focused on ensuring that multicast data frames from the source are arriving at the internal interface of the AED for the VLAN. At the receiving site, site group troubleshooting must verify that a receiver has expressed interest in the group by sending an IGMP membership report. IGMP snooping must have the correct ports to reach the receivers from the OTV AEDs internal interface, through any L2 switches in the path. In the transport network, the delivery group must be functional so that any OTV ED acting as a source host successfully sends the multicast-in-multicast OTV traffic into the transport for replication and delivery to the correct OTV ED receivers.

For multicast sent by Host A to be successfully received by Host C, some prerequisite steps must occur. The OTV AED's internal interface must be seen by the L2 switch as an mrouter port. This is required so that any IGMP membership reports from a receiver are sent to the AED, and any multicast traffic is also flooded to the AED's OTV internal interface. To achieve this, OTV sends a *dummy* PIM hello with a source IP address of 0.0.0.0 on the internal interface for each VLAN extended by OTV. The purpose is *not* to form a PIM neighbor on the VLAN, but to force the detection of an mrouter port by any attached L2 switch, as depicted in Figure 14-12.

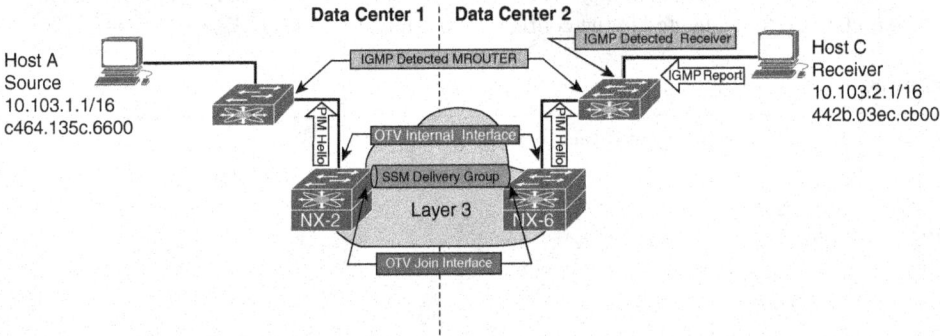

Figure 14-12 *OTV Dummy PIM Hello Messages*

An Ethanalyzer capture of the PIM dummy hello packet from NX-6 on VLAN 103 is shown in Example 14-49.

Example 14-49 *Dummy PIM Hello Captured in Ethanalyzer*

```
! Output omitted for brevity

Type: IP (0x0800)
Internet Protocol Version 4, Src: 0.0.0.0 (0.0.0.0),Dst: 224.0.0.13 (224.0.0.13)
  Version: 4
```

```
  Header length: 20 bytes
  Differentiated Services Field: 0xc0 (DSCP 0x30: Class Selector 6; ECN: 0x00:
 Not-ECT (Not ECN-Capable Transport))
    1100 00.. = Differentiated Services Codepoint: Class Selector 6 (0x30)
    .... ..00 = Explicit Congestion Notification: Not-ECT (Not ECN-Capable
Transport) (0x00)
  Total Length: 50
  Identification: 0xa51f (42271)
  Flags: 0x00
    0... .... = Reserved bit: Not set
    .0.. .... = Don't fragment: Not set
    ..0. .... = More fragments: Not set
  Fragment offset: 0
  Time to live: 1
  Protocol: PIM (103)
  Header checksum: 0x3379 [correct]
    [Good: True]
    [Bad: False]
  Source: 0.0.0.0 (0.0.0.0)
  Destination: 224.0.0.13 (224.0.0.13)
Protocol Independent Multicast
  0010 .... = Version: 2
  .... 0000 = Type: Hello (0)
  Reserved byte(s): 00
  Checksum: 0x572f [correct]
  PIM options: 4
    Option 1: Hold Time: 0s (goodbye)
      Type: 1
      Length: 2
      Holdtime: 0s (goodbye)
    Option 19: DR Priority: 0
      Type: 19
      Length: 4
      DR Priority: 0
    Option 22: Bidir Capable
      Type: 22
      Length: 0
    Option 20: Generation ID: 2882395322
      Type: 20
      Length: 4
      Generation ID: 2882395322
```

Example 14-50 shows the IGMP snooping status of the L2 switch in Data Center 2 after receiving the PIM dummy hello packets on VLAN103 from NX-6.

Example 14-50 *NX-6 Detected as an MROUTER Port by IGMP Snooping*

```
DC2-Layer2-sw# show ip igmp snooping mrouter vlan 103
Type: S - Static, D - Dynamic, V - vPC Peer Link
    I - Internal, F - Fabricpath core port
    C - Co-learned, U - User Configured
    P - learnt by Peer
Vlan  Router-port  Type    Uptime    Expires
103   Po3          D       3d09h     00:04:58
103   Po1          SVP     3d09h     never
```

When Host C's IGMP membership report message reaches NX-6, it is snooped on the internal interface and added to the OTV mroute table as an IGMP created entry. Remember that any switch performing IGMP snooping must forward all IGMP membership reports to mrouter ports.

Example 14-51 shows the OTV mroute table from NX-6 with the IGMP created (V, *, G) entry and Outgoing Interface (OIF) of Port-channel 3 where the membership report was received.

Example 14-51 *OTV MROUTE State on NX-6*

```
NX-6# show otv mroute

OTV Multicast Routing Table For Overlay0

(103, *, 239.100.100.100), metric: 0, uptime: 00:00:38, igmp
 Outgoing interface list: (count: 1)
  Po3, uptime: 00:00:38, igmp
```

NX-6 then builds an IS-IS message to advertise the group membership (GM-Update) to all OTV EDs. NX-2 in Data Center 1 receives the IS-IS GM-Update, as shown in Example 14-52. NX-6 is identified by the IS-IS system-id of 6c9c.ed4d.d944. The correct LSP to check is confirmed with the output of **show otv adjacency,** which lists the system-id of each OTV ED IS-IS neighbor.

Example 14-52 *OTV IS-IS MGROUP Database on NX-2*

```
NX-2# show otv isis database mgroup detail 6c9c.ed4d.d944.00-00
OTV-IS-IS Process: default LSP database VPN: Overlay0

OTV-IS-IS Level-1 Link State Database
 LSPID              Seq Number   Checksum  Lifetime  A/P/O/T
 6c9c.ed4d.d944.00-00 0x00000002 0xFA73    1119      0/0/0/1
  Instance    : 0x00000000
```

```
    Group-Address :   IP Multicast : Vlan : 103    Groups : 1
          Group   : 239.100.100.100 Sources : 0
  Digest Offset : 0
```

Note At this point only Host C joined the multicast group, and there are no sources actively sending to the group.

NX-2 installs an OTV mroute entry in response to receiving the IS-IS GM-Update from NX-6, as shown in Example 14-53. The OIF on NX-2 is the overlay interface. The *r* indicates the receiver is across the overlay.

Example 14-53 *OTV MROUTE Entry on NX-2*

```
NX-2# show otv mroute

OTV Multicast Routing Table For Overlay0

(103, *, 239.100.100.100), metric: 0, uptime: 00:00:47, overlay(r)
 Outgoing interface list: (count: 1)
  Overlay0, uptime: 00:00:47, isis_otv-default
```

Host A now begins sending traffic to the site group 239.100.100.100 in Data Center 1. Because of the PIM dummy packets being sent by NX-2, the L2 switch creates an IGMP snooping mrouter entry for the port. The L2 switch forwards all multicast traffic to NX-2, where its received by the OTV internal interface. The receipt of this traffic creates an OTV mroute entry, as shown in Example 14-54. The delivery group (S, G) is visible with the addition of the *detail* keyword. The source of the delivery group is the AED's OTV join interface, and the group address is one of the configured OTV data-groups.

Example 14-54 *OTV (V, S, G) MROUTE Detail on NX-2*

```
NX-2# show otv mroute detail

OTV Multicast Routing Table For Overlay0

(103, *, *), metric: 0, uptime: 00:01:02, overlay(r)
 Outgoing interface list: (count: 1)
  Overlay0, uptime: 00:01:02, isis_otv-default

(103, *, 224.0.1.40), metric: 0, uptime: 00:01:02, igmp, overlay(r)
 Outgoing interface list: (count: 2)
  Eth3/5, uptime: 00:01:02, igmp
```

```
    Overlay0, uptime: 00:01:02, isis_otv-default

(103, *, 239.100.100.100), metric: 0, uptime: 00:01:01, igmp, overlay(r)
 Outgoing interface list: (count: 2)
  Eth3/5, uptime: 00:01:01, igmp
  Overlay0, uptime: 00:01:00, isis_otv-default

(103, 10.103.1.1, 239.100.100.100), metric: 0, uptime: 00:09:20, site
 Outgoing interface list: (count: 1)
  Overlay0, uptime: 00:01:00, otv
   Local Delivery: s = 10.1.12.1, g = 232.1.1.0
```

The OTV mroute is redistributed automatically into IS-IS, as shown in Example 14-55, where the VLAN, site (S,G), delivery (S,G), and LSP-ID are provided.

Example 14-55 *OTV MROUTE Redistribution into OTV IS-IS*

```
NX-2# show otv isis ip redistribute mroute
OTV-IS-IS process: default OTV-IS-IS IPv4 Local Multicast Group database
VLAN 103: (10.103.1.1, 239.100.100.100)
AS in LSP_ID: 6c9c.ed4d.d942.00-00
[DS-10.1.12.1, DG-232.1.1.0]
```

The redistributed route is advertised to all OTV EDs through IS-IS. Example 14-56 shows the LSP originated by NX-2, as received by NX-6.

Example 14-56 *OTV MGROUP Database Detail on NX-6*

```
NX-6# show otv isis database mgroup detail 6c9c.ed4d.d942.00-00
OTV-IS-IS Process: default LSP database VPN: Overlay0

OTV-IS-IS Level-1 Link State Database
LSPID            Seq Number  Checksum Lifetime  A/P/O/T
 6c9c.ed4d.d942.00-00*  0x00000002  0x0110   1056      0/0/0/1
  Instance   : 0x00000004
  Active-Source :    IP Multicast : (103 - 10.1.12.1, 232.1.1.0) Groups : 1
            Group  : 239.100.100.100 Sources : 1
            Source : 10.103.1.1
  Digest Offset : 0
```

Note The **show otv isis internal event-history mcast** command is useful for troubleshooting the IS-IS control plane for OTV multicast and the advertisement of groups and sources for a particular VLAN.

NX-6 updates this information into its OTV mroute table, as shown in Example 14-57. The *s* indicates the source is located across the overlay.

Example 14-57 *OTV (V, S, G) MROUTE Detail on NX-6*

```
NX-6# show otv mroute detail

OTV Multicast Routing Table For Overlay0

(103, *, *), metric: 0, uptime: 00:00:42, igmp, overlay(r)
 Outgoing interface list: (count: 2)
  Po3, uptime: 00:00:42, igmp
  Overlay0, uptime: 00:00:41, isis_otv-default

(103, *, 224.0.1.40), metric: 0, uptime: 00:00:42, igmp, overlay(r)
 Outgoing interface list: (count: 2)
  Po3, uptime: 00:00:42, igmp
  Overlay0, uptime: 00:00:40, isis_otv-default

(103, *, 239.100.100.100), metric: 0, uptime: 00:00:40, igmp, overlay(r)
 Outgoing interface list: (count: 2)
  Po3, uptime: 00:00:40, igmp
  Overlay0, uptime: 00:00:38, isis_otv-default

(103, 10.103.1.1, 239.100.100.100), metric: 0, uptime: 00:08:58, overlay(s)
 Outgoing interface list: (count: 0)
   Remote Delivery: s = 10.1.12.1, g = 232.1.1.0
```

The **show otv data-group** command is used to verify the site group and delivery group information for NX-2 and NX-6, as shown in Example 14-58. This should match what is present in the output of **show otv mroute**.

Example 14-58 *Verify Site Group to Delivery Group Mapping*

```
NX-6# show otv data-group

Remote Active Sources for Overlay0

VLAN Active-Source   Active-Group    Delivery-Source Delivery-Group  Joined-I/F
---- --------------- --------------- --------------- --------------- ----------
103  10.103.1.1      239.100.100.100 10.1.12.1       232.1.1.0       Eth3/41
NX-2# show otv data-group
Local Active Sources for Overlay0
VLAN Active-Source Active-Group Delivery-Source Delivery-Group  Join-IF State
---- ------------- ------------ --------------- --------------- ------- ------
103   10.103.1.1    239.100.100.100 10.1.12.1       232.1.1.0       Po3     Local
```

OTV EDs act as source hosts and receiver hosts for the delivery groups used on the transport network. An IGMPv3 membership report from the join interface is sent to the transport to allow the OTV ED to start receiving packets from the delivery group (10.1.12.1, 232.1.1.0).

Verification in the transport is done based on the PIM SSM delivery group information obtained from the OTV EDs. Each AED's join interface is a source for the delivery group. The AED joins only delivery group sources that are required based on the OTV mroute table and the information received through the IS-IS control plane. This mechanism allows OTV to optimize the multicast traffic in the transport so that only the needed data is received by each OTV ED. The use of PIM SSM allows specific source addresses to be joined for each delivery group.

Example 14-59 shows the mroute table of a transport router. In this output 10.1.12.1 is NX-2's OTV join interface, which is a source for the delivery group 232.1.1.0/32. The incoming interface should match the routing table path toward the source to pass the Reverse Path Forwarding (RPF) check. Interface Ethernet3/30 is the OIF and is connected to the OTV join interface of NX-6.

Example 14-59 *MROUTE Verification in the Transport Network*

```
NX-5# show ip mroute 232.1.1.0
IP Multicast Routing Table for VRF "default"

(10.1.12.1/32, 232.1.1.0/32), uptime: 00:02:29, igmp ip pim
 Incoming interface: Ethernet3/29, RPF nbr: 10.1.13.1
 Outgoing interface list: (count: 1)
  Ethernet3/30, uptime: 00:02:29, igmp
```

Note Multicast troubleshooting in the transport network between OTV ED sources and receivers follow standard multicast troubleshooting for the delivery group. The fact that OTV has encapsulated the site group within a multicast delivery group does not change the troubleshooting methodology in the transport. The OTV ED are source and receiver *hosts* for the delivery group from the perspective of the transport network.

OTV Multicast Traffic with a Unicast Transport (Adjacency Server Mode)

Deployments that rely on a unicast transport network can also forward multicast traffic across the overlay for extended VLANs. This is achieved by encapsulating the site group multicast packet into an IP unicast OTV packet across the transport network as depicted in Figure 14-13. If multiple remote sites have interested receivers, the source site OTV

ED must perform head-end replication of the traffic and send a copy to each site, which becomes inefficient at scale.

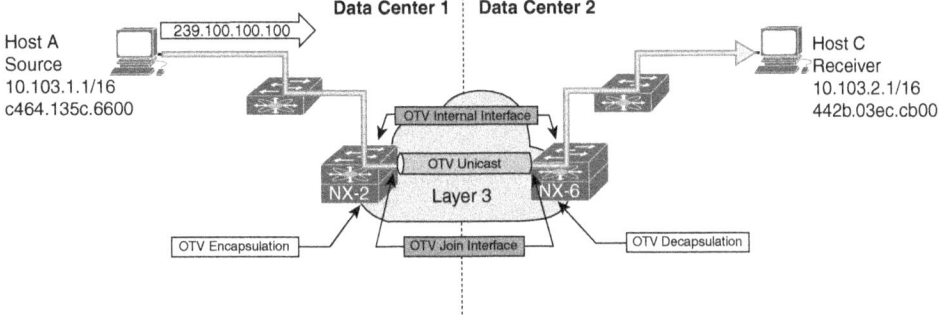

Figure 14-13 *Multicast Traffic Across OTV with Adjacency Server Mode*

In this example, Host A and Host C are both members of VLAN 103. Host A is sending traffic to the site group 239.100.100.100, and Host C sends an IGMP membership report message to the Data Center 2 L2 switch. The L2 switch forwards the membership report to NX-6 because it is an mrouter port in IGMP snooping. The same PIM *dummy hello* packet mechanism is used on the OTV internal interface, just as with a multicast enabled transport. The arrival of the IGMP membership report on NX-6 triggers an OTV mroute to be created, as shown in Example 14-60, with the internal interface Port-channel 3 as an OIF.

Example 14-60 *OTV (V, *, G) MROUTE Detail on NX-6*

```
NX-6# show otv mroute detail

OTV Multicast Routing Table For Overlay0

(103, *, *), metric: 0, uptime: 00:03:25, igmp, overlay(r)
 Outgoing interface list: (count: 2)
  Po3, uptime: 00:03:25, igmp
  NX-2 uptime: 00:03:24, isis_otv-default

(103, *, 224.0.1.40), metric: 0, uptime: 00:03:25, igmp
 Outgoing interface list: (count: 1)
  Po3, uptime: 00:03:25, igmp

(103, *, 239.100.100.100), metric: 0, uptime: 00:03:23, igmp
 Outgoing interface list: (count: 1)
  Po3, uptime: 00:03:23, igmp
```

The OTV mroute is then redistributed automatically into IS-IS for advertisement to all other OTV EDs, as shown in Example 14-61. The LSP ID should be noted so that it can be checked on NX-2, which is the OTV ED for the multicast source Host A in Data Center 1.

Example 14-61 *OTV MROUTE Redistributed into OTV IS-IS on NX-6*

```
NX-6# show otv isis ip redistribute mroute
OTV-IS-IS process: default OTV-IS-IS IPv4 Local Multicast Group database
VLAN 103: (*, *)
Receiver in LSP_ID: 6c9c.ed4d.d944.00-00
VLAN 103: IPv4 router attached
VLAN 103: (*, 224.0.1.40)
Receiver in LSP_ID: 6c9c.ed4d.d944.00-00
VLAN 103: IPv4 router attached
VLAN 103: (*, 239.100.100.100)
Receiver in LSP_ID: 6c9c.ed4d.d944.00-00
VLAN 103: IPv4 router attached
```

Note There is a PIM enabled router present on VLAN 103, as indicated in Example 14-61 by the (*, *) entry.

Because IGMP packets are not forwarded across the overlay, the IS-IS messages used to signal an interested receiver are counted as IGMP proxy-reports. Example 14-62 shows the IGMP snooping statistics of NX-6, which indicate the proxy-report being originated through IS-IS. The IGMP proxy-report mechanism is not specific to OTV adjacency server mode.

Example 14-62 *OTV IGMP Proxy Reports*

```
NX-6# show ip igmp snooping statistics vlan 103
Global IGMP snooping statistics: (only non-zero values displayed)
 Packets received: 1422
 Packets flooded: 437
 STP TCN messages rcvd: 21
VLAN 103 IGMP snooping statistics, last reset: never (only non-zero values
  displayed)
 Packets received: 1350
 IGMPv2 reports received: 897
 IGMPv2 queries received: 443
 IGMPv2 leaves received: 10
 PIM Hellos received: 2598
 IGMPv2 leaves suppressed: 4
 Queries originated: 4
 IGMPv2 proxy-reports originated: 14
```

```
 IGMPv2 proxy-leaves originated: 4
 Packets sent to routers: 902
 vPC Peer Link CFS packet statistics:
IGMP Filtering Statistics:
Router Guard Filtering Statistics:
F340-35-02-N7K-7009-A-vdc_4#
```

Following the path from receiver to the source in Data Center 1, the IS-IS database is verified on NX-2. This is done to confirm that the overlay is added as an OIF for the OTV mroute. Example 14-63 contains the GM-LSP received from NX-6 on NX-2.

Example 14-63 *OTV IS-IS MGROUP Database Detail on NX-2*

```
NX-2# show otv isis database mgroup detail 6c9c.ed4d.d944.00-00
OTV-IS-IS Process: default LSP database VPN: Overlay0

OTV-IS-IS Level-1 Link State Database
 LSPID            Seq Number   Checksum Lifetime   A/P/O/T
 6c9c.ed4d.d944.00-00 0x00000005   0x7579   820       0/0/0/1
  Instance     : 0x00000003
  Group-Address :    IP Multicast : Vlan : 103     Groups : 2
           Group   : 239.100.100.100 Sources : 0
           Group   : 224.0.1.40    Sources : 0
  Router-capability :    Interested Vlans : Vlan Start 103 Vlan end 103
IPv4 Router attached
  Digest Offset : 0
```

The IGMP Snooping table on NX-2 confirms that the overlay is included in the port list, as shown in Example 14-64.

Example 14-64 *IGMP Snooping OTV Groups on NX-2*

```
NX-2# show ip igmp snooping otv groups
Type: S - Static, D - Dynamic, R - Router port, F - Fabricpath core port

Vlan Group Address    Ver Type Port list
103  224.0.1.40       v3  D    Overlay0
103  239.100.100.100  v3  D    Overlay0
```

The OTV mroute on NX-2 contains the (V, *, G) entry, which is populated as a result of receiving the IS-IS GM-LSP from NX-6. This message indicates Host C is an interested receiver in Data Center 2 and that NX-2 should add the overlay as an OIF for the group. The OTV mroute table from NX-2 is shown in Example 14-65. The *r* indicates the receiver is reachable across the overlay. The (V, S, G) entry is also present, which indicates Host A is actively sending traffic to the site group 239.100.100.100.

Example 14-65 *OTV MROUTE Detail on NX-2*

```
NX-2# show otv mroute detail

OTV Multicast Routing Table For Overlay0

(103, *, *), metric: 0, uptime: 00:12:22, overlay(r)
 Outgoing interface list: (count: 1)
  NX-6 uptime: 00:12:21, isis_otv-default

(103, *, 224.0.1.40), metric: 0, uptime: 00:12:21, overlay(r)
 Outgoing interface list: (count: 1)
  NX-6 uptime: 00:12:21, isis_otv-default

(103, *, 239.100.100.100), metric: 0, uptime: 00:12:21, overlay(r)
 Outgoing interface list: (count: 1)
  NX-6 uptime: 00:12:21, isis_otv-default

(103, 10.103.1.1, 239.100.100.100), metric: 0, uptime: 00:12:21, site
 Outgoing interface list: (count: 1)
  NX-6 uptime: 00:10:51, otv
   Local Delivery: s = 0.0.0.0, g = 0.0.0.0
```

Note The OTV mroute table lists an OIF of NX-6 installed by OTV. This is a result of the OTV Unicast encapsulation used in adjacency server mode. The delivery group has values of all zeros for the group address. This information is populated with a valid delivery group when multicast transport is being used.

NX-2 encapsulates the site group packets in an OTV unicast packet with a destination address of NX-6's join interface. The OTV unicast packets traverse the transport network until they arrive at NX-6. When the packets arrive at NX-6 on the OTV join interface, the outer OTV unicast encapsulation is removed. The next lookup is done on the inner multicast packet, which results in an OIF for the mroute installed by IGMP on the OTV internal interface. Example 14-66 shows the OTV mroute table of NX-6. The site group multicast packet leaves on Po3 toward the L2 switch in Data Center 2 and ultimately reaches Host C.

Example 14-66 *OTV MROUTE Detail on NX-6*

```
NX-6# show otv mroute detail
show otv mroute detail

OTV Multicast Routing Table For Overlay0
```

```
 (103, *, *), metric: 0, uptime: 00:03:25, igmp, overlay(r)
  Outgoing interface list: (count: 2)
    Po3, uptime: 00:03:25, igmp
    F340-35-02-N7K-7009-A-VDC2 uptime: 00:03:24, isis_otv-default

 (103, *, 224.0.1.40), metric: 0, uptime: 00:03:25, igmp
  Outgoing interface list: (count: 1)
    Po3, uptime: 00:03:25, igmp

 (103, *, 239.100.100.100), metric: 0, uptime: 00:03:23, igmp
  Outgoing interface list: (count: 1)
    Po3, uptime: 00:03:23, igmp
```

With adjacency server mode, the source is not advertised to the other OTV EDs by NX-2. This is because there is no delivery group used across the transport for remote OTV EDs to join. NX-2 only needs to know that there is an interested receiver across the overlay and which OTV ED has the receiver. The join interface of that OTV ED is used as the destination address of the multicast-in-unicast OTV packet across the transport. The actual encapsulation of the site group multicast frame is done using the OTV unicast point-to-point dynamic tunnel, as shown in Example 14-67.

Example 14-67 *Dynamic Tunnel Encapsulation for Multicast Traffic*

```
NX-2# show tunnel internal implicit otv detail
Tunnel16390 is up
  Admin State: up
  MTU 9178 bytes, BW 9 Kbit
  Tunnel protocol/transport GRE/IP
  Tunnel source 10.1.12.1, destination 10.2.34.1
  Transport protocol is in VRF "default"
  Rx
  663 packets input, 1 minute input rate 0 packets/sec
  Tx
  156405 packets output, 1 minute output rate 0 packets/sec
  Last clearing of "show interface" counters never
```

Advanced OTV Features

Since its initial release as an NX-OS feature, OTV has continued to evolve. The next section in this chapter discusses some of the advanced features of OTV that allow it to be customized to meet the needs of different network deployments.

First Hop Routing Protocol Localization

First Hop Routing Protocols (FHRP), such as Hot Standby Routing Protocol (HSRP) and Virtual Router Redundancy Protocol (VRRP), are commonly used to provide a redundant default gateway for hosts on a VLAN. With OTV the VLAN has been extended across the overlay to multiple sites, which means that a router in Data Center 1 could form an HSRP neighbor with a router in Data Center 2. In addition, hosts in Data Center 2 could potentially use a default router that is physically located in Data Center 1, which results in unnecessary traffic crossing the overlay when it could be easily routed locally.

FHRP isolation is configured on the OTV EDs to allow each site's FHRP to operate independently. The purpose of this configuration is to filter any FHRP protocol traffic, as well as ARP from hosts trying to resolve the virtual IP across the overlay. A configuration example from NX-2 is shown in Example 14-68.

Example 14-68 *FHRP Localization Configuration on NX-2*

```
NX-2# show running-config
! Output omitted for brevity
feature otv

ip access-list ALL_IPs
  10 permit ip any any
ipv6 access-list ALL_IPv6s
  10 permit ipv6 any any
mac access-list ALL_MACs
  10 permit any any
ip access-list HSRP_IP
  10 permit udp any 224.0.0.2/32 eq 1985
  20 permit udp any 224.0.0.102/32 eq 1985
ipv6 access-list HSRP_IPV6
  10 permit udp any ff02::66/128
mac access-list HSRP_VMAC
  10 permit 0000.0c07.ac00 0000.0000.00ff any
  20 permit 0000.0c9f.f000 0000.0000.0fff any
  30 permit 0005.73a0.0000 0000.0000.0fff any
arp access-list HSRP_VMAC_ARP
  10 deny ip any mac 0000.0c07.ac00 ffff.ffff.ff00
  20 deny ip any mac 0000.0c9f.f000 ffff.ffff.f000
  30 deny ip any mac 0005.73a0.0000 ffff.ffff.f000
  40 permit ip any mac any
vlan access-map HSRP_Localization 10
    match mac address HSRP_VMAC
    match ip address HSRP_IP
    match ipv6 address HSRP_IPV6
    action drop
```

```
vlan access-map HSRP_Localization 20
   match mac address ALL_MACs
   match ip address ALL_IPs
   match ipv6 address ALL_IPv6s
   action forward
vlan filter HSRP_Localization vlan-list 100-110

mac-list OTV_HSRP_VMAC_deny seq 10 deny 0000.0c07.ac00 ffff.ffff.ff00
mac-list OTV_HSRP_VMAC_deny seq 11 deny 0000.0c9f.f000 ffff.ffff.f000
mac-list OTV_HSRP_VMAC_deny seq 12 deny 0005.73a0.0000 ffff.ffff.f000
mac-list OTV_HSRP_VMAC_deny seq 20 permit 0000.0000.0000 0000.0000.0000

route-map OTV_HSRP_filter permit 10
 match mac-list OTV_HSRP_VMAC_deny

service dhcp

otv-isis default
 vpn Overlay0
  redistribute filter route-map OTV_HSRP_filter
otv site-identifier 0x1
ip arp inspection filter HSRP_VMAC_ARP vlan 100-110
```

Recall the topology depicted in Figure 14-1. In Data Center 1 HSRP is configured on NX-1 and NX-3 for all VLANs. HSRP is also configured between NX-5 and NX-7 for all VLANs in Data Center 2. The configuration in Example 14-68 is composed of three filtering components:

- VLAN Access Control List (VACL) to filter and drop HSRP Hellos
- ARP Inspection Filter to drop ARP sourced from the HSRP Virtual MAC
- Redistribution Filter Route-Map on the overlay to filter HSRP Virtual MAC (VMAC) from being advertised through OTV IS-IS

FHRP isolation is a common source of problems due to incorrect configuration. Care should be taken to ensure the filtering is properly configured to avoid OTV IS-IS LSP refresh issues as well as duplicate IP address messages or flapping of the HSRP VMAC.

Multihoming

A multihomed site in OTV refers to a site where two or more OTV ED are configured to extend the same range of VLANs. Because OTV does not forward STP BPDUs across the overlay, L2 loops form without the election of an AED.

When multiple OTV EDs exist at a site, the AED election runs using the OTV IS-IS system-id and VLAN identifier. This is done by using a hash function where the result is an *ordinal value* of zero or one. The ordinal value is used to assign the AED role for each extended VLAN to one of the forwarding capable OTV EDs at the site.

When two OTV EDs are present, the device with the lower system-id is the AED for the even-numbered VLANs, and the higher system-id is the AED for the odd-numbered VLANs. The AED is responsible for advertising MAC addresses and forwarding traffic for an extended VLAN across the overlay.

Beginning in NX-OS 5.2(1) the dual site adjacency concept is used. This allows OTV EDs with the same site identifier to communicate across the overlay as well as across the site VLAN, which greatly reduces the chance of one OTV ED being isolated and creating a dual active condition. In addition, the overlay interface of an OTV ED is disabled until a site identifier is configured, which ensures that OTV is able to detect any mismatch in site identifiers. If a device becomes non-AED capable, it proactively notifies the other OTV ED at the site so it can take over the role of AED for all VLANs.

Ingress Routing Optimization

Egress routing optimization is accomplished with FHRP isolation. Ingress routing optimization is another challenge that needs to be considered in some OTV deployments. OTV allows a VLAN to be extended to multiple sites providing a transparent L2 overlay. This can result in a situation where more than one site is advertising the same L3 prefix to other sites, which may cause suboptimal forwarding.

Figure 14-14 shows that NX-11 has Equal Cost Multipath (ECMP) routes to reach the 10.103.0.0/16 subnet through either NX-9 or NX-10. Depending on the load-sharing hash, packets originating behind NX-11 reach either Data Center 1 or Data Center 2. If for example the destination of the traffic was Host C, and NX11 choose to send the traffic to NX-9 as next-hop, a suboptimal forwarding path is used. NX-9 then has to try to resolve where Host C is located to forward the traffic. The packets reach the internal interface of NX-2, which then performs an OTV encapsulation and routes the packets back across the overlay to reach Host C.

A common solution to this problem is to deploy OTV and Locator-ID Separation Protocol (LISP) together. LISP provides ingress routing optimization by discovering the location of a host and using the LISP control plane to advertise its location behind a specific Routing Locator (RLOC). LISP also provides options for supporting host mobility between sites. If a full LISP deployment is not required, LISP with Interior Gateway Protocol (IGP) assist can be used to redistribute routes from LISP into an IGP protocol.

Advanced OTV Features   941

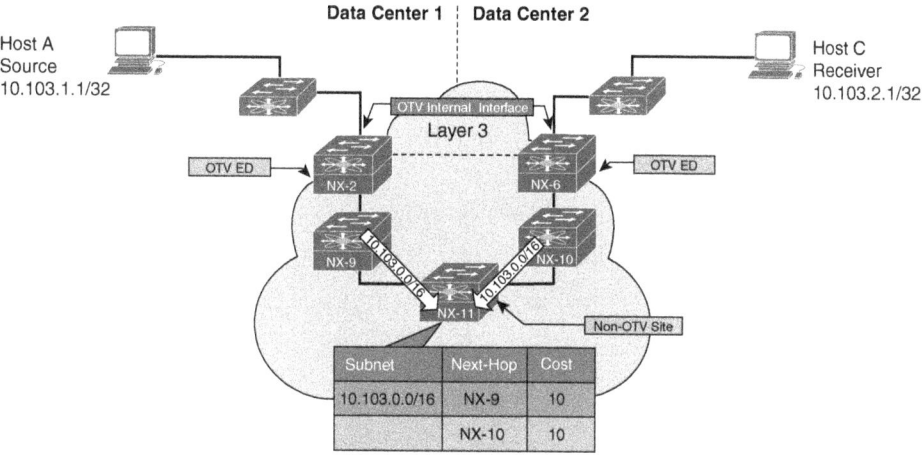

Figure 14-14 *Suboptimal Routing Behavior*

Another solution to this problem is to advertise more specific, smaller subnets from each site along with the /16 summary to the rest of the routing domain. Routing follows the more specific subnet to Data Center 1 or Data Center 2, and if either partially fails, the /16 summary can still be used to draw in traffic. Assuming OTV is still functional in the partially failed state through a backdoor link, the traffic then relies on the overlay to cross from Data Center 1 to Data Center 2. The best solution to this problem depends on the deployment scenario and if the two OTV sites are acting as Active/Standby or if they are Active/Active from a redundancy perspective.

Note   For more information on LISP, refer to http://lisp.cisco.com.

VLAN Translation

In some networks, a VLAN configured at an OTV site may need to communicate with a VLAN at another site that is using a different VLAN numbering scheme. There are two solutions to this problem:

- VLAN mapping on the overlay interface
- VLAN mapping on an L2 Trunk port

VLAN mapping on the overlay interface is not supported with Nexus 7000 F3 or M3 series modules. If VLAN mapping is required with F3 or M3 modules, VLAN mapping on the OTV internal interface, which is an L2 trunk, must be used.

Example 14-69 demonstrates the configuration of VLAN mapping on the overlay interface. VLAN 200 is extended across the overlay. The local VLAN 200 is mapped to VLAN 300 at the other OTV site.

Example 14-69 *VLAN Mapping on the Overlay Interface*

```
NX-2# show running-config interface overlay 0
interface Overlay0
 description Site A
 otv join-interface port-channel3
 otv control-group 239.12.12.12
 otv data-group 232.1.1.0/24
 otv extend-vlan 100-110, 200
 otv vlan mapping 200 to 300
 no shutdown

NX-2# show otv vlan-mapping
Original VLAN -> Translated VLAN
-------------------------------
     200 -> 300
```

If F3 or M3 modules are being used, the VLAN mapping must be performed on the OTV internal interface, as shown in Example 14-70. This configuration translates VLAN 200 to VLAN 300, which is then extended across OTV to interoperate with the remote site VLAN scheme.

Example 14-70 *VLAN Mapping on the L2 Trunk*

```
NX-2# show running-config interface Ethernet3/5
interface Ethernet3/5
 description 7009A-Main-VDC OTV inside
 switchport
 switchport mode trunk
 switchport vlan mapping 200 300
 mtu 9216
 no shutdown
```

OTV Tunnel Depolarization

L3 routers with multiple ECMP routes to a destination apply a load-sharing hash function to choose an exit interface for a particular flow. A flow is typically the 5-tuple, which consists of the following:

- L3 Source Address
- L3 Destination Address
- Layer 4 Protocol
- Layer 4 Protocol Source Port
- Layer 4 Protocol Destination Port

A problem typical to tunneled traffic is that it may become polarized as it traverses a multihop L3 ECMP network. These flows are referred to as elephants because they are typically moving a lot of traffic and can saturate single links of interface bundles, or of ECMP paths. Tunneled traffic uses a fixed 5-tuple because of the tunnel header and consistent source and destination address. This causes the input to the hash algorithm to stay the same, even though multiple diverse flows could be encapsulated inside the tunnel.

This polarization problem happens when each layer of the transport network applies the same hash function. Using the same inputs results in the same output interface decision at each hop. For example, if a router chose an even-numbered interface, the next router also chooses an even-numbered interface, and the next one also chooses an even-numbered interface, and so on.

OTV provides a solution to this problem. When using the default GRE/IP encapsulation for the overlay, secondary IP addresses can be configured in the same subnet on the OTV join interface, as shown in Example 14-71. This allows OTV to build secondary dynamic tunnels between different pairs of addresses. The secondary address allows the transport network to provide different hash results and load-balance the overlay traffic more effectively.

Example 14-71 *Secondary IP Address to Avoid Polarization*

```
NX-2# show running-config interface port-channel3
interface port-channel3
 description 7009A-Main-OTV Join
 mtu 9216
 no ip redirects
 ip address 10.1.12.1/24
 ip address 10.1.12.4/24 secondary
 ip router ospf 1 area 0.0.0.0
 ip igmp version 3
```

The status of the secondary OTV adjacencies are seen with the **show otv adjacency detail** command, as shown in Example 14-72.

Example 14-72 *OTV Adjacencies with Secondary IP Address*

```
NX-2# show otv adjacency detail
Overlay Adjacency database

Overlay-Interface Overlay0 :
Hostname              System-ID     Dest Addr      Up Time   State
NX-4                  64a0.e73e.12c2 10.1.22.1     00:03:07  UP
    Secondary src/dest:     10.1.12.4     10.1.22.1           UP
```

```
HW-St: Default
NX-8                   64a0.e73e.12c4 10.2.43.1    00:03:07 UP
     Secondary src/dest:    10.1.12.4    10.2.43.1         UP
HW-St: Default
NX-6                   6c9c.ed4d.d944 10.2.34.1    00:03:06 UP
     Secondary src/dest:    10.1.12.4    10.2.34.1         UP
HW-St: Default
```

Note OTV tunnel depolarization is enabled by default. It is disabled with the **otv depolarization disable** global configuration command.

When OTV UDP encapsulation is used, the depolarization is applied automatically with no additional configuration required. The Ethernet frames are encapsulated in a UDP packet that uses a variable UDP source port and a UDP destination port of 8472. By having a variable source port, the OTV ED is able to influence the load-sharing hash of the transport network.

Note OTV UDP encapsulation is supported starting in NX-OS release 7.2(0)D1(1) for F3 and M3 modules.

OTV Fast Failure Detection

OTV's dual adjacency implementation forms an adjacency on the site VLAN as well as across the overlay for OTV EDs, which have a common site identifier. When an OTV ED becomes unreachable or goes down, the other OTV ED at the site must take over the AED role for all VLANs. Detecting this failure condition quickly minimizes traffic loss during the transition.

The site VLAN IS-IS adjacency can be configured to use Bidirectional Forwarding Detection (BFD) on the site VLAN to detect IS-IS neighbor loss. This is useful to detect any type of connectivity failure on the site VLAN. Example 14-73 shows the configuration required to enable BFD on the site VLAN.

Example 14-73 *BFD for OTV IS-IS on the Site VLAN*

```
NX-2# show otv adjacency detail
! Output omitted for brevity
feature otv
feature bfd


otv site-vlan 10
```

Advanced OTV Features

```
otv isis bfd

interface Vlan10
 no shutdown
 bfd interval 250 min_rx 250 multiplier 3
 no ip redirects
 ip address 10.111.111.1/30
```

The status of BFD on the site VLAN is verified with the **show otv isis site** command, as shown in Example 14-74. Any BFD neighbor is also present in the output of the **show bfd neighbors** command.

Example 14-74 *Confirm BFD Neighbor on the Site VLAN*

```
NX-2# show otv isis site

OTV-ISIS site-information for: default

 BFD: Enabled [IP: 10.111.111.1]

OTV-IS-IS site adjacency local database:

 SNPA       State Last Chg Hold   Fwd-state Site-ID       Version BFD
 64a0.e73e.12c2 UP  00:00:40 00:01:00 DOWN    0000.0000.0100 3
Enabled [Nbr IP: 10.111.111.2]

OTV-IS-IS Site Group Information (as in OTV SDB):

 SystemID: 6c9c.ed4d.d942, Interface: site-vlan, VLAN Id: 10, Cib: Up VLAN: Up

 Overlay   State  Next IIH  Int  Multi
 Overlay1  Up     0.933427   3    20

 Overlay   Active SG    Last CSNP        CSNP Int Next CSNP
 Overlay1  0.0.2.0      ffff.ffff.ffff.ff-ff 1d14h   00:00:02

 Neighbor SystemID: 64a0.e73e.12c2
 IPv4 site groups:
  0.0.2.0
```

For the overlay adjacency, the presence of a route to reach the peer OTV ED's join interface can be tracked to detect a reachability problem that eventually causes the IS-IS neighbor to go down. Example 14-75 shows the configuration to enable next-hop adjacency tracking for the overlay adjacency of OTV EDs, which use the same site identifier.

Example 14-75 *Configuring OTV Next-Hop Adjacency Tracking*

```
NX-2# show run otv
! Output omitted for brevity
feature otv

otv-isis default
  track-adjacency-nexthop
  vpn Overlay0
    redistribute filter route-map OTV_HSRP_filter
```

Example 14-76 contains the output of **show otv isis track-adjacency-nexthop**, which verifies the feature is enabled and tracking next-hop reachability of NX-4.

Example 14-76 *Verify OTV Next-Hop Adjacency Tracking*

```
NX-2# show otv isis track-adjacency-nexthop
OTV-IS-IS process: default
  OTV-ISIS adjs for nexthop: 10.1.12.2, VRF: default
    Hostname: 64a0.e73e.12c2, Overlay: Overlay1
```

This feature depends on a nondefault route, learned from a dynamic routing protocol for the peer OTV ED's join interface. When the route disappears, OTV IS-IS brings down the adjacency without waiting for the hold timer to expire, which allows the other OTV ED to assume the AED role for all VLANs.

Summary

OTV was introduced in this chapter as an efficient and flexible way to extend L2 VLANs to multiple sites across a routed transport network. The concepts of MAC routing and the election of an AED were explained as an efficient way to solve the challenges presented by other DCI solutions without relying on STP. The examples and end-to-end walk-through for the control plane, unicast traffic, and multicast traffic provided in this chapter can be used as a basis for troubleshooting the various types of connectivity problems that may be observed in a production network environment.

References

Fuller, Ron, David Jansen, and Matthew McPherson. *NX-OS and Cisco Nexus Switching*. Indianapolis: Cisco Press, 2013.

Krattiger, Lukas. "Overlay Transport Virtualization" (presented at Cisco Live, Las Vegas 2016).

Schmidt, Carlo. "Advanced OTV—Configure, Verify and Troubleshoot OTV in Your Network" (presented at Cisco Live, San Francisco 2014).

draft-hasmit-otv-04 Overlay Transport Virtualization, H. Grover, D. Rao, D. Farinacci, V. Moreno, IETF, https://tools.ietf.org/html/draft-hasmit-otv-04, February 2013.

draft-drao-isis-otv-00 IS-IS Extensions to Support OTV, D. Rao, A. Banerjee, H. Grover, IETF, https://tools.ietf.org/html/draft-drao-isis-otv-00, March 2011.

RFC 6165, Extensions to IS-IS for Layer-2 Systems. A. Banerjee, D. Ward. IETF, https://tools.ietf.org/html/rfc6165, April 2011.

RFC 7348. Virtual eXtensible Local Area Network (VXLAN): A Framework for Overlaying Virtualized L2 Networks over L3 Networks. M. Mahalingam et al. IETF, https://tools.ietf.org/html/rfc7348, August 2014.

Cisco. Cisco Nexus Platform Configuration Guides, http://www.cisco.com.

Wireshark. Network Protocol Analyzer, www.wireshark.org/.

Chapter 15

Programmability and Automation

This chapter covers the following topics:

- Introduction to Open NX-OS
- Shells and Scripting
- Applications
- NX-API

Introduction to Automation and Programmability

What is automation? This question can be answered differently as it applies to various industries, such as robotics, process management, and information technology (IT). This chapter discusses automation in the specific context of computer networks. To start understanding automation, first consider an example. Assume that the network of an organization consists of 100 nodes, all running the same software and hardware. After months of testing and software validation, the network operations team agrees to upgrade the software to a newer release. The team then spends nearly 2 months working day and night to complete the upgrade. Soon after the upgrade, the network faces a massive outage and the network collapses. The root cause is found to be a software defect. The software also has a configuration command as a workaround that helps in service restoration. Now the network operations team has two options:

- Upgrade to a release that has the fix for the defect
- Apply the configuration workaround

Either option is time consuming, but the second one, applying a configuration workaround, involves the least amount of time. Applying a workaround on 100 nodes is not an easy task, however. This is where automation comes into play. If the process of provisioning and validating the successful application of the configuration can be automated, the workaround or fix can be quickly deployed on all the nodes in the network, possibly at the same time.

Network automation is simply defined as the process of recording certain steps using a script, a programming language, or an application and then replaying those recorded steps across the network at a designated time or at specific time intervals without human intervention. Network automation not only saves time, but also prevents the possibility of human error after the scripts are validated. The automation and orchestration methodologies leverage the pragmatic interfaces of the devices present in the network infrastructure to help reduce provisioning time and accelerate service delivery.

Programmability, on the other hand, refers to the capability of an entity to be programmed. Programmability enhances the *capability* of the programmable device to be extended or modified. The acts of programming an entity and interacting with it are different, a distinction that is often misunderstood. An application or script can interact with the network device without extending or modifying any of its existing capabilities. Manageability and programmability are distinct from one another because they serve different purposes:

- **Manageability:** Allows an entity to be managed in terms of how it can be operated, provisioned, administered, and maintained

- **Programmability:** Enables an entity or device to be extended or modified, to add new features and properties that enhance its capability

The following sections discuss in detail the multiple automation and programmability tools available with NX-OS to give network engineers more control and flexibility in performing various actions and running third-party applications.

Introduction to Open NX-OS

NX-OS has always been built on top of a Linux kernel. However, until recently, much of the underlying Linux operating system was not fully exposed to the user. The latest Nexus 9000 and Nexus 3000 series of switches run what Cisco has named *Open NX-OS*, beginning with NX-OS Release 7.0(3).

One reason Linux has achieved success in all aspects of computing and networking is its flexibility and vast user support community. With Open NX-OS, Linux applications can run on the switch to complement the feature-rich NX-OS operating system without a wrapper library or customization. The major components of Open NX-OS are listed here:

- **Kernel version 3.4:** This is a 64-bit kernel that provides a balance of features and stability.

- **Kernel stack:** The user space Netstack process that previous versions of NX-OS used has been replaced with the kernel stack. This allows the interfaces on the switch to be mapped to the kernel as standard Linux netdevs and namespaces. Interfaces are managed using standard Linux commands such as **ifconfig** and **tcpdump** from the Bash shell.

- **Open package management:** Tools such as RPM Package Manager (RPM) and Yellowdog Updater, Modified (YUM) aid in installing or patching software on the switch and provide extensibility.

- **Container support:** Linux containers (LXCs) run directly on the platform and provide access to a Centos 7–based Guest shell. This enables users to customize their switch in a secure and isolated environment.

Open NX-OS provides the foundation for a true DevOps-managed data center switch by providing Linux capabilities such as modularity, fault isolation, resiliency, and much more.

Note For more details on Open NX-OS architecture, refer to the book *Programmability and Automation with Cisco Open NX-OS*, at Cisco.com.

Shells and Scripting

A *shell* is a text-based user interface that enables the user to perform administrative tasks and interact directly with the operating system. The shell is commonly used to perform various administrative tasks, such as executing filesystem operations, starting and stopping processes, creating user accounts, executing scripts, and configuring the system. The concept of a shell dates back to the early days of the UNIX operating system. After years of evolution and refinement, the shell is a key functional component in modern operating systems.

The NX-OS operating system provides a shell more commonly known as the command-line interface (CLI). As the practice of automation through scripting and network management techniques has evolved, the capability to have direct shell access to the underlying Linux operating system of NX-OS has become desirable. The following section provides examples of the NX-OS Bash shell, the Guest shell, and Python capabilities. These powerful tools enable the automation of many operational tasks, reducing the administrative burden.

Bash Shell

Bourne-Again Shell (Bash) is a modern UNIX shell, a successor of the Bourne shell. It provides a rich feature set and built-in capability to interact with the low-level components of the underlying operating system. The Bash shell is currently available on the Nexus 9000, Nexus 3000, and Nexus 3500 series platforms. The Bash shell provides shell access to the underlying Linux operating system, which has additional capabilities that the standard NX-OS CLI does not provide. To enable the Bash shell on Nexus

9000 switches, enable the command **feature bash-shell**. Then use the command **run bash** *cli* to execute any Bash CLI commands. Users can also move into shell mode by using the NX-OS CLI command **run bash** and then can execute the relevant Bash CLI commands from the Bash shell. Example 15-1 illustrates how to enable the bash-shell feature and use the Bash shell command **pwd** to display the current working directory. To check whether the bash-shell feature is enabled, use the command **show bash-shell**. Example 15-1 also demonstrates various basic commands on the Bash shell. The Bash command **id -a** is used to verify the current user, as well as Group and Group ID information. You can also use **echo** commands to print various messages based on the script requirements.

Example 15-1 *Enabling the bash-shell Feature and Using Bash Commands*

```
N9k-1(config)# feature bash-shell

N9k-1# show bash-shell
Bash shell is enable
N9k-1# run bash pwd
/bootflash/home/admin
N9k-1#

N9k-1# run bash
bash-4.2$ pwd
/bootflash/home/admin

bash-4.2$ id -a
uid=2002(admin) gid=503(network-admin) groups=503(network-admin)
bash-4.2$
bash-4.2$ echo "First Example on " 'uname -n' " using bash-shell " $BASH_VERSION
First Example on  N9k-1  using bash-shell  4.2.10(1)-release
```

Note It is recommended that you become familiar with the UNIX/Linux bash shell commands for this section.

On NX-OS, only users with the roles network-admin, vdc-admin, and dev-ops can use the Bash shell. Other users are restricted from using Bash unless it is specially allowed in their role. To validate check roles are permitted to use the Bash shell, use the command **show role** [**name** *role-name*]. Example 15-2 displays the permission for the network-admin and dev-ops user roles.

Example 15-2 *network-admin and dev-ops User Role Permissions*

```
N9k-1# show role name network-admin

Role: network-admin
  Description: Predefined network admin role has access to all commands
  on the switch
  -------------------------------------------------------------------
  Rule    Perm    Type       Scope                Entity
  -------------------------------------------------------------------
  1       permit  read-write

N9k-1# show role name dev-ops

Role: dev-ops
  Description: Predefined system role for devops access. This role
  cannot be modified.
  -------------------------------------------------------------------
  Rule    Perm    Type       Scope                Entity
  -------------------------------------------------------------------
  6       permit  command                         conf t ; username *
  5       permit  command                         attach module *
  4       permit  command                         slot *
  3       permit  command                         bcm module *
  2       permit  command                         run bash *
  1       permit  command                         python *
```

With the NX-OS bash-shell feature, it becomes possible to create Bash shell scripts consisting of multiple Bash commands that execute in sequence on the underlying Linux operating system. The Bash script is created and saved with the extension *.sh*. The Bash shell also gives users traceability options, which is useful for debugging purposes while executing a shell script. This is activated by using the option -x along with the **#!/bin/bash** statement. Example 15-3 illustrates how to create a shell script and verify its execution with script debugging enabled via the -x option.

Example 15-3 *Creating and Debugging Bash Shell Scripts*

```
bash-4.2$ pwd
/bootflash/home/admin

bash-4.2$ cat test.sh
#!/bin/bash
echo "Troubleshooting Route Flapping Issue Using Bash Shell"
counter="$(vsh -c "show ip route ospf | grep 00:00:0 | count")"
echo "Printing Counter - " $counter
if [ $counter -gt 0 ]
```

```
then
        echo "Following Routes Flapped @ " 'date'
        vsh -c "show tech ospf >> bootflash:shtechospf"
        vsh -c "show tech routing ip unicast >> bootflash:shtechrouting_unicast"
else
        echo "No Flapping Routes at this point"
bash-4.2$ /bin/bash -x test.sh
+ echo 'Troubleshooting Route Flapping Issue Using Bash Shell'
Troubleshooting Route Flapping Issue Using Bash Shell
++ vsh -c 'show ip route ospf | grep 00:00:0 | count'
+ counter=0
+ echo 'Printing Counter - ' 0
Printing Counter -  0
+ '[' 0 -gt 0 ']'
+ echo 'No Flapping Routes at this point'
No Flapping Routes at this point

bash-4.2$ vsh -c "clear ip route *"
Clearing ALL routes


bash-4.2$ /bin/bash -x test.sh
+ echo 'Troubleshooting Route Flapping Issue Using Bash Shell'
Troubleshooting Route Flapping Issue Using Bash Shell
++ vsh -c 'show ip route ospf | grep 00:00:0 | count'
+ counter=16
+ echo 'Printing Counter - ' 16
Printing Counter -  16
+ '[' 16 -gt 0 ']'
++ date
+ echo 'Following Routes Flapped @ ' Tue Nov 21 20:21:15 UTC 2017
Following Routes Flapped @  Tue Nov 21 20:21:15 UTC 2017
+ vsh -c 'show tech ospf >> bootflash:shtechospf'
+ vsh -c 'show tech routing ip unicast >> bootflash:shtechrouting_unicast'
bash-4.2$ exit
N9k-1# dir bootflash:
! Output omitted for brevity
    1175682    Nov 21 20:21:17 2017  shtechospf
    2677690    Nov 21 20:21:19 2017  shtechrouting_unicast
```

In addition, the Bash shell is used to install RPM packages on NX-OS. Use the **yum** command from the Bash shell to perform various RPM-related operations such as install, remove, and delete. Example 15-4 demonstrates how to view the list of all installed packages on the Nexus switch, as well as how to install and remove a package. In this example, the BFD package is installed and removed. Note that when the package is removed, the feature becomes unavailable from the NX-OS CLI; the packages determine which features are made available to NX-OS.

Example 15-4 *Installing and Removing RPM Packages from the Bash Shell*

```
bash-4.2$ sudo yum list installed | grep n9000
base-files.n9000                    3.0.14-r74.2                installed
bfd.lib32_n9000                     2.0.0-7.0.3.I6.1            installed
bgp.lib32_n9000                     2.0.0-7.0.3.I6.1            installed
container-tracker.lib32_n9000       2.0.0-7.0.3.I6.1            installed
core.lib32_n9000                    2.0.0-7.0.3.I6.1            installed
eigrp.lib32_n9000                   2.0.0-7.0.3.I6.1            installed
eth.lib32_n9000                     2.0.0-7.0.3.I6.1            installed
fcoe.lib32_n9000                    2.0.0-7.0.3.IFD6.1          installed
isis.lib32_n9000                    2.0.0-7.0.3.I6.1            installed
lacp.lib32_n9000                    2.0.0-7.0.3.I6.1            installed
linecard2.lib32_n9000               2.0.0-7.0.3.I6.1            installed
lldp.lib32_n9000                    2.0.0-7.0.3.I6.1            installed
ntp.lib32_n9000                     2.0.0-7.0.3.I6.1            installed
nxos-ssh.lib32_n9000                2.0.0-7.0.3.I6.1            installed
ospf.lib32_n9000                    2.0.0-7.0.3.I6.1            installed
perf-cisco.n9000_gdb                3.12-r0                     installed
platform.lib32_n9000                2.0.0-7.0.3.I6.1            installed
rip.lib32_n9000                     2.0.0-7.0.3.I6.1            installed
shadow-securetty.n9000_gdb          4.1.4.3-r1                  installed
snmp.lib32_n9000                    2.0.0-7.0.3.I6.1            installed
svi.lib32_n9000                     2.0.0-7.0.3.I6.1            installed
sysvinit-inittab.n9000_gdb          2.88dsf-r14                 installed
tacacs.lib32_n9000                  2.0.0-7.0.3.I6.1            installed
task-nxos-base.n9000_gdb            1.0-r0                      installed
telemetry.lib32_n9000               2.2.1-7.0.3.I6.1            installed
tor.lib32_n9000                     2.0.0-7.0.3.I6.1            installed
vtp.lib32_n9000                     2.0.0-7.0.3.I6.1            installed
bash-4.2$ sudo yum -y install bfd
Loaded plugins: downloadonly, importpubkey, localrpmDB, patchaction, patching,
protect-packages
groups-repo                                    | 1.1 kB    00:00 ...
localdb                                        | 951 B     00:00 ...
patching                                       | 951 B     00:00 ...
thirdparty                                     | 951 B     00:00 ...
Setting up Install Process
Resolving Dependencies
--> Running transaction check
---> Package bfd.lib32_n9000 0:2.0.0-7.0.3.I6.1 will be installed
--> Finished Dependency Resolution
```

```
Dependencies Resolved

================================================================================
 Package         Arch              Version               Repository        Size
Installing:
 bfd             lib32_n9000       2.0.0-7.0.3.I6.1      groups-repo       483 k

Transaction Summary
================================================================================
Install     1 Package

Total download size: 483 k
Installed size: 1.8 M
Downloading Packages:
Running Transaction Check
Running Transaction Test
Transaction Test Succeeded
Running Transaction
  Installing : bfd-2.0.0-7.0.3.I6.1.lib32_n9000
1/1
starting pre-install package version mgmt for bfd
pre-install for bfd complete
starting post-install package version mgmt for bfd
post-install for bfd complete

Installed:
  bfd.lib32_n9000 0:2.0.0-7.0.3.I6.1

Complete!

N9k-1(config)# feature bfd
Please disable the ICMP / ICMPv6 redirects on all IPv4 and IPv6 interfaces
running BFD sessions using the command below

'no ip redirects '
'no ipv6 redirects '
bash-4.2$ sudo yum -y erase bfd
Loaded plugins: downloadonly, importpubkey, localrpmDB, patchaction, patching,
protect-packages
Setting up Remove Process
Resolving Dependencies
--> Running transaction check
---> Package bfd.lib32_n9000 0:2.0.0-7.0.3.I6.1 will be erased
--> Finished Dependency Resolution
```

```
Dependencies Resolved

================================================================================
 Package      Arch           Version             Repository              Size
================================================================================
Removing:
 bfd          lib32_n9000    2.0.0-7.0.3.I6.1    @groups-repo            1.8 M

Transaction Summary
================================================================================
Remove        1 Package

Installed size: 1.8 M
Downloading Packages:
Running Transaction Check
Running Transaction Test
Transaction Test Succeeded
Running Transaction
  Erasing    : bfd-2.0.0-7.0.3.I6.1.lib32_n9000                           1/1
starting pre-remove package version mgmt for bfd
pre-remove for bfd complete

Removed:
  bfd.lib32_n9000 0:2.0.0-7.0.3.I6.1

Complete!

N9k-1(config)# feature bfd
                       ^
% Invalid command at '^' marker.
```

Guest Shell

The network paradigm has moved from hardware, software, and management network elements to extensible network elements. The built-in Python and Bash execution environments enable network operators to execute custom scripts in NX-OS environments using the Cisco-supplied APIs and classes to interact with some of the major NX-OS components. However, in some scenarios, network operators want to integrate third-party applications and host the application on NX-OS. To meet those needs, NX-OS provides a third-party application hosting framework that enables users to host their applications in a dedicated Linux user space environment. Network operators must use the Cisco Application Development Toolkit (ADT) to cross-compile their software and package it with a Linux root file system into a Cisco Open Virtual Appliance (OVA) package. These OVAs are then deployed on the NX-OS network element using the application hosting feature.

NX-OS software introduces the NX-OS Guest shell feature on the Nexus 9000 and Nexus 3000 series switches. The Guest shell is an open source and secure Linux environment for rapid third-party software development and deployment. The guestshell feature leverages the benefits of the Python and Bash execution environments and the NX-OS application hosting framework.

The Guest shell is enabled by default on Nexus 9000 and Nexus 3000. You can explicitly enable or destroy the guestshell feature on NX-OS. Table 15-1 describes the various guest shell commands.

Table 15-1 *Guest Shell Feature Commands*

Command	Description
guestshell enable	This CLI installs and enables the Guest shell service. When this command is enabled, you can enter the Guest shell using the **guestshell** command.
guestshell disable	This command disables the guest shell service. Access to the Guest shell then is also disabled.
guestshell destroy	The CLI deactivates and uninstalls the current guest shell. All system resources associated with the Guest shell return to the system.
guestshell reboot	The CLI deactivates and reactivates the current Guest shell.
guestshell run *command-line*	The CLI is used to execute a program inside a Guest shell, return the output, and exit the Guest shell.
guestshell sync	The CLI deactivates the current active Guest shell, syncs its root file system contents to the standby RP, and then reactivates the Guest shell on the active RP.
guestshell upgrade	The CLI deactivates and performs an upgrade of the current Guest shell using the OVA that is embedded within the booted system image. Upon successful upgrade, the Guest shell is reactivated.
guestshell resize	The CLI allows modification to the default or existing parameters related to the Guest shell, such as CPU, memory, and root file system parameters.
guestshell	The CLI is used to enter the Guest shell.

When the Guest shell is up and running, you can check the details using the command **show guestshell detail**. This command displays the path of the OVA file, the status of the Guest shell service, resource reservations, and the file system information of the

Guest shell. Example 15-5 displays the detailed information of the Guest shell on a Nexus 9000 switch.

Example 15-5 *Guest Shell Details*

```
N9k-1# show guestshell detail
Virtual service guestshell+ detail
  State                  : Activated
  Package information
    Name                 : guestshell.ova
    Path                 : /isanboot/bin/guestshell.ova
    Application
      Name               : GuestShell
      Installed version  : 2.1(0.0)
      Description        : Cisco Systems Guest Shell
    Signing
      Key type           : Cisco release key
      Method             : SHA-1
    Licensing
      Name               : None
      Version            : None
  Resource reservation
    Disk                 : 250 MB
    Memory               : 256 MB
    CPU                  : 1% system CPU

  Attached devices
    Type             Name          Alias
    ------------------------------------------
    Disk             _rootfs
    Disk             /cisco/core
    Serial/shell
    Serial/aux
    Serial/Syslog                  serial2
    Serial/Trace                   serial3
```

If the Guest shell does not come up, check the log for any error messages using the **show logging logfile** command. To troubleshoot issues with the Guest shell, use the command **show virtual-service [list]** to view both the status of the Guest shell and the resources the Guest shell is using. Example 15-6 displays the virtual service list and the resources being utilized by the current Guest shell on the Nexus 9000 switch.

Example 15-6 *Virtual Service List and Resource Utilization*

```
N9k-1# show virtual-service list
Virtual Service List:

Name                        Status              Package Name
--------------------------------------------------------------------
guestshell+                 Activated           guestshell.ova
N9k-1# show virtual-service

Virtual Service Global State and Virtualization Limits:

Infrastructure version : 1.9
Total virtual services installed : 1
Total virtual services activated : 1

Machine types supported    : LXC
Machine types disabled     : KVM

Maximum VCPUs per virtual service : 1

Resource virtualization limits:
Name                        Quota   Committed   Available
--------------------------------------------------------------------
system CPU (%)               20         1          19
memory (MB)                  3840       256        3584
bootflash (MB)               8192       250        4031
```

> **Note** If you cannot resolve the Guest shell problem, collect the output of **show virtual-service tech-support** and contact the Cisco Technical Assistance Center (TAC) for further investigation.

Python

With the networking industry's push toward software-defined networking (SDN), multiple doors have opened for integrating scripting and programming languages with network devices. Python has gained industry-wide acceptance as the programming language of choice. Python is a powerful and easy-to-learn programming language that provides efficient high-level data structures and object-oriented features. These features make it an ideal language for rapid application development on most platforms.

Python integration is available on most Nexus platforms and does not require the installation of any special license. The interactive Python interpreter is invoked from the CLI on Nexus platforms by typing the **python** command. On Nexus 9000 and Nexus 3000 platforms, Python can also be used through the Guest shell. After executing the **python** command, the user is placed directly into the Python interpreter. Example 15-7 demonstrates the use of the Python interpreter from both the CLI and the guest shell.

Example 15-7 *Python Interpreter from CLI and the Guest Shell*

```
N9k-1# python
Python 2.7.5 (default, Nov  5 2016, 04:39:52)
[GCC 4.6.3] on linux2
Type "help", "copyright", "credits" or "license" for more information.
>>> print "Hello World...!!!"
Hello World...!!!
N9k-1# guestshell
[admin@guestshell ~]$ python
Python 2.7.5 (default, Jun 17 2014, 18:11:42)
[GCC 4.8.2 20140120 (Red Hat 4.8.2-16)] on linux2
Type "help", "copyright", "credits" or "license" for more information.
>>> print "Hello Again..!!!"
Hello Again..!!!
```

Note Readers are advised to become familiar with the Python programming language. This chapter does not focus on writing specific Python programs, however; instead, it focuses on how to use Python on Nexus platforms.

In addition to the standard Python libraries, NX-OS provides the Cisco and CLI libraries, which you can import into your Python script to perform Cisco-specific functions on the Nexus switch. The Cisco library provides access to Cisco Nexus components. The CLI library provides the capability to execute commands from the Nexus CLI and return the result. Example 15-8 displays the package contents of both the Cisco and CLI libraries on NX-OS.

Example 15-8 *Cisco and CLI Python Libraries on NX-OS*

```
>>> import cisco
>>> help(cisco)
Help on package cisco:

NAME
    cisco

FILE
    /usr/lib64/python2.7/site-packages/cisco/__init__.py

PACKAGE CONTENTS
```

```
            acl
            bgp
            buffer_depth_monitor
            check_port_discards
            cisco_secret
            dohost
            feature
            history
            interface
            ipaddress
            key
            line_parser
            mac_address_table
            nxapi
            nxcli
            ospf
            routemap
            section_parser
            ssh
            system
            tacacs
            transfer
            vlan
            vrf

! Output omitted for brevity
>>> import cli
>>> help(cli)
Help on module cli:

NAME
    cli

FILE
    /usr/lib64/python2.7/site-packages/cli.py

FUNCTIONS
    cli(cmd)

    clid(cmd)

    clip(cmd)
```

Noninteractive Python scripts are created and saved in the bootflash:scripts/ directory and are invoked with the **source** [*script name*] command. Another option is to utilize the Guest shell to create and invoke a Python script. The first line of your Python script must include the path to the Python interpreter, which is /usr/bin/env. Example 15-9 provides a sample Python script to configure a loopback interface and also to list all the interfaces in UP state on the Nexus switch. This script is created and invoked from within the Guest shell environment.

Example 15-9 *Python Script to Print All Interfaces in UP State*

```
#!/usr/bin/env python

import sys
from cli import *
import json

cli ("conf t ; interface lo5 ; ip add 5.5.5.5/32")
print "\n***Configured interface loopback5***"
print "\n***Listing All interfaces on the device in UP state***\n"
intf_list = json.loads(clid ("show interface brief"))
i = 0
while i < len (intf_list['TABLE_interface']['ROW_interface']):
        intf = intf_list['TABLE_interface']['ROW_interface'][i]
        i += 1
        if intf['state'] == 'up':
                print intf['interface']

sys.exit(0)
[admin@guestshell ~]$ python test.py

***Configured interface loopback5***

***Listing All interfaces on the device in UP state***

mgmt0
Ethernet1/4
Ethernet1/5
Ethernet1/13
Ethernet1/14
Ethernet1/15
Ethernet1/16
Ethernet1/19
Ethernet1/32
Ethernet1/37
Ethernet2/1
```

```
port-channel10
port-channel101
port-channel600
loopback0
loopback5
loopback100
Vlan100
Vlan200
Vlan300
```

A Python script can also be invoked from an Embedded Event Manager (EEM) applet as part of the action statement. Because multiple actions can be performed per event, multiple Python scripts can be called at different action steps, providing flexibility in the logic used to build the EEM applet. Example 15-10 illustrates the configuration of an EEM applet that triggers the previous Python script from an action statement. In this example, because the Python script is configured within the Guest shell, the Python script in the EEM script is invoked from the Guest shell. If the Python script is present in the bootflash:source/ directory, the command **action** *number* **cli source python** *file-name* must be used.

Example 15-10 *Python Script Invoked from an EEM Applet*

```
N9k-1(config)# event manager applet link_monitor
N9k-1(config-applet)# event syslog pattern "IF_.*DOWN:"
N9k-1(config-applet)# action 1 cli guestshell python test.py
N9k-1(config-applet)# exit
```

NX-SDK

The NX-OS software development kit (NX-SDK) is a C++ plug-in library that allows custom, native applications to access NX-OS functions and infrastructure. Using the NX-SDK, you can create custom CLI commands, syslog messages, event handlers, and error handlers. An example of using this functionality would be creating your custom application to register with the route manager to receive routing updates from the routing information base (RIB) and then taking some action based on the presence of the route. Three primary requirements must be met for using NX-SDK:

- Docker
- Linux environment (Ubuntu 14.04 or higher, Centos 6.7 or higher)
- Cisco SDK (optional)

Note NX-SDK can also be integrated with Python. Thus, Cisco SDK is not required for Python applications.

The NX-SDK must be installed before it can be used in the development environment. The installation steps follow:

Step 1. Pull a docker image from https://hub.docker.com/r/dockercisco/nxsdk

Step 2. Set the environment variables as follows for a 32-bit environment:

   1. export ENXOS_SDK_ROOT=/enxos-sdk

   2. cd $ENXOS_SDK_Root

   3. source environment-setup-x86-linux

Step 3. Clone NX-SDK toolkit from GitHub.

   1. git clone https://github.com/CiscoDevNet/NX-SDK.git

Explore the API after forking the NX-SDK from GitHub and use it to create custom application packages to be installed on the Nexus switch.

Note When creating custom applications, refer to the documentation and custom sample application code available as part of the NX-SDK.

Once the applications are built, use the *rpm_gen.py* Python script to automatically generate the RPM package. The script is present in the /NX-SDK/scripts directory. When the RPM package is built, the RPM package can be copied to the Nexus Switch in the bootflash: directory, where the package is then installed on the Nexus switch for further use. Example 15-11 demonstrates the installation steps for an RPM package on the Nexus 9000 switch. This example demonstrates the sample RPM package named *customCliApp* that is available as part of the NX-SDK kit. To start a custom application, first enable **feature nxsdk**. Then add the custom application as a service using the command **nxsdk service-name** *app-name*. You can check the status of the application using the command **show nxsdk internal service**.

Example 15-11 *Installing a Custom RPM Package*

```
N9k-1# conf t
! Output omitted for brevity
Enter configuration commands, one per line. End with CNTL/Z.
N9k-1(config)# install add bootflash:customCliApp-1.0-1.0.0.x86_64.rpm
[####################] 100%
Install operation 1 completed successfully at Sun Nov 26 06:12:49 2017


N9k-1(config)# show install inactive
Boot Image:
        NXOS Image: bootflash:/nxos.7.0.3.I6.1.bin
```

```
Inactive Packages:
        customCliApp-1.0-1.0.0.x86_64

Inactive Base Packages:

N9k-1(config)# install activate customCliApp-1.0-1.0.0.x86_64
[####################] 100%
Install operation 2 completed successfully at Sun Nov 26 06:13:40 2017

N9k-1(config)# show install active
Boot Image:
        NXOS Image: bootflash:/nxos.7.0.3.I6.1.bin

Active Packages:
        customCliApp-1.0-1.0.0.x86_64

N9k-1(config)# feature nxsdk
N9k-1(config)# nxsdk service-name customCliApp
% This could take some time. "show nxsdk internal service" to check if your App
is Started & Runnning
N9k-1(config)# end
N9k-1# show nxsdk internal service

NXSDK Started/Temp unavailabe/Max services : 1/0/32
NXSDK Default App Path       : /isan/bin/nxsdk
NXSDK Supported Versions     : 1.0


Service-name    Base App      Started(PID)    Version    RPM Package
---------------------------------------------------------------------------
customCliApp    nxsdk_app1    VSH(not running)  1.0      customCliApp-1.0-1.0.0.x86_64
! Starting the application in the background
N9k-1# run bash sudo su
bash-4.2# /isan/bin/nxsdk/customCliApp &
[1] 8887
N9k-1# show nxsdk internal service

NXSDK Started/Temp unavailabe/Max services : 2/0/32
NXSDK Default App Path       : /isan/bin/nxsdk
NXSDK Supported Versions     : 1.0


Service-name    Base App      Started(PID)    Version    RPM Package
---------------------------------------------------------------------------
customCliApp    nxsdk_app1    VSH (8887)      1.0        customCliApp-1.0-1.0.0.x86_64
! Output omitted for brevity
```

Note In Example 15-11, the RPM package is installed using the Virtual shell (VSH). The RPM package can also be installed from the Bash shell.

If any failure or erroneous events occur with the custom application installation, you can check the NX-SDN event history logs using the command **show nxsdk internal event-history [events | error]**. Example 15-12 displays the event history logs for NX-SDK and highlights the logs that indicate the successful activation and startup of the application customCliApp.

Example 15-12 *NX-SDK Event History*

```
N9k-1# show nxsdk internal event-history events
! Output omitted for brevity
Process Event logs of NXSDK_MGR
06:16:16 nxsdk_mgr : Added confcheck capability for 1.0, en 1, counter: 1
06:16:16 nxsdk_mgr : Adding confcheck capability for 1.0, en 0, counter: 0
06:16:16 nxsdk_mgr : Done: start service customCliApp nxsdk_app1
06:16:15 nxsdk_mgr : Heartbeat sent while start service customCliApp, nxsdk_app1
06:16:14 nxsdk_mgr : Feature nxsdk_app1 not enabled, State: 2, Error: SUCCESS
(0x0), Reason: SUCCESS (0x40aa000a)
06:16:14 nxsdk_mgr : Config service name customCliApp
06:16:14 nxsdk_mgr : App: /isan/bin/nxsdk/customCliApp is linked to libnxsdk
06:16:14 nxsdk_mgr : App: /isan/bin/nxsdk/customCliApp, MaJor Version: 1,
Minor Version: 0
06:14:30 nxsdk_mgr : Received CLIS Done Callback
06:14:30 nxsdk_mgr : Initialized with all core components
06:14:30 nxsdk_mgr : Initialized with sdwrap
06:14:30 nxsdk_mgr : Request all commands from CLIS
06:14:30 nxsdk_mgr : Initialized with CLIS
06:14:30 nxsdk_mgr : All core components for NXSDK_MGR are UP
06:14:30 nxsdk_mgr : Core component "clis(261)" is Up
06:14:30 nxsdk_mgr : Received feature enable message from FM
06:14:30 nxsdk_mgr : Started NXSDK_MGR mts thread, pid 6864
06:14:30 nxsdk_mgr : Started NXSDK_MGR mq mts thread, pid 6865
06:14:30 nxsdk_mgr : NXSDK_MGR Main Done: await join before exiting
06:14:30 nxsdk_mgr : nxsdk_mgr_create_threads: ok
06:14:30 nxsdk_mgr : Query sysmgr for core comp status: clis(261)
06:14:30 nxsdk_mgr : Done with NXSDK_MGR stateless recovery
```

Note In addition to the event history logs, you can collect the output of **show tech nxsdk** if custom applications are failing to install or are not working.

NX-API

NX-OS provides an API known as the NX-API that enables you to interact with the switch using a standard request/response language. The traditional CLI was designed for human-to-switch interaction. Requests are made by typing a CLI command and receiving a response from the switch in the form of output to the client terminal. This response data is *unstructured* and requires the human operator to evaluate the output line by line to find the interesting piece of information in the output. Operators that use the traditional CLI interface to automate tasks through scripting are forced to follow the same data interpretation method by *screen-scraping* the output for the interesting data. This is not only inefficient, but also cumbersome because it requires output iteration and specific text matching through regular expressions.

The benefit of using the NX-API is the capability to send requests and receive responses that are optimized for machine-to-machine communication. In other words, when communicating through the NX-API, the request and response are formatted as *structured* data. The response received from the NX-API is provided as either Extensible Markup Language (XML) or JavaScript Object Notation (JSON). This is much more efficient and less error prone than parsing the entire human-readable CLI output for only a small percentage of interesting data. NX-API is used to obtain output from **show** commands, as well as to add or remove configuration, thus streamlining and automating operations and management in a large-scale network.

Communication between the client and NX-API running on the switch uses the Transport Control Protocol (TCP) and can be either Hypertext Transfer Protocol (HTTP) or Hypertext Transfer Protocol Secure (HTTPS), depending on the requirements. NX-API uses HTTP basic authentication. Requests must carry the username and password in the HTTP header. After a successful authentication, NX-API provides a session-based cookie using the name nxapi_auth. That session cookie should be included in subsequent NX-API requests. The privilege of the user is checked to confirm that the request is being made by a user with a valid username and password on the switch who also has the proper authorization for the commands being executed through the NX-API.

After successful authentication, you can start sending requests. The NX-API *request object* is either in JSON-RPC or a Cisco proprietary format. Table 15-2 describes the fields present in the JSON-RPC request object.

Table 15-2 *JSON-RPC Request Object Fields*

Field	Description
jsonrpc	A string specifying the version of the JSON-RPC protocol. It must be exactly "2.0".
method	A string containing the name of the method to be invoked. NX-API supports either of the following: "cli": **show** or configuration commands "cli_ascii": **show** or configuration commands, output without formatting

Field	Description
params	A structured value that holds the parameter values to be used during the invocation of the method. It must contain the following fields: "cmd": A CLI command "version": NX-API request version identifier
id	An optional identifier established by the client that must contain a string, a number, or a NULL value. If the user does not specify the id parameter, the server assumes that the request is simply a notification and provides no response.

Figure 15-1 shows an example JSON-RPC request object used to query the switch for its configured switch name.

JSON-RPC Format

```
[
 {
  "jsonrpc": "2.0",
  "method": "cli",
  "params": {
    "cmd": "show switchname",
    "version": 1
  },
  "id": 1
 }
]
```

Figure 15-1 *JSON-RPC Request Object*

The second type of request object is the Cisco proprietary format, which is either XML or JSON. Table 15-3 provides a description for the fields used in the Cisco proprietary request object.

Table 15-3 *Cisco Proprietary Request Object Fields*

Field	Description
version	Indicates the current NX-API version.
type	A string containing the type of command to be executed: cli_show: Used for **show** commands. cli_show_ascii: Used for **show** commands. Output is unformatted. cli_conf: Used for noninteractive configuration commands. bash: Used to execute noninteractive Bash commands on devices on which the Bash shell has been enabled.
chunk	Used to chunk the output of large **show** commands. A value of 0 indicates no chunk output; a value of 1 indicates that the output can be returned in multiple chunks.

Field	Description
sid	Valid when the response message is chunked. To retrieve the next chunk of a message, the user should send a request with the sid set to the sid in the previous response message.
input	The input can be one or multiple commands. Multiple commands should be separated with " ;" (a blank character followed by semicolon).
ouput_format	The expected output format of the request message (XML or JSON).

Figure 15-2 shows an example Cisco proprietary request object in both JSON and XML formats. This request object is used to query the switch for its configured switch name.

JSON Format

```
{
 "ins_api":{
   "version":"1.0",
   "type":"cli_show",
   "chunk":"0",
   "sid":"1",
   "input":"show switchname",
   "output_format":"json"
 }
}
```

XML Format

```
<?xml version="1.0"?>
<ins_api>
   <version>1.0</version>
   <type>cli_show</type>
   <chunk>0</chunk>
   <sid>sid</sid>
   <input>show switchname</input>
   <output_format>xml</output_format>
</ins_api>
```

Figure 15-2 *Cisco Proprietary Request Objects*

The request object is sent to the switch on the configured HTTP (TCP port 80) or HTTPS (TCP port 443) port. The received request object is validated by the web server and the appropriate software object is provided with the request. The response object is then sent back from the switch in either JSON-RPC or Cisco proprietary formats to the client. Table 15-4 provides the field descriptions of the JSON-RPC response object.

Table 15-4 *JSON-RPC Response Object Fields*

Field	Description
jsonrpc	This string specifies the version of the JSON-RPC protocol. It is exactly "2.0".
result	This field is included only for successful requests. The value of this field contains the requested CLI output.

Field	Description
error	This field is included only on an errored request. The error object contains the following fields: "code": An integer error code specified by the JSON-RPC specification "message": A human-readable string that corresponds to the error code "data": An optional structure that contains other useful information for the user.
id	This field contains the same value as the id field in the corresponding request object. If a problem occurred while parsing the id field in the request, this value is null.

Figure 15-3 shows an example JSON-RPC response object.

JSON-RPC Response Object

```
{
  "jsonrpc": "2.0",
  "result": {
    "body": {
      "hostname": "NX02"
    }
  },
  "id": 1
}
```

Figure 15-3 *JSON-RPC Response Object*

Table 15-5 describes the fields included in the Cisco proprietary response object.

Table 15-5 *Cisco Proprietary Response Object Fields*

Field	Description
version	The current NX-API version.
type	The type of command being executed.
sid	Session ID of the current response (valid only for chunked output).
outputs	Tag enclosing all of the commands' output.
output	Tag enclosing a single command output. If the type is cli_conf or bash, it contains output from all of the commands.
body	The body of the response to the command requested.
code	The error code of the command execution. Standard HTTP error codes are used.
msg	The error message associated with the error code.

Figure 15-4 shows an example Cisco proprietary response object in both JSON and XML formats.

JSON Format

```
{
  "ins_api":{
    "type":"cli_show",
    "version":"1.0",
    "sid":"eoc",
    "outputs":{
      "output":{
        "input":"show switchname",
        "msg":"Success",
        "code":"200",
        "body":{
          "hostname":"NX02"
        }
      }
    }
  }
}
```

XML Format

```
<?xml version="1.0"?>
<ins_api>
  <type>cli_show</type>
  <version>1.0</version>
  <sid>eoc</sid>
  <outputs>
    <output>
      <body>
        <hostname>NX02</hostname>
      </body>
      <input>show switchname</input>
      <msg>Success</msg>
      <code>200</code>
    </output>
  </outputs>
</ins_api>
```

Figure 15-4 *Cisco Proprietary Response Objects*

Multiple commands can be sent in a single request. For the JSON-RPC request object, this is done by linking an unlimited number of single JSON-RPC requests into a single JSON-RPC array. For the Cisco proprietary request object, up to 10 semicolon-separated commands can be linked in the *input object*. With either request object type, if a request fails for any reason, the subsequent requests are not executed.

The NX-API feature must be enabled in the global configuration of the switch using the **feature nxapi** command, as shown in the output of Example 15-13.

Example 15-13 *NX-API Feature Configuration*

```
NX-2# conf t
Enter configuration commands, one per line. End with CNTL/Z.
NX-2(config)# feature nxapi

NX-2# show nxapi
nxapi enabled
HTTP Listen on port 80
HTTPS Listen on port 443
```

Note The default HTTP and HTTPS ports are changed using the **nxapi http port** and **nxapi https port** configuration commands.

When the NX-API feature is enabled, you may authenticate and begin sending requests to the appropriate HTTP or HTTPS port. NX-OS also provides a sandbox environment for testing the functions of the API; this is accessed by using a standard web browser and connecting through HTTP to the switch management address.

Troubleshooting problems related to NX-API typically involve the TCP connection used to deliver the request and response messages between the switch and the client. The NX-OS ethanalyzer capture tool is used to troubleshoot connection issues from the client and confirm that the TCP three-way handshake is completed (see Example 15-14).

Example 15-14 *Ethanalyzer Capture of the Client Connection*

```
NX-2# ethanalyzer local interface mgmt capture-filter "tcp port 443" limit-captured-
  frames 0

Capturing on mgmt0
192.168.1.50 -> 192.168.1.201 TCP 52018 > https [SYN] Seq=0 Win=65535 Len=0
MSS=1460 WS=5 TSV=568065210 TSER=0
192.168.1.201 -> 192.168.1.50 TCP https > 52018 [SYN, ACK] Seq=0 Ack=1
Win=16768 Len=0 MSS=1460 TSV=264852 TSER=568065210
192.168.1.50 -> 192.168.1.201 TCP 52018 > https [ACK] Seq=1 Ack=1 Win=65535
Len=0 TSV=568065211 TSER=264852
192.168.1.50 -> 192.168.1.201 SSL Client Hello
192.168.1.201 -> 192.168.1.50 TLSv1.2 Server Hello, Certificate, Server Key
Exchange, Server Hello Done
192.168.1.50 -> 192.168.1.201 TCP 52018 > https [ACK] Seq=518 Ack=1294
Win=65535 Len=0 TSV=568065232 TSER=264852
192.168.1.50 -> 192.168.1.201 TLSv1.2 Client Key Exchange, Change Cipher Spec,
Hello Request, Hello Request
192.168.1.201 -> 192.168.1.50 TLSv1.2 Encrypted Handshake Message, Change
Cipher Spec, Encrypted Handshake Message
```

After confirming that the TCP session from the client is established, additional information about the NX-API communication with the client is found with the **show nxapi-server logs** command. The server logs in Example 15-15 show the connection attempt, as well as the details of the request that was received. The execution of the CLI command is also shown in the log file, which is helpful in identifying why a particular batch of commands is failing. Finally, the response object sent to the client is also provided.

Example 15-15 *NX-API Server Logs*

```
NX-2# show nxapi-server logs
ngx_http_cookie_set:627 2017 November 17 07:18:25.292 : creating cookie
ngx_http_ins_api_post_body_handler:549 2017 November 17 02:18:25.292 : Input
```

```
Message {
  "ins_api": {
    "version": "1.0",
    "type": "cli_show",
    "chunk": "0",
    "sid": "1",
    "input": "show switchname",
    "output_format": "json"
  }
}
parse_user_from_request:41 2017 November 17 02:18:25.292 : cookie had user
'admin'
parse_user_from_request:55 2017 November 17 02:18:25.292 : auth header had user
'admin'
pterm_idle_vsh_sweep:667 2017 November 17 02:18:25.292 : pterm_idle_vsh_sweep
pterm_get_vsh:710 2017 November 17 02:18:25.292 : vsh found: child_pid = 10558,
fprd = 0x98d0800, fpwr = 0x98d0968, fd = 14, user = admin, vdc id = 1
pterm_write_to_vsh:446 2017 November 17 02:18:25.292 : In vsh [14] Writing cmd
"show switchname | xml "
pterm_write_to_vsh:522 2017 November 17 02:18:25.302 : Cmd 'show switchname | xml
' returned with '0'
pterm_write_to_vsh:627 2017 November 17 02:18:25.302 : Done processing vsh output
(ret=0)
_ins_api_cli_cmd:288 2017 November 17 02:18:25.302 : Incorrect XML data,
replacing special characters
_ins_api_cli_cmd:304 2017 November 17 02:18:25.302 : found ns vdc_mgr and copied
it to blob vdc_mgr len 7
pterm_write_to_vsh:446 2017 November 17 02:18:25.302 : In vsh [14] Writing cmd
"end"
pterm_write_to_vsh:522 2017 November 17 02:18:25.304 : Cmd 'end' returned with
'0'
pterm_write_to_vsh:627 2017 November 17 02:18:25.304 : Done processing vsh output
(ret=0)
ngx_http_ins_api_post_body_handler:675 2017 November 17 02:18:25.304 : Sending
response {
    "ins_api":    {
        "type":     "cli_show",
        "version":    "1.0",
        "sid":    "eoc",
        "outputs":    {
            "output":    {
                "input":    "show switchname",
                "msg":    "Success",
                "code":    "200",
```

```
                    "body":    {
                        "hostname":     "NX02"
                    }
                }
            }
        }
    }
}
```

Note Any activity from the NX-API is logged in the switch accounting log just like in the traditional CLI. The username associated with the NX-API is listed in the accounting log as *nginx*.

In addition to the NX-API server logs, NX-OS has a detailed **show tech nxapi** command that provides the server logs in addition to the nginx web server logs from the Linux process.

Summary

Automation and programmability are the defining building blocks for the future of networking. Open NX-OS was conceived to meet the future needs of SDN and the desire for users to natively execute third-party applications directly on Nexus switches. Open NX-OS provides the architecture that allows network operators and developers to create and deploy custom applications on their network devices. Integration of the powerful Bash shell and Guest shell has made it easy to create scripts for automating tasks on Nexus switches. This chapter covered in detail how you can leverage the Bash shell and the Guest shell to deploy third-party applications. Integration of Python with NX-OS enables you to create dynamic applications that enhance the functionality and manageability of Nexus switches. In addition to Python support, Cisco provides the NX-SDK, which supports building applications in both the C++ and Python languages and compile them as RPM packages. Finally, this chapter covered NX-API, an API that enables users to interact with the Nexus switch using standard request/response language.

References

Programmability and Automation with Cisco Open NX-OS: https://www.cisco.com/c/dam/en/us/td/docs/switches/datacenter/nexus9000/sw/open_nxos/programmability/guide/Programmability_Open_NX-OS.pdf

NX-SDK: https://www.cisco.com/c/en/us/td/docs/switches/datacenter/nexus9000/sw/7-x/programmability/guide/b_Cisco_Nexus_9000_Series_NX-OS_Programmability_Guide_7x/b_Cisco_Nexus_9000_Series_NX-OS_Programmability_Guide_7x_chapter_011010.pdf

Index

Symbols

* (asterisk) in RegEx, 683
[] (brackets) in RegEx, 680
^ (caret) in RegEx, 679
[^] (caret in brackets) in RegEx, 681
, (comma) utility, 41
$ (dollar sign) in RegEx, 679–680
- (hyphen) in RegEx, 680–681
() (parentheses) in RegEx, 681–682
. (period) in RegEx, 682
| (pipe) in RegEx, 681–682
+ (plus sign) in RegEx, 682
? (question mark) in RegEx, 683
_ (underscore) in RegEx, 677–678
(*, G) join from NX-4 and NX-3 example, 865
802.1D standards, 219–220

A

access ports, 203–204
accounting log, 45–46, 91
ACL Manager, 570–576
ACLs (access control lists), 569–570
   ACL Manager, 570–576
   for BFD in hardware example, 700–702
   BGP network selection, 577
   formats example, 571–572
   IGP network selection, 576–577
   to match traffic on NX-1 example, 810
   for permitting BGP traffic example, 613
   programming and statistics for DAI example, 346–348
   statistics example, 572–573
   verifying, 613–615
action-on-failure for on-demand diagnostic tests example, 107
activating maintenance mode with custom profiles example, 730–731
active interfaces, verifying, 402–403
active query in EIGRP, 441–442
Active state, 604
Active/Standby redundancy mode, 29–34
AD (administrative distance), 600

address assignment (IPv6), 357–362
    DHCPv6 relay agent, 357–359
    DHCPv6 relay LDRA, 360–362
address families, 598–599
adjacency internal forwarding trace example, 162
adjacency manager clients example, 165
adjacency server mode in OTV, 907–912, 932–937
adjacency verification in OTV, 888–898
advanced verification of EIGRP neighbors example, 423
advertising community value example, 685–686
AFI (address-family identifier), 598–599
aggregate-address command, 634–635
allowed VLANs, 206
AM (Adjacency Manager), 160–175
anycast RP, configuring and verifying, 830–841
anycast traffic, 734
architecture of NX-OS, 8–9
    feature manager, 14–16
    file systems, 19–25
    kernel, 9
    line card microcode, 17–19
    Messages and Transactional Services (MTS), 11–12
    multicast architecture, 741–743
        CLI commands, 743
        CPU protection, 745–747
        implementation, 747–750
        replication, 744–745
    Persistent Storage Services (PSS), 13–14
    system manager (sysmgr), 9–11

area settings mismatches
    in IS-IS, 539–541
    in OSPF, 473–474
areas
    in IS-IS, 508–509
    in OSPF, 453
ARP (Address Resolution Protocol), 160–175
    ACL configuration and verification, 348–349
    dynamic ARP inspection (DAI), 345–349
    entry for multicast source example, 796
    event history example, 163–164
    event-history logs and buffer size example, 92
    ND-Cache event-history example, 916–917
    in OTV, 915–917
    synchronization in vPC, 291–292
    table example, 162
ARP-ND-Cache, 915–917
ASM (any source multicast), 785–787
    configuring, 787–788
    event-history and MROUTE state verification, 789–795
        platform verification, 795–799
    verifying, 788–789
ASN (autonomous system number), 597–598
ASN mismatch, 412–413
AS-Path access lists, 684
assert message (PIM), 778–779
asterisk (*) in RegEx, 683
asynchronous mode in BFD, 691–692
asynchronous mode with echo function in BFD, 693

attach module CLI usage from supervisor example, 18–19
attribute modifications for route-maps, 586
attributes (BGP), 637
authentication
   in EIGRP, 416–419
   in FabricPath, 302
   in IS-IS, 544–546
      on overlay interface, 905–907
   in OSPF, 478–482
automation, 949–950. *See also* programmability
   Open NX-OS, 950–951
   shells and scripting, 951
      bash shell, 951–957
      Guest shell, 957–960
      Python, 960–964
AS (autonomous system), 597
autorecovery (vPC), 289
auto-RP
   configuration on NX-3 example, 817–818
   configuring and verifying, 813–820
   event-history on NX-4 example, 819–820
   listener configuration on NX-2 example, 818–819
   mapping agent configuration on NX-4 example, 815–816

B

backup Layer 3 routing in vPC, 292–293
bad BGP updates, 622–623
baseline configuration

EIGRP (Enhanced Interior Gateway Protocol), 399–401
IS-IS (Intermediate System-to-Intermediate System), 518–520
OSPF (Open Shortest Path First), 456–458
bash shell, 51, 951–957
best path calculation in BGP, 636–639
BFD (bidirectional forwarding detection), 689–691, 944–945
   asynchronous mode, 691–692
   asynchronous mode with echo function, 693
   configuring and verifying sessions, 693–707
   control packet fields, 691–692
   with echo function configuration and verification example, 702–703
   event-history logs example, 696–697
   failure log example, 703
   failure reason codes, 703
   feature status example, 695
   for OTV IS-IS on site VLAN example, 944–945
   over port-channel example, 706–707
   over port-channel (micro session configuration) example, 706
   over port-channel per-link configuration example, 704–705
   session-based event-history example, 697–699
   transition history logs example, 699–700
bfd per-link command, 704–705
BGP (Border Gateway Protocol), 597–598
   address families, 598–599
   attributes detail example, 652–653

best path calculation, 636–639
best path selection example, 638–639
configuration and verification, 605–609
convergence, 646–649
event-history example, 674–675
event-history for inbound prefixes example, 666
event-history for outbound prefixes example, 667
filter-lists example, 670, 672–673
flaps due to MSS issue example, 628
and IBP redistribution example, 633–634
IPv6 peer troubleshooting, 621–622
keepalive debugs example, 619
logs collection, 687
loop prevention, 599–600
message sent and OutQ example, 625
messages
    KEEPALIVE, 602
    NOTIFICATION, 602
    OPEN, 601–602
    types of, 601
    UPDATE, 602
multipath, 640–643
neighbor states, 602–603
    Active, 604
    Connect, 603–604
    Established, 605
    Idle, 603
    OpenConfirm, 604
    OpenSent, 604
network selection, 577
path attributes (PA), 599

peer flapping troubleshooting, 622
    bad BGP updates, 622–623
    Hold Timer expired, 623–624
    Keepalive generation, 624–626
    MTU mismatches, 626–630
peering down troubleshooting, 609–610
    ACL and firewall verification, 613–615
    configuration verification, 610–611
    debug logfiles, 618–619
    notifications, 619–621
    OPEN message errors, 617–618
    reachability and packet loss verification, 611–613
    TCP session verification, 615–617
policy statistics for prefix-list example, 667–668
policy statistics for route-map example, 675
regex queries
    for AS _100 example, 678
    for AS _100_ example, 678
    with AS 40 example, 680
    for AS 100 example, 678
    for AS 300 example, 679
    with asterisk example, 683
    with brackets example, 680
    with caret example, 679
    with caret in brackets example, 681
    with dollar sign example, 680
    with hyphen example, 681
    with parentheses example, 682
    with period example, 682

broadcast optimization in OTV 981

with plus sign example, 682

with question mark example, 683

route advertisement, 631

with aggregation, 634–635

with default-information originate command, 636

with network statement, 631–633

with redistribution, 633–634

route filtering and route policies, 662–663

communities, 684–686

with filter lists, 669–673

looking glass and route servers, 687

AS-Path access lists, 684

with prefix lists, 663–669

regular expressions, 676–683

with route-maps, 673–676

route processing, 630–631

route propagation, 630–631

route refresh capability example, 656

route-map configuration example, 673–674

router ID (RID), 601

scaling, 649–650

maxas-limit command, 662

maximum-prefixes, 659–661

with route reflectors, 657–659

soft reconfiguration inbound versus route refresh, 654–657

with templates, 653–654

tuning memory consumption, 650–653

sessions, 600–601

table for regex queries example, 677

table on NX-2 example, 662–663

table output after prefix-list configuration example, 665

table output with route-map filtering example, 674

table with filter-list applied example, 670–671

template configuration example, 654

update generation process, 643–646

wrong peer AS notification message example, 617

BiDIR (Bidirectional), 799–803

configuring, 803–804

terminology, 800

verifying, 805–811

blocked switch ports

identification, 225–227

modifying location, 229–232

bloggerd, 47

bootstrap message (PIM), 777–778

bootup diagnostics, 98–99

Bourne-Again Shell (Bash), 951–957

BPDU (Bridge Protocol Data Unit), 220

filter, 244–245

guard, 243–244

guard configuration example, 243

brackets ([]) in RegEx, 680

BRIB and URIB route installation example, 648

bridge assurance, 250–252

configuration example, 250

engaging example, 251

brief review of MST status example, 237–238

broadcast domains, 198. *See also* VLANs (virtual LANs)

broadcast optimization in OTV, 877

broadcast traffic
   multicast traffic versus, 734-735
   in OTV, 917-918
BSR (bootstrap router), configuring and verifying, 820-830
   on NX-1 example, 822-823
   on NX-2 example, 826-827
   on NX-3 example, 825-826
   on NX-4 example, 824-825
buffered logging, 88-89

C

candidate RP advertisement message (PIM), 779
capture filters in Ethanalyzer, 65-67
capturing
   debug in logfile on NX-OS example, 90
   LACP packets with Ethanalyzer example, 265
   packets. *See* packet capture
caret (^) in RegEx, 679
caret in brackets ([^]) in RegEx, 681
CD (collision domain), 197-198
cd command, 20
changing
   LACP port priority example, 269
   MST interface cost example, 240
   MST interface priority example, 241
   OSPF reference bandwidth on R1 and R2 example, 503
   spanning tree protocol system priority example, 228-229
checking
   for feature manager errors example, 16
   feature manager state for feature example, 15

IS-IS metric configuration example, 555
Cisco and CLI Python libraries on NX-OS example, 961-962
Cisco proprietary request object fields, 969-970
Cisco proprietary response object fields, 971
classic metrics
   on all Nexus switches example, 436
   versus wide metrics
      in EIGRP, 433-439
      on NX-1 example, 435
clear bgp command, 654-657
clear ip mroute command, 748
CLI, 39-44
collecting show tech-support to investigate OSPF problem example, 45
comma (,) utility, 41
commands
   access port configuration, 203
   aggregate-address, 634-635
   bash shell, 951-957
   bfd per-link, 704-705
   clear bgp, 654-657
   clear ip mroute, 748
   CLI, 39-44
   conditional matching options, 583-584
   configure maintenance profile, 728-730
   debug bgp keepalives, 618-619
   debug bgp packets, 623
   debug bgp updates, 671-672
   debug ip bgp brib, 643-645
   debug ip bgp update, 643-645
   debug ip eigrp packets, 405-406

debug ip ospf, 464
debug ip pim data-register receive, 790
debug ip pim data-register send, 790
debug isis, 529–530
debug mmode logfile, 731
debug sockets tcp pcb, 156–157
default-information originate, 636
ethanalyzer local interface, 65
ethanalyzer local read, 68
feature bfd, 693
feature netflow, 74
feature nxapi, 972
file system commands
    dir bootflash: 21
    dir logflash: 24
    list of, 20
    show file logflash: 24–25
Guest shell, 957–960
IGMP snooping configuration parameters, 758–761
install all, 719
install all kickstart, 714–718
maxas-limit, 662
maximum-prefix, 659–661
for multicast traffic, 743
no configure maintenance profile, 728–730
no system mode maintenance, 724–725
python, 50, 960–961
redirection, 39
run bash, 51
show accounting log, 45–46
show bfd neighbors, 694–695, 704–705
show bfd neighbors detail, 702–703

show bgp, 606–607, 638–639
show bgp convergence detail, 648–649
show bgp event-history, 647–648
show bgp event-history detail, 642–643, 646, 665–667, 674–675
show bgp ipv4 unicast policy statistics neighbor, 675
show bgp policy statistics neighbor filter-list, 672
show bgp policy statistics neighbor prefix-list, 667–668
show bgp private attr detail, 652–653
show bgp process, 607–609
show cli list, 42–43
show cli syntax, 43
show clock, 82
show copp diff profile, 188
show cores, 29
show cores vdc-all, 108
show diagnostic bootup level, 99
show diagnostic content module, 101–103
show diagnostic ondemand setting, 106–107
show diagnostic result module, 103–105
show event manager policy internal, 85–86
show event manager system-policy, 84–85
show fabricpath conflict all, 310
show fabricpath isis adjacency, 304–305
show fabricpath isis interface, 303–304
show fabricpath isis topology, 306

show fabricpath isis vlan-range, 305–306
show fabricpath route, 307
show fabricpath switch-id, 303, 315
show fabricpath unicast routes vdc, 308–309
show fex, 126–128
show forwarding distribution ip igmp snooping vlan, 765
show forwarding distribution ip multicast route group, 797
show forwarding internal trace v4-adj-history, 162
show forwarding internal trace v4-pfx-history, 172–173
show forwarding ipv4 adjacency, 162–163
show forwarding ipv4 route, 173–174
show forwarding route, 173–174
show glbp, 386–388
show glbp brief, 386–388
show guestshell detail, 958–959
show hardware, 98
show hardware capacity interface, 113
show hardware flow, 76–77
show hardware internal cpu-mac eobc stats, 118–119
show hardware internal cpu-mac inband counters, 123
show hardware internal cpu-mac inband events, 122–123
show hardware internal cpu-mac inband stats, 119–122
show hardware internal dev-port-map, 797–798
show hardware internal errors, 114, 124
show hardware internal forwarding asic rate-limiter, 184–185
show hardware internal forwarding instance, 309
show hardware internal forwarding rate-limiter usage, 182–184
show hardware internal statistics module pktflow dropped, 116–118
show hardware mac address-table, 764
show hardware rate-limiter, 745–746
show hardware rate-limiters, 181–182
show hsrp brief, 373–374
show hsrp detail, 373–374
show hsrp group detail, 377–378
show incompatibility-all system, 713–714
show interface, 110–112, 193, 194, 203–204
show interface counters errors, 112–113
show interface port-channel, 261–262
show interface trunk, 204–205
show interface vlan 10 private-vlan mapping, 216
show ip access-list, 572–573
show ip adjacency, 165–166
show ip arp, 161–162, 796
show ip arp inspection statistics vlan, 345–346
show ip arp internal event-history, 163–164
show ip arp internal event-history event, 92
show ip dhcp relay, 337–338
show ip dhcp relay statistics, 337–338
show ip dhcp snooping, 342

show ip dhcp snooping binding, 342–343
show ip eigrp, 404
show ip eigrp interface, 402, 415–416
show ip eigrp neighbor detail, 410–411
show ip eigrp topology, 395, 398
show ip eigrp traffic, 405
show ip igmp groups, 845–846
show ip igmp interface, 853–854
show ip igmp interface vlan, 768–769
show ip igmp internal event-history debugs, 769
show ip igmp internal event-history igmp-internal, 769–770
show ip igmp route, 769
show ip igmp snooping groups, 845–846
show ip igmp snooping groups vlan, 764
show ip igmp snooping internal event-history vlan, 766
show ip igmp snooping mrouter, 854–855
show ip igmp snooping otv groups, 935
show ip igmp snooping statistics, 864–865
show ip igmp snooping statistics global, 767
show ip igmp snooping statistics vlan, 767–768, 934–935
show ip igmp snooping vlan, 757, 763–764
show ip interface, 374
show ip mroute, 770–771, 794–795, 892–893, 932
show ip mroute summary, 894

show ip msdp internal event-history route, 837–838
show ip msdp internal event-history tcp, 837–838
show ip msdp peer, 835–836
show ip ospf, 461
show ip ospf event-history, 464–465
show ip ospf interface, 461, 475–476
show ip ospf internal event-history adjacency, 47
show ip ospf internal event-history rib, 169–170
show ip ospf internal txlist urib, 169
show ip ospf neighbors, 458–459
show ip ospf traffic, 463
show ip pim df, 805–806, 809
show ip pim group-range, 829–830
show ip pim interface, 782–783, 852–853
show ip pim internal event-history bidir, 806
show ip pim internal event-history data-header-register, 840–841
show ip pim internal event-history data-register-receive, 790
show ip pim internal event-history hello, 783–784
show ip pim internal event-history join-prune, 792–793, 806–807, 808, 846–847, 858, 865
show ip pim internal event-history null-register, 790, 791, 840–841, 857
show ip pim internal event-history rp, 819–820, 827–828
show ip pim internal event-history vpc, 857, 865–867
show ip pim internal vpc rpf-source, 856–857, 866–867

show ip pim neighbor, 781
show ip pim rp, 814–819, 822–827
show ip pim statistics, 783, 828–829
show ip prefix-list, 580–581
show ip route, 171, 419–421
show ip sla configuration, 324
show ip sla statistics, 323
show ip traffic, 154–156, 611–612
show ip verify source interface, 349–350
show ipv6 dhcp guard policy, 369–370
show ipv6 dhcp relay statistics, 358–359
show ipv6 icmp vaddr, 378–379
show ipv6 interface, 378–379
show ipv6 nd, 355–356
show ipv6 nd raguard policy, 364
show ipv6 neighbor, 354
show ipv6 snooping policies, 369–370
show isis, 525–526
show isis adjacency, 520–523
show isis database, 558–560
show isis event-history, 530–531
show isis interface, 523–525, 526–527
show isis traffic, 528–529
show key chain, 417, 546
show lacp counters, 262–263
show lacp internal info interface, 263–264
show lacp neighbor, 264
show lacp system-identifier, 264
show logging log, 88
show logging logfile, 959
show logging onboard internal kernel, 148

show logging onboard module 10 status, 23
show mac address-table, 198–199
show mac address-table dynamic vlan, 796, 919–920, 923
show mac address-table multicast, 764
show mac address-table vlan, 305–306
show maintenance profile, 727–728
show maintenance timeout, 726
show module, 96–98, 708
show monitor session, 56–57
show ntp peer-status, 82
show ntp statistics, 83
show nxapi-server logs, 973–975
show nxsdk internal event-history, 967
show nxsdk internal service, 965–966
show otv adjacency, 889, 906–907, 910
show otv arp-nd-cache, 916
show otv data-group, 931
show otv internal adjacency, 890
show otv internal event-history arp-nd, 916–917
show otv isis database, 899
show otv isis database detail, 900–902
show otv isis hostname, 899
show otv isis interface overlay, 906
show otv isis internal event-history adjacency, 898
show otv isis internal event-history iih, 896–897
show otv isis internal event-history spf-leaf, 902–903

commands 987

show otv isis ip redistribute mroute, 930, 934
show otv isis mac redistribute route, 903–904
show otv isis redistribute route, 921–922
show otv isis site, 895–896
show otv isis site statistics, 904–905
show otv isis traffic overlay0, 904, 906
show otv mroute, 928, 929
show otv mroute detail, 929–930, 931, 933
show otv overlay, 888
show otv route, 902, 923
show otv route vlan, 921
show otv site, 889–890, 895, 911–912
show otv vlan, 891–892, 920
show policy-map interface, 114
show policy-map interface control-plane, 189–190
show policy-map system type network-qos, 194–195
show port-channel compatibility-parameters, 272
show port-channel load-balance, 273–274
show port-channel summary, 260–261, 272, 704–705
show port-channel traffic, 273
show processes log pid, 29
show processes log vdc-all, 109–110
show queueing interface, 114
show queuing interface, 193, 194
show routing clients, 167–168
show routing event-history, 647–648
show routing internal event-history msgs, 169–170

show routing ip multicast event-history rib, 770
show routing ip multicast source-tree detail, 868–869
show routing memory statistics, 171
show run aclmgr, 572
show run all | include glean, 161
show run copp all, 186
show run netflow, 76
show run otv, 908–909, 917–918
show run pim, 781
show run sflow, 79
show run vdc, 137
show running-config, 45
show running-config copp, 188–189
show running-config diff, 43–44
show running-config mmode, 730
show running-config sla sender, 324
show sflow, 79–80
show sflow statistics, 80
show snapshots, 725–726
show sockets client detail, 157–158
show sockets connection tcp, 615–616
show sockets connection tcp detail, 157
show sockets internal event-history events, 616–617
show sockets statistics all, 159
show spanning-tree, 225–227, 237–238, 281–282
show spanning-tree inconsistentports, 246, 252
show spanning-tree interface, 227
show spanning-tree mst, 238–239
show spanning-tree mst configuration, 237

show spanning-tree mst interface, 239–240

show spanning-tree root, 222–224, 225

show spanning-tree vlan, 897–898

show system inband queuing statistics, 150

show system internal access-list input entries detail, 190

show system internal access-list input statistics, 340–341, 348–349, 359, 367–368, 700–702

show system internal access-list interface, 339–340, 367–368, 700–702

show system internal access-list interface e4/2 input statistics module 4, 573–574

show system internal aclmgr access-lists policies, 574–575

show system internal aclmgr ppf node, 575–576

show system internal adjmgr client, 164–165

show system internal adjmgr internal event-history events, 167

show system internal bfd event-history, 695–699

show system internal bfd transition-history, 699–700

show system internal copp info, 191–192

show system internal eltm info interface, 195

show system internal ethpm info interface, 175–178, 195

show system internal fabricpath switch-id event-history errors, 310

show system internal feature-mgr feature action, 16

show system internal feature-mgr feature bfd current status, 695

show system internal feature-mgr feature state, 15

show system internal fex info fport, 128–130

show system internal fex info sat port, 128

show system internal flash, 13–14, 24, 88–89

show system internal forwarding adjacency entry, 173–174

show system internal forwarding route, 173–174

show system internal forwarding table, 350

show system internal mmode logfile, 731

show system internal mts buffer summary, 145–146

show system internal mts buffers detail, 146–147

show system internal mts event-history errors, 148

show system internal mts sup sap description, 146–147

show system internal mts sup sap sap-id, 11–12

show system internal mts sup sap stats, 147–148

show system internal pixm info ltl, 765

show system internal pktmgr client, 151–152

show system internal pktmgr interface, 152–153

show system internal pktmgr stats, 153

show system internal port-client event-history port, 179

show system internal port-client link-event, 178–179
show system internal qos queueing stats interface, 114–115
show system internal rpm as-path-access-list, 672–673
show system internal rpm clients, 588–589
show system internal rpm event-history rsw, 588, 672–673
show system internal rpm ip-prefix-list, 589, 668–669
show system internal sal info database vlan, 350
show system internal sflow info, 80
show system internal sup opcodes, 147
show system internal sysmgr gsync-pending, 32
show system internal sysmgr service, 10
show system internal sysmgr service all, 10, 11, 146
show system internal sysmgr service dependency srvname, 142–143
show system internal sysmgr state, 31–32, 710–711
show system internal ufdm event-history debugs, 171–172
show system internal vpcm info interface, 318–320
show system mode, 720–722
show system redundancy ha status, 709
show system redundancy status, 29–30, 708–709
show system reset-reason, 29, 110
show tech adjmgr, 167
show tech arp, 167
show tech bfd, 704
show tech bgp, 687
show tech dhcp, 362
show tech ethpm, 179
show tech glbp, 390
show tech hsrp, 379
show tech netstack, 617, 687
show tech nxapi, 975
show tech nxsdk, 967
show tech routing ipv4 unicast, 687
show tech rpm, 687
show tech track, 334
show tech vpc, 294
show tech vrrp, 385
show tech vrrpv3, 385
show tech-support, 44–45, 320, 749–750
show tech-support detail, 124, 141
show tech-support eem, 87
show tech-support eltm, 195
show tech-support ethpm, 130, 195
show tech-support fabricpath, 310
show tech-support fex, 130
show tech-support ha, 719
show tech-support issu, 719
show tech-support mmode, 731
show tech-support netflow, 78
show tech-support netstack, 160
show tech-support pktmgr, 160
show tech-support sflow, 80
show tech-support vdc, 141
show tunnel internal implicit otv brief, 890–891
show tunnel internal implicit otv detail, 922, 937
show tunnel internal implicit otv tunnel_num, 891
show udld, 247–248

show udld internal event-history errors, 248–249
show vdc detail, 137–138
show vdc internal event-history, 140–141
show vdc membership, 139–140
show vdc resource detail, 138–139
show vdc resource template, 131–132
show virtual-service, 959–960
show virtual-service tech-support, 960
show vlan, 201–202, 214
show vlan private-vlan, 210–211
show vpc, 280–281, 284–285, 314–315
show vpc consistency-parameters, 285–286
show vpc consistency-parameters vlan, 286–287
show vpc consistency-parameters vpc, 287
show vpc orphan-ports, 288
show vpc peer-keepalive, 282–283
show vrrp, 380–381
show vrrp statistics, 381–382
show vrrpv3, 383–384
show vrrpv3 statistics, 384–385
soft-reconfiguration inbound, 654–657
source, 963
system maintenance mode always-use-custom-profile, 728–730
system mode maintenance, 720–722
system mode maintenance dont-generate-profile, 730–731
system mode maintenance on-reload reset-reason, 726–727
system mode maintenance timeout, 726
system switchover, 711–712
test packet-tracer, 71–72
communities in BGP, 684–686
community PVLANs, 207, 212–215
comparing before and after maintenance snapshots example, 725–726
complex matching route-maps example, 585
conditional matching, 569
  with ACLs, 569–570
    ACL Manager, 570–576
    BGP network selection, 577
    IGP network selection, 576–577
  with prefix lists, 580–581
  with prefix matching, 578–579
  route-maps, 582–584
    command options, 583–584
    complex matching, 585–586
    multiple match conditions, 584–585
configuration checkpoints, 48–49
configuration rollbacks, 48–49
configure maintenance profile command, 728–730
configuring
  ARP ACLs, 348–349
  ASM (any source multicast), 787–788
  AS-path access list, 684
  auto-RP configuration on NX-3, 817–818
  auto-RP listener configuration on NX-2, 818–819
  auto-RP mapping agent configuration on NX-4, 815–816

BFD (bidirectional forwarding detection)
  with echo function, 702–703
  for OSPF example, 694
  over port-channel per-link, 704–705
  sessions, 693–707
BGP (Border Gateway Protocol), 605–609
  route-map, 673–674
  table output after prefix-list, 665
  template, 654
BiDIR (Bidirectional), 803–804
BPDU guard, 243
bridge assurance, 250
BSR (bootstrap router)
  on NX-1, 822–823
  on NX-2, 826–827
  on NX-3, 825–826
  on NX-4, 824–825
console logging example, 88
CoPP NetFlow, 78
custom maintenance profiles example, 728–730
DAI (dynamic ARP inspection), 345–346
DHCP relay, 336–337
DHCP snooping, 342
DHCPv6 guard, 369–370
dynamic ARP inspection, 346
EEM, 85–86
EIGRP (Enhanced Interior Gateway Protocol)
  baseline configuration, 399–401
  with custom K values, 414
  with modified hello timer, 416
  with passive interfaces, 404–405
  stub configuration, 424
error recovery service, 244
ERSPAN, 59
FabricPath, 300–302
FEX (Fabric Extender), 126
FHRP localization configuration on NX-2, 938–939
filtering SPAN traffic, 57
GLBP (Gateway Load-Balancing Protocol), 386
HSRP (Hot Standby Routing Protocol), 372–373
HSRPv6, 377
IP SLA ICMP echo probe, 323
IP SLA TCP connect probe, 328
IP source guard, 350
IPv6 RA guard, 364
IPv6 snooping, 367
IS-IS (Intermediate System-to-Intermediate System)
  baseline configuration, 518–520
  L2 route-leaking, 564–565
  metric transition mode, 555
  with passive interfaces, 528
  routing and topology table after static metric configuration, 552–553
jumbo MTU system, 193
L1 route propagation example, 560
L2 and L3 rate-limiter and exception, 184–185
LACP fast and verifying LACP speed state example, 270
Layer 3 routing over vPC example, 294

loop guard, 246
with maximum hops example, 425
maximum links example, 267
minimum number of port-channel member interfaces example, 265–266
MST (Multiple Spanning-Tree Protocol), 236–237
multicast vPC
  on NX-3, 851–852
  on NX-4, 850–851
NetFlow, 73–77
  flow exporter definition, 75–76
  flow monitor and interface, 76
  flow monitor definition, 76–77
  flow record definition, 74–75
  sampler and interface, 78
NTP, 81–82
NX-1 redistribution, 431, 488, 567
NX-1 to redistribute 172.16.1.0/24 into OSPF, 489–490
NX-2 redistribution, 587
NX-2's PBR, 592–593
NX-3 anycast RP with MSDP, 832–833
NX-4 anycast RP with MSDP, 834–835
NX-API feature configuration, 972
NX-OS BGP, 606
on-reload reset-reason, 726–727
OSPF (Open Shortest Path First)
  baseline configuration, 456–458
  to ignore interface MTU example, 470
  network types example, 476
  with passive interfaces, 462–463

OTV (Overlay Transport Virtualization), 882–885
  adjacency server on NX-2, 908–909
  ED adjacency server mode on NX-4, 908
  internal interface, 882
  IS-IS authentication example, 905
  join interface, 883
  next-hop adjacency tracking example, 946
  overlay interface, 885
packet tracer, 71–72
PIM (Protocol Independent Multicast)
  anycast RP on NX-4, 840
  ASM on NX-1, 788
  auto-RP candidate-RP on NX-1, 814–815
  BiDIR on NX-1, 803–804
  sparse mode on interface example, 781
  SSM on NX-2, 843–844
  SSM on NX-4, 844–845
  static RP on NX-3, 812
PIM RP, 811–812
  anycast RP, 830–841
  Auto-RP, 813–820
  BSR (bootstrap router), 820–830
  static RP, 812–813
port down upon MAC move notification example, 242–243
port-channels, 259–260
promiscuous PVLAN SVI example, 216
route-maps, 586
sample distribute list configuration, 427

sample MST configuration on NX-1, 236–237
sample offset list configuration, 428
scale factor configuration, 190, 191–192
scheduler job example, 50
sFlow, 79
SPAN (Switched Port Analyzer), 55–56
SPAN-on-drop, 61
SPAN-on-latency, 61
SSM (source specific multicast), 843–845
syslog logging, 90
trunk port, 204
UDLD, 247
unicast RPF, 351–352
URPF (Unicast Reverse Path Forwarding), 351–352
VDC (Virtual Device Contexts), 133–134
virtual link, 484
vPC (virtual port-channel), 278–280
  autorecovery example, 289
  peer-gateway example, 291
vPC+, 311–314
vPC-connected receiver, 861–869
vPC-connected source, 849–861
VRRP (Virtual Router Redundancy Protocol), 380
VRRPv3 migration, 382
confirming
  BFD neighbor on site VLAN example, 945
  IS-IS interfaces, 523–526
  OBFL is enabled on module example, 23
  OSPF interfaces, 460–461
  redundancy and synchronization state example, 31–32
confusing EIGRP ASN configuration example, 412
Connect state, 603–604
consistency checkers, 49–50
  vPC, 283–287
console logging, 88
control plane (OTV), 885–886
  adjacency server mode, 907–912
  adjacency verification, 888–898
  authentication, 905–907
  CoPP, 912–913
  IS-IS topology table, 898–905
  multicast mode, 887–888
convergence in BGP, 646–649
convergence problems, 439–441
  active query, 441–442
  stuck in active (SIA) queries, 443–446
CoPP (control plane policing), 179–192
  classes, 745
  NetFlow configuration and verification example, 78
  strict policy on Nexus example, 186–188
copy command, 20
core interfaces (FabricPath), verifying, 303–304
corrupt BGP update message example, 623
count or wc utility usage example, 40
count utility, 40
CPU protection, 745–747
creating and debugging base shell scripts example, 953–954

CSMA/CD (Carrier Sense Multiple Access/Collision Detect), 197

custom maintenance profiles, 727–731

D

DAI (dynamic ARP inspection), 345–349
   ACL programming, 346–348
   ARP ACLs, 348–349
   configuring and verifying, 345–346

data plane (OTV)
   ARP resolution and ARP-ND-Cache, 915–917
   broadcasts, 917–918
   encapsulation, 913–915
   multicast traffic with multicast enabled transport, 924–932
   multicast traffic with unicast transport, 932–937
   selective unicast flooding, 918–919
   unicast traffic with multicast enabled transport, 919–924

Dead Interval Time, 476–478

debug bgp keepalives command, 618–619

debug bgp packets command, 623

debug bgp updates command, 671–672

debug bgp updates output example, 671–672

debug commands with filter example, 649

debug filters, 47–48

debug ip bgp brib command, 643–645

debug ip bgp update command, 643–645

debug ip eigrp packets command, 405–406

debug ip ospf command, 464

debug ip pim data-register receive command, 790

debug ip pim data-register send command, 790

debug isis command, 529–530

debug log file and debug filter example, 47–48

debug logfiles, 47–48, 90, 618–619

debug mmode logfile command, 731

debug sockets tcp pcb command, 156–157

debugs for BGP update and route installation in BRIB example, 644–645

decimal format, converting to dot-decimal, 473

dedicated OTV broadcast group example, 917–918

default FA in OSPF type-5 LSA example, 490

default-information originate command, 636

delete command, 20

dense mode (DM), 771–772

dependencies in feature manager, 14

deployment models for OTV, 881

deployment of community PVLANs on NX-1 example, 213

deployment of isolated PVLAN on NX-1 example, 209–210

detailed VLAN 115 IGMP snooping group membership example, 764

detecting inconsistent port state example, 251

determining current supervisor redundancy state example, 29–30 determining the SoC instances on module 3 of NX-2 example, 797–798

DF election message (PIM), 779–780

DHCP (Dynamic Host Configuration Protocol)
  relay configuration example, 337
  snooping ACL programming example, 343–345
  snooping binding database example, 343
  snooping configuration and validation example, 342

DHCP relay, 335–341
  ACL verification, 339–341
  configuring, 336–337
  verifying, 337–338

DHCP snooping, 341–345
  ACL programming, 343–345
  binding database, 342–343
  configuring, 342

DHCPv6
  guard configuration and policy verification example, 369–370
  relay ACL line card statistics example, 359
  relay statistics example, 358–359

DHCPv6 Guard, 368–370

DHCPv6 relay agent, 357–359

DHCPv6 relay LDRA, 360–362

diagnostic tests. *See* GOLD (Generic Online Diagnostic) tests

diff utility, 40

different OSPF areas on Ethernet1/1 interfaces example, 472

different OSPF hello timers example, 477

dir bootflash: command, 21

dir command, 20

dir logflash: command, 24

DIS (Designated Intermediate System), 516–517, 543–544

disabling BGP client-to-client reflection example, 658

discontiguous networks in OSPF, 482–485

display filters in Ethanalyzer, 65–67

displaying
  active EIGRP interfaces example, 402
  EIGRP neighbors example, 401
  IS-IS neighbors example, 521
  IS-IS neighbors with summary and detail keywords example, 521–522
  OSPF neighbors example, 459

distribute list, 426–427

dollar sign ($) in RegEx, 679–680

domains (vPC), 275–276, 280–282

dot-decimal format, converting decimal to, 473

drop threshold for syslog logging example, 190–191

DRs (Designated Routers), 452, 474–476

dummy PIM hello captured in Ethanalyzer example, 926–927

duplicate multicast packets, 870

duplicate router-ID example, 471

duplicate router-ID in OSPF, 485–487

duplicate system-ID example, 539

duplicate System-ID in IS-IS, 546–549

dynamic ARP inspection configuration and verification example, 346

dynamic tunnel encapsulation
    for multicast traffic example, 937
    for NX-6 example, 922

E

EBGP (external BGP), 600, 640–643
echo command, 951–952
EEM (Embedded Event Manager), 47, 50, 83–87, 107, 964
    configuration and verification example, 85–86
    system policy example, 84–85
    with TCL script example, 86
egrep utility, 41–42
egress multicast replication, 744–745
EIGRP (Enhanced Interior Gateway Protocol), 393–394
    adjacency dropping due to retry limit example, 410
    adjacency failure due to holding timer example, 415
    configuring
        baseline configuration, 399–401
        with custom K values example, 414
        with modified hello timer example, 416
        with passive interfaces example, 404–405
    convergence problems, 439–441
        active query, 441–442
        stuck in active (SIA) queries, 443–446
    interface level authentication example, 418
    neighbor adjacency troubleshooting, 401–402
        ASN mismatch, 412–413
        authentication, 416–419
        connectivity with primary subnet, 409–412
        Hello and hold timers, 414–416
        K values mismatch, 413–414
        passive interfaces, 403–405
        verifying active interfaces, 402–403
        verifying EIGRP packets, 405–409
    packet debugs example, 406
    packet types, 399
    path attributes for 10.1.1.0/24 example, 428–429
    path metric calculation, 396–398
    path selection and missing routes troubleshooting, 419–421
        classic metrics versus wide metrics, 433–439
        distribute list, 426–427
        hop counts, 424–425
        interface-based settings, 430
        load balancing, 421
        offset lists, 427–430
        redistribution, 430–432
        stub routers, 421–424
    process level authentication example, 419
    reference topology, 394
    route-maps, 587
    stub configuration example, 424
    terminology, 394
    topology for 10.1.1.0/24 network example, 440–441
    topology for specific prefix example, 398
    topology table, 395–396

traffic counters with SIA queries and replies example, 444–445

traffic statistics example, 405

ELAM (embedded logic analyzer module), 19

email utility, 42

Empty echo, 249

emulated switches

   in FabricPath, 310–311

   verifying, 315

enabling

   authentication on FP ports example, 302

   bash-shell feature and using bash commands example, 952

   BFD feature example, 693

   FabricPath feature example, 301

   FP core ports, FP VLAN, and CE edge ports example, 301

   MAC address lookup mode example, 757

   NetFlow, 74

   vPC ARP synchronization example, 292

encapsulation in OTV data plane, 913–915

encrypted authentication in OSPF, 480–482

entering bash shell example, 51

EOBC status and error counters example, 119

EPLD (electronic programmable logic device), 26

error recovery service configuration and demonstration example, 244

ERSPAN (Encapsulated Remote SPAN), 57–60

   configuring, 59

   session verification, 59–60

Established state, 605

Ethanalyzer, 63–71

   capture and display filters, 65–67

   capture example, 68

   capture of client connection example, 973

   capture of IGMP messages on NX-2 example, 767

   GLBP (Gateway Load-Balancing Protocol) and, 388–390

   HSRP (Hot Standby Routing Protocol) and, 375–376

   for HSRPv6, 379

   IPv6 Neighbor Discovery, 354–355

   multicast traffic examples, 871

   write and read example, 69–70

ethanalyzer local interface command, 65

ethanalyzer local read command, 68

EtherChannels. *See* port-channels

Ethernet protocol, 197

EthPM (Ethernet Port Manager), 175–179

event history logs, 16, 46–47, 92, 749–750, 789–795

   ARP (Address Resolution Protocol)

     buffer size example, 92

     ND-Cache event-history example, 916–917

   auto-RP on NX-4 example, 819–820

   BFD (bidirectional forwarding detection), 696–697

     session-based event-history example, 697–699

   BGP (Border Gateway Protocol), 674–675

     for inbound prefixes example, 666

     multipath example, 643

for outbound prefixes example, 667

update generation example, 646

BiDIR join-prune

on NX-1, 808

on NX-4, 807

BiDIR on NX-4 example, 806

for hello messages example, 784

hello packet visibility from IS-IS, 530–531

IGMP (Internet Group Management Protocol)

internal events example, 770

snooping VLAN event-history example, 766

IS-IS (Intermediate System-to-Intermediate System), event-history indicates different areas example, 540

and MROUTE state verification, 789–795, 799

MSDP on NX-4, 837–838

null register on NX-4 example, 841

NX-1 and NX-2 example, 536–537

NX-1 IGMP debugs example, 769

NX-1 IS-IS adjacency with MTU mismatch example, 538

NX-1 OSPF adjacency with MTU mismatch example, 469

NX-2 OTV IS-IS IIH example, 896

NX-4 OTV IS-IS IIH example, 897

OSPF (Open Shortest Path First), with mismatched area flags example, 473

OTV (Overlay Transport Virtualization)

IS-IS adjacency event-history example, 898

IS-IS SPF event-history example, 903

for RP from NX-4 with BSR example, 827–828

RPM (Route Policy Manager)

client for prefix-lists example, 668–669

viewing, 588

spanning tree protocol, viewing, 234

SSM join-prune

on NX-2, 847

on NX-4, 847

UDLD example, 248–249

examining

accounting log example, 45–46

interface MTU example, 538

interface's MTU example, 470

MTS queue for SAP example, 12

NX-2's L2 detailed LSPDB example, 559–560

exclude utility, 42

executing

command with multiple arguments example, 41

consistency checker example, 49

external OSPF path selection for type-1 networks example, 497

external routes

on NX-2 example, 432

in OSPF, 495–499

F

FabricPath. *See also* vPC+

advantages of, 294–296

authentication, 302

configuring, 300–302

devices, 310

emulated switches, 310–311
packet forwarding, 297–300
terminology, 296–297
topology information example, 306
verifying, 303–310
    core interfaces, 303–304
    IS-IS adjacency, 304–305
    software table in hardware, 308–309
    switch-IDs, 303, 310
    topologies, 306
    in URIB, 307
    VLANs (virtual LANs), 305–306

failure detection in OTV, 944–946. *See also* BFD (bidirectional forwarding detection)
feature bash-shell command, 951–952
feature bfd command, 693
feature dependency hierarchy, 142–143
feature manager, 14–16
feature netflow command, 74
feature nxapi command, 972
feature sets, installing, 15
FEX (Fabric Extender), 2–3, 124–130
    configuring, 126
    detail example, 127–128
    internal information example, 128–130
    jumbo MTU settings, 193–194
    verifying, 126–128
FHRP (First-Hop Redundancy Protocol), 370
    GLBP (Gateway Load-Balancing Protocol), 385–390
        configuring, 386
        Ethanalyzer and, 388–390

HSRP (Hot Standby Routing Protocol), 370–379
    ARP table population, 375
    configuring, 372–373
    Ethanalyzer and, 375–376
    HSRPv6, 376–379
    multicast group, 374
    verifying, 373–374
    version comparison, 371
localization, 938–939
VRRP (Virtual Router Redundancy Protocol), 380–385
    configuring, 380
    statistics, 381–382
    verifying, 380–381
    VRRPv3, 382–385
FHS (First-Hop Security), 362–370
    attacks and mitigation techniques, 363
    DHCPv6 Guard, 368–370
    IPv6 snooping, 365–368
    RA Guard, 363–364
file systems, 19–25
    commands
        dir bootflash: 21
        dir logflash: 24
        list of, 20
        show file logflash: 24–25
    flash file system, 21–22
    logflash, 23–25
    onboard failure logging (OBFL), 22–23
filter lists, 669–673
filtering routes
    in BGP, 662–663
        AS-Path access lists, 684
        communities, 684–686
        with filter lists, 669–673

1000 filtering routes

looking glass and route servers, 687
with prefix lists, 663–669
regular expressions, 676–683
with route-maps, 673–676
in OSPF, 487

filtering traffic
Ethanalyzer capture and display filters, 65–67
multicast traffic, 748–749
SPAN (Switched Port Analyzer), 57

firewalls, verifying, 613–615

flapping peer issues. *See* peer flapping (BGP) troubleshooting

flash file system, 21–22

flow exporter definition, 75–76

flow monitor definition, 76–77

flow record definition, 74–75

FNF (Flexible NetFlow), 72–73

Forward Delay, 220

forwarding addresses in OSPF, 488–494

forwarding loops
BPDU filter, 244–245
BPDU guard, 243–244
detecting and remediating, 241–242
MAC address notifications, 242–243
unidirectional links, 245
bridge assurance, 250–252
loop guard, 245–246
UDLD (unidirectional link detection), 246–250

FSM (Finite State Machine), 602–603

G

GIR (Graceful Insertion and Removal), 719–727

GLBP (Gateway Load-Balancing Protocol), 385–390
configuring, 386
Ethanalyzer and, 388–390

global EIGRP authentication, 418–419

GOLD (Generic Online Diagnostic) tests, 98
bootup diagnostics, 98–99
diagnostic test results example, 103–105
EEM (Embedded Event Manager), 107
runtime diagnostics, 100–107

graceful consistency checkers, 284

graceful convergence (LACP), 270

granular verification of EIGRP packets with ACL example, 409

granular view of MST topology example, 239

Guest shell, 957–960

guest shell details example, 959

gunzip command, 20

gzip command, 20

H

hardware crashes, 108–110

hardware forwarding verification on module 3 example, 799

hardware interface resources and drops example, 113

hardware internal errors example, 124

hardware rate-limiters for glean traffic example, 161, 167

hardware troubleshooting, 95–98
GOLD (Generic Online Diagnostic) tests, 98
bootup diagnostics, 98–99

EEM (Embedded Event Manager), 107
runtime diagnostics, 100–107
health checks, 108
   hardware and process crashes, 108–110
   interface errors and drops, 110–115
   packet loss, 110
   platform-specific drops, 116–124
health checks, 108
   hardware and process crashes, 108–110
   interface errors and drops, 110–115
   packet loss, 110
   platform-specific drops, 116–124
hello message (PIM), 775
Hello packets
   in IS-IS, 513–514
      authentication, 544–546
      visibility, 530–531
   in OSPF, 450–451
      visibility, 465
Hello Time, 220, 476–478
Hello timers
   in EIGRP, 414–416
   in OSPF, 476–478
high availability. *See also* BFD (bidirectional forwarding detection); FHRP (First-Hop Redundancy Protocol); vPC (virtual port-channel)
   custom maintenance profiles, 727–731
   GIR (Graceful Insertion and Removal), 719–727
   ISSU (in-service software upgrade), 713–719

   stateful switchover (SSO), 707–712
   VDC policies, 133
high-availability infrastructure, 28–29
   in-service software upgrade (ISSU), 34–35
   supervisor redundancy, 29–34
historical information of FIB route example, 172–173
history
   of Nexus platforms, 1–2
   of NX-OS, 1–2
HM (health-monitoring) diagnostic tests, 100–105
Hold Timer expired, 623–624
hold timers in EIGRP, 414–416
hop counts, 424–425
HSRP (Hot Standby Routing Protocol), 278, 370–379
   ARP table population, 375
   configuring, 372–373
   Ethanalyzer and, 375–376
   multicast group, 374
   verifying, 373–374
   version comparison, 371
HSRPv6, 376–379
   configuration example, 377
   group detail example, 378
   virtual address verification example, 379
HWRL (hardware rate limiters), 179–192, 745–747
hyphen (-) in RegEx, 680–681

I

IANA (Internet Assigned Numbers Authority), 597
iBGP (internal BGP), 600
   multipath, 640–643

ICMP echo probes, 322–324
id -a command, 951–952
identifying
    active EIGRP interfaces example, 403
    EIGRP example AS, 413
    if passive IS-IS is configured for a level example, 526–527
    if passive OSPF interfaces are configured example, 461
    matching sequence for specific prefix pattern example, 580–581
    member link for specific network traffic example, 274
    root ports example, 223–224
    root ports on NX-4 and NX-5 example, 224–225
Idle state, 603
IEEE 802.1D standards, 219–220
IGMP (Internet Group Management Protocol). *See also* vPC (virtual port-channel)
    created MROUTE entry on NX-1 example, 769, 771
    event-history of internal events example, 770
    IGMPv1, 750
    IGMPv2, 751–752
    IGMPv3, 752–756
    state on NX-3 example, 863–864
    state on NX-4 example, 862–863
    verifying, 761–771
IGMP snooping, 756–761
    MFDM entry example, 765
    OTV groups on NX-2 example, 935
    statistics on NX-4 example, 864–865
    status for VLAN 115 example, 763–764
    VLAN event-history example, 766

IGMPv1, 750
IGMPv2, 751–752
IGMPv3, 752–756, 846
IGP (Interior Gateway Protocol), 576–577
IIH (IS-IS Hello) packets, 513–514, 544–546
in-band management (VDC), 134–136
in-band Netstack KLM statistics example, 150, 152
include utility, 42
incompatible OSPF timers example, 477
incomplete configuration of route-maps, 586
indication of EIGRP K values mismatch example, 414
ingress routing optimization, 940–941
initializing VDC (Virtual Device Contexts), 134–136
instability in OTV MAC routing table example, 902
install all command, 719
install all kickstart command, 714–718
installing
    custom RPM package example, 965–966
    feature sets, 15
    NX-SDK, 965
    and removing RPM packages from bash shell example, 955–957
inter-area routes in OSPF, 495
interfaces. *See also* passive interfaces
    EIGRP
        authentication, 418
        settings, 430

error counters example, 113
errors and drops, 110–115
FabricPath, verifying, 303–304
IS-IS
   confirming, 523–526
   link costs, 549–553
OSPF
   area number mismatches, 471–473
   confirming, 460–461
   link costs, 500–504
PIM, verifying, 780–785
PktMgr statistics example, 153
port-channels
   consistency, 271–272
   establishment troubleshooting, 272
priority. *See* port priority
queueing statistics example, 114–115
status
   object tracking for, 330
   reflecting UDLD error example, 248
STP cost, 221–222

internal flash directories example, 88–89

internal interfaces (OTV), configuring, 882

inter-router communication
   in IS-IS, 511
   in OSPF, 450

intra-area routes in OSPF, 494

I/O module MFIB verification on module 3 example, 798

IP SLA (Service Level Agreement), 321–322
ICMP echo probes, 322–324
object tracking, 331
statistics example, 323
TCP connect probes, 328–329
UDP echo probes, 324–325
UDP jitter probes, 325–327

IPFIB process, 171–175

IPSG (IP Source Guard), 349–350

IPv4 services, 335
DHCP relay, 335–341
   ACL verification, 339–341
   configuring, 336–337
   verifying, 337–338
DHCP snooping, 341–345
   ACL programming, 343–345
   binding database, 342–343
   configuring, 342
dynamic ARP inspection (DAI), 345–349
   ACL programming, 346–348
   ARP ACLs, 348–349
   configuring and verifying, 345–346
IP Source Guard (IPSG), 349–350
Unicast Reverse Path Forwarding (URPF), 351–352

IPv6 services, 352
address assignment, 357–362
   DHCPv6 relay agent, 357–359
   DHCPv6 relay LDRA, 360–362
First-Hop Security (FHS), 362–370
   attacks and mitigation techniques, 363
   DHCPv6 Guard, 368–370
   IPv6 snooping, 365–368
   RA Guard, 363–364
Neighbor Discovery (ND), 352–356
   Ethanalyzer capture example, 355
   interface information example, 355–356

peer troubleshooting, 621–622
RA guard configuration example, 364
snooping, 365–368
IS-IS (Intermediate System-to-Intermediate System), 507
areas, 508–509
configuration with passive interfaces example, 528
database for area 49.1234 example, 563
database with L2 route leaking example, 565–566
DIS (Designated Intermediate System), 516–517
event-history indicates different areas example, 540
hello debugs example, 529–530
hierarchy in, 507–508
IIH packets, 513–514
interface verification example, 523–525
inter-router communication, 511
L2 route-leaking configuration example, 564–565
LSPs (link state packets), 515–516
MAC addresses, 512–513
metric transition mode configuration and verification example, 555
mismatch of interface types example, 543–544
missing routes troubleshooting
duplicate System-ID, 546–549
interface link costs, 549–553
L1 to L2 route propagations, 556–561
metric calculation, 553–556
redistribution, 566–567
suboptimal routing, 562–566

neighbor adjacency troubleshooting
area settings mismatches, 539–541
baseline configuration, 518–520
checking adjacency capabilities, 541–543
confirming interfaces, 523–526
DIS requirements, 543–544
IIH authentication, 544–546
MTU requirements, 537–539
passive interfaces, 526–528
primary subnets, 535–537
unique System-ID, 539
verifying neighbors, 520–523
verifying packets, 528–535
NET addressing, 509–510
OSPF, compared, 508
OTV control plane, 885–886
adjacency server mode, 907–912
adjacency verification, 888–898
authentication, 905–907
CoPP, 912–913
IS-IS topology table, 898–905
multicast mode, 887–888
packet types, 511–512
path selection troubleshooting, definitions and processing order, 517–518
protocol verification example, 525–526
routing and topology table after static metric configuration example, 552–553
TLVs, 512

topology for area 49.1234 example, 563

topology table with mismatched metric types example, 554–555

traffic statistics example, 529

verifying adjacency in FabricPath, 304–305

isolate and shutdown maintenance mode example, 721–722

isolated PVLANs, 207, 208–212

ISSU (in-service software upgrade), 34–35, 713–719

J

join interfaces (OTV), configuring, 883

join-prune message (PIM), 776–777

json utility, 42

JSON-RPC request object fields, 968–969

JSON-RPC response object fields, 970–971

jumbo MTU system configuration example, 193

K

K values mismatch, 413–414

Keepalive generation, 624–626

KEEPALIVE message, 602

kernel, 9

L

L1 adjacency is affected by L1 IIH authentication on NX-1 example, 545

L1 IIH authentication on NX-1 example, 545

L2 and L3 rate-limiter and exception configuration example, 184–185

LACP (link-aggregation control packets), 256–258

advanced configuration options, 265–268

interface establishment troubleshooting, 272

port-channel configuration, 259–260

system priority, 268–271

verifying, 262–265

LACP fast, 269–270

last utility, 40–41

Layer 2 communications

multicast addresses, 738–739

overview, 197–199

troubleshooting flowchart, 253

Layer 2 overlay. *See* OTV (Overlay Transport Virtualization)

Layer 3 routing

backup routing in vPC, 292–293

multicast addresses, 739–741

over vPC, 293–294

LDRA (Lightweight DHCPv6 Relay Agent), 360–362

license manager, 15

licensing, 28

line card interop limitations, 141–142

line card microcode, 17–19

listing files on standby supervisor example, 22

load balancing, 421

Local Bridge Identifier, 220

locate UUID for service name example, 11

logflash, 23–25

logging, 87–90
    accounting log, 91
    BGP logs collection, 687
    buffered logging, 88–89
    console logging, 88
    debug logfiles, 90
    event history logs. *See* event history logs
    levels, 87
    syslog server, 90
long-lived software releases, 26
looking glass servers, 687
loop guard, 245–246
loop prevention
    with BGP, 599–600
    in route reflectors, 658–659
loop-free topologies. *See* STP (Spanning Tree Protocol)
LSAs (link state advertisements), 453–456
LSPs (link state packets), 515–516

M

MAC addresses
    address table example, 316
    in FabricPath, 305–306
    host C example, 919–920
    host C on NX-6 example, 923
    in IS-IS, 512–513
    multicast source example, 796
    for multicast traffic, 738–739
    preventing forwarding loops, 242–243
    redistribution into OTV IS-IS example, 903–904, 921–922
    viewing, 198–199

    in vPC+, 315–316
maintenance mode (GIR), 719–724
maintenance mode timeout settings example, 726
maintenance profiles, 727–731
maintenance software releases, 25
major software releases, 25
manageability, 950
match route-map command options example, 634
Max Age, 220
maxas-limit command, 662
maximum-prefixes in BGP, 659–661
MD5 authentication in OSPF, 480–482
member interfaces (port-channels), consistency, 271–272
member links (vPC), 277
messages
    BGP (Border Gateway Protocol)
        KEEPALIVE, 602
        NOTIFICATION, 602
        OPEN, 601–602
        types of, 601
        UPDATE, 602
    PIM (Protocol Independent Multicast)
        assert message, 778–779
        bootstrap message, 777–778
        candidate RP advertisement message, 779
        DF election message, 779–780
        hello message, 775
        join-prune message, 776–777
        register message, 775–776
        register-stop message, 776
        types of, 773–774

metric calculation
  for common LAN interface speeds example, 433
  for EIGRP paths, 396–398
  in IS-IS, 553–556
MFDM verification on NX-2 example, 797
minor software releases, 25
mismatched OSPF hello timers example, 478
missing path of only one route example, 426
missing routes troubleshooting
  EIGRP (Enhanced Interior Gateway Protocol), 419–421
    classic metrics versus wide metrics, 433–439
    distribute list, 426–427
    hop counts, 424–425
    interface-based settings, 430
    load balancing, 421
    offset lists, 427–430
    redistribution, 430–432
    stub routers, 421–424
  IS-IS (Intermediate System-to-Intermediate System)
    duplicate System-ID, 546–549
    interface link costs, 549–553
    L1 to L2 route propagations, 556–561
    metric calculation, 553–556
    redistribution, 566–567
    suboptimal routing, 562–566
  OSPF (Open Shortest Path First)
    discontiguous networks, 482–485
    duplicate router-ID, 485–487
    filtering routes, 487
    forwarding addresses, 488–494
    redistribution, 487–488
mkdir command, 20
modification of spanning tree protocol port cost example, 231–232
move command, 20
MRIB creating (*, G) state example, 770
MROUTE entries
  clearing, 748
  from NX-3 and NX-4 after IGMP join example, 860
  from NX-3 and NX-4 after SPT join example, 859
MROUTE state
  on NX-1 after SPT switchover example, 794–795
  on NX-1 with no receivers example, 791
  on NX-2 after SPT switchover example, 794
  on NX-2 with Active Source example, 790
  on NX-4 after SPT switchover example, 794
  on NX-4 with receiver example, 792
MROUTE types, 924
MROUTE verification, 789–795
  on NX-2 example, 795
  in transport network example, 932
MSDP (Multicast Source Discovery Protocol), 831–838
  event-history on NX-4 example, 837–838
  peer status on NX-4 example, 835–836
  SA state and MROUTE status on NX-3 example, 836–837

MST (Multiple Spanning-Tree
Protocol), 236
  configuring, 236–237
  tuning, 240–241
  verifying, 237–240
MTS (Messages and Transactional
Services), 11–12, 144–148
  message stuck in queue example, 146
  OBFL logs example, 148
  SAP statistics example, 147–148
MTU mismatches, 626–630
MTU requirements
  in IS-IS, 537–539
  in OSPF, 469–470
MTU settings, 192–195
MTU verification
  under ELTM process example, 195
  under ethpm process example, 195
multicast enabled transport
  multicast traffic with, 924–932
  unicast traffic with, 919–924
multicast mode in OTV, 887–888
multicast source tree detail on NX-4
and NX-3 example, 869
multicast traffic, 733–735
  Ethanalyzer examples, 871
  IGMP. *See* IGMP (Internet Group
Management Protocol)
  Layer 2 addresses, 738–739
  Layer 3 addresses, 739–741
  with multicast enabled transport,
924–932
  NX-OS architecture, 741–743
    CLI commands, 743
    CPU protection, 745–747
    implementation, 747–750
    replication, 744–745

PIM. *See* PIM (Protocol Independent
Multicast)
  terminology, 735–738
  with unicast transport, 932–937
  vPC (virtual port-channel), 848–849
    duplicate packets, 870
    *receiver configuration and
verification, 861–869*
    reserved VLAN, 870
    *source configuration and
verification, 849–861*
multicast vPC
  configuring
    on NX-3, 851–852
    on NX-4, 850–851
  IGMP interface on NX-4 example,
853–854
  PIM interface on NX-4 example,
852–853
  source MROUTE entry on NX-3 and
NX-4 example, 855
  source registration from NX-3
example, 857
multihoming in OTV, 939–940
multipath (BGP), 640–643
multiple match options example
route-map example, 585
multiple match variables example
route-map example, 584
multiple subnets in VLANs, 203

N

naming conventions for software
releases, 25–27
native VLANs, 206
ND (Neighbor Discovery), 352–356

neighbor adjacency troubleshooting
   EIGRP (Enhanced Interior Gateway Protocol), 401–402
      ASN mismatch, 412–413
      authentication, 416–419
      connectivity with primary subnet, 409–412
      Hello and hold timers, 414–416
      K values mismatch, 413–414
      passive interfaces, 403–405
      verifying active interfaces, 402–403
      verifying EIGRP packets, 405–409
   IS-IS (Intermediate System-to-Intermediate System)
      area settings mismatches, 539–541
      baseline configuration, 518–520
      checking adjacency capabilities, 541–543
      confirming interfaces, 523–526
      DIS requirements, 543–544
      IIH authentication, 544–546
      MTU requirements, 537–539
      passive interfaces, 526–528
      primary subnets, 535–537
      unique System-ID, 539
      verifying neighbors, 520–523
      verifying packets, 528–535
   OSPF (Open Shortest Path First)
      area settings mismatches, 473–474
      authentication, 478–482
      baseline configuration, 456–458
      confirming interfaces, 460–461
      connectivity with primary subnet, 468
      DR requirements, 474–476
      interface area number mismatches, 471–473
      MTU requirements, 469–470
      passive interfaces, 461–463
      timers, 476–478
      unique router-ID, 471
      verifying neighbors, 458–460
      verifying packets, 463–467
neighbor states
   in BGP, 602–603
      Active, 604
      Connect, 603–604
      Established, 605
      Idle, 603
      OpenConfirm, 604
      OpenSent, 604
   in OSPF, 451–452
neighbors (PIM), verifying, 780–785
NET addressing in IS-IS, 509–510
NetFlow, 72–73
   configuring, 73–77
      flow exporter definition, 75–76
      flow monitor definition, 76–77
      flow record definition, 74–75
   sampling, 77–78
   statistics, 77
Netstack, 148–160
   socket accounting example, 159
   socket client details example, 158
network automation, 950
network broadcasts, 198
network communications, Layer 2
   overview, 197–199
   troubleshooting flowchart, 253
network hubs, 198

network QoS policy verification example, 195
network sniffing, 53–57
  Ethanalyzer, 63–71
  packet tracer, 71–72
  SPAN (Switched Port Analyzer), 54–57
    configuring, 55–56
    ERSPAN, 57–60
    filtering traffic, 57
    SPAN-on-Drop, 61–62
    SPAN-on-Latency (SOL), 60–61
    verifying, 56
network statement BGP route advertisement, 631–633
network switches, 198
network types in OSPF, 474
network-admin and dev-ops user role permissions example, 953
next-hop adjacency tracking, 946
Nexus 2000 series, 2–3
Nexus 3000 series, 3–4
Nexus 5000 series, 4
Nexus 6000 series, 4–5
Nexus 7000 series, 5–6
  hardware rate limiters example, 746
  in-band events example, 123
  in-band status example, 120–122
  packet flow drop counters example, 116–118
Nexus 9000 series, 6–7
  in-band status example, 120–122
Nexus core files example, 108
Nexus in-band counters example, 123
Nexus interface details and capabilities example, 111–112
Nexus platforms

history of, 1–2
Nexus 2000 series, 2–3
Nexus 3000 series, 3–4
Nexus 5000 series, 4
Nexus 6000 series, 4–5
Nexus 7000 series, 5–6
Nexus 9000 series, 6–7
Nexus process crash example, 109–110
no configure maintenance profile command, 728–730
no system mode maintenance command, 724–725
no-more utility, 42
normal traffic flow to NX-6's loopback 0 interface example, 593
NOTIFICATION message, 602
notifications in BGP, 619–621
NTP (Network Time Protocol), 81–83
  configuring, 81–82
  statistics, 83
NX-1 and NX-2 detect bad subnet mask example, 468
NX-1 and NX-2 event-history example, 536–537
NX-1 and NX-2 routing table for adjacency example, 412
NX-1 and NX-3's routing table example, 564
NX-1 configuration to redistribute 172.16.1.0/24 into OSPF example, 489–490
NX-1 detects NX-2 as neighbor example, 410
NX-1 does not detect NX-2 example, 537
NX-1 external OSPF path selection for type-2 network example, 498–499

NX-1 IGMP debugs event-history example, 769

NX-1 IGMP interface VLAN 115 state example, 768–769

NX-1 IS-IS adjacency event-history with MTU mismatch example, 538

NX-1 OSPF adjacency event-history with MTU mismatch example, 469

NX-1 redistribution configuration example, 431, 488, 567

NX-1 stuck in INIT state with NX-2 example, 535

NX-1's routing table example, 420

NX-1's routing table with missing NX-4's 10.4.4.0/24 network example, 547

NX-1's routing table with missing NX-4's loopback interface example, 485–486

NX-1's spanning tree protocol information example, 226

NX-2 and NX-4's routing table after L1 route propagation example, 561

NX-2 OTV IS-IS IIH event-history example, 896

NX-2 redistribution configuration example, 587

NX-2 VLAN 115 IGMP snooping statistics example, 767–768

NX-2's LSPDB example, 558

NX-2's PBR configuration example, 592–593

NX-3 anycast RP with MSDP configuration example, 832–833

NX-3 external OSPF path selection for type-2 network example, 499

NX-3's LSP after enabling route propagation example, 561

NX-4 anycast RP with MSDP configuration example, 834–835

NX-4 OTV IS-IS IIH event-history example, 897

NX-6 detected as MROUTER port by IGMP snooping example, 928

NX-API, 968–975
  Cisco proprietary request object fields, 969–970
  Cisco proprietary response object fields, 971
  feature configuration example, 972
  JSON-RPC request object fields, 968–969
  JSON-RPC response object fields, 970–971
  server logs example, 973–975

NX-OS
  architecture of, 8–9
    feature manager, 14–16
    file systems, 19–25
    kernel, 9
    line card microcode, 17–19
    Messages and Transactional Services (MTS), 11–12
    Persistent Storage Services (PSS), 13–14
    system manager (sysmgr), 9–11
  BGP (Border Gateway Protocol)
    configuration example, 606
    peering verification example, 607
    process example, 608–609
    table output example, 607
  component logging level example, 89
  detection of forwarding loop example, 242
  high-availability infrastructure, 28–29
    in-service software upgrade (ISSU), 34–35
    supervisor redundancy, 29–34

history of, 1–2
licensing, 28
management and operations
   accounting log, 45–46
   bash shell, 51
   CLI, 39–44
   configuration checkpoint and rollback, 48–49
   consistency checkers, 49–50
   debug filters and debug log files, 47–48
   event history logs, 46–47
   python interpreter, 50
   scheduler, 50
   technical support files, 44–45
multicast architecture, 741–743
   CLI commands, 743
   CPU protection, 745–747
   implementation, 747–750
   replication, 744–745
pillars of, 1–2, 8
Python interpreter example, 50
Software Maintenance Upgrades (SMUs), 27–28
software releases, 25–27
system component troubleshooting, 142–143
   ARP and Adjacency Manager, 160–175
   EthPM and Port-Client, 175–179
   HWRL, CoPP, system QoS, 179–192
   MTS (Message and Transaction Service), 144–148
   MTU settings, 192–195
   Netstack and Packet Manager, 148–160

virtualization
   Virtual Device Contexts (VDCs), 35–37
   virtual port channels (vPC), 37–39
   Virtual Routing and Forwarding (VRF), 37
NX-SDK, 964–967
event history example, 967

O

OBFL (onboard failure logging), 22–23
object tracking, 329
   for interface status, 330
   for route status, 330–331
   with static routes, 334
   for track-list state, 332–333
offline diagnostics, 107
offset list configuration example, 428
offset lists, 427–430
on-demand diagnostics, 105–107
on-reload reset-reason configuration and verification example, 726–727
OPEN message, 601–602, 617–618
Open NX-OS, 950–951
OpenConfirm state, 604
OpenSent state, 604
ORIB entry for host C on NX-6 example, 923
orphan ports (vPC), 288
OSPF (Open Shortest Path First), 449
   adjacency failure example, 475
   areas, 453
   configuration with passive interfaces example, 462–463
   Designated Routers (DRs), 452

encrypted authentication example, 480–481
event-history with mismatched area flags example, 473
hello and packet debugs example, 464
Hello packets, 450–451
interface output example, 461
interface output in brief format example, 460
inter-router communication, 450
IS-IS, compared, 508
LSAs (link state advertisements), 453–456
missing routes troubleshooting
  discontiguous networks, 482–485
  duplicate router-ID, 485–487
  filtering routes, 487
  forwarding addresses, 488–494
  redistribution, 487–488
neighbor adjacency troubleshooting
  area settings mismatches, 473–474
  authentication, 478–482
  baseline configuration, 456–458
  confirming interfaces, 460–461
  connectivity with primary subnet, 468
  DR requirements, 474–476
  interface area number mismatches, 471–473
  MTU requirements, 469–470
  passive interfaces, 461–463
  timers, 476–478
  unique router-ID, 471
  verifying neighbors, 458–460
  verifying packets, 463–467
neighbor states, 451–452
neighbors stuck in EXSTART neighbor state example, 469
network types, 474
path selection troubleshooting, 494
  external routes, 495–499
  inter-area routes, 495
  interface link costs, 500–504
  intermixed RFC 1583 and RFC 2328 devices, 499–500
  intra-area routes, 494
plaintext authentication example, 479
route distribution to URIB example, 169
routing table example, 456
traffic statistics example, 463

OTV (Overlay Transport Virtualization), 875–877
(V, *, G) MROUTE detail on NX-6 example, 933
(V, S, G) MROUTE detail on NX-2 example, 929–930
(V, S, G) MROUTE detail on NX-6 example, 931
adjacencies with secondary IP address example, 943–944
adjacency server configuration on NX-2 example, 908–909
adjacency server mode dual adjacency example, 911–912
adjacency server mode IS-IS neighbors example, 910
advanced features
  fast failure detection, 944–946
  FHRP localization, 938–939
  ingress routing optimization, 940–941

OTV (Overlay Transport Virtualization)

    multihoming, 939–940
    tunnel depolarization, 942–944
    VLAN mapping, 941–942
  configuring, 882–885
  control plane, 885–886
    adjacency server mode, 907–912
    adjacency verification, 888–898
    authentication, 905–907
    CoPP, 912–913
    IS-IS topology table, 898–905
    multicast mode, 887–888
  data plane
    ARP resolution and ARP-ND-Cache, 915–917
    broadcasts, 917–918
    encapsulation, 913–915
    multicast traffic with multicast enabled transport, 924–932
    multicast traffic with unicast transport, 932–937
    selective unicast flooding, 918–919
    unicast traffic with multicast enabled transport, 919–924
  deployment models, 881
  dynamic unicast tunnels example, 891
  ED adjacency server mode configuration on NX-4 example, 908
  flood control and broadcast optimization, 877
  IGMP proxy reports example, 934–935
  internal interface configuration example, 882
  IS-IS (Intermediate System-to-Intermediate System)
    adjacencies on overlay example, 889
    adjacency event-history example, 898
    authentication error statistics example, 906
    authentication parameters example, 906
    database detail example, 900–901
    database example, 899
    dynamic hostname example, 899
    LSP updating frequently example, 901–902
    MGROUP database detail on NX-2 example, 935
    MGROUP database on NX-2 example, 928–929
    overlay traffic statistics example, 904
    site adjacency example, 889–890
    site-VLAN statistics example, 904–905
    SPF event-history example, 903
  join interface configuration example, 883
  MGROUP database detail on NX-6 example, 930
  MROUTE
    detail on NX-2 example, 936
    detail on NX-6 example, 936–937
    entry on NX-2 example, 929
    redistributed into IS-IS on NX-6 example, 934
    redistribution into OTV IS-IS example, 930
    state on NX-6 example, 928

overlay interface configuration example, 885
overlay IS-IS adjacency down example, 907
partial adjacency example, 895
routing table with selective unicast flooding example, 918–919
site VLAN, 882
SSM data-groups example, 925
supported platforms, 878
terminology, 878–880

out-of-band management (VDC), 134–136

output of RR reflected prefix example, 659

overlay interfaces (OTV)
configuring, 885
IS-IS authentication on, 905–907
verifying, 888–898

P

PA (path attributes), 599
packet capture, 53–57
Ethanalyzer, 63–71
packet tracer, 71–72
SPAN (Switched Port Analyzer), 54–57
configuring, 55–56
ERSPAN, 57–60
filtering traffic, 57
SPAN-on-Drop, 61–62
SPAN-on-Latency (SOL), 60–61
verifying, 56

packet loss
reasons for, 110
interface errors and drops, 110–115
platform-specific drops, 116–124
verifying, 611–613

Packet Manager (PktMgr), 148–160

packet processing filter (PPF), 575–576

packet tracer, 71–72

packets. *See also* messages
EIGRP (Enhanced Interior Gateway Protocol)
types of, 399
verifying, 405–409
FabricPath, 297–300
IS-IS (Intermediate System-to-Intermediate System)
IIH, 513–514, 544–546
LSPs, 515–516
types of, 511–512
verifying, 528–535
LACP. *See* LACP (link-aggregation control packets)
OSPF (Open Shortest Path First)
types of, 450
verifying, 463–467

parentheses () in RegEx, 681–682

partial configuration of route-maps, 586

passive interfaces
in EIGRP, 403–405
in IS-IS, 526–528
in OSPF, 461–463

path changed for 10.1.1.0/24 route example, 427

path check after L2 route leaking example, 566

path metric calculation in EIGRP, 396–398

path modification on NX-6 example, 429–430

path selection troubleshooting
   EIGRP (Enhanced Interior Gateway Protocol), 419–421
      classic metrics versus wide metrics, 433–439
      distribute list, 426–427
      hop counts, 424–425
      interface-based settings, 430
      load balancing, 421
      offset lists, 427–430
      redistribution, 430–432
      stub routers, 421–424
   IS-IS (Intermediate System-to-Intermediate System), 517–518
   OSPF (Open Shortest Path First), 494
      external routes, 495–499
      inter-area routes, 495
      interface link costs, 500–504
      intermixed RFC 1583 and RFC 2328 devices, 499–500
      intra-area routes, 494

Path-MTU-Discovery (PMTUD), 626–627

PBR (policy-based routing), 591–594

peer flapping (BGP) troubleshooting, 622
   bad BGP updates, 622–623
   Hold Timer expired, 623–624
   Keepalive generation, 624–626
   MTU mismatches, 626–630

peer link (vPC), 277

peer-gateway (vPC), 289–291

peering down (BGP) troubleshooting, 609–610
   ACL and firewall verification, 613–615
   configuration verification, 610–611
   debug logfiles, 618–619
   notifications, 619–621
   OPEN message errors, 617–618
   reachability and packet loss verification, 611–613
   TCP session verification, 615–617

peer-keepalive link (vPC), 276–277, 282–283

period (.) in RegEx, 682

Persistent Storage Services (PSS), 13–14

pillars of NX-OS, 1–2, 8

PIM (Protocol Independent Multicast), 771–772
   (S, G) join events and MROUTE state example, 868
   anycast RP configuration on NX-4 example, 840
   ASM (any source multicast), 785–787
      configuring, 787–788
      event-history and MROUTE state verification, 789–795
      platform verification, 795–799
      verifying, 788–789
   auto-RP candidate-RP configuration on NX-1 example, 814–815
   BiDIR, 799–803
      configuring, 803–804
      DF status on NX-4 example, 805–806
      event-history on NX-4 example, 806
      interface counters on NX-4 example, 807–808
      join-prune event-history on NX-1 example, 808

join-prune event-history on NX-4 example, 807
MROUTE entry on NX-1 example, 809
MROUTE entry on NX-2 example, 811
MROUTE entry on NX-4 example, 805
terminology, 800
verifying, 805–811
DF status on NX-1 example, 809
Ethanalyzer capture of PIM hello message example, 784–785
event-history for hello messages example, 784
event-history for RP from NX-4 with BSR example, 827–828
global statistics example, 783
group-to-RP mapping information from NX-2 example, 830
interface and neighbor verification, 780–785
interface parameters on NX-1 example, 782–783
join received from NX-1 on NX-2 example, 793
join sent from NX-1 to NX-2 example, 793
message types
  assert message, 778–779
  bootstrap message, 777–778
  candidate RP advertisement message, 779
  DF election message, 779–780
  hello message, 775
  join-prune message, 776–777
  list of, 773–774
  register message, 775–776
  register-stop message, 776
neighbors on NX-1 example, 781
null register event-history on NX-4 example, 841
RP configuration, 811–812
  anycast RP, 830–841
  Auto-RP, 813–820
  BSR (bootstrap router), 820–830
  static RP, 812–813
RPT join from NX-4 to NX-1 example, 792
RPT join received on NX-1 example, 792
SPT joins from NX-2 for vPC-connected sources example, 858
SSM (source specific multicast), 841–843
  configuring, 843–845
  verifying, 845–848
static RP on NX-3 configuration example example, 812
statistics on NX-4 with BSR example, 828–829
trees, 772–773
vPC (virtual port-channel)
  forwarder election on NX-3 and NX-4 example, 866–867
  RPF-source cache table on NX-3 and NX-4 example, 856–857
  status on NX-4 example, 867
ping test and show ip traffic command output example, 612
ping with DF-bit set example, 629
ping with source interface as loopback example, 611
pipe (|) in RegEx, 681–682
PktMgr (Packet Manager), 148–160

plaintext authentication in OSPF, 478–480
platform FIB verification example, 173–174, 176–178
platform-specific drops, 116–124
plus sign (+) in RegEx, 682
PMTUD (Path-MTU-Discovery), 626–627
port priority
  LACP, 268–269
  modifying, 232–233
port-channels, 255–258. *See also* vPC (virtual port-channel)
  advanced LACP options, 265–268
  advantages of, 255–256
  configuring, 259–260
  LACP in, 256–258
    interface establishment troubleshooting, 272
    system priority, 268–271
    verifying packets, 262–265
  member interface consistency, 271–272
  traffic load-balancing troubleshooting, 272–274
  verifying status, 260–262
Port-Client, 175–179
portfast, 232–235
PPF (packet processing filter), 575–576
prefix advertisement using network command example, 632–633
prefix lists, 580–581, 663–669
prefix matching, 578–579
prefix-list-based route filtering example, 664
primary subnets
  EIGRP connectivity, 409–412
  IS-IS connectivity, 535–537
  OSPF connectivity, 468
process crashes, 108–110
programmability, 950. *See also* automation; shells and scripting
  NX-API, 968–975
  NX-SDK, 964–967
  Open NX-OS, 950–951
promiscuous PVLANs, 207
  community PVLANs and, 212–215
  isolated PVLANs and, 208–212
  on SVI, 215–217
PSS (Persistent Storage Services), 13–14
PVLANs (private VLANs), 207–208
  communication capability between hosts, 208
  community PVLANs, 212–215
  isolated PVLANs, 208–212
  promiscuous PVLANs on SVI, 215–217
  trunking between switches, 217–218
PVST (Per-VLAN Spanning Tree), 220
PVST+ (Per-VLAN Spanning Tree Plus), 220
pwd command, 20, 951–952
Python, 960–964
  with EEM example, 87
  interpreter from CLI and guest shell example, 961
  invoking from EEM applet example, 964
  printing all interfaces in UP state example, 963–964
python command, 50, 960–961
python interpreter, 50

Q

query modifiers. *See* RegEx (regular expressions)
question mark (?) in RegEx, 683
queue names (MTS), 146

R

R1 routing table with GRE tunnel example, 139–140
R1's and NX-2's IS-IS routing table entries example, 554
R1's and NX-3's IS-IS topology table with default metric example, 551
R1's routing table with 1 gigabit link shutdown example, 502
R1's routing table with default interface metrics bandwidth example, 550
R1's routing table with default OSPF auto-cost bandwidth example, 502
RA Guard, 363–364
rate-limiter usage example, 183–184
reachability, verifying, 611–613
redirection, 39
redistribution
  in BGP, 633–634
  in EIGRP, 430–432
  in IS-IS, 566–567
  in OSPF, 487–488
redundancy switchover example, 711–712
RegEx (regular expressions), 676–683
  asterisk (*), 683
  brackets ([]), 680
  caret (^), 679
  caret in brackets ([^]), 681
  dollar sign ($), 679–680
  hyphen (-), 680–681
  list of, 676
  parentheses (), 681–682
  period (.), 682
  pipe (|), 681–682
  plus sign (+), 682
  question mark (?), 683
  underscore (_), 677–678
register message (PIM), 775–776, 790
register-stop message (PIM), 776, 791
replication, 744–745
reserved VLAN, 870
resolved and unresolved adjacencies example, 165–166
resource templates (VDC), 131–132
restoring connectivity by allowing BPDUs to process example, 252
reviewing OSPF adjacency event history example, 47
RFC 1583 devices, 499–500
RFC 2328 devices, 499–500
RID (router ID)
  in BGP, 601
  in OSPF, 471, 485–487
rmdir command, 20
Root Bridge Identifier, 220
root bridges, 219
  election, 222–224
  placement, 228–229
root guard, 229
Root Path Cost, 220
root ports
  identification, 224–225
  modifying location, 229–232

route advertisement in BGP, 631
    with aggregation, 634–635
    with default-information originate command, 636
    with network statement, 631–633
    with redistribution, 633–634
route aggregation in BGP, 634–635
route filtering
    in BGP, 662–663
        communities, 684–686
        with filter lists, 669–673
        looking glass and route servers, 687
        AS-Path access lists, 684
        with prefix lists, 663–669
        regular expressions, 676–683
        with route-maps, 673–676
    in OSPF, 487
route leaking in IS-IS, 564–566
route policies in BGP, 662–663
    communities, 684–686
    with filter lists, 669–673
    looking glass and route servers, 687
    AS-Path access lists, 684
    with prefix lists, 663–669
    regular expressions, 676–683
    with route-maps, 673–676
route processing in BGP, 630–631
route propagation in BGP, 630–631
route reflectors in BGP, 657–659
route refresh in BGP, 654–657
route servers, 687
route status, object tracking for, 330–331
route-maps
    attribute modifications (set actions), 586
    in BGP, 673–676
    conditional matching, 582–584
        command options, 583–584
        complex matching, 585–586
        multiple match conditions, 584–585
    explained, 581–582
    partial configuration, 586
    PBR (policy-based routing), 591–594
    RPM (Route Policy Manager), 586–590
routing loop because of intermixed OSPF devices example, 500
routing protocol and URIB updates example, 170
routing protocol states during maintenance mode example, 722–724
routing tables
    with impact example, 422
    of NX-1, NX-2, NX-3, and NX-4 example, 557
    of NX-1 and NX-6 example, 424–425
    of NX-2 and NX-4 example, 486, 548
RP configuration (PIM), 811–812
    anycast RP, 830–841
    Auto-RP, 813–820
    BSR (bootstrap router), 820–830
    static RP, 812–813
RPM (Route Policy Manager), 586–590, 668–669
RSTP (Rapid Spanning Tree Protocol), 220–221
    blocked switch port identification, 225–227
    interface STP cost, 221–222
    root bridge election, 222–224

root port identification, 224–225
tuning, 228–235
    port priority, 232–233
    root bridge placement, 228–229
    root guard, 229
    root port and blocked switch port locations, 229–232
    topology changes and portfast, 232–235
verifying VLANs on trunk links, 227
run bash command, 51, 951–952
runtime diagnostics, 100–107

S

SAFI (subsequent address-family identifier), 598–599
SAL database info and FIB verification for IPSG example, 350
sampling
  with NetFlow, 77–78
  with sFlow, 78–80
SAP (service access points), 11, 147
scale factor configuration example, 190, 191–192
scaling BGP (Border Gateway Protocol), 649–650
  maxas-limit command, 662
  maximum-prefixes, 659–661
  with route reflectors, 657–659
  soft reconfiguration inbound versus route refresh, 654–657
  with templates, 653–654
  tuning memory consumption, 650–653
scheduler, 50
scripting. *See* shells and scripting
secondary IP address to avoid polarization example, 943

section utility, 42
selective unicast flooding, 918–919
sessions (BGP), 600–601
set actions for route-maps, 586
setting static IS-IS metric on R1 and R2 example, 552
sFlow, 78–80
  configuring, 79
  statistics, 80
shells and scripting, 951
  bash shell, 951–957
  Guest shell, 957–960
  Python, 960–964
short-lived software releases, 26
show accounting log command, 45–46
show bash-shell command, 951–952
show bfd neighbors command, 694–695, 704–705
show bfd neighbors detail command, 702–703
show bgp command, 606–607, 638–639
show bgp convergence detail command, 648–649
show bgp convergence detail command output example, 648–649
show bgp event-history command, 647–648
show bgp event-history detail command, 642–643, 646, 665–667, 674–675
show bgp ipv4 unicast policy statistics neighbor command, 675
show bgp policy statistics neighbor filter-list command, 672
show bgp policy statistics neighbor prefix-list command, 667–668

show bgp private attr detail command, 652–653
show bgp process command, 607–609
show cli list command, 42–43
show cli list command example, 42–43
show cli syntax command, 43
show cli syntax command example, 43
show clock command, 82
show command output redirection example, 40
show copp diff profile command, 188
show cores command, 29
show cores vdc-all command, 108
show diagnostic bootup level command, 99
show diagnostic content module command, 101–103
show diagnostic content module command output example, 102–103
show diagnostic ondemand setting command, 106–107
show diagnostic result module command, 103–105
show event manager policy internal command, 85–86
show event manager system-policy command, 84–85
show fabricpath conflict all command, 310
show fabricpath isis adjacency command, 304–305
show fabricpath isis interface command, 303–304
show fabricpath isis topology command, 306
show fabricpath isis vlan-range command, 305–306

show fabricpath route command, 307
show fabricpath switch-id command, 303, 315
show fabricpath switch-id command output example, 303
show fabricpath unicast routes vdc command, 308–309
show fex command, 126–128
show file command, 20
show file logflash: command, 24–25
show forwarding distribution ip igmp snooping vlan command, 765
show forwarding distribution ip multicast route group command, 797
show forwarding internal trace v4-adj-history command, 162
show forwarding internal trace v4-pfx-history command, 172–173
show forwarding ipv4 adjacency command, 162–163
show forwarding ipv4 route command, 173–174
show forwarding route command, 173–174
show glbp and show glbp brief command output example, 387–388
show glbp brief command, 386–388
show glbp command, 386–388
show guestshell detail command, 958–959
show hardware capacity interface command, 113
show hardware command, 98
show hardware flow command, 76–77
show hardware internal cpu-mac eobc stats command, 118–119
show hardware internal cpu-mac inband counters command, 123

show hardware internal cpu-mac inband events command, 122–123

show hardware internal cpu-mac inband stats command, 119–122

show hardware internal dev-port-map command, 797–798

show hardware internal errors command, 114, 124

show hardware internal forwarding asic rate-limiter command, 184–185

show hardware internal forwarding instance command, 309

show hardware internal forwarding rate-limiter usage command, 182–184

show hardware internal statistics module pktflow dropped command, 116–118

show hardware mac address-table command, 764

show hardware rate-limiter command, 745–746

show hardware rate-limiters command, 181–182

show hsrp brief command, 373–374

show hsrp detail command, 373–374

show hsrp group detail command, 377–378

show incompatibility-all system command, 713–714

show interface command, 110–112, 193, 194, 203–204

show interface counters errors command, 112–113

show interface port-channel command, 261–262

show interface trunk command, 204–205

show interface trunk command output example, 205

show interface vlan 10 private-vlan mapping command, 216

show ip access-list command, 572–573

show ip adjacency command, 165–166

show ip arp command, 161–162, 796

show ip arp inspection statistics vlan command, 345–346

show ip arp internal event-history command, 163–164

show ip arp internal event-history event command, 92

show ip dhcp relay command, 337–338

show ip dhcp relay statistics command, 337–338

show ip dhcp snooping binding command, 342–343

show ip dhcp snooping command, 342

show ip eigrp command, 404

show ip eigrp interface command, 402, 415–416

show ip eigrp neighbor detail command, 410–411

show ip eigrp topology command, 395, 398

show ip eigrp traffic command, 405

show ip igmp groups command, 845–846

show ip igmp interface command, 853–854

show ip igmp interface vlan command, 768–769

show ip igmp internal event-history debugs command, 769

show ip igmp internal event-history igmp-internal command, 769–770

show ip igmp route command, 769

show ip igmp snooping groups command, 845–846
show ip igmp snooping groups vlan command, 764
show ip igmp snooping internal event-history vlan command, 766
show ip igmp snooping mrouter command, 854–855
show ip igmp snooping otv groups command, 935
show ip igmp snooping statistics command, 864–865
show ip igmp snooping statistics global command, 767
show ip igmp snooping statistics vlan command, 767–768, 934–935
show ip igmp snooping vlan command, 757, 763–764
show ip interface command, 374
show ip mroute command, 770–771, 794–795, 892–893, 932
show ip mroute summary command, 894
show ip msdp internal event-history route command, 837–838
show ip msdp internal event-history tcp command, 837–838
show ip msdp peer command, 835–836
show ip ospf command, 461
show ip ospf event-history command, 464–465
show ip ospf interface command, 461, 475–476
show ip ospf internal event-history adjacency command, 47
show ip ospf internal event-history rib command, 169–170
show ip ospf internal txlist urib command, 169

show ip ospf neighbors command, 458–459
show ip ospf traffic command, 463
show ip pim df command, 805–806, 809
show ip pim group-range command, 829–830
show ip pim interface command, 782–783, 852–853
show ip pim internal event-history bidir command, 806
show ip pim internal event-history data-header-register command, 840–841
show ip pim internal event-history data-register-receive command, 790
show ip pim internal event-history hello command, 783–784
show ip pim internal event-history join-prune command, 792–793, 806–807, 808, 846–847, 858, 865
show ip pim internal event-history null-register command, 790, 791, 840–841, 857
show ip pim internal event-history rp command, 819–820, 827–828
show ip pim internal event-history vpc command, 857, 865–867
show ip pim internal vpc rpf-source command, 856–857, 866–867
show ip pim neighbor command, 781
show ip pim rp command, 814–819, 822–827
show ip pim statistics command, 783, 828–829
show ip prefix-list command, 580–581
show ip route command, 171, 419–421

show ip sla configuration command, 324
show ip sla statistics command, 323
show ip traffic command, 154–156, 611–612
show ip verify source interface command, 349–350
show ipv6 dhcp guard policy command, 369–370
show ipv6 dhcp relay statistics command, 358–359
show ipv6 icmp vaddr command, 378–379
show ipv6 interface command, 378–379
show ipv6 nd command, 355–356
show ipv6 nd raguard policy command, 364
show ipv6 neighbor command, 354
show ipv6 snooping policies command, 369–370
show isis adjacency command, 520–523
show isis command, 525–526
show isis database command, 558–560
show isis event-history command, 530–531
show isis interface command, 523–525, 526–527
show isis traffic command, 528–529
show key chain command, 417, 546
show lacp counters command, 262–263
show lacp internal info interface command, 263–264
show lacp neighbor command, 264
show lacp system-identifier command, 264

show logging log command, 88
show logging logfile command, 959
show logging onboard internal kernel command, 148
show logging onboard module 10 status command, 23
show mac address-table command, 198–199
show mac address-table dynamic vlan command, 796, 919–920, 923
show mac address-table multicast command, 764
show mac address-table vlan command, 305–306
show maintenance profile command, 727–728
show maintenance timeout command, 726
show module command, 96–98, 708
show module command output example, 96–97, 708
show monitor session command, 56–57
show ntp peer-status command, 82
show ntp statistics command, 83
show nxapi-server logs command, 973–975
show nxsdk internal event-history command, 967
show nxsdk internal service command, 965–966
show otv adjacency command, 889, 906–907, 910
show otv arp-nd-cache command, 916
show otv data-group command, 931
show otv internal adjacency command, 890
show otv internal event-history arp-nd command, 916–917

show otv isis database command, 899
show otv isis database detail command, 900–902
show otv isis hostname command, 899
show otv isis interface overlay command, 906
show otv isis internal event-history adjacency command, 898
show otv isis internal event-history iih command, 896–897
show otv isis internal event-history spf-leaf command, 902–903
show otv isis ip redistribute mroute command, 930, 934
show otv isis mac redistribute route command, 903–904
show otv isis redistribute route command, 921–922
show otv isis site command, 895–896
show otv isis site statistics command, 904–905
show otv isis traffic overlay0 command, 904, 906
show otv mroute command, 928, 929
show otv mroute detail command, 929–930, 931, 933
show otv overlay command, 888
show otv route command, 902, 923
show otv route vlan command, 921
show otv site command, 889–890, 895, 911–912
show otv vlan command, 891–892, 920
show policy-map interface command, 114
show policy-map interface control-plane command, 189–190
show policy-map interface control-plane output example, 189–190
show policy-map system type network-qos command, 194–195
show port-channel compatibility-parameters command, 272
show port-channel load-balance command, 273–274
show port-channel summary command, 260–261, 272, 704–705
show port-channel traffic command, 273
show processes log pid command, 29
show processes log vdc-all command, 109–110
show queueing interface command, 114
show queuing interface command, 193, 194
show role command, 952
show routing clients command, 167–168
show routing event-history command, 647–648
show routing internal event-history msgs command, 169–170
show routing ip multicast event-history rib command, 770
show routing ip multicast source-tree detail command, 868–869
show routing memory statistics command, 171
show run aclmgr command, 572
show run all | include glean command, 161
show run copp all command, 186
show run netflow command, 76
show run otv command, 908–909, 917–918
show run pim command, 781
show run sflow command, 79

show run vdc command, 137
show running-config command, 45
show running-config copp command, 188–189
show running-config diff command, 43–44
show running-config diff example, 43–44
show running-config mmode command, 730
show running-config sla sender command, 324
show sflow command, 79–80
show sflow command output example, 80
show sflow statistics command, 80
show snapshots command, 725–726
show sockets client detail command, 157–158
show sockets connection tcp command, 615–616
show sockets connection tcp detail command, 157
show sockets internal event-history events command, 616–617
show sockets internal event-history events command example, 617
show sockets statistics all command, 159
show spanning-tree command, 225–227, 237–238, 281–282
show spanning-tree inconsistentports command, 246, 252
show spanning-tree interface command, 227
show spanning-tree mst command, 238–239
show spanning-tree mst configuration command, 237
show spanning-tree mst interface command, 239–240
show spanning-tree root command, 222–224, 225
show spanning-tree vlan command, 897–898
show system inband queuing statistics command, 150
show system internal access-list input entries detail command, 190
show system internal access-list input statistics command, 340–341, 348–349, 359, 367–368, 700–702
show system internal access-list interface command, 339–340, 367–368, 700–702
show system internal access-list interface e4/2 input statistics module 4 command, 573–574
show system internal aclmgr access-lists policies command, 574–575
show system internal aclmgr ppf node command, 575–576
show system internal adjmgr client command, 164–165
show system internal adjmgr internal event-history events command, 167
show system internal bfd event-history command, 695–699
show system internal bfd transition-history command, 699–700
show system internal copp info command, 191–192
show system internal eltm info interface command, 195
show system internal ethpm info interface command, 175–178, 195
show system internal fabricpath switch-id event-history errors command, 310

show system internal feature-mgr feature action command, 16

show system internal feature-mgr feature bfd current status command, 695

show system internal feature-mgr feature state command, 15

show system internal fex info fport command, 128–130

show system internal fex info sat port command, 128

show system internal flash command, 13–14, 24, 88–89

show system internal forwarding adjacency entry command, 173–174

show system internal forwarding route command, 173–174

show system internal forwarding table command, 350

show system internal mmode logfile command, 731

show system internal mts buffer summary command, 145–146

show system internal mts buffers detail command, 146–147

show system internal mts event-history errors command, 148

show system internal mts sup sap description command, 146–147

show system internal mts sup sap sap-id command, 11–12

show system internal mts sup sap stats command, 147–148

show system internal pixm info ltl command, 765

show system internal pktmgr client command, 151–152

show system internal pktmgr interface command, 152–153

show system internal pktmgr stats command, 153

show system internal port-client event-history port command, 179

show system internal port-client link-event command, 178–179

show system internal qos queueing stats interface command, 114–115

show system internal rpm as-path-access-list command, 672–673

show system internal rpm clients command, 588–589

show system internal rpm event-history rsw command, 588, 672–673

show system internal rpm ip-prefix-list command, 589, 668–669

show system internal sal info database vlan command, 350

show system internal sflow info command, 80

show system internal sup opcodes command, 147

show system internal sysmgr gsync-pending command, 32

show system internal sysmgr service all command, 10, 11, 146

show system internal sysmgr service all command example, 10

show system internal sysmgr service command, 10

show system internal sysmgr service command example, 10

show system internal sysmgr service dependency srvname command, 142–143

show system internal sysmgr state command, 31–32, 710–711

show system internal ufdm event-history debugs command, 171–172

show system internal vpcm info interface command, 318–320
show system mode command, 720–722
show system redundancy ha status command, 709
show system redundancy status command, 29–30, 708–709
show system reset-reason command, 29, 110
show tech adjmgr command, 167
show tech arp command, 167
show tech bfd command, 704
show tech bgp command, 687
show tech dhcp command, 362
show tech ethpm command, 179
show tech glbp command, 390
show tech hsrp command, 379
show tech netstack command, 617, 687
show tech nxapi command, 975
show tech nxsdk command, 967
show tech routing ipv4 unicast command, 687
show tech rpm command, 687
show tech track command, 334
show tech vpc command, 294
show tech vrrp command, 385
show tech vrrpv3 command, 385
show tech-support command, 51, 320, 749–750
show tech-support detail command, 124, 141
show tech-support eem command, 87
show tech-support eltm command, 195
show tech-support ethpm command, 130, 195
show tech-support fabricpath command, 310
show tech-support fex command, 130
show tech-support ha command, 719
show tech-support issu command, 719
show tech-support mmode command, 731
show tech-support netflow command, 78
show tech-support netstack command, 160
show tech-support pktmgr command, 160
show tech-support sflow command, 80
show tech-support vdc command, 141
show tunnel internal implicit otv brief command, 890–891
show tunnel internal implicit otv detail command, 922, 937
show tunnel internal implicit otv tunnel_num command, 891
show udld command, 247–248
show udld internal event-history errors command, 248–249
show vdc detail command, 137–138
show vdc detail command output example, 137–138
show vdc internal event-history command, 140–141
show vdc membership command, 139–140
show vdc resource detail command, 138–139
show vdc resource detail command output example, 138–139
show vdc resource template command, 131–132
show virtual-service command, 959–960

show virtual-service tech-support command, 960
show vlan command, 201–202, 214
show vlan command example, 201–202
show vlan private-vlan command, 210–211
show vpc command, 280–281, 284–285, 314–315
show vpc consistency-parameters command, 285–286
show vpc consistency-parameters command example, 285–286
show vpc consistency-parameters vlan command, 286–287
show vpc consistency-parameters vlan command example, 286–287
show vpc consistency-parameters vpc command, 287
show vpc consistency-parameters vpc vpc-id command example, 287
show vpc orphan-ports command, 288
show vpc peer-keepalive command, 282–283
show vrrp command, 380–381
show vrrp statistics command, 381–382
show vrrpv3 command, 383–384
show vrrpv3 statistics command, 384–385
SIA (stuck in active) queries in EIGRP, 443–446
SIA timers output example, 444, 446
site VLAN for OTV, 882
SM (sparse mode), 772
SMUs (Software Maintenance Upgrades), 27–28
sniffing. *See* network sniffing

soft reconfiguration inbound in BGP, 654–657
software releases, 25–27
SOL (SPAN-on-Latency), 60–61
source command, 963
SPAN (Switched Port Analyzer), 54–57
  configuring, 55–56
  ERSPAN, 57–60
  filtering traffic, 57
  SPAN-on-Drop, 61–62
  SPAN-on-Latency (SOL), 60–61
  verifying, 56
SPAN-on-Drop, 61–62
SPT switchover on NX-4 example, 793
SSM (source specific multicast), 841–843
  configuring, 843–845
  verifying, 845–848
SSO (stateful switchover), 707–712
stateful restarts, 29
stateless restarts, 29
static joins, 748
static routes, object tracking with, 334
static RP, configuring, 812–813
status of overlay example, 888
STP (Spanning Tree Protocol), 218–219
  forwarding loops
    BPDU filter, 244–245
    BPDU guard, 243–244
    detecting and remediating, 241–242
    MAC address notifications, 242–243
    unidirectional links, 245–252

IEEE 802.1D standards, 219–220
MST (Multiple Spanning-Tree Protocol), 236
   configuring, 236–237
   tuning, 240–241
   verifying, 237–240
port states, 219
port types, 219
portfast enablement example, 235
RSTP (Rapid Spanning Tree Protocol), 220–221
   blocked switch port identification, 225–227
   interface STP cost, 221–222
   root bridge election, 222–224
   root port identification, 224–225
   tuning, 228–235
   verifying VLANs on trunk links, 227
terminology, 219–220
stub routers, **421–424**
subnets in VLANs, 203. *See also* primary subnets
suboptimal path selection example, 562
suboptimal routing in IS-IS, 562–566
supervisor redundancy, 29–34
suspend individual (LACP), 271
suspending vPC orphan port during vPC failure example, 288
SVI (switched virtual interface), promiscuous PVLANs on, 215–217
switching from maintenance mode to normal mode example, 724–725
syslog
  configuring, 90

with LSAs with duplicate RIDs example, 486, 487
with LSPs with duplicate system IDs example, 547
with neighbors configured, 472
server, 90
triggered loop guard example, 246
sysmgr (system manager), 9–11
system component troubleshooting, 142–143
   ARP and Adjacency Manager, 160–175
   EthPM and Port-Client, 175–179
   HWRL, CoPP, system QoS, 179–192
   MTS (Message and Transaction Service), 144–148
   MTU settings, 192–195
   Netstack and Packet Manager, 148–160
system maintenance mode always-use-custom-profile command, 728–730
system manager state information example, 710–711
system mode maintenance command, 720–722
system mode maintenance dont-generate-profile command, 730–731
system mode maintenance on-reload reset-reason command, 726–727
system mode maintenance timeout command, 726
system priority (LACP), 268–271
system QoS (quality of service), 179–192
system redundancy HA status example, 709

system redundancy state example, 709

system switchover command, 711–712

System-ID in IS-IS, 539, 546–549

T

tar append command, 20

tar create command, 20

tar extract command, 20

TCAM (ternary content addressable memory), 573–574

TCN (topology change notification), 232–235

TCP connect probes, 328–329

TCP sessions, verifying, 615–617

TCP socket connections example, 615

TCP socket creation and Netstack example, 157

TCPUDP component (Netstack), 156–160

technical support files, 44–45

telnet to port 179 usage example, 616

templates in BGP, 653–654

test packet-tracer command, 71–72

threshold for track list object example, 333

timers in OSPF, 476–478

TLVs (type, length, value) tuples, 512
   in IIH, 514
   in LSPs, 516

topologies
   after SIA replies example, 445
   EIGRP topology table, 395–396
   IS-IS topology table, 898–905
   verifying in FabricPath, 306

track object with static routes example, 334

track-list state, object tracking for, 332–333

traffic load-balancing (port-channels) troubleshooting, 272–274

trees in PIM, 772–773

trunk ports, 204–205
   allowed VLANs, 206
   configuring and verifying, 204
   native VLANs, 206
   PVLANs and, 217–218
   verifying VLANs on, 227

tuning
   BGP memory consumption, 650–653
   MST (Multiple Spanning-Tree Protocol), 240–241
   RSTP (Rapid Spanning Tree Protocol), 228–235
      port priority, 232–233
      root bridge placement, 228–229
      root guard, 229
      root port and blocked switch port locations, 229–232
      topology changes and portfast, 232–235

tunnel depolarization, 942–944

Tx-Rx loop, 249–250

Type 1 vPC consistency-checker errors, 283–284

Type 2 vPC consistency-checker errors, 284

Type-1 networks, external OSPF routes, 496–497

Type-2 networks, external OSPF routes, 497–499

U

UDLD (unidirectional link detection), 246–250
   configuring, 247
   empty echo detection example, 249
   event-history example, 248–249
UDP echo probes, 324–325
UDP jitter probes, 325–327
UFDM process, 171–175
UFDM route distribution to IPFIB and acknowledgment example, 172
underscore (_) in RegEx, 677–678
unicast flooding, 198
   with multicast enabled transport, 919–924
   in OTV, 877
   selective unicast flooding, 918–919
unicast forwarding components, 167
unicast routes from NX-2 for VLAN 215 and VLAN 216 example, 858
unicast RPF configuration and verification example, 351–352
unicast traffic, 734
unicast transport, multicast traffic with, 932–937
unidirectional links, 245
   bridge assurance, 250–252
   loop guard, 245–246
   UDLD (unidirectional link detection), 246–250
unique router-ID in OSPF, 471
unique System-ID in IS-IS, 539
update generation process in BGP, 643–646
UPDATE message, 602
URIB (Unicast Routing Information Base), 167–171
   clients, 168
   route installation, 647–648
   verifying FabricPath, 307
   verifying vPC+, 316–317
URPF (Unicast Reverse Path Forwarding), 351–352
UUID (Universally Unique Identifier), 9

V

VDC (Virtual Device Contexts), 35–37, 130–131
   configuring, 133–134
   initializing, 134–136
   internal event history logs example, 140–141
   management, 137–142
   out-of-band and in-band management, 137
   resource templates, 131–132
verifying
   access port mode example, 203–204
   access-list counters
      in hardware example, 574–575
      in TCAM example, 573–574
   ACLs (access control lists)
      on line card for DHCP relay example, 339–340
      statistics on line card for DHCP relay example, 340–341
   active interfaces, 402–403
   AED for VLAN 103 example, 920
   anycast RP, 830–841
   ARP ACLs, 348–349
   ARP ND-Cache example, 916
   ASM (any source multicast), 788–789
   Auto-RP, 813–820

BFD (bidirectional forwarding detection)
  with echo function, 702–703
  neighbors example, 694–695
  sessions, 693–707
BGP (Border Gateway Protocol), 605–609
  ACLs and firewalls, 613–615
  configuration, 610–611
  reachability and packet loss, 611–613
  TCP sessions, 615–617
BiDIR (Bidirectional), 805–811
BPDU filter example, 245
BSR (bootstrap router), 820–830
community PVLAN configuration example, 214
configuration incompatibilities example, 713–714
connectivity
  after virtual link example, 484–485
  between primary subnets example, 411
  with promiscuous PVLAN SVI example, 216–217
  between PVLANs example, 214–215
contents of logflash: directory example, 24
CoPP (control plane policing)
  EIGRP example, 407–408
  IS-IS example, 532
  NetFlow, 78
  OSPF example, 465–466
current bit-rate of OTV control-group example, 894
DAI (dynamic ARP inspection), 345–346

detailed dynamic tunnel parameters example, 891
DHCP relay, 337–338
DHCPv6 guard configuration and policy, 369–370
EEM (Embedded Event Manager), 85–86
EIGRP (Enhanced Interior Gateway Protocol)
  hello and hold timers example, 415–416
  neighbors, 423
  packets, 405–409
emulated switch-IDs example, 315
ERSPAN session, 59–60
FabricPath, 303–310
  core interfaces, 303–304
  IS-IS adjacency, 304–305
  software table in hardware, 308–309
  switch-IDs, 303, 310
  topologies, 306
  in URIB, 307, 309
  VLANs (virtual LANs), 305–306
FEX (Fabric Extender), 126–128
filtering SPAN traffic, 57
forwarding adjacency example, 163
FP core interfaces example, 303–304
FP MAC information in vPCM example, 318–320
hardware forwarding on module 3, 799
hardware rate-limiters on N7k and N9k switches example, 181–182
hardware statistics for IPv6 snooping example, 367–368
HSRP (Hot Standby Routing Protocol), 373–374
HSRPv6 virtual address, 379

IGMP (Internet Group Management Protocol), 761–771
IGMP snooping example, 757
IGMPv3 on NX-4, 846
ingress L3 unicast flow drops example, 62
interface's OSPF network type example, 475–476
I/O module MFIB on module 3, 798
IOS devices after NX-OS metric transition mode example, 556
IS-IS (Intermediate System-to-Intermediate System)
  adjacency example, 305
  interface, 523–525
  interface level type example, 542
  metric transition mode, 555
  neighbors, 520–523
  packets, 528–535
  process level type example, 541
  protocol, 525–526
  system IDs example, 549
isolated PVLANs
  communications example, 211–212
  configuration example, 210–211
keychains example, 417
LACP (link-aggregation control packets), 262–265
LACP speed state, 270
Layer 3 routing over vPC, 294
local and remote FP routes in URIB example, 316–317
maintenance and normal profile configurations example, 727–728
maximum links, 267
MFDM on NX-2, 797
missing 172.16.1.0/24 network example, 493–494

MROUTE, 789–795
MROUTE in transport network, 932
MROUTE on NX-2, 795
MST (Multiple Spanning-Tree Protocol), 237, 240
MTU
  under ELTM process, 195
  under ethpm process, 195
multicast routing for OTV control-group example, 893
NET addressing example, 541
network QoS policy, 195
new path after new reference OSPF bandwidth is configured on R1 and R2 example, 503–504
no services pending synchronization example, 32, 34
NX-OS BGP peering, 607
on-reload reset-reason, 726–727
optimal routing example, 493
ORIB entry for host C example, 921
OSPF (Open Shortest Path First)
  area settings example, 474
  encrypted authentication example, 481
  neighbors, 458–460
  packets, 463–467
  packets using Ethanalyzer example, 467
  packets with ACL example, 467
  plaintext authentication example, 479
OTV (Overlay Transport Virtualization)
  IS-IS adjacencies, 888–898
  next-hop adjacency tracking example, 946
  site adjacency example, 896

packet tracer, 71–72
PBR-based traffic example, 593
PIM ASM platform, 795–799
PIM interfaces and neighbors, 780–785
platform FIB, 173–174, 176–178
platform LTL index example, 765
port priority impact on spanning tree protocol topology example, 232–233
port-channel status, 260–262
PPF database example, 575–576
promiscuous PVLAN SVI mapping example, 216
PVLAN switchport type example, 211
redistributed networks example, 567
remote area routes
  on NX-1 and NX-4 example, 483
  on NX-2 and NX-3 example, 482–483
RFC1583 compatibility example, 500
root and blocking ports for VLAN example, 226–227
SAL database info and FIB for IPSG, 350
site group to delivery group mapping example, 931
site-ID of OTV IS-IS neighbor example, 890
site-VLAN spanning-tree example, 897–898
size and location of PSS in flash file system example, 13–14
software table in hardware for FP route example, 308–309
SPAN (Switched Port Analyzer), 56
spanning tree protocol root bridge example, 223

SSM (source specific multicast), 845–848
state and available space for logflash: example, 24
suboptimal routing example, 491
sysmgr state on standby supervisor example, 33
total path cost example, 230–231
trunk port, 204
UDLD switch port status example, 247–248
URPF (Unicast Reverse Path Forwarding), 351–352
VLANs on trunk links, 227
vPC (virtual port-channel)
  autorecovery, 289
  autorecovery example, 289
  consistency-checker, 283–287
  domain status, 280–282
  peer-gateway, 291
  peer-gateway example, 291
  peer-keepalive link, 282–283
vPC+, 314–320
  emulated switches, 315
  MAC addresses, 315–316
  show vpc command, 314–315
  in URIB, 316–317
  in vPCM, 318–320
vPC-connected receiver, 861–869
vPC-connected source, 849–861
VRRP (Virtual Router Redundancy Protocol), 380–381
which OTV ED is AED example, 892
viewing
access port configuration command example, 203
and changing LACP system priority example, 268

contents of specific file in logflash: example, 24–25

CoPP policy and creating custom CoPP policy example, 189

debug information for redistribution example, 590

detailed version of spanning-tree state example, 234

EIGRP (Enhanced Interior Gateway Protocol)
  authentication on interfaces example, 417
  passive interfaces example, 404
  retry values for neighbors example, 410–411
  routes on NX-1 example, 420–421

IIH authentication example, 545–546

inconsistent ports example, 252

inconsistent spanning tree protocol ports example, 246

interface specific MST settings example, 240

keychain passwords example, 481, 546

LACP (link-aggregation control packets)
  neighbor information example, 264
  packet counters example, 263
  time stamps for transmissions on interface example, 263–264

MAC addresses on Nexus switch example, 199

nondefault OSPF forwarding address example, 492

number of classic and wide EIGRP neighbors example, 438

number of RPM clients per protocol example, 588–589

OSPF (Open Shortest Path First)
  password for simple authentication example, 480
  RID example, 471

port-channels
  hash algorithm example, 273
  interface status example, 262
  summary status example, 260

RPM (Route Policy Manager)
  event-history example, 588
  perspective example prefix-lists, 589

STP (Spanning Tree Protocol)
  behavior changes with vPC example, 281–282
  event-history example, 234
  port priority example, 232
  spanning tree protocol type of ports with bridge assurance example, 250–251

traffic load on member interfaces example, 273

VLANs (virtual LANs)
  allowed on trunk link example, 206
  participating with spanning tree protocol on interface example, 227

vPC (virtual port-channel)
  orphan ports example, 288
  peer-keepalive status example, 282
  status example, 280–281

virtual link configuration example, 484

virtual service list and resource utilization example, 960

virtualization
    Virtual Device Contexts (VDCs), 35–37
    virtual port channels (vPC), 37–39
    Virtual Routing and Forwarding (VRF), 37
VLANs (virtual LANs), 200–201
    access ports, 203–204
    creating, 201–203
    IGMP snooping group membership example, 764
    loop-free topologies. *See* STP (Spanning Tree Protocol)
    mapping
        on L2 trunk example, 942
        in OTV, 941–942
        on overlay interface example, 942
    multiple subnets in, 203
    PVLANs (private VLANs), 207–208
        communication capability between hosts, 208
        community PVLANs, 212–215
        isolated PVLANs, 208–212
        promiscuous PVLANs on SVI, 215–217
        trunking between switches, 217–218
    reserved VLAN, 870
    site VLAN for OTV, 882
    trunk ports, 204–205
        allowed VLANs, 206
        native VLANs, 206
    verifying
        in FabricPath, 305–306
        on trunk links, 227
vPC (virtual port-channel), 37–39, 274–275
    ARP synchronization, 291–292
    autorecovery, 289
    backup Layer 3 routing, 292–293
    configuring, 278–280
    domains, 275–276
    IGMP snooping state on NX-4 example, 854–855
    Layer 3 routing, 293–294
    member links, 277
    multicast traffic, 848–849
        duplicate packets, 870
        receiver configuration and verification, 861–869
        reserved VLAN, 870
        source configuration and verification, 849–861
    operational behavior, 277–278
    orphan ports, 288
    peer link, 277
    peer-gateway, 289–291
    peer-keepalive link, 276–277
    status with consistency checker error example, 284–285
    topology, 275–276
    verifying
        consistency-checker, 283–287
        domain status, 280–282
        peer-keepalive link, 282–283
vPC+
    configuring, 311–314
    verifying, 314–320
        emulated switches, 315
        MAC addresses, 315–316
        show vpc command, 314–315
        in URIB, 316–317
        in vPCM, 318–320
vPCM (vPC Manager), verifying vPC+, 318–320

VRF (Virtual Routing and Forwarding), 37

VRRP (Virtual Router Redundancy Protocol), 380–385

configuring, 380

state and detail information example, 381

statistics, 381–382

verifying, 380–381

VRRPv3, 382–385

VRRPv3, 382–385

W

wc utility, 40

well-known multicast addresses, 741

wide metrics

versus classic metrics in EIGRP, 433–439

on NX-1, NX-2, and NX-3 example, 437–438

on NX-1, NX-2, NX-3, and NX-6 example, 438–439

on NX-1 and NX-2 example, 436–437

X

xml utility, 42

Y

yum command, 954

Exclusive Offer – 40% OFF

Cisco Press Video Training
livelessons

ciscopress.com/video
Use coupon code **CPVIDEO40** during checkout.

Video Instruction from Technology Experts

Advance Your Skills

Get started with fundamentals, become an expert, or get certified.

Train Anywhere

Train anywhere, at your own pace, on any device.

Learn

Learn from trusted author trainers published by Cisco Press.

Try Our Popular Video Training for FREE!
ciscopress.com/video

Explore hundreds of **FREE** video lessons from our growing library of Complete Video Courses, LiveLessons, networking talks, and workshops.

Cisco Press   ciscopress.com/video

ALWAYS LEARNING   PEARSON

REGISTER YOUR PRODUCT at CiscoPress.com/register
Access Additional Benefits and SAVE 35% on Your Next Purchase

- Download available product updates.
- Access bonus material when applicable.
- Receive exclusive offers on new editions and related products.
  (Just check the box to hear from us when setting up your account.)
- Get a coupon for 35% for your next purchase, valid for 30 days.
  Your code will be available in your Cisco Press cart. (You will also find
  it in the Manage Codes section of your account page.)

Registration benefits vary by product. Benefits will be listed on your account page under Registered Products.

CiscoPress.com – Learning Solutions for Self-Paced Study, Enterprise, and the Classroom
Cisco Press is the Cisco Systems authorized book publisher of Cisco networking technology, Cisco certification self-study, and Cisco Networking Academy Program materials.

At **CiscoPress.com** you can
- Shop our books, eBooks, software, and video training.
- Take advantage of our special offers and promotions (ciscopress.com/promotions).
- Sign up for special offers and content newsletters (ciscopress.com/newsletters).
- Read free articles, exam profiles, and blogs by information technology experts.
- Access thousands of free chapters and video lessons.

Connect with Cisco Press – Visit CiscoPress.com/community
Learn about Cisco Press community events and programs.

Cisco Press

ALWAYS LEARNING   PEARSON